SOUTH AFRICAN

PRACTICAL PROBLEM SOLVER

READER'S DIGEST

SOUTH AFRICAN

PRACTICAL PROBLEM SOLVER

SUBSTITUTES, SHORT CUTS AND INGENIOUS SOLUTIONS

The Reader's Digest Association
South Africa (Pty) Limited, Cape Town

SOUTH AFRICAN
PRACTICAL PROBLEM SOLVER
was edited and designed by
The Reader's Digest Association, South Africa (Pty) Limited,
Cape Town.

The Reader's Digest Association
South Africa (Pty) Limited,
130 Strand Street, Cape Town 8001

Editor: Tim O'Hagan
Designer: Jo-Anne Goodwill
Research Editors: Judy Beyer, Pat Kramer
Project co-ordinator: Carol Adams
Indexer: Sandie Vahl

ISBN 1-874-912-25-4

The publishers wish to thank the following who,
as contributors and consultants, assisted in preparing this book.

Contributors and consultants
Marty Anderson
Ann Arnott
Vivian Baard
Pauline M J Bradshaw
William Barker
Brian Johnson Barker
Therese Hoehlein Cerbie
Phillippa Cheifitz
Rita G Christopher
Thomas Christopher
Sarah Clayton
Donna Dannen
Kent Dannen
Alan Duggan
Gene Hamilton
Katie Hamilton
Signe Hammer
Lorna B Harris
Sherwood Harris
Merle Henkenius
Penny Hinkle
John H Ingersoll
Peter H Johnson
Joe Koemer
Frank B Latham
Nick Lee
Malané Lutzeler
Neilah Miller
Margaret Moore
Boyd Norton
Cinda Siler
Jennifer Godbold-Simpson
Elizabeth Tener
Frank X Wamsley
Jeff Yablonka

Illustrators
Lyn de la Motte
Stephen Gardner
John Gist
Linda Gist
Ed Lipinski
Marianne E Markey
Ray Skibinski
Mario Stasolla
Victoria Vebell
Jeanette Venter
Mary Wilshire

Recipe testing and development
Therese Hoehlein Cerbie
Ben T Etheridge
Sandra Gluck
Ann L Rafferty

CONTENTS

ABOUT THIS BOOK

Here is a remarkable reference book to help you conquer the everyday difficulties that confront us all. This book approaches those commonplace problems in five ingenious ways.

Problem solver's dictionary offers effective and imaginative solutions to more than 1,000 problems, from dripping taps to telephone sales calls. Look up your problem as you would a word in a dictionary. If you don't find it right away, turn to the index at the back of the book; the answer may be under another subject heading.

Charts & checklists presents solid information in concise packages, touching on everything from getting organized to getting married. This diverse collection of lists, charts and quizzes provides essential advice, money-saving tips and illuminating self-evaluations.

Common things with uncommon uses is arranged alphabetically and reveals how familiar household items can be used in creative ways to solve hundreds of commonplace problems.

Recycling & renewing tells you how to prevent waste and save money by converting potential discards into attractive furnishings. Illustrated step-by-step instructions show you how to give your home and garden a face-lift by using your imagination with a variety of old household accessories.

Formulas & recipes gives you the secrets for making your own health and grooming aids, a variety of household cleaners, culinary delights and gifts – while saving money in the process.

1. PROBLEM SOLVER'S DICTIONARY

You may not find a cure for all the world's woes in these pages, but you'll find plenty of inventive, common-sense ways to deal with the sort of problems that bedevil day-to-day life. Some examples: what to use when you don't have the right tool, how to cope with emergencies, ingenious short cuts to make your chores less tedious.

A

Abdominal flab

1. Proper posture can do wonders for the way your stomach looks. Stand up straight, put your shoulders back, and tuck in your abdomen and buttocks.
2. Breathe correctly: deeply, from the diaphragm.
3. Pull in your abdominal muscles and hold for several seconds. Make the exercise part of your routine; do it while you're brushing your teeth or sitting at your desk, or whenever you're stuck in traffic or waiting for a bus or train.
4. If you don't have a bicycle, try this bicycle exercise: lie on your back. Put your hands underneath your buttocks for support and bend both knees up to your chest. Extend one leg straight up toward the ceiling. As you bend it in a pedalling motion, extend the other. Repeat this between 10 and 20 times.
5. Do a set of bent-leg curl-ups as shown below, that is, on your back. Inhale, and then as you exhale, slowly curl your head and shoulders upward and slide your hands up your thighs toward your knees. Pause. Inhale, and while exhaling slowly curl down to a resting position. Repeat slowly 10 times.
6. While doing any exercise, contract your abdominal muscles to keep yourself in alignment. During an abdomen-toning supine exercise, keep the small of your back on the floor: otherwise your hip flexors will take on the abdomen's work.

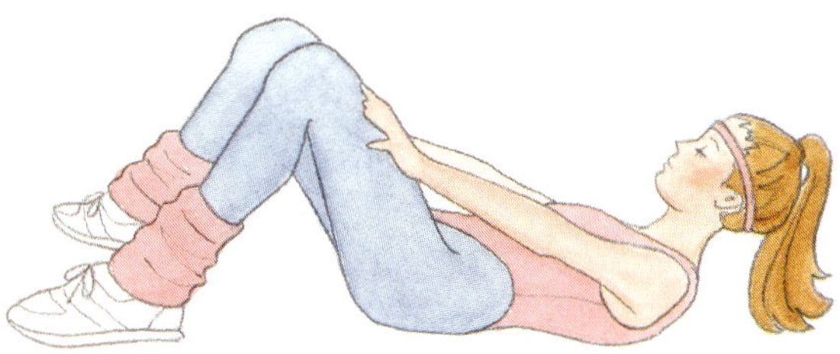

Bent-leg curl-up: this exercise fights flab, strengthening the abdomen and back.

Abrasive paper

1. Are you out of sandpaper? Look under your kitchen sink for abrasive nylon pads, with or without sponge backing. Or try steel wool; back it with a piece of canvas or a sponge to protect your hands.
2. A pumice stone – the kind which is used to smooth calluses from hands and feet – is good for smoothing wood and plastics.
3. An emery board is handy for tight, hard-to-reach areas. And because it's flexible, it's great for contours and curved surfaces.
4. Save old sanding belts and discs; cut them up for hand sanding.
5. For rough sanding, use a brick or a piece of concrete block. The weight helps provide the necessary pressure. Try them on wood, plastic and masonry surfaces. (You'll end up with many scratches that will need additional smoothing.)
6. Smooth large areas, such as a tabletop, by first spreading out a good amount of fine, clean sand or ground pumice. Then wrap a sanding block in canvas or other tough cloth and rub with it in the direction of the wood grain; tap it clean frequently.

Adult children at home

1. Set a clear time limit on how long an adult son or daughter may live at the family home.
2. To reduce the inter-generational friction, write out a contract outlining the rules for sharing facilities, food, expenses and chores. All wage earners living at home should pay their own way as well as share the household duties.
3. Adult children should get and pay for their own telephone lines.
4. Co-ordinate your social plans by setting up a family calendar or bulletin board. (A parents' night at the concert might be a good time for an adult son or daughter to have a dinner party at home, for example.)
5. To accommodate excess books, baggage, furniture and out-of-season clothing, rent some storage space. This could range from a cupboard or small room to a garage. For your own convenience, ensure that the storage area is accessible 24 hours a day.

Aggressive pets

1. Does your bird peck at you when you're filling its water dish? Try using a long-stemmed watering can. And make sure that you keep your fingers out of the cage!
2. If your cat tries to attack your bird, suspend the cage from the ceiling or place it on a pedestal.

Spray an aggressive cat with a plant mister. Or smack the floor next to the animal with a rolled-up newspaper. Be sure to follow this up with positive reinforcement.
3. Dogfight? Don't yell; make a loud noise – press your car hooter, ring a bell or beat on a frying pan. If this fails, douse the combatants with a hose or with buckets of water.

An aggressive dog is always potentially dangerous. But if your dog misbehaves in a non-threatening manner around a new baby, the postman or anyone else, you may be able to modify its behaviour with positive reinforcement. Try showering it with attention and various treats when the disliked person is present. The dog may gradually begin to enjoy the person's presence.

Airline delays

1. Avoid delays by checking up on the airline and on the flight you're considering. Newspapers sometimes publish the timetables of various airlines, and you can call the airline itself to find out the on-time record of a specific flight.
2. Carry a portable phone so that you can notify people who are waiting for you that you'll be late.
3. Find out why your flight is being delayed. If it's something that affects only your flight, such as a mechanical problem, you can ask the airline to reschedule you on another flight.
4. Be assertive and persistent. If you don't get satisfaction from a travel agent, ask for a supervisor.

Airline tickets

If possible, pay for your ticket with a credit card. That way the ticket number will be on the receipt and flight insurance will probably be included in the price.

Read your ticket immediately to see if there are restrictions, and to make certain that all information is correct. Policies on exchanges and refunds vary among airlines.

Make a photocopy of your ticket or write down the number. Keep this record in a safe place; it will help you get reimbursed if the ticket is lost.

In that eventuality, file a lost ticket application immediately. On most domestic flights, you will be asked to buy the replacement at the full fare even if you held a discounted ticket; you may, however, plead your case with the airline's supervisor. Many international flights will issue replacement tickets, provided you agree to reimburse the airline if the lost ticket is recovered or used.

Airsickness

1. If you're subject to this problem, reserve a seat over a wing. Fly well rested and wear loose clothes. Eat light, easily digestible food before and during the flight; avoid alcohol and cigarette smoke. As soon as you're seated, direct the air from the vent above you toward your face.
2. If your child is susceptible to airsickness, bring his favourite games, toys and puzzles for distraction.
3. Instead of motion sickness medications, try chewing a little fresh root ginger or crystallized ginger. Vitamin B6 is said to help – 25 milligrams every two hours for adults and 10 milligrams for children.
4. As soon as you begin to feel in any way dizzy or nauseated, recline your seat and close your eyes or stare at a fixed point.
5. Be sure to breathe deeply through your mouth. Alternately tense and relax your body.

Air travel

1. You may be able to travel at greatly reduced rates by carrying letters or a package for a courier or some other company. Check through the Yellow Pages under "Courier Service" and also see under "Air Freight Agents". Some listed companies though, don't use freelancers.
2. If you're an old-age pensioner, use an airline that offers concessions to senior citizens.
3. If they are available on your particular route, travel on late-night, "no frills" flights.
4. Save time at your destination by travelling with hand luggage only.
5. Make a standby reservation by waiting for a last-minute cancellation – it is inconvenient, but there may be a substantial saving.
6. Investigate "frequent flyer" programmes and other travel organizations that claim to offer substantially reduced fares.
7. If you can, avoid travelling by air if you have a bad cold, flu or sinus infection or blockage.

Alarm clock

1. An electronic timer can serve as a backup alarm for home or travel. You can get one that times up to 10 hours and, with three separate channels, can even work as a "snooze alarm".
2. Ask a friend or relative to give you a morning wake-up call – and offer to return the favour.
3. Set an automatic timer to turn on all the lights, the radio and the TV in your bedroom for the time you want to get up.

Alcohol

If your alcoholic drink is too strong and there's no room in the glass for any more mixer, you can float a thin slice of cucumber on the surface; it will absorb much of the harsh taste. Floating long slivers of cucumber in a punch bowl will tend to mellow punch in the same way.

Remember that although the taste may be mellower, the alcohol content is not significantly reduced, so special care should be taken with stronger-than-usual drinks, particularly if you intend to drive afterwards. Remember, too, that "fizzy" mixers such as soda water and cola tend to speed up the rate of alcohol absorption by your body. A "safe" rate of drinking is reckoned to be the equivalent of about one ordinary tot per hour.

Allen key

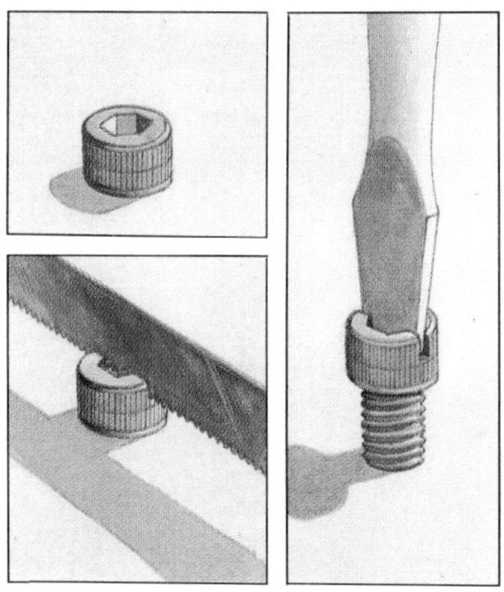

Lacking an Allen key, you can still tighten or remove an Allenhead screw; just try different sizes of plain screwdrivers until you find one that fits the opening.

Or, if the Allen screw protrudes above the work surface, use a hacksaw to cut a slot in the top; then use a standard screwdriver to tighten or remove it. Or grip the head of the screw with a pair of locking-grip pliers to loosen.

Allergies

Many people in South Africa have severe physical reactions to such allergens as pollen, dust, foods, feathers, insect venom, animal dander and medications.

HAY FEVER

This is the most common allergy. Its familiar symptoms: sneezing and a stuffy, runny nose. It's usually a fairly mild reaction to pollen and can be treated with over-the-counter or prescription antihistamines.

Removal of the irritant is the best cure. If that isn't possible – in pollen season, for example – stay indoors with the windows closed. Run the air conditioner, if you have one, without cooling if necessary.

ANAPHYLACTIC SHOCK

This is the most severe form of allergic reaction. It can develop in minutes or even seconds after contact with an allergen, or it may appear half an hour or more later or even progress suddenly from an apparently mild allergic reaction.

The face, chest and back become flushed, itchy and burning; skin rashes may appear. The face, tongue and lips may swell and the lips turn bluish. Breathing is laboured and wheezing. The pulse becomes weak. Pale skin, dizziness, nausea and headache may follow. Finally, the person may lapse into a coma.

Honeybee venom is a potent allergen to some people.

The victim needs an immediate injection of adrenaline.

If he has a treatment kit with a syringe of adrenaline, help administer a dose; follow the instructions on the kit, injecting into a muscle or under the skin – not into a vein. Take him straight to a casualty department or call an emergency medical service.

Altitude adjustment

Planning a holiday in the mountains? To avoid altitude problems, take it easy during your first day. Don't work out or do aerobic exercise. Drink plenty of water but no alcohol. If you begin to feel sick (headache, dizziness or nausea), go to bed and rest.

Serious mountain climbers need to take further precautions to help prevent altitude sickness. If you have a heart or lung condition, consult your doctor before you go. Even if you're in good health, ask about prescription drugs that prevent the symptoms of altitude sickness.

If your destination is higher than 2,500 metres, spend the first day at an intermediate level. Then proceed upward at a daily rate of 150 to 300 metres, resting often and drinking at least four litres of water a day. If you're already used to living at a high elevation, you can probably ascend or descend as much as 1,500 metres with few problems.

Breathing pure oxygen will relieve the discomfort, as will descending to a lower level to rest. If you develop a nosebleed or headache or feel dizzy or nauseated, immediately descend 700 to 900 metres; get medical attention promptly.

Anchor

Going canoeing or rowing? Take along an old basketball net, a net shopping bag or even a sturdy hessian bag. When you arrive at your anchorage, fill it with rocks and close the ends with cord, wire or a mountain climber's snap-link carabiner. (For salt water, use a brass snap shackle.) Attach a rope, lower the net to the bottom, and you have a handy, disposable anchor.

Antiseptics

1. Soap and warm water are your first line of defence against germs; wash minor scrapes, burns, cuts and blisters thoroughly.
2. If you want to try an alternative to a pharmacy-bought antiseptic, liberally apply the juice from the pulpy centre of a fresh aloe leaf directly to the skin.
3. Another domestic application is crushed raw, fresh garlic or the freshly extracted juice of garlic. This can be applied to gauze (not directly to the skin); garlic contains allicin, a powerful germ killer.
4. Hydrogen peroxide, available at pharmacies, is inexpensive and can be used full strength.
5. Various non-prescription topical antiseptic ointments are good for cuts and have the added advantage of preventing the dressing from sticking to the wound. Use them with caution, however; they can sometimes produce an allergic rash. If the wound does not heal after a couple of days you should consult a doctor.

Ants

Ants enter houses in search of food, warmth and shelter. When they find food, they establish a trail that leads back to their nest outside. Follow the trail to the point of entry into the house and seal it off completely, if possible, with caulk.

Destroy and wipe up every ant you find. Locate nests and destroy them by pouring several litres of boiling water into the entrances. Then stir up the soil and repeat the process.

Some organic ant repellents may also be effective: ants dislike walking on powder – scatter talcum powder, cream of tartar, borax or powdered sulphur at entry points.

A safe but effective product on the market is a trap for ants. This is a small enclosed box which contains some poisoned food.

The food is transported back to the nest by foraging ants, and poisons those inside. A second kind of trap works on the principal of trapping the ants in water.

Apartment & house plants

The key to success in indoor gardening is finding the appropriate plants for the available light. Consult a reliable house plant guide or the people from whom you buy your plants to find out a particular plant's needs.

Professionals use a light meter to match the plant to the location; you can substitute a 35-millimetre camera with a built-in light meter and adjustable f-stops and shutter speeds.

Set the camera's ASA/ISO dial to 100 and the aperture ring to f4. Focus on a white mat card at least 30 centimetres square, in the spot where you plan to keep the plant. Move closer, taking care not to block the light, until the card fills the viewfinder. Then adjust the shutter speed until the correct exposure is indicated.

The reading on the shutter equals the intensity of the light: strong light, 125 to 500; medium light, 60 to 125; low light, 30 to 60.

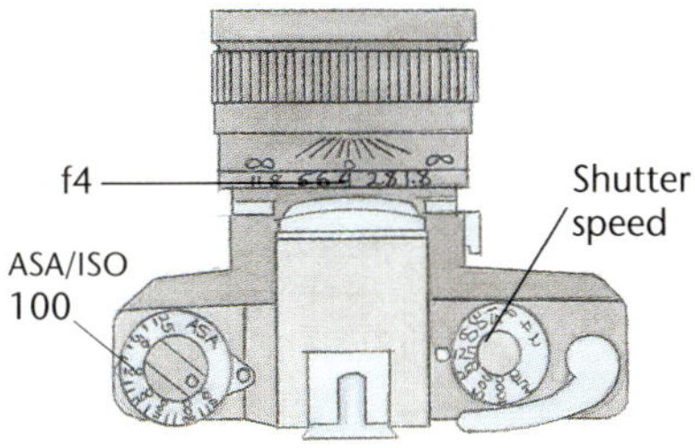

Aphids

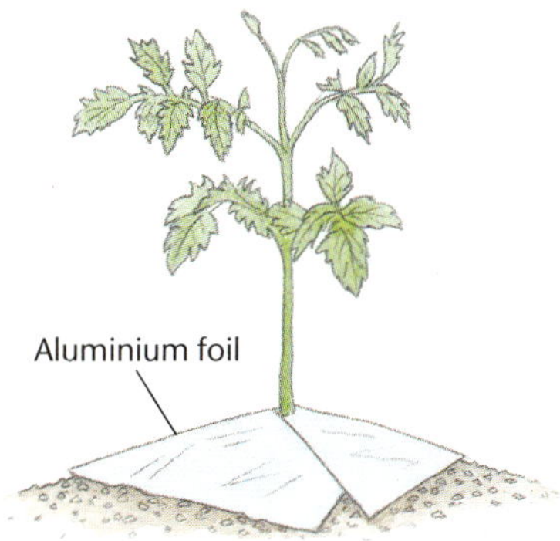

1. Wash aphids off house plants under a gentle flow of tap water. Spray a large infestation with a solution of mild detergent in water. Or dab the leaves with a cotton ball dipped in methylated spirits. (Make sure that you do not use methylated spirits on such delicate plants as African violets, however.)

2. Outdoors, use an aluminium foil mulch; the reflection confuses the insects and drives them away.

3. Interplant vegetables with aphid repellent plants, such as onions, garlic and chives.

Appetite control

1. Avoid crash or fad diets. A sensible goal for a diet is a weight loss of 500 grams to one kilogram a week.

2. Eat foods low in fat and high in complex carbohydrates (fruits, vegetables, grains and legumes). Animal fat readily turns to human fat.

3. Don't skip a meal; try to eat five or six small meals a day instead of three big ones – you won't feel as hungry, and your body will use more energy in digestion.

4. Eat slowly, savouring each bite. It takes about 20 minutes for the feeling of fullness to register; wait that long before eating more.

5. When you feel hungry between meals, have a sugarless cup of tea; caffeine inhibits the appetite.

6. Be sure to exercise regularly; not only does it burn up kilojoules, but it can also make you feel temporarily less hungry.

LOOK BEFORE YOU LEAP

Common diet myths

□ The only way to lose weight is to eat less. Not necessarily. A dieter may lose weight in the short term but may regain much of it. Exercisers, however, tend to keep it off.

□ A kilojoule is a kilojoule is a kilojoule. Not so. All kilojoules are not created equal. About 25 percent of the kilojoules from starches such as pasta, whole-grain bread or potatoes are burned up for energy. Not so with fat. If you switch from a high-fat diet to a diet rich in complex carbohydrates, you should lose weight in time.

□ Margarine is less fattening than butter. False. Margarine and butter both have about 35 kilojoules per pat. The difference is that butter contains saturated fat, which is high in cholesterol, while soft margarines (especially those made from polyunsaturated vegetable oils, may actually help lower the blood cholesterol level).

□ Starches are fattening. Also false. The only things that make starches fattening are the butter, sour cream and rich sauces that people like to put on them.

7. After about three weeks of dieting, you may stop losing weight altogether until your body accepts its new norm. The trick is to get past this three-week mark without gaining back what you've lost. When you finally reach your ideal weight, maintain it for at least three weeks to establish a new norm.

Appetite loss

IN CHILDREN

If a toddler seems to have lost his appetite, he may just be growing more slowly than before. Don't force him to eat.

Give him as much as he wants at meals; cut down on snacks so that he'll be hungry at mealtimes.

IN TEENAGERS AND ADULTS

1. Check that you're getting the recommended dietary allowances of the B vitamins and zinc, which stimulate the appetite.
2. Make sure that you eliminate all caffeine, an appetite suppressant.
3. Try eating faster; you may be able to beat the brain signal that, 20 minutes after you start eating, says you're full.
4. See a doctor; loss of appetite may be caused by illness.
5. A prolonged appetite loss in an adolescent girl could be anorexia nervosa, which needs specialist care.

IN OLDER PEOPLE

1. At about the age 65, many people lose some sense of taste and smell, and the appetite suffers. Try stimulating it with a good variety of strongly flavoured or spicy foods, such as curry or chilli; older people often tend to find such foods more palatable than youngsters do.
2. Try to vary the texture, colour and temperature of your food; this may compensate for the lack of flavour.
3. Savour each bite. Chewing slowly and moving the food around in the mouth before swallowing increases contact with the taste buds and, via the back of the mouth, with odour receptors in the nose.

Appliance fires

1. If flames are shooting out of an appliance, or if you see smoke or smell burning odours coming from one, immediately pull out the plug or shut off the main power (p.162). If the appliance continues to burn, douse it with an ABC fire extinguisher (p.81). Do not use water under any circumstances. If the appliance is still burning after one minute, telephone the fire department at once and get out of the house.
2. If smoke comes from your oven, check to see if you left any food inside. If not, try cleaning the oven. (A continuous-cleaning oven normally smokes a little.)
3. If grilling creates smoke, food may be too close to the heat. Or fat may not be draining properly; if you use foil or a disposable grilling pan, cut slashes in it to allow fat to drip into the pan below.

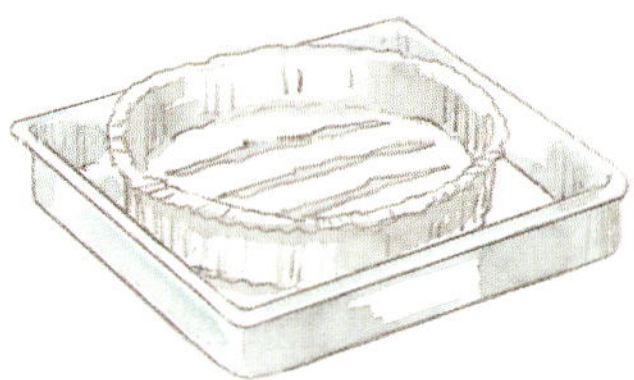

4. If smoke comes out of the microwave, interrupt the cycle, eliminate the problem, and restart the cycle. To be on the safe side, never leave an appliance operating when you are away from home.

Appointments

There is no such thing as being fashionably late for an appointment. If you are habitually late, you are guilty of wasting others' time and will certainly lose respect. Here are some habits that will help you become a more punctual person:
1. Give yourself extra time – just in case you're delayed by weather, traffic or other circumstances.
2. Keep only one diary; carry it between home and workplace.
3. Use a watch, a calculator or an electronic "secretary" with a beeper to remind you when to leave.
4. If possible, take scheduled transportation, such as a train, so that you'll have to depart at a set time.

LATENESS IN OTHERS

1. Ask a chronically late person to call you just before he leaves.
2. Avoid meeting him for scheduled events, such as movies. If you really must do so, plan to meet early, perhaps for a meal.
3. If your doctor or dentist is known to overbook patients, call first to see if she's running late.

Aspirin sensitivity

1. Paracetamol, the active ingredient in most aspirin substitutes, doesn't irritate the stomach, and so it's safe for people with ulcers. Asthmatics can also take it.

IN TIMES GONE BY

The history of the first wonder drug

Before there was aspirin, there was willow bark. About 400 B.C., Hippocrates, the "father of medicine," advised chewing it to ease the pain of childbirth. For centuries people all over the world knew of, but did not understand, its power to treat headache, fever and inflammation.

Enter chemistry. In Germany in the 1820's, the magic chemical was isolated and named salicin. Later in the century, acetylsalicylic acid was developed, but no one knew what to do with it. Meanwhile, people still took a rude form of the drug that, they said, burned in their stomachs like fire ants.

Then a young chemist at Bayer and Company tried acetylsalicylic acid on his arthritic father. Aspirin was born.

Why it was named aspirin is a subject of debate. One theory holds that the word was derived from *Spiraea*, the plant from which salicin was actually isolated. Aspirin first appeared in stores at the turn of the century.

Although paracetamol does reduce fever and pain, it doesn't reduce inflammation. What's more, it can't help prevent heart attacks as an aspirin every other day may.

2. Aspirin substitutes with ibuprofen can reduce inflammation considerably, and may be somewhat effective against heart attacks, but they also may irritate the stomach (although somewhat less than aspirin). To reduce inflammation, ulcer sufferers can take aspirin that is specially coated to dissolve in the small intestine, rather than in the stomach.

Caution: Children and teenagers should not take aspirin when they have a virus because of the danger of Reye's syndrome, a rare but often fatal disease linked to viral infections and aspirin. Paracetamol and ibuprofen are quite safe alternatives.

Asthma

1. If someone is having an asthma attack, he will cough, wheeze and have difficulty breathing; reassure him and try to keep him calm.

2. To ease breathing, have him sit up and lean slightly forward, resting on his elbows. Or turn on the hot water in the bathroom and have him sit and breathe the moist air.

3. Give him his prescribed medication along with various liquids to prevent dehydration.

4. If the medication doesn't bring immediate relief, take him – quickly but calmly – to the nearest hospital emergency unit.

EXERCISE AS TREATMENT

Although some type of physical exercise is usually recommended for asthmatics, if it is too strenuous it can trigger an attack – especially outdoors during cold weather or spring.

Indoor swimming is best for most asthmatics. Aerobic exercise is also good; a physically fit person gets more oxygen into his body – important during an asthma attack.

An asthmatic should begin his exercises with a slow 15-minute warm-up and finish with an equally slow cool-down. (See *Warm-up & cool-down exercises*, p.224.)

To help keep his airways open, he should exercise in one- to two-minute spurts, breathing through his nose to filter the air somewhat.

Atomizer

1. If your atomizer gets clogged, unscrew it from the bottle, raise it, and let the perfume drain out of the stem.

Immerse the atomizer in water. Pump a few times, take it out of the water, and pump until no more water sprays out.

2. Any small spray bottle, available in pharmacies, can be a short-term substitute for a perfume atomizer. But be sure not to leave perfume in a plastic container; the plastic will interact with its ingredients.

Attics

1. Think hard – what's stored in your attic? If you can't remember, it's time to take stock. Make a list and post it near the entrance. From then on, whenever you store or remove items from the attic, note the changes.

2. If your attic is unfinished, create a floor by nailing down two or more plywood panels. To support walking and storage safely, the panels should be at least 20 millimetres thick and span at least three ceiling joists.

3. No electrical wiring in the attic? Battery-powered lights, found in most hardware stores, provide an easy means of illumination.

4. Short on cupboard space? Install a wooden rod or a metal conduit between rafters, for hanging out-of-season clothing. Drill through the rod and secure it with lag bolts. Or use pipe straps or pipe clamps to hold it against the rafters.

Attic ventilation

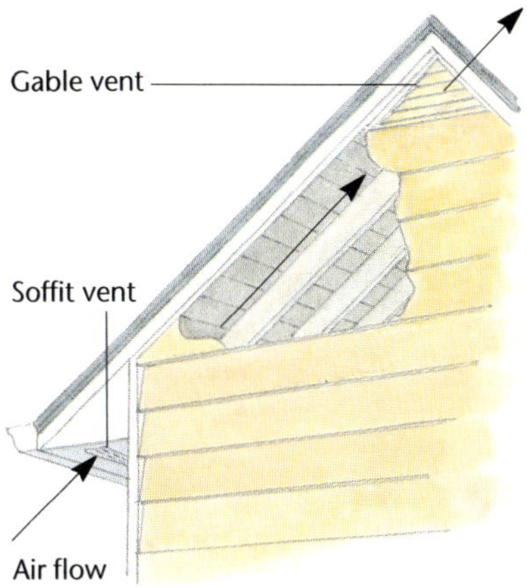

An unventilated attic can cause serious moisture problems in the walls and ceilings of the entire house. To increase overall airflow, use an electric fan at least 500 millimetres across. Set it at the entrance of the attic, so that it draws air up from the house. If the opening is a ceiling cutout, lay the fan across it.

LONG-TERM IMPROVEMENTS

You can buy soffit vents, or you can make your own from screening. With a jigsaw, cut a round hole in the soffit between rafter and joist. Cut a piece of fine mesh about 15 millimetres larger on all sides than the opening, and staple it over the hole. For a neat appearance, frame it with wood.

A cupola on the roof ridge should be more than an attractive detail; it can help exhaust hot, stale air. Cut an opening in the ridge (but not the ridge board) beneath it.

To further improve the airflow, you can install an electric ventilating unit in the cupola.

Keep all vents clean and free of debris. Gable vents are a favourite place for birds and wasps to build nests; staple a piece of fine mesh over the exterior of these vents to keep them clear.

Avocados

1. You can keep a bowl of mashed avocado from darkening by burying the pit in it until time to serve.

Or press a piece of plastic wrap flat on the surface of the bowl and smooth out any air bubbles.

2. To keep sliced or cubed avocado from discolouring, sprinkle with lemon or lime juice. You can coat larger pieces with softened butter, margarine or mayonnaise before refrigerating; they should keep fresh for three to four days.

3. Avocados ripen almost twice as fast if sealed in a brown paper bag and stored in a warm (not hot) place. For even faster results, put an apple in the bag, too. Even a cut avocado will ripen this way, but first coat its cut surfaces as described above.

Awnings

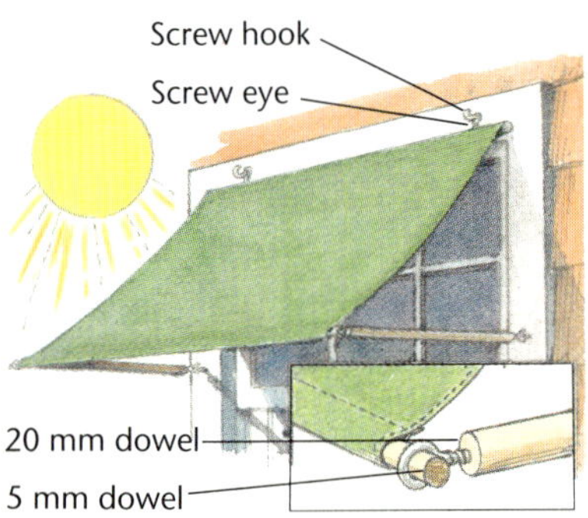

Instead of an old-fashioned, pulley-operated awning, install a single piece of canvas attached to a wooden pole at top and bottom. Secure the top above your window with hooks, and attach the lower pole to the wall, as shown. Or you can create a natural awning by constructing a trellis above your window and growing a flowering vine or ivy on it.

B

Babies' names

The name you choose for your child must last a lifetime, so it had better be pleasing – to him and to you.

1. Make sure the initials don't spell something which sounds strange (the American general, Ulysses S. Grant, changed his name from Hiram Ulysses at West Point because he was tired of being called HUG).

2. Think of the possible nicknames.

3. Try to imagine calling the name at the top of your voice to summon the child home.

4. If you'd like a namesake but don't want to be known as Big Mary or Big Bill, give the child a variation of your name, perhaps a foreign version.

5. Choose a suitable name that can grow with the child and continue to give pleasure at every stage of the namebearer's life.

6. Vary the number of syllables to create a pleasant rhythm.

7. If you select a poetic or unusual name, give the child a choice: a commonplace middle name.

Baby fitness

As infants develop their basic co-ordination and reflexes in their first few months, parents can provide soothing and stimulating activities to help them. Try not to push your baby; her own movements will let you know what's good for her.

Even in the baby's first days, eye-head and eye-hand co-ordination can be helped a lot by brightly coloured mobiles and toys to look at, as well as friendly people to interact with. After the first month, you can foster body awareness and confidence simply by holding your baby in different positions. Carefully support your child in the bath so that she will enjoy the water and start to become aware of the feeling of her muscles.

You can massage your baby. Use no more pressure than your hand's weight with the palm open. Stroke smoothly outward in slightly circular motions; this relaxes tension, soothes cramps, and lets your baby develop a sense of her body.

To stretch and strengthen your baby's arms and legs, place her on her back; raise one arm smoothly above her head while bringing the other down by her side, then reverse the action. Always make sure your baby's head is well supported.

Keeping her legs straight, gently bend one knee toward her stomach, then straighten the leg again. Alternate legs – and let her participate as much as she wants to.

Backaches

Most people will be stricken with back pain of some sort or other at some time in their lives. In South Africa, millions of working days are lost each year because of it.

Fortunately, however, back pain seldom lasts for more than a few days or weeks, and often goes away on its own. If the pain persists, you should see a doctor in case there is a serious underlying cause.

Back pain usually has a simple physical cause – such as inflamed or strained muscles, restricted joints or pressure on nerves. It can keep recurring, and may not necessarily be helped at all by conventional treatment with painkillers, such as aspirin and paracetamol, or anti-inflammatory drugs, such as steroids.

To avoid the cost and discomfort of treating back pain, here are some useful tips on how to avoid it:

1. Avoid any sudden strain; try to exercise regularly to limber the back and strengthen its supporting abdominal muscles.

2. If you sit for long periods, make sure your back is properly supported. Place a small roll in the arch of your lower spine (at belt height) to maintain its normal S-curve. (Stuff the inside of a paper towel roll with rags and strengthen it with masking tape.)

3. When lifting, never bend down from the waist – lower and raise yourself at the knees.
4. Balance items you carry evenly on both sides of your body and hold them close – or use a backpack.
5. Sleep on your back if possible, with knees raised on a pillow.
6. For a firm bed, place a bedboard between the mattress and the box spring. (Cut a sheet of 20-millimetre plywood, 25 millimetres smaller all around than your mattress, and sand its edges.)

TREATMENT

1. Limit activity or stay in bed for at least 48 hours.
2. Depending on which works better for you, apply either heat or a cold pack for 15 minutes at a time every couple of hours over a period of two days. (Keep an athlete's soft cold pack in the freezer or use a bag of frozen peas; both will mould easily to your back.)
3. Aspirin or ibuprofen will help combat both pain and inflammation; paracetamol, only pain.
4. To minimize chronic minor back pain, tip your pelvis back, then forward, until you find the position of least pain; maintain it.

Back exercises

Strengthening and stretching all the muscles of your lower back will help you to prevent lower back strain. The exercises which follow progress from gentle to strenuous. Do only what's comfortable; stop exercising if you feel any pain. If you've had back problems, consult your doctor.

PELVIC TILT

Lie on your back with both of your knees bent. Keeping your spine against the floor, squeeze your buttock muscles as hard as you can, pull your stomach muscles in, flatten the small of your back to the floor, and hold for five seconds. Your pelvis will tilt slightly upward of its own accord: don't try to raise it. Repeat 10 times.

CAT STRETCH

Kneel on your hands and knees. Then arch your upper back slowly upward, contract your stomach muscles, and let your head drop. Hold the position for five seconds. Follow this by raising your head and reversing the action, until you return to the kneeling position. Try to avoid pushing your pelvis forward to create a swayback. Repeat five to 10 times.

HIP ROLL

Lie on your back, both arms outstretched for support. Raise your knees toward your chest and then roll them gently from side to side, keeping your shoulders on the floor if you can. Roll 10 to 20 times.

BACKWARD LEG RAISES

Lie flat on your stomach, resting your head on folded arms. Keeping your pelvis on the floor, slowly raise one leg from the hip until your foot is 15 centimetres above the floor. Repeat five to 10 times with each leg.

SINGLE LEG RAISES

Lie on your back, knees bent, arms crossed under your head, and both elbows touching the floor. Straighten one leg, then slowly raise it as high as you can. Hold it five seconds, then lower slowly. Repeat five to 10 times.

DIAGONAL REACH

Start on your hands and knees. Slowly extend your right arm in front of you; at the same time, raise your left leg straight out behind you. Stretch and hold for five seconds; then return to your original position. Do the same with your left arm and right leg. Repeat 10 times.

Cat stretch: Arch your upper back upward while contracting your stomach and letting your head drop. Hold for five seconds.

Then raise your head and reverse the action until you return to the kneeling position. Avoid pushing your pelvis forward.

IN TIMES GONE BY

Victorian backaches

Consider the Victorian corset. Made of heavy canvas, with vertical stays of whalebone or steel, it encased a woman in a rigid cage from hip to bust. Many little girls got their first one at age three or four; by adolescence they were wearing adult versions, tightly laced up the back to achieve something close to Scarlett O'Hara's 42-centimetre waist.

Ladies of the time were thought to be so delicate that their muscles couldn't hold them upright without assistance. The corset made this myth a reality. By the time girls were ready for adult corsets, their back and abdominal muscles had atrophied so badly that many couldn't sit or stand without one.

Backpacks

To make a temporary backpack for carrying your lunch on a short hike, bringing home various treasures from a backpacking adventure or transporting other light objects, just close the waist of a long-sleeved tracksuit or jacket with pins or string.

Knot the sleeve ends securely together to form a strap. Then stuff your cargo inside the makeshift backpack, slip the strap over your shoulders, and you're on your way.

Backseat drivers

To deal with one of these pests:

1. Try using humour ("Hey, do you want to *cause* an accident?") or distraction ("Please add up the kilometres to the turnoff").

2. Turn up the volume on the radio or tape deck, without saying it's to drown out unwanted advice.

3. Sing while you drive. You may even inspire your passenger to sing along with you.

4. Take the other passengers aside before setting out and ask them to keep up an active conversation.

Bad breath

1. Brush your teeth with a paste of bicarbonate of soda and water to keep your breath fresh. Bicarbonate of soda neutralizes the acids in which the bacteria that cause bad breath and tooth decay flourish. (A mouthwash of hydrogen peroxide and water is also antibacterial.)

2. Chew fresh parsley after eating. It contains an antiseptic that kills bacteria in the mouth. It's effective against garlic and onions too, as are mint leaves and cloves. (Suck, don't chew, the latter.)

3. Floss daily to dislodge decaying food particles. If your gums are red, swollen and sore, see your dentist.

Bait & switch

You see a bargain price advertised for a specific product, and so you go into the store to purchase it. There you discover that the advertised item is out of stock, but the store just happens to have a slightly more expensive version.

That's called bait and switch, and it's illegal unless the ad specifies that only a limited supply is available. Look for such a disclaimer before rushing off to the store. If the advertisement doesn't include one and you encounter what is clearly a bait-and-switch technique, call your local Consumer Council.

Bait and switch also rears its head in home improvements. You get an amazingly low estimate, only to find at the last minute that important and costly details have been left out.

Never commit yourself until you have a written estimate from several contractors detailing the work to be done, listing the materials to be used and supplied by the contractor, and setting a limit on how much the cost may exceed the estimate.

Ask each contractor for the names of people in nearby areas for whom he has done similar work; then call and check out the references.

Baking ingredients

Margarine or vegetable fat generally works as well as butter in most cakes and quick breads, although the finished product may look and taste somewhat different.

If you're out of cake flour, replace each cup called for with one cup minus two tablespoons of sifted all-purpose flour. For one cup of self-raising flour, substitute one cup all-purpose flour plus 1½ teaspoons baking powder and ½ teaspoon salt.

Here are some other substitutes:

□ For 30 grams of baking chocolate: mix three tablespoons cocoa powder with one tablespoon softened butter, margarine or sunflower oil.

□ For one cup of whole milk: ½ cup evaporated milk plus ½ cup water.

□ For a whole egg: two yolks mixed with one tablespoon water.

□ For one teaspoon of baking powder: ¼ teaspoon bicarbonate of soda and ½ teaspoon cream of tartar. Or use ¼ teaspoon bicarbonate of soda plus ½ cup buttermilk or sour cream (omit ½ cup of another liquid from the recipe).

□ For one cup of granulated sugar: one cup honey or maple syrup (omit ¼ cup of the liquid that is called for in the recipe).

□ For ½ cup of brown sugar: ½ cup white sugar plus two tablespoons golden syrup. Keep in mind, however, that both this and the granulated sugar substitute will tend to make your baked goods heavier.

Ballpoint pen

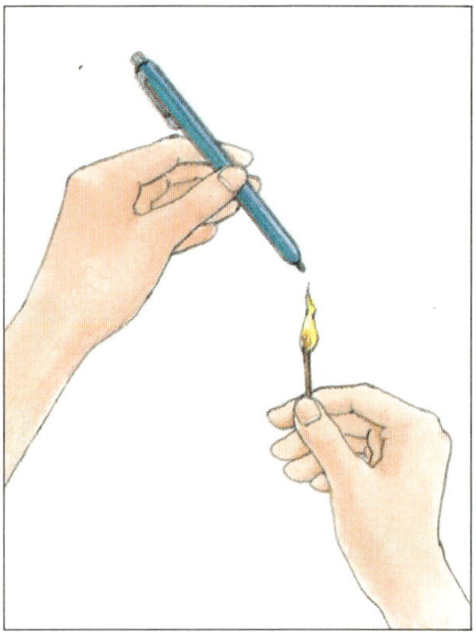

Has your ballpoint pen clogged up? Get the ink flowing by holding a lighted match under the point. Keep rotating the pen so that the plastic doesn't melt.

Bandages

Bandages are useful for treating a variety of injuries and conditions. They hold dressings or splints in place, keep a wound clean and free of infection, maintain pressure on a dressing to help control bleeding, and provide support for an injured limb. In an emergency you can improvise a bandage from cotton, calico and almost any other clean material.

1. Before you begin, ensure that the injured part is supported in the position in which it is likely to remain.
2. Apply the bandage with sufficient firmness to control bleeding or restrict movement, but not so tightly that it ends up blocking the patient's circulation. Check regularly to make sure the bandage doesn't become too tight as the tissues swell. If you're dealing with an injured limb, there's an easy way of monitoring circulation: simply leave fingernails or toenails exposed and press a nail until it becomes white. If it quickly regains its pink colour after pressure is released, it means the blood is circulating satisfactorily. If not, check the bandage.
3. As a general rule, apply a bandage only when the patient is sitting or lying down.
4. Stock your first aid cabinet with a variety of prepared bandages in different sizes: plasters in varying shapes, rolls of gauze in 2,5- and five-centimetre widths, gauze pads, one-centimetre-wide surgical adhesive tape and several widths of elastic wrapping bandage. This assortment should equip you to bandage minor wounds and provide protection in more serious situations until medical help arrives.
5. Change bandages at least once a day, or whenever soiled or wet. After a week, most cuts will have healed enough to dispense with plasters.

MINOR CUTS AND WOUNDS

1. For less serious cuts and wounds that are bleeding very little or have stopped bleeding altogether, use a plaster. Choose one of the right size and shape for the injury, and ensure that the gauze covers the entire wound, or you could reopen the cut when removing the plaster. If the injury is on a finger, elbow or toe, rather use a flexible fabric bandage.

After cleaning and drying the area, wrap the plaster fairly tightly to close blood vessels. Within an hour, clotting will prevent further bleeding and you can take off the first dressing. Replace it with a clean one, more loosely applied.

2. Use a plaster to draw together the sides of a small open cut so that it will heal with the minimum of scar tissue. Apply one side first, then tug gently as you apply the other side while ensuring that the edges of the cut are aligned. Don't pull too hard or the edges of the cut will curl inwards.

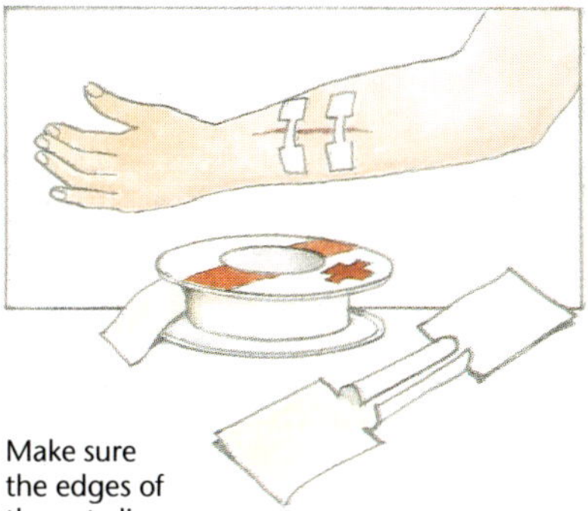

Make sure the edges of the cut align before applying the bandage.

However if the cut is more than 2,5 centimetres long, or the patient has a deep cut across a joint or a cut that is potentially disfiguring – for example, on the lip, nose or eyebrow – then consult a doctor as soon as possible. Apply a plaster in the meantime.
3. Scrapes need be covered for only a day or two, by which time they will probably have formed scabs. A scab has been described as nature's bandage: it seals the wound while allowing air to reach it. Elbow and knee scrapes are best bandaged with a gauze pad held loosely in place by two strips of adhesive tape so that the joint can bend freely. Gauze may stick to an oozing abrasion; to remove it, soak the area in clean water for a few minutes until the gauze can be pulled away easily and painlessly. Then gently pat the area dry.
4. Bandages can also be used to relieve the pain of minor joint injuries such as twists, sprains and bruised fingers. Once the doctor assures you that the injury isn't serious, provide a wrapping of gauze to support the joint and to remind you not to move it. Otherwise use an elastic wrapping bandage, following your doctor's instructions or those on the package. You should support a bruised finger with a tongue depressor, held firmly in place by a four-centimetre-wide strip of gauze wrapped crisscross around the finger and secured by a wrap and tie at the wrist.

Basting

1. Spare yourself the nuisance of picking out stitches; try basting with water-soluble thread, which disappears under a steam iron.
2. For seams, use a glue stick; apply dabs at five-centimetre intervals to join the seam allowances.
3. For trims, zips and pockets, lay a basting tape sticky side down along a seam; lift off the paper covering and position the other fabric on top. (Don't worry; both glue and tape wash out.)

Bathing on camping trips

Take along a waterproof vinyl bag for heating water by solar energy. Fill it in the morning, set it in the sun, and you'll have warm water for a sponge bath by evening. The plastic bladder from a boxed wine dispenser works well. And it comes complete with tap.

Bathroom safety

An ordinary family bathroom can be a hazardous place if you don't exercise care.
1. Are you scalded in your shower when someone turns on the cold tap or flushes the toilet? Install a mixing valve with a built-in regulator.
2. Be sure not to touch the light switch or operate any electrical appliance when your hands or feet are wet, as you could receive a shock.
3. At all times avoid taking electric heaters, radios or other mains appliances into the bathroom – there's good reason for caution in this wet, potentially dangerous environment.
4. For safety's sake, ensure that a locked bathroom door can be opened from the outside. If there's a bolt on the inside, remove it.
5. Protect yourself from falls on slippery surfaces with carpeting or rub-

ber-backed non-skid mats on the floor and suction-type mats or non-skid tiles in the bathtub and shower.
6. If there's an elderly or handicapped person living in the house, affix grab bars securely to the wall at convenient locations beside the bath, shower and toilet.
7. Make sure that the shower enclosure is made from shatterproof glass.
8. Don't store prescription drugs in an unlocked bathroom cabinet; even ordinary headache tablets can be deadly to young children if taken in large enough quantities.
9. Store cleaning materials out of children's reach.

Bathtub drains

Most of us have had to deal with clogged bathtub drains at some time of our lives, and wished there were an easier way. There is – it's called preventive maintenance. Try and get into the habit of removing and cleaning the stopper assembly now and again. Don't wait until the outflow becomes completely blocked before taking action.
1. You might be able to clear a blocked drain by using a plunger to dislodge the debris (the vacuum will be increased if you close off the overflow drain with a piece of cloth).
2. If that doesn't work, insert a piece of thin, flexible wire into the drain hole or overflow opening and jiggle it to dislodge the blockage.
3. A chemical drain cleaner may help to reduce the build-up of soap and stray hairs in awkward-to-reach areas but don't overdo it or the powerful solvent could corrode the system.
4. Always rinse the drain thoroughly after using a chemical cleaner and make sure that you follow the manufacturer's instructions.

Bathtub rings

To avoid bathtub rings, don't use oily bath preparations; use a water softener if you live in a hard water area; be sure to rinse the bathtub immediately after bathing.

If a ring does form, wipe it off with undiluted ammonia (wear rubber gloves) or a wet sponge generously sprinkled with bicarbonate of soda; rinse clean and wipe dry. For a more stubborn stain, scour with automatic dishwashing detergent or rub with a cloth dipped in vinegar.

Batteries

1. To avoid buying batteries that have been on the store shelf too long, buy from an outlet that has a high turnover – a toy store, for example. Pick from the centre of the stack.
2. Shop for the best price; there are few real differences among brands.
3. Choose zinc carbon batteries for clocks, torches and calculators. Use heavy-duty zinc carbons for small radios and penlights; save alkaline batteries for items such as tape recorders, photo flashes and toys.
4. Store batteries away from hot spots in the house or car and keep them out of the sun. Best of all, store them in the refrigerator, wrapped in a plastic bag to keep moisture out. Let them warm to room temperature before using.
5. Remove batteries from items that you hardly ever use. Bundle them together with a rubber band and store in a plastic sandwich bag. Don't allow them to touch metal objects during storage or they may lose power.
6. When putting torches into a backpack, put a slip of cardboard between torch contacts and battery to prevent it being switched on in the pack.
7. If you can avoid it, don't mix old batteries with new. New ones can put stress on old ones, causing them to leak acid.

Beauty creams

Are you spending a fortune on basic cosmetics? Why not make them at home instead, using simple ingredients that are readily available from your local pharmacy? The only other things you'll need are a stove, a double boiler and a few pretty jars for your home-made cosmetics.

Your skin type will determine the choice of beauty preparation: an oily skin will probably need no more than a light moisturizing lotion to protect it from the elements, whereas a dry skin requires a dense, oily cream.

Most of the beauty creams we buy in shops are based on emulsions – tiny globules of oils or waxy substances suspended in water.

Most common among them are lanolin, a wax that combines with water to hold moisture near the skin; glycerine, an oily liquid with very good emollient (skin-softening) properties; mineral oil, a lubricator and softener; beeswax, a mixer and emulsifier; and Vaseline, a softener.

Try these recipes:

LIGHT MOISTURIZER

This is really the easiest one of all. Simply mix equal parts of glycerine and rosewater or any herbal water. To turn it into a soothing, pleasant smelling aftershave lotion, add a dash of witch hazel or bay rum.

SKIN-SOFTENING BODY CREAM

Mix 250 millilitres (one cup) Vaseline and 12 millilitres (2½ teaspoons) lanolin in the top of a double boiler and heat gently; you'll notice small globules of lanolin forming on top of the melted mixture.

Warm 500 millilitres (two cups) water and five millilitres (one teaspoon) glycerine in a separate pan, then combine the two mixtures, adding the water to the oil. Allow to cool. When it starts to solidify, add a few drops of a non-oil-based perfume or essence. When completely cool, drain off excess water and put the cream in a jar. This recipe should yield about 250 millilitres (one cup) of cream.

CLEANSING CREAM

Put 500 millilitres (two cups) mineral oil and 125 millilitres (½ cup) beeswax into the top of a double boiler and heat gently until the beeswax melts. Allow the mixture to cool to 500°C. In a separate pan, heat about 250 millilitres (one cup) water to

500°C and add 22 millilitres (1½ tablespoons) powdered borax, stirring gently until it dissolves. Then slowly pour the water and borax mixture into the oil and wax mixture, stirring constantly to mix.

Cool the mixture until it starts to solidify, then pour it into jars. This will make about 750 millilitres (three cups) cleansing cream.

Bedding plants

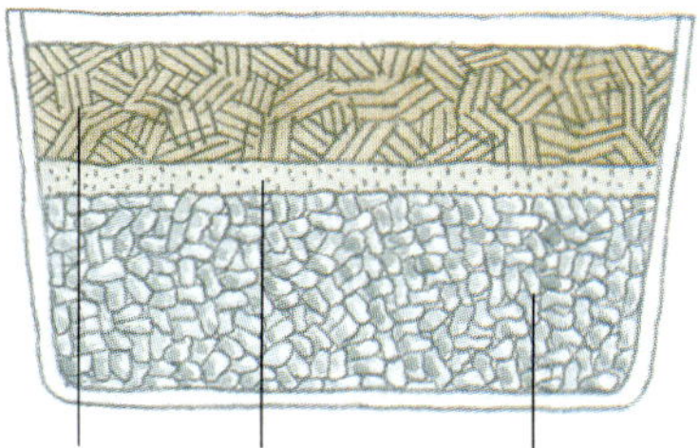

Instead of consigning all bedding plants to a fixed place in the garden, make them portable so that they can do double duty or more. Let them brighten a party on your patio one night and adorn your front steps the next morning.

1. To save strain, choose containers that are strong but light, such as fibreglass pots or ones with wheels; even a large timber tub is easy to move if it's set on casters. Or you can use an old wooden wheelbarrow; its big wheels make it both portable and very decorative.

2. To lighten the load of a large container, fill it to within 25 centimetres of the top with styrene chips or a similar foam-based packing material; sprinkle this with a five-centimetre layer of cat litter for drainage, and top with potting soil.

3. To save further kilograms, you can blend three parts of a soilless potting mixture with one part potting soil and one part peat moss.

Beds

Company coming and you don't have enough beds in the house? If the couch alone won't solve the problem, consider using sleeping bags, air mattresses or pads of thick foam rubber. All are easy to store when not in use.

A futon – a cotton-filled, pliable mattress – is another alternative, although more expensive. You may consider it worth the cost because it can be shaped into a low couch for extra seating when it is not being used as a bed.

To make a double bed, place two air mattresses or futons side by side and hold them together with a fitted double sheet. (Foam rubber is not rigid enough for this.)

For more comfort and to prevent sliding during the night, place temporary beds on a thick rug.

For babies, a playpen will do. Or take a drawer from a chest of drawers and pad it, checking to see that there are no splinters in the wood. A third choice is a padded laundry basket.

Bedsores

1. An air mattress – or even a thick sheepskin pad over a standard mattress – relieves pressure and prevents bedsores. Pads or pillows under sensitive points help too.

2. Be sure to change a bedridden person's position every two hours.

3. Moisturizer and 100 milligrams of vitamin C, taken every day, help sustain proper skin tone.

4. Three 85-gram servings of protein a day help maintain muscle tissue and accelerate healing if bedsores begin to develop.

5. Bedsores are easier to prevent than to treat. If you notice any red spots on the skin, keep pressure off the area and call a doctor.

Bedtime rituals

Most children love bedtime rituals. They ease the transition from play to sleep and provide a reassuring pattern. But what happens when the pattern must be broken?

1. If both parents will be absent, the person left in charge should know the routine. List bedtime activities on a big chart and instruct the child to help the adult tick them off.

2. Before leaving, why not tape-record a special good night. A simple, "We love you, sweet dreams, see you soon" in the parents' own voices can be very reassuring.

3. When special guests visit, find ways to include them in the ritual. A guest might pour the milk, turn down the covers, tell a little story.

IN TIMES GONE BY

The evolution of the bed

For most of us, a bed is not only the place where our lives begin and end, but also the place where we spend about one-third of the time between those milestones.

Early beds were probably little more than pits lined with leaves, reeds, or other natural cushions. Later, to keep out crawling insects and animals, latticed thongs were attached to an elevated wooden frame and topped with skins. The ancient Egyptians went much further; their beds were usually topped with a mat, linen sheets and woven blankets. A footboard even prevented sleepers from sliding down their beds, which were tilted upward at the head. A separate hard headrest protected the coiffure.

It was not until about 3,500 BC, in the royal palaces at Sumer in Babylonia, that the bed got its own room. Such luxury, however, was reserved for the master of the house. He occupied the bedroom; his wife, children, servants and guests slept elsewhere – on couches or the floor.

The Greeks were the first to use headboards, against which the wealthy laid embroidered silk pillows. The Romans, who were good farmers, invented the first true mattress: a sack stuffed with straw, wool or feathers. Water beds, developed in the early 19th century for hospital patients with bone fractures or bedsores, made a big splash in the 1960's and are still popular, along with bunk beds and other variations.

4. If you're caught away from home without a beloved teddy bear, improvise a floppy animal from a pillow, or try stuffing knotted socks or a soft turtleneck shirt to make a substitute cuddle object.

Bedtime stories

Instead of reading from a storybook, try improvisation. One parent begins a story and after a few minutes turns the narrative over to the other, who, after a few more turns in the plot, lets the kids pick it up.

Most children's favourite themes are invariably familiar people or animals, who may live in other worlds but are actually their family, friends and pets and, coincidentally, even have their names.

A parent who's away from home can participate in the story hour by telephone or, prior to leaving, can tape-record several segments for the stay-at-homes to complete.

An alternative: prepare a picture story about your trip or your dinner out. Make your own drawings or cut out illustrations from magazines and then write a simple text to tell what Mommy or Daddy is doing.

Bedwetting

1. Don't scold or punish your child for a wet bed; it will only make him feel guilty. Be patient; praise him for his dry nights and encourage him to keep a record of them.
2. Restrict fluids before bedtime, but only within reason.
3. Wake the child for a trip to the bathroom before you go to bed. Or try setting an alarm clock to remind him to get up himself.
4. A shower curtain makes a good mattress cover.
5. If bedwetting persists, you should consult a paediatrician.

Beetles

1. Beetles, termites and spiders may come into the house on firewood. Vacuum them up and destroy them. Keep your firewood outside and away from the house. Inspect each log carefully.
2. Flying insects head for bright lights at night. To keep them at bay replace white outdoor bulbs with yellow ones, and use screen doors.
3. Carpet beetles can damage many kinds of fabrics. Thoroughly vacuum rugs, dark corners, mouldings and under furniture, then remove and dispose of the vacuum bag. Clean pet bedding regularly and seal all floor cracks. Store clothes (dry-clean them first) in insect-proof bags or boxes, along with some mothballs or flakes.
4. Garden beetles can be controlled; clean up debris to remove winter hiding places. Before resorting to insecticides, remove as many beetles as possible by hand. Wear rubber gloves to protect yourself from the secretions of some beetles as these can cause skin irritations. Try planting beetle-repellent plants, such as mint, among your vegetables.

To protect developing melons and squash, cover with paper bags, stapled or pinned shut. Or use pantihose sections tied off at both ends.

Bellows

Having trouble getting a campfire started? Use your lungs as a bellows. Blow through a hollow tent pole section or the rubber tubing from a first aid kit. Both will enable you to direct and concentrate the air where it is needed most.

Hold the tent pole section with a sock, glove or washcloth to protect your hands from the heat, and blow through a cupped hand to avoid direct contact with your lips. Blow gently so that the fire doesn't flare in your face – and *don't* breathe in through the tube.

Bicycle chains

1. Paraffin is the best cleaner for a greasy bicycle chain. To keep the chain from squeaking, clean it every two months and lubricate it with a lightweight bicycle oil or a spray lubricant designed for the purpose.
2. If your chain breaks and you can't fix it right away, lower the seat and push along with your feet.

Bicycle lock

You can make a lock from two metres of vinyl-covered steel cable, two U-bolts and a padlock, available from most hardware stores.

At each end of the cable, make a loop and secure it firmly with a U-bolt; strip or epoxy the threads so that the nut can't be removed (see *Nuts & bolts*, p.145).

Run the cable through the frame and wheels and around the bike rack or a sturdy post. Padlock the loops together.

If you must leave your bike unlocked, remove the handlebars or front wheel and take it with you.

Bicycle riding

1. Keep a whistle on a chain around your neck and use it instead of a hooter; it's louder and shriller.
2. Having some trouble climbing hills? Maybe you're hunching over the handlebars; this constricts your breathing. Sit up straight instead.
3. On wet roads brake lightly now and then to whisk water off your brakes – especially after you've gone through a puddle and before you start down a hill.
4. If you skid, don't try to move your wheel; be sure to keep it in whatever direction you're going. Similarly, on a loose surface, let the bike drift the way it wants.
5. In the country, sharp curves often have loose gravel and holes. Brake to reduce speed before you get to a curve, not while you're on the loose surface. Keep as far to the left as possible to avoid cars that may suddenly move into your lane as they round the corner.
6. Consider lining your cycling helmet with felt in cold weather. For further warmth, why not try pushing a thick, folded section of newspaper under your shirt to help insulate you against cold winds?

Bicycle tyre

You can repair a tyre – in no time at all – with two kitchen spoons, some fine sandpaper, contact cement, talcum powder and a thin piece of rubber or soft plastic.

For patches, cut small squares of rubber from an old tyre tube or bathing cap. Coat one side with contact cement and let it dry.

Remove the wheel and push in the tyre with your thumbs just enough to angle the spoons, 12,5 to 18 centimetres apart, under its edge. Work them around, pulling the edge of the tyre over the rim.

Take the tube out of the tyre and look for the puncture. Check inside the tyre for any sharp stones or debris. Put your ear to the tube; can you hear the air escape? If you can't find the leak, inflate the tube and submerge it in water; bubbles will locate the hole.

Dry the tube and rough up the area around the hole with sandpaper. Coat it with a reliable contact cement and apply the patch, sticky side down. Sprinkle talcum powder liberally over the patched area so that the tube won't stick to the tyre wall.

If you inflate the tube a little, it will be easier to put back in the tyre. Begin remounting the tyre by first inserting the air valve into the rim, then work the tyre back onto the rim with your thumbs. (If this proves to be difficult, you can use the spoons – but with care. They could well puncture your newly repaired tube.)

When the tyre is back on the rim, inflate it and replace the wheel.

Bill paying

1. Many banks offer bill-paying services to their customers. Discuss the procedure to be followed with your bank. You can then use your computer to communicate with the bank: call in your merchant code numbers and the amounts to be paid.
2. Pay your bills at the office (on your own time, of course); you might even have them sent there.
3. Put everything you need in a large envelope and take it to a pleasant environment – a park or tearoom.

Binoculars

Want to see something far off more clearly? Close one eye and bring your hand, shaped into a circle, up to the other eye. Or look through one end of a cardboard paper towel roll or similar tube. The small channelled opening acts as a lens.

Birdcalls

1. You can recognize many birds by their calls – sunbirds, starlings and doves, for example. If you can't, use a field guide to identify them.
2. A good way to attract birds is to make squeaking noises by kissing the back of your hand.
3. The time to hear most birds sing is during the breeding season. If you are really keen, purchase a cassette tape of local birdcalls and study it, together with a field guide. Most birds are quiet at midday and in midsummer.

Bird feeder

1. Make a funnel to load a bird feeder by cutting off the bottom of a plastic milk jug. Unscrew its cap and hold it upside down when you're ready to fill the feeder with seed.
2. Fill a nylon-mesh bag, the kind onions or grapes are packaged in, with bread crumbs.
3. Tie a string around the top of a pine cone; roll the pine cone first in room-temperature bacon fat or peanut butter and then in birdseed or bread crumbs.

Birds as pests

Birds can devastate a fruit or berry crop in a twinkling. If you don't want to go to the trouble of covering your trees or bushes with the netting that's normally used to thwart them, try one or more of these tactics:
1. Let your cat wander loose among the trees or in the berry patch. Tie a bell to its collar so that it won't bring home any dead birds.
2. Put a stuffed animal – a teddy bear, for example – in the branches. Move it every few days; birds quickly get used to stationary objects.
3. Plant a mulberry tree as a trap crop. Birds go for mulberries before

hitting other fruits. Plant it well away from the house, however, since its fruit is messy.

4. Staple brown paper bags around bunches of ripening grapes; cut a vent hole at each corner.

Birth certificate

Keep a copy of your birth certificate in your home or office, as well as in your safe deposit box.

To get a copy, take your identity book to the nearest office of the Department of Home Affairs. A computer printout of your birth certificate can be supplied on request. If you do not have an identity book, you can apply for a copy of the certificate, which may take some time to arrive.

If no birth certificate exists for you – either because your birth was not registered or because the records were destroyed – apply to the Department of Home Affairs for late registration. You will have to provide some proof of identity, for example, a baptism certificate or early school records. If you are 15 years of age or older, you will have to apply for an identity book at the same time.

Biscuits

1. Let crumbly biscuit dough – the kind that is made with a lot of butter or margarine – rest and soften for an hour at room temperature. It will then be quite easy to roll.

2. To keep biscuits from burning, bake them at 1°C lower than the recipe calls for and add a minute or two to the baking time. As extra insurance, doublepan the biscuits: stack two baking sheets together with the biscuits on the top sheet.

3. Need to soften tough biscuits? Put them in an airtight tin or jar with a piece of fresh bread or a wedge of apple. Or wrap a wet paper towel in aluminium foil and place it in the tin on top of the biscuits.

4. To keep biscuits crisp, cool them on wire racks and transfer at once to an airtight canister.

5. When the children ask for biscuits and the tin is empty, improvise by baking bits of marshmallow on crackers. Make them even better by adding some chocolate chips. Store extras in the freezer.

6. Use the crumbs at the bottom of the jar as a topping for ice cream.

7. To pack biscuits for mailing, use unsalted popcorn in a cardboard box (fill it to the top). It's great padding. Just mix the biscuits in loosely.

Bites

In South Africa, people are probably more exposed to bites than they are in most countries around the world. Spiders, snakes, ticks, mites, beetles, mosquitoes, dogs and even sharks are on the long list of potential offenders.

Most bites are not serious, but if you are in any doubt about the consequences, be sure to consult a doctor as soon as possible.

If someone has been bitten by an animal or by another person, your first priority is to stop any severe bleeding. Then wash the wound thoroughly with soap and water.

Rinse under running water for five minutes and cover with a sterile dressing or clean cloth.

To prevent the risk of infection, be sure to immobilize the area of the bite with a bandage or a splint, and take the victim to the nearest doctor or hospital emergency unit for appropriate antibiotics and possible antitetanus treatment.

Black tie

When an invitation says "black tie", the only article of a man's attire (other than a white shirt) that doesn't have to be black is – the bow tie! Whatever the tie's colour, the cummerbund should match.

In summer he may substitute a white, print or solid colour dinner jacket. A woman can wear a long gown or a dressy short one.

A man can always rent a tuxedo. At the end of the year and during the festive season, when there are usually a lot of social functions, dances, graduations and weddings taking place – you may need to book one well in advance. To buy a tuxedo at less than the cost of a new one, try secondhand clothes stores. One advantage: the adjustable-waist trousers guarantee an adequate fit.

Bleach spots

1. If the garment is dark, disguise the spot by rubbing it with a permanent marker or a crayon that matches the fabric's colour.

2. Dip a light-coloured garment in diluted bleach to even the colour.

3. Sew an applique over the spot.

4. Dye the garment a darker colour or tie-dye it.

Blenders

1. If liquid leaks from around the cover, place strips of aluminium foil over the jar's edges before putting on the cover. The foil acts as a seal.

2. Prolong the life of your blender by whirling away any food particles caught under the cutting blades (a strain on the blades will eventually stop the motor from turning). Place a few drops of mild detergent and a cup of warm water in the blender jar and pulse at high speed for a few seconds. Repeat with clear water to rinse. If gummy food residue remains, bend the end of a bottle brush to reach under the blades.

3. When a blender no longer cuts in the kitchen but its blades still turn, retire it to the workshop for tasks such as mixing paint or plant food.

Blood stains

1. Put a paste of water and cornflour or talcum powder on fresh spots; let dry and brush off. Or cover fresh or dried stains with meat tenderiser and add cool water. After some 15 to 30 minutes, sponge off with cool water.

2. Fresh blood on leather? Dab on a little hydrogen peroxide. After it bubbles, wipe it off.

3. If you prick your finger while sewing and get blood on the fabric, wet a long piece of white cotton thread with saliva and place it across the spot. The thread will absorb the blood.

Blushing

1. You may be able to disguise a blush by combing your hair onto your face, wearing lighter make-up, and dressing in blush-coloured clothes so that there will be less contrast with your face.

2. Or you may get relief by meditating: close your eyes, relax, and think of some place far away.

3. If worst comes to worst, employ distraction – pretend you've lost your purse or keys; look anxious and flustered while you search your handbag and your pockets.

Board games

1. Various bottle caps and coins make good counters. Try using different colour crayons, tabs of adhesive-backed paper or even child-sized round plasters to indicate the sides.

Check your sweet drawer: fruit drops or coloured mints also work as counters. Each player uses a different colour to distinguish the pieces. And when you take an opponent's piece, you can eat it.

2. Lost dice? Mark sugar cubes with a ballpoint pen; they won't last long in play, but they're easy to replace. Be sure the numbers on opposite faces add up to seven.

Or you can substitute two cardboard spinners. Trace circles on a piece of cardboard, divide each into six equal sections, and number the sections. Make two arrows and attach them to the centres of the circles with staples, straight pins or tacks. Spin both arrows for each turn.

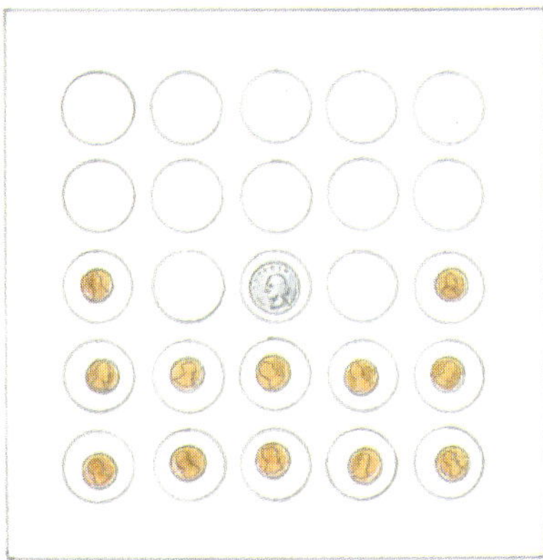

3. To make a simple board game called Indian and Rabbits, draw 25 circles in five rows of five each on a cardboard square. Place ten 20-cent pieces (the rabbits) across the bottom two rows of circles and one on each end of the centre row. Put a 50-cent piece (the Indian) in the middle of the centre row.

One player controls all the rabbits; the other controls the Indian. A rabbit or the Indian may move one circle up, down or across on each turn. To win, the rabbits must corner the Indian, or the Indian must capture all but one rabbit. The Indian captures rabbits by jumping over them, as in draughts. The Indian may make more than one jump in a turn if all the jumps are in a straight line.

Boating mishaps

1. Sometimes the vibrations of high-speed power boats cause the powder in dry fire extinguishers to compact so tightly that they won't work even when the pressure gauge indicates they are ready. To make sure your fire extinguisher will work when you need it, try occasionally hitting it lightly with your hand or against the side of the boat or quayside several times to loosen the powder.

2. You may be able to plug a small leak temporarily with rags, cotton or towels. It's better to carry an all-purpose damage-control device, resembling an umbrella, that will plug a hole at least until a permanent repair can be made.

3. For a larger leak or a hole, first try plugging from the inside with pillows or a mattress. If that doesn't work, make a damage-control device with a tarpaulin and four lengths of rope as shown above.

Tie a rope to each corner of the tarpaulin. Secure three corners on the damaged side of the boat and bring the fourth rope under the craft and tie it on the other side.

Body bulges

WOMEN

1. Avoid tight-fitting undergarments; they can emphasize or even create bulges. Minimize bulges with a one-piece undergarment, such as a slip or body suit that has a fitted top or a built-in bra.

2. Add a bright scarf or large jewellery; accessories can deflect the eye from bulges by attracting attention.

3. For a skirt that shows thigh bulges, try tying a large scarf (be sure to co-ordinate colours) around your hips. If your skirt buttons down the front, unbutton the bottom one or two buttons; the skirt will fall more gracefully.

MEN

1. To cover that paunch, wear full-cut rather than form-fitting clothes. A loose sweater is good for casual wear. A waistcoat that matches your suit can have a slimming effect.

2. Pockets should not have flaps. Pants should have a belt. Stay away from heavy textures, such as nubby tweeds and sharp colour contrasts.

Bookcases

For a quick, attractive bookshelf, lay boards across bricks, glass blocks or concrete blocks.

Plastic milk crates – the kind that milk cartons are carried in – can be stacked to make a colourful set of shelves for a child's room. Most of these cartons belong to dairy companies and must be paid for, but you can find similar units for sale in many home centres. (With diligence and a bit of luck, you may even locate some old-fashioned wooden crates at a flea market or country antique shop.)

Some plastic milk crates are designed to interlock. If yours aren't, secure them with twist ties, strips of cloth or plastic tape. For neatness, choose a matching colour.

Bookends

1. To make a bookend in a minute, snip off the hook of a wire coat hanger with wire cutters and bend it at a 90° angle. Slip one end of the folded hanger under the books.

2. Draw a line across an unwanted long-playing record just to one side of the label. With a hair dryer, heat the record on both sides along the line until you can bend it.

Books

1. Dog-eared corners in your books? Put a sheet of paper on top and press with a warm iron.

2. Mend torn pages by using a starch paste to glue Japanese tissue over the tears. Sandwich newly repaired pages between sheets of waxed (on both sides) paper so that they won't stick to other pages.

3. Water spilled on a book's pages? A frost-free freezer will draw out the moisture and unstick the pages.

If water has damaged too many books to fit in the freezer, call a local wholesale meat distributor or food company, and see if you can arrange to rent freezer space.

4. Clean leather bindings with saddle soap or neat's-foot oil. Apply sparingly and gently with your fingers or a piece of felt, cheesecloth or chamois. Wait several hours, then repeat.

5. Protect your books with covers made of strong paper. Shape the cover, then seal with adhesive tape – don't let the tape stick to the book.

6. Clean books with your vacuum's dusting-brush attachment, a shaving brush or a soft paintbrush.

7. Run a dehumidifier in a damp room containing books. Wipe mould and mildew off the bindings and pages with a clean soft cloth. Do not allow the cloth to touch more than one page – fold it over or use lots of little pieces of cloth. This is to prevent the spread of the mould. If the pages are still mouldy, wipe with an alcohol-dampened cloth, then fan the pages dry. Pure alcohol diluted 50 percent with water should be used. Use sparingly to prevent the pages from from becoming soggy. Or sprinkle cornflour on the pages and brush it off after a few hours.

8. To remember to return library books before you owe a fine, keep a running list of the due dates on your refrigerator. Alternatively, keep your library books in a prominent place in your home, where you are likely to see them daily.

9. If you lend a book to a friend, write, "Please return to (your name)" on the inside front cover. Keep the jacket, along with a notation of the borrower and the date; it will remind you to ask for the book to be returned after a reasonable time.

Boots

1. To dry boots fast, heat a pan of clean round pebbles in the oven, pour them into the boots, and shake until the stones cool. (First test the boot lining by holding a hot pebble in one place for a few seconds.)

2. Blow warm air on wet rubber boots with a vacuum-cleaner blower attachment or your hair dryer.

3. To remove salt stains, wipe the boots with a solution of one cup water and one tablespoon vinegar.

4. Rub rain spots off suede boots with an emery board.

5. What do you do when you're caught on a bad day without your boots? Wear leggings by cutting off the feet of old, worn-out knee socks. For walking a very short distance, try fastening plastic bags over your shoes with rubber bands.

Bores

A bore has been defined as a person who finds himself more interesting than he finds you. If cornered by one, don't bother trying to be polite; he won't notice anyway.

1. Entertain yourself by asking irrelevant questions and counting the seconds until he manages to work his way back to his pet topic.

2. Create a diversion: spill a drink; get hiccups or the giggles; notice a long-lost friend across the room.

3. Smile, nod now and then, and recite poetry in your head. If the bore is someone important (your boss, for example), use the magic phrase "I see" from time to time.

4. Open a magazine, a book, your pocket calendar or a small calculator. Give it your utmost attention.

5. Walk away.

Bottle & jar caps

1. Run hot water over a recalcitrant jar cap to expand it. Then, for additional grabbing power, wrap the cap with a rubber band.

2. To loosen the stop from a decanter, wrap a hot, wet cloth around the neck of the bottle. If necessary, let a few drops of water trickle into the neck and around the stopper to dissolve whatever might be holding it tight. Quickly drain off the water so that it doesn't touch the contents of the bottle.

3. To remove a bottle or jar cap without an opener, use an oil-filter wrench (for large jars), an adjustable wrench or the strikeplate opening of a doorframe (the plate that receives the latch). Remember too, that the handle of a corkscrew often serves as a bottle opener. Or you can use needle-nose pliers, a screwdriver or the teeth of a key to pry up the folds of the cap one at a time.

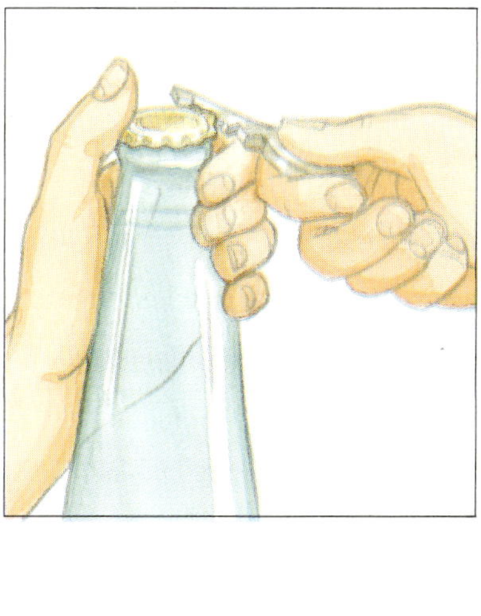

Bottles

To clean a narrow-necked bottle, fill it with equal parts water and detergent or ammonia. Add some uncooked rice and swirl the solution until the bottle is clean.

For cloudy stains, pour in vinegar and some coarse sand. Every half hour for up to five or six hours, shake and swirl the mixture around until the stain disappears.

Braaiing

The sociable South African braai is essentially an outdoor pleasure. To preserve this ambience, ensure that all the ingredients and equipment you'll need are ready to hand before you start cooking. Using gas or electric equipment, you can even braai indoors. Do not use charcoal indoors, except in a specially designed fireplace, or you may run the risk of carbon monoxide poisoning.

1. Never use petrol or any other chemical fire-starter.

2. Lay your fire so that the spread of coals will be slightly larger than the area of the cooking grid.

3. Keep a screen handy as a shield against the wind. Almost anything will do, from a piece of roofing iron, to sacking stretched on a rough wooden frame.

4. Once your fire is burning well, don't disturb it. The ashes you knock off will form cold spots and cause uneven cooking.

5. Once you've cleaned the grid, smear it with vegetable oil or wipe with pieces of cut-off fat before laying your meat on it for cooking.

6. Whatever heat you decide to use, wait until the stage of flames and thick smoke has passed.

7. For each adult, allow from 350 to 450 grams of meat on the bone or about 230 grams filleted. Make cuts at five centimetre intervals along the fatty border of the meat to prevent the piece curling as it cooks.

8. Add salt and seasoning at the last moment before cooking, otherwise it tends to dry the meat.

9. Never pierce the skin of boerewors – you'll lose all the juice and most of the flavour. Forks are out – use flat or blunt tongs.

10. Arrange your cooking programme so that steaks can be eaten about one to two minutes after cooking. A steak "kept" after braaiing loses its flavour, but boerewors doesn't.

11. Always be sure to braai fish over a low heat or medium if wrapped in aluminium foil.

Bra & slip straps

Straps keep falling down? Before you put your bra on, tie them together across the back with a shoelace, string or ribbon.

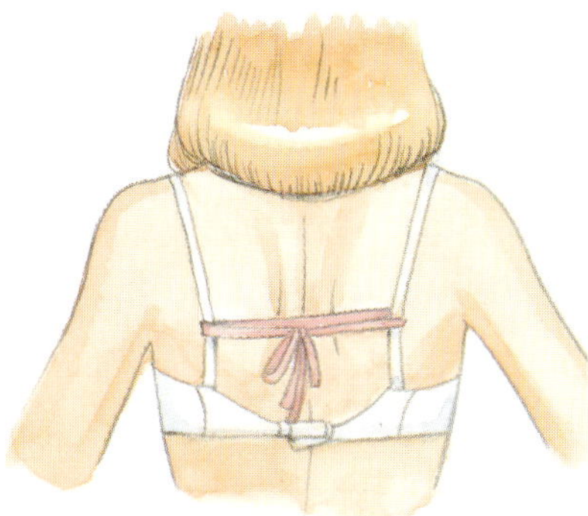

For a permanent solution, sew a piece of thin elastic between them.

If you don't want straps to show with a wide neckline, sew small Velcro strips on the top of each one and on each inside shoulder seam of the dress or blouse. Or carefully pin your strap to your blouse with small brass safety pins.

Bracelet

1. Need a bracelet to match a special outfit? Wrap one of yours in matching fabric or ribbon.

2. Make your own bracelet by removing both ends from an empty tuna tin, smoothing down any jagged metal with a metal nail file, and twisting or gluing on yarn, fabric and ornaments. You should use rubber cement or epoxy.

3. For a particularly festive look, dab papier-mâché on a band made from a

strip of cardboard. When the papier-mâché is dry, paint it in bright colours.
4. Save old belts. For a bracelet that's sure to attract attention, fasten several buckles together on a single belt strap. Cut off the excess strap, and "fasten" your bracelet with the original belt buckle.

Brass

1. To remove the tarnish from unlacquered brass fittings, nameplates and other small objects, submerge them overnight in a solution of equal parts water and ammonia; then rub with extra-fine steel wool or a soft brush.
2. For stubborn tarnish, rub with a paste of salt and vinegar or use a salted lemon rind. Toothpastes – both regular and gel – also work.
3. If the brass is covered with lacquer, clean it with mild detergent and water, then rinse and wipe dry. Avoid harsh abrasives, which can wear through the lacquer.
4. In all cases, rinse afterward in clear water and buff dry with a soft cloth or chamois.

Bread baking

1. Save the water when you boil peeled potatoes; it will provide food for yeast and make for a better-flavoured bread. Heat the water to a temperature of 40°C to 46°C before dissolving the yeast in it.
2. To get dough to rise, you need a draught-free spot with a temperature of 24°C to 27°C. Try putting the bowl of dough, lightly covered, in a cupboard above a water heater, on top of the refrigerator or on a television set or fish-tank light.
3. A quick fix for bread burned in baking or reheating is to scrape off the black spots with a kitchen grater. For severe burns, simply cut off the damaged part and eat the rest.

Bread crumbs

1. Instead of relying on the usual store-bought dry bread crumbs, you can use crushed cornflakes, unsweetened bran cereal or matzo meal. Or make crumbs from toasted white bread: crush the slices with a rolling pin or an empty bottle or buzz them to fine crumbs in an electric blender or food processor.
2. Cracker crumbs can also double as bread crumbs but contain more sodium, so taste for saltiness as you prepare a recipe.
3. Freshly made bread crumbs will keep for a week or more in a tightly closed jar in the refrigerator.

Breast-feeding

If full-time breast-feeding is impossible, the best substitute is expressed breast milk given from a bottle. Second best is a commercially prepared formula.

A good time to introduce a bottle is when the baby is four to six weeks old. Some babies may take two weeks or longer to become comfortable with bottle-feeding.

Practise expressing your milk – either manually or with a breast pump – before returning to work or various other duties. In order to have adequate milk for bottle-feedings, you'll need to pump two or three times in the course of the day.

If you're away from home, take along a vacuum bottle filled with ice cubes; empty it when you want to store the milk. At home, store expressed milk in 250-millimetre plastic (not glass) bottles.

If you plan to use the milk within 48 hours, place it in the refrigerator. For longer storage, you should use the freezer; it should remain good for at least three months.

When you're ready to use the frozen milk, thaw it in the refrigerator for several hours, use a microwave oven or hold it under warm running water for a few minutes. Shake the bottle well before feeding.

Caution: Thawing in a microwave oven may overheat the milk; test it before giving it to the baby.

Breathing exercises

Increasing the volume of oxygen in your lungs can help relieve tension.

DIAPHRAGM BREATHING

Stand straight or lie flat on your back and place your hands flat against your diaphragm with your little fingers along your waistline. Inhale slowly through your nose, pulling the air down into your lungs. You will feel the bottom of your lungs fill, which concentrates airflow. Exhale through your mouth. Repeat five times.

Y MOVEMENT

Stand or lie flat on your back, arms crossed in front, with each palm resting on the opposite thigh. While

---

DID YOU KNOW . . . ?

Breast-feeding myths

Advice to nursing mothers has been rich and varied – and often contradictory – over the years. Here are some examples from various times and places:

If you eat peanuts, your milk will dry up (although some tribes in Africa believe that peanuts increase the flow).

Some people insist that eating chocolate will stop your milk; others, that it will produce more.

In many places it has long been believed that drinking beer or milk will increase your milk supply; in America it is believed that oatmeal helps.

Eating like a cow, nature's premier milk producer, is advised in some quarters: drink lucerne tea or eat lucerne sprouts. (But farmers don't allow cows to graze near apple orchards – eating apples causes their milk to dry up.) There are more examples: if you nurse in a car, the baby will get gas; ditto if you eat cabbage. An onion in your stomach will give your baby colic. If you rock while nursing, you'll shake up the milk.

If a mother becomes nervous, angry, frightened or sexually stimulated, her milk will turn sour.

---

inhaling deeply through your nose, slowly raise both arms above your head, uncrossing them and turning the palms to face each other. As your shoulders open and your lungs expand, your arms will push outward at an angle. Reverse the movement as you exhale, bringing your shoulders forward to the starting position.

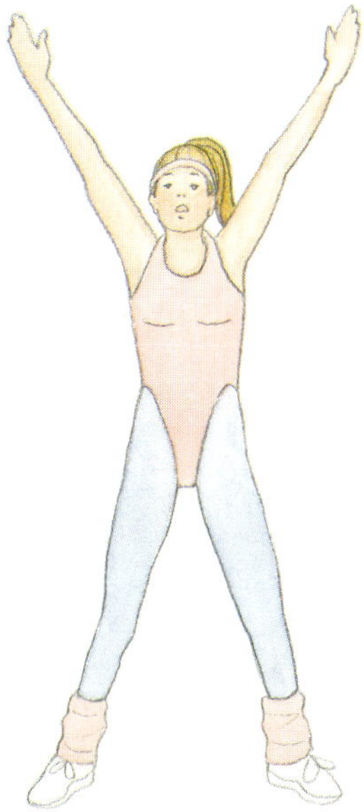

Brick & stone cleaning

1. Scrub paint specks and mortar smudges from brick surfaces with a piece of broken brick that's the same colour as the brick you are cleaning. Don't use the face of the brick; it is harder than the core and can cause scratches. Use the broken surface.

This technique works for other masonry surfaces too. Use a bit of stone to clean stone and a concrete block fragment for concrete blocks.

2. Here's an easy way to rinse surface dirt and grime from a brick or stone wall. Position a lawn sprinkler to spray directly against the wall. Leave it on for several hours during two or three consecutive days.

3. Lift out fresh oil and grease stains with dry powdered cement or cat litter. Spread a layer of the material over the stain, allow it to soak up the oil, and sweep the area clean. Repeat the process, if necessary.

On a vertical surface, hold a piece of plastic over the stain and attach the side and bottom edges with duct tape. Fill the pouch with powdered cement or cat litter and tape the top edge firmly closed.

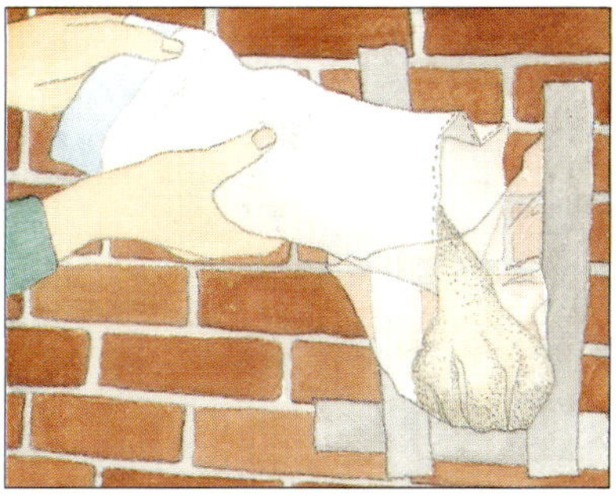

Brushes

1. A soft-bristled baby brush is great for cleaning the delicate fabric on lampshades and curtains.

2. When you are dusting walls or bookshelves, place an old wet towel or some damp newspaper under the area being cleaned, and leave in place for ten minutes. The falling dust will stick to it. Do the same when drilling holes in brick walls.

3. Whenever you vacuum or dust, carry a small hand broom or unused paintbrush with you to get into the hard-to-reach places.

Bulbs

1. If you're the kind of serious gardener who plans for the long term, save money on expensive lily bulbs by harvesting bulbils, the tiny dark bulbs produced on the stem between the leaf axils. Pluck them just after the flowers have faded.

Plant them in containers of potting soil just below the surface, spacing them well apart so that you won't have to thin them before they're established. They will take a long time to flower – three to four years. Don't bother to propagate in this way from hybrid lilies, since the resulting blossoms are unlikely to resemble those of the parent plant.

2. Don't think of bulbs solely as spring bloomers. Plant the traditional tulips, daffodils, snowdrops and hyacinths for that season, but also consider putting in dahlias and gladioli for summer, crocuses for autumn and early flowering narcissi for the colder months.

Cannas and day lilies will bloom throughout winter in the warmer parts of the country. Cyclamen, amaryllis and other bulbs can brighten window sills on gloomy winter days throughout South Africa.

Bumper stickers

Before you put that bumper sticker on your car, make sure that you'll be able to remove it – apply it over a layer of car wax. You will also find it much easier to peel off if you remove it within a month.

Remove an old bumper sticker from chrome by scraping off the top layer of paper or vinyl with a sharp knife or a single-edged razor blade. (Try not to scratch the surface.) The adhesive beneath should come off with methylated spirits; if that doesn't work, use paint thinner. If the sticker is on a painted surface, test a tiny patch to make sure the paint doesn't dissolve.

Burglar alarms

1. Even if you don't have a big, scary dog, post a "Beware of the Dog" sign. Wire a recorded bark to your doorbell, or carry a small recorder with a taped bark to set off when you answer the door.
2. Two dogs – one inside, one out – remain the best burglar deterrent.
3. A bunch of cowbells hung on a garden gate cannot be silenced and provides gentle warning of visitors, without offending friends. They also invariably trigger off any intelligent watchdog. Crunching footsteps on a gravel pathway effectively serve the same purpose.
4. Even if you can't afford an alarm system, paste security-system stickers on the windows. Instruct your children to tell no one that the system doesn't exist.
5. Turn on outdoor lights or wire infrared or sound-activated detectors to switch them on if intruders come within range.

Burglaries

1. If you come home and see an open door or household objects out of place, turn around at once and leave quietly. Notify the police from a neighbour's home.

Watch your home from a safe distance – don't try to stop the burglar when he leaves. Get a good description and write down the licence number of his vehicle. (See *Witnessing a crime*, p.233.) Stay out of your home until the police arrive to make sure nobody else is inside.
2. If you hear a burglar entering your home or prowling around, collect your family in a room with a strong door and a good lock; call the police if possible, or wait until the intruder leaves before seeking help.
3. If you confront a burglar face-to-face or wake up to discover one in your room, stay quiet and cooperate. Screaming may only frighten or anger an already scared or irrational burglar into violence.

AFTER A BURGLARY
The police need a full description of all stolen items. For that reason, it's wise to photograph and list all your valuables (including serial numbers) long before a crisis arises, and be sure to keep the inventory in a safe-deposit box. (See also *Insurance claims*, p.117; *Safe-deposit box*, p.176; *Valuables*, p.220.)

Burned cookware

To effectively clean burned food from pots or pans, wet the burn, sprinkle with salt, and let stand for 10 minutes. Scrub well.

Or cover the burned area with a paste of bicarbonate of soda and water. Leave it on overnight, then scour. (Be aware, however, that bicarbonate of soda and other alkaline substances will etch the surface of an aluminium pan if they are left on for more than an hour.)

For stubborn burns, scrape off as much burned food as possible with a wooden spoon and fill the pot halfway with water. Add a strong detergent or scouring powder, boil for 10 minutes, and let stand overnight. Then scrub.

Burns

The seriousness of a burn depends on three things: how deep it is, how much of the body it covers, and the age and health of the victim. Babies, children under the age of five, and adults over 60 are especially vulnerable; a burn that's moderate to a young adult could be fatal to them.

First-degree burns are superficial; the skin becomes slightly reddened and swollen. The pain is similar to that of sunburn.

Second-degree burns penetrate the first layer of skin and damage the second. The skin is red, mottled and blistered; pain is intense.

Third-degree burns damage all layers of the skin, usually leaving charred, black areas or dry, white ones. There may be extreme pain or, because of nerve damage, very little pain after the initial acute pain. Such burns are always serious, as they are easily infected.

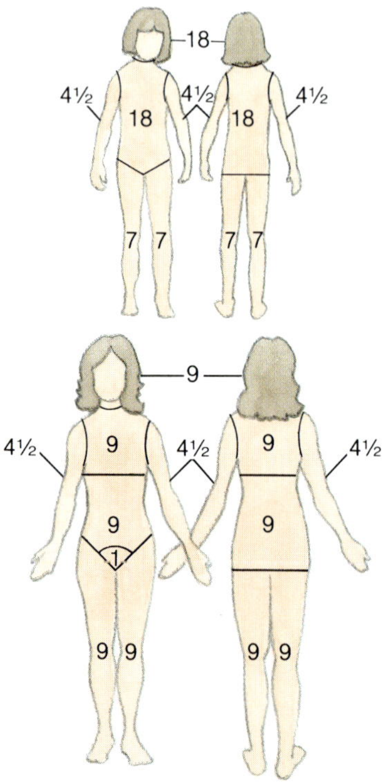

Use this guide to estimate the amount of burn damage; it divides areas of the body into portions or multiples of nine percent.

1. Wet down, remove, smother or cut away any smouldering clothes. Pour cold water over tar, wax or grease; don't try to remove it. If the skin and clothes are still hot, and the burn seems to be first or second degree, immerse the area in ice or cold water or apply a cool, wet dressing for no longer than 10 minutes. If the burn appears to be third degree, immerse it in water only if it's still burning.
2. Facial burns or soot in the nose or mouth indicate that the person has inhaled smoke. Check that the victim has no breathing problems.
3. Apply a loose, dry, preferably sterile dressing to all third-degree

burns and to second-degree burns over more than nine percent of the body. If the burns are extensive, wrap the person in a clean sheet. *Don't put anything else on the burn.* Take the person to an emergency unit.

If the burn is minor – second degree on less than nine percent of noncritical areas of the body or first degree on less than 18 percent – apply a loose dressing, moistened only with cool water to help relieve the pain. Be careful not to break any blisters. If there's tar, grease or wax on the skin, cover with a loose, dry dressing, and take the person to the emergency unit of the nearest hospital.

Burping a baby

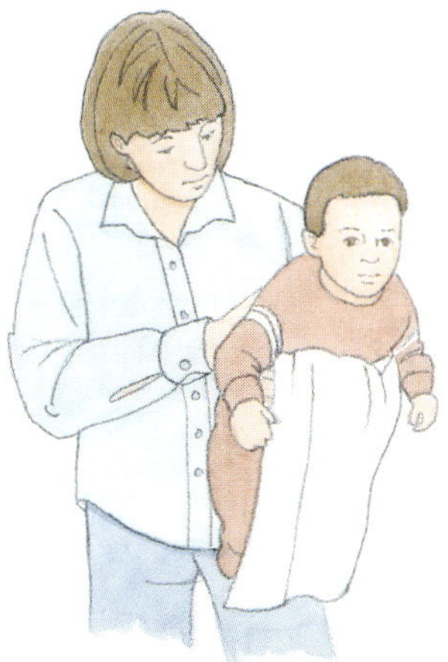

If your baby needs burping but you need to move around and keep one of your hands free, try one of these walking-burping techniques:

1. Set the baby on your hip, facing outwards, with one of your arms securely around his tummy. The slight pressure of your arm plus the movement of your walking will help bring up the wind.

2. Strap on your "front pack" and put the baby into it, arranging a clean cloth to catch any milk that comes up with the burp.

3. If the baby is over four months old and can hold up his head, put him in a backpack carrier – the movement of your walking will eventually help a burp develop.

Business lunches

When initiating a business lunch, especially with a new person, be sure to state the reason, even if it's only to share information and get to know each other. This will prevent misunderstandings and give both of you a chance to prepare.

The one who suggests the lunch should be ready to pay the bill. But if you're asked to lunch informally by someone who is obviously not on an expense account, offer to share the bill. No matter who had what, split it down the middle. Lunch is lunch.

To pay the bill unobtrusively, speak to the waiter or maitre d' privately before lunch to make sure the bill is given to you and not your guest. If you forget to settle this matter before lunch, excuse yourself to use the cloakroom, and speak to the waiter on the way.

You can even arrange to pay the bill while you are away from the table. (Paying by credit card is less obvious than by cash.)

If you entertain at one restaurant regularly, the staff will help make your lunches smoother. Phone in advance for reservations. Give your name and company, the day and time, the number of people, and the table you'd like. After lunch, discreetly tip the waiter (usually 10 percent of the bill). After doing this a few times, you'll find that you get a consistently high standard of service from the waiter who serves you.

Butter

1. Margarine can effectively replace butter in most recipes, but not in those for shaped, rolled or batter biscuits; its greater shortening power makes the biscuits spread out over the baking sheet.

Sunflower oil or lard can substitute for butter in all dishes except baked goods, although the amounts will be different: one tablespoon butter equals ¾ tablespoon sunflower oil or lard; one cup butter equals ⅞ cup sunflower oil or lard.

2. Butter won't burn as quickly in a sauté pan if you add a drop or two of olive oil.

Buttermilk

No buttermilk? Use plain low-fat yoghurt. Sour cream works, too, but not in cakes – too much butterfat.

OTHER SUBSTITUTES

1. Stir a tablespoon of lemon juice or vinegar into one cup whole milk and let it stand for a few minutes.

2. Mix one cup milk with 1¾ tablespoons cream of tartar.

Buttons

TEMPORARY MEASURES

1. When a button pops, stay "decent" with a safety pin hidden under the buttonhole until you can replace the missing button.

2. Fasten a pretty brooch in place of the missing button.

3. Tack the button to the fabric with the wire from a twist tie.

PERMANENT ALTERNATIVES

1. Use button-sized Velcro circles and squares. Position each piece with a pin, then hand- or machine-stitch around the edges.

2. Cut "buttons" any size you desire from iron-on Velcro tape. Follow the package directions for attaching them to the fabric.

3. Buy snaps or hooks and eyes that are anchored to tapes. Cut off as many fasteners as you need; stitch the tape edges to the fabric.

4. Try snap fasteners; they're sold in lots of finishes. Attach them with a fastening tool or a hammer.

C

Cabbage caterpillars

To thwart these pests, slip sections of old pantihose over young cabbage heads. Knot the tops and pull the hose down to soil level. They will expand as the plants grow.

Or lightly dust leaves with a powdered mixture of ½ cup salt and one cup flour; apply while the plants are wet with dew.

Cakes

1. Slip your hand inside a plastic sandwich bag before greasing a cake tin with butter. No mess!

2. To find out if a cake is done, insert a wooden toothpick in the centre. If it comes out clean, the cake is ready. Or press the centre with your finger; the cake is cooked if the top springs back, leaving no imprint.

3. Cakes leavened with beaten egg whites – such as angel food, chiffon and sponge cakes – often fall while cooling. To minimize the chances, invert the tin as soon as it comes from the oven and let the cake cool upside down. Don't worry about it falling out of the tin; egg white-based cakes have to be loosened with a spatula.

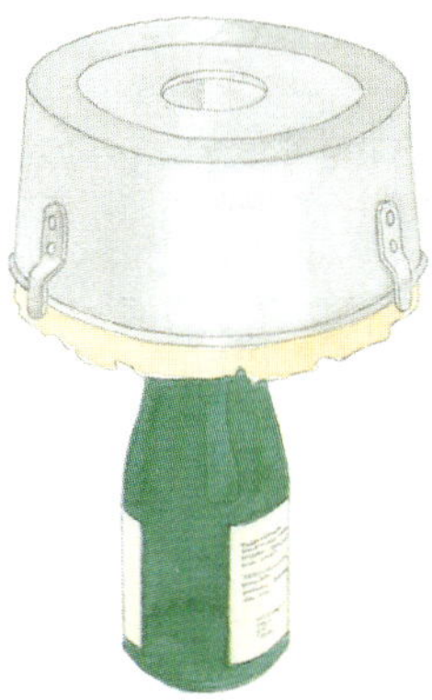

Most angel cake tins have three "feet" at the top, so that the tin can be inverted without squashing a risen cake. If yours lacks feet or if the cake has risen too high, place the centre of the inverted tin over a glass bottle.

4. Because microwaved cakes often come from the oven sticky, uneven and unbrowned on top, make sure that you microwave only those cakes that will be iced or those that have crumb toppings.

5. To decorate a cake, turn a self-sealing plastic sandwich bag into a pastry bag. Store icing in it, refrigerated, until the cake is ready. Then snip off a bottom corner and pipe away. For better control insert a plastic decorating tip.

6. You can use a paper doily as a stencil. Position it on top of the cake and sprinkle icing sugar generously over it. Then carefully lift the doily.

7. When time is short, bake one large, single-layer cake instead of a double cake. It's quicker to ice.

8. A cut cake will stay fresh longer if you place half an apple inside the cake keeper or storage tin.

Calamari

Calamari, or squid, rates very highly on the menu of most seafood lovers in South Africa.

The eight suckered arms, elongated body and two long tentacles of the local calamari species (*Loligo vulgaris reynaudi*) may appear unappetising but, properly prepared, they make a mouth-watering meal. The average South African squid is about 15 to 30 centimetres long.

Squid are caught mainly off the eastern Cape coast of South Africa. The fishermen mostly lure them with bright lights, then catch them with special jigs.

Mediterranean cooks have always given squid its rightful place on the dinner table but in South Africa, until quite recently, it was more commonly known as chokka, used principally as fisherman's bait. Calamari can be bought either fresh or frozen from your local supermarket.

Usually, it is cleaned and sliced into rings, ready for cooking. Make sure you thaw it completely before cooking. Marinating with lemon juice will add to its overall flavour.

Here's a quick and easy way to prepare fresh calamari:

1. Wash thoroughly. Drain.

2. Pull the body and head apart. Remove ink sac, cut tentacles and arms off, discard head and entrails, horny beak and long transparent "pen" inside the body.

3. Cut off lateral fins, and chop into bite-sized pieces.

4. Neatly slice the body into rings, one centimetre thick.

5. Deep-fry for 15 seconds with or without crumbs.

Another cooking method is to stew the calamari for about 20 minutes. You can also chop up the fins, tentacles and arms and fry them or use them as a stuffing.

Calcium

Calcium is the chief component of bones and teeth, but about one percent of the body's store of this mineral plays a vital part in regulating the muscles, in blood clotting and the transmission of nerve impulses.

Calcium is most needed during childhood and adolescence and, by women, during pregnancy and breast-feeding.

Foods rich in calcium include milk and cheese, dark-green vegetables (except spinach), citrus fruits, dried peas and beans and small fish eaten with the bones, such as sardines.

Calcium is adequately absorbed by the body only in the presence of Vitamin D, which is found in milk, egg yolk, liver and tuna. A deficiency of calcium, although very rare, can contribute to rickets and other bone deformities when Vitamin D is also in short supply. In the elderly, long-standing calcium deficiency may lead to osteoporosis or brittleness of the bones. A healthy adult on a normal, balanced diet should not require supplementary calcium. The mineral is a frequent component of stones (calculi) of the urinary tract, but no firm conclusions have been drawn with regard to intake.

The daily recommended dietary allowance (RDA) for calcium intake by adults is 800 milligrams; for adolescents 1,200 milligrams; and for pregnant women 1,600 milligrams.

Calculators

A basic calculator is not just for balancing chequebooks and figuring out budgets – it has a wealth of helpful, perhaps unexpected, uses.

Before you begin, check your calculator's accuracy. Enter nine's all the way across. Divide by 81. The answer should be 12345678.

IN THE CAR

1. Calculate your petrol mileage. Note the odometer reading when you fill the tank; the next time you fill up, divide the kilometres you've driven by the number of litres you've used.

2. Check your speedometer's accuracy on a highway that has markers posted every kilometre. Driving at a steady speed, count the seconds between two signs. Divide that number into 3,600, the seconds in an hour, to get the speed in kilometres per hour.

IN THE SUPERMARKET

1. Curb impulse buying by tallying the amount of your grocery order on a calculator as you shop.

2. Comparison shop: you can compute the unit cost of an item by dividing the price by the number of grams marked on the container.

AT SALES

1. Find out how much you'll pay on an item marked "reduced 60 percent", even if your calculator lacks a percent key. Multiply the price by the discount (,60); subtract the discount for the sale price.

2. Convert fractions to decimals by dividing the top number by the bottom number. If an item is ⅓ off, the discount is ,33 or 33 percent.

IN HYPERMARKETS

Work out the cost of new carpeting. Measuring in metres, multiply the length of the room times the width to get the square metres, and multiply that times the cost per square metre. If you're painting walls instead, calculate the area in the same fashion in order to buy the right amount of paint.

IN A RESTAURANT

If friends want to split the bill, add up each person's share; to calculate the tip, multiply the before-VAT total by 10 to 15 percent.

IN A PHONE BOOTH

Use the calculator as a notepad to take down a phone number – but use the decimal point, not the minus sign, as the hyphen!

FOR FUN

Punch in 0.7734 and turn upside down to see HELLO.

Calendar

1. Co-ordinate family activities on a centrally located calendar with a big square for each day. Assign coloured pens or markers to family members, or use them to differentiate specific activities: for example red ticks on the days you have the lift club, blue dots to indicate refuse removal days. Encourage everyone to record any activities affecting family life.

2. Use your home computer as a calendar; programme it to display each day's activities, which you and other family members have previously entered into it.

3. Set up a countertop tickler file and keep it in the kitchen, hall or other main area. Purchase a cardboard accordion file and number its compartments one to 31, or get a large-format file box with 31 numbered dividers.

With this file you can organize many family activities: the list of items to buy at the hardware store on Saturday; dry-cleaning receipts; questions to ask your child's primary school teacher; Tuesday's theatre tickets. Drop the slips or tickets in the appropriate slot; then check the file each morning. Store next month's items in a separate compartment at the beginning or end of the file.

Callipers

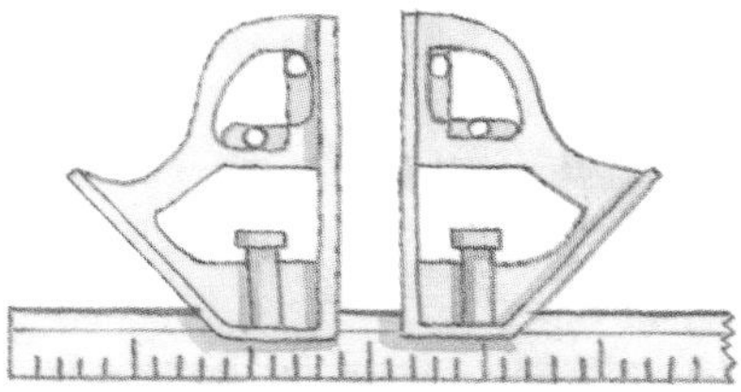

To measure the outside diameter of a round object, use a C-clamp, a pair of locking-grip pliers or an adjustable wrench. Set the jaws to the width of the object and measure the space between them.

If you have a couple of combination squares, slide both heads onto one ruler, face to face, as shown. Fit the heads against the object in question, then read the ruler.

Or use a cloth measuring tape to determine the circumference of a pipe or other cylinder; divide by pi (3,14) to arrive at the diameter.

Calluses

Usually found on the sole of the foot, calluses are hard, slightly raised and insensitive areas of skin produced by abnormal friction or pressure.

To find out what's causing your calluses, look at the shoes you wear: are they badly fitting; do they cause abnormal pressure on your feet?

Avoid calluses by wearing comfortable, roomy shoes, and, if necessary, insert padding to reduce discomfort. They can be removed gradually by softening the skin in warm water and gently using a pumice stone to rub away the dead skin, or your doctor may refer you to a chiropodist, who will shave away some of the thickened outer layers of skin.

Camera filters

Need a haze filter for that lovely scenic shot? You may already have the best one in your camera bag – a polarising filter.

Normally used to darken blue skies, polarizing filters also cut down haze in distant scenes. On a single-lens reflex camera, rotate the polarizing filter until you see the best effect.

A diffusion filter adds a dreamy feeling and soft edges to portraits and scenic shots. Don't have one? Lightly smear Vaseline on any ultraviolet or polarizing filter. Wipe it off later with tissues and methylated spirits.

Cameras

Protect your camera with a plastic bag.

Raise the bag for picture-taking.

PROTECTION FROM THE ELEMENTS

Carry a supply of plastic bags in your camera pack. An inverted bag with the corners snipped off and the camera straps threaded through will give some protection against rain or snow. Let the bag hang over the camera, open end down; slide it up to take a picture. For more waterproofing, tape the edges of the holes to the strap with vinyl tape.

A self-sealing storage bag, used as above, or a refuse bag, edges folded over and sealed with paper clips, will protect your camera from dust.

OVERRIDING AUTO EXPOSURE

Most cameras adjust automatically to give the right exposures. Sometimes, however, the lighting will fool your camera into the wrong exposure – for example, if there's a strong backlight. If you suspect this, review the instruction manual; you can probably override the automation.

On some point-and-shoot cameras, you can change the film speed to fool the camera. For example, changing from a speed of 100 to 200 will reduce the exposure, giving you deeper blue skies in outdoor scenes.

Camp baking

An inexpensive two-litre ring mould and a camp stove can be used to bake quick breads and biscuits.

Mix the dry ingredients in a plastic bag at home. Add water in camp; hold the bag shut and mix the contents by squeezing and kneading. Slit the bag slightly and squeeze the batter into the greased mould.

Set the mould on the stove, placing its hole over the burner; to avoid burning the dough's edges, adjust the stove to a small flame. Cover with an upside-down frying pan.

If your stove produces only a wide-spreading flame, nestle the ring mould inside another of the same size to distribute the heat more evenly. If wind keeps blowing the flame to the side, rotate the stove often.

Baking time depends on altitude but averages 80 percent of the baking time for a package mix.

Camp cooking

1. Most campsites have a fire ring or small fireplace where you can braai your meat or fish, or make a potjie. Game reserves and National Parks in southern Africa usually supply firewood or charcoal at a reasonable price. This wood may be too large for a small cooking fire, so take an axe or other chopping tool along with you when you go camping.

2. A lightweight camp stove, available at most stores which cater for outdoor camping or backpacking, is quite indispensible for quick boiling and prolonged heating. It is faster, cleaner, and easier to cook with than a fire; it also causes less wear and tear on the landscape. If you do make a fire, spread the coals out for low, easily controlled heat.

3. You can devise cooking pots from 100-, 250- and 750-gram coffee cans that nest inside each other. Pack pliers to lift hot cans.

4. Supermarkets sell many freeze-dried foods at less than half the price charged by camping stores. Combine macaroni, noodles or rice with instant soup mix for a satisfying camp meal. Other common standbys, such as powdered fruit drinks, instant potatoes, spaghetti dinners and puddings, work well too.

5. A large coffeepot has a variety of uses, including boiling vegetables and heating water for washing. Because water boils at lower temperatures at high elevations, you will have to boil your foods for a longer period at high altitudes. Experiment with cooking times.

6. Cooking with a stove inside a tent can cause headache, nausea, dizziness or even death from carbon monoxide. In bad weather set the stove just outside the tent door under the rain-fly overhang while cooking from inside the tent.

Some tents are designed with partitions for this purpose.

Caution: Always refuel a stove outside the tent and away from all open flames. And don't ever throw used fuel canisters in the fire.

Campfires

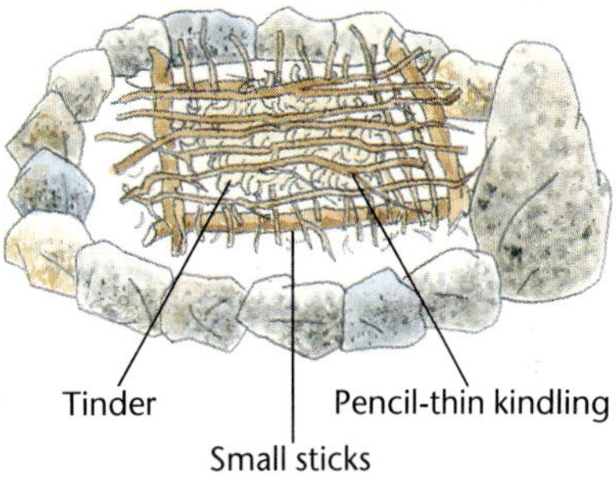

Campfires are prohibited in many wilderness areas. Even where legal, they're dangerous and troublesome. If you must build an emergency fire and a fireplace is available, use it.

Otherwise, clear away organic material down to the bare ground within a one-metre radius. Assemble rocks into a circle larger than the cooking pots you intend to use.

Collect several dozen dry dead twigs and break them into kindling no more than half-a-metre long. Use a penknife to slice two fistfuls of very thin shavings. Then assemble the materials as shown. Light the shavings from the windward side and feed more shavings into the flame, one at a time, until the fire is vigorous. (If it's windy, shield the flame with a flat rock.) Build a teepee of larger wood pieces around the tinder, as shown.

Before you leave, be sure to return the rocks to their original locations, sooty side down. Douse the ashes with water until they are completely cold, then cover them with dirt.

Carry matches in a waterproof tube and some old candle stubs or birthday candles. In wet weather a candle will help to sustain a flame.

Caution: Some parts of southern Africa – particularly the coastal regions – are buffeted by very strong winds in summer. Before you make a fire (even if a fireplace is available), consider the threat of wind-borne sparks starting another fire that could have disastrous consequences.

Camping aids

1. A reclining lawn chair is more comfortable than a picnic bench and is much easier to move.
2. A waterproof tarpaulin, draped over a rope, will shelter your cooking area from rain and midday heat.
3. A soiled pillowcase makes a good laundry bag. Put several on each pillow and peel them off for use.
4. Sleeping bag liners extend the time between washings. To make one, fold a sheet lengthways and sew the open side and bottom closed.
5. Sheets on top of the bags protect them from dirty footprints.
6. One-rand coins and a couple of 50-cent pieces are useful for vending and washing machines, telephones and showers. Stow them in 35-millimetre film canisters.

Camping in rainy weather

1. Have your outer clothing waterproofed by a dry-cleaner.
2. Rain gear works better and feels more comfortable when it fits loosely. Air spaces provide ventilation and allow your body to dry.
3. Any camper who has endured the tedium of a rainy day knows that a paperback book can be important first aid for boredom.

Various travel-sized board games (such as draughts, chess, backgammon, Scrabble) and a pack of cards are also lightweight, easy-to-carry protection against the dreary monotony of a soggy campsite. Writing postcards and letters helps you recall the best moments of your trip and takes your mind off the rain.
4. Suspend a waterproof tarpaulin over a picnic table on a rainy day to create a welcome airy shelter for family activities outside the cramped confines of a tent or caravan. Anchor the corners with wooden pegs.

Camping meal planning

Eating outdoors is half the fun of camping, but it takes some planning. Consider not only the weight and bulk of the food you carry but also its kilojoule content (hauling a pack may burn 13,400 to 16,000 kilojoules a day, more than twice what's needed to swing in a hammock).

Also consider storability. Among the foods that won't spoil if left unrefrigerated for a few days are hard cheese, hard salami, biltong, dried fruit, sliced carrots and celery, margarine and pita bread.

Try new camping foods at home; a campsite is a poor place to discover that an anticipated delight tastes more like sawdust.

Plan major meals in advance and pack all the ingredients in double plastic bags for extra protection. Use colour codes to distinguish breakfasts, lunches and dinners; place coloured paper between the inner and outer bags or mark the bags with indelible pens.

If you are camping, anticipate rainy days when you won't want to cook outside; take along a few one-pot, add-hot-water dinners to heat at the tent door. Complement these with light snacks – pretzels, salted biscuits and some biltong. For those cold, rainy mornings, plan a breakfast that doesn't need cooking: fresh or dried fruit, rich breads, various cheeses, muesli and smoked fish.

IN TIMES GONE BY

Weather forecasting

Most adages about the weather – many of them in rhyme – are grounded in centuries of observation by farmers and seafarers who were finely tuned to their surroundings. We can still take some of the old sayings seriously today:

A circle round the moon,
'Twill rain soon.

Ice crystals in high cirrostratus clouds refract moonlight, so that there appears to be a halo around the moon. Those clouds, in turn, foretell advancing cold fronts that bring storms.

Sky red in the morning
Is a sailor's sure warning;
Sky red at night
Is the sailor's delight.

Dry air supports more dust than humid air and hence reddens the light. When the sky is red to the west – just after sunset – you can suppose that fine weather is on its way, since air currents in the southern hemisphere move from west to east. But when the predawn sky looks red to the east, the dry weather has passed you by, and rain may be coming.

Swallows fly high,
Clean blue sky;
Swallows fly low,
Rain we shall know.

Low atmospheric pressure and high humidity, both harbingers of rain, make it difficult for insects to fly high; so swallows fly closer to the earth to prey on them. Other signs of low pressure and probable rain: smoke that curls down from a chimney, soot that falls into the fireplace, clouds forming at low altitudes, and strong ground odours rising from ditches and marshes. In South Africa hot, dry Berg winds are another sign of impending rain — particualrly along the eastern and western seaboards.

Camping: where to go

Southern Africa's wide open spaces, magnificent scenery and abundance of game parks and nature reserves all contribute to the ever-increasing popularity of camping in this country. The larger game parks offer campers the use of restaurants, shops and swimming pools. They usually have information counters with comprehensive details of local attractions, from bird watching and fishing, to canoeing and sailing. Many parks, especially on the coast, are fully booked during the December and January holidays, so try to make your reservation in advance.

Detailed information on camping sites throughout the country is provided in the South African Tourist Board (Satour) publication: *South Africa – Where to Stay*. This comprehensive guide is available at 12 Satour offices nationwide.

Most of southern Africa's larger towns have publicity associations or travel agents that will gladly give you brochures (some with maps) describing game parks, nature reserves and the many holiday resorts that offer camping facilities.

Alternatively, you can consult any one of the many travel guides available at booksellers and stationers throughout the country.

Particularly recommended are T V Bulpin's *Discovering Southern Africa*, the Reader's Digest's *Illustrated Guide to Game Parks and Nature Reserves of Southern Africa* and the *Guide to Hiking Trails*, by Willie and Sandra Olivier.

Campsite lighting

When your trusty torch fails, you can fall back on these emergency short-term substitutes:

1. Car headlights can provide light for 10 to 15 minutes without the battery dying.

2. Make a lantern of an open tin can; punch a few holes for air and stick a candle on the inside seam. For a handle, thread wire through holes in the side opposite the seam.

Campsite noise

Some campers seem to think that loud conversation or a loud radio is acceptable in the outdoors. Nothing could be further from the truth.

Try politely informing such folks that you are trying to learn the difference between the songs of certain species of warblers.

Another subtle hint: in the evening, tell your noisy neighbours that you plan to rise early (for bird watching, of course), and that you'll try to be quiet. But you want them to know that if they do hear you stumbling about, it's just you, not a jackal.

Campsite washing

Wear large latex gloves over wool gloves to keep your hands warm and dry while hauling water or washing clothes or dishes in cold weather.

LAUNDRY

1. In *Travels with Charley*, John Steinbeck wrote of putting water, detergent and dirty clothes in a refuse bin and securing the lid. Using an elastic rope, he hung it from a clothes pole in his camper and let road motion do the job. Later, he rinsed the clothes in a stream.

2. To dry socks, shut a car window on them and let them blow in the wind. Or tie wet clothes to a backpack; they'll dry as you hike.

DISHWASHING

1. Let fire-blackened pot bottoms stay black; they'll heat much faster and more evenly.

2. Absorbent babies' nappies are generally lightweight and make excellent camp towels.

3. Fine grains of sand stirred firmly in greasy bowls and pans make a good scouring powder.

4. Thoroughly wash cookware and dishes to avoid digestive disorders.

Candle moulds

Tin cans, cardboard milk cartons, heavy glass mugs and plastic foam cups make good candle moulds. Oil the inside of the mould lightly to make removing the candle easier; reinforce a milk carton with masking tape wound around the middle and across the top.

For a wick, knot a piece of light string to a pencil and lay the pencil across the top of the mould. Weigh the loose end with a nut, bolt, screw or paper clip so that it hangs straight.

Candles

1. To make a candle burn longer and drip less, you should give it a light coat of clear varnish.

2. Melting some wax into the holder is the usual way to get a candle to fit snugly. A cleaner method is to wrap the base of the candle with string or strips of paper towels, making sure they don't show.

3. To remove melted wax from candle holders easily, place the holders in the freezer for an hour or two.

Cane furniture

To clean dust from the crevices of cane furniture, use the brush attachment of a vacuum cleaner.

Sponge dirty cane with a solution of warm water and mild detergent or ammonia; rinse and wipe dry. Apply liquid wax occasionally.

To prevent drying out and splitting, take cane furniture outside once a year and wet it down with a fine spray from the garden hose. Or give it a quick shower in the bathroom.

Let dry slowly, out of the sun. If any bindings come loose, rewrap them and tack in place.

To support the sagging seat of a cane chair temporarily, tack padded plywood to the underside. Or try brushing water onto the underside to shrink and straighten the cane.

Canes & crutches

CANES

A cane is the right height if the hand holding it is at hipbone level and the elbow is slightly bent.

For the best support, hold the cane on the side opposite the injury or weakness – 15 centimetres to the right or left of the "good" foot, as shown.

CRUTCHES

A crutch is at the right height if there's a three-finger-wide space between its top and the armpit.

The armpits and the shoulders shouldn't carry the weight – let the hands and the wrists do that. Keep your elbows slightly bent and rest your armpits on the crutches only briefly, when swinging the uninjured leg through.

EMERGENCY ASSISTANCE

1. Lay the arm on the injured person's good side over your shoulder, grasp the wrist, and put your other arm around his waist.

2. A broom can serve as a crutch; a plain broom or mop handle, as a staff.

3. A thick stick, an umbrella or a croquet mallet makes a useful cane.

Can openers

If you can't find one:

1. Open canned liquids with the triangular punch end of a beer can opener; punch on both sides so that air can enter for easier pouring.

You can also use the triangular punch all the way around a can, but beware of sharp edges.

2. Puncture the can with a sharp rock, a penknife or a screwdriver; then work it open with pliers or some other tool (not your hands).

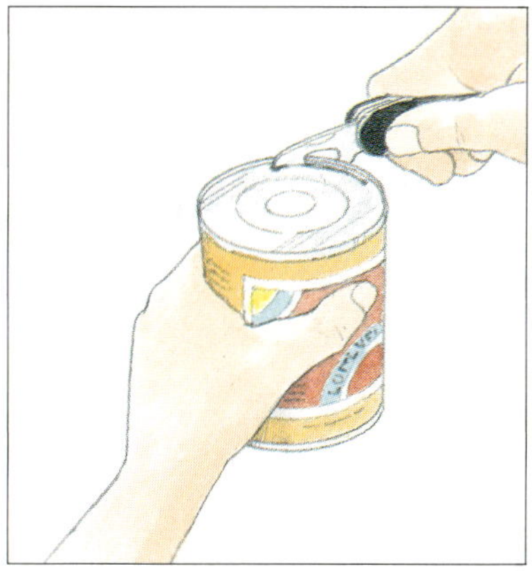

3. Multipurpose camping knives often have can openers.

Plunge the sharp point of the U-shaped tool inside the rim, hook the other end on the outer edge, then work it firmly, up and down, full-circle around the can. (The tool is made for right-handed people.)

Caution: Watch out for any metal scraps that fall into the can.

Car accelerators

If you let up on the accelerator, but the engine keeps racing, shift immediately into *Neutral* and brake gently until you can pull off the road safely.

Push the accelerator to the floor, then let it go suddenly. If the pedal is still stuck, turn off the engine; do not drive any further.

Then look under the bonnet to see if some object is stuck against the throttle linkage; free it if possible. Perhaps the throttle return spring has broken; if so, you can temporarily repair it by bending the end into a hook and reattaching it.

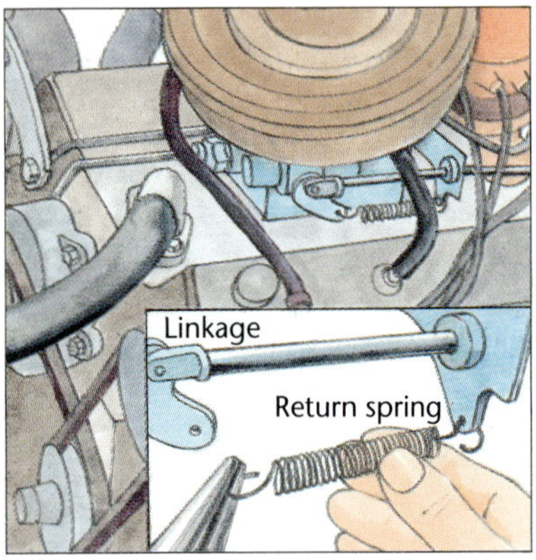

Caravanning

More and more South Africans are turning to caravan holidays as a cheaper, more adventurous alternative to staying in hotels or holiday apartments. More than 800 caravan parks around the country offer clean, secure, well-kept surroundings, with facilities of a high standard.

Most of the caravan sites at seaside resorts, national parks and the smaller game reserves offer hot and cold showers, laundry and ironing facilities, ablution blocks and braaiing areas.

Many of these sites offer restaurants, swimming pools, tennis courts, golf courses and other forms of recreation. For full details of available caravan parks, you can contact any one of the South African Tourism Board's offices nationwide.

If you don't have a caravan, you can rent a caravan and a car to tow it, by consulting your local Yellow Pages, or by contacting your nearest South African Tourism Board office.

Before you leave for your holiday carefully check the towing hitch of your vehicle. Have the caravan's brakes checked, and make sure that the tyres are in good condition. Also see that the brake lights, registration plate light and the indicator lights are working properly.

If your view on the interior rear-view mirror is impeded in any way, have outside mirrors fitted. An essential part of your travel kit is a pair of warning triangles which you should place not less than 45 metres in front of, and behind, your vehicle in the event of a breakdown.

While towing a caravan observe these basic rules:

1. Pull off slowly and change down gears early on hills.
2. Keep in the left-hand lane of a highway, except when overtaking.
3. Avoid sudden braking.
4. On downhill runs, always keep the car in gear.
5. Don't let the caravan drift off the road onto gravel verges; this could lead to dangerous swaying with serious consequences.

Car batteries

If your car battery is dead, jumper cables and a working car (with a battery the same voltage as yours) can get you driving again.

1. Bring the cars nose to nose but be sure that they do not touch.
2. Set the vehicles' handbrakes; put both transmissions in *Park* or *Neutral*; turn off both ignitions and all electrical accessories.
3. Connect one jumper cable from the positive terminal of the dead car to the positive terminal of the live car.
4. Connect the other cable to the negative terminal of the live car and to an unpainted bolt on the dead car's engine, away from the battery. Make sure that the cables are away from all fans, belts and pulleys.
5. Immediately start the live car, then the dead one.
6. Remove the cables in the reverse order of the way you attached them.
7. Drive the car for at least half an hour to recharge the battery.

Caution: It is hazardous to smoke while jump-starting a car.

Car bonnets

If the bonnet of your car suddenly flies up, don't slam on the brakes in panic; slow down and pull off the road. Steer the car by sticking your head out the window or peeking through the opening between the bonnet and the dashboard. (Prepare for this emergency in advance by raising your bonnet to see which is the better vantage point.)

If the bonnet latch is broken, not just incorrectly closed, tie the bonnet shut with a piece of rope and get it fixed immediately.

Car brakes

If your brake warning light is on, check to see if the handbrake has been released.

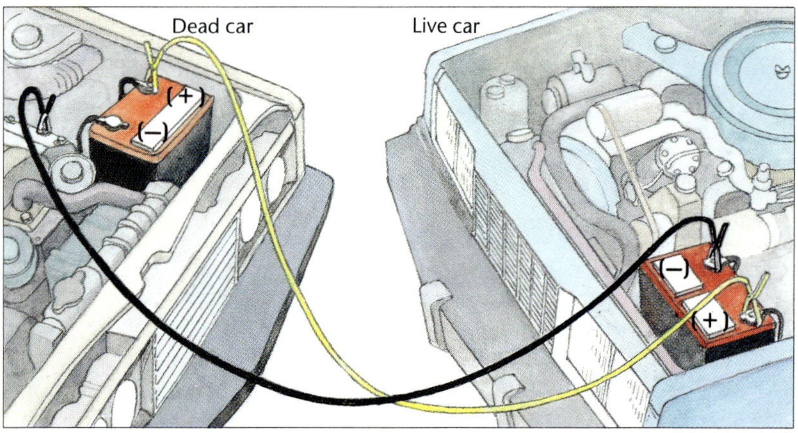

If the warning light comes on when you hit the brake pedal, there may be something wrong with the main braking system. Don't panic. You probably have enough braking power to slow and stop the car.

1. Turn on the hazard lights, then head off the road to stop. Keep in mind that you'll need more distance than usual for braking; you may have to press the brake pedal harder and it may depress farther.

2. Pump the brake pedal rapidly to build up pressure. If that doesn't work, use the handbrake or change to a lower gear so that engine drag slows the car. When the car has slowed to a virtual stop, pull onto the shoulder of the road and turn off the ignition.

3. If none of these measures halts the car, you may have to sideswipe something – a curb, a hedge, even a parked car – to stop it. Press your hooter and flash your lights to alert other drivers to your emergency.

Car doors

STICKING DOORS

Before going to the expense of getting a sticking door realigned, try lubricating its hinges with an aerosol penetrating solvent (sold in hardware stores). This lubricant will also effectively take the squeaks and groans out of the hinges.

WEATHERSTRIPPING

Don't wait until the rain is dripping into your car and the windows are difficult to move up and down before taking care of the weatherstripping. Instead, prevent it from cracking and tearing by applying a spray vinyl-and-rubber protectant every time you wash the car.

LOCKED BACK DOORS

Can't open a back door from the inside? Perhaps someone activated the child-safety lock. This tiny mechanical lever, which is hidden inside the jamb when the door is closed, is a special feature put on many cars to prevent small children from opening the door. Simply open the door from the outside and trip the lever to the open position.

Career advancement

1. Make yourself visible to the people who count; identify the influential people in your department or division (they may not be the ones with the formal power) and look for opportunities to work with them, even if it means extra hours.

2. When the boss is away, resist the temptation to slack off; work at your normal pace or even harder. You'll gain a reputation as a disciplined self-starter. If your boss gives you a job before he leaves, make it your business to have it completed upon his return. He'll be grateful for his lightened load.

3. People with contacts throughout the company have a better chance of promotion. Join in company activities – the sports club or the company's social planning committee.

4. Make your good work known to higher-ups by circulating to them any complimentary letters you receive from customers or clients. If appropriate, include a cover memo with a good word about your boss and/or department. You'll make your team and yourself look good, and you'll reassure your boss that you're not trying to steal his thunder.

5. Learn all you can about the business you're in. Don't limit your contribution to your own speciality.

6. Take night courses in a field outside your own discipline.

Career changes

1. What do you really like to do? You might be happy pursuing your hobby as a full-time career.

2. Which activities do you find most fulfilling? Do they involve working alone or with others? Solving new problems or making systems work? Negotiating or giving orders? The answers may help you find the career that you are best suited for.

3. Before leaving your company, ask the personnel department about jobs in other departments or divisions that you're qualified for.

4. If you want to investigate other fields, try to continue the work you've been doing on a part-time, freelance or consultant basis.

5. Many universities have programmes geared towards older students, including those who work full-time. Consult the faculties – they can advise you on the suitability of courses.

6. If you're thinking about a new profession but you're not sure it's right for you, do volunteer work in the field to find out more about it.

Car fires

If you suspect a fire, pull off the road and turn off the ignition and lights; in so doing, you stop the flow of petrol and electricity, which may be enough to stop the fire.

Get everybody out of the car. If the fire is near the petrol tank, try to stay at least 200 metres away and warn approaching cars and pedestrians of the danger.

Call the fire department or emergency service (or ask a passing motorist to do so) immediately. Do not open the car's bonnet or try to fight even a small fire yourself.

IN THE PASSENGER COMPARTMENT

Every car should have a fire-extinguisher with a capacity of at least 1,5 kilograms "dry powder" or "vaporizing liquid" to fight small interior fires that might be caused by stray ash or an electrical malfunction. Keep the extinguisher *in* the car, under the front seat or in the glove compartment. In the time it would take to retrieve the extinguisher from the boot, the fire could be out of control.

Car hooters

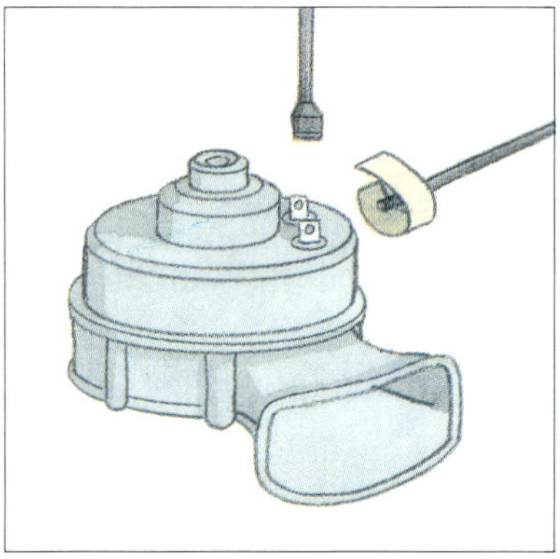

If your hooter won't stop blowing:

1. Turn off the engine, open the bonnet, and locate the hooter – the noise will guide you!

2. Disconnect or cut the wires leading to the hooter and tape the exposed metal ends.

3. If you can't get at the hooter wires and you know where the fuse box is, you can pull out the fuse. (Usually the thickest wire.)

4. Or disconnect the earth lead of the battery. Reconnect before starting up the car.

Car jacks

It's best to jack up a car on level, firm ground. If you must do so on a slope, put large rocks or wedges on the downhill side of the tyres.

In an emergency you can use a hubcap or wheel cover to support a jack on soft ground. Many newer cars don't have hubcaps, however, and others have wheel covers made of plastic or thin metal that may be ruined by such use. (Still, a wheel cover may be a small price to pay to get back on the road.)

A better solution is to carry a couple of boards with you. Ask a timberyard for scraps of 40-millimetre wood: one about 200 millimetres square to use as a base under the jack and another, about 150 millimetres x 200 millimetres, to use as a chock for the tyre being changed, to prevent the car from rolling off the jack. (If you're caught without a chock on the road, you can use a brick or a rock.)

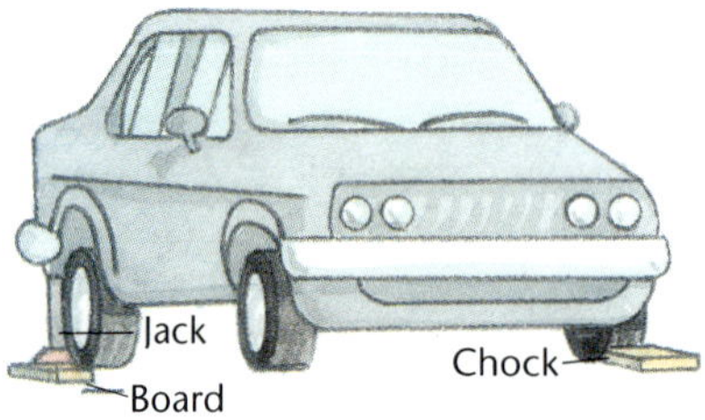

Carpenter bees

Carpenter bees, which bear a resemblance to big bumblebees, have a nasty habit: they bore tunnels into wooden doorframes, windowsills, outdoor furniture and all exposed external timber work.

To control the pests, look for piles of sawdust under their entrance holes, which are about one centimetre in diameter. When you see a bee emerge from the hole, squirt it with methylated spirits from a pump sprayer, which will kill it quickly.

To repair damage to wood, first blow fine powdered earth (known as diatomaceous earth) into the hole to flush out the insects. Then seal the hole with caulking compound or wood putty.

Carpets

1. To even out carpet wear, you should rearrange your furniture occasionally, redirecting the flow of traffic. Use scatter rugs in front of your favourite chairs. Turn all rugs and loose carpets regularly.

2. To revive the dents left by furniture legs, hold a steam iron about 15 centimetres above the spot until the fabric is moist. Then work the fibres back and forth with the edge of a large coin or the back of a comb. Prevent such dents by often shifting furniture a few centimetres.

3. Prevent static shock by spraying carpets with a solution of one part liquid fabric softener to five parts water. The solution can also be applied with a sponge or cloth.

4. To revive the colour of a rug, first vacuum; then, using a sponge or cloth, apply a solution of one part white vinegar to three parts boiling water. Dampen only the pile, taking care not to wet the backing. When the rug is dry, rub it lightly with fine bread crumbs, then vacuum.

5. To make your own rug shampoo for nylon or other synthetic-fibre rugs, add one tablespoon ammonia and a generous amount of mild detergent to a large bowl of warm water; mix vigorously, preferably with an egg beater, to make suds. Rub the suds lightly over the carpet, let dry, then vacuum.

6. Cornflour can also act as a rug cleaner. Sprinkle it on, let stand for five to 30 minutes, then vacuum.

7. To deodorise a carpet, liberally apply bicarbonate of soda (between two and three kilograms for a three-by-four metre rug). Let stand for at least 15 minutes (overnight for strong odours), then vacuum.

Carpet stains

Scrape off any solids. Blot up liquids quickly, dabbing lightly with a clean white towel or paper towel.

1. To remove greasy stains, apply a non-flammable dry-cleaning agent to the spot with a white towel; work gradually from the edges towards the centre. Don't scrub; dab gently until the spot comes clean. (Always pretest any cleaning agent on an inconspicuous part of the carpet and let it dry before continuing.)

Coat less stubborn greasy stains with aerosol shaving cream or carbonated water. Use a hair dryer to speed drying, then vacuum.

Or sprinkle a greasy stain with bicarbonate of soda, cornflour or talcum powder. Leave on for at least six hours, then vacuum.

2. To remove water-soluble stains, try applying some detergent solution (½ teaspoon of mild detergent per 500 millilitres water), working from the edges to the centre of the stain. Place several layers of white tissues or paper towels over the spot and weight down with books or pots and pans; let stand about one hour. Replace with fresh tissues or towels and leave overnight. Then fluff up the carpet pile with your fingers.

3. To remove excrement, urine or vomit stains, try this: after scraping off the solids, apply a detergent solution (½ teaspoon mild detergent per 500 millilitres water) and blot. Then use an ammonia solution (one tablespoon per cup of water) and blot. Follow with a solution of equal parts white vinegar and water (pretest on an inconspicuous place; vinegar can remove some dyes). Blot, flush with water, and blot again.

Car registrations

By law, all motor cars in South Africa must be registered and licensed, and a clearance certificate disc must be displayed on the windscreen before the vehicle is driven.

If you buy your car from a dealer, he will probably have it licensed and registered for you, but you will have to complete and sign a notice of transfer of ownership and an application for registration and licensing. These must be sent, with the appropriate fees, to the registering and licensing authority in your area.

If the car is new, you will need a certificate stating the vehicle's mass. If the car is a second-hand model, a current certificate of roadworthiness is required.

A second-hand car retains the previous owner's registration number, provided that the car remains in the same registering area.

Carrots

Mix a packet of carrot seeds with a cup of *unused* coffee grounds. Not only does the extra bulk make the tiny seeds easier to sow, but the coffee aroma is said by some gardeners to repel soil pests and other pests, too.

You can also add a few radish seeds to the blend. While the carrots may take three weeks to sprout, the radishes will be up in a matter of days to mark the rows. When you harvest the radishes, you'll be thinning the carrot seedlings and cultivating the soil at the same time.

Car security

1. Most motor cars manufactured currently have individualised identification numbers etched onto each window at the factory. Older motor cars or those with windows that need replacing may be sent to specialist companies for marking.

2. Don't leave valuables visible in the car.

3. Sharply turn the front wheels of the car to lock the steering wheel. Make sure you set the gear lever in *Park* on an automatic-transmission car; on a manual, leave the car in gear. Engage the handbrake.

4. Close all windows tightly, including the sunroof. Lock the car and pocket the key, even if you're only stepping away for a few minutes or you're parked in your own driveway.

5. Vary your routines – don't park in the same place every day, for the same length of time. Whenever possible, park your car in the middle of the block so that it will be more difficult for a thief to tow away.

6. Always drive with all doors locked, and in traffic and at intersections keep windows at least three-quarters closed to foil snatch-thieves.

7. Avoid parking in a low-traffic, dimly lit area, such as the remote sections of a shopping mall, where a thief can work undetected.

8. When travelling away from your home town, pack up any valuables and take them inside at night. Your licence plates are a drawcard to thieves, and indicate that your car may have saleable contents.

9. Special locks, alarms and assorted disabling devices are among the many antitheft devices available for cars today. Invest in one – and use it regularly (especially if you have a new or desirable car).

Carsickness

If you're prone to carsickness, get plenty of rest before you set out on a long car trip. Eat a light, easy-to-digest meal and make sure you wear comfortable, light clothing.

To be on the safe side, always try to carry waterproof plastic or paper bags (such as restaurant doggie bags) and a damp washcloth or premoistened hand towels.

Take along bland food and beverages: unbuttered popcorn, crackers or plain biscuits, water, juice or carbonated drinks, such as ginger ale or soda water.

Sit in the front seat and turn on the air conditioner to keep heat and humidity low. (Both are factors in motion sickness.)

If disaster seems imminent, open a window and breathe deeply. (See also *Airsickness*, p.9.)

Car-starting problems

1. Check the fuel gauge to make sure there's petrol in the tank.

2. Try the headlights. If they seem dim or don't work at all, the battery may be either weak or dead. While this is a problem that usually occurs in winter, it can happen at any time (see *Car batteries*, p.36).

If the battery is weak but not completely dead, you may be able to start a car with a manual transmission by getting it pushed; the working car should have bumpers the same size and height as your car's.

3. If nothing happens when you turn the key and the car has an automatic transmission, be sure the gear lever is firmly in *Park* or *Neutral.* Jiggle the gear lever in each position as you try

to start the engine. If it then starts, you probably have a faulty safety switch; take the car in for a service soon.
4. If you flood the engine trying to start the car (you'll smell petrol), wait five minutes; then hold the accelerator to the floor and turn the starter for 10 seconds. If this doesn't work the first time, wait at least five minutes and repeat the procedure. Never pump the pedal; you'll only flood the engine more.

Car warning lights

OIL-PRESSURE LIGHT

If your car's oil-pressure light stays on longer than a moment as you start up or if it glows steadily as you drive, turn off the engine. This light is a warning that you may not have enough oil to lubricate the engine – a condition that can cause serious damage to the engine very quickly.

Check the oil level; add oil if it's needed. If the oil is at the correct level or the light stays on after you add oil, the problem probably is the light circuit. To be on the safe side, have the car towed to a garage.

ALTERNATOR LIGHT

If the alternator light goes on, the battery is expending more energy than it is actually receiving; don't shut off the engine – you may not be able to restart it. Turn off any unnecessary electrical equipment and drive to a service station. In the meantime, keep an eye on the temperature gauge. If the car overheats, pull off the road to stop. (See also *Car brakes,* p.36.)

Cats

1. If your cat acts like an unwelcome alarm clock, feed it before you go to bed. Or install a bird feeder outside a window, well away from your bedroom; your pet may be mesmerized by the birds and let you sleep.
2. In winter cats like to snuggle up in a warm place, such as a car engine. You might save your pet's life by banging on the bonnet or pressing the hooter before starting up.
3. Run a damp cloth along your cat's coat to pick up shedding hair. Or gently brush with a soft-bristled hairbrush – some cats love it.
4. To discourage your cat from jumping on beds, sofas and other pieces of furniture, squirt it gently with a water pistol each time you spot it in a place that's off-limits.
5. A pine log makes a good scratching post. For toys, try balled-up aluminium foil, ping-pong balls, old knotted socks, paper bags, empty thread spools and plastic pill bottles filled with rice. Avoid string, thread, yarn and rubber bands – your cat may swallow them.
6. A clean cardboard box can serve as a cat bed. Cut an opening into one side for easy access. Then for comfort and warmth, line the box with a pillow, blanket or towel.
7. To help prevent hair balls, add a teaspoon of bacon fat or sunflower oil to one meal daily.
8. To keep your cat from licking or biting at its wounds, isolate its head by securing a circular cardboard collar around its neck.

9. Trouble getting that pill down your cat's throat? Try coating it with butter first. If the medicine is liquid, use an eyedropper to squirt it into your pet's throat.

Caulking compounds

1. A good substitute for conventional caulking in this country is foam-rubber weatherstripping (actually made of vinyl or neoprene). Often sold as foam tape, it comes in square, rectangular or round strips. Use a thin wood shim, a large screwdriver or a blunt putty knife to pack the strips.

Other usable materials include strips of styrofoam (polystyrene), fibreglass insulation and cotton rope. Seal holes and oddly shaped openings with wads of aluminium foil or well-chewed sugarless bubble gum.
2. When faced with cold-weather caulking chores, leave the caulk cartridges indoors, near a heating source, until ready for use. On extremely cold days you can wrap an electric blanket around the caulking gun. Set the control on *Low.* The surface to be caulked should be heated too; use a heat lamp, heat gun or large floodlight.
3. Save the small plastic tip that you cut off a new caulking cartridge; it makes a perfect plug to seal a partially used cartridge. Insert it pointed end first into the nozzle and cover with masking tape.
4. For a neat job of caulking around countertops, plumbing fixtures and various other interior surfaces, start by outlining the caulking area with masking tape. Apply a bead of caulking and smooth it with the back of a plastic spoon. Wait for it to get tacky (about 10 to 20 minutes), and then remove the tape.
5. To apply caulking in hard-to-reach areas, use a length of clear plastic tubing. Force the tubing over the open nozzle of the caulking cartridge and secure it firmly with duct tape.

Make sure you hold the tubing as you would a pencil while you squeeze the caulking gun's trigger.

Ceilings

1. Acoustic ceiling tiles offer a decorative way to conceal an unsightly ceiling. Those that you staple in place are the simplest to install, but you must nail up furring strips first. A better solution is to install a complete system, in which a metal grid is fastened to the ceiling to hold the tiles.
2. A suspended ceiling is a good way to conceal wiring, pipes and duct work. The panels can easily be removed to allow access for repairs. For a customized look, replace the drop-in panels with panels of hardwood-veneer plywood.
3. Wallpaper on the ceiling? Why not? First, patch all holes and cracks and remove peeling paint; then sand. Self-adhesive wallpaper makes the job easier. In any case, ensure a strong, lasting bond by pressing each wallpaper strip up against the ceiling with a clean, dry paint roller, working from the middle toward both ends.
4. It's hard to paint over water stains: they usually reappear within a few days. One solution is to seal the stained area with pigmented shellac or a stain-killing sealer before you start painting.
5. Use semi-gloss enamel for kitchen and bathroom ceilings; it's easier to clean than flat paint.
6. Wooden beams can lend a rustic charm to a living room that needs atmosphere. Fake beams of lightweight polyurethane foam are easy to install, and many look authentic. Or you can make your own beams using standard-dimension timber. Screw a mounting strip to the ceiling; then build a U-shaped box beam to fit snugly over it and nail it in place. For a weathered look, rough up the edges with a knife, chisel or axe.

TEXTURED CEILINGS

1. The best way to clean ceilings that have a highly textured finish is with a vacuum cleaner; use the dust-brush attachment to avoid damaging the surface. Sweeping the ceiling will also work, but use only a soft-bristled floor brush.
2. Here's how to remove dust from small areas, such as those found around light fixtures, that attract dust. Remove the crusts from several slices of fresh, doughy white bread, roll the bread into a ball, and roll the ball along the dusty surface.

Cellulite

If the skin on your thighs, knees or buttocks looks dimpled – even if you aren't overweight – you have cellulite. Your best bet is a well-balanced diet and regular exercise – to reduce body fat and to tone the skin. (The more fat you have, the more dimpling there will be.)

DIET

Avoid crash diets; when you regain the weight, your skin may stretch, making cellulite worse than it was before. Instead, try to cut back on fatty and salty foods and add fibre to your diet. Drink six to eight glasses of water daily.

EXERCISE

Aerobic exercise is best, especially walking and swimming. Spot calisthenics may tone and shape problem thighs. Do 10 repetitions with each leg for each exercise.

Chair substitutes

You're having a party, but you have more guests than chairs. Aside from asking your neighbour for a loan, what else can you do?

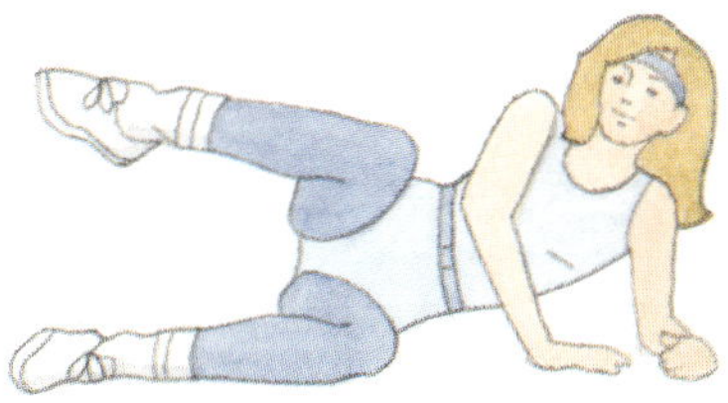

Flex right foot; raise and lower top leg 10 times. Repeat with foot pointed.

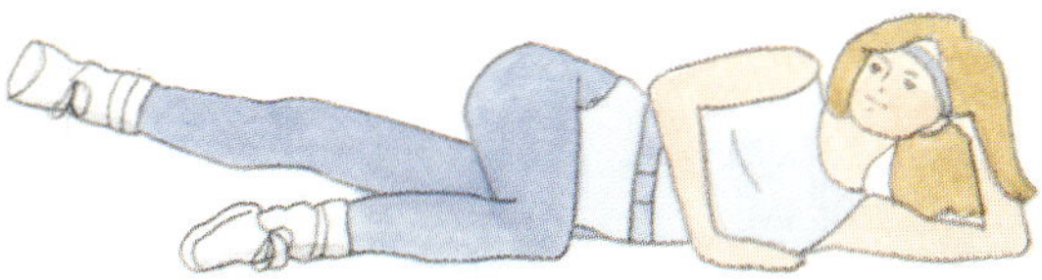

Flex foot; raise and lower left leg 10 times. Repeat with foot pointed.

LOOK BEFORE YOU LEAP

Cellulite myths

Purveyors of expensive "solutions" to the cellulite problem sometimes say that the culprit is a different kind of fat from the stuff that is found elsewhere on your body. Or worse, that the condition is caused by "toxic" fat – a sort of swamp of suet trapped in abnormal, chronically inflamed tissue through which blood and lymph fail to flow as they should.

In fact, cellulite is caused by normal fat laid down unevenly under thin skin. The chief cause is heredity, which determines whether – and where – normal fat is to be deposited.

There is no sure cure for the condition, and no proof that special creams, scrubbers or massage have any effect. Surgical liposuction may remove fat, but it may also create or worsen skin dimpling. If you have it, you probably have it for life, but ask your doctor if there is anything you can do about it.

Avoid "cures" designed to release the nonexistent "trapped toxins". Saunas to sweat them away, electrical devices to loosen them, crash diets to melt them, and body-wrapping tapes – all are equally ineffective.

1. Stacked two or three high, floor cushions can make a person feel like a raja. They stand up to hard use if you cover them with nylon, densely woven cotton such as corduroy or other tough fabrics.

2. For a children's party, make a picnic bench by nailing a 22 x 296 millimetre plank to two sawhorses or wooden crates. To prevent the children getting splinters, sand the board and cover it with a blanket or adhesive plastic, as used for covering shelves. Or turn sturdy metal or plastic wastepaper baskets over; pad each "seat" with a towel or old cushion, and decorate with fancy paper.
3. Don't forget the garden. Patio chairs can be brought indoors and dressed up with cushions.
4. Use a coffee table for dining. With colourful placemats adding a festive touch, guests won't mind sitting on the floor (or on cushions). Let your guests know your plans beforehand so that they can dress appropriately.
5. Rent folding chairs.

Chandelier cleaning

You don't have to take a chandelier apart to clean it.

First, turn the light fixture off and let it cool. Then cover the light sockets with plastic sandwich bags and secure with rubber bands or twist ties. Cover half the chandelier with a plastic sheet and spread another sheet on the floor.

Spray the uncovered half with window cleaner or a commercial chandelier cleaner and carefully wipe each piece clean. Repeat for the other half.

A quicker, easier way: liberally spray the chandelier with a solution of dishwashing liquid dissolved in hot water. Let it drip-dry for a few hours over a plastic sheet.

Chapped lips

The skin on your lips is much more sensitive than the rest of your face; it cracks easily in cold air, sun or wind. When this happens, resist the temptation to pick the peeling skin.

PREVENTION

1. Even though licking your lips seems to provide relief, resist the temptation; they're more likely to chap as they dry.
2. Apply a lip ointment at night; during the day use one that contains a sunscreen.
3. When reapplying lipstick, don't wipe off the old coat; doing so can cause irritation. At night gently remove traces of lipstick with Vaseline or cold cream.

Charcoal starter

Try this ignition sleeve for sure-fire charcoal lighting: first, punch holes around the lower edge of a clean five-litre can with a beer can opener; then remove both ends of the can. Punch two holes at the top and attach a handle of coat-hanger wire.

Set the sleeve in the braai and place one or two sheets of loosely wadded newspaper inside. Fill the sleeve with charcoal briquettes and light the newspaper through the punched holes at the bottom. When the coals are aglow, lift the sleeve from the braai with tongs, leaving the burning coals behind. You can also use a smaller container and surround it with briquettes; they'll light after the sleeve is lifted from the hot coals.

Or you can fill a milk carton with briquettes and light it at the bottom. The briquettes will be aglow by the time the carton burns away.

Cheese grater

1. To avoid skinning your knuckles, use a hand-held cheese grater with a drum and turning crank.
2. If need be, you can use a strong four-pronged fork as a cheese grater; just scrape away. Or place small cubes of Parmesan or other hard cheeses in a blender or food processor and buzz for a few seconds.
3. Brush a little cooking oil (or spray a little non-stick cooking spray) on a grater before using it; the oil will facilitate the grating, and make cleaning

a lot easier. Try to keep an old toothbrush at hand to scrub off any cheese that clogs the holes.

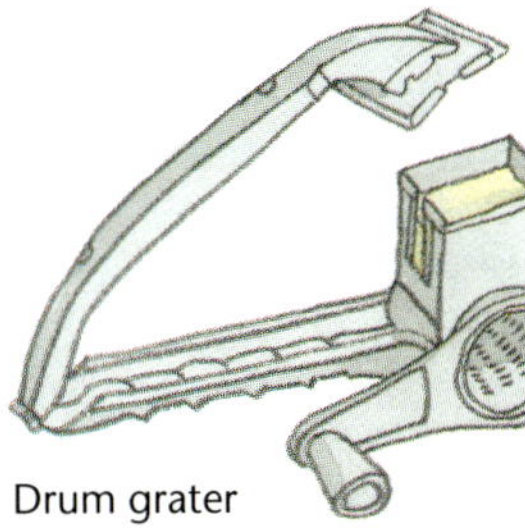

Chequebook balancing

Make sure that you balance your chequebook as soon as your statement arrives. You have a limited time to notify the bank of any errors.

1. Compare each cheque with the statement, put the cheques in numerical order, and mark them off in your chequebook.

2. Add up those cheques that haven't cleared. Subtract this total from the bank's total, then add any deposits not on the statement.

3. Deduct any service charges from your chequebook total; add any interest payments.

If your chequebook and statement don't balance, try subtracting the smaller number from the larger. If the result can be divided by nine, you've probably transposed figures – written 142 instead of 124, for example. If you still don't come out even, recheck your arithmetic carefully.

Cheques

A cheque is simply a written instruction to a bank to transfer money from the current account of one of its clients to the person or company named on the cheque. The person or company to whom the cheque is payable is known as the "payee" and the person who writes out and signs the cheque is called the "drawer".

If you make a mistake when filling in the cheque, you may cross out the error and correct it, but the correction must be accompanied by your signature above or below or next to it.

SECURITY

Fill in cheques carefully. When inserting the amount in words and figures, don't leave spaces that dishonest people can fill in afterwards to obtain more money than you intended them to have. If you write 'not negotiable' across the face of a cheque, the amount can be paid only into the account of the person to whom the cheque is made out (the payee). When you receive a cheque that is to be deposited, write 'for deposit only' on the back before you endorse it. Never sign a cheque before all the details have been completely filled in.

BOUNCED CHEQUES

Most banks will arrange to advise you when you run the risk of an overdraft. A charge is made for this service. A bank is entitled to refuse payment if a cheque is wrongly completed – where you've inadvertently filled in last year's date, for instance, or where the amounts in words and figures don't agree.

STOPPING PAYMENT

This means telling the bank not to pay out when the cheque is presented for payment – such as when you're paying for a product or service that has turned out to be faulty. You should instruct the bank in writing. You are not obliged to exclude the bank from liability if it overlooks your instruction and pays out after all, and you may cross out and sign any clause to this effect.

Stopping payment on a cheque for an amount that is legally due may result in prosecution for fraud.

DATING CHEQUES

As a rule, banks don't pay out on cheques until the date written on them. A cheque dated more than six months earlier than the date of presentation is regarded by the bank as 'stale', and will not be paid out.

LOST CHEQUES

If your chequebook is lost, advise your bank immediately. You can then stop payment on all cheques in the book and, where necessary, reissue fresh cheques to replace those that are stopped.

BANK STATEMENTS

You may obtain a bank statement of your cheque account (current account) as often as you like – but a charge is made for each. A statement is usually issued monthly.

Chewing gum

1. To remove chewing gum from a rug or carpet, harden it with an ice cube and scrape it off with a blunt knife. To avoid wetting the rug, put the ice in a plastic bag.

2. To remove gum from hair, work a little cooking oil or peanut butter into the gum and hair, then pick or comb the gum out. Or harden the gum with ice and "crack" it off the hair. Follow with an oil treatment.

Chicken breasts

1. Don't give up if your favourite recipe calls for chicken breasts and the store is out of them. Sliced turkey breast, pork or veal schnitzel are equally delicious in virtually any chicken dish.

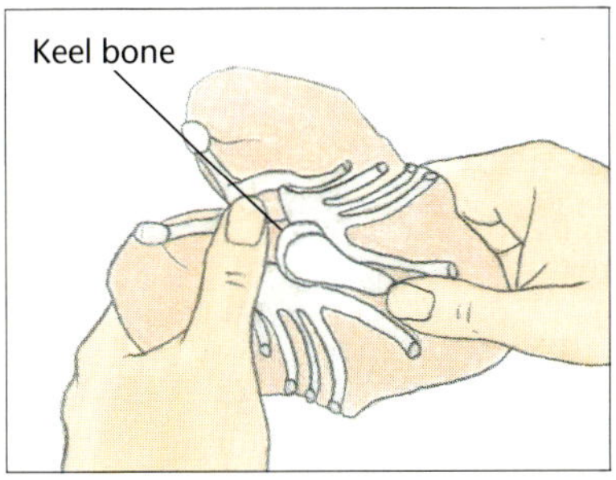

2. It would be advisable to invest in a 15-centimetre boning knife and bone chicken breasts yourself. First, thoroughly wash and dry the chicken breast and place it, skin side down, on a cutting board. Cut down the centre to expose the dark, spoon-shaped bone and the white cartilage.

With one thumb at the top of the bone and the other thumb at the base, bend the breast back firmly until the bone snaps. Running your fingers under the cartilage and bone, pull out the bone.

Insert the tip of the boning knife under the first long rib and gently free the meat from the bones, letting your knife slide flat along the rib cage. Repeat on the other side.

Pull up the wishbone and cut it free, slicing close to the bone. Cut the breast in half down the centre and remove the tendons underneath. Finally, pull off the skin and slice the breast. Freeze the surplus chicken and make stock with the bones.

Chickenpox

1. To relieve the irritating itch, apply calamine lotion to the affected areas of the body.
2. Or try a cool bath with several handfuls of bicarbonate of soda or ground oatmeal in the water.
3. Smooth on aloe vera gel (slice a freshly cut aloe leaf lengthways, or buy the gel in a health food store).
4. To keep children from scratching, put gloves on their hands.
5. In severe cases, ask a doctor for an antihistamine prescription.

Children's crafts

Many household throwaways can be turned into children's crafts.

PUPPETS
Paint faces on worn socks for hand puppets; cut the fingers off old knitted gloves for finger puppets.

For a milk carton puppet, cut off the carton top and slice the carton across the middle on three sides. Cut finger holes in the back. Make puppet hair and faces with yarn or markers and glue on paper cutouts as ears.

VASE
Cover an empty bottle with torn pieces of masking tape. Rub over the surface with a crayon or shoe polish.

SPACE HELMET
Remove the bottom of a two-litre plastic cooldrink bottle, and cut a face hole in the side. Make a cardboard visor with openings for the eyes; attach it to the helmet with hairclips or paper clips or, better still, a stapler. Decorate with pipe cleaners, paper cutouts and wire ties wound around the neck of the bottle.

SPACESHIP
Cut one of the top flaps of a cardboard box into a T-shaped handle; remove the other flaps and cut them into the shape of tail fins.

Glue the fins on the sides; add buttons and bottle caps for a control panel; and attach paper cups or the rolls from toilet paper or paper towels for rocket exhaust pipes.

ETCHINGS
Save plastic-foam trays – the type used to package meat, fruits and other consumer products in supermarkets. Trace a picture on the tray and rub paint over the surface. Press a piece of paper onto the tray and lift it off.

FURRY ANIMALS
Draw an animal's outline on dark paper and fill in with white glue. Stick on plastic-foam packing beads, then spray-paint. Colour individual beads for features.

TREASURE CHEST
Glue magazine pictures onto an old lunchbox, overlapping them to create a collage.

Milk carton puppet

Children's friends

1. Don't worry if your child is content with just one or two friends – we can't all be social butterflies. But if he's concerned, you can help by making your home an inviting place for young people to gather.
2. If your child's "best friend" is "stolen" by a third child, help her realize that she shouldn't restrict her attachments, that she should get along with lots of people.
3. Young children sometimes invent imaginary friends – it's not a sign of mental instability but an indication of an active imagination. Don't squelch or ridicule it in your child; nurture it.
4. Even if you don't like the way your child acts in the company of certain friends, don't criticize them. Consider inviting them to your home for meals, letting them sleep over, and including them in family occasions. You will learn a lot about your child, and you will be able to show by example what kind of language and manners you find appropriate.

Children's parties

If you have qualms about giving a birthday party for an active six-year-old, think about buying or hiring some of the vital party ingredients.

THE PLACE
Consider renting a room in a church or synagogue, YMCA, school or day-care centre. It will be more childproof than your home.

THE FOOD
Order any or all of the food – pizza, fried chicken, birthday cake – or have the whole party handled by a professional caterer.

Take the guests out. Many fastfood outlets and family restaurants provide birthday meals, including a decorated cake and special attention for the birthday child.

THE ENTERTAINMENT
Take the kids to a movie, the zoo, a rugby match, a park where they can

play softball or frisbee, the ballet or a skating rink. Alternatively take them on a hike; visit the beach or try fishing or swimming.

INVITATIONS

You can buy invitations, of course, but you and your children may enjoy making them together so that you can build up considerable anticipation for the coming party. One simple design is illustrated below.

If sending by post, make sure a cutout invitation fits your available envelopes. Or make fold-over invitations and seal them with stick-on dots (available at stationery stores in many colours). Use extra dots as "balloons" next to each address.

Children's quarrels

There's no doubt about it: young children enjoy fighting with their sisters and brothers. And children who learn to handle such quarrels may be better able to deal with challenges outside the home. Even so, you may wish to promote peace.

Don't even try to mediate routine squabbling – you probably won't be able to find out who started it anyway. But if a fight sounds serious or if a child is being physically hurt, don't hesitate to separate the combatants. If a fight breaks out in the car, pull over, and explain that you can't drive when you are being distracted by fighting.

Do try to understand the big picture of why the children fight and make adjustments as necessary. Is one of the children insecure? (Perhaps he needs a bit more time alone with a parent.) Do fights tend to erupt before suppertime? (Maybe they're just hungry.) Are they bored? (Try to keep them busier with more activities.) Do you need a few new rules? (No hitting; hands off Sally's toy cars!)

Do call a family meeting to draw up a list of rules of behaviour that everyone agrees to live by.

1. Require two squabbling siblings to wash a window – one on the inside, the other on the outside – making faces at each other as they work.

2. Request a written report on the fight from each of the combatants. Write a response to each report.

3. Ask the combatants to imagine three better ways to settle an argument. Post the suggestions on the refrigerator and refer to the list when the next fight erupts.

Chilli peppers

1. Be sure to wear rubber gloves when handling jalapeno, cayenne or other hot peppers. Never rub your eyes; oils in the peppers can irritate and burn your skin.

2. To peel fresh chilli peppers, first roast them under the grill or on a long fork over a gas flame. Turn often until the skin is charred all over, then immediately seal in a plastic or brown paper bag for 15 minutes. The skin will then peel off easily under cold running water.

Chimneys

1. To prevent chimney fires, clean your fireplace chimney at least once a year and your wood-burning stove chimney at least twice a year. In both types, a buildup of materials (chiefly creosote) can pose a real danger. Only specialist outlets carry chimney brushes; be sure to get the right size. Or you can hire a professional chimney sweep. To save costs, tie an old wire and plastic lavatory brush securely to a length of strong, green cane, tape paper over your fireplace, and do the job yourself.

2. An open-top chimney is an invitation for trouble. Block out bats, birds, mice and other animals with a chimney screen. Use a square of 15-millimetre galvanized steel mesh. With tin snips, cut out the corners to form a cross with four equal sides, as shown. Fold up the sides to make an open-ended box and wire the edges together. Then push the screen you've created, open end down, into

DID YOU KNOW ... ?

Birthday superstitions

Many of the cherished rituals performed during children's birthday parties actually have their origins in ancient superstitions.

☐ Wishing on candles: the offering the ancient Greeks made to Artemis – the protector of the young and the goddess of the moon, the hunt and childbirth – was in the form of a round cake with a candle on top. German bakers, who invented the modern birthday cake during the Middle Ages, encircled the cake with lit candles. Over the years, the birthday cake itself came to be decorated with one candle for each year of life. Some people add an extra candle "to grow on".

☐ Playing games: a birthday begins a new year, and games of power and skill – physical and mental – give the birthday child a chance to demonstrate increased strength and wisdom.

☐ Birthday spankings: inflicting a little pain chases away evil spirits and ensures good luck for the coming year. In some countries, guests give the birthday child whacks, punches or pinches – but all are given for good luck.

☐ Gifts to the guests: the small prizes concealed in birthday crackers – such as rings and coins – are tokens for telling fortunes in some families. Guests may also get various charms.

the flue. Not only will it keep out animals, but it will also block airborne cinders and sparks – an especially important consideration for a home that has a thatched roof.

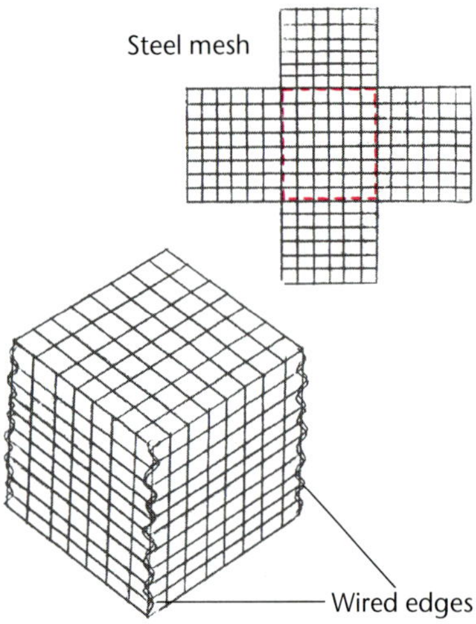

Chipped porcelain enamel

1. To conceal nicks and scratches, use specially formulated enamel paint. First, scrub the damaged area thoroughly to remove all traces of soap and grease. Then wipe with nail polish remover and let dry before applying the paint.

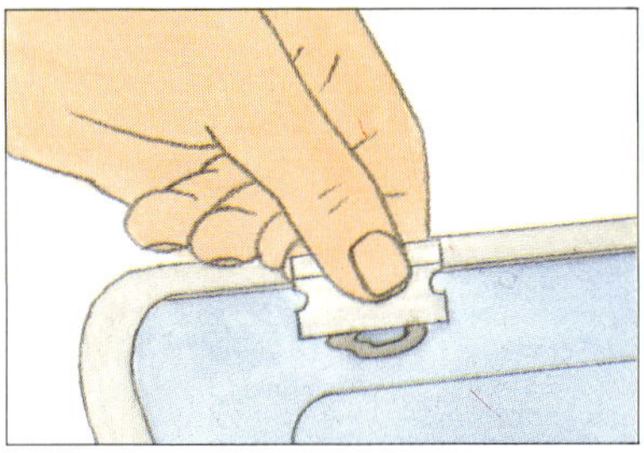

2. Repair large chips and cracks in a porcelain fixture with two-part epoxy resin paste or special tubed porcelain repair paste. The colour match may not be perfect, and some epoxies weather to a yellowish hue when old.

First, scrub the area around the blemish with fine-grit sandpaper to remove all rust and soap deposits. Then, using a clean cloth, wipe with nail polish remover. Next, mix the resin and hardener and add the colour (available at some art supply shops) until it matches the fixture. Using a single-edged razor blade, fill the crack with the epoxy compound. Pour alcohol on your finger and – using a very light touch – smooth the repaired surface.

Chocolate

Nothing but cocoa in the cupboard, and you need 30 grams of dark cooking chocolate? No problem! Just blend three level tablespoons unsweetened cocoa powder with one tablespoon margarine or vegetable fat. (For 30 grams semi-sweet baking chocolate, use the same mixture with three tablespoons sugar.)

Chocolate stains

Blot up or scrape off the excess chocolate. Apply a solution of ½ teaspoon mild detergent in half a litre of water; blot with a clean white towel. If the stain remains, apply a solution of one tablespoon ammonia in one cup water; again blot with a clean white towel. If the stain still remains, use a 50-50 solution of white vinegar and water, then blot again. If the stain is on a carpet, dry it by stacking several white towels over the spot and weighting them down with a heavy object. Let stand for several hours.

Cholesterol

You can protect your arteries and lower your risk of heart disease by maintaining a cholesterol level of 1,93 grams per litre of blood.

But beware: your cholesterol level may vary naturally by as much as 20 percent – that is, a test that shows a level of five millimoles/litre may indicate a high of six or a low of four. Also, lab results are commonly out by about 10 percent, which could make the difference between a borderline and a serious problem. To be sure, have at least three tests done and compare the results.

For many people, a change in diet is enough to correct high cholesterol levels. The basic dietary strategy is low fat (very low saturated fat), low cholesterol and high fibre (see *Low-fat diet*, p.130).

1. Restrict the total fats in your diet to 30 percent of your daily kilojoules, and the saturated fats to 10 percent. Instead of fatty beef, pork and lamb, eat salmon, tuna, mackerel and herring, whose unsaturated oils may reduce cholesterol.

2. Cook with mono-unsaturated and polyunsaturated fats. Sauté with olive oil; bake with sunflower oil; use olive or sunflower oil in salad dressings. Try to avoid palm-kernel and coconut oils and hydrogenated (hardened) vegetable oils – all saturated, all used in canned and packaged foods.

3. Use low-fat dairy products. Non-dairy creamers may contain more saturated fat than low-fat milk does; put powdered skim milk in your coffee instead.

4. Consume no more than 250 to 300 milligrams of cholesterol per day – about the amount in a single egg.

5. Increase your consumption of oatmeal, oat bran, apples, oranges, carrots and broccoli – each contains a special kind of fibre that helps reduce cholesterol.

6. A regular exercise programme may also help, but be sure to start out slowly. If all else fails, drug therapy may prove effective.

Chopsticks

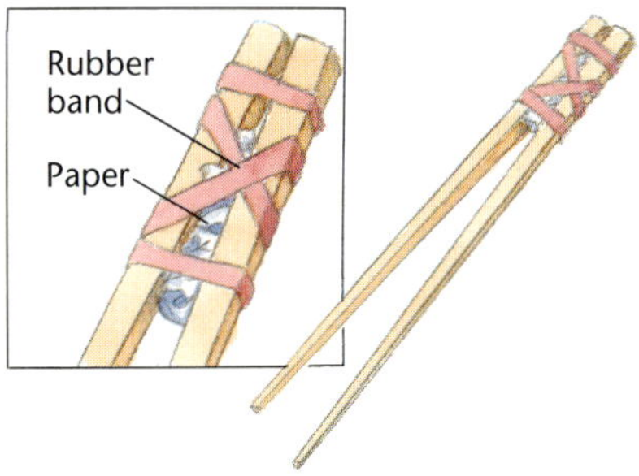

Do you find chopsticks quite unmanageable? Here's how you can tame them: wind a rubber band around the square ends, as shown, and slip a small wad of folded paper between them. Then slip a loop of the rubber band in front of the paper and you've created a hinge.

Chores and children

If you are thinking of giving chores to your children, start when they are young. Be patient, firm and flexible. Praise generously.

1. Ask the kids to help you make a list of what it takes to keep the household running smoothly, from cleaning the goldfish bowl to clearing the dust behind the TV set.

2. Then assign the labour, noting everyone's particular skills, interests and outside commitments. Rotate the jobs everyone hates – and be sure to take your own turn.

3. Consign jobs that fall outside the weekly routine to a "chore jar", to be dipped into by family members in need of spending money. Write a job description and assign a salary to each chore.

Christmas trees

When buying a fresh tree, choose one with pliable needles and branches; test its freshness by dropping it on the cut end – few needles should come off. Consider buying a small potted cypress tree which can be placed in the garden during the year, and brought inside for the festive season.

To prolong your tree's freshness, saw off the bottom centimetre or two of the trunk and put the base in water as soon as possible. Then spray the branches – be sure they are dry before you put on the decorations.

To help a tree absorb water better still, use a long drill bit to bore a hole up through the centre of the trunk. Pack firmly with cottonwool balls; they'll act as a wick.

Keep the tree in the coolest part of the room, away from sunlight, heaters and fireplaces. When refilling the stand, use cool water with a few aspirins added. (See also *Christmas tree fireproofer*, p.389.)

If you buy a live potted tree, wrap wet towels around the root ball. Be sure to keep them moist. Protect the carpet, rug or floor with a heavy plastic sheet. Keep the tree away from heat or draughts.

Chrome

1. Clean chrome with any of the following: soda water or mineral water, spray window cleaner, bicarbonate of soda, vinegar (cider or white) or lemon peel. Or use a solution of one part clear ammonia to 16 parts water.

2. To remove insects from your car's bumper, try rubbing with a soap-impregnated scouring pad that is moistened with cola. For rust spots, rub with crumpled aluminium foil.

Cigarette smoke

Allergic? Don't provide ashtrays. Politely explain your problem, then don't be afraid to get tough; ban smoking in your house, your office – and, of course, your car.

IF YOU SMOKE OR LIVE WITH A SMOKER

Invest in air purifiers or install a permanent air ionizer or a smoke filter. Remember to clean or replace the filtering mechanism regularly. Place a bowl containing potpourri in every room, as well as a few hen-and-chicken (spider) plants – they are said to be natural air purifiers.

FOR TEMPORARY TOBACCO ODOURS

Before party guests arrive, set out a few bowls of vinegar or a mixture of two tablespoons ammonia in one cup of water; their odour will help mask the strong smell of smoke. Burn scented candles; they will clear and gently perfume the air. Consider putting solid room deodorisers near air conditioners, or attach scented fabric-softener sheets over the grilles.

When your guests have gone, open the doors and windows and whoosh out lingering smoke with a towel moistened with a vinegar-and-water solution. Turn on any extractor fans and the air conditioner, if you have one. Wash all ashtrays.

WHEN THERE'S SMOKE IN THE CAR

Empty the ashtrays after each use and clean them thoroughly. Then put a layer of bicarbonate of soda or pebbles in them to smother butts and ashes. Or make the ashtrays unusable; fill them with hard sweets or change for parking meters.

Clamps

1. A vice will stand in for clamps if you're gluing a small object. Protect your work from the jaws with plywood scraps. Another quick solution is locking grip pliers.

2. Use weights to secure the joints of large items such as bookshelves. Keep the work out of the way so that you don't accidentally knock it over.

3. Use a tourniquet to secure the corners of a newly glued drawer or the joints between rungs and chair legs. Canvas or heavy cotton fabric strips won't cut into your work as twine might. Stick a baton under the strip (a pencil will do) and twist it until the strip is taut. Tape one end of the strip to keep it tight.

4. For an adjustable clamp, cut two 400-millimetre lengths of 50 x 75 millimetre timber strips. Drill two holes through each end as shown – 75 millimetres from one end and 230 millimetres from the other – both larger than the diameter of a 300 millimetre-long machine bolt. Insert two such bolts, one through each set of holes, using washers on both ends; the bolts should run in opposite directions.

Secure with wing nuts. Position the open end of your clamp over the work and tighten the nuts.

Adjustable clamp

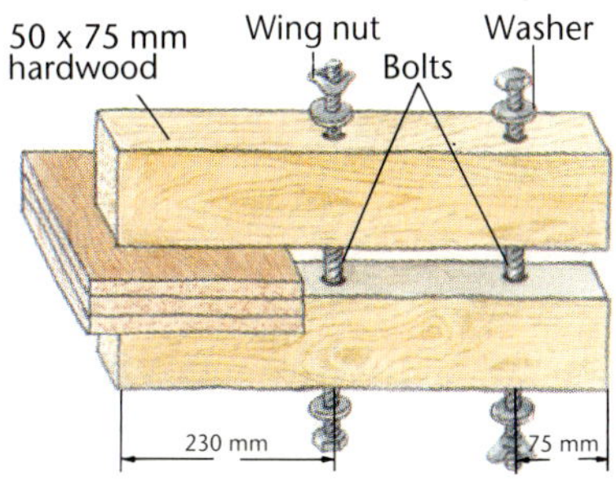

Clasps

Putting a new clasp on a necklace or bracelet can be a relatively simple procedure. To replace a screw-type clasp on a string of beads, work on one end at a time.

Snip off the old clasp, leaving as much cord as possible. If there's no knot next to the last bead, make one. Then thread the cord through the link in the new clasp and knot the link against the last knot in the string.

Trim the cord, leaving a length equal to the width of the last bead. Apply water soluble glue to the cord end and let it dry until it is stiff.

Then use jeweller's pliers to insert the cord end through the hole in the last bead. Leave only the knot showing. Dab epoxy cement on the knot and let it dry.

Cleaning

1. Automatic-dishwasher detergent works well on refrigerators, stoves, floors, walls and glass. Dissolve ¼ cup in 4,5 litres of very hot water; wipe with a dry cloth afterwards. Wear rubber gloves, and test first to make sure that what you're cleaning is colourfast.

2. Remove ugly crayon marks from your painted walls by scrubbing with toothpaste or an ammonia-soaked cloth. Rinse and dry.

3. Methylated spirits will clean the caulking around bathtubs; it also shines chrome and glass. Liquid chlorine bleach (¼ cup to 4,5 litres of water) will also clean caulk.

4. Clean the toilet bowl while you're away by pouring in ¼ cup bleach and leaving it until you return. (Don't use bleach if you're already using a tank-held cleaner that's released when the toilet is flushed; the two may react chemically.) To avoid clogging and odours, pour one cup bicarbonate of soda down the bowl weekly.

5. Can't get to that dirt in the corner? Make a pointed tool by cutting an old whisk broom at a 45° angle.

Clogged drains

First try a plunger (p.158). If it fails, use a wrench to remove the plug on the bottom of the trap (or remove the trap itself) and try to dislodge the blockage with your fingers or a bent wire coat hanger. Don't forget to place a bucket under the trap before you open it.

Caution: Chemical drain cleaners are dangerous; they can burn your skin and damage the plumbing. If you use one and it fails to work, call a plumber – don't keep working on a drain with chemical cleaner in it.

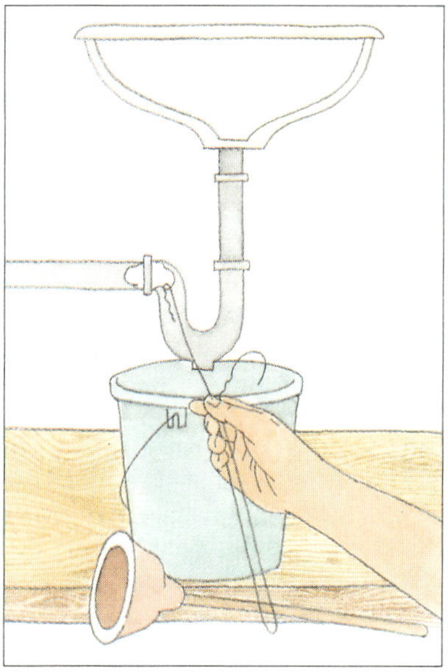

Clogged shower heads

If your shower has become erratic, spitting water in peculiar patterns, chances are that the openings in the shower head are clogged with mineral deposits.

Unscrew and disassemble the entire shower head, keeping the pieces in order for easy reassembly. Soak the parts in vinegar overnight, then scrub off the encrusted minerals with steel wool or a wire brush. Poke open the small holes in the faceplate with a pin.

Clogged toilets

1. If you think you can reach whatever is clogging your toilet, put on a rubber glove and try to fish it out. If necessary, reach in deeper with a bent wire coat hanger.

2. Next, try a plunger (p.158). Give it several tries. If water rushes out, victory! Before flushing, pour in a bucket of water to make certain the toilet drains.

3. If the plunger fails, try using a hose. You can try it with the nozzle, but if your water pressure is good, it is safer to remove any fittings and the nozzle – if they come off in the toilet, retrieving them will be a messy business and might be impossible if they are flushed along the waste pipe. First use the hose as a rod, without a jet of water, pulling and prodding. When the obstruction feels broken up, turn on the water and blast it loose.

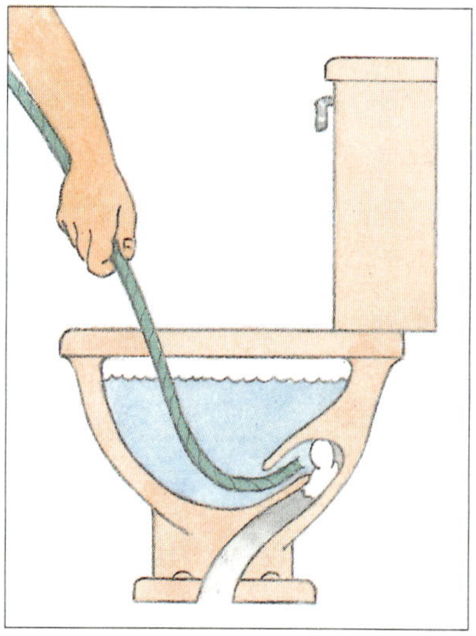

Close-up photography

1. A cluttered background can spoil a close-up photo. One solution is to use a piece of black velvet or other solid-colour fabric about 600 millimetres square. When photographing flowers, for example, drape the cloth over distracting bushes and branches. The flowers will stand out against a dark background.

Another alternative is a small wall mirror, angled to reflect blue sky as a background for flowers.

2. Inexpensive, lightweight alternatives to macro lenses and extension tubes are close-up diopter lenses. Like filters, they screw onto the front of a 35-millimetre camera lens or onto a zoom lens. They come in a range of magnifying powers: +1 allows a normal lens to focus on objects 50 centimetres away; +2 to about 33 centimetres. Coupling a +1 and a +2 together yields a +3 diopter, focusing to about 25 centimetres.

3. When you are using an electronic flash unit for close-up photographic work in a studio or at home, it is usually necessary to soften the light which the flash emits. Fix an ordinary white polystyrene cup over the flash. The light filtered through the polystyrene is less harsh than the direct flash, which can "white-out" a close-up photograph.

4. You can also use a polystyrene cup to mute an electronic flash for portrait photography – you will have to arrive at the correct exposure by trial and error.

Clothes dryers

Dryer won't run? Check the plug, then the circuit breaker or fuse. Next, make sure that the electricity hasn't been shut off.

The door safety switch may be stuck. This small button or lever, usually located in the rim of the opening, prevents the dryer from operating when the door is open. Jiggle it, then see if the dryer will run. If it doesn't, call a service technician.

DRYER FIRES

A dryer-related fire is usually caused by a dirty lint filter or exhaust duct or by drying such inappropriate items as foam-rubber pillows.

Keep the dryer door closed and immediately shut the door to the room where it's located. Turn off the electricity if possible. Call the fire department right away.

IF ALL ELSE FAILS

Speed up line-drying with a fan. A hair dryer works on thin fabrics, such as lingerie. If you have a hose-type hair dryer, slip a plastic dry-cleaning bag over the garment, put the hose in the bottom, and tie the bag around it.

Clothes storage

1. Develop the habit of hanging up your clothes as you take them off – except of course for those garments that are to be washed. Allow them to air and, if necessary, brush them before putting them away.

2. When hanging a garment, close the fasteners and arrange collars and sleeves neatly.

3. Use substantial wooden hangers for trousers, suits and coats. A piece of plastic foam glued to the crosspiece will prevent trousers slipping and will reduce the cross-leg crease. Make padded hangers for lighter garments by gluing on strips of plastic foam or by binding with clean rags.

4. Drawers tend to stay tidier if you make some compartments in them with cardboard boxes, cut to the right height. Use boxes also on very deep or high shelves that may otherwise be difficult to keep tidy. Cut away a section of the front of each box so that you can see what is inside. They can act as handy sliding drawers.

5. Plastic bags are suitable for storing synthetic fabrics, but wool, cotton and silk should not be stored in plastic for more than a month or two. Use old white sheets instead.

Clothes washing machines

If the washing machine doesn't run, check the plug first, then the circuit breaker or fuse. Next, see if tap is turned on. (Turn it off when the washing machine is not in use; constant pressure exerted on the hose eventually makes it leak.) Are the control switches properly set?

DRAINAGE PROBLEMS

1. If the washing machine isn't draining, the hose may be kinked or clogged – perhaps a sock has worked its way into the line. Refer to the owner's manual to see if you can correct the problem yourself.

2. There may have been a dip in voltage; wait 20 minutes for the motor to cool off and try again.

3. Otherwise, pull the plug, wring out the clothes, and bail or siphon out the water.

NOISY VIBRATIONS

1. Loud shaking during a spin cycle is usually a sign that the load is unbalanced, probably with bulky items. Stop the washing machine, rearrange the load, and continue the cycle.

2. Too much foam can also cause such vibrations to occur. Use less detergent next time or switch to a low-foam washing powder.

3. Are the levelling legs properly set? If not, adjust them.

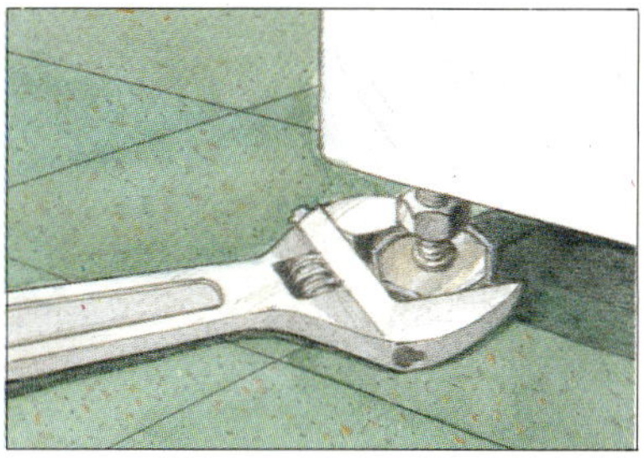

4. Is the drain hose secured? If not, tighten the clamp.

5. Inspect the floor under the machine; it may not be sturdy enough to give solid support.

6. If a new washing machine is sounding noisy, look inside for packing materials that may have been left around the basket.

IF ALL ELSE FAILS

1. Fill a sink or bathtub with water and detergent. Imitate the washing machine's churning with a plunger.

2. Put white and colourfast cottons into a pot of simmering water and detergent for 15 minutes.

3. To remove excess water, wring out the clothes or place them on a towel on a firm surface and run a rolling pin over them. Roll delicate garments in a towel.

CLOTHING PROBLEMS

1. Undiluted chlorine bleach may damage fabric. Use it only as recommended on the container and by the washing machine manufacturer.

2. If there's lint all over your freshly washed clothes, you may be overloading your washing machine. Lint may also result from poor drainage (see above), too little detergent, undissolved granular detergent, or incorrect use of a fabric softener.

Clouds

Fluffy white clouds sailing across a blue sky indicate continuing fair weather. But if they mass to form anvil-shaped clouds, be prepared for an electric thunderstorm, even if the sun is shining brightly.

Striped frosty clouds high in the sky indicate the probability of light rain; dark, layered clouds overhead mean steady rain or snow.

If you are ever completely lost at sea, look for the patches of stationary woolly clouds that usually form a little to the windward side of an island.

Clutter

1. Keep periodicals in baskets. Cull magazines and newspapers often; cut out the recipes and articles you want to save and file them in folders labelled by subject.

2. Set out bedside baskets for reading material. Place dishes on bureaus to collect loose change, other pocket items and jewellery.

3. Provide special bins for records, tapes and games in rooms where the family likes to relax; insist that users return these notorious clutter culprits to their "homes".

4. Throw out any old medications and cosmetics.

5. To keep bathroom countertops tidy, install bins for extra supplies – and any items that won't fit in medicine cabinets.

6. Outdoors, keep a plastic refuse bin in the garage or in the garden for playthings. Install pegboards in your garage or toolshed for gardening supplies and sports equipment.

7. Above all, de-junk your whole house. Room by room and in stages, go through all your various possessions. Throw away, give away or sell duplicates and anything else that you don't use or that is unusable.

Coasters

You can make your own coasters for furniture legs with the scrap ends of carpeting or cork samples available from a flooring supply dealer.

Nubby-textured carpet works best; it is more durable than plush or velvet and less expensive. Trace the shape from another coaster, then cut the coaster to size.

Cockroaches

Cockroaches lay their eggs in little brown satchel-shaped pouches that look like seeds. Look for the egg cases in dark, damp, warm places: under sinks, behind stoves and refrigerators, even in curtain pleats and inside curtain rods. Scrub them away or vacuum them up with the crevice nozzle of your vacuum cleaner and discard the dust bag.

To prevent infestation, dust cracks – especially under appliances, skirtings and cupboards – with organophosphates or pyrethrins.

One of the most effective commercial controls is a bait that has chlorpyrifos as the active ingredient. Place several bait traps in the kitchen and wherever cockroaches congregate; the pests are attracted to the bait, take some, and go off to die.

Coffee

1. To make instant coffees taste and smell just like the real thing, cover the cup or mug with a saucer after you've added the hot water, then let the brew steep for a full minute.

2. To preserve its fresh flavour, always store ground coffee in the refrigerator or freezer.

3. Freeze strong leftover coffee in ice cube trays. When you want a cup, put a couple of cubes in a mug, top up with water, and heat in a microwave.

4. Stretch 500 grams of coffee by adding 75 grams of prepared chicory; it increases the yield by about 10 cups. If the pleasant bitterness of chicory suits your taste, add still more – up to 250 grams.

5. Instead of decaffeinated coffee, try one of the coffee substitutes on the market. They are made from roasted grains, nuts or chicory. Their taste can be mellowed by adding a vanilla bean to the grounds.

Coffee and caffeine

The "pep" that you get from drinking coffee (and certain teas, cocoa and cola) comes from a very common ingredient – caffeine. You'll also find it in many prescription medicines and patent remedies.

Caffeine belongs to the group of chemicals called xanthines, which are potent stimulants of the central nervous system. Here's what caffeine does to the system:

Just a small dose acts as a stimulant, increasing awareness and counteracting fatigue. A little more can cause constriction of the blood vessels of the brain, an irregular heartbeat and symptoms that include general restlessness and irritability, muscle spasm and headache.

Heavy caffeine intake, equal to eight cups of coffee or 1,000 milligrams of caffeine daily, can lead to dependency, in the same way as over-use of alcohol or other drugs can. In addition, researchers around the world have carefully examined the role of caffeine in heart attacks, stomach ulcers and cancers of the stomach and urinary tract.

Although no firm conclusions have been drawn, it's sensible to avoid too much caffeine. A moderate caffeine intake is safe for normal, healthy adults, with the exception of pregnant women and feeding mothers.

Avoid caffeine if you have a family history of diabetes, coronary heart disease or high blood pressure. Children's intake of caffeine, found in various colas and chocolates, should also be strictly controlled.

Coffee grinders

1. Grind only as many beans as you need each time you make coffee. For drip pots, including automatic coffee makers, grind them as fine as possible; for percolators, a coarse grind is better. Keep the grinder spotless, brushing out any stray bits of bean after each use.
2. While electric grinders do the fastest job, an old-fashioned metal or heavy ceramic mortar and pestle still gives the finest grind and will never break down or wear out. But be prepared to work hard; the process is slow and tedious.
3. Don't try grinding coffee beans in your blender or food processor; you'll more than likely blunt and bend the blades and possibly stall or burn out the motor.
4. You can wrap some coffee beans in a dishcloth and pound them with a hammer. Use more beans than you ordinarily would – the "grind" will be quite coarse.

Coffeepots

Making do without a regular coffee or filter pot:
1. Line a funnel or a strainer with a coffee filter (a white paper napkin will do). Spoon in two level tablespoons of finely ground coffee for every 150 millimetres of water, then set over a heatproof jar and pour the boiling water through.

Or simply use a jug or saucepan. First warm it with hot water and empty it; then spoon in the measured coffee. Pour in freshly boiled water, stir, cover, and allow to steep for about four minutes.
2. You can serve Turkish coffee even without the traditional long-handled copper coffeepot. Grind the coffee beans – mocha is a good choice – to a very fine powder and spoon into a saucepan (one heaped teaspoon per cup is about right). Add cold water and plenty of sugar and bring to a boil. Simmer the coffee until frothy, then serve in your smallest cups. Be sure to let the grounds settle in the cup before drinking.

Coffee stains

To remove a coffee stain from fabric or a rug, try one of these methods:
1. Dip a white cloth into a beaten egg yolk and rub the yolk into the stain. Then rinse with clear water.
2. Rub prewash stain remover into the stain, then rinse with water.
3. Apply a solution of ½ teaspoon mild detergent in 500 millilitres of water; blot with a white towel. If the stain remains, apply a 50-50 solution of water and white vinegar and blot.

Colds

1. If you're catching a cold, ask your doctor whether you should take decongestant tablets to reduce the severity of its symptoms.
2. To relieve the scratchy, burning throat that signals the start of a cold, dissolve one teaspoon of salt in half a litre of very hot water; let it cool down, then gently inhale the solution from a small dish, or squirt it into your nose with an eyedropper.

THE FULL-BLOWN COLD

1. Take aspirin or paracetamol for cold-related aches and fever. Give youngsters under 18 paracetamol.
2. Rest as much as possible. Sleep helps recharge your immune system – and staying in bed prevents you from spreading your germs.
3. Avoid exercise; your strength and endurance are low, and you're more likely to injure a muscle. Exercising with a fever is especially dangerous because it can cause heat exhaustion.
4. Drink lots of fluids to replenish those you've lost. In addition to water, drink plenty of citrus juices; the acid they contain may make your throat inhospitable to the viruses causing your cold. Avoid colas, coffee and tea; they contain caffeine, a diuretic that causes you to lose body fluids.
5. To soothe a sore throat and help shrink swollen tissue, gargle every two hours with a solution of ¼ teaspoon salt in one cup warm water.

NASAL CONGESTION

1. Saltwater nose drops may help relieve a stuffy nose. Boil ½ cup water, let it cool, and dissolve ¼ teaspoon salt in it.

IN TIMES GONE BY

The cold war

Traditional folk wisdom says that if you leave a cold alone, it lasts seven days; if you treat it, it will go away in a week.

Nonetheless, people have sworn by such "cures" as this: hang your hat on the bedpost, drink gin until you see two hats, then pull the covers up until the siege is over.

In parts of North America, people rubbed camphor and whisky on their congested chests; in Victorian England they used hot, wet cloths sprinkled with turpentine.

Today millions gulp down vitamin C tablets to combat colds. It probably doesn't hurt, but there's no firm evidence that it does any more good than eating an orange a day.

2. If you prefer medicated nose drops or sprays, don't rely on them for any longer than three days; longer use can cause the "rebound effect", which increases congestion.
3. Hot chicken soup helps dissolve mucus. In addition, the water and salt in the soup prevent dehydration, important when your nasal tissue is unpleasantly dry.
4. A strong cup of peppermint tea has much the same effect. Pour half a litre of boiling water over 10 grams of dried leaves; steep for five to 20 minutes. (Adding honey helps soothe a sore throat.)

Cold sores

A virus known as *Herpes simplex* is the culprit that causes these small blisters (fever blisters) to occur around the mouth. If you have cold sores, don't regard yourself as exceptional – well over 50 percent of the adult population have had the infection at some time or another.

Cold sores are most common in children between the ages of six months and five years. The first attack may cause an illness resembling influenza, with the victim having a slight fever.

Cold sores may cause ulceration of the lips, the lining of the cheeks, the gums and the tongue. Recurring cold sores, known as secondary sores, may be reactivated by fever, sunburn, colds or menstruation.

The painful stage of cold sores lasts about 10 days, but it may take up to three weeks for the ulcers to heal.

To ease the pain or discomfort of cold sores you should:
1. Rinse the mouth thoroughly with a mouthwash recommended by your local pharmacist.
2. Sip iced water.
3. For troublesome sores apply the antiviral ointment acyclovir.

Cold-weather starting

If you're having trouble getting your car engine to turn over in cold weather, the problem is probably a weak battery. To forestall the problem, check your battery before cold weather sets in. At the same time, make certain that the clamps are securely connected, and that the terminals are not corroded.

To clean top-post battery terminals, first remove the clamps: loosen the bolts and twist the clamps back and forth – you may even have to tap them lightly with a hammer before they'll move. Then plug the vent holes with a rag or cover them with masking tape. Scrub both the clamps and the terminals with a wire brush. Before you reattach the clamps, apply a thin coat of Vaseline at the connection to retard further corrosion.

To clean side-terminal batteries, loosen the retaining bolt until each cable comes off; clean all surfaces with a wire brush. Replace the cables and tighten the bolts.

If cold, damp weather starting is a constant headache, water-protect the engine. With engine hot, clean it with engine cleaner. Run to dry completely, then spray all electric cables, distributor and battery leads with a silicone sealer.

Colic

Some colicky babies seem to cry less if they sleep in a very quiet environment and are handled very gently by their parents.

Others are soothed by monotonous sounds or motion, such as rocking.

Although not always convenient, a car ride is frequently quite effective treatment for a colicky baby. For times when this is impossible, many baby's accessories stores sell a small motorised device that attaches to the crib springs and simulates the vibration of a moving car.

Try giving the baby a fennel or anise solution. Boil 125 millilitres of water for about 10 minutes; add one teaspoon fennel tea or aniseed and ½ teaspoon sugar; reboil for one minute, then strain into a bottle.

Colitis

Also known in this country as ulcerative colitis, this is severe inflammation of the large bowel.

Typical symptoms are cramps low in the abdomen and the frequent passing of loose stools that show blood and mucus. Diarrhoea may become quite severe – with bowel actions up to 20 times a day, sometimes producing only watery, bloodstained stools. Bloody, mucoid stools may also be produced in various cases of parasitic infestation such as amoebiasis, but the cramping and frequency tend to be much more pronounced in colitis.

To manage colitis:
1. Try to follow a diet that excludes vegetable roughage and raw fruits. Taking simple preparations for the relief of diarrhoea may also help.
2. Avoid stress or anxiety – both are known to aggravate the condition.
3. During severe phases, rest in bed as much as you can.

The presence of blood, pus or mucus in the stools may be caused by a variety of conditions, so consult your doctor when this occurs.

He may send you for specialised investigations, and follow up by prescribing certain medicines. Colitis may clear up spontaneously, or continue with periodic remissions.

Collections

1. Look carefully around the house to see if you already have the makings of a "pop culture" collection for your children, that can grow in value: Masters of the Universe figures, teddy bears, theme mugs or old rock 'n roll records. To add to your stock, shop around at flea markets.

2. Pick a theme to organize a shell, rock or pressed-flower collection: colours, interesting shapes or geographical areas, for example.

3. A collection of small objects disappears against a white background. Paint shelfbacks a dark colour or line them with dark paper.

Wooden printer's trays – the kind that were used to store lead letters – are ideal for displaying a collection of tiny objects. These could include seashells, miniature dolls, precious stones and other miscellaneous collectors' items. Consider searching antique shops for original trays and flea markets for modern versions. After cleaning, rub with furniture oil, polish or coat with a polyurethane varnish.

4. Stamps, coins and antiques often grow in value, but they're easier to buy than to sell. Dealers seldom pay more than half the retail value.

Colour in the home

The way colours are combined in a room sets a mood and sometimes creates illusions. Light colours on walls make a room seem larger; dark colours make it cosier. Reds, oranges and yellows bring a noticeable excitement, vibrancy and cheer; blues, greens and purples are generally soothing and serene.

1. Start with the colour of a favourite decorative element such as a rug, a chair, a vase or even a painting. The simplest way to use that colour is monochromatically – with shades or tints of the same hue.

2. You'd like more drama? Why not try adding other colours. Related colours (such as blue, blue-green and green) invariably tend to yield natural harmony to the surroundings. Colours from opposite sides of the spectrum (red and green, perhaps) produce a complementary scheme that works best if one colour predominates and the other provides accents. Since complementary colours are difficult to balance, test them out in smaller, proportional amounts first.

3. To ensure buying paints, wallpapers, fabrics and carpets that co-ordinate, assemble a portable swatch book for each room. With each purchase, add a snippet large enough to show its colour or mix of colours. Bear in mind that the colours in small or mat-finish samples will look darker in a big or sunny room.

4. Paint, stain and home dyes can be mixed to the exact colour you want. Paint can be custom-coloured by the dealer, or you can mix "universal colorants" (generally sold in tubes at paint supply stores) and use the blend as the pigment for tinting white paint. Darker colours may require a tinted base paint.

Whichever colour you use, test a small amount first. Don't judge it until it has had at least a day to dry. Then mix an ample supply – the colour will be hard to duplicate.

5. Blend two or more commercial fabric powder or liquid home dyes to create the exact shade you want. Fabric dyes work best on all sorts of natural fibres (cotton, linen, rayon, silk, wool), on nylon and acetate and on blends. Polyester and acrylic do not accept dyes, but blends containing them will reach an even tint of the chosen hue, although not a particularly deep shade.

Combs

1. To prevent static electricity, use a wooden comb.

2. You can also use a plastic fork.

3. An Afro-comb works much better than an ordinary comb for very curly hair, whether natural or permed. To provide lift for curly hair without using an Afro-comb, you can try one of these items: a pen, a comb handle, a toothbrush, an unsharpened pencil or even a chopstick.

Compasses

If you are lost and don't have a magnetic compass, you can find your bearings by fixing the approximate direction of north with your analogue watch. Point the number 12 on the dial directly at the sun. In the southern hemisphere, north lies halfway between the 12 and the position of the hour hand. In southern Africa, for most of the day, the sun is on a roughly east-west line to your north.

The needle of a magnetic compass points to magnetic north which, in South Africa, is about 23 degrees west of true north. This difference, known as the angle of declination, is shown on most topographical maps. Place your compass on the map with the long edge of the base plate connecting where you are with where you want to go. Turn the bezel (the dial) until the orienteering arrow lines up with magnetic north, as shown on the map. Hold the compass in front of you and turn your body until needle and orienteering arrow line up. The long line of the base plate and the direction-of-travel arrow, are pointing in the direction you want to go.

When taking a compass reading, keep clear of iron-containing metals, such as fences, vehicles and wires.

Compost bins

1. A large drum makes a good compost container.

First, remove both ends to make an open cylinder. Then set it upright in a corner of the garden and fill it gradually with compost material. When the drum is full, let the compost age for about three to six months, then lift it to release a pile of garden-ready humus.

2. In a small garden or on a rooftop or terrace, you can conceal compost neatly in odourproof plastic. Line a refuse bin with a thick, durable plastic bag. If the compost material is dry, such as autumn leaves, add 4,5 litres of water and 750 millimetres of lawn fertilizer. Seal. All in all, the composting process should be complete in three to four months.

Compost material

1. Use your kitchen leftovers to feed your plants. Fill a compost bin gradually with alternating 15-centimetre layers of kitchen waste (no meat scraps, grease or bones), garden debris (no weed seeds) and soil. Add a sprinkling of high-nitrogen fertilizer – a 3.2.1 formulation is ideal – to each layer. (A little lime will also help, but don't add it if you're going to use the compost to side-dress acid-loving plants such as azaleas.) Let the mixture age three to six months, and douse it regularly with a hose.

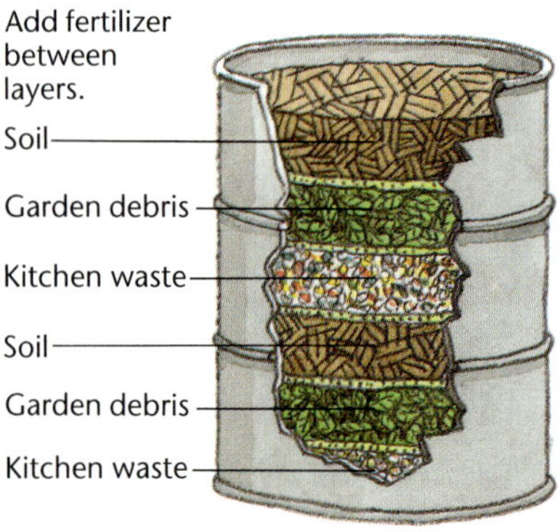

2. Such rural compost ingredients as animal manure and spoiled hay may be difficult to come by.

Look carefully around your town for suitable industrial by-products instead: shredded cardboard and newspaper, weathered sawdust from the timberyard, mill wastes of wool and silk, hair clippings from the barbershop. All can be prime fuel for the compost heap.

Try to avoid using old ashes from a coal fire, dog or cat droppings or shredded magazines; they may contain sulphur oxides, disease organisms or inks that are bad for plants. And avoid cooking grease; it not only attracts animals but it also tends to slow the composting process.

Computations

Stuck without your trusty calculator? Here are a few easy ways to double-check your arithmetic.

ADDITION

A quick and easy way to check your addition is to add up the digits in each number and then add up the digits in each sum; you should keep the process going until each number is reduced to a single digit. Then add together the single digits above the line; their total should equal the single digit in your sum.

Example: 9,236 + 5,347 = 14,583

9 + 2 + 3 + 6 = 20;	2 + 0 = 2
5 + 3 + 4 + 7 = 19	
1 + 9 = 10;	1 + 0 = 1
1 + 4 + 5 + 8 + 3 = 21;	2 + 1 = 3

It's even easier if you "cast out the nines". Eliminate all nines and digits adding up to nine – they (take this on faith!) don't affect the outcome.

Example: 9,236 + 5,347 = 14,583

~~9~~ 2 ~~3~~ ~~6~~ = 2
~~5~~ 3 ~~4~~ 7 = 1
~~1~~ ~~4~~ ~~5~~ ~~8~~ 3 = 3

SUBTRACTION

To make sure you've subtracted correctly, add together the result and the number you subtracted – you should get the number you started with.

MULTIPLICATION

Divide the answer by one of the numbers being multiplied. You should get the other number.

DIVISION

Multiply the answer by the number you divided by; if you come up with the number you originally divided, you get an A!

Computers

When you can't get your computer to work, don't panic – the problem may be easy to remedy.

1. Check all the cables and connections; one of them may have worked itself loose.

2. Did you turn everything on? The monitor? The printer?

3. Did you put a disk in upside down or backward? Quit the programme and start it up again.

4. Did you skip a key step?

5. Is a special function key in the wrong position?

6. If all else fails, you should refer to your user's guide.

DISKS

Treat your floppy disks with extreme care. Heat, fingerprints, magnetic sources (telephones, stereo speakers, televisions, motors), writing directly on or clipping something to a disk – all these things and more can destroy their contents.

FATIGUE

If you find it tiring to work (or play) at your personal computer for long periods of time, check these points:

1. Is the console too high, forcing your shoulders and upper arms into a somewhat strained position?

2. Is your chair the right height, with good support for your back?

3. Is there glare on the screen from the sun or room lighting, causing unnecessary eyestrain? (Wearing a visor may help if the problem is bright overhead lighting.)

Concrete floors

Here's how to remove dirt stains from a concrete floor: spray with a garden hose and sprinkle on scouring powder. Wait 20 to 30 minutes, then scrub with a stiff-bristled scrubbing brush. Rinse and sweep up the residue.

For grease or oil stains, cover with a layer of powdered Portland cement and saturate the powder with paint thinner or petrol. Spread a sheet of plastic over the area and let stand overnight. The next day, sweep the powder away.

To make future cleaning easier, apply a liquid concrete sealer to the floor with a paint roller.

Constipation

Despite their popularity, laxatives and enemas are seldom the answer; they may even make constipation worse because many of them can be habit-forming.

1. Double your consumption of fibre-rich foods. But remember, all fibre is not the same. Wheat bran, wholewheat bread, pasta, brown rice and other wholegrain foods contain the fibre that works best on constipation. The fibre in oats, beans, apples, broccoli and various other fruits and vegetables helps somewhat less.

2. To get your system operating smoothly and help the fibre work, you should drink one to two litres of water a day – at least a glassful with any wholegrain food. And take a daily half-hour walk, jog or swim.

3. Don't ignore the urge to defecate; that in itself can cause constipation. So can antacids, diuretics and hypertension medication. If constipation persists, see your doctor.

Contact lenses

Many soaps leave an oily film on your hands that transfers to your lenses when you touch them. To check your soap, run a finger down a mirror after washing your hands. If you make a streak, use a different type of soap before handling your lenses.

LOST LENS

If a contact lens accidentally falls into a sink, be sure to turn off the running water immediately and close or cover the drain. If the lens has fallen down the drain, act quickly. Place a bowl under the trap and open the clean-out plug with a wrench. With luck, the lens will fall into the bowl with the other debris.

If your contact lens falls on the floor, darken the room and sweep a torch slowly and methodically back and forth across the area. The lens will glint in the beam, even if it has fallen into a pile rug. Or use a small lamp, as shown.

Contests

The chances of you winning a magazine or television competition or a sweepstake are remote – as high as one in a million. There are ways, however, of bringing the odds down.

1. If the rules permit, enter the contest over and over again. Send in each entry form separately, and try to post them on different days and in different weeks.

2. To reduce your competition, enter contests that run for only a short time. The best time is summer, when a great many other potential contestants are on holiday.

3. Follow the contest rules to the letter – and be especially sure that your entries are postmarked before the deadline.

4. Watch for contests that allow you to send in a facsimile of the entry form. If you make yours on bright-coloured cardboard, you will improve your chances of having it drawn. Pleat or fold your entry into an intricate shape so that it stands apart from others in the drum.

5. Subscribe to a magazine which gives various tips and details on current contests.

CONTESTANT BEWARE

1. When entering competitions, read the fine print carefully, and don't commit yourself unnecessarily.

2. Stay away from any contest that guarantees a prize to everyone; the prize is usually worthless.

3. Take note of the prize date. Some prizes aren't awarded for several years; others are of far less value than the purchase required for eligibility.

Contraception

A range of drugs, chemical preparations and artificial contraceptive devices is commonly available with or without prescription in South Africa. For those who prefer natural contraception, there are several options, including abstinence.

ARTIFICIAL METHODS

1. With the spiralling increase in reported AIDS cases in the world, the condom has become widely used as a contraceptive device. It is an easy-to-use, reliable barrier against sexually transmitted diseases and is available in most pharmacies and some supermarkets. This tube-shaped latex rubber sheath may be used with a lubricating cream, and should be carefully examined for durability or defects before use.

2. The diaphragm and cap used by the female are effective when used with spermicide. This device must be fitted by a doctor or nurse, and the user taught to insert and remove it.

3. Spermicidal foam, gel and sponge are easy to use but expensive – and effective for about one hour only.
4. An intrauterine device (IUD) is an excellent contraceptive, and needs no attention once fitted into the uterus by a doctor or nurse.
5. The contraceptive pill is almost 100 percent effective if taken as directed, and it has the advantage of reducing premenstrual tension. On the downside however are numerous possible side effects (including possible weight gain).
6. The morning-after pill is effective for up to 72 hours after unprotected intercourse but is not suitable for routine use, as it may cause nausea and other side effects.

NATURAL METHODS
Here are several natural ways of preventing conception:
1. The rhythm method, which requires long periods of abstinence.
2. *Coitus interruptus*, or withdrawal before ejaculation – which is risky.
3. Temperature method, whereby the woman ascertains when ovulation takes place, by recording her temperature every morning.

For detailed information on the use of these and various other methods of contraception, speak to your doctor or pharmacist.

Convulsions

Your companion suddenly becomes rigid and then begins jerking violently – he is having a convulsion or fit. What can you do?
1. Try to assist him to the floor or the ground, well away from potentially dangerous objects.
2. Loosen restrictive clothing.
3. Stand by to protect him from injury. Don't try to hold him down or place anything in his mouth. Most people neither bite nor swallow their tongues during a seizure, but they may choke on anything that's in their mouths (even objects as large as a small wallet).

A convulsion, whether epileptic or from some other cause, may last from one to several minutes. The victim may drool and foam at the mouth; his lips and face may turn bluish.
4. After the convulsion is over, remove any vomit from his mouth. Then keep him resting comfortably on his side, with his head down to allow him to breathe easier and to prevent choking.

Cooking oils

1. To cut down on cholesterol, substitute polyunsaturated vegetable oils and margarines for saturated fats and solid fat. (Be careful of substitutes in baking, however; they don't always work.)
2. Look for soft tub margarine; the softer it is, the less saturated fat it contains. If possible, choose a margarine that lists sunflower oil as the first ingredient.

If the first ingredient is qualified as "partially hydrogenated", or if palm-kernel or coconut oil is one of the ingredients, you should rather choose another brand.
3. You can make chips in the oven by brushing potato slices with a little olive oil and baking them at about 190°C for 20 minutes. Turn three times during the cooking process, brushing each time with a little more oil. The chips, or "fries", will have considerably fewer grams of fat than the deep-fried kind.

Cookware

1. Some common items can do double duty in the kitchen.

A wok makes an efficient steamer. A plastic fruit basket or an old aluminium-foil pie plate with holes punched in the bottom can serve as a makeshift colander.

Used coffee cans are perfect for baking banana and other quick breads. And a Swiss-roll pan can stand in as a roasting/baking pan.

If you're caught without a fish poacher, use a roasting pan. Put a wire cooking rack or an inverted saucer under the fish and cover the top with foil.
2. For minimum cleanup, nothing beats baking in foil packets; they're ideal for braising steak and for simply seasoned chicken breasts, minced beef, fish and vegetables. Layer ingredients on one half of a large piece of heavy-duty foil. Dot with butter or margarine, add herbs or seasonings of your choice, and fold over the foil. Seal the edges tightly, then fold over once more. Seal again, leaving little room for expansion.

Try a favourite campfire dinner at home. Place a minced beef patty, two potato slices, a slice of tomato, a thin onion slice, and a pat of butter on foil. Season, seal and bake at 180°C for 45 minutes to one hour.

Cooling

Need a cool-down in the scorching heat of a South African summer?
1. Install a ventilator fan in your attic, if you have one. Under a blazing sun, attic air can be as much as 10°C hotter than the air outside.
2. Position portable or window fans to blow hot air out. For cross-ventilation, open windows at the top and bottom and on all sides of the house.
3. Install ceiling fans. They're both nostalgic and practical as they stir up a gentle breeze.

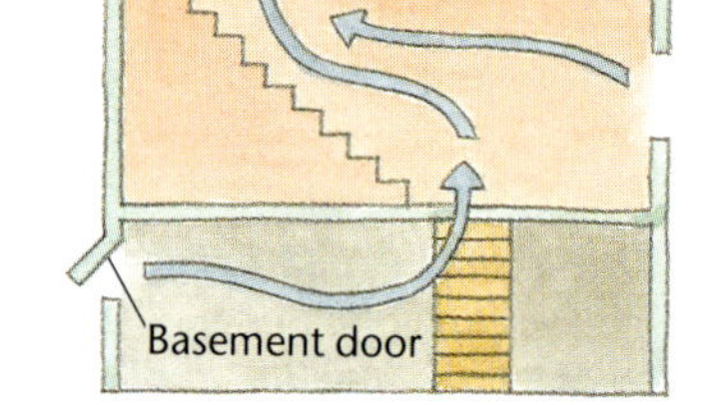

4. Even on a windless summer day you can cool a house without air conditioning by taking advantage of the "stack effect" – a draught that rises through the house. The aim ultimate-

IN TIMES GONE BY

The art of keeping cool

Those of us who routinely trek from an air-conditioned car to an air-conditioned office, shop, or factory may find it hard to believe, but before 1902 – when Willis H. Carrier installed the first air-cooling system in a New York printing plant – people somehow managed to survive without air conditioning.

In hot climates, families learned to build shelters that shielded the sun's rays and took advantage of cooling breezes. Thatched huts, for example, kept out the sun overhead while filtering the wind through thinner wall weavings.

Tomb paintings tell us that the ancient Egyptians mounted what appeared to be wind vanes above their roofs to catch breezes, a method still practised in Pakistan. Several thousand years ago, East Indians hung wet grass mats over openings at night so that breezes could flow through, cooling interiors by evaporation.

In African lands bordering the Sahara, in many Mediterranean locales, and in the American southwest people built with adobe, stone, and stucco, which produced what is now called thermal lag. The masonry roof and walls were thick enough to absorb and retain the day's heat, keeping interiors cool. At night, when the air cooled, the masonry released its heat to warm the interior.

For many people, the best way to get relief from the heat was to take a trip to the mountains or the seashore. But the wealthy were sometimes able to buy comfort. Roman emperors, for example, imported snow from the Alps in summer, and Middle Eastern rulers had slaves fan them with palm fronds. And no less a consultant than Leonardo da Vinci was engaged by one Milanese duchess, who kept her boudoir cool with the inventor's foot-powered fan.

By the late 19th century, form had become as important as function. One cooling device, shown here, consisted of a metallic statue crowned with an urn. The urn was filled with ice, which chilled the air just below the ceiling and dripped cold water through the statue into a basin filled with plants and fish.

ly is to get the cool air from your basement to replace the hot air that naturally rises. Just keep your basement door open and open a path all the way to the attic.

5. Use awnings, solar screening, roof overhangs or various types of shutters to block sunlight. Interior shades, venetian blinds, curtains and tinted glass are helpful, but don't work as well as devices that completely prevent sunlight from getting through the window to begin with.

Be aware too that any heat which is trapped between the glass and interior shading will eventually circulate through the room.

6. Keep heat out by insulating to the maximum and caulking potential air leaks, just as you would to keep heat in during winter.

7. Deciduous trees on the south, east or west help cool a house if they don't block breezes.

8. Choose white or light-coloured roof shingles to reflect heat.

Cork retriever

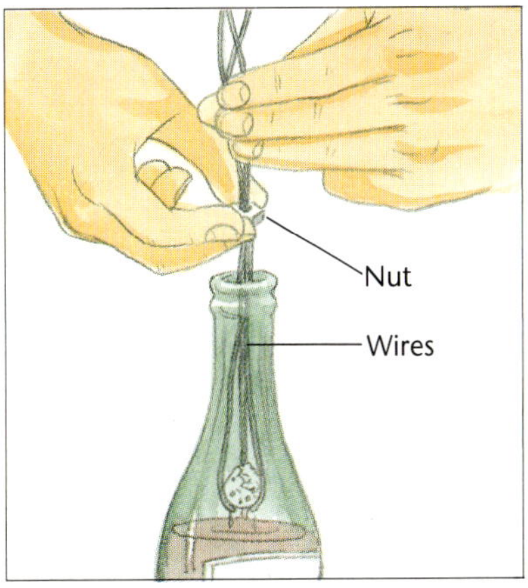

If a large piece of cork falls into a bottle of wine, twist three pieces of stiff wire together at one end and make hooks at the other ends. Push this "claw" into the bottle and grasp the cork with it. Tighten the grip by slipping a ring or nut down the wires as far as possible, then draw out the offending piece.

Corkscrew

1. Can't find your corkscrew? Open a bottle of wine with a large screw hook or eye; use a mixing spoon or sturdy stick to pull it out.

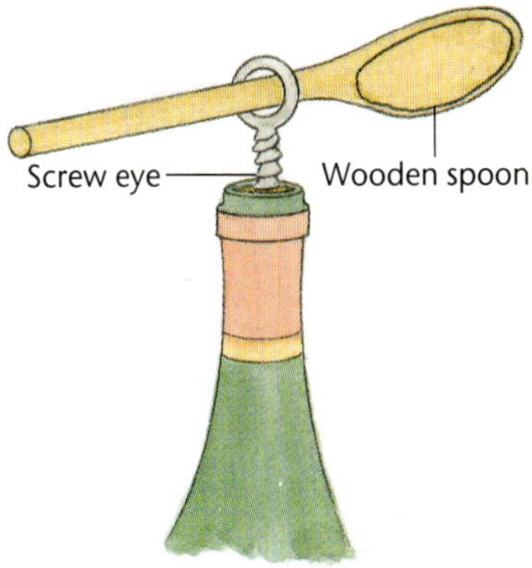

Or drive a plain screw into the cork and grip the head firmly with a pair of pliers. Pull the screw and cork up.

2. To ease out a stubborn cork, dip a cloth in very hot water and wrap it

around the neck of the bottle; it will expand the glass.
3. If a cork refuses to budge or breaks in the neck, try pushing it into the bottle, then pour out the contents.

Coughs

1. For a cough from a cold, dissolve one tablespoon each of lemon juice and honey in a small glass of warm water and sip it.

If you prefer something stronger, combine equal parts of lemon juice and honey. Take ½ to one teaspoon at bedtime. Either mixture will help loosen irritating mucus.
2. Make a soothing "stew" by boiling quartered oranges and lemons in a little water and then adding extra lemon juice and honey to taste. Take hot at bedtime.
3. To soothe the throat so that you can sleep, take one teaspoon honey at bedtime; let it trickle down your throat. (See also *Cough syrup*, p.391.)

CPR (Cardiopulmonary resuscitation)

This emergency technique to revive people whose hearts have stopped beating or who are not breathing has three major steps, known popularly as the ABC's of CPR:
1. Clear the *Airways*.
2. Look and listen for signs of *Breathing* by watching the chest, or put your head close to the mouth or nose. If the victim is not breathing, apply artificial respiration.
3. Check to see if the patient has *Circulation* – feel for a pulse at the side of the neck, the temples or the underside of the arm near the armpit. If the heart is not beating apply chest compression.

ARTIFICIAL RESPIRATION

1. Lie the patient on his back on a firm, hard surface. Tilt the head by gently pressing on the forehead and lifting the chin. Don't tilt the head too far back. Clear any obstruction from the airways with a finger. Look and listen for signs of breathing.
2. If the patient is not breathing, pull the lower jaw open with one hand and pinch the nostrils shut with the other. Take a deep breath and, covering the patient's mouth with your own, blow into the casualty's lungs twice. Watch the casualty's chest fall.
3. Breathe once into the casualty's lungs every five seconds (every three seconds for a child), until he starts breathing on his own. Be persistent and don't stop until help arrives.

CHEST COMPRESSION

Place the heel of one hand on the centre of the patient's breastbone, and place your other hand on top of the first. Press quickly and firmly 15 times in succession, then inflate lungs twice by artificial respiration. Check for a pulse on the carotid artery after a minute. Continue this cycle at a rate of about 80 presses a minute (apply more lightly 80 to 100 times a minute for children).

Cracking walls

1. To conceal ugly wall cracks that appear just below the ceiling, fill the crack and then cover it with a self-adhesive wallpaper border. These borders come in a variety of widths and are available in several different colours and patterns.

Wood mouldings – crowns, baseboards, chair rails and so forth can also serve this purpose.
2. To fill hairline cracks, use a proprietary quick-drying spackling compound. First, enlarge the crack slightly by raking it with the edge of a filling knife or old screwdriver. Brush away all dust and debris. Dampen the crack with a wet sponge and apply the spackling compound with a flexible-blade putty knife. Once it has dried, sand it flush with a medium-grain sandpaper.

Large or recurring cracks can be repaired the same way, but two important additional steps are required. First, cover the crack with adhesive-backed fibreglass joint tape. Then force joint compound into the tape and crack with a 10- or 12-centimetre-wide putty knife. Allow this first application to dry, then apply another layer of compound with a 20-centimetre-wide putty knife. Once the compound has dried, sand the repair with medium sandpaper.
3. Cover badly damaged walls with wood panelling or heavily embossed wallpaper, which hides surface imperfections much better than standard wallpaper.
4. Resurface with decorative wallboards. Nail directly into the studs, or cement the wallboard in place with construction adhesive. Then tape and sand the seams.

Crank calls

The most effective way to deal with a crank call is to hang up, depriving the crank of any satisfaction he may derive from harassing you. Instruct children and babysitters to do the same. If the calls continue, leave the phone off the hook for a while. The next time the caller disturbs you, blow a whistle into the mouthpiece.

If the calls persist or if they are threatening, record the time and date of each call. This will help the police apprehend the offender if you decide to file a formal complaint with the phone company.

Cream

For one cup of heavy cream, substitute ¾ cup whole milk and ⅓ cup melted unsalted butter. (Don't use in ice cream or mousse, however – the butter will lump.)

If you're counting kilojoules, replace one cup of heavy cream (2,550 kilojoules) with a cup of canned evaporated milk (1,462 kilojoules). An extra bonus: evaporated milk has far less cholesterol, too.

Credit cards

1. Keep the number of your credit cards to a minimum to curb impulse spending and to reduce your risk if they're lost or stolen.
2. Remember that a card's rate of interest doesn't necessarily indicate its true cost. You must also consider the cardholder fee and the grace period – if any – before interest is charged.

Make sure you pay interest only on the amount left unpaid at the end of a billing cycle; on some cards, unless your bill is paid up, interest is charged on all new transactions as well.

SECURITY
1. Sign new credit cards as soon as they arrive. Cut up the old ones and throw them away.
2. Carry your credit cards separately from your wallet. Make sure that you keep a record of their numbers and the telephone number of each company in a secure place.
3. Avoid placing credit-card orders from a telephone in a public area.
4. Never sign a blank receipt.
5. Destroy all carbons and void all incorrect receipts.
6. Save all receipts to compare with your monthly statement.
7. Don't let the credit card out of your sight in a strange supermarket, shop or restaurant. Insist on paying for your purchase or meal at the cash desk yourself.

Croup

1. A child with croup can breathe more easily sitting up.
2. A humidifier or vaporizer may help. For temporary relief, turn on a hot shower and sit with the child in the steam-filled bathroom.
3. If the child is having serious difficulty breathing, has secretions in his mouth, or is not relieved by the measures above, call your doctor or take him to a hospital emergency unit as soon as possible.

Cupboard clutter

1. Use your cupboards for everyday things – not for long-term storage.
2. Coats take up space; put them on a coat rack near the door.
3. Whenever you take a piece of clothing off a hanger, put the hanger in the centre of the rod, where it will be easy to find when needed.
4. To conceal open shelves at the top of the cupboard, install a decorative window shade.
5. To keep cupboards clean, dry and fresh smelling, place unwrapped bars of soap in them. Or make moth-repellent sachets from dried lavender, whole peppercorns, powdered orris root and a 50/50 mixture of rosemary and mint. (Get the ingredients from your local supermarket or a health food shop.) If you can't find sachet bags, make your own with pantihose.

Cupboard doors

Want to hide unsightly or makeshift storage areas? Use your ingenuity to come up with decorative substitutes for cupboard doors.
1. Build shelves on bedroom walls and cover them with matching curtains. Or try positioning handsome Japanese-style shoji screens at one end of a long room.
2. Hang bamboo or plastic roll-up blinds from the ceiling to conceal a small kitchen area. Or suspend a blind at the end of a long corridor and stow the ironing board and vacuum cleaner there.

Cup stains

Remove coffee or tea stains from your china cups in one of the following ways. Then rinse thoroughly and dry.
1. Scrub with salt or a paste of bicarbonate of soda and water, or a 50-50 mixture of salt and white vinegar.
2. Place in a denture-cleaning solution and soak overnight.
3. Let stand overnight in half a cup of household bleach in two litres water.

Curdling

Curdled cream sauce? Push it through a fine sieve with a spoon.

To save a Hollandaise sauce, add two tablespoons boiling water; beat with a wire whisk until smooth. Or set the pan in a bowl of ice water; whisk until smooth, then warm very gently over barely simmering water, whisking constantly.

Curfews

Children often perceive curfews as rules made to be broken, but in fact they should teach responsibility. Discuss the subject with your children until you agree on a sensible, flexible policy. (It's OK to bend the rules for special events.) If you suspect you're being conned, consult other parents about their kids' curfews.

Insist that your children phone if they'll be late. Five or 10 minutes past curfew doesn't really deserve a reprimand, but an hour or more requires an explanation and, possibly, corrective action.

Curtains

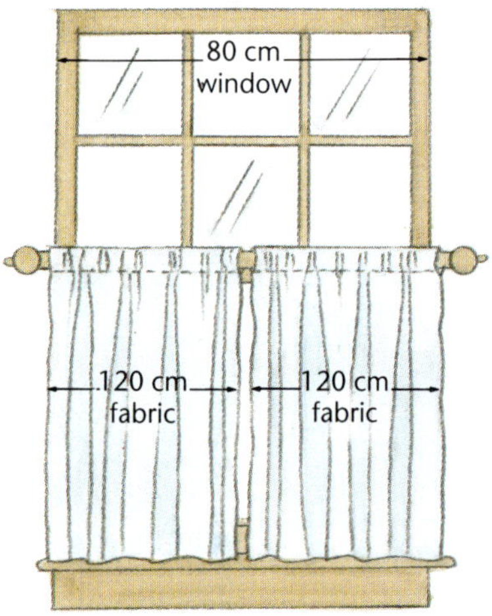

Bedspreads, tablecloths, quilts and sheets can make good curtains and may well be cheaper than store-bought fabric.

Choose a colour and pattern to match the room's decor.

To determine how much fabric you'll need, measure the distance from the top of the window frame to where the hem will fall. Add eight centimetres at the top for a four-centimetre pocket that the rod can slide through. Add another five to 10 centimetres for a hem (the heavier the fabric, the deeper its hem). For width, triple the distance across the area you plan to cover.

Cut flowers

There are a number of simple ways in which you can keep your cut flowers fresh as long as possible.

1. Always cut the blooms from your flower garden either very early in the morning or late in the afternoon. Then put them in a bucket of water for the whole day or night before arranging them.

This will allow them to fill their stems and be crisp and turgid by the time you want to actually arrange them. Some flowers, such as hydrangeas, arums and cannas should be totally immersed in water.

2. Some flowers last better if given special treatment immediately after cutting. Flowers with hollow stems, such as dahlias, Iceland poppies, delphiniums and larkspur, should have about five to 10 centimetres of their stems dipped in boiling water. The stems of woody plants like hawthorn, flowering quince or prunus, should be split or crushed, and a little of the bark on the end of the stems should be scraped off.

Seal the ends of plants like poinsettias, which exude a milky sap, by singeing them with a flame from a candle or match.

Daffodils, narcissus and agapanthus also have sticky sap. To make sure that they last well in water, you should wash away the sap or it may block the stems, causing the flowers to wilt quickly.

3. To keep foliage fresh – with the exception of furry or felty foliage – immerse it completely in a bath of water. Ferns should have their stems singed after soaking in water and just before being used in an arrangement.

Cuts & abrasions

The seriousness of a cut depends on how large it is, how deep it is, and how much it bleeds.

Although painful, small cuts and abrasions are seldom very dangerous. Wash them gently with mild soap and water, then apply an antibiotic cream if available; cover the cut with a large plaster or a reasonable substitute.

SEVERE BLEEDING

When treating deep cuts, the first priority is to control bleeding.

1. Apply firm pressure through a pad directly to the wound.

2. Elevate an injured arm or leg, unless it is fractured or dislocated or you suspect spinal injury.

3. If direct pressure and elevation don't stop the bleeding, locate a point where a major artery crosses bone near the surface (you can feel a pulse) and apply firm pressure to the artery.

Pressure points highlighted in red

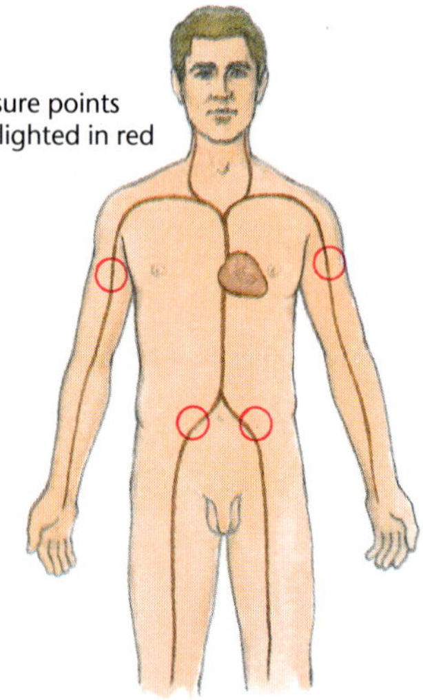

4. When bleeding has stopped or lessened considerably, place a clean cloth directly over the wound, completely covering it; put a clean bulky dressing on top.

Wrap strips of cloth tightly over the dressing and on each side of the wound. Be sure to seek medical help as soon as possible.

Cuttings

A hanging bag of soil makes a space-saving medium for rooting stem cuttings from various plants.

Mix enough peat moss and perlite or vermiculite (available at any garden centre) in equal parts to fill a 20-litre plastic bag. Moisten the mixture thoroughly and then fill the bag with it. Poke small holes in the bottom for drainage.

Close the bag with stout cord and hang from a tree in a sheltered spot or elsewhere where there is a waterproof floor; a shaded patio or stoep is ideal. In winter hang the bag indoors to protect it from the cold.

Poke holes in the sides of the bag and gently insert your stem cuttings. Mist the cuttings daily, letting water run down the stems to remoisten the rooting mixture. When the cuttings have rooted, slit the bag open with a sharp knife.

Cutworms

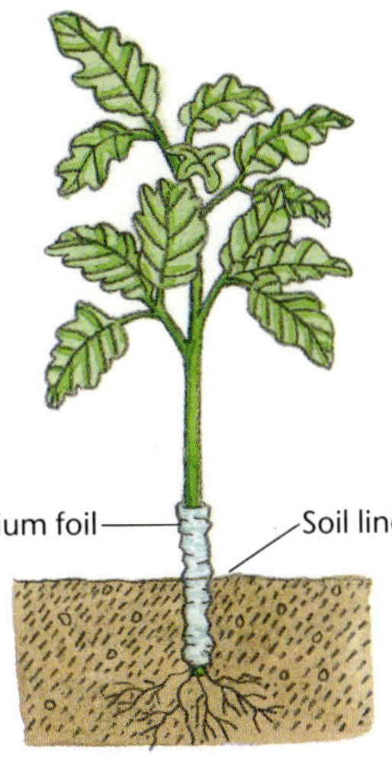

The usual method of foiling cutworms – placing a bottomless can or plastic cup around young plants – guards only against worms outside the barrier. A better control is to wrap the stem of a seedling with aluminium foil before setting it out. Plant with five centimetres of foil below the ground and five centimetres above. Wrap loosely so that the stem has room to grow.

D

Dampness

Lingering dampness eventually leads to mould. Get rid of the source of water, then use one of these methods to dry out a damp area:

1. Vent moisture from a laundry room or bathroom with an oscillating fan. Fans are rated according to the volume of air they move: measure the room to be vented, and check the specifications which come with the appliance. Preferably buy a bigger fan than strictly meets your needs.

2. In the kitchen, keep a window open and use the stove's extractor fan when cooking or boiling water. If dampness is damaging walls or ceilings above a sink or steamy area, paint with an oil-based gloss or semi-gloss enamel paint.

3. If the damp problem is minor, hang a desiccant (a moisture-absorbing chemical) near damp areas in confined places, such as bedroom cupboards. More serious damp problems should be tackled at the source of the problem – from foundations or roof, or the outside. New plastic damp-proofing paints (such as "Raincote", for example) work wonders in preventing water coming through.

4. Install a dehumidifier. It works, but it's as expensive as a good TV set. Moreover, it throws off heat, and unless the collected water is piped to a drain, you have to empty the water pan once or twice a day.

5. If part of an exterior wall is damp, cut away nearby branches and shrubs. This will increase airflow and allow sunshine to keep the area dry and free of mildew.

Debt

Does more than 35 to 40 percent of your annual gross income go to cover your debts? For example, if you earn R60,000, are you paying more than R24,000 on a mortgage bond, instalment loans and various credit card purchases? If so, you should consider taking immediate steps to reduce your indebtedness.

1. Stop the debts from growing – cut up your credit cards; postpone the purchase of that new car.

2. Cut back on open-ended lines of credit, such as bank credit cards or current accounts with overdraft facilities, where the monthly payments vary according to the unpaid balance. Make all minimum payments on time, then add something extra to reduce the balance.

3. Apply windfalls, such as bonuses or tax refunds, toward paying off these open-ended accounts. If anything's left over, pay off as much as possible on other loans.

4. If you cannot pay your debts, inform you creditors immediately and try to come to an agreement with them on a lower rate of repayment. This is particularly important in the case of your mortgage bond. Discuss the problem immediately with the manager of the bank or building society. Although every application is dealt with on its merits, you may be able to negotiate a temporary arrangement, such as the payment of only the interest on the bond.

Decks

Rust spots which are caused by nails, screws and corroding hardware will discolour a stained deck. Using a wire brush, remove as much rust as you can from the metal and the surrounding wood. If any rust spots remain on the wood, bleach them by scrubbing thoroughly with oxalic acid, available in pharmacies.

Use a small artist's paintbrush to coat the metal with a rust converter. Let the repair dry thoroughly.

Deep-frying

When trying out this method of cooking food rapidly in very hot oil, use a heavy, deep pan. If the family likes the taste, you might go on to acquire a thermostatically controlled deep-fryer, which is convenient but by no means essential.

Make sure that you use a polyunsaturated oil such as sunflower oil rather than animal fat – it's odourless, tasteless and non-smoking at the right frying temperature.

At sea level, this is between 180°C and 190°C and decreases by 1,5 degrees for every 330 metre rise in altitude. Set the thermostat when the oil is cold, or place a deep-fry thermometer in the cold oil. If you do not have a thermometer, use the bread-cube test.

Cut a 2,5-centimetre block of white bread and drop it into the hot oil. If it browns in about 60 seconds, the oil temperature is right for deep-frying. If the bread cube starts to brown in less than 40 seconds, the oil is too hot, and the temperature setting should be reduced accordingly.

Over-hot oil will result in food being browned on the outside, and underdone on the inside, while cooking with oil that is too cold will produce oily, soggy food.

Food portions should be of even size up to four-centimetres thick, and blotted dry with a paper towel before being placed in the oil. Excessive surface moisture will cause violent spitting of the oil.

Remember that large batches of food placed in the oil at once will cause the oil temperature to drop, and cooking will be incomplete.

When removing the cooked food, allow it to drain in single layers on a wire tray or paper towel.

Each batch of cooked and drained food can be kept warm for a short period in an oven at 120°C until ready to serve.

Deep-frying oil should not be used more than three times before being discarded. Sunflower oil that reaches 'smoke point' – the temperature at which a bluish, hazy tinge appears above the oil – should also be discarded after use. Repeated heating or over-heating of sunflower oil produces chemical changes that can make it unhealthy to consume.

Dehydration

Heat, overexertion, illness and long bouts of vomiting or diarrhoea can cause the loss of body fluids and salt. Infants, small children and the elderly are the most vulnerable.

If you suspect dehydration, drink lots of water or juice; in summer or after heavy exercise, drink cool water with enough salt to make it taste slightly salty. If these measures don't help, seek medical advice. (See also *Heat exhaustion*, p. 106.)

Dentist visits

Fear of the dentist is old-fashioned. With today's techniques and materials, dentistry need not be painful. Seek out a dentist who seems sensitive to your fears and who will explain exactly what he's going to do before he does it.

To conquer anxiety in the chair, try to relax, breathe slowly and deeply, and focus on something else, such as counting backward from 100. Or try distraction – bring a cassette player with earphones to drown out the noise of the drill.

Agree on a special signal with your dentist beforehand to indicate the onset of pain.

Try not to convey your anxiety to your children. Ask your paediatrician to recommend a dentist who specialises in preventing both cavities and fear of dentistry.

Deodorant

1. Try plain bicarbonate of soda. When you've dried yourself after your bath or shower, pat a little under your arms; the moisture still on your skin will help it stick. If it isn't soft enough, mix it with cornflour.

2. Mash a sturdy dark-green leaf of cos lettuce to extract a drop of chlorophyll. Spread the liquid under your arms and let it dry.

3. If you have persistent body odour, try a different brand of soap. Some soaps contain chemicals that cause odour when they react with certain people's body chemistry.

Depth gauge

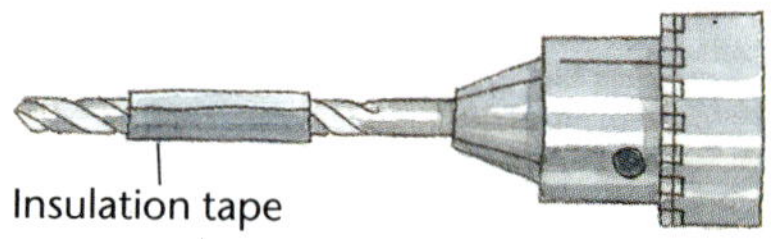

Wrap a small strip of masking or insulation tape around a drill bit so that the exposed part of the bit equals the desired depth of a hole. Or mark the bit with a grease pencil.

Alternatively, you can use a block of wood as a gauge; position it care-

IN TIMES GONE BY

Common sense about common scents

It's not perspiration that causes body odour – it's the action of bacteria on our perspiration and body oils. People didn't know this until fairly modern times, and so for centuries they tried to overpower their own smell by dousing themselves with stronger odours.

The ancient Egyptians, though they knew nothing of bacteria, understood all about countering the odours they caused. True, they regularly applied perfumes and oils made from citrus fruits, spices and wood resins. But they also were fastidious about daily bathing, and they regularly removed their underarm hair – which offers bacteria an expanded surface on which to grow.

Later societies, in their own efforts to smell sweet, copied the Egyptian formulas and added powders and bicarbonate of soda to the deodorant list. But somehow, with rare exceptions, cleanliness was overlooked by most of humanity.

Around the turn of this century, it even became stylish for women to flaunt a slight aroma of the upper body. It was romantically called *bouquet de corsage*, and these ladies thought men found it attractive. Perhaps. But the style soon passed.

fully beside the drill so that the chuck will butt against it when the desired depth is reached.

Diabetic emergencies

Insulin shock (too much insulin in the blood) starts very quickly. The usual symptoms are a damp, pale, clammy skin; a strong, rapid pulse; sweating; hunger; dizziness; headache; convulsions; aggressiveness; fainting; or occasionally coma.

Give the person some sugar, honey, sweets, fruit juice or a soft drink right away – make sure that it is sweetened with sugar, not a sugar substitute. Do not try to give an unconscious person anything; get him to a hospital quickly or call an emergency medical service.

Diabetic coma (not enough insulin in the blood) develops more slowly than insulin shock, over several hours or days.

The symptoms are thirst, abdominal pain, vomiting, restlessness, confusion and a gradual lapsing into stupor and coma. The skin is dry, red and warm. There may be a sweetish smell of acetone, like nail polish remover, on the breath. Whether the person is conscious or not, take him to a hospital emergency unit or call an emergency medical service.

If you're not sure whether a conscious person is in the first stages of diabetic coma or is going into insulin shock, ask. Most diabetics will know. If you're still in doubt, give sugar and call for help.

Diarrhoea

The cause may be a viral or bacterial infection, food poisoning or an inflammatory disease. Or it could simply be stress or overindulgence in food or drink.

An infant under three months old can quickly become dehydrated from a bout of diarrhoea; call a doctor immediately. A breast-fed baby should continue to be nursed; a formula-fed baby should be given half-strength formula thinned with water.

Give a child clear liquids and gelatine desserts. As the diarrhoea tapers off, gradually introduce binding foods in the so-called BRAT diet (Bananas, Rice cereal, Apple sauce and Toast).

An adult should be treated in much the same way. If the diarrhoea persists for several days, however, and the person hasn't eaten and drunk enough to balance the loss of fluids and nutrients, dehydration becomes a threat.

If thin, watery stools last longer than three days, contain blood or mucus, or are accompanied by fever and vomiting, call a doctor.

Dimmer switches

To install a dimmer switch, first be sure to shut off the power at the mains (see *Power shutoff*, p.162). Remove the faceplate of the existing switch, and remove the faceplate of the dimmer by taking off the wheel. Unscrew the screws holding the switch mechanism to the wall box.

The switch should connect the "live" (red) wires only. Unscrew the clamps holding the wires to the old switch. Insert the braided end of the red wire into the empty post clamp on the dimmer, and tighten the grub screw. Join the black dimmer wire and the black wire from the wall with a cable strip connector.

Finally, remount the switch and replace the faceplate.

Dinner parties

For a dinner party with a different twist, try one of these ideas:

1. Throw a theme party featuring food, beverages, music and decor from a foreign country or a distant part of southern Africa. Or, for the sake of variety, turn it into an international buffet.

2. Ask each guest to prepare and serve one course at his or her own home. Your job will be to co-ordinate the transportation.

3. Serve elaborate but substantial finger food, such as stuffed croissants or chicken croquettes with a tantalising savoury dip.

For a change, prepare a fish supper, such as smoorsnoek or fish bobotie, with salads.

4. Have a pot luck picnic: ask everyone to bring a favourite dish.

5. Supply the grill and beverages and ask each guest to please bring one item for a braai.

Dishwashers

Your dishwasher stopped working? The timer may just be at a normal pause in a cycle; wait a few minutes to see if the action resumes.

Make sure you've latched the door and set the timer dial and cycle selector properly. Check the fuse or circuit breaker. See if the water is turned off anywhere on the line.

On a portable model, the electric cord may not be plugged in securely or the hot-water tap may be off. Check the door latch. Look for a kink in the hose.

LEAKS

Many leaks are caused by objects blocking the water inlet. Remove, clear blockages and reassemble.

You may have used too much detergent, or your particular brand may generate excessive foam, forcing water out. Stop the machine and add a cup of vinegar to neutralize the foam.

If that doesn't do the trick, remove the racks and bail out the water. Let the motor dry thoroughly before turning it on again.

DRAINAGE PROBLEMS

A little water at the bottom of a dishwasher is normal. (It keeps the seals from drying out.) If there's a lot of water, be sure the strainer at the bottom isn't clogged and the rubber drain hose isn't kinked. If the water drains through a refuse disposer, check that it's empty.

DIRTY GLASSES

The most common cause of spots or film on glasses is hard water deposits. Soak the greasy item in white vinegar for 15 minutes; if the film disappears, hard water is the problem. To prevent a recurrence, increase the amount of detergent, be sure the water temperature is at least 65°C, and use a rinse additive to help water "sheet" off.

If the clouding can't be removed with vinegar, use less detergent, a lower water temperature and a rinse additive; turn off the machine before the drying cycle.

Dizziness & fainting

Fear, anxiety, pain, the sight of blood or injury and a stuffy, overheated room can all cause dizziness and fainting.

To prevent fainting, have a dizzy person sit and place his head between his knees. Or if he has a heart problem, difficulty in breathing, or any serious injury, have him lie down with his feet elevated.

If a person faints, try to prevent him from injuring himself in the fall. Lay him on his back and raise his legs. If he doesn't revive in a few minutes, seek medical help.

Elderly people who faint should see a doctor right away; such an occurrence can be a sign of a serious medical problem.

Dog & cat bites

Although a dog bite may look more serious, a cat bite is more dangerous – there are more bacteria in a cat's mouth, and the risk of infection, therefore, is much greater.

Wash a dog or cat bite with soap and water, rinse under running water for at least five minutes, and cover with a dressing or a clean cloth. Try not to move the affected area until the bite has been treated by a doctor.

Although rare today, rabies can still be found in stray dogs and in such wild animals as dassies, polecats, jackals and bats. It can even be transmitted if a rabid animal licks an open wound. Because the disease is fatal unless treatment begins at once, it's important to identify the source of a bite as soon as possible.

An animal's behaviour won't necessarily offer any clue to whether or not it has rabies. If possible, check a dog's collar for a rabies vaccination tag or ask its owner about its shots. If it's an unfamiliar animal, arrange to have it impounded and observed. (See also *Bites*, p. 22.)

Dog baths

1. Be sure to take your dog for a walk before bathing it so that it won't go outside wet.

2. Put a steel-wool pad in the bathtub drain to collect hairs.

3. If your dog fears baths, let it watch you take one yourself. But be prepared – it may jump in with you.

4. To keep soap out of a dog's eyes, gently apply a thin layer of Vaseline over its eyebrows and around its eyes.

5. To minimize soap film, add vinegar or lemon juice to the rinse water. Rinse your pet thoroughly.

6. To prevent your dog from splattering you, wash its head last – a wet head makes the dog want to shake itself dry. Dry your dog immediately after its bath.

7. Use a blow dryer. Set it on warm, not hot, and hold it at least 15 centimetres away from your pet.

Dog chasing

Cyclists and joggers can take a few precautions to protect themselves against being chased by dogs.

1. Speak to the dog in a commanding but calm tone.

2. Carry a stick and use it to keep the animal at bay. Don't hit the dog – just make it keep its distance.

3. If you can't outdistance a pursuing dog on your bike, dismount and use the bike as a shield. If necessary, try squirting the dog in the eyes with your water bottle.

DID YOU KNOW . . . ?

Canine trivia

☐ Some experts believe that a dog can be trained to understand as many as 400 words.

☐ Dogs have better night vision than humans because of the arrangement of the rods at the back of their eyes and a membrane called the tapetum, which acts like a reflector. That's what causes the shine in a dog's eyes when it looks into a car's headlights.

☐ The well-known saying that one dog year is equal to seven human years is not true. A one-year-old puppy is equivalent in development to a 15-year-old human; a two-year-old dog, to a 24-year-old human. Thereafter, each year could be compared to four human years, so that its age at 10 approximates 56 human years.

☐ A cold, wet nose says nothing about a dog's health.

☐ The fastest dog is the greyhound. It can run 53 km/h and cover 5,4 metres in a single stride.

☐ The tiniest, at about 1,8 kilograms, is the Chihuahua. The largest is the St. Bernard; it can weigh up to 90 kilograms.

☐ A dog's hearing is far more sensitive than a human's, particularly at higher frequencies. Dogs also use their ears to communicate, varying the position to signal fear, anger and so forth.

☐ Newborn puppies cannot see or hear, but they can smell, and this sense leads them to their mother's milk. Some studies indicate that a dog's keen sense of smell may be 100 times as developed as its owner's.

4. Keep dog treats, such as biscuits, in your pocket. Throw one in the direction of an approaching dog – as far as you can.
5. Squirt highly diluted ammonia from a water gun.
6. Carry a pop-up umbrella to open in the animal's face.

Dog hair

1. To collect loose hairs, put your dog on an old sheet or towel before you brush it.
2. To remove burrs, crush them with pliers or soak the tangle in sunflower oil, then comb them out.
3. To get rid of sticky substances such as tar, saturate the area with sunflower oil. After 15 minutes apply dog shampoo; rinse immediately.
4. Allow paint or gum to harden, then snip off the hair that holds it.
5. To clean a dog brush, move a toothpick through the rows.

Dog leash

If you have to take the dog for a walk and you can't find its leash, try one of these substitutes:
1. A rope or length of clothesline. Tie a secure bowline or other nonslip knot around the dog's collar. Make a loop for the handle and wrap it with insulation tape.
2. A long leather belt. Run the end beneath the collar and then through the buckle.
3. A pair of pantihose. Pull one leg under the collar and tie the feet together with a reef knot.

Dog parasites

1. Keep fleas at bay by bathing the dog regularly with a dog shampoo.
2. Keep the dog's sleeping area as clean as possible. Fleas spend most of their lives in the dog's blankets and in cracks in his kennel or basket. Bedding should be washed every time the dog is bathed and his sleeping area sprinkled with flea powder.
3. Fleas are repelled by the smell of pennyroyal (a herb obtainable at your local nursery) – attach one or two sprigs to his collar.
4. Attach a flea collar to the dog – but keep a close watch for a possible allergic reaction in the neck area.
5. If the problem persists, consult a veterinarian before resorting to drastic action such as dipping.
6. After you have exercised your dog, check his coat for ticks. When you remove an embedded tick be sure to remove the head as well – dab with alcohol and pull the entire tick out with a pair of tweezers.

Doorknobs

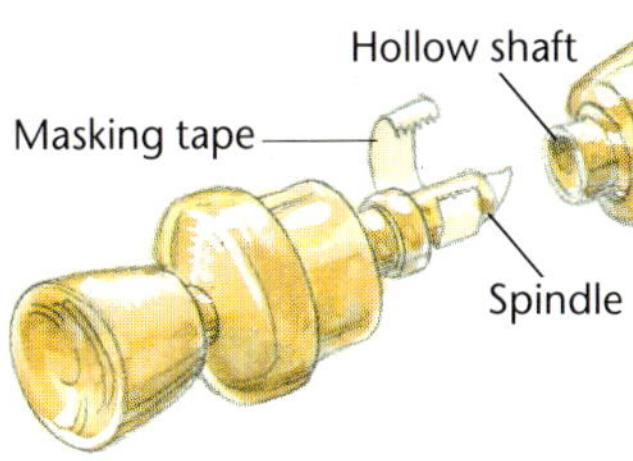

A loose doorknob is probably the result of wear – the inside of the knob's hollow shaft has become slightly enlarged. Remove the knob, wrap the hollow shaft in a soft cloth, and tap it very gently with a hammer in several places to crimp it a bit; be careful not to crush it. Then slip the knob back onto the spindle and make sure that it fits snugly.

Alternatively, you can wrap the spindle with masking tape and then force the doorknob back onto the spindle. One or two layers of tape will usually suffice to ensure that the knob fits tightly.

Doors

1. When a door refuses to stay open, check the hinges. If one has shifted or a hinge screw has pulled loose, reset the hinge in its original position and tighten the screws.

If a screw cannot be tightened because the hole has been stripped or enlarged, remove it, pack the hole with wooden toothpicks, reinsert the screw, and tighten securely.
2. To silence a door that's a slammer, adhere a strip of foam rubber to the edge of the doorstop moulding. Peel-and-stick foam weatherstripping tape works well. A short length of foam rubber near the top and bottom of the moulding will often suffice. You can also try a narrow strip of cork.
3. To keep a door from slamming against the wall when it opens, make a simple doorstop from window-sash chain. Attach one end to a screw eye on the face of the door and the other to one on the top of the frame.
4. Here's a really easy-to-make door bumper for a child's room: put a rubber ball in a sock and hang it from the inside doorknob.
5. The self-closing hinges on many kitchen cabinet doors make them slam shut. Muffle the noise with bumpers made of silicone caulk:

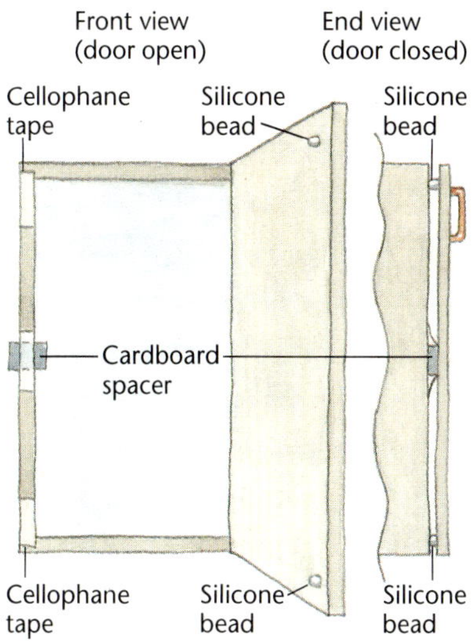

Put two small dollops of caulk – each about the size of a pencil eraser – on the inside corners of each door, one at the top and the other at the bottom. Then place strips of cellophane tape on the cabinet where the silicone makes contact. Smear each tape strip with a thin film of Vaseline to keep the caulk from sticking when the door is closed. And, to act as a spacer, tape a small piece of cardboard to the cabinet between the tape strips. Close the door, let the silicone dry overnight, then peel off the tape and cardboard.

Down payments

To save money on a major purchase, be sure to pay for it outright or make the largest down payment you can afford. Because if you borrow less, you'll pay less interest.

The savings may be greater than you realize. For example, if you buy a R30,000 car at 19 percent and make a 10 percent down payment, you'll pay R10,440,36 interest over three-and-a-half years. But if you make a 50 percent down payment (R15,000), you will pay only R5,788,22 interest over the same period – a savings of R4,652,14 or almost 45 percent.

Few, if any, investments in South Africa offer a higher rate of return than the interest you pay on a loan. Therefore, if you intend to buy a relatively expensive item, you should consider withdrawing money from your savings account so that you can make a larger down payment.

Drainage testing

1. To test how well your garden soil drains, dig holes a metre deep at different locations around your garden and fill them with water. Then observe what the water does.

If it drains away immediately, your soil is too sandy for most plants; dig in some compost, peat moss or other organic matter to help it retain water.

If it stands for 30 minutes to one hour, the drainage is ideal for vegetables and flowers.

If it remains in the hole for several hours, your soil is poorly drained – a heavy clay or fine silt. Either dig in some sand, peat moss, manure or compost, or construct raised beds (p.169) of improved soil.

2. An easier, though less reliable, drainage guide is natural vegetation. The presence of water-loving plants such as arum lilies willows and gums indicate poorly drained soil; proteas, pincushions and other indigenous plants indicate good drainage.

Draughts

Cold convection currents drop to the floor from windows, through gaps in windows and glass doors, then move across your feet. To prevent them, insulate walls and ceilings to the maximum. In very cold rooms, add your own "storm panes" to windows. With a stapler or masking tape, fix clear plastic or shrink-wrap to windows, then shrink to a neat pane using a hair dryer. These can be taken down in summer.

Air leaks and cold traps are the main source of draughts in the house. There are six vulnerable spots:

ROOMS LOWER THAN THE REST

Any room lower than the rest of the house acts as a "sump" – when all the windows are closed, the coldest air tends to flow down to the lowest room, and stays there. To reverse the process, heat the lowest room first – hot air rises.

PASSAGES

These can provide a conduit for cold air, and enable air to move from warm areas of the house to colder spots. If they are dingy, consider building skylights to let in sunshine during the day. To isolate draughty passages, install thick curtains, or hang a kelim rug on a pole near the ceiling, that reaches to the floor.

WINDOWS AND DOORS

Caulk between casings and sidings around all your windows and exterior doors. Try to use silicone, Butyl or acrylic for durable protection. Install weatherstripping around all windows and doors.

UNUSED ROOMS

Close off the room; stuff the crack under the door with old towels or a strip of carpet.

FIREPLACES

Shut the damper after you are certain the fire is out.

ATTICS

Be sure to insulate around the access door. Use foam or fibreglass to insulate around plumbing vent pipes and other openings.

Drawers

1. When a drawer won't pull out properly, the chances are that something inside is projecting above the sides. All you have to do is remove the drawer above, then empty and re-pack the sticking drawer.

2. A loose nail in the drawer frame may also be the culprit; if so, hammer it down.

3. If a wooden drawer drags, sand its runners lightly and then rub them with a candle or a bar of soap. Or if the wood has swollen in damp weather, lightly sand or plane the front lip of the drawer and along the tops of the sides and back.

4. If a wooden drawer pulls out too far, the chances are that you need to reattach or replace either the glue blocks that secure the bottom or the stop that is on top of the rail – below the drawer – at the front of the chest.

5. Replace a split bottom with thin plywood, or mend it with a canvas strip and white glue.

6. When the bottom of a wooden drawer sags, flip over the drawer. If the bottom fits into a groove in the back of the drawer, you must disassemble the frame to fix it. Wrap a cloth around a mallet and tap apart the dovetail joints at the corners of the drawer. Slide the bottom out, scrape off the old glue, and reassemble the drawer with the bottom upside down.

7. If nails hold the sagging bottom to the back, pull them out with pliers. Break the glue blocks from the bottom with a chisel and mallet. Slide out the bottom and return it upside down. Then renail the bottom to the back and glue the blocks back in place.

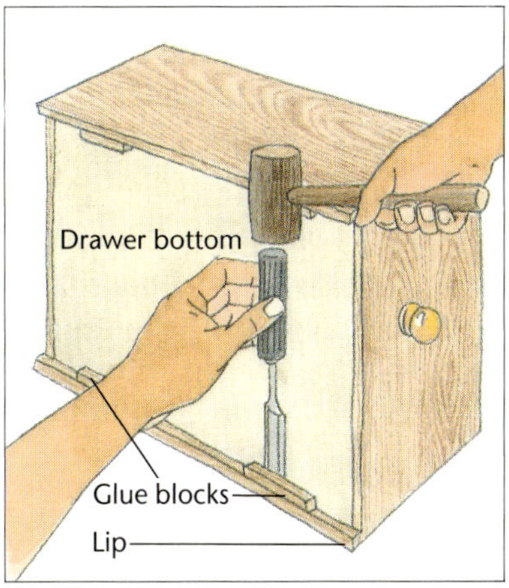

Drawstrings

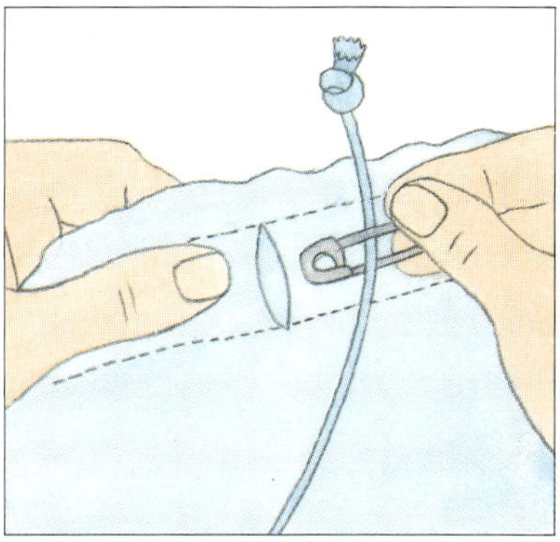

1. If a drawstring frequently does a disappearing act into its casing, double-knot the tips. Or harden the tips with a few drops of household cement for easy retrieval.
2. If you lose a drawstring, substitute a shoelace, ribbon or fabric tubing; you can attach a safety pin on one end to help feed the replacement through the casing.

Drills

If you don't have an electric drill, use a finishing nail or push drill to make a pilot hole and then try one of these alternatives. All make for slow work, but they'll do the job.
1. Lock the shaft of a bit upright in a metal vice. Position the starter hole over it and turn the work.
2. If you lack the appropriate bit for a pilot hole, snip the head off a finishing nail and use it instead.
3. Insert the bit into the collar of an old-fashioned doorknob and tighten the setscrew.

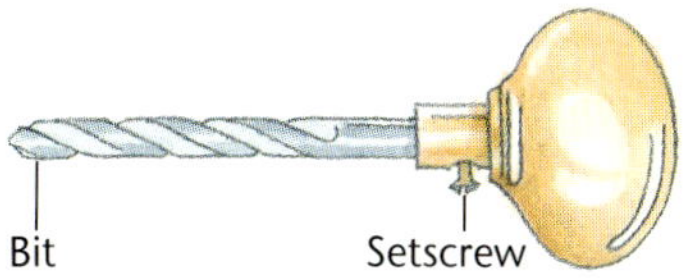

Dripping taps

Modern taps are less prone to leaking than older designs, because the washer is larger. When they do, you can usually repair them by replacing the washer at the base of the headgear, which unscrews with the tap itself in one unit.

If the tap leaks from around the shaft, it may be possible to unbolt the whole assembly and replace worn rubber O-rings. Before going to this trouble, check whether your plumbing supplier has the parts. It may be easier to replace the entire top, known as a "tap headgear".

To avoid going without water, sketch the tap or take a snapshot with you when buying parts.

PILLAR TAPS
A single tap – hot or cold – is eventually prone to leaks, usually caused by a worn washer.

First be sure to shut off the water at the nearest stopcock. With a screwdriver or pliers, remove the colour-coded cover (if applicable). Unscrew the tap handle, either from the side or the top. Wrap a cloth around the cover, and unscrew, using the pair of pump pliers. This exposes the headgear. Using the pump pliers again, unscrew the headgear.

At the base of the headgear (this is sometimes left inside the tap) is the "hopper". Unscrew the nut, and then replace the washer – or replace with the new hopper-washer assembly. Finally, reassemble.

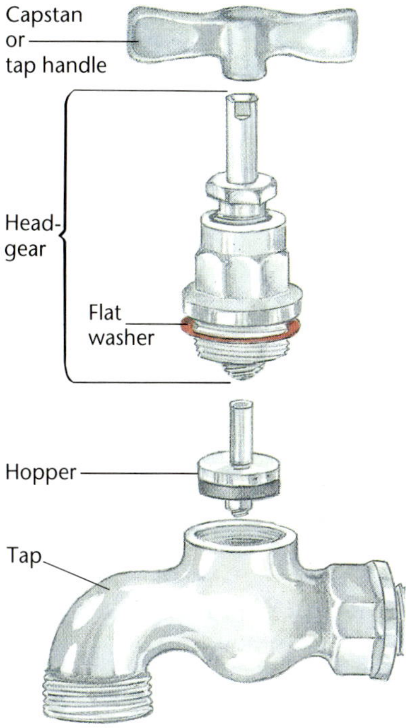

Driver's licence

If you lose your driver's licence – generally affixed to your Book of Life – contact your local Department of Home Affairs for a temporary licence until your duplicate Book of Life arrives. Be sure to telephone the department beforehand to find out what you need to take with you.

Drug interactions

Anyone who takes more than one drug at a time – prescription or over-the-counter – or who drinks alcohol while taking medication may suffer side effects from their interaction or cumulative effect. The elderly are especially vulnerable. Here's how to help prevent this problem:
1. Keep an updated list of all the drugs and vitamins you take; go over it with your doctor whenever a new medication is suggested.
2. Ask your doctor to check a drug interaction data base before prescribing a new medication.

3. If you develop new symptoms at any time, especially after starting a new drug, call your doctor or put all your drugs into a bag, take it to her office, and ask her to carefully review your medication.
4. Ask for a full drug review at every checkup – and take samples of all your drugs along whenever you see a new doctor.
5. Look for a pharmacist who will keep a complete record of all the drugs that you take, your allergies to foods and drugs and your doctors' names and addresses. When a new medication is prescribed, a check of this record will immediately identify incompatible drugs.

Drunk drivers

In South Africa, drunk drivers are responsible for thousands of motor vehicle accidents every year, involving needless injury and death to hundreds of innocent victims.
1. If you intend to drink alcoholic beverages at a party, designate someone else as the driver. If you're going alone, arrange a ride home.
2. If an intoxicated person is about to get behind the wheel of a car, reason with him not to drive. If that doesn't work, take his car keys away and call a taxi for him or find someone who will give him a ride home. If you're already in motion when you realize the driver is drunk, insist that he stop the car and let you or someone else drive. If he refuses, get out at the first opportunity and call the police. Give them your location, a description of the car and driver and the licence plate number. You may lose a friend, but you may also save a life.
3. If you see a car weaving toward you, assume the driver is drunk and be prepared to take evasive action.

Dry-cleaning odours

It's your dry-cleaner's obligation to deliver your clothes odour-free. The petroleum-based solvents once used in the process did cause an unpleasant aroma, but those days are gone.

If your garments smell, take them back and complain. It may not be the operator's fault; fabrics are often treated with selected chemicals to give them body – but these give them an odour, too. Have the clothes recleaned; if the problem isn't solved, return them to the shop.

Occasionally, dry-cleaned clothes tend to smell because the unit malfunctions or because the drying cycle is too short.

Again, have the clothes recleaned immediately. If the condition persists, change cleaners.

In all cases, remove the plastic covering. Nearly all odours evaporate quickly with an airing out.

Dry skin

1. To prevent dry skin, try drinking ordinary water: it's always accessible, and costs you nothing. Drink six to eight glasses a day and eat foods high in water content, such as fruits and leafy vegetables.
2. Bath in mildly salted water (½ cup of salt per tubful) to rehydrate your body, then apply a cream or lotion that will act as a moisturizer.
3. For an easy facial, mash a banana, add a tablespoon of honey, and smooth the mixture on your face. After 15 minutes, rinse off with warm or lukewarm water.

Dual careers

Do you and your working spouse spend too little time together? Why not try the following:

Choose a day when you're both free – Sunday is probably best – and go over your respective diaries, looking for a time when you can schedule dinner, a movie or a romantic evening at home. Make a firm date together, and don't cancel unless there's a very good reason.

Not only will this private time together let you relax and enjoy each other's company, but in addition it will lend both of you energy and emotional support for facing your professional challenges.

HOUSEHOLD TIMESAVERS

You and your spouse will find more time to devote to each other if you take the following shortcuts:
1. Do one-stop shopping whenever possible, seeking out hypermarkets or shopping malls that sell clothing, rent videos, provide automated banking machines and so forth.
2. Stock up on non-perishables.
3. Look for essential items you can buy through mail-order (sometimes advertised on television and in newspapers and magazines).
4. Deal with stores that take phone orders and deliver.
5. Enlist the children to help you with the chores around the house (see *Chores and children*, p.47).
6. Hire neighbourhood teenagers or pensioners to do chores and run errands. Give the babysitter some extra money to wash dishes, iron clothing and perform other household chores.

Dusting

Your aim is to pick up dust, not displace it. For dustcloths, spray discarded cotton towels, T-shirts or nappies with a little furniture polish. Avoid using a feather duster for ceilings – rather cover a broom with a flannelette cloth.

Starting at the top and working downward, use slow, even strokes. If you'll be dusting for some time, coat your nostrils with Vaseline to prevent a scratchy throat.

To carry all your supplies from one room to another, just wear a multi-pocketed apron or use a firm plastic bucket with a handle. You can include a bag for collecting debris.

Spray an old cotton or woollen sock with furniture polish and wear it as a glove to dust tables and chairs.

Don't bother dusting knick-knacks one by one. Just soak them all together in a bowl with detergent. Use your hair dryer to dry them.

You can use soft tissues to dust small picture frames.

Wax your dustpan so that dust won't cling. Shake mops and dustcloths inside a sack or outdoors.

Hard-to-dust things and places – pleated lampshades, carved furniture and crevices – are easy to clean if you blow the dust out with a hair dryer. An empty squeeze bottle used as an air pump also does the trick.

To get at narrow spots behind cupboards or under the refrigerator, dampen an old sock, slip it over one end of a metre-long flattened stick and secure it with a rubber band.

E

Ear popping

Avoid travelling by plane if you have a cold, flu or allergy; you may develop painful ear or sinus problems. If you must fly, take an oral decongestant an hour before takeoff and landing, or use a nasal spray before and during descent.

If your ears start to pop or you get earache, try one of the following: swallow, chew gum, suck on a hard sweet, sip a liquid or yawn. Don't sleep during takeoff and landing; you won't swallow often enough to keep your ears clear.

For babies, nursing or sucking a bottle or dummy will help, especially during ascent and descent.

Earrings

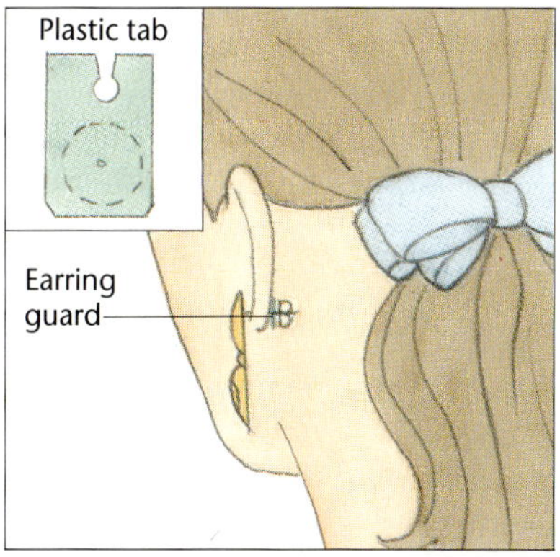

1. To keep pierced earrings from flopping forward and to balance heavy ones, make an earring guard. Fold a small piece of transparent tape so that the sticky side is covered. (You may want to cut it into a circle.) Or cut a circle from the plastic tab that seals a loaf of bread.

Poke a pinhole in the centre of this tab; then insert the earring through your earlobe and the tab. Finally, secure it with the earring back.

2. If you lose an earring, put the remaining one on a chain to wear as a pendant, turn it into a brooch with a pin (sold in craft stores), or make a ring out of it.

3. To keep track of your pierced earrings and display them at the same time, attach a piece of hessian to a dowel and hang it next to your dressing table. Your earrings will slip into the hessian easily, and you'll have a pretty wall hanging as well.

Ears

1. Something in your ear? Don't probe it – you may drive the object deeper and damage the eardrum. Instead, ask someone to look inside the ear with a torch or strong light. If there is no bleeding and the object is small, irrigate the ear with tepid water from a syringe. If it is large or embedded, seek medical help.

2. If there's an insect in the ear, keep calm, sit down and shine a torch in to attract it. An alternative is to float the insect out by pouring warm olive or baby oil gently into the ear.

EARWAX

Small glands in the outer ear canal continually produce wax which protects the sensitive ear lining from infection. Never probe your ear canal with anything smaller than a fingertip. If wax builds up, lie on your side and put a few drops of lukewarm water into your ear; after 10 minutes, shake water out. Repeat with olive oil.

RINGING IN THE EARS

1. Check for earwax buildup.

2. Try to eliminate caffeine and stop taking aspirin.

3. Avoid loud noises.

WATER IN THE EAR

Here's one simple way to rid your ear of water: turn your head so that the ear points downward, and gently pull the ear upward and backward.

EARACHES

For temporary relief, take aspirin or paracetamol and lie with your head raised and your ear resting on a hot water bottle or hot compress.

PIERCED EARS

To prevent any infection, you should gently swab newly pierced earlobes with alcohol twice a day. Apply an antiseptic ointment with a cotton-wool swab nightly. To avoid an allergic reaction, make sure the posts are gold or surgical steel.

Earthquakes

Although earthquakes are not common in South Africa, the possibility of one occurring cannot be ignored. In 1969, for instance, an earthquake shook the Tulbagh-Ceres area of the southwestern Cape, causing extensive damage, killing nine people and injuring many others. That earthquake registered 6,5 on the Richter scale and triggered rock slides in the surrounding mountains.

IF YOU'RE INDOORS

Stay indoors. Get under a table, desk or any other protective cover, or stand in a doorway or an inside corner next to an interior wall. Keep well away from any windows, mirrors, glass, bookcases, light fixtures, tall cabinets and fireplaces.

IF YOU'RE OUTDOORS

Get into an open area; avoid buildings, walls, power lines and trees. If you're in a car, stop immediately – but stay inside until the tremors stop. Try to avoid bridges.

AFTERWARDS

1. Be on guard for smaller aftershocks that can cause more damage.
2. Apply first aid to any injuries.
3. Check the house for structural damage, fires and damage to electrical appliances.
4. If you smell gas, open all doors and windows, turn off the main gas valve and leave the house.
5. If electrical wires are shorting or fixtures have loosened, shut off the power (p.162).
6. Until public water supplies are declared safe, boil all tap water for at least 10 minutes.

If water pipes are damaged, shut off the water supply (see *Water leaks*, p.227). Get emergency drinking water from the toilet tank (not the bowl), water heater or ice-cube trays. Don't flush the toilet until you know that the sewer lines are intact.

Eating utensils

UTENSILS FOR THE DISABLED

Specially designed eating utensils are available for the disabled. These include built-up crockery for those who have difficulty gripping, and a rocking knife for people who have the use of only one hand. For more information on these products, you can contact Clinical Services, PO Box 24072, Claremont 7735.

SUBSTITUTE UTENSILS

In an emergency, a number of items can serve as eating utensils. Before using any item, clean it thoroughly.
1. As a knife: a seashell edge, a nail file, a letter opener, the serrated edge of an aluminium foil box, a single-edged razor blade, scissors or even a sharp-edged rock.
2. As a fork: a twig, a skewer, a hairpin, comb or a pair of chopsticks.
3. As a spoon: a seashell, a small stone with a hollow, a coffee scoop.
4. As a plate: a serviette or paper towel, a piece of cardboard, aluminium foil, a plastic coffee tin lid or a flattened coffee filter.
5. As a bowl: a jar, a coconut shell, a perlemoen shell, a coffee filter, a Frisbee, a thermos flask top or a hollowed out stone.
6. As a cup: fold a square piece of paper as shown; turn corner A over to meet corner B and crease firmly. Then turn corner D up to meet line BC, so that the new edge is parallel with the bottom edge.

Turn corner C over to corner E. Fold the two top corners (at B) outward and down. Tuck in A. Squeeze gently to open.

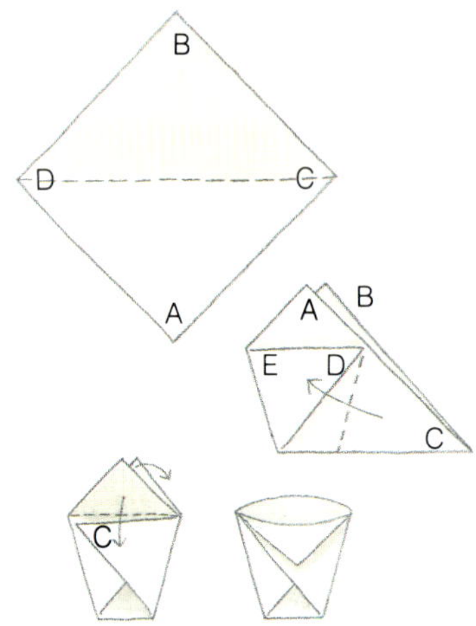

IN TIMES GONE BY

The evolution of eating utensils

The earliest spoon undoubtedly was a cupped hand.

The discovery of fire and cooking, however – and the danger of burning one's hands – led people to shape clay, carve wood and stone, and utilize the natural shape of shells.

The earliest knives, dating back 35,000 years, were chipped from stone. Because of their crudeness, they were used mainly to hack up food rather than to eat with.

Forks were originally single-pronged instruments, like knives. The Romans invented the two-pronged form, but eating with forks was still considered an affectation as late as the 16th century. By 1700, knives and forks became commonly accepted as eating utensils in Italy, France, England and America.

Eczema

Although eczema – an inflammation of the skin – may occur in several forms, the initial stages are often similar. Redness of the skin is generally followed by swelling, itching and the formation of blisters.

After bursting, the blisters 'weep' or discharge clear fluid, and may become infected, but finally dry with the formation of scabs. When the condition is chronic, thickened and reddish patches of affected skin may become covered with flaky scales. These thickened areas become dry, and then crack and bleed.

Contact eczema is caused by sensitivity to compounds such as cosmetics or even materials. It clears when the source of irritation is removed.

Atopic eczema occurs in children of families with a history of allergy (hay fever) or asthma. Cold and stress are sometimes precipitating factors. Most cases clear with age.

Seborrhoeic eczema occurs in areas of numerous sebaceous glands, such as the scalp, around the ears, in the armpits and groin, between the shoulder blades and under the breasts. It responds well to treatment but may recur.

Discoid eczema, circular patches of eczema, usually affects young adults and is commonly seen on the arms and legs. In most cases, it clears itself. Varicose eczema occurs on the lower third of the leg in later life, and may be associated with a skin ulcer.

The irritation of the early stages of eczema can be treated with calamine lotion. Thickened areas of chronic eczema may respond to zinc and coal-tar ointment, and using a bath oil regularly may also help.

Regular, vigorous washing, especially with medicated or approved coal-tar soap, will usually help to clear seborrhoeic eczema.

Varicose eczema must be protected from injury, and the foot should be raised on a stool whenever possible. If the condition persists, or lesions become infected, be sure to consult your doctor.

POINTS TO CONSIDER

1. Smallpox vaccination can be lethal to sufferers from atopic eczema. Consult your doctor if such a vaccination is required.
2. Most eczema improves and clears before adulthood.
3. Eczema is not contagious – you can't get it from someone else.
4. Wearing wool next to the skin can aggravate eczema.
5. Eczema is made worse by stress, so aim to create a calm and happy atmosphere.

Eggs

1. Test eggs for freshness by placing them in a bowl of cold salted water. Discard any eggs that float to the surface or turn their broad ends up – they're stale.
2. When you break an egg into a bowl, double-check its freshness – a fresh egg will have a rounded, yellow yolk and a firm white. A stale egg has a flat yolk and a runny white.
3. For a perfect poached egg, add a tablespoon of vinegar to the water. It helps set the white.
4. When you cook eggs in a microwave oven, prick the yolks first to keep them from bursting. And never microwave eggs in their shells – they'll explode and make a mess.
5. Pricking the shell will usually prevent it from cracking and leaking while the egg is being boiled. This is most easily done by using one of the inexpensive, patent utensils available from most supermarkets, but a finely sharpened wire nail will do as well.
6. To freeze eggs, either separate the whites and yolks, or mix whole eggs together. Freeze just the number of eggs you'll need for a special purpose and, to prevent the yolks from becoming gummy, add a quarter-teaspoon of salt or three-quarters of a teaspoon of sugar to each half cup.
7. If your recipe calls for only the whites, use the yolks to make mayonnaise, custards, puddings or cakes.
8. If you're left with whites after following a recipe, freeze them in an ice-cube tray before storing them in the freezer in a plastic bag. They can be thawed and used in meringues, souffles or icing, or you can add an occasional extra white while making scrambled eggs.

Elastic

1. To substitute a drawstring or cable cord for worn-out elastic, cut the cord 60 centimetres longer than the casing and knot both ends; brush clear nail polish or household cement on the tips to prevent fraying. Pin one end to an open seam and feed the other through the casing. (See also *Drawstrings*, p.67.)
2. To replace a waistband that has lost its stretch, snip open a seam across the casing and pull out the old elastic. Cut a piece of new elastic three centimetres smaller than your waistline. (Use non-roll elastic with vertical ribs to prevent twisting.) Pin one end at the open seam and work the other through the casing with a safety pin. Smooth out the elastic; then overlap the ends by one centimetre, sew them together and close the seam.

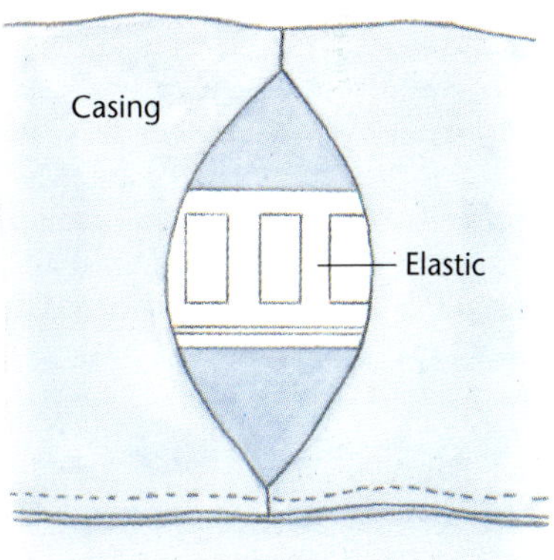

Electric blankets

The electric blankets available in this country – the fitted and the flat ones – are both capable of covering the mattress like a pad.

If you prefer non-electrical warmth, why not try an old-fashioned hot water bottle, which always does a good job of heating the bed before you climb into it?

Cotton flannel sheets help, too; even without a hot water bottle, they warm your skin more than smooth sheets do.

Electronic banking

1. No matter how technically proficient you may be, before you make your first transaction at an automatic teller machine (ATM), ask a bank official for a full explanation and demonstration of how it works.
2. If you can, choose a personal identification number (PIN) that's really secret: not your date of birth, address or telephone number. However, your bank may give you a computer-generated number as a PIN. Hide the number in a safe place and memorize it.
3. Wait until the ATM has turned itself off and you have received your bank card and printed receipt before walking away. Check the receipt to make sure that neither you nor the computer made a mistake.
4. Record each transaction in your chequebook as soon as possible so that you can balance your bank statement more easily. If the statement shows any inaccurate ATM transactions, notify the bank as soon as possible. The bank will be able to resolve the problem.
5. Lost your bank card? Be sure to report it immediately. The bank will charge you a minimal replacement fee for a new one.

Emergency calls

When you need outside help in an emergency, don't waste valuable and potentially life-saving time by having to search for the right telephone number. Make a list of emergency numbers and keep it next to your telephone. To make sure it *stays* next to the telephone, attach it to the table top, to the wall or even underneath the telephone base set. To prevent smudging from accidental spillage, cover the list with a sheet of tough, clear plastic. Try to be aware of the changes that are made on relatively rare occasions to particular groups of numbers. Notice of changes may be published in a local newspaper or may be sent with your telephone account. A list of numbers that will change during the currency of a telephone directory is published near the front of the directory. And in the alphabetical section of the directory, numbers that are to change are usually indicated by a symbol such as a dot or asterisk. Check your list of emergency numbers each time you get a new directory. Your list should include the following:
1. Your doctor – surgery and after hours' numbers.
2. Ambulance service – local authority service and private service. Check your medical aid or medical insurance. (The national ambulance emergency number is 10177.)
3. Hospital emergency unit.
4. Poisons information centre. If there is no separate information centre in your area, ask your doctor or hospital whom you should contact in an emergency. Ask now, before the emergency arises.
5. Police – both your local police station and the national Flying Squad number (10111).
6. Fire brigade – make sure that you have the number of the service that attends to fires in your ward or local authority area.
7. National Sea Rescue Institute – there are branches inland too, as at the Vaal Dam, for instance.
8. Your dentist's surgery or his after-hours number.
9. Your security service.

Employees' medical aid

Where membership of a company medical aid scheme is a condition of employment, you may not have much room to negotiate, but it's still worth finding out all about the scheme before you need to make a claim. You may find, for instance, that you need to 'top up' your medical aid by arranging additional medical insurance.

Company medical aid schemes usually pay out between 70 and 100 percent of the fee charged in accordance with the recognised scale of benefits. You must pay the balance.

Payments are made only up to certain set limits for each beneficiary each year. The limits are placed into separate categories that may include, amongst others, dentistry, psychiatry, medicines, maternity or optometry.

When you have 'used up' the available annual benefit in a particular category, you are personally responsible for settling further accounts in that category until the following year's benefits become available.

It's important to find out what the medical aid covers and what it excludes. What about pregnancy? Are your spouse and children included? What are the annual limits? If you have special health needs, you should check whether these will be met adequately.

Make sure that your needs are known to your employer – if enough company members need a certain coverage, the company may be able to modify the benefits accordingly.

Employment agencies

Don't expect an employment agent to provide career counselling. The bulk of his business is to fill vacancies for clients, not helping individuals find the right vocation.

Take the agent's assessment of your skills and potential with a grain of salt; he may even belittle you or mislead you about the current state of the job market so that you'll take the job he has available. If this happens, try another agency.

To help an agency find the right job for you, write a letter stating:
1. Your job objective, target industry, desired salary range and the geographical areas you'd consider.
2. Several of your proudest accomplishments (with the rands-and-cents results of each, if possible).
3. A description of your personality traits that make you ideal for the job, with examples.

You'll have to fill out an application form and submit a curriculum vitae.

When you get a job offer, negotiate the salary on your own; to serve his client, the agent may try to convince you to take less money. And don't be afraid to turn down a job if it's not right for you; the agent won't drop you – on the contrary, he will assume that if you've received one offer, you'll get another. (See also *Headhunters*, p.105; *Job hunting*, p.120; *Job interviews*, p.120.)

Empty-nesters

Some survival strategies if your children have left home for good:

1. Move into a smaller space; sell or store the excess furniture.

2. Expand your environment. Convert a former child's room into a den, home office or workroom.

3. Fill the void. Some young people who have left their homes in distant cities may need not only a place to live but a family to live with. You may gain a "perfect" substitute son or daughter who will gladly do household or other tasks in exchange for rent. Draw up a contract so that expectations are clear on both sides.

4. Extend your family. Develop new relationships, drive senior citizens, do voluntary work with children.

5. Expand your horizons – don't just sit at home waiting for the children to pay a visit. Enroll in a continuing education course, take up a hobby, travel or work for a charity.

Endurance building

Badly out of shape? Recuperating from an illness? Start rebuilding yourself slowly by walking up and down your block for two minutes. Walk five days a week, a little longer each time, until you can walk 15 minutes without stopping.

Gradually increase your speed until you can walk 1,5 kilometres in 15 minutes. Start your workout by walking slowly until your body is warm; slow down again towards the end to cool off. Finish up with stretches for flexibility (see *Warm-up & cool-down exercises*, p.224).

Gradually increase distance until you're walking five kilometres in less than 45 minutes. (This should take about 12 weeks after you achieve a 10-minute kilometre.)

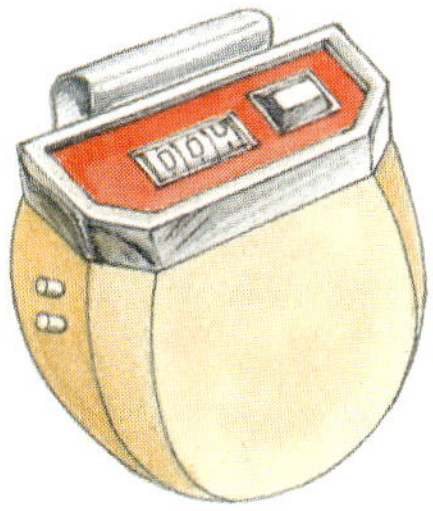

To measure your walking distance, wear a pedometer on a belt or a waistband.

THE GOAL

Now you're ready to start jogging, aerobic dancing, rowing or cycling three to five times a week for 30 minutes or so. Or just keep walking; aim for 10 to 12 kilometres at six km/h – when you reach 30 kilometres a week, you'll be in good shape.

Ultimately, your heart rate should increase to between 70 and 90 percent of your maximum rate (calculated by subtracting your age from 220). If you're sedentary, aim to increase your heart rate to 60 percent of your maximum.

Caution: If you're over 35, overweight, or have a family history of high blood pressure or heart disease, see a doctor before beginning any exercise programme.

If at any time you feel an irregular heartbeat or pain or pressure in your chest; if you're dizzy or lightheaded or if you vomit during or after exercise; if, after finishing your workout, you can't catch your breath in less than a minute, stop at once and seek medical help.

Eraser

1. Can't find an eraser? Twist a rubber band around your finger to erase pencil marks.

2. For special jobs on coloured paper – hand-lettered invitations and school projects, for example – cover errors with Tipp-Ex fluid or a dab of the acrylic paint used for model airplanes. Choose low-gloss paint and mix the colours until you have an exact match for the paper.

Evening attire

Going straight from the office to an evening affair?

1. If you're a woman, you can wear a simple dress or ensemble to work and bring accessories – earrings, bracelets, necklace – a pair of dressy shoes and an evening wrap, such as a brightly coloured shawl or silk blouse to wear as a jacket. A suitable length of black satin ribbon, four to eight

DID YOU KNOW . . . ?

The tuxedo rebellion

The year: 1886. The place: Tuxedo Park, New York.

As the story goes, tobacco tycoon Pierre Lorillard was bored with the formality of traditional tails. And so, for the annual Autumn Ball, he had his tailor make him several tailless jackets in the mode of the British riding coat popular among fox hunters. It was a daring idea, but Pierre lost his nerve and donned the standard formal costume.

His son, Griswold, however, possessed the audacity that Pierre lacked. He and his friends astounded the cream of society by appearing in short dinner jackets.

Tongues wagged for a while, but the desire for change must have lurked beneath the staid surface of society – or perhaps the famous Lorillard name worked some magic – because others were soon wearing the tailless "Tuxedo suits" that eventually became standard attire.

Accessories to the tuxedo also have their histories. A forerunner of the cummerbund, for instance, was worn in India as part of Hindu formal attire. The British liked the look and adopted the style for themselves.

The pleats were worn facing up, probably because dress trousers lacked pockets.

DID YOU KNOW?

Money talk

☐ The first specifically South African coinage was minted for the northern Cape mission station of Griquatown, in 1815.
☐ The pound, half-pound and five-shilling coins of the old Zuid-Afrikaansche Republiek, minted in Germany in 1892, were quickly withdrawn from circulation. Not only had the engraver, Otto Schulz, depicted the Voortrekker wagon on the crest with double shafts, but his initials appeared prominently on the bust of President Paul Kruger – and "OS", in Dutch and Afrikaans, spells "ox".
☐ Because of a shortage of coins in the 19th century, many shopkeepers in South Africa issued their own "good-fors" or tokens in cardboard and metal. These could be exchanged for goods and often circulated widely.
☐ During the South African War, legal tender was so scarce that the paymaster of the Border Scouts in Upington issued "notes" printed on the tails of khaki shirts.
☐ In 1898 some 215 threepenny pieces were struck – in gold – at the State Mint in Pretoria. These "Sammy Marks tickeys" are named after the pioneer Witwatersrand financier who was given special permission to mint them.

centimetres wide, can serve as a last minute belt or hair tie. The finishing touch: a showy silk tassel (available from curtaining shops) attached to the zip tab on a leather handbag.

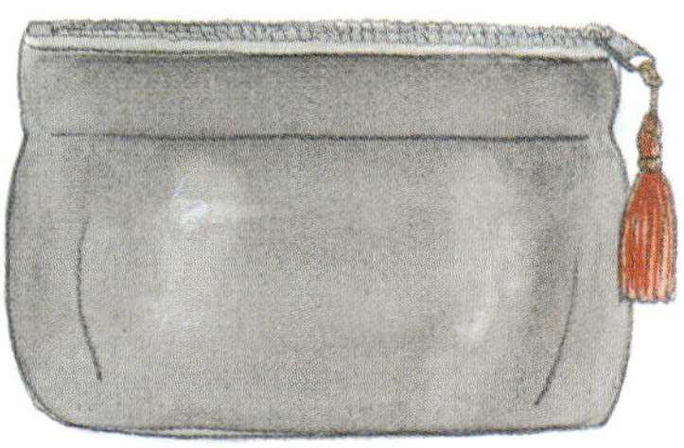

2. If you're a man, wear a dark suit to work and bring a clean shirt, fresh tie and perhaps a silk handkerchief, if that's your style. A flower in the lapel does wonders, too.

Exchanging currency

Learn a country's official exchange rate before you go; check with a travel agent, a large bank or the business section of your local newspaper. You'll usually get a better rate in the country itself, but take the equivalent of R500 with you – order it from your bank or exchange it in the airport before departure – for immediate incidentals such as tipping, phone calls and taxi fare.

In your host country, hotels, shops and independent exchange agencies generally offer the worst exchange rates; airports and city banks, the best – although in some countries officially tolerated black markets offer the best rates of all.

Traveller's cheques often get better rates than cash. If there is a difference of more than five percent between the posted buy and sell rates, you are probably getting cheated.

You must show your passport during currency transactions, and you may be required to show your receipts when you exchange your currency back into rands. Coins are usually not exchangeable.

Be aware of bank hours and holidays in the country you're visiting. Large railway stations and airports often have longer banking hours.

Bear in mind that the exchange rate on a credit card billing is based upon the rate in effect when the charge clears in South Africa, not when you make the particular transaction.

A pocket calculator is handy for converting prices when you shop.

Exercise cramps

WHILE RUNNING

1. If you feel a twinge in your abdomen, slow both your pace and your breathing rate; if necessary, stop. The pain should disappear when breathing returns to normal.
2. For relief from a cramp in your calf or thigh, do a "wall stretch": stand about a metre away from a tree or a wall and lean into it, bending your front knee while keeping your back heel on the ground. Hold for a count of 50 or until the cramp disappears. (See also *Stitch in the side*, p.196.)

WHILE SWIMMING

1. If you're in a pool, get out or go to the shallow end and do a wall stretch.
2. In a lake or in the sea, float on your back or stomach.

Straighten the cramped leg, and extend your toes forward as far as you can. Hold and count to 30 slowly, then relax.

Repeat until the cramp disappears.

Exercise equipment

1. Use 410-gram cans of soup or vegetables as hand weights for arm exercises. Alternatively, try one-litre soda bottles. (Don't open them immediately after use.) Hold one item in each hand and, with both arms at your sides, alternately raise each arm to shoulder level.
2. For ankle weights, fill socks with dry sand, small stones, raw rice, dried lentils or beans or clean cat litter. Weigh them (start with one kilogram) and tie them shut, leaving room in the toe so that you can fasten them around your ankles.

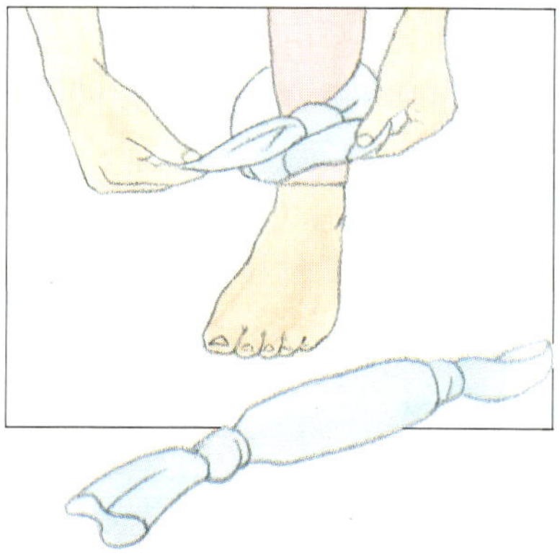

Lie on your back, with one knee bent and the other leg straight. Raise the straight leg as high as you comfortably can. Switch the position of both legs and repeat.
3. Squeeze a tennis ball or tightly rolled-up pair of socks in each hand to strengthen your grip.
4. To stretch your calves, sit on the floor with your legs straight, loop a

bath towel around the ball of one foot, and pull, resisting with your foot; repeat with the other foot.
5. Stand, holding a towel above your head, and pull on the ends.
6. Rest your ankle on the back of a chair in front of you, keeping the leg straight. Bend over, getting your face as close to your knee and your hands as close to your ankle as possible; hold for five seconds. Repeat with the other ankle.

Exercise mats

1. If you're not doing heavy tumbling, a bath or beach towel on a rug or a folded cotton or wool blanket will work well as a mat.
2. Or exercise on a firm mattress, preferably one resting on a bedboard, a platform bed or the floor.

Exercising gently

IF YOU'RE CHAIR-BOUND

1. Raise first one arm, then the other straight up over your head. With both arms overhead, reach for the sky with your right hand, then your left, five times each. Relax.
2. Let your head fall forward. Slowly tilt it to the right and let it rotate back, to the left, and then to the front. Repeat in the reverse direction. Don't force the action.
3. Shrug your shoulders high, then let them drop four times. Pull them backward, then push them forward four times.
4. With your feet firmly on the floor about half a metre apart, hold your arms straight out in front of you. Bend forward as far as you can, stretching out your arms. Return to the starting position. Twist to the right and bend as far as you comfortably can, then to the left. Repeat.
5. Hold the seat of your chair. Raise your right leg from the knee, wiggle your toes, and move your foot in a circle, first one way, then the other. Return the right foot to the floor and repeat with the left leg.
6. Raise one knee as high as you can, then let it drop and raise the other one. Repeat this action as vigorously as you are able to, "marching" in place 10 times.

IF YOU'RE BEDRIDDEN

1. Lie on your back on a firm mattress. Raise your head; with your chin close to your chest, turn your head slowly from side to side.
2. Lie on your back with your arms comfortably at your sides. Raise your right arm, cross it over your face, then return it to your side. Repeat with your left arm, three to five times each.
3. Lie on your left side, with your legs straight, your head resting on your left arm and your right hand flat on the mattress at chest level. Bend your right knee and pull it up towards your chest. Hold it there, resting on the mattress, for two to three minutes. Then roll over and repeat the action with the left leg.

Exercising on the go

1. Whenever possible, walk, jog or cycle to work. Carry your work shoes in a bag. (You can even carry a change of clothes in a small backpack and change at the office.)
2. If you take a bus or train, get off a kilometre before your stop and walk the rest of the way.
3. Use the stairs at work, instead of taking the lift.
4. Walk a kilometre before lunch.

WATCHING TV

Ride an exercise bike, bounce on a mini-trampoline, skip or run in place while you're watching your favourite programmes.

ON THE PHONE

Use wrist and ankle weights to do leg lifts and arm raises while you're talking on the phone.

DOING HOUSEWORK

1. For aerobic housecleaning, warm up with a light activity such as dusting or washing dishes, then proceed to vacuuming, sweeping or floor polishing for 20 to 30 minutes. Upbeat music may help keep you moving.
2. To pick up light items from the floor, stand with your feet apart, arms at your sides. Bend slowly from the waist and touch the floor, flexing your knees if you have to. Count to 10 before straightening.
3. To dust a high shelf, stand with your feet apart and hold the dustcloth in both hands, bending from side to side to wield it.

AT YOUR DESK

1. While sitting at your desk, lean slightly forward, grip the sides of your chair firmly, and alternately raise your left and right knees to your chest. Try not to strain.
2. While reading, put your foot through the handle of your handbag or briefcase; lift until your leg is horizontal to the floor.

Repeat the exercise 10 times without touching the floor. Then do it again with the other foot. (See also *Office exercises*, p.145.)

Exposure meter

If you've left your exposure meter at home or your camera's meter is broken or faulty, use the "Sunny 16 Rule". On a sunny day with distinct shadows, set the f-stop at f/16, then match the shutter speed as closely as possible to the film's speed; that is, 1/60 second for 64 ASA/ISO film or 1/125 for 100 ASA/ISO.

If it's cloudy but fairly bright with soft shadows, set the stop at f/11 and use the same formula. On a day without shadows, set at f/8.

Extension cords

Be careful when you choose an extension cord. Just because it happens to have several receptacle ends, don't take that to mean that it can carry more amperage than the outlet it's plugged into.

And be aware that the longer the cord, the greater the amperage drop. A 30-metre cord, for example, has to be heavier than a three-metre cord performing the same task. If an extension cord feels warm, consider that a warning. Replace it with a heavier cord or jettison an appliance or two.

Eye make-up

Well-chosen and carefully applied eye make-up can enhance your appearance and downplay imperfect facial features. With eye make-up, less is often more. For example, too much dark eyeshadow makes deep-set eyes appear to recede, while heavily applied make-up makes you look older.

Some rules to observe when applying make-up are:

1. Remove all traces of stale make-up with cottonwool soaked in eye make-up remover. Ensure that your make-up applicators are clean and dry.
2. If you have sensitive eyes, use a hypo-allergenic preparation. Contact lens wearers should consult their eye-care practitioner.
3. Use gentle, sweeping strokes when applying make-up – the skin around the eyes is delicate.
4. Don't overpluck eyebrows. Remove only straggly hairs from below the eyebrow curve.
5. Darken your eyebrows slightly with an eyebrow pencil to complement the colour of your hair.
6. Brush your eyebrows with an eyebrow brush – it softens them.

For colours that match your looks, follow these easy guidelines:

☐ Redheads are complemented by moss and olive green (green eyes), teal (blue eyes), warm copper, brown and amber (all eye colours). Use brown and charcoal eyeliner. Opt for brown or green mascara.
☐ Brunettes may use sapphire, emerald, purple and mauve. Keep colours muted by day; increase depth for night drama. Use black mascara for a dark skin and dark eyes, brown-black if you are fairer.
☐ Blondes should wear brown and pink (green eyes), pink and mauve (blue eyes), deep green and coral (brown eyes). Use soft brown or charcoal eyeliner and brown mascara.
☐ Dark-skinned beauties should use deep, glowing shades. Silver or gold highlighter adds evening glamour. A liquid black eyeliner and mascara will complete the effect.

Put on mascara last. Make sure eyelashes are free of powder, apply one layer of mascara, allow to dry, then apply another. Touched-up mascara may look clumsy. Clean off and start from scratch.

Finish the effect with a fine line drawn with an eyeliner along the base of the eyelashes.

Eye problems

STIES

A sore lump on the edge of your eyelid is a sty. Apply a hot, wet compress several times a day to bring it to a head, so that it can discharge its contents. If it remains for several weeks, see a doctor.

RED EYE

A bright red blotch in the white of your eye is usually a harmless haemorrhage caused by coughing, choking or rubbing the eye. It should disappear by itself in about a week; if it occurs again soon, or if you are bruising easily or experiencing headaches, see a doctor.

PINKEYE

If one (or both) of your eyes is red, teary and sticky, you may have pinkeye or conjunctivitis. This irritating condition may last for two or three weeks without treatment, so you should consult your doctor to make sure of the diagnosis. In the meantime, to soothe it, you can bathe the eye in warm water.

The disease is contagious. Wash your hands before and after touching your eyes and keep your towels and washcloths separate from those of the rest of the family.

Throw out all your old eye make-up. (Replace with new products once the infection is over.) See a doctor if the infection persists.

If your eyes are red, itchy, teary, and feel sandy but are not sticky, you may have noncontagious pinkeye. This condition may be due to allergies; use cold compresses to relieve the itching and try to avoid possible allergens. The condition may also be the result of chemical irritation; if so, use "artificial tears" (available without prescription at a pharmacy), and wear goggles while swimming.

BURNED EYES

If you burn your eyes, close them immediately. Ask someone to put moist sterile pads or other cloths over your eyes and secure with a bandage. Seek medical help right away.

CHANGE IN VISION

If all or part of what you see appears hazy, blurry, wavy or distorted; if you see spots or clouds, sudden flashes of light or black specks or threads drifting across your field of vision; if you experience a sudden partial or complete loss of vision, however brief, be sure to see your ophthalmologist immediately or go quickly to the closest emergency unit.

If the doctor finds nothing wrong, get a second opinion.

Eyes & foreign bodies

1. Even a tiny object – a speck of soot or a grain of sand – can irritate your eye. If you refrain from rubbing it, your tears may wash the object away.
2. If an object is on the surface of the white of the eye or under the lower lid, irrigate gently with sterile water, if available; otherwise, use tap water. Tilt your head and pour from the inner corner of the eye so that the water drains down towards the outer corner and out.

3. If the object is under the upper eyelid, grasp the lashes with your thumb and forefinger and fold them up over the tip of a cottonwool swab. If you can see the object, remove it with a moist, sterile cottonwool swab.

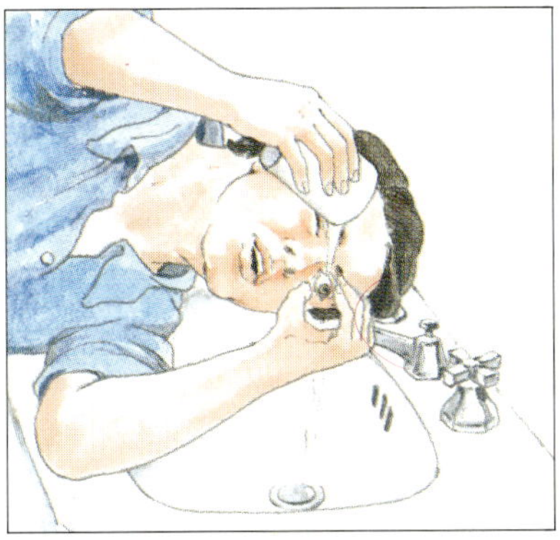

4. If the object doesn't wash out, it may be stuck to or embedded in the eye. Don't try to remove it; get to a doctor as soon as possible.

Eyestrain

PREVENTION

1. Do not position your computer screen under a bright fluorescent light or opposite a window.

Install an antiglare screen; reduce blur by cleaning it often and tuning the display to ensure that there's a high contrast between the characters and the background.

2. When reading or writing, light should come from over your shoulder – the right shoulder if you're left-handed, the left shoulder if you're right-handed.

3. Turn on a low light when watching TV and sit directly in front of the screen, two metres away.

4. Wear good quality sunglasses to protect your eyes from ultraviolet light, particularly when doing outdoor summer activities.

RELIEF

1. If your eyes feel tired and achy after prolonged close work, refresh them by refocusing on a distant object for several seconds.

2. Try to rest your eyes for about 15 minutes every hour or so.

F

Fabric care

1. Read and follow all care labels. If you buy your own fabric, make a note of its content and use only recommended cleaning agents.

2. Wash or clean all the pieces of a matched set together every time – the jacket and the trousers, all the living room loose covers, all the bedroom curtains and so on. Exceptions are sets in which one piece is a solid colour and the other a print.

3. Bleach generally whitens and brightens a washable fabric, but check the label to see whether chlorine or a milder oxygen bleach is called for. Drip-dry white fabrics, for example, often yellow when exposed to a chlorine bleach.

4. Always remove stains before laundering, or tell the dry-cleaner where and what the stains are. Light-coloured liquids such as ginger ale and perfume may leave no mark but in time or with heat may turn brown and stubborn. Blot up food stains on washable fabrics at once and sponge from the wrong side with soda water. Make sure you wash or dry-clean the article promptly.

Family photographs

If your family pictures are all forced smiles and stiff poses, try these tips to improve them:

1. Avoid poses. Everyone is uncomfortable in front of a camera. To make sure that your subjects look relaxed, snap them while they're active or unaware of your camera. On a family outing, sneak up to someone braaiing chops or setting the table. If he stiffens, ask him to describe what he's doing. Take his mind off the camera.

2. Use a zoom lens. A camera at close range can be intimidating. A zoom lens lets you stand back while zooming in for a portrait.

3. Watch the details. It takes only a second to check for cluttered or distracting backgrounds.

4. Beware of light. Bright sunlight is harsh and causes squinting and ugly shadows. Shade is softer and more flattering to skin tones.

5. Take two or three quick shots of the same person. Pros know that it's rare to get a perfect picture on the first try. Shooting several increases your odds of capturing the peak of action or the perfect smile. So bring plenty of film on family trips or outings.

6. To keep full-length shots from looking very amateurish, include the *whole* figure; be careful not to cut off the subject's feet.

7. Turn your favourite photographs into postcards by gluing them to index cards; trim with scissors, a razor blade or a penknife. Your friends and family will love finding pictures of themselves in the postbox.

Family relationships

Do you belong to a particularly close-knit family? If you make your home in Cape Town, and granny lives in Durban, brother Bill and his kids in Johannesburg, and sister Sue in England, it may be a long time between visits. But there are ways to build a family support system.

THE MAIL POUCH

Use a sturdy manila envelope to circulate messages among the family. Each recipient puts in something: a letter, photographs, newspaper clippings, three-year-old Lisa's drawing of the family dog, a brand-new recipe or even an audio or video tape. (Who but the family can truly appreciate a tour of the old house, the baby's gurgles or a braai at a close friend's farm?)

To keep the packet moving through far-reaching branches of the family tree, provide a routing list and pre-addressed labels.

As you add your latest contribution to the packet, be sure to remove material that has made the rounds, preserving it for your own personal archives if you like.

ALBUMS AND SCRAPBOOKS

1. Start a new photo album at the beginning of each year to provide a visual diary of your family life; add photographs or school photos sent by distant relatives.

2. Keep a scrapbook of notes, photographs and birthday cards from grandparents, aunts, uncles and cousins to remind your children of happy family relationships.

3. When youngsters go out on their own, give them an album of family photographs as the cornerstone of their own family archives.

STORIES

Telling tales – and preserving them on audio or video tape when possible – about relatives, distant and long gone, builds a sense of family and may create surprising relationships between the subject of the story and the audience. Black sheep Uncle George may really have been a rotter, but the spunk he showed in emigrating to Australia may serve as inspiration to a descendant yearning to follow her own star.

Fashions

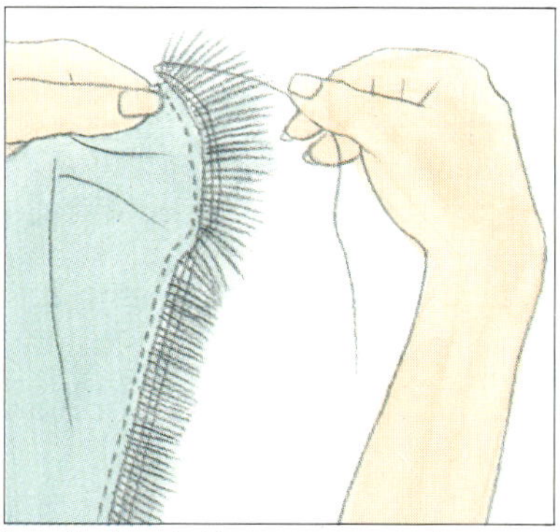

For a budget fashion accessory, make a fringed scarf from a length of fabric. Loosen thread at the edge of the fabric and pull; for a longer fringe, remove more threads.

1. No matter what the latest fashion is, ignore it until you know what basic lines suit you. If you can't tell by spending time in front of a mirror, ask a friend for an honest appraisal.

2. Experiment with colour. Hold fabric samples next to your face to see which colours are most flattering. Don't be a slave to fashion – if this year's colours don't look good on you, don't wear them.

3. To play it safe, choose classic styles for expensive items such as coats; go trendy with less costly separates and sportswear.

4. An alternative to making a big commitment to this year's styles is to follow the fashions only with accessories: shoes, belts, bags and jewellery. Scarves in particular can give clothes a fashionable lift.

You can make them from any lightweight fabric, new or old, and tie them at your neck or waist, or use them as turbans or shawls.

Fastening into concrete

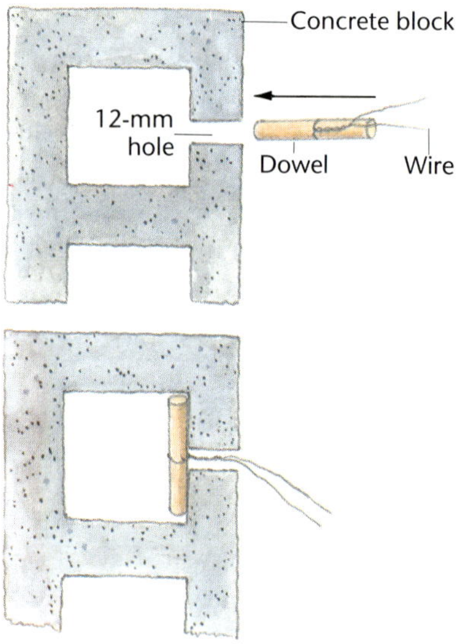

1. Here's a useful way of improvising a toggle bolt to fasten an object firmly to a hollow concrete-block wall. Make the "toggle" by wrapping a 300-millimetre-long piece of flexible wire around the centre of a 75-millimetre length of 10-millimetre hardwood dowel, as shown. Then, using a carbide-tipped masonry bit, bore a 12-millimetre hole into the block and force the dowel into it. Hold onto the wire's loose ends so that, after the dowel is trapped inside the concrete block, you can use them as twist ties to secure an object.

2. When screws driven into plastic or lead anchors loosen from solid concrete walls or floors, replace them with wood screws. First remove the anchor and clean out the hole. Then whittle a softwood plug to fit tightly into the hole. If necessary, wrap it with masking tape to ensure a snug fit. (A section of hardwood dowel, sanded to fit, can also be used.) Drive the plug into the hole with a hammer and cut off the protruding end flush with the surface. Bore a small pilot hole and drive in a wood screw.

3. If a screw loses its grip in a lead anchor, replace it with a larger screw. Or insert one or two lengths of lead solder into the anchor and then re-drive the screw.

4. To fasten wood furring strips to a concrete wall, make glue-in-place nail fasteners. First cut a 75-millimetre square piece of sheet metal and drive a nail through the centre. Then spread a generous amount of panel adhesive or construction adhesive on the back of the metal square and on the nail's head. With a twisting motion, press the plate onto the wall with the pointed end of the nail protruding. Install one such fastener every 400 to 600 millimetres. Once the adhesive has cured, hold the furring strip against the row of nails and hammer it down. Bend the nails over to secure the furring strip.

Fastening into metal

1. If a sheet-metal screw strips its hole, replace it with a larger screw or with a blind rivet.

2. Metal parts fastened together with nuts and bolts often loosen as a result of ongoing vibration. To prevent this, you should coat the bolt's threads with shellac or clear nail polish before threading the nut onto it.

A more permanent way to secure the nut is to crush the remaining threads with a hammer and punch or cold chisel after the nut has been tightened in place.

3. To hang light objects from metal columns or beams, use heavy-duty magnets and string or wire.

4. Here's a convenient way of replacing a threaded fastener in a metal component when you don't have the right size replacement:

Insert into the tapped hole a plastic expansion anchor that accepts machine screws and bolts. Then firmly drive in the appropriate fastener for the anchor.

5. Fasten objects to metal studs with self-tapping sheet-metal screws. Drill a small pilot hole for each screw.

To hang a heavy object from a metal stud wall, use a strong magnet to locate a stud, then drill through it and insert a toggle bolt.

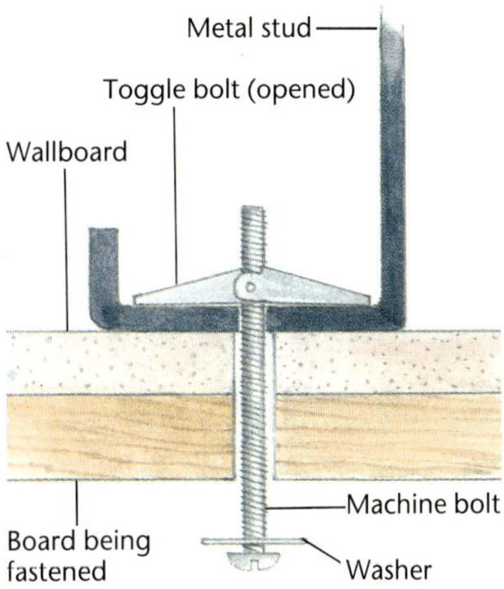

Fastening into wallboard

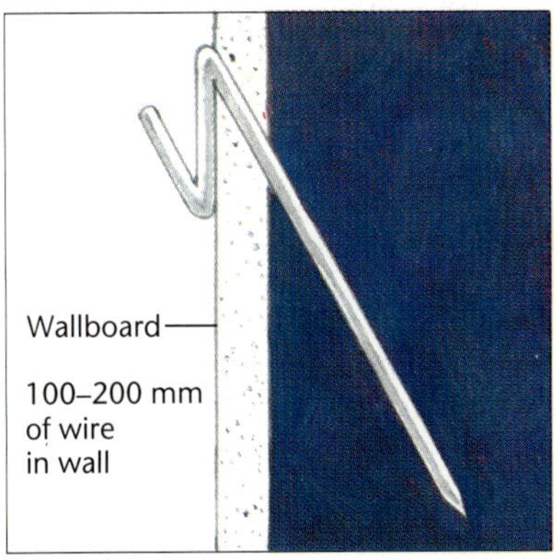

1. If you must attach an object to wallboard where there is no wood backing, such as a stud or joist, you should use hollow wall fasteners: plastic anchors, expansion anchors or toggle bolts.

2. Hot-melt glue – the quick-setting kind which is dispensed from an electric glue gun – is ideal for sticking wood, plastic and small metal pieces to wallboard.

3. To hang a lightweight item, such as a small picture frame or a calendar, make a hanger from a 200-millimetre length of wire clothes hanger. File a sharp point at one end of the wire and use pliers to make two bends at the other end, as shown. Then force the point into and through the wallboard at a sharp downward angle. Push about 100 or 125 millimetres of wire into the wall.

Fastening into wood

1. Save some elbow grease by rubbing a candle or a piece of soap on the threads of wood screws.

2. When nailing into hardwoods, bore pilot holes to prevent splitting the wood. If you don't have the appropriate bit, use a finishing nail as a drill bit (see *Drills*, p.67).

3. If you must screw into end grain, reinforce the joint with a hardwood dowel. Drill a hole and insert the dowel as shown.

4. If a wood screw strips its hole, replace it with a larger screw. Or insert a few wooden matchsticks or toothpicks and drive in the screw.

Or whittle a tight-fitting wooden plug. Apply glue around the inner edge of the hole and then drive in the plug with a hammer. Bore a pilot hole before driving the screw.

5. When fastening into wood, drive nails at a slight angle to increase their holding power. About two-thirds of the nail's length should enter the second board.

Fatigue

1. Tired all the time? See your doctor for a checkup; there may be a medical reason for your fatigue.

2. Give aerobic exercise a try. It can combat the fatigue caused by insomnia, anxiety, stress, premenstrual hormonal changes, and – believe it or not – inactivity. It tones up your body, pumps oxygen to your brain, and revs up the production of "feel-good" body chemicals.

3. Cut down on caffeine and alcohol; eliminate both after dinner. Caffeine may appear to give you energy, but the lift is short-lived; it will also keep you awake. Alcohol makes you temporarily drowsy but interferes with normal sleep patterns.

4. Review your eating habits; crash diets cause fatigue by producing nutritional deficiencies. The cure: a well-balanced diet.

5. Check your drugs. Antihistamines, diuretics, tranquillizers, pain relievers and antihypertensives can all cause fatigue. So can many drug interactions (p.67). Discuss the problem with your pharmacist and doctor.

6. If you're one of the many people who are prone to mid-afternoon energy slumps, try to schedule challenging, creative projects in the morning and save your routine chores for the afternoon. Alcohol-free, protein-based light lunches also tend to combat afternoon fatigue.

Fences

1. A living screen of fast-growing flowering vines offers a low-cost summertime alternative to conventional fencing or hedges. Dig a strip 600-millimetres wide along the perimeter of the area you want to enclose and set rough poles at two-metre intervals along the centre line. Staple a strip of chicken wire or plastic netting from top to bottom. Around the base of each pole, plant some seeds of a fast-growing flowering vine: morning glories, jasmine, honeysuckle and sweet peas are good choices. As the tendrils grow, fasten them to the wire with twist ties.

2. Instead of topping off a hollow metal fence post with an expensive cap, cram it with wadded newspaper or styrene chips; then fill the top 50 millimetres with concrete.

3. When painting a fence with a roller, hold an old dustpan at the bottom of the posts to keep the roller from touching the ground and picking up dirt. If necessary, you can use a shoe polish brush to touch up the posts at ground level.

4. If you're spray-painting a fence, protect plants by dragging a large piece of cardboard along the fence as a backdrop; a large appliance carton is ideal.

5. To treat an already painted fence post with a wood preservative, drill holes at a sharp angle on all four sides at the top, middle and bottom of the post. Use the longest drill bit you have – at least 250 millimetres. Pour the preservative into the holes until it overflows and let it soak in for a few hours. Then patch with wood putty.

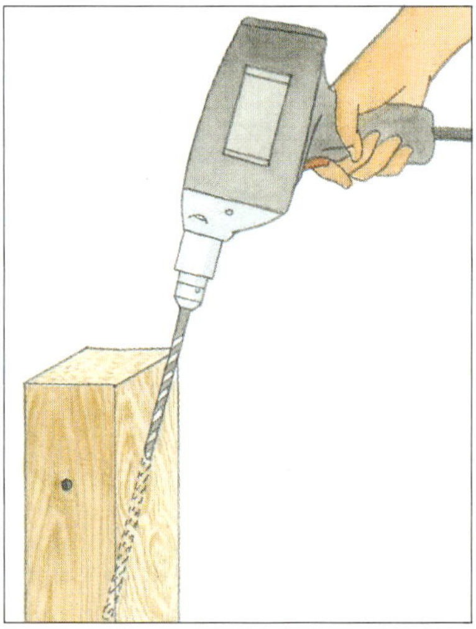

Fertilizers

1. Make your own fast-acting tonic for garden plants. Mix one teaspoon Epsom salts, one teaspoon bicarbonate of soda and ½ teaspoon household ammonia in 4,5 litres of warm water. Apply at a rate of one litre for a rosebush-sized shrub.

2. Mow regularly to keep grass clippings short. Leaving such clippings in place as a mulch not only saves the trouble of raking them but also returns nutrients to the soil, reducing the need for fertilizers.

3. "Shampoo" your lawn with a spray of biodegradable liquid detergent (30 grams in 45 litres of water for every 500 square metres of turf) to reduce surface tension in the soil and allow fertilizers to penetrate more effectively. Apply when the ground is dry – before summer rains start or after the winter rains stop in the western Cape.

4. To rebuild garden soil naturally, plant a "green manure". Agricultural lupins, legumes that manufacture their own nitrogen fertilizer, are a good choice. Sow 15 to 30 kilograms per acre, in the spring in cold inland areas or in the autumn in temperate areas. As the plants flower, mow and till the soil.

Fever

Except in a very young or a very old person, a fever up to 39°C is not ordinarily serious; aspirin or an aspirin substitute (p.12) will usually bring it down to the normal 37°C. In the meantime, get plenty of rest and drink lots of fluids. If temperature rises higher than 39°C, consult a doctor.

A sick child can develop a high fever very quickly; temperatures of 40°C are common in infants and small children but must be reported to a doctor nonetheless.

Fibreglass tubs

Never use harsh abrasive cleansers or scouring pads to scrub fibreglass; they scratch the surface, making it harder than ever to keep clean. Instead, use a fibreglass cleanser or an abrasive powder or liquid cleanser. Or rub with bicarbonate of soda and a sponge. Then, for a nice shine, rinse the tub thoroughly and dry it.

For stubborn stains, let the cleanser stand for a minute or so before removing it. Or apply paint thinner, then wipe it off with a dry cloth and rinse thoroughly.

Files & rasps

1. Coarse tungsten-carbide sanding sheets with steel backing provide a workable stand-in for files and rasps.

IN TIMES GONE BY

Old-time fertilizers

Before today's high-powered synthetic fertilizers came along, gardeners made do with what they found around the house and farm. Ashes from the fireplace were stashed away in a dry place, then worked into the soil a couple of weeks before planting time. (Not a bad idea today; hardwood ash is about 40 percent potash, a major plant nutrient.)

Gardeners who lived near the coast harvested seaweed to plough directly into the soil; they found that the seaweed enriched the soil and the high salt content killed weeds and hastened decomposition. Guano (the accumulated droppings of seabirds and bats) was imported by the shipload from various areas; it provided a plant-boosting yield of 10 percent nitrogen and 10 percent phosphorous. Other old-fashioned but still popular fertilizers include dried blood; bone dust; blood and bone meal as well as dried animal manures.

The standby of every gardener a century ago was "manure tea", used as a liquid fertilizer for houseplants, flowers, shrubs and trees. To make this tea today, fill a 50-kilogram hessian bag with equal parts fresh cow, horse and chicken manure, then sink it in a 200-litre steel drum of water. Let it stand for 30 to 45 days; remove the bag and then top up the drum with fresh water. The resulting tea-coloured extract has yet to be improved upon.

Coarse aluminium-oxide sandpaper also works but won't last as long. Both types will reduce wood, plastic or metal. To shape flat surfaces, try attaching a sheet to the workbench, nailing it to the sides to keep the nailheads out of the way. To reproduce the action of an angle file, wrap the sandpaper around a tapered stick.
2. For rough wood texturing or heavy stock removal, cut and flatten a section from the side of a tin can. Puncture the metal liberally with a nail, then turn it over and nail it to a block of wood. It won't last long, but it does the job until you can buy the right file.

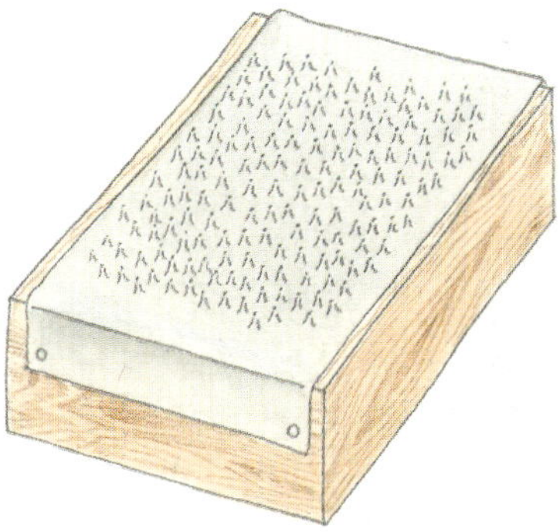

Fingernails

1. No emery board? Try the striking part of a matchbox.
2. For nail-mending paper, cut off a bit of a coffee filter or a tea bag.
3. When applying polish, rest your hands on an upside-down bowl.
4. To dry polish in a hurry, dip your fingers in a bowl of ice water (don't touch the cubes or the bowl). Or stick your hands in the freezer.
5. Do you tend to polish your finger as well as the nail? Moisten the end of a toothpick, wrap cottonwool or toilet paper around it, and saturate it with nail polish remover. Then dab away the polish.
6. To remove the ugly yellow stains caused by some polishes, try soaking your nails in lemon juice.
7. Ragged cuticles? Lubricate them with lip ice.

Or put a few drops of mineral, baby or vitamin E oil into a bowl and soak your fingernails.

Fire damage

1. Photograph or videotape all damage immediately to document the extent of the fire.
2. If firemen have broken doors or windows, have them boarded up.
3. Contact your insurance broker or insurance company for assistance with your claim.
4. Collect receipts for all costs related to your fire damage.
5. Before using electricity, have a licenced electrician check that everything is in safe working order.
6. Move damaged household goods to a safe place so that the insurance assessor can inspect them.
7. Use fans, blowers or dehumidifiers to dry out the house.
8. If it's very cold, drain the plumbing system and pour antifreeze down the toilets and drains to prevent the pipes from freezing.
9. Move all rugs and carpets (and their underfelt) outdoors to dry and eliminate odours.
10. Wipe off wood furniture: vacuum loose sooty residue from upholstery and all horizontal surfaces.
11. Don't let wet fabrics dry in place. Move them to an undamaged room to dry at room temperature.
12. Transfer artworks, manuscripts, photograph albums, books and other porous valuables to a freezer (if yours is too small, try a local frozen food company) until you can hire specialists to restore them.
13. Discard all food, beverages and medicines that have been exposed to high heat or otherwise damaged.
14. Send clothing to a dry-cleaner immediately and ask the attendant there to try to eliminate the smoky odour permanently.

Fire extinguishers

There are three categories of fire: each is extinguished differently.
1. *A* fires burn to ash. They are fuelled by wood, cloth, paper and some plastics. Water quenches them.
2. *B* fires bubble. They involve flammable liquids and grease. Most kitchen fires are of this type; do not use water on them – it will only splatter and spread the flames.

For oven or grilling fires, turn off the heat and shut the door. If meat catches fire, put a lid over it.

If the fire is on top of the stove, turn off the hotplate. Leave the pan where it is, and smother the flames with a lid. Or douse the fire with handfuls of bicarbonate of soda or salt.
Caution: Never put baking powder, sugar or flour on a fire.
3. *C* fires have a charge. They occur in electrical wiring or appliances. Unplug the appliance immediately or shut off the power (p.162). Extinguish the fire with an all-purpose, or ABC, fire extinguisher. (This can be used on all types of fires.) Pull its pin firmly, press the handles, point at the base of the fire, and then spray with back-and-forth passes.

Fireplace mess

Keep a whisk broom with your poker and shovel to make it easier to sweep up little bits and pieces of bark, firewood and ash.

Remove ashes from the fireplace as soon as they're cold to prevent them spreading throughout the rest of your home. With the damper closed, gently sweep up as much as possible into a dustpan. To make the job easier next time, spread aluminium foil beneath the grate; when the ashes are cold, simply gather up the foil and discard it. Vacuum the fireplace occasionally, using the crevice tool to clean out the corners. Wipe the fire irons with a damp cloth or buff them firmly with a metal cleaner; clean glass doors with a window cleaner or a solution of one tablespoon ammonia per litre of water.

Fireplaces

Fireplaces are inefficient because most of the heat rises up the chimney. In fact, some chimneys which draw too strongly may actually make the house colder by drawing heated air from the house up the chimney.

Installing glass doors with an adjustable air vent over the fireplace opening gives the fire enough air to burn while controlling the loss of already-heated air. And the doors guard against flying sparks. Close the air vent whenever the fireplace is not in use and before retiring.

Raise efficiency another notch by putting in a fireback – a cast-iron plate, sometimes decorative, that covers the back of the firebox. It reflects heat into the room.

You can also increase overall efficiency by installing a 'Jetmaster' fireplace. It burns anthracite or wood in a strong steel box and draws cold air in at its base, pumping warm air out at the top.

Fires

If you decide to put out a small fire, position yourself between the fire and your planned escape route. If after two minutes you can neither contain nor extinguish the flames, don't waste critical time. Close the doors and windows to confine the flames, gases and smoke, get out of the house, and call the fire department.

MAKING AN ESCAPE

1. Test each door for warmth (use the back of your hand). Do not open a door if it feels hot or if smoke is seeping out. Otherwise, proceed quickly and cautiously, staying low if there's smoke.

2. If you're in bed when the smoke alarm goes off, roll out and crawl to the door. If the door is not hot, proceed as above. If possible, cover your mouth and nose with a damp cloth.

3. Try to escape through a first- or second-storey window if the exit is blocked. If there's no rope or chain ladder, straddle the sill, then hang by your hands before dropping to the ground. If you must break a window, use a chair or drawer – anything but your hands.

AWAITING RESCUE

1. If you're trapped above the second floor, try to keep smoke and flames out by stuffing the cracks around the door and the air-conditioning ducts, if any, with damp sheets or curtains. (Do not use paper.) If a tap is nearby, fill a wastepaper basket and douse all doors and walls between you and the fire.

2. Position yourself near a window and signal by waving a brightly coloured cloth or a torch or by turning the light on and off rapidly. Keep the windows closed to prevent a fire-attracting draught. If necessary, crack a window at the top to let smoke out, at the bottom to admit fresh air in. Make sure you do not break the window – you may need to shut it, if there's smoke outside.

Fire safety

1. Be prepared: draw a plan of your home (including stairs, windows and doors) and plot two escape routes from each room. Study the plan with household members; assign someone to help young children, the elderly or the disabled. (As an extra precaution, apply special signs to the windows of their rooms so that firemen can locate and rescue them.)

2. Hold regular fire drills and designate a place you can all meet outside for a head count.

3. Make sure everyone needing to use a window for escape is able to reach and unlock it, remove the screen or storm window, and reach the ground safely.

Fires in public places

1. Note the location of the fire exits any time you're in a high-rise office building, theatre, restaurant or any other public place – no matter how brief the visit.

2. Don't use a lift if a fire breaks out; heat or power failure can make it stall or go to the floor that's burning.

IN HOTELS AND MOTELS

1. Immediately after checking into your room, go into the hall and locate the exits and fire-alarm box. Count the number of doors between your room and the exits.

2. Buy a portable smoke detector to hang on your door.

3. In case of fire, roll out of bed, take your keys and torch (make it a habit to keep them on a bedside table), and crawl to the door. Check to be sure that it isn't hot, open it cautiously, and follow your escape route. If the exits are blocked or filled with smoke, stay in your room.

Firewood

For the cleanest, most efficient fire, burn hardwoods rather than softwoods, and keep your fire hot as long as possible, so that it leaves only ashes instead of wasteful charcoal.

To protect indigenous trees, most firewood available commercially is from exotics, the harder woods being wattle, Australian blackwood, Port Jackson, willow and rooikrans.

For a delicate fragrance, throw a few incompletely opened pinecones on the fire. The wood of South African-grown pine is relatively soft and fast burning, so keep plenty in reserve if you're using pine.

If you have to store firewood logs outdoors, place each layer at right angles to the one below it, and pack the logs with the bark upwards, to shed as much rain as possible.

If you have no firewood, make a tight roll of newspaper and bind it with wire. It needs a hot fire to get it going, but once alight it is clean burning and long lasting.

On trails, you usually have a choice between fuel stoves or firewood provided at approved campsites.

Not many woods are poisonous, but some are so toxic that they should not be used even as firewood. These are tamboti, common in lowland Natal and the northern Transvaal, and oleander, an exotic species often planted along highways.

Fireworks

1. Buy only labelled, top-quality fireworks; store in a cool, dry place well away from all flammable materials.
2. Light fireworks outdoors, one at a time, in an open area.

Never ignite a firecracker indoors or in a bottle. Avoid high-explosive firecrackers; some are equal to a quarter stick of dynamite or more.
3. Keep everyone at a distance and out of harm's way when lighting fireworks; aim rockets and set off roman candles, wheels or snakes away from people and houses.
4. Never pick up a "dud"; it could explode at any moment. Keep a water bucket nearby for emergencies and for disposal of used fireworks.

WATERWORKS

As an alternative to fireworks (especially in view of their potential danger), present a night-time display of colourful waterworks. Ask your guests to wear swimsuits and hand out torches covered with coloured cellophane. Turn on your sprinklers, then light up the water as it sprays in all directions; play recorded patriotic

marches – or Tchaikovsky's *1812 Overture*, which actually ends with cannon fire.

Fish bait

1. South Africa is mainly a saltwater fishing nation. Unfortunately, there are now legal limits on baits for saltwater fishermen because of overexploitation, and enthusiasts should contact the Department of Environment Affairs to check the current legislation.
2. The bait most commonly used along our coastal waters includes redbait, found on the rocks above and below the level of the low-water spring tide mark; bloodworms, found under the sand on the beach and in river estuaries; musselworms, which live among colonies of black mussels; wonderworms, coral worms, prawns and moonlight worms which occur in the sand. Smaller species of fish found along our coastline, or the young of some of the bigger species, are also used as bait to attract larger fish.

Generally, one type of bait will serve as a lure to a wide variety of fish, and it is mainly personal experience and hearsay from old fishermen that will guide you in your selection.
3. For freshwater angling, you can use bait such as mealie meal dough (which lures most types of fish), earthworms, crabs, frogs, crickets and flying ants. Once more, experience will teach you the best bait for each type of fish.
4. It is generally advisable to use fresh bait, although some fish do prefer stale bait at certain times. It can be stored in the refrigerator or frozen – but remember to place it in a container along with a sample of its environment so that the bait does not lose its natural smell.

Fish cleaning

1. Before cleaning a fish, wipe it instead of washing it; water causes a slick coating to form. If you do have to handle a slippery fish, rub your fingers first with salt.
2. You can remove the innards of a fish with one quick jerk, since the tongue, gullet, gills and intestines are connected.

First, using a small, very sharp knife, cut through the gristle that holds the gills to the skull at the roof of the mouth. Then feel for the bony ridge next to the gill plate on the outside of the fish; cut along the outside of this ridge, extending the cut all

the way to the tip of the lower jaw. Repeat on the other side of the head.

Again insert the knife into the fish's mouth, this time cleanly severing the strip of gristle that connects the tongue to the jawbone.

Next, keeping your cut very shallow, slit the belly cleanly from the gill line to the anal vent. Finally, holding the fish lengthways, put your fingers into the slit under the jaw, grab the tongue, and pull downward strongly and quickly. The innards should all come out in a clump. If necessary, you can cut around the anal orifice to disconnect them.

Fish-hook

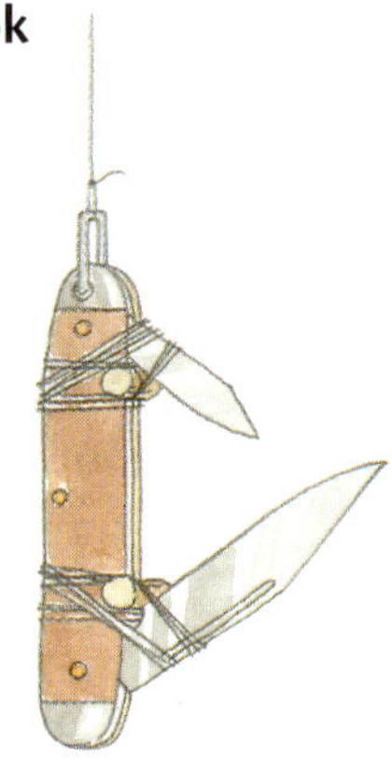

Need a fish-hook? In a pinch, even a penknife can become a hook for a large fish. Prop the blade partly open with a piece of wood and tie it in place. Use a smaller blade at the other end to form a barb.

For smaller prey, try using a safety pin, a piece of wire, bent finishing nail or even a paper clip. Or carve a hook from bone or hardwood as the American Indians did, binding on a sharp thorn for a barb.

Fish poaching

1. You don't need a fish kettle to poach fish; your roasting pan will do fine. Place the fish on the rack, cover with water or stock, and simmer very gently for 10 minutes per 25 millimetres of thickness at the middle.

2. To keep a poached fish from breaking as you transfer it from cooking pan to serving dish, cook it on muslin or greased aluminium foil. Cover the rack of the kettle or roasting pan, making sure enough material extends over the edge so that you can get a good grip. Hold the material taut as you lift the fish from the pan and slide or roll it onto a serving dish.

Fish stuffing

You can stuff a fish with your own mixtures of chopped onion, celery, herbs, bread crumbs or cheese. Mushrooms also make a good filling. If a big enough cavity is left after cleaning the fish, simply stuff it and close tightly with skewers or sew shut with heavy duty thread.

1. If you must make more room for stuffing in a cleaned fish, take out the spine and ribs. Make a slit along the length of the spine with a sharp kitchen knife, cutting on the thicker side (often the darker side) of the fish. Lift the flesh with your fingers and, with the tip of the knife, release it from the ribs. Turn the fish over, cut down the other side of the spine, and repeat. If you haven't already removed the head and tail, cut through the bones at the head and just above the tail, then remove the spine and ribs in one piece. Close the openings with a skewer or heavy-duty thread.

2. To prepare fillets or steaks for baking, simply sandwich the stuffing between two of them; top with more stuffing if you like. Or spread the stuffing on a thin fillet and roll it up like a swiss roll; secure with toothpicks.

Fish tanks

To keep tropical fish happy, change about a third of the water in their tank every week. The simplest way is to make a siphon from an old hose or plastic tubing. Pinch the bottom tightly with your fingers and fill the tube with water from the tap; pinch the top closed and carry it to the tank. Insert

DID YOU KNOW . . . ?

Fish stories: the ones that didn't get away

Is the typical fishing scene still composed of a line with a worm on one end and a fool on the other? Probably not, since fishermen now use sophisticated tackle, special lures and all kinds of high-tech equipment. And angling has more active participants than any other sport in South Africa. But fish do still manage to get away, although some that have been caught have been record-setters.

The brown trout, for instance, averages around 1,5 kilograms but a veritable giant of about seven kilograms was taken in the Mzintlava River near Franklin, in East Griqualand, in 1913. The "angler", though, used a stockwhip and a technique not generally recommended, so this didn't count as an angling record.

Here are some other examples of monster catches:

Sea fishes

Kabeljou or kob	73,5 kg
Yellowfin tunny	107,5 kg
Elf or shad	10,3 kg
Galjoen (the national fish emblem)	6,5 kg

Freshwater fishes

Sharptooth catfish or barbel	31,80 kg
Carp	24 kg
Smallmouth yellowfish	7,83 kg
Tilapia or blue bream	3,26 kg

one end in the tank and the other in a bucket a metre below it. The water will flow from the tank to the bucket. When you've removed enough water, refill the tank with water that has been at room temperature for hours.

To start the siphoning without filling the tube with water, suck sharply on the loose end of the tube before putting it in the bucket. But do this carefully, or else you will end up with a mouthful of fishy water.

Fitness for the elderly

1. If you're not exercising regularly, ask your doctor if it would be advisable. If he thinks you should exercise, choose an activity, such as walking, cycling or swimming, that won't cause stress to your joints or tendons – and don't start out too strenuously (see *Endurance building*, p.73). Check with your local senior citizen organization health club for classes in aerobics and callisthenics tailored for older bodies. Whatever exercise you select, in order to reduce the chances of injury, warm up and cool down gradually (p.224).

2. If you have difficulty walking or are otherwise disabled, contact your doctor or local senior centre. They may give you an exercise routine, or advise you on fitness classes available in your area.

3. To keep fit mentally, stay involved. Church, family and voluntary activities; crafts, puzzles and games; and especially a wide circle of friends – all contribute to mental alertness.

4. If you live alone, adopt a pet, preferably one that's easy to look after. If a dog is too much to handle, consider a cat instead or perhaps a bird or fish.

Fitness on the road

IN AN AEROPLANE

1. Check to see if the airline magazine has details about exercises you can do on the aeroplane.

2. Exercise regularly in your chair (see *Office exercises*, p.145; *Exercising gently*, p.75).

3. Walk up and down the aisles for 15 minutes every hour or so; take the opportunity to stretch in the open spaces next to the rest rooms.

ON A DRIVING TRIP

1. Stop every two hours for five minutes of strenuous stretching and a brisk 15-minute walk.

2. Walk for at least 15 minutes before eating lunch and dinner.

AT HIGH ALTITUDES

The first day just take a stroll; after that, do your usual exercises but reduce the time by 15 percent for each 1,500-metre gain in altitude. If it's hot, don't exercise outdoors at all between 10 a.m. and 4 p.m.

AT THE HOTEL

1. If there's no exercise room or pool, ask at the desk for a list of local health clubs or get a street map so that you can walk or jog.

2. To find an aerobics class, look under "Health studios and gymnasiums" in the Yellow Pages.

3. Bad weather? Walk or jog in the halls. Or stair walk: up for one minute, down for 30 seconds.

IN YOUR ROOM

1. Pack a skipping rope, exercise tape and cassette player.

2. Run on the spot to the morning news or dance to radio music.

3. Stretch for 10 minutes morning and night, or pack 100 paper clips or hair grips, throw them in the air, and bend to retrieve each one.

Fleas

These parasitic, blood-feeding insects are more than just a nuisance and, as intermediate hosts of the dog tapeworm, may pass this infestation on to children, through their droppings and larvae. In hot weather, fleas develop through all the stages from egg to adult in about four weeks or eight weeks in winter. Although they prefer the higher body temperatures of domestic animals, they feed on humans when pets are absent.

1. Use a flea comb with very fine tines to remove fleas and their eggs from cats or dogs.

2. Spray your pet's coat with a nontoxic insect growth regulator, such as methoprene, every three to four months to stop larvae from developing into adults.

3. Apply a product containing citrus extracts (limonene) to the itchy areas of your pet. Another product available is "Program" – a drug which inhibits the physical growth of the fleas. It is available from veterinary clinics and pharmacies.

4. Thorough house-cleaning will help control fleas. Wash pets' blankets especially well, and then spray or dust them with insecticide.

5. Put flea powder in the vacuum-cleaner bag to stop flea infestation there, and vacuum rugs, furniture and skirtings frequently.

6. Keep pets well groomed and washed, using special shampoo, a collar or whatever your veterinarian recommends. Flea droppings show up on your pet as tiny, dark specks and flea eggs show up against a dark background as small, white spheres.

Flood action

1. If rising water threatens to flood your home, prepare for evacuation.

Fill your car's petrol tank and stock the car with food, water, warm clothes, blankets, torches and a first-aid kit with essential medications.

2. Rinse bathtubs, sinks and jugs with household bleach and fill with clean water for drinking.

3. Shut off the electric power (p.162) and any gas valves.
4. Open all the windows and doors of the house so that the floodwaters can drain properly once the flood starts to subside.

DURING THE FLOOD
1. Listen to a portable radio for information and instructions.
2. Don't drive through water; if the car stalls, abandon it and make your way to high ground.
3. If you're trapped at home, go to the highest point and wait for help.

Take emergency food and water, warm clothing and a torch.

If time permits, move portable valuables to the upper floors of the house.

AFTERWARDS
1. Check your home carefully for any injury to pets.
2. Carefully check your floors, foundations, walls, roof and chimney for any structural damage.
3. Throw out all food that has been touched by floodwaters.
4. Boil all drinking and cooking water for 10 minutes.

Flood damage

1. Before dealing with the effects of flooding – whether from an act of nature, a burst pipe or an overflowing bathtub – make sure you shut off your home's power (p.162).
2. Remove standing water with a submersible pump. (If the power is still off, rent a petrol-powered pump from a hire-out agency.)

Then scrape all remaining debris into piles with a squeegee or a 10-centimetre-wide strip of one-centimetre plywood screwed to an old broomstick. Shovel the piles of mud, sand and debris into buckets, and deposit them outdoors. If there's a lot of debris, shovel it out of a window into a rubbish bin, wheelbarrow or pick-up truck.
3. To dry out a room quickly, place fans in windows at the opposite ends of the room; put one on intake and the other on exhaust. Newspaper and old towels are invaluable in soaking up dampness from carpets, and from under bookshelves or beds. As the paper saturates, bundle it up and throw it away.
4. If trapped water has caused a ceiling to sag, punch drainage holes at the low points with an awl, an ice pick or a small screwdriver.

Floods

1. If your home is susceptible to flooding, backfill soil against the foundation so that the land slopes gradually away from the house.

Plant grass or shrubs to absorb water and prevent erosion.

For extreme situations, dig around the foundation and lay perforated PVC drainpipe on a gravel bed. Slope it so that the water will drain off.
2. Photograph and list all your household belongings (see *Valuables*, p.220); keep this inventory in your safe-deposit box.

Floors

1. To remove stains from resilient flooring, use a detergent that contains ammonia. Scrub lightly with a plastic scouring pad. If that fails, rub lightly with extra-fine steel wool. Then wax or polish.
2. "Erase" light scratches in resilient flooring by rubbing with a soft cloth moistened with paste floor wax. Or try rubbing with the edge of a large coin. If the flaw remains, place two layers of aluminium foil over it and press with a hot iron.
3. If you spill nail polish on resilient flooring, allow it to dry until tacky, then peel it off. Clean up any residue with nail polish remover.
4. Chewing gum stuck to the floor? Put an ice cube in a small cup and turn the cup upside down over the gum. When the gum is brittle, gently pry it off with a butter knife.
5. Never clean a wood floor with water; it can cause warping, and even worse, wood rot. Instead, use a dry dust mop. If necessary, wrap the mop with a damp, soft cloth that's thoroughly wrung out.
6. For wooden floors that need more thorough cleaning, use a proprietary liquid cleaning wax that contains a solvent such as turpentine. Be sure to ventilate the room.
7. The self-cleaning, solvent-based polishes available at your supermarket work by removing old wax and dirt. Change the applicator pad or cloth often to prevent unnecessarily spreading the dirt.
8. Seal stone, brick, slate and concrete floors with a masonry sealer, available from hardware stores and flooring centres. Unsealed masonry floors absorb cleaning agents. Clean with a mild solution of water and washing soda or detergent.

Flour sieve

Flour is sieved before use to make sure that it is fresh, dry and well-aerated. If the flour has become damp, you should dry it in a warm place before you use it, as it will make your pastry heavy.

If you don't have a sieve on hand, try one of the following alternatives (before you measure).
1. Put the flour in a medium-sized fine-meshed kitchen strainer and shake or stir until it sifts through.
2. Your food processor will give you extra-fluffy flour; just use the metal blade and blend twice in short five-second bursts.

Flower boxes

Wooden flower boxes provide far better insulation than plastic or metal planters, helping to protect roots against summer heat and unseasonable frosts.

Rot-resistant hardwoods, like jarra, are the best material for flower boxes. Less expensive pine must be treated after the box is assembled. Avoid commercial wood preservatives; their fumes may kill plants. Instead, char the interior of the box by painting it with petrol and setting it alight for 30 seconds. Smother the flames by turning the box over or covering it with a piece of plywood.

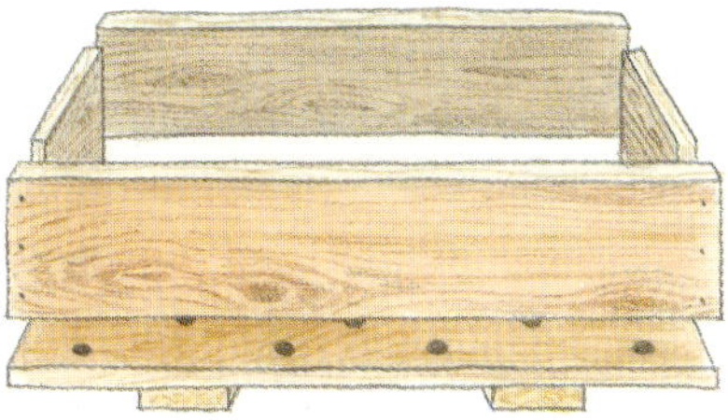

Exploded view of flower box construction.

Flower drying

Would you like to keep your house full of flowers right through the year? You can do it by drying your favourite blossoms in your microwave oven. Roses (including buds), geraniums, marigolds and zinnias dry well; impatiens and petunias don't. Whatever you use, cut the flowers late in the morning, after the dew has dried. And be aware that your dried flowers will come out a couple of shades darker; red roses become almost black, pink or coral ones become red.

1. Line a microwave-safe container with a bed of silica gel crystals (available at craft stores) and heat at *High* for three minutes to make sure the crystals are as dry as possible.
2. Pour 2,5 centimetres of warm crystals into a heavy glass tumbler wide enough to accommodate the flower you're drying.
3. Snip the flower stem so that only two centimetres remain attached to the flower, then stick the stem firmly into the crystals so that the blossom stands upright.
4. Gradually pour the remaining warm crystals down the side of the glass until the flower blossom is completely covered.
5. Microwave at *High* for one minute 45 seconds for rosebuds or up to four or five minutes for large, fleshy blooms (experiment with imperfect blossoms to judge precise timing).
6. Cool for 20 minutes, then gently pour off the crystals. Clean the flower petals carefully with a fine paintbrush, then mist lightly with an acrylic spray. Tape to florist wire to make a new stem.

Flowerpots

1. Look around the house for containers that would make good flowerpots. Pretty coffee mugs fit on a windowsill and make the perfect holder for herbs or small plants. Drill a drainage hole in the bottom with a carbon-tipped glass or masonry bit, or place 2,5 centimetres of gravel and some charcoal in the bottom of the container to keep the roots from becoming waterlogged.

Larger kitchen containers, such as bean pots, ceramic milk jugs and the old pot that sits abandoned at the back of the cupboard, are good choices, too.

2. Cleaning a plastic flowerpot requires nothing more than a stiff brush and hot soapy water, but the stains and ground-in dirt on an old clay pot may prove more stubborn. Soak the pot in a solution of ½ cup bleach per five litres of water for five minutes, then remove, rinse and scrub; repeat as necessary.
3. If a pot has housed a diseased plant, sterilize it before reusing by soaking it for a few minutes in boiling water or running it through a complete cycle in the dishwasher.

Flowers

You can make your own preservative to keep cut flowers fresh. To each litre of water add one tablespoon sugar, one teaspoon vinegar, one teaspoon mouthwash and three to four drops dishwashing detergent.

Before setting flowers in the water, remove two to five centimetres of stem by making a diagonal cut with a sharp knife (scissors crush the stems). Wash bowls and vases with hot soapy water before reusing; fill them with lukewarm water. Keep flower arrangements out of direct sunlight; store them in a cool room (4°C to 10°C) until ready to display. Although florists keep cut flowers in a refrigerator, the home refrigerator is not a good storage place, especially if it contains fruit; fruit releases ethylene gas, which will cause the flowers to age prematurely.

Flyswatter

Because flies are sensitive to air currents, a rolled-up newspaper is a poor substitute for a porous fly swatter. Instead, put some methylated spirits in a plant mister and spray the fly. The stuff kills on contact – but be aware that it may mar some finished surfaces. Or spray the fly with hairspray to immobilise its wings; then you can swat it with a newspaper.

Foefie-slides

You haven't lived until you've had a ride on a foefie-slide. A "foefie" is a stunt or a gimmick; the "slide" part of it makes it quite unlike anything you have ever done.

A foefie-slide can't be bought at the nearest corner store. You have to get a long steel cable (ask an electrician or your hardware dealer where you might get one), tie one end to a high, strong branch in a tree, take the stretch of cable over a mountain stream, river or dam, and tie the other end to a firm branch lower down on the opposite bank.

An essential item for the slide is a pulley with a steel strop to which a cross pipe is fitted for a handhold. This has to be fitted over the cable before both ends are tied.

Now you're ready for the most fantastic ride, which will either end in a splash in the water or a crash against the tree if you don't let go in time.

Points to consider when setting up a foefie-slide are:

1. Don't make the angle too steep or you will move too fast.

2. Try to keep the cable taut or else you will end up hanging motionless in the middle.

3. Instead of a cable you can use a strong steel wire with a pipe as a handhold.

4. Build your foefie-slide over water – it offers a safe and fun landing if you fall off prematurely.

Folding laundry

1. To reduce wrinkling of laundry, remove clothes from the dryer and hang them up as soon as possible. Since most of the laundry is stored in or near the bedroom, do your sorting on the bed. If the seams or pockets on jeans or other sportswear are slightly damp and puckered, pull on them and flatten them with your fingers; then let them air-dry before putting them away. This can often save you ironing time.

2. Fold towels lengthways first so that you don't have to refold them when you hang them on the rack in the bathroom.

3. Try this method for folding fitted sheets: (1) Fold in half, bringing the contoured ends together; at each corner align the contoured edges and invert one into the other. (2) Fold in half again, bringing one matched set of corners to the other; invert one set into the other set. (3) Then fold as usual, smoothing the edges as you go.

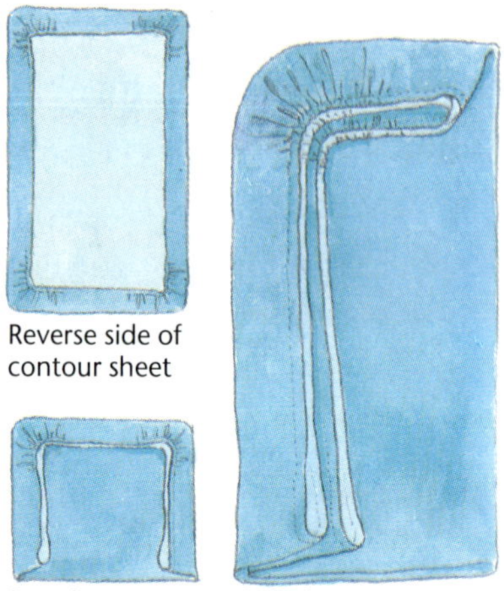

Reverse side of contour sheet

Step 1

Step 2

Food odours

1. To rid a plastic container of food odours, freeze it or expose it to sunlight for several hours. Or drop a lemon wedge into it, close it, and let it stand until the odour disappears. (It may take a few days.)

2. Freshen a lunchbox by moistening a piece of bread with white vinegar and leaving it in the closed box overnight.

3. Eliminate lingering food odours in the kitchen by baking orange peels at 180°C for several minutes.

4. Fast cooking may be the cure for the powerful aroma that Brussels sprouts, cabbage and broccoli can leave. Put them in a pot of rapidly boiling water and return it quickly to the boil. A few drops of vinegar in the water helps, too.

5. For a natural room deodoriser, you should keep an open jar of vanilla pods in the kitchen.

Food poisoning

When you eat contaminated food you will invariably develop diarrhoea and start vomiting. It normally does not last longer than 24 hours, but you won't be able to hold down any food or liquids. That will cause dehydration, more so in small babies and the elderly. It is therefore vital that you take a sip of water or weak tea every few minutes.

Even if your body absorbs just a drop at a time, it might save your life. Children might find Coca Cola, made flat by stirring in sugar, easier to stomach. *Never, ever drink milk.*

You can obtain an electrolyte solution from your chemist, a must for all medicine cupboards. Just a small amount of the appetising drink might keep you from a drip and a hospital bed.

Vomiting caused by nausea can be curbed by a tablet, or better still, by using a suppository. Both are available over the pharmacy counter.

Medication is seldom necessary for food poisoning. There are several products to stop an upset tummy, but you should not curb the diarrhoea before your body has rid itself of the contaminated food.

When, after the crucial 24 hours, you gradually start on a diet of bland solids, you should not attempt to eat any dairy products.

You should immediately consult your doctor if you suspect food poisoning in a small child. The same applies if the fever and abdominal pain persist and the diarrhoea contains blood or mucus.

Avoid canned foods that are soft, foul-smelling and that bubble. Never refreeze food and avoid food that has been left standing at room temperature, reheated, or fastfood "made this morning" but left in a warmer drawer until the evening.

Food processors

1. Don't ignore your food processor just because you can't face cleaning it. Check the instruction manual carefully; many models can be cleaned in the dishwasher.

2. The bowls of food processors have been known to crack right in the middle of processing. Don't remove the food; just tape the crack temporarily with several layers of masking

or insulating tape, then finish processing. Replace the bowl at the first possible opportunity.
3. To prevent leaks between an average size bowl and its cover, never use more than two cups liquid.
4. Don't think something's wrong with your processor if food is left on top of the disc after slicing or shredding. It's normal.
5. Avoid overprocessing foods: chop in short bursts. Check the food often to ensure it's not getting mushy.
6. Pastry scraps? Throw them into the processor along with some sesame seeds, honey, brown sugar or a zesty spice. Both kids and adults love biscuits made this way.

Food safety

1. Bacteria love to lurk in the cracks and little knife nicks on your cutting board. Use a brush to scrub the board vigorously with hot soapy water after each use. And don't let any meat, fish or poultry – raw or cooked – sit on the board for more than a few minutes.
2. Before you start to freeze uncooked poultry, remove it from the store package, rinse well, and rewrap with your own plastic wrap or freezer paper; this reduces the bacteria accumulated between processing and purchase. It's also a good practice to rinse chicken under cold running water before you cook it.
3. If you're grating lemon, lime or orange peel, scrub the fruits first under cold running water; they may have a residue of insecticide.
4. Don't leave homemade custards or other milk-based dishes in the refrigerator for more than two days. Yoghurt is an exception.
5. Once frozen meat or pre-cooked dinners have been thawed, do not refreeze them, as bacteria can develop very quickly.
6. In a hot climate carry an insulated cooler box in your car to ensure that cold foods get from the supermarket to the kitchen without spoilage.
7. You can also stow a freezer pack in a lunchbox. Or freeze the sandwiches overnight before you pack them in an insulated lunchbox – they will thaw nicely by the time lunch rolls around. (See also *Picnics*, p.155.)

Food storage for campers

Here are some ways to help you protect food and keep it fresh while you are camping.
1. Remove powdered foods from their original containers and repackage small quantities in double plastic bags. Between the two layers, slip in an identification label and the relevant mixing instructions.
2. Transfer spices from large containers into clean prescription bottles or plastic film canisters; label the containers and lids.
3. To protect eggs, carry them in a container filled with flour.
4. A stream can serve as a refrigerator; put the food in well-anchored waterproof bags.

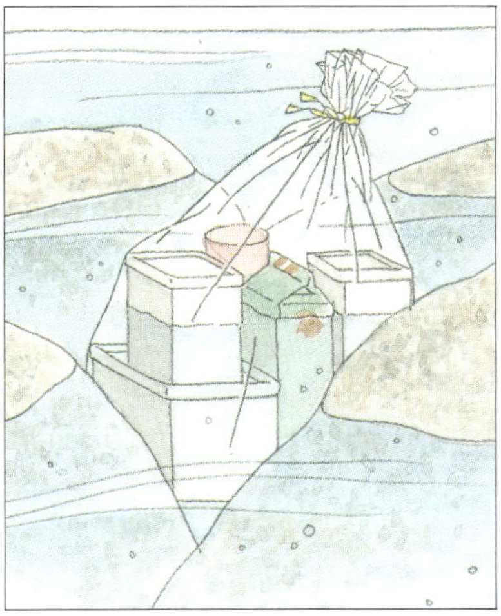

5. In camp remove food from backpacks and tents and leave zips and flaps open. Otherwise rodents will gnaw through them to investigate enticing aromas.

Foot odour

1. Soak your feet every night for 10 minutes in Burow's aluminium acetate solution (1:40 concentration), keeping your toes separated to ensure penetration; air-dry. If foot odour persists, double the strength of the solution. If you can't find Burow's at your pharmacy, use a solution of 25 millilitres vinegar in four litres water. Once the problem is under control, soak two or three times a week.
2. Dust your feet with talcum powder or bicarbonate of soda every day.
3. Be sure to wear clean, absorbent, lightweight wool or cotton socks and leather shoes; steer clear of synthetic fibres – they don't breathe.
4. Rinse socks in a solution of 25 millilitres vinegar in four litres water.
5. Avoid wearing the same pair of shoes two days in a row.
6. Air your feet as much as possible by wearing open sandals.

Foot problems

ATHLETE'S FOOT

Soak your feet in Burow's aluminium acetate solution (1:40 concentration) and rinse your socks properly in a solution of 25 millilitres vinegar in four litres water.

Apply an over-the-counter antifungal solution, cream or powder between your toes and on reddish, scaly areas of your feet twice a day for a month. Sprinkle antifungal powder in socks and shoes daily.

To prevent a recurrence, keep your feet dry and clean; if they tend to sweat, dust the inside of your shoes with antifungal powder and change your socks twice a day. Wear shower sandals in the changing room.

BLISTERS

Leave blisters alone to break spontaneously. Twice a day apply a compress of Burow's solution (1:40 concentration), then cover the blister with antibiotic cream.

BUNIONS

Elevate your feet and apply an ice pack: 10 minutes on, 10 minutes off, until swelling and pain dissipate. Or run cold water over your feet for two minutes at a time.

CORNS

Don't cut corns away – rub them with an emery board.

Cover a stubborn one with a pad on which you've put several drops of 10 percent salicylic acid solution or use a 40 percent salicylic acid plaster; after four or five days soak the foot in water and check to see if the corn has dissolved enough to lift off. Repeat the treatment if necessary.

Caution: If you're a diabetic, seek professional foot care for corns.

INGROWN TOENAILS

Soak the foot in a basin of lukewarm water with one tablespoon Epsom salts twice a day. Insert a piece of cottonwool soaked in baby oil under the nail and cover with a gauze pad. Repeat daily until the ingrown toenail has healed.

SORE FEET

Soak weary feet in a basin of hot water with two tablespoons Epsom salts or a handful of plain salt. Or rub them with ice cubes, towel-dry, and splash with cologne. Elevate them whenever possible.

Massage sore feet by rolling them over a tennis or golf ball. Or knead them, pulling each toe for 10 seconds, and then running the knuckles of a fist along the midsoles.

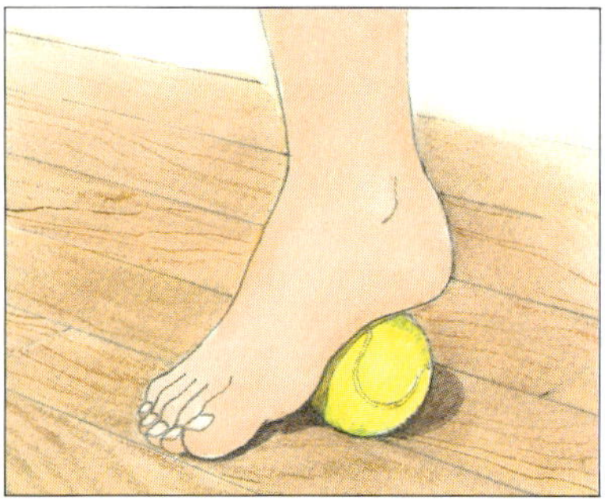

Footwear for sports

1. Your old-fashioned tackies are still fine for boating as long as they have a non-slip tread.

2. Try high-top basketball shoes for canoeing (and portaging); they'll provide extra ankle support when you need it most.

3. It's okay to play tennis in aerobic shoes (they give support for quick side-to-side movements), but don't do aerobics in tennis or running shoes – they lack sufficient cushioning under the ball of the foot.

FIT

1. Be sure your shoes have enough room for your toes to spread under your full weight; allow one centimetre between the end of your big toe and the tip of the shoe when you are standing on both feet. If your feet are wider than normal, ask your sports dealer what brands have different widths in the same sizes.

2. Shoes should be snug and supportive in the heel, but not tight. If you have narrow heels, buy shoes with extra lacing holes. Or loop each shoelace through the last hole on its own side and thread the opposite lace through the loop.

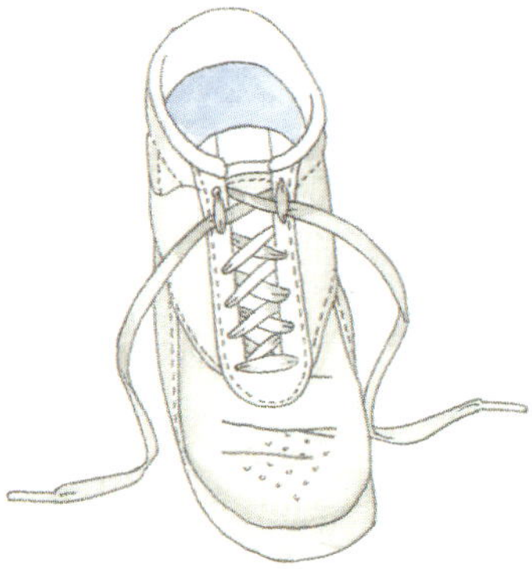

Forcing flowers

For a springtime display in midwinter, you can force flowers from a few branches of flowering quince, forsythia or pussy willow.

1. Anytime after the first of June, choose branches with the fattest buds (these are flower buds – the smaller ones produce only leaves). Cut the branches off with pruning shears.

2. Scrape the bark from the lower six to eight centimetres of each branch and split the end lengthways for five to eight centimetres.

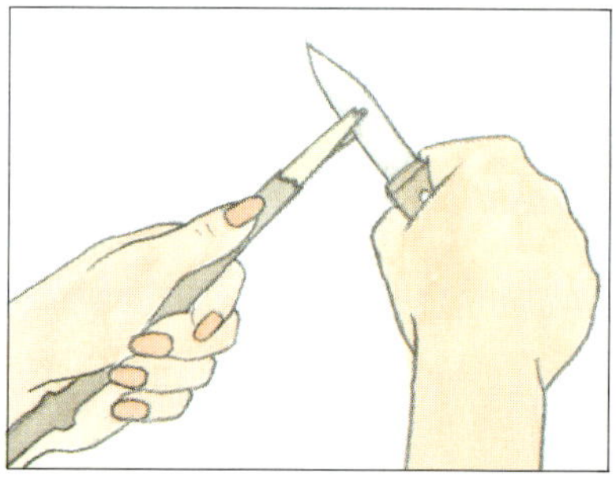

3. Plunge the whole branch into a bathtub full of room-temperature water for a few hours.

4. Arrange the branches in a vase or bowl of cold water and set it in a sunny room. (Ideally, the temperature should be 16°C to 18°C.) Mist the

DID YOU KNOW . . . ?

Footgear favourites: the story of canvas shoes

Actor Dudley Moore (whose feet are two different sizes) bought 30 custom-made pairs in one day, singer Mick Jagger got married in them, and comedian Woody Allen was spotted wearing them with a tuxedo. These modern miracles of comfort are really nothing new.

When – as Indian lore has it – members of a Brazilian tribe dipped their feet into the liquid latex of rubber trees some 300 years ago, they created what were, in effect, the world's first canvas shoes.

The vulcanizing process, developed in the 1860s, made it possible to manufacture rubber shoe soles. But it wasn't until just before the turn of the century that canvas-and-rubber shoes appeared. For years "sneakers" (named by the Americans for their noiselessness) were white or black, low or high cut, and maligned as unhealthy and informal.

In 1962 the first modern running shoe, with a comfortable wide front, a rippled sole, and a shockabsorbing wedge, was marketed. Innovations followed: designer colours, new sole patterns, "breathable" nylon uppers and more. Now technology has caught up with the running shoe. One model has a built-in microchip that measures speed, distance and kilojoules burned. Another, when plugged into a computer, tracks long-term performance. Some runners, however, still prefer the older models.

branches twice a week to protect the buds from drying out. They should bloom within two weeks or so.

You can also force apple, pear or flowering peach blossoms, but they'll take three or four weeks to bloom; don't cut them until six weeks before their normal flowering time.

Foreign phrases

Before visiting another country, it's best to learn at least the basics of the language; take a course, buy tapes, or borrow them from the library. But if there isn't time, take along a phrase book and dictionary or at least learn a few basics such as *Please, Thank you, Good day, Where is...*, and *Help, I need a doctor.*

Don't be afraid to use these phrases; a few words go a long way toward making friends and getting help.

Gestures and pantomime also help. Or carry a pocket-size electronic device that translates your phrase. For a real treat, hire an interpreter.

In a country that uses a different alphabet (Japan, for example), it is advisable to buy a map with both foreign and English place names. Before leaving your hotel, have someone write your particular destination in the native language. Carry the name, address and phone number of your hotel with you at all times (a printed matchbook or the hotel's business card is good for this). Keep a list of emergency phone numbers handy, including the police, local tourist board and South African embassy or consulate.

For any information concerning English-speaking medical practitioners in a foreign country, contact the company with whom you took out travel insurance.

Fractures

Even a slight force can cause a broken bone. Fracture victims often feel the bone break or hear a snapping sound.

There may be intense pain and tenderness – especially when there is pressure on the area of the break – with swelling and discoloration; the limb may look deformed or oddly angled. Or swelling and pain may not occur for hours.

Many fractures are impossible to detect without an X-ray. If any of these symptoms are present, however, assume there's a fracture and seek medical help.

WHILE AWAITING TREATMENT

1. Relieve swelling by placing an ice pack near the break (not on it).
2. Immobilize the injured part and move as little as possible.
3. If an ankle or a foot appears to be broken, take off shoes and socks and elevate the leg.
4. If bone has pierced the skin, cover the wound with a dry, clean dressing and apply pressure to control severe bleeding. (See also *Slings*, p.188; *Splints*, p.193.)

Freckles

1. If you don't like your freckles, stay out of the sun; it darkens them. And don't put lemon juice on them; it just increases the skin's overall sensitivity to the sun.
2. Cover them with liquid make-up.
3. Flaunt your facial freckles unashamedly! Even them out by dotting on rose-brown lip pencil and wear copper-toned lipstick, a little blusher and eyeshadow to set them off.

Free information

1. For information on a specific subject, look for the appropriate organization under "Associations" in the Yellow Pages directory.
2. If there's no Yellow Pages entry, ask staff at your library, town hall or information bureau whether they know of any place where you might find the right information.
3. When you're asking for written information from a voluntary or non-commercial organization, send a stamped and addressed envelope, all ready for their reply, with your request. It might get you faster service, and it will certainly be appreciated.
4. Call on the government – at all levels, from ministerial to municipal. Government departments collect and process an immense amount of information, and some of it is probably what you're looking for. State and provincial administration department numbers are listed at the back of the telephone directories.
5. Check your local newspaper's columns and community notice-boards for reference services.
6. To learn more about a place you're going to visit, contact the local visitors' bureau or chamber of commerce. Or you can write to the consular representative of a foreign country. Although travel agents can often be very helpful, don't expect them to provide an unlimited free information service if you're not buying tickets.
7. Make full use of the services of any organization you belong to – such as the Automobile Association.
8. Financial institutions publish a great many brochures advertising their services. Each is promoting itself, of course, but reading through all their literature will give you a good idea of what services are available, and an opportunity to compare them.
9. Expect service as well as goods when you spend money. If you buy seeds, ask about cultivating them. How do you cook the joint you've just bought? Are there free lessons with the camera you're thinking of buying? Buy where you get this sort of service.
10. Take advantage of free information leaflets, even if you don't think the subject is of any interest to you. You might find just the clue you were looking for.

Freelancing

Selling your art, writing or photography is difficult, but successful freelancing can be an eventful and rewarding full-time job, or it can be a good supplement to a more stable source of income.

To find a professional who can assess your talent and possibly help you break into the freelance market, take a course that relates to your chosen field at a local university, technikon or adult learning centre.

Evening courses for adults are often held at schools. These are advertised on school and local community boards and at your local library. Also join a writers', artists' or photographers' group; use advertisements to find fellow hopefuls with whom to form a support group; or consult the "Associations" list in your local Yellow Pages for the names of appropriate organizations.

The easiest places to gain an entry into the freelance world are through local newspapers, the advertising-supported newspapers that are distributed for free, and regional magazines.

Submit your work for no fee at first then, if successful, photocopy your published work to send to larger publications. Include a self-addressed, stamped envelope if you're anxious to get your work returned – don't send an original copy.

Once you've targeted a suitable publication, submit several ideas for stories, photographs or illustrations; try to capture the imagination of the editorial committee with an entertaining or unusual idea – make sure that it is in keeping with the general image of the publication. If it appeals, you may even get an assignment and a cash advance.

Be professional at all times. Use appropriate business cards and letterheads. Do your best on every project and include an invoice with each assigned submission. Be cordial but persistent as you follow up on projects you've had no word on or payments that are tardy.

Freezer odours

Unpleasant odours in the freezer can ruin a healthy appetite. To prevent them, package all foods in moisture-proof, airtight materials that are labelled for freezer use.

Do not use old bread wrappers, wax paper, margarine tubs or plastic supermarket bags.

CURE

1. Spread bicarbonate of soda on pans and place them on the freezer shelves.

2. Remove all food from the freezer and pack crumpled, slightly dampened newspapers on each shelf. Replace the newspapers every day or so until the odours disappear.

3. When defrosting, clean and deodorise the freezer with a solution of two tablespoons bicarbonate of soda in one litre warm water. If you have a frost-free freezer, wash the interior with a bicarbonate of soda solution at least once a month.

4. To get rid of the smell of spoiled food after a freezer failure, place bowls filled with used or unused coffee grounds inside the freezer.

Frost

1. An easy way to protect plants from light frost – such as that experienced on the highveld – is to sprinkle them the night before. Before you go to bed, wet them with a fine spray from the garden hose. (If you have an automatic sprinkler system, set it to spray once or twice more during the night.) The mist will crystallize on the surface and insulate the plant's foliage.

If you awaken to find that there was a frost you didn't expect, minimize the damage by spraying plants before the sun strikes their leaves.

2. To protect tender seedlings from a late-spring cold snap, cover them with miniature greenhouses; just cut the bottoms off plastic bottles or jugs and mound soil around the base of each container to hold it in place. On cold but sunny days, unscrew the caps for ventilation.

Frostbite

1. Superficial frostbite, or frost nip, can develop very rapidly in a cold wind. The skin turns whitish or mottled and feels firm to the touch. Warm the skin directly against the body and go indoors immediately.

2. If the flesh feels hard and cold and the skin turns greyish yellow to greyish blue, get medical help as soon as possible. Do not rub the frostbitten tissue or try to rewarm it or put any pressure on it.

3. If you're hiking, get to a warm shelter right away and call for help. While waiting, immerse the frostbitten area in warm water (no hotter than 43,3°C), being careful not to let the flesh touch the container. When the skin begins turning red or blue, gently pat it dry and cover with a clean cloth – preferably a sterile one – making pads between fingers and toes if they're affected. (See also *Hypothermia*, p.112.)

Fruit

1. If you have a big bunch of bananas or other fruit that you're afraid may ripen all at once, place a few in a brown paper bag with holes in it. The bag traps ethylene gas, making the fruit inside ripen almost twice as fast.

2. Fully ripened non-tropical fruit belongs in the refrigerator. Unripe fruit is best kept at room temperature in an open-weave basket that allows air to circulate.

3. If fruit has become overripe, don't throw it away. Purée it in a blender or food processor with a little lemon juice and spoon the resultant mixture over ice cream.

4. Strawberries retain more juice and absorb less water if you wash them before hulling. And always rinse the berries quickly in running water instead of soaking them.

Fruit flies

These tiny flies are attracted by fermenting or overripe fruits and vegetables, vinegar, fruit juices and yeast breads. To trap them, insert a paper or metal funnel into the mouth of a two-litre jar baited with bits of overripe fruit. They'll fly into the jar but won't be able to find their way out. Outdoors, promptly collect fallen tomatoes and other fruit from the garden and make sure that refuse bins are tightly closed.

Funnel

1. A better substitute than a rolled up, taped piece of cardboard is an empty food can – a 410-gram one will do fine, with a hole punched near the joint between the bottom and the side. (Don't punch the hole in the centre of the can or you'll have less control over the flow.) Hold the can at an angle while you pour through it.

2. Cut the bottom off a plastic cola bottle and turn it upside down.

Furniture polish or wax

Avoid build-up; apply polish or wax sparingly and no more than a few times a year. To prevent a build-up in the crevices of carved and decorative areas, put a small amount of polish or wax on a cloth before you wipe it onto the furniture.

If a build-up does occur, you can remove it by wiping the furniture with a soft cloth dampened with a solution of 300 millilitres white vinegar and 1,75 litres warm water.

HOMEMADE POLISHES

1. Use mineral oil. If you prefer a lemon-scented polish, add one teaspoon of lemon oil for every two cups of mineral oil.

2. Mix one litre boiled linseed oil with two cups turpentine. (Store in a covered container.)

3. Combine one part lemon oil and three parts olive oil.

Furniture scraper

If you don't have a steel-blade furniture scraper, you can use a scrap piece of window glass. Cut or break it into a rough rectangle about 8 x 12,5 centimetres. Cover three edges with masking tape to protect your hands.

To scrape, set the cutting edge on the wood and, using long strokes, pull the glass towards you at a 75° angle. Keep the pressure even so that the corners don't gouge the wood and the glass doesn't break in your hands.

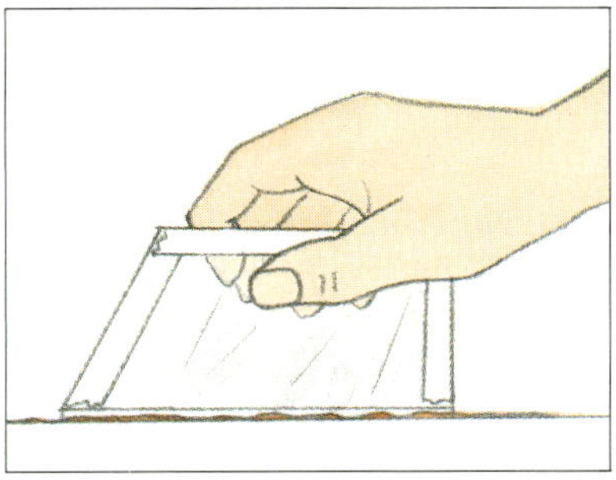

Furniture stains

1. To remove the white rings left by cups or glasses, rub with an abrasive. First, try cigarette or cigar ashes moistened with a little cooking oil; apply with your finger. If that doesn't work, try successively stronger steps: use table salt and a drop or two of water; mayonnaise, toothpaste and, finally, silver polish or car polish.

2. Erase superficial ink spots effectively by using fine steel wool and raw linseed oil.

Fuses

Most household circuits are protected by trip switches. If a switch trips repeatedly, unplug the appliance and plug in another. If it does not trip, the first appliance is faulty. If it still trips, the circuit is faulty: either is a job for an electrician.

Appliance fuses are either ceramic screw-ins, usually for stoves, or the cartridge type, typically for amplifiers or TV sets. Cartridge fuses are either "slow-blow" or "quick-blow". When changing a fuse, take the old one along: replacing with a wrong fuse can damage the appliance, or even cause a fire.

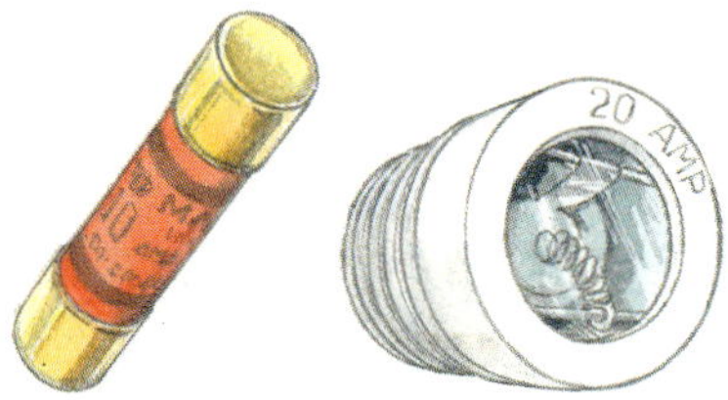

Cartridge fuse Screw-in fuse

Fynbos

The early Dutch naturalists at the Cape referred to the local vegetation as fynbos or "fine bush", because of the gracious, narrow leaves of many of the plants, notably the proteas and the heaths.

Today fynbos features in the gardens of thousands who live in the winter-rainfall regions of South Africa, particularly the western Cape. It's easy to grow, brings variety and colour to your garden, and can provide a haven for birdlife.

There are no less than 8,500 different species of fynbos that make up the Cape's floral kingdom, including more than 1,000 daisies, 600 irises and 400 lilies.

If you're planning to grow a fynbos garden, you should certainly consider such popular flowering plants as sugar bush proteas (*Protea repens*), pincushions (*leucospermums*), candelabra flowers (*Brunsvigia*), watsonias, wild hyacinth (*Lachenalia contaminata*), chincherinchees (*Ornithogalum thyrsoides*), common everlastings (*Helichrysum vestitum*) and the profusion of colourful ericas. Other recommended varieties are the king protea (*Protea cynaroides*) and the delicate red disa (*Disa uniflora*).

The Cape's floral kingdom also nurtures some rare species of plants, such as the marsh rose (*Orothamnus zeyheri*), the snow protea (*Protea cryophila*) and the beautiful blushing bride (*Serruria florida*), which came close to extinction, but which now graces the gardens of some fynbos lovers in the Cape.

A wide selection of fynbos is available at nurseries throughout the southern and western Cape (consult the Yellow Pages for details of nurseries in your area).

Many gardeners prefer to cultivate their own fynbos plants, growing them from seed and planting them out in March and April, before the advent of the winter rains.

Your local nursery or garden centre will advise you on planting procedures, pests and weather preferences.

G

Games for grown-ups

1. Badminton-volleyball. This is played by two teams over a volleyball net, using volleyball rules.

2. Frisbee golf. Use trees, basketball posts, poles and rocks as holes and designate tee-off spots. Throw a frisbee and keep throwing it from where it lands until you hit the hole. The person who takes the fewest throws to hit all holes is the winner. Assess a penalty point whenever the frisbee lands on a spot from which it can't be thrown.

3. Word spell. One person says a letter and the next person adds another letter to logically spell a word. Play continues around the room, with the object being not to complete a word; giving the last letter of any word costs you a point.

For example, if the existing letters are *t* and *a*, add a *c*, perhaps (for tack) or an *i* (for tail). A *b* (tab) or *g* (tag) would complete the word and penalize you one point – five points and you're out. In case of a challenge, you must identify the word you have in mind or lose a point. The winner is the last person still in the game.

4. Dictionary. The player who is "it" picks an obscure word from the dictionary and writes its definition on a card; the other players write what they think the word might mean.

The cards are shuffled and the definitions read aloud by the "it" player; then each player guesses which definition is correct.

The "it" player keeps score, awarding one point for guessing correctly and one point for fooling someone with a false definition. He, himself, gets five points if no one guesses the word. The game continues until each player has had a turn being "it".

5. Gomuku. This Japanese noughts and crosses game uses a grid of 19 horizontal and 19 vertical lines. One player places X's, the other O's on the intersections of the lines. The first to have five letters in a row wins.

Garbage bins

Prevent back strain: use your child's skateboard or wagon to take the filled bins out to the pavement.

CLEANING

1. Wash with ½ cup ammonia in four litres water. To disinfect, substitute ¾ cup bleach for the ammonia; let stand five minutes, then rinse.

2. To combat mould and bacteria, sprinkle ½ cup borax in each bin.

PREVENTING ANIMAL RAIDS

1. Pour bleach over the refuse to eliminate the odour of food.

2. Stretch bungee cords across the lids, hooking them onto the handles of the bin.

3. Strap or tie the bins to a post.

4. Slip broom handles or thin stakes through the handles and drive them into the ground.

5. Tie the bins together – they'll be harder to knock over.

6. Put the bins in a box with a lid fastened by a hasp.

7. Suspend the bins from a frame so that they are 45 centimetres above the ground. If an animal tries to break in, the bin will simply swing away.

Garbage disposers

1. "Sweeten" your disposer by running lemon or orange peels through it from time to time. Or, to sharpen the blades at the same time, make ice cubes (½ cup vinegar per tray of water) and run them through.
2. Never put your hand in a disposer to free a blockage. Instead, turn off the power and use a dowel or broom handle to turn the flywheel rotor in both directions. Remove debris with kitchen tongs.

Garden hose

1. You can temporarily plug a pinhole leak by jamming a round wooden toothpick into the hole. Snap the toothpick off flush with the hose's outer skin. Then wrap the hose with plastic insulation tape for 50 millimetres on either side of the leak. Stretch the tape tight over the hole but looser toward the ends, so that the bandage can flex as the hose bends. As the wood absorbs water, it will swell to seal the hole.

2. Never store a single garden hose by hanging it over a single nail or peg. The hose will sag and kink, and repeated kinking will crack the vinyl or plastic skin. Instead mount an old car tyre rim on the garage or toolshed wall to serve as a hose rack.

Gardening

You can get more plants out of your vegetable plot – and reduce pest damage at the same time – by interplanting a crazy quilt of vegetables in a wide row. Choose plants that can be sown in the same season and, for the fun of it, follow a theme. A salad row, for example, might consist of chives, radishes, garden cress, red and green leaf lettuce, chicory, dill and parsley.

First, prepare a row at least one metre wide. Combine all the seeds in a small jar (a peanut-butter jar is ideal). Then punch a dozen or more holes in the lid and screw it on. Using the jar as a shaker, sprinkle seeds sparsely over the whole row. Scratch the surface lightly with a hand cultivator to cover the seeds, then water with a gentle shower.

Thinning will be the only real chore. Widen the intervals between plants only as they actually need the room, since the less soil you leave bare, the less chance there is for weeds to invade.

A thick blanket of foliage also shades the soil, acting much as a mulch would.

The interplanting also helps keep garden pests in check; in traditional row gardens, insects find the crops they like and race down the rows, jumping from plant to plant. In your crazy quilt garden, they're more likely to concentrate on one plant at a time.

Be imaginative and choose other themes: a spaghetti sauce row, with tomato and pepper seedlings, basil and garlic; or a soup row, with carrots, leeks and beetroot.

Garden pests

You need look no further than your pantry, medicine chest or seed catalogue for an arsenal of rough-and-ready remedies for many pests.
1. Aphids, mealy bugs and other soft-bodied insects succumb instantly to a spray of full-strength methylated spirits. But don't spray young or tender plants or you may damage them.
2. Bait slugs with jar lids filled with at least one centimetre of beer or dry yeast mixed with water – they love the stuff and drown in it.
3. Kill mites with a spray of buttermilk from a plant mister.
4. Control onion maggots and bean beetles by scattering wood ash around plants or on the foliage.
5. Queen Anne's lace, fennel, sage and buckwheat attract a number of

IN TIMES GONE BY

Haste makes waste

Garbage disposal has always been a problem. The residents of ancient Troy left their rubbish on the floors of their homes or dumped them in the streets. On the Garden Route, early man occupied the Matjes River cave, near Plettenberg Bay, off and on over almost 11,000 years, and left layers of rubbish nine metres high.

The ancient Greeks organized the first municipal dumps in the western world, and Athens was the first city known to prohibit throwing refuse into its streets. In some South African towns, this practice continued unchecked well into the 19th century.

An attempt at "the regulation of nuisances" was made in 1781, when the Burgher Senate in Cape Town published a decree concerning the disposal of night soil. But the town's canals were still clogged with rubbish, and butchers continued to ply their trade on the beach, leaving the tide line littered with offal.

There was a distinct sign of improvement in 1814, when Hendrik Vos Jacobs announced a twice-weekly removal of household rubbish, which was to be carefully piled next to the front stoep of each house. It was only much later, after the formation of municipal councils, that taxes were applied to the proper removal and dumping of rubbish. And even then, the most reliable refuse removers in many centres were the pigs, in competition with out-of-town jackals.

The first municipality to operate successfully a sewage and water treatment scheme was Wynberg, now a part of Cape Town, in 1905. With this venture, recycling had begun. With every two urban South Africans generating about one kilogram of refuse per day in 1993, and the amount likely to rise to 1,5 kilograms or more by the year 2000, it seems that recycling will become a mandatory form of rubbish disposal.

beneficial insects such as hover flies, lacewings, ladybirds and parasitic wasps and flies. Sit back and let them do some pest-control work for you.

Garden produce

1. To save mature green tomatoes from an early frost, pick them and set them on top of the refrigerator to ripen at room temperature. Or wrap them individually in newspaper and store in a cool spot.
2. Keep bean weevils from ruining your dried kidney beans or limas: just dip the freshly shelled beans in boiling water for one minute before you spread them out to dry.
3. Instead of thumping your watermelons to check for ripeness, look for brown tendrils on the stem near the fruit and a yellow area instead of a white patch where the fruit touches the ground.

Both are signs that the melon is ready to pick.
4. When you harvest pumpkins, leave a 10-centimetre stem on the fruit to ensure that it stays succulent until cooking time.
5. Test potatoes before you store them by rubbing the skin; if it rubs off easily, the potato is probably too green for storage.
6. Don't wash or blanch freshly harvested peas before freezing them. Just shell them directly into a plastic freezer bag and seal; they'll stay separated, allowing you to dip into them as you need them.

Garden tools

1. A wide putty knife is great for scraping earth from spades and trowels. And it's unbeatable for transplanting your seedlings from trays, weeding between closely planted vegetables, and cultivating the soil in the crevices of a rock garden.
2. An electric drill will keep your garden tools polished and sharp. Use a wire brush attachment to scour rust from neglected tools (particularly if you're near the sea); a coarse aluminium oxide disc can put an edge back on a nicked axe or mower blade much faster than a file and whetstone. Do it quickly, so that the high-speed sanding doesn't heat the steel and ruin its temper.

After polishing and sharpening the tools, keep blades and teeth bright with a coat of oil; dirty oil from your car or power mower is as effective as any and costs you nothing.
3. For jobs too big for a trowel but too small for a spade or shovel, use an army entrenching tool. You can usually find them at shops which supply camping equipment.

Garlic

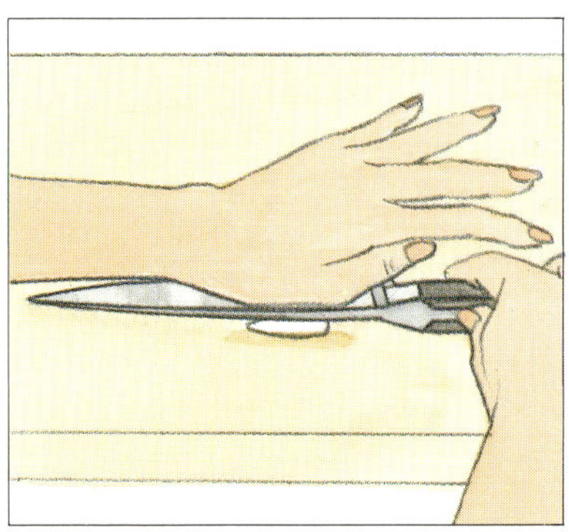

1. You can peel a garlic clove by placing the flat side of a knife over it and giving it a sharp rap with your hand or a utensil. The skin will come away easily.
2. If you want a subtle garlic taste, chop the cloves with a knife. Putting garlic through a press or mincing it in a food processor makes it considerably stronger because more oil is released as it is crushed.
3. If you don't have fresh garlic, substitute ½ teaspoon garlic salt for each clove and omit ½ teaspoon salt from the recipe.
4. To tame your breath after a garlic-rich meal, munch fresh parsley.

Gas burners

A professional should check your burner installation once a year or so. In addition, you can take these steps at any time to ensure safety:
1. Run the dust-brush attachment of your vacuum cleaner over the opening between the gas manifold and the burner heads to remove dust and carbon particles.
2. With the burner turned off, open the access door and examine the firebox and heat exchanger for soot deposits. If soot is present, either the burner or something in the gas lines is malfunctioning. Call a local service centre to locate and fix the problem, as well as to remove the soot for you (a dirty job).
3. With the burner switched on and the thermostat turned up for heat, the burners should ignite. If the pilot light is on and the burners fail to ignite, don't try a second time. Call for service. If the pilot light is out and doesn't relight after three or four tries, call for service.
4. If the burners come on as they should, open the access door and inspect the flames; they should form a solid blue bank. Significant amounts of yellow – especially yellow tipping – indicate a poor air/fuel mix. Something in the lines is at fault, and should be investigated. Turn off the burner and gas. Call for service.
5. In a power cut, or at any time, never use a portable gas cooker on a stove top. If the power comes on, the stove might heat up and explode the cylinder. In event of a gas fire, drag all other cylinders away from flames, vacate and call the fire brigade. Never use a match to search for leaks!

6. Ensure that gas-heated rooms, and especially showers with gas-heated water are always ventilated. Gas consumes oxygen in burning.

Gas odours

1. If a strong whiff of gas awakens you or greets you at the door, leave your home at once. Do not use your telephone or turn on any light fixture or appliance – an electric spark can cause an explosion. Call the gas company and fire department from a public telephone or a neighbour's home; don't return home until it is safe for you to do so.
2. If you smell a faint odour of gas near your stove, open the windows to clear the air and open the oven door. See if any burners were left on and turn them off. Check to be sure that all the pilot lights are lit.

When you're sure the smell is gone, carefully relight all pilot lights. If your stove has pilotless ignition, turn on each burner to test it. If a pilot light won't stay lit or the smell persists, call for service.

Gates

If a gate sags, try tightening the hinge screws. You may have to replace them with longer ones or with thicker screws of at least the same length as the originals. If necessary, drill right through the gatepost and secure the hinges with bolts. If the gate is still out of line, try realigning it with a turnbuckle and wire, running the wire from the upper hinge side to the lower latch side. Next, make sure you check the gatepost. If this is at an angle, try straightening it with a turnbuckle and wire attached to the next solidly anchored upright.

The most common reason for a wooden gate sagging is that its "pins" – screws or nails – have become loose, due to rusting or to shrinkage of the wood and expansion of the holes. The best way to cure this is to remove the gate, lie it flat and, making sure that its frame is square or true, tighten existing screws and fit new screws about two or three centimetres from the existing ones. Make sure that each vertical slat is attached to a diagonal brace. If the components of the gate are very loose but otherwise in sound condition, take them apart and reconstruct the gate, using waterproof glue and then driving in screws while each newly glued joint is held in a clamp.

When buying the hardware for a new gate, choose strong, rust-resistant materials. Brass is strong, non-rusting and attractive, and although very expensive, will almost certainly outlast the gate itself. For most jobs, galvanized and japanned (black lacquer coated) steel is more than adequate. T-shaped strap hinges take much of the strain of supporting a wider gate – say more than one metre wide. Self-closing hinges or simply a sturdy bolt, will help to keep pets or small children inside. Gate hardware often comes with screws, but it's usually a good idea to use longer ones than those supplied, if the thickness of your timber will allow it.

Getting & giving directions

You're lost in a strange place and you ask a stranger for help. She, familiar with the territory, gives you directions that only confuse you further. It has happened to all of us, but how do you make sure it doesn't happen to you again the next time?
1. Carry a map. It's easier to mark out a route than to describe it.
2. State your destination clearly. If possible, write down the name and address. Ask the person to locate it on the map, along with the place where you are. If you don't have a map, ask her to sketch the route.
3. Write down all instructions, including landmarks, and verify. Don't be shy to admit you don't understand a direction; ask for clarification.

GIVING DIRECTIONS

Remember that the person you're helping doesn't know the territory.
1. Be sure you understand where the person wants to go. If he speaks a foreign language, use a map or have him write down the address or name of his destination.
2. Use large, obvious landmarks as references rather than those that require familiarity with the place.
3. Try to estimate distances as best you can, whether in city blocks or country kilometres.
4. Make sure that the person understands. Have him repeat your directions back to you.
5. Draw a sketch.

Gifted children

1. Boredom and lack of challenge can be major problems for a gifted child. If your child's school has no special programme for the gifted, ask his teacher or principal to suggest alternatives. Correspondence courses are available and you could approach your nearest university for information concerning special courses for gifted children.
2. Look for gifted children's groups; your child will probably feel more comfortable with others like himself. Consider joining (or perhaps starting) a parents' group; contact your education department for information.
3. Classmates – and even adults – may perceive your child as odd. Be sure to let him know that you're proud of his achievements and that he shouldn't be embarrassed by his intelligence. Let him express and test his ideas at home.
4. Never use a gifted child's intelligence against him ("How could someone as smart as you do something so stupid?").
5. Emphasize that he doesn't have to do everything perfectly. (Gifted children can be too demanding on themselves.) Make sure that he knows you love him for himself, not for his brains or talent.
6. Even though your child may sound like an adult, he's still a child who needs a certain amount of guidance. Don't be afraid to set limits and don't be intimidated or manipulated – gifted children tend to challenge authority out of a need to learn.

7. If your gifted child has siblings, keep in mind that each child is unique and all are special. Avoid comparisons; help each to succeed in his or her own way.

Gifts at work

Occasional business lunches or inexpensive holiday gifts are usually acceptable; expensive, personalized gifts are best refused. Report them to your boss, then return them with a gracious thank-you note stating that accepting such gifts is against company policy.

If you're offered a gift from an organization you feel might be trying to buy your influence, ask your boss for guidance. Or check your company's personnel manual; it may instruct you to refuse certain gifts, to make a written declaration of gifts over a certain value, or to report all offers of gifts.

If your employer requires you to influence customers or suppliers through gifts or lavish entertainment, you'll be wise to move on; your own reputation may be at stake. The most appropriate and commonly accepted gifts to give and receive are samples of your company's products.

Gift wrap

1. If your wrapping paper is a bit too short to cover your package, turn the package at an angle and try wrapping it that way.

2. To premeasure a length of gift wrap from a roll, wrap string around the package and use it as a guide.

3. Aluminium foil is a good substitute for gift wrap; for a textured look, press it gently against a rough surface such as a stucco or brick wall.

4. Make your own printing block by cutting a simple design on a bar of soap or a halved potato (p.378). Then use it to decorate newspaper, paper bags or white shelving paper. Use an ink pad or pour out some paint on a paper plate or a clean plastic foam meat tray.

5. Save wrapping paper. When you have a large box to cover, use different pieces of your stored paper to create a patchwork look.

Glare on the road

To eliminate hazardous glare, extend your motor car's sun visors. Secure adhesive-backed Velcro to the visors and to pieces of cardboard or opaque plastic. Attach the extensions to the visors and move them around until you can comfortably see the road.

Glass

Never pick up broken glass with your bare hands – or approach it in your bare feet. Carefully sweep it into a dustpan, wrap it in newspaper, and throw it out.

To pick up tiny flecks of glass, wipe all around the breakage area with a paper towel smeared with moist bar soap. Rinse with a watersoaked paper towel and wipe dry.

Glassware

1. Use the bartender's method for speedy stemware washing: holding the base, pump the glass vigorously in very hot sudsy water, then quickly pump it in hot clear water (cooler water may shatter it); dry upside down on a cotton towel.

2. For extra-shiny, streakless glasses, add a little vinegar or borax to the final rinse water.

3. If glasses have hard water stains, rub them with a scouring pad dipped in vinegar.

4. Never use hot water, harsh soaps, ammonia or washing soda on silver- or gold-rimmed glasses.

5. A well-lathered old shaving brush cleans deeply etched or cut-glass especially well.

6. If eggs have dried on your patterned glass tableware, you can rub off the residue quite easily with a slice of lemon.

7. Handle glass ovenware very carefully. Avoid hard knocks and sudden exposure to heat or cold and keep it away from all water (even a moist countertop) while warm.

8. If glass cookware remains stained after washing, boil a solution of one part vinegar to three parts water in it for about 20 minutes.

Gloves

1. Need gloves in a hurry? Slip a sock over your hand and move your thumb away from your index finger; cut through the material in that space. Remove the sock and stitch along the cut edge.

2. Remove fresh spots from leather and suede gloves by rubbing them with stale bread.

3. Clean white kid gloves with powdered starch or tailor's chalk. Apply with a piece of silk, then shake the loose powder off.

4. For a stain on black kid, dab on indelible black marker, then rub in a few drops of olive oil.

5. To dry out wet plastic or rubber gloves, hang them by their fingers or put them over propped-up wooden kitchen spoons.

6. Clean oil stains on leather gloves by sprinkling with a little cornflour. Leave overnight and brush the cornflour off in the morning.

7. Make your gloves last longer – always pull them back into shape after removing them.

Glue

1. Most white glue and carpenter's glue are water-based. To clear a nozzle, unscrew it and soak it in warm water. (Tape the bottle closed so that the glue won't harden.) Once the glue in the nozzle softens, clean it out with a wooden toothpick.

2. Substitutes for glue on such lightweight materials as paper, fabric and cardboard include flour and water mixed to pancake-batter consistency; plain egg white (no yolk) applied with a brush; doublestick tape, which adheres to almost any clean, dry surface; and iron-on tape, which forms a surprisingly strong bond on fabrics.
3. When disassembling old furniture, soften the old glue with warm distilled white vinegar. Drip it directly into the joints with an eye dropper.
4. To unclog a tube, don't try to poke through the hardened glue with a nail or needle. You may damage the tube. Instead, bore into the clogged nozzle with a small drill bit. (Soak the bit in either lacquer thinner or nail polish remover first and clean off all the remaining glue afterward.)
5. Replace the cap to a tube of glue with a cuphook or screw eye. Then you can hang it up for storage.

Glued fingers

1. Quick-setting cyanoacrylate glues bond instantly. If your fingers get stuck together, dissolve the bond with a little nail polish remover or acetone. Most epoxies can also be dissolved this way.
2. If your skin is stuck with contact cement, dissolve the bond with lacquer thinner. Let it soak the cement for a couple of minutes and then slowly pull your fingers apart. If necessary, apply more thinner.

Golf clubs

Don't rush out and buy a set of clubs the moment you decide to take up golf. The professionals at most courses have a few sets for hire. Try these for several rounds and then, if you're sure you like the game, get advice from the professional or from a sports shop that specializes in golf equipment. Both these sources can analyze your swing and match you with the clubs most suited to your size, weight and action.

A steel-shafted golf club is usually the best, with the rigidity of the shaft matched to the club-head speed set up by your swing.

Although almost anyone can use standard-length clubs (because fingertip height above the ground is almost the same for all, whether tall or short), you need to select clubs that have the right lie.

The lie of a club is the angle of the shaft to the ground when the club head rests flat on its sole.

Rubber hand grips are less likely to become slippery when wet, and are easier to clean.

Clubs should be washed all over with warm water and a little detergent, and then wiped dry.

The rules allow a golfer to use 14 clubs, made up of four woods (which may, in fact, be all steel,) seven irons, two wedges and a putter.

If you can find good quality clubs, you should consider starting off with a half set (1 and 3 woods, 3, 5, 7 and 9 irons and a putter).

Golf jargon

Here's a guide to what the television announcers are saying:

Ace. A hole in one.
Address. To prepare to hit the ball.
Approach shot. A shot made from the fairway towards the green.
Albatross. A score three strokes under par.
Back nine. The last nine holes of an 18-hole golf course.
Birdie. To score one shot under par.
Blast. A hard trap shot.
Blind hole. A green that the golfer cannot see when driving or making an approach shot.
Bogey. To score one shot over par.
Bunker. A sand trap.
Carry. The distance a ball stays in the air after being hit.
Chip. A short, low approach shot.
Divot. A piece of sod dislodged by the player's stroke.
Dogleg. A fairway that bends.
Double bogey. To score two strokes over par.
Double eagle. To score three strokes under par.
Drive. The first shot toward the green, generally from a tee.
Eagle. To score two under par.

IN TIMES GONE BY

For love of a glove

Power, wealth, nobility, and even love – all these things and more were once symbolized by gloves. They seemingly carried the aura of the hands that wore them.

Not until early in the 17th century were gloves commonly worn by the average woman – but fine ladies had begun to sport fancy gloves as early as the Middle Ages. Still warm from a soft hand, a glove would be given to a knight as a token of love.

And off he would ride into battle, the intimate favour in his helmet, its mate with his mistress awaiting his return.

Dainty though it was, the feminine glove became a sign of strength to him – an amulet to ward off evil, an incentive for brave deeds, and a reminder of the sweet reward that would be his should he survive.

His own armoured glove, or gauntlet, was a different matter entirely. There was nothing dainty about it; its aura embodied strength, power, and honour.

It might be offered as a pledge in a court of law. And to "throw down the gauntlet" at another man's feet was to challenge him to combat, often mortal combat. It was a meaning that lasted for centuries; long after the knightly gauntlet had faded into history, perfumed dandies were challenging each other to duels at the drop of a soft kid glove as dainty as any lady's of the time.

Fairway. The area of well-mowed, hazard-free grass between the teeing-off area and the green.
Flagstick. A marker on the green indicating the location of the cup and the number of the hole.
Gimme. An easy putt conceded to a golfing opponent.
Green. The area of short, well-tended grass surrounding the cup.
Handicap. The number of strokes that are deducted from the score of a weaker player when he is competing against a more skilful opponent.
Hazards. The bunkers and water obstacles on the golf course.
Hook. A ball that veers in midflight to the left for a right-handed golfer, to the right for a lefty.
Iron. A club with a bladelike metal head; used for accuracy.
Lie. The position in which the ball stops after a stroke.
Links. A golf course (from the Scottish word for the undulating land by the sea where the early golf courses were built).
Par. The score an expert player in good weather is expected to make on a particular hole.
Putter. The club used for making short, accurate shots on the green.
Rim. To have a ball go around the edge of the cup and not drop in.
Shank. To hit the ball poorly. Slice. The opposite of a hook.
Tee. The little peg used to raise the ball off the ground before it is driven or teed off.
Trap shot. A shot from a bunker.
Wood. A club with a hardwood head, used for long shots.

Grandparenting

1. Set aside a cupboard or a room as a "family museum" to focus the younger generation's attention on their heritage; fill it with old pictures, letters, clothes, toys and furniture.
2. If you can't see your grandchildren regularly, phone and write often to remind them of their "roots". (Don't wait for them to phone you and don't be offended if they fail to – you're the one with the job to do.) Or bridge the distance by recording personalized bedtime stories that describe the family's past or family anecdotes.
3. When it comes to gift giving, it's natural for grandparents to be generous. But parents, the generation in between, should have some say about what you give their children. They must deal with such problems as favouritism, sibling rivalry, competition between two or more sets of grandparents, or just the feeling of being outdone by their own parents. Don't undermine their efforts by going overboard with extra treats.

Grants

Do you need money or equipment for a photography project, a community garden or theatre, a youth recreation hall? Grants for an amazing variety of projects are available from government and community agencies, foundations, large corporations and other organizations.

Here are a few tips on getting one:
1. Consult the many excellent reference books available at your nearest public library.
2. Once you have decided which grant to apply for, find out as much as you can about the organization providing the funds. Call and ask for a brochure or an annual report. Try to make personal contact with someone in the organization.
3. Keep your grant proposal clear, simple and brief, with the most important information at the beginning.

Explain how you're going to make the best possible use of the money. Include information on the support you already have for your project. Try to get some endorsement letters from people well known in the community or in your field. Once you have submitted your proposal, make an appointment to discuss it in person.
4. If you're turned down, consider applying to the same donor again. It often takes three or four tries to gain approval.
5. Apply for many grants. If you're lucky enough to be approved by two donors, decide which offer is better.

Explain the situation to the other source – you may be able to receive both grants, either in succession or at the same time.

Grass

Always grow grass types which are suited to your local area. Because of the cold, dry winters in inland areas, indigenous, winter-dormant grasses such as the various strains of kweek (*Cynodon*), are recommended.

Where it is possible to water during the winter months non-indigenous grasses such as bent grass or Kentucky blue can be grown successfully. In the warmer regions, warm climate grasses such as kikuyu, LM (Durban grass) and buffalo are a good choice.

Lawns consisting of a mixture of grasses are becoming popular. The mixtures normally consist of grasses which suit specific uses. There are special mixtures for shady areas, for example, as well as "evergreen" mixtures which will ensure that lawns remain green in winter as well as in the summer months.

Grass seed lawns usually require plenty of water, and are not as hard wearing as some of the spreading grasses which are grown by roots or turfs. (See also *Lawns*, p.123.)

Grass stains

1. Rub the stain with liquid detergent or a pad soaked in diluted alcohol; rinse thoroughly. If the stain still persists, try a little vinegar on it, a mild solution of hydrogen peroxide or – if safe for the fabric – bleach.
2. If you're in a hurry, dab the stain with a cottonwool swab soaked in water and a little bit of bleach. Be patient – it may take a few minutes for the stain to fade.
3. Cover a permanent stain with an appliqué or a patch.

Gravy

1. For extra flavour, stir a handful of diced carrots, celery and onions and a pinch of herbs into the drippings as they simmer; strain before serving. Or, if you don't have time to cut and chop, just add a stock cube. Or turn the gravy into a delicious epicurean treat with a splash of port, sherry or white muscadel.

2. Brown flour in the oven before using it to make gravy. It adds flavour and colour.

3. If gravy lacks body, stir in 1½ teaspoons of cornflour for every cup of liquid. Cook and stir until the mixture bubbles, thickens and clears (about three minutes – no longer or the gravy will begin to thin).

4. Remove all the fat from the surface of the gravy with a bulb-type baster. Or, time permitting, refrigerate the gravy overnight, then lift off the congealed fat.

If you need the gravy right away, quickly chill it on ice or in the freezer. You can also blot up fat by placing several thicknesses of paper towels flat on the surface of the gravy. Repeat as needed.

5. Freeze leftover gravy in ice-cube trays. Wrap the frozen cubes tightly in aluminium foil and reheat as needed or add to soups.

Grease spots

1. In a hurry to remove a grease stain? Apply shampoo, then rinse and blow-dry.

2. Absorb the grease from a rough-textured fabric with cornflour; for a smooth fabric, use mealie meal. Leave on the spot for up to 12 hours, brush off, then wash the fabric.

3. Use soda water to remove grease stains on double-knit fabrics. Talcum powder works on polyester; rub into the spot with your fingers, let stand for 24 hours, then brush off thoroughly. Repeat if necessary.

4. Get rid of grease stains on white shoes with nail polish remover. (Be careful not to remove the shoe's finish.) For other colours, rub on cleaning fluid with a soft cloth.

5. Wash car grease from hands with laundry detergent and water. Paraffin works, too – but wash immediately with warm, soapy water.

6. To remove old, greasy heel marks from vinyl or linoleum floors, try silver polish or white appliance wax.

Green salads

Fresh salads supply vitamins, minerals and roughage, make a visually attractive display and serve as an appetite stimulant. Green salads may include almost any combination of leafy, green vegetables, such as lettuce, cress, endive, chicory, parsley, spinach and cabbage.

Whatever ingredients you choose, they should be chilled, clean, crisp and dry, and served on a cool or chilled plate. To freshen the ingredients, place them in iced water about half an hour before you start preparation. Add the dressing just before serving, and then little by little so as to moisten the salad – too much dressing will make it soggy. Most salads tend to look their best when they are arranged on a bed of lettuce leaves, either whole or shredded.

A good, simple salad consists of lettuce leaves tossed in a dressing made fragrant with freshly chopped herbs like mint, chives, thyme, parsley, dill or chervil.

For variety, mix the ordinary crisp leaves with leaves of the softer butter lettuce, and experiment with taste and texture by using any suitable greens in season.

Ingredients can be cut into various attractive shapes – celery can be "curled", for instance, and you can make radish "roses". Be sure that you don't cut them so small that ingredients can't be recognised on sight.

Spring onions, avocado, green peppers, chives, sprouts, onions, celery and radishes make tasty and attractive looking garnishes. Always use one of the salad ingredients for garnishing, and keep the garnishes simple.

Greeting cards

1. To preserve a greeting card, coat it with a light film of hair spray.

2. Use last year's Christmas cards to make this year's postcards. Tear a card apart and cut the front to postcard size. Glue it to a blank card if it is not thick enough. Draw a line down the middle of the back and write your message on the left side and the address on the right.

3. If you find a card with the perfect message but you don't like the art, glue gift-wrapping paper or your favourite photo over the front.

4. Make gift tags by cutting down last year's greeting cards, folding them, and punching a hole in the corner for a colourful ribbon.

5. For an attractive greeting card, use a leaf as a stencil. Affix it to a sheet of stiff white paper or a note card, then spray-paint. After the paint dries, just strip away the leaf.

Grey hair

1. Since grey hair tends to be dry and wiry, keep it well trimmed for manageability and to prevent split ends. For a more youthful look, avoid a rigid, overdone hairstyle.

2. If you're just beginning to turn grey and would like to conceal it, try highlighting your hair; the grey will blend in with the newly lightened strands of hair.

3. Downplay the grey by lightening your original hair colour a shade or two. A general rule of thumb: lighten rather than darken as you age; it's more flattering, less harsh.

4. A quick way to help cover grey: stir one tablespoon cider vinegar into four litres warm water. Use as a final rinse after shampooing.

5. Your grey hair may look better than you think. Try to enjoy it rather than change it.

Grills

1. Line a grill with heavy aluminium foil to reflect heat upward; it also makes cleaning easier.

2. A wire cake rack can replace a light camping grill. Stove or refrigerator shelves can support pots over a fire, but don't let refrigerator shelves touch the food – they may emit toxic elements at high temperatures.

3. Use an old Boy Scout trick to make a "tennis racket" grill. Find a green forked stick and wire the ends of the fork together (or use long shavings from green wood). Use short green sticks to lace the meat into this circle before holding it over the campfire. If the meat is going to take a while to cook, you can use stones to prop the grill over the fire.

4. Rub a cooking grate with fat trimmings or bacon to keep meat from sticking to it.

Grout

1. Remove old grout with a beer can opener. Use the pointed end to scratch out the grout, taking care not to damage the surrounding tiles.

2. After regrouting, use a spray bottle to apply liquid silicone sealer to the dried grout lines; it helps prevent staining and makes the grout more water-resistant.

Guarantees & warranties

1. Before making a major purchase, read the guarantee or warranty (the terms are interchangeable).

2. Store all your warranties, along with proofs of purchase and dated receipts, in a separate file. If you misplace a warranty, call the store where you bought the merchandise and ask for a copy or have them read the terms over the phone.

3. You needn't send in a warranty card to be covered by its provisions. (You won't be notified, however, if the manufacturer recalls the item.) Even if you lose the warranty, your merchandise is covered, as long as you have proof of purchase.

4. If both seller and manufacturer have failed to deal with the faulty product to your satisfaction, discuss your problem with the Consumer Council, who may advise you to take your case to the small claims court.

Gum disease

1. To prevent this major cause of tooth loss, clean your teeth after every meal and at bedtime with a soft, rounded, nylon-bristled brush; work in circles, keeping the bristles at an angle to the gum line. Instead of toothpaste, you can use a pea-soup-thick mixture of bicarbonate of soda and water once a day.

2. If you can't brush after every meal, rinse with a mouthwash or a solution of one teaspoon bicarbonate of soda in 125 millilitres water. At the very least, swish water around your mouth after you have eaten.

3. Floss at least once a day (preferably at bedtime) to remove plaque and unseen food particles from between the teeth.

4. Massage your gums regularly with a toothbrush or a clean fingertip to stimulate blood flow.

5. Eat a low-sugar diet rich in calcium and vitamins A, B and C.

6. If your gums bleed, are swollen and sore or contain pus, see a dentist immediately. (See also *Dentist visits*, p.62; *Toothbrush*, p.213.)

Gutters

1. Try clearing debris-clogged gutters and downpipes with a garden hose. First push it up the downpipe and turn the water on hard to loosen any blockage. Then move to the roof and, with another high-powered blast, push debris along the gutter toward the downpipe.

2. No need to climb onto the roof to inspect gutters. Instead, tape a hand-held mirror to the end of a garden rake or other long-handled tool.

3. To prevent your gutters from clogging, cut leaf guards from steel-wire mesh or plastic mesh, both sold at hardware stores. Use tin snips to cut the mesh into strips about 150 millimetres wide, then bend them lengthways down the middle to bow them slightly so that they will fit into the gutters.

4. L-shaped aluminium flashing, or drip edge, can be used to divert rainwater from a section of roof directly above a doorway. Slip it under the second course of shingles and angle it to one side to direct water away from the door. Hold it in place with a couple of nails; cover the heads with roofing cement. Be sure to position the flashing so that it extends at least 600 millimetres beyond the doorway on each side.

H

Hacksaw

1. If you don't have a hacksaw and need to cut a thin piece of metal, use the edge of a file or wood rasp to make a groove, then bend the metal back and forth until it breaks.
2. Grind through hard metal with an abrasive wheel in your electric drill. (Wear eye protection!)

Haemorrhoids

1. It's quite easy to avoid bouts of constipation (p.55); a high-fibre diet – rich in fresh fruits and vegetables as well as wholegrain or bran breads and cereals – and plenty of non-alcoholic liquids every day will soften the stool and eliminate the need to strain.
2. Make sure you wash and dry yourself gently with soft tissues.
3. Apply a cloth or tissue soaked with cold water or witch hazel to the affected area for five to 10 minutes; to soothe the pain of a particularly severe attack, use an ice bag.
4. Take a long, soothing soak in a steaming hot bath to relieve painful muscle spasms.
5. Buy over-the-counter astringent suppositories to help soothe and shrink the haemorrhoids.

Hair

1. No time to shampoo? Put clean pantihose over your brush and run it through your hair to remove dirt and oil. Or work a mixture of ½ cup bran and one tablespoon bicarbonate of soda into your hair and brush out.
2. To cure hair-spray buildup, vigorously work one tablespoon bicarbonate of soda into your lathered hair when shampooing.
3. You can rinse oily hair with a 50-50 mixture of water and lemon juice or vinegar.
4. Out of cream rinse? Add a little fabric softener to your final warm water rinse.
5. For a conditioner, saturate dry hair with warm safflower oil. Cover with a plastic bag and hot damp towel; leave on for two hours and rinse off. Or try a rum and egg conditioner: beat two yolks, add one tablespoon rum, and beat again; leave on 30 minutes, shampoo and rinse.
6. Prevent sun and saltwater damage by applying a small amount of coconut oil, wheat-germ oil or Vaseline to hair ends.
7. If your hair is limp after conditioning, rinse with one cup water mixed with ¼ cup vinegar.
8. Make an aromatic hair spray from a lemon or, if you have dry hair, an orange. Boil one piece of fruit (quartered) in two cups of water until one cup remains; cool and strain. Keep in a spray bottle in the refrigerator.
9. Did chlorine turn your blond hair green? Rinse with soda water, tomato juice or several aspirins in warm water. (See also *Grey hair*, p.101.)

Hairbrushes

To clean hairbrushes (and combs too), soak them in about two litres of warm water with a few tablespoons of ammonia, then rinse and let dry. A mixture of a tablespoon of borax, a tablespoon of detergent and two litres of water works well too. Pull hair from the brush with a comb.

Hair dryers

1. If your dryer suddenly stops working, it may have just overheated; wait a few minutes and try it again.
2. On a sunny day, take the opportunity to sit and read or catch up on correspondence while the sun dries your hair.
3. Put a net over your hair and sit in front of a fan.
4. Attach the hose to the exhaust port of a cylinder vacuum cleaner.

Hairstyling

1. No hair rollers in the house? Cut a few narrow strips of cloth from an old shirt or clean rag and then knot them in the middle.

Roll a section of damp hair around the knot and use the loose ends of the cloth to tie the curl in place, or secure it with a hairgrip. For larger curls, cut

IN TIMES GONE BY

Battling the bane of baldness

□ The Egyptians, in an attempt to stimulate hair growth, used to anoint their heads with fat taken from snakes or crocodiles.
□ In Greece, Hippocrates applied a mixture of opium, rose oil and unripe olives in an effort to reforest his pate. (The fringe of hair over the ears and around the back of a bald man's head is popularly known as the Hippocratic wreath even today.)
□ Romans who were too poor to buy wigs painted hair on their scalps – evidence of the desperate measures men will take.
□ Men through the ages have massaged their scalps with rum, vodka, red pepper, ginger, the boiled flesh of moles and even horse manure. For all their ingenuity, their hair remained as sparse as ever. Even minoxidil, the locally applied drug approved for distribution in the late 1980s, can't guarantee results, although its introduction was celebrated by worried men the world over.

a paper towel roll into four sections and roll the hair around them.

2. To revive a perm, spray it with water from a plant mister and fluff with your fingers. For setting lotion, put flat beer in the mister and spray on damp hair.

Halloween costumes

Use household items and cast-off clothing to create Halloween costumes that don't cost money.

1. Transform old colanders, bowls and plastic containers into helmets and other hats. Cut a deflated rubber ball in half and spray-paint it silver for a robot's, spaceman's or knight's helmet. Turn thick work gloves into gauntlets by spraying them silver.

2. You can try using shredded cellophane as a wig.

3. A balaclava makes a good start for a lot of costumes; attach animal ears, yarn or jewellery. For a small child, use a baby-grower in the same way.

4. You can make white clown make-up simply by mixing two tablespoons of cornflour with one tablespoon of solid white margarine. Try adding some colour, if you like, with a few drops of food colouring.

5. For facial decals, cut stars, flowers or hearts from brightly coloured tissue paper. To make the glue, cook one large potato, with skin, until it's soft; let it cool. Rub decals on the potato and then stick them on dry, clean skin.

6. If you need extra padding for a costume, wear large pantihose and stuff with cushions or rags.

7. Would you like to go trick-or-treating dressed as a slice of pizza? It's easy to do. Start with a piece of carpet foam padding; cut it into a triangle as tall as you are. Spray the "crust" at the base of the triangle tan (allow for plenty of crust, because you'll have to fold some of it over your shoulders), then spray the rest of the triangle tomato-sauce red (or red and yellow if you like your pizza with cheese). Cut mushroom slices, green pepper strips and onion rings from plastic foam meat trays and paint them the appropriate colours. For salami, cut circles from a brown paper bag and paint them reddish-brown; they curl up just like the real thing and look wonderful. Glue the pieces on the pizza slice or, better still, attach them with Velcro glued to the slice and to the backs of the various pieces. Fold over the crust, cut a suitable hole for your head, and staple the crust together at your shoulders.

Hands

1. For dry hands, rub Vaseline or baby oil on at bedtime and sleep in cotton gloves or socks.

2. To wash away the grime of gardening or housework, sprinkle a little sugar on your hands as you lather with soap and water.

3. While rearranging items in the freezer, wear oven mitts to protect your hands from the cold.

4. When you wash your hands with soap, counter the drying effects of the alkali by adding a few drops of cider vinegar to the water.

5. To avoid soap, wet your hands, rub plain bran all over them, then rinse. On sensitive hands try a mixture of cornflour and lemon juice.

6. Remove light stains with a piece of grapefruit or lemon peel, heavier spots by rubbing with a pumice stone and lemon juice.

7. Protect chapped fingertips with fingercots (small latex caps available in pharmacies). Dab cream or ointment on each fingertip before donning them, then wear them as you go about your daily tasks.

Hanging laundry

1. No clothes pegs? Try clip-on earrings, hairgrips, paperclips or the pocket clasps of pens. (To avoid rust, put wax paper, plastic or cloth under metal clips.)

2. If you need a clothes pegs bag, use a hanging plant pot. Its drainage holes will keep rain from collecting and waterlogging the clothes pegs. An onion or potato bag – the mesh kind – will do the same. (See also *Plastic jugs*, p.319.)

3. To keep your hands warm on a winter's day, put a hot-water bottle in the clothes basket for occasional squeezes. Or wear cotton gloves covered with rubber gloves.

Hangovers

PREVENTION

1. In anticipation of a big night, take a gram or more of vitamin C for a couple of days; it may help clear the alcohol from your body.

2. Just before you go out – and also while you're partying – line your stomach with milk products.

3. Fill up on bulky foods, such as bread and pasta, to slow the absorption of alcohol into the blood.

4. Avoid red wine and such dark spirits as whiskey and rum; they contain more of the type of impurities that intensify a hangover.

5. Mix your drinks with fruit juice or plain water – carbonated water speeds the absorption of alcohol – or down a glass of water after every alcoholic drink.

TREATMENT

1. Before going to bed, take a B-complex supplement (50 to 100 milligrams) and drink at least half a litre of water or juice.

2. The morning after, drink more water and juice. (Sauerkraut juice neutralizes congeners.) Avoid caffeine; it dehydrates. Eat easy-to-digest foods for breakfast – cereal and milk, toast and fruit. (Skip difficult-to-digest eggs.)

3. Honey is a specific remedy for an alcohol-induced headache; take two tablespoons. Aspirin or paracetamol helps, too, but don't take the latter within eight hours of drinking alcohol. For an upset stomach, try mint tea or an antacid.

Hatchets & axes

A sharp hatchet or axe is safer than a dull one; it cuts cleanly, whereas a dull one may ricochet from a log to your leg. Use a fine, flat file or a grinding wheel to sharpen the blade before each use, then clean and oil the metal before you put the hatchet away. Store with the blade covered in one of these ways:

1. Make a wood or leather sheath and secure it against the blade with a rubber band or strip of inner tube.

2. Sink the blade into a sturdy block of softwood.

3. Wrap an oiled rag around the blade and tie it with twine.

4. Slice open a short scrap of garden hose and cover the cutting edge of the hatchet with it.

Hazardous waste

Many homes contain hazardous materials which are poisonous or inflammable. If you have no use for these products, dispose of them. Leftover paint, household cleaner, insect spray, weedkiller, glues and fuel are all hazardous wastes. Flushing them down the drain can damage sewage treatment systems; putting them out with the refuse sends them to the rubbish dump, where they eventually seep into groundwater.

If you can't use up a potentially hazardous product, think of someone who can. Schools, neighbours, churches or welfare organizations may be pleased to accept your extra paint, insect spray or cleaning solution. Call your local authority to find out how to get rid of your waste.

Leftover and out-of-date medicines are another form of hazardous waste. Clean out your medicine chest regularly and flush small quantities of medicines down the toilet. Some pharmacies have annual campaigns during which the public is urged to bring in old medicines for disposal. Never place old medicines in your rubbish bin.

Headaches

1. At the first sign of a headache, stop what you're doing and, if possible, lie down in a dark, quiet room with an ice bag or a cold pack on your forehead for 30 to 45 minutes.

2. Relax: ask someone to massage your neck, shoulders and upper back; take a hot bath; do relaxation exercises (see *Stress*, p.198).

3. Take aspirin or a substitute (p.12). To prevent a rebound headache, don't overdose the medication or take it after the pain is gone.

4. As long as the pain persists, eat very lightly and abstain from alcoholic beverages.

5. To identify and remove the cause of recurring headaches, keep a record: the date and time of each occurrence, what you were doing and with whom, what foods or beverages you had consumed, and any recent change in habits.

6. Most headaches are not serious. But if yours doesn't respond to simple self-treatment; if it includes fever, facial soreness and a nasal discharge; if it's accompanied by other symptoms or follows an accident or injury; or if it's piercing or localized, you should seek medical help. (See also *Migraine headaches*, p.135.)

Headboards

If your bed doesn't have a headboard, you can make your own and hang it on the wall.

1. Cut a piece of 12,5-millimetre hardboard to size. Paint or stain it, then hang it with heavy-duty picture wire or mount it with screws or toggle bolts. Dress it up, if you like, by gluing on an attractive geometric design in wooden strips.

2. To make a padded headboard, start with a base of 12,5-millimetre plywood or hardboard. Cut a 75-millimetre-thick layer of polyester batting 50 millimetres larger all around and a piece of tightly woven fabric 75 millimetres larger all around.

Lay the fabric wrong side up, place the batting over it, and put the wood on top. Every 250 millimetres or so, snip both the fabric and the batting from the edge of the material to the edge of the wood. Then, starting at the centre of a long edge, pull the batting over the wood and staple it in place, working alternately on opposite sides. Then do the same with the fabric, smoothing it as you staple it down. Mount the construction with picture hangers or bolts.

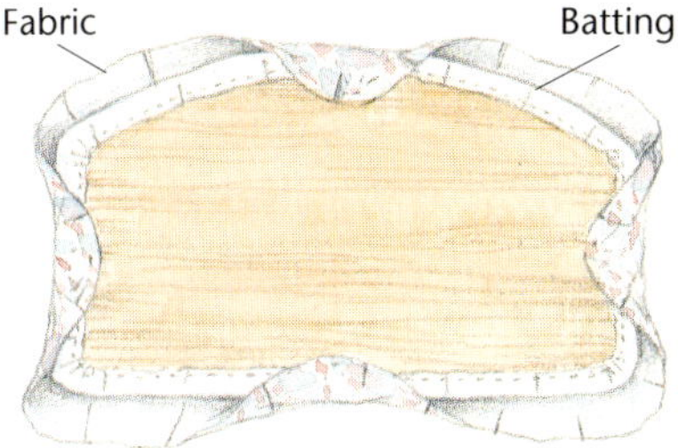

3. For a still softer effect, mount a pair of café curtain rods, one above the other, behind the bed and stretch fabric between them. To create generous folds, sew enough widths of fabric together to form a panel which is three times wider than the length of the rods.

4. If you trust your artistic talents, you can paint a headboard on the wall. Add black to the paint to put in grey shadows and give your creation dimension. If you'd like striations similar to wood grain, try using a feather to brush on vinegar paint – one part powdered pigment to two parts white vinegar.

Headhunters

A headhunter, known also as an executive search specialist, is not an employment agent. He's a recruiter, who is hired by companies to seek out candidates for high-level positions or specialized jobs. He finds people through research, networking and discreet telephone calls.

FINDING ONE

1. Ask industry colleagues to recommend you to the headhunters they work with.
2. Call a headhunter directly (it's best to say who recommended him), but be sure you're clear about the kind of job you want and what you have to offer in return.
3. Join an industry association and get your name published in its magazine or newsletter; headhunters often scan association directories and magazines for names.
4. Send your chronological curriculum vitae (see *Job interviews*, p.120) to headhunters specializing in your field of work.
5. Don't be surprised if they won't see you. They're paid by the companies who hire them and may not have time to spend counselling you.

USING ONE

1. Discuss your background and experience (don't lie about your salary or misrepresent yourself), and ask for an evaluation.
2. Question the headhunter in depth about any companies to which he sends you. (But do your own independent research as well.)
3. Discuss your career goals and ask for positive or negative feedback on your curriculum vitae.

UNSOLICITED CALLS

1. If a headhunter telephones you, ask for his firm's name, address and phone number right away. (Be suspicious if he won't tell you.) Check out the firm with your colleagues and look it up in a directory of executive search firms.
2. If the headhunter is vague concerning job information or asks a lot about your present firm and little about you, be suspicious – he may be trying to pump you for information about your employer. Be polite but firmly discreet.
3. If he uses high-pressure sales tactics or seems unresponsive to your needs, don't work with him.

Head lice

If you or the school nurse finds lice in your child's hair, eradicate them with an over-the-counter shampoo or rinse that contains pyrethrin, a safe, natural insecticide. Products containing lindane should be used with caution as it is readily absorbed through the skin, and can cause toxic side effects. It should not be used on infants, children under 10, the elderly or pregnant or lactating mothers.

Wash, dry-clean or spray with pyrethrin everything with which the child has come in contact.

Using a fine-toothed comb dipped in vinegar, check your child's hair, strand by strand, every night until you find neither lice nor their eggs or nits. To prevent a recurrence of head lice, tell the child not to share combs, brushes, hats or earphones.

Hearing loss

1. Safeguard your hearing – keep the noise down. To protect yourself from excessive noise made by others, carry earplugs or improvise with cotton or tissue paper. Wear earplugs or anti-noise muffs when operating noisy power equipment.
2. Keeping your diet low in fats may help prevent age-related hearing loss due to atherosclerosis, the accumulation of fatty deposits in the arteries, including those that lead to the ears (see *Cholesterol*, p.46).
3. Check your medications. Too much aspirin can cause ringing in the ears, as can antibiotics whose names end in -mycin. Talk to your doctor about the problem.

Heartburn

Although the burning sensation may be real enough, it has nothing to do with your heart. Heartburn – hot pain behind the breastbone – is a symptom of indigestion, and may be accompanied by regurgitation of partly digested food from the stomach into the oesophagus, by belching and a feeling of general discomfort. It almost always follows overeating or drinking, taking exercise too soon after eating, being overweight or wearing too-tight clothing. Severe heartburn of long duration may be a symptom of something more serious, such as a stomach ulcer or hiatus hernia, that will require medical attention.

You can do a lot yourself to relieve painful heartburn.
1. Avoid it, by eating smaller meals, for instance.
2. Cut down on alcoholic drinks and fatty foods and those that contain chemical preservatives.
3. Avoid condiments, especially the hot and spicy kind.
4. Drink only sparingly at meals, and avoid drinking immediately prior to sitting down to a meal.
5. Try to relax for about 20 minutes, both before and after a meal, and try to take the meal more slowly, chewing thoroughly.
6. Avoid irritants such as tea and coffee, smoking, aspirin and many other over-the-counter painkillers.

If you have an attack of heartburn, loosen all tight clothing, especially around the stomach, and rest in a comfortable chair.

Take half a teaspoon of bicarbonate of soda in a glass of water, and sip it slowly, or take one of the many patent antacids, either in tablet or liquid form. Be sure not to make a habit of taking antacids – your stomach contents are meant to be acid.

Heat exhaustion

When you overexert yourself or wear heavy clothing in very hot, humid weather, you run a real risk of heat exhaustion.

Among its symptoms are: cold, clammy skin; perspiration; dizziness, nausea and headache; rapid breathing and pulse; and faintness that may lead to unconsciousness.

If you see someone with these symptoms, have him sit or lie down in a cool spot immediately. Loosen his clothing and remove extra layers. Fan his skin. If he's alert, get him to drink up to a litre of water; if he's groggy and dazed, don't force fluids – you could cause choking.

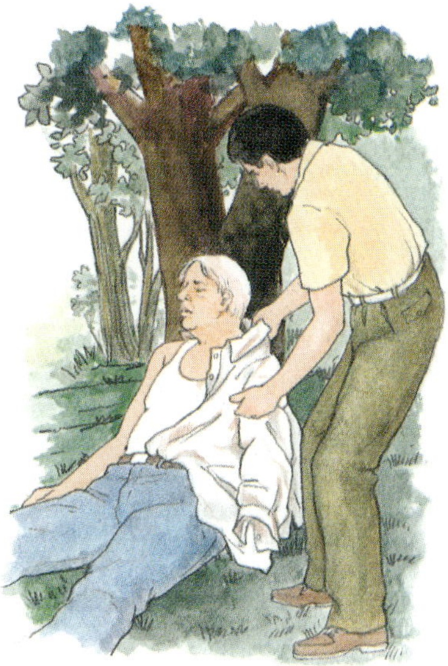

If the condition doesn't improve within 30 minutes, there is risk of heatstroke. Its symptoms: hot, dry, flushed skin; deep, then shallow breathing; rapid, strong pulse, followed by rapid, weak pulse; dilated pupils; unconsciousness; twitching muscles; and convulsions.

If you suspect heatstroke, get the person cooled off as fast as you can. Take extreme measures: soak towels and sheets in cold water and wrap them around his body. If ice is available, put it in plastic bags and place under his armpits, behind each knee, in the groin, on the wrists and ankles, and on the sides of the neck.

Call an ambulance or rush the victim, wrapped in wet cloths, to an emergency unit. If hospitalization must be delayed, immerse him in the coldest water possible; stay with him to prevent drowning.

Hedges

There's no instant cure for an overgrown hedge. It takes hard pruning and a few growing seasons to bring it under control. But there are ways to do the job while keeping the hedge healthy looking.

1. If the hedge has grown too dense, shear it back right next to the main stems on one side only. Let the hedge recover and put forth new growth for a year. Then shear the hedge back on the other side.

2. If the hedge has become too tall, cut back every second shrub to within a few centimetres of the ground. A thicket of new shoots should sprout around the severed trunks. You can then cut back the remaining shrubs the following year.

3. Don't prune a hedge into a vase shape, wider at the top than at the bottom. The lower part will be shaded, and the foliage will fall off while the upper growth flourishes and spreads. The result: a leggy hedge. Instead, prune so that the base is broader than the top.

Note: Plants such as privet, eugenia, hibiscus, myrtle, honeysuckle and pittosporum respond well to hard pruning. Needled evergreens, such as cypresses and pines, do not; replanting is the only way to rejuvenate such an evergreen hedge.

Hems

1. Instead of sewing a hem, use iron-on fusible web tape. Turn up the hem, press it, and trim the edge, then insert the tape about 50 millimetres from the hem's top edge. "Tack" it with light touches of a warm dry iron; to secure, press the hem with a steam iron (use the wool setting). Test before using on delicate materials.

2. For a temporary fix, attach a drooping hem with transparent, masking or adhesive tape. Or try a dab of chewing gum.

3. When lengthening a garment, sponge away the crease with equal parts white vinegar and water. If the crease leaves a dark line, try to eradicate it with spot remover. A white line is permanent; hide it under lace, braid or trim.

4. Instead of pinning up a hem, use paperclips – they won't prick your fingers. And for easy measuring, notch a piece of cardboard at the desired hem width; place the turned-up hem in the notch and move it along as you sew or pin.

Herbs

1. For a *bouquet garni* for soups, stews or sauces, make a bag from a 15 x 15-centimetre square of muslin or cheesecloth. Fill with parsley flakes, dried thyme and a crumbled bay leaf. Or try celery seed, fennel seed and dried basil, marjoram or tarragon. Taste the dish often as it cooks and remove the herbs when you like.

2. When you're substituting dried herbs for fresh, use less. A rule of thumb: one teaspoon dried herbs replaces one tablespoon fresh.

3. Crumble dried herbs between your fingers to release their flavour.

4. No tarragon? Use parsley – but increase the quantity by about 50 percent. If you're out of thyme, try using marjoram, oreganum or a bay leaf.

5. Thyme on your hands? If you have too many home-grown herbs at the end of summer, dry whole plants upside down in perforated paper bags; then use them to make herb wreaths or sachets. Or tie the dried bunches with a colourful ribbon, and hang them from hooks for a country kitchen atmosphere.

DID YOU KNOW . . . ?

A funny spasm that's nothing to laugh about

Hiccups are often the subject of humour, but a bout that won't go away can be painful, exhausting, or, at their worst, even fatal.

☐ There is no good time to get hiccups, but doctors agree that one of the worst is during surgery. A patient under general anaesthesia is, unfortunately, in no position to try one of the traditional remedies, such as being startled, breathing into a paper bag, or reciting a nursery rhyme backward.

☐ One Texas man endured long and frequent sieges for 22 years. Once he couldn't eat or sleep for four weeks. When he reached the point where he had lost nine kilograms, he checked himself into a hospital. It was later discovered that his spasms were a side effect of some medicine he had been taking for another ailment.

☐ The world record holder for non-stop hiccuping is Charles Osborne of Iowa, USA. He began hiccuping in 1922 while trying to lift a 159-kilogram hog on his farm. His hiccups continued throughout his life. Doctors say the physical strain ruptured a blood vessel, destroying a spot in the brain that inhibits hiccups.

Hiccups

If all your standard remedies for hiccups don't seem to be having an effect, give one of these a try:

1. Stand in front of a mirror and – taking short, shallow breaths – slip a cool spoon handle into your mouth and touch the uvula, the small lobe hanging at the back of the throat, until your hiccups stop.

2. Lie down with your head tilted as far back as possible and your mouth wide open.

3. Ask someone to gently press the protruding skin directly in front of your ear canals while you drink a glass of water. The hiccups should subside within a minute.

4. To help stop alcohol-related hiccups, eat a lemon wedge saturated with bitters.

Hiking boots

1. In an emergency you can make a hiking boot water-resistant by dripping candle wax onto the welt where the sole joins the upper. But to do the job right, use boot wax.

Set the boots and the tin of wax in the hot sun until they are warm, or you can warm them with an electric hair dryer. Then apply the wax evenly and rub it in with your bare hands; put an extra-thick application all around the welts. Warm the boots again until the leather has completely absorbed the wax. Repeat the procedure, then remove excess wax with a dry cloth. If the boots will be exposed to moisture often, reapply boot wax frequently. (A small amount of wax can be carried in an empty 35-millimetre film canister.)

2. To make boots warmer, why not use insoles? Or try putting heavy wool socks on over the boots. The bottoms of the socks will wear out quickly, but what remains will add considerable warmth. (See also *Boots*, p.24.)

Hinges

1. For a quick fix, nail a short piece of leather belt over a broken hinge – it's flexible and surprisingly strong. Apply lanolin to keep the leather from drying and cracking.

2. Replace a damaged or lost hinge pin with a snug-fitting common nail or a machine screw. Coat the replacement pin with lubricating oil.

3. Hinge screws often pull loose and lose their holding power. To repair this problem, whittle a wooden stick or dowel to fit tightly into the screw hole. Coat it with glue, and knock it firmly into the hole. When the glue is dry, cut the stick off flush with the hole and drive in the screw. As an alternative, you can jam several toothpicks or ordinary household matches into the hole and cut off the excess; glue is not needed.

4. Here's an easy way to silence a squeaky hinge. Cut a washer out of felt and saturate it with light oil. Then remove the hinge pin, put the washer on it, and reinsert it. Add more oil if the squeak ever returns.

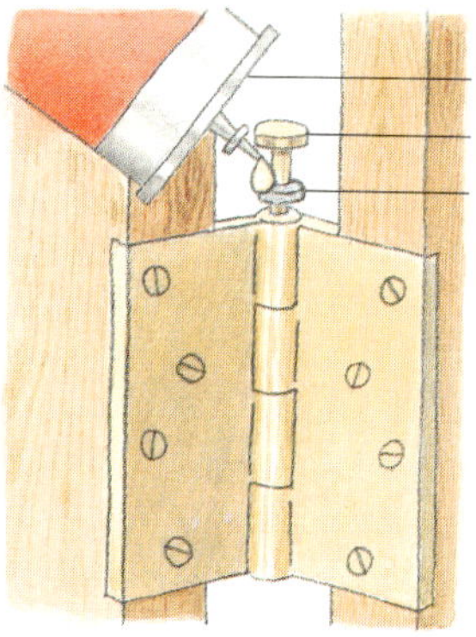

Holes in knitwear

1. Repairing a knitted garment? Place the unravelling part over the bristles of an ordinary household brush (or a hairbrush) – the bristles will hold the garment and prevent stretching.

2. To repair holes in a sweater, place fine net curtaining on the wrong side of it, then darn right through its holes.

3. For a quick fix when your sweater snags, pull the loose loops to the in-

Use a crochet hook or bent paper clip to draw snagged stitches inside a sweater.

side and secure them with a hairgrip or paperclip until you get home and can restitch.

Holes in pockets

1. For an emergency repair on an inside pocket, fold the damaged edge under and secure it with small safety pins or staples.
2. If a patch (exterior) pocket gives way, attach it with double-sided tape. (Don't put anything in the pocket until you can make repairs.) Or, if you can fold under the loose section, fasten it from the inside with safety pins or staples.
3. For a permanent repair, instead of stitching, insert fusible web tape between the two seam allowances of an inside pocket or between a garment and its patch pocket; press with a warm dry iron.

Home-buying

THE PRICE RANGE

A bank or building society may lend you up to 80 percent (rarely 100 percent) of the purchase price. You have to find the deposit, and be sure you can repay the loan, over a period of 20–30 years. Don't let the monthly repayment exceed more than 30 percent of your income.

The price asked is almost certainly higher than the seller expects to realize. Always make an offer of around 20 percent less than the asking price. You can always increase it.

THE NEIGHBOURHOOD

Find out which local authority administers the area.

Do local zoning regulations permit the existence of commercial or industrial development nearby? Or do they prohibit you developing the property as you want to?

Do you need to be close to schools, shopping malls or public transport? Are services such as telephones and waterborne sewage available?

Are rates and taxes high in relation to the services provided?

ATTORNEYS AND ESTATE AGENTS

Estate agents aren't essential, but if agents have been given the mandate to sell, you'll have to deal with them.

If no estate agent has been retained, it's cheaper to do the whole deal through an attorney.

Don't sign an offer to purchase until it's been examined and approved by your attorney.

Although estate agents represent the seller, they are obliged to disclose any latent (hidden) defects they know about, and must provide accurate information.

The estate agent's commission is usually built into the purchase price.

HIDDEN COSTS

Many first-time home buyers are not aware of all the expenses which are involved in purchasing real estate. Before you apply for a mortgage bond ask your bank, building society or attorney about: transfer duty or VAT, conveyancing fees, connection fees and deposits, homeowner's insurance, householder's insurance and mortgage bond insurance.

The bank or building society's fees for inspecting the house for structural soundness and the presence of notifiable beetle, as well as their valuation fee, are usually "built into" the amount to be repaid with the loan.

Home security

Good home security aims to keep you and your possessions safe by keeping burglars and other intruders out.

Dogs are reliable deterrents, but are not foolproof. Other options are electronic security devices or burglar bars. Both systems have their merits – and their failings.

Substantial, visible bars and security gates tend to discourage burglars more effectively than electronic systems, even one with a loud siren.

The casual opportunist, who is responsible for a large number of burglaries, knows that from the time the siren goes off – until someone arrives is ample opportunity to clean up and clear out.

The choice of system may depend on cost and maintenance fees, aesthetics, the situation of your house and your relationship with your neighbours. Consider these points before buying an electronic system.

Also consider the overall present security of your home. Take your name off the letter box. Thieves can look up your telephone number, ring it and, getting no reply, realize there's nobody home.

Check the walls around your property. Are they really high enough to prevent entry? Although height may be a deterrent, it is also a convenient screen for a burglar while he's breaking into your house. Consider putting a sturdy metal railing or spikes on top of lower walls.

Look at your garden. Could you trim some of the bushes to reduce shadowy hiding places?

Check your doors. Are they fragile, with hollow cores and flimsy frames? If so, replace them and reinforce their effectiveness with sturdy locks.

For added security use extra-long screws to anchor the hinges right through the doorframe into plugged holes in the masonry.

Doors should have solid panels. If glass panes are fitted, use dead-bolt locks that can be opened only with a key, whether from inside or out. Fill the slots of the lock's securing screws with hard-setting putty.

Chains that allow the door to be opened only a short distance are better than no protection at all, but most can be easily broken by a determined push from outside. It's much better to fit a wide-angled peephole so that you can inspect the caller from behind your locked door.

If you fit burglar guards, choose them carefully. Make sure that they are strong and durable. Many burglar guards are too fragile to do their job properly, and have insufficient strong points at which they can be attached to the window frame or (preferably) the wall.

Steel bars should be solid, and allow enough space for windows to be opened and closed comfortably.

And even if you have bars or a substantial security gate, keep your distance from strangers on the other side. Don't be lulled into a position where they can grab you and take your keys from you.

Homework

Compile your study roster, and set aside two hours daily for homework.

You need a quiet place, a comfortable chair and desk and good ventilation and lighting. Don't lie on your bed and don't listen to music.

Keep reference books handy, and try to work at a steady pace – it sustains concentration.

Outline priorities. Did you understand the day's classes? What's due tomorrow or the following days? Break projects into units. List items needed for a project.

Jot down what you want to accomplish that day. Start with the most difficult tasks. Try to finish homework given that day.

Take a five-minute break after 45 minutes of hard concentration.

You can scan an entire chapter or read to remember. Read, underline and take notes. Go over the chapter again. Write down main ideas and use mnemonics to remember them.

Horseradish

Folk wisdom suggests that planting horseradish at each corner of a potato patch repels potato moths and beetles. Even if you don't have a potato patch, grow horseradish anyway: the sauce you'll make from it is far zestier than anything you can buy.

Just scrub and peel the roots and purée them in a blender with an equal amount of white vinegar. Add a pinch of salt and refrigerate.

Caution: The plant is very invasive. To keep it from taking over your garden, enclose its bed to a depth of at least half a metre with bricks or sheet metal. Or grow it in a tub.

Hospitalization

1. If you have a choice of hospitals, consider your own needs. A large teaching hospital usually provides state-of-the-art care, but for simpler procedures you may feel more comfortable and get more individual attention at a smaller institution. Before making your decision, get the advice of your doctor and any family members or friends who may have received any treatment at the hospitals you're considering.

2. Before you are booked into the hospital, you will have to fill in an admission form issued by the hospital concerned. Read it through carefully before you fill it in. It serves in part to act as a consent form, showing your agreement to undergo the particular treatment or operation for which you are being admitted.

Don't sign anything until you are clear about what has been written – ask your doctor if you're unsure – and check that the form has been completed accurately. Remember that you have a right to refuse consent until all the different aspects of your proposed treatment have been explained to you.

3. In the case of an emergency, you can be treated at the emergency unit of any provincial hospital.

4. Provincial hospitals charge a daily rate for their services, based on your income. If you have to go to a private hospital where treatment is more expensive, and you are quite concerned about your financial situation, speak to your doctor – he may be prepared to negotiate a special fee.

5. Take a couple of small plastic shopping bags; they're handy for keeping things organized.

6. Ask your spouse, a relative or a friend to accompany you. Besides lending emotional support, they can see that you're comfortable by getting fresh water or pillows; they can even question the advisability of prescribed tests or drugs for you.

7. Don't feel you must play host to unexpected visitors when you're tired; ask them to come back another day – and to call beforehand. (See also *Surgery*, p.201.)

Hotels & motels

1. When you contact a hotel to make a booking, mention any special requirements you may need – for example, bringing a pet. Once arrangements have been made, it is advisable to confirm them in writing and to request acknowledgement of your letter. Bookings normally run from noon on the day of arrival to noon on the day of departure.

2. For low rates at downtown locations, check into a YMCA/YWCA. If you're under 21, try a youth hostel.

3. Consider bed-and-breakfast alternatives; many guidebooks describe the ever-growing options, from a room with a shared bath in a private home to a well-appointed suite.

4. Travelling abroad? For information on such unique accommodation as homes, villas, farmhouses and canal boats, contact your travel agent who will advise you.

5. House or apartment swapping is a possibility for a longer trip; put an advert in the classified section of the newspaper of your intended destination. Or take advantage of listings from the tourist board. Travel agencies can often help you find approved listings, too.

Hot-water bottles

1. Half-fill a self-sealing, heavy-duty plastic bag with hot (not boiling) water. Seal it inside a second bag and wrap in a towel.

2. Fill a screw-top glass jar with hot water, tighten the lid, check for leaks and wrap in a towel.
3. Heat a clean brick in the oven and wrap in a towel.

House guests

1. When inviting house guests, let them know what time you expect them to arrive and to leave. Mention in your invitation any activities that call for special clothes, such as tennis or swimming.
2. If someone is notorious for staying longer than scheduled, arrange an activity for the day after their preset departure time and inform the guest of your other plans.
3. Ask your guests if they have food and drink preferences or allergies.

THE ROLE OF THE GUEST

1. Bring a small gift – wine, flowers or a homemade cake. Or bring toys to leave behind for the children.
2. Adjust to the schedule of the house. If you're an early riser, try to remain in your room until your hosts are up and about. If you really must have a cup of coffee, move very quietly around the kitchen.
3. Instead of asking if and how you can help, simply observe. Work out what needs to be done and do it. A guest pitches in by helping clean up after meals, sweeping stoeps and occasionally buying the groceries.
4. Offer to bring or buy one night's dinner. If you plan to stay for three nights or longer (usually not a good idea), take your hosts out or cook for them, but give them enough warning so that they won't already have planned that meal.
5. Keep the guest room neat and clean even when the door is closed. On the last day of your stay, remove and fold your soiled linen and remake the bed with just the blanket so that the guest room looks presentable after you leave.
6. Ask permission before making any long-distance calls and arrange to reimburse your host. Don't overstay your welcome.

Household insurance

If you have a mortgage bond on your house, the lender will probably insist that you insure it for at least the value of the loan and premium payments are often "built into" the monthly bond repayment.

Even if no bond exists on your home, it makes sense to insure it against damage or loss – by fire, for example. A homeowner's insurance policy covers damage to the structure of your home and to certain fixtures. A typical policy covers house and outbuildings, walls, fences and gates, light fittings, hot water system, sanitaryware, fitted carpets and fitted cupboards and even swimming pools.

Among the risks covered are fire, lightning, earthquake, flood and falling trees. Damage caused to the structure of the home by burglars is also covered, but loss of moveables is not covered (see below).

The policy usually includes public liability insurance – that is, cover against claims resulting from people, other than those who live there, who are injured on your property.

Because most building costs and property prices are constantly rising, it is important to review your insurance policy regularly. If you are under-insured, you will not be paid out the full amount of your claims, even for only partial loss or damage.

A householder's insurance policy covers moveables inside the home, such as furniture, TV and electronic equipment and clothing. Special collections, like stamps, jewellery and books may have to be valued and insured separately. They are insured against being stolen or damaged by intruders. An all-risks policy should be taken out to cover items that you regularly use out of the home, such as cameras, jewellery or firearms.

House plant food

To supplement complete fertilizers with an extra dose of nitrogen, you can add a little gelatine to the water once a month.

Empty an envelope of *unflavoured* gelatine into one cup of boiling water, stir until the gelatine dissolves, and mix with three cups of cool water. Apply immediately; discard any leftover liquid.

House plant pests

Control spider mites, aphids, thrips and whiteflies with a spray of two tablespoons biodegradable liquid detergent in five litres of water. Coat the leaves top and bottom. One treatment may not kill all the insects, so spray a second time in three to seven days. Small plants without flowers can be dipped into the solution to ensure better coverage.

For a persistent infestation, purée two hot peppers and two or three cloves of garlic in a blender; add three cups water and two tablespoons biodegradable liquid detergent, then strain into a spray bottle.

Caution: Soap can injure leaves in very hot weather; don't use these treatments during a heat wave.

House plant polish

Plant polish, whether store-bought or homemade, plugs the leaf pores and does your indoor greenery more harm than good.

For a healthier sheen, bathe plants twice a month with two tablespoons of biodegradable detergent dissolved in a litre of water. Wash both sides of the leaves to remove dust, and add a small dose of weak tea to the solution to enhance their colour.

Housing for the elderly

A nursing home is not necessarily the next stop when you're no longer able to live on your own at home. There are many different housing arrangements that will let you retain your independence.

1. For those who are slightly disabled, living at home may still be quite feasible with help from qualified housekeepers, paid companions and visiting nurses. Meal delivery and transportation services are also available in many places.

2. If you choose to remain at home, install extra telephone extensions to make it easier to call for help if you have a problem. Fit a security system with a "panic button" that can be pushed for emergencies.

3. If loneliness is more of a problem to you than frailty is, consider a group living arrangement. Shared housing offers companionship, security and financial assistance. Take care to choose someone with whom you are compatible. Advertise in the newspaper or on your church or local community noticeboard.

4. You may prefer living on your own in a retirement community. Many such communities – generally offering small cottages with a bedroom, sitting room, bathroom and kitchen – provide meals, care for the ill and frail, sports facilities and transport arrangements.

5. Or you may choose to live with relatives. To guard against losing your independence, perhaps part of the home could be converted into a self-contained "granny flat". Local centres for the aged may offer outside stimulation to combat boredom.

6. When looking for a home for an elderly person, investigate the various types of care offered. Some homes offer residential services only, while others provide medical care for the ill and frail. For a list of homes for the aged, contact the South African Council for the Aged or your local welfare organization.

Humidifiers

1. To add moisture to the air in your home, place pans of clean water on top of your radiators (if you have them) or other heat sources.

2. For a temporary infusion of moisture, try showering with the bathroom door ajar.

3. In cold weather, asthmatics or patients recovering from bronchitis can gain great relief and real benefit from the humidifying effect of a tumble drier – and it gives off heat as well.

Take care that the lint filter is clean, or the benefit could be nullified, however. Bring the tumble drier out of the laundry, and use with damp clothing straight from the washing machine, adjusting the heat setting for comfort.

Another means of adding humidity is to simply boil a kettle in the room – but auto-switching kettles will not meet this need. Make sure the kettle is filled, and kept topped up.

Hydrangeas

A native of Asia and the Americas, the hydrangea is widely known in South Africa as the Christmas flower, because it is in full bloom at the height of the festive season.

There are over 20 different varieties, some of which grow more than two metres in height.

The range of flower colours include pink, rose-red, white, shades of blue and mauve. Hydrangeas grow best in semi-shade, and should be protected from the afternoon sun.

Water generously, especially from the months of November to March, which is the flowering season.

Hydrangeas growing in alkaline soil will always be pink, while those growing in acid soil will always be blue. This applies no matter what colour the flowers were when you bought the plants.

If your soil is close to neutral, however, you can intensify the colours or even change the growing colours from blue to pink or pink to blue.

For blue flowers, you should add aluminium sulphate (alum). Dissolve about 100 grams of alum in seven litres of water and feed this quantity to each plant just before and during the flowering season.

For pink flowers, the soil must be made less acid by the addition of lime, starting with the same quantities as used with alum, and controlling the results by the colours obtained.

You can also buy specially prepared colour-changing compounds from your nearest nursery.

When cutting blooms for the vase, make sure that the small florets in the middle of the flowering head are fully open, or the cut blooms will soon wilt and die.

Hypertension

1. You should learn to check your blood pressure. Buy an inexpensive blood-pressure monitor (available at pharmacies), then take it to your doctor's office to check its accuracy as well as your own technique.

2. Keep a running chart of your readings to show your doctor. Make sure that you record the date, the time, location, body position (standing or sitting), circumstances (stress, medications and other special factors).

3. To maintain a normal weight, eat a well-balanced, nutritious diet and exercise regularly.

4. Limit your sodium to three grams a day. (A can of soup or a frozen entrée may have one gram!)

5. Ration your alcohol intake. Make sure that you drink no more than two beers, two glasses of wine or 75 millilitres of spirits per day.

6. Eliminate caffeine from your diet for a couple of weeks to see if it affects your blood pressure.

7. Get a pet. Caring for, playing with, talking to, and even just watching pets can reduce stress and blood pressure to some extent. Birds and fish are particularly soothing.

Hypothermia

Hypothermia has caused the death of thousands, from mountaineers in the mist to vagrants in cold alleys. It can also happen on a warm day, by swimming in icy water. When your body temperature drops to 35°C or below, hypothermia will set in.

Symptoms are shivering, cold skin, slurred speech and, eventually, confusion and lethargy before you slip into unconsciousness.

It is essential that a victim be rewarmed. Move him into shelter and remove all the wet clothing. Wrap all but his face in anything available. Newspaper provides excellent insulation. Get out of the wind, light a fire. Cover the victim with your own body.

Ideally you should summon medical help.

If there is no pulse, administer cardiopulmonary resuscitation. If there is no breathing at all, apply mouth-to-mouth resuscitation.

Never rub or massage the limbs or put them in hot water. Provide hot, sweet liquid but not alcohol.

You can take several precautions to prevent hypothermia. Rest well and eat a high carbohydrate meal before you set off into the cold. Munch chocolate. Don't smoke or use alcohol.

Be sure to dress warmly. Three layers of thinner clothing are better than one thick jersey. Air is trapped and warmed between the layers. A waterproof outer suit will prevent heat from escaping, while the wind chill cannot penetrate. Remember to cover your head and hands, and, most important, keep moving.

I

Ice cream

1. Ice cream retains its texture and quality best at –18°C; put a thermometer in your freezer and adjust the setting accordingly.

2. Ice cream picks up freezer odours easily, so be sure to store it in a sealed plastic container.

3. To soften a litre of ice cream for easy serving, you can place the container in a microwave oven on *Defrost* for 40 seconds.

4. It may help to know that if you replace ice cream with sorbet, you'll be eating less butterfat but consuming more sugar.

Ice cream cones

Before you scoop ice cream into a cone, drop a jelly bean in the bottom; it helps forestall drips.

With a bit of ingenuity, you can serve up an ice cream treat without relying on store-bought cones. Here are some ideas:

1. Make an ice cream wafer by putting a scoop between two oversize biscuits or splitting a brownie in half and filling it.

2. Hollow out a cupcake to make a little edible bowl.

3. Use a pancake to make an ice cream treat with a difference (hold one end of the pancake tightly closed to keep it from dripping).

4. Enclose the scoop in a pita bread pocket. It's better than you think; just make sure the bread isn't the garlic-flavoured kind.

5. Surprise the kids with cones made from dried fruit rolls. Roll into cones and store them upside down in the freezer for at least 15 minutes before filling them with ice cream. Warn the kids that this cone loses its shape quickly, and they'll have to clean the mess unless they eat fast. For less mess, you can place a scoop of ice cream on a sheet of dried fruit and roll it into a cylinder; fold the ends over. Keep in the freezer until needed.

IN TIMES GONE BY

I scream for ice cream

No one really invented ice cream – not even Dolley Madison, the woman who served it to the President of the United States of America, long before it became one of the world's favourite desserts. Rather, ice cream evolved.

History records that iced drinks were served in King Solomon's time. Later, the Roman Emperor Nero is said to have had snow retrieved from the mountains and served with fruits, juices, and honey. At the end of the 13th century Marco Polo returned from the Far East with a recipe resembling today's sherbet. Most historians believe it was probably this recipe that evolved into ice cream in Italy sometime during the 16th century.

Ice cream was first served to the general public at Café Procope in Paris in the late 1600s (the café, like the dessert, is still there). But almost 200 years passed before it was really made available to all; it happened after the invention of insulated ice houses and the hand-operated ice cream freezer.

The first wholesale ice cream appeared in Baltimore in 1851, and before long, ice cream vendors were setting up shop.

By 1874 a soft drink concessionaire in Philadelphia had introduced the ice cream soda.

If an ice cream vendor at the 1904 World's Fair in the United States hadn't run out of bowls, we might never have seen the birth of the ice cream cone. As the story goes, he had some Middle Eastern waffles at hand, and when he folded them into cornucopia shapes and filled them with ice cream, he started a fad that's still going strong.

Ice cubes

1. Need extra ice cubes for a party? Freeze water in clean egg cartons, then transfer the ice to sandwich bags, and store in the freezer.

2. You won't get bubbles in your ice cubes if you use bottled spring water – non-carbonated. Or if you boil tap water, cool it, then freeze.
3. A full freezer works best, so fill up the empty spaces.

Giant ice cubes, made by filling loaf tins or plastic bags with water, do the job. They're great for picnics, too; just pop them into the cooler bag.

Illness away from home

1. Planning a foreign holiday? A month or so before you leave, have thorough physical and dental examinations, get all the required inoculations, and request copies of all your prescriptions, including those for your spectacles. As an additional safeguard, ask your doctor to write out the generic names of all your medications so that a foreign pharmacist can recognize them.
2. Pack a small first aid kit containing bandage materials, disinfectant, antibiotic ointment, diarrhoea medicine, motion sickness pills and aspirin or a substitute (p.12).
3. Carry a short medical history in your wallet, and wear a tag indicating any life-threatening allergies or conditions such as diabetes.

For a small fee you can join the Medic Alert Foundation of South Africa; you'll receive a membership card and a bracelet or necklace engraved with your identification number, any critical medical conditions you have, and the organization's internationally recognized symbol and local telephone number.

A doctor or anyone else who may find you ill or unconscious, can call the foundation on the toll-free number 0800-222-366 from anywhere in South Africa.
4. Ask your travel agent about special insurance options that will cover unforseen medical costs such as consulting a doctor or taking out a prescription. Carry your insurance card, your agent's name and phone number and several claim forms.
5. If you get sick while abroad, contact the South African embassy or your travel insurance company for names of English-speaking doctors who will be able to understand you.

Immunization

Children are routinely immunized to protect them from the very serious diseases of tuberculosis, diphtheria, whooping cough, tetanus and polio.

The vaccine against polio is given by drops, and the others are injected. Among other vaccines that may be given, especially to children, are those for mumps, measles and rubella (German measles). A vaccine has also been devised against hepatitis B. Shorter-term immunity can be obtained from typhoid, yellow fever, cholera, rabies and influenza.

Many vaccines are given in doses of graduated strengths, so that it is often necessary for a child to receive more than one vaccination against the same disease. However, for increased effectiveness, and to avoid upsetting children unnecessarily, some vaccinations are given as combined doses.

Immunization in South Africa follows a standard pattern. Newborn babies should receive BCG (anti-tuberculosis) and polio vaccines. At three, four-and-a-half and six months, babies are given their DWT (anti-diphtheria, whooping cough and tetanus) and polio vaccines.

Six-month old babies "at risk" are also given a measles vaccine, although it is more usual for this to be given at the age of nine months. Immunization against measles may be given in combination with mumps and German measles vaccines at the age of 15 months. DWT and the fourth polio vaccine – a "booster" – are given at 18 months. Children between five and six years old, receive the fifth polio dose (another booster), immunization against diphtheria and tetanus (DT) and BCG. Measles vaccine may be given six weeks or longer after the BCG, if the child has not yet had measles or been previously immunized against this disease.

The immune status of children is checked in their first school year, when a DT booster and polio vaccine may be given, and again four years later. BCG immunization may also take place on either occasion.

Children should be immunized before admission to school because disease can spread very rapidly in the confined space of a classroom.

The Public Health Act provides for the exclusion from school of children with infectious diseases, the period of exclusion depending on the particular disease.

Your doctor or the nearest neighbourhood clinic will advise you on all matters concerning immunization, including what reactions to expect after a vaccine.

If the reaction includes a high fever, pain or discomfort and convulsions, call your doctor immediately.

Immunization may be necessary for people who travel out of the country. Consult your travel agent or doctor for more details.

Income tax returns

To keep your tax return problem-free, take these steps.
1. Double check all calculations – errors will be picked up by the tax office, and you could be the loser.
2. Make sure your taxpayer's number and ID number are correct, and remember to date and sign the return.
3. Answer all questions. If you have no response to a question, write "N/A" (not applicable).
4. Remember to attach all IRP5 certificates, as well as other documents to support your claims, to the appropriate page of your return.
5. Make sure you haven't omitted any sources of income, including the gross amounts of all investment income. Tax exemptions will be calculated by the Receiver of Revenue, who may also cross-check your figures with those provided by your employer, bank or other sources.
6. Check that you have the same figures on your return and on your supporting documents.
7. Post your return to reach the tax office before the deadline, to avoid

having to pay interest on tax due or a prescribed fine.

8. If you've sent off your return, and then discover that it contains an error, write to the Receiver of Revenue immediately to point this out.

Incontinence

This once-forbidden subject is no longer taboo, nor should it be a cause for embarrassment. In most cases incontinence can be successfully managed or even cured.

1. The first step is a medical diagnosis of the underlying cause. If the pelvic and bladder muscles are weak, they can be strengthened with a regimen of simple exercises or biofeedback methods. If the prostate has become enlarged, surgery may restore proper bladder function. In addition, medications and bladder pacemakers can sometimes aid in regulating the bladder.

2. For incontinence that can't be managed medically, absorbent pads, lined underwear, collecting bags and catheters are available.

3. Bladder and bowel incontinence can be difficult to cure, especially amongst the elderly, and careful examination is necessary. Consult your local doctor.

Indigestion

1. To relieve gas, drink mint tea. Steep 15 grams of fresh leaves in half a litre of boiled water for 20 minutes.

2. Instead of a commercial antacid, try one teaspoon bicarbonate of soda in a glass of water (not recommended for those who must restrict their intake of sodium).

Caution: A heart attack may be mistaken for indigestion. If you are in doubt, seek medical help fast.

PREVENTION

1. Stop smoking and chewing gum. Cut out aspirin, alcohol, caffeine and carbonated drinks. Forego foods that don't agree with you.

2. Make time for stress-free meals. Try eating four or five small meals slowly instead of gulping two or three large ones.

3. Relax, sitting up, for 15 to 30 minutes after every meal.

4. Sleep with the head of your bed slightly elevated.

Indoor plants

You don't need expensive and temperamental house plants to add greenery to your home. Many of the vegetables you bring home from the supermarket will sprout and brighten a windowsill. And kids love to watch them grow.

1. Cut the top couple of centimetres off a beetroot, parsnip or turnip and completely trim off the greens. Line an earthenware ashtray or other low container with pebbles and fill it with water. Set the flat cut end of the vegetable on the pebbles. Over the next few days, change the water whenever it gets cloudy. The resultant forest of greens will last for a month or more.

2. Slice the leaf crown and two centimetres of flesh off the top of a pineapple. Set it in moist sand and keep it watered. When roots form, plant in potting soil that has some peat moss mixed in and – presto! – you have a plant that will last for years.

3. To germinate apple, grapefruit, orange, lemon or seeds, sow them in small flats of potting soil and keep well watered. When they're a few centimetres tall, transplant them to larger pots and watch them grow into lush (but probably fruitless) trees. Loquats, pomegranates and tropical fruits such as pawpaws, litchis and mangoes can also be started this way.

4. You can easily turn a carrot into a hanging display of fernlike feathery foliage. Just cut an extra-large carrot in half (the top half must still have its leaves). Hollow out the centre of the top half, leaving the outer wall intact. With a stout needle, run a thread through the wall of this "basket" and hang it, leaves down, in a sunny window. Fill it with water and keep it filled – if it dries out, it will shrivel. Before long, delicate foliage will emerge and all but hide the carrot.

5. That old standby, the indoor tree grown from an avocado pit, usually turns into a slender stem weighted down by a little pom-pom of leaves. The reason: it's not pinched back and pruned hard enough. Don't be afraid to start over occasionally; cut the plant back to an eight- or 10-centimetre stem. You'll force new root growth to take place and get a bushier, healthier plant.

Influenza

1. For aches, fever or a headache, take some aspirin or paracetamol (p.12) with a glass of water.

2. Drink 225 millilitres of fluids every two hours to prevent dehydration from fever. Dilute apple juice or flat ginger ale with water. Avoid citrus juices if you feel nauseated; milk if you are vomiting or have diarrhoea.

3. Don't starve a fever. Eat small, bland meals – cottage cheese, yoghurt, apple sauce, bananas, dry toast, baked or boiled potatoes. Don't worry if you're not hungry for three or four days, but when your appetite returns, eat a high-protein, high-kilojoule diet rich in vitamins B and C (see *The Balanced diet,* p.254).

4. If you have a sore throat (p.192), drink hot liquids, gargle with salt water and chew cloves.

5. For a runny nose, sip hot tea with a dash of honey and take a decongestant if you wish.

6. For a dry cough, use a humidifier (p.112) and suck on cough drops or hard sweets (see *Coughs,* p.58).

7. Stay in bed – or at the very least reduce physical activity – as long as you can (at least until your temperature returns to normal again); resuming your regular activities too soon will encourage a relapse.
8. Don't drive; flu impairs reaction time almost six times as much as moderate alcohol intake.
9. If you're over 65; if you have a chronic disease; if you feel especially ill or the fever lasts more than four days; or if your fever is accompanied by a stiff neck, severe headaches, irritability and confusion, see a doctor. (See also *Colds*, p.51.)

Informal attire

1. A woman who gets an invitation for an evening party that says "informal" should wear a smart dress; a man, a dark suit.
2. If the invitation says "casual" or is for a daytime event, and you're unsure what to wear, phone your host and ask. If the answer is vague, ask what the host plans to wear.

Ink stains

1. For ballpoint pen marks on fabric, try a pen eraser. If this doesn't work, saturate the spot with hair spray or nail polish remover (test on an inconspicuous piece of fabric first); then blot, first with a cloth dampened with the solvent and then with a dry cloth. Or you can apply Vaseline to white cotton fabric, then rub gently in a warm detergent solution.

The spot may also be sponged with methylated spirits or turpentine, then rubbed with a detergent solution. As a last resort, use chlorine bleach on bleachable fabrics.
2. For felt-tip marks on fabric, gently rub liquid detergent into the stain or sponge with methylated spirits before washing in a detergent solution. If unsuccessful, try sponging the stain with dry-cleaning solvent or diluted chlorine bleach (if safe for the fabric).

FROM LIQUID INK
1. If the ink is still wet, pour salt on the stain and brush off after a few minutes; repeat if necessary.
2. Soak the stain with methylated spirits, then blot with a soft cloth.
3. Work concentrated ammonia into the stain, then vinegar; rinse.
4. Sponge the stain with water, then with a solution of mild detergent and a few drops of vinegar; wait 30 minutes before rinsing.
5. Rub liquid detergent over the stain, then rinse.

LOOK BEFORE YOU LEAP

Are your house plants killers?

You may find it merely annoying when your cat chews on the house plants. Your poor cat may find it fatal.

Most people know that oleanders are poisonous, but so are some innocent-looking favourites: caladiums, dieffenbachias, elephant's ear, monsteras, philodendrons, and even English ivy.

Not only cats, but also toddlers, can be attracted to house plants – especially those with flowers or berries. Besides oleanders, hazardous flowers include moonflower, (*Datura candida*), every part of which is toxic, birds-of-paradise, and lantanas, which bear berries that are poisonous while they are green.

A popular indoor plant, especially at Christmas time, the Jerusalem cherry (*Solanum pseudocapsicum*) has berries that look invitingly edible – but don't partake! And keep the plant well out of the reach of pets and children.

Many popular flowering bulbs, especially the spring flowering types, are toxic: daffodil, narcissus, hyacinth and amaryllis bulbs may look like onions but are dangerous if ingested.

If you have any doubt about a plant's toxicity, ask your florist or nursery owner for its botanical name. Then call the nearest poison control centre (you'll find the number at the beginning of the white pages of your telephone book) to find out if it's safe.

In-laws

1. Get the jump on potential conflicts. As soon as you become an in-law, circulate a questionnaire – make it as humorous as possible – covering potentially thorny issues, such as what to call your in-laws, where holidays will be celebrated, who will help after a grandchild is born, and what family occasions you are expected to attend or to host.
2. Some relationships are permanent. Your son is your former mother-in-law's grandson, no matter how many times you divorce and remarry. The same is true of aunts, uncles and cousins. Don't discourage such family relationships, however you feel about your former in-laws. They can enrich the lives of your children.

Insect bites & stings

Most insect bites and stings are not serious unless the victim is allergic to the particular toxin. The most frequent exception is the bite of the female *anopheles* mosquito that causes malaria. Don't enter malarial areas unless you have already started a recommended course of anti-malarial drugs. The treatment must begin one week before you begin your journey and continue for four weeks after you have left the malaria zone.

Tick bites may have serious consequences, but you can generally avoid them by wearing suitable clothing, such as a pair of long trousers tucked into thick stockings and long-sleeved shirts when walking through tick-infested countryside. Examine your body for ticks when undressing.

To reduce the chance of being bitten by mosquitoes, use an insect repellent. These are available in various forms – gel, stick, spray or cream – from your pharmacy. Natural substitutes include oils of citronella and pennyroyal, available at health stores. Mix them with vegetable or baby oil – a few drops to about 25 millilitres of oil. Rub repellants on your body and spray your clothes and bed linen, if this is necessary.

Some cosmetic preparations are thought to attract biting insects, so try to avoid using perfumes and highly scented soaps and suntan products. Plain clothes, preferably with long trousers and long sleeves, are the most suitable. Don't camp at the edge of rivers or lakes. Mosquitoes breed in stagnant water, and waterside campers are particularly prone to attack.

If the sting of a bee or wasp is visible, carefully remove it, preferably with tweezers. Bathe the site of a sting in cold water, and clean the surrounding area with an antiseptic. Apply calamine lotion to relieve irritation.

Avoid scratching, as this usually makes matters worse by introducing an infection. If you know you are allergic to insect stings or bites, ask your doctor about emergency medication that you can keep handy.

Insomnia

1. Cut back on smoking, chocolate, caffeine and alcohol, especially in late afternoon and evening.
2. Avoid heavy meals close to bedtime – a snack of hot milk and crackers may be helpful.
3. Do not exercise strenuously just before going to bed – heavy exercise at this time could keep you awake.
4. Spend less time in bed. Get up at the same time every morning, but go to bed later. Start with a half hour later; if necessary, keep pushing back your bedtime until you can doze off readily without becoming tense.
5. Don't sleep late or take naps during the day.
6. Turn your alarm clock towards the wall so that you don't keep checking the time.

Insulation

1. Make sealers for the cracks at the bottoms of doors by filling socks (or long strips of material sewn together) three-quarters full of sand or cat litter. Knot the tops and decorate, if you like, as mice or dachshunds.
2. On a particularly cold night, insulate a window by taping clear plastic

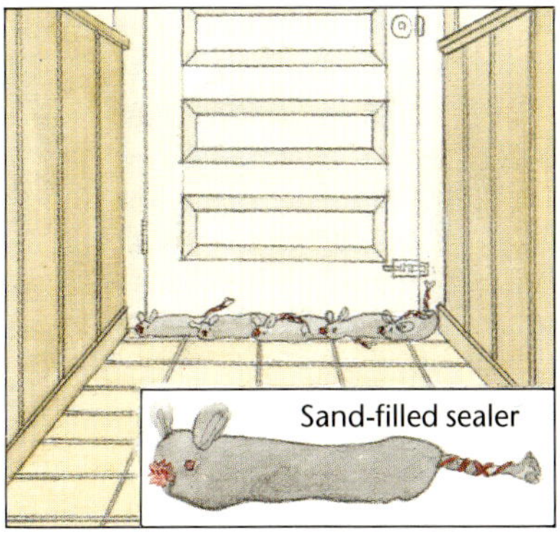

Sand-filled sealer

– even food wrap – to the frame. (See also *Draughts*, p.66.)

Insurance claims

1. List everything covered by your householder's policy, including all relevant serial numbers and, if at all possible, sales slips to show the cost and date of purchase.

Photograph the most valuable items and note their value and the date on the back of each photograph. In the case of loss, contact your insurer immediately. Contact the police if the loss is the result of a crime.
2. After a fire, make a detailed description of the damage done to your home; if the list is disputed, the insurance company's assessor may prepare an alternative list. When you receive a cheque for the repairs, you will be asked to sign a receipt that payment has been made "in full and final settlement" of your claims. Check this form thoroughly before you sign it.
3. The accounts of doctors, dentists and various other medical practitioners can be submitted directly to your medical aid society, provided that their fees are in accordance with the society's scale of benefits. Or you can pay the doctor yourself before claiming what is due to you from the medical aid society.
4. Be sure to disclose any pre-existing conditions on your health insurance application; the policy may be invalidated if you make a claim for treatment of a condition you haven't previously reported.
5. To get the best settlement on a car insurance claim, keep all receipts for maintenance; take periodic photographs of the car to demonstrate its condition before the accident.
6. Keep the information on how to file claims with all your policies.

Insurance costs

To prevent incurring extra charges, pay all your premiums annually.

MOTORCAR

1. The cost of motorcar insurance depends on the type of cover you require and on how much of a risk you are to the insurer. Different companies have different criteria for assessing risk, but all take into account factors such as your age, your driving record, your job, the type of car, where it is garaged, what it is worth and what it will be used for.
2. Once a quotation has been given, you may find that the monthly premiums are too costly. The insurer may then reduce the high premium rate if you agree to an increase in the first amount payable by you in the event of a claim.

MEDICAL

Membership of a medical aid scheme may be offered as an option when you join a company, although some employers insist on it as a condition of employment.

If your company does not provide medical cover, you might consider joining a medical scheme fund individually. This is expensive, and you may consider taking in its place personal medical insurance, which offers policies covering personal accidents and hospitalization.

Ironing

1. When ironing a variety of fabrics, start with the iron at its lowest setting and work up to the highest. Go with the weave of the cloth so that you don't stretch the fabric. To prevent a shine, iron dark fabrics, rayons and acetates on the wrong side.

2. If you're travelling and don't have an iron, hang your just-unpacked clothes in the bathroom and run hot water in the shower. Close the door and let the steam smooth out the wrinkles. This method works especially well with wool.
3. If you have an iron but no board, cover a counter with newspapers and then a towel. Or put newspapers into a pillowcase and use it as your ironing board. Or place a towel over the corner of the bed.
4. Place a piece of aluminium foil, shiny side up, between the ironing board and cover pad; it will reflect heat for a faster job.
5. Interrupted from your ironing? Throw sprinkled clothing into a plastic bag and put it in the refrigerator or freezer for a while.

The bag holds in moisture and the low temperature prevents mildew. (Remember to let frozen clothes thaw before ironing!)
6. To press a wrinkled ribbon, keep the iron stationary and pull the ribbon underneath it.

IN TIMES GONE BY

This is the way we pressed our clothes

Ironing is still a chore, but today's lightweight, thermostatically-controlled irons make the task a lot easier than it used to be.

In ancient Greece, where crisp clothing was a sign of status (and drip-dry fabrics did not exist), a heated rod resembling a rolling pin was used to put pleats in linen robes. The Romans fought wrinkles in their clothes as fiercely as they fought their foes – they hammered them out with a flat metal mallet, usually wielded by slaves.

By the 10th century, the iron had evolved into a mushroom-shaped glass object that the Vikings rolled back and forth on dampened fabric. Europeans in the 15th and 16th centuries used either a flatiron heated over a fire or, in wealthier homes, a hot box iron containing coals or a hot brick. Gas-heated irons were introduced in the 19th century, but they sometimes leaked or exploded, setting a house on fire.

In 1882, an electric iron was patented in the United States. Later, temperature-controlled irons arrived, and were widely used. But the real breakthroughs in the war against wrinkles came in 1926, when the steam iron hit the market, and in the 1960s, when easy-care drip-dry fabrics were introduced.

Itching

1. For quick relief, place a wet tea bag or a cold witch hazel compress directly on the itchy area.
2. If skin is not broken, apply a cooling lotion made from ½ cup water, ½ cup methylated spirits and three to four drops oil of peppermint. Store in a tightly capped bottle and shake well before using.
3. For all-over relief, crumble one cup finely ground oatmeal into lukewarm bath water as it flows from the tap. Be careful getting in and out of the bathtub – it will be extremely slippery. Soak 15 to 20 minutes and gently pat dry so that a thin coating of oatmeal remains on your skin.
4. For itchy, dry or chapped skin, a mineral oil bath (two to 75 millilitres per bathtub of lukewarm water) or a salt bath (½ to one cup per tub) works wonders. (Mineral oil or salt will also make the bathtub slippery, so be careful.) After the bath, smooth on aloe vera gel from the centre of a freshly sliced aloe leaf – you can also buy it at a health food store.

J

Jams

To make jam, choose fresh, but not over-ripe fruit.
1. Peel, remove pips and cut into small pieces. For best results, cook not more than eight 250-millilitre cups of fruit at a time.
2. Put fruit into a large, heavy enamel or stainless steel pot and add water – about half a cup for every four cups of fruit (you don't need to add water to grapes, berries or tomatoes).
3. Cook fruit until tender, stirring frequently to prevent sticking. Add sugar – about ¾ cup for every one cup of fruit and stir until dissolved. Boil the mixture rapidly until it starts to thicken. Most fruits reach the jam stage within five to 15 minutes or at 4°C above the boiling point of water.
4. Scoop off any foam that forms on the jam.
5. To test for doneness, dip out a metal spoonful of syrup, let it cool slightly and tip it slightly over the pot. If the syrup droplets merge as they slide off the spoon, the jam is done.
6. Pour warm jam into sterilized jars. Make sure they are dry.
7. When the jam has cooled, cover it with a round piece of paper dipped in brandy or a layer of melted paraffin wax. Screw on the lid. Store in a cool, dry place.

Jars

Battling to open the lid of a jar? The easiest way to break the seal – but only if you don't want to re-use the lid and jar – is simply to pierce the lid with a can opener.

Alternatively, try putting the lid under hot running water. The resultant expansion may be enough to allow you to loosen the obstinate lid. Another way of loosening a lid is to knock gently along its side, and then to twist it off manually.

For really stubborn lids, use the inner tube of a bicycle wheel to give your hand greater traction while turning the lid. Or try a tourniquet-type of opener, using canvas webbing and a screwdriver for leverage.

To help prevent the lid sticking, ensure that the inside of the lid and the neck of the jar are clean before you close it.

Jet lag

1. Alternate a "feast day" (high-protein breakfast and lunch, high-carbohydrate dinner) with a "fast day" (soup and salad) for three days before departure; during those days don't drink any caffeine except between 3:00 and 5:00 p.m. On flight day eat sparingly and drink caffeine only in the morning if you're flying west, between 6:00 and 9:00 p.m. if you're headed east.

2. Preadjust your bedtime. If flying east, go to sleep an hour earlier each day for each time zone you're crossing; if flying west, move bedtime later in the same fashion.

3. When flying east over several time zones, try to take a morning flight instead of an overnighter. On arrival your "body time" will still be mid-afternoon; local time will be early evening. Eat dinner and go to bed late by local time. The next morning you'll feel rested.

4. Flying west is easier. In fact, you may avoid jet lag altogether if you take a late flight, stay awake during the trip, then go to bed as soon as you reach your destination.

5. A dose of Vitamins C, E and B-complex are believed to alleviate the side effects of air travel.

6. Drink lots of fluids before and during the flight, but avoid any kind of alcoholic beverages.

7. Go outside into sunlight as soon as possible after arriving. Take a brisk walk or jog; moderate exercise may help your body adjust faster (see *Fitness on the road*, p.85).

Jewellery allergies

1. To prevent inflammation when having your ears pierced, make sure a stainless steel needle is used. Wear only stainless steel post earrings until the earlobes heal.

2. If you have a reaction to a ring, earrings or spectacle frames, clean them with methylated spirits, then use clear nail polish to coat the part that touches the skin. Reapply the polish when it wears off. Another way to lessen irritation is to apply over-the-counter hydrocortisone cream to the affected parts before you put on the jewellery or frames.

3. Nickel, a component in some jewellery metals, causes an allergic reaction in some people; if you suspect you're one of them, wear pure copper or non-metal jewellery.

4. Try to avoid wearing tight-fitting metal watchstraps or bracelets. Wrap a handkerchief or other absorbent fabric under a watchstrap or bracelet during humid weather or exercise.

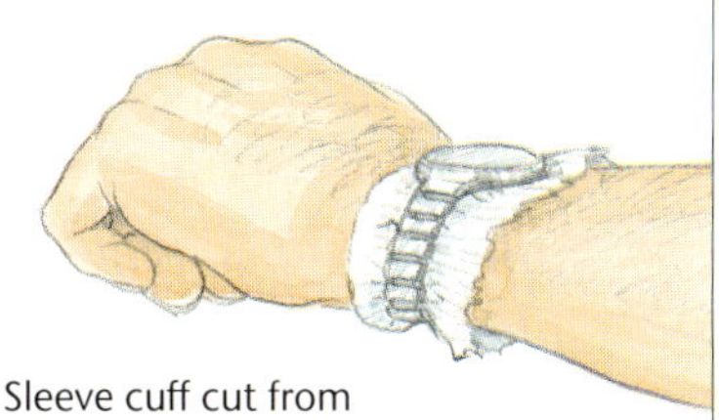

Sleeve cuff cut from long-underwear top or cotton pullover.

Job burnout

Do you find you've reached the point – whether from overwork, stress or just plain boredom – where you don't enjoy your job anymore? Here are some ways which might help you to get the zest back:

1. Redefine your job. Write up a realistic job description and discuss it with your boss, stressing that you want to adjust your duties so that you can be more productive.

2. Develop and sell a new project. Write a memo to your boss explaining why your idea is worthwhile, what kind of help you would need, and how long it would take. Even if the project doesn't work out, you'll have done something different, and you'll probably be remembered for your earnest attempts.

3. Develop a life outside work – take up a hobby or do voluntary work. If necessary, take some time off to think and gain perspective.

4. If you're still burned out, perhaps it's time to find a better setting for your skills or to consider making a career change (p.37).

DID YOU KNOW . . . ?

A few nuggets about gold

- ☐ To produce one fine ounce of gold, an average of about 3,3 metric tons of ore must be processed.
- ☐ All of the gold ever mined could fit into a cube with 16-metre sides.
- ☐ South Africa is the world's largest producer of gold.
- ☐ Gold is so valuable that refineries clean their roofs and chimneys periodically to recover the specks that have accumulated there.
- ☐ The Romans serrated the edges of gold coins to prevent people from shaving off tiny bits.
- ☐ Gold doesn't tarnish or corrode. Coins from sunken ships often are as shiny as new, even after centuries beneath the sea.
- ☐ Gold is so malleable that one fine ounce can be hammered into a gold leaf that covers 130 square metres, or pulled into an extremely fine wire 80 kilometres long.
- ☐ Pure gold (24 carat) is so soft that it must be mixed with another metal to make it durable enough for fashioning jewellery. It turns reddish when mixed with copper, bluish when mixed with iron, and it forms white gold when nickel is added.
- ☐ Gold is important to the American space programme. During astronaut Edward White's historic space walk, a gold-plated cord was his lifeline; today gold wire and tubing are vital to the space shuttle.

Job hunting

1. A good employment agency can be of great assistance. Choose one which is reputable.
2. Invest in an answering machine or an answering service so that you can get messages from prospective employers or employment agencies.
3. Inform your friends, business associates and former employees that you are looking for a job. Keep in contact with those who may be able to help you – keeping a low profile will ensure that you are forgotten.

RESEARCHING A PROSPECT

1. If you hear of a position that interests you, investigate the company – read newspaper and magazine articles about it, and study its annual and quarterly reports.
2. If possible, talk to people who work for the company. Find out its position in the industry, what its main problem areas are, and how it treats its employees. Does the company promote from within its ranks? Does it offer education for its employees? Does it help them advance?
3. Visit the company if it is practical to do so. Do the employees look enthusiastic? Do they talk positively about their work?
4. Write a letter to whoever is in a position to hire you.

Indicate your knowledge of the company, state how you could help it reach its goals, and request an interview. Say that you'll follow up by phone in about a week. Then do so.

IF YOU HAVE A JOB

1. Ask agents or prospective employers to leave only their first name if they phone you at work. Or have them phone you at home.
2. Do not look for work during company time. Schedule interviews after work or during lunch hour.

Job interviews

1. Prepare a curriculum vitae for each interview, tailoring your stated objectives to suit the available job. (This is easier if your cv is on a computer disk.)
2. Create two basic curriculum vitaes – a chronological one if you're working through agencies and a functional one, organized around your skills and experience, if you've had a number of jobs or are returning to work after several years.

PREPARATION

1. Choose four or five incidents from current and past jobs that show your accomplishments and work style. Create a success story for each one to help answer such questions as "What are your major accomplishments?" or "What is your relevant experience?"
2. Rehearse the interview with a friend or family member. Anticipate likely questions and practise telling your success stories without rambling. Ask for feedback.
3. Give yourself an extra hour or so to dress and get to the interview. If your hands tend to be clammy, use anti-perspirant on your palms.

THE INTERVIEW

1. Look the interviewer directly in the eye and follow her lead when shaking her hand.
2. Remember that you are making a choice as much as she is. Ask any questions necessary to decide if this is a job you really want.

Job loss

A job loss is almost always an opportunity disguised as a disaster. Keep in mind that you have several priorities: to handle the immediate crisis, to re-evaluate your career, and to make plans for your future.
1. Press for severance pay – many employers offer as much as two weeks' pay for each year of service. Find out about continuing with group medical aid at your own expense.
2. Losing a job can be a traumatic experience. Allow yourself to feel depressed and angry. Tell your family what you're experiencing and ask them for extra moral support during this difficult time.
3. Don't panic. If you can afford to take a holiday, do so – it may lend perspective. If you can't, give yourself little treats: eat lunch at a new restaurant or escape to the movies.
4. Then get busy. Re-evaluate what went wrong – be honest, but don't torture yourself. Did you hang on too long when you knew things were going badly? Was there poor chemistry between you and your boss or your colleagues? Were you less than fully committed to your job?
5. Make use of any contacts you may have built up over the years. (See also *Job hunting*, p.120.)

Jogging

1. Before you buy a new pair of running shoes, check the soles of your worn-out pair. If the outer edge of the heel is worn, your running style is to roll your feet outward; if the inner edge is worn, you roll your feet inward. Take the old pair to the store and ask a knowledgeable salesperson what kind of running shoe best suits your style.
2. If your cotton socks are lined with towelling, wear them inside out to reduce friction and help prevent blisters. Smearing Vaseline on your feet before running also helps; rub it on your inner thighs to keep your legs from chafing.
3. If you find jogging too jarring, try walking briskly on a regular schedule; it gives comparable benefits. Start moderately: walk a kilometre in 10 to 15 minutes five times a week. Gradually increase distance and time over the next few weeks (see *Endurance building*, p.73).
4. Try to find a congenial jogging partner. It's more fun to jog in company and there'll always be someone to help or give the alarm if misfortune should strike.
5. If you're in doubt about any aspects of your general health, or if you're over 35 years old, see your doctor before you take up jogging.
6. When choosing a venue for jogging, consider your safety first. Avoid an area where there is fast or heavy

traffic, to prevent the risk of an accident as well as the inhalation of exhaust fumes. At the other extreme, be wary of a lonely path through an area that could conceal a mugger.

Juggling

You'll achieve precise hand and eye co-ordination only by following the golden rule of juggling – never look at your hands. With hands at waist height, toss a ball from one to the other so that it follows an arc with its highest point or crest, at eye level. Keep your hands cupped so that the ball lands in the palm, and rolls off your fingertips as you gently flick upwards again.

Now try to keep the ball going around, rather than back and forth. Throw it up with your right hand, catch it with your left and keep it moving by tossing it back at waist height to your right hand. Now try it with two balls, starting with one in each hand, tossing with the right hand and passing the second ball from left to right as the first ball reaches its highest point.

Juice extractor

1. Gently squeeze cut citrus fruit over an inverted cup, using a saucer to catch the juice. (A small coffee cup works best for lemons.)
2. Put the halved fruit in a sealed plastic bag and squeeze it between the hinges of a door.
3. Try pliers or a nutcracker.

K

Keys

1. Carry two sets of car and house keys just in case one set gets locked inside. Keep a third set at home in something that can't be locked.
2. Colour code the faces of your keys so that you'll instantly know what lock each one opens.
3. If a duplicate key is difficult to insert or remove, try filing down its rough spots with an emery board.
4. If a key breaks in a lock, you may be able to extract it with a pair of needle-nose pliers or a fine, stiff wire. An alternative method is to insert a narrow coping-saw blade into the lock as shown. Catch the key with the teeth of the blade, then pull it out, keeping the blade parallel to the top of the keyway.

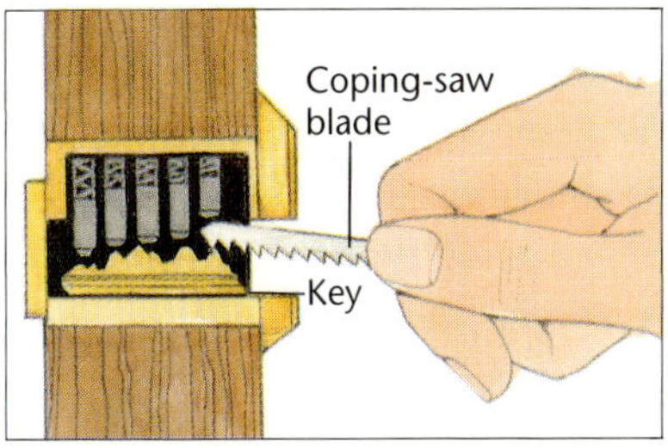

5. When a house key is hard to turn, squeeze a little powdered graphite into the lock and spread it around by jiggling the key back and forth. If you don't have any powdered graphite, scrape the point of a soft-lead pencil over the teeth of the key and insert it into the lock. Don't ever use oil – it will gum up the lock.
6. If you've lost the key to a locked drawer, first see if the drawer above is unlocked; if it is, remove it to get into the locked drawer below. If this approach is impossible, minimize damage by taking off the back of the desk or chest.
7. Make a copy of the manufacturer's code number imprinted on a new car key or its attached tag and keep it in a safe, handy place so that a locksmith can easily make a duplicate key in an emergency. If you lose the code, your car dealer may have a record; find out before asking a locksmith to make a car call.

Knee problems

If God had intended humans to be perfect, according to an old saying, he wouldn't have given us knees. Despite the fact that the knee is the body's biggest, heaviest and best protected joint, it is injured more often than any other. Many injuries can be prevented by taking these precautions:
1. If you're overweight, slim down to reduce stress on the joint, especially if you engage in such activities as jogging or playing tennis.
2. If you sit in one place for long periods, change the position of your legs often. Whenever possible, stand up and stretch your legs or take a short walk.
3. Avoid climbing stairs or bending your knees any more than is necessary. When working on something below waist level, sit on a stool or on the floor.
4. Avoid wearing high-heeled shoes or those that have thin, poorly cushioned soles.
5. When gardening, kneel on an old sofa pillow or a piece of foam rubber; shift your weight frequently from one knee to the other.
6. Relieve wear and tear on your knees whenever you exercise. Use a resilient surface for walking, jogging, playing tennis or doing any kind of aerobics. Wear flippers while swimming so that your calves and ankles will do much of the work. Avoid cycling in high gears.
7. To strengthen your knee muscles, do a set of knee curls daily. Lie on your stomach on an exercise bench or a bed so that your lower legs extend over the edge. Turn one foot inward to an angle of about 45°, slowly bend your knee to a 90° angle, and lift your upper leg as high as you can. Hold this position for about 10 seconds, then lower your leg slowly and let it

straighten. Repeat the knee curls 10 times with each leg.

8. Never ignore any knee injury, however slight it may seem. See a doctor as soon as possible. Meanwhile, follow the RICE rule: Rest, Ice, Compression and Elevation.

Knitting

1. You can use a pair of chopsticks or wooden dowels as substitutes for knitting needles, if you have to. Just sharpen the tips in a pencil sharpener and smooth them off neatly with an emery board.

2. Similarly, you can renew the blunted tips of knitting needles made of wood with a pencil sharpener or by rubbing them with fine sandpaper or an emery board.

3. Wooden knitting needles will work more smoothly if you rub them with a soap-filled scouring pad.

4. No stitch holder handy? Use a plastic straw.

5. To keep a ball of wool from unrolling while you work, put it in a tin with a lid; poke a hole in the lid to draw the wool through.

6. For stitch and row markers, attach the little plastic tabs used to close packages of bread.

7. Instead of wool, knit or crochet with one long fabric strip cut from an old T-shirt. Starting at the hem, cut the T-shirt horizontally into a continuous two-centimetre-wide strip. Tug on the strip and the cut edges will curl under neatly.

L

Ladders

1. Spray-paint the top two steps of a stepladder bright orange or red as a visual reminder to keep off them.

2. As a safety precaution, always keep your hips within the vertical rails of the ladder.

3. Before climbing an extension ladder, jump up and down lightly on the bottom rung a few times to make certain that the legs are firmly planted.

On muddy ground, drive a sturdy stake into the ground behind the ladder, as shown. Then tie a rope around the second rung from the bottom of the ladder, knot it tightly, and secure it to the stake.

4. When working high on a ladder against the house, lash the ladder through an open window so that it can't fall over. Tie one end of a rope to a rung about two-thirds of the way up, and the other end to a solid object inside the house. Or use a plank long enough to bridge the inside of the open window.

5. Because the hollow rungs of aluminium extension ladders weaken with wear, reinforce them before they fail. Insert a hardwood dowel into each rung; make sure it's long enough to extend six millimetres past the rail on both sides. Wrap tape around both ends to ensure a snug fit. (If you're painting, replace a dowel with one that extends half a metre or more beyond the rung – it makes a great place to hang the paint tin.)

Lamps

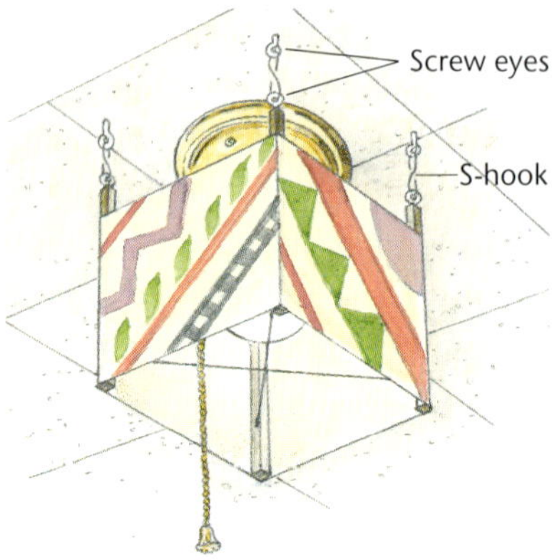

1. Dress up a bare ceiling bulb with a colourful box kite. Cut off one end of the assembled kite and insert screw eyes into the ends of the spines. Keep the sides at least 75 millimetres away from the bulb.

2. Do you need light fast? Clip photographers' lamps to a shelf, cabinet, desktop or wherever you need it.

3. If a light bulb shatters, turn off the switch or unplug the cord, press a wad of putty over the sharp edges, and twist the stub with it. A cut potato works, too.

Lampshades

Here are a few ways to spruce up an old shade:

1. Using a toothbrush, lightly spatter the surface with a shade of paint that matches or accents the colour of the room. (Practise your technique on newspaper first.)

2. For a rustic touch, glue on dried flowers or leaves.

3. Create silhouettes of recognizable shapes or free-floating patterns by gluing noodles, rice or paper stars inside the shade. Keep these objects well away from the bulb, which should be no more than 60 watts.

4. Custom decorate a flat-surfaced shade with stencils. Or glue a colourful old map around the outside and lacquer it when dry.

5. Transfer a needlepoint design directly onto a cloth shade. Use heavy yarns and double-tied knots.

6. To remove spots from a paper shade, use an art-gum eraser. Plastic or nylon shades can be washed in a tub with mild liquid detergent and water. Send silk and other fabric shades to the dry-cleaner.

7. Repleat a shade by simply gathering every two or three pleats with a decorative stitch or tassel.

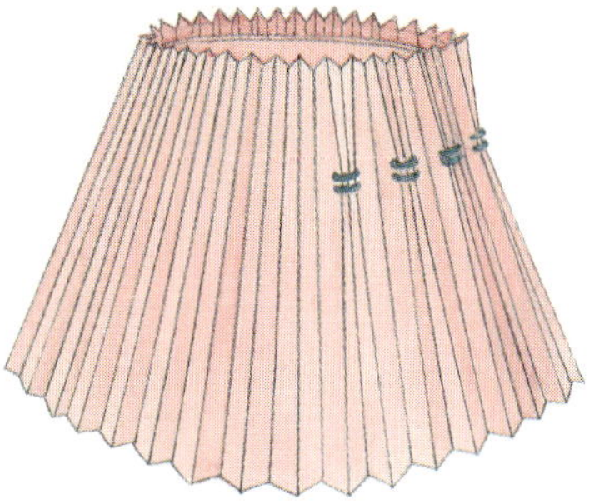

Laryngitis

1. Rest your voice; don't even answer the phone. Carry a pencil and paper to replace conversation.

2. Give up smoking.

3. Eat mild, easily swallowed foods; drink plenty of nonalcoholic liquids.

4. Stay in a humid atmosphere. Use a humidifier or inhale steam – sit in the bathroom with the door closed and the hot shower on, or fill a bowl with boiling water, lean over it with a towel over your head, and breathe in the steam.

5. If laryngitis lasts longer than 48 hours or is accompanied by a high fever, call your doctor.

Latchkey children

Fear, loneliness and boredom can be problems for children staying home alone after school. But careful preparation and training can help you and the child feel more comfortable.

TRAINING

1. When you go out together, let the child lock and unlock the door. Leave him alone for short periods, making sure he locks the door behind you.

2. Give the child a small task to accomplish while you are out of the house so that he gets used to functioning independently.

3. As you near the day when the child will be home alone after school until you return, you can both gain confidence with a regular "What would you do if...?" quiz. Keep this up even after the child is staying alone; it will help uncover lurking anxieties or problems.

SUPPORT SYSTEM

1. Identify which of your neighbours the child can telephone for assistance, companionship or a spare house key.

2. Telephone home at a set time each day or have the child telephone as soon as he gets home. If you can't be available by telephone, arrange for a relative, friend or neighbour to receive this check-in call and chat.

3. Stick up a list of important phone numbers or enter them in the memory dialing system of the telephone.

4. Leave the radio playing softly on the family's favourite station.

5. Install an answering machine to monitor incoming calls.

6. Assign a necessary but light task that will help the flow of family life: setting the table, making a salad, putting away laundry. This helps remind the child that family members are soon to return.

Lawn patches

When you dig a new planting bed or vegetable garden, use the upended turf to patch bare or damaged spots in your lawn. Such homegrown sod may not be as flawless as the commercial product, but it will match your lawn perfectly, making mends invisible.

1. Strip the turf from the new planting area by cutting it into neat 30-centimetre squares with a sharp spade and turning it over right in place. Shave most of the soil from the roots so that the pieces of turf are no more than five centimetres thick.

2. Store these patches of grass side up in a shady spot; keep moist until needed. They should stay fresh for three to four weeks in cool weather.

3. Prepare bare spots for patching by loosening the soil to a depth of 10 centimetres. If the gap in the lawn was caused by a herbicide or petrol spill, remove and replace the loosened soil. If salt or the neighbour's dog did the damage, neutralize the soil with a handful of gypsum.

4. Cut the turf pieces to size and fit them into the gap, sifting compost into the cracks to protect the roots from drying out. Water well.

Lawns

1. A lawn looks best when it forms a sweeping, unified background to trees, shrubs and other elements of the landscape. If you stud it with island beds of flowers and shrubs, it loses much of its aesthetic appeal.

2. Aerate your lawn often, not just once a year, by wearing golf spikes as you mow it.

3. Don't mow too short. Blades of grass are the turf's leaves, converting sunlight into food; if you leave them a little long, you'll significantly reduce the need for fertilizer.

4. If you have a large, high-powered rotary lawn mower, another adjustment can save hours of labour in autumn. Tape a piece of cardboard over the exit chute to block it; then mow the newly fallen leaves instead of raking them. They'll be pulverized, sifting back into the turf to serve as organic fertilizer for your garden.

5. Who says you have to plant grass? For a part of the garden that is usually only seen and not used, consider ground covers such as ajuga, English ivy, *polygonum sutera*, thyme or vinca. Not only are they ornamental, but they also don't need regular mowing. (See also *Grass*, p.100.)

Lawsuits

When a deal or even a marriage goes sour, or something that you've purchased doesn't perform as the salesman promised, you may consider hiring a lawyer and taking the case to court.

But there's another way to settle disputes, and it's cheaper and usually less time-consuming. It's called arbitration, and it consists of you and the other party in the dispute, each telling your own side of the story to a third person, the arbitrator, who then resolves the dispute.

Most arbitrations result from disputed contracts in which recourse to arbitration was provided for. This method of problem-solving is becoming increasingly popular.

Both parties must agree to have their differences settled by an arbitrator who is acceptable to both of them. Either or both parties may select the arbitrator. An arbitrator may also be appointed on application to a professional body, such as the Bar Council.

Although the arbitrator's decision is usually final, a contractor may appeal against such a decision, if the arbitrator has acted unfairly or irregularly.

Lawyers

1. A set means test will determine whether you qualify for free legal aid, but it is estimated that only about 20 percent of those who appear in the lower courts have legal representation. In the Supreme Court, a pro Deo (literally 'for God' or free) counsel is appointed to represent those who cannot afford one.

2. The rules and conditions that govern free legal aid are set out in the *Legal Aid Guide*, a book that is available free of charge from the Legal Aid Officer at some magistrate's courts or from the Director, Legal Aid Board, Private Bag X163, Pretoria 0001.

3. For some legal procedures, such as drawing up a will, or buying or selling property, you can obtain the necessary forms from a legal stationer. But even apparently simple procedures have serious pitfalls, and it is advisable to ask a lawyer to examine all the completed papers before you sign them.

4. If you need the services of a lawyer, ask him in advance what his fee will be and what services it will cover. You are entitled to negotiate for a lower rate or an extension of time in which to pay. Or simply shop around until you find the right combination of terms and legal expertise.

Learning disabilities

Some children of average or above average intelligence have difficulty learning and retaining information in the traditional fashion. Some early warning signs: hyperactivity; inability to concentrate; problems with discipline and changes in routine; lack of co-ordination; memory problems; and difficulties in speaking, reading and writing.

If your child exhibits any of these "symptoms", contact your family doctor to be sure there's no medical cause. If there isn't, speak to your child's teacher. An educational psychologist may be called in to assess the child and make recommendations, which may include remedial lessons as part of the school day or lessons with a private teacher.

For more help or support, ask your school administration about any local parents' groups or contact the South African Association for Learning and Educational Disabilities, c/o Division of Specialized Education, University of the Witwatersrand, Private Bag 3, Wits 2050. Alternatively, you can phone your local university – some run child guidance clinics.

DID YOU KNOW?

Famous people with learning difficulties

□ Leonardo da Vinci. Some people believe the mirror writing in his notes was a code; others say it was a symptom of dyslexia.
□ Hans Christian Andersen. The manuscripts of this writer contain amazing variations in spelling.
□ Thomas A. Edison. This brilliant inventor was taught by his mother after schools were unsuccessful.
□ Albert Einstein. This genius didn't talk until he was four or read until he was nine.
□ Woodrow Wilson. This president couldn't read until he was 11. His relatives considered him "dull" and "backward".
□ Auguste Rodin. "I have an idiot for a son," the sculptor's father once said. He did poorly in spelling and arithmetic – but his most enduring work is "The Thinker".
□ Winston Churchill. A duplicate of his original application, sent anonymously to his old school, was rejected as not up to the school's standards.

Leather

MAKING GARMENTS

1. For skirts, pants and vests, buy sheep nappa leather. It's easy to machine-sew with heavy-duty cotton or polyester thread, and is available in various colours.

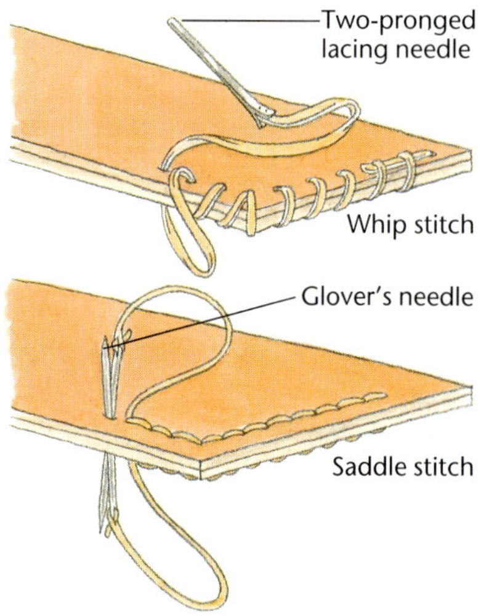

For sturdy outdoor garments, belts and handbags, buy veg shoulder leather (leather tanned with vegetable oils). Rent a professional sewing machine or put pieces together by punching holes along their edges with an awl and lacing thin thongs through the holes.

2. Before cutting leather or suede, check the hides for scars so that you can avoid them in laying out your

pattern. If you find thin spots, reinforce them with fusible tape.
3. Stroke suede to find the direction of the nap, mark it on the wrong side with a felt pen, then cut the pattern pieces so that the nap all goes one way. Otherwise, adjoining pieces won't match.
4. Instead of basting seams together on a leather garment, you can "pin" them with paper clips eight centimetres apart.

After you've finished stitching them, brush a little rubber cement onto the underside of the seam allowances and onto the adjacent leather. Let it dry completely, then press the seam allowances flat with your fingers; flatten further by tapping lightly with a wooden mallet. If you don't have a mallet, use a wooden block.

MAINTENANCE
1. If a leather coat gets wet, hang it on a padded hanger – not a hook – and let it dry away from direct heat. Wrinkles will generally straighten out overnight, but if they don't, press on the wrong side with a dry iron set on *Low*, using heavy wrapping paper as a pressing cloth.
2. Clean small spots or markings on smooth, glossy leather by rubbing with a damp sponge.
3. Erase scuff marks with wax shoe polish or mink oil. On suede use an eraser or a sponge.
4. When restitching leather gloves or slippers, use dental floss instead of thread. It lasts longer.
5. To clean a combination bag, such as canvas and leather, clean the non-leather portion first. Make bubbles with liquid dishwashing detergent and rub them into the material with a sponge or soft cloth (use only bubbles – don't immerse the sponge). Work on heavily soiled spots with a soft brush, such as a vegetable or nail brush, but brush vigorously.

To rinse, dampen a sponge in warm water and rub the surface until the bubbles are gone. Use saddle soap to clean the leather portions, then apply a neutral shoe wax or a wax the same colour as the leather.

Leaves

Sending leaves to the rubbish dump is a time-consuming nuisance and a waste of a valuable resource. Instead, "chunk mulch" the leaves. Stack them in an inconspicuous corner of the garden, wet them down and trample them. Over the winter they will settle further, compacting into a tight, solid mass. In the spring break the mass up into small chunks with a garden fork and spread it among shrubs, flowers and vegetables. It will serve as an attractive mulch for at least one season, then decompose to fertilize and condition the soil.

Leftovers

1. Don't throw out stale bread and rolls. Use them for bread crumbs, melba toast and croutons to serve with soups and salads.
2. Freeze leftover cooked fish until you want to use it in a salad. Thaw, flake and toss with onions, salad vegetables and a dressing.
3. Keep a special bag in the freezer for leftover vegetables. When you have enough for soup, thaw and purée in the blender with a cup or two of chicken or beef stock.
4. Or turn leftover vegetables into a salad. Toss with a vinaigrette dressing or mix with chopped onions, mayonnaise and herbs before mounding onto lettuce leaves.
5. For a terrific sandwich spread, grind some beef scraps and mix with mayonnaise or cream cheese; add mustard, horseradish or pickle relish.

Leg cramps

1. If you wake up with a painful cramp in your leg, try to flex first your toes and then your whole foot upward, toward your knee. Or bend your knee, grab your toes, and flex them toward you while pushing back with your foot. If this gives only partial relief, massage the sole of your foot under the arch, pressing firmly.
2. For a calf cramp, straighten your leg and flex your foot as far up as you can. Or put your toes on the floor and slowly lower your heel.

PREVENTION
1. If you sleep on your back, use an open-ended box or a frame to keep the weight of the covers off your feet. If you sleep on your stomach, let your feet hang free over the end or the side of the bed.
2. Drink lots of plain water (some find quinine water helps), and keep your diet rich in calcium, potassium, magnesium and the B vitamins (see *The balanced diet*, p.254).
3. Do wall stretches nightly: stand a metre from the wall and lean toward it, keeping your heels firmly on the floor; hold for one minute.

Lemons & limes

1. You can substitute ½ teaspoon vinegar (any kind) for one teaspoon lemon or lime juice in a recipe.
2. To get just a few drops of juice from a lemon or lime, prick one end with a fork or toothpick and squeeze. The fruit can be refrigerated and used again when more juice is needed.

Letters

The art of letter writing, as practised by previous generations, is rare in today's electronic world. But there are some occasions when only a letter, note or card will do. When you must write, keep these tips in mind:

PERSONAL
1. Don't write only about yourself and your family. Ask questions, even rhetorical ones. Even if you don't expect a reply, at least express interest in the recipient's welfare.
2. Avoid dwelling on dreary topics such as a minor personal illness.
3. Choose plain white blank cards for letters of sympathy.

Don't be mawkish, but do say that your thoughts are with the bereaved and then recall a fond personal memory of the deceased. Offer specific help, if possible – babysitting or shopping, for example.

4. Wait 24 hours before posting an emotion-packed letter – whether written in love or anger. Read it over and then decide if you really want to send it after all.

BUSINESS

1. If you're writing to a corporation, address your letter to a specific person. Phone the headquarters and ask who's in charge of the department you want to reach.
2. Letters of complaint should be straightforward, factual and polite. Try not to be too forceful. Expressing too much indignation or unjustified criticism will merely antagonize the reader. If possible, work a touch of humour into the letter; it can be effective in getting results.

Lettuce

1. Reviving wilted lettuce is easy. Just give it a quick dip in hot water, then a rinse in ice water that has a little salt or sugar added. Shake, then refrigerate for an hour.
2. Always make sure lettuce leaves are absolutely dry before tossing them with dressing; it won't cling to moist leaves.
3. If you have to dry a lot of lettuce – say, for a party – put the washed leaves in a clean pillowcase, tie it shut, pop it in a tumble dryer, and set on *Cool Air*.
4. Use your fingers to tear lettuce into bite-size pieces; a knife can cause the edges to turn brown.
5. Use extra lettuce leaves as a hot vegetable. Braised, sautéed or stir-fried, they make a surprisingly good side dish.

Level

1. To make sure a picture or mirror is level, hold a half-full glass of water against the top edge. The water surface will be level no matter how you tilt the glass.
2. For long-distance levelling, use a length of plastic tubing attached to a bottomless plastic jug, as shown. Pour water into the jug until it reaches

the desired height at both ends; mark the spot on the tube. No matter how far apart the ends are or how irregular the terrain is between, the water, when aligned with the mark, is at the same level.

Liability

1. The best precaution: an umbrella policy that gives you additional coverage if an accident occurs on your property.
2. Inspect your property regularly for hazards, such as broken railings or deeply cracked patios. Fix them as soon as you can; meanwhile, do your best to warn and protect others against harm. This does not guarantee you against a lawsuit – anyone can sue anyone for anything – but it greatly improves your chances of winning.
3. If you have an "attractive nuisance", such as a swimming pool or a trampoline, put up warning signs and a fence with a locked gate.
4. Clear fallen leaves and flowers from paths and under pergolas as soon as possible. If you have guests, warn them that the paths may be slippery underfoot.
5. Keep family pets inside or within a fenced-in area.
6. If, despite your efforts, a guest has too much to drink, take away his car keys and drive the person home yourself, call a taxi, or make him stay until he sobers up.

Life insurance

How much life insurance is enough? You can still follow the old rule of thumb that says coverage should equal four to five times your annual salary. Or, for greater precision, you can use this formula:

1. Set an income objective for your survivors – perhaps 70 percent of your current yearly income. Multiply this by the number of years you want them covered.
2. List all other financial resources your survivors can use, including your current assets – cash, securities, pension and so forth – as well as their own income. Subtract this amount from the amount required.
3. What remains is the amount of life insurance you should obtain.

Life preserver

1. Anything with buoyancy – a styrofoam ice chest, even an empty 4,5-litre jug, tightly sealed – can help a non-swimmer stay afloat.
2. If your trousers are made of a natural fibre – cotton or wool – take them off and knot the bottoms of the legs. Holding the waistband, swing the

Inflating trousers as a buoy gives arms a temporary rest from treading water.

DID YOU KNOW . . . ?

Lightning lore

☐ Lightning can and does strike the same place twice – at least, the higher the structure, the more likely it is to be hit. Statistically, an average home on moderately flat terrain in a moderately active thunderstorm region might be hit once in 100 years. But a structure 360 metres high might be struck 20 times each year.

☐ It is perfectly safe to touch a person who has been struck by lightning – he no longer holds an electrical charge.

☐ To learn how many kilometres away a thunderstorm is, count the seconds between a lightning flash and the ensuing thunderclap, then divide by five – that's how much slower sound travels than light.

☐ Lightning helps fertilize the soil. It converts nitrogen into an oxide, which, coupled with rainwater, forms a weak nitric acid (a compound of hydrogen, nitrogen and oxygen). Added to the minerals in the soil, this acid forms nitrates, which nourish plants.

☐ Lightning travels at speeds of between 160 and 1,600 km/second.

pants over your head and down onto the water. Then tuck the air-filled pants legs under your armpits to serve as a buoy.

Lifts

Holding a lift button in or pushing it repeatedly may satisfy you but does nothing at all for the lift. Its electronic circuitry can register only the first call.

The same is true when a lift passes you by. Modern lifts have load sensors that cause them to bypass floors once they've reached load capacity. Be patient; the lift will stop for you on its return.

New lifts have devices that are sensitive to pranks. If a prankster pushes all the buttons on his way out of your lift, the newer models will automatically cancel the calls. Just press the button for your required floor once more to get the lift moving again. Older lifts may have to stop at all floors. Just be patient.

Light bulbs

1. The familiar filament or incandescent bulb, is the commonest but least efficient kind, although some types are better than others. Generally, an incandescent bulb will last for 600 to 1,000 hours.

Incandescent bulbs get very hot – be careful not to exceed the wattage recommended for the fitting. A plastic lampshade will melt and fall to the floor if the bulb is too hot.

Be aware that incandescent bulbs will have a shorter lifespan if used horizontally or if jolted or shaken.

2. The most efficient lights are fluorescent tubes. They are costly, but a tube lasts an average of 9,000 hours and gives triple the light per watt of an incandescent bulb.

3. Do not switch fluorescent tubes on and off every time you enter and leave a room – the biggest strain is starting up when switched on.

4. For easy removal of an outdoor bulb, coat the threads with silicone spray before you screw it in.

Lighting

Add drama to a drab room by "painting" with light.

1. For an element of surprise, vary the light sources throughout the room. Mount small fixtures under a row of wall cabinets, inside a china display cabinet, on top of a bookshelf and so forth. Bounce light both upward and downward.

2. Vary the intensities as well; a 40-watt bulb here and there provides a nice, subtle touch. Or, for real flexibility, replace your lamps' on-off switches with dimmers.

3. Warm up a cold room with a floor lamp or a pendant fixture hung over a chair or sofa. This will change the whole atmosphere of the room.

4. Picture lights lend a soft glow while accentuating works of art.

5. In a child's bedroom, glue or paint glow-in-the-dark stars or creatures on the ceiling.

6. To make the most of a blank wall, project a floor spotlight up through the leaves of a large plant.

Lightning

Lightning tends to strike the tallest object around, then arc off to the side. If you get caught in a lightning storm and you're the tallest thing on the terrain, get to a low spot, squat down (preferably on something dry), and make yourself compact; hug your knees and tuck in your head (most fatalities occur when lightning strikes the head and exits through the feet or arms). Stay clear of hills, trees, fences, barns, cars and other conductors.

If you're playing golf, quit and go home – you are exposed to lightning on a golf course and the few places you may seek shelter serve as conductors for the lightning. If you're in your car, stay there. Lightning will arc across the metal shell, but you'll be safe inside.

Often you'll get advance warning of a strike. If your skin begins to tingle and your hair stands on end, stoop down. If someone near you is struck, keep her warm and try to revive her. Then send for a doctor.

Linen cupboards

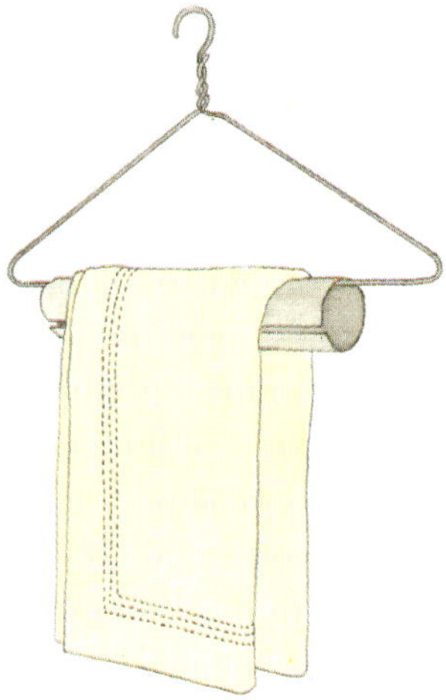

1. To keep table linens from creasing, install a rod just beneath a low shelf and hang the linens on hangers padded with paper towel tubes.
2. Fold and store bed or bath linens by sets, not by size. That way, you can grab a complete set when you want it instead of having to pick through several stacks.

Lint

Since lint or fluff, is highly contagious, remove it before you put a garment in the cupboard.

1. Are you stuck without a clothes brush? Try wrapping a strip of cellophane tape several times around your hand, with the adhesive side out, and move it across the garment. Or use a damp sponge.
2. You'll find that lint is much easier to remove with a damp clothes brush than with a dry one.
3. To remove lint from velvet fabric, a sponge powder puff works well: on wool use a dry cellulose sponge.

Lipstick stains

Before washing a smeared garment with extra detergent, try one of these pretreatments:
1. Rub in some cold cream or white margarine, then rinse the stained area with soda water.
2. Use methylated spirits or salad oil.
3. Rub the stain with a generous amount of Vaseline.
4. Wipe with a slice of white bread, then brush away the crumbs.
5. If the garment is white, soak it in lemon juice; if it's coloured, dilute the lemon juice by half with water.
6. Place the stained area over a white towel, and sponge on a mixture of powdered soap and water.

Litter for cats

1. Instead of commercial cat litter, you can use sand, wood shavings or peat. Don't use sawdust. Watch your cat in case it develops an allergic reaction to one of these substitutes.
2. To deodorize any type of litter, mix one part bicarbonate of soda into three parts litter; cover the bottom of the litter pan with straight bicarbonate of soda.
3. Use cut-up plastic carrier bags as pan liners.
4. Better still, make a "pillowcase" for your litter pan: slip the whole pan into a heavy-duty refuse bag (or two thin ones – claws can punch tiny holes) before filling it with litter. When it's time to dispose of the contents, simply turn the bag inside out over the litter and lift it off.

Liver problems

The liver is the largest gland in your body, and is situated in the upper right part of your abdomen. Among its many functions – there are about 500 of them – the liver regulates the conversion and storage of foods and vitamins, controls some of the clotting mechanisms of the blood, and detoxifies the blood.

Hepatitis, or jaundice, a condition that may produce a yellowish discoloration of the skin and of the whites of the eyes, is caused by a group of viruses usually transmitted in food and drink. The most serious is hepatitis B, which is transmitted by sexual intercourse and blood and blood products. About 10 percent of hepatitis B cases are fatal, so you should consider immunization.

A blockage of the bile duct – usually by gallstones – causes obstructive hepatitis. Cirrhosis of the liver is the replacement of damaged liver cells by hard scar tissue, and is commonly caused by toxins, particularly alcohol. With any form of liver disorder, precise diagnosis can be established by blood tests.

Urine, faeces, saliva and blood of a patient infected with hepatitis should be considered infectious, and care should be taken handling them. Wash your hands thoroughly after physical contact with a patient.

If you suspect a liver problem, consult your doctor immediately. With any form of hepatitis, complete bed rest is essential, at least until the fever has subsided.

Your doctor will prescribe a course of treatment, which invariably will include the avoidance of certain foods and alcohol.

Locks

1. If your outside door has a window in or near it, install a double cylinder dead-bolt lock, which must be opened with a key from either side. That way, even if a burglar breaks the window, he won't be able to open the securely locked door.
2. Burglarproof your ground-floor windows by installing two or more strong bars across each one.
3. To prevent a sliding glass door from being opened, place a pipe or stick in the bottom track as shown.

To prevent anyone from lifting the door out of its track, set protruding screws in the top groove.

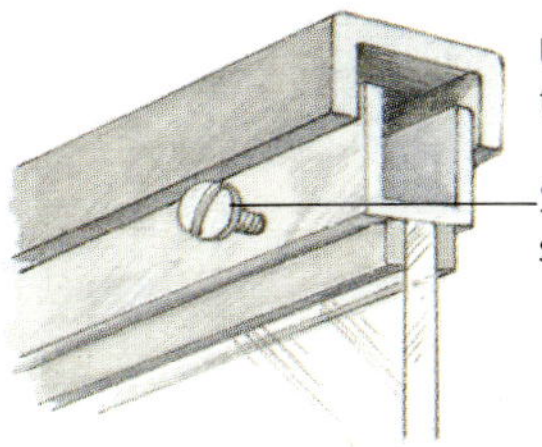

ON CARS

Don't try to force a car lock open – the key may break off. If a key won't turn in the lock at all, don't force it – try to manipulate it gently or wiggle it until it eventually turns.

Long-distance parents

Though you and your child may live far apart, whether because of divorce or some other cause, there are ways to ensure that the bond between you stays strong.

1. Regular telephone calls are a necessity, not a luxury. Phone every few days at least – often enough to know what tests are coming up in school and how your child does on them; to share her excitement over an upcoming birthday party or field trip and then get a full report after the fact; to discuss current films and TV shows. Prepare for each call: think about what was said the last time and have a list of fresh things to talk about. It's a good idea to phone at set times so that your child can be prepared, too.

2. If your child can read, send cards and newspaper or magazine clippings that amuse and provoke. These small gestures remind the child that she is in your thoughts.

3. Arrange for your child to visit you as often as possible. Then let her share your daily routine. Don't try to cram every minute with a special activity; having to keep up with an energetic father who tries too hard to entertain offspring can be hard work for a kid and is ultimately less satisfying to both of you than quiet time spent together.

4. Develop a set of rituals and routines that only the two of you share: reading favourite books at bedtime, eating at a neighbourhood restaurant, strolling in a nearby park, attending Sunday school.

5. Keep a "treasure box" for your child to open when you see her again: polished stones, stickers, souvenirs, photos and whatever small items she chooses to keep. Re-examining her treasures each time she visits will help give her a sense of continuity and make her feel all the more at home.

Lopsided house plants

All plants grow toward the light. To simplify the task of keeping them well rounded, place them on a lazy Susan, a revolving spice rack or a spinning barstool so they can be turned easily. **Caution:** Do not rotate a flowering plant that is about to bloom. The drastic change in light may cause the flower buds to drop.

Lost child

Getting lost is a part of nearly everyone's childhood. To keep it from becoming a real tragedy, prepare your children for the experience.

1. Teach them a family whistle, an easy-to-learn tune involving a phrase and a response. This can reduce panic and help you find each other in the aisles of a supermarket or in the bush.

2. Teach them how to use a public phone to make a reverse-charge call home. Have them practise.

3. Introduce them to a new environment (the shopping mall, the park) by showing how to get help. (Where's the policeman? The security guard? The nearest telephone?)

4. Make sure they always carry a copy of your address and phone number – both at home and at work. (See also *Runaways*, p.174.)

Lost in the outdoors

The first impulse of any lost person is to keep moving.

Wrong! The best strategy is usually to stay put and signal for help. Find a way to give three consecutive signals – shouts, whistle blasts or smoke columns, for example – to serve as an SOS. On a sunny day use a mirror to flash signals at low-flying planes; if you don't have a mirror, use a knife blade, a piece of glass or any reflective surface.

If you must find your way out of the woods, first sit down and get your bearings. Try to remember the last spot you knew where you were. Then try to recall landmarks, such as a distinctive rock or tree, between that spot and where you are now. Ask yourself: which way do the streams run? The roads? In which direction am I most likely to find help?

Choose a direction and stay on course by using a compass (p.54) or by walking from landmark to landmark. Within your line of sight, find two landmarks a good distance apart in the direction you wish to go. Before you reach the first, look for a third one that lies beyond the second.

As you set out, glance behind to establish the lie of the land in case you have to backtrack. If you stop to rest, sit or lie down facing the direction in which you are heading.

If you take a nap, scratch an arrow in the dirt to remind yourself of that direction when you wake up.

Lost luggage

Of the more than 480 million pieces of luggage handled by airlines annually, less than two percent are lost. But when you're looking for your luggage on an airport conveyer belt, this statistic is little consolation.

There is no way to guarantee that your luggage won't be lost or stolen, but there are ways to rig the odds in your favour – and to improve your chances of recovery.

1. Check in early; last-minute arrivals often mean lost luggage.

2. If you are making a connecting flight, try to use the same carrier. Choose a flight that allows adequate time for your luggage to be transferred. Consult the airline, your travel agent or the *World Airways Guide* for a minimum connecting time.

3. Use durable luggage with combination locks.

Standard suitcase locks are easily pried open. A combination lock is more secure.

4. Put your name, business address and business phone number inside and outside each bag. (A home address is an invitation to burglars.) Enclose a copy of your itinerary in each bag so that the airline will be able to locate you.

5. Remove tags from other flights.

6. Carry a list of each bag's contents. Keep all valuables, important documents, prescription medicine and eyeglasses in carry-on luggage.

7. Remember, most airlines pay only a nominal compensation based on the weight of your lost luggage. This is one of the main reasons luggage is weighed at the check-in counter.

8. If a bag doesn't show up, file a complaint at the airline counter immediately. If it isn't located within three days, chances are slim that it will ever turn up. Even so, keep all your documentation: it may take a while for you to be reimbursed.

Lost pets

1. Have your name, address and phone number engraved on a resilient tag and make sure that your pet wears it at all times. Alternatively, make an identity collar: write the information on a white elastic band with indelible ink, sew on a press stud, and fasten the band around the animal's neck.

If your pet always loses his identification tags, have an identification microchip inserted under the skin by a veterinarian. The Society for the Prevention of Cruelty to Animals (SPCA) keeps a complete computerised record of these microchips.

2. Always keep on hand a clear colour photograph of your pet and a list of its distinguishing markings.

3. If your pet is missing, search the neighbourhood, contact the Animal Welfare Society, SPCA, local police station and veterinarian. Put notices up in shops and check the lost-and-found columns of the newspaper. If your pet is a purebred, contact local pedigree clubs; they may have their own rescue committees.

4. If you find a pet with a licence tag, contact the local authority for the identification of the owner. Otherwise, call the local animal shelters and the police. Place a notice in the "found" section of the newspaper – most newspapers offer this as a free service to the public.

Low-fat diet

1. Buy minced beef labelled "extra lean". It has about half the fat of regular minced beef.

2. Avoid well-marbled beef. The lower grades tend to be less fatty, and the fat is more easily trimmed off.

3. Make soups and stews a day ahead so that you can extract the fat. After overnight refrigeration, it will have solidified on top.

4. The white meat of chicken has about half the fat of red meat.

5. Avoid products that list palm kernel oil or coconut oil as an ingredient. Both are high in saturated fat.

6. Skim milk has less than ¼ gram of fat per cup, while whole milk has more than eight grams. Skim milk is also lower in fat than one percent and two percent low-fat milk.

7. Instead of sautéing onions in butter or oil, poach them in a little chicken stock or beef stock before adding to a dish. (See also *Cholesterol*, p.46; *The balanced diet*, p.254.)

Low-sodium diet

1. The salt in ham and other cured meats can push your sodium consumption way above the daily recommended level of one to three grams (about 1½ teaspoons), so avoid the delicatessen counter.

2. Beware of canned or dehydrated soups, almost all of which are sky-high in sodium. Instead, make your own stock and freeze it for use in soups. A few cups boiled down to a glaze make handy stock cubes when frozen in an ice-cube tray.

3. Substitute lemon juice, vinegar, wine, herbs and spices for salt (dried dill, especially, has a vaguely "salty" flavour). Experiment with your own herbal blends in the kitchen as well as at the table. Throw out salt-cellars and use pepper mills to grind whole mustard seeds or black peppercorns over soups and salads. (See also *Salt substitutes*, p.177.)

Lubricating oil

1. Out of oil? Try liquid paraffin – but not in your car's engine. Cooking oils may also do for short-term projects but soon turn rancid.

2. For lubricating parts underwater – in a toilet tank perhaps – Vaseline is long-lasting.

3. To remove rust or corrosion, use vinegar, lemon juice or pepper sauce instead of penetrating oil.

M

Magazine subscriptions

1. Before you subscribe to a magazine, make sure that your letterbox is big enough to hold the magazine. It should also be securely locked and you should not be able to pull the magazine out of the letter slot.

2. If you're moving, notify every magazine you subscribe to at least four weeks in advance. Use the change-of-address form in the publication or send the address label from a recent issue and your new address.

3. If you're going away on holiday, ask a neighbour to clear your postbox every second day. This will prevent magazines from becoming damaged by overcrowding in your postbox.

Magic tricks

It may be true that the pen is mightier than the sword, but that other old saying, that the hand is faster than the eye, is certainly not true. In fact, when you're practising magic, don't even try to fool your audience by sharp, sudden movements.

The real art is misdirection – get your audience's attention fixed on some stage prop, your face or what you're saying, on anything, in fact, except the hand that's actually performing the 'magic'.

If you want them to look at something, look at it yourself. It follows, then, that you mustn't look at your hands, especially that 'magic' hand.

Learn one trick at a time and practise it, and your line of patter, in front of a mirror until you feel you could carry out the complicated movements blindfolded, but still absolutely smoothly and naturally.

Learning basic coin-palming is a good start for any sorcerer's apprentice. Here's a trick to practise:

Take a 50-cent coin between the thumb, and the index finger and middle finger of one hand. Now make as though you're going to take the coin with your other hand but, as this hand passes over the coin, push it deeper into the hand that's already holding it.

Now try to hold the coin in the palm of your hand, with the fleshy part of the ball of your thumb holding it up against the loose skin towards the edge of your palm. Relax the hand muscles to keep the coin in place and, later, you can mysteriously produce it by retrieving it with the first two fingers of the hiding hand.

You can time the moment of the coin's return to make it look as though you've produced it from almost anywhere in the room.

Magnifying glass

1. Turn a rounded wine glass or goblet on its side and hold it over the material you want to enlarge. Rotate the glass slightly to bring things sharply into focus.

2. Poke a small hole in a piece of paper and bring it up to your eye; things will appear larger. (See also *Binoculars*, p.21.)

Mailing

1. When mailing express, ask how much sooner the item will arrive compared with ordinary mail. You may find that the expense is not worthwhile. Priority mail is more expensive but an urgent letter will be delivered within 24 hours.

2. If you send post overseas at Christmas, remember that surface mail normally takes six to eight weeks – even longer over the Christmas period. Start checking overseas mailing dates with your local post office from about August or September.

3. Before you go on holiday, type addresses for postcards on gummed labels. You'll be more likely to send the promised cards.

4. A cigar box is perfect for mailing small items. You can also use an empty shoebox. (See also *Postal service substitutes*, p.161.)

Mail-order buying

The sale and purchase of items through the post is gaining popularity in South Africa and many other Western countries. Mail order is a quick, convenient way of buying a wide spectrum of consumer goods, without the hassle of driving to the store, queuing up at store counters and using precious time when it is in short supply. Before you buy on mail order, however, consider these points:

1. Check that the company through which you are purchasing a product is a member of the Southern African Direct Marketing Association. If you are in doubt, contact the association at PO Box 85370, Emmarentia 2029.

2. Deal only with companies which name a street address at which the goods may be viewed in their advertisement. Try not to buy from a mail order company which lists only a post office box number.

3. To protect yourself in case of disagreements, keep a copy of your order, noting the date it was placed and the name of the company representative. Also be sure to keep copies of the original advertisement, any cancelled cheques or credit slips and all correspondence you enter into.

4. When you return goods, be sure to address the return package correctly, and send it registered mail from the post office.

5. If you are not satisfied with the product, your first step is to complain to the company. If you are still not satisfied, there are a number of other options. You may try approaching the Southern African Direct Marketing Association, the advertising manager of the publication which carried the advertisement, the Advertising Standards Authority or the local branch of your Consumer Council.

Male menopause

Men don't really go through menopause, of course (p.134). But many experience some kind of psychological crisis in their 40's or 50's. The urgent awareness that there are goals yet to be reached and pleasures yet to be enjoyed – and that time will, indeed, run out – can lead to anxiety, depression, self-doubt and marital discord – even divorce.

If you're experiencing such feelings, remember that they are perfectly normal and that they, too, shall pass. Here, nevertheless, are a few tips to help you get through:

1. Don't become a cliché. The trappings of youth don't make you look younger, just faintly ridiculous.

2. Don't leave your wife for a younger woman. It's usually a mistake, and it's not really dealing with the cause of your unhappiness.

3. Don't worry about sex. You may not be 17 anymore (and aren't you glad?), but your body still works; problems in the bedroom are often the result of worrying about them. Consult your doctor to be safe.

4. If you hate your job, don't just sit around complaining. Either quit or don't – then get on with your life (see *Career changes*, p.37).

5. Get involved in voluntary work. Find out how you can teach reading to underprivileged people or perhaps read to a blind person. For a real change join an organization that provides the possibility of new adventures – a mountaineering or skydiving club or an informal hiking group.

6. Can a therapist help? Make an appointment with one and see.

7. Jog, walk or join a gym so that you get at least 30 minutes of heart-pumping exercise at least three times a week (with your doctor's permission, of course). You'll look better, feel better, and probably add years to your life in the bargain.

Marking gauge

Make your own marking gauge from a wooden ruler and a pair of locking-grip pliers.

Insert a small wood screw through the 2,5-centimetre mark on the ruler. Then, if you want to mark a parallel line eight centimetres from the edge of your work, for example, set the pliers at the 10-centimetre line. Hold

the nose of the pliers against the edge of the work with one hand; hold the end of the yardstick with the other. Keeping the yardstick square with the edge, pull it evenly toward you across the work surface, so that the screw scratches a line.

Marshmallows

1. To freshen stale marshmallows, seal them in an airtight tin or plastic bag with a slice of fresh bread for two or three days.

2. If a recipe calls for marshmallows by weight, use this guide: 16 large marshmallows or one cup melted marshmallows equals 125 grams.

3. Marshmallows are easier to cut with scissors than with a knife. Dip the scissors repeatedly in hot water so they don't gum up.

Matches

1. Starting a fire without matches is hard work, so carry reserves. If you must do so, however, first gather some dry tinder, such as dried leaves, twigs, pine cones, fluff from clothing, bits of rope end and pieces of rotten logs. Form the tinder into a nest, and shelter it from wind and moisture. Hold the flint edge of a waterproof matchbox or a dry hard stone as close to the tinder as possible. Strike it downward with the back of a knife blade or a small piece of steel to send sparks into the centre of the tinder.

Fan the smouldering tinder into a flame; add fuel gradually, starting with small, dry twigs.

2. On a sunny day use a magnifying glass, a camera or binocular lens or a pair of strong reading glasses to focus the sun's rays on the tinder.

3. When lighting a fire in windy or rainy weather, use a candle stub to conserve matches.

4. To waterproof "strike anywhere" kitchen matches, dip them in melted candle wax or paraffin.

5. To dry matches quickly, pull them through your hair.

6. If you're short of paper matches, you can double your supply. Insert the point of a sharp knife in the base of each match and slowly pull the halves apart.

Maths in your head

1. A quick way to do calculations is to drop the 0's at the ends of numbers, then replace them for your final answer. For example, to add 120 and 90, get the sum of 12 and nine and then add one 0.

2. Similarly, to break down complex problems, start with the big numbers. To multiply six times 348, for example, first multiply six times 300 (1,800), then six times 40 (240). Add the two to get 2,040 and tack on the result of six times eight (48) for a final total of 2,088.

3. Change kilometres to miles by dropping the last digit and multiplying by six: thus, 72 kilometres is approximately 42 miles.

4. Want an easy way to multiply by nine? Assign each finger a number, beginning with the little finger of your left hand (one) and ending with the right pinkie (10). Then, to multiply three times nine, for example, turn down the number three finger, making a space on your left hand. Count the fingers to the left of the space (two); then count the fingers to the right (seven). The answer: 27. (See also *Computations*, p.54.)

Mattresses

1. To keep a mattress from sliding around on its base, put a non-slip rug pad between the two.

2. To even out the wear, flip a new mattress over and reverse it end to end every three weeks for three months – then regularly every couple of months thereafter.

3. Don't use the handles on the mattress to lift it. They're not designed to take the full weight. You should use them only to move the mattress around while it's on the base.

4. Air a mattress in the sun occasionally for a fresh, clean odour.

Mayonnaise

1. To rescue mayonnaise which has begun to curdle, beat rapidly. If this fails, add a few drops of water and beat again.

2. Badly curdled mayonnaise can be reconstituted – beat an egg yolk until it is thick, then beat in a few drops of oil. Gradually add the mayonnaise to this mixture, beating continuously.

3. Mayonnaise stains are tricky as they contain both egg and oil. Sponge small stains with lukewarm water then wash. Sprinkle bicarbonate of soda on large stains. When the fizzing has stopped, rinse and dry. Finally wash as usual. The oil stain on non-washable fabric may have to be removed with carbon tetrachloride or stain remover.

Measuring

1. If there's no one to help you measure a long stretch with a tape measure, secure the end of the tape with masking tape or anchor it with a brick or a heavy wood block.

2. To find the circumference of a round object when you don't have a flexible tape measure, try this simple trick: cut a strip of paper and wrap it around the object. Mark the spot where the end of the paper overlaps itself. Then lay the strip out flat and measure it with a ruler.

3. To lay out an exact 90° angle, use the 3-4-5 ratio. From a common point, stretch out two long strings perpendicular to each other. Mark one string at three metres from the common point and the other at four metres. Stretch a tape measure from the three-metre mark on one string to the four-metre mark on the other and adjust the strings until the distance between the two marks is exactly five metres. The angle between the two strings will be 90°. (This method works for any unit of length and for any variation of a 3-4-5 ratio.)

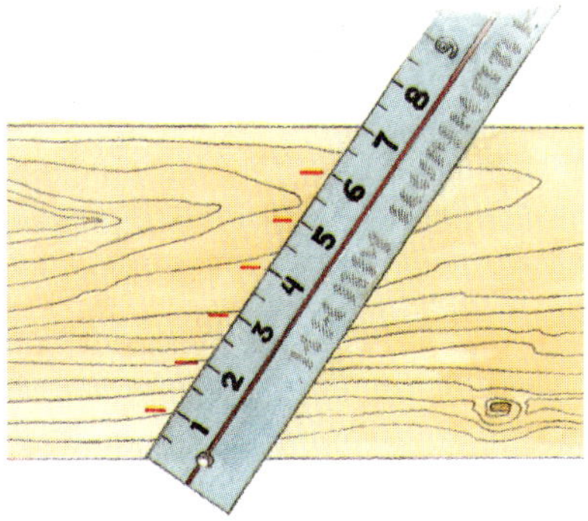

4. Here's how to divide a board into equal parts lengthwise. Lay a ruler diagonally across the width of the board so that the beginning (0) is at the left edge. Then adjust the other end of the ruler until the right edge of the board aligns with the number of parts desired. Mark off each of the centimetre graduations.

5. For fast, approximate measuring, use your own body. If you're of average size, the first joint of your index finger is about 25 millimetres long, your fist is about 100 millimetres wide, and the span from the tip of the thumb to the tip of the pinkie on your outstretched hand is about 275 millimetres. Your shoe is about 300 millimetres long.

Measuring cup

1. No measuring cup? A plastic medicine spoon which is supplied by pharmacies holds five millilitres or one teaspoon. Three spoonfuls is the equivalent of 1 tablespoon.

2. If you want to measure liquids, look around the kitchen for any containers marked in millilitres – for example, fruit juice boxes and milk cartons contain one litre or five cups.

3. A 410-gram can holds two cups.

4. A standard-size herb or spice bottle will hold 125 millilitres or ½ cup of liquid.

Meat mincer

1. Clear clogged holes in a meat mincer by rapping the mincer plate several times against the edge of the kitchen counter.

2. If your mincer is dirty or extra greasy, run a piece of bread through it, then wash it.

Medication schedule

1. Make up a week-by-week chart: write the days of the week down the short side of a large piece of paper, the hours of the day across the long side; fill in the dosages in the appropriate hours. Hang the chart near or inside your medicine cabinet and check off each marked box right after you take the medication.

2. Label the compartments of an ice-cube tray for all your waking hours. Each morning place pills or small slips of paper (representing liquid medicines) in their appropriate compartments. Discard the slips after taking the medicine.

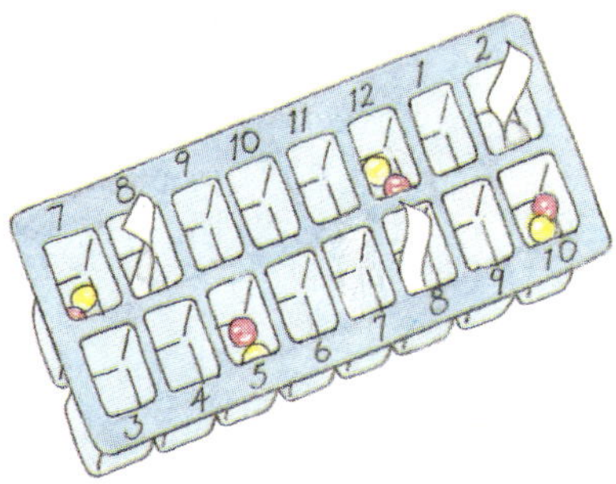

3. Wear a digital watch set to beep every hour. Carry your medications and schedule with you. When the beeper sounds, check your schedule and take your medicine.

4. To prevent confusion, write the name of each medication in bold letters on a label that will fit on the container. If it's possible, colour-coordinate the labels on your morning, afternoon and evening medicines.

Meetings

1. When it comes to meetings, keep in mind that less is more. Any meeting will be shorter and more productive if you invite only those people who are directly involved in the matters under discussion.

2. Whenever possible, schedule a meeting in the morning, when people are more alert. But avoid "first thing in the morning" sessions. The day before or after a weekend or holiday is also a bad time.

3. A few days before the meeting, put your agenda in writing and distribute it to all participants. Tell them how much time will be devoted to each topic, and allow extra time at the end just in case some topics run over the allotted time.

4. To stay on schedule, refer to the agenda as the meeting progresses. If someone gets long-winded, wait until he takes a breath and say, "I'm afraid we've run out of time on this topic, so let's summarize".

5. To keep participants on their toes, ask each one to give a brief presentation on their particular task.

6. To draw out a creative but shy person, tell her in advance that you'd like her ideas on a particular topic, then call on her. Or go around the table, asking each person in turn for a comment.

Memory

1. To remember the name of a person you've just been introduced to, first make sure that you've heard it properly. (Ask to have it repeated or spelled if you're not sure you understand.) Then call the person by name in your conversation and again when you say good-bye.

2. If you find it hard to keep the names of your friends' children straight, jot them down next to the friends' names in your address book. Do the same with business contacts you don't deal with often.

3. Establish a place for putting such easily misplaced items as gloves and keys. Much of what people think is bad memory is just bad organization.

4. Keep a pad and pencil handy near your telephone and in your handbag, pocket and car. If you write something down, you won't have to worry about remembering it. Make a habit of going over your list at a set time every day – say, right after breakfast.

5. Don't be afraid to talk to yourself. If the telephone rings while you're on your way out, put your car keys down and say out loud. "OK, keys, I'm putting you on the kitchen table." It might sound silly, but it will also help fix their location in your mind.

6. Use the same technique if you have medicine to take daily. Before you swallow your pill, say out loud. "I'm taking my pill now," and you won't wonder in an hour whether you've taken it or not. Or establish a signal to yourself; move a straight pin from your left lapel to your right, shift your watch from one wrist to the other, or transfer a specific object from pocket to pocket.

7. Give your lazy memory a regular workout by playing the type of quiz games that demand quick recall, or else try a card game (such as bridge) that requires carefully keeping track of the cards played.

8. To remember the main topics of a talk you're to give, associate each one with a room in your house. As you give your talk, picture yourself moving from one room to the next.

DID YOU KNOW . . . ?

Develop that memory!

'I've gone BLONC,' murmured the boy whose teacher asked him the names of the bastions of the old Castle at Cape Town. BLONC? He wasn't suffering a lapse of memory, but was using a clever mnemonic device to aid his memory. His response contains the first letter of each of the Castle's bastions – Buuren, Leerdam, Oranje, Nassau and Catsenellenbogen.

To remember the Great Lakes of North America, try HOMES – the lakes' (Huron, Ontario, Michigan, Erie, Superior) initials are all there. Want a quick way to recall the planets in order, from the sun? Take the first letter of every word in the following sentence: My Very Educated Mother Just Served Us Nine Pickles.

Mnemonics can be more than just a game. You can use them to help your own memory. Make up a sentence using the first letters of all the items on your shopping list for example: Eagles Become Panicky Before Showers for a list of eggs, bread, peanut butter and sugar. Or for errands at the cleaners, the market, the post office and the garage, try Clever Mothers Prepare Orange Gravy.

And how can you remember how to pronounce mnemonics in future? It's easy – just use the mnemonic "Drop the M".

Memory loss

Although older people are often forgetful, ageing itself is not the cause. Memory can be affected by medications, illness, alcohol, depression, stress or isolation. If you or an older relative becomes increasingly forgetful, visit a doctor to see if there is a physical cause and whether or not it can be remedied.

You can make life easier for someone whose memory is failing by organizing the household:

1. Label cabinet doors and drawer fronts with lists of their contents.

2. Paint hot water taps with bright red nail polish.

3. Hang a large-type list of emergency numbers by the phone. Or buy a phone with a memory.

4. Place an oversize hook next to the door for keys.

5. Put up a big wall calendar and mark it clearly with reminders of important dates.

6. Talk over upcoming events just before they occur.

Menopause

For most women the "change of life" is a brief, relatively painless event. Some, however, endure several years of hot and cold flushes, a degree of emotional upheaval and even occasional mental confusion.

If you're having such difficulties, be honest with your family and friends.

Tell them what you're experiencing; they can't be supportive if they don't understand the problem. It might be especially helpful to discuss what you're feeling with an older woman.
1. Stay cool during hot flushes – switch off the heater and wear easy-to-remove layers of loose, comfortable cotton clothing.
2. For nighttime hot flushes, buy absorbent, soft cotton sheets and nightclothes. Keep a spare nightgown and a thermos of ice water at the ready on the bedside table.
3. Keep two athlete's cold packs in the freezer; hold them against your cheeks when a hot flush begins.
4. Continue or, after checking with a doctor, start regular aerobic and relaxation exercises.
5. Ask your doctor about hormone replacement therapy. (See also *Osteoporosis*, p.146.)

Menstrual cramps

1. At the first sign of cramps, start taking ibuprofen or aspirin. (Some women tend to get prompt relief with ibuprofen; others may find that they must take it for at least four to five days before they feel relief.)
2. Instead of going to bed when you feel the pain, get some exercise – take a walk, ride a bicycle or do a few minutes of yoga.
3. Give yourself a heat treatment: a warm bath or a hot-water bottle on your lower back or your abdomen.
4. Some women get relief by taking B complex vitamins, vitamins C and E, zinc, calcium and magnesium. Check with your doctor.
5. Get a soothing lower-back massage. Or ask a friend or relative to apply acupressure: rub the mid-back, one centimetre to the right of the spine, for three to four minutes. (You may get three to six hours of relief.) If you're alone, press on a point two thumb widths above the wrist joint on your inner arm, in line with your middle finger.
6. Eat a healthy, low-fat, low-salt, high-carbohydrate diet with plenty of fibre. (See also *PMT* p.159.)

Mice

1. If you have a mouse problem, move objects around periodically to disorient the creatures; they're easier to trap as they move about investigating the rearrangement.
2. If you use standard snap traps, don't fall for the old cartoon cliché of baiting them with cheese. Use bits of peanut butter, oatmeal or cooked bacon instead; mice seem particularly fond of them.
3. To catch a mouse alive, try this trick: when you see the creature running around a room, open a black umbrella and hold it on the floor at an angle that allows the mouse to run in (it helps if someone else can chase the mouse). Your prey, drawn to dark places, will probably head straight for the umbrella. Then quickly close it, go outside, and set your prisoner free.

Microwave ovens

1. Find the hot and cold spots by spreading a layer of trimmed white bread slices edge to edge over the microwave floor. Set on *High*, and watch the browning process through the glass door.
2. To test whether a dish is microwave safe, place it in the oven next to a glass measuring cup of water; turn on *High* for one minute. If the water is warm, you know the oven is working. If the dish is cool, it's OK to use; if it's hot, don't even consider using it for cooking in the microwave.
3. To get full cooking power, wipe out the oven after each use – especially around the door seal – using a mild detergent or bicarbonate of soda solution. Soften stubborn dirt with steam by boiling a cup of water in the oven; then clean with a plastic (not steel wool) scrubbing pad.
4. To give microwaved meat an appetizing browned look, brush it first with soya sauce mixed with a little water (use a pastry brush).
5. To get rid of lingering food odours or a stale smell, place a thick slice of lemon on a paper towel and microwave it on *High* for one to one and a half minutes; let stand overnight.
6. If greasy residue or food inside the oven catches fire, keep the door closed, turn off the oven, and disconnect the cord at the plug or shut off the power (p.162).
7. If you're worried about high electricity costs, economize by preheating food in a microwave on *High* before completing the cooking in a regular electric or gas oven.

Migraine

The warning: flashes of light, dizziness and nausea. The affliction: an intense, throbbing pain on one side of your head.
1. If you sense the warning stage, take your medication and drink a cup of hot coffee (not decaffeinated).
2. Immediately pain strikes, pour cold water over your head, take a cold shower, or use an ice or cold pack.
3. Lie down in a dark, quiet place and imagine a beautiful scene. Listen to soothing music. (To develop a "relaxation response," try to do this exercise for 30 minutes twice a week for five weeks.)
4. Give yourself (or ask someone to give you) a gentle scalp, neck and shoulder massage.

PREVENTION
1. Try to discover and eliminate the cause of your migraines by keeping a diary (see *Headaches*, p.105). Common culprits are red wine, hot dogs, bacon, pork, salami, monosodium glutamate, yeast, chocolate, mature cheese and cigarettes.

2. Maintain a routine: try to wake up at the same time each day, eat regular meals, and exercise daily.
3. Wear sunglasses in the sun and avoid looking directly at bright lights. (See also *Pain relief*, p.149.)

Mildew

To prevent mildew, keep things clean and dry.

BATHROOMS

1. Use an old toothbrush to scrub the mildew from grout. For stubborn stains, cover with a paste of scouring powder that contains bleach and let stand for several hours; scrub and rinse off.
2. After using the shower, keep the shower door or curtain open while you wipe down the walls and let them air-dry. Then close the curtain or door so that it, too, can dry.
3. To effectively clean a fibreglass shower cubicle, gently scour the walls with bicarbonate of soda on a damp sponge, then rinse and dry.
4. Got a mildewed shower curtain (p.185)? Just soak it in the bathtub in water softener.

BOOKS

1. Put a piece of charcoal in a closed bookcase to absorb moisture.
2. For damp pages, sprinkle cornflour throughout the book; brush it off several hours later, after the moisture has been absorbed. If the pages are mildewed, brush the cornflour off outdoors to keep mildew spores out of the house.

BASEMENTS

Check the drainage around the outside of the house and seal up all cracks so that moisture can't get in.

CLOTHES

To remove mildew from a washable fabric, wet the area and rub it with detergent. Wash in the hottest water recommended for the fabric, using chlorine bleach if the fabric will tolerate it. If not, soak in a non-chlorine bleach solution, then wash.

CUPBOARDS

1. To increase air circulation, keep the door ajar. Consider replacing a solid door with a louvred one.
2. Keep items susceptible to mildew, such as shoes and luggage, on wire racks or perforated shelves so that air can circulate around them.

MATTRESSES

1. If possible, take a mattress outside and brush off the mildew; if not, vacuum it and throw away the bag. Lay the mattress in the sun for several hours until thoroughly dry; if drying indoors, use a fan.
2. Platform beds are often affected by mildew. Buy one with slats, or drill a few holes in the platform for air circulation.

REFRIGERATORS

1. Wipe interior walls regularly with bicarbonate of soda.
2. If your refrigerator has a pan underneath, make sure that you clean it regularly and sprinkle some bicarbonate of soda inside.

Milk

1. If you're out of milk and need some for baking, try using the same amount of fruit juice. It works surprisingly well for many quick breads and butter cakes. Or use buttermilk (add half a teaspoon bicarbonate of soda per cup). If you prefer to use skim milk, add two teaspoons of sunflower oil per cup.
2. Milk in paper cartons picks up refrigerator odours. Close the carton flaps with a clothes peg – the spring type works best.
3. If milk starts to go sour, salvage it for use in cake batter, pancake batter or biscuit dough; just add half a teaspoon bicarbonate of soda to the dry ingredients. Sour milk also makes a good substitute for buttermilk.

Mirrors

1. Never spray cleanser directly on a mirror – the drips could seep onto the silver backing and damage it. Instead, spray it on a clean soft cloth or paper towel and wipe the mirror.
2. Make your own cleanser. Fill a spray bottle with water and a little vinegar, methylated spirits or ammonia. Avoid strong ammonia solutions and abrasives.
3. To hide a scratch in the silver backing of a mirror, cover the spot with a piece of aluminium foil, shiny side forward. Paint with clear shellac and let dry.

DID YOU KNOW . . . ?

The mystique of mirrors

The reflected image – it entranced Narcissus in a pool of still water, and it has lost none of its fascination since. But mirrors serve more than vanity. They've inspired superstition and ingenuity throughout history.

☐ Ancient Egyptians were using mirrors around 3,000 BC. These small, hand-held mirrors were made of polished gold, silver or bronze.

☐ The Chinese hung mirrors on their front doors so that evil spirits, seeing their horrid reflections, would be frightened away.

☐ The Greek mathematician Archimedes used huge mirrors to save his native city of Syracuse. They reflected the sun onto an attacking fleet of Roman ships, which burned in the intense heat.

☐ In wealthy Venetian homes during the 16th century, homeowners encouraged servants to be careful by telling them that breaking a mirror would result in seven years bad luck – and they had the power to make the curse come true.

☐ Silver is used in mirrors because it reflects about 95 percent of the light that falls on it. Also, its neutral colour accurately reflects skin tones and make-up hues.

☐ A special mirror, patented in America in 1974, has an adjustable lower half that permits the viewer to appear as slim as he wishes.

Moles

1. Discourage these little diggers by burying bottles up to their necks in the earth – moles dislike the sound of the wind whistling across the protruding bottlenecks.
2. Repel moles by dropping such noxious items as dog waste or rags soaked in olive oil or creosote into their tunnels. They hate it.
3. Moles can damage roots as they tunnel through the garden. Worse still, mice use their tunnels to gain access to tender bulbs and root vegetables. Protect plants by lining planting holes with shade-cloth.

Moonlighting

Need a second job to make ends meet? You'll have more zest for moonlighting if your part-time job is built on hobbies or interests you already enjoy.

Try to find work you can do in your own time, perhaps even at home. There are some enjoyable possibilities: selling, writing, fund-raising or conducting surveys over the phone; babysitting; selling cosmetics or home products; tutoring or giving lessons; teaching a course at a technikon or trade school; selling property; proofreading; word processing on your home computer; bookkeeping for a local company; boarding or grooming pets; growing plants; running a bed-and-breakfast inn.

Check with your employer first. If there's no conflict of interest, you're not legally or ethically obliged to tell your boss about your outside activities – but he'll probably appreciate your honesty. And some firms forbid employees to freelance, particularly for competitors.

Mops & brooms

1. Always clean a dry dust mop before you store it. To avoid making a dust cloud, put a damp paper bag over the head of the mop before shaking it. Wash a very dirty mop in soapy water and rinse. Or, if the head is removable, put it in a mesh bag and toss it into the washing machine. Hang to dry in an airy place.
2. Rinse and squeeze a wet mop after each use. Store with the head up; a string mop can be hung head down if its strings are well off the floor. Keep the door to the storage cupboard open slightly until the mop is dry. For best results, hang a sponge mop outside in the shade to dry, a cotton string one in the sun.
3. Never store a wet mop in a bucket; it may go sour or mouldy. If this happens to a cotton string mop, soak it for a few minutes in a weak bleach solution (half a cup chlorine bleach in four and a half litres of water). Rinse several times and let dry.
4. Trim a cotton mop occasionally with a pair of strong scissors.
5. When you store a broom, hang it so that there's no pressure on the bristles. You don't need a special broom and mop holder; just attach screw eyes to the tops of the handles.
6. To prevent a floor mop or broom handle from marring furniture as you clean under it, wrap the lower part of the handle with velvet ribbon.
7. To neaten an old, frayed broom, soak the bristles in warm water for a few minutes, then wrap several heavy rubber bands around them until the broom is dry.

Mortar repairs

1. To prevent mortar from crumbling, brush on a masonry sealer. It will repel water, which damages mortar by freezing and expanding.
2. If patches of mortar need re-pointing and you can't find a mason willing to do such a small job for a reasonable price, try this. Wait until you see a new building going up in the neighbourhood and ask one of the masons if he'd like to earn a few extra rands during his lunch hour.
3. Mortar becomes unworkable after an hour. Mix an amount which can be used up in that time. For small jobs, use a proprietary mortar mix to which you simply add water.

Mortgage bond default

You've always paid your mortgage bond on time but suddenly you can't – perhaps you've fallen ill or lost your job. Tell your lender the situation; you may be allowed to make interest-only repayments for a specified period, though you will have to make increased payments as soon as you can to clear the arrears which have built up. Each case is assessed on its merits and if your payments have been irregular, you may have a problem.

If your mortgage is foreclosed, your house will be sold by auction (probably to the lender) for the amount outstanding on the mortgage plus any incurred costs. You'll get nothing.

The prudent thing to do, therefore, if foreclosure is a real threat, is to sell your house, pay off the lender, and put the leftover cash in an interest-bearing account.

Mosquitoes

1. Check all such innocent indoor breeding places as flower vases; change the water daily. And don't forget the catch pan under the refrigerator in the kitchen.

2. Clear blocked drains and areas of standing water outside. Keep fish in your pond.
3. If you're camping in an area where mosquitoes are pests, use mosquito nets. Check that the net is tucked in all around and has no holes. For additional protection, impregnate the net with permethrin (0,2 gram per square metre every six months).
4. Expose as little skin as possible, wear long-sleeved shirts and long trousers with socks and shoes.
5. Use a suitable insect repellent on the skin. A number of products are available in neighbourhood supermarkets and pharmacies.
6. Relieve the itchiness of a mosquito bite by dabbing on calamine or antihistamine lotion or taking antihistamine tablets.
7. In parts of Asia, South and Central America and southern Africa (including parts of the Transvaal and Natal), a mosquito bite can result in malaria. If you intend to visit a malaria-infested area, consult your doctor, who will prescribe antimalarial drugs. Follow the instructions for the antimalarial drugs strictly. The course of tablets must be started one week before you leave, so see your doctor well before your trip. The course must also be continued for four weeks after your return.
8. Since mosquitoes in some areas have become resistant to the normally prescribed antimalarial drug (chloroquine), be specific about the areas you intend to visit. Contact the Department of Health Services and Welfare for additional advice.

Mothball odour

1. Hang clothes outdoors on a windy day. To prevent a garment from blowing away, place it on two hangers with the hooks facing in opposite directions; secure with clothes pegs.
2. Let the clothes air for a few hours, then tumble them in a warm dryer.
3. Keep sachets or empty perfume bottles in drawers or cupboards.
4. Hang a pomander or herbal potpourri in the cupboard. For a simple and cheap remedy, string six bay leaves together and hang in your storage area.

Mothball substitutes

Use cheesecloth bags, clean baby booties or pantihose to make moth-repellent sachets. Fill with any combination of the following items: dried lavender, aromatic pipe tobacco, whole peppercorns, or a mix of equal parts dried mint and rosemary.

Moustaches & beards

1. To help you decide which style of moustache or beard suits your face, have an ordinary black-and-white portrait taken, get several large prints, and draw various styles of facial hair with a felt-tip marker. Be aware, however, that nature will also have a say – your whiskers will grow the way they want to, so make the most of your own attributes.
2. Since wet hair stretches, always trim your moustache when it's dry.
3. To give your moustache a nice flat appearance, cut the top hairs shorter than those at the bottom.
4. To shape your moustache more easily, apply moustache wax or a little hair-styling mousse.
5. Remove after-meal crumbs from your moustache with a toothbrush. A firm-bristled toothbrush also works well for grooming beards.

Mouth ulcers

1. To lessen the irritation, try to avoid citrus fruits, nuts, chocolate, spicy foods and very hot foods.
2. To kill the bacteria that make the sore more painful and long-lasting, rinse with a mouthwash, hydrogen peroxide (diluted up to half-and-half with water) or aloe gel (from the centre of a fresh aloe leaf).
3. To counteract the acid environment in which the bacteria thrive, rinse with milk of magnesia or a solution of bicarbonate of soda and water.
Caution: Do not swallow any of the above solutions.

Moving heavy objects

The key to moving something heavy by yourself is to use more brain than brawn. First make sure the item – including any protruding parts – will fit through openings and around corners. Then give careful thought to how you can do the job with the least strain. Once you decide on a strategy, be patient; going slowly may take time, but it may also prevent injury. If necessary, get help. Here are some useful tips:
1. In general, pushing is easier and more effective than pulling.
2. Make a big box lighter by removing all or some of its contents.
3. If you are throwing the object out or if you can reassemble it, take it apart and move it piece by piece.
4. When pushing something across the floor, put newspapers, blankets or cardboard under it. You'll protect the floor from scratches, and the thing will slide more easily.
5. To move a large object, such as a refrigerator, get behind it, lean it toward you, and walk it slowly from side to side.
6. To carry a box on your back, wrap a strap around it; a belt, beach towel or blanket will do. Or make a loop of strong rope; put one length around the box and hook the other around one bottom corner so that it passes under the box. Put your hands in the free ends of the loop.
7. If you often have to move heavy objects around, invest in a pallet truck. It will save you time and effort.

STAIRS

1. To get an object down a flight of stairs, use two boards as a ramp; slowly slide the object down the boards as you back between them.
2. Or lay the burden on a quilt or heavy blanket; control the descent with your shoulder as you back down, lifting the leading edge of the "skid" slightly with both hands.
3. If circumstances permit, slide the object down the banister. Place it gently on a blanket to avoid scratching the woodwork.

DOLLIES

1. To get a dolly under a heavy object by yourself, put the dolly against the wall, then walk or slide the object to it; the wall will keep the dolly from scooting away.

2. Improvise a dolly with a shopping trolley, a child's cart, a skateboard or roller skates.

3. Instead of a proper dolly, use pipes, poles or unopened tin cans. As those in the rear become free, move them to the front.

FURNITURE

1. To move a couch or anything else with legs, lay it on its back or side and slide it.

2. Take the drawers out of a desk or dresser to lighten the load.

3. To move a bulky chair, put the seat on your head and stand upright with the back on your back.

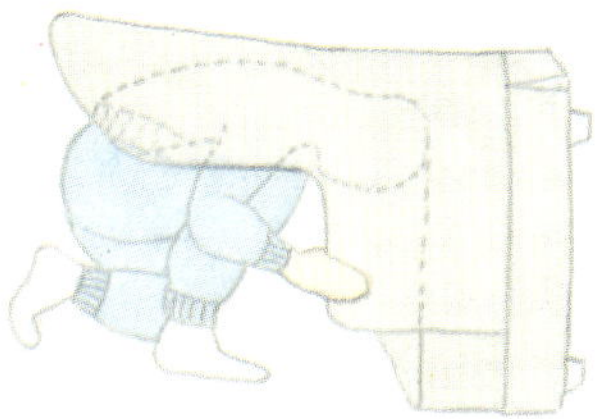

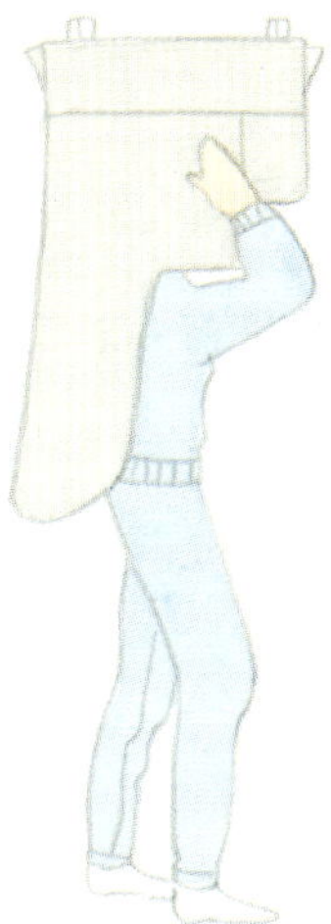

Mugging

1. If you think you're about to be mugged, stay calm and consider your options: acquiescence, stalling for time, talking your way out, screaming "help", or, ultimately, resisting.

2. If resistance appears to be your only choice, don't be squeamish about it – hurt your attacker any way that you can. Kick the groin or the instep; scratch at the eyes (a handful of keys or the teeth of a comb can do a lot of damage); bite; or go for the hands (the thumb and the pinkie are especially vulnerable). But don't get too involved in the battle; all you want is a chance to get away.

PREVENTION

1. If you live in a block of flats, put just your first initial and surname on the postbox or door buzzer (if your apartment block has them); if you live alone, add a fictitious roommate's name. If a threatening stranger follows you into the foyer, push all the buzzers to summon neighbours.

2. Never get into a lift with someone who looks suspicious. Stand next to the control panel. If you are unhappy with a person who gets into the lift, push the open door button and get out immediately or at the next floor.

3. Lock all the windows and entry doors. Install a peephole (p.152). Ask any meter readers and repairmen for identification before letting them in; if you still have any doubt, phone their place of business to double-check their identity.

4. Travel with a companion and steer clear of dark, empty buildings, poorly lit streets, dangerous neighbourhoods and lonely areas.

5. Walk confidently at a steady pace, close to the edge of the pavement and facing traffic. If you think someone is following you, cross the street. If the suspicious person does the same, walk quickly to a busy, well-lit area or go to an occupied house or shop and phone the police. As a last resort, throw a rock through a shop window to set off its burglar alarm.

6. Drive with your all your car doors locked and windows closed. Keep your handbag out of sight.

7. Park in a well-lighted area; look around before getting out and check inside the car before getting in. (See also *Rape*, p.170.) Lock all doors and windows immediately.

Mulching

To make black plastic sheeting even more effective as a mulch in your own vegetable garden, add a coat of aluminium paint. By reflecting sunlight away from the soil and onto the plants' foliage, this shiny coating keeps the soil as much as 2°C cooler, even in the heat of the summer, and promotes stronger growth. (In trials, it has increased the yield of squash plants by 60 percent and maize by 200 percent.) In addition, it repels aphids and thrips.

A coat of red paint has a similar effect on tomatoes, boosting their yield 20 percent over plants mulched with ordinary black plastic. A white mulch is good for potatoes. Green plastic is best for early spring crops.

Muscle aches

Muscle stiffness and soreness is likely to follow unaccustomed or excessive exercise. Only if the pain is severe should you take an analgesic such as paracetamol, and then only if your doctor has approved even its occasional use for this condition.

Heat will help to relax the muscles, so try a hot bath or shower, applying a heating pad or hot towel, or a massage with a heat-producing liniment. Gentle exercise, especially in the mornings, will help get stiff muscles back in working order.

Painful swelling may well be a sign of a pulled muscle. Immobilize the muscle until it is no longer painful, and treat it with an ice pack, followed by light binding with a crêpe or elastic bandage. If pain and swelling have not subsided after about 48 hours, or if they are intense, call your doctor.

When a muscle cramps suddenly, gently massage it, and try to stretch it. A cramp in the hand can be relieved by gently pushing back the fingers, and limb cramps can generally be relieved by pulling the limb straight. The commonest cramps affect the foot and calf muscles, especially when you're sleeping on your stomach. Walking about will bring relief by increasing circulation, and you may be able to prevent night-time cramping by raising the foot of your bed or by changing your usual sleeping position.

Mushrooms

1. Keep mushrooms from getting mouldy or mushy during storage by leaving them unwashed. Wrap them loosely in paper towels, refrigerate in plastic or paper bags, and use as quickly as possible.

2. Slicing mushrooms is easy if you use an egg slicer. Cut downward from the rounded side of the cap. The fresher the mushrooms are, the better this method works.

3. Cook frozen mushrooms straight from the freezer to prevent them from becoming slimy.

Musical instruments

Homemade musical instruments can be more fun – and easier to construct – than you think. Make them with your friends and organize a little rainy-day band. Who knows? It may be your ticket to fame and fortune.

1. Make a rhythm bass from a metal washtub, a broom handle and some sturdy twine. Turn the tub upside down and punch a nail hole in the centre of the bottom. Push a small bolt through and secure it with a nut, using washers top and bottom. Tie one end of the twine to the top of the secured bolt.

Notch one end of the broomstick and groove the other about two centimetres from the end. Fit the notched end over the tub edge, then tie the free end of the twine around the groove at the opposite end.

As you hold the broom handle upright, the twine should be fairly taut. Now put one foot on the edge of the tub and pluck away, varying the tone by changing the tension in the twine. As you gain virtuosity, you can also change the pitch of the note by holding the twine at various places along the broomstick.

2. For a simple rubber-band zither, use four 25-millimetre nails, a 15-centimetre length of wood two and a half centimetres wide with a hole cut in the centre, and an aluminium pie plate. Drive one of the nails about two centimetres from the edge, centred on one side of the wood, then hammer the remaining three along the other side. String rubber bands of different thicknesses from each of the three nails to the single nail. Put the instrument on top of the inverted pie pan to give it a resonating chamber.

3. Play the jug. A large earthenware one looks best and gives the most resonant tone, but you can also use a large glass cooldrink bottle or even a tomato sauce bottle.

Hold the jug straight up and pucker your lips against the neck; arch your upper lip slightly over the opening. Then blow gently across the opening, adjusting your lips until you get a sound. One note is all you can play – the jug is a rhythm instrument. To change the note, add to or remove water from the jug or bottle.

4. A few ballpoint pens can yield a homemade harmonica. Take out the ink cartridges and use the plastic casings. Plug the small holes at the points with clay; add more clay for a high note, less for a lower one. Line the "pipes" up and fasten them to two ice cream sticks with a couple of rubber

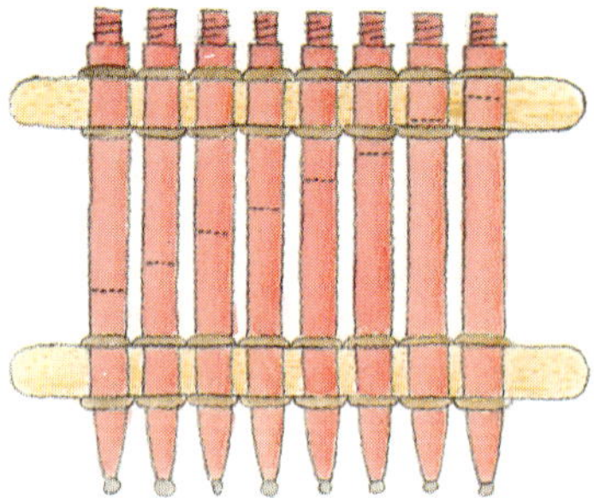

bands. Then play a tune; it takes a bit of practice, but keep trying.

With practice, your group can play real songs, but you're probably better off letting a piano or guitar carry the melody and using these instruments as accompaniment.

Mussels

Black-shelled mussels are found all along the South African coastline, attached to rocks in the intertidal zone. You can easily pluck them off with your hands.

White mussels are found in intertidal sands along certain stretches of the coast. To collect them, dig into the sand with your bare hands (instruments such as spoons and spades are prohibited) or wade into the surf and twist your feet firmly into the sand to feel for them.

Gather medium-sized mussels for the best flavour and most succulent texture. Never overcook mussels, they will toughen.

1. To prepare, scrape the surface of the shells and leave the mussels in cold water for about 30 minutes to purge them of sand.

2. Cover the bottom of a heavy-based pan with one and a half centimetres of water or white wine, and steam the mussels until the shells open. Be sure to discard unopened mussels. Remember to remove the "beards" of black mussels, and serve with lemon juice and pepper.

To marinate mussels simmer them in oil, wine, lemon juice, onion, herbs and pepper. Add salt only after tasting. Marinate the cooked mussels in the refrigerator for at least an hour before you serve.

N

Nail biting

1. When you're tempted to nip at your nails or cuticles, keep your hands busy – doodle, knead an eraser or finger some worry beads.
2. Give yourself a weekly manicure; the neat appearance may deter you from biting your nails.
3. Buy your young nail biter a manicure set as well.

Nailing

1. Caught without a hammer? Pound home a nail with the back end of a hatchet. Or try using a small crowbar. Or hold a flat metal plate (a hinge, perhaps) on the nailhead and hit it with a piece of wood.
2. A quick solution to the problem of driving picture-hook nails into plaster or plasterboard has been used by generations of homemakers: find an old steel-tipped, high-heeled shoe and pound the nail home with the stiletto heel.
3. Don't try to hammer with wrenches, planes or other shop tools. You could render them useless. A nail can gouge a smooth metal surface and crack a cast-iron wrench body.
4. To keep from hammering your fingers, hold a tack with tweezers, a hairclip or a paper clip until you get it started.

Nail polish

1. Only apply nail polish to scrupulously clean nails which are dry and free of soap.
2. Cut a sponge into small triangles and use these to keep your toes apart when you are applying nail polish. This will prevent smudging.
3. If your nail polish is always chipping, use a light colour – the chip will not be so noticeable and it will be easier to touch up.
4. Nail polish stains can be removed by using acetone or non-oily nail polish remover, but be sure to check first on a seam that the material will not be damaged as acetone melts some artificial fibres.

Use small pieces of cottonwool and work inwards to prevent the stain from spreading, changing the cottonwool frequently. Remember, acetone is highly inflammable. Dab any remaining colour with a little methylated spirits.
5. If the stain has hardened, soften with a few drops of carbon tetrachloride (check first on an invisible seam to see that the fabric will not be damaged), then apply acetone.
6. For longer lasting nail polish, keep the bottle in the fridge.
7. Thin nail polish which has thickened by placing the bottle in a pot of boiling water for a minute or two.
8. A drop of nail polish on a snag in your stocking will stop an unsightly ladder from forming.
9. Dab a drop of nail polish in a discreet place on your possessions when loaning them out.

Nail punch

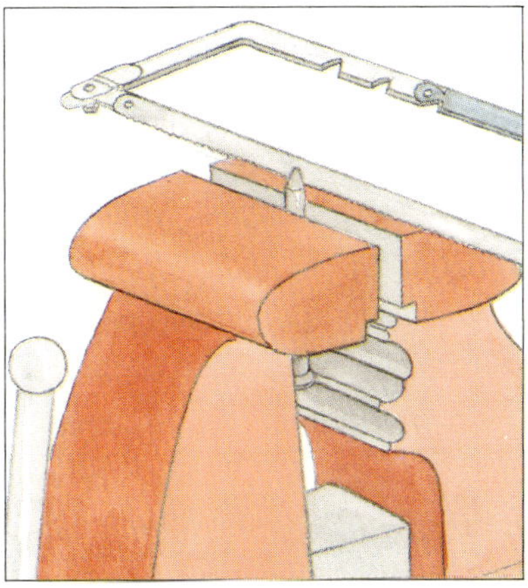

For a homemade nail punch, lock a 75-millimetre nail in a vice (without crushing the head), point up. Using a hacksaw, cut off the tip neatly and square, then smooth the cut edges with a metal file. You now have a handy nail punch that does a good job at embedding finishing nails of the same diameter or larger, since the diameter of the shaft matches that of the heads of finishing nails. Don't get it mixed up with your normal nails.

Neckache

1. If you feel an ache coming on, shrug your shoulders several times.
2. Try taking a long, hot shower, and let the spray hit the back of your neck for 10 to 15 minutes.
3. While reading or watching TV before bedtime, rest a hot-water bottle against your neck.
4. Using your fingertips, knead the back of your neck from the earlobes down to the shoulders; lightly massage the vertebrae. Finish off with brisk chopping movements, using the little-finger side of your flat, stiff hands – but not too hard.
5. Exercise your neck. Stand or sit erect, with your arms relaxed, or lie flat on your back, with your knees bent. Slowly turn your head to the right without feeling strain or pain; hold for five seconds, then turn to the left. Repeat the exercise five times.

Necklaces

1. To prevent metal costume jewellery from tarnishing, store a piece of white chalk with it.
2. To avoid tangled necklaces, hang them from adhesive-backed plastic hooks on your dressing table mirror or from a tie rack on the inside of the cupboard door. Don't throw them all together in a jewellery box.
3. Make a necklace from fishing swivels. String them together with satin cord, knotting the cord between each swivel. Add beads between swivels to make a more colourful necklace.
4. Do you want to clean non-plastic costume jewellery? Immerse it in methylated spirits for five minutes. Then rinse in warm water and dry with a lint-free cloth. Soak rhinestone pieces in straight liquid detergent for 15 minutes; rinse in warm water and dry with a flannel cloth. Do the same for metal jewellery, but dilute the detergent with warm water.

Needle & thread

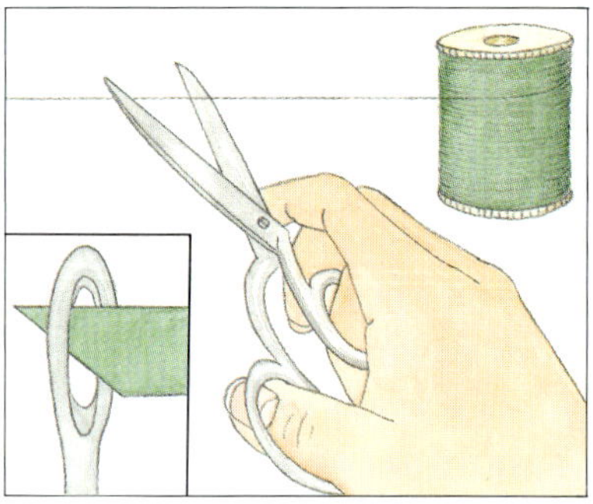

1. To make threading a needle easier, cut the thread diagonally.
2. Keep your needles extra sharp by storing them in a steel-wool pad.
3. Out of thread? In an emergency use dental floss or, on heavy clothing, five-kilogram fishing line.
4. If you can't quite match the colour of a fabric, buy thread a shade lighter than the cloth.
5. Try unravelling an edge of the fabric you're about to mend to get some thread that is a perfect match.
6. There's no need for a needle and thread with iron-on fusible tape; the tape is 35 millimetres wide and it is mainly used for hems, although it could be used for any sewing task which requires that the fabric be held firmly in place.

Needlecraft

1. Knit a rug from pieces of old fabric cut lengthways into thin strips. Sew the ends together and press the edges in for a neater look. Use a simple knit stitch and big needles.
2. To make a patchwork quilt quickly, arrange your patches on panels of fusible web (sold by the metre in fabric shops) and iron them down. Peel the paper backing from the web panels and iron them onto a bedsheet. Use the zigzag stitch on your sewing machine to conceal the patches' raw edges. Add filler and backing, and quilt as usual.

Neighbours

Neighbours need not be nuisances. Here are some tips on building good relationships:
1. If your neighbours are willing, exchange home phone numbers and find out how to reach them at work in case of emergency.
2. Invite your neighbours over occasionally. Make sure they know the layout of your house or apartment and make an effort to learn theirs. Such knowledge could be important in a crisis.
3. When a new family moves in, welcome them with a basket of biscuits and a list of the names and phone numbers of their new neighbours and nearby shops. Offer to collect post and newspapers and to keep an eye on their home while they're on holiday. Be friendly, but don't make a nuisance of yourself; some people are more private, and prefer to keep their distance from neighbours.
4. Organize an annual block party or neighbourhood family day. (Ask the police if the street can be closed to traffic for a few hours.) Have everyone bring something – food, beverages or entertainment. Have a chat to neighbours you don't know well.
5. Join the local neighbourhood watch system, if there is one. The essential idea of the neighbourhood watch is that neighbours undertake to keep an eye on one another's properties. Safe houses are also established – homes which children and the elderly particularly can approach if they need help. For details contact the South African Neighbourhood Watch at PO Box 4024, Randburg 2125.

Networking

This is the modern term for what your parents meant when they said, "It's not what you know, but who you know". Whether you're trying to find a job, change careers or get a promotion, the fundamental premise applies – you need help to achieve your goal. Here are some tips:
1. Ask friends, neighbours, relatives and former colleagues if they know anyone who works in the field you're interested in. If so, write to or phone the person to request a brief interview (be sure to mention the name of your contact). If she's too busy to meet with you, invite her to lunch.
2. When you meet, don't simply announce that you're networking or

IN TIMES GONE BY

A labour of love

(From *The Standard Book of Quilt Making and Collecting*)

That kindly, ancient lady, Marguerite Ickis, reminisced as she passed work-worn fingers over a quilt she had pieced together while her family was growing up: "It took me more than 20 years, nearly 25, I reckon . . . in the evenings after supper when the children were all put to bed. My whole life is in that quilt. It scares me sometimes when I look at it.

"All my joys and all my sorrows are stitched into those little pieces. When I was proud of the boys, and when I was downright provoked and angry with them. When the girls annoyed me or when they gave me a warm feeling around my heart. And John, too. He was stitched into that quilt and all the 30 years we were married.

"Sometimes I loved him and sometimes I sat there hating him as I pieced the patches together. So they are all in that quilt, my hopes and fears, my joys and sorrows, my loves and hates.

"I tremble sometimes when I remember what that quilt knows about me."

looking for a job. Instead, ask about her work, her company, and how she got where she is.

3. Avoid getting too personal. Your attitude should make it clear that your interest is in business.

4. Mention your skills in passing, but don't sell yourself. Bring a curriculum vitae in case it's requested.

5. At the end of the conversation, ask for the name of another person you could contact. Follow up soon with a thank-you note.

6. Remember that whenever a person recommends you, she is putting her reputation on the line. Never abuse the privilege, and always offer to return the favour.

7. If someone's lead works out, treat her to lunch, and make it clear that you know you owe her one.

New baby

Forestall jealousy among siblings before a new baby arrives.

1. Discuss all the responsibilities of keeping a helpless infant alive, the resultant changes in daily routine, and the ways the kids can help. Emphasize that the situation won't be permanent, but will gradually change as the baby develops into a self-sufficient human being.

2. Make sure that the older children know that they'll have certain perks and powers along with their new responsibilities in the family.

3. Make a scrapbook of baby pictures clipped from magazines; borrow videotapes from other families with new babies. Do a sales job, not a con job – show crying and messy nappies as well as the cute stuff.

4. Raise the issue of the sex of the baby gently. Start out with his personality: though helpless, he'll be a distinctive new person – not a copy of anyone and not an object to be moulded. Make a game of imagining who he might turn out to be.

5. Involve the children in choosing a name for their new sibling (see *Babies' names*, p.14). Let them help make birth announcements.

6. Before you confront the kids with the new baby, let them welcome Mother. They'll have missed her.

New pet

1. Don't take home a puppy or kitten less than eight weeks old or you may encounter some behaviour problems later in your pet's life.

2. When you're picking up a puppy or kitten that you've bought from a breeder, take a soft piece of fabric with you. Rub it on the fur of the animal's mother and siblings to catch their scent. Then put the fabric in your new pet's bed.

3. If your pet cries at night, it may still miss its mother. Wrap a ticking clock in a towel and put it in the animal's bed. Or wrap a hot-water bottle for it to cuddle against.

Newspaper clippings

1. To prevent yellowing, dissolve a milk of magnesia tablet in two litres of soda water. Let the mixture stand overnight. Stir well and soak your clipping in the solution for one hour; blot with a paper towel and place on a screen to dry.

2. If clippings have been stored in a damp place, remove mildew by drying them in the sun. (On a rainy day try the low setting on a hair dryer or an electric fan.) Then sprinkle cornflour over them to absorb what moisture remains. (See also *Photographs*, p.154.)

Night blindness

Avoid bumping into the furniture when you step into a dark room. Wait a minute or so to let your eyes adjust to the dark.

Then focus your gaze slightly off-centre – your eyes' light receptors are concentrated on the sides of the retina, so peripheral vision is better than direct vision in dim light.

Noise

1. If you're regularly awakened by early morning traffic, refuse trucks or barking dogs, make use of white noise – a low, constant sound that screens the din but isn't loud enough to keep you awake. An air conditioner does the trick in summer, an electric fan in winter. Or make a continuous tape of chirping crickets, running water or another soothing sound. Compact discs of morning or evening sounds are also available at some record shops.

2. For white noise in your garden, install a splashing fountain.

3. If you work in a place where you must shout to be heard one metre away, the noise around you may be causing permanent hearing loss. Wear anti-noise muffs or earplugs.

4. Don't listen to headphones for more than three hours at over 100 decibels, which is about the loudness of a car hooter.

5. You can reduce the noise in your home or in a particular room, by fitting double glazing in the windows. This also acts as a very efficient thermal insulator. A partition between yourself and a noisy neighbour can be sound-proofed with cork tiles or acoustic tiles. Placing a cupboard against the wall will also absorb much of the sound.

6. Although there is currently no legislation to enforce noise control, various avenues are open to those who feel they have a justifiable complaint. Contact your local Department of Environment Affairs, Traffic Department (for noisy motor cars) or your local police station or municipality if you are plagued by a neighbour's loud stereo equipment. Effects of loud noise can range from a transient ringing in the ears to pain, sound distortion or hearing loss. (See also *Hearing loss*, p.106.)

Noisy pipes

1. If a loosely-mounted pipe vibrates against a roof beam or against outside walls, wrap it with felt or secure it with extra pipe hangers or a U-shaped strap cushioned with a piece of rubber.

2. If you hear rattling when the water turns on and off quickly, it could be a worn or faulty tap washer. Turn off the water supply, remove the tap headgear, and replace the washer on the hopper (see *Dripping taps*, p.67).

3. Sometimes the hammering and banging can only be stopped by installing shock-absorbing air chambers at points in the system, usually in the roof space around the plumbing. This is a job for skilled plumbers – and the shock absorbers are not always available. Shop around for professional help. (See also *Pipes*, p.157.)

Non-stick cookware

To remove grease buildup and stains from a non-stick pan, mix one of these solutions: three tablespoons non-chlorine bleach and one teaspoon liquid dishwashing detergent in one cup water; or three tablespoons automatic dishwasher detergent in one cup water. Simmer for 20 minutes in the pan; then wash, rinse, dry and reseason the pan.

Nosebleeds

1. Sit down, lean forward and firmly pinch the fleshy part of your nostrils shut for at least 10 minutes.

2. If the bleeding doesn't stop after 20 minutes, hold an ice pack or athlete's cold pack to your forehead and

the bridge of your nose while continuing to pinch the nostrils.

3. As a last resort, pack the bleeding nostril with sterile gauze and leave for 30 to 60 minutes.

4. If the nosebleed doesn't stop, or if you begin to feel faint, ask someone to take you to your doctor or to an emergency unit. A doctor may apply a local anaesthetic and then try to staunch the bleeding by packing your nostrils with gauze, or by using a special inflatable balloon. It may be necessary to have a minor blood vessel cauterized.

5. If nosebleeds persist, see your doctor, who may order special tests, such as a blood count, in addition to checking your blood pressure.

6. There is often no apparent cause for nosebleeds, but they are quite commonly associated with colds, vigorous sneezing or nose-blowing, a head injury, pressure changes, sinusitis and high blood pressure.

Nursing homes

Guilt feelings may keep you from placing a loved one in a nursing home long after the move is needed. But remember that even love and care can run to excess; if keeping your ageing relative at home causes severe deprivation and ruins your family life, it is not good for either of you.

Perhaps the most difficult problem you'll face will be bringing up the subject in the first place. But it is imperative to face this emotionally charged situation honestly.

Listen to your relative's concerns; he will be more reassured if you let him air his fears. His major worry is likely to be abandonment. You must be very firm about the nursing home being part of your continuing care – not the end of it.

Another key step is to come to terms with any revulsion you yourself feel for nursing homes. Try to visit several homes in your area, keeping in mind that they are designed to help

IN DAYS GONE BY

Accommodating the aged

Old people in some non-industrialized societies have had it better than their counterparts in the rest of the world.

Aged members of the San (Bushmen) of southern Africa, for example, have long been valued for the advice they could offer to the active food producers in the group. In Bali the oldest people enjoyed the highest rank because they were living repositories of information; they enjoyed control over the community.

The Yakut nomads of Siberia, on the other hand, were not so generous to the aged. Living on the edge of starvation, parents tended to neglect their young children; when the children grew up, they were hostile to the needs of their ageing parents.

In the Western world, old people reap the benefits of their years of work through pensions from their governments and former employers. (Germany started the ball rolling by initiating old-age pensions in 1889. The United States was relatively late; the Social Security Act was passed in 1935.)

But the value of the accumulated experience of the elderly is too often discounted as new technology makes the old ways of doing things obsolete.

Still, old people in the West can probably be glad they live where they do. Some Eskimos, after all, faced with food shortages and harsh winters, still abandon old people who become too feeble to care for themselves.

severely disabled people and must be judged on that basis. Try to focus on how well they keep their elderly patients functioning.

If possible, take your relative along. First reactions will probably be negative, but in time you are both likely to see which of the homes you visited will be most suitable.

Since people in nursing homes live in close quarters, find one that offers a compatible environment. Note the religious, ethnic and cultural groups in each home that you visit; if religion is important to your relative, give priority to nursing homes run by his denomination.

Another important consideration is proximity to family members. Frequent visits will reassure your relative that your love and concern are strong.

Nutcrackers

No nutcracker handy?

1. Wrap a nut in a towel and pound it with a rock, hammer or mallet.

2. Squeeze the nut with a wrench, a pair of pliers or a vice.

3. Put it on the hinge side of a door, then shut the door slowly.

4. Hold the nut at the top edge of a drawer and slam the drawer shut, but watch out for your fingers.

Nuts

1. Mature walnuts, pecans, chestnuts and macadamias fall to the ground by themselves; if necessary, gently shake the tree, but protect your head. The outer covering of the almond splits when it is ready to be picked.

2. If you have a huge crop of nuts, keep them fresh and prevent weevils from ruining them by freezing for up to a year in polythene bags.

3. Nuts will crack more easily and won't break up as much if you heat them in a covered glass dish of water in a microwave oven for two minutes. Drain, cool, then crack.

Nuts & bolts

1. To keep a nut from working loose, slip a locking washer over the bolt before applying the nut or tighten a second "jam" nut over the original one to lock it in place.

2. Another method: crush the exposed threads with pliers or a cold chisel. Or coat them with silicone caulk, epoxy glue or a proprietary nut-locking chemical before tightening the nut.

3. The best way to remove a rusted or "frozen" nut is with penetrating oil, sold at hardware stores. Let the solution seep in and then, using a wrench large enough to give good leverage, work off the nut with a series of short, sharp jerks rather than an extended pull. (See also *Lubricating oil*, p.130.)

4. Or heat the nut with a gas torch or even a few kitchen matches. The metal may expand enough to let you work it loose.

5. To prevent nuts from rusting to bolts in the first place, dip them in shellac before use. They will always come apart.

6. If you find there's no way to remove a nut, destroy it. Rent or buy a nut splitter, a kind of ring-held cold chisel. Position the ring over the nut and turn the screw with a wrench. Or hold a cold chisel against the nut and give it a few hefty blows with a hammer. Though split, the nut may still have to be wedged off with a crowbar. Don't forget to have a replacement at hand before you begin.

O

Office exercises

Exercising at your desk or computer terminal will help relieve tension. Whenever time permits, try one or more of the following:

1. Inhale deeply through your nose and then exhale through your mouth. Repeat six times.

2. Raise your arms high above your head; stretch one hand toward the ceiling, then the other, and then both together; relax. Repeat twice.

3. Clasp your hands behind your head to keep it still and press back your neck muscle to loosen and stretch it. Hold for 10 seconds and relax. Repeat five times.

4. With your arms by your sides, push your shoulders back as if to make your shoulder blades meet; hold five seconds and relax. Now push your shoulders forward; hold five seconds and relax. Repeat this set of exercises three times.

5. Hold your arms straight out at the sides, with your palms up, and slowly rotate them in small circles; do 20 forward, then 20 backward.

6. For your hands, wrists and fingers, hold both arms straight out in front with the palms down. Keeping your fingers straight, gently bend your hands back at the wrists as far as you can, then bring them forward. Now spread your fingers as wide as you can; hold for five seconds, then make a tight fist.

Office politics

1. The best way to deal with the office rumour mill is to listen with interest but never pass on what you hear. That way you can benefit from inside information without getting a reputation as a gossip.

2. To prevent colleagues from stealing credit for your ideas, put them in writing; send a copy to your boss.

3. Even if you dislike a colleague, never let it show. The ability to get along with co-workers – including those you don't care for – is a measure of your professionalism.

4. Though flattery may occasionally get you somewhere, in the long run it usually backfires. If someone is shallow enough to reward an employee for buttering him up, he probably won't last long – and neither will you if you become his yes-man.

Office romance

Depending on how you look at it, the office may be the best or the worst place to find someone special. On the one hand, it's an ideal setting in which to get to know someone well. On the other hand, mixing business and pleasure can jeopardize your job, your relationship or both.

1. Before getting involved with a co-worker, weigh the risks carefully – a relationship with the boss is especially dangerous. If you do decide to start dating a co-worker, keep your behaviour at work strictly professional – don't call each other by pet names, don't display affection publicly, and don't spend hours chatting on the phone or in the halls. And don't discuss the details of your romance with co-workers.

2. No matter how discreet you both try to be, sooner or later teasing or gossip is bound to begin. If you're not prepared to accept this, don't start a new relationship.

3. Bear in mind that romances often go sour, and if this one does, you and your co-worker will still have to face each other every day.

4. Also bear in mind that if you get married, your company may forbid you to work in the same department.

Oily skin

1. To help normalize skin, avoid spicy foods, reduce oils and fats in your diet, and drink six to eight glasses of water daily.

2. For a refreshing facial, fill a spray bottle with tepid water and one teaspoon of salt, then spray the solution on your face. Blot dry with a towel. For a quick steam, heat a wet towel in the microwave and form a tent over your face.

3. Here's a quick facial mask: mix three tablespoons each of mineral water and fuller's earth and apply the paste to your face. After 20 minutes rinse with warm water. Or try a paste of warm water and oatmeal on your face for 10 minutes.

4. If you're out of astringent, mix cider vinegar or lemon juice with a little cool water and splash some on your face; cover your hair and close your eyes. Wipe with cottonwool. During the summer, freeze the solution in an ice-cube tray; run a cube over your face when you feel hot.

5. To remove make-up, mix a teaspoon of powdered skim milk with warm water; apply with cottonwool, wipe with tissues, and blot dry.

Older drivers

1. If you are worried about your own driving ability, enroll at a driving school for a refresher course. Phone driving schools in your area and explain that you want to learn to cope with, for example, fast-moving traffic on highways. Study the official learner's licence booklet to renew your licence. Copies are sold at your local bookshop. Or try the library.

2. Steer clear of potentially dangerous situations. Devise alternative routes to shopping centres and doctors' offices to avoid busy intersections and highways. If you're in the market for a new car, buy a white, beige or yellow one so that other drivers can see you more easily.

3. When you have decided to stop driving, don't relinquish your independence. Look for other ways to get around: explore bus routes and scout out dependable taxi services. Many churches and senior centres provide transportation for older people. Some shopping centres also organize buses for non-drivers. Check with the public relations officer of your local shopping centre.

Only child

1. Take extra care to see that an only child has plenty of opportunities to play with others. Ask friends and relatives who have children to come over often and make sure your child gets to spend a lot of time with them. Make young friends feel like part of the family; put an extra bed in your child's room to encourage sleep-overs.

2. Don't gang up on an only child when disciplining or criticizing him; it tends to make him feel he's one against the world and to envy children who have siblings to side with. Instead, you and your spouse should take turns at the unpleasant chore. (Praise, on the other hand, is reinforced when both parents join in.)

3. Make time for silly behaviour now and then: a pillow or water pistol fight can be fun for everyone.

Osteoporosis

Just ingesting calcium may not stop bones from growing thinner during and after menopause. What seems to work is calcium, taken with plenty of regular exercise. (Although men are less prone to osteoporosis than women are, they should also follow these suggestions.)

1. Dairy products, broccoli, spinach, sardines, pilchards and citrus fruit are excellent, easily accessible sources of calcium (see *The Balanced diet*, p.254). If your diet doesn't fulfil your needs, take a supplement.

2. To absorb calcium, you need 400 units of vitamin D daily; two litres of milk or adequate exposure to the sun will do the job. It's best to avoid calcium supplements containing vitamin D, which can be toxic in high doses.
3. Avoid smoking, alcohol and caffeine, and reduce salt intake; all interfere with calcium absorption. So do some drugs; check with your doctor. (Women should also ask their doctor or physician about oestrogen replacement therapy.)
4. Weight-bearing exercise – walking, jogging, dancing, tennis – for half an hour three times a week prevents loss of bone mass and may increase it. Before starting an exercise programme, check with your doctor; then, if she approves, begin slowly and build up gradually (see *Endurance building*, p.73).
5. Prevent falls and possible broken bones by "trip-proofing" your home – nail down throw rugs, provide adequate lighting, and install grab bars and non-slip decals in the bathtub.

Outdoor cooking

1. You can turn an old metal wheelbarrow into a mobile braai. Punch 1 centimetre holes in the bottom and sides, line with a layer of stones, and cover with charcoal. An old oven shelf can serve as a grill (don't use refrigerator shelves; they might contain poisonous cadmium).
2. Season a new iron hibachi to prevent rust. First, check that there are no wooden parts. Then rub all surfaces with sunflower oil and set the hibachi on a baking sheet in a 120°C oven. Leave for half an hour, turn off the heat, and let the oven cool. Finally, remove the hibachi and firmly wipe off excess fat.
3. To find out if the coals are hot enough to braai steaks, hold your hand two centimetres above the grill for a count of three. If the heat's unbearable, the fire is ready.
4. To prevent flare-ups when you braai, make an aluminium foil drip pan and set it under the meat.
5. Another way to prevent flare-ups: spread lettuce leaves on the hot coals before you braai fatty meat (the outer leaves from the head you're using for the salad will do nicely). The lettuce will blacken but won't ignite.
6. Don't forget that you can braai vegetables as well as meat. Wrap onions, mealies or sliced potatoes (all dotted with butter or margarine or brushed with braai sauce) in heavy-duty foil. Grill onions and mealies over medium coals for 30 minutes, turning often; place foil-wrapped potatoes directly on the coals for 45 minutes, turning once. Put chunks of baby marrow or aubergines on skewers, brush with oil, and grill for 10 minutes over medium coals, turning often to prevent burning.
7. Flies hate basil, so keep a pot of the herb close to the dining table. Crush a few leaves to release the oils. A bonus: fresh basil leaves to chop into your salad.

Ovens

1. If your electric oven isn't working, first check to see that all the controls are set properly. If they are, see if a fuse has blown or a circuit breaker has tripped.
2. Never try to use a commercial oven cleaner in a self- or continuous-cleaning oven. Check your instruction booklet carefully to see which type of oven you have.

If you accidentally apply a commercial cleaner, clean the oven thoroughly before using it once more. Apply full-strength white vinegar to the oven surfaces with a sponge, then rinse with warm water. Next, for a self-cleaning oven, run a full self-clean cycle. For a continuous-cleaning oven, heat the oven to 200°C for one hour. Rinse either type with warm water after it has cooled. Consult the manufacturer before you attempt any of these methods.

Oven thermometer

You can check your oven's accuracy with this simple test: after preheating, lay a sheet of plain white paper on the centre oven rack and leave it for five minutes. The paper's colour will now correspond to the stove's temperature: pale biscuit, 150°C or less; light brown, 180°C to 200°C; golden brown, 200°C to 230°C; dark brown, 230°C to 250°C; black means the temperature is over 250°C.

Overheated engine

Overheating can ruin a car engine very quickly, so if the temperature gauge starts edging up, take immediate action. (By the time the warning light on the dashboard comes on, the problem is already serious!)

Turn off the air conditioner and turn on the heater (it draws off engine heat). If you stop for a minute or more in traffic or at lights, shift into *Neutral*, and rev the engine. Make sure that you stay as far behind the car ahead of you as possible to keep its hot exhaust away from your radiator.

If this doesn't stop the temperature rise, pull off the road at your first opportunity. Raise the bonnet (be careful; the bonnet and the engine compartment are hot) and see if there is something obviously wrong, such as a snapped belt, a broken fan, a coolant leak or insects or debris coating the air conditioning condenser or the radiator.

If there are no obvious reasons for the overheating, wait at least an hour for the engine to cool, then check the coolant level in the radiator. If it is low, let the engine idle while you top it up (plain water will do if necessary). If there is no cap on the radiator, add coolant to the reservoir if it's empty. As soon as possible, have the system drained and filled with the appropriate radiator coolant. (See also *Radiator hose*, p.168.)

Overindulgence

Are you afraid you may eat or drink too much at a friend's party? Here are some survival strategies:

1. Never go to a party hungry. Eat a light, high-carbohydrate snack (salad and pasta or wholewheat bread) beforehand so that you won't be tempted to overeat.

2. At a buffet, put only one course on your plate at a time, beginning with the salad. This may satisfy your hunger before dessert is served.

3. When you are offered a drink, ask for a little alcohol in a tall glass of water or fruit juice; find out if there is alcohol-free beer or wine, or drink soda water with a twist of lemon.

4. When your alcoholic beverage is half gone, refill the glass with ice.

Overspending

The compulsive spender is often the last to recognize that he has a problem, but if your cheque book refuses to balance or your total debt is more than 20 percent of your annual take-home pay, here are some constructive actions you can take:

1. If shopping is your social exercise, look for new friends who play cards or golf.

2. When you feel a sudden urge to go on a spending spree, telephone a frugal friend and ask her to talk you out of it.

3. Go on a crash "spending diet" for a month. Shun shopping malls; shut off TV commercials; avoid glossy "consumer" magazines and catalogues. Then count all the cash you've saved.

4. Cut up your credit cards and use your cheque account only for essential purchases. Make all purchases with cash or money orders.

5. When shopping is absolutely necessary, make a list and buy only the items that appear on it.

6. Once you've got your spending under control, open a savings account and deposit 15 to 20 percent of your pay; restrict yourself to withdrawing the accrued interest.

Oysters

1. If you intend taking the oysters from the sea yourself, remember there are strict regulations applicable to oysters. For details, write to the Department of Environment Affairs, at Private Bag X2, Roggebaai 8012.

2. You can tell if an oyster is fresh because its shell is firmly closed or snaps shut when tapped. If it's already opened, check for a clean, sea-sweet odour and clear liquid.

3. A "drunken" oyster is much easier to open than a sober one. Carbon dioxide does the trick; after five minutes in soda water, its muscles relax and the shell is a cinch to open.

4. Caught at the shore without anything to prise them open? Set oysters on hot rocks close to the fire – they'll open themselves. Or wrap them in wet seaweed and lay them on hot coals for a minute or two.

5. Cook opened oysters quickly on low heat so that they don't become tough. The best way is to poach them gently in hot milk or sauce, just until the edges curl.

6. If you're grilling oysters, steady them in the pan by setting them in coarse salt or propping them with crumples of aluminium foil.

P

Packing clothes

1. To reduce wrinkles, fold your garments in tissue paper or wrap them in plastic bags. For shirts or blouses, wrap several layers of them around a piece of cardboard.

2. Or interfold clothing; place one end of a long garment face down and even with an inside wall of the suitcase and let the other end hang out. Then lay shorter items vertically on top of it and fold the end over. Alternate layers so that the garments cushion one another.

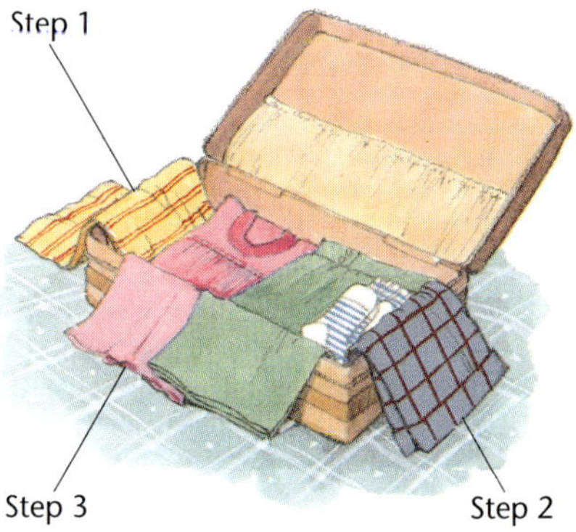

3. Tuck small items, such as socks and handkerchiefs, into collars and along fold lines.

4. Don't fold clothes that are going into a duffel bag; roll them.

5. In a three-section suitcase put the heaviest items in the middle.

6. In any bag make sure that heavy items are on the bottom when the luggage is upright. Don't overstuff.

7. In a hanging bag put the delicate clothes in first. Centre garments on hangers and bring their sleeves slightly to the front.

8. Need an extra bag? Use a department store or dry-cleaner's garment bag as a hanging bag. Use a child's book bag or rucksack for personal items. On short trips a picnic basket is all you need for carrying frequently used items.

Pain relief

1. Laugh. Really! A hearty laugh causes the release of endorphins, the body's natural pain relievers. If you're lacking humour in your life, see if you can rent comic videotapes or read humour magazines or joke books. Invite friends over to tell jokes or form a comedy club.

2. Tension and stress tend to intensify pain. Take up meditation or join a meditation group. Get a massage or do relaxation exercises (see *Stress*, p.198), but don't strain the painful part of your body.

3. Explore hypnotherapy; it teaches you to screen out pain effectively with pleasant images. Give it a try! (See also *Aspirin sensitivity*, p.12.)

Paintbrushes

1. To keep from flooding the rim of a paint tin, remove the excess paint by tapping the bristles against the inside of the tin.

Also, if you punch several nail holes around the groove inside the rim, any paint that does drip in will drain neatly back into the tin.

2. For hard-to-paint objects, such as narrow pipes, try making a painting mitt. Put a plastic bag over your hand and cover it with an old towel. Secure with a rubber band around your wrist – but not too tight as you don't want to cut off circulation.

3. If you take a short break while painting, there's no need to clean the brushes or rollers. Just wrap the wet bristles in plastic food wrap.

4. To soften a paintbrush that's stiff with dried latex paint, soak it in a 50-50 solution of vinegar and water for 10 minutes.

5. To protect cleaned brushes for long-term storage, wrap the bristles in brown paper cut from a grocery bag and secure with a rubber band or tape. Store brushes flat or hang them by their handles; standing them up will bend the bristles out of shape permanently. Be kind to your brushes and they'll be kind to you.

6. Don't throw away an old paintbrush with ruined bristles. Snip about 25 millimetres off the tip and use the brush for dusting. Or cut the bristles to stubble – about 16 millimetres long – for a handy scrubbing brush.

Painter's tray

Need a tray for a roller?

1. Try a shallow baking pan. Line it with aluminium foil for easy cleaning up. Or use a foil baking pan.

2. Line a shallow cardboard box with a plastic refuse bag.

3. Coat the roller with a brush.

Painting

1. For a drop cloth, it's much better to use canvas or heavyweight cloth instead of plastic; it will absorb any paint that might otherwise be tracked through the house. If you must use plastic, cover it with old newspapers.

2. Before painting a window frame, rub a bar of candlewax on the glass next to the woodwork. Then scrape dried paint off with a putty knife or a single-edged razor blade.

3. If you prefer to use tape to mask a painted area, remember to remove it before the paint dries. If you forget to do so, cut along the edge of the tape with a single-edged razor blade or penknife; otherwise you'll peel off the fresh paint.

4. When touching up small areas with spray paint, mask them with rubber cement. Then just peel away the rubber film after the paint has dried.

5. To prevent "skin" from forming on the surface of paint, seal the lid tightly and store the tin upside down. The paint will form an airtight seal around the lid. Or lay a sheet of plastic food wrap or aluminium foil on the paint's surface before closing the tin.

6. To mask adjacent surfaces while painting trim or moulding, you can use an old metal venetian blind slat. A piece of sheet metal or thin cardboard also works effectively.

Paint roller

1. To make use of a roller encrusted with dried paint, wrap a strip of towelling tightly around it. Secure each end with a rubber band.

2. If you don't have a roller, make a painting pad by gluing a piece of thick carpet to a block of wood. It'll do for simple jobs.

Paint solvent

Solvents such as paint thinner, turpentine and alcohol can easily be reused. Pour the used solvent into a large jar and cap it tightly. In a couple of days, when the paint solids and resins have settled to the bottom, carefully pour the clean solvent into another container and save it for your next job.

Paint stains

1. To make cleaning up easier, apply a thin layer of Vaseline to your hands and face before painting.

2. To remove dried latex paint from clothing, soak the garment in a solution of warm water and detergent for about two hours. Then brush it gently with a toothbrush. Repeat the process, if necessary.
3. As a last resort for a paint-spattered carpet, carefully snip off the stained fibres. (See also *Brick & stone cleaning*, p.27.)

Pantihose

1. To prevent snags, soften rough hands with lotion before handling pantihose or wear cotton gloves while putting them on.
2. Tie the ankles of pantihose that have runs so that you can quickly recognize them as "for slacks only."
3. If your pantihose seem a bit short as you put them on, wet your hands and smooth the legs upward. Next time stretch the legs first.
4. Do your pantihose tend to tear at the toe? Before putting them on, stretch out the toe area. Or spray it with hair spray or rub it with paraffin after each washing.
5. Pantihose tend to last longer if you hand-wash them; for an extra thorough cleaning, add two tablespoons of ammonia to the water and detergent in the basin.

When machine-washing, put hosiery in a mesh bag and use the delicate setting. It's best to let hosiery drip-dry, but if you must use the dryer, set it on *Low* and remove the pantihose as soon as the legs and top are dry; the elastic may still be damp, but it will air-dry quickly.

Pants

1. To keep your pants' legs smooth when you are away from home, lay them between the mattress and the springs and press them while you sleep. Or hang them in a steamy bathroom. (Don't forget to pack clothes pegs for converting ordinary hangers into pants hangers.)
2. Before buying new pants, make sure they fit properly. If they wrinkle upward, the crotch length is too short; if they wrinkle horizontally, they're too tight across the front.
3. To keep knees from wearing out, put iron-on patches on the insides before wearing pants the first time.
4. Iron-on fusible tape will secure a split seam temporarily.
5. When you are putting hems in pants, finish one leg completely, then use it to mark the length of the other. Double-check by measuring the length at the inseam.

The hem should cover the instep in front and extend about 1 cm over the heel of the shoe at the back.

Parked cars

Worried that you won't be able to locate your car after parking it?

Keep a bright cloth in the glove compartment of the car so that, when parking, you can tie it to the radio aerial. Or carry a distinctive device attached to a suction cup for the roof. It's also helpful to jot down your vehicle's location on a slip of paper. But don't write "next to the big van" – the van may be gone when you return.

CHILD SAFETY

Toddlers have been known to release a parking brake, put a car in gear, and even start one. Never leave a child alone in a parked vehicle.

SUMMER DANGERS

On a 30°C day, the temperature inside a closed car can rise to 39°C within 10 minutes, presenting serious hazards.
1. Cassette tapes and camera film may deteriorate. Remove them if it's hot or if you will be parked for more than a few hours.
2. Perishable foods will deteriorate within an hour. Milk-based dishes can spoil even faster.
3. To keep interior fabrics from fading, cover the front windshield with cardboard shades. The side windows can also be shielded with side window shades. A number of designs are available, the most common is attached by means of suckers. Good shades can reduce the temperature inside quite considerably.

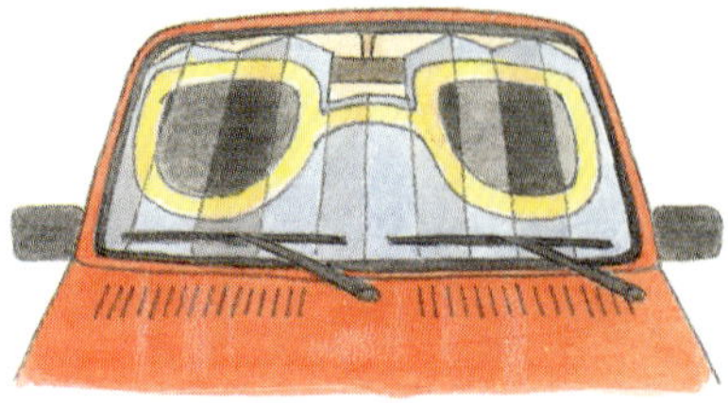

Use imagination to decorate a sunscreen.

4. Never leave your pet in a parked car in warm weather – even in the shade with the windows open. The animal can die from heat and stress.

Part-time jobs

1. Consider turning one of your skills into a part-time business. Are you a good baker? You might supply cakes to a local restaurant. If you're good at fixing things, you might find work doing odd jobs.
2. If you happen to know someone else who is also looking for part-time work, see if the two of you might be able to split a full-time job. (See also *Moonlighting*, p.137; *Temporary employment*, p.208.)

Party decorations

1. For a special birthday or anniversary, decorate the room with enlargements of flattering old photos of the guest of honour.
2. If you're serving foreign cuisine, ask a travel agency or the local consulate of the appropriate country for posters and travel pamphlets, and spread them out as a tablecloth. Add little flags to flower arrangements.
3. If you forget to buy decorations, a platter of colourful fruits or vegetables can make any table festive.
4. For a children's party, how about an arrangement of stuffed animals or toys down the middle of the table? The arrangement probably won't last very long, of course.

5. For a really unusual decoration, use a shower curtain as a tablecloth and a watering can filled with flowers as a centrepiece.
6. For help or ideas, look under "Party arranging and decor services" in the Yellow Pages and consult library books.

Party guests

1. Keep three lists: an A list of fascinating people, a B list of good listeners who can also converse easily, and a C list of people to whom you are personally or socially obligated.

Then, when you plan a party, draw from all three lists to balance personalities and interests. Recombine old friends, and always invite someone new to keep things interesting.
2. If there is a guest of honour, tailor the guest list to her personality.
3. If you're entertaining a newcomer, try to have at least one other person present whom he knows, and invite guests who share common interests with him. Give everyone some information about the newcomer so that they will have various points of departure for conversation.
4. Never invite a roomful of people who share the same occupation unless you want an evening given over to shop talk.
5. If you are having a special group – office people, fellow golfers or the like – tell your other friends so that they won't be offended at not receiving an invitation.
6. At a small dinner party arrange the seating for complementary personalities and interests. Place people with opposing views next to each other for lively conversation (but only if you're sure they'll restrain themselves).
7. Anyone hosting a party has the right to stand firm against people trying to bring uninvited friends or children. If a potential guest says, "I can't come unless I bring my child" (or my poodle, for that matter), tell the person that you will miss them and that you hope they will be able to come next time.

Passports

1. Apply for your passport well before your departure date. Normally it takes about a week to process it, but there are seasonal peak periods when it may take longer. If you need a passport immediately as a result of an emergency, make sure that you have all the correct documentation and explain your situation. Your passport can be ready within an hour, depending on your circumstances.
2. Have your two passport photos and application form certified (the simplest method is to take it to your local police station) before you visit the passport office. This will save you a lot of time.
3. Passports are worth a lot of money on the foreign black market. Don't ever leave yours with anyone or use it as collateral. If a hotel requires you to leave it overnight, get a receipt from the desk clerk.
4. To prevent theft, always carry your passport in a front inside coat pocket or in a document pouch worn under your shirt. Or leave it in a hotel safe-deposit box. Never leave a passport in your hotel room.
5. Be sure to make several photocopies of your passport in case of theft or accidental loss. Leave one at home, another in a separate section of your luggage, and carry extra copies of your passport photo.
6. If you are unfortunate enough to lose your passport abroad, report the loss as soon as possible to the nearest South African consulate. The consulate will issue you with a replacement.

Pattern cutting

1. If you can't find a tracing wheel to transfer a pattern, check the kitchen drawers – a pizza cutter or a pastry wheel may do the job.
2. Protect the cutting surface beneath the pattern with felt, a flattened cardboard box, a magazine or thick newspapers. An added bonus: you can pin the fabric and pattern down to prevent slippage.
3. To strengthen pattern pieces you want to preserve for frequent use, iron fusible tape onto the edges. Store them, rolled up, in cardboard tubes.
4. Create your own pattern: take apart a favourite worn-out garment with a seam ripper and press each piece out carefully.

Peeling paint

1. Scrape off peeling paint with a wide putty knife, a kitchen spatula or even an outdated credit card. Then sand to a feathered edge. Apply a prime coat and let it dry. Then apply two finish coats.
2. To reach peeling paint on ceilings, tape a wide putty knife or spatula to a broom handle. Replace it with a paintbrush or roller to paint.

3. Remove peeling paint from metal with steel wool or a wire brush (remember to scrub firmly). Then apply a metal primer and two coats of rust-resistant paint.

4. To scrape away peeling paint and dispose of it at the same time, use the bare end of your vacuum cleaner's extension wand.

Peepholes

Don't depend on a door chain when checking to see who's at the door; most aren't strong enough to prevent a forced entry. The safest way to find out who's outside is with a peephole or door viewer.

Although you can simply install a swinging cover over a hole in the door, you're better off with a wide angle peephole that gives you a sweeping view of the exterior. Position it at a convenient height for the shortest adult in the family.

If you don't want to put a hole in your door, you can mount a mirror above or beside the door or on a nearby window frame at an angle that reflects a visitor's image.

Peer pressure

Although we experience peer pressure throughout our lives, it is strongest during childhood, especially adolescence. It takes a secure, independent person to "just say no" – whether to drugs, alcohol, petty theft or other dangerous group activities. You can help.

1. Remember that peer pressure does have its positive side; it can help instill generosity, empathy and social skills in people.

2. Encourage your child to associate with friends who share your family's values and standards. Once a child has firmly identified with one peer group, he or she may find it difficult to break away and join another.

3. Don't argue over things that are superficial and harmless. If your son wants an outrageous haircut so that he "fits in," let him have it. Save your energy for more important issues.

4. Try to remember what you went through when you were young. Tell your child about your experiences, even if they're embarrassing.

5. Stay in touch with the parents of your child's friends so that you can work together to set standards.

6. Tell your child she can use you as an excuse if she doesn't want to go along with the group.

7. Some circumstances – the divorce of parents or the death of a grandparent, for example – can be extremely stressful; at such times a child may be more in need of peer support and therefore more susceptible to peer pressure. Help your child talk about his feelings with you or a counsellor.

Encourage him to spend time with friends, and provide them with space, privacy and time for conversation.

Pencil & paper

If you have to take down a phone number, address or message and can't find a pencil or paper, try one of the following:

1. Use your fingernail, a paper clip or hairclip to make a deep impression on a piece of paper. Later, rub the indentations with a pencil and the message will reappear.

2. You can write with lipstick, eyeliner, nail polish or a spent match on serviettes, newspaper, tissue paper or gum wrappers.

3. Try "braille": use a pin to poke tiny holes in a piece of paper to form letters or numbers.

4. If you have a pen or pencil but no paper, write the number on an inconspicuous part of your clothing – the back of your tie, the label of your jacket, the instep of your shoe sole.

5. Trace the number on a dirty or frosty windowpane until you find a pencil to write it down. Or wet your finger and dip it in dust or dirt to use as "ink".

6. If you're near a phone, call your own answering machine and tell it whatever it is you're trying to remember. You'll have it on tape.

7. Try singing a phone number or address to a familiar tune. Sing it over and over in your head until it gets stuck there.

Pencil sharpener

1. No pencil sharpener? Use a wood plane. Pull the pencil against the blade, turning as you go.

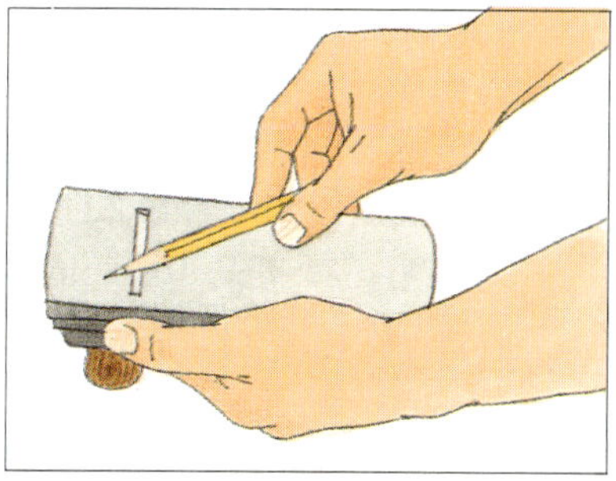

2. Try a potato peeler.

3. To hone the point of the lead itself, you can rub it across sandpaper, an emery board or the friction strip of a matchbox.

4. If you're desperate, break the pencil in two. You'll probably be left with a usable, if jagged, edge.

5. Glue a small plastic pencil sharpener to the bottom edge of your workbench, desk or telephone table. This way, you can sharpen a pencil one-handed, leaving the other hand free.

Perfume

1. Be careful of "nose fatigue". If you've been wearing the same perfume for a long time, you may not smell it as easily as others do. If the scent is obvious to you 30 minutes after application, you've probably overdone it; dab alcohol or a paste of bicarbonate of soda and water on the perfumed area, then wash off.

2. For a light touch, spray your perfume in front of you, then walk through it.
3. To make your favourite fragrance last longer, apply it after your shower or bath, while your skin is damp.
4. To co-ordinate scents, spray a little perfume onto your bath powder, close the container tightly, and allow to dry.
5. Lost the stopper for your perfume bottle? Try a pencil eraser.
6. Never leave perfume in direct sunlight; you should keep it in the refrigerator to help prevent evaporation and deterioration.

Perlemoen

1. Strict laws govern the harvesting and sale of this delicacy in South Africa. Before you take perlemoen from the sea, you must obtain a licence from an office of the Receiver of Revenue or from a magistrate's office. Only four perlemoen, with a minimum diameter of 11,4 centimetres, may be taken out of the sea in a day per person.
2. Make sure that you are not diving in a declared marine reserve.
3. The perlemoen you dive out are for personal consumption only and may not be sold. If you buy fresh perlemoen from a legal supplier, keep the invoice and receipt as proof of this.
4. The closed season runs from 1 August to 31 October and you may not harvest perlemoen during this period. The Department of Environment Affairs has a free booklet available which lists the regulations regarding perlemoen and other protected marine life. Write to the department at Private Bag X2, Roggebaai 8012.

Pesticides

Pesticides are divided into three main groups; contact, stomach or systemic insecticides. It is very important to use the right kind of pesticide and to follow the manufacturer's instructions.
1. Contact poisons kill only creatures they touch, either at the time of spraying or soon afterwards. They can be used for both chewing pests such as caterpillars and sucking pests such as aphids.
2. Stomach poisons kill pests which have eaten the leaves which have been sprayed. They can also be used for chewing and sucking pests. A number of popular garden pesticides are combinations of contact and stomach poisons.
3. Systemic pesticide is invariably absorbed by the plant through its foliage and into the sap stream. Pests which then suck out the sap, absorb a lethal dose. Systemic pesticides are particularly effective against all sucking insects such as aphids and stinkbugs, as well as mites such as red spider and citrus psylla.

Pet allergies

Many people suffer from allergies sparked off directly by household pets. If you suffer from such an allergy, consider the following:
1. Brush your pet outdoors or ask someone else to do it.
2. The animal should be thoroughly wiped down daily with a damp towel, and its living quarters or box thoroughly cleaned. If you must do these things yourself, wear a dust mask and wash your hands afterward.
3. Keep your pet off the furniture and vacuum the carpet daily. Make your bedroom a pet-free sanctuary.
4. Don't keep a cat's litter box in your bathroom (urine contains allergens); rather put a hooded box in a seldom-used cupboard.
5. If your allergy to cats or dogs gets the best of you but you can't live without a pet, consider a bird, a fish tank or a terrarium with frogs, toads, lizards or snakes.

Pet odours

1. In many cases, regular bathing with a shampoo formulated to reduce odours will do the trick.
2. Tartar buildup can cause bad breath. Take your dog or cat to the vet for dental cleaning.
3. Ear infections, anal gland infections and dermatitis can also produce bad odours; check with your vet.
4. The problem may be hormonal odour – designed by nature for sexual attraction. Neutering the animal is the only solution.
5. If carpeting or upholstery smells after a pet "accident", sprinkle it with bicarbonate of soda and allow it to take effect for several hours. Brush off the excess, then vacuum.

If that fails, sprinkle carpet deodoriser on the carpet and vacuum. You should use a commercial preparation to remove stubborn odours from soft furnishings.
6. The sight of other cats in your garden may be causing your male to spray. Close the curtains when you go out or spot an interloper.
7. If your cat tends to spray the furniture, protect the upholstery with a protective spray so that it won't absorb the odour. If he favours one spot, attach a matching piece of fabric that you can detach and clean. (Recurrent spraying may be a sign of a medical problem; check with your vet. She may also be able to suggest effective behavioural modification training.)
8. If possible, keep all pet paraphernalia – beds, toys, litter boxes – in rooms with hard floors and hard-surfaced furnishings. Upholstery and carpeting absorb odours.
9. A cat will pick up the scent of other animals when it stays at the vet, and your other cats may attack it when it returns home. Put a natural fragrance on your pets for several days.

Pewter

1. If you don't have pewter polish, use wood ash moistened with water. Or rub with raw cabbage leaves and buff with a soft cloth.
2. Remove corrosion from old pewter with fine steel wool dipped in linseed, olive or sunflower oil.
3. If pewter cookware doesn't come clean with soap and warm water, try a paste of methylated spirits and whiting (a fine abrasive powder available in hardware stores).

Phobias

1. All phobias represent a fear of losing control. To conquer yours, don't flee from it or the situation that brings on an anxiety attack. Accept it and control it; watch it happen and rate its intensity on a scale of one to 10.

2. If you feel an attack coming on in a public place, try to act as though you're not anxious at all. Breathe normally but more slowly; focus intently on something specific, such as a window display or the directions printed on a package.

3. Develop a ritual that gives you the illusion of being in control. If you're afraid to fly, for example, always carry a good-luck charm and sit in the same seat on the plane.

4. Find a sympathetic person, preferably a recovered phobic, to help rid you of your phobia.

5. Try to get an audiotape designed to counter your fears through self-hypnosis or relaxation. Do relaxation exercises (see *Stress*, p.198).

Photo film

1. You can keep your film supply fresh in a sealed plastic bag in a refrigerator. Or put the bag in the freezer – you'll actually extend the film's expiry date by a few months. Let it warm to room temperature before using.

2. If you intend taking a lot of photographs on your holiday, keep your films organized to avoid chaos. Mark your films with a code as you finish them. For example, KP may stand for Kruger Park and PR for Pilgrim's Rest. Alternatively, number the films and keep a list of the contents of each roll of film in a notebook. This will enable you to sort out your films when you return home.

3. If film gets jammed in your camera, you can rescue the pictures already on the roll by making a "darkroom" with a dark-coloured jacket or coat. Put the garment on back-to-front so that your hands stick through the ends of the sleeves. Then turn it inside out and lay it on a table in front of you without removing your hands.

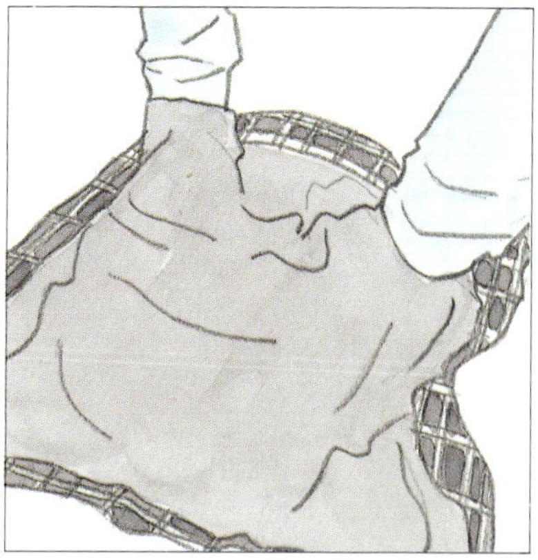

Place the camera inside and have someone pile clothing or pillows around the edges to further block the light. Open the camera, remove the film, and rewind it by hand.

Photo flash

1. For softer lighting (especially for portraits), make your own flash diffuser from translucent white plastic shopping bags. Hold the plastic over the flash with tape or a rubber band; leave the flash sensor uncovered so that the automatic exposure will work. For manual operation, exposure correction is necessary; it's usually an increase of one f-stop, but run some tests to be sure.

2. Slide-type switches for flash units sometimes get nudged to *On* in a camera bag, resulting in drained batteries. Put a strip of insulation tape over the switch. Then peel it partway back to use the flash.

Photographs

If your photos are fading, your album itself may be the culprit. Cheap albums have high-acid paper that eventually disintegrates and gives off harmful fumes; the effect is increased if plastic sleeves enclose the page. Moreover, the adhesive that holds the pictures to the page can also cause a degree of fading.

Keep important pictures in sealed polyethylene bags (don't use other kinds of plastic) with a small bag of moisture-absorbing silica gel (like the one that came packed with your new camera) in each. Store colour prints in a dark place; light accelerates fading, as do heat and humidity.

Protect slides in the same way. Where you store pictures is very important, too. You should avoid attics (too hot) and basements (too damp). A cupboard in the middle of the house has the most stable and moderate temperature and humidity.

Pickpockets

1. Carry cash and credit cards in separate wallets and pockets. If possible, divide your cash between your wallet and pocket.

2. Keep your wallet in an inside coat pocket or a front pants pocket.

3. Keeping your hands in your pockets keeps a thief's hands out.

4. The smaller your handbag, the smaller target it is for a pickpocket. Grip the bag tightly, close to your body and in front of you; if it has a flap or outside pocket, keep that toward your body. An open-top handbag invites trouble.

5. Make a list of the identification numbers for your credit cards, driver's licence, employee badge, cash cards and so on, as well as the numbers to call in case of theft. Keep one copy at home and another in a locked compartment at work.

6. Never flash money or jewellery in public – at a newsstand or bus stop, for example.

7. When shopping, be especially alert at store entrances, on escalators and in lifts, in bargain or demonstration areas or anywhere that large crowds gather. Also be on the lookout at the checkout counter, where you might temporarily put down your handbag and parcels.

8. Before using an automatic teller, take a good look around. If you see someone suspicious, go elsewhere. While using one, stand close so that no one knows the extent of your transaction. And when you leave, walk half a block or so in the wrong direction, then turn back to see if you've been followed.

COMMON SCAMS
Pickpockets often work with accomplices who create distractions while the thief robs the "mark". Here are some common ruses:
1. "Watch out for pickpockets!" Be wary when you hear someone shout this; your natural response, to reach for your money, alerts the pickpocket to its location.
2. The accident: perhaps someone's foot slips getting off the bus in front of you, or perhaps she drops packages in a crowded lobby; in either case, the momentary confusion is all the pickpocket needs.
3. The fight: an argument breaks out and people jostle each other getting out of the way; when it's all over, you're the loser.
4. "Oh, I'm sorry!" Someone rushing through a busy airport or train station bumps into you or spills food on you, then stops to help you up or brush you off; then he rushes off again – with your wallet.

Picnics

1. No cool box? Line your picnic basket or box with cold beverages and pack the food in the centre. But remember that the cold cans are no substitute for ice; use this trick only if you have a short way to travel and your food is unlikely to spoil.
2. Plastic cloth or a clean shower curtain makes a good picnic spread. Spills are easy to wipe up.
3. Carry your food to the picnic site in cardboard boxes; turn them upside down after removing the contents, line them up, and cover with your plastic cloth or blanket. *Voila!*, a miniature table.
4. A card table with the legs cut off makes a good picnic table for you and your family at the beach.
5. To keep ants out of food, use dome-shaped screens to cover your plates between servings; they are available at hardware and kitchen stores. Or use foil or plastic wrap.
6. Concerned about food poisoning? Avoid egg salad, potato salad, fish and pasta dishes, especially on hot days. Instead, make sandwiches out of lunch meats, canned meats or cheese. And use mustard (a fairly good preservative because of its acid content), butter or margarine instead of mayonnaise.
7. For greater protection against contamination, freeze the sandwiches. You can freeze puddings and yoghurt, too – stir first to distribute the fruit. Keep your cool box filled with ice (replenish if necessary) and keep your travelling time short. (See also *Food safety*, p.89.)
8. Want some cooked mealies or hot soup without a fire? Lift the bonnet of your car, start up the engine, and put a pot of water on top of the radiator. It will boil fairly soon.

Picture frames

1. Make back-to-school frames for portraits of the kids. Mount each photo on stiff cardboard with double-stick tape, leaving a six-millimetre margin all around. For a frame, glue wooden pencils to the margins.
2. To make random frames look like a set, spray-paint them all one colour or use co-ordinated mats.
3. Reinforce a wobbly frame with a staple gun; drive two staples across the back of each mitred joint.
4. For a substitute picture frame, try a shallow wicker basket with the centre cut out.

Pictures

Anything that will hang fairly flat can take the place of a picture.
1. Quilts, rugs and flags make attractive wall hangings. Tack or staple the top edge to a strip of lath or a lightweight batten. Or wrap it around a dowel or wooden curtain rod (available at hardware stores), and slip-stitch the back hem. Hang with picture wire or a decorative cord.
2. Do you enjoy putting jigsaw puzzles together? When you've finished one, slide it onto a glued sheet of 50-millimetre plywood.

Using two boards, force the pieces tightly together, first from the sides, then from the top and bottom. Cover it with wax paper, another piece of plywood and some weights until the glue sets. Then varnish the surface or apply spray fixative before framing.

LOOK BEFORE YOU LEAP

Watching out for scams and swindles

To protect yourself from con artists, remember a simple rule: if something sounds too good to be true, it probably is. Here are some common come-ons:
☐ Lucky winner: a telephone caller informs you that you've won an expensive prize, but he needs your credit card number to "verify" your identity. On your next bill you discover that you've been charged several hundred rands for the "free" prize.
☐ Holiday sensation: a letter offers you a free trip, but when you call for reservations, you learn that all the "free" days are booked. For a small fee, however, your trip can still be arranged. By the time the charges are totalled, you've taken an expensive holiday.
☐ Make a million: a "financial adviser" touts a sure-fire investment, often in commodities or precious metals. But once you put up your money, the cash vanishes, along with the counsellor.
☐ Something for nothing: that's what the letter promises. But you must visit a new resort community to pick up your prize. When you arrive, you get a high-pressure sales pitch to buy a holiday home.

3. Let the room's function suggest appropriate decorations. In an entrance hall, for example, you could use hats or canes. In a living room musical instruments, historic newspapers or antique embroidery tools might work.

In the dining room display doilies, baskets or serviette rings. In the kitchen hang decorative pots, a spice rack or a shelf of glass jars. In the TV room hang maps to locate places that are in the news. Add interest to a child's bedroom with colourful kites or a bookcase filled with dolls, model aeroplanes or stuffed animals.

Pie crust

1. To prevent the edge of a pie crust from browning too quickly, fold narrow strips of aluminium foil over it. Another trick is to trim the edge off a disposable aluminium pie plate that's a little larger than the pie you're baking. Place this collar over your pie crust and bake.

2. The liquid in fruit pies can make the crust soggy. Prevent the problem by brushing the bottom crust with beaten egg white and letting it air-dry for 10 to 15 minutes before filling. Set the pie on a piping hot baking sheet in a preheated 200°C oven and bake for 10 minutes; then reduce the heat to the specified temperature and continue baking.

3. To keep pie crusts from baking unevenly, leave ample space between the pans and make sure they are at least five centimetres from the oven walls. Never block airflow by covering the baking rack with aluminium foil; instead, partially cover the rack below to catch any drips. Preheat the oven to the correct temperature and resist the temptation to peek before baking time is up.

4. For flakier crusts, keep everything cold. Use ice water and well-chilled butter or margarine for mixing. Chill the dough before rolling it out (a marble slab is best for rolling because it stays cool). Use two knives or a pastry blender to cut the fat into flour – not your warm fingers.

Pigeons

Get tough with pigeons. Don't rely on inflatable cats, owls or snakes. These urban pests may become accustomed to them. Try one of these methods:

1. Replace each nest with a colourful solid object, such as a red brick or a painted rock.

2. Screen the birds out of wall recesses and window ledges with shade-cloth or plastic netting, sold at hardware and garden stores.

3. Run a strand of wire across a ledge at about half the height of a pigeon's breast. This will halve the amount of space available to them, and the birds will hate it.

4. Urge your neighbours to stop feeding them.

Pills

1. A pill that sticks in your throat may be caught in the tiny fleshy pocket between the upper throat and the larynx. To prevent this from happening, drink a full glass of water each time you swallow a pill.

2. Coat pills with butter or margarine to help them slip down. Or if your doctor approves, crush them and mix into apple sauce or ice cream.

3. If your child is having difficulty swallowing a pill, coat it with banana or embed it in a bite-size piece of the fruit. Or have her eat a few bites of banana after taking the pill. (See also *Medication schedule*, p.133.)

Pimples

1. Clear up a sudden single blemish quickly with an over-the-counter benzoyl peroxide gel (five percent).

2. To treat bigger breakouts, wash your face gently with warm water and a mild soap; rinse thoroughly and pat dry. Apply a benzoyl peroxide gel once a day (start with two-and-a-half percent). If after two weeks you see no improvement, apply it twice a day or use a five percent concentration.

IN TIMES GONE BY

Pigeons in peace and war

Airmail service started long before the aeroplane. Some 2,500 years ago, Cyrus the Great of Persia used homing pigeons to carry messages. Guided by an uncanny ability to find their way (which a modern ornithologist called "one of the classic puzzles in all of biology"), these tiny feathered messengers have played important roles in history ever since.

☐ In the first Olympic games, in 776 BC, a victorious athlete sent news of his triumph to his father by tying a purple ribbon to a pigeon's foot. Romans later used pigeons to relay the results of gladiatorial contests – and possibly to place bets before word of the results arrived by foot.

☐ Caesar conquered Gaul with the help of these avians, which can fly 900 kilometres without water.

☐ During the World War I Battle of the Argonne Forest, a pigeon named *Cher Ami* lost an eye and a leg while carrying a message that saved an American unit from being fired on by its own troops. The intrepid bird was awarded the Distinguished Service Medal, and its body was later stuffed and displayed at the Smithsonian Institution in Washington, DC.

☐ In World War II, the pigeon *G.I. Joe* flew 32 kilometres in 20 minutes and saved a British battalion, despite being shot through the wing. This feathered hero won a medal from the lord mayor of London.

☐ The French Army still keeps a pigeon corps in case communications are disrupted by nuclear holocaust. The birds can deliver a message some 800 to 900 kilometres away in a day.

3. Here's some single-pimple camouflage: use a little green eye shadow to neutralize the redness, then cover with foundation.
4. When shopping for new skin products, look for water- or glycerine-based moisturizers, sun lotions and foundations that won't clog your pores. Check the labels for the worst oils: any compound with lanolin or isopropyl myristate. If you're in doubt, test a product by dabbing it on a clean brown paper bag or a piece of bond paper; wait 24 hours and check for an oily ring.

PREVENTION
If you are subject to skin blemishes, here are some hints:
1. Be careful not to touch – or allow objects, such as the telephone, to touch – your face.
2. Avoid eating foods containing iodine (iodized salt, asparagus, kelp and shellfish, for example) or hormones (beef, liver and kidneys, for example). Watch out for the word iodide on multivitamin labels.
3. Prevent flare-ups by learning to relax (see *Stress*, p.198). Exercise also reduces stress, but be sure to take a shower immediately afterwards to prevent workout breakouts.

Pipes

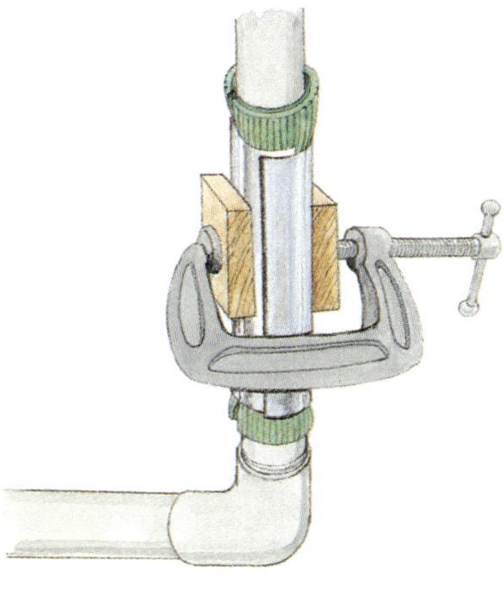

Did winter burst or crack any of your water pipes? Don't thaw them until you've put temporary patches on the damaged sections.

1. For an emergency patch on drain lines, slit a rubber hose and slip it over the pipe. Cover it firmly with a metal sleeve (you can make one by cutting a tin open along its seam) and secure with pipe clamps or car-hose clamps (or use two blocks of resilient wood and a C-clamp).
2. In areas with severe winters, wrap a layer of old felt carpet underlay around external pipes, and tie in place with heavy tinfoil and wire or nylon string. This will also save energy used to heat water.

THAWING
After you have patched the broken spots, open the tap nearest the frozen area. Then melt the ice.
1. If the pipe is metal, thaw it slowly, using a hair dryer, a heat lamp, a household iron, electric heating tape or an electric heating pad. Always start at the open tap and work toward the frozen area.

Never let the pipe get too hot to touch – it may well explode if the water inside boils. Keep looking for cracks and fix them as you go.
2. If the pipe is inside a wall, set a heat lamp about 150 millimetres from the wall.
3. With plastic pipe, wrap towels or rags around the affected area and pour boiling water over them until the ice melts.

LEAKS
First, shut off the water supply (see *Water leaks*, p.227). Then clean and dry the pipe.
1. Patch a leaky joint in a waste pipe with two coats of epoxy. Let the first harden before applying the second; let the second harden before turning on the water.
2. Repair a pinhole leak in a waste pipe by wrapping plastic insulation tape around the pipe, extending it about 150 millimetres on both sides of the hole.
3. For a larger leak in a waste pipe, cut a section of rubber hose and wrap it around the pipe; secure at 25-millimetre intervals with car-hose clamps or heavy-duty wire.

Caution: Any repairs to leaky pipes are temporary. Be sure to replace all defective pipes, valves and fittings as soon as possible.

Planing wood

1. If your plane isn't working as smoothly as it should, it may be that gummy wood resin has collected on the sole. Remove it with paint thinner. To keep the resin from collecting in the first place, apply paste wax regularly to the sole.
2. Always plane with the grain, not against it. To determine which way that is, look at the edge of the wood; the grain's pattern will be angled, not straight. "With the grain" means in the uphill direction of this pattern.

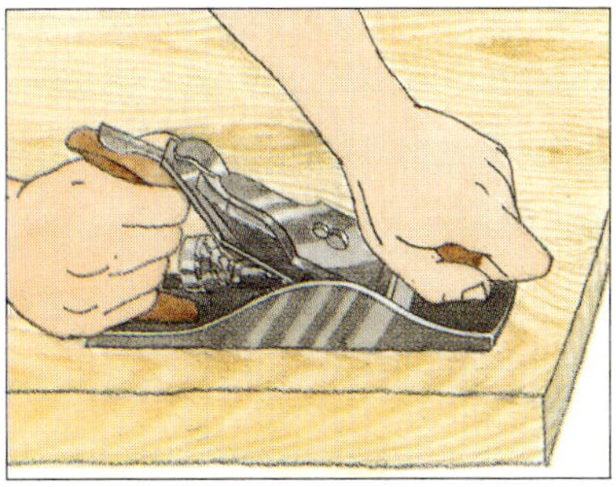

3. To keep from splintering the edge of your work, clamp a scrap board to it and plane them together.
4. To ensure a square edge, attach a guide to the sole of the plane. Choose a piece of wood that is at least as long as the plane, and position it flush with the edge of the plane iron so that it forms a square that can move along the face of the work. Clamp it firmly in place or drill two holes through the sole and screw it on.

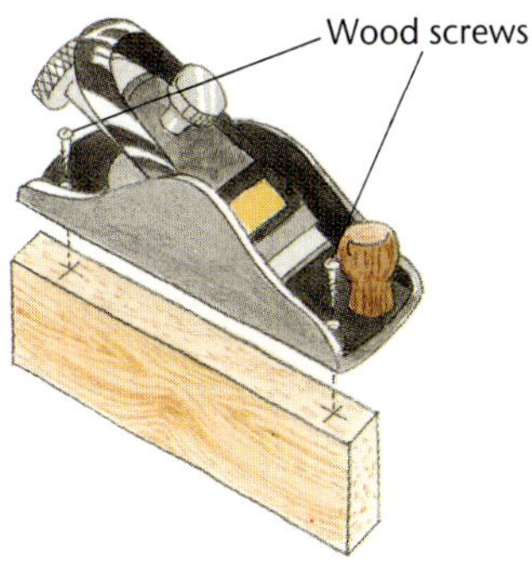

Plant markers

1. Instead of marking rows with the traditional empty seed packets on stakes, make far more durable labels out of plastic picnic knives. Use the plain white kind; their blades offer a good flat surface for inscriptions. Record plant variety and planting date with an indelible marker; then push the knife, handle downward, into the soil at the head of the row.
2. Wooden frozen sucker sticks, labelled with an indelible marker, also make good plant markers.

Playground equipment

1. Children can jump and slide on a 4 x 5-metre sheet of heavy polyethylene wetted down with a garden hose. Spread it on a slope and leave the hose running at the top corner. Move the sheet every hour to prevent damage to your lawn.
2. A section from a big log makes a fine play horse. So does a section of large ceramic water pipe; children can crawl through it, too.
3. For maximum fun as well as good drainage, build a bottomless sandbox. Make a frame of planks; reinforce the joints by driving stakes on both sides of each corner. Within the frame dig a pit 600 millimetres deep and line the sides with creosote poles, but leave the bottom uncovered. Order building sand from a building materials supplier. Cover with plastic or canvas when not in use to keep pets and water out.
4. A small, but neat and compact sandpit can be made using a fishpond mould. These can be bought at nurseries. Place the pond mould on the ground and, using a sharp instrument, mark the outline of the pond. Dig out this section of soil to the necessary depth and insert the mould into the hole. This fishpond mould is ideal if you only have a patio – simply remove the brick paving or quarry tiles, and place the pond in an unobtrusive corner.

Pleats & creases

1. Before washing pleated clothes, turn them inside out; remove them before the final spin.
2. To drip-dry a garment quickly, roll it up lengthways in a dry towel and squeeze out all excess water from one end to the other; then hang to dry.

IRONING
1. To hold pleats in place while pressing them, put a sheet of coarse sandpaper beneath.
2. For sharp creases, turn pleats inside out and iron them over a damp cloth, moving from top to bottom. For longer-lasting pleats, lightly spray the edges with starch before ironing.
3. To prevent any pleats underneath from marking the fabric on top, insert strips of brown paper and fasten them under the folds with paper clips, being careful not to snag the fabric.

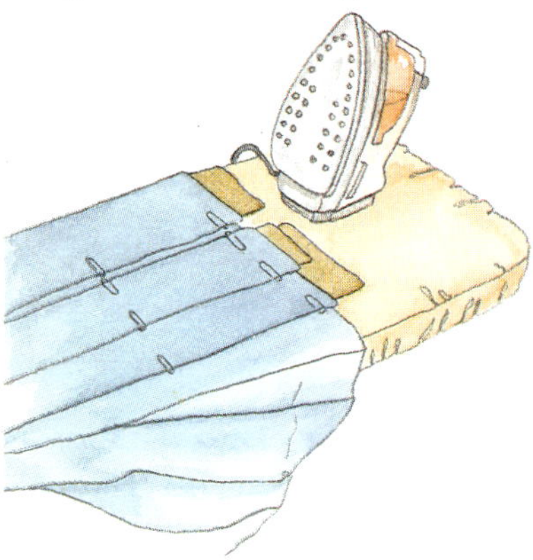

4. You can also press pleats by keeping the garment under your mattress overnight. (Keep in mind that the garment's sides will also be creased.)
5. To pleat curtains without ironing, fold them while they're wet and hang them from trouser hangers.

Plumb bob

1. Use a child's toy top as a plumb bob. Suspend it point down on a string; add weight by dropping a few metal washers over the string.
2. Or make a plumb bob from an empty frozen juice can. Mark dead centre on the bottom; puncture it and insert a tapered nail with a small head through the hole as your marker. Poke two holes exactly opposite each other at the top of the can, just under the rim, and form a short yoke with a piece of string. Fill the can with sand and suspend it from a string.

Plunger

Can't find your plunger? Try one of these remedies to unclog your sink:
1. Bail the water out, then pour lots of boiling water down the drain.
2. Cup your palm over the clogged drain and "squoosh" it up and down until the sink clears.

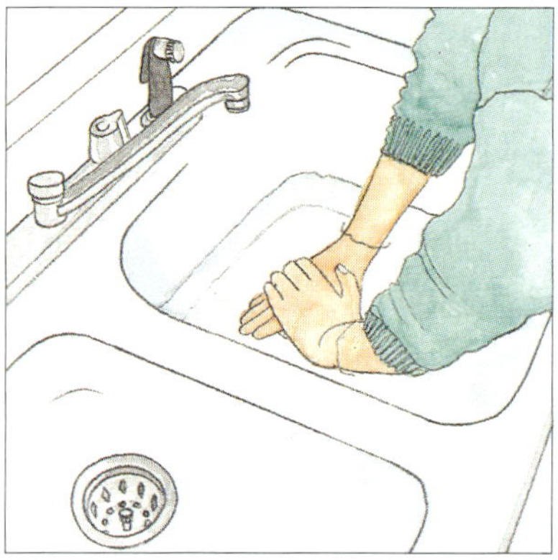

3. Shove a hose down the drain as far as it will go. Then attach it to a tap and turn the water on full blast for just a second or two. Bail out the sink if necessary and repeat. (See also *Clogged drains*, p.48.)

Plywood

1. Store plywood flat to deter warping. If you must store it on edge, rest it on wood blocks so that the bottom edge won't absorb moisture.
2. To keep all edges from absorbing moisture, rub with a bar of beeswax or a candle.
3. When cutting plywood with a handsaw, place the finished side face up so that any splintering will occur on the bottom. If you're using a circular saw or sabre saw, place the finished side face down.
4. To prevent splintering, cover the cutting line with masking tape, then mark the line on the tape.
5. Or score the cutting line with a utility knife – just deep enough to penetrate the top veneer. Then make the cut; any splinters will break off cleanly at the scored line.
6. Finish plywood edges with edging veneer. Or use adhesive plastic, such as that used for lining cupboards.
7. Plywood occasionally blisters as the top veneer delaminates from the core layer. To fix this, slit the blister with a single-edged razor blade and squirt a little glue inside. Spread the glue under the blister with a toothpick. Then cover the area with wax paper and weight it down overnight with large books.
8. Don't toss out a sheet of plywood just because it's warped. Try moistening the concave side, then lay the sheet flat with weights on top. If that doesn't work, save it for small pieces.

PMT

1. If you're beset by premenstrual tension or PMT, keep a symptoms diary for two to three months; record when your periods begin and end, how you feel (bloated? headache?), and what foods you crave. Report your findings to your doctor.
2. To combat mood swings, irritability and fatigue, eat a low-fat, high-carbohydrate diet (p.130). Include four helpings of whole-grain breads and cereals a day and plenty of leafy green vegetables and fresh fruits; replace fatty red meat with lean fish and chicken or turkey.
3. Instead of three large meals a day, eat a small meal every three hours to stabilize your blood sugar level. Cut out sugar and caffeine; they cause volatile blood sugar levels.
4. Even if you crave potato chips, pretzels and ham, skip them to limit your intake of salt and prevent bloating; use herbs, lemon juice and vinegar as seasoning (see *Low-sodium diet*, p.130).
5. Do aerobic exercise – take a brisk walk, dance or skip – for 20 minutes every day or for 30 minutes four times a week. Ask a friend to join you.

Poisoned pet

Drooling, panting, vomiting, persistent diarrhoea, burns on the mouth, lack of co-ordination, convulsions and coma are all signs of poisoning.
1. Be prepared. Buy a comprehensive pet book that lists common poisons and their antidotes, and also keep a supply of activated charcoal and hydrogen peroxide, both of which are available at pharmacies.
2. Try to determine what your pet ingested. The container's label may list an antidote.
3. Call your vet immediately. If you can't reach him, call a veterinary hospital or poison emergency unit, which should be listed under Emergency Services in the front of your telephone directory.
4. If you're unable to reach professional help and you don't know the antidote, give two teaspoons of activated charcoal mixed with water or milk. See a vet as soon as possible.
5. If the substance is corrosive (contains acids, alkalis or petroleum distillates), do not induce vomiting. Give your pet milk, whipped egg whites or water to dilute it.
6. If you're sure that the poison is non-corrosive and you need to induce vomiting, give your pet a dose of hydrogen peroxide (28 grams per nine kilograms of body weight). Or use a solution of warm water and one teaspoon of salt.
7. Let your pet drink as much water as it wants. However, don't give it anything by mouth if it's unconscious or convulsing.
8. When you go to the vet, take the toxic substance and any packaging that has a label. If you don't know what the animal ingested, take any suspect material – loose pills, solvents, pesticides. If your pet has vomited, bring a sample.

Poisonous plants

Direct contact with a number of plants may cause skin irritations, such as itchy rashes, blisters or an outbreak of red lumps on the skin.

The best known irritant is poison ivy. Other plants in South African gardens, which are known for causing an allergic reaction in some people, include euphorbias, naboom, poinsettia, primula, rainbow leaf and wax leaf. The last two are also members of the poison ivy family.
1. If you find you've been exposed, quickly rub the crushed leaves and

stems of busy lizzie or any other type of impatiens over the area. Its juices counteract the irritant, but won't cure a rash once it has begun. (Ironically, this plant often grows in the same habitat as poison ivy.)

2. As soon as possible, flood the affected area with methylated spirits to remove the plant's juices from the skin. If this isn't available, use running water to wash it off.

3. Rinse or wash all contaminated clothing and tools as well.

4. Once the rash appears, apply compresses soaked in cold water or Burow's solution (1:40 concentration) for 10 minutes three times a day. After air-drying (do not rub with a towel), soothe the rash with calamine lotion or over-the-counter hydrocortisone cream. A soothing skin wash can also be made from an infusion of ajuga and elderberry leaves, while the sticky juice and pulp from the aloe vera plant can also soothe rashes and skin irritations.

5. But if the rash affects the face or genital area or if it spreads widely, seek medical treatment.

ELIMINATING POISONOUS PLANTS

1. Mix one-and-a-half kilograms salt with four litres soapy water; spray the solution on the plant's leaves, flowers and stems.

2. To pull out a few small shoots, slip your hand into a plastic bag; after uprooting the plant, carefully cover it with the bag. Close and toss into the rubbish bin.

3. Never burn these plants or their leaves; smoke carries the irritant.

Poisons

The symptoms of oral poisoning are burns or stains around the mouth; abnormal breathing; foaming at the mouth; pain in the mouth, throat or stomach; nausea; vomiting; diarrhoea; convulsions; and shock.

If these symptoms are present, call your nearest poison emergency unit (look in the front section of your phone book under Emergency Services). Be ready to tell the size, weight and age of the victim; the name of the substance ingested; how much and when; and whether the person has vomited.

ON THE SKIN

If a dry chemical, such as an acid, gets on skin, brush it off thoroughly, then flood the exposed flesh with a gentle stream of cold water for at least 10 minutes. Remove all contaminated clothing, jewellery and shoes and wash the skin beneath with soap and water. Go to a doctor or to an emergency unit immediately.

IN THE EYE

If a chemical or caustic agent gets into an eye, immediately flood it with cold water for 20 minutes. Run the water from the inside corner of the eye toward the outside, holding the lid open. If only one eye is affected, be careful not to let the water run into the other eye. If both eyes are affected, flood both by pouring water straight down onto the bridge of the nose. After washing, cover both eyes (even if only one is affected) with moist pads, and get to an emergency unit.

FOOD POISONING

Prolonged vomiting and diarrhoea two to 18 hours after eating generally indicate food poisoning. The symptoms continue until the digestive system is empty, usually not longer than 24 hours after eating.

The victim may feel ill for another 24 hours. If he develops a fever over 38°C, if vomiting and diarrhoea persist for 48 hours, or if at any point he becomes completely unresponsive or starts having a seizure, seek medical help immediately.

CARBON MONOXIDE

Headache, dizziness, nausea and drowsiness are the first signs of carbon monoxide poisoning. Get yourself or the victim outside into fresh air, or open all doors and windows and turn off the source of the fumes. If the victim remains groggy, call an emergency medical service and request that they bring oxygen.

Popcorn

1. Popcorn won't pop ? The kernels may have dried out. Soak them in water for about five minutes, then drain and try again. Or freeze them for a day or so.

2. In fact, the freezer is the ideal place to store popcorn – don't even thaw the kernels before putting them in the popper; the additional moisture will actually improve their overall popping performance.

3. Unbuttered popcorn has fewer kilojoules than most snack foods. Try sprinkling it with dried crushed herbs or spices of your choice.

4. You can also keep kilojoules down if you use a hot-air popper; it pops without oil.

Portaging

1. A canoe can be carried by one person more easily than by two, since no two people have exactly the same gait. When two people are sharing the job, the one with the shorter stride should take the lead.

2. Before a long portage, pad the centre thwart with foam rubber to reduce shoulder discomfort. You can also wear your life jacket as extra protective padding.

3. To relieve your shoulders without setting the canoe down, rest its end in

a tree fork or on a stump or large rock for a few minutes.

4. To lift a canoe, roll it on its side with the interior facing away from you. Then lean over, grasp the centre thwart with both hands (your stronger arm reaching farther), and lift the canoe onto your thighs while rolling it toward you. Straighten your knees and face forward as you raise the canoe above your shoulders, ducking your head in front of the thwart. Settle the canoe on your shoulders and firmly grasp the gunwales. Periodically shift the weight from shoulder to shoulder.

5. If you have a partner, have her lift one end of the canoe while you back into the carrying position.

6. To lower the canoe, reverse the lifting procedure.

Positive reinforcement

To get the response you want from people and pets, give them what they want: praise and rewards.

1. Compliment your child regularly for good behaviour. Favourite foods, special activities (perhaps a trip to the movies or the video store) and inexpensive toys can all be used as rewards. Some parents use tokens, such as stars or stickers, that can be exchanged for a treat – for example, 20 tokens for a doll or a board game. You can even use positive reinforcement when your child misbehaves; after a tantrum, for example, praise him for being back in control.

2. Don't ever take your spouse for granted. If he or she has agreed to take on an unpleasant chore or done a special favour, show your appreciation: put a note under a pillow or plan a special dinner.

3. Try positive reinforcement in the form of a compliment, a cup of coffee or a small gift to your postman, co-workers and friends.

4. Pavlov's dog wasn't the last animal to respond to conditioning. Praise, petting and treats will teach your pet appropriate behaviour.

5. Don't forget yourself! If you're having trouble finishing a project or sticking to an exercise programme, promise yourself specific rewards (a new jersey, a dinner out) for goals you have achieved.

Postal service substitutes

Looking for fast delivery service at a reasonable price?

1. The major cities all have a number of independent delivery firms. Check the Yellow Pages in your telephone directory under "Delivery Service". Phone around for quotes before you make a decision.

2. A private mailing service centre can do the job for you (see *Mailing*, p.131). You can also have your post sent directly to them.

3. Fax machines are the quickest way to transmit words and images around the world: 20 seconds via ordinary phone lines. Your easiest access to a fax machine is probably through a store which offers copying services. Check the stores in your neighbourhood, or consult the Yellow Pages in your telephone directory. If you have made a prior arrangement, the fax can be sent to another copying service store in the recipient's city. Be sure to include the fax number of your service so that a reply can be sent if necessary. If you intend to use a fax machine regularly, it might be worth your while to investigate buying or leasing a fax machine for your own home.

Potato blight

If blight tends to attack your potato plants every year, change your way of watering your plants. It's moisture in the leaves that promotes the destructive early and late blights. So be sure to irrigate the plants by watering the surface of the soil, or only water overhead early in the day, so that the foliage is dry by nightfall.

Also make sure you select only government-certified seed potatoes for the best results. Left-over kitchen potatoes give poor crops. Rewarding, disease-resistant types include BP 1, Up-to-Date and Van der Plant.

Potato skins

Slices of baked potato skins can be crisped in the oven for a healthy snack. Or try stuffing halved skins with cheese, meat, fish or vegetables; if you wish, mix the filling with the potato pulp.

1. Plan ahead. Before you bake the potatoes, prick the skins only where you plan to cut them into slices or halves. Then there won't be extra holes for the filling to leak through.

IN TIMES GONE BY

Stamps of approval

The saga of South Africa's postal services goes back to 1500, when Pedro de Ataide placed a letter in an old shoe and hung it in the branches of a milkwood tree at Mossel Bay.

From then on it was customary for passing ships to leave written messages on the shores of Table Bay, safely tucked in waterproof pouches under suitably inscribed stones. Numbers of these "post office stones", dating from the early 16th century to 1635, survive as treasured exhibits in museums.

The internal postal service took a while longer to get going. A "packet service" to the Netherlands was created. In 1792, the first post office was opened at the Castle in Cape Town. The present postal service is said to have grown from this.

Letters for conveyance were rubber-stamped either "Paid" or "To pay", but perhaps the most noteworthy event took place in 1853, when the Government of the Cape of Good Hope issued its first adhesive stamps to indicate prepaid postage. These stamps, the famous 'Cape triangulars', with their figure of Hope sitting demurely by an anchor, are among the most sought-after items in the fascinating (and often expensive) world of philately.

2. When you scoop out the pulp with a spoon, leave a little next to the skin so that the skin won't burn or tear when recooked.
3. To store cooked potato skins (filled or not), freeze them on a baking pan. Then stack them in freezer bags, seal, and keep frozen until you're ready to use them.

Power failure

Given advance warning, you can do a lot to ease the problems of sudden power failure. Even without warning, a cut need not be a major disaster for your household.

BEING PREPARED

1. Stock up on torches and batteries, and be sure to include at least one high-powered lantern. Have a transistor radio on hand.
2. Make sure you have plenty of candles (in hurricane-type holders to minimize the danger), and perhaps some paraffin lamps and a camp stove. Don't keep fuel in the lamps or stove, but know where to find it.
3. Keep two two-litre milk cartons filled with water in your freezer.
4. If you don't have a fireplace, invest in a safe gas-fired heater, or for a slightly smaller outlay and a rustic smell, a paraffin heater. Make sure you know how to use them, and lay in fuel.
5. Maintain an emergency supply of canned and dry foods, as well as a few containers of fresh water. Replace them regularly.
6. If you cook with electricity, have a substitute stove on hand – a charcoal grill or wok, a camp stove, even a paraffin stove – but make sure you have adequate ventilation whenever you use it.

WHEN A POWER CUT OCCURS

1. If you receive advance warning of a power cut, go grocery shopping in good time (the tills cannot work without power), and fill up the car (pumps also need electricity). Take care at traffic lights – treat all "dead" intersections as four-way stop streets.
2. Fuel your oil lamps or lanterns; make sure they work properly. Place them, as well as candles in holders, throughout the house, making sure they're in the open on non-combustible surfaces. For safety, place each on a "doily" of foil.
3. Move one of the two-litre cartons of ice from the freezer to the refrigerator; leave the other in the freezer. At the same time, remove enough food for immediate needs – fresh for today, frozen for tomorrow. Then leave both appliances closed for the duration of the power cut.
4. Shut off all air conditioners, ovens, microwaves, computers, television sets, stereos and so forth. Such devices could draw a sudden rush of excessive amperage when power is restored, tripping circuit breakers, blowing fuses and possibly damaging circuitry.
5. When not in use, store gas cookers and heaters outside in a storeroom, if possible. Protect from moisture.

Power shutoff

Know where to find the electric service panel in your house. It's usually in the kitchen, the garage or a utility room, and it should be easily accessible. It will be equipped with a main disconnecting switch.

Never place a gas cooker on the stove when cooking during a power cut – there is always the chance that the stove will be switched on, and the gas cylinder forgotten. It can explode with enough force to demolish the entire room and cause death or serious injury to your family.

CIRCUIT BREAKER PANELS

These have no fuses and are really the easiest to shut off. Simply open the panel door and flip the main disconnect switch at the top of the vertical row of breakers. It should be clearly marked *Main.*

PULL OUT FUSE BLOCKS

These are easily identified by their square shape and small front-side handles. To shut off the power, grasp the block handle and pull the entire block out of the panel. This procedure is safe so long as you keep your fingers out of the opening after the block has been removed. To restore the power, just press the block back into its slot.

Pregnancy exercises

1. Because your joints are looser and your centre of gravity is off balance, you should avoid strenuous activities such as high-impact aerobics, skipping, basketball and squash.
2. Swimming, walking and stationary cycling are all good exercises if not done too strenuously. Check your pulse rate to be sure that it stays at a safe level (consult your doctor).
3. You can jog if you are accustomed to it, but watch out for back strain. Drink plenty of water, don't get overheated or overtired, and don't exceed the pulse rate which should have been suggested by your doctor.
4. Here's a pelvic tilt to strengthen abdominal and back muscles: lie flat on your back, knees bent, feet comfortably apart. Rest your hands on your lower abdomen. Inhale; feel the floor with your lower back. As you exhale, gently pull in with your abdominal muscles, squeeze your buttocks, and raise your pelvis from the waist, keeping your upper back on the floor. Return to the flat position, inhale, and repeat. Work up to 10

Cat-stretch exercise: exhale as you slide forward from the starting position. Then gently press your chest down.

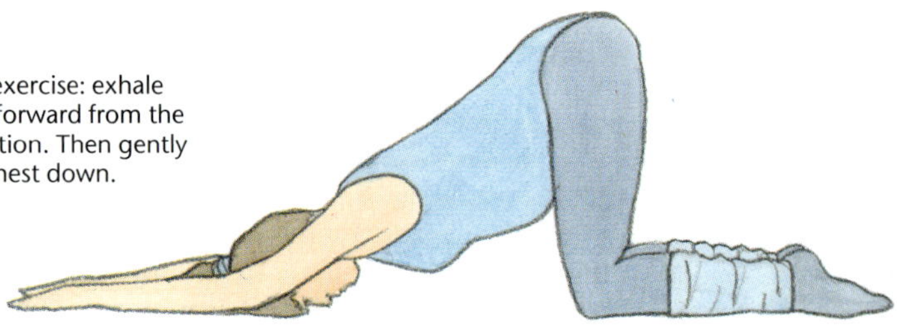

repetitions. You can also do bent-leg curl-ups (see *Abdominal flab*, p.8).

5. After the fourth month add this cat-stretch exercise: kneel with your buttocks resting on your heels, your torso folded over your knees, your forehead resting on the floor, and your arms stretched out in front of you. Inhale. Then exhale, raising your hips high and sliding your chest and arms forward as you do so. Gently press your chest down, keeping your hips still. Resume the original position. Repeat five times.

6. This exercise to tone your pelvic muscles can be done as long as you're comfortable: sit on the floor, legs crossed, back straight (against a wall if you like), and hands draped loosely over your knees. Close your eyes, relax your jaw, and tighten the vaginal muscles deep inside your pelvis. Hold for five seconds; release. Repeat five to 10 times. Do 30 to 40 repetitions per day.

7. Always do exercises that are specially designed for pregnant women. With your doctor's approval, you can do stretching and conditioning exercises throughout your pregnancy if you don't have complications. After the fourth month, change your position (from back to side, for example) every 10 minutes.

8. If you experience swelling in your legs and ankles due to water retention and increased weight, avoid wearing high-heeled shoes and don't sit cross-legged. To counter the condition, do ankle circles: lie on your back with your knees bent; raise one leg perpendicular to the floor, the knee slightly bent; rotate your ankle five times in each direction. Repeat with the other leg.

Pregnancy tests

There are two types of home test kits, and both use urine samples. One, which claims to work within a day of a missed menstrual period, turns a dipstick blue if a hormone secreted in the urine after conception is present. With the other, done nine days after a missed period, the urine creates a thick precipitate in combination with the test solution if the results are positive. Although both are reliable, most doctors prefer the former test because its results are easier to interpret.

Both tests can be affected by heat, cold, vibrations and foreign materials. So, whichever test you choose, repeat it a few days later.

Price stickers

Can't get a price sticker off? First, peel away as much paper as you can. Next, soften the residue. On glass apply vinegar, hair spray, window cleaner or nail polish remover; on plastic or painted surfaces, a hot rag or hair dryer; on fruits and vegetables, sunflower oil. Scrape off the softened residue with a dull knife, a coin, a letter opener or your fingernail.

Privacy

Don't feel guilty if you regularly require some time alone to relax and refresh yourself.

1. Keep hours that are slightly different from those of the rest of your family: rise earlier to recharge your energy and clear your head, or stay up a little later at night.

2. Invest in an answering machine and turn it on to screen calls even when you're at home.

3. Set aside your own private area in the house as a sanctuary.

4. Arrange a "Do not disturb" signal – a sign on the door, a special hat on your head – to let your family know you're in a private mood.

5. Go for a long walk. Or if you prefer to be alone in a crowd, go to a concert, a movie or a museum.

6. Learn to respect other people's privacy as well. Knock before opening a door; never consider opening others' post, read their diaries, or listen in to their phone conversations.

Product failure

1. Do you often find you buy products that are duds? Avoid the problem by shopping carefully. Many products fail because people buy the wrong model or have unreasonable expectations. (A weed-eater light enough for a child to use may not have the power to trim heavy underbrush.) Before making a purchase, read the operating instructions and warranty to make sure the item will do what you want. You won't be able to return it if it did its job, even though it was not the job you had in mind.

2. If you have a legitimate complaint and get no satisfaction from the store where you bought the product, write to the managing director of the company that manufactured it. Enclose a copy (not the original) of the sales receipt and warranty, if you have them, along with a letter detailing the problem and identifying the store. As a last resort, contact the local branch of the Consumer Council; enclose a copy of the letter you sent to the manufacturer. (See also *Guarantees, warranties*, p.102.)

Profanity

1. Since "Darn!" and "Gosh!" hardly make the grade as satisfying substitutes for profanity, rack your brain for creative euphemisms. Like the writer W. C. Fields, who coined "Godfrey Daniel!" you can probably come up with a curse that amuses rather than offends.

2. If you feel that you must occasionally use real profanity to underscore something you say, remember that your expletive will carry more weight if it's the only one in a given diatribe; repeated use makes the word lose its power to shock.

3. If you're talking with someone whose profanity offends you and there's no easy escape, try facial language first – look mildly shocked or troubled. If that doesn't work, laughingly say: "I don't know if my ears can take that language!" If that doesn't work, ask him directly to curb his tongue, as you find it offensive.

4. If your child uses profanity, explain to him why he shouldn't. Tell him that swear words are usually a crutch for not-so-smart people who can't think of a more precise word to express what they mean. If he continues to use it, discipline him – don't play cute games with him, like making him pay 20 cents every time he swears; that's only likely to make the problem more of an issue than it actually should be.

Property rates

Municipal and other property rates are assessed according to the valuation which is attached to your property by an experienced valuator employed by the local authority. You can get your rates reduced if you can prove that the official valuation of your property is unjustifiably high. This is the usual sequence:

1. An announcement appears in local newspapers and official gazettes that a new valuation of a particular area is to be made.

2. New valuations are open for public inspection at a stated place, and objections are invited. The objections must be lodged according to the procedure set out – usually within 21 days of notification.

3. A valuation court sits in each municipal division to hear objections, and to make decisions on amending the new valuation.

4. The most effective way to object is for property owners of a particular ward to share the costs of engaging an attorney to present their case. If the appeal succeeds, all valuations in that ward are reduced.

5. You may also appear before the valuation court as an individual property owner. You must prove that your house has been valued higher than similar houses in the same area, or that the valuation was based on incorrect facts – such as the wrong floor area, for instance.

6. If you decide to object individually, ask the town clerk's office or local authority's valuation department for details of the procedure.

7. Prepare your case carefully, and remember that a valuation court may actually decide to adjust a particular valuation upwards!

Prostate enlargement

After a man nears his 50's, the walnut-size prostate gland around his urethra may begin to grow, sometimes enlarging to the size of a lemon or lime and blocking the urinary tract. Symptoms include a frequent urge to urinate and a diminished stream of urine. If your doctor suggests surgery, ask him to explain about such alternatives as hormones, radiation or balloon dilatation.

Pruning shears

1. Your pruning shears will cut more efficiently if you clean the blades after each use with a toothbrush dipped in paraffin, then wipe with a light lubricating oil.

2. To restore the cutting edge, disassemble the shears by unscrewing the pivot nut and removing the pivot bolt. Sharpen by stroking a medium-grit oilstone along the cutting edge of the blade. Move from the pivot end to the tip, matching the original bevel as closely as possible (never hone the inside face of the blade, except to remove the burr left by sharpening). Repeat the process with a fine-grit stone. Reassemble the shears.

3. Use bonsai shears for pruning roses and other small ornamentals. The unusual configuration of their blades leaves a concave cut that heals more quickly than the flat cut of regular shears.

Bonsai shears

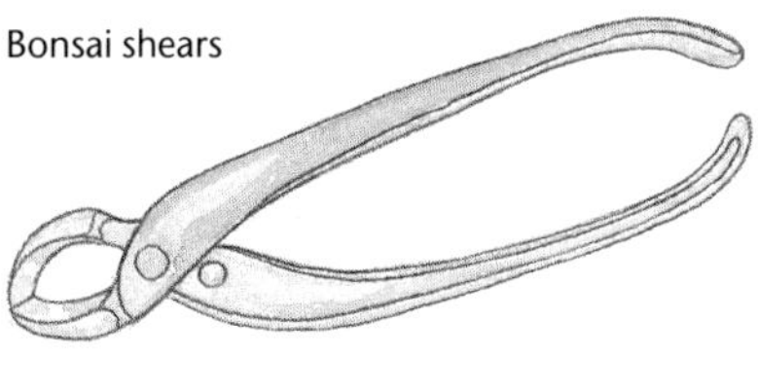

Public speaking

Are you afraid to give a speech? Most people are. Here are some ways to cope with the anxiety:

1. Be well prepared but don't try to memorize your speech. Whether you read it (10 double-spaced typewritten pages usually equal about 20 minutes of speech) or make notes and speak extemporaneously, you should try to rehearse your speech once or twice.

2. Grab the audience's attention by opening with a joke, a moving personal story or a relevant anecdote. Don't make it too controversial; if you antagonize your audience right away, you may never win them back.

3. Organize your speech by asking yourself: "If I could leave my audience with one main idea, what would it be?" Then focus on that idea, supporting it with no more than four secondary points. All of your facts and anecdotes should relate to at least one of these points.

4. When you arrive at the room, make sure that the sound system is working properly.

5. Take advantage of your pumping adrenalin. Use the energy and excitement to help project your ideas forcefully. But calm yourself with a few deep breaths before you start making your speech.

6. Oddly enough, if you acknowledge your nervousness to the audience, there's a good chance that you'll defuse it.

7. Don't worry about being boring. Focus instead on the importance of what you're saying. You're there to communicate ideas – not to be judged on your performance.

8. Watch your posture. If you stand straight, you'll automatically feel and look more self-assured.

9. A comforting fact – most audiences report that they notice little anxiety in speakers. So don't compound your anxiety by thinking everyone can see your trembling legs.

Puffiness

1. If your hands are puffy, hold them over your head for a couple of minutes; repeat at least three or four times a day. Elevate swollen feet for a minimum of 15 minutes.

2. If too much sun causes your lips to swell, use a sunblock specifically designed for lips. Also wear a wide-brimmed sunhat, and try to keep in the shade as much as possible.

AROUND THE EYES

1. Since moisturizers plump up the skin, apply them sparingly around your eyes or use a specially formulated eye cream.

2. The culprit may be water retention; cut down on salt and eat more bananas and grapefruit, which are natural diuretics. Raise the head of your bed or sleep on two pillows to keep your head elevated.

3. Apply soothing compresses of cold milk, borage tea or a mild astringent around the eye.

4. Throw away your frosted eyeshadow – it accentuates puffiness.

Pulley

1. Make your own clothesline pulleys by slipping short lengths of vinyl pipe over smaller steel pipes or wooden dowels or even large spikes driven into trees or posts.

2. The same pipe-over-pipe trick works as a weight-hoisting pulley. In this case, the inside pipe must be strong, smooth, and solidly mounted – between rafters in a garage, for example. Drop your rope over the outside pipe, attach a strong hook, and haul away.

Punch

Nails of different sizes can serve as punches for most sheet metal work, the size being dependent on the job. A nail set will also work, but only if you want a large hole.

Punching bag

1. For a lightweight bag, put a soccer ball or basketball in the waist section of a pair of nylon pantihose and knot the waist. Using the legs, tie it to a hook or beam.

2. For a heavy bag, you can stuff a duffel or heavy-duty laundry bag with rags or laundry and hang it securely from a beam or firmly mounted ceiling hook. Or use a tightly rolled foam mattress. Always make sure that you use some form of padded glove to protect your hands.

Q

Quackery

1. Be wary of exaggerated claims – a guaranteed, fast, easy, painless, miracle cure that sounds too good to be true probably is.

2. Question claims that a product is ahead of its time or that the medical establishment is trying to suppress it or persecute the people promoting it. You should think twice before being lured to a foreign country for an expensive "cure".

3. Suspect any unspecified "scientific studies" by "satisfied users".

4. Don't assume that an advertisement in a reputable publication is a clear endorsement; most publications don't screen their ads.

5. If you have questions about dubious drugs and mail-order devices, call your doctor, the foundation or society for a particular disease or the local consumer protection agency.

6. On your first visit to a doctor, be sure to inspect his office walls. A licensed doctor will often display a diploma from an accredited medical school and certification by the South African Medical and Dental Council. Check any unfamiliar or suspicious credentials – as rare as they may be, there are cases on record of impostors posing as doctors.

Quarantining pets

1. Many countries (including Australia, Britain, Ireland and Israel) require that an animal be quarantined for up

IN TIMES GONE BY

Quacks and others – some got rich quick

Unscrupulous people found out centuries ago that, by trading on fear or greed, they could sell almost anything, and at almost any price. Even cigarette smoking has been touted as being medically beneficial.

In 1901, when bubonic plague struck the Cape, a local newspaper carried this advertisement: "It is a generally accepted fact that smoking is a great protection from the plague. That being the case, the public are strongly advised to smoke Taddy's Myrtle Grove cigarettes."

A peculiarly South African cure-all seems to be the "snake stone" – a flattish, porous stone about the diameter of an old-fashioned penny. It impressed the Swedish physician Thunberg so much in 1793, that he wrote: "The genuineness of a snake stone is tested by its adhering to the palate when placed in the mouth."

A snake stone, placed on a snakebite wound, is said to adhere itself to the wound and suck out the venom. When "gorged", it apparently falls off, and the victim is saved. Snake stones formerly changed hands at very high prices, and one was shown on SATV in 1993.

The most enduring get-rich-quick scheme in rural South Africa is probably the issue of the Kruger Millions – which may never have existed anyway.

Typically, a farm labourer will mention to his employer that he has a friend who knows the whereabouts of boxes full of golden Kruger pounds. Sometimes, there's even a (genuine) sample coin to ensure that the bait is taken.

The farmer then arranges to meet the friend at night, hands over a large amount of cash and receives a bucket supposedly full of golden coins. The top layers look authentic in the moonlight, but turn out to be gold-painted coins, under which is a pile of worthless lead washers.

Gold and silver led some gullible people to part with their money in the early days of the Cape settlement. Profiteers would announce they had discovered gold or silver deposits in the Cape Peninsula and then sell off portions of land for exorbitant prices.

One enterprising merchant reported a rich seam of gold on Table Mountain. In the ensuing rush he made a fortune by selling his land to naive "diggers".

to 6 months before entering. This experience can be very stressful to a pet. If your pet is old or sickly, consult a vet to see if it can withstand quarantine. If at all possible, leave the animal at home with a trusted friend.
2. If you must take your pet with you, contact the foreign consulate well in advance to reserve a space in a quarantine facility. Try to arrange for one that will be near you and allows visits. Find out whom to contact in case problems arise.
3. If allowed, provide your pet with a toy and something that has familiar scents on it – a blanket or a pillowcase stuffed with old clothing from each family member.
4. When your pet is released, take it to a vet for a checkup. Find out what it has been eating. An abrupt change in food could make the animal sick – the vet may suggest a transitional diet.

Quarrels

The best way to end a quarrel is not to start one. However, if you find you're about to quarrel with a loved one, try one of these releases:
1. Stop and count how many deep breaths you can take in three minutes.
2. Call someone – it doesn't matter who it is so long as you trust her – and talk about your feelings. The point is not to involve an outsider in the quarrel but to give yourself a release and perhaps a fresh perspective.
3. Escape to the bathroom for at least 15 minutes with an apple and a good book. Chewing often relieves tension, and so does reading.
4. Try to write down everything you're feeling at the time. Try to express your frustration on paper. If you find it difficult to write, try singing, painting or moulding clay.
5. If you still want to fight, beat up a pillow, go for a fast walk, or engage in some other vigorous physical activity, such as swimming.
6. A sure-fire way of easing the hurt which quarrels sometimes cause is to try to put yourself in the other person's shoes and to look objectively at what you are saying.
7. You can help a quarrel fizzle out by avoiding the use of the word "you" as much as possible, and looking positively at ways in which you can *both* sort out the problem.

Quarry tiles

Quarry tiles are hard, durable, generally unglazed, and available in a variety of earthy tones including red, brown, buff and black. They make an ideal floor surface, either indoors or outdoors, where a hard-wearing but informal or rustic effect is desired.

They are usually about 13 millimetres thick or thicker, and are available in a variety of sizes, the most popular of which is probably 115 x 240 millimetres – about the size of a common stock brick.

Lay the quarry tiles on a concrete screed using as adhesive a 3:1 mixture of Portland cement with fine plastering sand. Quarry tiles rarely have lugs to ensure even spacing when being laid, but small pieces of 3-millimetre hardboard will serve perfectly as temporary spacers.

Suitable shades of grouting compound should be available from the dealer who supplied the tiles.

Grouting compound spilt on the surface of the tiles should be wiped off immediately with a damp cloth. Rub the tile until it is dry to ensure that no stain remains.

Cement on tiles can be removed easily within 24 hours of laying the tiles, by cleaning properly with spirits of salt. This is dilute hydrochloric acid, which should be further diluted one in three parts with tap water. To prevent the acid from attacking the grouting material or from seeping between the tiles, make a "snake" from modelling clay and press it down around the edge of the tile.

When grouting or working on newly laid tiles, kneel on a rigid board about one metre square. This will spread your weight and prevent tiles from being displaced.

Don't forget to start in the area furthest from the door, and work towards the exit.

Questionnaires

Many questionnaires ask for much more information than you're legally required to give. Here's what you do and don't have to answer:
1. On warranty cards you don't have to answer the questions about income, age and housing. This is just market research. In fact, you don't even have to send in the card – all you need for your guarantee is proof of purchase (see *Guarantees, warranties*, p.102).
2. If you don't want unsolicited telephone calls, don't include your telephone number.
3. Telephone surveys? Again, this is market research. If you want to spend your time answering questions for free, go ahead. But you don't have to give any information at all.
4. When you apply for a mortgage bond, a scholarship, credit, insurance or a bank loan, be prepared to answer fully all questions about your health and finances. If there's a personal question you're not comfortable answering, consult a lawyer.
5. Unfortunately, in South Africa you may have to answer questions which may not relate directly to your ability to do the job. Such questions may concern race, sex, marital status or even future marriage plans. You may be asked how many children you have, your present age or date of birth, weight, physical handicaps, the person with whom you live, home ownership or rental status and outstanding debts.

If you feel strongly about answering some of the questions put to you, explain your problem politely, but firmly, to the interviewer.

Quiche

The quiche, an open tart with an egg-based savoury filling, has its origins in France, but has rapidly become a worldwide favourite. It is easy to prepare, convenient to store (it freezes well), and offers an endless variety. This is one dish where you can allow your culinary creativity free rein.

The crust is made of unsweetened shortcrust pastry – remember that thinner pastry enhances the flavour of the ingredients in the filling. Roll out and line a greased pie dish.

To prepare the quiche filling, make a simple white sauce.

1. Melt one generous tablespoon of butter in a saucepan over a low heat.

2. Slowly add ½ cup of flour, stirring constantly to avoid lumps.

3. Once a paste has been formed, add one cup of milk. Stir continuously until the sauce thickens, then remove from the heat and stir in three well-beaten eggs.

4. Now add your savoury fillings. Choose from a selection of asparagus, salmon, ham, bacon, mushroom, cheese, broccoli, spinach or whatever takes your fancy.

5. Season to taste with salt, pepper and a dash of mustard.

6. Grate cheddar cheese on top and bake in a moderate oven heat for 25 to 35 minutes, or until golden brown and set.

7. Garnish with a sprig of fresh herbs and serve immediately with a fresh green or tomato salad.

Quilting

A quilt is a warm bedcover with a padded interlining. At its best, however, the quilt is an art form rich in visual and tactile expression. You don't need to be an artist to create something of lasting beauty using this medium. All you need is a sensitivity to colour and line and patience.

If you look closely at a quilt, you will note a linear pattern made by tiny running stitches. These have a decorative purpose, but also serve to hold together the three layers - the top, the backing and the middle layer of padding, without which it would be a bedspread rather than a quilt.

You will find that hand quilting is quite different from machine quilting. The latter is best suited to many contemporary designs and heavier fabrics. If you like working in small units, try the quilt-as-you-go technique, which simplifies the quilting of a large area by dividing it into smaller, more manageable sections.

You will need the following equipment: a hoop or frame, plain tape to pin to the edges of the quilt to hold it in a frame, a thimble and a good stock of short fine needles.

Choose top and backing fabrics similar in weight, and wash them before you begin. When you select padding, make sure it is bonded, or it will creep through the top layer. If you use synthetic filler, don't iron the quilt, or it will flatten.

Although you can buy quilting templates, they are very easy to make yourself. Essentially, they consist of outlines which you can fill with extra details if desired. These are traced onto the fabric.

Although quilting with a sewing machine is quicker than hand stitching and the stitches are stronger, be sure to work on a large table so that the quilt doesn't slip and ruin your stitching. Work in small units, finishing each before you move on.

Once your quilt is complete, you can finish it by bringing the backing over to the front to make a self-binding, or fold the edges of the top and backing inwards and hold them together with a running stitch. You could also use a separate binding of a contrasting colour to finish.

Quitting a job

Be very careful not to alienate your boss when you leave. You may need his reference down the road.

1. Give more than the notice stipulated in your letter of appointment. If you're in the middle of an important project, ask your new boss if you can stay until it's finished. Whether she says yes or no, she'll certainly respect your commitment to your work and your old employer.

2. Your letter of resignation is part of your permanent personnel file. Keep it simple and factual. If you're quitting because you are unhappy, don't put your gripes in the letter.

3. Offer to train your replacement. If a new person has not yet been hired, leave a list of things she should know and your telephone number. Make copies for your boss and successor.

4. Tell your most important contacts you're leaving and give them the name of your replacement.

Quotation marks

Here's how to use these helpful punctuation marks:

1. When you write, use quotation marks to enclose a cited speaker's or writer's exact words; use them to set off the titles of short works, such as stories, magazine articles, poems and songs, and to draw attention to words and phrases used in a special way (irony and jargon).

2. For a quotation within a quotation, use single quotation marks. For example: John said, "I wonder who wrote, 'To be great is to be misunderstood.' Rachel thinks it was Emerson." If the first and second quotations end together, put a single quotation mark, then double quotation marks: John said, "I wonder who wrote, 'To be great is to be misunderstood.'" Do the reverse – double followed by single quotation marks – if the first and second quotations begin together.

3. Where should other punctuation go? A full stop or comma should always be placed inside quotation marks if a complete sentence is quoted. When you use an exclamation point or question mark, however, it's a different matter; if the punctuation is part of the quoted matter, it goes inside; otherwise it should follow the quotation marks.

4. If a quotation has more than one paragraph, begin each paragraph with quotation marks but use them to close only the final one.

R

Radiator hose

If a leaky radiator hose is causing your car to lose coolant and its engine to overheat, you can usually fix the leak temporarily so that you can drive to a service station.

1. Let the engine cool thoroughly. The coolant is well above the normal 100°C boiling point, and opening the radiator cap prematurely will release a scalding gush of water.

2. When the radiator cap is cool to the touch (20 to 30 minutes), place a cloth over it and turn anticlockwise until you hit a stop – about one-quarter turn – then let go. This will release the remaining pressure, and the cloth will catch any steam and hot coolant. Keep your face averted.

3. If the leak is at the hose connection, retightening the hose clip may do the job temporarily. Don't tighten the clip too much or it will cut through the hose.

4. If the leak is not at the hose connection, look for the leak in the hose and patch it, using insulation tape or even tied rags.

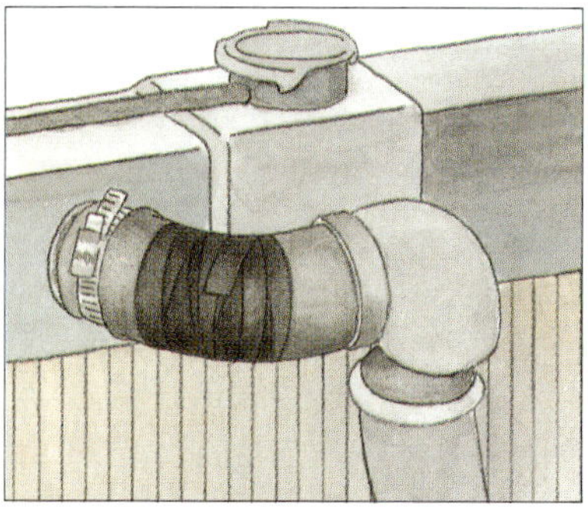

5. Then start the engine and fill the radiator with plain water. Replace the radiator cap, but tighten it only to the first stop so that pressure won't build up again.

6. Put the heater on *High*, and drive at moderate speed to the nearest garage or service station.

REPLACING A HOSE

You may find that the hose clip is "frozen" to the hose (or the hose to the hose neck) by corrosion or rust. Don't try to pry it loose – you could damage the connection at either end, causing a leak.

1. Put some penetrating oil on the hose clip to loosen it.

2. If it's a squeeze- or spring-type hose clip, squeeze and wiggle it with pliers. It should come loose.

3. For a screw-type hose clip, insert the tip of a screwdriver beneath the clip and gently work it around.

4. If the hose is stuck to the hose neck, don't pull. Twist it left to right until it releases. If that doesn't work, cut the hose off beyond the hose neck, slit the remaining piece of hose lengthways, and peel it off.

Radiators

1. In order to work efficiently, a radiator needs an unhampered airflow as the car moves forward. This flow of air is hampered when the fins of the radiator core become clogged with insects, as often happens on long, cross-country trips, especially at night. Clean the fins, using a soft brush, and spray with water from the back to the front (to avoid spraying the dirt back into the engine).

2. Check that the motor vehicle's number plate is not placed too high, blocking the radiator.

3. On long journeys, keep a bottle of radiator sealant in your boot – a leaking radiator can be sealed temporarily until you can reach a service station to have the damage assessed.

4. When you drain a radiator, be aware that the solution may be poisonous if it contains antifreeze. Should the antifreeze still be usable, drain the coolant through a fine sieve (not a kitchen sieve) and re-use.

Radio aerial

1. Aerial broken? If there is a hollow end protruding, you can make a substitute from a wire coat hanger. Using pliers, disengage the coiled joint beneath the hook. Then cut off the hook, straighten the hanger, and jam the coiled end into the aerial hole.

2. If the reception on your car radio is getting weak or ceases but the exterior portion of the aerial is not broken, it's one of three problems: a defective aerial, a bad aerial connection or a broken radio. To find out which, use this test. Pull the aerial cable plug out of the jack in the back of the receiver. (If it's not accessible from under the dashboard, remove the moulding, take out some of the screws, and pull the radio forward.)

Then insert a straightened hanger or a 600-900 millimetre piece of wire through the centre of the aerial hole and lean it against the outer edge of the hole. If the radio begins to pick up AM stations, however poorly, the problem is in the aerial, its mounting or the connection. If there's no improvement, the problem is the radio.

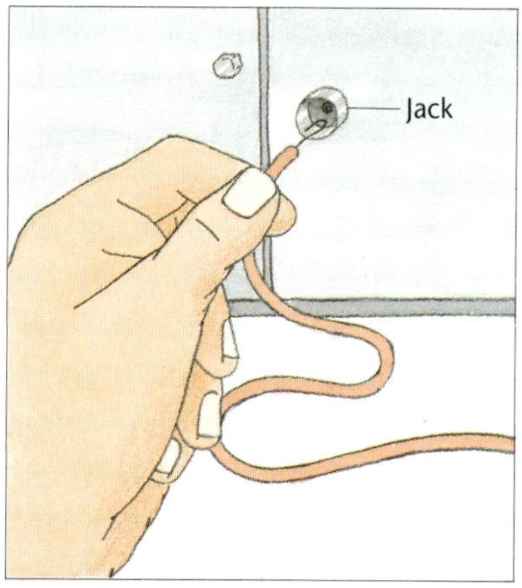

Radio (cordless) telephones

To exploit the security value of a cordless telephone, programme a preset button to call the "Flying Squad" or your security company. Keep the unit fully charged, and extend battery life by leaving the unit "off" when using it within earshot of a wired receiver. You can flick the switch to "on" and answer if a call comes through.

Most cordless telephones have a limited range, although the signal should penetrate several walls. Position the transmitting unit in a line-of-vision with the telephone, whether it's in the bathroom, workshop or lounge, for example.

Raincoats

1. There's little that can substitute for a proper raincoat, but in an emergency you can transform a plastic refuse bag into a poncho. Cut a hole in the bottom for your head, and openings in the sides for your arms. Use a smaller plastic bag as a hood.
2. Remove spots from a raincoat with bicarbonate of soda or scouring powder; rub on with a moistened cloth and rinse well.
3. To make a water-repellent finish last longer, hand-wash rainwear instead of dry-cleaning it. You'll know it's time to renew the finish when even a light rain soaks in (usually after a couple of dry-cleanings).

Rain spatters

Rainy day? Moisten a few paper towels so that you can wipe those dirty splotches off pantihose and trouser legs before they have a chance to dry. Wear dark patterned tights or trousers that won't show the dirt. Keep extra pantihose at work for days when the damage is beyond remedy.

For rainy days when you have to walk to work, wear old shoes with good insulation inside and out. Carry your good shoes in a bag or satchel, and change into them at the office. Keep your old shoes for the wet walk home after work.

Rainwater storage

There are several inexpensive ways to collect rainwater for non-drinking use. Almost any well-cleaned container will do for storing rainwater, once you've collected it. There's always a chance that someone may drink the collected water, so avoid using containers that have held poisons, especially those used as agricultural sprays.

The most convenient way to collect rainwater is as run-off from a roof. Check that gutters and downpipes are free of blockages, and then shorten a downpipe by cutting it with a hacksaw. Wear a mask over your mouth and nose if you have to cut an asbestos pipe, and be careful not to breathe in any of the dust.

Once the downpipe has been shortened, re-attach the elbow or attach a length of flexible PVC pipe to lead to the container. To avoid damage to foundations when the container overflows, set it a few metres away from the building, and on a slope that allows overflow to run away.

To conduct water into the container, make a funnel from a plastic bottle by cutting off the base of the bottle. Prevent excessive solids entering the container and blocking the outlet, by making a loose ball of fine wire mesh and pushing it into the cut-off bottle.

You can create a linked series of containers by leading an overflow pipe from one container to the next. Such a series of containers can be placed one on top of the other, or in a line. If they are in a line on level ground, make sure that each point of attachment of the overflow pipes is slightly lower than the previous one, to avoid buildup of back pressure and subsequent wastage.

Raised-bed planting

If your raised vegetable beds are infested with slugs and snails, it may be because you've enclosed them with boards or stones – ideal havens for the pests. Build the beds the Chinese way instead.
1. Using stakes and string, divide your garden into 150-centimetre-wide beds separated by 60-centimetre-wide paths.
2. Turn the soil inside the beds to a depth of about 30 centimetres, removing all stones and roots. Work in plenty of compost, manure, peat and sand so that the beds rise above the surrounding ground.
3. Rake the beds flat and smooth, and shape their sides. Do not frame them with boards or stones. Dig narrow trenches between them and the paths to catch water runoff.
4. You can remove the string from around the beds, but leave the stakes in place; they'll keep the hose from dragging across your plants as you water them.
5. Unlike a conventional garden, these raised beds won't need annual tilling. Just add a layer of compost and, if necessary, a dose of lime every autumn and turn it under with a fork.

Raises

Do you want a raise but don't know how to ask?
1. Try to determine what your job is worth. Ask friends in similar positions if they're willing to swap information in confidence. Check the employment ads and consult any professional organizations you belong to. Make allowances for factors that affect salary: your geographical location, your education (an advanced degree may be worth more money), the number of people you supervise, and the budget for which you are responsible (salary is usually commensurate with responsibility).
2. Lay your groundwork. Routinely give your supervisor any memos or documents that demonstrate your achievements. Pass on any compliments you get (but don't overdo it).
3. Always try to ask for slightly more money than you think you can get. You'll allow the boss to feel she's saved money by giving you slightly less, and you'll probably be offered what you want. You may even get what you ask for.
4. Time your request wisely. Obviously your chances are better after you've scored some kind of success or when the company is doing well. (Although, surprisingly, many people have received big raises during shake-ups, when a company was anxious to keep things stabilized and didn't want to lose valuable employees.) If a performance review shows that your work has improved, take it as an opportunity to ask for extra compensation.

5. Sometimes it's best to take on new responsibilities or projects and wait to ask for a raise (and perhaps a new title) until after you've carried them out successfully.
6. If a raise is less than you want, ask for a review in six months. If possible, set goals that, when met, will entitle you to the increase.

Rakes

1. Never leave a rake lying with the teeth upright: a child might spike a foot, or an unwary person step on the teeth and be hit in the face by the handle flying up.
2. To fight rust on your steel rake and make it easier to clean, spraypaint it with metal paint. Spray on an undercoat of metal primer first.
3. A little wire mesh over the head of a garden rake keeps stones from bouncing over the top; tack or staple it about 30 centimetres up the handle.
4. As a substitute for a lawn rake, you can secure some wire mesh to an old broom. Or use your power mower (see *Lawns*, p.123).

Rape

Rape – unlawful sexual intercourse with a female under the age of 16 years, or sexual intercourse with a woman without her consent – is the most commonly committed violent crime in South Africa. In 1993, a rape took place every 90 seconds of each 24-hour day.

If you're ever raped, don't touch anything that could affect the evidence. Don't change your clothes, and don't wash. Immediately phone someone you can trust and who can help you physically and psychologically. Phone a friend, minister of religion, your doctor or the police, tell them what happened and ask to be taken to a hospital.

Lay a charge of rape as soon as possible, even if you don't know who the rapist is. Preliminary evidence can be taken almost anywhere, even at the hospital. If you hesitate about laying the charge, your attacker's defence counsel may suggest that this casts doubt on whether rape actually took place. It is also important that your evidence be corroborated, especially by trained medical staff, so allow yourself to be examined as soon as possible after the rape.

Rape is a particularly cruel and vicious crime, and its victims suffer severe psychological and emotional trauma. Where pregnancy results from rape, an abortion may be legally carried out and, while this may bring some relief, it also brings further long-term problems – particularly psychological.

Correct counselling after rape, as well as before and after an abortion, is important. Your doctor may be able to suggest a helpful professional therapist, or you can contact Life Line or a women's organization in your district, such as Rape Crisis or People Opposing Woman Abuse (POWA).

Be aware of the danger to yourself, even at home. If you're alone, keep external doors locked and, if windows provide unobserved access, keep them locked as well. Consider fitting bars and safety gates.

Do your gardening when a husband, male friend or fierce dog are nearby. Try to avoid going out alone at night and don't travel along lonely routes on your own.

Make sure you keep your car doors locked with windows open only a centimetre or two at all times. If you have to park in a lonely or unfamiliar place, look around carefully before you get out of your car.

If you're attacked and there are people about, scream and try to break away towards them. If you're caught alone, try to talk your way to safety. Say you're menstruating, that you have a venereal disease, or that your husband is nearby. Assess your own situation, and do remember that each offender's reactions will be different.

Rats

1. Bait several traps but don't set them. Just leave them out for a few days, replenishing the bait as needed, until the rats in a shed or storeroom get used to them as a food source. Then set them.
2. Secure refuse bins so that they don't leak or lose their lids when pushed over. Keep them on a rack 30 to 45 centimetres off the ground and at least one metre away from walls.
3. Plug cracks and holes in outside walls with wads of steel wool, then permanently seal with shade-cloth or heavy-gauge sheet metal.
4. Here's an old-fashioned barrel trap for getting rid of a shed full of rats. Fill a barrel or oil drum halfway with water; stretch heavy, stiff paper over the top of the open barrel and secure with staples or duct tape. Place the barrel next to a table or some other object that rats can climb on. Spread food on the paper for four or five nights running until the rats expect a nightly meal. Then cut an X in the paper with a razor blade. The unsuspecting rats will fall through the paper into the barrel and drown.
Caution: Keep cats or other climbing pets confined on the night you set your trap.

Razor bumps & nicks

1. To prevent them, shower before shaving or steam your face over a basin of hot running water before applying shaving cream. Shave in the same direction the hair grows, using a light touch and long strokes; avoid going over the same area of your face more than twice.
2. Rinse a nick with cold water, then press hard. If the bleeding persists,

apply a styptic pencil or hydrogen peroxide on a cottonwool bud. (Alternatively, use lemon juice or a bicarbonate of soda paste.) For deep nicks you should apply an antibiotic ointment or cream.

3. To loosen ingrown hairs that can cause bumps, clean your face with a loofah sponge. If you have just one or two such hairs, pluck them out with a sterilized needle or a pair of tweezers; if you have more, consider using a depilatory cream.

4. No shaving cream? Use soap or baby oil instead.

IN TIMES GONE BY

Stubble trouble

The quest for a clean-shaven face has driven men to experiment with many kinds of razors.

☐ Prehistoric men shaved with clam shells, shark's teeth, sharpened pieces of flint or knives.

☐ In the fourth century BC the Egyptians smoothed their faces with gold and copper razors – items that have since been found in their tombs by archaeologists.

☐ A widely used straight, or "cut-throat" razor – a long steel blade that folded into a handle – was made in Sheffield, England, in the 18th century. Although it offered an incomparably close shave, it was hazardous when wielded by an unskilled hand.

☐ The first crude "safety razor" – a sharp blade that was set into a wooden casing so that it couldn't slice the shaver's skin, was manufactured in 1762.

☐ In America during the early 1900s, King Camp Gillette collaborated with the inventor William Nickerson to design a safety razor with disposable blades. It first went on sale in 1903, and despite a wide array of improvements, its basic design has changed very little since.

☐ In 1928 Joseph Schick patented an electric razor that provided the first dry shave. Today men can choose from a variety of hightech models, including those with rotary blades and microscreens.

Reaching things

1. Can't reach something on a high shelf? Use braai tongs.

2. Push and pull objects out of tight spots with a yardstick or straightened wire coat hanger. Place sticky tape or gum on the end to pick up light items.

3. If an ordinary match won't reach the wick in a hurricane lamp, light a strand of uncooked spaghetti.

Reading

1. If you haven't enough time for the reading you'd like to do, scan the first and last paragraphs of an article or the first and last pages of a book's first chapter to decide if it's worth your while to read what's in between.

2. Set time limits on your reading material and sort it accordingly: a high-priority pile for newspapers and news magazines that become dated quickly; a medium-priority pile for material that should be read for your job or your investments; a low-priority pile for material that has no time frame, such as cookery books, novels or travel magazines.

3. Don't try to read everything – sometimes it's enough to know that you have an article on file in case you need specific information sometime in the future.

4. Make an appointment with yourself to do your reading; if necessary, get up half an hour earlier, go to bed half an hour later, or schedule reading for your quiet time.

5. If you're looking for something other than a best-seller, ask your librarian for advice; he may ask about your interests or refer you to one of several guides to the classics.

6. Don't throw away all those paperback books; set up an exchange at work. If you find you don't like a book you borrowed, there's no need to feel guilty – you haven't spent a cent; just return it for another.

7. If your child resists "good" books, consult a children's librarian or a sympathetic, well-informed bookseller. She may be able to interest him in books you don't know about.

SCANNING FOR SPEED

1. Let your eyes follow your hand as it brushes down each page. Practise focusing on a line as a whole rather than one word at a time.

2. Run your fingertip or a bookmark under every line as you read it, to focus your attention and prevent your mind from wandering.

3. As you scan, mark the passages you'd like to return to.

Record keeping

Is tax season a nightmare? If you keep good records, you'll find everything in order when you need it.

1. Find out what you can deduct; check with an accountant, tax specialist or the Receiver of Revenue's office.

2. Then buy a spiral-bound calendar. Every night jot down all your tax-deductible travel, entertainment and meal expenditures; note the time, date, place and the nature of the business conducted. Keep all receipts.

3. Keep all your receipts in 20 x 25 centimetre envelopes organized by category: medical expenses, office supplies and so forth.

4. Pay all your bills by cheque. When you balance your bank statement, place the cancelled cheques for deductible expenses in the appropriate envelopes.

5. Keep a separate, clearly labelled envelope for records of any share sales or other capital gains. (See also *Income tax returns*, p.114.)

Recycling

Many of the everyday objects we use and discard can actually be used again – not necessarily in their same form or composition, but after being recycled. Recycling is the conversion of waste into new products and, to be most effective, needs careful organization and community co-operation.

If you want to start a recycling programme, first find out who will buy or accept particular types of waste. Check the classified advertisements in your newspaper, and look under "Recyclers" in the Yellow Pages. Once you know exactly what is required, build up a network of "supplier" households and businesses that generate the waste materials you want to see recycled. If you can persuade suppliers to separate their waste – by keeping paper apart from plastic, for instance – your work will be greatly reduced. You will still have to arrange final sorting and, possibly, delivery to several destinations.

If you cannot meet the quantities or conditions required by commercial recyclers, consider joining an existing recycling campaign. Contact schools and service clubs, such as Lions and Round Table, to find out whether they administer a recycling campaign. A number of charities advertise that they will accept or even collect certain types of material for recycling. Almost all glass bottles are accepted for recycling by some stores of the larger supermarket chains, which even pay a few cents per bottle. Glass, probably the most durable and hazardous of non-toxic wastes, can also be disposed of in the large blue "igloos" in many towns.

For any further information on recycling, contact the National Committee to Co-ordinate Recycling, PO Box 1378, Pinegowrie 2123.

References

1. If you didn't get along well with your former boss, ask someone else with whom you've worked for a reference – preferably someone with a managerial title.

2. If you know that a former employer had reservations about certain aspects of your work, tell him that you've improved in those areas. He might be willing to think again and give you a recommendation on the basis of your strengths.

3. If you've never held a paid job, ask former teachers or supervisors to recommend you for a particular job or for voluntary work.

4. To avoid alienating a referee, always phone first and ask if she would be willing to recommend you. Follow up with a thank-you note.

Refinishing

1. To darken bare wood, soak a plug of tobacco in half a litre of ammonia for a week. Strain the liquid through an old pair of pantihose before mopping it onto wood.

2. You can turn bare oak from light brown to driftwood grey by rubbing it with household ammonia; the tannic acid in the wood reacts with the solution to change the colour to a shade of grey permanently.

3. Never apply shellac in high humidity. The finish clouds as vapour condenses on the surface.

4. To disguise an unsightly furniture scratch, rub bits of pecans or Brazil nuts into the wood.

Refrigerators

1. Should your refrigerator or freezer conk out, check for a loose plug, a tripped circuit breaker or blown fuse or a temperature control accidentally turned off. If these are all in order, test the electrical outlet with a lamp. If it lights, the problem is in the appliance or its cord; if not, the outlet or house wiring is at fault. Until you can get it fixed, plug the unit into another outlet, but be sure any extension cord you use is rated the same amperage as the unit.

2. Water on the floor? Perhaps the drain tray is placed incorrectly or is cracked and needs replacing. Or maybe the drain tube is clogged; if so, flush hot water through it.

COOLING PROBLEMS

1. Make sure the temperature control is turned on. If it is, change it to a colder setting; wait 24 hours before adjusting it again.

2. Check the condenser coils at the base or the back of the refrigerator; if dust has gradually collected on them,

the unit won't cool properly. Clean thoroughly with your vacuum's crevice or brush tool.

3. Check to see that the door is sealed tightly. If the gasket is torn, dried out or obviously damaged, replace it. If it's in good condition, the refrigerator is probably improperly positioned on the floor; adjust the levelling legs or rollers.

Reservations

1. If you are making a reservation directly with the hotel, phone during normal business hours. If you intend staying at a hotel which is part of a chain, phone the central booking office. Some have toll-free numbers.

2. Always ask for the confirmation number or name of the person taking the reservation.

3. Ask if there are any special price packages available.

4. Have your details repeated back to you. Ensure that they have spelt your name correctly – this can be vital in the case of computerized reservations. Double check all special requests, such as those you may have made for babies' cots, kennels for pets or on-site babysitters.

5. Ask about the cancellation policy. Apart from forfeiting your deposit, you may be charged a non-arrival fee.

6. Always give the manager or staff an opportunity to solve a problem immediately, rather than writing a letter of complaint afterward.

7. If you are not able to settle your dispute with the hotel, contact The South African Tourism Board, Private Bag X164, Pretoria 0001.

IN A RESTAURANT

1. To avoid getting a bad table, find out the number of a table you like and ask for it specifically when you phone for a reservation. If you haven't been to the restaurant, specify your preferences and hope for the best.

2. If your table isn't ready when you arrive, you may get it faster by becoming a slight pest; rather than going to the bar to wait, stay put and keep asking when your table will be ready.

3. If you're not happy with your table, ask for a better one. If the restaurant is crowded, it helps to tip the maître d'.

Restaurants

1. If you dine out frequently, join a discount dining programme. Speak to friends who belong, or enroll through a participating restaurant.

2. When dining out with the children, consider a buffet. It will probably be cheaper than a full-course meal and will be more likely to please a variety of tastes and appetites.

3. If a waiter spills food or a beverage on you, you're entitled to be reimbursed for any dry-cleaning expenses; be sure to get the name of the waiter and one witness.

4. To get a waiter's attention, wave your hand or call "Waiter!" Never snap your fingers.

5. If a waiter is taking too long to bring the bill, as soon as he looks in your direction, stand up as though you are going to leave.

6. If you complain to the waiter about something and you're still not satisfied, insist on speaking to the manager or owner.

Retirement

Whether or not you retire early, you will have to be prepared for a drop in income. Even if you worked for a firm for 40 years, for example, you would probably only get a pension of two thirds of your final salary. Work out how much money will cover your living expenses, and consider where you could cut down, taking into account the erosive effect of inflation on savings. Selling up and moving to a new town can be expensive. Don't forget to take these removal expenses into account.

1. Check with your company's personnel department to find out how early retirement would affect your pension payouts.

2. See how your investments could be rearranged to provide income instead of long-term growth.

3. Work out how much money you would have if you started spending your savings and selling off your capital assets. To decide at what rate, look at a life-expectancy table. If you're 65 and expect to live 15 more years, you should plan to sell or spend $\frac{1}{15}$ of your capital per year; if you estimate 25 more years, plan to sell off $\frac{1}{25}$. Don't forget to take the effects of inflation into account.

4. Add in the money you would save if you kept just enough life insurance to allow your survivors to maintain their standard of living and pay estate duties, any leftover debts and your funeral expenses.

5. Now add it all up. Could you live comfortably on the results?

Rice

1. To prevent rice from becoming sticky, add a few drops of cooking oil or a teaspoon of butter or margarine to the cooking water.

2. For snowy white rice, add a few drops of lemon juice or vinegar to the cooking water.

3. If your rice turns out like wallpaper paste, use it in a casserole, in soup or to stuff peppers. Try again, using less water. Fluff the rice gently with a fork before serving.

4. Save electricity and time by cooking large quantities of rice and freezing it in small dinner-size batches. Cook straight from the freezer by pouring boiling water over the rice and simmering for a minute or two.

5. Make your own flavoured rice by replacing the water with stock and herbs. Chicken stock with mushrooms and onions is tasty.

6. If the salt in your salt cellar is damp and cannot be shaken out, place a few uncooked rice grains in the cellar. They will keep the holes unblocked. Alternatively, replace the salt.

7. When rice boils over, blow on the surface of the pot. This will cool the surface down briefly and stop it boiling over, giving you a chance to take the pot off the hotplate.

Roof gardens

Before starting a garden on the roof of your block of flats, consult your landlord and offer to share the cost of an architect's or engineer's inspection to make sure the roof can take the extra weight. Here's how to keep the weight down:

1. Lay a thick sheet of plastic on the roof to protect it from seepage and plant roots. Then construct a box frame of planks placed on edge and set it on top of the plastic. Reinforce the corners with angle irons.

2. Fill the frame with organic matter – grass clippings and finely shredded mealie cobs are suitable; vermiculite or perlite will serve as an alternative. (Beware of using peat moss, which becomes very heavy when wet.)

3. Water thoroughly and add 60 gm of 2.3.2 fertilizer per square metre. Water again lightly, then set out plants and sow seeds. (Herbs, onions, radishes, lettuce, cucumbers, brinjals, green beans, peas, strawberries, peppers and dwarf varieties of tomatoes will all thrive in this attractive roof garden in the sky).

4. Keep the surface of the "soil" evenly moist until germination, then increase watering to 10 litres daily. Feed with a soluble fertilizer every fourth or fifth watering.

Roof leaks

1. In an emergency, protect a damaged roof with a plastic drop cloth. Lay the plastic over the damaged spot, tucking its top edge under a course of shingles above that spot. Tack the plastic down or weight it with bricks or sandbags.

2. Patch a small damaged spot with sheet metal or an asphalt shingle. Spread some roofing cement on the underside of the patching material, then force the patch under the shingle course directly above the leak.

3. To catch water dripping into an attic from a leaky roof, nail a small wood block to the bottom of the rafter nearest the leak. Then place a bucket under the block.

Roofs

1. Here's how to give yourself secure footing when you are working on a steep roof. Secure one end of a long rope to a sturdy, stationary object, such as a tree or stoep, on the far side of the house. (If you use a car bumper, make sure the keys are in your pocket!) Then tie the other end to a weight, such as a large bolt, and toss it over the roof ridge. Lay a ladder on the far side of the house, from the roof ridge to the gutter. Thread the rope between the top two rungs and tie it to the bottom rung.

2. When working on any pitched roof, use a safety line. Secure a rope as described above and tie the loose end around your waist, allowing enough slack to let you work freely but not so much that you could fall over the roof's edge.

3. For traction when working on a roof, wear soft rubber-soled shoes or tackies, not slippery soles.

4. To move about the roof safely, crawl on your hands and knees.

5. During winter, in winter rainfall areas of the country, you should take great care when repairing tiled south-facing roof slopes. Moss growing on steep pitches can become hazardously slippery.

Roommates

1. Looking for a roommate? When you interview a stranger, take along a friend whose judgment you trust. Chat about smoking, neatness, TV, music and your social activities to make sure your habits and personalities are compatible.

2. When you move in with a new roommate, work out certain rules for bathroom times, overnight guests, shut-off times for the TV and stereo, division of expenses and housekeeping chores and refrigerator use.

3. Separate telephones and answering machines will help ensure that things run smoothly.

4. If you live with more than one person, post weekly maintenance duties for each. The refrigerator door is a good place for the list.

5. Develop a civilized method of airing problems and don't let annoyances fester. Humour can go a long way towards working things out.

Rose propagation

To start a new rosebush from your favourite variety, snip a perfect rose along with 30 centimetres of stem that has at least five leaf clusters. Set the stem immediately in water and leave it there for an hour or longer (up to two days if you want to enjoy the bloom). Prepare a bed in a sheltered, shaded spot. Dig to a depth of 45 centimetres and then add one part builder's sand to each part soil.

To prepare the cutting for rooting, snip off the blossom and cut off the top of the stem at an angle one centimetre above a bud. Cut the bottom of the stem off square one centimetre below the bottom leaf cluster. Strip off all but the topmost leaves, then dust the bottom of the cutting with powdered rooting hormone for softwood (available at nurseries).

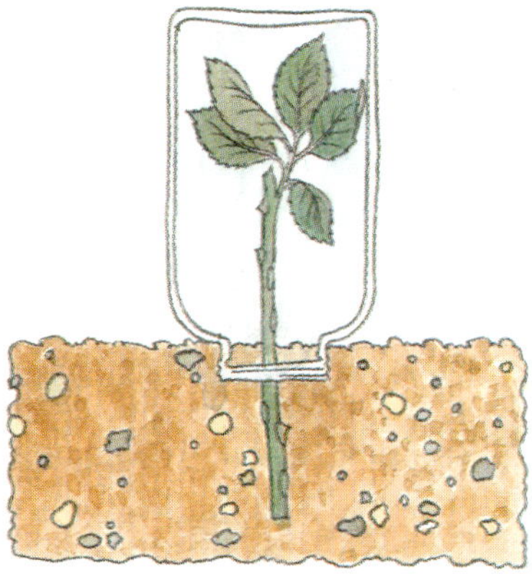

Plant this almost bare stick in the prepared soil to a point just below the second leaf scar from the top. Firm the soil around the cutting, water well, and cover with an inverted fruit jar. If water droplets gather inside the jar, prop it on stones so that air can enter.

The appearance of a second new leaf means that the cutting has started to root. Let it grow undisturbed for eight or nine months before transplanting the new rosebush.

Runaways

1. Little runaways, usually newly independent pre-teen primary schoolchildren, tend to head for the park

DID YOU KNOW . . . ?

Roses in myth and history

□ Myths about roses abounded in ancient Greece and Rome. One was that roses were originally white until Venus, the goddess of love, pricked her foot on a rose thorn as she hurried to save her imperilled lover. A drop of her sacred blood fell on the bush's flower, dyeing it the deep, lustrous red we see in roses today.

□ The rose gave its name to the cycle of prayers known as the rosary, literally "a rose garden". Rose petals may actually have been joined together to form the first rosary "beads".

□ The 15th-century conflicts between the English royal houses of York and Lancaster are known as the Wars of the Roses because the men of York supposedly wore a white rose as their badge while those of Lancaster wore a red one. But, in fact, Lancaster did not adopt the red rose as its badge until the wars were over.

□ In the 1870s Pretoria, now known as the Jacaranda City, was called the City of Roses. Roses, especially rambling roses, grew in many gardens, over hedges and alongside roads.

near the house or to a friend's house, and they generally make it home by suppertime or bedtime. In fact, you may miss the drama of the occasion and think they're just visiting.

2. An older runaway presents a more serious problem. You, the parent, may have little or no warning, especially if communication has failed during the turbulent early teen years. Watch for such signs of discontent as loss of interest in schoolwork, withdrawal, depression and unexplained bursts of anger. And pay special attention to your teenager when there is a major change in the family: death, remarriage, impending divorce or a move to another town.

3. If your child has run away, your task of finding him may be made easier if you know what has been going on in his life.

Make sure that you are fully aware of your child's extra-curricular programme at school; make a point of meeting his friends, and keep a list of all their phone numbers; find out the names of any youth clubs, nightclubs, shopping centres, games halls and other places he likes to frequent.

4. Inform the police and your local welfare officer that your child is missing. Be ready to provide a recent photograph as well as a full description of the child and the clothes he was wearing. Have the photo published in your local newspaper or, if your think he might have travelled further afield, in national newspapers. Search the neighbourhood and your child's favourite haunts.

Rust

The best defence against rust is prevention. The second best: treatment as soon as spots appear.

1. To protect your metal workshop equipment or any metals exposed to the elements, apply two coats of clean synthetic resin mixed with lamp black or any coloured pigment. Spray moving parts with a moisture-displacing silicone spray lubricant.

2. Rub small patches of rust with a typewriter eraser. It removes spots and won't scratch the surface.

3. To keep iron and cast-iron garden furniture rust-free, scrape or use a wire brush to get down to the bare metal. Paint with a rust-preventative primer followed by a premium top coat. Renew the top coat where needed each spring. Pay particular attention to any metal that is in contact with plants or soil.

CARS

1. Most new cars have extensive rustproofing. Beware if your dealer tries to sell you more. It's a rarely needed additional expense.

2. Protect the underbody of your car from rust by cleaning off the dirt and caked mud which has stuck to the car. Wash with a powerful hose to remove the road film and any adhering mud. Check the underbody box sections and clean out all mud or leaves with a stiff wire brush. Then, using a hosepipe, flush with water.

3. Place the car on a lift or safety stand and make sure that all drain holes are clear; they're on the underside of each door and in the frame or unit body. Also, to keep water out, make sure access holes placed in the sides of doors are firmly plugged.

4. Chips and scratches let moisture in under the paint surface. Make sure that you fix them immediately. Scrape away loose paint and rust with the corner of a single-edged razor blade, then wipe the spot with rust converter (a product that combines a rust inhibitor with a primer, thus eliminating a step). Wash with a mild detergent, rinse well, and dry thoroughly. Then, using an artist's paintbrush, apply the primer that is recommended for your car's model and colour. Let dry, then apply the correct paint. Don't be worried if the colour doesn't match exactly – that's a minor problem compared to rust damage.

Rust stains

Non-washable garments must be drycleaned, but washable fabrics with rust stains can be treated in one of several ways:

1. Rub a paste of salt and vinegar into the stain; let stand for 30 minutes, then wash as usual.

2. Soak the rust stain in lemon juice, then dry the garment in the sun to bleach out; rinse thoroughly.

3. Work a paste of cream of tartar and hot water into the stain; let set, then wash as usual.

4. Boil five stalks of rhubarb (cut into 1-centimetre pieces) in one cup of water until soft; pour the hot liquid over the stain. Wash as usual.

S

Safe-deposit boxes

1. Keep all valuable documents in a safe-deposit box: birth, adoption, marriage, divorce and death certificates; real estate deeds; military papers; share, bond or savings certificates; a copy of your will; a household inventory; and all insurance policies except those for life insurance. Keep an up-to-date list of the box's contents at home.
2. If you lose one of the keys to your box, the bank will provide a new one for a small fee. If you lose both keys, the bank may have to get a locksmith to drill the lock – a procedure which could prove costly.
3. Check your home owner's policy to see if it covers the contents of your safe-deposit box, or ask the bank if it offers insurance.
4. For more privacy, space and accessibility, consider renting a private safe which is housed in a specially constructed strongroom. This facility is available at certain banks.
5. When a box renter dies, the bank will only allow the executor of the will to open the security box. Therefore it is important that you keep all documents that your family may need in the event of your death – your will, funeral insurance, cemetery plot deed and life insurance policy in a safe place at home. The will is particularly important since the bank will not allow the executor to open the box without it.

Safes

If you don't have a safe and need a place to hide cash, jewellery or other small valuables, avoid the obvious.
1. Put them in a frozen vegetable box in the freezer or in a cream carton or the cavity of a green pepper. (Avoid the foods thieves are likely to sample, such as ice cream or fruit.)
2. Wrap them in plastic and store in a vacuum cleaner bag.
3. Hide them in a hollowed-out hardcover book.
4. Keep them in empty detergent boxes stored under the sink or in the laundry room's cupboard.

Safety gates

1. If you don't like the look and inconvenience of safety gates in your home, hang stable doors between rooms instead; close the bottom section whenever you want to restrict your toddler's travels.
2. You can substitute a screen door for a solid door in your child's room; ensure that the lock is on the outside. That way you'll be able to see what the child is up to every time you pass.
3. When a friend brings a crawler or toddler to visit your normally child-free home, you can improvise temporary safety gates from mattresses or tables turned on their sides. Or for a longer visit, hinge window screens or pieces of plywood to the doorjambs; equip the unhinged side with a hook and eye. The preferred type of safety gate has a straight top edge and rigid mesh screen.

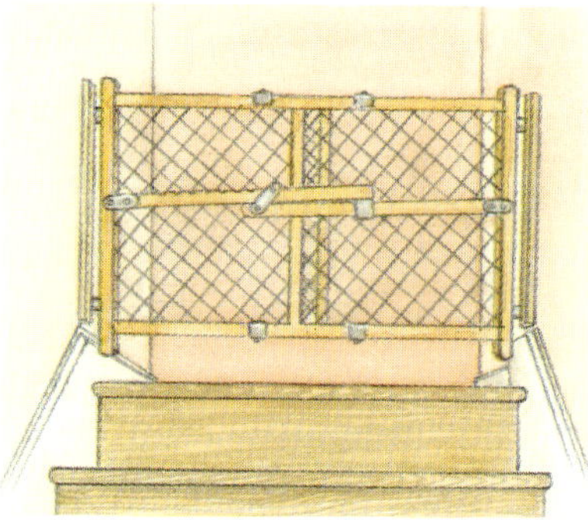

Safety in the home

Misadventure in the home is likely to be more serious for young children and the elderly; young children because their curiosity can lead them into serious danger, and the elderly because falls are likely to have grave consequences. A faulty electrical system, of course, is a hazard to all, and if there is any suspicion of a fault in an appliance or in the wiring, call in a competent specialist for an inspection before you use it.

A great many "ordinary" household substances are potentially hazardous. The long list includes *all* medicines, bleaches, detergents, ammonia, aerosols, spot removers and various other cleaning materials, paraffin, petrol, pesticides and herbicides, paint removers and thinners (including nail polish remover), and especially drain cleaner and stove cleaners. Store these items in cupboards that are locked and out of reach. Never store poisons or harmful substances in any container that your child may associate with food. A notorious example is paraffin used for window cleaning, which is sometimes stored in cooldrink bottles.

Ask at your hardware store about safety latches. These attachments, designed to prevent toddlers from opening drawers and cupboards, are relatively inexpensive and are easy to fit. Install these latches on cupboards containing glassware and other objects, such as matches, knives, sharp tools and scissors, that could hurt an inquisitive child.

Expired or unwanted medicines, including drugs sold over the counter, should be disposed of. The safest way to do this is to take them along to your pharmacist and tell him that you no longer require them.

Check your garden and even flower vases for poisonous plants, which include poinsettias, oleanders, moonflowers and arums. If you are not sure whether a plant is poisonous, ask a gardening specialist. He can probably refer you to an authoritative local source if he doesn't know himself.

To ensure safety on the floor, check carefully that loose mats have non-slip backings, and that all handholds on stairs are firm and solidly fixed. And if windows are unbarred, especially upstairs windows, ensure that they are firmly locked when there are small children about. Do not allow children to bounce or jump on a bed or near a window – they could bounce right out.

Saffron

Dried marigolds

Substitute homegrown marigolds (*Calendula officinalis*) for saffron. Their pungent flavour and colour are similar. Let the flowerheads air-dry or dry them in a microwave (p.87), then grind the petals into a fine powder with a mortar and pestle. Use in pastries, fish stews and Spanish paella, adding a pinch more than you would of saffron.

Sagging stoep

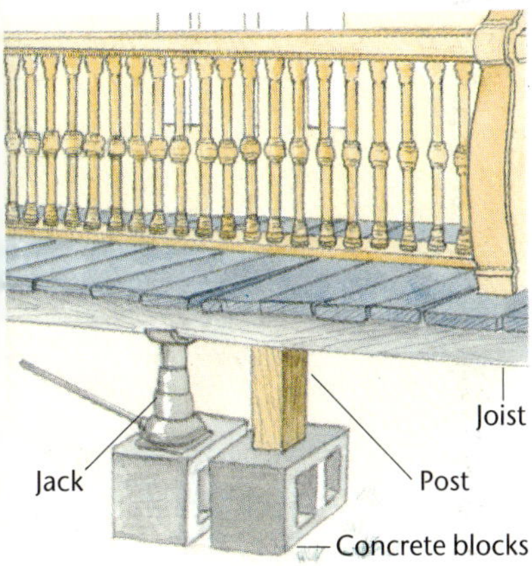

With the help of a car jack, you can install a temporary brace until you have a chance to make proper repairs on a sagging stoep. Place a sturdy board on a concrete block as shown. Position the jack securely under the header joist.

Make sure that the jack remains plumb while you raise the stoep (stand clear in case the jack slips). Then cut a strong, square post to fit between the joist and a board atop another concrete block. Put the post in place and remove the jack carefully and slowly.

Sales slips

Lost the sales slip for merchandise you want to return?

1. If the price sticker is intact, it will sometimes be accepted as proof of purchase in lieu of a receipt.

2. If you have an account, most stores will let you return the item in exchange for credit.

3. Stores where you don't have an account will usually give a credit voucher for the amount of your returned purchase.

4. Exchanging a gift can be a problem, but if you keep the container and packing material, they might help you convince the store manager to refund the purchase price.

Salt substitutes

Try this blend of herbs: one teaspoon garlic powder and one teaspoon each of dried basil, origanum and dried lemon rind. Use a mortar and pestle to grind them together; transfer to a salt cellar. Add a few grains of rice to keep the mixture dry.

For a spicier blend, use one teaspoon each of ground cloves, black pepper and crushed coriander seed, plus two teaspoons paprika and one tablespoon rosemary.

Sanding

1. Use fine sandpaper to roughen finished wood before applying new enamel or varnish. Sand between coats, too.

2. When you are sanding, be sure to wear rubber gloves (neoprene gloves will do in an emergency) to protect your skin and keep oily fingerprints off the wood.

3. To sand chair rungs and table legs, cut a strip of sandpaper and apply masking tape to the back as reinforcement. Then pull the paper back and forth around the rung or leg.

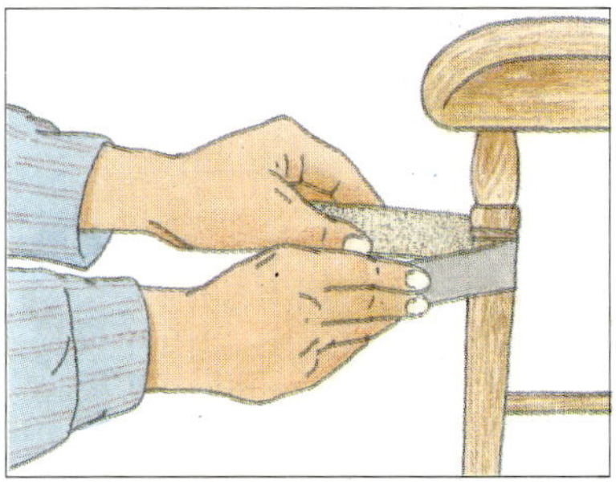

4. At carvings and turnings, fold the sandpaper and fit the folded edge into the curve so that the grit smooths both faces at the same time. Use fine steel wool to get all the way into deep crevices in the wood.

5. Make a tack cloth to wipe sanded wood clean of dust: dip cheesecloth in water, wring it out, dip it in turpentine, and shake it dry. Then drip varnish onto the cloth from a brush, fold it, and knead until the varnish is evenly spread. Store the rag in a jar or in plastic wrap. If it dries out, moisten it again with water and turpentine.

Saving money

1. Treat your savings as a necessity like food and clothing. Aim to build up a readily available emergency cash reserve – enough to cover such essentials as groceries, mortgage and car payments, and service accounts for at least three months.

2. Instead of relying on your self-discipline, arrange with your bank manager to automatically transfer a specific amount every month from your current account to an interest-bearing bank account.

3. If you get 13 salary cheques a year, use 12 of them – one a month – for the family budget: put the extra salary cheque or bonus, into your savings account – try not to spend it.

4. Or use the "loose money" system. At the end of each day, put all your loose change in a jar; once a week, deposit the accumulated coins in your savings account.

5. Try not to supervise your children's saving and spending too strictly or critically. Let them learn to handle their own money.

Letting them learn lessons with small amounts will save them expensive lessons later in life.

DID YOU KNOW?

Get-rich strategies of the early Dutch

Among some of the early Dutch settlers in southern Africa, it was a practice to attain wealth by marrying a rich widow, rather than by saving money. Cash was scarce and financial arrangements were shaky.

Although banking transactions of a sort took place at the Cape from the early days of settlement, the first state bank, the Bank van Leening, was established only in 1793. Sometimes known as the Lombard Bank, this bank lent paper money for up to 18 months at five per cent.

Following the second British occupation, Cape banking was placed on a slightly firmer foundation, although it was only in 1836 that the state monopoly on banking was ended. Between that year and 1873 at least 30 town and divisional banks opened.

Unfortunately, by 1892, about half of them had failed utterly, ruining their investors. Not surprisingly, many people mistrusted banks, and preferred to secrete their cash somewhere about the homestead, or to invest in livestock.

Somewhat more secure savings schemes were introduced in later years with the advent of building societies and other institutions, including the Post Office Savings Bank, which started in 1911.

Meanwhile, tales of misplaced or buried family fortunes of gold and silver are still to be encountered across the country.

Saws and sawing

Two kinds of handsaws are generally used around the home – those with a flexible blade, and the smaller, rigid type braced with a metal strip along the back of the blade. The flexible saws (panel saws) are used for cutting wood to rough dimensions, while those with the stiffened blades (tenon saws) are used for fine work, such as cutting joints.

Panel saws, which include rip saws and crosscut saws, are usually about 51 centimetres long and are known as ten-point saws – they have 10 cutting points per two-and-a-half centimetres. Tenon saws (about 25 centimetres long) are among the most popular of the rigid saws, with 14 or more points per two-and-a-half centimetres. Dovetail saws (about 20 centimetres long) are also popular.

Hacksaws (up to 30 centimetres long) are used for cutting metal, while coping saws (usually 16,5 centimetres long) are used for cutting curves in wood. Both are held rigid in metal frames and use disposable blades.

The pad saw or keyhole saw is used for cutting holes in panels, the sawn hole usually starting from a hole made with a brace and bit.

USE AND MAINTENANCE

A handsaw should cut readily under its own weight on the forward thrust. Riding over the wood without cutting or veering to one side, indicates that the saw is blunt.

You can set and sharpen a saw yourself, but these functions are probably best left to the expertise of a "saw doctor" who can be contacted through many hardware stores.

Wipe the saw blade with light machine oil before you store it, but be sure to wipe it dry before use.

To reduce friction when sawing, rub the blade with a bar of dry soap or a candle before you start. If the saw blade still binds despite having been rubbed with soap, open the kerf (the cut made by the saw) slightly by inserting a screwdriver into the end.

Try to avoid having to saw through a knot or rocking the saw to change the angle of the stroke.

To protect the teeth of your handsaw when it's not in use, slide the cutting edge into a slit length of old garden hose. A motorcar inner tube stretched (not tightly) around the circumference of a circular saw will protect the teeth.

Scale insects

Get rid of a scale infestation on your houseplants by dabbing the insects, which look like tiny brown army helmets, with methylated spirits on a cottonwool bud. (Mealy bugs, scales' woolly white relatives, succumb to the same treatment.) Then set the plants in the sink and wash gently with a spray of tepid water to eliminate any newly hatched insects that may have escaped your notice.

Scatter rugs

1. To keep a scatter rug in place, put a rubber bath mat under it.

2. To make a scatter rug lie flat, shellac the underside. When dry, apply a mild solution of laundry starch; let dry before using.

3. Prevent rag rugs from curling by rinsing them in a mild solution of starch and water.

4. To wash scatter rugs properly, place them in a bathtub half filled with warm, soapy water and scrub vigorously with a broom. Place smaller rugs in a washtub and use a plunger to agitate the water.

5. If your nylon bathroom rugs are matted, wash with soap or detergent, then add ½ cup vinegar or fabric softener to the rinse water.

Scissors

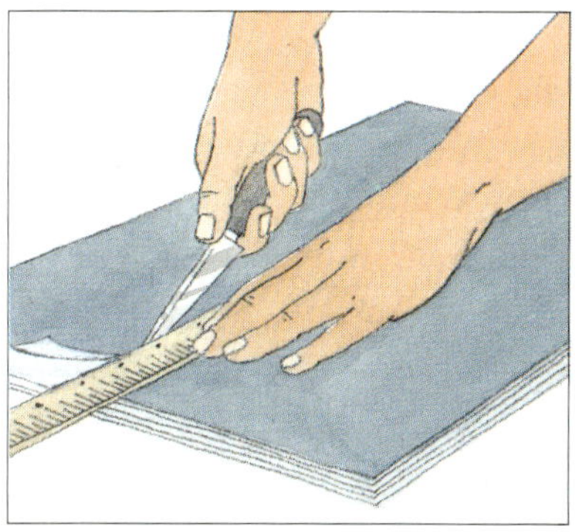

1. No scissors at hand? Hold a metal-edged ruler firmly on the paper and draw a sharp knife or single-edged

razor blade along it. Be sure to have padding underneath to protect the tabletop from being damaged.
2. Never cut paper with your haircutting scissors or dressmaking shears; it dulls the keen edge needed for cutting hair or fabric.
3. If your scissor blades are binding, tighten the screw.

Scratches in wood

1. To keep lamps and other tabletop accessories from scratching furniture, line the bottom with felt, cork or another soft material; attach it with rubber adhesive, double-sided tape or cold glue.
2. A scratch on bare wood can be rubbed out with medium sandpaper. Sand with the grain, not across it.
3. To hide scratches on furniture, use a crayon that matches the colour of the finish.
4. To hide scratches and fill nicks in shellac and other clear finishes, use clear nail polish.
5. For shallow scratches on a wood floor, buff the area lightly with extremely fine steel wool, rubbing with the grain. Then apply two coats of furniture polish; buff each coat with a soft cloth. Rewax three or four times a year to prevent future scratches.

Screen door spring

Don't throw out a broken spring. You can probably repair it.
1. If the break is in the snubber (the length of chain between the spring and the door), replace the broken link with a split-ring key holder.
2. If the problem is a broken bracket on the jamb or the door, replace it with a large screw eye. After screwing it in, pry it open slightly, insert the end of the spring or chain, and pinch the eye shut with pliers.
3. If the mounting bracket is pulled out, don't try to drive the screws back into the old holes. Reposition the bracket and drive larger screws into a new spot.
4. To improvise temporarily, replace an irreparably broken spring with a large rubber band or piece of elastic until you can get a new one.

Screens for doors

1. If you don't want passers-by looking in, apply a coat of white paint thinned down with turpentine to your door screens. You can still see out.
2. To prevent moisture from rotting wood frames, remove the moulding and apply caulking compound to the groove. Replace the moulding again and remove any excess caulking.
3. To keep metal screen door frames shiny, apply a coat of clear lacquer.
4. Fix a dented screen by pushing the strands back in place with a pencil, an awl, a knitting needle or a chopstick.
5. If one or two strands are broken, seal the hole with several coats of shellac varnish or clear nail polish; let each coat dry properly before applying the next.
6. To repair a large hole, cut a patch out of the same type of screening 25 millimetres wider and longer than the hole. Unweave each edge for about 10 millimetres, then bend the wires at

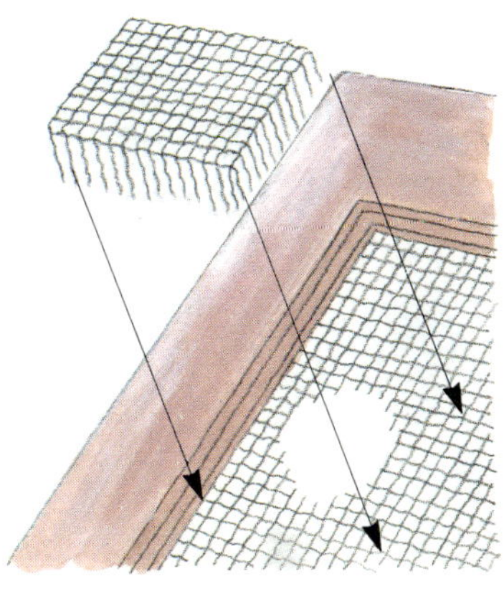

right angles to the patch. Push the bent strands into the screen holes and fold them toward the centre. Sew the patch in place with nylon thread; then seal with a few coats of shellac or clear nail polish.
7. Mend a long rip by sewing it with thin wire or nylon thread.
8. Repair damaged plastic and fibreglass screens with patches of the same material; seal with tubed glue.
9. Repair tent screens by sewing on patches of netting or pantihose.
10. In fact, pantihose can make a good temporary patch on any type of screen; secure it with tape.

Screwdriver

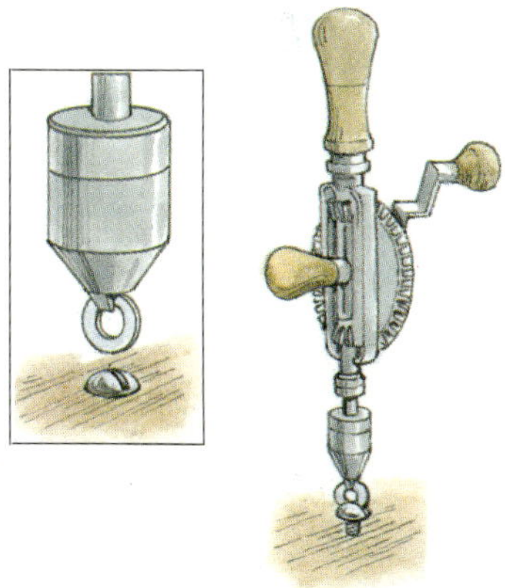

Here are some make-do solutions when you don't have a screwdriver.
1. Tighten a steel washer into the chuck of a hand drill or brace and insert the edge into the screw slot. (This is a good idea as well when you want to exert some leverage on a screw.) You can use a variable speed power drill, too.
2. Check out penknives around the house. Some may have a screwdriver blade. Or you can break the tip off an old knife blade.
3. A nail file can tighten a tiny screw – in spectacles, for example.
4. House keys will sometimes fit a slotted screw. But use them only on screws which are loose because key metal bends easily under pressure.
5. Or try a used hacksaw blade, the blade of a small pry bar, a paint scraper, a putty knife or the blade of a can opener or bottletop opener.

Screws

1. Can't remove a screw because the slot is ruined? If the head is above the workpiece, use a hacksaw to cut a new groove at a right angle to the original slot. Exert pressure evenly, not jerkily, with a screwdriver to ease out the screw.
2. Or remove the screw by gripping the head with locking-grip pliers.
3. If you need to remove a broken flathead screw, slice a new slot with a small drill and a tiny abrasive wheel. A friendly dentist may help if you are stuck. Or cut a new slot with a few sharp blows on a cold chisel the same width as the screw.
4. If a screw is rusted in place, try dropping a little oil or hot paraffin onto it.

Sea stings

The most common marine stings are from bluebottles, whose long, stinging tentacles can cause intense local pain and joint and muscle pain. Jellyfish in southern African waters have only mild stings that set up minor skin irritations. Other stinging creatures to watch out for are fireworms and stingrays. The latter can inflict a painful stab if you touch it.

In preparation for a trip to the seaside, assemble a first-aid kit containing antiseptic ointment, disposable ice packs, aluminium acetate spray, cottonwool, waterproof plasters and sterile gauze pads; over-the-counter paracetamol and antihistamine tablets or cream, methylated spirits, a pair of tweezers and a needle.

If a bluebottle stings you:
1. Rinse the skin well with water and remove any tentacles left on the skin (not with your fingers!). Apply an ice pack, and spray the sting with aluminium acetate spray, if available. A swab soaked in vinegar can also be used to neutralise the pain.
2. Take a painkiller, such as paracetamol or aspirin and an antihistamine, to reduce the swelling.
3. When the stinging has been widespread, shock may develop, with dizziness, nausea and clamminess. Lie down, cover yourself with a blanket or towel, and get someone to call for medical help.

If sea urchin spines break your skin, they will probably cause redness, swelling and burning pain. Pull out any visible spines with a pair of tweezers; wash with water, then apply a cold compress and an antiseptic ointment. If several spines are embedded or you feel intense pain, see a doctor.

Security blankets

Don't worry if your small child develops a close attachment to a special object, even if it's worn and ugly. Make sure it's always available when he needs it – at Grandmother's house, in a shopping mall or on holiday. Don't try to take it away or substitute a newer, cleaner version. Your child likes the way his old blanket, nappy or stuffed animal smells, tastes and feels; its familiarity is what makes it appealing. But to be on the safe side, get a duplicate in case the original gets lost.

If you accidentally leave the treasured object behind on holiday, explain that a holiday is a special time and that it will be waiting when you get back. Then help your child find a suitable substitute that will give some degree of comfort, especially at bedtime; try making a doll or puppet out of a sock or glove. Perhaps cuddling in your jacket, pullover or a cosy comforter will do the trick. (See also *Bedtime rituals*, p.19.)

Seed germination

1. For fast germination, soak seeds in water overnight before planting. To speed the process even more, add a drop or two of detergent; it reduces the water's surface tension, helping it to penetrate the seed's coat. An easy way to soak is to empty each seed packet into a different cup of a polystyrene egg carton, then fill each with the detergent solution.
2. Heating bean and pea seeds in the microwave not only increases the chances of germination but also enhances subsequent growth. The recommended power level varies with the oven, but it's always at the low end of the scale – four 15-second treatments with a cooling period after each, for example. Never warm the seeds to more than 48°C or they won't germinate at all.

Seed planting

Ensure proper spacing and eliminate the need for thinning with a homemade seed tape. An added bonus: the seeds will sprout faster.

Lay a strip of damp paper towelling on top of a strip of plastic wrap, then set out the seeds at the intervals recommended on the original seed packet. Cover with another strip of damp towelling, roll the paper and plastic up together, place in a plastic bag, and store in a warm place (the top of the refrigerator is ideal).

As soon as roots begin to emerge, take the tape to the garden and unroll it onto a well-tilled bed, peeling the plastic away. Cover with a layer of soil and water thoroughly but gently. Don't worry about the paper – it acts as a mulch to inhibit dehydration, then soon dissolves to reveal a perfectly spaced row of young seedlings.

Self-adhesive mounts

To remove a self-adhesive hook, drip vinegar behind it. Scrape any residue off the tile with your fingernail or a blunt knife. On a painted or plastic surface soften stubborn residue with a warm rag or hair dryer. On unpainted surfaces use alcohol, mineral spirits, cleaning solvent, lacquer thinners, aerosol hair spray or nail polish remover (acetone); test first on an inconspicuous area.

Sensitive skin

If your skin is easily irritated by the elements, by alcohol and other cosmetic ingredients, by chemicals in synthetic fabrics, or by shaving, consider these recommendations:

1. Stay well away from alkaline soaps, masks, grainy cleansers, alcohol-based astringents, acetone products such as nail polish remover and anything with fragrance.

2. Bathe in tepid or cool water, using mild superfatted soap; pat dry (no rubbing!), then apply a moisturizer containing urea or lactic acid to your damp skin.

3. "Breathable" natural fabrics are the best choice for clothing, but if you prefer synthetics, launder them several times before wearing to remove potential irritants.

4. Give your hands extra protection when you are washing dishes or clothes by wearing cotton liners inside your rubber gloves.

5. Don't assume products labelled "for sensitive skin" are necessarily safe for you. Test a new product on a small area of your inner arm daily for a week; if your skin reacts, don't use it. Look for products containing non-irritating allantoin, petrolatum and zinc oxide.

Septic tank overflow

Is the grass greener over your septic tank? Worse still, do your drains empty slowly or smell foul? If so, call your local municipality, and have your tank pumped out immediately.

If it's too late and your system is overloaded, whatever you empty or flush down a drain will rise in your lowest plumbing fixtures. (Don't add water – it will only make matters worse.) All your upstairs bathroom drains may seem clear, but if you use them, you'll cause an awful mess in the basement laundry sink or ground floor toilet.

If the municipal service can't come at once, a plumber may be able to dig down and break up the layer of semi-solid scum blocking the inlet pipe, giving you temporary restricted use of the plumbing.

PREVENTION

1. If possible, measure the level of solid waste in your septic tank regularly by removing its cover and probing with a long towel-wrapped pole. The sludge will leave a dark stain on the end; a layer which is more than 30-45 centimetres deep requires pumping. Generally, the tank should be emptied every two to five years. Cleaning intervals vary and depend on tank size, usage volume and the soakaway's soil type.

2. Keep all chemicals out of your septic tank. When buying toilet cleaning products, check for the words: "safe for septic tanks".

3. Instead of chemical bowl cleaners, add four litres of white vinegar to the water in the toilet bowl; let it sit for a few hours, then flush it down.

4. To keep the decomposition process active, flush 30 grams of dry yeast down the drain monthly.

5. Don't pour liquid fat or grease down the kitchen drain.

6. Never introduce tissues, newspaper, paper towels, cigarette stubs, sanitary towels or tampons or any kind of wrapping material into your septic system.

Sex education

1. Give short, simple answers to the questions your child asks about sex. Let her reaction to what you say determine whether to provide additional information. Be factual and to the point; don't overload her with facts she didn't ask for.

2. Listen carefully to all your child's questions. If she asks where she came from, find out – before you launch into a lecture about how babies are made. She may just want to know the name of the hospital or city where she was born.

3. As time goes on, don't restrict your answers to factual information; also try to communicate your attitudes and values. Children need help in coping with their sexual feelings and defining responsible sexual behaviour.

4. An easy way to introduce your children to the mystery of sex is to arrange for them to witness the birth of a litter of puppies or kittens.

5. For children who are over the age of eight, use the plots of TV programmes and the lyrics of certain songs as springboards for conversations about sex. "What does the woman find attractive in that man?" "What do those lyrics mean to you?"

6. If you and your adolescent find it difficult to discuss sexual matters, write her a letter describing the risks and responsibilities involved in sexual behaviour and stating your personal values.

Sexual harassment

IN THE STREET

1. People who shout obscenities, whisper unwanted endearments or make obscene gestures may be capable of physical violence. The best response is to ignore them completely and keep moving to a safe, well-lighted place. If the offender pursues you, call the police.

2. If you are constantly harassed at a particular building site, contact the contractor or the company constructing the building.

IN THE WORKPLACE

1. Confront the harasser. Appeal to his or her professionalism and make it clear that you object to the advances. If they continue, send your tormentor a letter by registered post, expressing your feelings and mentioning that you will complain to your employer and may even consider laying a charge with the police.

2. Keep a dated, written record of all incidents. Save all notes or letters.

3. If necessary, file a written complaint with your employer; if you work for a corporation, address it to the human resources department or the managing director of the company. Make sure that you include the date, place and details of all incidents. If you're a union member, your representative may handle the problem for you.
4. If there is no immediate investigation, if the harasser is your employer or a responsible official, or if the behaviour persists, contact your attorney or legal aid office.

IN A BLOCK OF FLATS
1. If a building employee is harassing you, send a letter of complaint to the landlord, the superintendent and the managing agent; keep a copy. If you are living in housing provided by a local authority, lodge a complaint with that authority.
2. Document your case meticulously; write down exactly who said what to whom and when.
3. Talk to your neighbours; this may be happening to others. Perhaps you can take action as a group.

Shaded garden

If your garden lacks sunshine throughout the year, don't give up on colour. Just think in terms of foliage rather than flowers.

Coleus, familiar as houseplants, make a brilliant massed display in a shady corner. Hostas, hardy perennials of the lily family, bear leaves in muted shades of blue, gold, green and white; they thrive in a damp, cool, woodland setting.

Caladiums, a subtropical favourite, are at their best in filtered sun, sporting arrowhead-shaped leaves marbled and veined in red, pink, green and white. Though not winter hardy inland, they adapt well to hanging baskets or tubs and can overwinter quite successfully indoors.

Vivid ground covers include dead nettle, a type of mint whose green leaves are splashed with silver, and variegated lilyturf, with grasslike green-and-white-striped leaves. Two other lilyturf varieties, Big Blue and Munroe White, offer less dramatic foliage, but bear showy flowers of blue or white in late summer.

Shaded lawns

The right choice of grass seed and a little extra care are all it takes to keep a shaded lawn full and green.
1. Plant chewings fescue, creeping red fescue or turf-type tall fescues if you live in an arid area. If you live in a region of high rainfall or if your soil is poorly drained, Kentucky bluegrass will be a good choice.
2. To fill in bare patches, try overseeding with a fast-growing ryegrass. You'll have to reseed every spring, since ryegrass won't last from year to year in the shade.
3. Thin trees instead of removing them. An experienced tree surgeon can remove 40 percent of a tree's leaf surface without harming it, and the extra light will do wonders for the grass underneath.
4. Raise your mower blade to a height of six centimetres before mowing a shaded part of the lawn; you'll leave more leaf surface to trap light.
5. Water no more than once or twice a week – and water deeply. Wetting only the surface of the soil encourages tree roots to grow upward, where they compete with grass for water and nutrients. (See also *Grass*, p.100; *Lawns*, p.123.)

Sharks

Although shark attacks are rare, the possibility of one occurring is always there, particularly in the subtropical coastal waters of southern Africa.

If you want to find out more information about sharks and shark attacks, or the prevalence of sharks in a particular area, you can telephone the Natal Sharks Board (their number appears in the Durban telephone directory). Alternatively, talk to lifeguards at the beach where you intend to swim. As a general rule, however, you should observe the following:
1. On the Natal and Transkei coasts, swim only at protected beaches or within demarcated swimming areas. Listen to instructions from lifesavers.
2. Stay out of the water if you have an open cut or scratch; sharks are thought to be attracted to blood.
3. Avoid swimming in deep water or too far from shore; sharks are more likely to congregate there. Also avoid bathing near seal colonies, as seals are a food source favoured by Great White sharks.
4. Never swim at night, at dusk or before dawn.
5. Avoid swimming in murky water, especially near river mouths.
6. Never swim with a speared fish tied to your belt.
7. To discourage a particularly inquisitive shark, use a shark billy – a thick, metre-long stick with a loop for your wrist at one end and a circle of nails, pointing outward, at the other; keep the shark at bay by poking it sharply on the snout.
8. Be aware of the possible presence of sharks, and, if you are diving, carefully scan your submarine environment frequently – many shark attacks occur without the victim even seeing the shark.
9. Swim with at least one other person to keep a watch for danger.

Sheet metal

If you lack tin snips, try one of these methods for cutting sheet metal easily and safely:
1. Use a hacksaw. Put the sheet on a flat bench or table with the saw line slightly overlapping the table edge. Position the blade at a 45° angle and keep the teeth in constant contact with the metal. If the waste section is sizeable, support it on another table or bench or have a partner hold it. Wear work gloves – the edges of newly cut metal are sharp.
2. Use a cold chisel to cut a small piece. Lock the metal in a vice with the cut line level with the top of the jaw. Hold the chisel against the edge of the metal at a 45° angle to the jaw top and hammer it along the length of

the piece. The waste will curl back like an orange peel.

3. You can also slice a large piece with a cold chisel. Lay the metal on a hardwood bench or table with the cut line even with the edge; then clamp a length of straight steel or hardwood on top. Hold the chisel at a 45° angle to the bench or table edge and hammer along the length of the metal. Scrap should safely peel down toward the floor.

Shelves

1. A clear pine plank 22 x 300 millimetres should span 1500 millimetres without sagging under a light load such as clothes, toys or pans; under a heavy load, such as books or records, it should span about one metre. For 10-millimetre plywood the limit is 650 millimetres under a light load, 450 millimetres under a heavy one; for thicker ply, this length can stretch.

2. You can make a removable shelf, by mounting folding brackets on the wall. Pull them down and place a board on top when needed.

3. Build a set of shelves from boards and coffee tins. Paint the tins or cover them with matching wrapping or leftover wallpaper.

4. Clay flowerpots work well for medium-weight loads. They look especially nice if you top each "column" of pots with a potted plant.

5. For a more colourful look, use glass blocks or large jars as shelf supports, filling them with marbles or some other bright objects.

6. Hang shelves with rope from a beam or hooks attached to the ceiling or wall. Drill pairs of holes at the ends of the boards and at all support points, 25 millimetres from the edges. Knot the end of a length of rope for each hole and slip a washer onto it; then feed the ropes up through the holes in the bottom shelf and knot them again on top.

Repeat the process. Just be sure that when you hang the shelves the ropes are firmly anchored; they may have to bear a lot of weight.

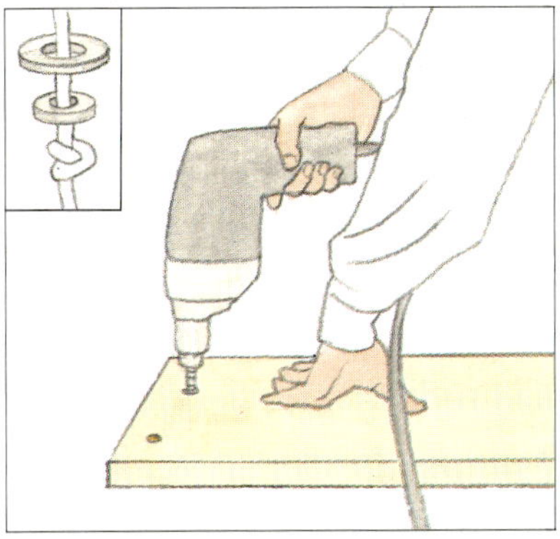

7. Or instead of using rope, hang the shelves with punched metal plumber's tape. Screw or nail two or three strips to each end of the shelves and suspend from a beam.

8. For lighter-duty shelves, you can use heavy cord or fishing line; instead of knotting the cord or line, double-wind it through each pair of holes like a sewing stitch.

Shiny clothing

1. If the knees or elbows on worsted-wool garments become shiny from wear, try steaming them; hang them in the bathroom while running hot water in the shower.

2. To prevent sheen, always press heavy cotton, wool, acetate, rayon, linen, drip-dry and dark fabrics on the wrong side. Or use a pressing cloth.

3. To get a high sheen on polished cotton, add half an envelope of unflavoured gelatin to the last rinse.

Shoe heels

1. Touch up scuffed heels quickly with a felt-tip pen or use a cottonwool bud to dab on ink, acrylic paint or motor vehicle paint. On white heels, use toothpaste.

2. Protect and shine wooden heels with lemon oil or clear nail polish. If they're badly scratched, sand and stain with furniture polish.

3. Rebuild worn rubber heels with athletic shoe-repair material (available at sporting goods stores). Make an outline of the original shape of the heel with masking tape, angling the tape outward slightly to make sure the material will cover heel edges. Fill with the repair material and let dry. Trim with scissors or a razor blade. The stuff will dry clear, so you'll have to colour it with shoe polish or a felt-tip marker.

Shoehorn

No shoehorn? Use a tablespoon, a soup spoon or a rubber spatula. Or use the narrow end of a silk tie to ease your heel into the shoe.

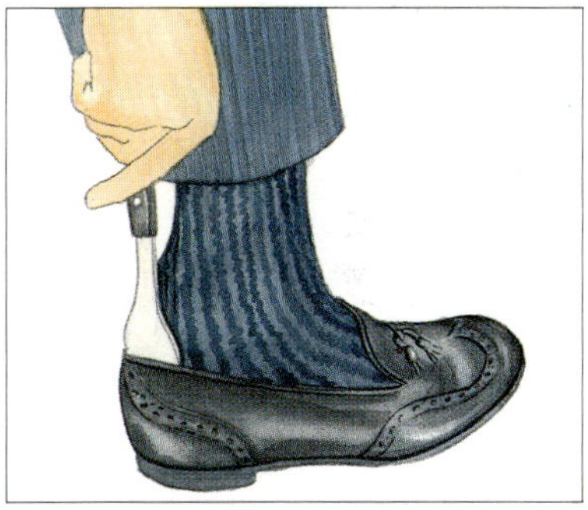

Shoelaces

1. Here's a method to retie a broken shoelace. Remove the lace, join the two pieces together with a reef knot, and estimate where the knot will fall in the laced shoe. Put the knot there and lace from that point outward in both directions.

2. If you're not quite sure what size shoelaces your child needs, count the pairs of holes in one shoe and multiply by three. For adults, multiply by at least six.

3. If the plastic tip of a shoelace is broken, wrap the tip with transparent tape. Or dip it in glue, hot paraffin or clear nail polish.

4. No shoelaces? Use string, yarn or twine. For women's shoes, ribbon makes a pretty substitute, especially if it's lace or satin.

Shoe polish

1. In the absence of proper shoe polish, there are a number of other options: you can shine your leather shoes with floor wax, spray furniture polish or spray window cleaner; you can even use a banana peel. On patent leather try Vaseline, spray window cleaner or castor oil.

2. For a high shine, squeeze a few drops of lighter fluid into your solid shoe wax – it will spread more easily and penetrate better. Or rub lemon juice into the leather after it's polished, then buff.

3. To get an even shine on white shoes, wipe them with methylated spirits, then polish.

4. To keep fresh polish from smearing clothing, let it dry, then rub with wax paper or spray with hair spray.

5. Recycle all your soft fabrics, for example, flannel pyjamas, socks or towels into shoe buffers.

6. Hard to get polish in that space between the uppers and the soles? Use a cottonwool bud.

7. To clean suede shoes, first remove the dust with pantihose or your vacuum cleaner's dust-brush attachment. Then hold the shoes over steam to raise the nap; brush lightly and let dry. Brush again.

8. Cover spots on black suede by sponging a little black coffee on them; on white suede, use chalk.

9. Remove stains from leather with a cloth and cleaning fluid.

10. Take spots off the white rubber on tackies with steel wool dipped in detergent or mild abrasive.

11. To remove salt rings from your boots, brush with a solution of one tablespoon vinegar in one cup water.

12. Cover unsightly scuff marks on white leather shoes with typewriter correction fluid.

13. If your shoe polish brush starts to become caked, soak it overnight in paint solvent.

14. If your only polish gets hard, heat it gently in the oven or add a few drops of turpentine or mineral spirits to soften it.

15. To keep your hands clean while polishing shoes, wear old gloves or cut the pockets out of old trousers and use them as mitts. They will also keep your fingernails clean.

Shoes

1. Slippery soles? Sand them or apply bath appliqués, small strips of adhesive tape or repair patches such as those used for bicycle tubes.

2. Cold feet? Make liners from pieces of sturdy quilted fabric, felt or scraps of thin carpet. First, make a pattern by tracing your feet on paper, then cut out the liners and slip into your shoes.

3. Keep your canvas shoes smelling sweet; sprinkle a little talcum powder, baby powder or bicarbonate of soda into them occasionally to absorb any moisture.

4. Deodorize any type of shoe with a little bicarbonate of soda.

5. Make your shoes water-repellent with a light coat of floor wax. Use Vaseline for galoshes. (See also *Hiking boots*, p.108.)

6. If the sole of your shoe separates from the upper, reattach it temporarily with a silicone or plastic sealer used for weatherstripping.

7. To prevent expensive leather shoes from cracking after they've been wet, apply a liberal coating of saddle soap while they're still damp. Let it dry away from the heat, then remove any excess saddle soap.

8. Soften dried leather shoes by wetting the outside with warm water and rubbing with castor oil, glycerine or paraffin sprinkled on a soft cloth.

Shopping addiction

Don't let "Born to Shop" bumper stickers fool you into thinking that compulsive shopping is something to be laughed off. It's not. A steady flow of credit card charges can put you in serious debt more quickly than you can imagine. If you're not a compulsive shopper but still feel that you should pull the reins in, try these tips:

1. Don't ever shop without a list.

2. Try to avoid sales; the temptation to overbuy is too great.

3. Keep a small notebook where you list everything you buy, even the morning paper. You'll find it harder to spend if you know you must write down each purchase.

IN TIMES GONE BY

Magic slippers

Since the earliest times, people from various cultures all over the world have regarded shoes as symbols of fertility and prosperity.

☐ In ancient Egypt, Palestine and Assyria, the seller of land gave a sandal to the buyer as a gesture of goodwill and as a seal of purchase.

☐ In India an old shoe placed upside down on the roof assured a couple good fortune.

☐ Childless Chinese women borrowed shoes from the shrine of the mother goddess to help them become pregnant.

☐ For good luck, the Scots threw a shoe after a sailor departing for his first voyage or after anyone starting a new venture.

☐ In ancient Anglo-Saxon weddings the father of the bride transferred his authority to the groom by handing him one of his daughter's shoes – it was this ritual that gave rise to the modern-day custom of attaching old shoes to the bridal carriage.

4. Resist temptation when you reach the till. This is where specific articles are placed to tempt you into impulse buying at the last minute.
5. Get someone else to do your shopping for you – perhaps you could offer to reciprocate.
6. Never shop when you are feeling hungry. Have a light snack before you leave home so that you can view the food objectively without your mouth starting to water.
7. Don't hang around after you have finished shopping – especially if you are in a shopping centre – get into your car and go straight home.
8. If you really can't control yourself when you are paying with a credit card, leave your card at home and only carry enough money on you to pay for the items on your list.

Shopping lists

Here's an easy way to speed up your weekly grocery shopping – and save money by curbing impulse buying.

Make a permanent list of the items you regularly buy; arrange them in the order in which they're set out in the supermarket, proceeding from aisle to aisle. If the fresh produce area is normally your very first stop, for example, list the fruits and vegetables you routinely buy, such as apples, oranges, carrots and lettuce; then leave some blanks for less frequently purchased goods.

Make lots of photocopies of the list and always keep one on the refrigerator door; mark items as soon as a need arises. When you go to the store, take the list; your shopping is organized as soon as you walk in.

Shovel

1. Plenty of garden tools are handy for breaking up the soil – a hoe, cultivator, pickaxe, metal rake, tiller, edging tool or pitchfork – but not much good for moving earth into a wheelbarrow. That takes a shovel. If you don't have one, lay out a square of hessian or heavy plastic; then, once the soil is loose, use a hoe or edging tool to heave dirt onto the square. Pull up the four corners and empty the soil into the wheelbarrow.
2. Make a handy scoop for small jobs like working with plant containers. Cut the bottom out of a two-litre plastic milk or orange carton, then cut out the side beneath the handle. Now you have a durable scoop that's easy to grab hold of.

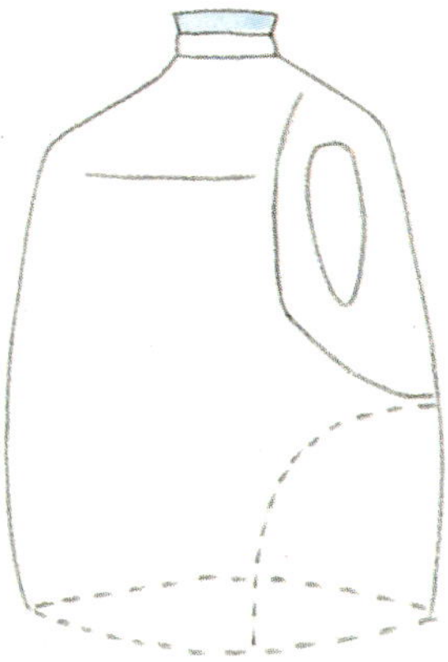

Shower curtains & doors

1. Make your plastic shower curtain more pliable by dipping it in warm water to which you have added a few drops of mineral oil.
2. Protect your new shower curtain by hanging the old one behind it to take the soaking. Wash both frequently to prevent mildew.
3. Shower curtains will dry faster if you spread them out.
4. To remove mildew (p.136) from bleachable shower curtains, use a solution of chlorine bleach and water.
5. To remove water and soap marks from glass shower doors, rub with a sponge dampened with vinegar. Or gently scrape with a single-edged razor blade.
6. If the doors don't slide smoothly, first clean the tracks with a brush and blunt knife or screwdriver; use a cottonwool bud or toothbrush to reach nooks and crannies. Then wash with ammonia or a strong detergent solution. After the tracks dry, spray with a silicone lubricant. (Shield the bathtub – the spray will make it slippery.) Try to remember to wipe the tracks dry every time you have had a shower.

Sibling rivalry

1. To encourage affection between siblings, arrange for them to enjoy things in common, such as holiday traditions and summer trips. Shared experiences and memories help build friendships that can withstand occasional angry flare-ups.
2. After a new baby arrives, give each older child some private time with you every day, away from the younger sibling and free from household distractions.
3. Encourage older children to use their experience to help younger ones. Commend their co-operation.
4. To prevent feelings of resentment and competition, never compare one child with another or hold one up as an example to another.
5. Give undivided, unconditional love and attention to each child at scheduled and unscheduled times, focusing on each one's strengths and individual accomplishments.
6. Designate special days other than birthdays – half-birthdays, for example, to mark the six-month plateaus – for each child. Hold a family celebration, complete with little gifts, and serve the favourite cake or dessert of the centre of attention.
7. "Who gets to ride in the front seat?" "Which TV programme will we watch?" To eliminate competition, have each child take turns making these decisions for a week.

Siding

1. Mildew can discolour any siding, particularly wood. It usually grows in the shade, appearing as dark grey or black spots that spread over larger areas. To treat a mild case, scrub with a solution of one part water and four parts household bleach. For a more stubborn case, use one cup trisodium phosphate (TSP) and one cup bleach in four litres of warm water; scrub the surface with a stiff brush, let dry on the surface, then hose it down.
2. Stained-wood siding fades and discolours after exposure to sun and rain. To get an even tone, restain it, let

it dry, and apply a clear wood preservative. Do this regularly.

3. Warped siding can be pulled tight against the house with galvanized thin-shank screws. Bore pilot holes to prevent splitting the siding. Or nail the warped siding back in place with galvanized ringed-shank nails.

4. To clean and rinse siding in one step, tape a garden hose to the head of a wide broom, using insulation tape at two or three places along the handle. Position the hose nozzle near the top of the broom head, just above the bristles. Try to ensure your hose is attached to a tap where the water pressure is high. The higher the pressure, the greater the overall cleaning effect will be.

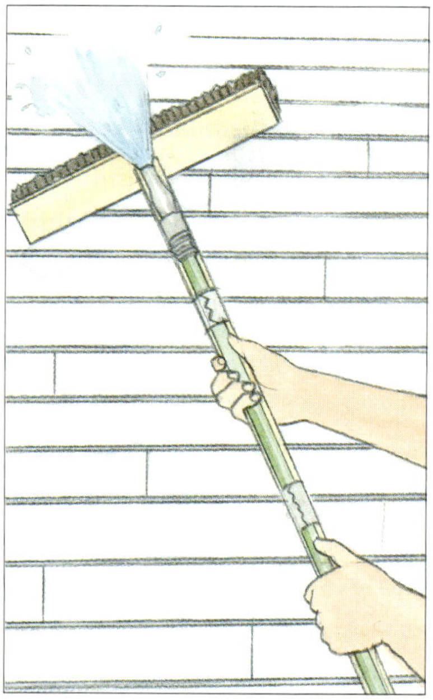

Sieves & colanders

1. Improvise a makeshift strainer for liquids from the legs of clean pantihose. Stretch the fabric across the bottom of a wide-necked funnel, hold it in place, and pour.

2. No colander? Punch holes in the bottom of an aluminium pie plate.

3. Use a fine sieve to smooth out the lumps in icing sugar; just push it through with a wooden spoon. The same remedy works for lumpy custard, sauce or gravy.

Silencer noise

A small hole in your silencer probably won't do any damage, but the noise is quite offensive and probably illegal. Worse, poisonous carbon monoxide can seep into your car. Get the leak fixed as soon as possible.

Small holes (no larger than three millimetres) in the silencer or tail pipe can often be repaired with special putty (available at motor vehicle parts stores). For larger holes (up to 25 millimetres) you can buy inexpensive heat-resistant "bandages."

You may be able to cover the hole temporarily by slicing open a tin and holding the material in place with wire or clamps, but such a patch probably won't last more than 80 kilometres, so don't leave it too long.

Silk flowers

1. To get more for your money and greater flexibility in your arrangements, buy stems with more than one flower. Cut off the blossoms and make a stem for each by twisting wire onto the cut end and covering it with green florist's tape.

2. For fragrance, hide a free perfume sample card in the arrangement.

3. To clean, dust each blossom with a soft brush, wipe it off with a damp cloth, or blow the dust off with an ordinary hair dryer.

4. For a more thorough cleaning, disassemble the arrangement and swish each flower in warm water and mild detergent. Rinse well and stand in tall vases or jars to air-dry.

Silver

With proper care, you can safeguard silver against tarnishing, pitting or scratching. Be especially gentle with silver plate, as the plating wears off easily, leaving nasty marks.

1. Always wash silver and silver plate by hand with mild detergent – never in the dishwasher. Then dry with a chamois cloth or soft towel.

2. Don't leave silver overnight with food on it. If you can't wash it right away, at least rinse off all the food. You can let it stand in clear water overnight, but don't add detergent.

3. If you don't have specially treated cloth bags or a silver chest for storage, thoroughly dry each piece, then wrap airtight in plastic wrap. Place alum or camphor with the silver to discourage tarnish (keep it away from children and pets).

4. Never let rubber come in contact with silver – it causes tarnish.

5. Don't let egg, fruit juice, olives, perfume, eau de cologne, salad dressing, salt, sulphur or vinegar stay on silver for any length of time – they cause stains and corrosion.

6. Clean silver salt cellar lids frequently to keep them from corroding. To remove corrosion caused by salt, soak for five minutes in a solution of hot vinegar and salt, then wash and dry with a soft cloth.

7. If you put cut flowers in silver bowls, change the water often to prevent unsightly deposits at the water line. Remove the flowers as soon as they begin to wilt.

8. If you keep fruit in a silver container, use a liner.

9. If you run out of silver polish, use one of the following homemade substitutes: a paste of water and cornflour, cigarette ashes or bicarbonate of soda; or toothpaste. Or let silver stand in sour milk or buttermilk overnight (you can substitute one cup whole milk mixed with one tablespoon white vinegar or lemon juice).

10. Polish with brisk up-and-down strokes, not across or in circles. For hard-to-reach crevices, use a soft brush – silver scratches easily.

11. Use a pipe cleaner with polish on it to clean between fork tines. Or put polish on a string and pull it back and forth between the tines.

12. To remove old scratches, make a paste of putty powder and olive oil; rub on with a soft cloth and polish with a chamois cloth.

13. To avoid water marks on your silver, do not leave it to air-dry. Use a soft cloth to dry it immediately you take it out of the water.

Skewers

1. If you sometimes try to turn a braai skewer and find that the food doesn't turn with it, solve the problem by using two-pronged skewers. Or simply thread the ingredients onto two skewers instead of one.

2. You've prepared the ingredients for shish kebab but the skewers can't be found? Cut new ones from unpainted wire coat hangers. Or look in the toolbox for some heavy-gauge wire. Or slice the food into small pieces and stir-fry it instead. (Just be sure to cook the meat – especially pork and chicken – longer than you cook the vegetables.)

3. When camping, don't be tempted to make improvised skewers from the branches of unknown trees – they might be poisonous.

Skidding

If you go into a skid, don't slam on the brakes suddenly – it only makes the skid worse. Instead, take your foot off the accelerator and turn the wheel gently in the direction of the skid. When the front wheels start gripping, begin to steer again (be prepared to counter another skid in the opposite direction). Very gently apply light accelerator pressure.

Skin care

Skin is the area of the body where the ageing process shows first. To preserve your skin in a healthy condition for longer, it is important that you care for it adequately from childhood. The establishment of a regular beauty routine is important. You should also be aware of the damage the sun's harmful rays can cause.

BASIC SKIN CARE

Wash the skin thoroughly with toilet soap every day to promote hygiene. Use a loofah to remove dead skin cells, particularly on the heels and elbows. Use a mild soap or cleansing lotion on the face to clear skin pores and prevent dryness.

If you have a problem skin, you should consult a specialist for advice on medicated cleansing products. An astringent dabbed onto the skin after cleansing will help to close pores.

Dry the skin thoroughly and apply a moisturizer, preferably one with a built-in sunscreen.

SUN PROTECTION

In this country, where sunshine is almost a daily commodity, you should take adequate precautions. Here are some points to consider:

1. Wear a wide-brimmed hat whenever you are exposed to the sun. In addition, use a barrier cream with a high protection factor to screen out ultraviolet rays.

2. Take particular care if you have blue or green eyes or fair skins that freckle easily. If you are olive- or dark-skinned, don't be fooled into thinking that because you can't see sun damage, it isn't occurring.

3. Always remember to replace barrier cream after a swim. Even the shade of an umbrella is not enough to prevent the sun's reflected rays affecting you.

Don't think you are immune from sunburn on a cloudy day – you can still burn when clouds are about.

4. If a freckle or blemish becomes enlarged or changes colour, contact a dermatologist at once to have the area checked. Skin cancer in its early stages can be cured completely, but may be serious if left unattended.

Skipping rope

A brisk 10-minute workout with a skipping rope can be as good an exercise as a 30-minute jog. You can use a piece of clothes line (about two metres will do – measure it by stepping on the middle; the ends should come to about mid-chest).

For handles, tie knots in the ends and wrap insulation tape 10 to 15 centimetres in front of each knot. If you have no rope (but only if you skipped as a child and remember how), you can skip with a phantom rope – no rope at all.

Always skip on a carpet or mat, and wear cushioned aerobic or jogging shoes with arch support. Start with the rope hanging to the floor behind you, your arms angled out 15 to 25 centimetres from your hips. Twirl the rope forwards from the elbows.

Start out skipping with your feet together; as you gain skill, try alternate-foot jumps. Your feet should come only a few centimetres off the floor. For variation, lift your knees high in front or kick up high behind.

Skip for 30 seconds, then rest for 30 seconds. Do this 10 times. Gradually

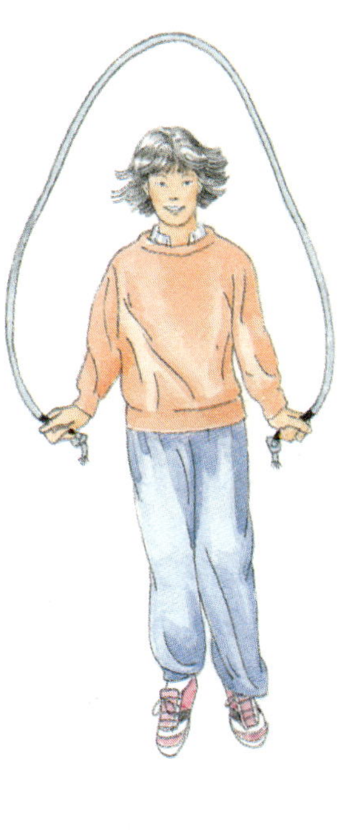

increase the skipping and rest times to 60 seconds each, for a total of 20 minutes, then gradually lengthen the total time until your heart rate is in your aerobic target range for 20 minutes (see *Endurance building*, p. 73).

Skylights

A skylight – a window in your roof – lets in roughly five times as much light as a vertical window of the same size, so it is a good way to make dark corners warm and bright.

A ventilating skylight is one that opens to expel heat and stale air. A glass skylight can be easily cleaned with ordinary window-cleaning preparations, but only a mild detergent (such as a dish-washing solution), should be considered for acrylic or polycarbonate panes.

These synthetics benefit from an occasional light polish with liquid car wax. Avoid abrasives (such as rubbing compound) and plastic pads; use only a soft cloth. Leaks between the frame and the roof are best plugged with roofing cement, and then smoothed to remove depressions in which water might gather.

Before applying the new cement, make sure that you remove all loose or cracked pieces of the old sealant. If the skylight itself leaks, you may need to obtain a new seal or gasket from the supplier.

Sleeping bag

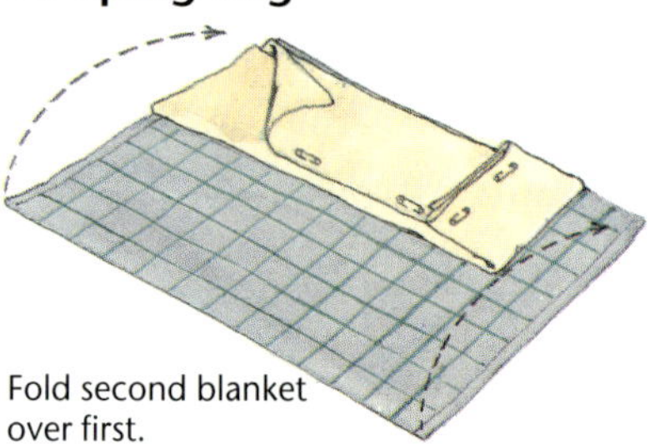

Fold second blanket over first.

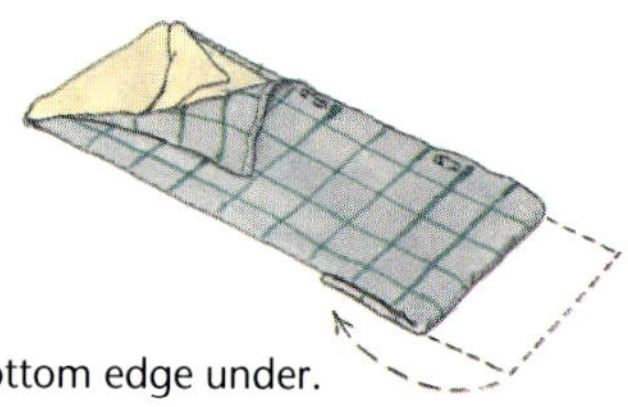

Tuck bottom edge under.

If you have two blankets, you can improvise a sleeping bag. Fold one in thirds lengthways and pin the free edge with large safety pins. Then fold up eight or 10 centimetres at the bottom and pin it. Lay it on the other blanket, as shown, and fold the second blanket over the first, pinning the edges firmly together. Tuck the bottom under.

Slides

1. You can scan your slides more easily if you store them in plastic slide sheets instead of boxes. Just make sure they're made of polyethylene (see *Photographs*, p.154). The sheets hold 20 slides and are punched to fit three-ring binders.

2. For safe storage, slides should be kept in a cool, dry place – not the attic or the basement. Heat and humidity are the enemies of colour dyes in slides and prints.

3. Dusty slides? To prevent scratching, use a soft camel's-hair brush, the kind that's used to clean camera lenses. Dust lightly and gently, starting from the centre.

4. Save money by mounting your slides yourself. Frames can be bought cheaply, and the only other equipment you need is a pair of smooth-nosed tweezers and a sharp pair of scissors. If you're not sure that your hands are steady enough, use a pair of white cotton gloves to avoid transferring fingerprints.

5. Label each slide, either with a self-adhesive strip or a felt-tip pen that won't smudge on the plastic frame. To keep the label brief, use a code system linked to a typed list with the full descriptions.

6. If you're giving a slide show, do *all* the setting up before your guests arrive. This includes focusing, arranging slides in trays or cassettes in an interesting sequence, and ensuring that you have a spare projector bulb right on hand.

7. If you're buying a hand-held viewer, get the type that allows you to look at a framed slide, as well as at strips of film.

Sliding glass doors

Although they are an attractive feature and a convenient entry point, especially to pool areas and pretty back gardens, sliding glass doors do present a few problems, several of them to do with security and safety.

1. If you're ordering a new door, the usual choice of frame is between aluminium or wood. Aluminium should require less overall maintenance.

2. Sliding doors are usually fitted with inexpensive (and fairly ineffective) locks. Specify a double-cylinder lock that can be operated only with the key. Back this up with one or more deadlocks fitted to the sliding frame, with the bolts sliding home into the standing frame.

3. Unless the sliding door is at a regular entry point, don't have keyholes or handles fitted to the outer side.

4. To prevent children and guests walking into closed doors, stick a row or two of decals about one metre above floor level. A row stuck higher up, or a set of wind chimes on the outside, will help warn off birds.

5. To insulate your glass doors, fit lined curtains or blinds that are made of a thick, non-conductive material. Allow blinds or curtains generous overlap at the ends of the frame.

6. To prevent an existing door being slid open from the outside, wedge a strong piece of wood in the lower channel, between the sliding frame and the end of the standing frame.

7. To remove the sliding frame, lift it up into the headspace in the top of the standing frame, then tilt the bottom outwards. To prevent burglars doing this, drive self-tapping screws into the upper member of the sliding frame from the inside, just below the top groove on the standing frame. Let the screws protrude so as to effectively block upward movement of the sliding frame.

Slings

1. Loop a towel or long scarf around an injured arm; pin or tie the ends securely around the victim's neck.

2. Put a fairly tight jacket on the victim, leaving the injured arm out of its sleeve. Then button or zip the jacket around the arm, elevating the hand eight centimetres above the elbow.
3. Put an oversize, long-sleeved shirt, jacket or cardigan on the victim; support the injured arm by pulling up the bottom of the garment as shown and buttoning it at the top.

Slugs & snails

1. If you live near the coast, you can try using salty seaweed as a slugproof and snailproof mulch.
2. Spread a full circle of marble dust around seedlings. The soft bodies of slugs and snails can't tolerate it.
3. Sprinkle salt on slugs to kill them. Stage an evening raid in the garden, salt cellar in hand; sprinkle each slug once, then again in five minutes. Or spray them with a 50-50 solution of vinegar and water.
4. Keep snails out of trees by wrapping an eight-centimetre band of thin copper sheeting around the trunks; the pests get a weak electrical shock when they crawl on it.

Small claims court

Small claims courts have been set up in the larger centres to make it easier and cheaper for people to have their cases heard. These courts deal only with claims up to about R2,000 – the amount is not firmly set because certain technical adjustments can be made by the court.

The only cases that can be heard in a small claims court are those that deal with:
- Debt arising from a signed document or from an instalment sale
- Non-delivery of property (such as a new appliance that you've paid for but not received)
- Removal of someone – an obstinate tenant, for instance – from your land or property
- Any other matter up to R2,000

Cases that a small claims court will *not* hear include anything to do with divorce or separation, wills, defamation, wrongful arrest or imprisonment, seduction, breach of promise to marry, malicious prosecution and mental capacity.

Only an individual may bring a case to the small claims court, but cases may be brought *against* a company or an individual.

The parties are not allowed legal representation, and the procedure consists of questioning by the Commissioner for Small Claims (usually a qualified lawyer or retired magistrate) to arrive at the truth.

Witnesses may be produced by either party, and evidence is given under oath.

A number of criteria must be fulfilled before you may take action through a small claims court:
1. You must have written proof that you are owed money.
2. You must send your debtor a written demand, by registered post, that he settle the outstanding amount.
3. If he has not done so after 14 days, you must call on the clerk of the small claims court of the district in which the debtor lives or works, with a copy of your demand.
4. A summons must be delivered to the debtor – either by you or the messenger of the court. If your debtor settles his debt, the matter is ended, but if he intends to defend the case, or does not respond, a date will be set for the hearing.

At the hearing, both you and your debtor are allowed to put your cases by presenting documents and calling witnesses. The Commissioner will then reach a decision and make an order of court.

If your debtor has not paid within 10 days of being ordered to do so by the court, report this to the clerk of the court. You will then have to draw up a sworn statement that will form the basis of a new hearing in a magistrate's court.

Smoke detectors

1. The best location for a home smoke detector is on or near a ceiling close to the sleeping area, away from corners, windows and doors. The top of a stairwell is also good.
2. If cooking causes false alarms, put a shower cap over the detector while you're in the kitchen. It's so obvious that you'll remember to take it off right after you've finished eating.

3. Never paint your smoke detector. Twice a year dust or vacuum it and change the battery.

Smoking

Quitting smoking isn't easy, but it may be the most rewarding thing you ever do. If you've failed before, the following suggestions may help you succeed once and for all:

DID YOU KNOW . . . ?

"A little night music"

The British novelist Anthony Burgess once noted: "Laugh and the whole world laughs with you; snore and you sleep alone."

□ About one in every five adults snores occasionally.

□ Problem snoring is more common in men, but women and children snore, too. And so do cats, dogs, horses, and many other animals.

□ Historically, snorers are in good company: Plutarch, Winston Churchill, and 20 of the first 32 United States Presidents were known to be nocturnal nuisances. Once when hospitalized, Teddy Roosevelt snored so loudly that most of the patients in his wing asked to be moved.

□ One woman, whose husband snored incessantly, became so irritated that she whacked him with a club. She was later found guilty of assault and battery. A fireman once shot a co-worker in the leg during an argument over snoring.

□ While snorers have tried everything from surgery to self-hypnosis to chin straps, a dependable cure for the sonorities has yet to be found.

1. Investigate your options – from "cold turkey" and nicotine gum to acupuncture, and various group programmes. Be prepared to try several methods or combinations of methods (prescription nicotine gum, for example, works best in conjunction with a group programme).

2. Be prepared for withdrawal symptoms: anxiety, restlessness, irritability, lethargy, impatience, confusion and lack of concentration are common. So are coughing, headaches, insomnia and appetite swings. Go for a run, take a brisk walk or do aerobic exercises to make you forget about your withdrawal symptoms and to burn energy.

3. Try using the buddy system. Join forces with another smoker who wants to quit and give each other moral support.

4. Enlist a former smoker to help you through the rough times and focus you on the benefits of quitting.

5. Get rid of all ashtrays, matches and lighters. Spend more time in places where you can't smoke.

6. Get your teeth cleaned; resolve to keep them free of nicotine stains.

7. Keep your mouth and hands busy: chew a piece of sugarless gum, nibble raw vegetables and fruits, drink liquids through a straw, play with a lucky coin.

8. Put the money you used to spend on cigarettes in a special bank account; use the proceeds to reward yourself for every week you succeed.

9. If you fail, try again. Most smokers need three or four tries.

Snakebites

Snakebite in South Africa is, in spite of popular opinion, neither common nor invariably fatal. The main groups of venomous snakes are:

□ Adders

□ Cobras and mambas

□ Tree snakes (boomslangs)

The following steps should be taken following a snakebite:

1. Check that the skin has actually been penetrated. If not, there is no danger at all.

2. Try to identify the snake. If it has been killed, make sure you keep the body for identification.

3. Keep the victim as still as possible and raise the affected limb (the leg or foot are the most common bite sites).

4. If cold packs are available, try to keep the area of the bite cool with them, until help arrives.

5. Transfer the victim to the nearest place where snake antiserum is available and administer it by injection as soon as possible.

6. If you are not able to reach medical assistance within 30 to 45 minutes, a tourniquet may be used. However, if the victim has been bitten by a back-fanged boomslang or an adder, do not use a tourniquet as these snakebites cause swelling and bruising of the limb. A tourniquet may be used for front-fanged snakebites (for example, cobra, mamba and ringhals) to delay the spread of the venom into the blood stream.

Use a lightweight band, such as a handkerchief or a strip of clothing, and tie it around the limb between the bite and the body. Do not tie too tightly and check it every 10 minutes – a band that is too constricting may cause gangrene to set in.

7. Do not try to suck the venom out of the bite or cut it open. Both actions will simply increase the blood circulation around the wound.

8. If the victim loses consciousness but is still breathing normally, place her on her stomach with one knee slightly raised and the corresponding arm bent so that the point of her elbow is in line with her shoulder (this is called the recovery or unconscious position). Wait for help.

9. If her breathing stops, begin mouth-to-mouth resuscitation. Don't leave the victim alone.

The antiserum supplied by the South African Institute for Medical Research is effective against most snake venoms, except boomslangs and vine snakes for which special antivenoms are available.

Snoring

For those of you who are troubled by your own or others' snoring, here are some interesting insights:

1. Caused by the vibrating of the soft palate while breathing through an open mouth, snoring was once considered merely as an irritating habit rather than a medical problem. It is now, however, accepted as a possible symptom of "sleep apnoea", during which the snorer may stop breathing for as long as 90 seconds at a time – depriving the body of oxygen and contributing to high blood pressure.

2. Other main causes of snoring are obesity, alcohol abuse and smoking. Do not drink, smoke or eat heavily before bedtime.

3. If you snore only when sleeping on your back, sew a tennis ball to the back of your pyjama top.

Snorkelling masks

1. To prevent your mask from fogging over, spit in it; rub the spittle around and rinse the mask.
2. To clear the snorkel tube of water as you ascend after a breathheld dive, tilt your head well back and exhale just as your mask breaks the surface of the water. Keep exhaling forcefully as you roll your head forward to continue snorkelling.

3. If your breathing tube fills with water, don't breathe in. Wait until the top of the tube is above the surface, then blow the water out.

Socks

1. If holes always appear in the same place on your socks, check your feet for rough spots – pumicing them may save your socks. You should check your shoes, too.
2. Socks won't stay up? You may be drying them on too hot a setting, which damages the elastic fibres.
3. Where do socks disappear to so mysteriously? We don't know, but here are a few ways to cope. Some get stuck in an inaccessible part of the washing machine or dryer. Check with the manufacturer on how and where to look for them. Better yet, before washing, put all your socks in a zipped net bag, or tie the pairs together. Or buy socks of the same style and colour in quantity – you may even get a discount. Then you'll never have to worry about pairing them up.
4. If several people in your household wear socks that look alike, mark the toes with small coloured stitches or initial them with indelible ink.
5. Athletes are less likely to get blisters if they wear high-quality socks made of high-bulk synthetic fibres. They cushion the foot and draw perspiration away from the skin. Or buy socks specially designed for your sport. Aerobic socks are padded at the heel, ball of the foot and toes; tennis socks are padded under the foot to protect against blisters and excessive perspiration.

Soft drink can

If the pop-up tab breaks off and you don't have an opener, don't despair. Because the hole in the can's top is scored, you can open it by lining up the tip of a spoon with the hole and pressing down with your thumb. No spoon? Do it with the tip of a screwdriver or house key. (See also *Can opener*, p.35.)

Soil erosion

Try using plants to stop soil erosion. They're cheaper and longer-lasting than a retaining wall.

STEEP SLOPES

To combat soil erosion on a steep slope, cover the area with a layer of straw, hay, dried bush or any other organic mulch, and cover with chicken wire, firmly pegged down.

Plant small plants, ground covers or grass plugs between the mesh. The organic mulch retains moisture, prevents soil movement and helps the plants become established.

A similar but simpler way of stabilizing sloping ground is to establish pockets or basins on the slope. The soil excavated from the pocket is used to form a protective wall around the pocket, particularly on its downward side, and plants are then planted in the pockets.

MODERATE INCLINES

Here you should plant a ground cover. First, sow annual ryegrass for an almost instant cover, then plant a fast-growing perennial like wedelia or a creeping shrub like Wilton's Carpet through the rye. The next spring handweed the rye out or use a weedkiller so that the ground cover can grow unimpeded.

Soil testing

The type of soil in your garden determines how much water and fertilizer you should apply and even what kinds of plants you can grow. Plants in sandy or light soil need plenty of water and nutrients; those in heavy clay may well be killed by overwatering. To work out what kind of soil you have, try this simple test:

In your garden, dig a straight-sided pit about one-metre deep, exposing the layers of soil. The top layer, which will be some 30-centimetres deep, should be dark and full of organic matter. The next layer will usually be lighter in colour as it has less organic matter in it. If it is hard and compacted, it is clay; if coarse and gritty, it is sandy. Beneath this layer is the base parent layer from which the top two layers are derived.

To test for drainage, fill the pit with water. If it has all drained away after 24 hours, the drainage is good. If, after two days, there is still water in the hole, the drainage is poor.

Sore throats

1. Avoid irritation – if you smoke, take the opportunity to stop.
2. To numb the pain, make this icy honey-lemon drink: squeeze the juice of one lemon into 125 millilitres of water and mix in plenty of honey or sugar; add lots of ice, stir well, and sip through a straw. Other soothers: gargle with half a teaspoon of salt in 120 millilitres of water or suck throat lozenges. These are available from your pharmacist.
3. Be sure to keep the mucous membranes moist: drink plenty of non-alcoholic liquids and run a vaporizer in your bedroom.
4. Take aspirin or a substitute to relieve pain.
5. Consult a doctor if your sore throat is accompanied by a fever, white spots on your tonsils, swollen or tender glands in your neck, great difficulty in breathing or swallowing, persistent headache, foul breath, a stiff neck or pain on opening your mouth wide. Tell him if you have recently been exposed to someone with a throat infection.

Soundproofing

1. In a family room, carpet the floor, cover the walls with cork, and install acoustic ceiling tile.
2. A dropped ceiling – made of a suspended metal grid in which acoustic panels are supported – offers even better soundproofing.
3. Insulate a noisy hot water cylinder to ensure a quiet bath.
4. Place a clothes dryer, washing machine or dishwasher on a thick pad of carpeting or rubber.
5. Put a television or stereo against an outside wall so that it won't transmit noise to an adjacent room.
6. Put stereo speakers on foam rubber on shelves or low tables.

7. Use lined curtains to block out street noise.
8. Carpet stairs to quiet footsteps.

Sour cream

1. Use plain low-fat yoghurt in dip recipes that call for sour cream. To thicken the yoghurt, spoon it onto a piece of cheesecloth and suspend it over a bowl in the refrigerator overnight to drain off the whey.
2. For a less kilojoule-laden potato topping, whirl low-fat cottage cheese or ricotta in a blender to smooth out the lumps, then stir in chives or chopped parsley. Alternatively, use low-fat yoghurt mixed with chopped basil, Parmesan cheese and freshly ground pepper.

Soy sauce

1. Try diluting soy sauce with an equal quantity of water to lower the sky-high sodium content. Or buy reduced-sodium soy sauce.
2. If sodium isn't a concern, a good soy sauce substitute is *tamari*, made from fermented soyabeans.
3. As a substitute in cooking, use three parts teriyaki to one part water.

Spectacles

1. When buying a pair of reading glasses, whether over-the-counter or prescription, keep in mind that glass lenses are less likely to scratch than plastic, but they can shatter and they do weigh more. Shop for tempered lenses that fit securely in the frame.
2. If you lose the hinge screw that holds an earpiece to the frame, use a small safety pin or paper clip for a quick fix.
3. Make your glasses fit more securely on your face by tightening the hinge screws with a jeweller's screwdriver. This is the tiny screwdriver that comes with a sewing machine. Alternatively, try the point of a paring knife or letter opener.
4. If a lens breaks cleanly, you can hold it together temporarily with a little transparent tape at the top and bottom of the crack.
5. Clean lenses with soapy water or a drop of vinegar, vodka or methylated spirits. To prevent scratches, do not rub plastic lenses until you've rinsed off all dirt.
6. Do your glasses fog up when you come in from the cold? Before heading out on a chilly day, just rub a thin coat of soap on the lenses. Then polish them until they are clear – instant waterproofing!
7. Do the lenses tend to pop out of your half-glasses? In an emergency, put chewing gum or any other sticky substance in the corner of the lens to hold it in place.
8. To secure a loose lens in a pair of full-frame glasses, look for a setscrew near the hinge; if your glasses are so equipped (some are not), tighten the screw to secure the lens. (See also *Magnifying glass*, p.131.)

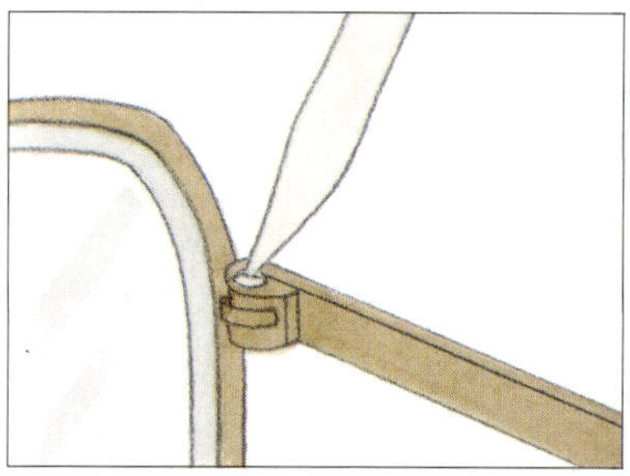

Spelling

1. Remember the old rhyme: "I before E, except after C, or when sounded like A, as in neighbour and weigh"?

Well, even this rule has its exceptions – many are in the sentence: "Sheik, seize the weird words either and neither at your leisure".

2. Ask a skilled speller to check what you've written; see if there's a pattern to your misspelling.

3. Use mnemonic aids to remember difficult words. For example: there's *a rat* in *separate*; there's an *end* in fr*iend*; the princi*pal* is your chief school *pal*; but a princi*ple* is a ru*le*.

4. Play word games and hold family spelling tests to help your children improve their spelling.

5. But note: some language experts believe that good spelling isn't a measure of intelligence and application but rather is an innate neuromuscular skill – that is, it can't be acquired. If, after trial and many errors, you still can't spell, the problem may be in your genes. If so, keep a dictionary always at hand: at home, on your desk, in your computer, in your briefcase or handbag.

6. No dictionary? Try looking up a word in the Yellow Pages, an encyclopaedia or the index of a book.

Spiders

Apart from the potentially deadly button (or black widow) spider, most of the great variety of spiders found in South Africa are harmless to man. They spin their intricate silken webs in cracks and crevices, behind cupboards and across corners, and serve us well by trapping and destroying household pests such as flies. So don't be tempted to spray them with insecticide, but rather trap them in a jar and set them free in your garden where they can feed on other insects to their hearts' content.

Symptoms of button spider poisoning occur within 10-20 minutes of the bite and include general redness of the skin around the wound, dizziness, stomach cramps, nausea, vomiting, sweating, anxiety, pains in the chest and, later, unconsciousness.

Apply an ice pack to the bite for a brief period to hinder the spread of the venom and get the victim to a hospital as soon as possible (Provincial hospitals have stocks of button spider antivenom.)

Take the spider with you, if you can, for positive identification.

Splinters

1. Can't see a splinter? Use a magnifying glass or apply a drop of iodine to stain it. Then remove it with a pair of tweezers and thoroughly cleanse the area with soap and water or hydrogen peroxide.

2. If the splinter resists, anaesthetise the area with an ice cube, wash it with soap and water and carefully use a sterilized needle to lift the skin and expose the end of the splinter. Remove it with a pair of tweezers.

Splints

Almost anything can serve as a splint. The lighter in weight it is, the better, so long as it can keep the fractured limb immobile.

1. A magazine works well; wrap it around the limb and secure it with cloth strips, tape or rubber bands. A thick newspaper will also do.

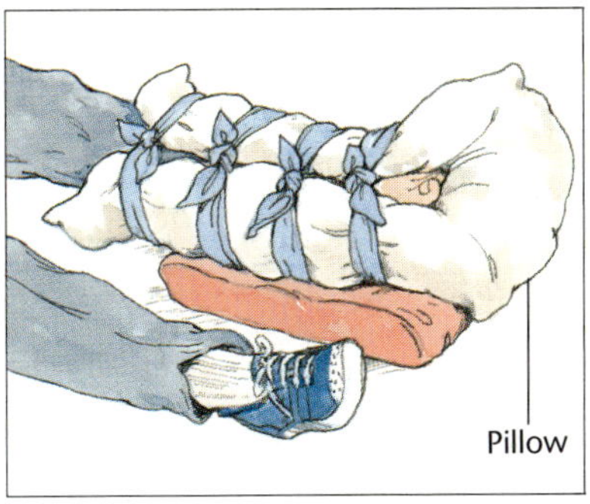

2. Other quite usable objects include pieces of timber, plywood or stiff cardboard; broom handles, umbrellas or boat paddles – even such soft items as pillows or blankets. Using a roller bandage or wide strips of cloth, fasten the splint snugly (but not so tightly that you cut off circulation) in several places above and below the fracture. Or try wrapping continuously upward from the end of the affected limb.

3. If nothing is available, bind a fractured arm firmly to the victim's chest, a broken leg to the uninjured one. In all cases, get the victim to a doctor or hospital emergency unit as quickly as possible. (See also *Fractures*, p.91; *Slings*, p.188.)

Spring fever

Does the end of winter leave you feeling lazy, listless and depressed? Here are some important ways to cure the blues and put you in harmony with the new season:

1. Get plenty of extra rest and make a special effort to eat a low-fat, low-carbohydrate, high-protein diet (see *Low-fat diet*, p.130; *The Balanced diet*, p.254).

2. Pack away your winter clothing; spring's lighter fabrics and colours may give you just the psychological lift you need.

3. Alter your daily routine: get up earlier than usual, take a different route to work, discover new places to eat lunch.

4. Instead of saving your holiday days for summer, use one or two now

DID YOU KNOW . . . ?

Matching your wits against words

Even champions have been stumped by the words on this list. Try holding a spelling game at home to see how many of these tricky, tough-to-spell words will baffle your family as well.

afflatus	condominium	ichthyology	mnemonic
atelier	dentifrice	incandescence	persiflage
bacchanalia	encomium	lavender	quidnunc
badinage	esoteric	meringue	quietus
cedilla	exorcism	minuscule	ratiocination
codicil	haemorrhage	miscible	sarcophagus

to do something enjoyable that you don't ordinarily have time for.
5. Brighten up your environment: wash the windows, open the curtains, buy something new for your home.
6. Start to work enthusiastically on your garden: plant seeds indoors, lay out vegetable beds, begin tilling the soil as soon as it's dry enough.
7. Find excuses for getting outdoors more: walk to work, watch the sun go down, count the stars at night.

Squaring a corner

No framing square? Try one of these methods to check for square:
1. To check a bookshelf or cabinet, measure diagonally from the upper left-hand corner to the lower right-hand one, then from the upper right corner to the lower left. If the work is square, the two measurements will be exactly the same.
2. Place a large book in the corner. If the work is square, both edges of the book will be exactly parallel to the two sides they touch.
3. Use a spirit level and a plumb line. Make sure the top of the work is exactly level, then hang the plumb line from the top.

Squeaking floor

To keep wood shims from shifting, spread glue on both sides.

1. For a quick fix, sprinkle talcum powder or powdered graphite between the squeaking boards. Or if that doesn't work, squirt in some liquid wax.
2. Rearrange furniture in order to change the traffic pattern in the room.
3. To silence a squeak from above, drill pilot holes and drive ringed-shank flooring nails through the floorboards into a joist.
4. If the floor is accessible from below, drive thin wood shims (cedar shingles tend to work best) between the underside of the squeaking boards and the top of the joist.

Squeegee

1. If the blade is nicked or damaged, reverse it. If it cannot be removed, smooth the edges with some fine sandpaper.
2. To clean car windows, cut a section of windscreen wiper blade and hold it with a large bulldog clip.
3. You can also use an old rubber dish-draining mat. Cut off the end several centimetres back from the lip so that you can hold it comfortably.

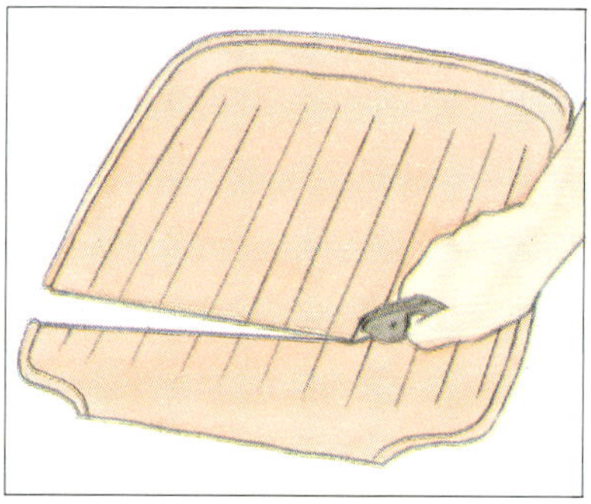

4. Clean rinse water from window glass or your glazed ceramic tiles with rolled-up newspaper.

Stain removal

A number of chemical stain removal preparations are available, yet many still prefer to use tried-and-tested remedies. These are often less expensive than their modern-day equivalents.

Linen: to remove recent fruit stains, hold the fabric tightly stretched over a tub and pour boiling water over the stained area.

This must be done before any soap is applied. Salt poured onto spilled wine or fruit juice will absorb much of the stain.

Blood stains can be stubborn. The best solution here is to wash the affected garment immediately in tepid water and soak it overnight in a specialized washing powder.

To remove coffee stains, sponge with a solution of borax, or loosen dried stains with a glycerine solution.

Grease spots on fabric: lay the stained area face down on a piece of woollen cloth. Cover with brown paper and iron with a hot iron for five to eight seconds.

Rub with a piece of brown paper. Or try dabbing the stain with turpentine, rub dry and then hang outside.

Grease stains on carpets: mix a little soap in a bucket of warm water, adding 30 grams of borax. Wash the area well with a clean cloth.

Fatty marks on steps: pour a boiling mixture of washing soda and water on the spot. Add fuller's earth made into a paste with boiling water. Leave the application overnight.

Ink stains on linen: dab the soiled part with lemon juice mixed with salt (blue ink) or ammonia (red ink).

Stairs

1. To put a slip-resistant surface on concrete stairs, mix sand into masonry paint and coat the treads with it. Stir often as you work.
2. On uncarpeted steps, apply a non-slip adhesive-backed strip about 25 millimetres from the front edge of each tread.
3. When carrying a large object, such as a basket of laundry, it's safest to walk slowly backwards up the stairs; drag the load with one hand and hold the banister with the other.
4. To silence squeaky stairs, nail the treads to the top edge of the risers with ringed-shank nails. Be sure to bore pilot holes first.
5. For a temporary tread, cut a piece of 16-millimetre plywood to fit and nail it in place.
6. If a staircase has very little headroom, install a small mirror on the front of the low spot. When people see their reflection, they'll duck, instead of banging their heads.

Stamps

1. If your postage stamps get stuck together, place them in the freezer for an hour or two. They'll usually come apart and be usable.
2. To remove a stamp from an envelope for collecting purposes, put it in the freezer overnight; then take it out and slide a knife between it and the envelope.
3. Or cut off the corner of the envelope with the stamp and float – don't immerse – it in lukewarm water until the paper comes off. Dry the stamp on blotting paper, then flatten it between the pages of a book. Or lay a thin paper over the stamp and run a moderately hot iron over it.
Caution: Be sure not to put an antique stamp in water because the ink might run. And don't use steam to loosen such a stamp: it might be ruined as a collector's item.

Staples

1. If you don't have a working stapler, try fastening papers at the corners with a dab of rubber cement or small squares of double-stick tape.
2. If you're missing a staple gun, tap staples into woodwork or upholstery with a tack hammer.
3. To remove stubborn staples from a wall or bulletin board, try needle-nose pliers or tweezers.

Static electricity

1. Take the crackle out of your carpet with a mixture of one part liquid fabric softener and five parts water. Put it in a spray bottle, mist the carpet, and let dry.
2. To fight static electricity in clothing, add fabric softener to the final rinse. If a clinging petticoat is the problem, starch it.
3. If you're already dressed, rub your petticoat or stockings with a fabric softener or a wire hanger. Or spray with hair spray.

Staying awake

1. Get up and move around; talk to other people.
2. Splash your face with cold water. Open the windows.
3. Drink beverages that contain caffeine and eat high-protein foods. Stay away from potato chips, muffins, biscuits, crackers, cake and sweets; far from being a "quick energy fix", these high-carbohydrate foods will make you sleepier.
4. Chew on a peppermint or a hot pepper; your body may rouse itself to the irritation.
5. If it's absolutely necessary to stay up for a couple of days, it may work to take a nap during the first 24 hours; a nap on the second day, however, may leave you feeling groggy.
6. If you feel drowsy while driving, open the windows and let the fresh air blow on your face. Sing along with the music on the radio or talk back to the disc jockey. If you're still sleepy, pull over and have a short rest. Do not drive unless you're alert.
7. If you have to change from one work shift to another, keep the same daily routine, regardless of what the clock says; eat breakfast before you go to work, break for lunch in the middle of your shift, and have dinner at the end of your work "day".

LOOK BEFORE YOU LEAP

For want of a nap, much can be lost

The French emperor Napoleon, who averaged less than four hours of sleep per night, believed that only fools and invalids required more sleep. But then history taught him a lesson.

When the little colony of Haiti rebelled against French rule in 1802, Napoleon dispatched a large army to quell the local uprisings. Though they were greatly outnumbered, the rebels feigned attacks night after night, depriving the French soldiers of their sleep. The tired soldiers eventually withdrew, and Haiti became a sovereign state.

For most people, lack of sleep has far less devastating consequences, but sleep deprivation can result in some serious side effects nonetheless.

After only 24 hours without sleep, you will start feeling irritable and have difficulty concentrating. After about two or three sleepless days, most people's memory and judgement will start to deteriorate, and ordinary mental and physical tasks will become a struggle to perform. If you stay awake long enough, you may even hallucinate or display other signs of mental illness.

Stereo systems

1. If your tapes don't sound quite as good as they used to, it's probably a good time to clean the playback heads on your tape recorder. (A once-a-month cleaning is wise.) Although you can use methylated spirits on a cottonwool bud, it's best to buy a special cleaner from an electronics supply store.
2. To clean the stylus on your turntable, put a little methylated spirits on a fine camel's-hair brush and move it gently along the cartridge from back to front. Never move the brush sideways or front to back.

SPEAKERS

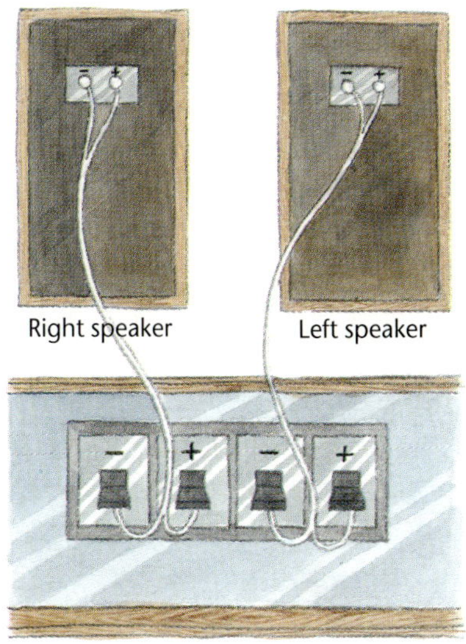

1. If a speaker stops working, make sure that all the connections are secure. If it's still dead, disconnect the jack or wire that goes into it from the back of the amplifier or receiver and connect it to the working speaker (after removing its own connection). If that speaker continues to work, the silent speaker needs to be repaired. If the second speaker ceases to work, the problem is in the wire or the amplifier; to find out which, reconnect the speakers and reverse the jacks or wires on the back of the amplifier. If the dead speaker now works, your amplifier needs repair; if it doesn't work, replace the jack or wire.

2. Does the speaker's sound cut out when you're using the turntable? Check the stylus while a record is playing; if it veers to the left or right, it may be missing one of the channels from the record. Replace it.

TURNTABLES

1. Does your turntable hum? See if the grounding wire (a thin black or green wire) is securely attached to the grounding post on the back of the receiver or amplifier.

2. Or try moving the turntable away from the speakers and other stereo components; it may be picking up vibrations. If you can't move it, place it on a piece of foam rubber.

Stings

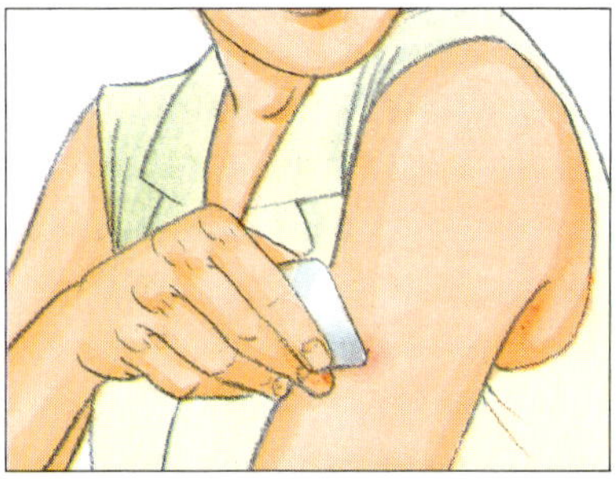

Insect stings – even multiple stings – are seldom very serious. The only notable exceptions are those stings which cause allergic or anaphylactic shock in people who have a particular allergy to them. The allergy is usually towards bee or wasp stings.

Remove the sting by gently scraping it with the blunt edge of a knife blade or with a credit card – if using tweezers, take care not to squeeze the poison bag. Apply a paste of meat tenderizer and water to the sting site as quickly as possible to reduce pain and swelling and to slow the rate of absorption of the poison.

To relieve the itch, apply ice packs, followed by an antihistamine cream; if not available, use calamine lotion. (See also *Insect bites*, p.116.)

Stitch in the side

1. Breathe deeply in and out to oxygenate your blood and energize the cramped muscle.

2. Dig your fingers firmly into the muscle at the point where you feel pain – usually on the left-hand side of the abdomen – then massage the spot by digging and rubbing.

3. If the stitch was caused by fatigue, rest is the best cure.

4. Mineral depletion is often the problem. Prevent a recurrence by eating a banana and some salt in the morning (for potassium and sodium). Pay attention to your calcium intake; it helps regulate muscle contractions. Drink lots of water.

Stitch removal

1. In a chain-stitch seam, all you do is cut a single loop and unravel the whole line of stitching.

2. The quickest way to remove a conventional machine stitch is with a seam ripper – or try using a razor blade – but be careful not to cut the fabric. The slow but sure way is to pull the seam apart gently and snip the individual stitches with tiny sharp-pointed scissors.

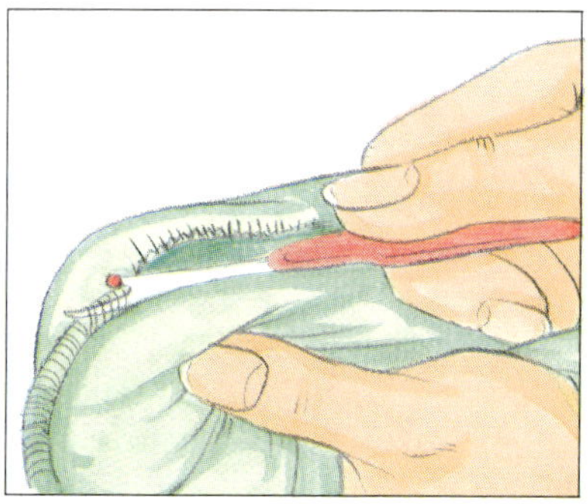

3. Overlocked seams look complicated, especially those using four or five threads in ladders of chains and loops. But you can cut them simply by running a seam ripper along the fabric's edge, underneath the outer row of loops.

Stolen car

1. Thieves quite often repaint cars and change the vehicle identification number (VIN) so that owners can't identify them. Foil them by having the VIN etched onto all the windows – a thief is less likely to steal a car on which all the windows would have to be replaced. You should find the VIN on the chassis and on a metal plate riveted onto the body of the car, usually in the engine compartment.

2. To help identify your car should it be stolen, drop business cards down the window channels.

3. In order to report the theft to the police, keep a record of the year, make and model of your car, as well as the VIN; make copies of the licence and registration.

Storage space

1. In one section of your cupboard install two rods, one about a metre above the other. Use them for short items such as shirts and skirts.

2. Hang handbags, belts and scarves from the cupboard rails with plastic shower curtain hooks or store in plastic holders with pockets.

3. Place storage boxes in the wasted space at the cupboard bottom. Make your own from wooden drawers; add hinged tops to keep out dust.

4. Storage boxes generally work well under the bed. They'll be much easier to pull in and out if you put them on wooden rollers.

5. You can store frequently used items in clear plastic boxes or wire baskets on cupboard shelves.

6. Attach hooks, towel racks or shoe bags to the cupboard walls or door for miscellaneous items.

7. In children's cupboards place rods within the kids' reach and use the

upper space to store out-of-season clothing. To encourage neatness, use plastic storage bins or label boxes with pictures of what's supposed to go in them.

8. Make a child's cupboard from an old chest with a hinged top. Screw short legs to whichever end will be the bottom. Stand the chest up and put a rod across the inside and a knob on the "door". For safety, remove all locking devices; use a magnetic catch to keep the door closed.

9. In an entrance hall where there's a staircase, hinge the tread of the bottom step; use it to store boots, umbrellas and sports equipment.

10. If there's space above or below your kitchen cabinets, enclose it and install sliding doors. Use the upper "mini-cabinets" for rarely used items, the lower ones for things you use all the time.

11. In your holiday home use metal storage compartments to keep out mice and other pests. Or line wooden compartments with aluminium sheeting or foil.

12. If you have a basement make a rack to fit under the steps and use it to store window and door screens.

13. In the dining room turn a windowsill into a bar and build a storage chest under it.

14. In the attic build triangular storage units to fit under the eaves.

15. If your living room fireplace sticks out into the room, build in a set of floor-to-ceiling bookshelves or cabinets on both sides.

16. Suspend a pegboard in the kitchen, pantry, garage or workroom for hanging cooking utensils and tools. The pegboard hooks are slotted through the holes and are capable of supporting substantial weights, including cast-iron pots.

17. Where there happen to be cupboards under stairways, install a small shelf under each step. Use the shelves for storing small articles.

Storm damage

1. Has hail broken windows in your home? For an energy-efficient quick fix, carefully knock out the rest of the glass and then staple a sheet of four-millimetre polyethylene to the frame, inside and out.

Or cover the screen window with a double thickness of polyethylene and put it in place while the broken window is being reglazed.

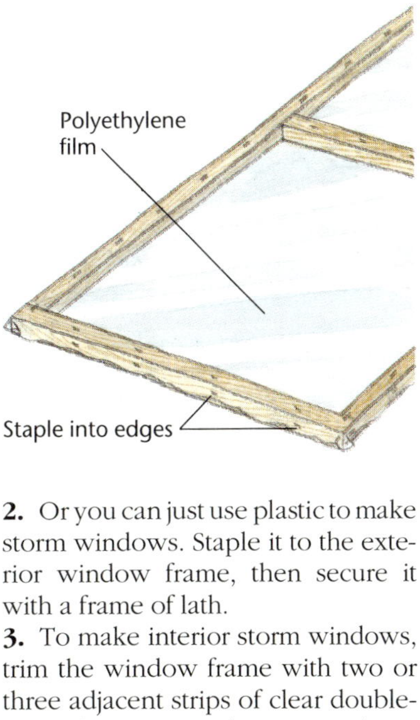

2. Or you can just use plastic to make storm windows. Staple it to the exterior window frame, then secure it with a frame of lath.

3. To make interior storm windows, trim the window frame with two or three adjacent strips of clear double-stick plastic tape. Then cut a plastic sheet slightly larger than the frame and press it onto the tape; be sure to start at the top, stretching the plastic to eliminate wrinkles.

4. If you have installed a traditional storm window and condensation starts to form on the house window, the storm window needs caulking. Apply latex caulk around it to form an airtight seal.

5. Before taking down storm windows in the spring, mark each one with a letter or number keyed to its proper place. This will simplify installation next autumn.

Stoves

Consider the following when purchasing a new stove:

1. Gas stoves usually cost less to operate and allow faster control of the heat. Electric stoves, on the other hand, give off less waste heat and are easier to clean.

2. Freestanding stoves are easier to move and cheaper than their built-in counterparts. However, most built-in stoves usually feature a separate hob and oven, and these allow greater flexibility when designing a kitchen.

3. Clean the surface of the stove while it is still warm, and the grease spatters have not yet hardened. Use soapy water and a cloth or sponge.

4. Wipe the inside of the warm oven with a soapy cloth or paper towels. If spills in the oven have hardened, stand a saucer of ammonia in the oven overnight and clean it the following morning with a soft cloth and soapy water.

5. Clean oven racks by placing them on an old towel in a large bowl and soaking them in a solution of ammonia and water overnight.

6. Save energy by adjusting a gas flame so that it just touches the bottom of the pot, and does not curl up around the base.

7. On an electric stove, use an element that is the same size as, or slightly smaller than, the pot.

8. Arrange oven racks before you turn on the oven. Every time you open the oven door, up to 12 degrees of heat is lost.

Strains & sprains

Both strains and sprains hurt. To tell the difference between them, look for swelling and discoloration; a sprain will have both.

To treat either injury, you should elevate and immobilize the affected part, and apply an ice pack as often as can be tolerated for about 24 hours to reduce swelling and pain. If you are in any doubt about the victim's condition, call a doctor.

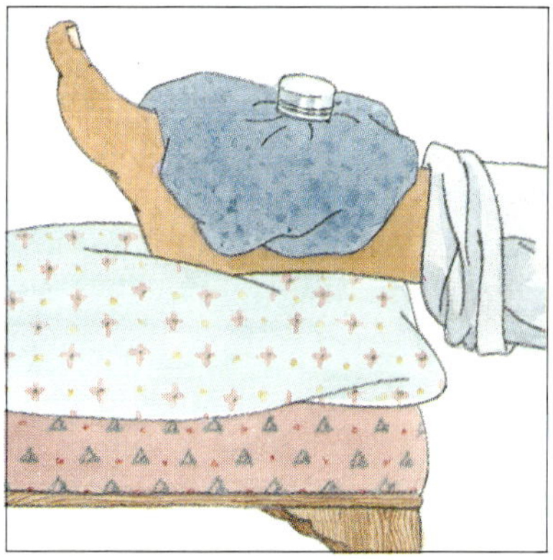

Strengthening exercises

1. For arms and shoulders do hip raises. Lie on the floor on one side. Raise your upper body, supporting it with your arm. Push your hip up to straighten your body, then bend your elbow as you lower yourself to the floor. Repeat three to six times on each side.

2. Or do modified push-ups. Stand about a metre away from a strong desk, table or counter – preferably one that has a rounded edge. Lean forward and support your weight with your hands on the edge, keeping your arms straight. Then bend your arms, keeping your body straight until your chin or chest touches the edge. Push back to the starting position and repeat five to 20 times.

3. For legs: try semi-squats. Stand with hands on hips directly in front of a straight chair. Bend your knees slowly until the backs of your thighs just touch the front edge of the chair at mid-thigh (or as low as you can without pain), raising your arms straight in front as you bend. Rise to the starting position. Repeat five times; work up to 30 or more rapid repetitions. As you get stronger, remove the chair.

4. For calves: hop, first with feet together, then on alternating legs, then stepping forward on alternating legs as if walking. Repeat each five times; work up to 25 times.

5. To build up endurance for hiking, go for long walks with a weighted backpack, increasing the weight as you grow stronger. Two-, five- or 10-kilogram bags of cat litter or dry pet food work well.

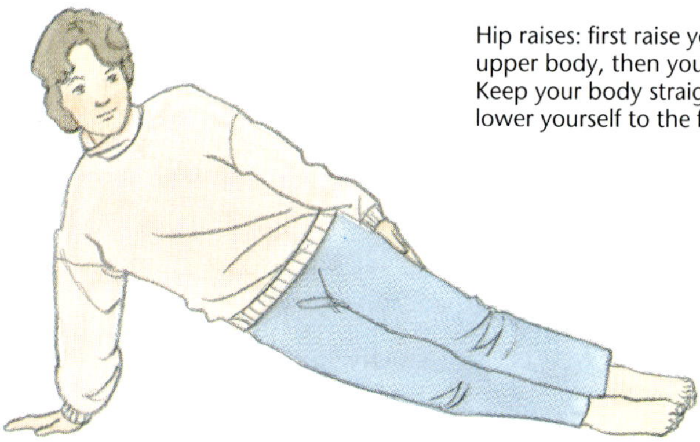

Hip raises: first raise your upper body, then your hip. Keep your body straight as you lower yourself to the floor.

Stress

Are you feeling tense, restless, anxious or irritable?

1. Clear your mind. Sit comfortably away from noise and distractions, close your eyes, and focus on a peaceful thought, a tranquil setting or a neutral word. Try to recall, minute by minute, the finest hour of the happiest day of the best holiday you ever had. Or just listen to yourself breathe. After five to 10 minutes, you'll feel refreshed.

2. Schedule at least 30 minutes daily for relaxation – listen to soft music, read, write, think or dream.

3. Breathe deeply for a few minutes several times a day or whenever you begin to feel tense. Clasp your hands over your abdomen and inhale slowly and deeply through your nose, extending your abdomen as far out as it will go. Hold your breath for several seconds, then exhale slowly through your mouth. (See also *Breathing exercises*, p.26.)

4. Loosen up tense muscles by doing stretching exercises.

5. Practise progressive relaxation on a daily basis. Sit in a comfortable chair or lie on your back with your arms resting limply at your sides; now close your eyes. One by one, tense up and relax each muscle area in your body, beginning with your head and gradually working your way down to your toes. As you progress, try to isolate individual muscles. (See also *Insomnia*, p.117.)

Stretchers

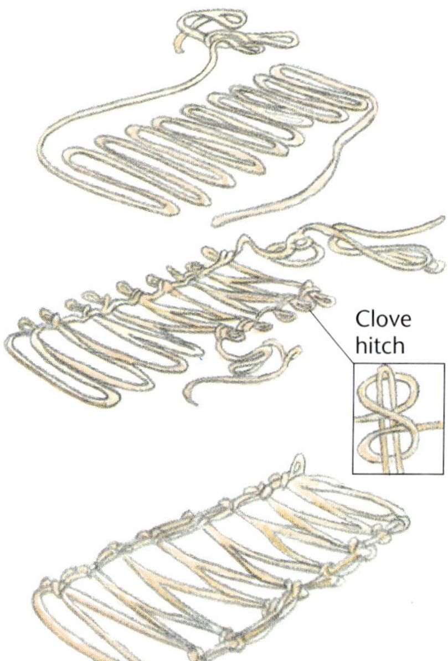

In an emergency you can use a door, surfboard or blanket as a stretcher, but there are other options available, if need be.

1. Place approximately 50 metres of rope on the ground and make 16 loops about as long and as wide as the person you intend to carry. Work the rope ends down the sides as shown, using a clove hitch to tie the loops together; thread what's left of the rope ends through the closed loops, then tighten all the loops.

2. Button or zip a coat or several jackets; turn inside out and run two poles (or broom handles, pipes or oars) through the sleeves.

Caution: Before using a makeshift stretcher, test it with an uninjured person. It may need more padding.

Stretching exercises

To reduce muscle tension and feel more relaxed, try these stretching exercises. Do each one slowly and stop when you feel tension in the muscle – but before the onset of pain. Hold a position, but never bounce; you could injure a muscle.

1. Arms, shoulders and back: kneel down, bend over, and rest your forehead on one forearm on the floor. Reach forward with your other arm, grab a couch leg or other firm object, and pull, feeling the tension in your arms, shoulders, upper back and sides. Hold for 15 seconds and release. Repeat with the other arm.

2. Arms and shoulders: raise your arms straight above your head, with your wrists intertwined and your palms together, so that the right palm faces right and the left palm faces left. Inhale as you stretch your arms up and back. Hold for five seconds, then lower your arms and relax. Repeat up to 10 times.

3. Sides: stand with your feet a shoulder-width apart. Raise one arm above your head, palm in. Rest the palm of your other hand against your thigh. Bend sideways from the waist, sliding your hand down your thigh and bringing your arm over, until you feel a pull from hip to shoulder. Hold for a count of five. Straighten. Alternate five times on each side.

4. Hamstrings: stand with your feet shoulder-width apart and your knees slightly bent. Bend over slowly, letting your arms and head dangle; keep your belly pulled in. Stop when you feel tension in your back or in the backs of your thighs and knees. Hold and count to 30, letting yourself relax. Imagine that the backs of your legs are turning to soft butter.

5. Calves: stand at arm's length from a wall, hands flat on the wall, arms straight. Bend your elbows and lean toward the wall, keeping your back and legs straight, until you feel tension in your calf muscles. Hold for 20 seconds, then push upright. Repeat three times. The ultimate goal is to hold for one minute with your head against the wall.

6. Groin: lie flat on your back with your legs raised, the heels resting against a wall, and your buttocks about 10 centimetres away from it. Now slowly separate your legs, letting your heels slide apart and down the wall until you feel a stretch in your groin and inner thighs. Hold for 30 seconds; then relax and pull your legs together. Repeat twice.

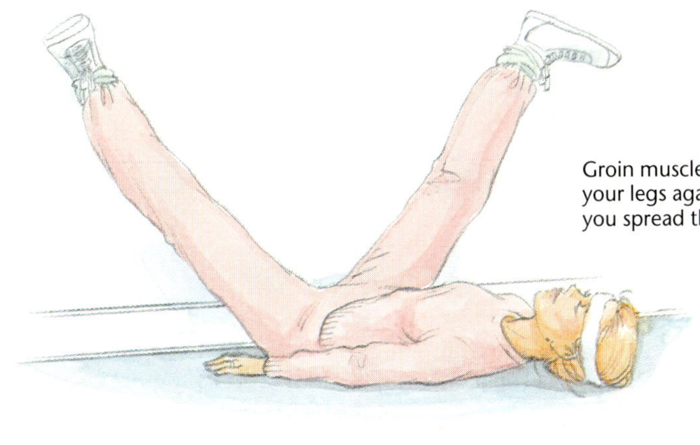

Groin muscles: support your legs against a wall as you spread them apart.

String

1. To loosen a knot, twist the string to compact it while pushing toward the knot from both sides. If necessary, ask someone to open the knot with a pencil tip or nail while you push. Or use your teeth.

2. Keep string neat by putting it in a dispenser. Make your own from a can or jar; punch a hole in the lid for the string to feed through. Or roll short pieces of string into an ever-increasing ball. Secure the loose end with a small piece of adhesive tape.

3. You can wrap short lengths of string around a fishing reel. Or use a toilet paper tube with a notch cut in one edge to secure the loose end.

Stringing beads

1. For heavy beads use fine fishing line or dental floss.

2. If you're using string, dab clear nail polish on one end. Let it dry before starting to string.

3. To keep the whole strand from coming apart if the string breaks, tie knots between the beads.

4. To keep beads of varying sizes in order while restringing, stick them to a strip of tape. Or lay them in the crack of an open book or magazine.

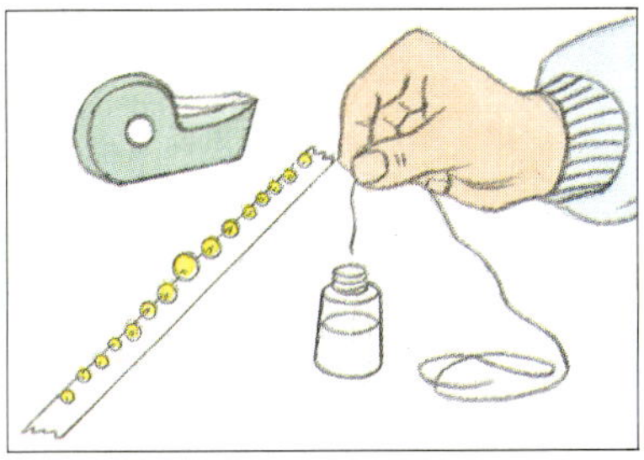

Stuck car

1. If you're stuck in mud or sand, be sure not to accelerate hard to try to pull away. The spinning of the wheels will simply bury them deeper and make gripping more difficult.

2. Place rocks, branches or sacking under the driving wheels for traction and point the wheels straight ahead. Engage first or second gear and gently

try to ease the car forward. Any passengers can help by pushing the car forward. They must, however, stand at the sides of the car and not at the back, in case it rolls back into them.

3. If you are stuck in beach sand, try "rocking" the car to create a track. Engage first gear and try to get it to move forward a few centimetres, then engage reverse gear and move backwards. Repeat until the car is able to mount branches beneath the wheels.

Sunburn

Sunburn is caused by overexposure to the sun's rays. It can vary in intensity from a mild case of reddened skin, itching and tenderness to a severe burn, where the victim's skin becomes extremely painful, bright red, swollen and blistered. Sunburn is usually at its worst some 48 hours after exposure.

1. For quick relief, take a cool oatmeal bath, then smooth on a thin layer of mild hydrocortisone cream (available from your pharmacy) or try calamine lotion. Apply cool compresses or sponge the area gently with cold water for 10 to 15 minutes several times a day. Antihistamine creams are not effective.

2. To prevent dehydration, try to drink plenty of non-alcoholic liquids.

3. Take aspirin or paracetamol to relieve general discomfort.

4. Leave blisters open to the air. Do not burst them.

Caution: If there is extensive pain, blistering or swelling or if the victim has a high fever, consult a doctor.

Sundials

The advantage of a sundial: it doesn't have to be wound or plugged in. The drawback: it can't be used at night or on cloudy days.

To make one, plant a straight or forked stick firmly into the ground at high noon; tilt it slightly southward (in the southern hemisphere) so that you get a shadow. Put a rock or line of pebbles at the tip of the shadow. Then set an alarm clock for each hour; when it rings, place another rock or line of pebbles at the shadow's tip. Repeat until sundown, then resume at sunrise until you've come full circle.

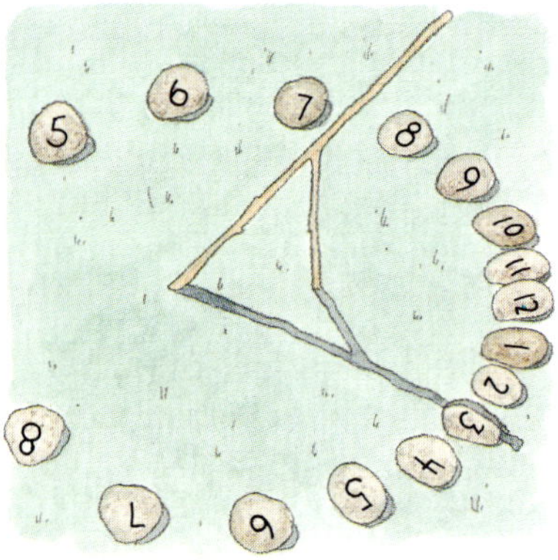

Ideally, a sundial should be laid out on the day of the spring or autumnal equinox. It will be accurate only on those two days.

Sunglasses

1. For maximum protection, look for the label: "Absorbs UV up to 400 nm"; this indicates that the sun's most damaging rays will be blocked.

2. Caught without your sunglasses? Make Eskimo-style goggles: bend a strip of cardboard lengthways, then cut two slits along the fold for your eyes and a nose slot. Attach with ribbon or string. (Don't pull your "sunglasses" flat; the triangular shape shades your eyes.)

Sunscreens

Sunscreens should be used regularly from early childhood to prevent lifelong skin damage (altered texture, wrinkling, discoloration, pronounced blood vessels and cancerous lesions) that may be caused by prolonged exposure to the sun.

1. Here's a formula for judging their effectiveness: determine how many minutes it takes your skin to begin to burn when unprotected. Multiply that number by the sun protection factor (SPF) printed on every commercial lotion. Divide the result by 60 to find how many hours of protection you can expect. If you would normally burn in 30 minutes, for example, an SPF 8 lotion should protect you for about four hours.

2. The most protective sunscreens are usually the most expensive. If you feel that the sunscreen with an SPF of 24 is too expensive, you might wish to buy one with an SPF of 12 and apply it more often. If you burn easily or intend being out in the sun for an extended period, consult your dermatologist or doctor. He may recommend a complete sunblock, such as zinc oxide.

3. Also take into account the sun's intensity; the higher in the sky it is, the more direct the rays are. You need a higher SPF number at midday than you do in the morning or evening, a higher number in the tropics than farther south.

4. What type of ingredients should you look for in various sunscreens? In the past, some doctors favoured the use of PABA (para-aminobenzoic acid) derivatives; however, a number of people showed allergic reactions to them, so doctors started recommending PABA-free sunblocks. Sunscreens should also be waterproof and non-stinging and give good broad-spectrum protection (not just against UVA and UVB rays).

5. Even a sunscreen labelled "waterproof" may come off while swimming. Remember to reapply it.

6. Never use a sunscreen that is more than a year old. Some have expiry dates – go by them.

7. Don't rely on "natural" lotions like sesame oil, cocoa butter or mixtures of vinegar and olive oil. They're not effective. (See also *Burns*, p.28.)

Support groups

You no longer have to be alone with your problems; for almost every difficult personal situation, physical affliction, fear and addiction, there is a mutual help or support group. By joining one, you'll gain the understanding of many other people who have gone through similar experiences, and get practical help in dealing with your problem.

FINDING ONE

The names of various organizations may be found by contacting your local hospital, church, the Citizens' Advice Bureau or the Department of Health Services and Welfare. Here are some of the groups offering help:

1. Aged: The South African Council for the Aged, PO Box 591070, Kendray 2100.

2. Aids: Department of Health Services and Welfare; Life Line (nationwide toll-free number 0800-012322).

3. Child abuse: South African Police Child Protection Unit (offices in all major centres or contact your local police station).

4. Childline (nationwide toll-free number 0800-123321).

5. Citizens' Advice Bureau (offices in most major centres).

6. Life Line (offices in most centres).

Surgery

1. Be sure there are no alternatives to surgery. Talk to your doctor and, if necessary, get a second opinion.

2. Be sure to choose your surgeon with care. You should check that he is registered with the South African Medical and Dental Council (SAMDC). Although this seems distrustful, cases have been discovered where unqualified people have been practising medicine for years. Your local public library should have a list of medical practitioners published annually by the SAMDC.

3. Ask the doctor about the extent of the operation, its risks, side effects and probable results. Ask how much the surgery will cost. If you feel that the cost is exorbitant, try to negotiate a lower amount.

4. Surgery requires the consent of the patient or, in the case of a minor, the consent of the parents or legal guardians.

Your doctor has a legal duty to inform you directly of all aspects of the impending operation. Such information should be in writing, particularly if major surgery is involved.

Sign any consent forms only after you are satisfied that all your questions have been answered.

Consent for surgery which does not involve a general anaesthetic is legally binding on anyone who is 14 years or older. If a general anaesthetic is required, consent is binding on patients 18 years or older.

5. Ask your surgeon for the names of others who have had similar operations. Call one or two and ask how they felt after the operation.

6. Make sure that your doctor is aware of any allergies or other physical conditions you have or have had. Have you ever had a negative reaction to an anaesthetic? Are you taking a course of drugs? If you are a smoker, you may be asked to kick the habit temporarily to allow for normal breathing during surgery.

7. If there's a possibility that you'll need blood during or after the operation, eliminate any risk of infection by asking your doctor for details about donating your own blood beforehand. Blood for transfusions can be stored in a blood bank for up to 42 days after it has been donated.

8. Ask the doctor to place any intravenous tubes in your non-dominant arm, away from the elbow, so that you'll be able to manoeuvre more easily.

9. Ask your doctor or physician exactly where the incision is to be made; then, if you wish, use a felt-tip pen to mark that place on your body before you go into surgery. (See also *Hospitalization*, p.110.)

Survival in the wild

You need three things to keep you alive in the wild: water, food and shelter. Cynics often add luck to the list but you can reduce your dependence on luck by preparing yourself thoroughly for any trip, whether on foot or by vehicle, through rough, inhospitable or lonely terrain.

Your basic equipment must be in good condition. This means that you and your vehicle, should be in the required state of fitness.

Your survival kit should include several full water bottles, emergency rations, water-purification tablets, waterproof matches, a sharp knife, space blanket, a torch, whistle, mirror for signalling, a first aid kit and emergency flares.

Rather than buy a prepared first aid kit, look at those that are commercially available, and make up your own, incorporating the most useful ideas from each.

Other useful items include an eight-metre length of light line and a few lightweight but heavy-duty garden refuse bags for making a lean-to. If possible, take along a spade, a gas stove, fuel, a compass and maps.

Before you set out, make sure that someone knows the details of your intended route and estimated times of arrival for each stage.

If you're stranded overnight, look for shelter close to your route or build a lean-to. Insulate yourself by padding your clothing with dry leaves or grass. You'll get most heat from a fire if you can build it near a sheltered rock face, and lie in between.

Caves and overhangs should be avoided in stormy weather because they tend to attract lightning. When visibility is adequate, you can consider your next move. Use your whistle, mirror or a flare to attract the attention of searchers.

Avoiding excessive fluid loss is especially vital in desert conditions. If you're lost, move and drink only at dawn or at night, and find shade for resting during the day. Keep your head and neck covered. Mark your position by spreading clothing or equipment on the ground.

Swimming emergencies

1. If you tire far from shore, don't panic. Float on your back. If there are people around, wave one arm slowly from side to side to attract attention. Start for shore when you regain strength. Don't push yourself; float when you need to rest.

2. If you're tangled in kelp or seaweed, relax, gently shake your arms or legs, and move slowly away with the current. If you're stuck, roll the seaweed down your arm or leg like a sock, or merely pluck it off your body.

3. Let heavy surf help you get to shore. As a wave approaches from behind, turn your body sideways to it, so that you can watch its progress while you tread water. Try to ride with the wave's upward movement. If the wave breaks on you, hold your breath until it passes over; then either resume a back float or ride behind it toward shore.

4. Body-surf on smaller waves: start swimming as one approaches. As it catches you, straighten your body, thrust your arms out in front, and hold your head up, tucking your chin in. Ride the wave, kicking to keep up with it. Rest when the crest passes.

5. If you get caught in an undertow, take a deep breath, relax, and let it carry you under and out. You'll bob up in time to breathe again. Body-surf back to shore.

6. If you get caught in a riptide (a current moving out to sea), let it carry you out. As soon as it slows down, swim sideways (riptides are usually only about six metres wide). Then swim toward shore, moving at a wide angle away from the tide.

RESCUING OTHERS

1. Never get close enough to a panicked swimmer for him to be able to grab you. Instead, reach out with a long stick or your leg while maintaining a firm hold on a boat or dry land. Or throw a coil of rope or something that floats, ideally a life buoy.

2. If the victim is beyond reaching or throwing distance, try to go out with a floating support, such as a canoe or surfboard; a rowing boat is best. When you get near the victim, turn the boat and approach stern first. Let the victim hold on to the stern as you row to safety.

3. Only as a last resort should you attempt a swimming rescue – and then only if you are a very good swimmer. If you have a shirt or towel, swim to the victim while holding it in your teeth. When you are just beyond arm's reach, take the shirt in one hand and flip the other end to the victim. Tow him to shore.

If all else fails, grasp his hair, collar or chin. If he grabs you, try to break his hold. Or take a deep breath and sink with him – he'll let go. Kick away before trying again.

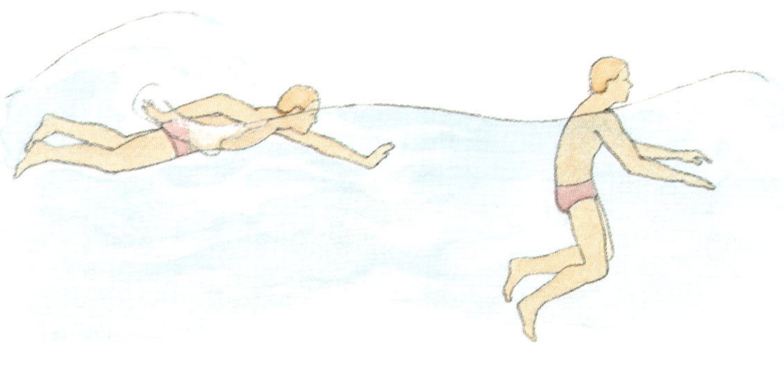

Swimming pools

1. To save any wear and tear on an above-ground pool with a plastic liner, cut up a rubber dish mat and put the pieces under the legs of the ladder where they meet the liner.

2. If your child's pool has a small hole or crack, let it dry and then patch both sides with waterproof tape.

3. Attack the mud and gravel problem by placing a small plastic tub of water next to your pool. Ask children to step in it before they decide to jump into the pool.

4. If your fence isn't keeping trespassers out of your pool, try planting thorny plants around it.

5. Ensure that your sunken pool is kept clean by banning food and drink from it. Clean the surface regularly with a pool net to stop leaves blocking the filter. Install an automatic pool cleaner, if possible.

POOL GAMES

1. Float an inflated bicycle inner tube in the water and use it as a target for balls. Or fly-cast into it, using a bolt or a sinker instead of a hook.

2. Enjoy water basketball? Just bolt a standard backboard, equipped with a hoop and nylon net, to strips of angle-iron. Attach them to the end of the diving board with two C-clamps.

IN TIMES GONE BY

The world's smallest bathing suit

In 1946 French couturier Jacques Heim created the world's smallest bathing suit – two tiny cloth triangles joined at the hips and topped by a narrow bra. That same year the United States announced that it would begin peacetime nuclear testing by dropping an atomic bomb on a small island in the Pacific known as Bikini.

Both events, though unrelated, inspired French manufacturer Louis Reard, who had copied Heim's design, to dub his creation the "bikini", hoping its impact on the fashion world would be as explosive as an atomic bomb.

Before long American GI's stationed in Europe brought bikinis home for their wives and girlfriends – who were thrown off beaches for wearing them. Not until the 1960s did the teeny-weeny garments become socially acceptable on South African shores.

3. Let small children go fishing. Make fish out of metal canning lids; tape over sharp edges and tie on bright plastic tails. Give the kids poles that have magnets for hooks.

Caution: Don't let children play around any pool unattended. Always empty a small pool when not in use. Keep the fence gate locked in the absence of adult supervision.

Swimsuits

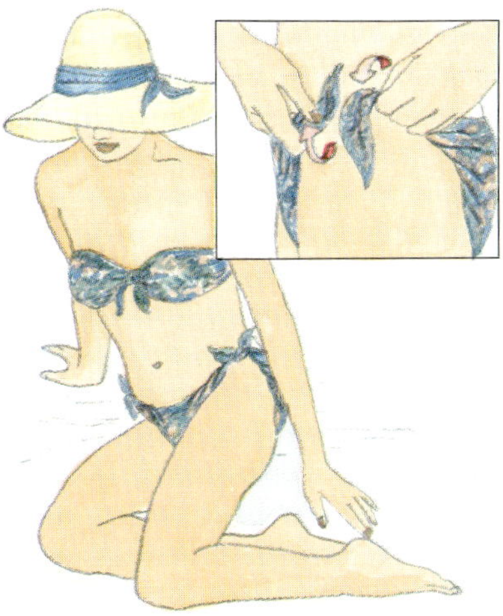

It's easy to make your own bikini. All you need are three sizeable scarves and a little ingenuity. A sewing machine helps, too, or at least a needle and thread; but you could probably make do with small safety pins.

THE BOTTOM

Fold two scarves in half to form triangles. Then fold back the tips (the bottom of the V) about five centimetres and sew them down. Sew both sections together to form the crotch. Tie the loose ends at the sides, as shown.

THE TOP

1. Fold the remaining scarf into a triangle, then a wide band. Place it against your back, then tie it in front; adjust the width as needed.

2. If the scarf is long enough, you can make a halter top. Put the scarf around your neck, cross it over your bust, then tie the ends in the back.

T

Table linens

1. Stored linens will discolour if all of the dirt – especially food or body oils – isn't removed first with proper laundering. Use hot water and adequate detergent, and make sure all stains are completely out.

2. Sun-drying helps reduce discoloration in linens.

3. If your linens have discoloured, a mild solution of chlorine bleach and water will do wonders.

4. To remove wax, place a white facial tissue, folded four times, over the spot and press with a warm iron. Repeat with a clean tissue if necessary.

5. Instead of ironing linen serviettes, just smooth them out, still wet from the washing machine, onto a table or countertop. They'll dry crisp and neat. Spread a damp tablecloth over a flat, non-wooden surface.

Table manners

1. If you can't get at your food with a knife or fork without making a mess – when eating spareribs, mealies or crayfish, for example – go ahead and use your fingers. Otherwise, when in doubt, follow your host's example or consider the formality of the situation.

2. If you've bitten into something that can't be swallowed – gristle, a pip or a fish bone, for instance – remove it from your mouth the way it went in (generally with your fork) and put it on the side of the plate.

3. Hair in your soup? Insect in your salad? In someone's home, either remove the interloper and eat your food, or leave it untouched – but refrain from commenting on it. In a restaurant, send the food back.

4. If ashtrays are on the table, you can assume it's all right to smoke; otherwise, ask if anyone minds. Never smoke while others are eating; only between courses.

Tables

1. If the sides of your drop-leaf table rattle against the legs, put a small plaster or foot pad at each point of contact. (If they're visible, paint them to match the wood.)
2. For a toddler's birthday party, use a long coffee table and short stools. If necessary, put books under each leg to elevate it. Be sure to cover with a plastic tablecloth.
3. Restored packing cases or crates can make interesting coffee or occasional tables.
4. Or use two stained or painted trestles to support an old but attractive door, and cover with a tablecloth.
5. Or place a sheet of heavy glass on top of a matched set of pedestals such as inverted urns, clay flowerpots or heavy baskets.
6. Shade a wooden picnic table with a big outdoor umbrella. Drill a hole in the centre of the tabletop, put the umbrella through it, and secure the bottom in a weighted umbrella stand.

Talcum powder

You can use either cornflour or fuller's earth as a good substitute for talcum powder.

Tangled cords

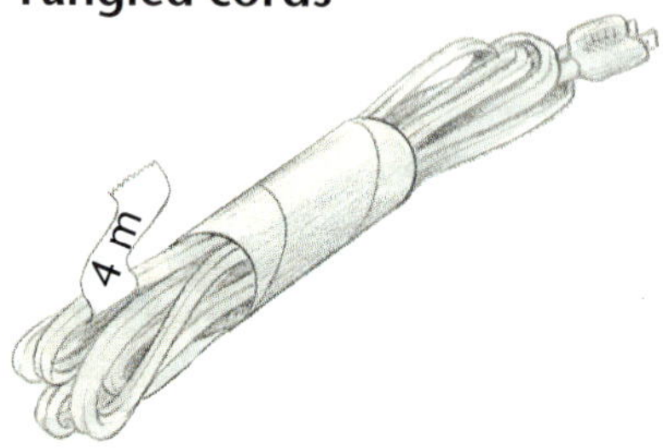

1. To store extension and appliance cords neatly, fanfold each one separately, wrap it securely with masking tape, and label it. You can also keep folded cords in serviette rings or in toilet paper tubes.
2. Alternatively, hang your extension cords from a tie rack.
3. When you are storing appliances that have cords permanently attached, avoid kinks by fanfolding the cord. Hold it together with a twist tie or a rubber band.
4. To store your cord, tie a length of string behind the plug. Roll up the cord, wrap the string around it, tie a bow and hang it on a hook.

Tape

1. If you're having trouble finding the end of a roll of tape, just slide a credit card along the roll until it catches. A knife or single-edged razor blade will also work.
2. If tape is difficult to peel off a roll, put a drop of paint thinner on the end and wait 30 seconds.
3. To mark the end of a roll, insert a small paper clip under the sticky side of the tape.
4. Need a lot of short pieces of tape that are the same length? Use a single-edged razor blade to cut into the roll through several layers of tape. Then peel off one piece after another.

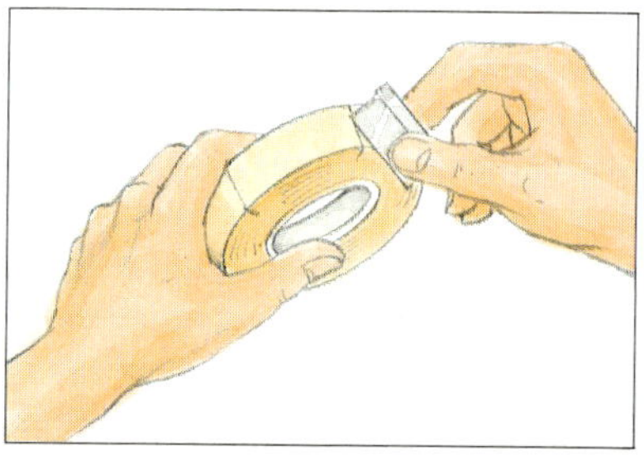

Tapes and CD's

1. Don't touch audio or video tapes with your fingers; you'll leave grease marks and particles of grit.
2. Don't store tapes on top of televisions, amplifiers, speakers or VCR's.

IN TIMES GONE BY

Minding your manners

□ "Refrain from falling upon the dish like a swine while eating, snorting disgustingly and smacking the lips", cautioned one 13th-century book.
□ Another warned: "A number of people gnaw a bone and then put it back in the dish – this is a serious offence." (The proper way to discard a bone, as all refined folk knew, was to throw it on the floor.)
□ Scratching while at the table was pointedly frowned upon even though fleas and lice were everywhere. "Thou must not put either thy fingers into thine ears or thy hands to thy head. The man who is eating must not be cleaning by scraping with his fingers at any foul part", wrote Fra Bonvincino da Rival in *The Fifty Courtesies for the Table* in 1290.
□ Other etiquette writers in the Middle Ages frowned on the common practice of blowing one's nose into a tablecloth or coat sleeve. They also advised their readers not to blow their noses into their fingers while seated at the table.
□ Then, as now, propriety at the dinner table was a concern of the upper classes. But the proprieties put forward by medieval makers of manners differ sharply from today's codes of conduct. Among the worst offences in modern times are talking with a mouth full of food, waving a fork or spoon in the air for emphasis, and eating with elbows on the table.
□ And one more: it's considered rude to look down upon a person whose manners are less than perfect.

All these machines generate magnetic fields that could erase the recordings.
3. In the car keep tapes off a hot dashboard; they'll get brittle.
4. If you bring a videotape in from the cold, let it warm to room temperature before you play it. This gives moisture a chance to evaporate. VCR's are sensitive to moisture, and even a small amount can do damage.
5. If a compact disc gets warped, heat it with a hair dryer; then put it on a flat surface between two pieces of wax paper. Weight it down with a heavy book or two and leave it in place for several hours. Repeat the process if necessary.

Tape splicing

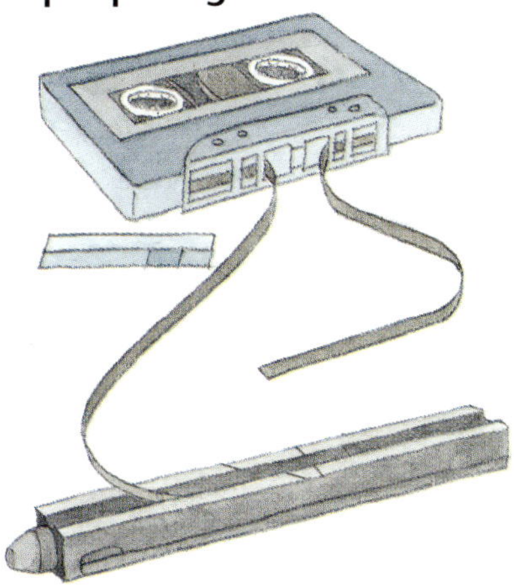

1. The most foolproof way to edit or repair an audiocassette tape is with an inexpensive kit sold by electronics dealers; it includes picks for retrieval, splicing tape and a rewinding device. But if you find that the tape is badly tangled in the cassette, don't force it; seek professional help.
2. Splicing videotapes is not recommended; even professionals won't try it. So use prevention: make a copy of valuable tapes and play only the copy. "Exercise" the master tape twice a year by running it fast forward through the player, then rewinding.

Taxis

In South Africa the minibus taxi industry has taken off in leaps and bounds. Those who used to be tied to the public transport system are now able to reach their destinations a lot more quickly and, in many cases, more cheaply.

Unfortunately, the drivers of some minibus taxis have given the minibus taxi industry here a tarnished image through careless driving and a lack of regard for the rules of the road. Traffic authorities are looking at this problem, and steps are being taken to improve the general standard of driving.

DRIVING A TAXI

If you wish to apply for a permit to start a taxi service, you must contact the National Transportation Commission or your local road transportation board. The board will demand a roadworthy certificate for the vehicle you intend to use as a taxi. It is an offence to operate a taxi service without a permit or to ignore the details of the permit.

USING A TAXI

1. When using a taxi, check the fares charged. The tariffs are laid down by the transportation board, although the owner of the taxi may increase his rates after an increase in the price of petrol, for example. Even then, however, this new increase may not exceed ten per cent of the former price.
2. When you get into a taxi, remember that the law does not require minibus taxis in this country to carry passenger liability insurance. Does the vehicle look roadworthy?
3. When waiting for a taxi, stand at a bus stop, a taxi-rank or at a spot where it is convenient for the taxi to pull off onto the side of the road. Don't hail a taxi at a point where it may block the flow of traffic. A taxi driver can refuse to stop for you if this means he is breaking the law. Stopping in a no-stopping area or overloading his vehicle would qualify as contraventions of the law.

Teachers

1. Among the pet hates of teachers are: talking in class, disrespect for school property, sloppy schoolwork, habitual tardiness and children chewing gum.
2. If your child says, "The teacher hates me", don't merely brush off the comment; discuss the situation sympathetically and get the facts. While it is true that children often exaggerate, the teacher may have had a bad day or may be more demanding than most. It is also true that personality conflicts sometimes exist. If so, your child needs your help and support.
3. Don't just storm into the teacher's classroom. Write a note asking for a meeting, and indicating the topic you want to discuss. During the meeting, focus on identifying and solving your child's problem, not on correcting what you think the teacher and the school are doing wrong. If possible, have your child participate in at least part of the meeting.
4. If things still don't improve, you can go to your child's counsellor and, if necessary, the principal.
5. If you decide to drop the matter, explain to your child that you're not abandoning him but are backing off to see if the situation will work itself out. Be prepared to help him cope – and to get involved again if things don't improve.

Teething

1. Rub a little anaesthetic gel (available from your pharmacy) on the baby's gums.
2. Dip your finger in ice-cold water and massage the baby's gums.
3. Let the baby chew on something cold: a chilled teething ring; an ice cube wrapped securely in a clean cloth; a large, cold carrot. Remember that teething may be quite uncomfortable, but it is rarely very painful. Any signs of fever or severe pain tend to indicate a simultaneous illness. Contact your doctor.

Telephone answerers

A telephone answering machine relays your message to a caller, records the caller's message and, at your prompting, plays back the caller's message. Most models allow you to hear the caller as he leaves his message, so that you can decide whether to answer at once. Some have a remote-control device that allows you, with the aid of an electronic 'page', to dial your number from outside and listen to the recorded incoming messages.

Telephone answering machines are operated through a 15-amp power socket. Most models carry a nine-volt battery that will operate for a limited time if the main power source fails. Although you don't need a licence to install or operate an answering machine, ensure that it is a Telkom-approved model.

The vendor should be able to produce an approval certificate, and the machine should have detailed operating instructions.

When you are recording your message, don't reveal your name, whereabouts or any other personal details. Simply give your number – which the caller knows, anyway – and say that you can't come to the telephone, but will return the call as soon as possible. Never ask callers to leave the date of their calls. Until you're accustomed to it, arrange some simple device to remind you to set the machine when you go out.

Telephone calls

1. Can't hear the telephone ringing when you're upstairs or in the garden? Put the phone in a metal pan or on top of a ceramic tile.

2. If someone rings you by mistake and asks who you are or what number he has dialled, don't tell him – you never know who it is or what he really wants. Instead, ask what number he was trying to reach and tell him he has made a mistake.

3. What to do if you are busy on a call, and you hear that there's another one waiting? If you have the facility, tell the waiting caller you'll call her back unless it's an emergency.

4. If you enjoy long phone chats but worry about wasting time, keep some paperwork near the phone.

5. If you have a toddler who loves to dial the phone but doesn't know the meaning of "expensive long-distance call", hold the receiver buttons down with a rubber band. (See also *Crank calls*, p.59.)

Telephones

1. If your telephone doesn't work, make sure that all the cords are properly connected: at the wall jack, on the telephone, and between the handset and the phone. If the phone is a plug-in type, test it by switching it with a working phone in your house or a neighbour's; if the instrument then works, call your local Telkom repair service (the relevant emergency telephone repair numbers appear in the front of your local telephone directory).

2. During the flu season or anytime someone is ill at home, be sure to wipe the mouthpiece, receiver and the handpiece with some methylated spirits. This should destroy lingering germs and keep the telephone clean.

3. To prevent the chance of an electrical shock, never use the telephone while you are in the bathtub, the shower or the swimming pool.

4. When you are making a long distance call, find out from your nearest Telkom office when the rates are cheaper. Telephone calls which are made at night are generally cheaper than those calls made during peak daytime hours.

5. If you find it difficult to read the numbers on your push-button phone, write larger numbers on masking tape and stick them on the buttons.

Telephone sales calls

1. There are many organizations, including time-share sales groups and charities, which try to sell their goods by telephone. You may be asked to buy an item in aid of a certain charity, or you may be invited to discuss the possibility of buying into a time-share scheme. If you agree, the more responsible telesales agents will call you again to double-check the arrangements or to confirm the order.

2. Once you have agreed verbally to buy the product, you will have entered into a contract with the company. If the product reaches you and it is not satisfactory or it is not what was originally described by the agent, you must return it to get a refund. Keep your cheque or postal order counterfoil as proof of payment. By agreeing to attend a meeting to dis-

DID YOU KNOW...?

Telephone tunes

☐ For a clever birthday greeting, call on a push-button phone and play *Happy Birthday* by pushing the following buttons in the appropriate rhythm:
1-1-2-1-#-6; 1-1-2-1-#-3;
1-1-#-#-8-4-1; #-#-6-4-2-1

☐ Here are a few other telephone tunes you can play – but always dial someone's number first, or you may find yourself paying for a call to Brazil or Singapore:

Oh! Susanna: 4-8-6-9-9-#-8-7-4;
4-8-#-#-8-1-8; 4-8-6-9-9-#-8-7-4;
4-8-6-6-0-0-4

Old MacDonald Had a Farm:
6-6-6-7-8-8-7; 9-9-0-0-4;
4-6-6-6-7-8-8-7; 9-9-0-0-4

Old Folks at Home (Swanee River): 3-2-1-3-2-1-#-4-5;
6-1-4-2; 3-2-1-3-2-1-#-1-4;
6-5-4-2-2-4

cuss the benefits of buying into a time-share scheme, however, you have not committed yourself to actually spending any money.

3. If you are tired of having your dinner interrupted, or you simply don't want to listen to the telesales caller, be quite firm but polite. Say, "No, thank you, I'm not interested" and put down the receiver.

4. If you have any complaints about telesales callers, contact the Southern African Direct Marketing Association. The Share Blocks Control Act and the Property Time-sharing Control Act contain strict regulations covering time-share interests and the responsibilities of both the seller and the purchaser. If you feel that you have been swindled, contact your lawyer.

Telephone services

When applying to have a telephone installed, ask what services are available to suit your particular requirements. Your existing installation, too, can be modified to suit changed circumstances. Modifications to the basic installation may cost extra at the time they are ordered, and also increase the monthly rental.

Apart from the various types of telephone system, you can order an extension telephone, additional jacks without an extension telephone to enable you to move the telephone from room to room, a telephone with an extra bell (or even with a siren or klaxon), a light to indicate the phone's ringing, an amplifier for the hearing-impaired and an extension cord up to six metres long. Telkom offers a reminder service, to help avoid being disconnected for omitting to pay your account. If you're going away you can have your telephone service temporarily suspended, although you'll still be liable for rent during this period.

To save on travel costs, you can contact Telkom's teleconference service, which can connect up to six participants from around the country or overseas. Person-to-person and fixed-time calls may also be arranged. Remember that, as a general rule, only those numbers starting with 0800 are toll free.

Television addiction

Here are some tips on kicking the couch potato habit:

1. Don't change channels aimlessly. Select specific programmes to watch, and just as soon as they're over, turn off your television set.

2. Unplug the set. Store it in a cupboard or back room and bring it out only when there's something special to watch.

3. To help judge the quality of your viewing time, write yourself a brief report on each show as soon as it's over. Say what it was about, what you learned from it, and what satisfaction it gave you. Be honest. Then read the reports weekly and write down what else you could have been doing with your time.

4. Instead of watching your favourite team's game on television, attend it in person. You will certainly rediscover the thrill of crowd participation and be reminded that TV makes much of life seem secondhand.

5. Don't use TV as a babysitter. Help your kids select the programmes they can watch each day and don't be swayed if they beg for more.

6. Have other entertainment handy when children plead boredom. Play cards or board games with them until they get used to the idea of generating their own fun.

Televisions

1. The only maintenance you should ever do on your television set without consulting a specialist repair service is to clean the tuner and the face of the picture tube. If your picture is grainy, jiggle the tuner button. If the picture clears, remove the channel selector button, spray tuner cleaner (from your electronics dealer) into the opening. The picture should take about half an hour to settle. Do not open the back of the set and be careful not to block the ventilation slots or place the set near a computer or a heat source.

2. Do you see snow on your TV when you play a VCR tape? Tack or glue a sheet of aluminium foil to the shelf between your VCR and your TV to reduce interference.

3. For clearer viewing, spray the TV screen at least once a week with window or spectacle cleaner; dry with a soft tissue or paper towel.

Temper tantrums

Normal and inevitable, your child's occasional temper tantrum has more to do with frustration than with temper in the usual sense.

1. Keep calm; getting angry will only make things worse.

2. Sometimes it's best to ignore the tantrum. Tell your child that you can see she's angry and that you'll talk about the problem once she calms down. Then pick up a magazine or do a chore, but stay within sight in case she needs comforting. And as soon as the child's tantrum subsides, make sure you keep your word.

PREVENTION

1. Children's frustrations are often rooted in their own helplessness. You can give your child more control over her life by letting her make certain decisions: which cereal to eat, which jersey to wear, which stuffed toy to sleep with, and so on.

2. Sometimes, however, you'll find that decision-making itself leads to tantrums; if this is your child's problem, simplify her life by making matter-of-fact statements. Say, for example, "When we have our coats on, we'll go to the shop", rather than "Would you like to wear your blue coat or your red jacket?"

3. Try to anticipate some of the situations that provoke temper tantrums. If they happen when she's hungry, give her an extra-nutritious snack or serve her meals earlier; if they tend to occur when she's tired, encourage her to take a longer nap or help her to find a quiet activity such as looking at books or colouring in.

Temporary employment

1. Most of the big centres have employment agencies that specialize in temporary placements, from clerical work to manual labour. Consult the Employment – Temporary (Commercial), and Employment – Temporary (Industrial) listings in your local Yellow Pages.

2. Think seasonally. Hotels and restaurants hire extra employees during peak tourist periods. Farms need help at harvest time; department stores need people at peak holiday periods.

3. Look for businesses with high employee turnover – restaurants, telesales services, taxi companies. (See also *Moonlighting*, p.137.)

Tennis jargon

Here's a guide to what the television announcers are saying:

Ace. A legitimate serve that cannot be returned.

Advantage. The first point scored after deuce.

Approach shot. A hard-hit ball deep into the opponent's court, giving the hitter a chance to rush the net.

Backspin. The effect on the tennis ball when a hitter's stroke makes it rotate in the opposite direction of its flight, causing it to bounce backward or to stop suddenly.

Base line. The line marking the end of the court, behind which a player must stand to serve.

Base line strategy. A plan in which the player avoids the forecourt, and stays close to the baseline.

Chop. A sharp spin which is given the ball by slicing down and under it with the racquet.

Cross court shot. A ball that is hit diagonally across the net from one side of the court to the other.

Deuce. A tied score of 40-all; since a game must be won by two points, a player must win two consecutive points to prevail.

Double fault. A point lost by a server for hitting two consecutive faults.

Drop shot. A shot that drops abruptly over the net.

Fault. A service that fails to clear the net or that lands outside the proper service court.

Foot fault. A fault called when the server's foot touches or goes beyond the baseline while serving.

Forecourt. The section of the court nearest the net.

Half-volley. The playing of a ball as soon as it bounces off the ground.

Let serve. Net point on service; not a fault if it hits the proper service court – the ball is served again.

Lob. A ball that is hit high above the opponent's head.

Love. Zero.

Match point. The point that, if won, will give a player the match.

Net point. A ball that hits the net and goes over; it remains in play except on the serve.

Passing shot. A ball hit along the side line deep into the corner of the opponent's court.

Rush the net. To move quickly forward, in the hope of volleying.

Seeding. The ranking of competitors by actual or potential ability.

Service court. The two subdivisions of each forecourt; a server must place the ball within the opponent's cross-court service court.

Set. A unit of a match; to win a set, a player must win at least six games with a margin of at least two games.

Smash. A ball hit hard with an overhand motion.

Volley. To return the tennis ball before it bounces.

Tennis racquets

1. Have your racquet strung to the tension that suits you best. The lower end of the tension range gives more power; the higher gives more control. If you're not satisfied with your racquet tension, take it to your sports shop for adjustment.

2. Check the tiny plastic grommets in the head of the racquet. A cracked or broken one will cut into the string that goes through it, causing it to snap. Have faulty grommets replaced.

3. At the end of every game, examine your racquet strings and adjust them with your fingers if they are out of line. Strings that are not properly aligned are more likely to break.

4. Look for an old wooden racquet at a sale to start a beginner playing tennis; it will give better ball control than a metal one.

Tent pegs

1. Carry pegs in a separate bag to avoid damaging the tent.

2. Try using 15-centimetre aluminium spikes for lightweight, inexpensive pegs.

3. To anchor lines in sand, tie them around sticks, rocks or sacks of sand. Then bury them.

4. To reduce wind stress, tie an elastic cord between the tent pegs and the guy lines.

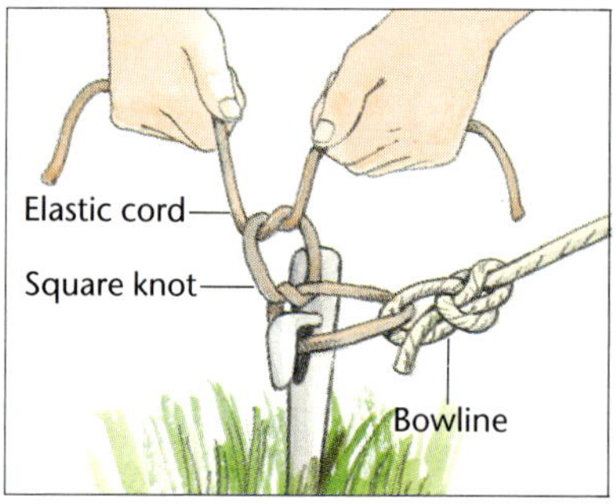

Tents

You can improvise a fair-weather tent with a 3 x 3-metre waterproof tarpaulin, a three-metre rope and a couple of poles, two ponchos and shoelaces. Keep in mind that this tent is a fragile one, unable to withstand high winds or heavy rain.

1. Drive a pole into the ground so that it stands erect.

2. Centre the tarpaulin over the pole and lash a shoelace around the top.

3. Weight one edge of the tarpaulin down with rocks.

4. Place the other pole under the opposite edge of the tarpaulin to form a door; lash with the other shoelace.

5. Guy the top of the front pole to the ground with the three-metre rope. (If you don't have a peg to secure the guy rope, you can tie the end to a stick and then bury it.)

6. Secure the sides of the tarpaulin with more rocks.
7. Drape both ponchos over the door, hanging them by their hoods from the pole.

Test taking

1. Before an exam or test, get a good night's sleep, eat a high-protein meal, and bring some sweets to suck when your energy flags.
2. Read all instructions twice before you begin, just to be on the safe side. When reading the questions, underline such key words as *not* and *except.*
3. Budget your time. Divide the total number of questions by the allotted number of minutes to determine how long to spend on each question. If you find you're taking too long on one, leave it and go on.
4. If you can make an "educated guess" between two or three choices on a multiple-choice question, do so: the odds tend to favour you – even if the exam has a built-in penalty for incorrect answers. But if you haven't a clue, don't guess wildly between five or six choices.
5. On true-or-false tests, questions that contain an *always* or a *never* are likely to be false; those that say *usually, sometimes,* or *often,* are likely to be true.
6. Begin with the easiest essay question and work up to the most difficult. (Sometimes a bit of incubation time helps.) If you don't have time to complete an essay, try writing an articulate outline, and add the explanation: "Ran out of time".

Theatre tickets

1. Most theatre tickets have to be bought from a central booking office, although the box office at the theatre may offer some of the seats. You may phone the central booking office to find out whether seats are available for a specific show, but bookings are not taken telephonically. The booking agent will check which tickets are available and will show these to you on her seating plan of the theatre.
2. Once you've purchased tickets, you can't get a refund unless the show is cancelled unexpectedly. Try selling your tickets to friends or advertise them on your office notice board.

Thermal underwear

1. In terms of efficient body insulation, thermal underwear comes tops, and is also lighter than exterior wear.
2. Remember that while cotton next to the skin can be super-warm if it's dry, it gets cold when wet from rain or sweat. Wool stays warm, as do some of the lightweight modern fabrics with "wicking" qualities to absorb pervasive moisture.
3. A hat – preferably woollen – can save your life in the outdoors. A significant fraction of body heat can be lost through the head.

Thermostats

1. To save on electricity bills, install an automatic thermostat control on your hot-water cylinder. By programming the control to switch off the heat while everyone is out during the day, or at night, you can save anything between seven and 12 percent on your heating bills.
2. To test the thermostat on your oven, place an oven thermometer in the centre of the oven and set it at 180°C. Check the reading when the oven light goes off. If the reading does not tally with the temperature at which you set the oven, pull off the temperature control knob and adjust it one notch left or right (usually clockwise to lower the setting and anti-clockwise to raise it). If you need to turn it more than two notches, have the thermostat replaced.

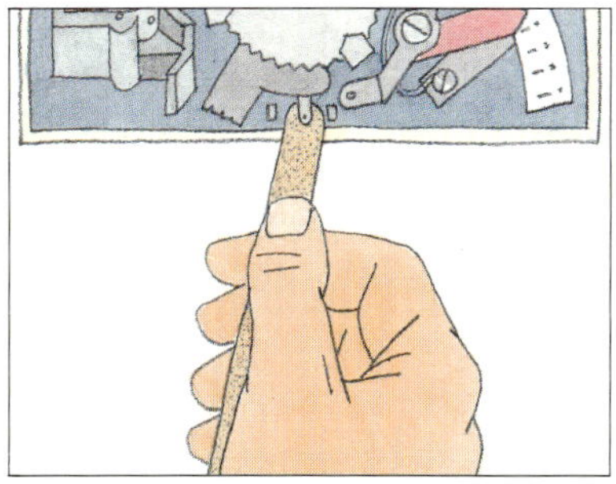

Thunderstorms

1. Is your preschool child afraid of thunder? Buy him a drum and tell him to bang it every time a thunderclap sounds or just have him yell "Boom!" back at the thunder. It will give him a sense of power.
2. Condition him by occasionally playing "thunderstorm". Turn on a recording of thunder, dim the lights in the house, and let him imitate lightning with a torch.
3. If your child is old enough, explain the connection between lightning and thunder; tell him how to work out how far away the storm is (see *Lightning lore,* p.127) and make a game of tracking it.
4. If your dog is afraid of thunder, the following routine may calm its fears. First, have the dog sit or lie down and give it a treat. Then turn on a recording of thunder very softly and give another treat. Increase the volume gradually, rewarding the dog with a treat or praise with each raise. Finally,

decrease the volume slowly until there's no sound. Repeat the artificial storms often.
5. When a real thunderstorm occurs, have the dog sit or lie down and reward it with treats for non-fearful behaviour, just as you did in the practice sessions. If the animal shows signs of anxiety, don't discipline it.

Tiles

CERAMIC TILES

1. Before you start cleaning bathroom tiles, run the shower on *Hot* for five minutes to steam the dirt loose.
2. For stubborn stains, apply a paste of scouring powder and water and leave for five minutes. Scrub with a nylon scouring pad, rinse thoroughly, and wipe dry.
3. To keep all the grout joints on countertops clean longer, wash with a solution of one to two tablespoons chlorine bleach in two litres of water. Dry thoroughly, then apply an acrylic sealer or several coats of wax polish, allowing time between each coat.
4. Remove mildew and make tiles sparkle by sponging with a solution of ammonia and water.
5. Remove soot from fireplace tiles with a mixture of lemon juice and salt, then wash.

CORK TILES

1. Cork floor tiles have good insulation properties, but the tiles should be coated with at least one, preferably two, coats of urethane varnish to make them durable.
2. Do not swamp cork tiles when you wash them with a mild detergent in warm water. Make sure that you do not use an abrasive.

ACOUSTICAL TILES

1. Clean with the dust-brush attachment of your vacuum cleaner.
2. Remove stains with mild soap and water; don't let the tiles get too wet.

ASPHALT VINYL TILES

1. If smudges don't come off floor tiles easily, rub with superfine steel wool and soap.
2. For easier cutting, heat tiles for one-and-a-half minutes under an infrared lamp. Heat rubber tiles for about one minute.

Timers

If you haven't got a timer and your watch is broken, don't give up; as long as you have a television, radio, record or tape player or telephone, you have plenty of substitutes around the house.
1. TV programmes are usually half an hour, one hour or two hours long. Prime-time shows generally run 12½ minutes between commercials.
2. Most commercials on TV and radio are 30 seconds long, with an occasional 15- or 60-second one. Many programme breaks are four commercials, or two minutes, long.
3. Music videos and popular songs usually last three to four minutes; an album or tape side, about 20 minutes.
4. A telephone ring and pause is about three seconds.

Toasters

1. If you can't reach that broken roll or slice of toast in the toaster, use dry wooden chopsticks.
2. If your toaster's broken, use the griller in your stove or hold the bread with tongs over a surface burner or heating element.
3. Or wrap buttered bread in foil and iron both sides; it doesn't brown, but it's warm and crunchy.

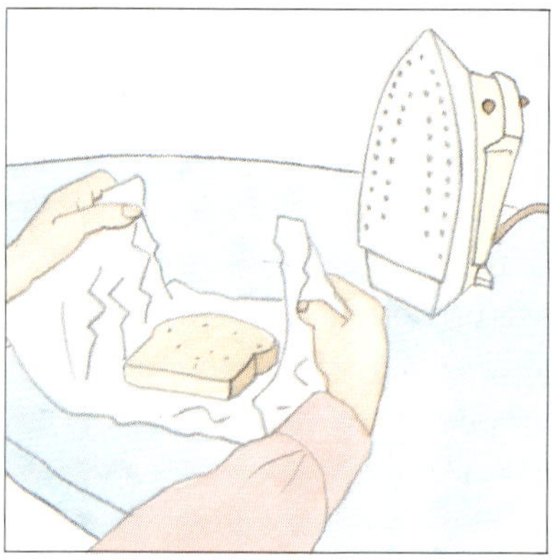

Caution: Do not stick anything into a toaster if the power is on.

Toilet leaks

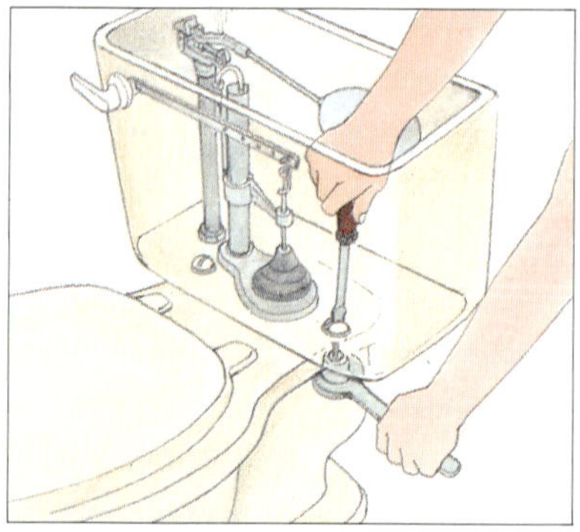

1. Condensation may be the cause of moisture around the bolts from the tank to the bowl. Or perhaps the bolts are loose. The most common source of leaking is a perished rubber elbow, connecting the L-shaped pipe from the cistern to the pan. This is white or black, and to seal properly must stretch over both the pipe and the pan inlet. To replace it, first drain the cistern by flushing with the stopcock closed, then unbolt the L-pipe. Then reassemble in reverse sequence.
Caution: Overtightening may crack the toilet cistern.
2. Moisture at the base of a toilet may mean that the bowl is cracked or that one of the seals between the toilet and the drain is faulty or worn. While waiting for the plumber, you can minimize the leakage – drain the tank and bowl as directed above.
3. An older toilet with a wall-hung tank may leak around the slip nuts at either end of the pipe joining the tank to the bowl. Drain the tank and unscrew each nut. Wrap the exposed threads with plumber's tape, and then retighten the nut.

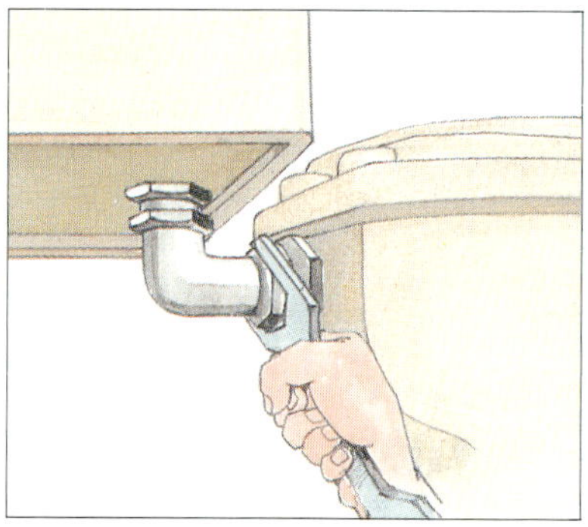

Toilet problems

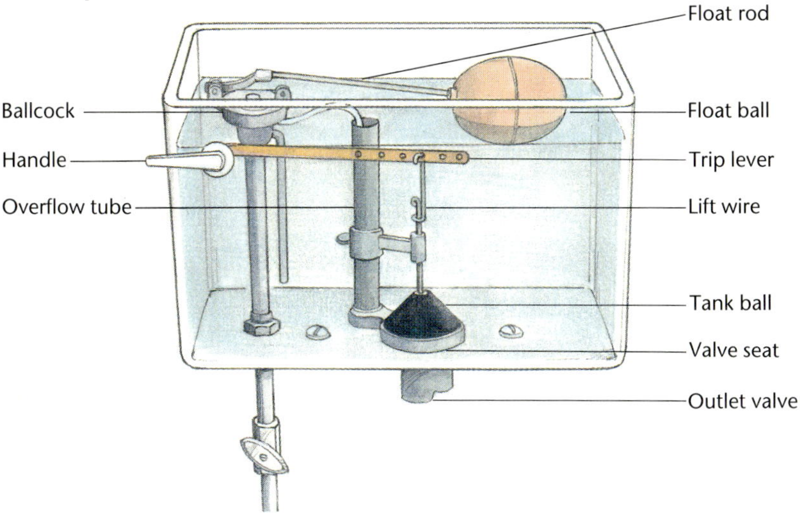

If the toilet fails to flush, remove the tank lid and study the linkage from flush handle to flush valve.

1. If the handle is too loose, use a wrench to tighten it on its shaft and at the setscrew holding it to the trip lever. (You can temporarily replace a broken handle with a pair of locking-grip pliers or a C-clamp.)

2. Reconnect or replace the lift chain or wire if necessary. Fishing line is a temporary expedient.

3. Make sure that the tank ball or flapper is securely screwed or hooked to the lift chain or wires.

INCOMPLETE FLUSHING

The water in a toilet cistern should be 20 millimetres lower than the top of the overflow tube.

1. If it's too low, raise the level by bending upward the rod that connects the ball to the ballcock. Do this carefully, to avoid placing stress on the ballcock. Various mechanisms are all triggered by the rising water, stopping further inflow.

2. If the water level is correct, check as you flush to see if the lift wires pull the ball clear of the outlet valve; if not, reposition the wires. If the ball is porous and soggy, replace it.

CONSTANTLY RUNNING WATER

1. If the tank doesn't fill, gently scour the valve seat (the outlet to the bowl) with fine steel wool, and wash the ball. Replace a sodden ball or flapper. Make sure that the lift wires are properly aligned.

2. If the tank is full and water still runs down the overflow tube, lower the water level by bending the float rod or adjusting the float cup downward. Unscrew the float ball and shake it; if it leaks, replace it. (First, drain the tank by turning off the water and flushing the toilet.) If, after filling the tank, water still runs, the ballcock leaks. Replace its diaphragm or washer or the ballcock; follow manufacturer's instructions.

Toilet training

Never use force to toilet train your child, and don't scold him if he refuses to use a potty or wets himself. Both strategies could retard bladder control and eventually cause emotional problems.

Usually children are able to indicate their intentions at 12 months of age; at about two years they have adequate muscle control to get to the toilet on time; and at three, they can stay dry all night if taken to the toilet before bedtime. Girls are generally dry sooner than boys.

When a child has an upset tummy, is teething or the weather turns cold, temporary "accidents" might occur. On the other hand, refusal to use the toilet is often caused by constipation.

When your child is a year old let him sit on a potty. Play this "game" at the same time every day, preferably after a meal and certainly only when you and he can relax. If he refuses, try again after a week or two.

If he is successful, praise him, discuss his "work of art" and let him empty it into the toilet. You could also let him use the toilet.

Tomatoes

1. Make the most of bland supermarket tomatoes by buying them a few days ahead of time and ripening them, stem side up, at room temperature. Make sure you never store them in the refrigerator.

2. To speed ripening, place tomatoes in a paper bag with a banana. Punch a few holes in the bag first.

3. You can use your own vine-ripened tomatoes for cooking right through the winter months. Just quarter the newly harvested, washed fruits and freeze them on baking trays. Then store in freezer bags. When you defrost them, their skins will easily peel right off.

4. To make peeling ripe tomatoes easier, plunge them into simmering water for 20 seconds and remove with a slotted spoon. Plunge into cold water and pull the skin away with your fingers. To microwave, bring one cup of hot water to the boil on *High*, then add a tomato for 30 seconds; peel as above. (See also *Vegetable varieties*, p.221.)

5. To firm up soft tomatoes, plunge them into a container of ice-cold water for a few minutes.

Tomato paste

1. You can substitute a tablespoon of tomato sauce for a tablespoon of tomato paste. Or use a quarter cup tomato sauce, reducing the liquid in the recipe by three tablespoons.

2. If you do have leftover paste, it can be saved and refrigerated in a camper's reusable squeeze tube. Or spoon it into an ice-cube tray, freeze it, and store the cubes in a freezer bag.

Tomato plants

1. You can prevent common problems by buying varieties with the letters V, F, N or T on the label. V means resistance to (but not immunity from) verticillium wilt; F, to fusarium wilt; N, to nematodes (rootknot eelworms); and T, to tobacco mosaic virus.
2. If you smoke, dip your hands in milk before handling tomato plants. It retards the growth of tobacco mosaic virus, which may have been left on your hands.
3. For plants that keep producing throughout the growing season, choose an indeterminate variety. For a heavier crop in the space of a few weeks, choose a determinate variety.
4. When you buy at the nursery, be sure to look for seedlings with thick stems and large root systems (the clues are a deep container and dark green leaves). Avoid plants that are already in bloom; they've been in pots too long and are stunted.
5. To help your transplants get off to a quick start, you should trench-plant them. Remove the young plant from its container and pinch off all but the top clump of leaves. Then lay it on its side in a shallow trench and cover the roots and stem with soil, leaving the tuft of leaves exposed. The sun will warm the shallow soil to encourage faster growth, and the heat-loving tomatoes will respond by sprouting roots along the stem.

6. Encourage bigger yields by injecting fertilizer into the root zone. Use five-centimetre plastic pipe to stake your tomatoes – a two-metre length if you intend to train the tomatoes to a single stake; 150-centimetre lengths to anchor a tomato cage. Fill the pipes with water to irrigate; add a soluble fertilizer when the first fruits form, and repeat at three-week intervals. (See also *Vegetable varieties*, p.221.)

Tool grips

1. To make hand grips for a shovel or spade, slit two pieces of radiator hose lengthways, slip them over the wooden handle, and hold them in place with PVC tape. Ask your local garage or service station – they might give you a piece of used hose.
2. For a rake or hoe, just slide a couple of 100-millimetre sections of the hose over the wooden handle. They should fit snugly; if they don't, secure them with insulation tape. Position the hose sections to match your natural hand grips. You'll find raking and hoeing more comfortable, particularly if you also wear work gloves.

Tool storage

1. Keep tools organized: frame a sheet of perforated hardboard with planks, and screw it to the garage or workshop wall. Then position your tools and put hooks or pegs of the appropriate sizes in place. Paint a white outline of each tool on the hardboard so that everyone can put it back where it belongs.
2. Lay an aluminium grilling pan in a drawer to store files and chisels – its corrugated bottom makes a cradle for each tool. Or glue lengths of half-round moulding on the bottom of a drawer to make divisions.
3. To separate small items, groove the sides of an open-ended wooden box and slide in muffin tins to serve as storage drawers for nails, screws, washers, bolts, hangers or any other small items.
4. To prevent the engine of your power mower from rusting during off-season storage, rid the tank and fuel lines of petrol by running the engine until it stops.

Brush off any debris, then coat bare metal parts with motor oil. Remove the spark plug and pour in a spoonful of motor oil. Hand-crank the engine to get oil into the cylinder. Cover, but do not seal the engine.

Toothache

1. Saturate a small piece of sterile cottonwool with oil of cloves or make a paste of powdered cloves and water; pack the cottonwool or paste in the sore tooth's cavity or place it on the surface. Be warned: the cloves may do more than just numb your toothache: they may also sting your lips and tongue.
2. If your tooth has only just begun to ache, you should try drinking warm liquids.
3. Try to gargle hourly with lukewarm salt water, and take aspirin or an aspirin substitute (paracetamol) every four hours.
4. Try trigger-point pressure: with your index finger, press gently all over your face, neck and head; when you find an especially sensitive area, press hard for 10 seconds and release.
5. Massage the web of skin between your thumb and index finger with an ice cube. Rubbing that part of the right hand will affect the right side of your mouth; the left hand, the left side. (This may sound strange, but it really does work.)

Toothbrush

No toothbrush? Use a clean cotton-wool ball, a bit of towel or your finger; rub in the toothpaste or bicarbonate of soda with your tongue.

Tooth knocked out

1. Telephone your dentist or go to the local hospital.
2. Try to stop the flow of blood from the wound. Make a small pad from sterile gauze and get the casualty to bite down on it.
3. Try to reinsert the tooth. If you cannot do this, it is absolutely vital to keep the tooth moist – keep it in your mouth or wrap it securely in a saliva-soaked cloth.
4. The dentist must implant the tooth within hours of the accident, so get to him as soon as you can.

Tooth stains

1. Lighten stains by rubbing with bicarbonate of soda; rinse thoroughly.
2. If your teeth tend to stain easily, avoid tea, coffee, cola drinks, red wine, grape juice, liquorice, curried foods and cigarettes.

Towel racks

1. If the bar of your towel rack is broken or missing, use an adjustable curtain rod as a substitute.

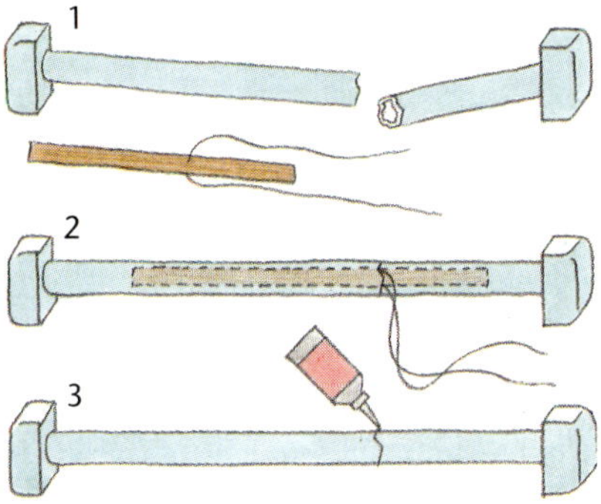

2. If the bar is hollow, try this: find a piece of wooden dowel wide enough to almost fill the hollow of the broken bar. Cut it slightly shorter than the longer piece of broken bar. Drill a hole in the middle and hang a length of thread through it (1). Put the long piece of the bar in its holder and slip the dowel inside. Then put the other piece of the bar in place and pull on the thread, sliding the dowel over to bridge the break (2). Pull the thread out and apply glue to the broken bar ends (3). Let dry for 24 hours.

Toys

Tired of buying expensive toys?
1. Most school-aged children love playing with magnifying glasses, torches, magnets, bells, wooden beads and other such items. Preschoolers enjoy empty cardboard boxes or tents made by throwing a sheet or bedspread over a table.
2. Make a "tunnel" by lining up two rows of straight-backed dining room chairs and covering them with sheets or blankets. Or sew a piece of canvas all the way around the edge of a beach umbrella to convert it into a special hideaway for your youngsters and their friends.

3. Don't throw away a once-used fancy dress costume – make a lifesize doll to wear the outfit. To make the pattern for the doll, have your child lie on a large piece of paper while you carefully draw her outline on it. Cut out the pattern on a double layer of fabric. Sew the fabric together, and stuff; draw a colourful face or appliqué features onto the doll and then dress it in the costume.
4. If plastic toys become misshapen, soak them in hot water for several minutes, then work them back to their original form.
5. Vacuum stuffed toys; use the upholstery-brush attachment. If they're really dirty and can't be machine-washed, put them in a large paper bag with plenty of cornflour; shake vigorously, remove the toys, and gently brush off the cornflour.
6. To extend the life of cardboard games, coat them with shellac.
7. To prevent rust and keep colours bright, coat metal toys or painted toys with clear varnish or shellac.

Transplant shock

Transplanting damages the fine root hairs that take up a plant's water and nutrients. Give them time to recover by moving trees and shrubs when the plants don't need much water – before the leaves appear in spring or after they drop in autumn.

If the soil is dry, water the yet-to-be-transplanted tree or shrub thoroughly several days ahead of time; the moisture will help keep the earth intact around the roots.

After replanting, spray evergreen foliage with an anti-transparent (available at most nurseries). This gluey liquid plugs the leaf pores temporarily, retarding dehydration.

To help flower and vegetable seedlings survive transplanting, slip the plants from their containers upside down, keeping the soil intact around the roots, and dip the stems and leaves in a bucket of anti-transparent before planting.

Spray newly laid sod with anti-transparent, too, to keep the grass from browning before it can send roots down into the soil.

Travel emergencies

Most travel emergencies brought on by mechanical failure are avoidable, so have your car well serviced and examined before you set out. If there is a breakdown, get your car well off the road. Once you've stopped, switch on the hazard flashers to warn approaching traffic. If you're mechanically minded and it's safe to get out of the car, try to remedy the problem. When you can't get off the road, switch on the flashers and, if you have one, place a warning red triangle by the roadside about 75 metres behind your car. If there's a serious risk of collision, place yourself in a safe position to signal oncoming traffic to slow down. Depending on your personal safety, it might be best simply to collect your more portable valuables and hitch a lift to the nearest town. Try to stay together with your passengers. If you don't like the look of the people who stop, merely ask them to advise the garage, the police or the Automobile Association, and wait for a safer-looking lift.

When illness on the road obliges you to take medicines, make sure that, if you're the driver, they won't cause drowsiness or any other dangerous condition. If there's no hospital in a strange town, go to the most respectable-looking hotel and ask for the name and telephone number of the local doctor whom they call when their out-of-town guests need medical attention.

When a public conveyor misplaces your luggage, fill in a claim form at once, even if staff assure you your goods are not lost. Ask about provision of overnight necessities. Be sure that you have adequate medical and accident insurance when abroad. Buying your ticket with your credit card may cover you automatically, but ask for a written statement to this effect, and keep it with you.

Travel for the elderly

Among the various discounts that are a benefit of growing old are the special travel allowances offered by many public conveyors. Some of these discounts are very substantial, and apply not only to travel by train, bus or aircraft, but also, in some instances, to hotel tariffs. Discounts are usually granted to pensioners and people over the age of 60 years.

Before you make any reservations for your next trip, find out where you can get the biggest benefits, but do remember to ask about restrictions that might, for instance, limit you to travel only at certain times or between certain centres.

Among organizations that can help you take advantage of special offers is the Association of Retired Persons and Pensioners. Many other groups, such as senior centres and church groups, also arrange travel discounts.

When travelling, take extra sets of spectacles and dentures, as well as copies of important prescriptions. Keep these, and your medicines and documents, in your hand luggage.

To avoid overtaxing yourself, arrange meals, naps and bedtimes as close as possible to your normal routine and, if you're in doubt about your ability to undertake a particular trip, have a complete physical check-up before arranging your travels.

Travelling abroad

1. Research before making reservations. Get information about foreign destinations from the public library or a travel agent. Don't only read about the scenic spots; find out about immunizations, currency, public holidays, opening and closing times and the practicalities of commuting.
2. Buy a good guidebook and a foreign dictionary or phrase book (see *Foreign phrases*, p.91).
3. Arrange for a passport (p.151) and round-trip transportation. Check with a country's consulate, its embassy or your travel agent about applying for a visa. If you plan to drive, get an international driver's licence from your Automobile Association.
4. Make a hotel reservation (p.172) for your first night and confirm it before departure; take any confirmation letters with you.
5. If you're going to Europe, you should consider buying a Eurail pass; it gives you discount railroad transportation across most of Europe. You can buy one only in this country, so get yours before you depart.
6. Pack lightly; make a list of everything in your suitcase and carry it with your passport. Such a list is handy when making a claim for lost luggage.
7. If you're taking any electrical appliances, carry a current converter and a plug adaptor.
8. If you take prescribed medication regularly, take enough with you to last the whole holiday. Take a copy of your prescription as well.
9. Try to fit unobtrusively into any country's culture. Smile and show appreciation or enthusiasm; don't make negative comparisons.
10. Find out what is taboo for picture-taking; always ask permission before photographing anyone.
11. Make sure you keep receipts for your purchases to show customs, and to reclaim any value-added tax when you leave the country.
12. If you plan to stay in any country longer than a month, check that your insurance will cover you for your length of stay.
13. Carry the address and telephone number of the local South African diplomatic office; if you have any trouble, contact officials there.
14. Remember, however, that while in another country you are subject to its laws. Learn the local laws and be sure to obey them.
15. Reconfirm your return transportation at least 72 hours before departure. (See also *Exchanging currency*, p.74; *Illness away from home*, p.114.)

Travelling alone

1. Before leaving on a trip, read about your destination and map out a tentative itinerary; without plans you might have too much time on your hands and get lonely.
2. Always carry full identification; don't forget to include the name and telephone number of a close friend or family member and the address of your hotel.
3. To discourage unwanted advances, wear a decorative ring on the third finger of your left hand so that you can slip it around to resemble a wedding band.

4. Before you consider tipping the porter, be quite sure your hotel room is suitable – that it is in a safe location (preferably near the lift), and that it has strong, functional locks on the door and windows.
5. Always double-bolt your door locks. If there is a peephole, use it before opening the door. Never sleep with balcony doors open. The *Do Not Disturb* sign may discourage prowlers, but it will also keep the maid from entering your room.
6. When you arrive at your destination, take a city tour to acclimatize yourself and get the opportunity to meet friendly people who may be looking for companionship.
7. If you are looking for company, ask about local 'meet the people' programmes; contact local chapters of any professional, fraternal or social organizations that you belong to; or else, try to seek bed-and-breakfast lodgings, where you'll be likely to meet congenial people.

DINING ALONE

1. Make sure the hotel you stay in has a dining room. If you get cold feet about going out alone at night, at least you won't have to eat in your room. On the other hand, it's always a good idea to bring along an immersible water heater and tea bags or instant coffee so that you can economize with an occasional take-away meal in your room. You might even carry a few packets of freeze-dried meals, available in camping supply stores.
2. If you want to eat at a popular restaurant but fear rejection, make a reservation for before or after peak time. If you're still given a tiny table near the kitchen, firmly ask for a better location or use your hideaway as a vantage point for observing the local scene.

CHILDREN ALONE

Children aged from two years to about 13 years who are travelling alone by air, must pay the applicable children's fare plus the full adult fare for an accompanying hostess. Unaccompanied children under the age of two years must pay the full adult fare. Check with your travel agent.

Airlines must always be advised ahead of time when a child will be travelling alone. The child should board the plane early and be escorted from it by airline personnel; someone must be present to meet her on arrival. Whatever the mode of travel, don't leave the terminal until you've seen the bus, train or plane depart with the child aboard.

Travelling and pets

Travelling is stressful for pets, but sometimes it can't be avoided. Here are some tips:

SHIPPING PETS

1. Many animals escape from carrying cases – even "locked" ones. Fasten the doors with twist ties for extra insurance, then wrap bungee cords around the case from front to back and side to side. Don't ship your pet in a wicker or cardboard case; neither is sturdy enough.
2. In cold weather put a blanket in the case – one with your scent on it. For long trips the polyester fur fabric sold in some pet stores is an especially good insulator.
3. If the top can be removed from the case, let your pet use it as a bed for a few days before travelling. The animal won't feel as threatened.

LEAVING THE PET BEHIND

1. If you're leaving an animal with friends or in a kennel, supply its regular bedding, toys and dishes. Your pet will feel more secure.

2. In case of an emergency, give the person looking after your animal the name of your vet.
3. Cats usually do best in their own homes with someone coming in to feed them. Be sure to keep the cat locked up while you're packing. They often panic and run away.
4. If a cat is destructive and you must leave it with friends, save wear and tear on both. Buy a cage, large enough for the cat and its dishes, bed and litter box.
5. Large cages also work well for dogs that bark or destroy furniture. A nervous dog perceives most sounds and smells as threatening; the cage makes it feel more secure.
6. If you plan to leave a pet in a kennel, make sure well ahead of time that it has all its vaccinations or it may not be accepted.

TRAVELLING WITH YOUR PET

1. Wicker pet carriers are draughty. In cold weather line the bottom and sides with newspaper.
2. If your pet is unaccustomed to being in the car, take it on short drives before you leave.
3. If your pet is a particularly anxious traveller, ask your vet to prescribe a special tranquillizer.
4. Check before taking your pet on any kind of public transportation – some carriers will allow an animal in a case; some won't. In hot weather put a cool, damp cloth on top of the case. (See also *Parked cars*, p.150.)

Travelling with children

1. Always carry a kit with snacks, drinking straws, a night light, paper towels, towelettes, first aid supplies and a baby's bottle, if applicable.
2. Give each older child a backpack and let him carry whatever he needs to amuse himself: books, paper and crayons, games and so forth.
3. Avoid highly salted foods – they make children drink more, necessitating more pit stops.
4. Ask restaurants to bring young children's dinners out as soon as they're ready. The children will stay

occupied, and you'll probably have their food cut up by the time your meal arrives.

5. Instead of expensive souvenirs, encourage children to collect shells or stones. Arrange them in a nice display when you get home.

6. Childproof your hotel or motel room as soon as you arrive: tape bathroom locks open, remove any breakables or hazards, and lock dangerous windows. Don't leave children alone in a hotel room.

If you need a babysitter, ask at your hotel or the consulate. Ensure that she speaks English.

BY AEROPLANE

1. If you are flying with an infant, call the airline ahead of time: it may provide a bassinet and assign you a bulkhead seat with room to put it at your feet. Ask to board early.

2. Always try to book night flights; children are more likely to sleep.

3. Try giving your infant a bottle or dummy just before the plane takes off and lands: the sucking will invariably ease the pressure in the baby's ears. Give older children chewing gum or a boiled sweet.

4. If your child has a cold, consult your doctor before flying – the pressure of take off and landing can damage eardrums.

BY CAR

1. Tie toys to your child's car seat so that they don't fall to the floor.

2. If your toddler is teething, tie a bagel to a string and attach it to his wrist. It will keep him occupied, and perhaps he won't put other things in his mouth.

3. On a long car trip, take an extra map and a coloured pencil and let the kids mark your progress. Then they won't ask about it every few minutes.

4. Take a tape recorder and cassettes with favourite stories or songs. Include blank tapes so that the children can make up their own plays.

5. Try these car games:

Dog catcher. One player counts all of the dogs on the left side of the road; the other counts dogs on the right.

Spotting a white horse doubles your score. If you spot a graveyard on your opponent's side of the car, he loses all his points.

Special cars. Have younger children look for yellow moving vans, horse trailers, cement mixers and so on. Award one point to the first child who spots a special car. Older children can try to spot particular makes of car or add the number of people in cars passing in the opposite direction.

Travelling without children

Before you go away, even on a short trip, leaving your small child behind, take steps to ease his anxiety:

1. Include the child in discussions about the trip so that he understands why it is necessary.

2. Act out the departure and the return home: stage a little drama in which everyone says good-bye with hugs and kisses and smiles. Then go out the door with a suitcase, wait a while, ring the bell, open the door, and cry, "I'm home!" Again, hugs, kisses and smiles.

3. Prepare a travelogue in advance, using illustrations cut from magazines (let the child help) to show where you'll be, how you'll get there, and what you'll do. Make the trip sound interesting and safe.

4. Mark the calendar to show when you'll leave and when you'll return. Let the child mark off the days one by one. Leave an envelope for each day you'll be gone, with stories, little love notes, jokes, riddles and gifts. Or record tapes of songs you and the child sing together.

Trees

As trees are by far the largest and most permanent features in the garden, they must be chosen very carefully to suit their required uses, and to avoid any problems at a later date. A tree in the wrong place will need constant trimming back and may eventually have to be cut down completely.

SIZE

Before planting any type of tree, ask your local nurseryman what height and width the tree is likely to grow to. Trees grown under ideal conditions will grow bigger and faster than those growing under adverse conditions, such as low rainfall and strong wind.

Typically large-growing trees include London plane, Cape syringa, jacaranda and flamboyant. Because of their large potential size, they are not a good choice for small gardens or confined areas.

If you're looking for a smaller tree consider planting a Chinese elm or pride of India. In very small areas, such as a townhouse garden or patio, a large shrub, trained to a tree-shape, is ideal.

EVERGREEN OR DECIDUOUS

There is constant debate about the merits of trees which keep their leaves all year – the evergreens – and the ones which drop their leaves in autumn and are dormant in winter – the deciduous trees.

It is a fallacy to think that evergreen trees will make no mess in the garden. Actually they will shed a few leaves all the time, and often quite a large amount of foliage at the beginning of the new growing season.

Deciduous trees, on the other hand, only drop their leaves in the late autumn. Many of them also have the added advantage of turning exquisite autumn colours, especially in the colder parts of the country.

SHADE
For summer shade choose a tree with a wide-spreading crown, such as a Chinese elm, rather than an upright growing type such as a conifer.

Trees with light, open foliage provide more attractive summer shade in areas which don't get too hot, but in very hot regions, heavy foliaged trees will provide a cool outdoor living area. Remember, however, that most lawn grasses will not grow well under heavy shade. If the shade tree is to be planted fairly close to the house, use a deciduous tree so that you get plenty of sunlight in winter.

PRIVACY AND PROTECTION
Trees planted in strategic positions in the garden will provide you with both privacy from neighbours and passers-by, as well as protection from wind and the noise of traffic. In this instance, thick, dense evergreens are the best choice.

ROOTS
Because of their size, trees have a big root system. Most types have deeply penetrating roots, but some have surface roots which can cause damage to paving and other hard surfaces, as well as block drains. Other trees will produce new growth – suckers – if their roots are damaged. These quickly develop into thickets of small trees.

To avoid any possible problems, never plant a large-growing tree closer than five metres to a building or swimming pool or a smaller tree closer than three metres.

UNSUITABLE TREES
Many trees are unsuitable for the average suburban garden because of their size and aggressive root systems. Ironically, a lot of these unsuitable trees are imports from other countries that have spread like wildfire in South Africa. Such unwanted trees include: black locust, blue gum, cluster pine, Carolina poplar, grey poplar, silver wattle, black wattle and Port Jackson, as well as Canary Island date palm. If you have any of these trees on your property, remove them.

Tripod

To keep your photographs from blurring, use a beanbag as a tripod. It moulds itself to rocks, tree branches or the rim of a car window while the camera rests firmly on top. Use it for timed exposures, low-light shots and ground-level close-ups of flowers.

Make or buy a beanbag about 250 x 300 millimetres with a zip or Velcro closure on one end. Carry it empty and fill it with beans, rice or pebbles when needed.

Tulips

1. To keep cut tulips from drooping, add a few drops of vodka to the water in the vase.
2. When dividing your tulip bulbs, plant the smallest ones in an out-of-the-way place; they'll take a few years to flower.

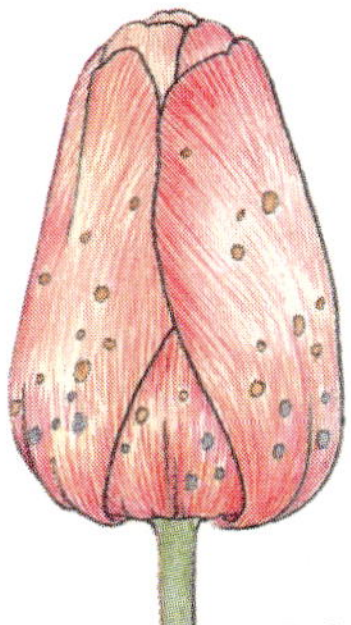
Tulip fire

3. Spotted petals and foliage are invariably signs of a fungus called tulip fire (*Botrytis tulipae*). Destroy all diseased plants; lift the remaining bulbs from the soil and dust thoroughly with the fungicide PCNB, available at most nurseries.

Turkey

1. When you are selecting this traditional Christmas meal, it is important to remember that the younger and fleshier the turkey, the better its texture and taste will be.
2. How much should your turkey weigh? Allow at least 450 grams per person unstuffed, 500 grams stuffed.
3. You can store a frozen turkey for up to a year at 0°C or below. But a fresh turkey should be cooked within a day of purchase.
4. Frozen birds that weigh six kilograms or less can be thawed, still wrapped, in the refrigerator. Allow one to two days. Do not defrost a larger turkey in the refrigerator – the process takes too long, and bacteria can develop.
5. To defrost a large turkey, submerge it completely in a pot of cold water. This method is also good in an emergency for smaller birds. Check that the wrapping has no tears and change the water often. Allow four to five hours for a four-to-six kilogram bird; 11 to 12 hours for a 10-to-12 kilogram bird.
6. Cooking a turkey on a rotisserie is a nice alternative to roasting. Be sure to truss the bird compactly so that it doesn't slip on the spit.
7. Before cooking a turkey in an oven bag, put a tablespoon of flour into the bag and shake it around; this will keep the bag from bursting. Be sure to follow the manufacturer's directions to the letter.

Tweezers

1. If it hurts to tweeze your eyebrows, numb the area by pinching it for 15 seconds or by rubbing it with an ice cube.
2. When your tweezers don't grip properly, you can tighten the legs by putting a pencil between them and bending the tips together. Or just try

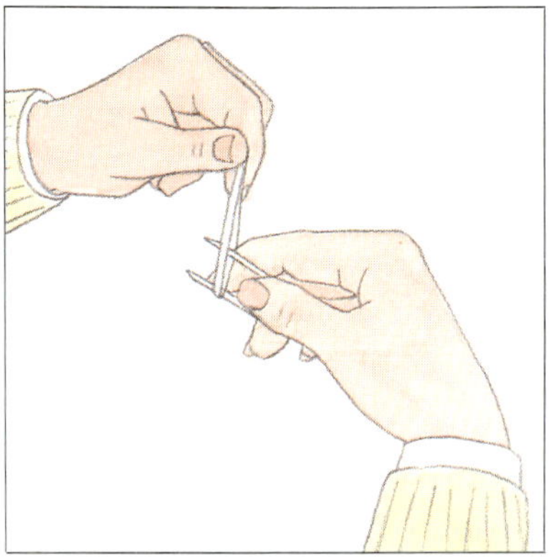

twisting a small rubber band firmly around the tips.
3. For household emergencies, use needle-nose pliers, tongs or the metal clasps on manila envelopes in place of tweezers.

Twine

Need to tie something in a hurry and there's no twine around?
1. Knot your shoe or tackie laces together and you'll have about a metre of cord.
2. Try using heavy leather laces or a leather belt to tie up a car's tail-pipe or silencer until you can get to a garage. Or, if your car has a six- or eight-cylinder engine, remove a long spark plug wire (the engine will still run) and use it as an emergency cord.

Twins & triplets

Here are various ways to encourage a healthy sense of individuality in matching sets of children:
1. Give them very different names (Ann and Rachel, for example, rather than Karen and Corinne). Refer to them by name, not as "the twins" or "the triplets".
2. Avoid dressing them alike after their first birthday. If they're given matching outfits, don't use them on the same day. If they want to dress alike, however, don't prevent them from doing so, but provide each with a varied wardrobe and a separate place to keep it.
3. Allow each child the chance to choose her own toys.
4. Spend some special time alone with each child every day.
5. For their birthday, bake two (or three) cakes and sing "Happy Birthday" two or three times.

Tyre changing

1. Are you unable to loosen frozen or rusted wheel nuts? Apply penetrating oil, vinegar, lemon juice or hot pepper sauce. The next time you rotate the tyres or change one, coat the threads with an anti-seize compound.
2. If one wheel has lost its nuts, borrow one nut from each of the other wheels; make sure that you replace them as soon as possible.
3. Be sure to turn the socket spanner or wheelbrace in the right direction – consult your instruction booklet.
4. More force can be applied by pushing a socket spanner down, not pulling it up. If possible, try using your foot.
5. A cross-shaft nut spanner, available at most motorcar parts suppliers, gives more leverage than a single-shaft socket spanner. For additional leverage, you can fit a piece of pipe over one arm of the wrench. (See also *Car jacks*, p.38.)
6. Keep in mind that you will make your task a lot easier if you loosen the wheel nuts slightly before the car is jacked up.

U

Ulcers

Suffering from ulcers? Try some of these ways to make your restricted diet tastier and more interesting:
1. Mix fresh-pressed cabbage juice, often prescribed for peptic ulcers, with carrot or celery juice; it's more palatable that way.
2. Purée half a cup of fresh, frozen or canned vegetables, and blend the result with a cup of thin white sauce to make a tasty soup.
3. Try using a little freshly minced lean meat (grilled or baked but not fried) in casseroles or soufflés to stimulate the appetite.
4. Don't avoid dinner at a friend's house because you're on a restricted diet. Ask if you can bring your own precooked meal for reheating.
5. Coffee and tea may be taboo, but well-diluted fruit juices are permitted. Mix and match grapefruit orange and prune juices. You can also make soothing milk-based drinks from milk and canned fruit or fruit juice; just sweeten with some honey and whirl together in a blender.
6. Even the blandest bill of fare can be improved by making it look better. Serve small portions on pretty plates. Dress it up with bright bits of pimento, parsley sprigs and showy decorations. Use your best china, napkins and place mats.

Umbrellas

1. Has the fabric come loose from the tip of a rib? You can fix it in an emergency by inserting a paper clip or safety pin through the cloth and then through the hole in the tip. When you get home, you can whipstitch the cloth to the hole.
2. Is a rib bent? Bend it back very gradually so that you don't break it. And don't straighten it too much – it's supposed to be curved.

3. To fix a loose handle, remove it and apply epoxy glue to the shaft. Quickly replace the handle: let dry for at least 24 hours.

4. When buying an umbrella, check for sturdiness by pressing on the ribs – they shouldn't give.

5. To repair a broken rib, tape a small piece of wire coat hanger across the broken part with masking or PVC tape.

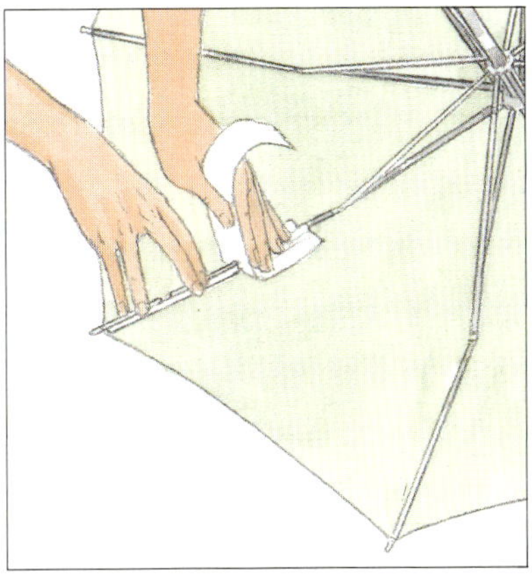

IN TIMES GONE BY

Real men don't carry umbrellas

☐ The Egyptian pharaohs sat under ceremonial umbrellas, which were said to bring them power from heaven.

☐ In ancient Greece and China, parasols were used in religious ceremonies. And in Japan, the emperor was followed by an attendant with a red sunshade, symbolizing absolute power.

☐ In Europe, however, umbrellas were used only by women until some 300 years ago. Men wore hats and got drenched.

☐ Robert Louis Stevenson felt that an umbrella displayed a lack of character – too much concern about getting wet.

☐ Carrying an umbrella also betrayed a lack of social status; it suggested you did not own a carriage. Another good reason not to carry one was that the early models weighed some four-and-a-half kilograms. Furthermore, the oil-soaked cotton wasn't very waterproof.

☐ It wasn't until the 16th century, when the pope decided that the umbrella was a symbol of honour, that they gained favour in European society. Even so, the first Englishman to tout a rain shield, one Jonas Hanway, suffered public ridicule. And coachmen steered through puddles in order to splash him with mud.

☐ When the fashionable "Beau" MacDonald began carrying a silk umbrella in 1778, his sister refused to be seen with him. Nevertheless, he persisted, and others soon followed suit. Men had finally worked out that one umbrella costs a lot less than catching a taxi every rainy day.

Unwanted visitors

Are you one of those people who is subjected to unannounced visits by others just wanting to chat or settle down for a long social visit? If you are, here are some common-sense tips:

1. Don't be afraid of telling the truth. If someone arrives unexpectedly and you are tired or busy, say so and suggest that you get together at a more convenient time.

2. If, however, you don't enjoy the person's company, don't feel obliged to encourage another visit – cutting the relationship short will probably save wear and tear on both parties in the long run.

3. What about dinner guests who linger too long? Since considerate people would be embarrassed to overstay their welcome, the nicest thing is to say, "I wish I weren't so tired so we could talk more". If that doesn't work, you can always resort to making an important phone call.

4. How do you discourage co-workers from dropping in? Put a few books and papers on the chairs in your office so that there will be no place to sit; they won't stay as long.

Upholstery

1. Don't let zips on chair and sofa cushions fool you – the fabric will probably shrink unless it's cleaned in place. If the fabric is washable, you can scrub it with a solution of mild detergent, warm water and a dash of white vinegar or chlorine bleach. Work on one section at a time, removing the suds with a wet rough cloth.

2. Repair a cigarette burn by darning it with matching yarn.

3. Mend a rip by placing adhesive or iron-on tape on the underside of the fabric, sticky side up. Press the edges closed; trim off stray threads.

4. If new upholstery isn't in the budget, drape your chair with fabric, quilting, a tablecloth or a bedspread. Secure it to the underside of the frame with upholstery tacks. Cover worn spots with crocheted doilies, lacy handkerchiefs or matching pieces of suede or leather. Just tack them down with a few quick stitches.

5. To prevent soiled and worn spots, have matching covers made for the back and arm rests that can be removed and laundered.

6. Is your wooden chair uncomfortable? Pad the arms and the slats on the back by wrapping with polyurethane foam; then cover with fabric. For trim, you can sew on strips of contrasting fabric or ribbon.

7. Plump a matted-down cushion by tumbling it in a clothes dryer for five minutes. Include a few bath towels for proper balance.

8. Keep seat pads in place by sewing ties onto the back corners. Or use some Velcro.

9. Make your own seat pad by cutting a piece of 35-millimetre-thick polyurethane foam to size and covering it with fabric.

V

Vacuum cleaners

1. If your vacuum cleaner isn't picking up dirt as well as it used to, see if the hose or wand is clogged. Look carefully through both ends; if you are unable to reach the clog with your hand, use a thin stick or the end of a straightened wire coathanger.

2. Never pick up cigarette butts with your vacuum. Not only could they clog the machine, but a smouldering one could be dangerous.
3. Before you consider replacing the old dust-bag jacket on an upright vacuum cleaner, first try repairing it with iron-on patches.
4. If the hose attachments stick when you're pulling them apart, rub the joints with wax paper.
5. The rule of thumb for vacuuming: pass over the rug three times for light cleaning and at least seven times for heavy cleaning.

Valuables

1. Hire a professional appraiser to value all jewellery, antiques and rare objects; then make sure that your insurance covers the full value of what you own.
2. To enable you to identify your property if it's ever stolen, mark it indelibly with a code such as your driver's licence or insurance policy number. Use waterproof paint on the bottom of ceramic or wooden pieces, and use an engraving tool (available at hardware stores) to mark metal and

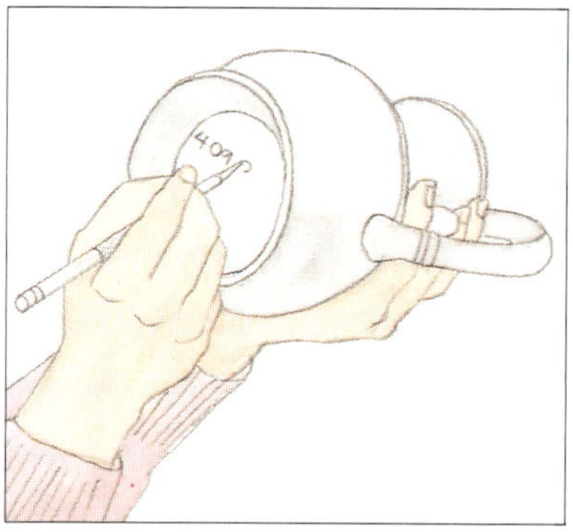

glass objects. Club together with a couple of friends to buy one engraving tool which can be shared.

MAKING A HOUSEHOLD INVENTORY
1. Compile a complete written inventory of your most valuable household belongings; keep one copy at home, another in your safe-deposit box, and a third with your insurance agent. Although making the inventory may be tedious, it will be extremely valuable if you're ever the victim of theft, fire, flood or some other disaster.
2. Catalogue each room; open every drawer and cupboard and carefully list anything of value. Write a description of each piece (including its serial number and brand name), the date you bought it, and its price. Keep receipts and appraisals for very valuable items.
3. If you wish, you can also photograph or videotape each room to supplement your written inventory and prove ownership. But pictures don't replace lists because some small items may be overlooked, and details like carving may not show up. (See also *Household insurance*, p.111; *Insurance claims*, p.117; *Safe-deposit boxes*, p.176.)

Varicose veins

1. Exercise your legs regularly: jog, walk, cycle or swim.
2. Don't sit or stand for long periods of time. When you do sit, avoid crossing your legs at the thighs.
3. Avoid wearing too tight boots, girdles, socks or pantihose. Wear support stockings and sturdy-soled shoes with 2,5-centimetre heels; no tackies, flat shoes, high heels or thin soles.
4. If your legs feel especially tired, give them a gentle, soothing massage, starting at the ankles.
5. Keep your weight down; eat a high-fibre, low-sodium diet (p.130).
6. Ask your doctor about non-surgical removal of varicose veins. One method involves lasers; another, chemical injections into the veins.

Vases

1. If there's a whitish film on the inside of your vase, try soaking it in vinegar or a mild solution of chlorine bleach and water.
2. To remove water rings, rub them with salt. If the vase is narrow and you can't reach them, fill it with a strong saltwater solution and shake until clean; then wash.
3. Coat the inside of a leaky vase with hot wax and let harden. Or, if the vase is opaque, put a glass inside it to hold water.
4. Many household effects make pretty vases. Teapots, wine carafes, copper kettles and jugs are especially nice. Put single stems in a wineglass or goblet. Let wildflowers or daisies spill out of a basket (first put them in a small waterproof container that won't show). For dinner parties use small bottles and put a tiny bunch of violets at each place setting.
5. If your vase has a wide mouth, crisscross the opening with transparent tape – it will hold your arrangement in place.

VCR's

Most VCR care is simply preventive maintenance; once a problem occurs, there are no established do-it-yourself remedies – take the unit to an authorized service centre.
1. Record on high-quality videotapes only. Cheap tapes harm the recording heads – as will any tape after about 100 hours of use.
2. Cover your VCR when not in use to keep dust and debris out of the vents

and to prevent children from putting things in the cassette slot.

3. Moisture can ruin a VCR. Don't rest a container of coffee, cooldrink or any other liquid on the machine and don't use liquid cleaning products on its exterior. If you live in a humid area, buy small packets of silica from an electronics supply store and put them on top of the VCR to absorb moisture. When the packages are soaked, bake them dry in the oven and reuse.

4. If your picture is snowy and the sound is fuzzy, it's time to clean the tape heads; follow the manufacturer's instructions. If you use many rented tapes, you may need to clean the heads fairly often. (See also *Televisions*, p.207.)

Vegetable peelers

1. For maximum efficiency, push the blade away from you when using a peeler with a swivel blade; pull it towards you if the blade is rigid.

2. Use a vegetable peeler to make neat chocolate curls for your desserts. Using tongs, hold 30 grams of unwrapped baking chocolate over a steaming kettle to soften it slightly. Or place it on a plate in the microwave on 50 percent power for 15 to 20 seconds. Dip your peeler in hot water and draw it across the edge or bottom of the chocolate.

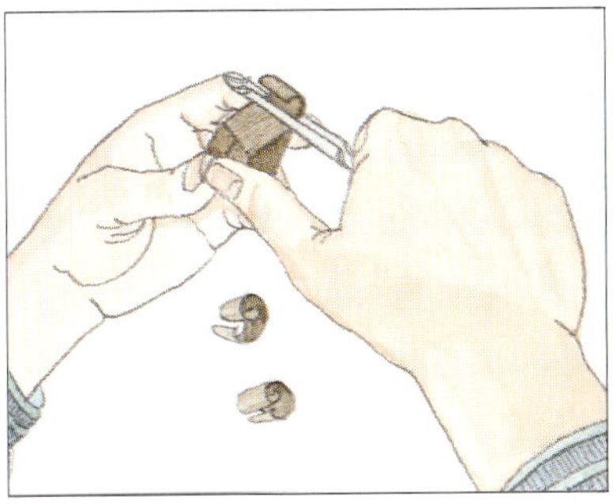

Vegetable steamers

1. For a make-do steamer, use an electric frying pan with 2,5 centimetres of water in it. Place the food on a heatproof plate and balance it on some kind of stable platform – a bottling jar ring, perhaps, or an empty tuna can with both ends removed. Then cover, leaving a small air vent so that any condensed steam doesn't drip onto the food.

2. Or make a steamer from two thicknesses of foil and set it over a few centimetres of water in a saucepan. Jab small holes in the foil with a sharp pencil and tightly crimp the edges over the rim of the pan. Place the food inside, cover and steam.

Vegetable varieties

If your homegrown vegetables aren't up to scratch, you may be planting the wrong varieties. Believe it or not, the details on seed packets *do* make a difference. Read the information on the seed packet carefully and look for those varieties that are best suited to your conditions.

1. Vegetables can be divided into three groups – cool season, warm season and intermediate vegetables. The seeds of cool season and intermediate vegetables will germinate at temperatures of between 15°C and 20°C, while seeds of warm season vegetables germinate at a temperature of 20°C or higher. The seeds of warm season vegetables which take a long time to mature, for example, eggplants and peppers, should be germinated in warm, sheltered boxes, then planted out when the weather warms up.

Quicker growing vegetables, such as beans, tomatoes and cucumbers, can be sown successively over the months to provide you with a constant supply of fresh vegetables.

2. Beware of commercial varieties, tailored to the needs of large-scale growers and packers. Their characteristics, such as tough skin and long shelf life, are pointless in the home garden, and usually take precedence over taste and texture. All seeds sold in small picture packets by garden stores and nurseries tend to be the home-garden types. Always buy your seeds from a reputable source – seed that is kept too long in a store will loose its freshness and may not germinate as well as it should.

3. Look at other local vegetable gardens to see what varieties do well in your area. Ask your local nurseryman for advice, or contact the local extension office of the Department of Agriculture. (Look under *Agriculture* in the Government Departments section of your telephone directory).

4. Don't let your vegetables grow until they are huge; rather pick them when they are young and succulent. Large plants sometimes tend to lose their flavour.

Vetkoek

1. Vetkoek are traditional fried cakes enjoyed with butter and jam or filled with savoury or curried mincemeat.

2. Sift together 250 millilitres cake flour, 15 millilitres baking powder and two millilitres salt. Add one beaten egg and 125 millilitres milk. Mix well. Heat cooking oil – at least five centimetres deep – in a frying pan. Drop tablespoons of the mixture into the hot oil and fry until golden brown. Drain on absorbent paper.

3. To make 100 vetkoeke use one litre of water, 500 millilitres milk, four eggs, 125 millilitres white sugar, 2,5 kilograms cake flour, 25 millilitres baking powder, 15 millilitres salt and a 25 gram cake of yeast. Heat the water and the milk. Beat into the eggs and sugar. Crumble the yeast and add. Leave for 15 minutes. Sift the dry ingredients together, add to the yeast mixture and knead well. Cover and leave in a warm place for 60 minutes to rise. Roll out the dough two centimetres thick. Fry in hot sunflower oil until golden brown.

4. The vetkoek may be eaten immediately or they can be frozen. The batter may be stored in the refrigerator and kept until needed.

5. For variety, bran can be mixed into the dough or some of the flour substituted with whole-wheat flour.

Videotaping

1. For good-quality home movies, take a few minutes to plan your shots. Better yet, jot down a rough shooting script. Have it tell an interesting story; show preparations for a trip, for example, and then the departure. After filming the holiday's main highlights, attach an ending – perhaps something humorous about arriving home exhausted.

2. When you are shooting, do what the professionals do: try to hold the video camera as steady as possible. Pan slowly and smoothly, without too much repetition.

3. Don't overdo zooms; too many are visually disturbing. Use them to emphasize something important, like a close-up of a child's face blowing out birthday candles.

4. Don't make scenes interminably long; linger on one angle for only eight to 10 seconds before you switch to another view.

Vines and creepers

Afraid you'll plant a vine or creeper in the wrong place? Learn how it grows and you'll know how best to use it in your garden.

TWINING TYPES

Wisteria, canary creeper, morning glory, honeysuckle, glorybower, Carolina jasmine and mandevilla vines wrap their stems around their host. Because they can choke a tree, confine them to a trellis, pergola or fence.

TENDRIL TYPES

Granadillas, ornamental grape, coral creeper and perennial sweet peas pull themselves aloft with delicate tendrils. They clamber up a tree or shrub harmlessly if thinned by periodic pruning, and provide the host with a bonus period of bloom or a colourful autumn foliage display.

HOLDFAST TYPES

Light-stemmed self-clinging creepers, such as Virginia creeper and Boston ivy, literally tend to glue themselves to exterior walls with resinous holdfasts. They will not really damage the wall's mortar. But heavy-stemmed self-clinging creepers such as ivy and tickey creeper could cause damage.

Vinyl tiles

Vinyl tiles are resistant to wear, water, denting and most household chemicals. In full sunlight, though, some colours will tend to fade.

Before you try covering an unsightly wooden floor with vinyl tiles, first check that there is not excessive springing of any of the boards, or weakness of the underfloor supports.

The slight movement that is normal with a suspended floor will eventually produce some lifting or loosening of tiles, but this can be greatly reduced, or even eliminated, by first attaching sheets of hardboard to the floor and then laying the tiles on the hardboard. A parquet or wood-block floor should also first be overlaid with hardboard before tiling. Before you lay tiles, make sure that the floor surface is free of dirt and dust which may prevent proper adhesion.

Vision loss

1. Look for large-print books which are available in most public libraries, or order them from a bookstore. Or try audiocassettes of recorded books, movies and periodicals. Audio tapes can also be borrowed from *Tape Aids for the Blind* who have branches in all the major cities.

2. Investigate the many household items that are now designed with large print, for example, watches, clocks and software for computers. In addition there are many new magnifying devices, ranging from a simple enlarging glass with a light attached, to a closed circuit television that enlarges the image many times.

3. Seek out a specialist to teach you how to make the best of your impaired eyesight. Contact the local branch of an association for the blind, which will probably be able to point you in the right direction.

Vitamins

Essential for health, vitamins are present in small quantities in the food you eat, and a well-balanced diet supplies all you need. Vitamins regulate metabolism, which is the way your body breaks down and uses the various foods it takes in.

A lack of vitamins can lead to a number of illnesses. A serious deficiency of Vitamin C – obtained from fresh fruit and vegetables – can cause scurvy, formerly widespread among sailors. Other vitamin deficiencies may cause severe headaches, stunted growth or infertility.

As an example of high vitamin content, a medium-sized orange contains about 50 milligrams of Vitamin C, compared with a paltry 10 milligrams in an average apple.

Here are the 13 major vitamins, all of which are listed with their recommended daily amounts (RDA) and convenient sources.

- ☐ Vitamin A (RDA 0,75 milligrams): many vegetables, full-fat dairy produce and liver.
- ☐ Vitamin B1 (RDA 1,3 milligrams): a variety of wholegrain cereals, brown rice, brewer's yeast, seafood, meat, nuts and pulses.
- ☐ Vitamin B2 (RDA 1,5 milligrams): wholegrain cereals, meat, fish, pulses, brewer's yeast, green vegetables, eggs and cheese.
- ☐ Vitamin B3 (RDA 18 milligrams): rice, cereals, brewer's yeast, meat, fish, nuts, pulses, eggs and cheese.
- ☐ Vitamin B5 (RDA 4–7 milligrams) and Vitamin B6 (RDA 1-2 milligrams).
- ☐ Vitamin B9 (RDA 0,3 milligrams): meat, vegetables, yeast, fruit.
- ☐ Vitamin B12 (RDA 2 micrograms): meat, fish, egg yolk, cheese, various fortified cereals.
- ☐ Vitamin C (RDA 30 milligrams): raw fruits and fruit juices (especially citrus), vegetables.
- ☐ Vitamin D (RDA 10 micrograms): liver, oily fish, egg yolk, full-fat dairy products. It is also produced by the action of sunlight on the skin.
- ☐ Vitamin E (RDA 10 micrograms): vegetable oils, cereals, nuts, pulses, green vegetables, egg yolk.
- ☐ Vitamin K (RDA 140 micrograms): produced in the large intestine, and found in green vegetables, potatoes, eggs and wheat germ.

DID YOU KNOW . . . ?

Volunteers who man our lifeboats

The South African coastline is regarded by mariners as one of the most dangerous in the world. The coastal waters from Alexander Bay in the west to Kosi Bay in the east are littered with the bones of broken ships and sailors who went down with them.

In 1967, recognizing the dangers of sailing in our coastal waters, the Society of Master Mariners called for the establishment of a rescue service to help people and ships in peril on the sea.

In June of the same year, the National Sea Rescue Institute (NSRI), an entirely voluntary organization, was founded.

After 25 years, the approximately 650 active voluntary crewpersons of the NSRI operate 22 stations, including one in the Transvaal (at the Vaal Dam), using craft that range from rubber ducks to inboard-engined boats of up to 14 metres in length.

By mid-1993 the NSRI had saved more than 1,292 lives, assisted 11,169 persons, towed in 2,698 craft, and assisted a further 1,325 craft.

These rescue operations, usually mounted in appalling weather conditions, are not exempt from risk to the coxwains and crews who man the boats. But in the spirit of Wolraad Woltemade, the South African folk hero who rode his horse into the waves of Table Bay to save the crew of a sinking ship in 1773, NSRI crews go about their business with commitment and dedication.

Although crews give their time and expertise freely, costs are high, and the fuel bill for answering a single call – which may turn out to be anything from a complicated rescue to a cruel hoax – could easily run to several thousand rands.

The NSRI does not charge for its services, so these and other costs are met by donations, bequests, legacies, various sponsorships, relatively small grants from the state and from local authorities. Fundraising campaigns include an annual street collection.

□ Biotin (RDA 0,2 milligrams): part of the Vitamin B complex, and found mainly in egg yolk, liver, wheat germ, nuts and brewer's yeast.

Caution: Excessively high doses of vitamins A and D may be toxic.

Volunteering

Want to work with a voluntary group but don't know where to start?

1. Check with the local library, where civic groups often leave pamphlets describing their activities.

2. Scan the classified pages of the newspaper for small display ads placed by non-profit organizations.

3. Consider your interests – would you like to read to sick children, deliver meals to the needy or serve in a charity store? Find out which organizations need these services, and approach them. Don't volunteer for anything you know you will dislike.

Vomiting

1. To prevent dehydration after a bout of vomiting, drink as much fluid as you can keep down. Avoid drinks that contain caffeine; it may irritate your stomach. Once the liquids stay down, ease back into eating solid foods, beginning with dry toast, clear soup, gelatine, apple sauce and jelly.

2. Support a child's body and forehead while he vomits, then wipe his face with a cool moist cloth and help him rinse his mouth and brush his teeth. If he's frightened, explain that his stomach is just getting rid of something it dislikes.

3. Call a doctor if there is abdominal pain, bloating or constipation, or if vomiting persists for more than a day – or 12 hours in a baby. (See also *Airsickness*, p.9; *Hangovers*, p.104.)

W

Walkers

These tubular frames, used conventionally to help babies learn to walk, can be used for other purposes too, so before you discard yours, consider the following:

1. To make carrying odds and ends easier, attach a small wicker bicycle basket to the front of the walker. Run an elastic loop or a sturdy rubber band through the wicker to hold a glass of liquid firmly inside. (To ensure maximum safety, you can use a covered container or a cyclist's plastic water bottle.)

2. Tie a plastic supermarket bag to one side of the frame to hold tissues and other light items; a second bag tied securely on the other side can serve as a wastebasket.

3. Door-closing problems? Run a cord from the knob to a screw eye on the hinge side; then just pull the cord to close the door behind you.

4. If something is out of reach, use a pair of long tongs; suspend them from the walker frame with string.

5. For comfort, and to prevent your hands from slipping, wrap the top bar of the walker with friction tape.

Wallboard

1. To repair wallboard tape that has pulled away from the wall, wet the back slightly to make it flexible. Then squeeze on a little cold glue and spread it with a toothpick. Press the tape to the wall, hold a sheet of wax paper over it, and apply pressure with a hardcover book or board for about 3 or 4 minutes.

2. Hammer a popped wallboard nail back into the wall stud and drive another nail a few centimetres above or below it. Fill nailhead dimples with spackle; when dry, sand lightly and repaint. Or pull popped nails and replace with drywall screws.

Wallflowers

Getting wallflowers (shy guests) off the wall and into your party takes tact. Here are some tips:

1. Ask the shy guest to help you to serve the hors d'oeuvres or the drinks – you'll get a helping hand and he'll have a good reason to circulate among the other guests.

2. Introduce the timid soul to another person who looks lost; give them both some useful information about each other so that they can start a conversation: "Dick, I'd like you to meet John Smith visiting from Pretoria, where he practises law. John, this is our neighbour, Dick Jones, who teaches at the high school."

3. If you are having a small party, take the trouble to brief your guests ahead of time on who else is coming. It will help break the ice. If one person isn't participating, ask her something about her special interest so that she can have the spotlight for a while.

4. You can do a lot to keep people mingling by arranging the room properly: place the drinks at one end, the food at the other. And don't provide too many chairs; if potential wallflowers have to stand, they'll be more likely to move around and chat.

Wallpaper

1. To keep the wallpaper around a baby's crib clean, staple clear, non-adhesive vinyl over it.

2. To dust papered walls, tie a duster over your broom and work from the top down.

3. To remove pencil marks and other non-greasy spots from non-washable papers, use an artgum eraser or a slice of fresh rye bread.

4. To remove greasy spots, crayon marks and food stains, apply a paste of cleaning fluid and fuller's earth, cornflour or talcum powder. Let dry and brush off. Repeat the treatment until the spot is gone.

5. Wipe off fingerprints with a damp cloth, then sprinkle the moist area with fuller's earth; let it dry and then brush it off.

6. To prevent splash marks when you're washing skirting boards or other woodwork, mask wallpaper with a wide ruler, venetian blind slat or piece of rigid plastic.

7. When you save scraps of wallpaper for patching, tack them to a wall in the attic or cupboard. When you use them for repairs, they won't look so brand-new.

8. Patches that have cut edges tend to show, so don't cut the paper – tear it instead. The feathered edges won't be so noticeable.

9. If you don't have any wallpaper left for making patches, just touch up the damaged spots with some matching paints.

HANGING WALLPAPER

1. Make a resting place for the sticky paste brush by slipping a length of coat hanger through the bail eyes on your bucket. Then set the bristles on the wire and the handle on the side of the bucket.

2. To smooth out air bubbles under freshly applied paper, try using a paint roller.

3. If you are papering over old wallpaper, be sure to cover any grease spots with a sealer so that they won't bleed through.

4. Use leftover wallpaper for wrapping paper, book covers or for lining cupboard drawers.

Wallpaper removal

1. To make old wallpaper easier to remove, first slash it diagonally with a single-edged razor blade or a knife every 300 millimetres. Then mix a 50-50 solution of vinegar and warm water in a spray bottle, and squirt it behind the cut edges. Let the glue soften for a few minutes, then scrape off the paper with a broad, flat putty knife or metal spatula. (Tape the tool firmly to a broom handle for scraping near the ceiling.)

2. To strip a small area of stubborn paper, cover it with a clean cloth and press with a steam iron to soften the glue. If your iron won't produce steam when held vertically, wet the cloth before ironing.

Warm-up & cool-down exercises

If you exercise strenuously without warming up, you can injure muscles. If you stop exercising without cooling down, your blood pressure can drop suddenly and cause dizziness, nausea and irregular heartbeat; this can be life-threatening to someone with a heart problem. Check with your doctor before starting an exercise regime.

1. The first step in warming up is to raise your body temperature and increase your muscle flexibility. Jogging in place and slow aerobic activities are both good. So is a fast

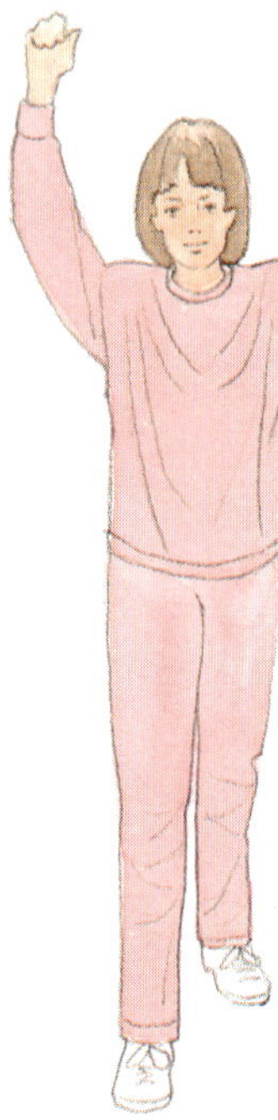

Warming up

walk: step out briskly, heel first; swing your arms and shake them vigorously as you walk to stimulate your circulation. Lengthen your stride and gradually increase your speed as you warm up.

2. Once your muscles have warmed up, do at least five minutes of stretching exercises (p.199). If you're warming up to run, choose exercises that will stretch the groin, hamstrings, calves and quadriceps. If you're preparing to lift weights, concentrate on the muscles of your upper body, particularly those of your shoulders. A good book on your sport should include some specific suggestions for stretching exercises.

3. After a workout, the best way to cool down is to stay in motion while gradually reducing your effort; walk briskly or jog slowly for five to 15 minutes in order to stabilize your blood pressure and steadily slow your heart rate.

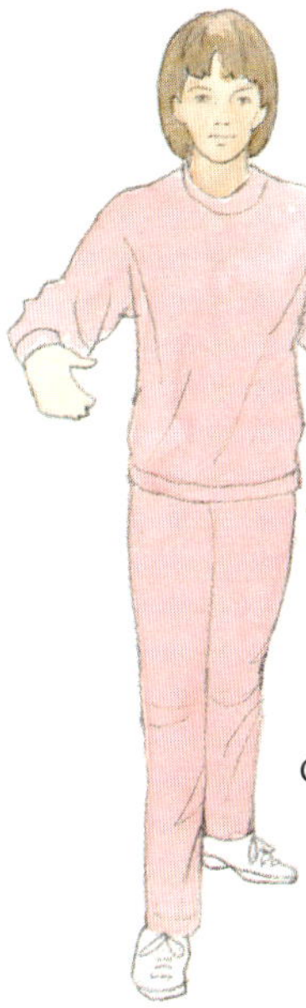

Cooling down

LOOK BEFORE YOU LEAP

The hazards of exercising

Exercise is not always a good thing. Too much too soon can cause injuries.

□ Running injuries are most frequent in people who log more than 50 kilometres a week. Sports medicine experts say 30 to 40 kilometres is quite enough to keep you in top physical condition.

□ No pain, no gain – right? Wrong! Strenuous exercise may cause some discomfort, but pain is a warning to back off before you injure yourself.

□ Never take salt tablets before exercising – they can cause nausea and vomiting. To counter salt loss, drink salty liquids or add a little extra table salt to your food.

□ Many people are seriously injured working out on weight machines because they don't use them properly. Get instructions first and be sure they come from a qualified instructor.

□ The myth that you shouldn't drink water while exercising is not only wrong but dangerous. Working out when you're dehydrated puts extra strain on your heart and muscles. Drink a glass of water before you start and have more if you feel thirsty.

□ Don't proceed as usual in very hot, humid weather – you could get heatstroke. Ask your doctor for guidelines for your age and fitness level.

□ If you haven't played a sport in a long time, don't start up at your former intensity. Start slowly to build up strength and endurance.

□ Exercise can be addictive. Beware if you continue to exercise despite injuries, if you find it hard to sleep even though you're exhausted, if exercise is interfering with your work or social life, or if you feel guilty or out of control when you miss a workout.

Warped wood

1. To prevent warping, saw two 6-millimetre-deep lines along a board's length in the bottom or back surface. Space the lines over the whole width; they act as stress-release gaps and allow the board to expand and contract without warping.

2. If warpage causes a board to pull its nails free, replace them with screws; clamp the board back in place before driving the screws.

3. For even greater holding power, bore holes through the board and bolt it down.

4. To correct a warped board, place it, concave side up, on some wet towels near (but not on) a radiator or other source of heat. Put heavy weights on each end of the board and let it sit for several days, rewetting the towels as necessary. (If the board is sealed with a finish, sand it off so that the board will absorb moisture.)

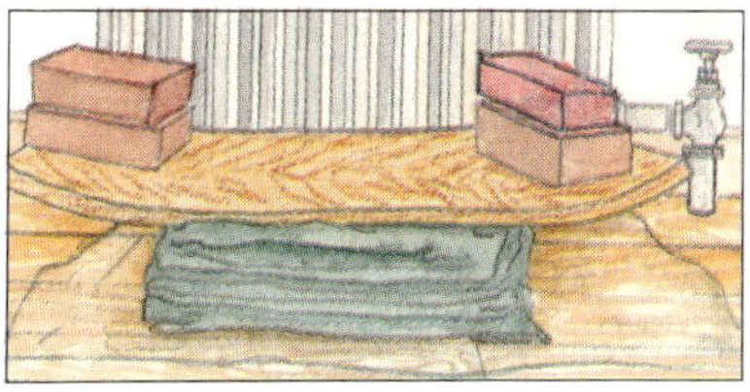

Warts & moles

Although they may look similar, warts and moles are unrelated skin conditions. To be sure which you have, consult your doctor before attempting any self-treatment.

Warts vary in size, shape, roughness and colour and tend to grow mainly on the face, neck, hands, forearms, legs and feet; almost always harmless, warts very often disappear all by themselves within six to 24 months.

To treat a wart that has been so diagnosed, soften it overnight with a plaster moistened with a 30 percent salicylic acid solution; then soak the wart for 30 minutes in Epsom salts and hot water and file it gently with an emery board or a pumice stone.

Or squeeze the contents of a gelatine capsule of vitamin A and one of fish oil onto the wart twice a day for two to five months.

Moles, small dark spots, can occur anywhere on the body.

If you are subject to moles, examine your skin monthly with a hand-held and full-length mirror.

Look carefully for growths which are larger than a pencil eraser and those that have an irregular raised surface, an asymmetrical outline and a mottled colour; also look for colour changes, scaliness, oozing, bleeding, itching, tenderness and a bump or nodule. If you spot any of these features, or if after 35 you begin to develop dark, smooth spots, see a doctor immediately.

Wasps and hornets

The solitary wasps that go about their business are unlikely to do you any harm at all and, in fact, benefit the gardener and householder by controlling small pests. Any wasp accidentally trodden on or molested will sting and, unlike a bee, sting repeatedly, but trouble is most likely to come from the social wasps which, typically, build their paper-like nests in hollows and hedges, and from the yellow-and-black European wasp.

To get rid of a nest, spray it at night with a suitable insecticide. If possible, avoid using a light, block entrances to prevent wasps escaping, and wear protective clothing.

Although wasp stings are painful, their effect is usually short-lived, but people subject to allergies should be on their guard. Hornets? – there aren't any in South Africa, but the name is often given to large wasps of the genus *Belonogaster*.

Waterblommetjies

Waterblommetjies, also known as Cape pondweed (*Aponogeton distachyus*), are delicately flavoured plants which have become an important part of traditional Cape cooking.

They grow wild in Cape ponds, dams and ditches, and are also commercially grown and harvested.

You can buy canned waterblommetjies throughout the year, but fresh ones are available in supermarkets and at roadside stalls only in spring, when the plant flowers.

Here are some tips for buying and preparing waterblommetjies:

1. When you buy from a roadside seller, ask where the plants were grown – it is important to establish that they were not grown in polluted dams or ditches.

2. Trim off the tough stems and wash waterblommetjies very well to get rid of grit and any other dirt.

IN TIMES GONE BY

Warts and all

□ Contrary to folklore, warts are not caused by frogs, toads or the water used to boil eggs; the ugly lumps come from viruses that are passed from person to person.

□ Perhaps because many warts simply disappear in time, an air of mystery has always surrounded them. People have tried to make them vanish by covering them with spiderwebs, raw potatoes or dandelion sap. Some have believed that they could give their warts to an enemy by rubbing the blemishes with a pebble, wrapping the pebble in a piece of paper with the person's name on it, and then throwing it away. Others have thought that their parents or friends could "buy" warts for a penny, yet not be afflicted.

□ One early wart remedy called for dousing a door hinge with vinegar after seeing a shooting star. Another was to rub a wart with an apple and then bury it; as the fruit rotted into the earth, the wart could disappear.

3. Soak the cleaned waterblommetjies in salty water for three to four hours (or overnight).

4. To season, add lemon juice or a handful of chopped wild sorrel – widely regarded as a weed. If you can't find any sorrel, try using a sour apple instead.

5. Don't stick to the traditional waterblommetjie bredie – try waterblommetjies in other dishes. For example, surprise your guests with a waterblommetjie quiche.

6. If you do intend making a bredie, allow for a cooking time of about two and a half hours.

Water conservation

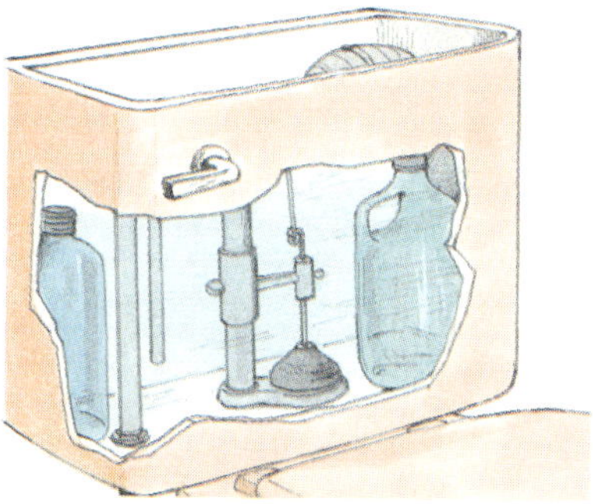

1. At about 10 to 20 litres a flush, the toilet is your household's worst water waster; to save as much as five litres a flush, displace some water in the tank with rocks, a brick or a plastic jug of sand. Don't overdo it, or you'll cause an incomplete flush.

2. Take shallow baths and short showers or install a water-saving showerhead. Run your dishwasher only when it is full of cutlery and crockery.

3. Rinse dirty dishes in a pan instead of under running water.

4. Collect rainwater for irrigation.

5. Keep your plants alive with "grey water", the waste that would usually go down the drain. Use water from the washing machine or the bathtub only, and only if you've used bar soap or soap flakes (no detergents, bleach, borax or softeners).

Run a hose from the drain to a plastic refuse bin; carry the water to your plants in a bucket.

Caution: Don't use grey water on food crops and don't use water in which you've washed nappies. Cover the storage container outdoors so that the water doesn't become a breeding ground for mosquitoes.

Water divining

While some people scorn water diviners, others swear by them. In some areas it is said that wherever you drill, you will hit underground water, so the diviners really cannot miss. But elsewhere, in really dry areas, using their magic, knowledge of local geology and intuition, diviners have been known to find water where geologists and other experts have drilled dry hole after dry hole.

Some contractors you might hire to sink a borehole or a well-point will not start drilling unless the diviner has told them where to drill. Not all diviners and borehole contractors have the same success – consult with neighbours to find those who have a good track record in your area.

Whether you follow his or her directions or not, paying a water diviner a few rands can be entertaining. To locate underground water, some rely on "vibrations" which they feel in their feet or in the palms of their outstretched hands. Others hold a Y-shaped stick, of willow wood in both hands, with the third arm of the stick pointing at the sky. As they find the spot to drill, the stick flips over, appearing to gain a power of its own, and points downward. Others are far more low-key, just walking around the property and pointing out likely spots to try.

Without maps of the underground terrain, a geologist (and perhaps some diviners too) studies surrounding surface geology, notes vegetation, and tries to establish where neighbours have found water.

Water hazards

1. Do not leave any basins or buckets of water within reach of toddlers. Nappy sterilizing buckets should have the lid firmly attached.
2. Fish bowls, aquariums and outside fish ponds should all be covered.
3. Never leave a child unsupervised in a bath or plastic swimming pool, even if the water is shallow.
4. The fencing of swimming pools is regulated by local authorities, but use common sense as well. Keep chairs, tables and anything else which a child may stand on away from the fence.
5. Prevent a burn from hot bathwater by always running the cold water first. Then heat the bathwater to the required temperature.
6. Keep children away from boiling water – even the steam can cause a nasty burn.
7. Water conducts electricity – avoid electric shocks in the bathroom by never operating an appliance with wet hands. Unplug and store all appliances before children use the bathroom. Plug points are illegal in bathrooms in South Africa.

Water leaks

Your first step in any leaking-water emergency should be to cut off the water supply at your home's main *Shut-off* valve so that the flood won't get worse while you look for the trouble spot. If you use city water, your main shut-off valve is the one nearest the meter. If you have your own well, the main valve is near the water storage tank.

Once you've located the source of the leak, look for a shut-off valve for the branch line to that part of the house (it's usually located where it branches off the main line) and shut it. Most sinks, toilets, showers and bathtubs have their own shut-off valves for both the hot and cold water. As soon as you isolate the problem area, you can restore the water supply to the rest of the house while making your repair or waiting for the plumber.

Water purification

1. To purify water, first filter it. Fill a clean sock with successive 25 millimetre layers of fine gravel, crushed charcoal and sand. Pour water into the sock and let it drain into a cup. Then boil the water for five minutes (one minute longer for each 300 metres above sea level).
2. If you use purification tablets, allow one hour for them to take effect. Follow the directions on the bottle carefully; dosage can vary significantly with temperature.

SOLAR STILL

While on camps you can make a solar still that produces several cups of pure water a day.
1. Dig a bowl-shaped hole a metre in diameter and 750 millimetres deep.
2. Set a clean bucket or bowl in the centre of the hole.
3. Secure a large piece of clear plastic over the hole with earth or rocks. Then place a rock in the middle of the plastic so that the sheet's lowest point is directly above the container. Solar heat will penetrate the plastic and bake moisture out of the soil. The water will condense on the lower side of the plastic and run down to drip into the container; night cuts accumulation in half.
4. Try to delay collection as long as possible; opening the still lets out moisture-laden air, which takes some 30 minutes to resaturate.
5. When the soil is baked dry, rebuild the still in another spot. Hollows and dry riverbeds are likely to have wetter soil than high ground.
6. You can use the same method to purify salty or polluted water, even urine, or to extract moisture from plant materials. Just put the water source off-centre in the hole and let the sun work its wonders.

Water retention

If bloating and swelling are recurring problems for you, consult your doctor to see if there is cause for concern. If not, you should consider taking the following measures:
1. Decrease your salt intake; avoid all canned and processed foods, from soup and salami to salted nuts and potato chips (see *Low-sodium diet*, p.130). It may help to cut back on sugar and caffeine as well.
2. Try to eat foods that are natural diuretics: typical examples of these are apples, cucumbers, parsley, beetroot, watercress, asparagus, strawberries and grapes.

3. Exercise regularly – swim, cycle, jog, go hiking or walk briskly – to improve your circulation.
4. Wear support stockings.
5. Elevate your feet for 20 minutes during the day and an hour or two before going to bed.
6. Avoid extreme stress (p.198); it can sometimes activate a water retaining hormone.
7. If your doctor prescribes diuretics, use them with caution; they can cause potassium deficiency. Instead (believe it or not), drink lots of water; it won't add to the bloat but rather will make your kidneys work harder. (See also *Puffiness*, p.164.)

Water softener

1. Today's built-in water softeners are not for everyone; they add sodium to the water. So if you're on a no-sodium diet, don't use one. If on a low-sodium diet, check with your doctor and take into account the original hardness of the water.
2. Eliminate "telltale grey" from your laundry by using a heavy-duty liquid detergent and adding half a cup borax or washing soda to the wash water. A litre of white vinegar in the final rinse water will help remove the last traces of soap scum. Don't do this too often, however; the enamel in washing machine tubs is not acid-resistant.
3. To rid your washing machine of hard water buildup, fill it with water, add one cup white vinegar, and let it run – without laundry – through a complete cycle.

Water taste

Various water-filtering devices are available on the market. It is not worth buying elaborate filters to filter all the water you use, but you might afford a small, portable filter-jug to screen drinking water.

Filtered water can be used in kettles, which will last far longer until they need to be cleaned out, because the filtering will remove dissolved salts. This makes it valuable to kidney sufferers too.

1. If the odour, taste or colour of your water suddenly seems strange to you, call your local authority or municipality immediately to query whether all is normal.
2. If you have your own well or borehole, carefully watch for surrounding sources of pollution, such as the fuel tanks at petrol stations, leaks from septic tanks and sewers or leaching from dump sites.
3. There is a danger of contaminating the pipes anytime you break into the plumbing system. After any plumbing work, be sure to run the taps for a while to scour them out before drinking.
4. You can use a swimming pool test kit to measure pH (acidity/alkalinity) and also the amount of chlorine in the water, from about one part per million to about five parts per million.

Weatherstripping

1. Through-the-wall air conditioners are quite notorious for inadequate weatherstripping. To seal, wad up aluminium foil and, using a ruler or putty knife, pack it around the unit, especially the gap underneath. Then seal with PVC tape.
2. Firmly wipe rubber weatherstripping with a thin film of household oil from time to time. This will keep it flexible longer. It also keeps the weatherstripping from sticking to the door or window on hot days. (See also *Insulation*, p.117.)

Use masking tape as a temporary seal for draughty windows. Just stick the tape to both the sash and the frame.

Weddings

If you're planning a wedding and are worried about the cost, relax. Here are some ways to cut costs and still have a day to remember:
1. A beautiful location doesn't have to be expensive. You could have the ceremony on the beach, aboard a yacht, in a park, in a garden, at an historic site, or, of course, in a church, mosque or synagogue.
2. Instead of renting a room, hold the reception at home. Make a festive – if not waterproof – tent by sewing strips of brightly coloured fabric or parachute silk together. Then tie it to the trees. Or lash tent flies or canopies to poles and set them up in clusters or against the side of the house. For an evening wedding why not string the garden with a gala canopy of tiny white lights?
3. Ask a music student to play at the ceremony. For the reception, hire a local discotheque or make your own dance tapes.
4. Rather than serving a sit-down meal, plan an afternoon wedding and serve high tea or cocktails and hors d'oeuvres. Champagne punch costs less than champagne and domestic brands less than imported. Look for someone who makes wedding cakes at home; the cake will probably cost less than one from a bakery, and should taste just as good – maybe a lot better.
5. Hire a professional photographer to take formal shots, but ask friends who are photo buffs to take the candid shots at the reception. Develop and print the film yourself.
6. Make your own floral arrangements and bouquets with blossoms from your garden or with flowers from a friend's garden. Alternatively, buy them yourself from a neighbourhood flowerseller.
7. Scout second-hand boutiques for the wedding dress. You can often find beautiful gowns that are relatively inexpensive that way.
8. Instead of printed invitations, ask someone who does calligraphy to write them by hand. Or ask an artistic

friend to design an invitation that reflects the personalities or interests of the couple.

Weeds

1. Want to get rid of weeds without using herbicides? Till and fertilize soil well in advance, then cover it with a sheet of black plastic. The plastic will absorb sunlight to warm the soil; when the weed seeds germinate, it will smother the unwanted seedlings. Some six to eight weeks later, the bed will be ready to uncover and plant with flowers or vegetables.
2. Make sure you don't sow weeds in your garden. Compost horse and cow manure before adding it to your soil (p.54); in the process you'll destroy any seeds the animal may have ingested. Because lawn cuttings may be full of weed seeds, don't put them directly onto the soil as a mulch but compost them first.
3. Weed on a 10-day schedule. Till the soil 10 days before planting and hoe out any seedlings that appear in the interval before you sow your crops. Clean up again 10 days after planting, when the weeds are still small and easy to uproot. Ten days later work the soil yet again. For fast-growing and late-season crops, this should be all the weeding you'll need to do for a while.

Weevils

If a package of flour, cornflour, nuts, cereal or birdseed is seriously infested, discard it immediately. To get rid of a minor infestation, place the foodstuff in the deep freeze for four days or in the oven long enough so that the internal temperature remains at 50°C for 30 minutes. (To prevent overheating, prop the oven door open a few centimetres.)

You can guard against re-infestation: clean out cupboards by vacuuming and scrubbing them thoroughly. Remove and replace shelf paper. Keep foodstuffs in tightly closed clear containers so that the pests can be seen without removing the lid.

Wheelchair access

1. Make a ramp from planks covered with 16-millimetre plywood. Store it in the garage and use it to cover stairs, rough terrain or sand when you need wheelchair access.
2. To make it easy for a wheelchair to pass through narrow interior doorways, pop the hinge pins and remove the door. Keep the area behind other doors clear of wastebaskets, furniture and other items that might impede easy opening.
3. Tape down the latches on doorknobs so that doors can be pushed open and closed.
4. Tie short lengths of rope to the handles of sliding doors and refrigerators so that they can be pulled open without difficulty.

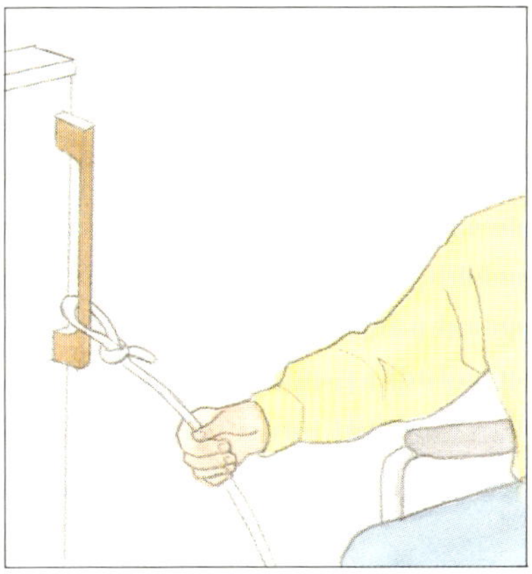

5. Take up all loose rugs, carpets and hallway carpet runners to provide a smooth floor surface. (See also *Walkers*, p.223.)

Whipped cream

1. For a substitute, whip a cup of nonfat dry milk powder in a cup of ice water for five minutes. Use it quickly, before the "cream" collapses.
2. Over-whipped cream can sometimes be salvaged by whipping in one or two tablespoons of evaporated milk. Or you can keep whipping, and pretty soon you'll have some sweet butter; drain off the liquid before using the butter on scrumptious hot scones or crumpets.

Wicker

1. Remove dust from wicker by vacuuming with the dust-brush attachment. To remove grime, wash with a solution of two tablespoons ammonia to five litres of water; use a paintbrush or a toothbrush to get at hard-to-reach places. Rinse well; air-dry in the shade, not direct sunlight.
2. To prevent wicker from drying out, wet it down at least once a year. Don't leave it outdoors when not in use – sunshine dehydrates wicker; water rots it.
3. Never strip paint from wicker or it will get brittle. Repaint instead, using spray paint.
4. For a smooth finish, remove any threadlike fibres from wicker by singeing them off with a gas torch before painting. Keep the flame moving so that you don't burn the reed.

Widowhood

Adjusting to the loss of a spouse takes time, no matter how well you manage the first few days or weeks or how much help you get. Not only must you absorb your grief, but you must learn what it is like to be single again.
1. Give yourself permission and time to mourn. Filling each day with activity will only delay and perhaps compound the grief.
2. Don't panic if you think you're losing your mind; grief, with its often accompanying lack of sleep, can cause erratic behaviour and many unusual feelings. If you weren't mentally ill before, you're not likely to become so now, even though you are under severe stress.
3. Beware of the temptation to rely on tranquillizers or alcohol to numb the pain; they will only postpone it and make matters worse.
4. Avoid making irreversible decisions during the first year; if you are contemplating a change, try it out first. Instead of quitting your job, ask for a leave of absence; consider renting your house rather than selling it.
5. Since stress may weaken your immune system, be extra careful: eat

balanced meals, exercise regularly, and report any physical problems to your doctor immediately.

6. It may help to talk to others who have felt what you are feeling now. If you don't know any widowed people and would really like to talk to a sympathetic listener, phone Life Line (see your telephone directory).

7. If you feel that your children aren't doing enough for you, it may be that they need more parenting than they did before. This is a difficult time for everyone; it helps to share your feelings with them.

Wigs & hairpieces

1. When the time comes to cut your long hair, why not save it for a perfectly matched hairpiece? Plait your hair, cut the plait off, then restyle your hair. Or cut your hair first, secure one end of the cuttings with a rubber band, and make a plait. When you want long hair, attach the plait to the underside of your own hair with hairclips and a small comb.

2. To get a wig of the right style, buy one with long hair and take it to a salon to have it custom-cut.

3. Need a wig stand? Use a cooldrink bottle with a roll of toilet paper over its neck.

4. If you have a wobbly wig stand, glue the bottom to an unwanted long-playing record.

5. The easiest way to hide baldness is with a hairpiece. Ask a friend who has one that looks good where he got it or consult a hair stylist or dermatologist. Most people need at least two so that one can be worn while the other is being cleaned and restored.

6. If you've lost hair because of illness or medical treatment, you may be entitled to reimbursement for your hairpiece under your medical aid plan. You'll need an explanatory letter from your doctor and the invoice from the wig manufacturer.

7. Avoid scalp irritations – keep your wig or hairpiece scrupulously clean by using a proper wig cleaner. Wash and condition your scalp or hair daily.

Wilderness sanitation

1. Don't bury leftover food at your campsite, particularly in areas where wild animals are common. The animals will just dig it up and perhaps bother the next camper in the vicinity. Carry out cans, bottles and food wastes when you leave.

2. Bury human faeces 10 to 25 centimetres deep. Save overlying sod to hide the hole. In areas of little soil, follow local recommendations for shallow burial and cover waste with whatever soil is available. Keep a small trowel next to the toilet paper at the campsite.

3. For a latrine that will be used by more than one person and have to decompose more waste, lengthen rather than deepen the hole.

4. Be sure that toilet areas are at least 50 metres from any watercourses, hiking trails and campsites.

5. Carry your own roll of toilet paper – in a small plastic bag – in your rucksack. Make sure that soiled paper is well buried, or burn it.

6. Improvise a toothbrush by chewing the end of a green (non-poisonous) twig. Use salt for toothpaste.

Wills

Your legally valid will provides instructions about what you wish to happen to your property after your death. If your will is not valid, or if you die without a will, your property is divided according to the laws of intestate succession, which may mean – if you have no blood relatives, for instance – that a large part of your estate, or even all of it, will go into the state coffers.

These laws also apply to any of your property not specifically mentioned in your will.

Any person of at least 16 years, who understands the consequences of his actions, may leave a will. The person leaving the will – the testator – must sign it at the end or, if it is longer than a single page, at the end of each page. Two witnesses must sign each page in the presence of the testator and each other. It is usual to appoint an executor, who is the person who will see to it that the terms of the will are carried out.

Alterations to the will, including deletions or the addition of a codicil (a new term added after the will has been signed), must be signed by the testator and two witnesses. Witnesses must be at least 14 years old.

A legacy means the specific item, whether property or cash, that you leave to a specified person or legatee.

Heirs are those who are nominated to receive the bulk or residue of your estate, after provision has been made for legacies, and debts and estate duty have been paid.

Keep the wording of your will plain and very clear. For instance, if you want a sum of money to be divided among your children, some of whom are stepchildren, you should specify "children and stepchildren" and, preferably, state the name of each one. You can buy will forms from legal stationers. If you choose to write your own will, ask your attorney to examine it.

Winch

1. If you need to lift the engine out of a car, and don't have several people to help you, the safest mechanism is a sturdy block and tackle, rigged to the rafters of your garage. If you have any doubt that the beam will not take the strain, push the car outside, and rig a tripod made from three gum poles at least 12 centimetres thick, with its apex securely roped together over the engine compartment of the car.

The pulley set is suspended from the apex of the tripod. You will need help – once the engine is out, one person will hold it suspended, while the other pushes the car back. If the engine is small, lower it onto a wheelbarrow. Alternatively, let it down onto a freight pallet (you can pick these up for nothing at many factories).

2. If the weight of whatever you need to haul resists moving when pulled, attach a block and tackle, and then use the method the Egyptians used to shift blocks of stone for the pyramids: roll the load slowly over the gumpoles, which roll like roller bearings beneath it.

3. To haul a car out of a ditch or a motorboat onto dry land, fix a block and tackle to a hefty tree trunk and the hauling end to the car or boat. Get some help if you can't pull it alone.

Windows

1. To keep windows from frosting over during winter, sponge them with salt water and wipe dry.

2. If your windows tend to fog up, wipe them with soap rubbed on a moist cloth; rinse and dry, then go over them with a glycerine-dampened cloth.

3. Hold a cracked pane together temporarily with adhesive tape.

4. For more privacy in a room, try frosting the window: brush it with a solution of one tablespoon Epsom salts in one cup beer. "Defrost" with concentrated ammonia.

5. To loosen sticky windows, lubricate the channels with silicone spray, a bar of soap or a candle.

6. When painting or varnishing windows, leave the metal channels and fittings alone. When dry, slide the windows up and down a few times or open and shut the casements to make sure nothing sticks.

7. To break a paint seal, force the blade of a putty knife between the sash and the frame; slide the blade up and down the length of the window and across the top and bottom until the window opens easily.

Window blinds

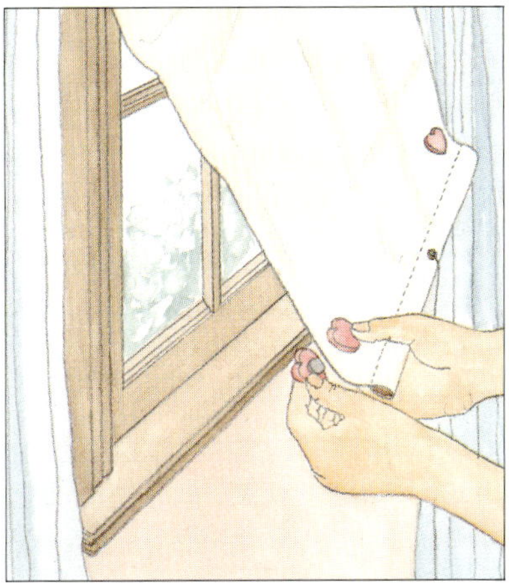

1. If a window blind tends to curl up at the bottom, you can usually weight it with matched pairs of refrigerator magnets or lead sinkers.

2. A towel can make an adequate temporary blind; secure it to the frame with drawing pins. Dark-coloured towels do the best job of blocking the sun's rays; lightweight white ones give a translucent glow.

3. Resurface worn blinds with new fabric affixed with rubber cement or spray-on adhesive. Bed sheets, cut to fit, are ideal for the purpose. Be careful to smooth on the new fabric so that there are no air bubbles, or the blind will wrinkle when it rolls up. Work on a clean, flat surface.

4. To remove stains and smudges from a window blind, lay it on a flat surface and clean the blemishes with an artgum eraser or a dough-type wallpaper cleaner.

5. If a blind won't stay down, easing the tension usually helps. Roll the blind up, remove it from its brackets, and unroll it by hand; then replace it in the brackets and roll it up again.

6. To put a window blind in a frame that is rounded or odd-shaped at the top, install the brackets at the base and a small pulley at the top; then run a cord through the pulley to raise and lower the blind.

Window treatment

1. Festoon fabric across the top of a frame, hanging it from knobs or tie-backs mounted at the corners. Then drape it in deep pleats down the sides. If the window is wide, loop or tack the fabric around a rod or wooden pole to make a decorative hanging around the window.

2. If you want to ensure total seclusion, make folding screens of light plywood. Cover them with fabric or wallpaper and hinge them to the inside of the window frames.

3. Make "stained glass" windows with glass paints and leading, available at some crafts shops. After painting your design on the window pane, outline its elements by squeezing strips of leading directly from the tube onto the window.

4. In winter have your kids decorate their windows with paper snowflakes. Take a square sheet of paper, fold it in half lengthways and then up into quarters. Fold again into thirds,

as shown in the illustration, and trim off the irregular corners at the bottom. To create a pretty snowflake pattern, make cuts in one of the folded edges – the closer you cut to the opposite edge, the more delicate the design will be. Unfold the snowflake and tape to the window.

Windscreens

1. Remove the haze which normal windscreen cleaning fluid will not shift, by applying full-strength household vinegar. Rinse with water and wipe dry.
2. Foggy windscreen? A blackboard duster works better than cloth.
3. Deal with smearing by cleaning the windscreen and the wipers with methylated spirits on a soft cloth. Clean the windscreen first.

Windscreen wipers

Are your wipers doing a poor job? Before buying new blades, clean both the glass and blades thoroughly. If you've had your car cleaned at the car wash, you may have to use a mild household abrasive cleaner to remove any silicone wax. If that doesn't do the trick, try the following:

1. Water beads are usually the result of grease or silicone buildup. Clean the windscreen with the solvent used for removing grease or silicone from the car's bodywork.
2. To end smearing, clean wiper blades with a cloth dipped in a 50-50 solution of water and methylated spirits. Wipe the windscreen with household vinegar.
3. If the wipers are smearing in only one direction or if they chatter, the blades may be frozen. Warm them between your hands or use a hair dryer; if that doesn't help, dip them in warm water.
4. Chattering may also be caused by a bent wiper arm. In this case, stop the wipers in midstroke to see if they are parallel to the windscreen. If an arm is bent, straighten it with two pairs of pliers until it remains parallel to the glass when released. If the tip of the arm is bent, remove the blade before you straighten the arm. The problem may also be corroded joints. Free them up with penetrating solvent.
5. Streaking may occur when the nozzle of the windscreen sprayer is blocked; insert a needle to clear it. Or the windscreen washing fluid may not be spraying in the wiper's path; straighten the nozzle with needle-nose pliers or a screwdriver and keep checking until the spray pattern is on target. Some types of nozzle aren't adjustable; don't force them.
6. If the blade on the driver's side isn't working, switch it with the one on the passenger's side.
7. Before driving in the rain, rub your wiper blades with bicarbonate of soda – you'll see better.

DID YOU KNOW . . . ?

In vino veritas

□ An old wives' tale said that the cure for rabies was to drink a glass of wine containing a few hairs taken from a rabid dog. Hence our folk remedy of taking a drink to cure a hangover – "the hair of the dog that bit you".
□ Dom Perignon, a Benedictine monk, discovered in the 17th century how to create and retain the natural sparkle in champagne. Upon his first sip he is said to have called out to his brothers: "Come quickly! I am drinking stars!"
□ According to legend, the shape of the first wine chalice was inspired by the breasts of Helen of Troy. Centuries later the buxom Marie Antoinette of France had champagne glasses made in the shape of her breasts. Today the narrower tulip-shaped and flute glasses are preferred because they prevent champagne from losing its bubbles as quickly.
□ Jan van Riebeeck, first commander at the Cape, ordered vine stock from Holland as early as May 1652 (remember, he only arrived in April), but it took three years for healthy plants to arrive. These were planted, and on 2 February 1659 Van Riebeeck wrote that the first wine had been produced.
□ The average wine consumption in South Africa is 11 bottles per person a year. The average person in France drinks more than 110 bottles annually.
□ South Africa has 4,731 farmers who grow grapes for wine production. The wine is produced at 70 co-operative cellars and 82 estate wineries.

Wine

1. To decide how many bottles you'll need for a dinner, follow this rule: a standard bottle is generally ample for three people, a half-bottle for two.
2. If you intend serving two dinner wines, remember this simple protocol: white before red, young wine before old. And a dry wine always precedes a sweet one; the sweet taste will linger. Save your sweet wines to serve with dessert.
3. Uncork red wines an hour before drinking so that they can "breathe" and develop flavour; then serve at room temperature. Chill whites and rosés but don't uncork them until you're ready to serve.
4. Don't throw out wine left in the bottle. Recorked, it will keep in the refrigerator for a few days.
5. Even if you don't have a cellar, any dark corner with some humidity and no vibration can be turned into a wine storage area. A dark cupboard, a fireplace with a blocked-off chimney or a corner of a well-insulated garage will all do. Keep the temperature as close to 10°C as possible.
6. If you don't have a wine rack, use empty cardboard liquor cases with dividers; some bottle stores are quite happy to give them away.
7. Most bottles of wine are stored horizontally to ensure that the cork stays moist. Ensure that the cork is completely covered when you store your wines. If the cork is allowed to dry, there is a risk of that great spoiler of wines – air – entering the bottle.
8. Although cork is the traditional closure for wine bottles, the humble screwcap is more efficient, and is likely to be more widely used in future as

cork sources are unable to keep up with demand.

9. However small or modest your private "cellar" may be, keep a cellar record book. You'll be surprised what interesting reading it will make after only a year or two.

Be sure to keep a note of prices, vintage (it doesn't always appear on the label), dates bought and consumed, and comments on tasting.

10. When buying wines, particularly a rare or expensive wine, hold the bottle to the light to check the level of the wine. If it has been well stored, the bottle should be almost as full as it can be. A level that has dropped well below the cork suggests that the wine may be oxidized and therefore undrinkable.

WINE WITH FOOD

If you're serving fish and light meats, such as chicken or veal, choose a dry white wine or a light-bodied red. Generally, the more delicately flavoured the fish or meat is, the lighter the wine can be.

For red meats, such as roast beef or steak, red wines are a popular choice. They also taste good with dark-meat birds, such as duck, and with various pastas and cheese-based dishes. Sweet wine or late harvest is usually served with desserts, but some prefer it simply on its own.

When serving any wine observe these simple rules:

1. All white and pink wines should be served chilled.

2. Medium-dry as well as dry sherries should be served slightly chilled.

3. Nearly all other red wines are served at room temperature.

Wine stains

1. If you spill wine on your clothing or a tablecloth, blot it up immediately with an absorbent cloth, then sponge with soda water or cool water. If the fabric is washable, stretch the stained area over a pot (hold it in place with a heavy rubber band), put salt on it, and pour boiling water through from 30 centimetres above. (If boiling water would harm the fabric, just cover the stain with moistened salt.) Wash normally with detergent.

2. On non-washable fabrics, cover the stain with a pad moistened with a mixture of detergent, water and a few drops of vinegar; then rinse. Dry-clean as soon as possible.

3. If red wine is spilled on your carpet, sponge it with soda water. Or cover the stain with salt and let it absorb the wine; vacuum the residue. If a stain remains, wipe gently with a solution of detergent, water and a few drops of white vinegar.

Wires

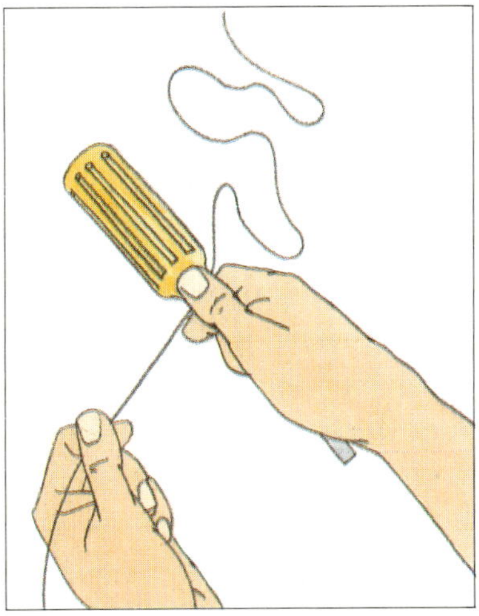

1. Avoid electrical wires housed inside walls that you might need to drill to hang pictures or shelves. Avoid drilling above or below light switches or below wall sockets.

2. Straighten kinks in thin electrical wire by drawing it between your thumb and a screwdriver handle as though you were combing long hair. After a few passes, the wire will have a long, uniform curve that makes it easy to roll into coils.

Withered plants

Foliage wilting in the garden? It's not necessarily a sign of dry soil; it may just be a reaction to hot summer wind. If the plant revives at sunset, everything's fine. But if the foliage still droops in the morning, water at once. Don't flood the garden; sprinkle only until the soil is moist to a depth of 12 to 15 centimetres. Then stretch some water-soaked hessian sacking between stakes to shade the wilted plant until it revives.

To revive a withered house plant, plunge its pot into a bucket of tepid water. Let it soak until bubbles stop rising from the soil. Drain the excess water and set the plant in a humid spot such as a bathroom or greenhouse. Or cover the plant with a transparent plastic bag, supporting the plastic with a frame of stakes or coat hanger wire so that it doesn't touch the plant. Secure the bag to the pot's rim with twine or a large rubber band.

Witnessing a crime

1. When you see a crime being committed, call the police at once; don't assume that someone else already has. And don't feel intimidated – there's no need to give your name or address over the telephone when describing what you've seen. Or, if you have any information about a crime, you can phone the Crimestop toll-free number – 0800-111213 – and give your information anonymously.

2. Don't linger near the scene of a crime. Wait at a safe distance for the arrival of the police.

3. If you see a street crime from indoors, call the police, then open a window and shout that the police are on their way. (Move away fast.)

4. To help the police, write down a description of the criminal or criminals while your memory is still fresh (height? build? hair and skin colour? clothing?) and the make, model, colour and licence number of the vehicle if you know them. Jot down exactly what happened from beginning to end, then doublecheck yourself by going over the story backward, from the end to the beginning.
5. If you hear screams or other loud or unusual noises coming from a neighbour's home, telephone the police. Don't try to investigate or interfere yourself.

Wobbly furniture

1. First, check to see that all screws and bolts are tight.
2. For a quick fix on a glued joint like that of a chair rung, pull the dowel out of the socket as far as you can (take care not to break another joint). Soften the old glue and scrape it from both the dowel and its socket. Apply wood glue all around the dowel, shove it back into the socket, and wiggle it to spread the glue. Wipe off any excess with a damp cloth and apply a tourniquet clamp until the glue is dry.

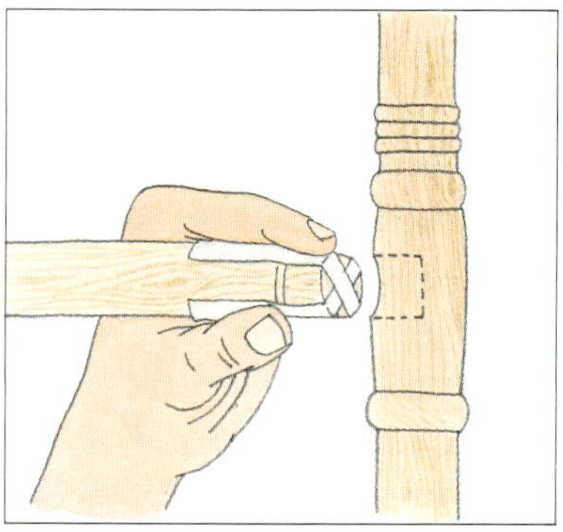

3. If a screw or dowel is loose because the wood has dried out and the hole is too big, push glue-dipped flat toothpicks in beside it to tighten the fit. Or wrap the end with a piece of paper before pushing it into the joint. Or cut two strips of cloth a bit narrower than the dowel's tip and hold them over it before inserting in the glue-primed hole; use a razor to trim off any visible cloth.
4. If a table or chair leg is shorter than the others, force it into a glob of wood putty placed on a piece of wax paper.

When it's even with the other legs (check with a spirit level), use a knife to scrape away excess putty. Then let the putty dry, sand it smooth, and finish as you wish.

Wood filler

1. Save the sawdust when you are doing heavy sanding on a woodworking project. Mixed with cold glue it makes a good-as-store-bought crack filler. If mixed with clear epoxy, it makes a durable, waterproof filler that will not shrink.
2. If you do buy filler, choose one based on a fine clay or silex for interior work, and solvent-based varieties (which are waterproof) for any exterior work.
3. If you are going to stain your woodwork, use a woodfiller that will accept stain; alternatively, choose a filler the shade of the stained wood you are filling.

Wood-finishing

There are several ways to ensure that the surface of a prized or handworked piece of furniture is properly protected or beautified. Whichever course you follow – sealing with lacquer or varnish or an oil finish – the most important ingredient of all is probably patience.

Everything except new items will require attention to the existing finish, which is usually best stripped away. In some cases, though, even an imperfect finish is preferable to revealing the bare wood. This is especially true of antique furniture that has acquired a distinctive patina or gloss through many years of wear and use.

A gentle wash with a mild detergent is all that should be attempted. Oil the surface sparingly with tung oil or a synthetic-resin oil.

When you've stripped an old surface and made the necessary repairs, allow time for the wood to dry evenly, then sand with fine (120) paper, finishing with very fine grit – 220 for softwoods and 280 for hardwoods.

Then wet the surface slightly with water, to raise the grain, and note the colour. This is close to what the appearance will be with a clear lacquer.

When the wood is dry, sand again with very fine paper and be careful to remove all particles of dust, using a vacuum cleaner and a tack cloth.

If the wood has a pleasing grain, it will be enhanced by a penetrating oil finish. Apply the oil freely and rub well, applying more oil to localized patches that show a dull appearance. Remove excess oil after one hour, and repeat oiling and rubbing after at least 24 hours. A third application may be required after a further 24 hours, and should be gently rubbed with 0000 steel wool that has been dipped in the oil. Wipe dry, and do not use for at least 24 hours.

When veneer has to be replaced, lay a matching veneer over the damaged section, line up the grain and cut a boat-shaped piece, larger than the damaged section, through old and new veneers.

Peel away the damaged veneer, and remove old glue and dust. Apply contact glue to the exposed wood and to the patch, and press the patch firmly in place. It may be necessary to build up the level of the patch with several layers to allow for loss of thickness when sanding.

Oil and polish slowly to match the existing finish.

For a very hard, durable finish that will completely seal the surface, use lacquer to varnish.

Wood floors

On waxed floors you should always remove food or dried milk stains with a damp cloth, water stains with superfine steel wool, and heel marks with fine steel wool dipped in floor cleaner or mineral spirits.

For alcohol spots use boiled linseed oil, silver polish or a cloth dampened with ammonia.

Harden old crayon marks, chewing gum or candle wax with an ice cube in a plastic bag, then scrape off with a blunt knife or your fingernail. Or pour cleaning fluid around the spot to loosen it. In all cases, after the floor has dried, rewax if necessary and polish to regain the shine.

Wood preservatives

Almost all timber – with the exception of a few hardwoods such as stinkwood, jarrah and mahogany – will rot when exposed to moisture outdoors, and so needs to be treated with a preservative. Although paint provides a protective, sealant covering, it is not a preservative, and painted wood is susceptible to a number of destructive agents, including fungi.

If you can't buy timber that has been impregnated under pressure with a protective solution, check the range of preservatives at your hardware store, and use the least toxic preparation for your particular purpose. Remember that preservatives can't penetrate moist timber, so apply them on a hot day, when the timber is likely to be dry. If possible, soak the timber, by standing it end-up in the preservative container.

Wrapping packages

1. Do you want that package tied really tight? Moisten the twine before tying; it will dry snugly.
2. Protect small items by hollowing out a firm bath sponge and fitting the object snugly inside.
3. Save any large paper packets or carrier bags – the paper is usually quite strong and ideal for wrapping parcels. Even a sugar packet, turned inside out, makes good, strong wrapping paper for a small parcel.
4. Not sure how much paper you'll need? Wind a piece of twine around the package and add five centimetres. Measure the length the same way.
5. To cushion an object in its packing box, use balled-up newspaper, yarn, old clothes or popcorn. Cushion small objects in cottonwool or tissues.

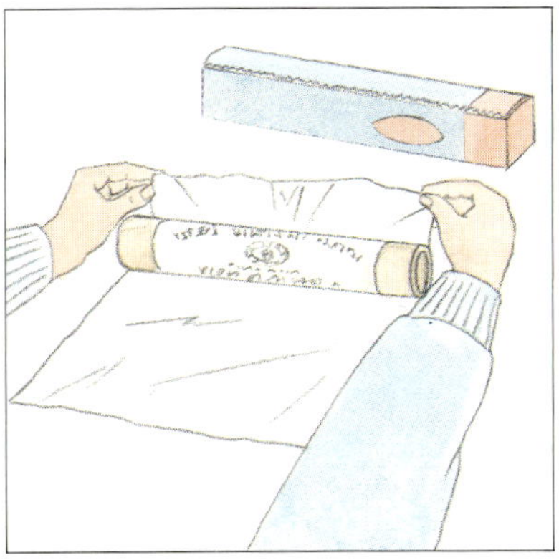

6. If you have papers to post that you don't want to fold, wrap them around the cardboard tube from a box of aluminium foil. Cover with paper or foil, place back in the aluminium foil box, wrap and post.

Wrench

1. When possible, pull rather than push a wrench handle; it's easier and more efficient.
2. The longer a wrench handle, the more leverage it will give. To add extra muscle, slip a piece of pipe over it. (But use common sense – too much pipe breaks tools.)
3. A series of sharp tugs works better than an extended pull in loosening a seized nut. For a really hard case, tap the wrench handle with a mallet or piece of planking.
4. To protect the finish of plumbing fixtures, cover the teeth of a pipe wrench with several layers of insulation or cloth tape.
5. If a wrench isn't available, try a set of locking-grip pliers. The next alternative is offset pliers, then standard slipjoint pliers. (See also *Belts*, p.289.)
6. To turn a large nut or secure a bolt head, try a C-clamp.
7. If nothing seems to work and the item is portable, lock the nut in a vice and turn the item itself.

Wrinkles

1. To slow the wrinkling process, apply a sunscreen whenever you go out, even during winter. Put sunscreen on children, too.
2. In dry areas, use a good moisturizing cream, particularly before retiring at night.
3. Prevent your skin from becoming weatherbeaten – protect it from harsh winds, intense cold and biting salt sprays from the sea.
4. Don't make faces: don't frown, squint, scowl, grimace or purse your lips. To prevent overusing facial muscles, stick cellophane tape on areas prone to wrinkling.
5. To prevent temporarily creasing your face, make a special effort to sleep on your back.
6. Make a short-term anti-wrinkle mask: apply a beaten egg white to your face for 10 minutes, then rinse off. Your face should look smoother for a few hours afterward.
7. Apply a cloth soaked in witch hazel to frown lines for five minutes at a time.
8. Rub a light eye cream on outer-eye lines. Then open your eyes wide, press the heels of your hands against the areas, and hold for a minute; repeat daily. (See also *Dry skin*, p.68.)

XYZ

Yoga

Much more than just "exercise", yoga is based on a Hindu system of integrated spiritual, mental and physical training, especially beneficial to those suffering from stress and stress-related problems. In Western countries, Hatha yoga, the form that accentuates the physical aspect of yoga, is the most popular.

Yoga is best learned from a qualified teacher, and should be practised regularly – preferably daily. Taking a shower before and after yoga adds to the relaxation. Try a few basic postures on your own.

Bow: Lie face down keeping the feet together. Bring your feet up until you can grasp your ankles. Breathe in and pull on your ankles to raise thighs, chest and head off the floor. Resting on your abdomen, hold arms straight and keep the pose for up to 10 breaths, then breathe out and release your legs.

Bridge: Lie on your back with arms at your sides, knees bent and legs slightly apart. Breathe in and raise your body from knees to shoulders. Interlock your fingers and stretch arms out straight on the floor, at the same time pushing with your feet to raise the bridge higher.

Tuck your shoulders beneath you, and lean first towards one, then the other. Breathe in with your abdomen and hold for a minute, then lower your body and straighten your legs.

Spinal twist: Sit with legs extended, then place your right foot on the outside of your left knee. Breathe out, turning your trunk to the right and reaching for your left ankle with your left hand, but try to keep your back straight by resting your right hand on the floor behind you. With each breath, twist a little further to the right, holding each position for one minute. Repeat by twisting to the left.

For information about yoga teachers, write to the Yoga Teachers Fellowship of Southern Africa, PO Box 6929, Brackendowns 1454.

Yoghurt

Here's a simple method for making your own yoghurt. You will need the following ingredients: five cups of skim or whole milk; ¼ cup skim milk powder; one tablespoon of starter (yoghurt culture). Dried culture is available at food stores.

Mix the milk and the powder, then heat it to just below boiling point. Allow the mixture to cool to 45°C before adding the starter. Incubate until it has reached the desired consistency, then refrigerate.

METHODS OF INCUBATING YOGHURT

1. Wrap the just-filled bottling jar in a wool blanket or down jacket.
2. Put it in a box along with a hot-water bottle, and pack crumpled newspapers loosely around both.
3. Turn an electric blanket to its lowest setting and wrap it around the jar containing the yoghurt mixture.
4. Set the jar in a metal box with a glowing Christmas tree bulb.
5. Put it in a gas oven with only the heat from the pilot light.
6. Turn on the TV and set the yoghurt jar on top.

Zen gardens

The aim of a Zen garden is to provide a peaceful, tranquil setting for contemplation and meditation. You do not need a huge garden – with careful planning, the corner of a patio can become a Zen garden.

1. Plan your garden before you start. Decide on the location and consider the proportions of the area – a sense of peaceful balance is your aim.
2. The central focus of the garden is the "shrine", which is made up of an arrangement of rocks. Search for three or four rocks which have pleasing shapes. They need not be huge – choose the correct size and shape for your site.
3. Place the rocks off-centre in an arrangement which is natural and attractive. Balance is the keyword.
4. For a really simple garden, lay down some gravel or cut the grass in front of the rocks.
5. If you have a big garden, you may decide to build an interwoven mixture of flowerbeds and gravel paths.
6. On a patio or in a small garden, enclose your Zen garden with plant containers to provide privacy.
7. Visit your local library and consult books on Japan and Zen Buddhist temples to familiarize yourself with the construction of the gardens.
8. For further information on Zen Buddhism, write to the Dharma Centre, Heldervue Homestead, 16 Prunus Street, Heldervue, Somerset West 7130.

Zips

1. To make a zip work smoothly, run a candle up and down the teeth. If it's really sticky, try using wax paper.
2. If you've broken the pull tab of your zip, use a safety pin or paperclip.

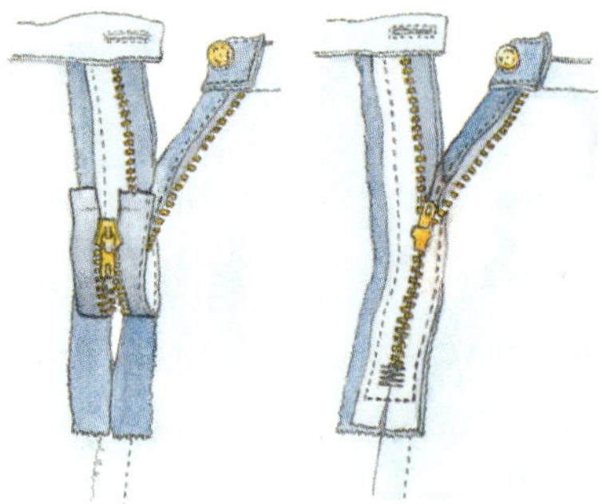

3. Has your zip pulled apart at the bottom? Carefully undo the stitching, remove the stop, and separate the zip completely. Put the sides back into the pull and zip it up. Then run a zigzag stitch across the bottom of the zip, creating a new stop.
4. Before inserting a zip, press the underside of the tape to smooth out the folds; if the teeth are plastic, be careful not to iron over them.
5. Preshrink tape that is not 100 percent polyester by submerging the zip in hot water for three minutes; then let the tape dry before pressing it flat.

2. CHARTS & CHECKLISTS

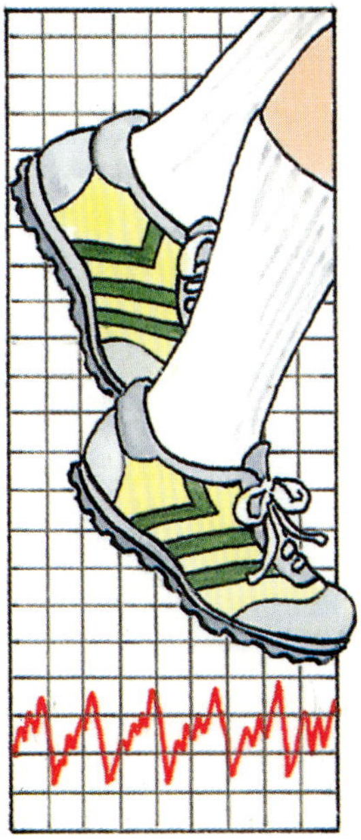

Do you want to get organized? Stay healthy? Prepare for a pleasant retirement? If so, the next 46 pages – filled with more than 80 charts, checklists and quizzes on these and many other subjects – can be important to you. Here you'll find facts at a glance on everything from tipping to tools, buying a home to selling one, stretching a budget to stretching a recipe.

The paper chase: organizing important papers

Financial documents	Shares 	Bonds 	Bank book 	Cancelled cheques 	Income tax returns 
Insurance policies	Life 	Health 	Homeowner's 	Car 	Valuables 
Certificates	Birth and adoption 	Marriage 	Divorce 	Citizenship 	Death 
Numbers	Medical aid 	Credit cards 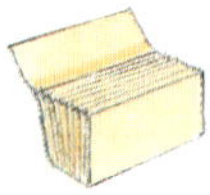	PIN numbers 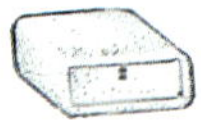	Personal ID 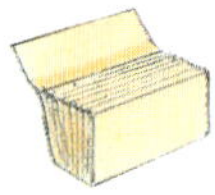	Bank accounts 
Legal documents	Will (copy)*  	Power of attorney 	Contracts 	Deeds 	Mortgages 
Personal documents	Personal property inventory 	Pension plans 	Academic diplomas 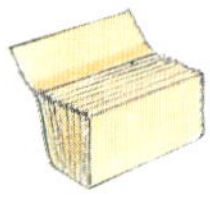	Passports 	Military discharge papers 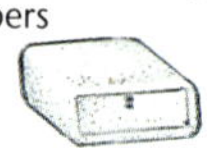

*Leave original with your lawyer.

KEY

Personal file	Safe-deposit box	Fireproof strongbox

A foolproof filing system

☐ For your own files, an alphabetical system will suffice. For a family file, use a colour-coded system. Or you can combine the two.

☐ Gather all the papers to be filed and make a list of general categories, such as receipts, contracts, correspondence and insurance.

☐ Make a separate folder for each category and label it. File each document in its appropriate folder.

☐ If an item falls under more than one category, make copies. Or note its location on index cards for other relevant folders.

☐ If any misfits remain that don't call for their own folders, store them in a *Miscellaneous* file.

☐ Within each folder, place items in chronological order, with the most recent item in front.

☐ Review the contents of a folder periodically; toss obsolete material into the nearest wastepaper basket.

☐ Staple material together – paper clips snag and rubber bands snap.

☐ If you don't have time to file regularly, keep items in a *To file* folder so that they don't get lost.

☐ If you remove material for an extended period, leave a note in its folder to remind you where it is.

☐ File business cards separately in a handy business card holder.

☐ Establish a weekly and monthly *Tickler* file to remind you of important deadlines.

Cures for the chronic procrastinator

- Break the chronic procrastinator's habit: whenever you catch yourself thinking, "I can do it later", stop and make a point of doing it then.
- Tell others about your goals so that you'll have extra motivation to accomplish them.
- Eliminate distractions, even if it means locking the door or taking the phone off the hook.
- Make plans that require you to complete your chores by a certain time or date.
- If a project is large or complex, break it down into smaller, more manageable parts.
- Ask yourself: "Is there an easier way to do this?"
- Don't wait until you have time to finish the entire task. Do as much as you can whenever you can.
- Set firm but realistic deadlines for yourself.
- Start with the simplest or the most enjoyable part of a job, even if it's not the first logical step. The rest will be a whole lot easier once you have gained momentum.
- Or try the opposite strategy: tackle the toughest part of the project first so that you can coast if your energy or enthusiasm runs out later on.
- Deal with smaller projects or problems as soon as possible, but in order of priority.
- Make a list of everything you have to do, and don't stop until you've checked off every item.
- Don't be a perfectionist; you can polish your work as much as you wish but only after you've made some headway.
- Don't interrupt yourself by starting another task before you've completed the first one.
- Remember that buckling down to a task, although it seems hard at first, really makes your life easier in the long run.
- Treat yourself to a small reward for each deadline you meet.

Protecting personal time

- Ask friends, relatives or co-workers to phone before they drop by.
- Post a list of where everything in the house is stored, and train family members to help themselves.
- Teach children that a closed door means "Do Not Disturb". If necessary, post the message on the door as well.
- Invest in a telephone answering machine.
- Interruptions provide a good excuse to avoid work; resist the temptation to extend them by prolonging a conversation.
- If you don't want to cut a telephone conversation short, keep small, easy projects nearby and complete them while you're talking.
- If you can't concentrate at home, take your work to the office, and don't tell anyone where you're going.
- If you don't have a receptionist at work, ask a willing co-worker to take your calls, and offer to return the favour when she's busy.

How to get out of the house on time

1995 — Week 1 — Tuesday 3 January

MORNING:	
0600	Make the bed as soon as you get up.
0630	Turn on the radio instead of the television.
0700	Schedule bathroom times for each family member.
0730	Allow extra time for unexpected delays.
0800	Save the newspaper for later in the day.
EVENING:	
1700	Put your keys in the same place every night.
1730	Put a clock in every room, including the bathroom.
1800	Prepare the next day's lunch before bedtime.
1830	Use disposable tableware if you don't have a dishwasher.
1900	Set the table for breakfast straight after dinner.
1930	Take your bath or shower before you go to bed.
2000	Lay out your clothes the night before.

INVESTING IN YOUR FUTURE

Type	Explanation	Sources	Advantages	Disadvantages
Annuity	Provides fixed income for life or for minimum number of years	Life assurance companies, brokerage firms	High returns for elderly, no risk	Interest taxable, non-transferable and cannot be used as collateral
Fixed deposit	Money deposited for specified period (from 31 days to five years) at fixed minimum interest rate	Banks, building societies	No risk, higher yield than ordinary savings	Penalty for early withdrawal; usually non-negotiable except with institution holding deposit
Preference shares	Shares owned in a public company	Banks, brokerage firms	Low risk; stable dividends paid before those of ordinary shares; from one third tax-free; easily converted to cash	Lower appreciation potential than ordinary shares
Ordinary shares	Shares owned in a public company	Banks, brokerage firms	Potentially high profits; from one third tax-free; easily converted to cash	High risk; wide daily fluctuations; brokerage fees
Real estate	Investment in land or buildings	Owner of deed; estate agents; brokerage firms	Hard asset; value usually appreciates; can yield regular income	Not liquid; possible management costs; large capital amounts needed
Debentures	Long-term, fixed interest bond issued by a public company	Banks, brokerage firms	High income, paid as interest; low risk; can usually be converted to ordinary shares	Income fully taxable
Unit trusts	Group long-term investment through a management company on the stock exchange	Banks, life assurance companies, brokerage firms	Potentially high returns; only interest portion taxable; easily converted to cash	Moderate risk; wide daily fluctuations
Participation mortgage bonds	Units in large loans on commercial and industrial properties, administered by financial institutions	Banks, brokerage firms	High income that fluctuates with inflation rate; low risk; negotiable and can be used as collateral	Income fully taxable; capital usually not redeemable before five years
Mortgage loans	Money lent against security of a bond on fixed property	Estate agents, brokerage firms	High income that fluctuates with inflation rate	Higher risk than participation mortgage bond scheme; not readily negotiable or usable as collateral; income fully taxable
Retirement annuities	Long-term savings for retirement	Life assurance companies, brokerage firms	Interest and capital untaxed until retirement; contributions tax-deductible up to set limits	Money locked-in until retirement; cannot be used as collateral; no surrender value
Endowment policies	Long-term savings for retirement	Life assurance companies; brokerage firms	Medium-rate tax-free returns; very low risk	Money locked-in for at least 10 years; tax penalty for early surrender
Loan stock	Issued, to raise loans, by the Treasury, public corporations such as municipalities, and some private companies	Banks, brokerage firms, Post Office (Treasury bonds only)	Usually medium-rate returns, depending on risk, which is lowest with Treasury bonds, highest with uncertain companies; fully negotiable and may be used as collateral	Interest fully taxable, except that Treasury bonds are tax-free up to a set limit
Subscription shares	Fixed-value investments issued by financial institutions	Banks, building societies, brokerage firms	Low risk; dividends enjoy tax privileges; interest rates usually free to rise; can be used as collateral	Cannot readily be converted to cash

Although the national economy and market conditions fluctuate, financial experts still agree on two basic rules: never buy medium- or high-risk securities before you have put aside the equivalent of at least six months' income in safe, liquid assets. When you can set aside money for investment, aim for diversity.

Your annual budget planner

INCOME

Your take-home pay ______
Spouse's take-home pay ______
Bonuses ______
Part-time work ______
Interest ______
Dividends ______
Tenant's rent ______

TOTAL INCOME R ______

EXPENSES

Housing
- ☐ Rent ______
- ☐ Mortgage ______
- ☐ Maintenance ______
- ☐ Repair ______
- ☐ Improvement ______

Utilities
- ☐ Telephone ______
- ☐ Gas ______
- ☐ Water ______
- ☐ Fuel ______
- ☐ Electricity ______
- ☐ Computer services ______
- ☐ TV and radio licences ______

Rates and Taxes
- ☐ Receiver of Revenue ______
- ☐ Property ______

Car
- ☐ Maintenance, repairs ______
- ☐ Petrol ______
- ☐ Licence ______
- ☐ Repayments ______

Insurance
- ☐ Retirement annuity ______
- ☐ Life ______
- ☐ Householder's ______
- ☐ Motor vehicle ______
- ☐ Medical aid ______
- ☐ Disability ______

Medical (not reimbursed)
- ☐ Doctor ______
- ☐ Dentist ______
- ☐ Prescription drugs ______
- ☐ Spectacles ______

Clothing
- ☐ New garments ______
- ☐ Laundry, dry-cleaning ______

Transportation
- ☐ Travelling expenses ______
- ☐ Garage ______
- ☐ Taxi ______

Recreation
- ☐ Dining out ______
- ☐ Books and magazines ______
- ☐ Movies, theatre ______
- ☐ Holidays ______
- ☐ Hobbies ______

Gifts
- ☐ Birthday ______
- ☐ Anniversary ______
- ☐ Seasonal ______
- ☐ Wedding ______

Tuition ______
Furnishings, appliances ______
Food & beverages ______
Loan repayments ______
Contributions ______
Regular savings ______
Veterinary expenses ______
Other

TOTAL EXPENSES R ______

Total income minus total expenses = R to save or invest.

QUIZ

Are you an overspender?

Do you spend money on the assumption that your income will rise?

Do you fail to keep an accurate record of your purchases?

Do you hide your purchases from your family?

Do you often fail to pay your monthly bills on time?

Do you own more than five credit cards?

Does having several credit cards make you feel richer?

Do you spend more than 20 percent of your income on credit card bills?

Do you tend to make only the minimum payment on your credit card bills?

Do you take cash advances on one credit card to pay the balance on another?

Do you often pay for groceries with a credit card?

When you eat in a restaurant, do you collect cash from friends and then pay the bill with your credit card?

Do you have trouble imagining how you would survive without any credit at all?

If you answered *yes* to four or fewer questions, you're probably not an overspender.

If you answered *yes* to five to eight questions it's time to pay off your debts and follow a strict budget.

If you answered *yes* to nine or more questions, consult a credit counsellor or financial planner for help in changing your spending habits.

Income tax countdown

If you receive an income tax return, or if your annual gross income, minus pension contributions, is R50,000 or more, you must complete and submit an income tax return.

You must also submit a return if you earn more than R2,000 in annual interest, if your income is derived partly or entirely from commission, or if you are registered as a provisional taxpayer.

What could be more satisfying than to have your income tax return completely organized, filled in, and signed well before the dreaded due date – usually early in June?

Remember, if you are completing your income tax return by yourself, and you need help or advice, the office of the Receiver of Revenue has staff who will be able to assist you free of charge. Telephone your local Receiver of Revenue for more information.

January

- ☐ Using salary slips, chequebook stubs, bank statements and receipts, estimate your taxable income and deductions.
- ☐ Using last year's tax tables – or the current ones if you can obtain a copy – roughly calculate what you can expect to pay in taxes. If you owe a large sum, try to pay tax-deductible expenses before the end of the tax year – the last day of February – to gain the deduction for the current year. Or, if you can, defer some income to beyond the end of February so that it need be counted only in the next tax year.

February

- ☐ Assemble your records for the current year's expenses.
- ☐ If you were exempt from PAYE or SITE in the current tax year, find out from your employer whether this will continue in the new tax year.
- ☐ If you moved to another town or district during the current tax year, check that you advised the Receiver of Revenue of your move, and ask whether you will be dealing with the same office.
- ☐ Consult your accountant about changes in the tax law, especially deductions, in the new tax year. Adjust your spending, investments and your files accordingly.

March

- ☐ Start keeping records for the new tax year.
- ☐ If you have not received IRP forms from your employer, and income tax certificates from your insurance company, bank or medical aid society to record deductible premiums paid during the current year, report the oversight to them.
- ☐ If you are preparing your own return, consult a current-year tax guide.
- ☐ Review your salary records, chequebook stubs, bank statements and receipts; make a list of expenses that you can claim as deductions.
- ☐ List your sources of income, including salary, interest, dividends, capital gains, professional fees and pensions.
- ☐ If tax forms haven't arrived in the post, advise your local tax office. You can find out the address at the local magistrate's court.
- ☐ Obtain all relevant information regarding income and deductions from your spouse or spouse's employer.
- ☐ Once you have all the documentation you need, make an appointment with your accountant or tax consultant.

April

- ☐ If you have valid reasons for doing so, apply for an extension of time for submitting your completed return.
- ☐ Provide your tax consultant with all necessary records and information.
- ☐ Sign the forms and be sure to make photocopies for your files.
- ☐ If you completed the forms yourself, be sure to keep copies of all calculations.
- ☐ Review completed tax forms for errors and omissions.

May

- ☐ Send your completed return, and all supporting documents by registered post to the Receiver of Revenue.

Where to complain

1. Salesperson or supervisor. Talk calmly; avoid anger.

2. Direct to the company or producer. If it's urgent, you can register your complaint by telephone (many companies have toll-free lines). In most cases, it's probably preferable to write, and send your letter by registered post. Ask the store manager to provide an address for the company. Alternatively, look at transaction documents or product labels – they may carry the telephone number or company address.

Keep your letter reasonably short, polite and to the point. Set it out in the format below.

> Your address
> Date
>
> The Manager
> Company name
> Company address
>
> Dear ________
>
> ☐ Item or service: date/place/make & model/serial number/nature of service
> ☐ Problems experienced/steps taken so far
> ☐ Resolution wanted – what you expect the company to do
> ☐ Expect a reply by _______ .
>
> Yours faithfully
>
> Your signature
>
> Your name printed clearly

3. Consumer advocates. Contact newspapers, periodicals, radio and TV stations.

4. Advice and aid. Most universities run legal aid clinics. Check with your local authority whether there is a Citizens' Advice Bureau in your town. The South African Co-ordinating Consumer Council issues a series of free brochures for the guidance of consumers.

10 CONSUMER CAVEATS

Do	Don't
. . . patronize local businesses; transient dealers can disappear if something goes wrong.	. . . write cash cheques. Write your cheque payable to the company, not to its representative.
. . . read all the fine print on the front and back of a contract. Get a full explanation – from an independent authority, if necessary – of any clause unclear to you.	. . . forget to shop around for prices and finance terms; ask whether delivery or installation will cost extra.
. . . keep and file your copy of any contract, warranty or large bill. Remember that in some stores, the till slip serves as your warranty – keep it, and keep your cancelled cheques.	. . . sign a contract with blank spaces in it; draw a line through them and initial each one.
. . . beware of any warranty or guarantee that tries to exclude your common law rights. Under common law, goods must be fit for the purpose for which they are sold.	. . . forget that the law allows you a five-day "cooling off period", after signing a credit agreement, in which you may cancel the agreement without suffering any loss.
. . . try to give preference to goods bearing the mark of the South African Bureau of Standards (SABS).	. . . be pressured into hasty decisions. If "this great offer expires in 24 hours", let it.

The address is: the South African Co-ordinating Consumer Council, Sixth Floor, Nedbank Plaza, cnr Church & Beatrix streets, Pretoria 0002, or telephone 012-3202000. Branch addresses of the Council are PO Box 881, Bellville 7535; PO Box 3906, Durban 4000; PO Box 6590, Bloemfontein 9300; PO Box 3544, Vereeniging 1939.

5. Trade and professional organizations. Ask at your library for addresses of bodies such as trade or professional organizations, that can help you as a consumer. Send a registered letter, similar to the one shown above, addressed to the secretary of the organization.

6. Small claims court (these cater for claims up to R2,000).

7. State or provincial licensing and regulatory bodies. If a company has a history of complaints against it, for fraud or for failing to comply with the terms of its licence, for instance, an official investigation may be launched.

8. Private attorney to file suit in civil court (for money amounts larger than those handled by small claims court). If you don't happen to know an attorney, or if a friend or colleague can't recommend one, you should consult the latest edition of Hortors Diary and Law List for Southern Africa at most larger public libraries. It is also available at most legal bookshops.

RESOURCES

Useful published references that can help you resolve unhappy transactions are:

☐ *You and your rights,* Reader's Digest South Africa (Pty) Ltd, Cape Town 1992.

☐ *The Help Directory,* Oxford University Press, Cape Town, 1991.

Are you a workaholic?

Does your life revolve around your job to the exclusion of family concerns, social pleasures and other interests? If so, you may be a workaholic. To find out, ask yourself the following questions:

1. Does your family complain that you're never home?
2. Do you lose sleep over certain work worries?
3. Do you get anxious about delegating work to your staff?
4. Has starting your workday early and ending it late become a habit?
5. Do you gobble your lunch while working at your desk?
6. Are you angry when co-workers don't work as hard as you do?
7. Is your work the only thing you find enjoyable?
8. Do interruptions in your workday annoy you?
9. When you have more work than you can handle, does it make you feel inadequate?
10. Do you find social events a waste of time?
11. Do you often work weekends?
12. Do you feel guilty when you take time off?
13. Can you leave work on your desk for the following day?
14. Do you always agree to take on more work?
15. Do you go to work when you're not feeling well?
16. Are you able to enjoy doing absolutely nothing?
17. Do hobbies interest you?
18. Do you find you get restless while on holiday?
19. If your doctor told you to slow down, could you?

If you answered *yes* to most of the first 15 questions and *no* to some of the questions between 16 and 19, you may be a workaholic. Do not, however, be alarmed. This is not necessarily unhealthy if work tends to give you real satisfaction. But it can be as dangerous as any addiction if it takes you unawares, and if you derive a lot of pleasure from nothing but work. If this is the case, try to slow down or look for a less demanding job.

Do you think you have the right work environment?

☐ Are your co-workers warm, friendly and courteous?
☐ Is your job so enjoyable that you do extra work after hours?
☐ Does your work constantly challenge your imagination?
☐ If you inherited a large sum of money, would you keep your present job indefinitely?
☐ Are your efforts appreciated to the full by your employers?
☐ Are you fairly paid?
☐ Does your day go by quickly?
☐ Is your job conveniently located?
☐ Are you allowed to take time off when personal emergencies arise?
☐ Are people promoted from within your organization?
☐ Is your work area pleasant?
☐ Are your special talents and skills utilized to the full?
☐ Is your boss very helpful, capable and encouraging?
☐ Do you feel that your boss shares responsibilities with you in the workplace?
☐ Does the benefits package match your needs?
☐ Could you transfer to another department if it made sense to do so?
☐ Do you believe that your superiors show integrity and sincerity in their dealings with you?
☐ Is your company concerned about the health and well-being of its employees?
☐ Is your routine varied enough to forestall boredom?
☐ Are your work hours right for you and your family?
☐ Does your work make a difference to the company?

If you answered *yes* to 15 or more of these questions, chances are you are well suited to the career you have chosen. If you didn't, you might consider changing careers, returning to university or a college of learning, or retiring early. A good place to start is a career planning course, which may put you on an exciting new path of personal growth and satisfaction.

Writing a convincing curriculum vitae (CV)

An accurate, well-documented curriculum vitae can go a long way towards securing a job. Whether you are new on the job market, or merely wish to change employers, put a lot of thought and time into developing your CV. It should be convincing and present your achievements honestly. Here are some points to remember when writing yours:

Use simple, clear language. Be brief – one page is enough.

Place your name, address and telephone number at the top.

Relate your curriculum vitae to the job being offered.

List former employers and the cities or towns in which they are located.

Give the dates of job changes and promotions. Describe the activities performed for each position.

Stress your achievements. Explain them with such action verbs as managed, taught, appointed.

Cite the universities you attended, graduation dates and degrees or diplomas earned.

Include your photograph and reveal your height and weight only if you are seeking work in the glamour, entertainment or certain sales professions.

Divulge your age and your present marital status.

Define your job objective clearly in your curriculum vitae or in a covering letter.

State special interests if they relate to the job you want.

Spell correctly and be careful to avoid grammatical errors.

Supply the full names, business addresses, telephone numbers and titles of references upon request.

Forget gimmicky curriculum vitaes – ones printed on coloured paper or delivered with flowers. They're generally inappropriate. Do, however, make sure that the overall presentation of your CV is businesslike, neat and ordered.

EVALUATING A COMPANY'S BENEFITS PACKAGE

Give careful thought to your needs and those of your family. Do you need a medical plan that covers dependents? Is leave time important? Does your spouse's benefits package fill missing gaps in yours? Are you concerned about a pension? Remember, there's no point in opting for benefits you won't use. Here are some questions to ask.

MEDICAL BENEFITS

- ☐ Is membership of the group medical aid plan compulsory, or will the company still pay its premium contributions if you negotiate your own cover?
- ☐ Is major medical insurance for catastrophic illness included?
- ☐ How about dental coverage? Does it cover orthodontics and dentures sufficiently?
- ☐ Are any mental health costs paid for?
- ☐ At what age do dependants cease to be covered?
- ☐ How much is the premium? Is there a maximum premium?
- ☐ Are the benefits limited?
- ☐ Will a pre-existing illness preclude you from coverage?
- ☐ What doesn't the plan cover?

LEAVE

- ☐ How much paid annual leave will you receive?
- ☐ Can it be taken any time during the year? Do you have to take it all at once?
- ☐ Can you take unpaid leave?

DISABILITY BENEFITS

- ☐ What percentage of your earnings, if any, would you receive if you became disabled, and for how long would you receive these benefits?
- ☐ How much of the disability insurance premium must you pay?

EDUCATION

- ☐ Are any education expenses reimbursed?
- ☐ Is there on-the-job training, or are work-related seminars provided or encouraged?

CHILD CARE

- ☐ Do child care facilities exist on the premises, or is there a referral service for children of staff?
- ☐ Are any child care costs incurred reimbursed?

HEALTH MAINTENANCE PROGRAMMES

- ☐ Are exercise facilities available?
- ☐ Is the cost of sports and health club activities reimbursed?
- ☐ Are there ongoing stop smoking, weight loss and stress management programmes?

FINANCIAL SAVINGS PLANS

- ☐ Is there group life insurance?
- ☐ Does the employer pay the premium for you?
- ☐ Is there a profit-sharing plan?
- ☐ Can you purchase company shares if they are available?
- ☐ Is a company car provided?

FLEXIBLE BENEFITS

- ☐ Can you tailor your own benefits package by, for example, taking cash instead of time off or choosing from a selection of medical plans?

PENSION PLANS

- ☐ Is there a pension plan, and can you make contributions to it?
- ☐ How long must you be employed before becoming eligible?
- ☐ At what age can you start receiving your pension?
- ☐ If you retire early, what percentage of your pension will you receive, and when will these payments begin?
- ☐ Will your pension include cost-of-living increases?
- ☐ Will you have lifetime medical coverage both for yourself and your spouse?
- ☐ If your spouse outlives you, how much of your pension will he/she receive?

Planning your retirement

Like a second career, a rewarding retirement requires advance planning and some important choices. But this time, *you're* the boss. There are no right or wrong answers in the following checklist. It's designed to help you decide which issues are most important to you.

1. For my continued well-being, I'll:
- ☐ Follow a nutritious diet.
- ☐ Exercise a little every day.
- ☐ Develop activities and hobbies.

2. My savings programme can be substantially improved by:
- ☐ Diversification.
- ☐ Regular contributions.
- ☐ Professional advice.

3. If I remain in my home, I'll:
- ☐ Replace old appliances now.
- ☐ Fix dim lighting, frayed rugs.
- ☐ Rent part of it for income.

4. For retirement living, I'd enjoy:
- ☐ The city/country/small town.
- ☐ Non-stop sunshine/four seasons.
- ☐ The seashore/the mountains.

5. After I retire, I plan to get from one place to another:
- ☐ By public transportation.
- ☐ Driving the family car.
- ☐ With the help of the children, friends and neighbours.

6. The most important legal documents I'll need will be:
- ☐ A contract to buy/sell my home.
- ☐ An up-to-date, valid will.
- ☐ Power of attorney for myself and my spouse.

7. If I leave my community:
- ☐ I'll travel for a while.
- ☐ Sell my house and move away for good.
- ☐ Rent for six months or so before I decide to move permanently.

8. Other than my spouse, the relationships that matter most will be:
- ☐ The children.
- ☐ Old friends and neighbours.
- ☐ A new and different social circle.

9. When I take a trip, I'll opt for:
- ☐ Independent travel/group tours.
- ☐ Africa/Europe/the UK.
- ☐ Cruises/going by car/camping.

10. If I volunteer my time, I may want to work for:
- ☐ The elderly/children/disadvantaged people.
- ☐ My favourite political causes.
- ☐ My church, mosque, synagogue or a welfare society.

11. I'll work until I'm 65 because:
- ☐ I want full pension benefits.
- ☐ I enjoy working.
- ☐ I don't want to stay home all day.

12. I want to retire early because:
- ☐ I don't like my job.
- ☐ My spouse wants us to move.
- ☐ I have lots of other things to do.

Building your nest egg

If inflation wasn't the problem that it is, the average South African family would be able to live quite comfortably after retirement on about 85 percent of its pre-retirement budget. But inflation can play cruel tricks with this formula. For example, if you're 65 and plan to retire soon on a budget of R30,000 a year, you'd probably expect to spend about R600,000 over a 20-year retirement. But given a 10 percent annual inflation rate, the same lifestyle will cost some R1,216,341!

By the same token, a 55-year-old planning to retire in 10 years time on the same R30,000 (at today's rates) will need not R600,000 to maintain the same standard of living for 20 years, but a staggering R3,348,383. Fortunately, your assets can grow at roughly the same – or even faster – rate.

To make a rough projection of your retirement income, add the pension you expect to receive to any income from your investments and savings. Deduct 25 percent (or whatever figure most closely approximates your tax bracket). If the result is about 85 percent of what you now spend, and you can handle some annual inflation, you are financially prepared to retire.

If your nest egg is smaller than you would like it to be, remember that you may be adding to it by selling your home, and that many families are able to live on their capital in carefully planned annual instalments. If there is a substantial gap between your projected income and your anticipated needs, here are some things that you can do about it now.

- ☐ Plan to retire later.
- ☐ Save more money now.
- ☐ Try for a higher after-tax return on your present investments.
- ☐ If you rent, make every effort to buy a house. The money you're spending on rent could go toward paying off a mortgage on property that is likely to appreciate in value.
- ☐ Consider a second job; or perhaps your non-working spouse can get a full- or part-time job, and earmark all that particular income for a retirement fund.
- ☐ Provide now for retirement annuities that will start paying out a lump sum of money to boost your pension at three-year intervals after your retirement, for example, at age 68, 71 and 74.

THE COST OF RETIREMENT

	Present annual expenses				
	R15,000	R20,000	R30,000	R40,000	R50,000
Age now	Cost of 20-year retirement @ 10% inflation				
50	R2,696,302	R3,595,070	R5,392,605	R7,190,139	R8,987,674
55	R1,674,192	R2,232,255	R3,348,383	R4,464,511	R5,580,639
60	R1,039,541	R1,386,055	R2,079,082	R2,772,110	R3,465,137
65	R608,171	R810,894	R1,216,341	R1,621,788	R2,027,235

RETIREMENT HOUSING OPTIONS

Type	Advantages	Pitfalls	Precautions
Trailer caravan	Low cost. Mobile.	Small space. Parks noisy during holiday seasons. Rapid depreciation.	Check construction quality. Visit prospective sites.
Flat (rental)	You can move relatively easily. Landlord does maintenance.	Rents increase. Possible insecurity of tenure – if block sold under sectional title, for instance.	Negotiate written lease carefully. Check general condition and fitted appliances. Submit a list of anything which is damaged or broken to the agent immediately. Keep a copy.
Flat (sectional title)	Ownership of real estate can be bequeathed, like a house. External maintenance done by management (body corporate). Value appreciates.	Annual levy escalates. Loopholes in contracts. Delays in completion.	Have your lawyer check all documents and ensure that sectional title register is open before signing. Check reputation and financial position of the developer.
Flat (share block)	Often only a small deposit required. External maintenance done by management.	Monthly levy escalates. You do not acquire title to any real estate. Entire block may be sold if managing company defaults.	Check that the scheme is legally registered. Have your lawyer check all documents before you sign.
Buy or build home	Privacy. Custom features. Space. Ownership of real estate that will probably appreciate.	Large amount of capital tied up. Troubles with contractors. Dishonest developers.	Check that zoning is as advertised and that seller has clear title. Have your lawyer check all contract documents before you sign.
Retirement community	Depending on the scheme, as for sectional title or for share block. Meals, daily maintenance and medical facilities often included.	Depending on the scheme, as for sectional title or for share block.	Check that the scheme is legally registered. Have your lawyer check all contract documents before you sign.

Enjoying your time

Once you stop working, you may be surprised at how much leisure you have. What are you going to do with all that time? In one survey, most retirees cited watching TV as their number-one activity, yet it ranked nearly last on their list of things they enjoyed doing.

People who reported the highest degree of satisfaction in retirement had developed both balance and variety in their daily routine.

Before you retire, make a list of all the activities – hobbies, voluntary work, travel, club membership, recreation, social gatherings and the like – that you enjoy or that you'd like to try for the first time. Ask the following questions about each activity and give it one point for every "yes" answer.

- ☐ Is it healthy?
- ☐ Is it mentally stimulating?
- ☐ Is it meaningful and gratifying?
- ☐ Is it relaxing, refreshing, fun?

The scores on your list will give you a good idea which activities are apt to be the most (and least) rewarding. They also show you whether all four important aspects of retirement living have been included in your plans. If they haven't you can consider other activities.

CONSIDERING A MOVE?

Reasons to stay. . .	Reasons to go. . .
☐ The crime rate in your community is not as bad as in others.	☐ Taxes and prices are lower in another place that attracts you.
☐ You enjoy the climate where you presently live.	☐ Your doctor recommends a different climate.
☐ You enjoy the friends and neighbours you have now.	☐ You fear that your neighbourhood is deteriorating.
☐ The cost of living is affordable where you are.	☐ You want to move closer to your children.
☐ You like your current doctor and hospital.	☐ You'd like a new lifestyle, new friends.
☐ The children and grandchildren can visit you.	☐ You want to be closer to modern health facilities.
☐ A trip now and then will satisfy any need to see new places.	☐ Another area has more chances for part-time work in your field.

QUIZ

How long will you live?

The average life expectancy for men and women in this country is at best a very general statistic. Individual life spans vary greatly; the reasons are sometimes genetic, but some are under a person's control.

To get a more precise idea of how long you may expect to live – and what you can do about it, find the average life expectancy for someone your age in the chart at right, then answer the lifestyle questions below.

Average life expectancy

Age	Women	Men
25	79	73
35	80	74
45	80	75
55	81	76
65	84	80

1. For every five years that your father lived past 70, add one year. Add one year for every five years your mother lived past 78. _____

2. If you are single, deduct one year for each decade you are unmarried after age 25. _____

3. If you are married, add five years. If there is an unusual amount of family strife, subtract two years. _____

4. If you live in a city, subtract two years. If you live in a small town or on a farm, add two years. _____

5. If you have been either poor or wealthy most of your life, subtract three years. _____

6. If you're over 40, subtract a year for every two kilograms above your ideal weight. Men only: deduct two years per two and a half centimetres that your waist measurement exceeds your chest measurement. _____

7. If you exercise moderately but regularly, add three years. If you regularly do vigorous exercise, add five years. _____

8. If you think you have a hard-driving, competitive personality or are often tense, deduct five years. Add five years if you're usually cheerful and easy-going. _____

9. If you drink heavily, subtract five years; very heavily, 10 years. If you take recreational drugs, subtract five years. _____

10. If you smoke a half to one pack of cigarettes daily, subtract three years. If you smoke one to one and a half packs, subtract five years; two packs, 10 years. _____

11. If you have regular medical and dental checkups, add three years. If you're often ill, subtract two years. _____

12. If your diet is high in fats, salt and sweets, deduct four years. If you eat a balanced diet with plenty of fruit, vegetables and low-fat proteins, add four years. _____

Your life expectancy _____

Stress in your life

Scientists rank the causes of stress by severity in Life Change Units (LCU's). Although some stress (up to 150 LCU's) is normal in the course of everyday life, too much can lower your body's resistance to infection, aggravate allergies and raise your blood pressure, increasing your risk of heart disease or stroke. More than 300 LCU's in a given year is considered a threat to health. (For various ways to cope with stress, see *Stress*, p.198.)

Event	LCU
Christmas	12
Holiday	13
Trouble with boss	23
Change in work duties	29
Child leaving home	29
Trouble with in-laws	29
Mortgage over R30,000	31
Career change	35
Death of a close friend	36
Change in finances	37
Change in financial state	38
Sexual dysfunction	39
Business readjustment	39
Birth of a child	39
Pregnancy	40
Retirement	45
Marital reconciliation	45
Loss of your job	47
Marriage	50
Personal injury or illness	53
Death of a family member	63
Jail term	63
Marital separation	65
Divorce	73
Death of a spouse	100

The well-stocked medicine cabinet

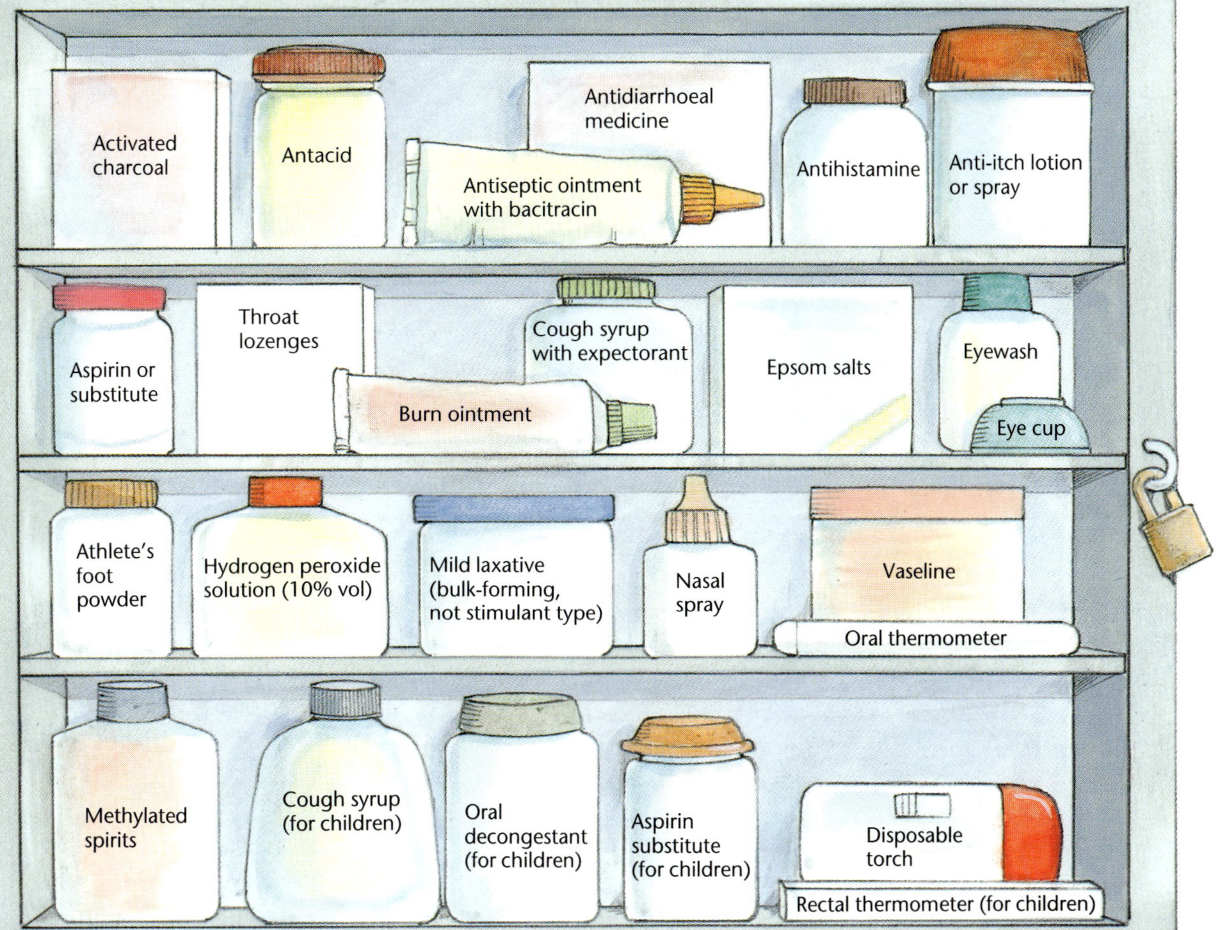

Don't keep medicines in the bathroom; warmth and humidity shorten their life. And you don't want to reach for nose drops at night and use mouthwash or something more harmful by mistake.

What you eliminate is important, too. Make sure you flush the following items away.

- ☐ Aspirin that smells vinegary.
- ☐ Prescription medicines from a former illness.
- ☐ Any medicine older than its expiry date.
- ☐ Over-the-counter medicines you no longer need.
- ☐ Any medicine without a label or not in its original container.

Health records to keep

FOR YOURSELF AND YOUR SPOUSE

- ☐ Any negative reaction to a drug.
- ☐ Allergies. Blood group.
- ☐ Medications you may have been taking regularly.
- ☐ Date of any illness.
- ☐ Frequent or chronic illnesses.
- ☐ Date of last eye examination.
- ☐ Date and reasons for any surgery or hospitalization.
- ☐ Last pap smear, mammogram.
- ☐ Dates of any immunizations.
- ☐ Date, nature, location of X-rays for last three years.
- ☐ Appointments for next physical and dental checkups.

FOR EACH CHILD

- ☐ Birth date and weight.
- ☐ Birth defects, if any. Blood group.
- ☐ Allergies; adverse reactions.
- ☐ Various types of immunizations given, with dates recording when they were given.
- ☐ Approximate dates of any childhood illnesses, such as measles and chicken pox.
- ☐ Types of infections (such as ear, eye): effect of medications on infections.
- ☐ Any serious injury or accident.
- ☐ Next appointments with paediatrician, dentist, ophthalmologist.
- ☐ Reports of school medicals.

Dealing with common ailments

Problem	Home care	Call the doctor for
Fever	Shake oral thermometer, leave under tongue three minutes No extra clothing or blankets, even if body is chilly Lukewarm sponge baths to lower body temperature 1 cup fluid (non-alcoholic) every two hours	Dehydration: dry, tight skin; lightheadedness; dry mouth; extreme thirst; dark or frequent urine Rash, headache, stiff neck, with irritability or confusion Severe abdominal pain or back pain. Listless behaviour Fever over 39°C or lasting three days or more. Vomiting or seizures Fever after new medication. Respiratory distress Cough with brown or green sputum. Earache or ear drainage
Back pain	For prevention and self-help, see p.14	Pain resulting from injury, especially at work Abdominal pain; painful or bloody urination Pain that travels down leg; weakness or numbness in legs or feet No improvement in three to seven days. Fever over 39°C Any severe pain during pregnancy
Headaches	Aspirin, massage, cold compresses for muscle-tension headache Decongestant, hot showers for sinus headache	Fever over 39°C or neck stiffness. Pain worse in morning Recent head injury, slurred speech, visual disturbance, numbness, weakness in arms or legs. Vomiting or convulsions Recurrent, unusually intense, or persistent (three days or more) pain
Heartburn, indigestion	Elevate head of bed No aspirin, caffeine, alcohol, smoking, irritating foods Take antacid	Severe chest pain; shortness of breath; pain felt through to back; heavy perspiration; sharp pains in arms and shoulders Bloody, black vomit or black stool Severe abdominal pain Abdominal pain that increases or is worse after meals Symptoms lasting more than two days; not relieved by antacids
Sprains	Elevate limb. Apply ice once an hour for 15 minutes, up to 24 hours Aspirin for pain as needed Apply heat for soreness after 24 hours While limb heals, use elastic bandage	Unsteady, misshapen, cold, blue or numb limb Sprain that resulted from serious accident, such as car crash or high fall Tenderness in particular area of bone (possible fracture) Pain lasting more than four days or requiring large doses of painkiller
Cuts	Control bleeding by pressure (10–15 minutes) Soap and water cleansing; rinse thoroughly Clean again with sterile gauze wet with antiseptic solution or spray Butterfly bandage, then adhesive strip Change dressing in 24 hours	Uncontrolled bleeding; unclosable wound Cut more than skin deep, more than two and a half centimetres long; deep cut on torso Loss of motion or numbness of digits. No tetanus immunization in five years Infection (pus, streaks, swelling, fever, redness) Cut not healed within three weeks. Persistent numbness
Cough, stuffy nose	Fluids; steam (see *Laryngitis*, p.123) Don't smoke. Suck cough drops. Try nasal spray or antihistamine Family members should wash hands often	Fever over 39°C for more than two days Chest pain, wheezing or shortness of breath Brown, green, bloody or purulent mucus Cough that lasts 10 days. Nasal congestion for two weeks
Vomiting, diarrhoea	Flat cola, ginger ale, water or rehydration solution; suck ice chips No aspirin products No antidiarrhoeal product for 5–6 hours after onset (let bacteria flush out) After nausea subsides, begin bland diet Diarrhoea in small babies may be life-threatening, particularly if accompanied by vomiting. Medical help should always be sought in these cases	Vomiting after head injury or accompanied by severe headache Yellow cast to skin or whites of eyes Abdominal pain, tenderness or distension; fever Dehydration (see *Fever*, above). Liquids not retained after 12 hours Stools that are black, bloody, or have "coffee grounds" look Symptoms that last three days or recur
Sore throat	Drink fluids. Don't smoke. Limit talking Saltwater gargle or over-the-counter anaesthetic solution Lozenges or sweets	Exposure to someone with strep throat Fever of 39°C or more, with no other cold symptoms Breathing difficulty; almost impossible to swallow Concurrent earache, chest pain. Skin rash Severe headache; difficulty bending head White spots on tonsils or large, ulcerated tonsils Swollen lymph nodes on neck for longer than three weeks

Finding the right hospital

It's wise to familiarise yourself with the hospitals in your community before you need one. The two basic kinds of general hospital found in this country are those that are run by private concerns and those that are run by the State or provincial administrations. In addition, a State or provincial hospital may also be a teaching hospital – that is, it is connected to the medical faculty of a university, and senior medical students obtain some of their practical training there.

If you belong to a medical aid scheme or do not require highly specialised treatment available only at a teaching hospital, you will probably be admitted to a private hospital or clinic.

If you need admission to a teaching hospital, it is unlikely that your own doctor will be able to treat you while you are under the care of the teaching hospital staff.

Here are some points to consider when looking for the right hospital:

☐ Be sure the hospital is fairly close by. Is there a 24-hour emergency unit? How long does it take a doctor "on call" to attend to you?

☐ A local State or provincial hospital can give you good care for less money than a private hospital or clinic normally would. If your financial situation is difficult, or if you do not belong to a recognized medical aid scheme, you should not hesitate to tell your doctor immediately. In many cases he may be able to minimize your costs.

☐ A teaching hospital or specialised medical centre may evaluate you and initiate treatment for a complex problem (such as some cancers or kidney or liver disease). Often, it may be possible for your own doctor to follow through closer to home.

☐ If you have children, ask your paediatrician which hospital has the best paediatric facilities. It may not necessarily be the one that best serves adult needs.

Questions to ask before surgery

Here are 11 commonly performed surgical procedures in South Africa, along with possible alternatives. If you're told that you need an operation, it's worth finding out what choices you have – perhaps a less major operation or another form of treatment. If you want a second opinion (some medical aid societies now require one), check column two for the medical professionals who act as consultants in a particular field.

The information on these pages is intended as a helpful home reference guide, and was compiled with the help of medical authorities. But it is not meant to be a substitute for your doctor's advice.

Procedure	Health professional	Surgery alternative	Other therapies
Back surgery	Neurosurgeon Orthopaedist Physiotherapist	Cortisone injections	Anti-inflammatory medications Exercise programme Heat applications Rest
Carotid artery surgery	Neurologist Neurosurgeon Vascular surgeon		Anticoagulants Aspirin therapy
Cataract surgery	Ophthalmologist	Intraocular lens implant	Corrective glasses Wait-and-see approach, if vision not badly impaired
Coronary bypass	Cardiologist Cardiothoracic surgeon	Angioplasty	Medications Diet Exercise programme
Gall bladder removal	Gastroenterologist General surgeon	Shock wave therapy	Dissolution therapy (with medication)
Haemorrhoidectomy	Colorectal surgeon Gastroenterologist General surgeon	Laser surgery Rubber-banding Cauterization	Creams; local care Stool softeners Bulk diet
Hysterectomy	Gynaecologist Oncologist	Dilatation and curettage Myomectomy	Hormonal therapy Wait-and-see approach
Joint surgery	Orthopaedist Physiotherapist	Arthroscopy	Magnetic resonance imaging for specific diagnosis
Pacemaker implant	Cardiologist specialising in arrhythmia		Medications
Prostate surgery	Oncologist Urologist	Orchiectomy Needle biopsy Open, transurethral or radical prostatectomy	Chemotherapy Hormone therapy Radiation
Removal of varicose veins	General surgeon Vascular surgeon	Injection therapy	Support stockings Diet Exercise

What should you weigh?

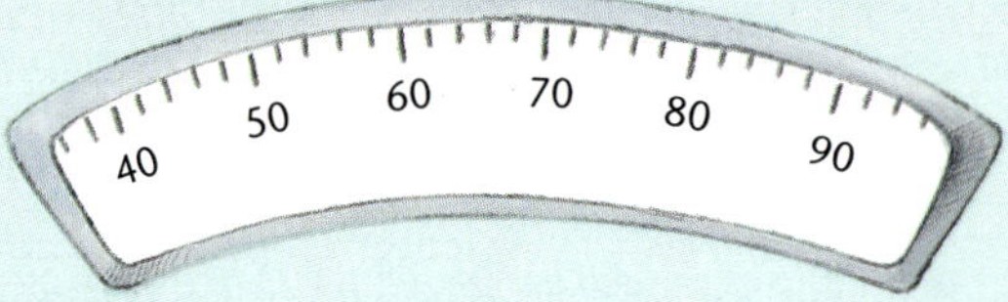

Women				Men			
Height	Small frame	Medium frame	Large frame	Height	Small frame	Medium frame	Large frame
147 cm	46,3–50,4	49,4–54,9	53,5–59,4	158 cm	58,1–60,8	59,4–64,0	62,6–68,0
150 cm	46,7–51,3	50,4–55,8	54,4–60,8	160 cm	59,0–61,7	60,3–64,9	63,5–69,4
152 cm	47,2–52,2	51,3–57,2	55,3–62,1	163 cm	59,9–62,6	61,2–65,8	64,4–70,8
155 cm	48,1–53,5	52,2–58,5	56,7–63,5	165 cm	60,8–63,5	62,1–67,1	65,3–72,6
158 cm	49,9–54,9	53,5–59,9	58,1–64,9	168 cm	61,7–64,4	63,1–68,5	66,2–74,4
160 cm	50,4–56,3	54,0–61,2	60,4–66,7	170 cm	62,6–65,8	64,4–69,9	67,6–76,2
163 cm	51,7–57,6	56,3–62,6	60,9–68,5	173 cm	63,5–67,1	65,8–71,2	69,0–78,0
165 cm	52,1–59,9	57,6–63,9	62,1–70,3	175 cm	64,4–68,5	67,1–72,6	70,3–79,8
168 cm	54,4–60,3	58,9–65,3	63,5–72,1	178 cm	65,3–69,9	68,5–73,9	71,7–81,7
170 cm	55,8–61,7	60,3–66,7	64,9–73,9	180 cm	66,2–71,2	69,9–75,3	73,0–83,5
173 cm	57,2–63,1	61,7–68,0	66,2–76,2	183 cm	67,6–72,6	71,2–77,1	74,4–85,3
175 cm	58,5–64,4	63,1–69,4	67,6–77,1	185 cm	69,0–74,4	72,6–78,9	76,2–87,1
178 cm	59,9–65,8	64,4–70,8	68,9–78,5	188 cm	70,3–76,2	74,4–80,7	78,0–89,4
180 cm	61,2–67,1	65,8–72,1	70,3–79,8	191 cm	71,7–78,0	75,8–82,6	79,8–91,6
183 cm	62,6–68,5	67,1–73,5	71,1–81,2	193 cm	73,5–79,8	77,6–84,8	82,1–93,9

To determine whether you have a small, medium or large frame, bend your elbow to form a 90° angle and have a friend measure from the inside to the outside of the bone. For women: 7 cm or more is a large frame; 5,7–7 cm is medium; less than 5,7 cm, small. For men: over 8,25 cm is a large frame; 6,4–8,25 cm is medium; less than 6,4 cm, small.

The weights above allow for 1,5 kg of clothing.

The benefits of exercise

The chart at the right tells you how seven medical experts rated 12 popular forms of exercise in terms of their benefits in four categories. With each expert allowed to give a maximum of three points for any one exercise, the highest possible score in any one category is 21.

Bear in mind, however, that strenuous exercises, such as squash, can be downright dangerous for anyone who has been sedentary and is out of shape. Be sure to check with your doctor before you begin any exercise programme. When you do start, ease into the programme gently, and build up your fitness level without too much strain. (See also *Endurance building*, p.73.)

Exercise	Weight control	Muscle tone	Digestion	Sleep	Total score
Jogging	21	14	13	16	64
Cycling	20	15	12	15	62
Swimming	15	14	13	16	58
Ice skating, roller skating	17	14	11	15	57
Squash	19	11	13	12	55
Basketball	19	13	10	12	54
Callisthenics	12	18	11	12	53
Tennis	16	13	12	11	52
Walking	13	11	11	14	49
Softball	7	5	8	7	27
Golf	6	6	7	6	25
Bowling	5	5	7	6	23

QUIZ

Test your fitness IQ

True or false?

1. Pregnant women should not exercise. ____

2. For most people, exercise is a better way to lose weight than dieting. ____

3. You can gain weight on an exercise programme. ____

4. If you're sweating profusely, you've had a good workout. ____

5. Eating a sweet just before you work out will give you extra energy. ____

6. It's natural to be out of breath after exercise. ____

---

1. False. They shouldn't overexert themselves, but moderate exercise is beneficial. Consult your doctor.

2. True. It's slower but better. Regular exercise controls appetite and improves muscle tone, bone strength and cardiovascular fitness. Low-kilojoule diets and appetite suppressants do none of these things.

3. Often true, because muscle weighs more than fat. But, paradoxically, you'll look thinner and your dress size or pants size will go down.

4. False. Sweating simply means you are too hot and your body is trying to cool off. It can be caused by humidity or warm clothes as well as exercise.

5. False. It will trigger your pancreas to produce insulin, and you'll soon feel tired and thirsty. Instead, try a complex carbohydrate, such as whole-grain bread or pasta, about two hours before you work out.

6. False. Gasping for breath is a sign of overexertion. You should be able to converse while you are exercising.

What's the right sport for you?

You will benefit from a sport only if you do it consistently. To find the one that will do the most for you, ask yourself . . .

- ☐ Does this sport require equipment? Do I have room for it and can I afford it?
- ☐ Is this exercise appropriate for my age and fitness level? Is it okay with my doctor?
- ☐ Is it fun only now and then, or can I see myself doing it regularly six months from now?
- ☐ Do I prefer a competitive group sport or exercising by myself?
- ☐ Where will I fit this into my daily or weekly schedule? Mornings or evenings?
- ☐ Must I travel to do it? Is the travel time manageable?
- ☐ Can I get better at this, develop my skills, as time goes on?
- ☐ Could I share the benefits of exercise by including other members of my family in my sports programme?

Maintaining all-round fitness

Three keys to a successful exercise programme are frequency, duration and intensity. Exercise shouldn't be painful, but it should make you breathe deeply and sweat. How you achieve that sweat is your decision. Any activity, from bouncing on a trampoline to running around the block, is acceptable, as it brings your heart rate up into the desired target area.

In general, exercise physiologists recommend that 20 to 30 minutes of sustained effort, sufficiently strenuous to maintain an elevated pulse rate, should be performed three or more times a week.

FREQUENCY

To gain the greatest benefit from your programme, plan to exercise three to five days a week. Three days is typical, with rest days in between. Five days will produce faster results if you are exercising for weight control. Deconditioning occurs when one stops exercising regularly: if you discontinue exercising for five weeks, you will lose almost 50 per cent of the fitness you have achieved. After 10 weeks, deconditioning will be total and you will be in the same condition as before you began – though reconditioning should be easier.

DURATION

With time allowed for warm-ups and cool-downs, plus the 20- to 30-minute stimulus period, your exercise should take under an hour. The stimulus time can be broken up into five-minute stints with brief rest periods – as long as the total stimulus period is 20 to 30 minutes. Swimmers doing sprints or walk-joggers are automatically doing this interval training. With high-intensity training, 10- to 15-minute stimulus periods will produce results.

INTENSITY

Few people know how fast to exercise. Most believe they must punish themselves to become fit. This is untrue. Exercise should be fun, and the golden rule is: "train, don't strain". The level of effort – that is, the appropriate amount of stress for your system – depends on your degree of fitness or your present work capacity. One determinant is maximum heart rate (ask your doctor or local health club for a chart that will accurately reflect your maximum heart rate).

Here's a good rule of thumb to remember while you are exercising: you should be able to converse with a fellow runner at the level you have set yourself.

Nutritional values of foods

For optimum health all year round, your body requires at least 40 nutrients, but you don't have to live with a calculator to keep track of them all if your daily meals include servings from each of the four basic food groups. Carefully check labels at the supermarket for food values (you should bear in mind that processed foods may contain extra sugar, sodium or fat). The chart below lists nutrients in many foods that are sold without labels.

Food	Grams	Food energy (kJ)	Protein (g)	Fat (g)	Calcium (mg)	Iron (mg)	Vitamin A (IU)	Thiamin (mg)	Riboflavin (mg)	Nicotinic acid (mg)	Vitamin B6 (mg)	Ascorbic acid (mg)
Fruits & Vegetables												
Apple, 1 small	160	392	0,32	0,64	11	0,32	85	0,03	0,02	0,16	0,077	10
Apricot, 1 medium	50	101	0,70	0,2	7	0,25	1306	0,02	0,02	0,3	0,027	5
Avocado, 1 small	125	843	2,5	19,13	14	1,25	765	0,14	0,15	2,38	0,35	10
Banana, 1 medium	80	307	0,8	0,40	5	0,24	65	0,04	0,08	0,4	0,462	7
Grapefruit, ½ medium	120	161	0,72	0,12	14	0,12	149	0,05	0,02	0,36	0,05	41
Grapes, medium bunch	250	743	1,75	1,5	28	0,75	183	0,23	0,15	0,75	0,275	28
Guava, 1 medium	75	158	0,60	0,45	15	0,23	594	0,04	0,04	0,9	0,107	138
Melons, spanspek, 1 medium	250	370	2,25	0,75	28	0,5	8060	0,1	0,05	1,5	0,288	108
Orange, 1 medium	130	256	1,17	0,13	52	0,13	267	0,12	0,05	0,39	0,078	69
Peach, 1 medium	150	270	1,05	0,15	8	0,15	803	0,03	0,06	1,5	0,027	11
Pear, 1 big	220	543	0,88	0,88	24	0,66	44	0,04	0,09	0,22	0,040	9
Pineapple, slice	85	176	0,34	0,34	6	0,34	20	0,08	0,03	0,34	0,074	13
Prunes, uncooked (10)	80	800	2,08	0,40	41	2	1590	0,06	0,13	1,6	0,208	2
Strawberries, sliced (125 ml)	85	108	0,51	0,34	12	0,34	23	0,02	0,06	0,17	0,05	48
Asparagus, canned tips (125 ml)	90	79	2,16	0,36	17	1,71	720	0,05	0,09	0,72	0,036	14
Beans, green, boiled, plain (125 ml)	120	126	1,92	0,24	60	0,72	648	0,08	0,11	0,6	0,068	14
Beetroot salad, cooked, grated with sugar (125 ml)	120	248	1,2	0,12	16	0,6	23	0,04	0,05	0,36	0,018	6
Broccoli, cooked, florets (125 ml)	75	82	2,33	0,23	66	0,6	1875	0,07	0,15	0,6	0,084	68
Brussels sprouts, cooked (125 ml)	100	151	4,2	0,4	32	1,1	520	0,08	0,14	0,8	0,180	87
Cabbage, raw, plain, grated (250 ml)	80	80	1,04	0,16	39	0,32	104	0,04	0,04	0,24	0,08	38
Carrots, raw, grated (125 ml)	80	141	0,88	0,16	30	0,56	8800	0,05	0,04	0,48	0,14	6
Cauliflower, raw, florets (125 ml)	80	90	2,16	0,16	20	0,88	48	0,09	0,08	0,56	0,197	62
Cucumber, raw, 5 slices	50	30	0,3	0,05	9	0,15	0	0,02	0,02	0,1	0,024	6
Mushrooms, boiled, plain (125 ml)	95	67	1,81	0,10	6	0,48	0	0,02	0,24	1,9	0,077	2
Onion, raw, chopped (125 ml)	65	103	0,98	0,07	18	0,33	0	0,02	0,03	0,13	0,098	7
Parsley, raw, chopped (1 tablespoon)	3,5	6	0,13	0,02	7	0,22	298	*	0,01	0,04	0,005	6
Peas, green, cooked, plain (125 ml)	85	252	4,59	0,34	20	1,53	459	0,24	0,09	1,96	0,078	17
Potato, boiled, plain, 1 medium	90	245	1,71	0,09	5	0,45	0	0,07	0,03	0,99	0,131	13
Potato, chips, French fried (250 ml)	120	1271	4,56	13,08	17	1,08	0	0,12	0,05	1,44	0,216	19
Potato, mashed, with whole milk and hard margarine (125 ml)	120	421	2,64	3,12	41	0,48	145	0,08	0,07	1,08	0,149	13
Potato, salad, with mayonnaise and egg (125 ml)	120	462	2,64	4,56	10	0,72	67	0,10	0,05	1,32	0,175	17
Potato, roasted in fat (1 medium)	90	493	1,53	7,2	5	0,45	0	0,07	0,03	0,99	0,131	13
Spinach, cooked, plain (125 ml)	90	86	2,70	0,27	84	1,98	7290	0,06	0,13	0,45	0,087	25
Squash, gem, boiled (½)	75	44	0,68	0,08	19	0,3	293	0,04	0,06	0,6	0,038	8
Tomato, raw (1 medium)	200	184	2,2	0,4	26	1	1800	0,12	0,08	1,4	0,220	46
Turnips, cooked (125 ml)	80	47	0,56	0,24	44	0,32	0	0,02	0,03	0,32	0,048	12
Breads, Cereals & Grains												
Bran, wheat, rounded tablespoon	10	87	1,41	0,55	11	1,29	0	0,09	0,04	2,96	0,138	0
Bread, brown, 1-cm thick slice	30	333	2,67	0,87	17	0,66	0	0,10	0,03	0,81	0,024	0
Cake, chocolate, iced, made with whole milk and hard margarine (1 piece)	150	2399	7,65	23,55	54	1,5	840	0,08	0,11	0,45	0,083	0
Cereal, Maltabella, cooked (250 ml)	250	453	2,75	1	5	1,25	0	0,13	0,05	1	0	0
Biscuits, home-made, plain, made with hard margarine (4)	80	1577	5,12	17,6	66	1,2	640	0,11	0,05	0,8	0,056	0
Macaroni, cooked (125 ml)	75	349	2,55	0,3	6	0,3	0	0,01	0,01	0,23	0,01	0
Popcorn, plain (500 ml)	18	291	2,29	0,9	2	0,49	0	0,02	0,40	0	0	0
Tart, lemon meringue, with short crust made with hard margarine (⅛ of 20 cm diameter)	125	1690	5,63	18,25	58	1,25	416	0,09	0,1	0,63	0,063	6
Dairy Products												
Cheese, blue-veined, (30 x 30 x 30 mm)	30	453	6,45	8,91	179	0,12	265	0,01	0,14	0,27	0,044	0
Cheese, Cheddar, grated (125 ml)	45	758	11,2	14,90	324	0,32	477	0,01	0,17	0,05	0,033	0
Cheese, cream, rounded tablespoon	40	584	3,04	13,96	32	0,48	571	0,01	0,08	0,04	0,019	0
Cheese, Feta, pieces (125 ml)	95	1048	13,49	20,24	467	0,67	0	0	0	0	0	0
Ice cream, cone, soft-serve	80	729	3,28	10,4	109	0,24	367	0,04	0,21	0,08	0,044	1

Food	Grams	Food energy (kJ)	Protein (g)	Fat (g)	Calcium (mg)	Iron (mg)	Vitamin A (IU)	Thiamin (mg)	Riboflavin (mg)	Nicotinic acid (mg)	Vitamin B6 (mg)	Ascorbic acid (mg)
Milk, whole (250 ml)	260	668	8,58	8,58	309	0,26	328	0,10	0,42	0,26	0,109	3
Milk, skim (250 ml)	260	380	8,84	0,52	320	*	0	0,10	0,36	0,26	0,104	3
Yoghurt, low-fat, plain, drinking (175 ml)	175	340	6,13	2,63	212	0,18	215	0,05	0,25	0,18	0,056	2
Fish, Poultry, Meat, Eggs, Legumes, Nuts & Seeds												
Calamari, fried in batter in sunflower oil (5 rings)	60	467	7,86	6,78	16	0,18	0	0,02	0,04	0,84	0,01	0
Clams, tinned (84 g)	85	188	7	1	47	3,5	0	0,01	0,09	0,9	0	0
Crab, tinned (125 ml)	70	296	12,18	1,75	32	0,56	*	0,06	0,06	1,33	0	*
Fish fingers, frozen, crumbed, fried in sunflower oil (1 finger)	30	293	4,05	3,81	14	0,21	*	0,02	0,02	0,42	0,063	*
Oysters, tinned, 5 large	50	159	4,25	1,1	14	2,8	155	0,01	0,10	0,4	0,019	*
Pilchards, tinned in tomato or chilli sauce (1 pilchard)	75	398	14,1	4,05	225	2,03	*	0,02	0,22	5,7	0	*
Shrimps, fresh, boiled (125 ml)	70	345	16,66	1,68	224	1,26	*	0,02	0,02	2,1	0,07	*
Sole, steamed, large	120	461	24,72	1,08	25	0,72	*	0,11	0,11	4,32	0	*
Tuna, tinned, water-pack (125 ml)	80	426	22,4	0,64	13	1,28	0	0,02	0,08	10,64	0,232	*
White fish, fried in sunflower oil	150	1070	28,05	16,2	50	0,9	5	0,12	0,02	4,8	0,419	*
Chicken, boiled, light meat with skin (medium breast)	110	927	28,71	11	14	1,1	106	0,04	0,12	7,59	0,297	0
Chicken, roasted, light and dark meat with skin (medium thigh)	65	650	17,75	8,84	10	0,85	105	0,04	0,11	5,53	0,26	0
Turkey, roasted, meat and skin (per slice)	30	261	8,43	2,91	7,8	0,54	0	0,02	0,05	1,53	0,123	0
Bacon, grilled or fried, 2 strips	20	482	6,10	9,84	2	0,32	*	0,14	0,06	1,46	0,055	0
Beef, minced, cooked (125 ml)	100	917	27,4	11,3	12	3,5	20	0,09	0,23	6	0,3	0
Beef, rump, roasted, trimmed (per slice)	270	2147	79,92	19,17	35	9,99	27	0,22	0,59	14,31	0,891	0
Biltong, beef, grated (125 ml)	36	306	12,35	2,27	7	1,84	*	0,03	0,12	1,37	0,17	0
Cold meat, corned, silverside (per slice)	20	146	6,46	0,98	2	0,64	*	0,01	0,06	0,78	0,066	0
Ham, cooked or tinned, lean (5% fat) (per slice)	30	164	5,82	1,50	2	0,24	0	0,28	0,07	1,44	0,138	0
Kidney, beef, cooked (125 ml)	130	936	33,28	10,01	21	10,4	1083	0,33	2,73	6,24	0,39	13
Liver, chicken, simmered (125 ml)	130	854	31,72	7,15	18	11,05	21288	0,20	2,28	5,85	0,754	21
Mutton, fat-trimmed, loin chop, grilled (medium)	50	464	13,9	6,15	5	1,05	*	0,08	0,15	3,60	0,11	0
Pork, cooked, leg, roasted, fat-trimmed (per slice)	30	277	8,49	3,3	2	0,24	3	0,25	0,11	1,59	0,114	0
Pork, loin chop, grilled, fat-trimmed (medium)	60	644	16,68	9,18	4	0,54	5	0,58	0,25	3,6	0,276	0
Steak and kidney pie (medium)	120	1619	10,92	25,44	64	3	642	0,14	0,18	2,04	0,07	0
Sausages, beef, dry, thin (30 cm)	100	2096	17,4	45,9	0	1,4	0	0,46	0,19	4,3	0,06	0
Sausages, boerewors, cooked, thick (13 cm)	60	995	8,28	21,78	0	0,68	0	0,22	0,09	2,04	0,03	0
Sausages, pork, cooked (9 cm long)	45	694	8,87	14,04	14	0,59	0	0,33	0,11	2,03	0,149	1
Tongue, ox, cooked (per slice)	80	973	15,6	19,12	25	2,4	*	0,05	0,23	3,28	0,072	2
Veal, cooked, roasted fillet, fat-trimmed (per slice)	250	2408	79	28,75	35	4	*	0,15	0,68	17,5	0,8	0
Venison, roasted (per slice)	30	250	10,5	1,92	9	2,34	0	0,07	0	0	0	0
Egg, large, boiled, shell removed (1)	50	331	6,05	5,60	28	1,05	260	0,04	0,15	0,05	0,057	0
Scrambled (25 ml liquid per egg), whole milk and hard margarine (1)	75	470	6,6	8,63	56	1,05	370	0,05	0,18	0,08	0,065	0
Almonds, shelled, chopped (250 ml)	130	3254	24,18	70,46	304	6,11	0	0,31	1,20	4,55	0,13	*
Beans, haricot, cooked (125 ml)	90	356	5,94	0,45	59	2,25	*	0,01	0,05	0,63	0	0
Beans, white kidney, cooked (125 ml)	100	405	7,1	0,3	19	1,7	*	0,14	0,07	0,7	0	0
Brazil nuts, shelled, chopped (250 ml)	120	3286	17,16	80,28	223	4,08	0	1,15	0,14	1,92	0,212	*
Cashew nuts, shelled, plain (250 ml)	140	3287	24,08	63,98	53	5,32	140	0,60	0,35	2,52	0	0
Peanuts, shelled, roasted (125 ml)	80	1949	20,96	38,96	58	1,76	0	0,26	0,10	13,68	0,33	0
Pecan nuts, shelled (250 ml)	120	3451	11,04	85,44	88	2,88	156	1,03	0,16	1,08	0,22	2
Soya beans, cooked (125 ml)	80	435	8,8	4,56	58	2,16	24	0,17	0,07	0,48	0	0
Sunflower seeds, dry, hulled (125 ml)	80	1875	19,2	37,84	96	5,68	40	1,57	0,18	4,32	1	0
Texturised vegetable protein, cooked, Toppers (125 ml)	120	456	8,64	2,64	56	4,44	0	0,3	0,11	0,53	0,412	12
Walnuts, shelled, chopped (250 ml)	120	3270	11,84	76,8	119	3,72	36	0,40	0,16	1,08	1,104	2

Asterisk (*) indicates that only traces of a nutrient are present.

Getting more for your food rand

Do you get nervous at the supermarket as you watch your receipt flowing from the cash register? Are you always wondering how you managed to spend so much money on so little? Here are some simple ways to stretch your food budget without sacrificing quality.

Food-borne illness

Food poisoning is unpleasant at best and can be life-threatening. It is usually caused by germs that inflame the lining of the stomach and intestines. Here are some useful tips to help you eliminate the risk of illness.

- ☐ Discard any food that smells or looks spoiled.
- ☐ Be sure to keep food either hot or cold. Bacteria thrive at room temperature.
- ☐ Scrub your hands with soap and warm water before preparing food and after handling raw fish, meat or poultry.
- ☐ Wash utensils and cutting boards after each use.
- ☐ Replace sponges, washcloths and kitchen towels as soon as they look or smell musty.
- ☐ If you're going to sneeze or cough, turn your head well away from food. Cover your mouth, then wash your hands.
- ☐ If you have broken skin on your hands or an infection, wear thin rubber or plastic gloves at all times in the kitchen.
- ☐ Make sure that you cover any cuts and sores on your hands with waterproof sticking plaster when you are working with food.
- ☐ Don't eat very rare meat, fish or poultry. Test for doneness with a meat thermometer.
- ☐ Don't let food stand on a counter to defrost. Thaw it in a microwave oven, the refrigerator or cold water. Cook immediately.
- ☐ Discard bulging or leaking tins.
- ☐ Cool leftovers in the refrigerator. Reheat solids thoroughly and boil sauces and gravies.
- ☐ Refrigerate perishables as soon as possible.
- ☐ Freeze food in small, shallow, closed containers. Never refreeze frozen food that has thawed.
- ☐ Take the "use by" date on packaged food seriously.
- ☐ Keep pets away from food and off the table.

Microwave do's and don'ts

☐ Make sure that you use ceramic and glass ovenware. If you buy new cookware, check that it's labelled "microwave safe".

☐ Never cook in metal containers. Aluminium foil is safe in some ovens but not others. Check your owner's manual.

☐ To avoid explosions, loosen the lids of frozen food containers, slit plastic food pouches, and pierce food with skin (such as chicken or potatoes) so that steam can escape during cooking.

☐ Do not deep-fry.

☐ Centre food in the oven and have the thicker, denser parts facing outward, toward oven walls.

☐ Follow the recipe and let food stand after you take it out of the oven; it's still cooking.

☐ Keep oven turned off when not in use (don't leave the oven rack inside). The door should close tightly.

☐ Don't stare at a microwave oven while it is operating. Just as your eyes can be damaged by staring at a naked light bulb for too long, they can also be affected by the microwave's heat.

☐ Periodically turn roasts, stir dishes towards the centre to distribute heat, and rotate dishes that cannot be stirred.

Perishable food storage

Freezer -18°C or lower			Refrigerator 1°C to 4°C	
Months Cooked	Months Uncooked	Items	Days Cooked	Days Uncooked
		Meat and poultry		
2–3	1–3	Bacon (opened package)	3–4	5–7
1	2–9	Chicken, whole/pieces	2–4	1–2
—	—	Eggs	—	7–35
—	1–2	Cold meat	—	3–5
		Beef		
4–6	6–12	Roast	4–5	3–4
2–3	4–6	Mince	3–4	1–2
2–3	12	Steak	3–5	2–3
2–3	1–2	Frankfurters	3–4	3–5
		Lamb		
4–6	6–9	Roast	3–4	2–3
2–3	6–9	Chops	3–4	2–3
		Pork		
4–6	4–8	Roast	3–4	2–3
2–3	3–4	Chops	3–4	2–3
2–3	1–2	Mince	3–4	1–2
2–3	1–2	Sausage	3–4	1–2
2–3	2–6	Turkey, whole/pieces	2–4	1–2
6–9	4–8	Veal roast	3–4	2–3
		Fish		
		Lean white fish		
1–2	4–6	Hake, angelfish, sole	2–3	1–2
		Oily fish		
1–2	2–3	Maasbanker, tunny, mackerel	2–3	1–2
3	3–6	Shrimp	2–3	1
		Dairy products		
—	6–9	Butter	—	7–14
—	6	Cheese, hard	—	90–180
—	—	Cheese, soft	—	14
—	—	Cream, light & heavy	—	10
—	1	Milk	—	3–5

The chart above lists the temperatures and times at which commonly used perishable foods can be stored for optimum safety, good taste and nutrition.

Handy helpers when supplies run short

Food	Substitutes	Stretchers
Baking powder 1 tsp.	¼ tsp. bicarbonate of soda plus ½ tsp. cream of tartar	—
Beer	—	Ginger ale, lemonade, tonic water
Bread crumbs	Cracker crumbs, wheat germ, cereal	—
Cake	—	Ice cream, fruit topping; mix broken pieces with custard
Cake flour 1 cup	1 cup less 2 tbsp. sifted all-purpose flour	—
Champagne	Sparkling wine	Fruit juices
Chicken	Veal, turkey	Onion, celery, rice
Chilli	—	Beans, rice, spaghetti, sweetcorn
Coffee	—	Roasted chicory or dandelion root
Cornflour 1 tbsp. (as thickener)	2 tbsp. all-purpose flour	—
Cream, 1 cup	¾ cup milk plus ¼ cup melted butter	—
Creamed sweetcorn	—	Milk and onion (for soup)
Egg 1 whole	2 egg yolks	Omelette with vegetables, cheese, poultry
Fish	—	Cut up, stir-fry with vegetables
Fruit juice, fruit punch	—	Soda water, ginger ale, tea
Gem squash	Pumpkin, butternut squash	Stuffing of leftover meat, rice
Gravy	Cream of mushroom soup with stock cube	Puréed vegetables, tomato sauce, mushrooms
Green pepper	Red pepper, yellow pepper	Stuffing of rice, leftovers
Honey 1 cup	1¼ cups sugar plus ⅓ cup water	—
Iced tea	—	Fruit juice, herb teas
Lemon juice 1 tsp.	½ tsp. vinegar; lime juice	—
Meat loaf	—	Crackers, rice, rolled oats, grated carrots, hard-boiled eggs, wheat germ
Milk, whole, 1 cup	1 cup skim milk plus 2 tsp. melted butter	Instant dried milk
Minced beef	Minced pork, veal or lamb	Grated squash or pumpkin, rice, pasta, wheat germ, unsweetened cereal, onion, green pepper
Noodles	—	Leftover vegetables, diced meats
Pudding	—	Vanilla wafers, sliced bananas, cubes of stale cake
Salad	—	Meat, fish, legumes, vegetables, avocado
Soups	—	Vegetables, pasta, legumes, tofu, sour cream, barley, yoghurt
Sour cream	Plain yoghurt	—
Spaghetti sauce	—	Extra meat, shellfish, vegetables
Steak	—	Cut up and stir-fry with vegetables or grill on skewer
Stews	—	Creamed sweetcorn, shredded wheat
Tartar sauce ½ cup	6 tbsp. mayonnaise plus 2 tbsp. sweet pickle relish	—
Tomato sauce or chilli sauce ½ cup	½ cup tomato paste plus 2 tbsp. sugar	—
Tomato sauce 2 cups	¾ cup tomato paste plus 1 cup water	Carrots, broccoli, green pepper
Tuna salad	White-meat chicken salad	Olives, relish, celery, pasta, eggs
Vegetables	—	Pasta, rice
Wine	—	Fruit juice

Spices & seasonings

ALLSPICE — Cakes, biscuits, pies, breads, puddings, fruit preserves, pickles, relishes, yellow vegetables.

BASIL — Tomatoes, tomato sauce, barbecue sauce, salads.

CELERY SEED — Meat loaf, beef, lamb and vegetable stews; bean salad.

CAYENNE PEPPER — Eggs, cheese, soups, curries, stews, seafood, chutneys.

CINNAMON — Cakes, biscuits, pies, puddings, coffee, dessert toppings, yellow vegetables, hot spiced beverages.

CLOVES — Ham, beetroot, pickling, beef marinades, hot spiced beverages, cakes, pies, puddings.

DILL — Salads and salad dressings, sour cream or mayonnaise dips, eggs, cucumbers, tomatoes, carrots, fish, cheese dishes.

GARLIC — Nearly all types of meat, fish, poultry, vegetables, sauces, stews, soups, salads and salad dressings.

HORSERADISH — Cocktail sauce, sour cream dips, ham, sausage, boiled beef, smoked fish, salad dressings.

MARJORAM — Bread, veal, lamb, seafood, poultry, green vegetables, potatoes, tomatoes.

NUTMEG — Cakes, biscuits, pies, puddings, eggnog, custards, creamed vegetables, stewed fruits, bean soups, poultry.

ORIGANUM — Tomatoes, tomato sauce, green vegetables, salads and salad dressings, beef, poultry, seafood, eggs.

ROSEMARY — Lamb, poultry stuffing, beef and pork roasts, tomato sauce, salads, seafood, turnips, potatoes, cauliflower.

SAGE — Veal, sausage, poultry, stuffings, cheese spreads, soups.

TARRAGON — Salad dressings, sauces, egg dishes, stews, poultry, seafood.

THYME — Fish soup, seafood, stuffing, poultry, meat, vegetables.

EQUIVALENTS FOR COMMON COOKING INGREDIENTS

Quantity	Ingredient	Equivalent	Quantity	Ingredient	Equivalent
500 g	Apples	2 large	500 g	Meat, minced	2½ cups
500 g	Bananas	3 large	500 g	Mushrooms	3 cups, quartered
500 g	Beans, dried	1 ¼ cups	150 g	Peanuts, shelled	1 cup
1 litre	Berries	3 cups	1 medium	Onion	½ cup chopped
1 slice	Bread	½ cup crumbs	6–8 tbsp. juice	Orange	½ cup pulp
100 g	Cheese, grated	1 cup	3 medium	Potatoes	1¾ cups mashed
30 g	Chocolate	1 square	150 g	Raisins	1 cup
250 ml	Cream	1 cup	1 cup uncooked	Rice	2½ cups cooked
500 g	Flour	4 cups	250 g	Spaghetti	3½ – 4 cups cooked
1 envelope	Gelatin	10 g	500 g	Sugar, icing	4 cups
1 tsp.	Herbs, dried	5 ml	500 g	Sugar, granulated	2½ cups
2–3 tbsp. juice	Lemon	¼ cup pulp	500 g	Tomatoes	5 medium
1 cup dry	Macaroni	2¼ cups cooked	500 g	Walnuts, in shell	1¾ cups chopped

FOUR TO THREE WEEKS BEFORE

- ☐ Decide on the particular type of party.
- ☐ Set budget.
- ☐ Draw up guest list. Post, telephone or personally deliver invitations.
- ☐ Hire help if needed.
- ☐ Rent equipment.
- ☐ Arrange entertainment.

TWO WEEKS BEFORE

- ☐ Decide on food and drink.
- ☐ Plan setup: bar, buffet, decorations.
- ☐ Choose utensils, dishes, glassware, table linens, serviettes, candles and any other supplies you may need.

ONE WEEK BEFORE

- ☐ Shop for non-perishable food, drinks and supplies.
- ☐ Order flowers.
- ☐ Prepare those dishes that can be frozen.
- ☐ Ask a friend or neighbour if they can help with the organization of the party.

FIVE TO TWO DAYS BEFORE

- ☐ Polish silver.
- ☐ Clean house.
- ☐ Make or buy ice.
- ☐ Arrange seating plan and write out place cards.
- ☐ Clean, press party attire.
- ☐ Choose music (if there's no entertainment).

ONE DAY BEFORE

- ☐ Buy all the perishable food you need.
- ☐ Set up bar and buffet table.
- ☐ Put out ashtrays and matches.
- ☐ Check bathroom supplies.
- ☐ Determine area for coats.

DAY OF PARTY

- ☐ Arrange decorations in the entertainment area.
- ☐ Set out uncooked foods.
- ☐ Prepare cooked foods.
- ☐ Set table (if a dinner party).
- ☐ Chill white wine.
- ☐ Do last-minute tidying up.
- ☐ One hour before: put ice, water, garnishes at bar. Open a bottle or two of red wine.

How much do you need?

It's a nuisance to run out of supplies during a party or to cope with too many leftovers afterwards. The amounts given here are meant for 20 guests. If you are having more or fewer people, simply divide or multiply by the appropriate number.

DRINKS

- 1 litre each vodka, gin, whisky and brandy
- 2 cases beer
- 6 bottles white wine
- 4 bottles red wine
- 2 litres each soda water, tonic, orange juice, tomato juice, cola, diet drinks, ginger ale
- 3 limes, 1 lemon
- 10 kg ice cubes

HORS D'OEUVRES

- 1 kg cheese
- 3 loaves bread
- 3 bags chips
- 500 g crackers
- 3 cups dip
- 1 kg nuts
- 2 kg raw vegetables or 150 finger foods (tiny sandwiches, frankfurters, sausage rolls and so forth)

DINNER

(Choose from among the following)

- 5 kg meat with bone
- 2,5 kg boneless meat
- 5 kg poultry
- 2 kg fish fillets
- 500 g pasta
- 5 cups rice
- 2 kg any vegetable
- 4 heads lettuce
- 2 kg fruit
- 2 cakes or 3 pies
- 40 petit fours
- 1,5 litres ice cream

Setting a place at your table

Nowadays people are having fewer formal dinner parties. The diagram below illustrates where all the elements in a rather informal place setting go. You may want to eliminate a soup spoon or a wineglass from the arrangement, depending on the menu you've selected.

1. Salad plate
2. Salad fork
3. Dinner fork
4. Dessert fork
5. Dinner plate
6. Serviette
7. Knife
8. Dessert spoon
9. Soup spoon
10. Butter plate
11. Butter knife
12. Water glass
13. Wineglass

Cheese choices

Cheese is an excellent protein food to serve when people are drinking alcohol. It works equally well as an hors d'oeuvre or a dessert.

☐ If you want to try before you buy, go to a store that sells cheese in bulk, rather than packaged, and ask for a sample to taste.

☐ Do not buy cheese which is so overripe that it smells of ammonia. However, total lack of aroma means that the cheese has been stored at too low a temperature or, even worse, has been frozen.

☐ Store cheeses in the door or vegetable compartment of the refrigerator. Rewrap leftover pieces tightly in plastic or aluminium foil.

☐ Take cheese from the refrigerator at least an hour before serving (except cottage or cream cheese).

☐ For dessert, combine apples and pears with Brie, Gorgonzola, Cheddar, mozzarella, smoked cheese or Port Salut. Oranges and naartjies go well with Stilton or cream cheese. Peaches complement Bel Paese, blue cheese or Camembert.

☐ A full red wine or a good white dessert wine, such as a Muscat d'Alexandrie, complements most cheese and fruit combinations. Save port for strong cheeses.

To satisfy everyone's taste, you should try to serve a wide selection with an assortment of savoury biscuits and dark bread.

SOFT AND SEMISOFT CHEESES

Bel Paese, Brie, Camembert, cottage cheese, Drakensberg, feta, Limburger and Rabiola.

FIRM AND SEMIFIRM CHEESES

Cheddar, Cheshire, Derby, Edam, Emmenthal, Gouda, Gruyère, Havarti and Leicester.

☐ Serve at least one pungent cheese for your adventurous guests: Blaauwkrantz, Danish Blue, Stilton, or Gorgonzola.

☐ Aromatic cheeses should be served on a separate board with their own serving knife so that they don't overwhelm milder cheeses.

☐ Use a wire cutter for blue cheeses to keep them from falling apart.

Tips on tippling

No one wants an inebriated guest – drunkenness at any function can be embarrassing, upset the other guests and ruin a well-intentioned get-together.

IF YOU'RE THE HOST

☐ Never urge drinks on guests, even if the punch or cocktail is your own special recipe.

☐ Keep a good supply of ice on hand and put plenty of ice in drinks.

☐ When you make the cocktails for your guests, measure the alcohol exactly with a tot measure.

☐ Have plenty of non-alcoholic beverages available and visible on the drinks table.

☐ Set out high-protein food, such as cubes of meat or fish, near the bar. Keep food bowls full throughout the evening.

☐ If you think a guest is getting tipsy, stop serving him liquor.

☐ If someone is obviously drunk, either call a taxi or drive her home yourself. Take away a guest's car keys if necessary. If there is no other solution, phone a police station and ask a policeman to take the guest home for you.

IF YOU'RE A GUEST

☐ Drink milk and at least 600 millilitres of water before you go to a party. Eat a snack before you leave home and eat when you get there as well.

☐ Sip your drinks slowly. Keep replenishing the ice in your drink.

☐ Ask for diluted drinks.

☐ Drink non-alcoholic beverages (but not carbonated drinks, which enhance the effects of alcohol) part of the time.

☐ Do not allow yourself to be pressurised into drinking alcohol if you would prefer a soft drink. If you find yourself in a situation where drinking a soft drink might invite some embarrassing comments from guests, have lemonade or soda water in a wineglass — few people will notice the difference.

Are you in love?

- ☐ Do you think about her every day? Sometimes phone just to ask her what she's doing?
- ☐ Do you have pretty much the same values, laugh at the same things, have fun together?
- ☐ How about the way he looks? What others consider a flaw – that gap between his teeth, for instance – do you think it's cute?
- ☐ Do you buy things you think she'd like, even give her something dear to you, such as an heirloom?
- ☐ Are you intensely curious about his family background, various interests and work, and do you want to show him some of the things that you've accomplished?
- ☐ Do you want to discuss everything important with her?
- ☐ Does he always seem to be involved in your plans for the future?
- ☐ Do you want to become a better person for her sake?
- ☐ Do you go to the theatre because he loves it, even though you don't?
- ☐ Do you feel a strong emotional and mental attraction to her most of the time? Do you really enjoy being affectionate?
- ☐ Do you find it easy to resist attractions to other people?
- ☐ Do you feel young, buoyant, glad to be alive? Do people keep asking you why you're so happy?

If you've answered *yes* to all or most of these questions, it may be the right time to move on to the *Wedding checklist.*

10 TIPS FOR A HAPPY MARRIAGE

1. FIGHT, BUT WITHIN LIMITS
Express your feelings, but don't explode. Encourage your partner to tell you when something's wrong. As tactfully as you can, try to get to the root of problems and resolve them.

2. HAVE YOUR OWN INTERESTS
If your life is totally focused on your spouse, you'll place a burden on him and limits on yourself. Keep in touch with your friends, pursue activities you enjoy, join organizations and take classes that interest you. Your mate is apt to find such a multifaceted person intriguing.

3. SUPPORT YOUR PARTNER
If she's worried about a speech she has to give, let her know that you care, even if you can't really help. Be proud of her achievements; remember that she's not your rival – her accomplishments can only reflect well on you.

4. BE AFFECTIONATE
Don't stifle an urge to hold hands or take his arm. Let him know that he's still attractive to you. And don't forget to say, "I love you" – perhaps the sweetest words in the English language. He won't get tired of hearing them.

5. MAKE TIME FOR EACH OTHER
No matter how busy you are, find time to be alone with your mate – whether you set aside a couple of hours on Sunday afternoon or go away for the weekend. Make "dates" with each other if you need to, and keep them.

6. APPRECIATE YOUR SPOUSE
Do you thank her when she does you a favour? Do you treat him as considerately as you would a friend? Do you compliment her enough? Sometimes we forget the basic courtesies when we live with someone.

7. KEEP THE GOOD TIMES IN MIND
When you're going through a hard period, bring up wonderful memories; sharing them will reinforce the bond between you and remind you of the things that made you love each other in the first place.

8. FORGIVE AND FORGET
Don't keep replaying the same fight. If your spouse has apologized for something, try not to bring it up again unless it seems helpful. If it keeps bothering you, ask yourself why. If you can't break destructive patterns, see a marriage counsellor. If your spouse refuses, go by yourself.

9. COMMUNICATE YOUR FEELINGS
If you say, "When you do that, I feel hurt (humiliated, angry)", you're explaining your own reactions rather than accusing your spouse. And if you remember to say, "I love it when you do that", it will encourage behaviour that makes you both happy.

10. GIVE IN SOMETIMES
Go to that movie just because he wants to. Eat potjiekos just because she wants to. Chances are that your compromises will even out in the long run – and besides, no one should be counting.

Your wedding checklist

Planning a formal wedding can test the fortitude of even the most organized mind. Here's a chronological checklist to minimize any last-minute crises on the happy day.

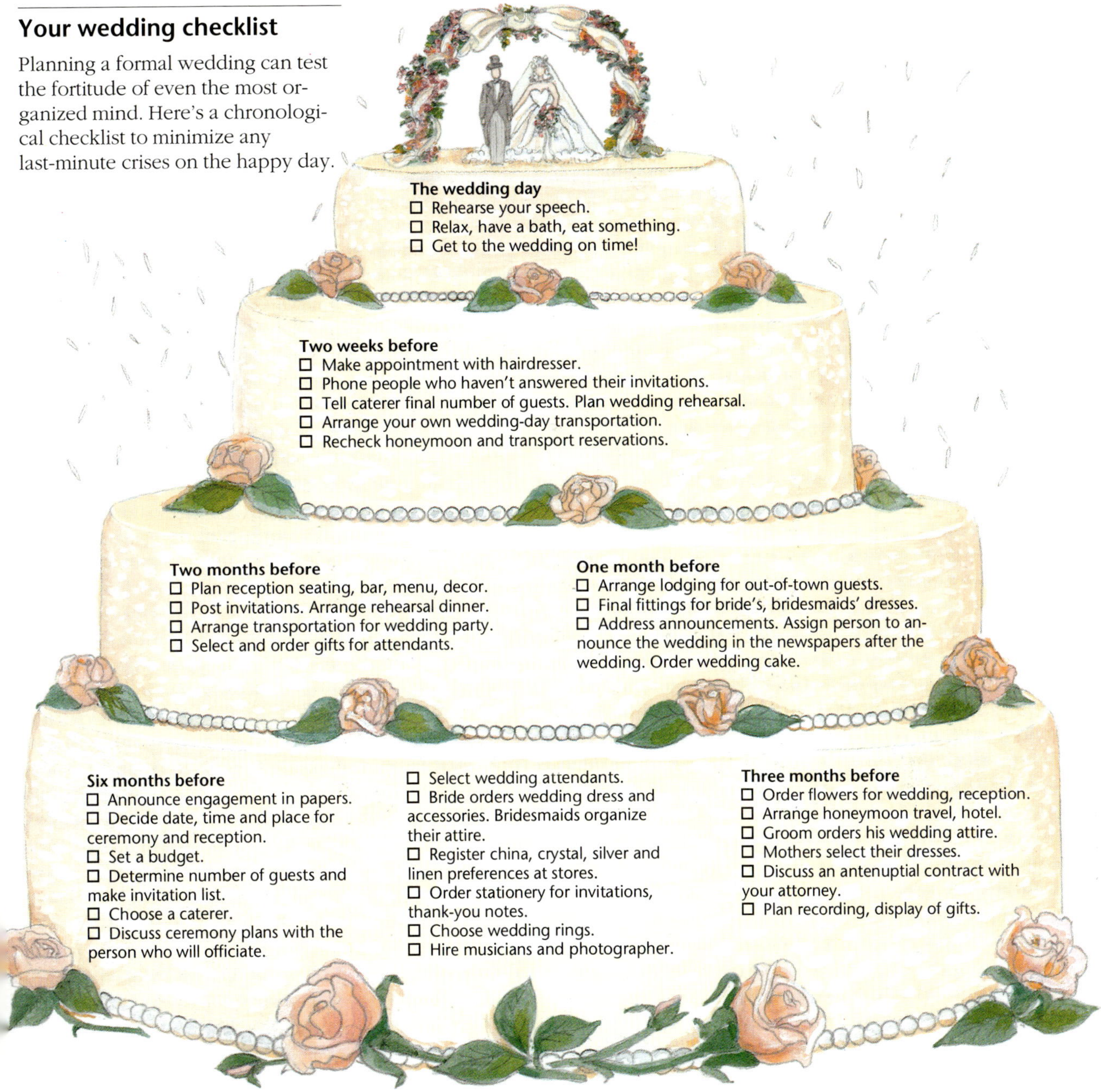

The wedding day
- ☐ Rehearse your speech.
- ☐ Relax, have a bath, eat something.
- ☐ Get to the wedding on time!

Two weeks before
- ☐ Make appointment with hairdresser.
- ☐ Phone people who haven't answered their invitations.
- ☐ Tell caterer final number of guests. Plan wedding rehearsal.
- ☐ Arrange your own wedding-day transportation.
- ☐ Recheck honeymoon and transport reservations.

Two months before
- ☐ Plan reception seating, bar, menu, decor.
- ☐ Post invitations. Arrange rehearsal dinner.
- ☐ Arrange transportation for wedding party.
- ☐ Select and order gifts for attendants.

One month before
- ☐ Arrange lodging for out-of-town guests.
- ☐ Final fittings for bride's, bridesmaids' dresses.
- ☐ Address announcements. Assign person to announce the wedding in the newspapers after the wedding. Order wedding cake.

Six months before
- ☐ Announce engagement in papers.
- ☐ Decide date, time and place for ceremony and reception.
- ☐ Set a budget.
- ☐ Determine number of guests and make invitation list.
- ☐ Choose a caterer.
- ☐ Discuss ceremony plans with the person who will officiate.
- ☐ Select wedding attendants.
- ☐ Bride orders wedding dress and accessories. Bridesmaids organize their attire.
- ☐ Register china, crystal, silver and linen preferences at stores.
- ☐ Order stationery for invitations, thank-you notes.
- ☐ Choose wedding rings.
- ☐ Hire musicians and photographer.

Three months before
- ☐ Order flowers for wedding, reception.
- ☐ Arrange honeymoon travel, hotel.
- ☐ Groom orders his wedding attire.
- ☐ Mothers select their dresses.
- ☐ Discuss an antenuptial contract with your attorney.
- ☐ Plan recording, display of gifts.

A wedding in a week

SIX DAYS BEFORE
- ☐ Arrange time, place (maybe a church hall).
- ☐ Find the person to officiate.
- ☐ Telephone people you want to invite (not too many).

FIVE DAYS BEFORE
- ☐ If you want reception at friend's home, get consent.
- ☐ Discuss legal requirements with an attorney.

FOUR DAYS BEFORE
- ☐ Decide on wedding attire. Order flowers if desired.

THREE DAYS BEFORE
- ☐ Buy the rings.

TWO DAYS BEFORE
- ☐ Buy food, liquor and any decorations you may need for the reception.

ONE DAY BEFORE
- ☐ Final details: shine shoes, borrow Mom's pearls.
- ☐ Relax and look forward to a new life with someone you love dearly.

A babysitter checklist

WHAT THE SITTER NEEDS TO KNOW

□ Time you'll be home.
□ Children's bedtimes.
□ What TV shows and snacks are allowed.
□ Whether to answer the door.
□ How to answer the phone; (it may be wise not to say that you're out).
□ Special instructions for infants or sick children.
□ Where things are: nappies, toys, food, books, fire extinguishers, torch, phone, first-aid supplies, fire exits, children's rooms.
□ How to lock and unlock windows and doors.

TELEPHONE NUMBERS

□ Where you can be reached:
□ Neighbour:
□ Doctor:
□ Police:
□ Fire:
□ Ambulance:
□ Poison control:

PROVISIONS FOR THE SITTER

□ Cool drinks, snacks.
□ Magazines, pillow.

Why a baby cries

Cause	Indications	What to do
Hunger	Two hours since last feeding. Baby may make sucking motions.	Give milk or formula.
Thirst	Hot day; baby perspiring.	Give water or diluted fruit juice.
Illness	Change in colour or appearance. Cold symptoms. Diarrhoea.	Consult medical book or paediatrician.
Fatigue	Baby missed nap or has had more stimulation than usual (for example company). Baby may yawn or put hands to eyes.	Put to bed. If baby can't sleep, rock or walk her.
Discomfort	Soiled nappy. Cold or hot room. Bathwater too hot or cold. Clothes tight or stiff.	Check for and change source of discomfort.
Wind/colic	Baby may pull up legs, scream, pass wind.	Burp baby. Lay him on his stomach and rub back. Carry, rock or take for a drive.
Needs contact	Stops crying when picked up.	Hold baby or put in carrier. Or position older baby so that she can see you.

Finding the right day care

ASK THE DIRECTOR

□ Is the day care centre registered? By whom?
□ What qualifications are set for the staff? How are references checked?
□ How is discipline handled?
□ What arrangements are made for sick children?
□ May I have references? The names of parents whose children have gone through the school, and parents of children now enrolled?
□ What is the children's daily routine? Are there other special programmes or activities?
□ What is the child-staff ratio? (Should be no more than 5:1 for children three to four years old; 7:1 for four- to six-year-olds.)
□ What are the fees? Can they be paid in instalments? Must they be paid in advance?
□ The answers to the above questions will help you narrow your selection and make a fairly accurate assessment of the available day care centres for your child. Make an appointment to visit two or three centres near you.

VISIT THE CENTRE OR SCHOOL AND OBSERVE

□ The attitude towards safety and cleanliness.
□ How the members of staff interact with the children.
□ Whether space, light, ventilation, heat are adequate.
□ Whether all the school's equipment seems sufficient and in reasonably good condition.
□ Whether the atmosphere is cheerful, and decorations are designed for or by children.
□ If the children look happy, relaxed, active.

TELEPHONE

□ The Department of Health Services and Welfare will give advice if you have any doubts. Ask if any complaints have been made against the centre or school.
□ The references which have been provided by the director.

Games for a rainy day

- ☐ Cut out pictures from magazines and glue them onto cardboard to make greeting cards for a child's friends or relatives.
- ☐ You can create a picture storybook on pages of coloured paper in the same way.
- ☐ If you have childproof musical instruments, such as tambourines, put on a record and let them play along.
- ☐ Invent your own instruments. Give children a lidded coffee tin or shoebox as a drum; chopsticks become drum sticks. Staple beans or buttons inside two aluminium pie plates for a tambourine.
- ☐ Have a cooking class: make some simple recipes together. The family can enjoy them at dinner.
- ☐ Act out a familiar fairy tale, or start making up your own story and let each child add a section in turn.
- ☐ Make necklaces by painting spools or pasta with acrylic or poster paints. String them together with yarn or cord. You might like to intersperse a few odd buttons.
- ☐ Put together a gift box for a favourite friend or relative; it can include the child's photo, poems or stories.
- ☐ Make costumes for next Halloween (see *Halloween costumes,* p.104).

You and your teenager

- ☐ Try not to overreact to a teenager's emotional highs and lows. They are quite normal, and are to be expected at this age.
- ☐ If your child isn't as willing to talk as he once was, or wants to be alone, don't take it personally. Respect his privacy, and don't barge into his room.
- ☐ Listen seriously to your child's opinions. If you disagree, refute an argument with the same logic and courtesy you would employ with an adult at a party or the office.
- ☐ Give her total responsibility in appropriate areas – for example, her appearance or room. She needs to learn to make her own decisions and to live with the consequences, good or bad.
- ☐ Avoid comparing him to yourself at his age.
- ☐ When conflicts arise, try not to blame or attack. Try to be generous and flexible. Stick to your basic standards, but be open to negotiation and compromise on less important points.
- ☐ Remember to praise good behaviour and admire her achievements.
- ☐ It's perfectly natural for a teenager to want acceptance by his peers. Try not to criticize his friends or, conversely, to compare him unfavourably to them.
- ☐ Make sure she receives accurate information about alcohol, drugs and sex. Encourage her to come to you or another trusted adult if she needs to talk about any matter that bothers her.
- ☐ If you're not sure how to deal with a problem your teenager has, or if there are difficult family problems, talk to the school principal or seek other professional help.

Seasonal home checkups

IN THE SPRING

OUTSIDE

☐ Check whether plaster or woodwork needs repainting or oiling to see it through the heat of summer.
☐ Patch holes in screens and screen doors.
☐ Check roof. Repair leaks; replace damaged tiles or shingles.
☐ Check for wood-boring beetles. Call exterminator if necessary.
☐ Clean out gutters and downpipes. If gutters sag, replace support brackets or add extra brackets.
☐ Check for branches and roots encroaching on house. Trim where necessary.
☐ If fascia and barge boards are loose, check for rot or sprung nails.
☐ If brickwork is damaged, add mortar where needed.
☐ See that all doors and windows open easily and close properly.
☐ Check that drains and gulleys are clear and free flowing.
☐ Increase hours of operation of pool pump.
☐ Inspect outdoor furniture and braai equipment. Check that children's play equipment is sturdy and safe.

INSIDE

☐ Open basement and attic windows to ventilate on sunny days.
☐ Check various stains and bulges on ceilings and walls. Wash if needed, or call in a qualified inspector.
☐ Check all household drains, and clean out if sluggish.
☐ Clean fireplace or anthracite burner, and consider having chimney cleaned.
☐ Unpack cupboards, allow them to air, and replace shelf liners.

IN THE AUTUMN

OUTSIDE

☐ Check mounting straps, screws, bolts for TV antenna.
☐ Inspect chimney for cracks and loose mortar. Examine flashing and, where needed, secure and add roof cement.
☐ Clean downpipes and gutters once the local deciduous trees are almost bare.
☐ Check for branches and roots encroaching on house. Trim where necessary.
☐ Check weatherproofing, and caulk around windows if necessary.
☐ Stow away portable outdoor equipment.
☐ Examine garden hoses and fittings, and stow away if area subject to severe frost.
☐ Patch and seal cracks in masonry and woodwork, especially where rats or other pests might take shelter.
☐ Decrease hours of operation of swimming pool pump.

INSIDE

☐ Close off unused rooms, to reduce the area that needs heating.
☐ Check that electrical outlets don't have too many plugs.
☐ Check that electrical wires are not worn, and that extension leads don't overheat when connected to heaters.
☐ Check doors and windows for fit, and install draught excluders where needed, especially at door leading to unheated garage.
☐ Decide where clothes can be dried indoors with least disruption to the normal household flow.
☐ Examine ceiling insulation and check lagging of waterpipes.
☐ Inspect fireplace or anthracite burner and remove any debris or flammable objects from their vicinity.

Selecting and working with contractors

☐ First, be sure to make a clear set of plans for your project. Unethical contractors will deliberately pitch their bids low, knowing that they will more than make up the difference in price on the extras or changes that inevitably occur when a contract is not clear.

☐ For small jobs that will take only one or two days, have a list of specific materials, colours, textures and finishes. For medium-sized work (three to five days), add drawings and detailed measurements.

☐ For any construction work that will take more than 15 days to complete, you should have detailed drawings done by a certified draughtsman or architect.

☐ Hire a contractor who is a member of the local master builders' association. These associations only accept membership after carefully screening the contractor. You can also complain to the association if you have problems later.

☐ Find work that you like in your community and ask the homeowner who did it. Ask your friends for recommendations too.

☐ Other good sources of information on a contractor's reputation are local estate agents and architects or draughtsmen, as well as neighbourhood hardware stores and building material suppliers.

☐ Solicit three or four written tenders. (An estimate is a guess. A tender is a legal document.) Make sure all tenders are for the same brands, grades and specifications you listed.

☐ Check with your local authority whether the work you want done requires that you should submit plans or obtain a permit. You, as owner, and not the builder, may be liable for any violations of the building by-laws.

☐ The contract you sign should spell out everything the contractor is to do (including weights, sizes and grades of materials; brand names and model numbers of appliances); the time in which he is to do it; and penalties for late completion.

☐ Include a provision limiting the cost overrun you'll accept. A maximum of 10 percent will encourage tenderers to be realistic.

☐ Your contract should specify who does the cleaning up, where things may be stored, and whether

The basic home tool kit

Because no one wants to call a repairman every time something needs doing around the house, it's wise to collect the tools you want before you need them. Always buy the best, even if you have to assemble your tool kit in stages. Cheap tools are harder to use, may collapse, and often need to be replaced.

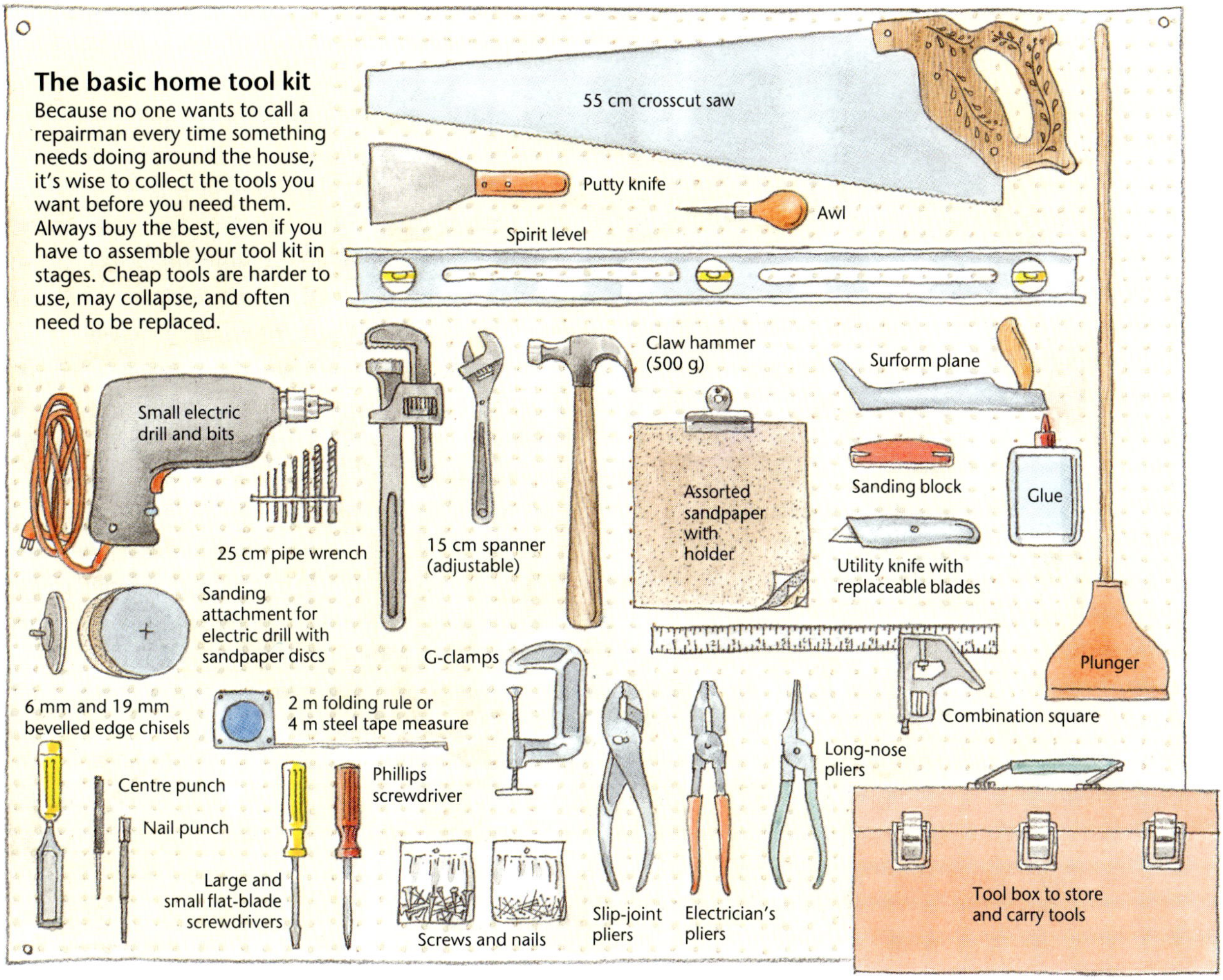

you want old appliances and timber saved or thrown out.

□ The contractor must agree in writing to install guaranteed items according to the manufacturers' instructions. All guarantees should be in writing and include the addresses of whoever is to honour them.

□ Decide whether you or the contractor will arrange insurance for loss of materials, damage to materials and to other property, worker's compensation and public liability. Check the policy for completeness and validity.

□ If your contractor doesn't pay his subcontractors or suppliers, they may be able to put a lien, or right of retention, on your home or on the materials supplied. You may be able to insert a "waver of lien" clause in your contract, or withhold payments for materials until you have seen proof that the contractor has actually paid for them. Alternatively, investigate buying materials yourself – it may work out cheaper, but it will take up a little more of your time.

□ Avoid changing your mind in the middle of a project. If you must do so, submit a written change order to the contractor, not a workman, and get his price in writing.

□ For small jobs, pay a maximum of 10 percent at the time of agreement and the balance on completion. For medium-sized jobs, 10 percent upon agreement, 25 percent when work begins, 25 percent on the third day, and the balance on completion. If you have any particular complaints, withhold 15 percent of the balance until the problems have been corrected. All financial arrangements must be clearly set out in the contract.

□ For large jobs, pay 10 percent at the time of agreement. After that, schedule 10 percent progress payments on a weekly or monthly basis – for completed work only. At no point should you or the contractor have more or less than 10 percent between what is completed and what is paid for.

□ Withhold the final 10 percent until at least 10 to 15 days after the job is finished and, if permission was required from the local authority, until the building inspector has approved it.

Safety tips for your home

Most accidents or fires that occur in the home are preventable (see *Fire Safety* p. 82). Here are many of the danger spots in the average South African home. Note that safety tips in one room may apply to other rooms as well.

Bedroom

Keep bulb wattage to that of lamp socket. If not known, limit to 60 watts.
Keep electric blankets smooth and flat. Don't tuck them under the mattress. Don't place on baby or anyone who can't tell you that blanket is too hot.
Freestanding heaters are dangerous. Keep them away from paper items, curtains, rugs, furniture, traffic paths. Keep children, pets away. Check stability, wiring label.
Have lamp and phone accessible from bed.

Avoid clutter on floor near bed.

Hallways, stairs and landings

Ensure good lighting with switc
at ground floor and each landin
Have smoke detector on each floor, one near bedrooms.
Keep clear of clutter or of furniture with sharp or protruding pa
Treads should have non-skid sur-
faces. For visibility, use five-centimetre white tape on edges.

Never leave anything on the stairs.

Install gates across bottom of stairs if you have small children.

Living room

Compare wattage on cords to that on appliances, lamps. Overloaded extension cords or outlets cause fires. Install cover plates on all outlets and switches. Call electrician if any outlet or plate is warm to the touch. Provide wide-rimmed ashtrays; don't empty them into wastepaper baskets.

Shield fireplace with screen or heat-tempered glass doors. (Keep area clear of newspapers.) Keep chimney clean; check often with torch for cracks. Leave air space around TV and stereo to prevent overheating. Keep fire, police, doctor, poison control numbers near the phone.
Don't run electrical cords under rugs or furniture or in traffic areas. Replace frayed, cracked or pinched cords.

Tack carpeting down.
Make sure balustrade is sturdy.

Tack down carpets; back rugs with slip-resistant coating or pads. Use non-slip polish on waxed floors.

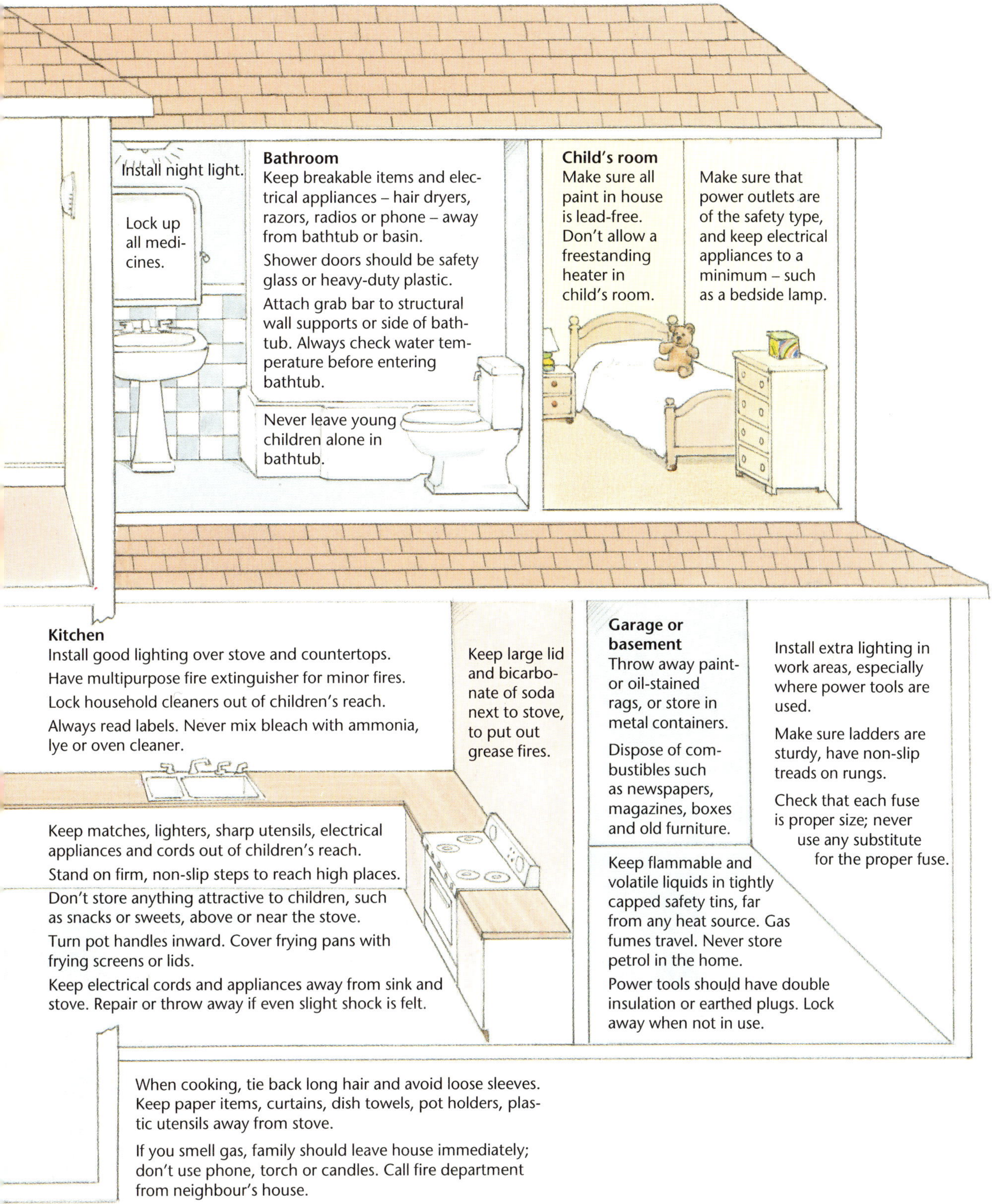

Install night light.

Lock up all medicines.

Bathroom

Keep breakable items and electrical appliances – hair dryers, razors, radios or phone – away from bathtub or basin.

Shower doors should be safety glass or heavy-duty plastic.

Attach grab bar to structural wall supports or side of bathtub. Always check water temperature before entering bathtub.

Never leave young children alone in bathtub.

Child's room

Make sure all paint in house is lead-free. Don't allow a freestanding heater in child's room.

Make sure that power outlets are of the safety type, and keep electrical appliances to a minimum – such as a bedside lamp.

Kitchen

Install good lighting over stove and countertops.

Have multipurpose fire extinguisher for minor fires.

Lock household cleaners out of children's reach.

Always read labels. Never mix bleach with ammonia, lye or oven cleaner.

Keep large lid and bicarbonate of soda next to stove, to put out grease fires.

Keep matches, lighters, sharp utensils, electrical appliances and cords out of children's reach.

Stand on firm, non-slip steps to reach high places.

Don't store anything attractive to children, such as snacks or sweets, above or near the stove.

Turn pot handles inward. Cover frying pans with frying screens or lids.

Keep electrical cords and appliances away from sink and stove. Repair or throw away if even slight shock is felt.

When cooking, tie back long hair and avoid loose sleeves. Keep paper items, curtains, dish towels, pot holders, plastic utensils away from stove.

If you smell gas, family should leave house immediately; don't use phone, torch or candles. Call fire department from neighbour's house.

Garage or basement

Throw away paint- or oil-stained rags, or store in metal containers.

Dispose of combustibles such as newspapers, magazines, boxes and old furniture.

Install extra lighting in work areas, especially where power tools are used.

Make sure ladders are sturdy, have non-slip treads on rungs.

Check that each fuse is proper size; never use any substitute for the proper fuse.

Keep flammable and volatile liquids in tightly capped safety tins, far from any heat source. Gas fumes travel. Never store petrol in the home.

Power tools should have double insulation or earthed plugs. Lock away when not in use.

Protecting your home

One of the most effective ways to protect your home is with an alarm system. You can install some systems yourself; others are best left to professionals. Your insurance company or the police may be able to provide advice.

Windows

Stick alarm-system labels, or beware-of-dog signs on windows – whether or not you have an alarm system or a dog.

To substitute for a lock, drill holes at a slightly downward angle through inside sash, about three-quarters of the way into outside sash at top corners of lower window. Insert eye-bolts or nails into holes.

Close curtains or blinds and lock all the windows if you're going out.

Place TV's, VCR's, and the like with illuminated parts facing away from window.

Have timers turn certain lights and the radio on and off at staggered times when you're away at night.

Leave radio on during day when you're out.

Install key locks on windows.

Fasten air conditioner securely to window frame or sill so that it can't be pulled out.

Doors

Solid wood or metal doors should fit snugly into frames.

Give a set of keys to trusted neighbours. Don't hide or hang them outside.

Be sure to mount dead-bolt locks securely to doorframes.

Replace glass or lightweight panels in doors or install double-cylinder locks with both inside and outside keys. Or cover glass panels with grillwork.

Consider having metal expanding doors fitted over the door which you usually open when someone knocks.

Install lights over doorways. Have house number lit and visible from street.

Install wide-angle peephole and chain lock. Have second peephole for children.

Never leave notes on door that indicate you're absent.

Don't install a pet door; a thief may have a child accomplice.

Ground-floor windows

Consider shatterproof glass for ground-floor windows, or substantial burglar-bars.

Shrubs and trees

Don't grow trees where they obscure windows or doors.

Keep shrub height below windows and use prickly plants, such as roses or cacti.

Basement windows

Install steel bar securely midway across basement windows so that intruders can't get through opening.

Postbox

Use only last name if you live alone.

Drainpipes

Plastic drainpipes are less likely than metal ones to support a climber.

Apply grease on the drainpipe.

Put cement between drainpipe and wall. (Check first to be sure this won't cause humidity build-up.)

Surround bottom of drainpipes with prickly plants.

Other precautions

Have lampposts or floodlights illuminate garden at night.

Place floodlights too high for burglars to reach. Infrared sensor will turn lights on when someone approaches.

Put ladders away after each use. If they are stored outside, padlock them to something immovable.

Keep trellises and picnic tables away from house.

Install a metal fence with a locking gate. (Solid fences shield burglars from view.)

Post crime-watch signs near street.

Dogs, even small ones, that bark at strangers are good deterrents to burglars.

Sliding glass doors

Use vertical-bolt locks or shatterproof glass for sliding glass doors. Or cut broom handle to fit in track so that doors won't slide.

Drill holes and insert screws along doorframe so that sliding doors can't be lifted.

Large wooden doors installed outside glass doors need not be closed or locked except in your absence.

Garage

Have a switch inside your house that can turn garage lights on and off.

Install peephole in door between house and garage.

Have chain with combination lock that prevents door from being lifted even if an intruder breaks a panel and unlocks door.

Padlock roller bracket on garage door to track or place obstruction in track to prevent intruder from lifting door.

Stoep

Keep stoep lit at night.

Remove deliveries promptly so that house doesn't seem unoccupied.

Plant	Light and care	Plant	Light and care
African violet Delicate flowers (white, blue, purple, bicolour) in rosette of leaves.	Diffused light. Add peat moss to soil. Keep pot on wet pebbles. Keep soil moist, not soggy. Clean leaves with lukewarm water; let dry in shade.	**Aloe** Juice in thin, long succulent leaves soothes burns but is toxic if ingested.	Maximum light. Use light sandy soil mix. Water when soil dries completely, once or twice weekly in summer, once or twice a month in winter.
Amaryllis Large flowers (white, pink to red) on stalk with long, thin leaves. Bulb is poisonous.	Maximum or moderate light. Water only during active growth period (spring to autumn), when soil dries. Feed monthly during this time.	**Asparagus fern** Needlelike leaves on thin, graceful stems.	Moderate light. Keep soil moist, not soggy. In spring and summer, give all-purpose foliage plant food monthly.
Begonia, wax Shiny foliage on fleshy stems. Numerous white, pink or red flowers.	Maximum to moderate light. Allow soil to become slightly dry between thorough waterings. Feed monthly.	**Boston fern** Cascading, lush. Various types include those with ruffled and lacy leaflets.	Moderate light in winter, diffused in summer. Use soil containing humus. Keep pot on wet pebbles. Keep soil moist, not soggy.
Coleus Green leaves variously marked with pink, red, orange and yellow.	Maximum light in winter, moderate in summer. Keep soil moist, not soggy. In spring and summer, give foliage plant food every two weeks.	**Grape ivy** Shiny, three-part leaves on climbing vine.	Moderate or diffused light. Keep soil moist, not soggy. Give all-purpose plant food every two to three months.
Jade plant Fleshy leaves on branching stems; sometimes has pink or white flowers.	Maximum light. Use light sandy soil mix. Water after soil is nearly dry.	**Philodendron, split-leaf** Sectioned glossy leaves are toxic.	Diffused light. Use soil containing humus. Keep soil moist, not soggy. Mist leaves regularly. In spring and summer, feed every month.
Devil's ivy Heart-shaped, waxy leaves, mottled with yellow. Poisonous if eaten.	Diffused light. Water when soil is nearly dry.	**Rubber plant** Broad oval leaves on tall stalk.	Maximum to diffused light. Keep soil moist, not soggy. Give all-purpose plant food every six months. Spray or wash leaves.
Schefflera (umbrella tree) Whorls of compound leaves on long stalks.	Moderate or diffused light. Water thoroughly when soil is nearly dry.	**Mother-in-law's tongue** Long, knife-shaped, leathery leaves grow vertically from the soil.	Maximum to minimum light. Water after soil is nearly dry. Give all-purpose plant food occasionally in spring and summer.
Hen and chickens Slender leaves, green with white stripes, cascading from rosette; spidery plantlets sprout along shoots.	Diffused light. Keep soil moist, not soggy. Give foliage plant food every two months. Plantlets can be cut and rooted.	**Crab cactus** Drooping jointed branches with clawlike notches bear showy pink blooms.	Maximum light, but diffused in summer. Use porous soil. In dormant period, water when soil is dry. During flowering, water after surface soil dries.
Velvet plant (purple passion plant) Purple hairs on jagged leaves give fuzzy texture.	Maximum light. Use soil containing humus; keep it moist, not soggy. Give foliage plant food once monthly.	**Wandering Jew** Cascading oval leaves are green and silver on top, purple underneath.	Diffused light. Keep soil moist, never soggy. In spring and summer, give foliage plant food once monthly.

Caring for your house plants

The chart above lists the needs of the most popular house plants. In the *Light and care* column, *maximum* means direct (not through glass) sunlight; *moderate* describes bright light but not direct sunlight; *diffused* light describes light found away from a strong source of light, and *minimum* means very low light or shade.

Weapons for weed-haters

□ When buying grass seed or runners, it's worth paying a higher price to a reputable dealer.
□ Feed and top-dress your lawn regularly to aid grass growth.
□ To deny weeds the light they need and to keep grass roots competitive, don't mow until grass has reached a height of five to seven centimetres.
□ Douse weeds that grow in the cracks of your paths with boiling water to which you've added salt.
□ If moss grows in your garden, it's a clue that your lawn needs better drainage, more frequent fertilization, and the addition of lime.
□ Find out which of your weeds are annual, biennial and perennial. Biennials will die if you pull out the tops. (This is also true of annuals in the summer and autumn.) Perennials must be completely eradicated.
□ Pull out difficult weeds with pliers; extract small patches with the forked end of a claw hammer.
□ Where you must weed by hand, wait until just after rain.
□ Avoid using weed-killing chemicals where they may also affect ornamental plants. Rather use your hoe or rake.
□ If you must use chemicals, wait for a windless day, and follow instructions carefully.
□ Adding lime to the soil discourages many weeds, but be sure not to overdose.
□ Thick clumps of weeds can be destroyed with boiling water. Pull out large amounts with a rake.
□ Some weeds, such as young dandelion greens and purslane, make a tasty salad.
□ If you own weedy land near your garden, make sure it's mowed properly at least twice a year. Goats and sheep love weeds but, if not fenced off, will also devour your favourite flowers.
□ Clover, English daisies, Queen Anne's lace, and a variety of other flowering weeds can be decorative in a well-tended garden. You may not need to rid the entire lawn of these weeds; in fact, some gardeners nurture them, but restrict them to a limited area and add them to flower arrangements indoors.

Safety tips for power mowers

Every year hundreds of people are injured in lawnmower accidents. To make sure you're not one of them, take the following precautions.
□ Carefully read and follow safety instructions in your owner's manual. (Some may be printed on the mower.)
□ Periodically check the machine. Make sure nuts, bolts and screws are tight, and remove grass, debris and excessive grease from the engine.
□ Fill the petrol tank outdoors while the engine is cold. Be sure to stay away from all heat sources (including cigarettes). Immediately wipe up any spills. Replace petrol cap securely.
□ Before mowing, clear the lawn of stones, wire, sticks and other objects that could be picked up and spun out by the blades. Set the blade height for at least five to seven centimetres. Never run a lawnmower over gravel.
□ Never wear running shoes, tackies or sandals when using a power mower. Sturdy shoes are best. Avoid loose clothing and jewellery. Tie back long hair.
□ Make sure the machine is on level ground when you start it. Stand clear of the blades.
□ Mow only when grass is dry; wet grass can make you fall and can clog the machine.
□ Allow no one, especially children and animals, in the area where you're working. If someone should approach you, turn off the engine.
□ Mow across, rather than up or down, a slope. You'll have better control, and if you should slip, you'll be less likely to fall toward the mower. Never make a sharp turn on a slope.
□ If you have a four-stroke petrol-powered mower, ask the agent whether it is safe to use on a steep slope. The angle of the slope may cause the oil to drain away from the big-end bearings, resulting in a seized engine.
□ Frequently remove debris from the blades with a stick. First, turn the engine off and wait for the blades to stop. Unplug an electric mower. With a petrol-powered mower, disconnect the spark plug.
□ Turn the engine off if you need to leave the mower unattended, even for a few minutes.
□ Always put the mower away after you use it. Let the engine cool off first.

WALK-BEHIND POWER MOWERS

□ When using a walk-behind power mower, never raise or tilt it once it's running. This not only exposes the blades to your feet, but it also poses a hazard to others nearby. Tilting a mower may also cause the blades to engage objects on the ground.

RIDING MOWERS

□ Check the safety features. The ideal safety feature is the switch that cuts the motor as soon as the operator rises from the seat.
□ Never carry passengers. Look behind you before you reverse, to be sure no one has strayed into the area.
□ Mow slowly and avoid holes and sudden drops, which could cause the machine to overturn.
□ Be sure the blade is disengaged and the transmission is in *Park*, before putting your foot on the ground.

Before you look for a house

Searching for a house to buy can be a long and arduous process. But the experience need not be too stressful. You can save time and effort in the long run by starting with a number of general enquiries about the area you like, finding out about its amenities, its possible disadvantages and the types of housing which are available.

DETERMINE YOUR PRICE RANGE

□ Shop for financing first. The amount of your loan will determine which houses you can consider.

GET TO KNOW THE NEIGHBOURHOOD

□ Drive, cycle or walk around an area that is new to you, to get the feel of the community. Make several visits, at different times of the day and week. Do not assume that streets which are quiet on a Sunday afternoon continue to be so for the rest of the week.

□ Visit the planning department of the nearest council and enquire about major development schemes to be carried out in the area.

□ Check how close the property is to any possible source of pollution – such as an oil refinery, cement factory or power station. If in doubt, consult neighbours.

□ Find out what form of public transport members of the family will have to use to get to work or school. Check the frequency of the services, and the times of buses and trains. If you plan to travel to work by car, drive over the route, preferably during the rush hour.

□ Check how many schools are in the area, and how close you are to them. Neighbours will most probably be able to tell you where the schools are, and may be able to pass on information about the reputation of a school. For a clearer picture of schooling standards, visit the school and talk to the staff.

Browse through back copies of the local newspaper to gain a knowledge of facilities and entertainment available in the neighbourhood. Newspapers will also give you a good idea of the social life of the area, as well as useful information about social, political and religious organisations.

□ Find out what the annual rates and taxes are in the area?

GETTING THE RIGHT AGENT

Before you buy a house, make sure you're dealing with a reputable estate agent.

□ Does the estate agent represent a company known to you or recommended by your friends? Will the agent give contactable references – that is, the names and addresses of satisfied clients?

□ Remember that the agent represents the seller; however, she owes the buyer honest disclosure of all known facts about a property.

INTERVIEW ATTORNEYS

A good attorney is vital when you intend buying a house. Find out:

□ If the attorney is experienced in handling local property transactions.

□ What services he will provide.

□ What his hourly or flat rate is.

□ If there will be additional costs.

INSPECTING THE HOUSE

Some sorts of inspection – checking for subsidence and structural soundness, for instance – are jobs for an expert: an architect or a valuer. If you apply for a mortgage loan, the property will be checked by a building society's inspector. If not, you can engage a valuer to value the property – his charge will depend on the value.

Hidden costs of home buying

Many first-time home buyers are not aware of all the expenses involved in purchasing property. Ask your banker, broker and attorney about the following, which can add from two to 10 percent to what you expected to pay.

□ Attorney's fee

□ Application fee for your mortgage

□ Appraisal fee on the house

□ Survey of the property

□ Engineer's inspection of the house

□ Credit report on you

□ Conveyancing fee

□ Bond registration costs

□ Interim interest

□ Life insurance, to cover the amount of the mortgage bond

□ Homeowner's insurance

□ Householders' insurance

□ Inspection of the house for notifiable beetle

□ Transfer duty

□ Occupational interest

□ *Pro rata* share of rates and taxes.

Paying for your house

Shopping for a mortgage bond is the most crucial step in the home-buying process. Talk to several

Monthly payments in rands on a fixed 30-year mortgage bond

Interest rate	R100,000	R120,000	R140,000	R160,000	R180,000	R200,000
16%	941	1,076	1,210	1,345	1,479	1,614
15%	885	1,012	1,138	1,264	1,391	1,517
14%	829	948	1,066	1,185	1,303	1,422
13%	774	885	996	1,106	1,217	1.327
12%	720	823	926	1,029	1,131	1,234
11%	667	762	857	952	1,047	1,143
10%	614	702	790	878	966	1,053
9%	563	644	734	805	885	966
8%	514	587	660	733	807	881

banks and building societies, and take the list of hidden costs (opposite) with you. Ask which of them will be charged. As the chart shows, even a "small" increase can add substantially to your monthly payments and leave you with less money to offer for the house you want. (See also *Down payments*, p.66.)

Evaluating a house

Once you know what you can afford and have found a neighbourhood you like, you can narrow the field to two or three houses.

☐ Ask yourself: do I want a house this new (or this old)?

☐ Determine that the house meets your basic space requirements – for example, if you plan a family or want a downstairs bedroom for an elderly parent.

☐ Have a competent builder or an engineer check the structural soundness of the house and the electrical and plumbing systems.

☐ Ask to see the owner's bills for electricity and water for the past 12 months.

☐ Ask to see the owner's bills for property rates and taxes.

☐ In rural areas have a plumber inspect the septic system. Have the borehole water tested for quality and for flow.

☐ Before you start negotiating the price, find out how much comparable houses in the neighbourhood have fetched recently.

Sprucing up

After you decide to sell your house, make it as attractive as possible to potential buyers. Avoid expensive or unusual renovations. Your goal is to make your house look bright, neat, cheerful and problem-free.

OUTDOORS

☐ Try to get rid of any clutter in the garden.

☐ Mow lawn, weed flower beds, prune shrubs, sweep paths.

☐ Spend about R300 to plant colourful flowers or shrubs where they can be seen from the street.

☐ See that outdoor lighting works.

☐ Have gates, fences painted and in good repair.

☐ Touch up exterior paint where needed. Give special attention to front door, garage door and woodwork around windows.

☐ See that roof is in good condition.

☐ Clean the pool.

INDOORS

☐ Put away any clutter. Storing extra furniture makes rooms look more spacious.

☐ Arrange storage areas and cupboards neatly.

☐ Fix leaky taps. Remove water or rust stains from basins and baths.

☐ Be sure the air conditioning is working smoothly.

☐ Have a spring cleaning: shampoo rugs, polish floors, wash walls and windows, wipe away fingerprints, smudges, dust, mildew.

☐ Replace burned-out or dim bulbs with higher-wattage light bulbs.

☐ Replace tired-looking shower curtains or kitchen curtains.

☐ Glue down any loose wallpaper.

☐ In the kitchen, clear off countertops, wipe cabinets, and clean the oven. Replace flooring if it's in very bad condition.

☐ Give your house the "sniff test". To get rid of food odours and pet odours, bake an apple or sprinkle vanilla in a warm oven on days when you're expecting buyers.

Buying a car – the costs

Before you buy a car, decide exactly what it will be used for, then study the costs of running it. If you intend using the car for shopping and local trips, rather than long, high-speed journeys, your costs may differ considerably.

However, certain essential costs of owning a car – registration, insurance, garaging and loss of interest on capital – remain the same, whether you drive 100 kilometres a week or 1,000. Petrol and maintenance costs, when viewed against the overall cost of car ownership, make up only a small percentage of costs, so if you want a car only for occasional weekend trips and holidays, it may be cheaper to rent one.

There are three principal ways of financing the purchase of a car – buying for cash, raising a loan and hire purchase.

CASH

This is normally the cheapest way – you save finance charges and should be able to negotiate a reasonable cash discount.

RAISING A LOAN

If you can, try to borrow money independently, rather than through the dealer or hire purchase bank. This enables you to pay cash for the car and still negotiate a cash discount. Several options are available, and all of them should be investigated thoroughly before you commit yourself.

1. See your bank manager about an overdraft, and ask what the applicable interest rate is. Favourable rates will be available to you if you have enough securities to deposit with the bank. The drawback is that the overdraft can be recalled with very little notice.

2. Borrow against a building society investment – interest rates charged on these loans are normally very favourable.

3. Borrow more money on the mortgage bond of your home. The building society or bank will consider your application in the light of the value of your property, the balance still owing, and whether they have funds available.

HIRE PURCHASE

In a hire purchase sale, you, the buyer, agree to buy the vehicle from the seller on an instalment basis, the seller retaining ownership until the final instalment is paid. However, you possess the vehicle and use it as if you were the owner.

You will have to pay a minimum deposit laid down by law when the agreement is concluded, and will be given a period in which to pay instalments on the purchase price of the item. This period is also laid down by law.

If you are satisfied that you can afford to buy on instalment sale, you may either:

1. Obtain finance from the dealer or supplier; or

2. Obtain finance from a bank or finance house, which means, in effect, that you can buy the vehicle for "cash" (as far as the dealer is concerned).

If you want to obtain credit through the dealer, you should ask the dealer what rate of finance charges you will pay – but you must be quite sure that the rate quoted is the true rate.

If finance is obtained from the dealer, the dealer will normally "discount" with a finance house. This means the finance house will take over the agreement, and instalments will be paid to it, rather than to the dealer. The finance company will pay the dealer the price of the vehicle, plus a small cut of the interest charged – say 3 or 4 per cent where a 30 per cent charge is levied.

Very often you will pay fewer finance charges on an instalment sale if you obtain cash direct from the finance house, which will not have to pay 3 or 4 per cent commission to the dealer. You will also probably be able to negotiate a discount for cash with the dealer.

Credit agreements must be in writing and signed by every party to the agreement. The written contract must state the names and addresses of the parties and the amount of the "initial payment" or "initial rental" (the deposit).

It must also describe the goods or service involved and any goods which form part of the purchase price, such as a trade-in.

Shopping for a used car

Because depreciation is less, the operating cost of a used car per kilometre, on average, is approximately half that of a new car. Here are some tips to help you tell the bargains from the lemons.

SHOP

for your car loan first. You will save time by knowing which cars you can afford.

CHECK

the going price of cars that you like, in the newspaper columns, car magazines and motor-trade publications that you may be able to obtain in your library.

DON'T

confine your shopping to used-car lots. Check trade-ins at new-car dealers as well as owners' ads, especially those from affluent suburbs.

BEST BUYS

are usually cars three years old or newer that have been driven between 15 000 and 25 000 kilometres.

AVOID

convertibles and luxury cars which won't be bargains. Small and medium sedans are easier to maintain and repair.

The visual inspection

- ☐ Always wait for a sunny day.
- ☐ Suspect any cosmetic paint job (check trim, rubber around doors for signs of overpainting).

□ Reject a car that's rusting badly. Check wheel wells, edges of doors, window trim.
□ See whether kilometres on the odometer match the figures on service stickers on the door post.
□ Examine underside for rust, broken frame, fluid leaks, new welding.
□ Push down hard on the bodywork above each wheel, then let go. If the car bounces up and down repeatedly, shocks are worn. Strut-type shocks are costly to replace.
□ Uneven wear on tyres or spare tyre may mean wheels need alignment or may indicate serious front-end problems or bad ball joints.
□ Be sure that windows and doors open and close properly.
□ Water stains in boot, around windows, on carpet, indicate leaks.
□ Beware of cars with cracked windscreens; they may not pass the roadworthy examination.
□ Open bonnet. Check engine block for cracks, oil leaks. Repaired wiring shows earlier electrical fault.
□ Check belts, hoses, cables for wear. Powdery residues on hoses indicate leaks.
□ Engine oil dipstick should read *Full*. Milky colour or flakes in oil indicate serious engine problems.
□ Open the radiator cap: look at the coolant. If it is rusty or strawberry coloured, radiator is corroded.
□ Turn the ignition on. Do all dashboard lights go on at once? Oil light should go off soon after engine starts if there is good oil pressure.
□ Check accessories. Do headlights work on both high and low beams? Is parking light OK? Do windscreen wipers and indicator lights function?
□ Start the engine; if it clanks when you start it or grinds or knocks when you rev it, reject the car. Blue or black exhaust smoke means the engine burns too much oil.
□ With the engine warm and idling, pull the automatic transmission dipstick; it should read *Full*. Fluid should be red; if it's dark or smells burnt, the car may need valve-train repair.

Test-driving a used car

□ While car is stationary, push the brake pedal briefly. If it sinks to the floor, there may be a leak in the hydraulic system. Make sure that you don't drive the car.
□ Map out a route that includes a city street, a parking lot, a bumpy road, a hill and a freeway.
□ On a street with little traffic, accelerate to 60 km/h. If the gears stick, grind or jerk, reject the car.
□ Brake gently and slow down to about 15 km/h. Car should not pull to either side; brakes should not squeak or grind.
□ When no driver is behind you, speed up to 25 km/h and brake hard. The car should stop at once without swerving; the brakes shouldn't squeal.
□ In an empty parking lot, test the transmission by shifting into *Reverse*, braking to a stop, shifting into *First*, braking at about 8 km/h, and shifting into *Reverse* again. Car should run smoothly.
□ Make some sharp right, left and U-turns. A car that doesn't handle well may have a faulty front suspension or steering linkage.
□ At 30 km/h remove hands from the wheel; after a minute, brake smoothly. If car didn't keep a steady course, have mechanic check the front end.
□ On a bumpy road, notice if the car sways, bounces or shimmies and shakes. If it does, don't buy it.
□ With front-wheel drive cars, listen for clattering noises from the CV (constant velocity) joints up front, especially when cornering.
□ Stop halfway down a hill, shift into *Neutral*, and set the parking brake. Does the parking brake hold when you remove your foot?
□ At a freeway, wait till way is clear, then pull away rapidly. If the car doesn't accelerate smoothly and progressively, or if smoke comes from the exhaust, the engine may need expensive repairs.
□ Make sure you can pass other cars easily.
□ At the end of the test drive, let the engine idle a few minutes before shutting it off. Raise the bonnet and look for leaks or seepage.
□ Examine the ground under the car. There should be no fluid drips except from the air conditioning, which normally drips clear water.

Before you make an offer

If a car has passed your visual inspection and test drive and you want to make an offer, here are some final steps to take.
□ Get the name of a reliable diagnostic centre, service station or mechanic from friends or the Automobile Association. The mechanic should do the following:

1. Perform a compression test and a cylinder power-balance test.
2. See that the car will pass the roadworthy examination.
3. Find out how much a used car warranty will add to the price, and exactly what parts and labour it covers. For what period or distance covered is it valid, and is it underwritten by the car's agents?

□ If buying from a private owner, ask for proof of regular servicing or of repairs he claims to have carried out. If no documents can be produced, check with the workshop he claims to have used.
□ When buying an older model – say 10 years or older – make sure that spare parts are still readily available at reasonable prices, and are likely to continue to be available.
□ Before you hand over any money, check that the chassis number and engine number match those on the registration certificate. If you suspect the seller, ask the police to run a stolen car check. A stolen car can be reclaimed by its owner.
□ Ask to see proof that the car has been fully paid – approach the financial institution which loaned the money to the original owner if necessary. A car which has not been fully paid for by a previous owner can be reclaimed.

Coping with car noises

Sound	Possible problem	Solution	Sound	Possible problem	Solution
Backfiring	Incorrect ignition timing; faulty ignition parts or valves	Have a mechanic check ignition and valve timing	Hiss	Leak in tyres, hoses or exhaust system	Check tyres or see a mechanic
Buzz	Loose dashboard or heater components	Tighten accessible clamps or screws	Clatter from front end	Worn steering components or, with front-wheel drive, worn CV joints.	See a mechanic
Clatter from engine	Insufficient oil level. Defective valves or lifters	Check oil level or see a mechanic	Rattle when engine accelerates	Wrong grade of fuel or engine needs tuning	Try higher octane petrol or get a tune-up
Clatter under car with rear-wheel drive	Faulty U-joints	See a mechanic	Roar as car accelerates	Rusted-out muffler or exhaust pipes	Have exhaust system inspected without delay
Clicking under bonnet	Fan blade may be striking radiator	Check fan and radiator for damage	Screech when braking	Worn or defective brake parts	Have brakes checked
Clicking from wheels	Loose hubcap or stone under hubcap. Bad wheel bearing	Check for stones. If none, see a mechanic	Squealing as car accelerates	An engine accessory drive belt is loose	Tighten or replace drive belt
Squealing as wheels turn	Power steering drive belt is loose	Tighten or replace drive belt	Whirring from starter	Fault in starter bendix	Clean bendix; check spring

Keeping your car on the road

You should scrupulously follow the maintenance schedule designed for your car as outlined in your owner's manual. Keep the manual in the vehicle's cubbyhole for easy access if an emergency crops up. Be alert for such problems as abnormal vibrations, steering-wheel pull, brake pedal softness or hardness, unusual noises or odours, and abnormal readings on dashboard gauges or warning lights.

Whenever you fill the petrol tank, make a habit of carefully checking the levels of oil, coolant and windscreen wiper fluid. Also check that the vehicle's petrol consumption is much the same as that which was promised by the dealer.

You should also keep an eye out for minor defects on the bodywork or on the interior – especially if your vehicle is brand-new.

Here are some guidelines for caring for most car makes.

EVERY MONTH

- ☐ Test lights.
- ☐ Check battery fluid level.
- ☐ Inspect ground under car for fluid leaks.
- ☐ Check tyre pressure.

3 MONTHS/5 000 KM

- ☐ Change engine oil and filter.
- ☐ Clean battery terminals, cables.
- ☐ Inspect exhaust system for leaks.
- ☐ Remove debris from radiator.
- ☐ Check the vacuum hoses and drive belts.

6 MONTHS/10 000 KM

- ☐ Check fluid levels (power steering, brake, transmission, rear axle).
- ☐ Check the protection strength of the coolant.
- ☐ Check hoses (radiator, heater, air conditioner).
- ☐ Check all drive belts for wear, cracks, oil damage.
- ☐ Inspect exhaust system for signs of rust-through; retighten clamps.
- ☐ Check front-wheel-drive axle boots for cracks and leaks.
- ☐ Examine battery cable terminals.
- ☐ Check air filter; replace if dirty. Rotate tyres.
- ☐ Check headlight aim.

12 MONTHS/20 000 KM

- ☐ Inspect brake lines for cracks; brake pads and linings for wear.
- ☐ Test parking brake (automatic transmission). Replace spark plugs.
- ☐ Lubricate lock cylinders; body points; door, bonnet, boot and fuel door hinges and locks.
- ☐ Check shock absorbers, wheel alignment.
- ☐ See that weatherstripping is snug around doors.
- ☐ Have radiator flushed and replace antifreeze.

4 YEARS/100 000 KM

- ☐ Replace drive belts, brake fluid, transmission fluids (gearbox and differential) and filters. Flush cooling system and then replace coolant hoses. Remember to add water-pump lubricant or antifreeze if required when refilling.

At an accident

On average, there are almost 400,000 accidents on South African roads each year. This is an alarming figure if one considers that in Britain, with a population more than double that of South Africa, the number of accidents annually is roughly the same.

About 29,000 of all accidents involve pedestrians, while about 24,000 involve motorcyclists. More than 91,000 people are injured each year, and about 12,000 die. Because of the high number of accidents in South Africa, many people find themselves indirectly involved by arriving on the scene, rendering first aid and helping casualties.

Here are some vital tips to heed at the accident scene:

1. Park your car well away from the accident – behind it, if possible. Turn on your hazard warning lights. At night, train your headlights on the damaged vehicles as well.

2. Be sure to leave your car with its front wheels turned towards the kerb so that if another car runs into yours, your car will be pushed off the road, not into you or the crashed vehicles.

3. If one of the crashed vehicles is on fire, keep clear. Its petrol tank could explode without warning.

4. Take charge of the accident scene if no one else has done so. If someone is already in charge, make yourself useful to him.

5. Warn approaching traffic in both directions. If other traffic is coming up behind you, flag it down, keeping well to the side of the road; at night use a torch or light-coloured scarf. Ask someone to stop traffic coming the other way.

6. Put a warning triangle, if one is available, about 90 metres behind the damaged vehicles, towards the nearside edge of the road. Ideally, put another the same distance away in the opposite direction.

7. Check the number of vehicles involved, and the number of victims, noting whether anyone is trapped.

8. Ask a passing driver or anyone living nearby to call an ambulance (if necessary) and the police from the nearest telephone. Tell him how many people are injured or trapped. Try to describe their injuries.

9. If you are telephoning the ambulance service and police, describe the accident location as exactly as you can. Say how many vehicles are involved, whether any vehicle is on fire, and whether anyone is trapped.

10. Immobilise the crashed vehicles immediately by switching off their ignition, but leave the key in the ignition in case the steering locks – the vehicle may have to be moved later.

11. Check that the handbrake of each car is on. If it is not, put it on.

12. Do not smoke, and warn others not to – even away from the cars. There may be petrol running in the gutter or leaking across the road from a ruptured fuel tank.

13. Do not move anyone unless he is in immediate danger – if there is a car on fire close by, for example, or if he is lying in leaking petrol which you think might catch fire. If you move an injured person, you risk aggravating his injuries; that risk is worth taking only to protect him from a greater risk.

If you're in an accident

1. Stop as soon as you safely can. Check for injuries to yourself and to any passengers or pedestrians.

2. Call an ambulance if necessary. Call the police. It is possible that they may come only if there is an injury, or if damage appears to be very serious.

3. Write down the names, addresses and telephone numbers of all those involved, including passengers and witnesses. Note if anyone was injured.

4. In addition, get the other car's licence plate number, name and address of its owner and whatever details you can about the other driver's licence, his insurance company and policy number.

5. Make a note of the time, weather and road conditions.

6. Take snapshots or make a diagram of the accident scene. Be sure to show the vehicles involved, the directions in which they were moving, any skid marks, and nearby road signs or traffic lights.

7. If a police officer arrives, note his name or badge number. Make every effort to co-operate, but be careful what you say. Avoid blaming yourself, directly or indirectly.

8. Don't sign any statements.

9. If you are taken to a hospital, write down its name and the names of all the doctors who treat you, in addition to their diagnoses. Even if you don't think you're hurt, consider going to your own doctor to get an evaluation.

10. If the police don't arrive, report the accident at the nearest police station within 24 hours, and ask for the incident number. You will need this when dealing with insurance claims. Only one of the parties involved must report the accident, so decide with the other driver.

11. Write down your impressions of the event as soon as you get home. Add subsequent recollections or medical symptoms.

12. Notify your insurance company as soon as possible; ask how to proceed, and especially how to fill out an accident report.

Don't get taken for a ride

- ☐ Shop around for a reliable local mechanic and workshop *before* you have an emergency.
- ☐ Ask your friends and neighbours (especially those with older cars that run well) for recommendations.
- ☐ Ask local used-car dealers which garages they use.
- ☐ Having small problems taken care of before they become big problems is a good practice and helps you assess the general reliability of a workshop.
- ☐ Make a written list of your car's symptoms and give it to the workshop foreman or, preferably, direct-

ly to the mechanic. (Keep a copy for your own reference.)

- ☐ Don't ask for a specific repair unless you're absolutely sure about the nature of the problem. You may end up paying for a repair you didn't need.
- ☐ If you don't feel that you can accurately describe what's wrong, ask the mechanic to go with you for a test drive.
- ☐ Insist on a detailed written estimate and the guarantee that no additional work will be done without your permission. Leave a phone number where you can be reached.
- ☐ When you pick up the repaired car, it's a good idea to test-drive it before you take it home.
- ☐ Request an itemised bill and a receipt in case the problem wasn't solved and you have to return the car for further adjustment.
- ☐ If items such as shock absorbers or a silencer system need to be replaced before their guarantee expires, instruct the workshop to keep the parts so you can use them to claim a refund from the supplier.
- ☐ Ensure that your choice of workshop will not invalidate the terms of any guarantee or warranty.
- ☐ The principal reason that so-called "pirate parts" are usually much cheaper than the car manufacturer's parts, is that they're often of inferior quality, so use them with caution.

Packing light

Want to avoid long waits at the baggage counter or, worse yet, lost luggage counter? Try to pack everything into carry-on bags. (Women can also fit some items into a large handbag.) Wear your heaviest clothes; wear layers unless it's too hot. Here's a checklist to help you choose which items you really need.

CLOTHES

- ☐ Walking shoes
- ☐ Smart shoes
- ☐ Jersey
- ☐ Waterproof jacket or raincoat
- ☐ Socks (can double as slippers)
- ☐ Nightwear that can double as dressing gown
- ☐ Two skirts, preferably reversible
- ☐ Jeans or shorts
- ☐ Three shirts or blouses (T-shirt can double as vest and beach covering)
- ☐ Bathing suit, reversible if possible
- ☐ Underwear

TOILETRIES AND OTHER ITEMS

- ☐ Medications and prescriptions
- ☐ Extra spectacles or a prescription
- ☐ Sunglasses
- ☐ Folding umbrella
- ☐ First aid items
- ☐ Toothpaste and toothbrush
- ☐ Dental floss
- ☐ Shampoo, soap, deodorant, cosmetics, sunscreen in small plastic travel containers

OPTIONAL

- ☐ Laundry detergent in travel-sized packets
- ☐ Paperbacks
- ☐ Magazines
- ☐ Camera and film
- ☐ Travel alarm
- ☐ Small cassette player or radio
- ☐ Travel-sized hair dryer

A car survival kit

Keep the following essential items on hand to ensure that you and your family are safe and comfortable on long driving trips.

IN THE CUBBYHOLE

- ☐ Owner's manual
- ☐ Registration
- ☐ Insurance details
- ☐ Automobile Association membership card
- ☐ Emergency phone numbers
- ☐ Coins for tolls and telephone
- ☐ Paper and pen
- ☐ Maps

FOR YOUR COMFORT

- ☐ Tissues
- ☐ Refuse bag
- ☐ Bottle opener
- ☐ Sunglasses
- ☐ Air cushion

FOR REPAIRS AND CLEANUPS

- ☐ Jumper cables
- ☐ Spare tyre
- ☐ Jack and wheelbrace
- ☐ Tyre pressure gauge
- ☐ Instant tyre inflator
- ☐ Small fire extinguisher (check expiry date)
- ☐ Tool kit – including a sturdy penknife, strong pliers, magnetic screwdrivers, adjustable spanner
- ☐ Duct or insulation tape
- ☐ Tow rope
- ☐ Reflective warning triangle
- ☐ Waterproof torch
- ☐ Waterproof matches
- ☐ Five litres of water
- ☐ Paper towels, rags

IN WINTER

- ☐ Ordinary blankets
- ☐ Non-perishable snack
- ☐ Tin of de-icer
- ☐ Windscreen washer fluid

FOR TRIPS IN REMOTE AREAS

- ☐ Shovel
- ☐ Rugs or traction mats
- ☐ Large polythene bag
- ☐ Foil space blanket
- ☐ Nylon washing line
- ☐ Compass
- ☐ Whistle
- ☐ Flares
- ☐ Mirror (for signalling)
- ☐ Empty petrol can
- ☐ Portable CB radio
- ☐ Brake fluid
- ☐ Motor oil
- ☐ Transmission fluid
- ☐ Drive belt
- ☐ Spare batteries
- ☐ Fuses, fuse puller
- ☐ Fuel filter
- ☐ Tyre pump
- ☐ Tyre repair kit
- ☐ Flexible copper electrical wire
- ☐ Fire-lighters
- ☐ Non-perishable foods (sweets, dried fruit, nuts)
- ☐ Snake-bite kit
- ☐ First aid kit
- ☐ Small hatchet

Travelling on a budget

Transportation costs and hotel bills are not the only major expenses an average traveller encounters. Here are a few ideas for saving money on your next trip.

- Try the tourist information office for package deals and discount tickets to various events.
- Cinemas often sell tickets at a discount on certain days and at certain hours; so do many museums that require admission.
- Peruse local newspapers to find free or inexpensive museums, concerts, walking tours and other attractions. Local events are also an enjoyable way to meet people.
- Avoid restaurant bills by preparing delicious picnics. Explore local markets and buy bread, cheese, vegetables, fruit and regional delicacies. Then have a lovely meal in your room or in a park.
- Pack an immersion heater for making soups and hot drinks.
- When you do eat at a restaurant, make lunch your main meal – it's usually cheaper than dinner. Have a snack or picnic for supper.
- Department stores often have inexpensive lunch counters.
- Look for popular neighbourhood cafés rather than dining at hotel restaurants, which tend to be more expensive and duller.
- Avoid making many telephone calls from your hotel, which will often add exorbitant surcharges. Whenever possible, phone only to give your number and have the person phone you back.
- Search for seasonal sales at various clothing stores. If you are travelling in the northern hemisphere, a pre-winter clothing sale will probably set you up with a supply of clothes for your summer at very reasonable prices.
- When shopping abroad, it is often appropriate – even expected – to haggle with a persistent vendor. If you're unsure, offer to pay about half the stated price and observe how the vendor reacts.

Tipping guidelines

RESTAURANT	Waiter	15% of pretax bill
	Wine steward	10% – 15% of wine bill
	Bartender	15% of bar tab
	Coat checker	At least R1,50 per coat
HOTEL	Bellboy	R3 per bag
	Doorman	R3 for any service
	Chambermaid	R3 per person per day
AIRPORT	Porter	At least R1,50 per bag
STATION	Rail porter	At least R1,50 per bag
TAXI	Taxi driver	15% of fare (but not less than R1)
SHIP	Cabin steward	At least R6 per day
RESORT	Pool attendant	R3 for any service
HAIR SALON OR BARBERSHOP	Hair cutter	10% – 15% of bill
	Shampooer	R3
	Manicurist	15% of bill
SHOE-SHINE STAND	Shoe shiner	At least R1

50 commonly misspelled words

If you see that you have been spelling a word or two on this list incorrectly, you have plenty of company. Lots of people forget that there's only one *n* in *inoculate*, and shouldn't be *embarrassed* (two *r*'s).

accommodate	esoteric	icicle	misspell	separate
advantageous	excerpt	icily	noticeable	sergeant
anonymous	exhilarate	incandescent	occurrence	siege
conscience	fulfil	inoculate	parallel	subtle
corroborate	guerrilla	irascible	plebeian	supersede
counterfeit	harass	iridescent	privilege	translucent
diarrhoea	heighten	lavender	receipt	vacuous
dilemma	haemorrhage	liaison	recipe	vacuum
ecstasy	homoeopathy	manoeuver	restaurateur	vilify
embarrass	hygienic	minuscule	rhythm	yield

Misused words and phrases

Some words are easy to confuse with others, especially those that sound similar to others or have similar spellings. The list below shows some of the words that are often misspelt, mispronounced or confused with others. The list will help you and your family use the word or phrase that is precisely correct.

All right is the correct form, not *alright.*

All together, altogether. *All together* means all at the same time. *Altogether* means entirely.

Between you and me. Never "between you and I". The preposition *between* requires an object – hence, *me.*

Canvas, canvass. Canvas is the heavy fabric; to solicit something, such as votes, is to canvass.

Cement, concrete. Cement is powdered rock and clay; mixed with water and gravel, it forms concrete.

Climactic, climatic. *Climactic* refers to a climax. If you're talking about the weather, it's *climatic.*

Cohort. A cohort is a band of people; the word is often misused to mean an individual companion.

Comptroller, controller. A comptroller is usually a governmental financial officer; a controller is a business financial officer. They're pronounced the same way – "controller".

Could care less. This phrase is quite often used erroneously. To express a total lack of concern, you should use couldn't care less.

Differ from, differ with. One thing differs from another. Two people who disagree about something differ with each other.

Disinterested, uninterested. A disinterested person is unbiased, impartial. An uninterested person is unconcerned, bored.

Faze, phase. *Faze*, meaning to disrupt or bother, should not be confused with *phase*, which is a stage.

Gibe, jibe. To gibe is to ridicule. To jibe is to move a sail or boom to the other side of the boat, to change the direction of a boat, or, more commonly, to agree ("The numbers don't jibe").

Incredible, incredulous. Something that's incredible is not believable; a person who's incredulous is disbelieving or skeptical.

Jail, prison. A jail confines those awaiting trial or sentencing and those convicted of misdemeanours and civil offences. A prison confines those convicted of serious crimes.

Noisome, noisy. *Noisome* means offensive; it has nothing to do with the words *noisy* or *loud.*

Prone, supine. If you're lying down with your face up, you're supine, but if your face is down, you're prone.

Tortuous, torturous. *Tortuous* means winding, like a tortuous road. *Torturous* means painful, like torture.

Troop, troupe. A troop is a group; a troupe is a company, usually referring to actors ("troupers").

Foreign flavours

An advantage of living in the African "melting pot" is that foreign words flavour our conversations and writings like exotic spices. At the left are some examples from German, French, Latin and Yiddish; can you match them with their English definitions?

1. pièce de résistance
2. crème de la crème
3. modus operandi
4. je ne sais quoi
5. mise-en-scène
6. caveat emptor
7. chef d'oeuvre
8. comme il faut
9. coup de grâce
10. fait accompli
11. wunderkind
12. tour de force
13. trompe l'oeil
14. raison d'être
15. roman à clef
16. cri de coeur
17. pied-à-terre
18. au courant
19. succès fou
20. bon vivant
21. pro forma
22. mot juste
23. idée fixe
24. mensch
25. tant pis
26. de trop

A. The blow bringing death to one who is mortally wounded; any finishing stroke

B. An illusion created so that the viewer may think the representation is reality, such as a window painted on a brick wall

C. Something already done and probably irreversible

D. Chief dish at a meal; most outstanding item in a group or series, especially in art

E. An obsession, a firmly lodged idea not subject to modification

F. The word or phrase that is precisely correct

G. Up-to-date, aware of current events

H. A person who enjoys living well

I. Appropriate or proper; applies especially to behaviour or dress

J. A heartfelt plea or protest

K. Excessive, superfluous

L. Hard to define or describe

M. Arrangement of actors in a play or film; an environment

N. Method of doing something; in police jargon, this is known as a criminal's M.O.

O. An honourable, responsible person

P. According to or as a matter of form

Q. The purpose of a thing or action

R. A novel with real persons or events thinly disguised

S. A second or temporary home

T. An exceptionally skilful act

U. Let the buyer beware

V. An unusual, total success

W. So much the worse

X. The best of its kind

Y. Child prodigy

Z. Masterpiece

Key

1-D
2-X
3-N
4-L
5-M
6-U
7-Z
8-I
9-A
10-C
11-Y
12-T
13-B
14-Q
15-R
16-J
17-S
18-G
19-V
20-H
21-P
22-F
23-E
24-O
25-W
26-K

Get well

Illness can be a lonely time. A short note can express your concern and cheer up someone who is convalescing.

Dear Sean

I understand from Nancy that you are doing well but cannot yet have visitors. We miss you at our weekly chess games! Perhaps when you're up to it, I'll bring a set to your room. In the meantime, you just concentrate on getting your rest and building your strength. I told Nancy to call if you or she should need anything.

Best regards
Chris

Thank you

When you want to convey your appreciation for a gift or event (such as a stay at someone's home), mention something specific about it that shows its value to you.

Dear Jim and Sally

Cecilia and I want to thank you for the lovely house-warming present. We had been wanting a rocking chair, so your choice was perfect. It will get plenty of use in the corner we've picked for it, especially after the baby is born!

We look forward to seeing you soon.

Sincerely,
Patrick

Condolences

Any letter of sympathy offers welcome support to someone who is bereaved. It's helpful to mention something personal about the deceased and to offer some small practical assistance when possible.

Dear Martha

I was very saddened to hear of the death of your father. I remember how friendly he was to me and my brother when we were children and came to visit; we were thrilled that he let us into his workshop and showed us a table he was building. I'm sure he will be greatly missed.

I know this is a difficult time, and if there is something I can do, please let me know. I would like to have you over for dinner whenever you feel ready.

Much love
Sharon

Congratulations

Enhance a friend's enjoyment of an important event, such as an engagement, a wedding, the birth of a baby or a career move, with a note expressing your goodwill.

Dear Laura

I heard from Sidney about your promotion. Congratulations! It is, of course, well deserved, and your company is lucky to have someone so creative and dedicated for the position. I should know, from our five-year stint together at Harringtons. I'll call you soon to arrange a celebratory lunch.

With best wishes
Paul

3. COMMON THINGS WITH UNCOMMON USES

If you hate to throw things away, if you delight in dreaming up new ways to use ordinary household items, you'll welcome the suggestions in this section. And you'll be amazed at the problems you can solve at the same time. Our list is by no means complete. So look around your home and see how many clever uses you can devise for objects that you once dismissed as useless.

A

Air compressors

1. Broom. Use blasts of air to clear dirt and leaves from the garage floor, driveway and pavements.

2. Film cleaner. Rather than scratch a slide or negative with a cloth or brush, blow dust off the surface.

3. Air pump. With an adapter, you can blow up balloons and inflatable toys, rafts and plastic pool chairs.

4. Spark plug cleaner. To prevent dirt from getting into cylinders, blow air around spark plug holes before you remove the plugs. As a precautionary measure, wear safety goggles and a face mask while working.

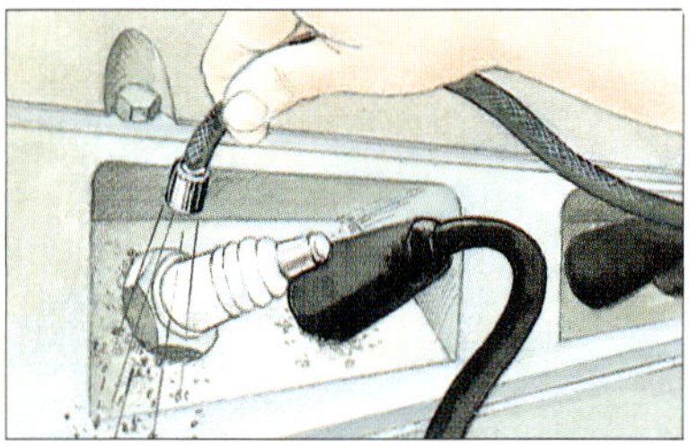

5. Dust and dirt remover. Blow out dust and crumbs from hard-to-reach places. (Place a wet towel behind them to catch the dust.)

6. Pesticide sprayer. Use the paint sprayer attachment to apply insecticide or herbicide to plants. Clean all parts thoroughly right after use.

7. Workshop cleaner. Blow sawdust around the workshop into an easily swept-up pile. As a precautionary measure, wear safety goggles and a face mask while working.

Aluminium foil

1. Sun box. Remove the top and one side from a cardboard box; line the other three sides with aluminium foil. Place plants in the box and set it near a window – the foil will reflect light, helping the stems to grow straight instead of bent toward the sun.

2. Heat reflector. Conserve energy by taping heavy-duty foil to insulation board and placing it behind radiators and ceramic heaters.

3. Foot warmer. Cover heated stones with foil, wrap them in a towel, and place them at the bottom of your sleeping bag to warm your feet while camping in cold weather.

4. Funnel. Roll a double thickness of heavy-duty foil into a cone shape.

5. Wallpaper. Cut foil into 30-centimetre squares; coat one side with wallpaper paste and apply in a haphazard, overlapping fashion.

6. Speciality cake tins. Make a teddy bear birthday cake, Valentine heart cake, Christmas tree cake or whatever shape cake you wish by forming a double thickness of heavy-duty foil into the desired contour within a large cake tin.

7. Fishing lure. Wrap foil around a hook or safety pin. Fringe the foil so that it covers the hook and wiggles as the line is reeled in.

8. Reflector. Glue foil to a matt board or heavy cardboard to make a reflector for photography. Make three identical panels and hinge or tape them together so that the reflector stands upright and is easy to carry.

9. Platter. Make a convenient disposable dish for picnics by covering some cardboard with heavy-duty aluminium foil.

10. Decorating tube. Instead of a pastry bag, use a tube of heavy-duty foil filled with free-flowing icing.

11. Paint masking. Crimp around doorknobs and wall phones before beginning to paint; remove when the walls are dry.

Ammonia

1. Furniture renewer. If an old piece of furniture is heavily stained, rub it with a cloth dampened with full-strength ammonia; when the cloth gets dirty, rinse it thoroughly in water, wring out and reuse.

2. Wax remover. Before waxing a very dirty floor, remove the old polish with a solution of one cup ammonia in five litres of water.

3. Jewellery cleaner. Soak gold jewellery in equal parts ammonia and lukewarm water for 10 minutes; rub with a soft brush and let it drain and dry without rinsing.
4. Silverware polish. Here's a quick way to a brighter shine: combine ammonia with paste polish, made of bicarbonate of soda and water, and apply with a soft cloth to your silver-plated and stainless steel cutlery.
5. Brass beautifier. Remove tarnish from solid brass by scrubbing it lightly with a soft brush dampened with a little ammonia.
6. Oil remover. When laundering sheets, towels and clothes, remove absorbed body oils by adding one cup ammonia to the usual amount of granular detergent. (Do not use ammonia with chlorine bleach.)

Aprons

1. Bib. Tie an apron around your youngster's neck for an instant bib.
2. Portable cash box. Turn up the bottom of an apron and stitch five pockets so that you can wear your cash box around your waist, keeping your coins and your banknotes separated. Alternatively, you can sew some extra pockets into a carpenter's apron. This is ideal for keeping parking meter money.

3. Ladder tool pocket. An efficient way to hold your tools while working on a ladder is to tack or staple a carpenter's apron to the top step.

Ashes

1. Children's make-up. For a ghoulish look, rub ashes all over the face and arms.

2. Fertilizer. Don't discard wood ashes; sprinkle them onto the compost pile or work them into your soil in the spring – but not around acid-loving plants, such as rhododendrons and azaleas. (Store ashes in a covered metal container, well away from buildings and flammable material; even apparently long-dead ashes, especially of hardwoods or coal, harbour hot embers that can burst into flame after the fire appears to have died completely.)
3. Glare reducer. Cut the glare and ultraviolet radiation reflected behind your sunglasses – moisten your fingertip with oil, dip it in ashes, and apply a dark line under your eyes.
4. Pewter cleaner. Moisten sifted ashes with water and rub on pewter with a soft cloth.
5. Grease cutter. When camping or braaiing, soak greasy pans and utensils in ashes mixed with water or make a thick ash-and-water paste — ideal for a dirty potjie.
6. Pest repellent. To discourage slugs and snails, build low ridges of wood ash around plants and between row crops.

Assorted tins

1. Sewing box organizer. A neat way to store press studs, sequins, buttons and beads is in individual small tins in your sewing box. Label the lids or glue on a sample of the contents for easy identification.
2. Stamp saver. Prevent stamps from sticking together by storing them in a small airtight tin.

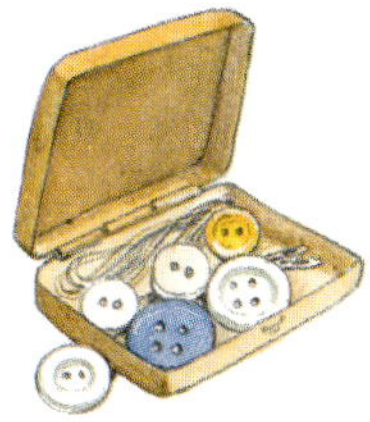

3. Emergency sewing kit. Keep a tin fitted with needle and thread in your handbag or pocket for on-the-spot repairs.

4. Birthday keepsake. Decorate the outside of a tin, line it with felt or silk, and insert a coin from the birth year of your friend.

5. Broken jewellery box. Keep all the little pieces safe and together in a tin.

6. Tangle preventer. Keep necklaces separate and untangled by storing each in its own small tin.
7. Workshop helper. Tins are useful for storing split-pins, glass cutters, self-tapping screws, washers and other small items.
8. Earring keeper. Prevent pairs of small earrings from straying; store them together in assorted tins.
9. Mini safe. Hide the keys to desks and drawers – it's unlikely that a thief

will suspect an innocent-looking tablet tin in your medicine chest.

10. Fuse cache. You'll always know where your spare car fuses are if you store them in a tin in the cubbyhole.

B

Baking pans

1. Dustpan. Cut out one side of an old cake pan with a coping saw. If you want a handle, drill two holes through the opposite side and bolt onto an old broomstick.

2. Utility tray. Here's a good way to store nuts, bolts, nails, screws and other workshop materials: bolt a muffin tin to the underside of a bench or shelf by one corner, using a washer as a spacer, so that the tin can be swung out as needed. Or attach cleats under your workbench or shelf to serve as runners for the rim of the muffin tin.

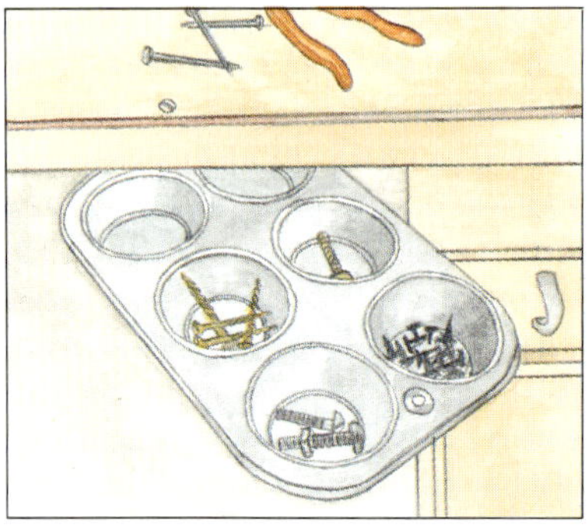

3. Serving tray. Avoid spills – use a muffin tin to carry cooldrinks.

4. Mealie catcher. Rest the stem end of a mealie cob in the centre of a tube pan; as you slide your knife down the cob, the kernels will fall into the pan.

5. Plant holder. Place a tube pan in the centre of your patio umbrella table and use it to hold cut flowers or decorative shade plants.

6. Water bowl. Does your dog make a habit of overturning its backyard water bowl? Drive a stake into the ground through the centre hole of a tube pan to keep it upright; or hang a sturdy bucket from a tree.

Balloons

1. Party invitations. Inflate brightly coloured balloons, then write out your invitations – very carefully – with a contrasting felt-tip pen. Deflate the balloons, put them in envelopes, seal, and post to your guests; in order to read your message, they'll have to reinflate them.

2. Mould. Use a balloon as a mould for a papier-mâché mask.

Banana peels

1. Fertilizer. Bury peels no more than 25 millimetres deep around rosebushes. If you have any more, add them to your garden's compost pile; they are an excellent source of phosphorus and potassium.

2. Bird food. Rotting banana peels will attract fruit flies, which will, in turn, attract birds.

3. Emergency shoe shine. For a spur-of-the-moment job, rub your leather shoes with the inside of the peel; then clean and buff with a paper towel or serviette.

Bar stools

1. Work stand. For access to all sides when painting or working with clay, set the piece on a swivelling bar stool.

2. High chair. A stool with a back can serve as a toddler's high chair; use a belt to secure the child.

3. Side table. Drape a circular tablecloth over a backless bar stool; top with a sheet of glass.

4. Plant stand. Paint a wooden stool and place a trailing plant on top.

5. Barber's chair. Seat your child on a bar stool to cut his hair.

6. Tomato cage. Remove the seat; push the legs into the soil and wrap them with strong twine to support small climbing tomato plants.

7. Lazy Susan. Place small serving bowls filled with snacks, appetizers or condiments on a revolving bar stool at a buffet.

8. Jack rest. Remove the seat and keep it in the boot of your car to use as a base for a jack should you have a puncture and need to change a wheel on soft ground.

Beer

1. Setting lotion. Try combing a small amount through your hair before you start styling it.

2. Insect lure. When entertaining outdoors, set open beer containers around the perimeter of the garden; stinging insects, such as bees, will be attracted to the beer rather than to you and your guests.
3. Marinade. To increase flavour and tenderness, marinate inexpensive cuts of meat in beer for an hour or so before cooking.

Belts

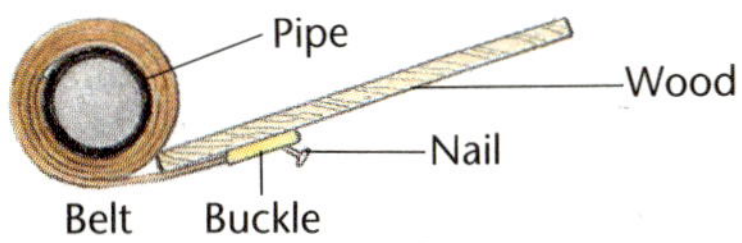

1. Strap wrench. Wrap a belt around a pipe or handle as shown and pull it tight; hook the belt buckle on a nail driven into a stout, short plank, then use the wood as a lever to overcome the jammed thread.
2. Luggage guard. Wrap an old belt around a suitcase and through its handle; buckle it to protect against rough handling or faulty latches.
3. Laundry carrier. Sort the laundry and bundle up each load with a belt for carrying to the laundrette.
4. Strop. Keep a leather belt in the kitchen for sharpening knives.
5. Book strap. An old belt can lash books together and provide a carrying handle as well; punch new holes if necessary.
6. Sling. Run a belt through a sturdy jacket sleeve, pull the sleeve on over the splinted forearm, run the belt around the back of the victim's neck, and buckle on the side.
7. Pet collar. Cut an old belt of yours to the correct length, punch new holes as needed, and add a metal ring to the buckle to attach identification and licence tags.
8. Organizer. Nail a belt to the wall in several places, leaving loops large enough to hold tools or utensils.

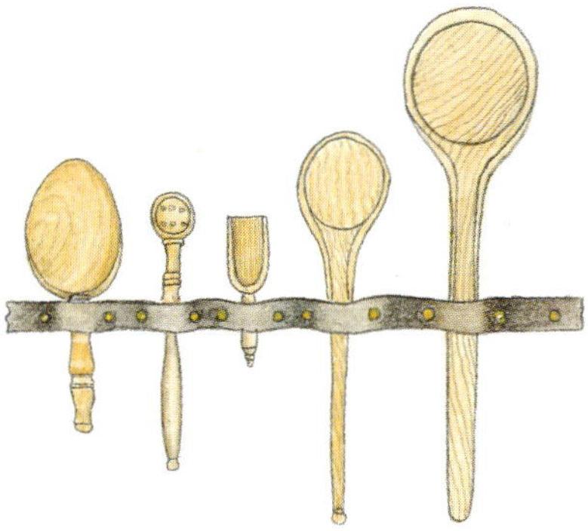

Bicarbonate of soda

1. Dishwasher deodorant. If you use your dishwasher less than once a day, you should toss a handful of bicarbonate of soda into the bottom between washes.
2. Wallpaper washer. Remove resistant smudges from wallpaper by rubbing them with a thick bicarbonate paste. (Test first in an inconspicuous corner.)
3. Furniture blancher. To spruce up white painted furniture, wash it with a solution of one tablespoon bicarbonate of soda in a litre of water.
4. Grill scourer. To remove grease and encrusted food from the rack, soak it in a solution of a quarter cup bicarbonate of soda per litre of warm water. For tough stains, put bicarbonate of soda on a damp sponge and scrub, working it into a paste.
5. Dog shampoo. To add softness and lustre to your pet's coat, put two tablespoons bicarbonate of soda in its bathwater. Bicarbonate of soda also works well as a dry shampoo for your dog; brush in, and then brush out.
6. Sting salve. A paste of bicarbonate of soda and water will ease the discomfort of bee stings.
7. Battery saver. Try to eliminate acid build-up on car battery terminals – apply a paste of three parts bicarbonate of soda and one part of water with a toothbrush; rinse with water and wipe dry. Wear safety goggles and rubber gloves to protect eyes and hands from splashed acid.
8. Skin emollient. For softer and smoother skin, add half a cup bicarbonate of soda to your bathwater.

Bicycle wheels

1. Trellis. Mount a bicycle wheel horizontally on top of a tall pole, then run strings from the rim or spokes to pegs planted firmly in the ground; train climbing peas or beans on the strings.
2. Tool hanger. Suspend a bicycle wheel horizontally and hang tools or utensils from the spokes and rim with bent steel S-hooks.
3. Mobile. Hang a bicycle wheel horizontally and suspend brightly coloured paper cutouts from it.
4. Drying rack. Dry your hand laundry by hanging it from a bicycle wheel suspended from the ceiling.
5. Christmas wreath. Cover a bicycle tyre with chicken wire, then weave evergreen boughs through it; attach a brightly coloured ribbon.

Blankets

1. Poncho. Fold a blanket in half, then cut and hem a slit in the centre to go over the head.
2. Insulation. Try inserting pieces of blanket inside pot holders, heat pads and place mats.

3. Hammock. Hang an old blanket between two trees.

4. Curtain padding. Sew a blanket between the curtain fabric and lining for fullness and insulation.

5. Quilt. Insert batting between two blankets and stitch together.

6. Pet stretcher. Place an injured pet in the centre of a blanket; ask someone to lift two corners at one end while you lift the other two.

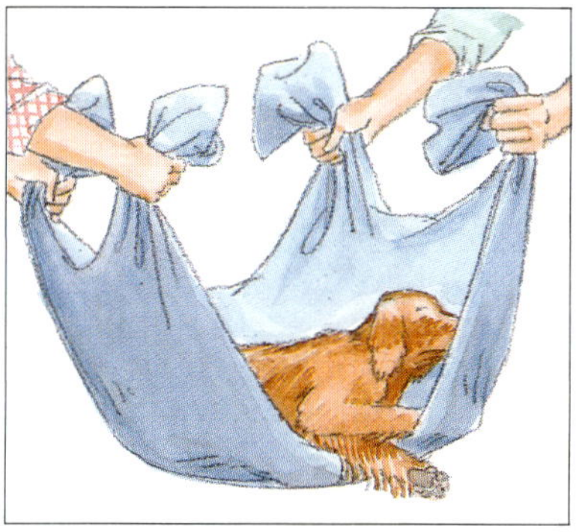

7. Mattress pad. Cut the blanket to the desired size, then sew on a strip of 25-millimetre-wide elastic across each corner to hold the pad firmly down onto the mattress.

Blue jeans

1. Draught dodger. Cut each leg in half lengthways. Stitch all four halves into tubes and fill with rags or sand; stitch closed and use to block winter draughts at windows and doors. Sew on eyes, ears, nose and tail, and you have a sausage dog.

2. Tackie bag. Cut 45 centimetres off one leg; close one end with stitches and make a casing for a drawstring at the other (or simply cut holes to thread cord through).

3. Patches. Save pieces of tattered jeans so that you have ready patches for a pair that's still worth saving.

4. Pillow. Cut off one leg, hem the raw edges, and tie one end tightly with decorative cord. Stuff the leg with old pantihose or other filler, then close the other end with a cord.

5. Tripod holder. Cut off a leg and stitch the bottom closed. (See also *Blue jeans*, p.342.)

6. Easel case. Stitch the legs closed, insert a drawstring at the waist, and sew a strap between one hem and the waist. Put the easel's legs into the jeans legs, supplies in the pockets, canvasses in the trunk.

Boards

1. Garden edging. Cut three boards 25, 30 and 35 centimetres high and sink them 15 centimetres into the ground; repeat the sequence for an undulating border.

2. Lock. Jam one end of a board under the doorknob and the other end tight against a carpeted floor.

3. Seesaw. Make a child's seesaw by placing the centre of a long 20-centimetre-wide board across a barrel or other firm support, such as a large pine log; sand the seesaw thoroughly, and paint with enamel to prevent splinters.

Book jackets

1. Place mat. Old book jackets make eye-catching table settings for informal dinner parties. Sandwiched in plastic they will last a long time.

2. Party hat. Fold into a cone or other hat shape and punch two holes for a string or an elastic.

3. Blotter. Protect your youngster's working area by using a book jacket as a desk blotter.

4. Container cover. Co-ordinate a room's decor by covering canisters, pencil holders and wastepaper baskets with book jackets.

5. Wallpaper. Paper one or several walls in the playroom or family room with colourful book jackets.

6. Notepaper. Take notes about the book you're reading on the inside of its jacket. Or, if you have to, use the jacket as stationery.

Books

1. Coffee table base. Place a thick sheet of glass with finished edges on top of several stacks of unwanted coffee table books.

2. Insulation. You can put book-filled shelves on exterior walls to help keep the heat in and the cold out and on the walls between rooms to muffle sound. A disused doorway can serve as the sides of a bookshelf.

3. Book end. Glue together three or four old books to make an extra-heavy book end.

4. Story wall. Rather than discard a book, cut pages from it, apply wall-paper paste, and use as a panel at the metre-high level of a bedroom or study wall.

5. Clamp. Hold just-glued surfaces together by weighting them down with a couple of books.

6. Doorstop. Glue together three or four unwanted old books to hold a stubborn door open.

Boots

1. Umbrella stand. Weight the bottom of an attractive old leather boot (a riding boot perhaps) or a tall rubber boot with pebbles or marbles and place near your home's front or back door.

2. Birdhouse. Take an old boot outdoors and hang it upside down. You may find that some birds will build a nest in the toe area.

3. Doorstop. Fill a boot with golf balls or pebbles.

4. Fish bucket. Keep your just-caught fish fresh: bring them home in a water-filled boot.

Borax

1. Fertilizer. Fill a shaker with borax and sprinkle on the soil all around beetroot plants.

2. Nappy freshener. Add half a cup borax along with the recommended amount of soap or detergent to a hot-water wash to eliminate odours and stains and make nappies absorbent.

3. China shiner. For an especially brilliant shine, rinse your fine china in a sinkful of warm water with half a cup borax added; thoroughly rinse again in clear water.

4. Flower preserver. Place a two and a half-centimetre layer of one part borax and two parts cornflour in an airtight container; put in one or two flowers and leave in a cool dry place. After seven to 10 days, pour off the mixture, and dust the flowers with an artist's soft brush.

5. Cat litter deodoriser. Blend six parts cat litter with one part borax to reduce odour in the litter box.

6. Cockroach killer. Small heaps in corners attract and kill them. Keep away from children and pets.

Bottle caps

1. Christmas decorations. Paint caps gold, drill a hole in each one, and hang on the Christmas tree with string or a hook. Or knot each on a string to make a garland.

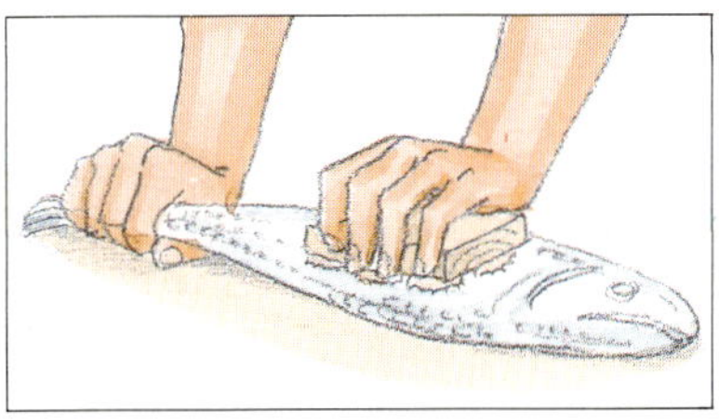

2. Fish scaler. Nail caps, fluted side up, onto a rectangular block of wood. Run the block up and down a fish to rid it of scales.

3. Mini paint tin. Mix small amounts of touch-up paint in a bottle cap.

4. Bird chaser. String a number of caps together and hang them in the garden. Birds will be frightened by the reflection.

5. Kids' cap beads. Paint bottle caps, punch a hole in the centre of each, and string them together on a piece of thin elastic or ribbon.

6. Trap. Fill bottle caps with ant or cockroach bait and set out where pests congregate.

7. Mud scraper. For a "doormat" that will scrape off even the stubbornest mud, nail bottle caps side by side, smooth side down, on a piece of plywood left outside the front door.

Bottles

1. Mole and rat repellent. When set in the ground near molehills with one and a half centimetres of their necks exposed, bottles will whistle in the wind and scare off moles. Half-filled bottles placed throughout the garden will do the same for rats.

2. Rolling pin. Who needs a rolling pin when you can fill a bottle with water, cap it, and roll out the dough?

3. Cruets. Use perfume, hair-tonic or other exotically shaped bottles as oil and vinegar cruets.

4. Bud vase. Remove the atomizer from an empty perfume bottle, wash thoroughly, and display a few small flowers in it.

5. Boot trees. Insert large cooldrink bottles into your boots to help them keep their shape.

6. Bowling pins. Paint the numbers one to 10 on clean plastic bottles and use an old rubber ball to bowl at home on a rainy day.

7. Cobbles. Cement in tops, packed edge down in steep paving.

8. Drill holster. To hold an electric drill or screw gun, cut the neck off a plastic bottle, then cut the bottle about halfway on the diagonal. Screw to the wall above your workbench or cut slits in the bottle so that you can put it on a belt.

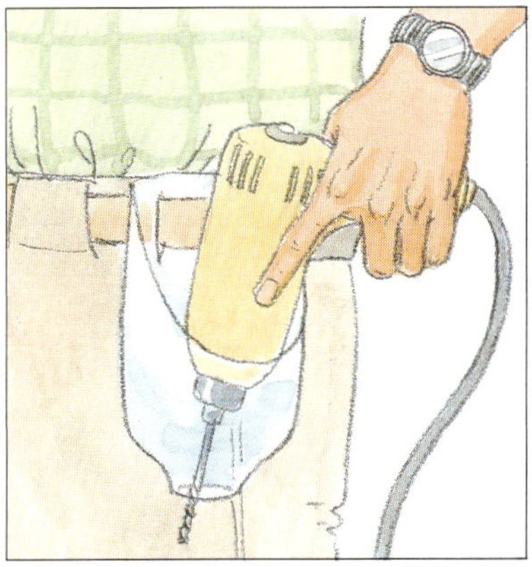

9. Bellows. When cleaned, a soft plastic detergent or tomato sauce bottle with a hole in its spout can serve as a bellows for encouraging a slow charcoal or fireplace fire.

10. Stopcock cover. Some stopcocks – where the water supply enters your property from the street – are beneath the ground. Prevent sand from falling into the hole and covering the tap by lining the hole with a disposable two-litre plastic cooldrink bottle. Cut off the neck, and with a screwdriver, loosen the black plastic base of the bottle. Cut the base off the bottle. Insert the tube into the hole over the stopcock, and cap with the black plastic base. If the hole is too deep for the bottle, use an offcut of 110-millimetre plastic waste pipe.

Bread

1. Fat absorber. A piece of bread in a grill pan will soak up any fat dripping from the meat and reduce the chance of smoke and fire.

2. Cake preserver. Fasten two slices of bread with toothpicks to the open faces of a cut cake to prevent drying out between tea times.

3. Bread bowl. Scoop out the centre of a round, crusty loaf and fill with an appetizer or a dip.

4. Edible place markers. Attach name tags to toothpicks and insert into rolls; place one at each setting.

5. Pipe wick. Before you start to solder a copper pipe, push a wad of white bread as deeply as possible into it to absorb any remaining moisture. When the water pressure has eventually been restored, the bread will dissolve and wash out.

6. Hand saver. Pick up broken glass with a piece of bread.

7. Velvet cleaner. A good way to clean a velvet evening bag is to brush it with a shaving brush, rub it lightly with fresh rye bread, then rebrush.

Bricks

1. Book end. Cover a brick with fabric or heavy wallpaper.

2. Desk organizer. Glue felt to the bottom of an airbrick and stick pencils and scissors in the holes.

3. Grill base. Place an old oven rack over four even stacks of bricks.

4. Garden border. Recess bricks to outline flower beds or to help prevent water runoff around trees.

Broom handles

1. Window washer. To reach upper windows without a ladder, attach a large sponge or a squeegee to the end of a broom handle.

2. Garden stake. Support a tall, top-heavy plant, such as a tomato, on a broom handle; sharpen one end for easy insertion into the ground.

3. Paintbrush stretcher. Attach a broom handle to a paintbrush with insulation tape.

4. Rolling pin. Cut to the size you need to roll out pie and biscuit dough.

5. Reach extender. Attach a screw hook to a broom handle to lengthen your reach so that you can get hold of those socks behind the washing machine or the basket on the highest shelf of a cupboard.

6. Wardrobe rod. Screw large screw hooks into beams in the wardrobe ceiling and rest a broom handle on them. Hang out-of-season clothing on broom handles attached to the ceiling joists with screw hooks.

7. Curtain rod. Cut a broomstick to the desired length and drill holes at both ends. Hang it from L-hooks fitted through the holes or finishing nails driven into the window moulding and bent upward with pliers.

8. Paint tin holder. Slide a broom handle into the rung of an aluminium extension ladder. Notch each end of the pole to keep the tin from sliding off.

9. Stoopless scoop. Prevent backache – pick up leaves and refuse with a stoopless scoop, made from two broom handles and a sturdy box, cut in half.

Brooms

1. Edger. When coating a driveway with tar emulsion, use an old broom as an edger in spots where your squeegee won't fit.

2. Bird guide. If birds fly in through open doors or windows, use a broom to assist them out so that they don't batter themselves against any glass windows as they try to escape.

3. Oiler. For those hard-to-reach places, dip a broom straw in oil and work it around the squeaky parts.

4. Dolly. Tip the heavy object so that one edge rests on the broom bristles. Ask someone to push the object while you pull the broom.

5. Textured paintbrush. Dip an old broom in paint to create special effects and unusual textures on a canvas or a wall.

Bubble pack

1. Rain bonnet. A bubble pack scarf will keep your hair dry.
2. Cooler. To help keep ice cream firm on the way to a picnic, wrap it with bubble pack.
3. Insulation. Glue to the inside walls of the dog's kennel to keep Rover warm on chilly nights.
4. Camping mattress. Thick bubble pack is light, waterproof and quite tough. Take a few sheets rolled up, and place on the ground under a sleeping bag to insulate and prevent dampness on camping trips.
5. Elbow and knee protector. Wrap bubble pack around your child's elbows and knees and secure it with tape to protect them from possible harm while rollerskating or skateboarding.
6. Picnic bench cushion. For pleasanter picnicking, stretch a length of bubble pack along the benches.

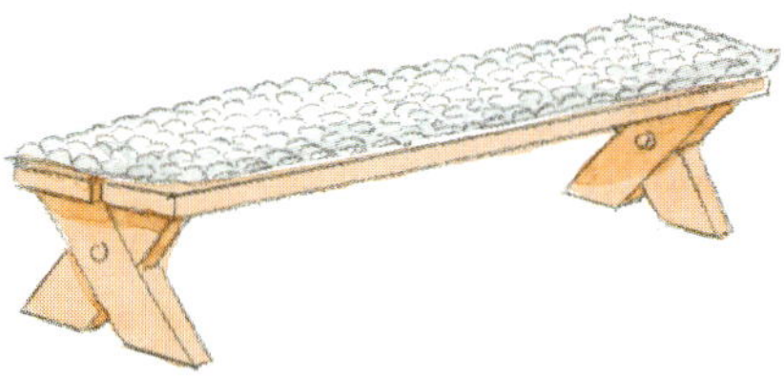

7. Stadium upholstery. Soften those hard stadium benches; take a layer or two of bubble pack with you.
8. Table pad. When repairing glass or china, you can help prevent breakages by covering the work surface with bubble pack.
9. Worry beads. Pop the bubbles to relieve tension.

Buckets

1. Mini stilts. Make working on a ceiling easier by attaching a pair of old shoes to two sturdy buckets without handles. Drive screws through the shoe soles and into wood blocks inside the buckets. Or punch holes in

the bucket bottoms and strap or tie the shoes down.
2. Christmas tree stand. Fill a bucket with wet sand or gravel and stand the tree in it.
3. Crayfish pot. If you don't have a large kettle, boil crayfish in an old metal bucket.
4. Shower. A perforated bucket makes an excellent campsite shower.
5. Paint tray. Use the lids from large plastic buckets as trays on which to put five-litre paint tins. The lids serve as platforms for the paint tins and will catch drips or serve as places to put paintbrushes.

Buckles

1. Scarf clasp. Pass a scarf through a pretty buckle and wear at the neck of a plain cardigan or dress.
2. Curtain ornament. Attach to a tieback as an added decoration.

Buttons

1. Doll's house decorations. Use buttons for decorative wall brackets for candles and lights, plates and wall hangings in your child's doll's house.
2. Poker chips. For an impromptu game, use buttons as chips, with each colour carrying a different value.
3. Beanbag filler. Instead of dried beans, use small buttons.
4. Game pieces. Substitute buttons for lost backgammon or bingo pieces. Or use them for a game of tiddlywinks on the carpet.
5. Christmas tree garland. Knot buttons on a sturdy length of string to give your Christmas tree an old-fashioned look.
6. Necklace. String attractive buttons, alternating large and small, on two strands of strong thread.

C

Calendars

1. Drawer liners. Take apart an old calendar and use its pages to line your desk drawers.
2. New Year's tablecloth. Pull apart the outgoing year's calendar and glue the months randomly to a large piece of paper for a pictorial summary of the year.

3. Jigsaw puzzle. Glue a favourite calendar picture onto a heavy piece of cardboard, then cut it into pieces.
4. Place mats. Use the pictures from beautifully illustrated calendars as place mats when setting the table for a special party.

5. Collage. Glue the pictures of a calendar on 61-millimetre plywood to make a collage of memories.

6. Greeting card. Glue a favourite old calendar picture on thin poster board for an inexpensive but attractive greeting card.

7. Wallpaper. Use calendar art to paper a powder room; protect and "antique" it with a coat of varnish.

Candles

1. Envelope sealer. Reseal an envelope with a few drops of melted wax from a lighted candle.

2. Egg decorator. Drip melted wax onto hard-boiled Easter eggs and then dye. Peel off the wax to reveal an intricate pattern.

3. Candle holder. Drip melted wax into the socket of a candlestick to hold wobbly candles in place.

4. Fire starter. Toss a couple of candle stubs into the kindling and light, but don't braai until all the wax has been burnt up.

5. Spade lubricant. Sticky clay soil will slide off your spade if you rub it down with a candle before using.

Can openers

1. Grout remover. Use the tip of a beer can opener to gouge old grout from between ceramic tiles.

2. Plumb bob. Suspend one from a string so that it hangs freely with its point down.

3. Screwdriver. Use the edge of a can opener handle, held sideways, to turn a large-slotted tap screw. Check that the handle is strong enough.

Cardboard boxes

1. Building blocks. Small children love making imaginary homes or houses out of movable items lying around. Get hold of a dozen or more cardboard boxes from your nearest supermarket or grocery store, dump them in the family lounge or playroom. Your children and their friends will have the ingredients for many fun-filled hours "building" easily-constructed homes.

2. Dust cover. Keep all dirt out of a small appliance, power tool or a typewriter – cut off the flaps of a box, put decorative adhesive plastic, such as that used to line drawers, on the sides and top, and use as a cover.

3. Table guard. Cut a large flat piece of cardboard to protect work surfaces from ink, paint, glue or knife and scissor nicks.

4. Mechanic's helper. Keep a piece of cardboard under your car's engine in the garage or carport. Not only will it keep the floor of the garage clean by catching drips, but the colour and location of the leaked fluids on the cardboard will help a mechanic identify potential problems. Engine or gearbox fluid is black, transmission fluid pinkish. Water stains indicate coolant leaks.

5. Gift of suspense. Place a friend's gift inside the smallest of a series of increasingly bigger cardboard boxes, each one specially wrapped.

6. Bed tray. Remove the top flaps and cut lap-wide arches from the two long sides; cover the top with attractive adhesive drawer-lining plastic.

7. In box. Cut off the top and one large panel from a cereal box; slice the short sides at an angle.

8. Puppet theatre. Stand a large cardboard box on end; cut a big hole in the back for puppeteers to crouch in and a smaller one high up in the front, folded in for the stage.

9. Magazine holder. Remove the top of a detergent box, then cut the box at an angle, from the top of one side to the bottom third of the other edge.

10. Place mats. Cut several 30- x 45-centimetre pieces of cardboard and cover them with colourful adhesive plastic, as used to line drawers. (See also *Liquor cartons*, p.310.)

Cardboard tubes

1. Megaphone. When you need to amplify your voice, talk through a cardboard tube.

2. Boot trees. Stick tubes into boots to hold their shape.

3. Knitting needle case. Prevent bending and breaking – store plastic needles in an empty cardboard tube.

4. Fluorescent light storage. Prevent breakage by keeping unused fluorescent lamps in cardboard tubes.

5. Light detangler. For trouble-free decorating next year, wrap Christmas tree lights around a tube and secure with tape or a rubber band.

6. Document holder. Before storing diplomas, marriage certificates and other documents, roll them tightly and insert them in paper towel tubes. This prevents creases and keeps documents clean and dry. Mothballs, in a perforated plastic bag, will deter fishmoths.

7. Linen press. After laundering tablecloths and serviettes, roll them around tubes so that they won't show creases where they were folded.

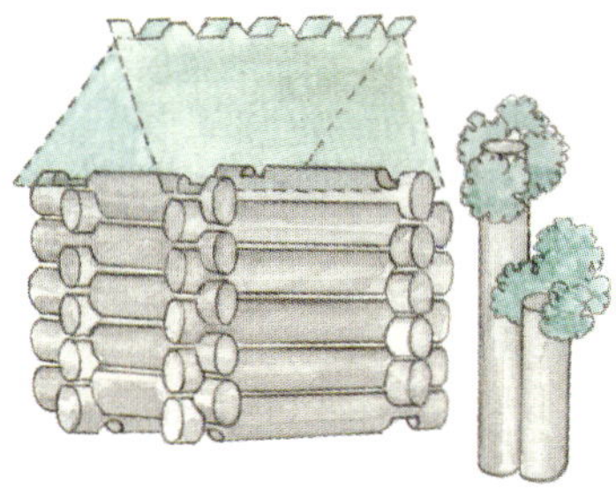

8. Play logs. Notch the ends with a knife and construct "log" cabins, fences and other toys.
9. Fabric keeper. Store leftover fabric scraps, tightly rolled, inside a tube. For easy identification, staple a sample of each fabric on the outside.
10. Kazoo. Cut three finger holes in the middle of a paper towel tube and attach wax paper with a rubber band to one end. Hum resonantly into the other end, plugging different holes to alter the pitch.
11. Plant guard. Prevent accidental scarring when cutting down weeds – cut a tube lengthways and put it around the trunks of young trees or plants; slip off afterward for use elsewhere, or leave in place.

Car jacks

1. Emergency accident repair. You can often pry a bent fender away from a tyre by placing a scissors or bottle jack between the fender and frame, then forcing the fender outward, as a temporary measure.
2. Mini crane. To raise a sagging deck for repair or to lift a grand piano for fixing a leg or straightening a rug, use a scissors-type car jack.

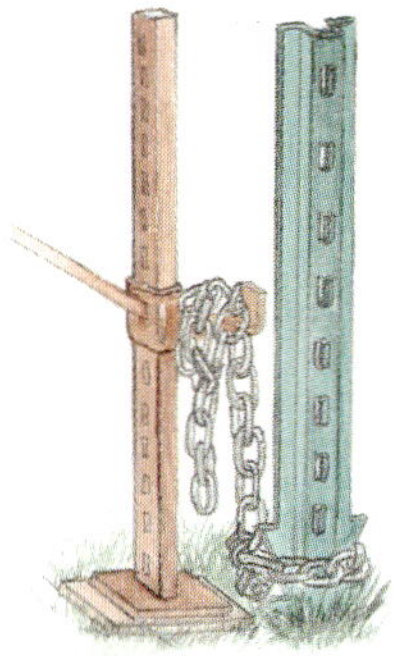

3. Post puller. Rather than use a spade, wrap a chain around the post, fastening the ends with a bolt or strong clamp. Lap the chain over the hook of a pillar jack and hoist the post out of the ground.

Car mirrors

1. Monitor. Mount a car mirror on the side of the house so that you can simultaneously watch youngsters in the front and back gardens.
2. Organist's friend. A car mirror attached to a wood block will enable an organist to keep an eye on the congregation or choir director while reading her music.
3. Signal. To signal fellow hikers on top of distant heights, carry a sturdy car mirror in your backpack.

Carpet scraps

1. Insulation. Cover the walls of a room with carpet scraps for soundproofing and temperature control.
2. Clatter killer. Cut pieces of carpet to fit under typewriters and sewing machines, on cabinet shelves and in toolboxes under spanners.
3. Bed bumper. Pad the corners of a sharp bed frame to prevent scraping or gouging the walls.
4. Foot warmers. Trace your feet on a piece of paper and use as a pattern to fit thin carpeting inside your boots, galoshes or work shoes.
5. Dolly. Set a heavy item on top of a piece of carpet and pull it by one of the corners.
6. Drop cloth. When doing messy repairs, protect the floor with old carpeting; if you're using a stepladder, make sure the piece is wide enough so that all four legs rest securely on it.
7. Exercise mat. Cut a piece of old carpet one metre wide and as long as you are tall. Roll it up when not in use.
8. Knee pad. Cut two pieces of carpeting 25 centimetres square; cut two slits or holes in each. Run old ties or scarves through the slits to tie the pads to your knees.
9. Buffer. Glue an old piece of carpet to a block of wood; use it to clean window screens, buff shoes or erase chalk from blackboards.

Car seats

1. Dog bed. Cut the foam-rubber padding from a car seat to the right size for your dog. (Ticks don't seem to like foam rubber.)
2. Furniture. Use old car seats as cheap recreation room or as tree house or Wendy house furniture.
3. Stoep swing. Hang an old back seat from four strong, well-secured ropes or chains.

Castor oil

1. Eye cream. Before going to bed, rub odourless castor oil all around the eye area.
2. Mole repellent. Drench molehills with a mixture of half a cup castor oil and eight litres of water.
3. Lubricant. Use it instead of mineral oil on kitchen scissors and other utensils that touch food.

Cat litter

1. Drying agent. Preserve flowers by placing them on a bed of cat litter in an airtight container for seven to 10 days. (See also *Flower drying*, p.87.)
2. Deodoriser. To remove unpleasant odours, sprinkle cat litter in rubbish bins, in the fireplace or on the floors of musty rooms; before pack-

ing a suitcase or a trunk, leave a litter-filled tin inside overnight.
3. Oil absorber. Sprinkle onto oil puddles and other spills on the garage floor. After the fluids have been absorbed, sweep it up.
4. Filler. Use to stuff dolls, toys, beanbags and draught excluders.

Caulk

1. Gasket. If the seal is torn on your refrigerator or dishwasher, repair it with caulk.
2. Shoe gum. Temporarily fill a hole in your sole with a dab of caulk; let dry before walking on it.

Chalk

1. Rust preventer. Place several pieces of chalk in the toolbox to eliminate moisture and prevent rust.
2. Marble polish. Wipe clean marble with a damp soft cloth dipped in powdered chalk; rinse with clear water and dry thoroughly.
3. Grease remover. Rub chalk on a grease spot on clothing or table linens, let it absorb the oil, then brush off. If the stain lingers, rub chalk into it again just before laundering.
4. Metal polish. Wipe metal with chalk dust on a damp cloth.
5. Repellent. Scatter powdered chalk around garden plants to repel ants and slugs.

Chamois

1. Photographer's helper. Wipe dusty photographs and camera lenses with a clean chamois.
2. Glove patch. Using leather glue, attach pieces of chamois to worn areas on work gloves.

Cheesecloth

1. Paint strainer. Remove the clots from an old tin of paint by straining it through cheesecloth.
2. Pressing cloth. When ironing delicate fabrics, press over a damp piece of cheesecloth – it leaves no lint and won't overwet your clothes.
3. Food tents. Protect your food from dirt and insects at outdoor parties – wrap a piece of cheesecloth around an old wire umbrella from which the handle is removed, and place over serving plates.

4. Sardine catcher. Cheesecloth makes a good fishing net.
5. Dry cleaner. To remove oil and dirt from your hair, cover your brush with cheesecloth.
6. Digital drape. If the light from your digital clock keeps you awake at night, cover it with a piece of cheesecloth – you'll still be able to see the numbers, but they won't be so bright.
7. Landscape cloth. To protect newly sown grass seed from wind and birds, cover with a layer of coarse-mesh cheesecloth weighted with rocks.
8. Shade. Drape over stakes to partly shade vegetable transplants.

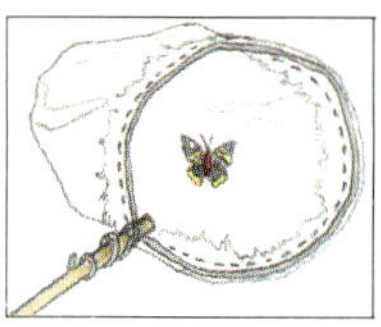

9. Butterfly net. Glue or staple cheesecloth to a hoop formed from a wire coat hanger.

10. Tea strainer. Strain freshly brewed tea into a cup or mug through a piece of cheesecloth.
11. Jam strainer. When making strawberry or gooseberry jam, pour the cooked fruit through three layers of cheesecloth to strain out seeds and skins, leaving a smooth jam.
12. Fat remover. To skim fat from soups or stews, wrap ice in cheesecloth and draw across the surface.
13. Vacuum attachment. Instead of removing the contents of a drawer to dust it, cover the nozzle of your vacuum with cheesecloth so that small objects aren't sucked into it.

Chewing gum

1. Valuables retriever. To recover a coin or piece of jewellery that's fallen down the drain, stick just-chewed gum to the bottom of a fishing weight; dangle it from a string in the weight's hole, let it take hold, then pull up.
2. Crayfish lure. Chew a stick of gum briefly; when it's soft but still has flavour, attach it to a crayfish line. Lower the line and wait for the crayfish to go for the gum.
3. Filler. Fill a crack in a wall or a clay flowerpot with well-chewed gum.
4. Window putty. Hold a loose pane of glass temporarily in place with a wad of chewing gum.
5. Hose sealer. Chewed gum will seal punctures in garden hoses.
6. Ear aid. On aircraft, chewing gum helps the ears adjust to altitude. Some doctors recommend chewing gum to help clear the blocked middle ear following infections.

Chicken wire

1. Dog repellent. Stake chicken wire flat around the perimeter of your garden – dogs will avoid it.
2. Rust repair. Push wire into a cleaned-out rust hole on your car; it will form a backing for the body filler.
3. Bulb protectors. To prevent rodent damage, line the bottom of a prepared bed with wire, plant the bulbs, and cover with soil.
4. Flower arranger. Compact wire together and place in the bottom of a vase to hold cut flowers.
5. Fence setter. To hold a fence post more securely, before setting it in concrete, wrap the base with chicken wire and nail it in place.
6. Insulation holder. After placing fibreglass batting between the roof and floor joists, staple chicken wire to the joists' edges to secure it.

Chlorine bleach

1. Bacteria killer. When refilling your humidifier, add one or two drops chlorine bleach per seven and a half litres of water to prevent bacteria growth.
2. Deodoriser. Remove odours from coolers and other closed containers with diluted chlorine bleach.
3. Mould exterminator. Apply bleach directly to the bath and shower to get rid of mould and mildew. Sponge mouldy ceilings with diluted bleach — wear gloves.

Christmas trees

1. Bird builder's garden. Leave tinsel, cotton and strips of wool on the branches of Christmas trees, and pile them in the garden. Watch how your neighbourhood birds collect nest-building material.
2. Holiday trimming. Insert the branches trimmed from a Christmas tree into a chicken-wire wreath, or wire them firmly together into evergreen swags to decorate mantlepieces or railings.
3. Bathroom freshener. Tie a bow on a freshly cut branch and hang in the bathroom for an evergreen scent. Spray with a plant mister frequently.
4. Animal deterrent. Cut off the branches and mulch flower beds and shrubs with them; they'll also serve to ward off animals.
5. Fire starter. Use dried-out sprigs to ignite kindling in a fireplace or on an outside braai. Don't overdo it – they burn furiously, and could start another, unwanted fire.

Citrus rinds

1. Suet bowl. Place a suet-birdseed mixture in an empty orange or grapefruit half; suspend with string from a back-garden tree or pergola.

2. Nail groomer. Press nail tips into the pithy side of a lemon rind to clean them after doing dirty garden chores.
3. Pan cleaner. To clean a blackened aluminium pan, boil citrus rinds in it. If any discoloration remains, rub with a steel wool pad.
4. Tea flavouring. Add citrus peel to tea leaves while they're brewing or put several small strips in a cup of just-boiled water with a teabag.
5. Deodoriser. Put small mesh bags filled with orange or lemon peels in drawers and cupboards.

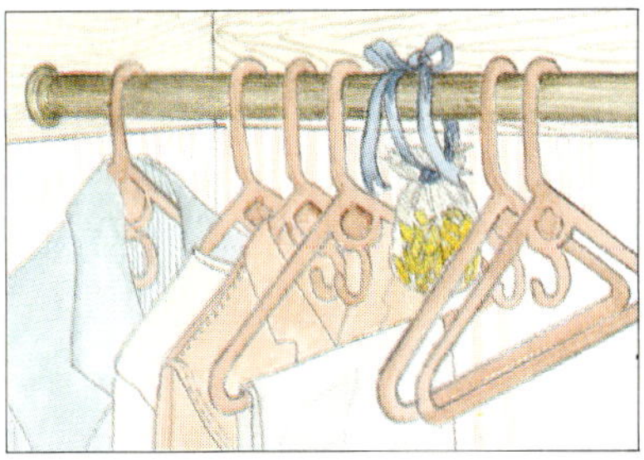

6. Potpourri. Add rinds to simmering cinnamon and cloves to fill your home with a wonderful aroma.
7. Cutting board freshener. Rub a lemon rind over your cutting board to clean and deodorise it.
8. Fireplace freshener. Add some citrus rinds to the fire for a spicy fragrance — best if the peelings are dry.

Clipboards

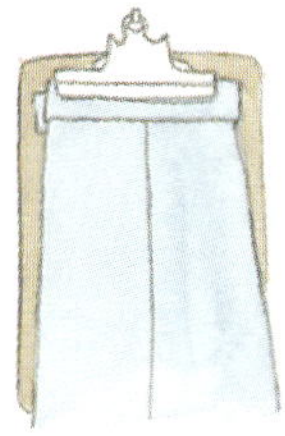

1. Pants hanger. Suspend a clipboard from a hook inside the wardrobe or on the bedroom door; hang trousers overnight by clipping the cuffs.
2. Place mat holder. Hang a clipboard inside a kitchen cabinet door and use the clamp for convenient place mat storage.
3. Recipe retainer. For easy reading of recipes cut from magazines and newspapers, attach a clipboard on the kitchen wall at eye level.
4. Travel aid. Before starting on a long trip, fold the map to the area in which you plan to travel; attach it to a clipboard and keep it nearby to check at rest stops.
5. Music holder. To keep flimsy pages upright, in place, and invulnerable to draughts, attach sheet music to a clipboard.

Clothes pegs

1. Clamps. When gluing a thin object, position spring clothes pegs around it until the glue sets.
2. Clipboard. Make a rack for small tools, toothbrushes or kitchen uten-

sils by screwing several clothes pegs onto a piece of wood.

3. Cord holder. To keep the vacuum cleaner cord from retracting while in use, clip a clothes peg to it after pulling it to the desired length.

4. Fastener. Close up packages of biscuits, snacks, cereal or seeds.

5. Paper clips. A spring clothes peg holds more than a paper clip does and is handier.

6. Bag holder. Nail two to your backyard fence to support a plastic leaf bag for easy filling.

7. Boot organizer. In crowded change rooms, clip your right and left boots together.

8. Note holder. Glue or screw to a surface to hold recipe cards near the food preparation area or messages on bedroom doors.

9. Spark plug reminder. Number clothes pegs and attach to spark plug cables before disconnecting them. Number from the front of the engine, adding D if it's on the driver's side, P for the passenger's side.

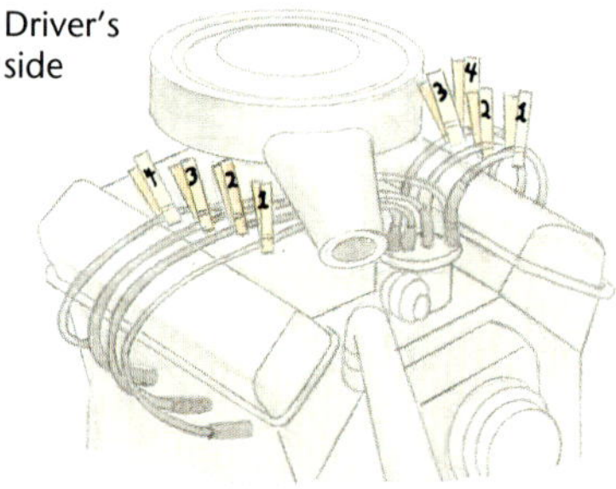

10. Cauliflower clips. Use clothes pegs to clip plant leaves together in hot weather, to help the flower form.

11. Christmas decorations. Make angels or toy soldiers by decorating clothes pegs; use the clips as legs.

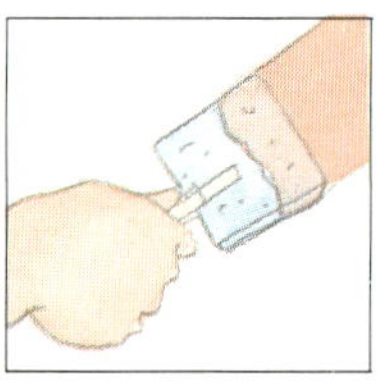

12. Paintbrush. Clamp a clothes peg over a small square of foam rubber and use for painting touch-ups.

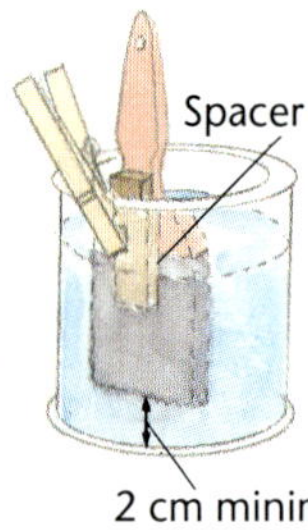

13. Paintbrush saver. Keep your paintbrush from sinking into the solvent residue when you clean it; clamp it to the container with a clothes peg.

14. Hem pins. There's no need to baste; while pressing the new hemline in place, hold it with clothes pegs.

15. Memory jogger. Clip a note on the sun visor or the steering wheel of your car as a reminder to turn off the headlights or take a package out of the boot.

16. Toothpaste stretcher. To avoid wasting any toothpaste, catch the bottom of a toothpaste tube with a peg and roll up.

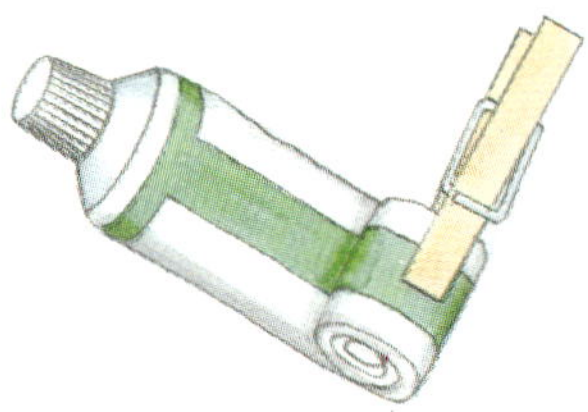

Coffee

1. Fertilizer. Work coffee grounds into the topsoil in your garden.

2. Dye. An inexpensive way to colour fabric brown is to soak it in strong black coffee – without sugar.

3. Bait carrier. Going fishing? Take your worms in a tin or paper cup of moist coffee grounds; they'll be easier to pull out.

Combs

1. Music maker. Fold a piece of wax paper over the teeth, hold it up to your lips, and hum.

2. Wallet guard. To make your wallet less accessible to a pickpocket, put a small comb, tines up, in your pocket; the tines will catch on the pocket edges and help secure the wallet. A comb also makes a potent slashing weapon, in a tight spot.

3. Vacuum brush cleaner. Save old combs to clean vacuum brushes.

4. Washboard. After immersing a stained fabric in soap and water, rub it across the teeth of a comb.

5. Back scratcher. Clip a comb to the end of a ruler with paper clips or spring clamps.

6. Nail holder. Avoid hammering your fingers – hold a small nail in place between the teeth of a comb.

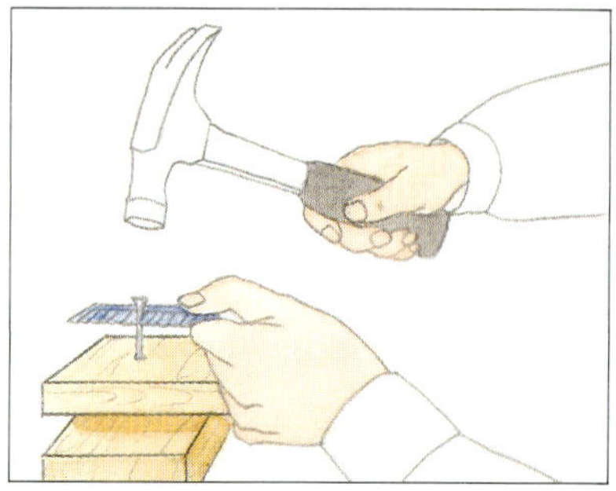

Concrete blocks

1. Anchor. Tie with a rope or chain and use to hold a rowing boat in place. Place in wind or tidal flows.

2. Traction. Place in the boot of your car to provide extra weight in winter.

3. Flower box. Make a plant container that drains well and is guaranteed not to tip over – fill the holes of a concrete block with soil and add flowers. Use a heavy potting soil to avoid it washing out through the bottom. Geraniums will love it.

Cooking spray

1. Spade slicker. Keep clay from sticking to the spade by applying cooking spray beforehand.

2. Grease repellent. To speed cleaning, spray tools and braai grills with cooking spray before use.

3. Debugger. Spray the car radiator with cooking spray before driving in the insect-infested summer months. Simply hose off the crushed insects; respray when the radiator dries.

Corks

1. Jewellery. Punch holes through the centres of several corks and string together; for variety, use different sizes and paint them.

2. Pincushion. Store needles in corks so that they won't prick you or get lost so easily.

3. Make-up. Burn the end and use the ashes as fancy dress make-up.

4. Trivet. Glue wine bottle corks together for a heat pad to protect the table surface.

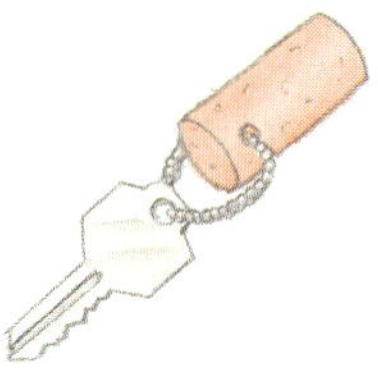

5. Key ring. Attach your boat key to a large painted cork; if it falls overboard, it will stay afloat and be visible.

6. Tugboat. Glue corks together to entertain a toddler in the bath.

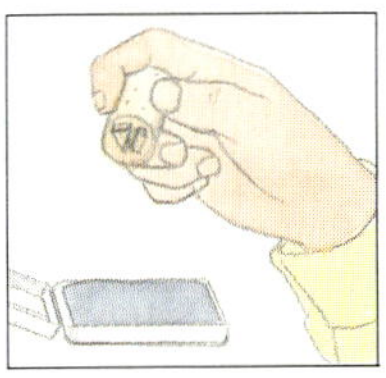

7. Stamp. Draw a design on the end, cut away the material outside the outline, and ink the cork on a pad.

8. Safety marker. String large corks on a yellow polypropylene line to define a special swimming area for small children.

9. Knife cleaner. Dip a dampened cork in scouring powder and pass it along the edges of a carbon-steel kitchen knife.

10. Scratch guard. Attach thin slices of cork to the bottoms of ashtrays, vases and lamps.

11. Recipe holder. Cut a slit in a cork and glue it to the lid of a recipe file box, place a card upright in it so that you can easily refer to it while cooking, without holding the page.

12. Rust preventer. Rub kitchen utensils and garden tools with a cork dipped in cooking oil.

13. Spike stopper. Make the "spike" at your telephone table, used for filing messages, safe for eyes and hands by corking the point. The cork can be removed between each message.

14. Rocking chair guard. To help prevent tipping, glue corks under both ends of each rocker.

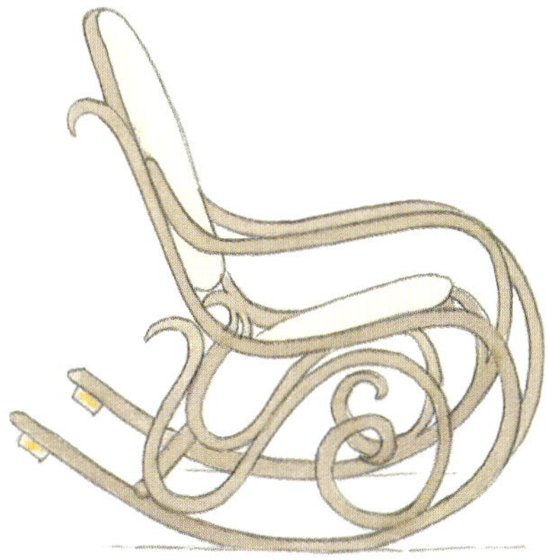

Cornflour

1. Window cleaner. For a nice polish on your windows, mix a little cornflour with ammonia and water.

2. Cockroach killer. Mix with plaster of paris (half and half) and sprinkle behind appliances or cupboards. The pests will "petrify" once they ingest the concoction.

3. Knot detangler. To help untie a stubborn knot, sprinkle it with a little cornflour to act as a lubricant.

4. Glove skid. Sprinkle cornflour inside your rubber gloves – they'll be much easier to put on and take off.

5. Pastry aid. Before you start rolling out the pastry dough, sprinkle the board and rolling pin with cornflour – it's quite tasteless and cleans up with no trouble at all.

6. Pet shampoo. To remove dirt and add fluff without bathing, rub cornflour into your pet's coat, then comb and brush out.

7. Baby powder. Apply sparingly when changing a baby.

Corsage

1. Autumn grasses. For an autumn wedding, use delicately tinged everlastings entwined with variegated ivy leaves to make long-lasting corsages for the bride and bridesmaids. To scent, sprinkle with lavender water.

2. Winning weeds. In spring, a host of tiny wayside and "weed" flowers appear, which can be very pretty when they are bunched with small roses or violets.

Cottonwool

1. Arm guard. To keep water from running down your arms when washing walls, wrap a strip of cottonwool, around your wrists and secure it loosely with rubber bands.

2. Summer refresher. Dab cottonwool balls in your favourite cologne, seal in a plastic bag, and store in the freezer. When you need a lift on a blistering summer's day, remove one of the balls and dab your wrists and neck for fragrant relief.

3. Deodoriser. To eliminate a sour odour in your refrigerator, dampen a handful of cottonwool with vanilla essence and place it on the middle shelf for a day.

4. Glove extender. Push bits of cottonwool into the fingertips of rubber gloves so that your nails don't poke through the ends.

5. Stuffing. Use as filler for dolls, toys, pillows and so forth.

6. Swab. Wrap cottonwool around a matchstick or toothpick; use to remove grit from delicate filigree and carvings. On dirty brass, smear on toothpaste and leave overnight. Then pick off with a cotton bud and an old toothbrush, and rinse.

7. Air freshener. Saturate a ball with cologne and place in the bag of your vacuum cleaner to sweeten the air while you are cleaning.

Cottonwool buds

1. Tape cleaner. Dip one or two cottonwool buds in head cleaner (this is available at most electronics supply shops) to clean the dirty heads on tape recorders and VCR's.

2. Crevice cleaner. Clean between phone buttons, in sewing machine and camera crevices, in shower door runners and in other tight spots.

3. Make-up applicator. A clean cottonwool bud is ideal for applying eyeshadow and removing mascara globs from around the eyes.

4. Insect flicker. Knock insects from house plants with an alcohol-moistened cottonwool bud.
5. Paint bud. Do touch-up paint jobs around the house and on the car. Buds also make good paintbrushes for children; they can use one for each colour and throw them all away at the end of the painting session.

Crayon stubs

1. Candle dye. Save stubs to melt with paraffin for making coloured candles for special occasions.
2. Sealing wax. Melt the remnants and use to seal envelopes.

Credit cards

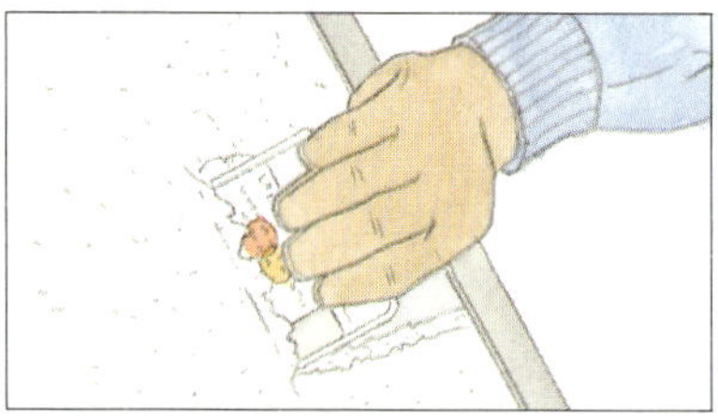

1. Scraper. When nothing else is handy, use a credit card to scrape grime from your windscreen.
2. Door key. If you accidentally lock yourself out, press the latch into the door by sliding an old credit card between the door and the frame. If the bevel faces the other way, cut the card into an L-shape, insert, and pull toward you.
3. Plectrum. Can't find your plectrum? Use the corner of your credit card instead.
4. Manicure tool. Clean your fingernails with a credit card.

Cucumbers

1. Rolling pin. If you don't have a rolling pin, roll out biscuit dough with a large cucumber.
2. Exercise equipment. Use the big ones as hand weights when doing arm exercises.
3. Juggling object. Try to keep two or three continuously in motion in the air. Start over a bed.

Cup hooks

1. Place mat hangers. Place a series of hooks inside a cabinet door or behind the dining room door.
2. Supports. Hang tools and utensils from cup hooks.
3. Miscellany haven. Use magnetic cup hooks in your kitchen, bathroom or car as temporary places to hang your keys, glasses or other items.

Curtain rods

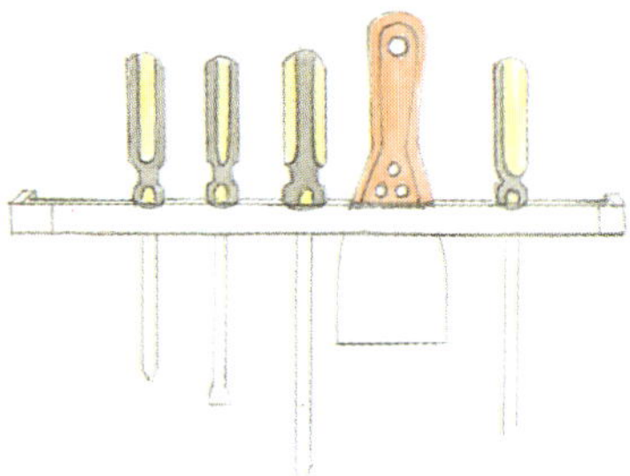

1. Workshop organizer. Fasten a short length to mounts on the wall. Store screwdrivers, chisels and other tools with handles, blade down, between the rod and the wall.
2. Garden stakes. Use old curtain rods to support garden plants.
3. Drying rack. Suspend on ropes over the washing machine and dryer.
4. Pointer. Use when calling children to attention.

Curtains

1. Play material. Old curtains are a boon for children, to play with inside or in the garden. Stretched between chairs, they become the walls and roof of a house. Worn, they become the regal cloaks of kings and queens, or the trappings of ghosts.
2. Paint catchers. Worn curtains can save cleaning in paint jobs: drape over furniture, and cover baths and basins while working.

D

Dandelions

1. Beverage. Clean and dry the roots of dandelions, roast in a warm oven until they turn dark brown, then grind and brew into a coffee-like drink; perk like coffee, using one teaspoon per cup of water. (This beverage is said to be diuretic.)
2. Salad greens. You can use tender young shoots for vitamin-rich salads. Alternatively, steam as a pot-herb. After flowers form, the greens are too bitter to eat.
3. Dye. Boil the flowers for a yellow dye, the roots for magenta.
4. Tonic. Steep two teaspoons of dried dandelion leaves in one cup of boiling water; strain and use as an appetite stimulant.
5. Timepiece-barometer. If dandelion flowers are wide open, you will know it's morning; if they are closed, however, it's late afternoon (or it's going to rain).
Caution: Do not use dandelions that have been treated with herbicides.

Dental floss

1. Umbrella salvager. Retie the loose material of an umbrella to its ribs with dental floss – it's a lot stronger than thread.
2. Cooking aid. Use unwaxed (and unflavoured) floss to truss poultry or to tie a rolled roast.
3. Jewellery string. Use dental floss in an emergency to restring beads and pearls.
4. Glove fixer. Cycling and sailing gloves always part along the stitching

first. Stitch them along the seams with dental floss, taking care to pierce the same holes used in manufacture, to avoid weakening.

5. Picture wire. Hang lightweight picture frames with dental floss – set against white walls, the floss is nearly invisible.

6. Cake knife. Split a cake into horizontal layers for icing, using floss instead of thread or a knife.

7. Moccasin saver. Replace worn stitching on your moccasins or other casual shoes with dental floss (use a large needle); to match the colour of the shoes, touch up the floss with a felt-tip marker.

8. Ornament hanger. Use with or without hooks to suspend the family's Christmas tree ornaments or decorations from thin branches.

9. Photo separator. When two photographs are stuck together, work a piece of dental floss between them and gently pull both ends from the top to the bottom.

10. Bait fastener. In the absence of fishing cotton or elastic, use unflavoured dental floss to secure bait to the hook. This will prove resilient in the roughest seas.

Dishwashing detergent

1. Shampoo. A mild dishwashing detergent cleans hair as well as many shampoos. Rinse thoroughly.

2. Car cleaner. Fill a nearly empty detergent bottle with water and keep in the cubbyhole for emergency treatment of spills.

3. Puncture finder. Mix with a little warm water and brush on a leaky tyre or tube; the bubbles will indicate the exact location of the puncture.

4. Bubble solution. Dilute the concentrate slightly and dip a bubble blower in it. For longer-lasting bubbles, add a few drops of glycerine to the solution.

5. Hand cleaner. Keep a bottle of detergent next to your garden tap – a drop or two will help to get most of the ground off your hands before you enter the house.

Doors

1. Folding screen. Hinge three together; decorate with paint or wallpaper if desired.

2. Bench. Place a solid door on concrete blocks.

3. Desktop. Looking for an ideal, economical work surface for your study or workroom? Flat, solid doors provide a sturdy surface for computers, typewriters and other large or bulky equipment. Some art teachers use them as working surfaces for their students. Doors are relatively cheap, therefore exposure to paint stains and scratches is not really a problem. (You can buy wooden or steel legs at your local hardware or department store or use filing cabinets or boxes of matching height.)

4. Work surface. Place an old solid door across a pair of sawhorses. It will easily absorb all the bumps and knocks handed out to it in the course of your work.

5. Table extender. Enlarge a small dining room table by placing a flat door on top. Put a pair of thin rubber gloves or a rubber pad on the table first to keep the door from sliding. Toss a tablecloth over the door to camouflage it. It's unlikely anyone will know the difference.

6. Raft. Attach two large pieces of plastic foam to an old door and you have an instant raft for your children. Be sure to test it for buoyancy before anyone decides to set sail.

7. Tree house. Two old doors laid side by side between sturdy branches can serve as a perfect base for a children's tree house. Make sure that you nail or tie the doors securely to the tree's branches.

8. Ramp. Use a flat solid wood or steel door as a ramp when wheeling furniture or other heavy objects up a step or an incline.

9. Transporter. If you want to move heavy items of furniture, such as a fridge or stove, without too much effort, use an old door with wooden rollers underneath. Place the furniture on the door and slide it along the rollers. Make sure you hold onto the items being moved.

10. Pathway. After a heavy rainstorm, lay old doors over soggy ground for easy walking. Or use it as a bridge for your wheelbarrow.

Dowels

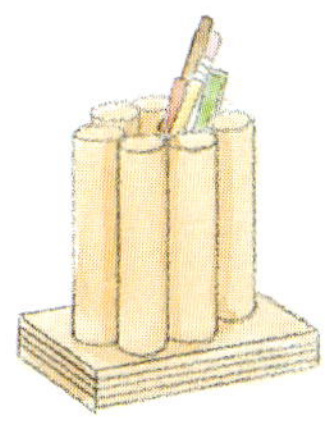

1. Pencil holder. Drill six-millimetre holes close together in a board, then glue and insert thin dowels.

2. Shelf extender. Nail 10-millimetre dowels along the edge of a shelf in the children's playroom to contain rolling toys such as miniature cars and marbles.

Drawers

1. Shadow box. Paint or paper the interior of a drawer and hang it on the wall to display trailing plants and favourite little knickknacks.

2. Rolling storage container. Fit old mismatched drawers with casters to slide under your workbench or bed for extra storage.

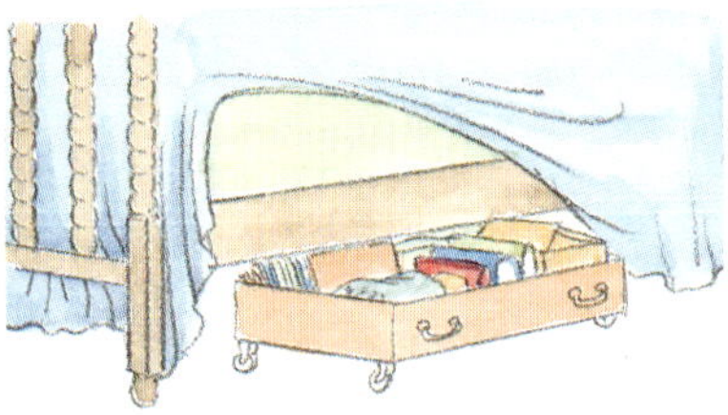

E

Eating utensils

1. Nail holder. Don't hammer your fingers; hold the nail between the tines of a fork.

2. Multipurpose tool. Use an old table knife as a spare screwdriver, a saw for cardboard, a putty knife or a file for odd jobs.

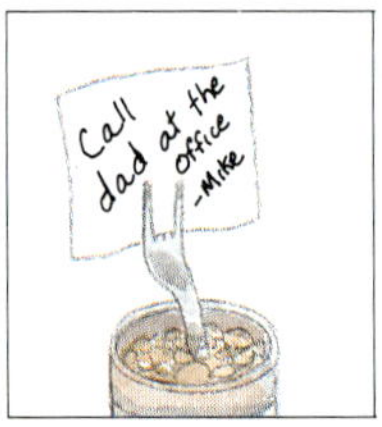

3. Message bearer. Anchor a fork in a pebble-filled soup tin and use to hold recipes or telephone messages.

4. House plant hoe. Bend the tines of an old fork at a right angle and use to aerate the soil of your potted plants.

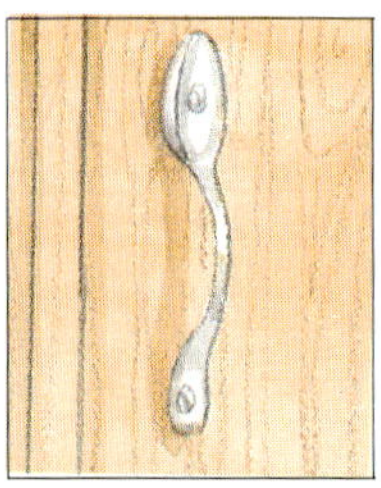

5. Cabinet handles. Bend the handle of a spoon; drill holes in the handle and in the centre of the bowl and screw to the cabinet door. Round off sharp edges.

6. Egg and spoon race. At the starting line, give each contestant an egg in a tablespoon; the first person to cross the finish line with an intact egg in the spoon is the winner.

Egg boxes

1. Desk organizer. Remove the top and place the box inside a desk drawer to hold paper clips, rubber bands and other small items.

2. Coin toss. Write a different number in each section and let your children compete for a high score by tossing coins.

3. Jewellery box. Store rings, earrings, chains and cuff links in the individual cups.

4. Fire starter. Place several cardboard egg boxes under the kindling wood in the fireplace.

5. Toy "centipede". Cut out the compartments and then string them together; make legs and antennae from pipe cleaners.

6. Christmas storage. Store small Christmas tree bulbs and fragile ornaments in empty egg boxes.

7. Seed starter. Punch a hole in the bottom of each cup, fill with potting soil, water, then drain overnight. Sow one or two seeds per cup and cover with plastic wrap; uncover when the seeds begin to sprout.

8. Palette. Children can mix paints neatly in an empty plastic egg box.

9. Game storage. Keep track of the small items in your children's games: use one box per game, label it with the name of the game, and keep it closed with a sturdy rubber band.

10. Ice cube tray. When you need extra ice for parties, fill plastic egg boxes with water.

11. Boxed sound. Egg boxes, mounted together on a door, a ceiling or on boards which can be moved, can deaden sound to studio levels.

Eggshells

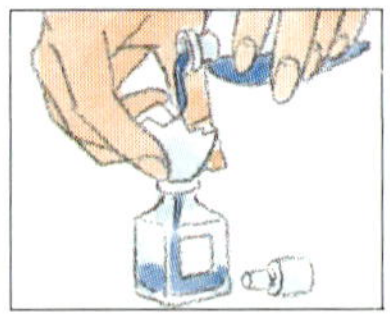

1. Mini funnel. Poke a hole in half an eggshell, then pour the liquid through it into a container.

2. Planter. Punch a tiny hole, add soil, moisten, and plant a seed. Support the eggshell in an egg box cup. Makes a novel gift.

3. Decoration. Poke a small hole in both ends of an egg; blow out the contents. Let the shell dry, then paint and decorate with beads, sequins and so on. To hang, glue ribbon or string to one end.

4. Fertilizer. Sprinkle crushed shells around garden plants to discourage slugs. Toss any extra eggshells into the compost heap.

5. Pot scrubber. When cleaning pots and pans while camping, a good substitute for steel wool is a handful of broken eggshells.

6. Mosaic. Paint the inside and outside of eggshells a variety of colours, then crush them in a paper bag. Draw a picture on cloth or paper and spread slightly diluted cold glue over it; now sprinkle a few appropriately coloured shells over the glue and protect with several coats of acrylic sealer.

7. Garden aid. Sprinkle rows of freshly planted seeds with crushed eggshells to keep birds away and to mark the rows.

Emery boards

1. Glass restorer. File rough edges on glassware with the fine-grit side of a damp emery board.

2. Pencil pointer. Glue an emery board under your workbench or desk to put a sharp point on pencils.

Erasers

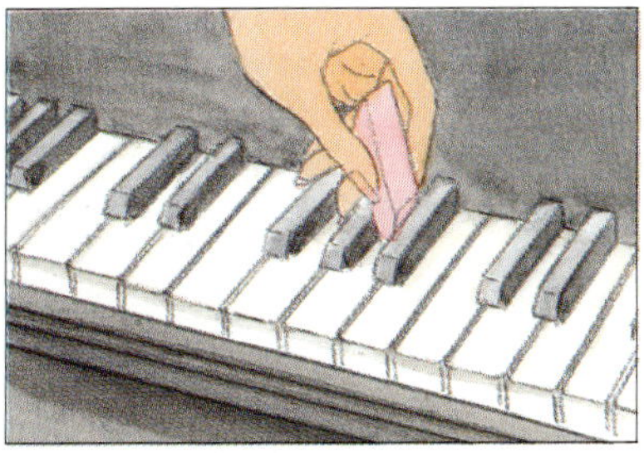

1. Key cleaner. Remove finger marks from piano keys with a rubber eraser; choose a size that fits easily between the black keys and gets into all the corners. For extra-tough spots, wrap the eraser with a cloth soaked in cleaning fluid.
2. Table stabiliser. Cut rubber erasers to fit the bottoms of table legs; fasten with adhesive or countersunk common nails.
3. Window cleaner. Give just-washed windows extra sparkle; wipe them with a clean blackboard eraser.

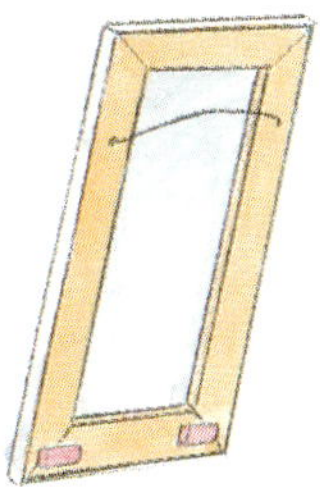

4. Wall saver. Glue rubber erasers to the bottom edge of the back of a frame; the frame will hang straighter, and it won't damage the wall.
5. De-skidder. Glue thin slices of a rubber eraser to the underside of a woven mat or sisal rug at its corners to keep it from slipping.
6. Household cleaner. Rub scuff marks from floors and fingerprints from woodwork with a rubber or an art-gum eraser.
7. Blade protector. Protect your knife – and yourself – by storing the tip in an eraser.
8. Rubber stamp. Draw a design on the flat side of a soft eraser, then outline it with the tip of a knife to a depth of about six millimetres. Carve away the waste, leaving the design.
9. Golf ball cleaner. On your next golf outing, take a rubber eraser with you to clean the ball at holes where there's no bucket.
10. Pincushion. Keep safety pins from drifting to the bottom of the dressing table drawer; stick the points into an eraser.
11. Upholstery cleaner. Rub lightly soiled cotton upholstery with an art-gum eraser.
12. Bit cushion. Store small drill bits, point first, in a large eraser.

Eyedroppers

1. Egg decorator. Apply dye to Easter eggs with eyedroppers.

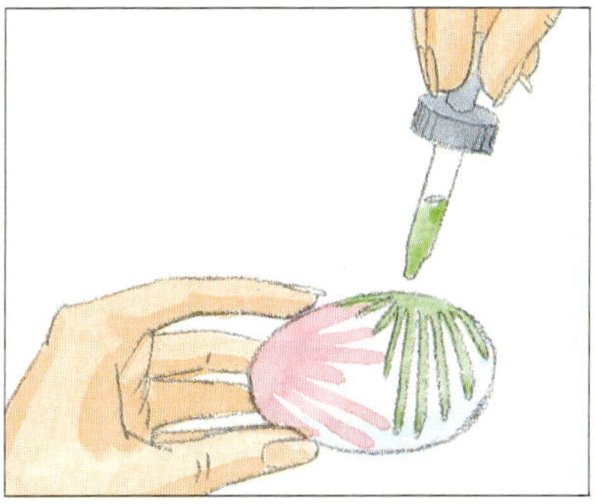

2. Glue dispenser. If the top of the glue container is clogged, use an eyedropper to dispense the glue.
3. Quicksilver catcher. Use an eyedropper to slurp up the mercury from a broken thermometer.
4. Puppy teat. Keep your eyedroppers in the kitchen to feed tiny puppies, birds or kittens.

F

Fabric softener sheets

1. Screen cleaner. Save used sheets of fabric softener to remove dust and static from TV and computer screens.
2. Deodoriser. Line the drawers and cupboard shelves in your house with fresh sheets.
3. Car freshener. Place several under the front seat to freshen stale air or eliminate smoke smells.
4. Shoe shiner. Buff shoes to a high gloss with a fabric softener sheet.
5. Static cutter. If you want to reduce static electricity in your hair, rub a sheet over your hairbrush.
6. Spectacle cleaner. Wipe lenses with a fabric softener sheet to clean them and prevent fogging.
7. Sewing aid. To prevent tangling, run your threaded needle through a sheet before sewing.

Fat

1. Cleanser. If your hands need a good cleaning after gardening or working on the car, rub in vegetable fat before using soap.
2. Bird food. Combine melted kitchen fat, bread crumbs and sunflower seeds in a paper cup. When the mixture hardens, peel away the cup and hang the contents from a tree in a mesh bag.
3. Screw driving. To penetrate surfaces easily, put vegetable fat on screw. Also inhibits rusting.

Filing cabinets

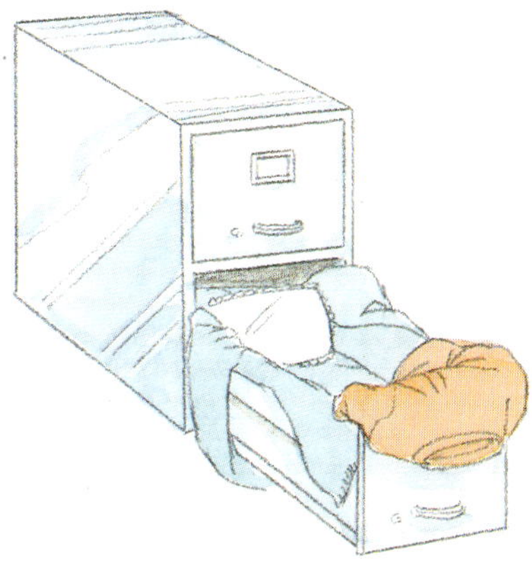

1. Crib. When your baby comes to visit the office for the day, empty the bottom drawer of a filing cabinet and pack in several pillows or jackets for a comfortable crib.
2. Desk base. Place a couple of two-drawer filing cabinets under a sturdy flat door for a desk.

Film canisters

1. Toolbox. Store small nails, screws, nuts or bolts inside.
2. Paperweight. Fill with sand and decorate with model paints.
3. Dry box. On camping and boating trips, film canisters will keep your banknotes dry.
4. Shakers. Drill holes in the lids of metal film canisters and fill with salt, pepper or spices. Now you have dispensers for picnicking.
5. Pillbox. Keep pills and vitamins in separate canisters when travelling; label with masking tape.
6. Candle mould. Tape a wick to the bottom of the canister and tie it to a toothpick across the top. Pour in hot paraffin wax and let harden.

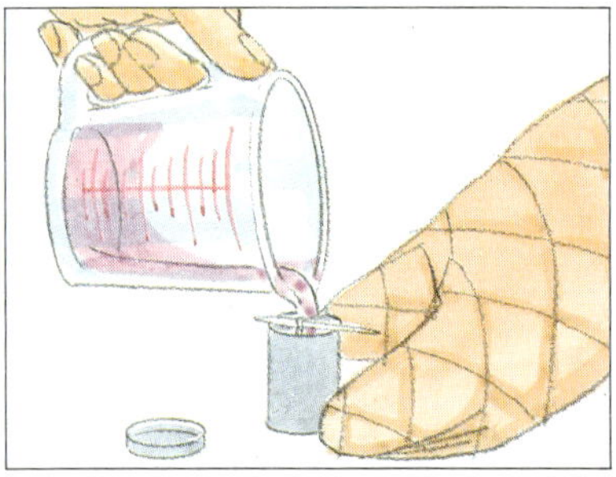

7. Organizer. Put paper clips, rubber bands and safety pins in individual canisters to keep them from tangling into bundles.
8. Coin holder. Use to hold change for telephones, buses, tolls, parking meters or laundry.
9. Jewellery box. Store your earrings and rings in a canister; put chains in individual canisters to keep them completely tangle-free.
10. Swimmer's helper. Carry your earplugs to the beach in a film canister. Then make a swap – put earrings and other small jewellery inside the canister so that they'll be protected from moisture and sand.
11. Battery holder. Use as a container for smaller batteries.
12. Stamp saver. Keep stamps unstuck and all in one place.
13. "Dry" ice cubes. Half fill with water, freeze, then cap tightly. Place several in a pitcher of fruit juice punch, lemonade or martinis to chill the beverage without diluting it.
14. Camping containers. A 35mm canister will hold seven teaspoons of sugar or jam, enough for a day trip.
15. Sewing kit. Put two needles, black and white thread wrapped around a piece of toothpick, a couple of buttons and several safety pins in a canister for emergency repairs.

Flowers

1. Wreath. Dry your garden's prettiest flowers (p.87), wrap clusters of three to five stems with wire, and attach to a straw wreath.

2. Potpourri. Dry garden flowers (p.87); place in an airtight container along with a few crushed fragrant leaves and spices and a drop or two of aromatic oil.
3. Flower salads. Put pansies, nasturtiums, violets, the leaves of carnations and rose petals in your salads.

4. Cake decorations. Dip fresh violet or rose petals in egg white, then place in a saucer of icing sugar; let dry on a wire rack, then arrange decoratively on your iced cake.

Foam mattress

1. Patio cushions. Cut an old mattress to fit patio chairs and cover with colourful fabric. Or stack the cushions for children to sit on.
2. Cushion filler. Cut or pull the foam into small pieces to use as a soft cushion filler.
3. Child's car seat. Let your small children sit on a comfortable piece of foam cut to fit the back seat of the car. This way they will also be able to see the passing view. Cover with a soft, absorbent fabric.
4. Package protector. To protect small or delicate packages in the post, cut a piece of foam, hollow out the centre and insert the package. Wrap with strong paper and post.
5. Frame saver. Before moving house, protect the corners of framed paintings and mirrors by covering with triangles of foam.
6. Baby's ball. Cut a solid cube of foam, 10 x 10 x 10 centimetres. Insert a bell into the middle and cover the foam with a different coloured fabric on each side.
7. Dog's bed. Cut an old foam mattress in half and use as a king-size bed for your dog. If your pooch chews the foam, cover with thick fabric.

Fries

1. Bubble and squeak. Don't throw away veggies left over from an evening meal. Keep in the refrigerator for a day and then fry them in butter with an egg or two for a super breakfast or a brunch.
2. Chinese. Try lightly-frying thinly sliced fresh vegetables in a hot pan for a Chinese treat.
3. French toast. Use up old bread: trim off the crusts, soak in a whipped mixture of eggs and milk, and then fry lightly on both sides. Serve plain or with maple syrup, jam or honey, or slice and pack into school lunch boxes to serve cold at break.

Frisbees

1. Biscuit tray. Turn upside down and fill with biscuits for your child's birthday party.
2. Birdbath. Punch through the Frisbee's edge at three points, insert wire plant hangers, and hang from a tree.

Frost

1. Jack Frost. On a cold night, leave a fine-spray sprinkler on in an orchard. If the mercury drops below freezing, by morning you will have a wonderland of icicles.
2. Nice ice drawing. Let the children write and draw in the frost that has formed during cold nights on windows or on your car windscreen. But make sure your radiator contains antifreeze before parking outside.
3. Battery water. The frost on the inside of your freezer is very close to distilled water. When defrosting, collect some and bottle it to top up your car battery when next needed.

Fruit

Sweet and sour. When making a potjie, toss in some dried fruit, two hours before cooking is complete. If some guests don't like fruit in stews, leave on the top.

Furniture polish

1. Tile saver. To prevent water spots and soap scum on shower walls, coat them with furniture polish.
2. Lubricating oil. You can use furniture polish to oil a squeaky door.

G

Garden hoses

1. Water mixer. To get just the right water temperature with double taps, slip a short section of hose over both taps, then make a V-shaped cut in the bottom middle of the tubing. Make sure that the cut is always above the level of the water.

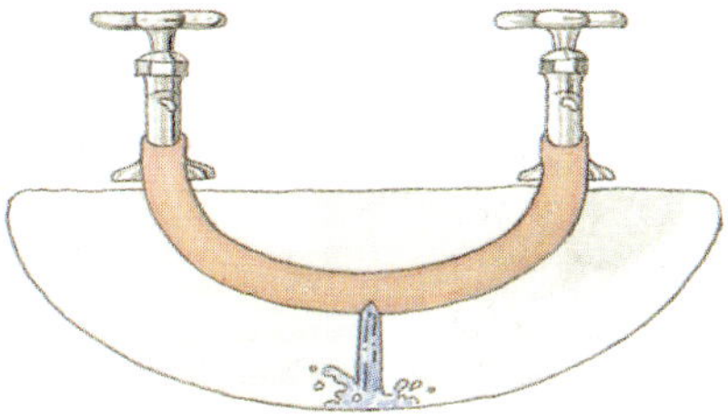

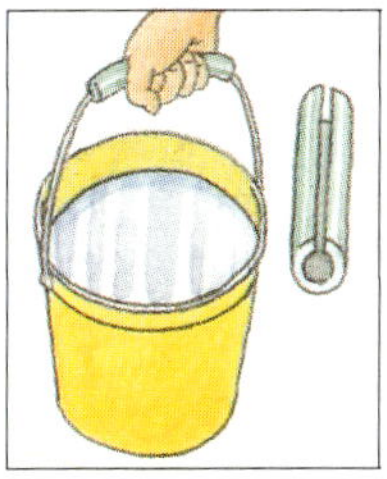

2. Bucket handle. For more comfortable carrying, slit a 10-centimetre length of old garden hose and slip it over the handle of the bucket.
3. Scary snake. Paint splotches on a short length of hose and leave it coiled in the garden to scare off animal intruders. Or twine it in the branches of a fruit tree to frighten birds when the fruits ripen.

4. Car door protector. Nail lengths of slit hose to the garage wall where the car door usually makes contact with the wall. It will protect the car and the wall.
5. Tree protector. Slit through one side of an old hose, then slip a section of it around the trunk of a very young tree to protect it from support ropes. Or put the hose around the ropes instead of the tree.
6. Blade guard. Slit a section of an old hose and slip it over the blade of an axe or a saw to protect the cutting edge and prevent injuries. Store safely in your garage or shed.

Gloves

1. Toy antlers. Stuff and use old gloves on children's fancy dress costumes or Christmas decorations.
2. Hand insulation. Keep one of your old gloves handy for unscrewing hot light bulbs.

3. Finger puppets. Create a cute face by sewing on buttons, yarn and rickrack or just paint one on. Insert your fingers to animate.

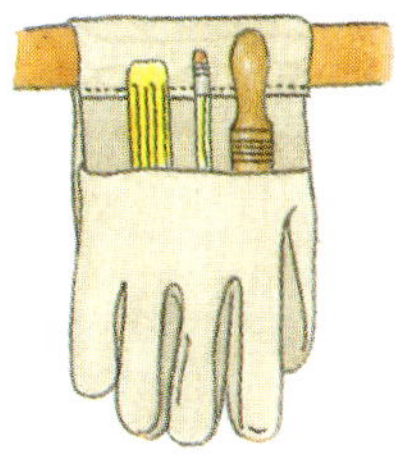

4. Tool holder. Cut off one side to the knuckles, fold over the other side, and stitch a tunnel to slip onto your leather belt.
5. Salvage. Cut up old leather gloves to make elbow patches or to re-cover leather buttons.
6. Venetian blind cleaner. Wearing soft cotton gloves sprayed with furniture polish, wipe each slat with one long stroke.

Greeting cards

1. Recipe tag. When sending home-baked goodies as a gift, write the recipe on the back of an old greeting card illustration.
2. Picture frame. Cut out a rectangle, oval or circle six millimetres

smaller on all sides than your picture; tape the picture inside and close.

3. Place mat. Glue greeting card pictures onto a 30- x 45-centimetre piece of cardboard; coat with clear varnish.

4. Christmas ornament. Punch a tiny hole in the top, then insert an ornament hanger.

H

Hair dryers

1. Wax remover. If candle wax drips onto a table, scrape off as much as possible with a blunt knife blade, soften the remainder with warm air from a hair dryer, then lift it up gently with a paper towel.

2. Invisible ink dryer. After writing a message on a piece of paper with lemon or onion juice, make it invisible by drying it on *Low*.

3. Invisible ink revealer. If you're the recipient of the secret message, make the writing visible again with a dryer set on *Hot*.

4. Traveller's aid. Hang just-washed garments on a towel rack or shower curtain rod and blow-dry.

5. Plaster remover. Ease a plaster off a wound by blowing hot air on it.

6. Paint dryer. Use to dry paint or varnish when in a hurry.

7. Heat leak detector. While someone holds a lit candle just inside a window, go outside with a hair dryer and blow air around the frame; if the flame wavers, the window is leaking heat. Repeat this procedure around every exterior door and window.

8. Fire starter. Fan the charcoal briquettes in an outdoor grill.

9. Duster. Blow dust off a high shelf or out from under an appliance.

10. Tackie dryer. If the toes of your tackies never seem to dry, aim the nozzle of a dryer, set on *Low*, into each shoe for about five minutes.

Hairgrips

1. Wire router. Secure speaker or phone wires to the skirting board. Clip the ends off the hairgrips so that they slide easily into the cracks.

2. Necklace. String hairgrips with coloured beads and knots of ribbon between them.

3. Ornament hanger. Slip through the ornament loop, then clip to the tree branch.

4. Apple bobbing. Let your guests bob for apples without getting wet. Insert hairgrips in the tops of a number of apples; leave part of each grip exposed and thread a string through it. Hang the apples from a broomstick suspended between two chairs.

5. Zip pull. Replace a broken one with a hairgrip.

6. Cuff links. Insert a hairgrip through both cuff-link holes; secure by twisting it or, if you wish, bending the ends into the shape of your initials with long-nose pliers.

7. Bookmark. Use hairgrips to mark your place in a book.

8. Peg. When propagating plants by layering, hold their stems down firmly with hairgrips.

9. Paper clip. Hold several pieces of paper together with a hairgrip.

10. Nail holder. Spare your fingers – use a hairgrip to grip a nail when hammering in tight spaces.

11. Invisible tie clip. Run the rear apron of your tie through the loop on the back of the front apron, then clip it to your shirt with a hairgrip.

Hair spray

1. Insecticide. Stop insects in their tracks with a shot of hair spray.

Caution: Do not use hair spray near an open flame.

2. Fabric saver. If hair colouring drips onto your clothing, spray it with hair spray, then dab it up with a towel.

3. Artist's fixative. Protect a child's pastel artworks and pencil drawings with hair spray.

4. Run stopper. If you get a run in your stocking, spray it immediately to prevent it from getting any longer.

5. Tarnish preventive. Spray it on freshly polished pieces of brass to retard tarnishing.

6. Flower extender. For longer-lasting cut flowers, give them a dash of hair spray; stand 30 centimetres away and direct it at the undersides of the leaves and petals.

7. Needle threader. Stiffen the end of the thread with hair spray.

Hammocks

1. Garden canopy. Make a simple frame and attach a flattened hammock to the top.

2. Utility tarpaulin. Cover roof rack commodities or small truckloads with an old hammock. Or gather branches and leaves in it.

3. Storage. Tie one up high in the storeroom to hold sleeping bags, out-of-season clothes and other lightweight items.

Handbags

1. Needlework tote. Keep your craft project in an old handbag (make sure that it's clean); store needles, thread, scissors and other essential supplies in its compartments.

2. Tool carrier. Keep a handbag filled with emergency tools in the boot of your car; the bag is light, rattleproof and easy to carry.

3. Clothes peg holder. Clip or slip the bag's handle over the line to keep your clothes pegs close at hand.

Handkerchiefs

1. Evening bag. Put your evening essentials in the centre of one and tie the corners diagonally.

2. Emergency sun hat. Tie knots in all four corners of a large handkerchief or bandanna and cover your head.

3. Smoke mask. If you're ever caught in a burning building, soak a handkerchief with water and tie it around your nose and mouth to filter out smoke and gas.

4. Bouquet garni. Tie herbs and spices in a handkerchief and put in soup or stew while cooking; remove from the dish before serving.

Hangers

1. Plant marker. At the end of each row of seedlings, insert a straightened hanger tagged with the plant's name and the planting date.

2. Green box. To convert a window box into a mini greenhouse, bend three or four small pieces of hanger into U's and place the ends into the soil; punch small holes in a dry-cleaner bag, wrap around the box, and place in bright light but not in sunshine. If you want to encourage your seeds to germinate, cover with brown paper.

3. Caulking tube stopper. Here's a way to prevent oozing from the tube once a job is done: cut a seven and a half-centimetre piece of hanger; insert one end into the tube after shaping the other into a hook so that you can easily pull out the stopper when you need to caulk again.

4. Christmas decorations. Cut and bend into star and angel shapes, spray-paint, and hang on the tree.

5. Bubble maker. To make extra-big bubbles, shape a hanger into a hoop with a handle, dip into the solution, and wave through the air.

6. Arm extender. If a utensil has fallen behind the refrigerator or you want to reach a cup or jug (preferably plastic) on a high shelf, straighten a hanger completely, except for the hook at the end.

7. Wicket. Replace a lost wicket in your croquet set with one made out of a coat hanger.

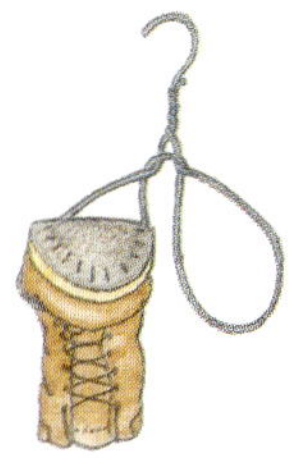

8. Boot dryer. To speed the drying of boots and other footwear, form two loops in a hanger, and hang with the boots inverted.

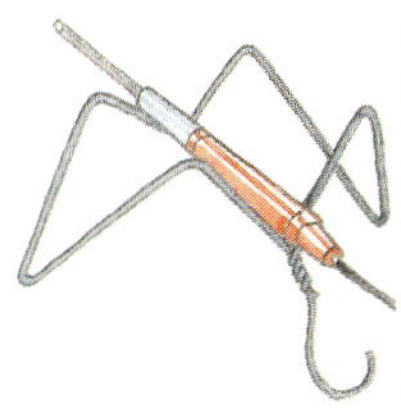

9. Soldering iron rest. Prevent a hot soldering iron from rolling away by placing it in a coat hanger rest as shown.

10. Plant hanger. Wrap a straightened hanger around a 15-centimetre to 25-centimetre pot just below the lip; twist it back on itself to secure it, then hang.

11. Wings. Use for making realistic wings on children's fancy dress and Christmas costumes.

Hatpins

1. Tack. Use them instead of drawing pins. Being longer, they hold better.

2. Stickpin. File down the point and attach to your lapel.

3. Ironing aid. Hold a difficult-to-press garment on the ironing board with several of them.

4. Upholstery securer. Keep upholstery covers from slipping off sofa arms with hatpins.

Hydrogen peroxide

1. Rust remover. Make a paste of cream of tartar and hydrogen peroxide and rub on to remove rust stains in sinks and bathtubs.

2. Scorch eraser. Remove (or at least lighten) ugly scorch marks by saturating them with peroxide.

3. Bleach. When whitening or brightening fabrics, substitute hydrogen peroxide for conventional bleach. It is gentler on fabrics.

I

Ice

1. Plant waterer. Put several ice cubes on house plant soil so that the moisture seeps in gradually. But don't let the ice touch the foliage.

2. Flavour negater. Before your child swallows an unpleasant-tasting medicine, have him suck on an ice cube for a few minutes so that his taste buds are numbed.

3. Indentation inflater. Put an ice cube in each dent left in carpeting by furniture legs – the moisture will plump up the fibres.

4. First aid. Pack crushed ice in a plastic bag around a twisted ankle: the cold will reduce internal bleeding and reduce swelling. Ice in a bag is also useful to stop nosebleeds: hold gently on the bridge of the nose, alternating with each temple and the nape of the neck.

Ice cream scoops

1. Beach toy. Give one to your child for making castles in the sand (or the back yard sandbox).

2. Trowel. When transplanting seedlings, use a scoop to make same-size planting holes quickly and easily.
3. Soil scoop. For mess-free repotting, use an ice cream scoop to add soil to the container.
4. Server. Scoop equal portions of rice or mashed potatoes onto the family's dinner plates.
5. Melon scoop. Use an ice cream scoop to make large melon balls.

Ice cream sticks

1. Stirrer. An ice cream stick neatly mixes small amounts of paint, putty and glue – and you can throw it away afterward without feeling guilty.
2. Ruler. In an emergency, draw a straight line with one.
3. Trivet. Glue a summer's worth of sticks together to form a square on which hot pots can safely rest.

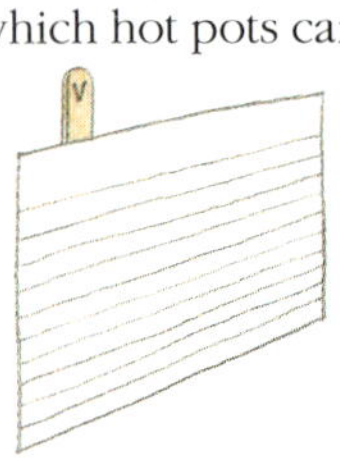

4. Index file marker. Cut to size if necessary, tape to an index card, and letter the top with a marker pen.

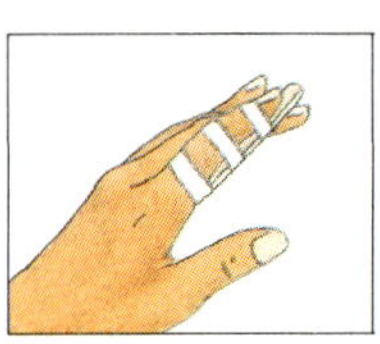

5. Splint. In an emergency, secure a stick to an injured finger with tape or strips of cloth.

6. Garden marker. Write the name of the plant and the date with indelible ink and insert it into the soil alongside.
7. Shim. Glue to the bottom corners or legs of a piece of furniture so that it stands level on the floor.
8. Insulator. If you have to check for the spark from a plug wire, hold it with two sticks; if the wire is leaking high-voltage current, you won't get shocked or burnt.
9. File. Glue sandpaper to one end and use for sanding.
10. Caulking trowel. Use a wet stick to spread caulk evenly around window and door frames.

Iodine

1. Furniture renewer. Dab some over scratches in mahogany furniture.
2. Water purifier. When camping in areas without a safe water supply, stir in six to eight drops of iodine per litre of drinking water; wait 20 minutes before consuming it.

J

Jar lids

1. Reflectors. Cover with reflective paint and place along paths and driveways to help visitors.
2. Biscuit cutter. Dip the lid in flour, then press it into the dough.
3. Food saver. To keep the remaining half of an apple or orange fresh for a day or so, place it face-down on a lid and refrigerate. To save a partially consumed glass of milk, cover it with a large lid and refrigerate. Cover leftover canned soup or fruit with a jar lid and refrigerate.
4. Coaster. Glue felt or cork inside a lid, then rest your cold drink in it.
5. Candle holder. On a camping expedition, use them to hold candles.
6. Frame. Paint the lid or cover it with a fabric remnant; cut a photograph to fit and glue it inside.
7. Paint palette. For quick touch-ups, pour paint into a lid and dip into it with an artist's brush.

Jars

1. Terrarium. Place a two and a half-centimetre layer of pebbles and charcoal chips and seven and a half centimetres of sterilized potting mix in a large jar. After planting, moisten slightly and place in a bright spot, uncovered, for a day, then cover.
2. Cocktail shaker. Use for mixing daiquiris, margaritas and other such liquid concoctions.
3. Piggy bank. Cut a slit in the lid with an old screwdriver or chisel.
4. Paint jars. Mix children's poster paint in small glass jars. When the children have finished painting, screw on the lid and put away for another time.

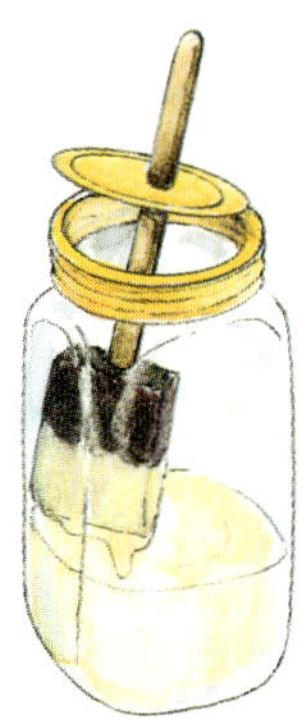

5. Glue pot. Drill a hole through a preserving jar lid to fit the handle of a disposable foam paintbrush. To let the brush hang in the pot, rest the lid on top of the screw-on ring. Wipe off excess glue which has been left on the ring.

6. Workshop storage. Nail lids to a rafter or the underside of a shelf in the workshop and screw in jars filled with nails, screws, nuts and bolts, which can easily be identified.

7. Washer. Put small hand-washables in a large jar and add detergent and water. Shake the jar one minute, let soak for three minutes, then shake again; rinse and air-dry.

8. Boat storage. Keep banknotes or matches dry by storing them in a screw-top jar; screw the lid to the underside of one of the seats.

9. Spare key storer. Place a spare house key in a glass jar, and seal with a lid. Bury the jar in your garden in a spot only your family can identify. No need to call the locksmith if you are locked out by accident.

K

Keys

1. Fishing sinker. With their pre-drilled holes, unidentified keys make great weights for fishing lines.

2. Curtain weight. To keep curtains hanging properly, try slipping old keys in the hems.

Knife holders

1. Fishing lure organizer. There's no need to poke around in your tackle box for lures – mount a magnetic knife holder inside to keep them all together.

2. Tool holder. Mount one on the workshop wall and attach screwdrivers, pliers and other small tools.

3. Sewing box organizer. Reduce the risk of injury – keep a magnetic knife holder inside your sewing box to hold scissors and loose needles and pins in one place.

4. Medicine chest neatener. You can use a magnetic knife holder to keep nail clippers, scissors and tweezers close at hand.

L

Ladders

1. Planting guide. Place a ladder flat on the soil and press down; repeat to make a series of parallel rows.

2. Sawhorse. Just lay an open stepladder on its side.

3. Utensil holder. Hang a section of ladder from the ceiling with ropes and suspend pots and pans from it.

4. Loading ramp. Place a ladder against the doorstep or the boot of the car and put boards on top.

5. Scaffolding. Place planks across the rungs of two ladders; adjust the height by using higher or lower rungs. When the height is no longer adequate, the ladders can be securely erected on top of weighted barrels, with each foot firmly planted in a barrel-centre. If working alongside windows, tie the ladders to a window frame for safety.

6. Clothing rack. Hang out-of-season clothing in a storeroom or attic by extending a long pole across the top rungs of two stepladders.

7. Trellis. Use an old ladder (preferably one with rounded rungs) to support climbing vines. Stand two facing each other and span a third across the top to make an arbour.

Laundry basket

1. Toy box. Store children's toys in brightly coloured laundry baskets – they'll be easy to find and pack.

2. Sled. Use a laundry basket for fun at the beach. Attach a piece of rope and pull toddlers along the sand.

3. Carrier. Keep a spare one handy at the top and the bottom of the stairs for transporting odds and ends from one floor to the other.

Leaves

1. Christmas table decoration. Paint or spray ivy leaves gold or silver, and use the sprigs to decorate the festive Christmas table.

2. Doily. When entertaining guests, serve cheeses, hors d'oeuvres or individual pastries on plates covered with shiny, non-poisonous clean leaves. Nasturtium, banana or any citrus leaves are ideal.

3. Place mat. Dry and press several leaves and arrange them between two sheets of clear adhesive plastic.

Lemon juice

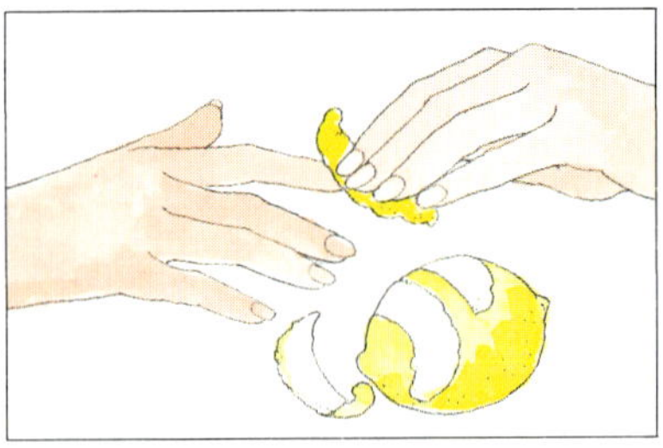

1. Fingernail treatment. Soak fingertips for five minutes in one cup warm water and the juice of half a lemon. After pushing back the cuticles, rub lemon peel back and forth against the nail.
2. Hair lightener. Comb lemon juice evenly through hair, then let it dry in the sun; repeat once a day for at least a week. Condition in between.
3. Bathroom cleanser. Rub stained enamel fixtures with a cut lemon; for stubborn stains, use a paste of lemon juice and borax.
4. Lettuce crisper. Soak soggy lettuce in a bowl of cold water to which you've added the juice of half a lemon; refrigerate for one hour.
5. Blemish healer. Dab a pimple with lemon juice several times a day.
6. Pore cleanser. Combine one litre boiling water, the juice of half a lemon and one to two tablespoons dried thyme or mint. Steam your face 30 centimetres above the mixture for 15 minutes, then rinse with very cold water to close the pores.
7. Sponge renewer. To salvage a soured sponge, saturate it with lemon juice, then rinse it thoroughly.
8. Apple preservative. Keep sliced apples from turning brown by coating the cut surfaces with lemon juice.
9. Piano prettifier. Rub a paste of two parts salt and one part lemon juice on piano keys; wipe off with a damp cloth, then buff with a dry one.
10. Air freshener. If the odour of fish lingers long after you've cooked it, place a pierced lemon in a 150°C oven for 15 minutes, leaving the oven door slightly open.
11. Hand deodoriser. Can't get rid of that fishy smell on your hands? Sprinkle powdered mustard on them, then add enough lemon juice to make a paste; rub in well, then wash with soap and water.

Lint

1. Tinder. Dispose of the lint from your tumbledryer by using it under kindling in the fireplace.
2. Filler. Use tumbledryer lint to stuff a small toy or pincushion.

Lip balm

1. Moisturizer. Rub it on your face to protect the skin while outdoors.
2. Face saver. Dab some on a shaving nick to stop bleeding.
3. Zip lubricant. Run a little lip balm up and down the teeth to ease the motion of a sticky zip.
4. Wax. Use it to groom moustaches or eyebrows.

Liquid starch

1. Piñata. Blow up a balloon and cover it with strips of newspaper soaked in starch.
2. Threader. Dampen the end of the thread with a bit of liquid starch before threading your sewing machine.

Liquor cartons

1. "Ski ball". Place a carton at an angle and erect a small ramp in front (a rubber mat over a pile of books will do). Assign numbered values to each section of the carton and roll golf or tennis balls up the ramp and into the box from a set distance.

2. Tool keeper. Put a topless box on the garage floor; cut off the tops and bottoms of two others. Stack the cartons so that the dividers match up and attach them to one another with insulation tape. Store a long-handled garden tool, such as a rake, in each divider.

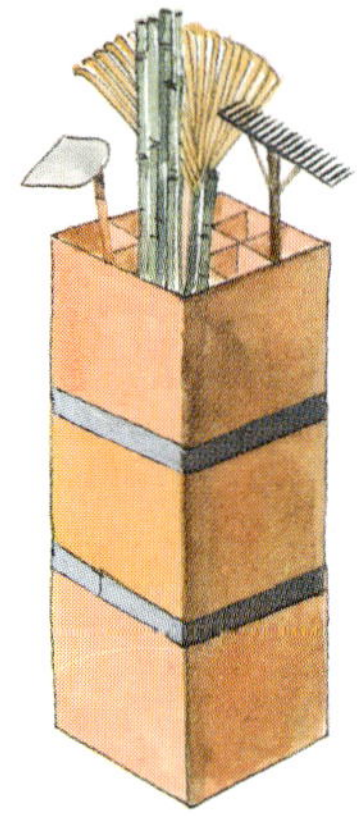

3. Art preserver. A clean liquor carton with its partitions intact is a good place to store rolled-up drawing papers and canvasses.

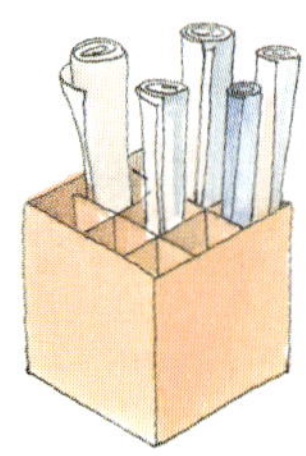

4. Ornament storage. Wrap those fragile Christmas ornaments or fine glassware individually with newspaper, then place several of them snugly in each of the carton's segments – they will be well protected.
5. Workshop organizer. A sectioned carton is an excellent place to store your dowels, mouldings, furring strips, weatherstripping, planks and metal rods of short length.
6. Glass protector. Keep fine crystal glassware or light bulbs, sorted by wattage, in individual segments.
7. Sports caddy. Keep one or two in your child's room or the playroom for neat storage of tennis racquets, hockey sticks, fishing rods, golf clubs and other sports gear. Decorate with adhesive shelf-lining plastic.

Liquorice

1. Ice breaker. At children's parties, instead of bobbing apples, set children the task of nibbling in pairs from each end of a string of liquorice. There will be strong competition between the groups and lots of laughs. Award prizes to the top three teams.
2. Medicinal. Taken in moderation, the sweet is a mild laxative.

M

Magazines

1. Stadium cushion. Wrap several thick magazines in a heavy-duty plastic bag and place between you and cold, hard wooden seats.
2. Funnel. Roll a large magazine into a cone, tape it, and use it to funnel dry substances into containers.
3. Truncheon. In a tight spot, open a magazine down the centre, roll into a long, tight tube, and fold this over. The fold makes a lethal knot of hard paper, the thin end a handle.
4. Boot trees. Roll magazines inside leather or rubber boots to keep the boots in shape.

Magnets

1. Petrol-cap holder. Attach a magnet near the opening to your car's petrol tank to hold the cap while you're filling up.
2. Drawer organizer. Place a magnet in your odds-and-ends drawer to keep pins and paper clips together.
3. Picker-upper. Use a magnet to pick up spilled pins, needles, tacks and staples.

Margarine tubs

1. Paint tin. Pour paint into an empty margarine tub for small touch-up jobs around the house.
2. Mould. Make individual moulded salads or desserts in them.
3. Pet dish. Take several of these lightweight and disposable containers along when you're travelling with your pet.
4. Baby bowl. Store leftover baby food in them. Or use them for feeding the baby away from home – you can even carry the food in them.
5. Piggy bank. Cut a slit in the lid.
6. Starter pot. Poke holes in the bottom, add potting mix, then sow seeds as recommended on the packet.
7. Storage bin. Clean and use to store odds and ends in the kitchen, garage, workshop or children's rooms. Ideal for wax crayons.

Mattresses

1. Gym pad. Hang one on the wall behind a basketball hoop to prevent injuries to players.
2. Party chairs. A mattress is better than chairs at children's parties.
3. Crash pad. Place one under a child's jungle gym to prevent injuries.
4. Trampoline. Keep an old one in the playroom for small children to bounce on.

5. Trundle bed. Keep an old mattress under the bed. When unexpected guests spend the night, pull it out and make it up – it will be much more comfortable than the floor.
6. Bumper saver. Nail one to the back wall of your garage, just in case.
7. Door protector. Nail a mattress to the side of the garage where the car door usually hits.

Mayonnaise

1. Ring loosener. Smear some on your finger to slide off a tight ring.
2. Furniture cleaner. Cover a water mark on finished wooden furniture with mayonnaise, then sprinkle with salt; using a clean cloth, rub the mixture in until the stain disappears, then buff until dry. Rewax if necessary.

Mesh bags

1. Salad spinner. Place washed lettuce leaves in a mesh bag, then twirl it around outdoors for several minutes. Even better on a string.
2. Flower arranger. Crumple one up and stuff it in a vase to anchor stems before arranging flowers.
3. Shoe scraper. In winter or when it's muddy, put a mesh bag over your doormat to give it a rough surface.

4. Bird feeder. Combine melted fat with birdseed, let harden, then place in a mesh bag and hang from a branch; the holes make the food visible, the scent attracts birds, and their beaks have easy access.
5. Lingerie bag. Place delicate underwear in a mesh bag so that it doesn't tangle with other clothes in the washing machine.
6. Dishwasher basket. Put baby bottle caps and teats in a mesh bag to

prevent them from flying all over the dishwasher when it's running.

7. Fish stringer. Put the fish in a bag and hang it in the water until you're ready to go home.

8. Soap on a string. On camping trips, carry your bar of soap in a mesh bag. Use the soap right in the bag.

9. Drain filter. To prevent clogging the drain, place a mesh bag over the shower drain to catch hair.

10. Harvester. String a heavy cord along the top of a bag and put freshly picked vegetables in it; hose dirt off the produce while it's still in the bag.

11. Fishing net. Bend a wire hanger into a ring as large as the bag's mouth and stitch the open edge of the bag to it. Lash this onto a short stick.

12. Scrub pad. Place a sponge inside a mesh bag, dampen, and use as a gentle but effective scrub pad for your car, braai or pots and pans. If you can't find a sponge, simply bunch up the bag and scrub.

13. Soap holder. Fold a small plastic mesh bag and put it in the bottom of the kitchen soap dish; it will keep the soap dry and also serve as an emergency pot scrubber.

14. Beach bag. Before you decide to leave the beach, put your children's spades, buckets, balls and other playthings in a mesh bag and dip it in the water so that you don't transport sand back home.

Methylated spirits

1. Chilli neutralizer. If your hands burn and sting after handling chillies, wash them thoroughly, then pour methylated spirits over them.

2. Windowsill cleaner. If your wooden windowsills are rain-spotted or discoloured, refresh them by wiping them with a little diluted methylated spirits on a soft cloth.

3. Bathroom cleaner. Keep a bottle of methylated spirits handy to shine chrome fixtures and to remove hair spray from the mirrors.

4. Knickknack polish. Carefully clean crystal and porcelain ornaments with a cloth dampened with methylated spirits.

Microwave ovens

1. Ironing aid. Sprinkle clothes lightly with water, place in a plastic bag, and microwave on *High* for one minute or until warm to the touch; iron immediately.

Caution: Make sure clothes have no metal parts.

2. Raisin rejuvenator. Place half a cup of dry raisins and one teaspoon water in a glass measuring cup; cover with plastic wrap and microwave on *High* for 30 seconds; stir, then let stand one minute.

3. Crisper. To freshen soggy potato chips, pretzels or crackers, microwave them on *High* for 30 to 60 seconds; let stand for two minutes.

4. Squash splitter. To cut gem squash easily, pierce the skin of an uncut squash with a fork, cook on *High* for one to two minutes, then cut it into halves, quarters or slices.

5. Compress warmer. Microwave a plastic-wrapped dampened washcloth on *High* for 15 to 30 seconds or until it's warm to the touch.

Milk cartons

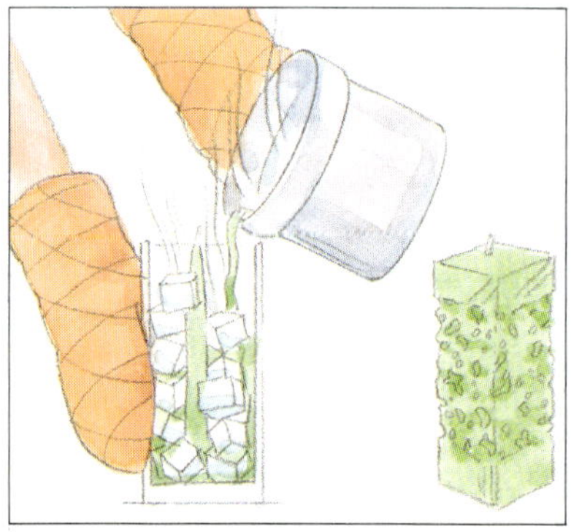

1. Candle mould. Coat the inside of a carton with cooking spray, put a thin candle in the centre, anchoring it with a base of melted wax, then fill with ice cubes. Pour in hot wax; when the wax cools, pour out the water and gently peel off the carton, leaving a delicate, lacy candle. Try adding food colouring to the hot wax.

2. Holding tank. Fill a clean carton with water to hold your fish while you're cleaning their aquarium.

3. Bunny air conditioner. During hot, humid weather fill empty milk cartons with water, freeze, and place in the bunny hutch to keep your pet rabbits comfortable.

4. Scrap sorter. Keep an empty carton next to the kitchen sink so that you can easily dispose of wet scraps, which could clog the drain. Throw all dry refuse in the rubbish bin.

5. Weight. Keep a tarpaulin down. Half-fill milk cartons with sand or stones. Punch a hole in top of each and loop a string through to tie to the grommets at the edge of the tarpaulin.

6. Toe guard. Do you enjoy camping outdoors? Help prevent yourself and fellow campers stubbing toes on unseen tent pegs in the dark. Put cut-off carton tops securely over the tops of protruding pegs.

7. Bird feeder. Combine melted suet and birdseed, pour into a carton, and insert a loop of string into the mixture. After it hardens, tear away the carton and hang from a branch.

8. Paint tin. Pour paint into the bottom half of a cut-off carton; discard when the job is finished.

9. Firelighters. Being waxed, milk cartons will burn furiously.

10. Block. Remove the spout end of a well-washed carton and cut slits at each corner to make four flaps. Fold the flaps, tape in place, and decorate.

11. Dustpan. Cut off the front and bottom of a carton, then slice the sides at an angle to sweep dirt in easily.

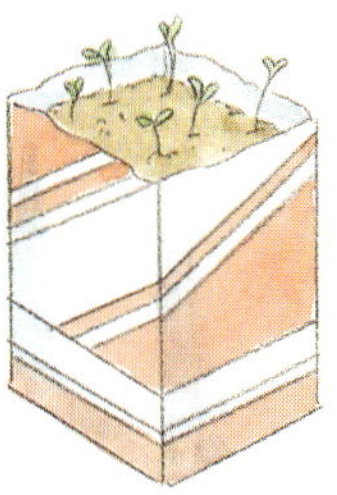

12. Seed starter. Cut the top off a carton, punch holes in the bottom, fill with potting mix, and sow seeds according to the instructions.

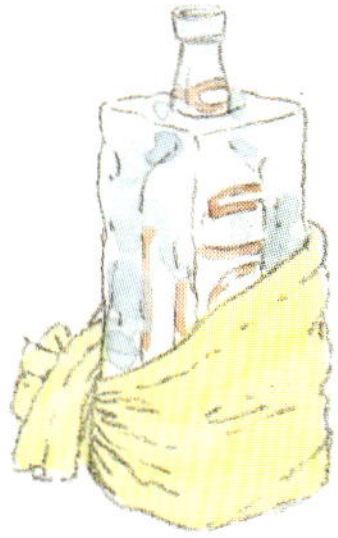

13. Cooler. Put a glass container of vodka, punch or lemonade inside one, fill with water, and freeze. Peel off the carton; to pour the beverage, wrap the icy bottle in a towel.

14. Vegetable collar. Cut off the top and bottom and push into the ground around tomatoes and peppers to discourage grubs and cutworms.

Mirrors

1. Handkerchief presser. Stick your just-washed cotton handkerchief onto the bathroom mirror; as it dries slowly in place, it will straighten itself out, as if ironed.

2. Reflector. Place mirrors along paths and driveways.

3. Tray. Use epoxy to glue a mirror to a piece of fibreboard.

4. Shelf. Put them on the bottom and back of your china cabinet to make your glassware sparkle.

5. Signal mirror. Using long and short flashes, send messages via Morse code.

6. Compact. Fit a small rectangular mirror (perhaps a piece of a broken one) inside the lid of a small tin.

7. Basement detective. If your basement seems damp, attach a mirror to one wall. Check it the next day; if it's moist or fogged over, the problem is condensation; if it's dry and the wall is damp, the problem is seepage.

8. Flush enhancer. Check under the rim of your toilet bowl with a small mirror; if the openings appear clogged, ream them out with a wire hanger, using the mirror again.

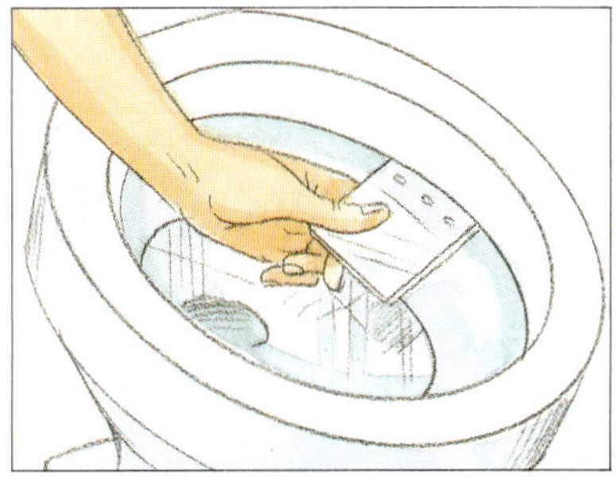

Mothballs

1. Storage. When washing woollens you're about to store, dissolve a few mothballs in the final rinse water.

2. Rust preventer. Place some in the toolbox to absorb moisture.

3. Rubbish bin deodorant. Put a couple of mothballs between the rubbish bin and the plastic refuse bag – at least the bin won't smell foul!

4. Pest deterrent. Place mothballs around holes and vents or in rubbish bins to discourage rats, dogs and other animal invaders.

5. Tarnish inhibitor. Place some in the silverware drawer or chest to help prevent discoloration.

Motor oil

1. Tool cleaner. Add used motor oil to a bucket of sand, then thrust the metal parts of garden tools into the mixture to clean them after use and help keep them rust-free.

2. Brush saver. After cleaning paintbrushes with turpentine, squeeze a little clean oil onto the bristles and wrap tightly with aluminium foil. Before using a brush again, rinse with a little more turpentine.

3. Body protector. To prevent corrosion from wet, muddy roads in winter, spray the underside of your car with used motor oil.

4. Concrete lubricant. To prevent sticking, brush onto wooden forms before pouring concrete.

Mousetraps

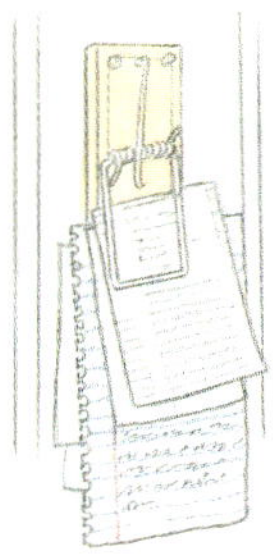

1. Wall clamp. Fasten a spring trap to your workshop or kitchen wall to hold frequently used but easily misplaced items, such as gloves, cloths or recipes.

2. Paperweight. Keep several spring mousetraps on your desk for organizing bills, receipts, business cards and other loose papers.

3. Glue clamp. If you're short of a spring clamp or two, a mousetrap or rat-trap will do the trick.

Mugs

1. Utensil container. Keep spoons, spatulas and other kitchen utensils in an attractive mug that has cracked and can't hold fluids anymore.

2. Planter. Even if it's chipped, a mug still makes a terrific container for small plants on the kitchen windowsill or bay window.

3. Pencil holder. Keep pens or pencils handy for telephone messages.

Mussel shells

1. Gravel. Try crushed mussel shells for an excellent pathway.

2. Paint palette. Use as disposable paint containers for small projects.

3. Fowl gravel. Crush and feed to hens as an egg-building tonic.

4. Garden trowel. A large mussel shell is an ideal tool for transplanting.

5. Jewellery holder. Glue small shells onto a large shell and use as a decorative container for brooches, chains and earrings.

6. Plant drain. Crush shells and use the fragments for drainage when repotting a house plant.

7. Seafood casserole. Cook and serve miniature seafood casseroles or devilled crab in them.

8. Wind chimes. Punch holes in shells, then run nylon line through them, knotting it to keep them evenly spaced; attach several strings of shells to a small piece of wood and hang.

N

Nail polish

1. Personaliser. Print names or initials on cups or glasses with bright nail polish.

2. Ornament paint. Decorate or touch up Christmas ornaments with a bit of nail polish.

3. Sealing wax. Seal letters with a dab of fingernail polish – it doesn't need warming in a flame, and it sticks just as well as wax.

4. Run stopper. Dab clear nail polish on a stocking or pantihose run to prevent it from growing.

5. Measure marker. Make the millilitre indicators on baby bottles or measuring cups easier to read by marking them with bright red or purple nail polish.

6. Brand. Paint your initials on wooden tool handles with nail polish. Before it dries, set a match to it and the polish will burn, leaving your brand in the wood.

7. Sealant. Keep a bottle or jar from leaking while you're travelling; apply a light coat of nail polish around the base of the cap.

Nails

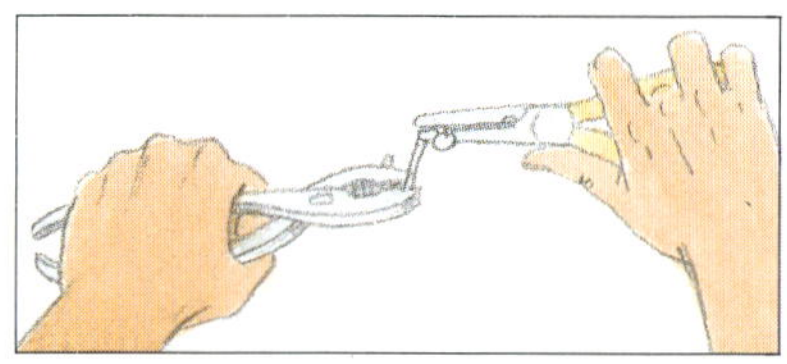

1. S-hook. Hold a thin nail with pliers and bend it into an S with a second pair; clamp a larger nail in a vice and hammer it into shape.

2. Weight. Use nails of various sizes as weights for a balance scale.

3. Potato baker. To shorten baking time, insert clean steel nails into potatoes before putting them into a conventional oven. Remember to remove them before serving!

4. Post setter. For a stronger hold, hammer a few long or bent nails partway into the base of a fence post before setting it in concrete.

Nappies

1. Bed pad. Sew several together for a thick, absorbent mattress pad for your baby.

2. Compress. Use nappies as hot or cold compresses for aching muscles or bruised limbs.

3. Cover. Wrap a hot-water bottle in a nappy to protect your skin.

4. Car waxer. Use one to apply and buff car wax and polish.

5. Drip catcher. If your roof has sprung a leak, put disposable nappies under it; they're an absorbent and quiet alternative to pots. Or put one in a bucket; it will absorb the sound while the bucket holds the excess water coming through.

Newspapers

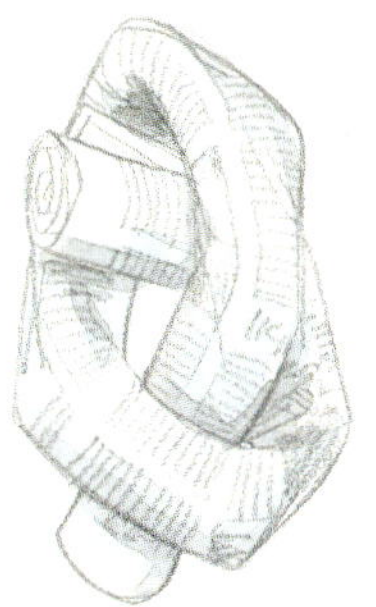

1. Fire starter. Overlap two or three sheets of newspaper to form a tight roll, then make an overhand knot. Half a dozen of these will get the most stubborn logs going. (See also *Firewood*, p.82.)

2. Oven cleaner. Use crumpled-up balls of newspaper to remove heavy grease, then wipe with a damp cloth or sponge.

3. Glass cleaner. After washing windows or mirrors with soap and water, crumple up newspaper and wipe the glass dry – it will sparkle and be streak-free.

4. Duster. For reaching those hard-to-dust places in the house, roll a sheet of newspaper into a tube and fringe one end.

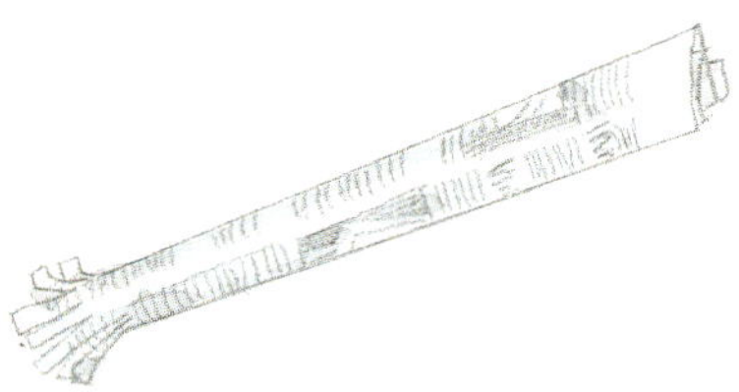

5. Cat litter. In an emergency, shred newspaper for the litter box.

6. Draught blocker. Keep out the cold by stuffing newspaper under doors and in the cracks of windows that won't close all the way.

7. Boot dryer. Stuff crumpled newspapers in wet boots or shoes and let dry overnight.

8. Deodoriser. Stuff wads of newspaper into shoes or boots to remove unpleasant odours overnight.

9. Window repair. Glue newspaper to both sides of a cracked pane of glass. When dry, chip away the putty, and the pane will come out without splintering and causing damage.

10. Plastic container sweetener. A piece of crumpled printed (no colours) newspaper sealed in a container overnight will remove most foul odours.

11. Luggage freshener. If your old trunks and suitcases haven't been used for a long time, stuff crumpled newspapers inside and leave for a couple of weeks.

12. Moplets. For cleaning up grease or sopping up paint remover, keep a supply of newspapers on hand in your workshop. Pile them up three centimetres or so thick, then cut them into quarters with a sharp knife. Stack the papers and drill a hole in one corner with an electric drill. Run a wire through the hole and hang from a convenient hook.

13. Tablecloth. For messy meals, set the table with newspapers.

14. Truncheon. Rolled into a long tube, and folded double, a newspaper makes a potent truncheon.

15. Mulch. Spread papers out flat or tear them into strips and place around plants. Water thoroughly to hold in place; if necessary, secure the papers with a few rocks.

16. Carpet padding. Place several thicknesses of newspaper under rugs and carpets.

17. Moth deterrent. Since moths appear to hate any form of newsprint, try packing out-of-season clothing in newspaper; roll papers inside rugs before storing.

Nutty putty

1. Exercise equipment. Knead it to strengthen your hands and forearms.

2. Caulking. Use to temporarily plug cracks around windows.

3. Tranquilliser. Play with it to calm your nerves – especially useful when you've just given up smoking.

4. All-purpose cleaner. Remove lint from clothes, erase pencil marks and clean computer keys.

Nylon line

1. Necklace cord. Restring beads or pearls without a needle.

2. Chandelier hanger. If the hook for a chandelier pendant is broken or lost, rehang it with nylon line.

3. Heavy-duty thread. Sew or repair dog leashes, pack straps, nylon mesh lawn furniture or window screens with nylon line. Don't use it on anything that needs ironing – it may melt.

4. Invisible trellis. Attach nylon line to the garage and to various pegs set in the ground.

5. Picture wire. Use it to hang pictures, wind chimes, mobiles and Christmas ornaments.

O

Olive oil

1. Chamois revitaliser. To renew an old piece of chamois, soak it for 15 minutes in a bucket of warm water to which you've added one teaspoon olive oil; be sure to stir the bucket every few minutes.

2. Eye make-up remover. Moisten a cottonwool ball with olive oil, dab onto the eye area, and wipe off. Olive oil will not damage the skin and is safely absorbed.

3. Leather softener. Rub it into dry leather with a soft, clean cloth; wipe off the excess.

4. Paint remover. If you get paint in your hair, dip a piece of cottonwool in olive oil and rub it gently over the unwanted colouring.

5. Body insulator. If you don't want to wear bulky clothes while exercising outdoors, cover your exposed skin with olive oil to stay warm.

6. Dry hair repair. Heat oil until warm, then apply liberally to hair. Cover with a plastic bag, then wrap in a towel; leave on for 45 minutes, then shampoo and rinse thoroughly.

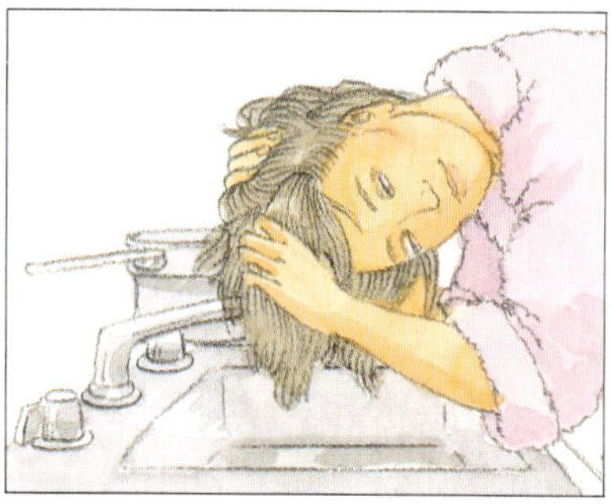

7. Hand softener. To treat hands, immerse them in a bowl of warm olive oil for about 10 minutes, then wipe off the excess thoroughly with paper towels.

8. Table ring remover. Rub a paste of equal parts olive oil and salt gently onto the mark with your finger; wipe it off with a dry cloth after two hours. Rewax if necessary.

9. Overflow inhibitor. Before boiling water, pour in a little olive oil.

Onions

1. Smelling salts. Briefly hold a cut onion under the nose of a person who is feeling faint. The onion may bring tears to his eyes, but will certainly help revive him.

2. Deodoriser. To remove the smell of paint from a cabinet, leave a sliced onion inside for several hours.

3. Dye. Boil red onion skins to make red dye, yellow skins for yellow dye.

4. Eye relief. Something in your eye? Chop up an onion and let your tears wash the foreign body out.

5. Knife renewer. Plunge a rusty knife into an onion two or three times, then wipe it clean with a rag.

6. Windscreen defogger. Rub a cut onion on the inside of your windscreen to prevent it from fogging up.

7. Athlete's foot soother. To relieve the itch, rub onion juice on the affected area.

8. Wart remover. Rub a stubborn wart with a raw onion dipped in salt; repeat until the wart disappears. (See also *Warts and moles*, p.225.)

Oven mitts

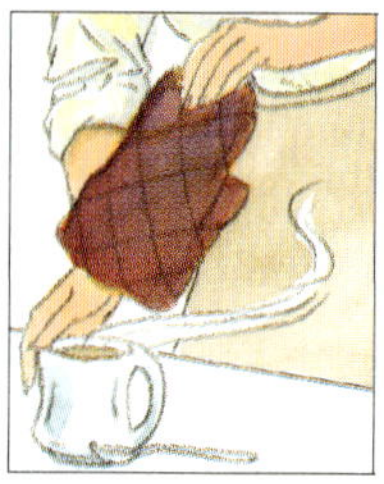

1. Beverage cozy. If you're called away, put your mug of tea, coffee or soup inside an oven mitt to keep it warm until you return.

2. Bulb changer. There's no need to wait to replace a burned-out light bulb – protect your hand from the heat in an oven mitt.

3. Duster. Use one side of the mitt for applying wax, the other for buffing.

4. Egg warmer. Keep boiled eggs warm for half an hour inside a mitt.

Overalls

1. Scarecrow. Save old overalls, rig on a cross-shaped scaffold and stuff with straw to protect crops and seedlings from birds. Also useful for keeping baboons from raiding agricultural crops. If you want to be a sensation with the neighbourhood kids, make the scarecrow for Guy Fawkes, and set it alight in a safe place.

2. Oversleeves. Keep legs and arms of old overalls, stitch on elastic cuffs, then use them to protect overalls when doing really dirty jobs, such as working under a car, or cleaning out the drains.

P

Paddling pools

1. TV lounge. To prevent spills on the carpet, let snacking children sit in an empty paddling pool while watching TV or eating.

2. Storage bin. Put toys, craft items and out-of-season clothing in a plastic paddling pool and slide it under a bed to tidy it away.

3. Cooler. Chill beverages for an outdoor party in a paddling pool half-filled with ice.

Paintbrushes

1. Puppet. Paint the base and handle then draw on a face; add a bow tie for the Mr, a bow for the Ms.

2. Glazer. Brush pie crusts with milk or egg white for a shiny golden finish.

3. Toaster cleaner. Use a fine brush to get into tiny crevices.

4. Duster. Wipe house plant leaves clean with a moistened paintbrush.

5. Baster. Brush a marinade or pan juices over poultry or meat to keep it succulent while roasting or braaiing.

Palm leaves

1. Shade cloth. Hung over a pergola and supported with wire, palm leaves can provide shade while creepers, bougainvillea or vines are growing.
2. Windbreak. Tie palm leaves tightly onto a wire fence. The gaps allow wind through, but will break most of its force and protect a garden.

Pantihose

1. Onion dryer. Push an onion into the foot and tie; continue knotting onions in the leg, then hang to dry. When you need one, simply cut it off.
2. Stuffing. For sturdy, washable filler for pillows, quilts and toys, cut up old pantihose.

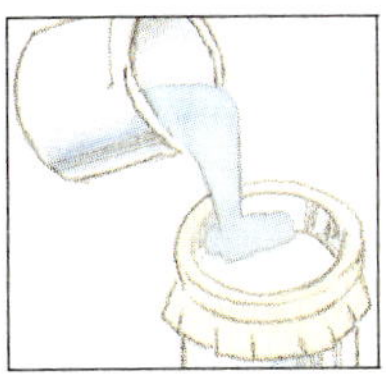

3. Paint saver. To get rid of the lumps, strain old paint through pantihose tied over the top of a receptacle.
4. Rubber band. Cut off the two legs, then slice them into segments about four centimetres wide. Use to hold boxes closed or to tie newspapers together.
5. Fanbelt. Keep a laddered pair of pantihose in the boot of your car, to tie up as a fanbelt and get you to the nearest garage.
6. Scrub pad. Moisten scrunched-up pantihose with warm water and a few drops of dishwashing detergent to clean non-stick cookware.
7. Photo enhancer. To add a misty, soft-focus quality to a photograph, fasten a piece of pantihose over the camera lens with a rubber band. To vary effect, use different tensions.

Paper bags

1. Lantern. Light up your pathway when guests are coming. Fill a bag halfway with sand and insert a candle.
2. Mealie saver. Protect ripening mealies from light frost, birds and mice by placing bags over the ears.
3. Fish cooker. Prevent fish from drying out – bake it partially, then place it in a greased bag and finish cooking in the oven.
4. Mailing paper. Instead of buying craft paper, cut up old paper bags.

Paper clamps

1. Music holder. Keep sheet music in place, songbooks open to the correct page.
2. Workshop hanger. Clamp paintbrushes, gloves or safety goggles and hang on a hook or nail.
3. Hair clip. Use to section off hair for cutting or styling.
4. Exerciser. Squeeze a large one again and again to strengthen your grip and to release tension.
5. Clipboard. A stout paper clamp, attached to the edge of a sturdy offcut of hardboard or plywood, becomes a useful clipboard. When the clamp loses its spring strength, it can easily be replaced.

Paper clips

1. Ornament hanger. Shape a paper clip into an S and carefully hook one looped end through the ball's opening; hang the other loop on the tree.
2. Soap bubble frame. Shape a big paper clip into an S, then, with needlenose pliers, pinch the larger loop to make a closed circle.

3. Money clip. Fold your banknotes in half, then hold them together with a jumbo paper clip.

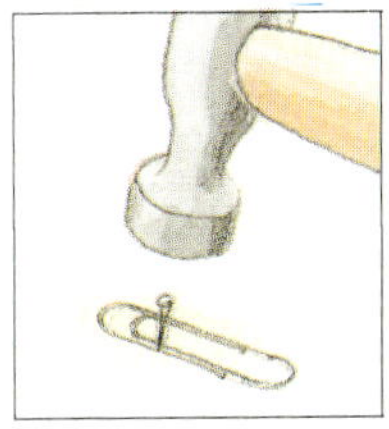

4. Brad holder. Avoid banging your fingers when hammering a small brad. Wedge the brad between the legs of a paper clip.

5. Watch setter. Use the tip of a straightened paper clip to press the tiny time-setting controls on your digital watch.

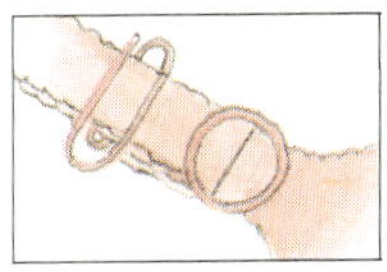

6. Bra strap repair. If the adjustable buckle breaks, you can substitute a paper clip.

7. Garland. Hook 100 or more clips together for glittery Christmas tree decorations.

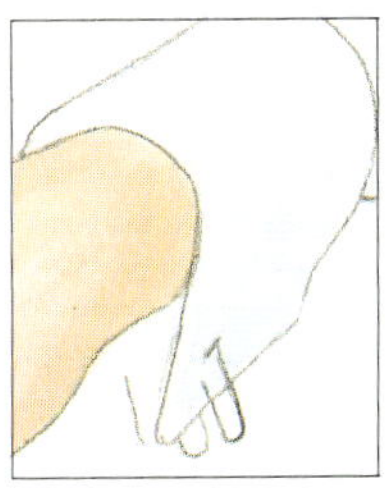

8. Cuff links. Partially straighten a paper clip and insert a looped end into each of the two cuff holes; then reshape the paper clip.
9. Bookmark. Finding your place in a book is easy when the page has been clipped.
10. Tie clip. Fasten both aprons of the tie to the shirt's front placket with a paper clip.
11. Collar stay. If you lose a stay, replace it with a paper clip; it will keep the tip of your shirt collar neatly in place. (Make sure that you remove the paper clip before laundering or it will rust.)

12. Unclogger. Clean the clogged holes of a shower head, a salt cellar, the nozzle of the windscreen washer of your car, or a sticky aerosol nozzle with a clip tip.
13. Chip clip. Keep bags of potato chips and other snacks fresh by closing them with a large paper clip.
14. Coin retriever. Reach coins that have fallen between the windscreen and dashboard with a large paper clip reshaped into a hook.
15. Pipe cleaner. Cover a straightened large paper clip with a strip of facial tissue or paper towel and run it through the length of the pipe stem.

Paper cups

1. Ice mould. Freeze water in cups, then peel the paper off.
2. Funnel. Poke a hole near the edge in the bottom.
3. Pouring cup. Crimp the rim to create a spout.
4. Tomato protector. Fend off cutworms and other pests by removing the bottoms of paper cups and sinking them into the soil around young plants. Better still, plant in the cup.
5. Oil funnel. Remove the bottom of a small paper cup. Crimp the small end if necessary to fit it into your car's oil filler and pour oil into the large end to avoid messing.
6. Wind vane. Remove the bottom and suspend the cup from a string so that it hangs horizontally; the wide end will tend to face into the wind.
7. Flash softener. To soften the effect of an electronic flash for portrait work, put a cup over the flash. Open aperture one stop.

Paper towels

1. Desilker. Peel the leaves from a mealie, then wipe it down from tip to base with a damp paper towel – the silk will come off easily.
2. Wax remover. Place a paper towel over melted wax on the carpet, then iron – the wax will melt into the towel. Repeat until all is removed.
3. Tea strainer. Did the bag break in your cup of tea? Layer two paper towels over another cup and carefully pour the tea through.

4. Potjie rust-stopper. Keep a paper towel soaked in cooking oil in a plastic bag. After each cook-up, smear the towel round the pot.

Paraffin wax

1. Thread strengthener. Pull a threaded needle over a piece of paraffin wax before sewing on a button.
2. Drawer glider. Remove a sticky drawer and rub a cake of paraffin wax up and down the edges and sides, especially where they appear rough from rubbing against the frame.
3. Lubricant. Rub paraffin wax on the shaft of a nail or screw for easier insertion into wood.
4. Window aid. Rub paraffin wax on window sash tracks to prevent sticking. Also rub it on rods so that curtain rings or hooks slide easily.
5. Rainproofer. After writing identifying details on garden markers, dip them in a pan of melted paraffin wax.

Peanut butter

1. Residue remover. Rub away the remains of price tags on pots, pans and other metal or plastic items with a dab of peanut butter.
2. Tar remover. To rid your car or your shoes of messy road tar, rub with peanut butter.
3. Wildlife bait. To lure a wild bird or small mammal into camera range, smear peanut butter on the spot where you want it to perch, making sure you keep the spread slightly out of view of the camera. Focus on that particular spot – your subject can't run off with the peanut butter as it can with nuts or seeds.

Pencils

1. Play logs. Slice off the eraser and tapered ends of a lot of old pencils. Glue them together to build a miniature cabin; cut up a disposable aluminium pan to make a tin roof.
2. Plant stake. To keep a small plant upright, insert a pencil into the soil next to it and tie them together.
3. Page turner. Use the eraser end for turning the pages of phone books.
4. Diviner. Insert a pencil eraser into a house plant's soil; if it comes out dry, get out your watering can.
5. Calculator puncher. The eraser end is ideal for pushing the small buttons of a pocket calculator.
6. Lock lubricant. If a lock becomes sticky, avoid oil. Rub the key thoroughly with a soft-leaded pencil, then insert and turn a few times to get graphite into the works.

Photographs

1. Headboard. Enlarge a simple photograph and mount it on a semicircle of one and a half-centimetre

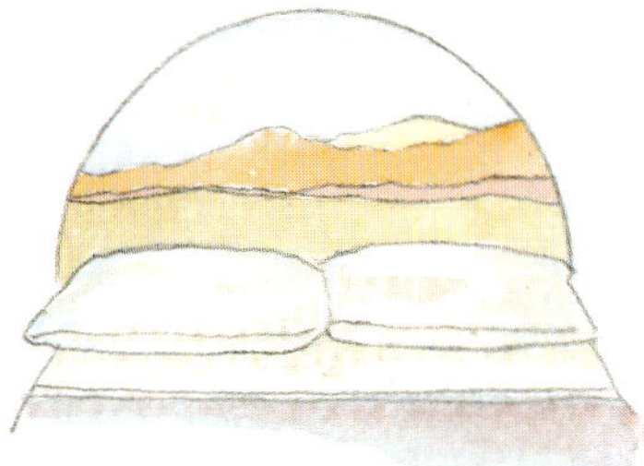

thick plywood the same width as the bed. It will strengthen the bed.

2. Paperweight. Make a cube out of a milk carton and fill it with sand for weight; tape pictures on all sides, then protect them with acrylic spray.

3. Wall hanging. Mount an assortment of various size prints on a clean window blind with contact or rubber glue.

4. Mobile. Glue photographs back to back on cardboard, then darken the edges with a marker. Suspend with nylon wire from three pieces of wire hanger.

Piggy banks

1. Paperweight. Fill with cents and place on top of papers.

2. Doorstop. A coin-filled piggy bank in front of a door will prevent it from blowing shut.

3. String dispenser. Place a small ball of string inside the piggy bank and slip the end through the slot.

Pillowcases

1. Sheets. Use standard-size pillowcases as sheets for baby's carry-cot.

2. Frost protector. Cover short tomato plants with old pillowcases whenever frost threatens.

3. Jersey saver. To help prevent pilling when washing jerseys, put them inside a pillowcase and tie with string before placing in the machine. (This also works well when machine-washing lingerie.)

4. Strainer. When you are making jam, separate the fruit juices from the seeds and pulp by pouring through a pillowcase.

Pipe cleaners

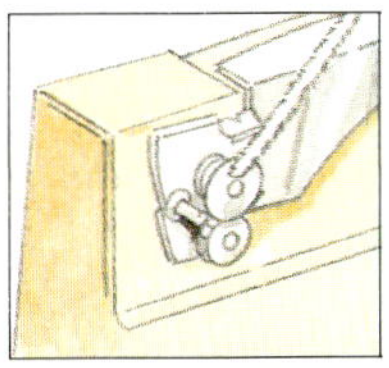

1. Mini scrubber. Remove the dirt from the wheel of a tin opener or clean the bobbin area of your sewing machine.

2. Gift decorator. Shape into a bow or a heart or whatever is appropriate, poke one end through a hole in the name tag, and affix to the package with transparent tape or a dab of glue.

3. Twist tie. Use a pipe cleaner to seal the top of a refuse bag.

4. Unclogger. Open and clean the ports in gas stoves, steam irons and aerosol containers.

5. Serviette ring. Shape them into circles, squares or hearts.

6. Plant tie. Secure small, fragile plants to stakes, or vines to trellises or other supports.

7. Chain cleaner. Use with grease-busting solvent or paraffin to clean thick sludge from between the links of a choked bicycle chain.

Plastic bags

1. Filler. Cut bags into strips and use to stuff outdoor cushions, bathtub toys and other items likely to get wet.

2. Shop apron. Cut the bottom off a large plastic bag with handles and put it over your head, slipping your arms through the handles.

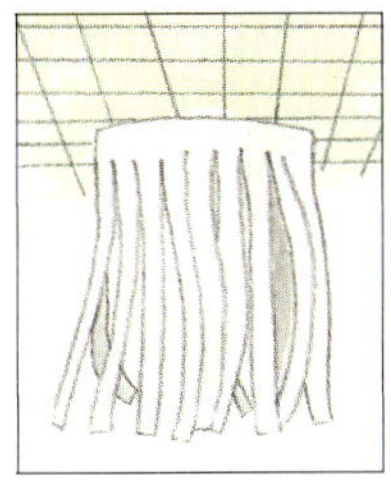

3. Streamers. Here's an easy way to hang party streamers – cut a bag into strips, starting from the open end and stopping short of the bottom.

4. Paintbrush protector. If you find that you're interrupted while painting, prevent the brush from drying out by slipping it into a plastic bag and tying it closed. Sealed like this, it will not dry out.

5. Liner. Tape pieces of plastic bags into the bottoms of picnic baskets, paint trays or boots.

6. Pastry bag. Fill a small plastic bag with icing or whipped cream, snip a corner, and squeeze.

7. Plant ties. Cut into two and a half-centimetre strips to secure plants to a pole or trellis.

8. Refuse collector. Suspend a plastic bag from a kitchen cupboard for temporary refuse collection.

Plasticine

1. Anchor. When repairing broken china or pottery, hold the pieces together on a bed of Plasticine (modelling clay) until the glue sets; when dry, remove the clay.

2. Gift. Enclose a small bottle or jar entirely with plasticine. Dot the exterior with tiny shells or stones. Fill with water, and put a few small flowers in the bottle. This is an easy Mother's Day gift for a child to make.

Plastic jugs

1. Hip bucket. Keep your hands free for harvesting. Cut a large hole from the side opposite the jug's handle and string your belt through it.

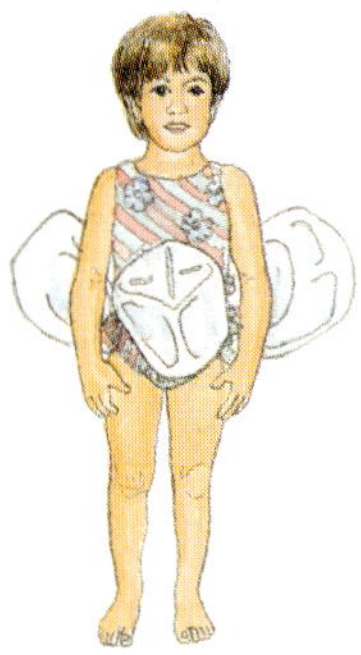

2. Water wings. Knot a sturdy rope through the handles of four empty, tightly capped five-litre jugs and tie them around the child's waist. **Caution:** Do not leave the child unattended.

3. Scoop. Cut diagonally across the bottom of a plastic jug and use it to scoop up dog food, sand or fertilizer.

4. Boat bailer. Cut off the bottom half of a plastic bleach bottle diagonally. Keep the cap on so that the water doesn't just slosh through.

5. Toss-and-catch game. Cut a plastic bleach bottle as shown. Using a tennis ball, toss and catch alone or you can use two containers and play with a friend.

6. Clothes peg holder. Cut off the top of a plastic jug, punch holes in the bottom to let out rainwater, and hang by its handle from the clothesline.

7. Weight. Fill two-litre or five-litre jugs three-quarters full of water and tie to the grommets in a tarpaulin or pool cover to hold it down on windy or stormy days.

8. Funnel. Cut a jug in half; remove the cap and turn upside down to use as an emergency funnel for motor oil, petrol or just about anything.

9. Emergency water carriers. For overland trips in remote areas, use plastic jugs to carry supplies of fresh water. Or keep spare jugs of water in the car to top up the radiator.

10. Buoy. Cap several jugs tightly and string them together to demarcate swimming and boating areas.

Plastic knives

1. Paint remover. Scrape paint splatters off acrylic bathtubs or other non-metallic surfaces that would be marred by a razor blade.

2. Filler knife. A plastic knife is ideal for small filling jobs.

3. Freezer cleaner. Scrape away the frost without damaging your freezer.

4. Biscuit cutter. A plastic knife will not damage Teflon coated pans.

5. Counter cleaner. Scrape up sticky bits of bread or pastry dough from a counter or breadboard.

Plastic lids

1. Drawer organizer. Store small nails, screws and other supplies in the tops of aerosol cans; attach them with contact cement to hardboard cut to fit your workshop drawers.

2. Sink stopper. Place a plastic lid, its rim facing down, over the drain.

3. Scraper. Cut a lid in half and use the straight edge to scrape batter from bowls or leftovers from plates.

4. Lens cap. Keep your eyes open for plastic lids that are just the right size to fit snugly over camera, binocular or telescope lenses.

5. Water tray. Place under plants to protect tabletops.

6. Frisbee. Try tossing a large lid with a flip of the wrist.

7. Hair clip. To keep your hair out of your face while cooking or cleaning, cut a large X in the centre of a plastic lid and poke your hair through it.

8. Hand shield. To keep paint from dripping onto your hand, slit an X in the centre of a lid and slide the paintbrush handle snugly through it.

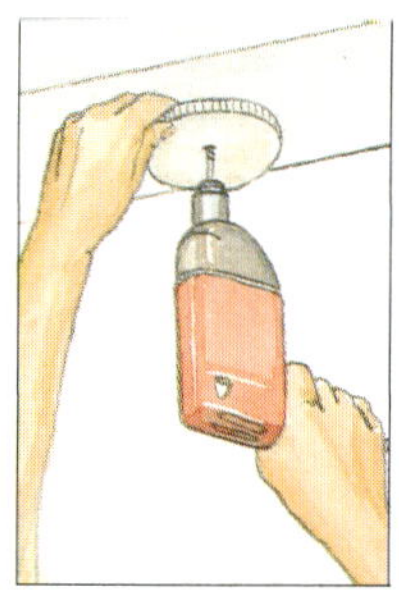

9. Dust buster. When making holes in drywall or plaster ceilings, drill through a plastic lid. Although the lid won't catch all the dust, it will protect your eyes and reduce cleanup.

10. Coaster. Protect tables on hot, humid days by placing plastic lids under icy drinks.

11. Stencil. Cut out numbers, letters or shapes for tracing.

Plastic mesh baskets

1. Orchid planter. Line a plastic mesh basket with sphagnum moss, add a little potting soil, plant an orchid, and hang with nylon line or yarn from a pergola.

2. Plant protector. Invert a basket and secure it firmly over small seedlings and plants to protect them from small animals.

3. Bulb cage. To foil rodents, set a mesh basket in a garden bed at the correct depth, place bulbs inside, and cover with soil.

4. Easter basket. Attach a pipe cleaner for a handle and fill with shredded paper "grass".

5. Bow saver. When posting a gift, protect the bow with an inverted basket from which the handle is cut off, or pack the whole gift in the basket.
6. String dispenser. Place twine inside two baskets, tie them together, and pull the twine through a hole.
7. Breadbasket. Cover the inside with aluminium foil or a serviette and serve bread or rolls in it.
8. Bubble maker. Dip the basket into a soap bubble solution and wave it in the air to make clouds of bubbles.
9. Colander. Drain pasta or wash fruits and vegetables under cold running water in the basket.
10. Frog. Turn a basket upside down in a bowl to hold flower stems in place while arranging.
11. Dishwasher basket. Put baby bottle caps and teats in a mesh basket; using rubber bands, secure another one upside down on top. Place in the upper rack of the dishwasher.
12. Party treats. Weave decorative ribbons through baskets to make party treats or sweet dishes.
13. Portable cage. Tape two together to carry small pets.
14. Mobile. Suspend one upside down over a crib and tie bells, scraps of ribbon or colourful fabric to it.
15. Seed starter. About two to three weeks before outdoor planting time, line baskets with newspaper, fill with potting mix, and sow four or five cucumber, squash or melon seeds in each; thin later to three plants. Plant the baskets outdoors, making sure soil is mounded over the basket.

Plastic tablecloths

1. Game board. Use checked tablecloths to play draughts or chess.
2. Shower curtain. Punch holes 15 centimetres apart and one and a half centimetres from one edge of a hemmed tablecloth. Insert shower curtain rings or loop strings through the holes and loosely tie to the curtain rod. To reinforce the holes, line the edge with PVC tape before punching.
3. Floor cover. Spread a plastic tablecloth beneath the baby's high chair to save on floor cleaning.
4. Leaf collector. Rake leaves onto an old plastic tablecloth, then grab the corners and tip it into a garden refuse bag for disposal or composting.
5. Window blind. Remove the roller and slat from an old blind. Cut a tablecloth exactly to the size of the blind; hem one end of the cloth to hold the slat firmly, and glue or staple the other end to the roller.
6. Drop cloth. Use them to protect rugs and floors when doing touch-up paint jobs or other messy chores.

Plastic trays

1. Plate. Save the plastic foam trays from packages of meat and other foods to use as camp dishes.
2. Plant saucer. Place trays under plants to catch runoff water.
3. Palette. Use them for mixing small amounts of paint.
4. Padding. Slip foam trays between plates or around other breakables when packing.

Plastic wrap

1. Book cover. Protect a dust jacket with a sheet of plastic wrap.
2. Seal. Place a small scrap of wrap between the neck and the screw top before closing your bottle of carbonated cooldrink.
3. Window repair. Tape plastic wrap over a small hole to temporarily block out wind or rain.
4. Paint saver. To prevent a skin from forming, place a layer of plastic wrap over a paint can before tapping its lid back in place.
5. Screw setter. To hold a screw in position, push its threads through a piece of plastic wrap. Then fit the screwdriver into the slot in the head and wrap the plastic back over the blade of the screwdriver.

Plungers

1. Chip catcher. When using a star drill overhead, catch falling chunks of plaster, cement or brick by placing a plunger cup over the shank. Cut a small-enough hole through the rubber to make a tight, slip-proof fit over the drill handle.

2. Dent remover. Try pulling out a shallow dent in a car door, boot or bonnet by pushing a wet plunger over the dent and pulling out sharply. This is most likely to be successful immediately after the dent is made.
3. Outdoor candle holder. Insert the handle into the ground and put a perfumed candle into the cup.

Postboxes

1. Train tunnel. Cut out both ends and run the tracks of an electric train set through it.
2. Garden caddy. Place one in a convenient spot in the garden to hold seeds and often-used tools.
3. Birdhouse. Set one in a tree or on a pole with the door open.
4. Breadbox. Clean and decorate a postbox thoroughly, then use it to hold bread or snacks in the kitchen.

Potatoes

1. Shoe restorer. If your badly scuffed shoes do not take polish, rub them with a raw potato, then polish.
2. Stain remover. Clean your hands with a slice of raw potato.
3. Black paint. Bake potatoes until they're dried out and black. Grind with a mortar and pestle; add linseed oil to make a paint-like consistency.
4. Itch reliever. For cool relief, rub a thin slice of salted raw potato on hives or insect bites.
5. Blackhead remover. Put warm mashed potatoes inside a cheesecloth pouch and apply to a stubborn blackhead several times a day to soften it for easy removal.

6. Compress. Potatoes retain heat or cold well. Boil one to use as a warm compress or refrigerate a cooked one for a cold compress.

Pots & pans

1. Oil catcher. Place an old five-litre (or larger) pot beneath the drain plug when you change your car's oil.

2. Birdbath. Set an old pan on top of a flowerpot in the garden and keep it filled with water.

3. Caddy. Leave those 25-kilogram sacks of fertilizer or grass seed in the garden shed and use a pot to carry what you need to the place in the garden where you are working.

4. Grill. Build your charcoal fire in a large discarded pot and cook on a wire cake rack placed over it. After you're finished, put the pot's cover on to smother the fire and save the charcoal for another braai.

5. Scoop. A pot with a handle works well as a boat bailer, dog food dipper or compost shovel.

Q

Quills

1. Pen. Cut the horny, hollow barrel of a feather into a point and dip into ink. This is ideal for italic printing, and gives a unique effect.

2. Duster. Use a large stiff feather to clean delicate bric-à-brac.

Quilts

1. Rug. Use a sturdy quilt as a floor covering in the baby's room.

2. Lining. Cut a piece to fit the inside of your silverware drawer – it will soundproof and scratchproof the interior, as well as make it look pretty.

3. Place mat. Use an old mat as a pattern, then trim the edges with bias binding to prevent fraying.

4. Dish separators. Cut pieces the size of your good china with pinking shears, and place between the stacked plates for protection.

Quivers

1. Holster. Carry a rolled canvas or an umbrella in one.

2. Camping aid. Transport beverage tins, tent poles or pegs to the camping site in a quiver.

Quoits

1. Furniture bumper. Before you begin to vacuum, put these flat plastic or wooden rings around furniture legs to protect them.

2. Coaster. Cut a piece of cork to fit inside one.

R

Razor blades

1. Stencil. Use the design of the cutout in a double-edged blade to decorate small boxes or plaques. Tape the edges of the blade for safety's sake

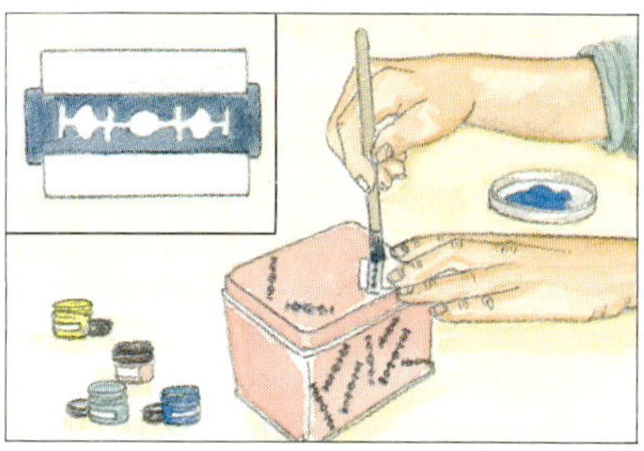

and apply the pattern with a felt-tip marker or a stiff-bristled brush, using a small amount of paint or ink.

2. Scraper. Remove paint, transfers or stickers from windows with a single-edged blade set in a holder or a double-edged blade set in a paper clamp to prevent injury.

Refrigerators

1. Dryer. Suspend an old refrigerator rack from the garage ceiling with a rope and hang laundry on it to dry.

2. Tool chest. Remove the door and store your tools and other workshop equipment inside it.

3. Root cellar. Remove the door from an old refrigerator. In a well-drained and reasonably sheltered part of the back garden, dig a deep hole large enough to hold the refrigerator box horizontally; line the hole with rocks, then lower the appliance gently into the ground. Alternate layers of sand or hay with root vegetables. Cover the opening with a section of plywood. Use concrete blocks to hold the plywood in place.

Rubber bands

1. Table stabiliser. Fasten two or more card tables together to form one long table by placing sturdy rubber bands around adjacent legs.

2. Clamp. When gluing something small, hold the parts together with a rubber band.

3. Gripper. Wrap around doorknobs, jar lids or tools to get a better handle on them.

4. Roll guard. Wrap one or several rubber bands firmly around a torch or screwdriver handle to prevent it from rolling. This will be a great help if you are working on tilted surfaces.

5. Garter. Use them to hold up socks or protect sleeves. But make sure they're loose enough not to cut off your circulation.

Rubber gloves

1. Hand warmer. When doing wet work on cold days, put rubber gloves over your garden gloves to keep your hands dry and warm.

2. Broom stabiliser. Slip a finger from an old glove over the end of a broom so that it won't fall down when propped against a wall.

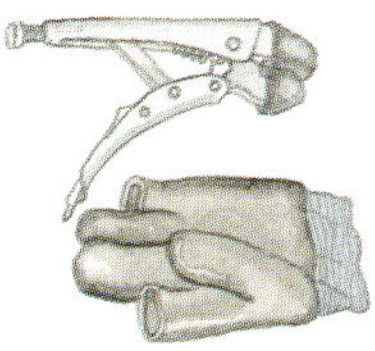

3. Pliers guard. To prevent ugly marks, cover the pliers' jaws with fingers from a ripped glove.

4. Pastry bag. Tie off all but one finger of a clean unlined rubber glove; fill it with icing, snip the tip, and squeeze.

5. Jar grip. Put on dry rubber gloves, hold the container in one hand, and twist the stubborn lid anticlockwise.

6. Ice pack. Fill with ice, then tie the cuff to prevent leakage.

Rubber jar rings

1. Bathtub mat. Lash rings together with strong thread or fishing line.

2. Skid guard. Sew one or more on each corner of a scatter rug.

3. Quoits. For a rainy-day indoor game, let preschoolers compete at tossing rubber jar rings over an upright post (perhaps the leg of an upside-down stool).

4. Table protector. Place under vases and lamps to protect furniture surfaces from scratches.

5. Party game. Warm and stretch a rubber ring to make it supple, then step into it and work it carefully up your body and over your head without breaking it.

Rubbish bin lids

1. Birdbath. Place a lid upside down on a somewhat smaller rubbish bin and fill with water.

2. Toy shield. Make your child a gladiator's costume for a neighbourhood fancy dress party; complete with rubbish-bin-lid shield.

3. Bag holder. Cut out the centre of a plastic lid, leaving a five-centimetre-wide rim. Place a refuse bag in the bin, and press the lid down over it. Fill the bag through the cutout.

4. Cymbals. Let your youngsters use pairs of metal lids as cymbals.

5. Jack rest. When using a car jack on soft ground, rest it on an inverted lid of a rubbish bin.

6. Leak pan. If your car is leaking oil or another fluid, put an upside-down plastic lid under the engine overnight. In the morning you'll see how much you lost – and of what. Water is obvious. Black oil is from the engine, pinkish oil from transmission.

S

Safety pins

1. Stitch counter. When knitting, use them to mark or hold stitches.

2. Chain. Hook them together to replace a broken pull chain until you can get a new one.

3. Missing link. Use a small safety pin to replace a broken clasp or link on a necklace.

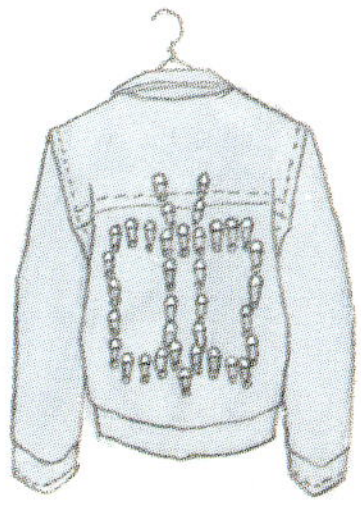

4. Embroidery. Add sparkle to pockets, blue jeans or the backs of jackets by "stitching" designs on them with large safety and nappy pins.

5. Rivet. If a rivet connecting a rib and a stretcher on your umbrella has broken, remove the stub with pliers or wire cutters and substitute a safety pin of the same gauge metal.

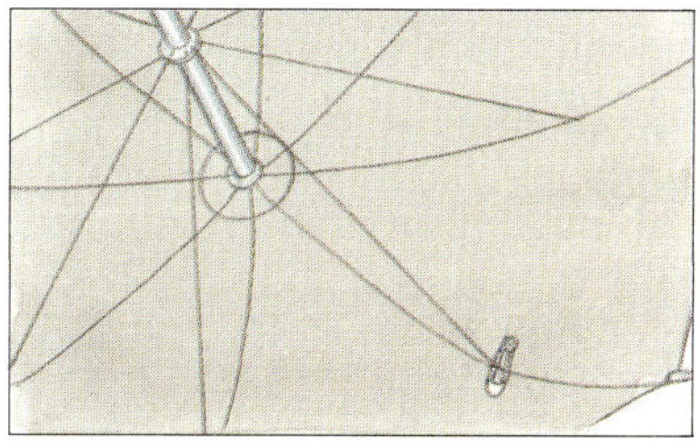

Salt

1. Stain remover. Combined with lemon juice, salt removes fruit stains from your hands.

2. Flower cleaner. Clean artificial flowers by shaking them in a large paper bag with half a cup of salt.

3. Drip-proofer. To prevent wax dripping onto the candlestick or the table, soak candles in salt water. Use two tablespoons salt for each candle and just enough water to cover.

4. Suds controller. If detergent is overflowing the washing machine, sprinkle salt on the excess suds to tame them.

5. Spill container. Cover fresh oven spills with salt, let stand for 15 to 20 minutes and wipe up. (Follow the same procedure when you drop grease or a raw egg on the floor.)

6. Herbicide. Kill weeds by spraying them with salt water.

Scarves

1. Handbag. Place your make-up, purse and other items in the centre of a square scarf and tie the four corners diagonally. (Make a tote bag from a larger scarf.)

2. Bag sling. If your grocery bag starts to give way, take off your scarf and loop it under the bottom of the bag to support it.

3. Belt. Make a solid-coloured dress look quite sensational or an old outfit look like new by twisting a scarf of a contrasting colour around your waist.

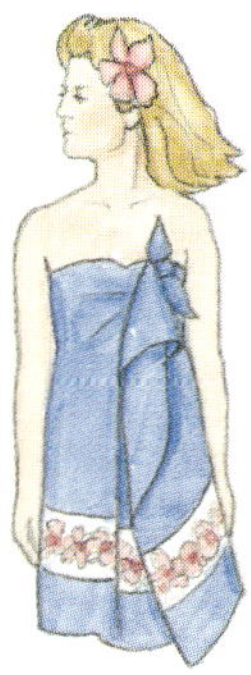

4. Sarong. Wrap a one and a half-metre square scarf under your arms at your waist or low on your hips; pull the fabric taut, then knot the top ends where you want the opening to fall.

5. Necklace. Fold a 60-centimetre-square scarf in thirds on the bias and knot several times.

6. Robe. Wrap a scarf around your shoulders and use it as a cover-up when travelling or on the beach.

Seeds

1. Artwork. On heavy paper, "paint" your design with white glue then drop seeds onto the glue and let dry. Use different types of seeds for colour and texture.

2. Jewellery. String fresh seeds with nylon line and a heavy-duty needle; then let dry.

3. Snack. Coat pumpkin, sunflower, melon or squash seeds with some oil, spread in a shallow pan, season and bake in a gently-heated oven for an hour or until they're dry. Or cook in the microwave for a minute, seasoned, oiled and covered.

Shampoo

1. Shaving cream. In the absence of real shaving cream, apply a small amount of shampoo to your wet skin and work up a lather.

2. Detergent. If you've run out of a gentle soap for hand-washables use shampoo instead.

Shaving cream

1. Lubricant. Spray both sides of the joint of a squeaky hinge with foamy shaving cream.

2. Upholstery cleaner. Rub a fresh stain on upholstered furniture with shaving cream, wipe with a damp cloth, then dry. (Test first in an inconspicuous corner.)

3. Defogger. To prevent your bathroom mirror from fogging up during cold weather, spread a little shaving cream on the mirror and wipe it off with a tissue.

Sheet music

1. Lampshade. Attach sheet music to an old lampshade, then brush with linseed oil and let dry thoroughly before turning on the light. (Be sure to use a low-wattage bulb.)

2. Wrapping paper. Wrap up a music lover's birthday gift with sheet music.

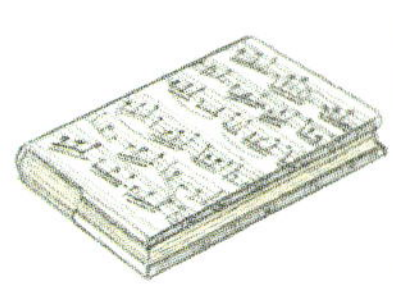

3. Book cover. If you've lost the jacket to a book, cover it with some sheet music.

4. Wallpaper. Paper a small room with sheet music, using mildew-resistant wallpaper paste.

Sheets

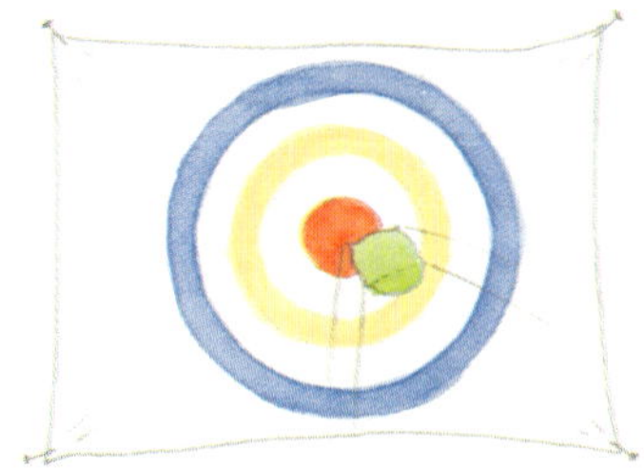

1. Bull's-eye. Hang an old sheet on the wall and draw a target on it; let youngsters try to score bull's-eyes with beanbags.

2. Tablecloth. Convert a patterned sheet into an attractive table covering.

3. Playsheets. Old sheets are wonderful for children's games. In one game, they are the robes of a king and queen; in another, stretched between patio furniture, a house; again, the sail of a galleon.

4. Leaf scoop. Rake leaves onto an old sheet, gather the corners together, and haul to the compost pile.

5. Drop cloth. Place old sheets over the furniture before painting a room, or under the table when having a children's party.

6. Banner. Advertise your jumble sale or wish a neighbour "Happy Birthday" by painting the message on an old white sheet.

7. Christmas wrap-up. After removing holiday decorations, wrap an old sheet around the Christmas tree so that you can carry or pull it out of the house without leaving a trail of pine needles.

Shoe bags

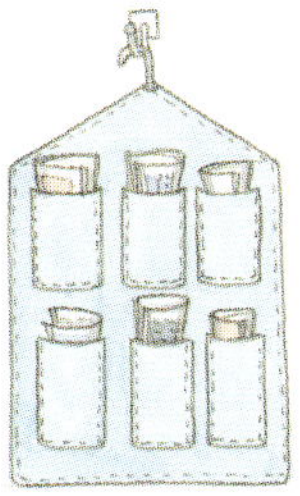

1. Magazine rack. Hang one from a hook on the bathroom door to hold magazines, paperbacks and other types of reading material.
2. Toy bag. Hang a shoe bag over the car window or attach it to the back of the front seat to provide storage space for travelling toys and games as well as books and snacks.
3. Kitchen caddy. Fasten a shoe bag to the back of the kitchen door to keep cleaning supplies all in one place for convenience.

Shoe boxes

1. Play bricks. Children can use them to build play houses and forts.
2. Birthing box. To reduce the risk of the mother rolling onto a newborn and smothering it, place puppies or kittens in a towel-lined shoe box while the others are being born.

3. Safe. Store keepsakes, cancelled cheques and other valuable items in one or more labelled shoe boxes.
4. Seed starter. Punch holes in the bottom of a box, cover with five centimetres of vermiculite, then plant.
5. Gift box. They're the perfect size for loaves of home-made bread, but you can also pack biscuits, biltong or other snacks in them.

Shoe polish

1. Wood stain. Mix two or more colours together to get just the right shade and apply with a dry cloth.
2. Paint. Touch up scratches and picture hook holes on wood-panelled or darkly-wallpapered walls.

Shower caps

1. Plant saucer. If a hanging plant doesn't have a suitable saucer, put a shower cap over the container's bottom while you water it.
2. Ice bag. Fill one with ice cubes and apply to an injury.
3. Hair helper. Wear one when you paint the ceiling.
4. Bowl cover. Use a clean one to cover leftovers in the refrigerator.

Shower curtain hangers

1. Cupboard organizers. Slip several of them over the end of your cupboard rod to hang handbags, umbrellas and belts.
2. Key ring. Keep rarely used keys in one place.

Shower curtains

1. Apron. Cut an old shower curtain into a cobbler's apron with pinking shears and attach ties at the top and the middle; wear it when doing extra-messy jobs around the house.
2. Ground cover. Position an old shower curtain under a tent or sleeping bag.
3. Poncho. Fold in half, snip an opening for your head, then trim the length as necessary.
4. Mulch. When landscaping with gravel or bark chips, place old shower curtains beneath the material to prevent weeds from growing through.
5. Raincoat. Toss them over the braai and outdoor furniture during sudden summer storms.
6. Babyproofer. Cut a generous square to protect the floor beneath the high chair; use leftover scraps to make bibs.
7. Tablecloth. Use one to cover the picnic table.
8. Tarpaulin. Throw a shower curtain over your wood pile to protect it from rain and dew.
9. Defroster. On wintry nights cover your windscreen with a plastic liner with magnetic hem.
10. Drop cloth. Since paint can't seep through, plastic shower curtains are better than sheets for covering floors and furniture.

Skateboards

1. Laundry cart. Keep a basket on top of a skateboard; fill with dirty washing; and simply roll the load over to the washing machine.
2. Decorative shelf. Support an old skateboard (or just its deck) with two shelf brackets in a child's room.
3. Paintmobile. Prevent backaches – when you are painting skirting boards and lower walls, sit cross-legged on a skateboard and roll along with your paint. You can also use a skateboard while grouting tiles.

Skirt hangers

1. Mat keeper. Hang place mats from a skirt (or slacks) hanger on the inside of a kitchen cabinet door.
2. Dryer. Use them to dry your children's artwork.

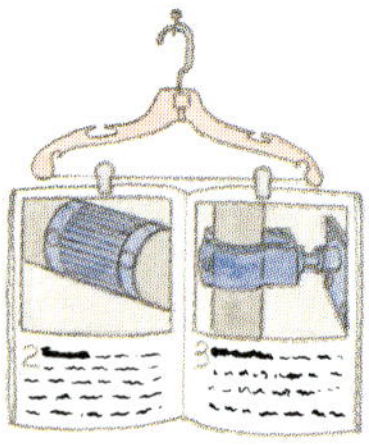

3. Place keeper. When you are working from printed plans, hold the page in place with a skirt hanger; hang it from a nail or wire.

Soap

1. Pomander. Place soap scraps in drawers or luggage to keep their contents smelling fresh.

2. Bee deterrent. If you are working near a hive, or where bees are busy, shower with a bar of green carbolic soap. Bees go for sweat-smell, but the smell of carbolic calms them.

3. Candle extender. To make your candles smokeless and long-lasting, soak them in thick soapsuds, being careful not to wet the wick; let them dry before lighting.

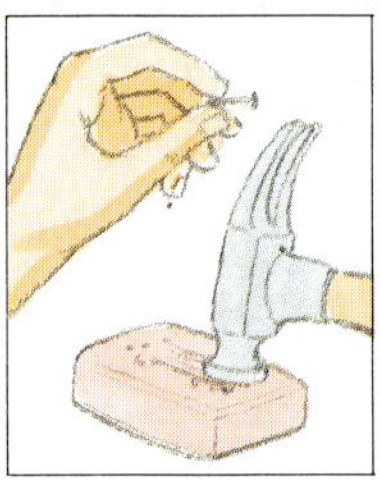

4. Magnetic hammer. When driving carpet tacks, rub the face of your hammer over a bar of soap, and your tacks will cling to it.

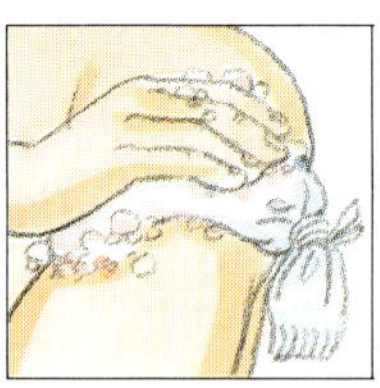

5. Soap mitt. Collect soap remnants in a cotton sock; tie with elastic or string and use when bathing.

6. Pincushion. Stick various pins and needles into a wrapped bar of soap to keep them all in one place with their points lubricated.

7. Tailor's chalk. Store a few dry slivers of soap in your sewing box and use them to mark darts and hems on washable material.

8. Bubble bath. Shave or grate to make flakes; store in a container by the bath.

9. Screw smoother. Scrape screws across a bar of soap before driving them into hardwoods.

Socks

1. Pet bandage. If your dog or cat has a wound on its leg, pull a clean old sock over the dressing to help hold it in place.

2. Scratch preventer. Before moving a piece of heavy furniture, slip socks onto the legs. Do the same on ladder tops so that you won't scratch the paint or siding.

3. Cozy. When interrupted, slip a thick sock over a baby bottle or a mug of coffee, tea or cocoa to help keep the contents warm.

4. Shoe keeper. Pull a pair of socks over your shoes while painting; remove them before leaving the room to avoid spreading paint.

5. Bath fragrance. Put potpourri into a cotton sock and toss it into the bathtub while the water is running; remove the mixture before you get in and dry it for reuse.

6. Buffer. Use them to apply wax and to polish shoes or cars.

7. Arm bib. Cut the feet off old socks and use the leg portions as sleeve protectors for messy little eaters.

Soda water

1. Soft drink. Add to fruit juice for a healthy and inexpensive beverage.

2. Rust remover. Pour over rusty nuts and bolts to loosen them.

3. Cleanser. Clean and shine porcelain fixtures by pouring soda water over them; no soap or rinsing is necessary, and it won't mar the finish.

4. Tummy tamer. Cold soda water with a dash of bitters works wonders on an upset stomach due to indigestion or a hangover.

Spectacle cases

1. Fishing companion. Keep hooks and lures in a safe, convenient place – slit open an old spectacle case and fasten them to the liner.

2. Pocket protector. Prevent pens and pencils from damaging your clothing by keeping them in an empty spectacle case in your pocket.

Spinnaker tape

1. Transfers. Let kids cut and stick their own designs onto tracksuits.

2. Camping aid. Patch tears in a tent or sleeping bag with tape.

3. Patch. Use the tape to repair work clothes or children's play clothes.

4. Identification. Cut out player numbers and letters for the name of the team and press them onto soccer or rugby shirts.

5. Decoration. Make hatbands from tape or adorn T-shirts with cut-out and pressed-on flowers.

Sponges

1. Sound soother. Insert dry sponges between large appliances and walls to reduce vibrations and eliminate rattling sounds.

2. Soaper. Make a sudsy scrubber for bathing or kitchen cleaning by slitting a sponge and inserting soap scraps.

3. Pincushion. Push pins and needles into a dry sponge.

4. Paint applicator. Use a sponge to add an unusual texture to walls and other surfaces.

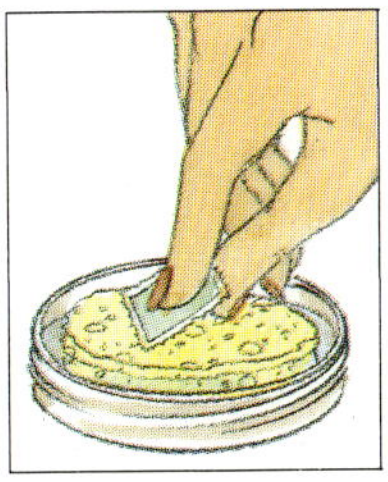

5. Sealer. Before posting a lot of greeting cards, "lick" the envelopes and stamps by whisking them over a damp sponge in a jar lid filled with water.

6. Produce preserver. Put a few water-soaked sponges in the vegetable drawer of your refrigerator to keep fruits and vegetables fresh for longer. Renew with fresh water daily.

7. Tie-down aid. When carrying surfboards or furniture on the roofrack of your car, first position a few sponges on the rack. It not only saves scratches, but helps hold the freight down at speed.

8. Knee pad. Sew pockets onto the knees of old pants and slip in small soft sponges.

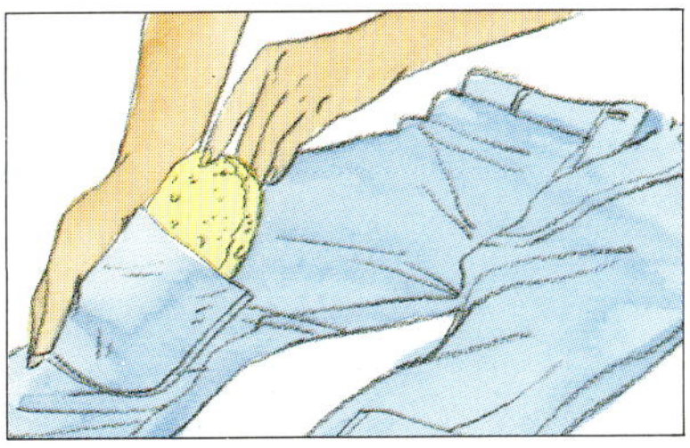

9. Blocks. Cut into wedges and squares and let your kids use them as building blocks.

Spray bottles

1. Athlete cooler. During the hot summer months, bring a trigger spray bottle of water to children's ball games. Spray any overheated athletes during the breaks.

2. Mister. Fill a trigger spray bottle with tepid water and treat house plants to a good misting.

3. Glass cleaner. Mix two tablespoons vinegar with one cup water in a trigger spray bottle.

4. Clothes dampener. Fill a trigger spray bottle with water and keep with your ironing supplies.

Squeeze bottles

1. Water gun. Fill and use for back yard "combat".

2. Fire controller. Use a water-filled squeeze bottle to damp down flames when braaiing outdoors.

3. Ice pack. Fill an empty bottle three-quarters full of water and freeze. Don't fill, it could burst.

4. Spotter. Put liquid laundry detergent in a squeeze bottle to pretreat grimy collars, cuffs and stains.

5. Condiment carrier. Clean small squeeze bottles and use to transport salad dressing, mayonnaise and other condiments that are not available in squeeze bottles.

Steel wool

1. Screw tightener. Wind strands of steel wool around the threads of a screw before you reinsert it into the old hole.

2. Tackie cleaner. A soapy steel wood pad and a little elbow grease will make those dirty tackies presentable again.

3. Clog preventer. When you are washing a dog in the bath or shower, put a ball of steel wool in the drain opening to catch stray hairs and to prevent clogging.

4. Pest control. Plug small cracks and holes in floorboards or in the ceiling with steel wool to help keep out rats and mice.

Straws

1. Stem stretcher. If you want to arrange short-stemmed flowers in a tall (preferably opaque) vase, slip the ends of the stems into drinking straws before placing them in the container.

2. Unclogger. Insert a straw into a tomato sauce bottle to break the surface tension and get the contents flowing properly.

3. Bubble mould. Shape into circles, rectangles, squares and triangles, dip into the bubble solution, and wave through the air.

4. Spout extension. When lubricating hard-to-reach spots, put a plastic straw into the end of the spout of the oil can.

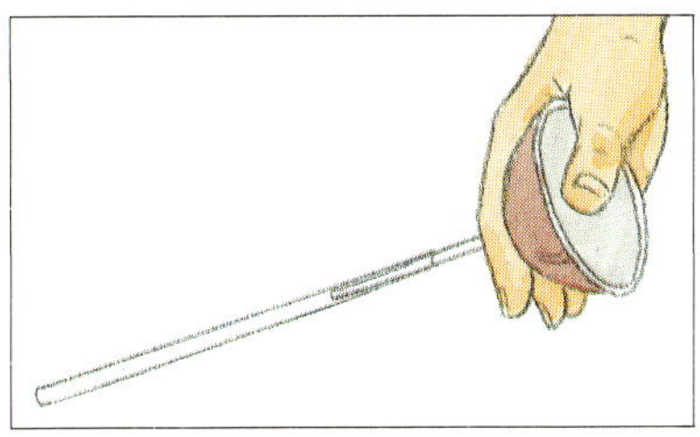

5. Dropper. Insert into liquid, then place your finger over the open end – the liquid will stay put until you decide to let go.

String

1. Slam-no-more. Loop a piece of string around both doorknobs, avoiding the latch, so that the door won't bang shut easily.

2. Schedule anchor. Punch a hole at the top of the weekly TV schedule, loop a string through the hole, then tape the string to the TV set, or hang it over the tuner.

3. Clothesline. When you're travelling, carry a length of string so that you can hang hand-washables over the bath to dry.

4. Leak silencer. Stop the tom-tom effect of a dripping tap by tying a string around the nozzle and dropping the end into the drain – the water will slide down the string and into the drain (silently).

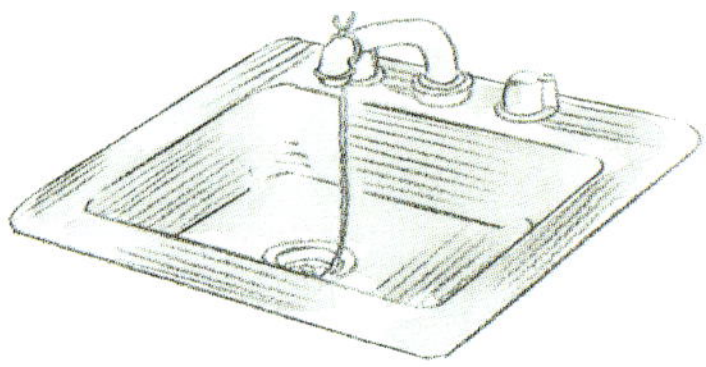

Stuffed animals

1. Draught-resister. In the winter, line them up along the bottoms of windows and doors for decorative insulation from the cold.

2. Scarecrow. Mount in gardens or on rooftops to scare off birds, or use as a deterrent to living animals. You can use durable plastic shopping-bags or onion or citrus net-bags.

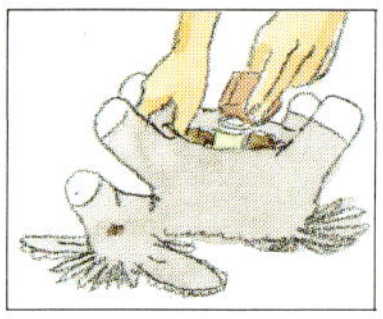

3. Safe. Cut open the underside, remove a small amount of stuffing, and insert your small valuables.

4. Hand puppet. Open the bottom and remove all the stuffing so that your thumb and fingers can reach the head and limbs; ring the opening with elastic.

5. Book end. Ideal for your childrens' bedrooms. Slit the back or underside of a pair of stuffed animals (such as teddy bears); remove some of the stuffing and fill with marbles or lead sinkers. Sew up the slit and glue a piece of an old rubber glove to the bottom to prevent the animals from slipping off.

Sunflower oil

1. Egg preserver. Store leftover egg yolks for up to four days in the refrigerator by placing them in a bowl and covering them with a film of flavourless sunflower oil.

2. Splinter easer. Gently soak the wounded area in sunflower oil for a few minutes before trying to remove the splinter with tweezers.

3. Grease buster. When your hands are covered in black grease, rub them thoroughly in sunflower seed oil. The dirt will float off, saving your hands from harsh scouring. Finish off by washing your hands with ordinary soap and water.

4. Conditioner. Massage lukewarm sunflower oil into dry hair; cover with plastic wrap for 30 minutes, then shampoo your hair and and rinse it out thoroughly.

5. Lubricant. Give your spade a heavy coating of sunflower oil to prevent clay or cement from sticking to it and weighing it down.

6. Skin smoother. Massage a generous quantity of oil into your skin; after 15 minutes remove the excess with a paper towel and have a bath. Be extra careful when you step out of the bathtub, since this luxurious bath is also slippery until towelled off.

7. Cholesterol reducer. Mix equal parts melted butter and polyunsaturated sunflower oil and refrigerate to make a healthier substitute spread.

T

Tape

1. Pedal light. For safer night-time cycling, attach reflective tape to your pedals' edges.

2. Drill depth. Wrap a few turns around an electric drill bit, when the depth is important, or to avoid going right through. As the drilled surface reaches the tape, you know you're deep enough.

3. Label. Cut masking tape to the desired length, stick it on, and write the information with a ballpoint pen.

4. Ant exterminator. Pick up an advancing line of ants with tape.

5. Comb cleaner. Press adhesive or transparent tape along the teeth, then lift it off and dip the comb in an alcohol or ammonia solution.

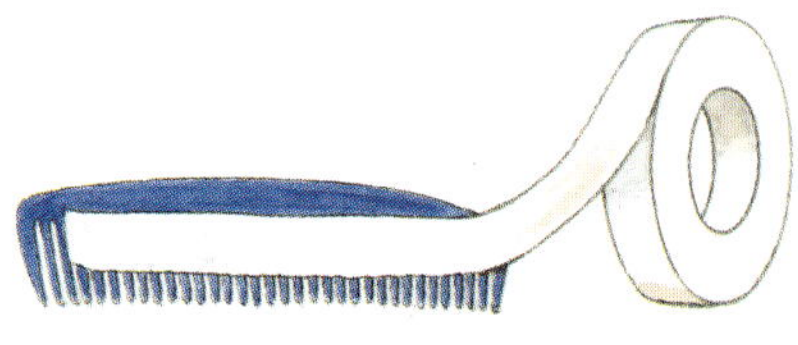

6. Court marker. Tape off your driveway or path for outdoor games.

7. Steady bit. When drilling glass, start through a square of PVC tape. The bit will be held from sliding around the surface.

8. Gripper. Wrap masking or insulation tape firmly around a knife or tool handle until it feels fat enough for a good grip.

9. Key finder. Put reflective tape on the tops of car or house keys so that you can distinguish them in the dark.

10. Sign letters. Make block letters or numbers; use reflective tape if you want the sign seen at night.

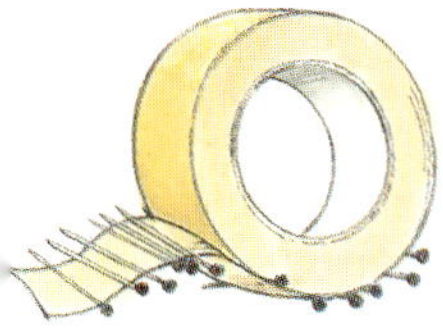

11. Nail caddy. Place nails or tacks between layers of tape so that they'll be instantly ready to use.

12. Hatshrinker. If your hat feels loose after a haircut, wrap adhesive tape around the sweatband.

13. Caster cover. To prevent marks on flooring, wrap caster wheels firmly with adhesive tape.

14. Tube hanger. To store all your sticky tubes of household cement or caulk, cut a strip of adhesive or insulation tape several centimetres long and fold it over the bottom of the tube, leaving a flap at the end. Punch a hole in the flap and hang the tube on a nail or hook.

15. Garage saver. To help you aim the car down the centre of the garage, stick reflective tape on the rear wall. Also put some on anything that seems to be in your way at night.

16. Crayon extender. Wrap masking tape around crayons to prevent them breaking.

17. Hand protector. To remove a broken window without cutting yourself, crisscross it on both sides with adhesive or masking tape, then gently tap the inside edges with a small hammer until the pane breaks free. Peel off the tape to remove any shards.

Tea

1. Facial. Don't throw out that used herbal tea bag. Empty its contents into a pot of boiling water, lean over it with a towel over your head, and enjoy a scented herbal facial sauna.

2. Eye lift. If your eyes are tired or swollen, place moist tea bags over them for at least 15 minutes.

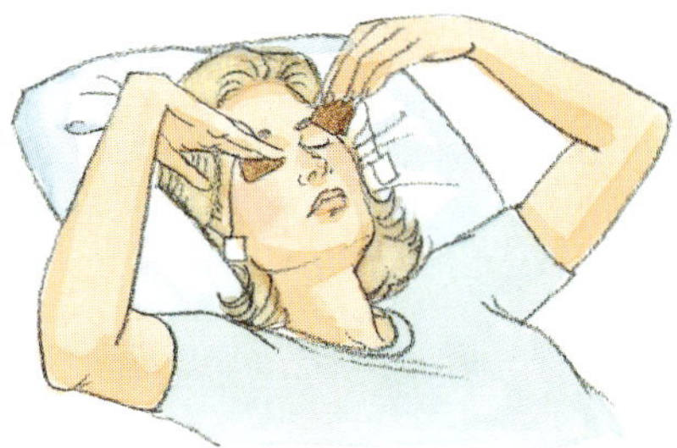

3. Plant invigorator. Help ferns and other house plants to thrive by watering them once a week with a weak solution of tepid tea.

4. Pet soother. If your dog breaks out in hot spots (wet, red skin eruptions), put cold, soothing wet tea bags on them, then see a veterinarian.

5. Poultice. Apply wet tea bags or loose tea leaves directly on a burn; cover with gauze to secure them.

6. Lacquer enhancer. Wash black lacquer pieces with strong tea, then wipe dry with a soft cloth.

7. Dust damper. To keep the dust from rising when you clean the fireplace, sprinkle moist tea leaves over the ashes first.

8. Dental aid. To help stop a gum from bleeding after an extraction, press a cool moist tea bag against it with your finger.

Telephone books

1. Origami. Cut pages into squares and fold into original pieces of art.

2. Confetti. Cut through several pages at once or consider running them through the office shredder.

3. Insulation. Lay them side by side over the floor of your young camper's back garden tent or over the bottom of the kennel.

4. Towel. Use the pages of an old phone book to remove the first layer of grime from your hands.

5. Booster seat. Slipcover an outdated phone book so that your youngster can reach the table.

Tennis balls

1. Garden border. Paint halves, then lay them side by side, keeping them in place with wire hangers cut and bent into small stakes.

2. Garden tool guard. As a safety measure when storing garden tools or other sharp-pointed tools, push old tennis balls onto their tips.

3. Massager. Put several in a tube sock, tie at the end, and use as an effective back massager.

4. Safe. Make a five-centimetre slit along one seam, then place jewellery and spare cash inside; store with other sports equipment to prevent possible detection.

5. Bumper. Attach to a string and hang from the garage ceiling so that the ball hits the windscreen when the car is parked the proper distance from the back wall.

6. Chair feet. Slit tennis balls and put them over the feet of a deck chair so that it doesn't fall through the spaces between the boards of a deck.

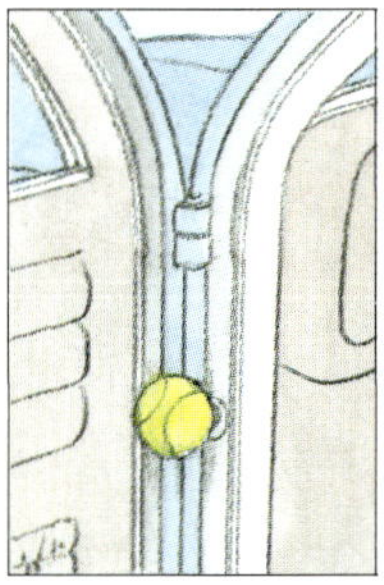

7. Battery saver. When keeping your car door open for an extended period of time, wedge a tennis ball into the door jamb so that it depresses the interior light switch.

8. Drip catcher. Before beginning a paint job, split a tennis ball and make a slit in the top of one of the halves; slip it onto the brush handle, concave side up, to prevent paint from dripping onto your hand.

9. Christmas wreath. Paint balls green; when dry, drill holes through each one and string onto a hanger shaped into a circle. Fill in with greenery and attach a bow.

10. Maraca. Punch a hole in a ball and put in some rice or beans; insert a dowel in the opening for a handle.

11. Doorstop. Cut one in half, then nail or screw it into the wall behind a swinging door.

12. Table mover. Place halves of tennis balls under each foot of a heavy table, and push.

Timers

1. Prompt. Use a timer to remind you to make a telephone call or to call again if you get a busy signal on your first try.

2. Organizer. When working in blocks of time, let a timer cue you to move on to the next task.

3. Memory jogger. Set one to remember to turn off the sprinkler or to turn on the TV for a programme.

4. Mediator. When your youngsters can't resolve whose turn it is to play with a toy, give each one 15 minutes with the plaything. When the buzzer sounds the turn is over.

Tins

1. Outdoor candle holder. Remove the label from an empty tin, punch holes in the sides, place a candle in the bottom, and light.

2. Floor patch. Nail tin lids to a wooden floor to plug knotholes and thwart rodent entry.

3. Plant protector. Remove both ends and push the tin into the earth as a collar to protect young garden plants from cutworms.

4. Pots. Different-size tins will nestle together compactly to provide cheap, disposable pots when you are camping; be sure to handle the tins with pliers or with a removable camper's pot-gripping tool when hot.

5. Amplifier. There's no need to open the door of the baby's room repeatedly to check on him. Just hold the open end of an empty tin against the door. It will amplify any noises from inside.

6. Table lock. For large dinner parties, lock card tables together by setting adjacent pairs of legs into tins.

7. Egg poacher. Remove the top and bottom of a tuna tin; place in a pan of simmering water and crack an egg into it.

8. Bird feeder. Wedge a small tin filled with suet between tree branches or posts.

9. Seeder. Perforate the bottom of a tin, fill it with grass seed, and shake over the lawn.

10. Rain gauge. Set open coffee tins around the garden. Check rainfall reports for your area – to calibrate your own gauges.

11. Reflectors. Remove the bottom of an empty tin; with tin snips, cut down the length of the tin on opposite sides, making two curved reflectors and windscreens for candles.

12. Pedestal. Fill several wide tins with rocks or sand, glue together, then screw a piece of wood into the bottom of the top tin before attaching it to the others. Place a plant, lamp or statue on top.

13. Miniature golf markers. Arrange tins with both ends removed so that the ball must go through them, go up a ramp into them or ricochet off a plank through them.

14. "Basket tennis". Play basketball with a tennis ball. Nail a coffee tin above the garage door, bottom open and top flipped up as a backboard.

15. Bread baking tin. Bake or steam bread in clean coffee tins.

16. Ash spreader. Punch holes in the bottom of a coffee tin. Fill with wood ashes and shake over soil.

17. Pigeonholes. Glue six or more tins together, paint them with bright enamel, and store silverware, office supplies, nails or other odds and ends in them.

Tissue paper

1. Biscuit keeper. Crush tissue paper and put it in the bottom of the biscuit tin to keep baked goods fresh.

2. Glass protector. When storing panes of glass in the workshop, separate them with sheets of tissue paper – the panes will be safer to pick up, and the paper will reduce the possibility of breakage.

3. Candle stabiliser. Prevent wobbling by stuffing several three and a half-centimetre rounds of tissue into the holder around the candle.

4. Sound effects. Taping a happening or a home play? Depending on how you crunch it near the microphone, tissue paper can sound like wind in the trees, a breaking wave or footsteps in a leafy forest.

5. Tracing paper. Tape it tightly over the drawing and work under a good light or on a sheet of glass placed over a light source.

Tongue depressors

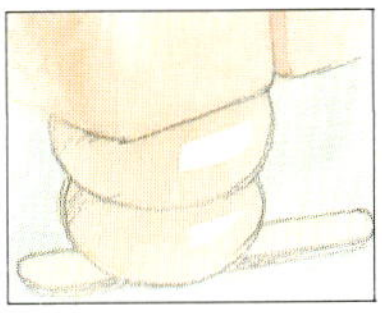

1. Shim. Place one or several under the short leg of a piece of furniture to keep it steady.

2. Sander. Glue sandpaper to one end and use it to file small objects.

3. Stirrer. Use one to mix a small quantity of paint or glue.

4. Splint. Secure one to an injured finger with adhesive tape.

5. Condiment spreader. Put one in each container of mustard, relish and other sauces at picnics and buffets.

Toothbrushes

1. Mini scrubber. Unblock small-appliance vents and get at patchy tile grout and dirty typewriter keys.

2. Crevice cleaner. Use with silver polish to remove tarnish from filigreed pieces or with furniture polish to remove dust in carved wood.

3. Manicure implement. Clean fingernails and toenails with a soft toothbrush and soapy water.

4. Motor cleaner. An old toothbrush dipped in paraffin is great for getting oily deposits out of hard-to-reach nooks and crannies.

Toothpaste

1. Brass cleaner. Cover dirty ornaments with toothpaste. Work into crevices with an old brush, and leave overnight. Rinse off the next day: repeat until the bright metal is exposed.

2. Surface restorer. Cover a stain or scratch on acrylic or plastic with toothpaste, let dry, then rub with a soft cloth.

3. Jewellery cleaner. Work it into jewellery grooves with a toothbrush, then rinse well and polish dry with a soft cloth.

4. Christmas decoration. Write holiday messages or draw festive pictures on your window with toothpaste. Afterwards, use it to clean the window – first with a wet cloth, then a dry one.

Toothpicks

1. Bookmark. Save your place in a book or magazine.

2. Glue applicator. Dip one end into glue or epoxy to apply just a drop for small jobs.

3. Plug. Dip the end of a toothpick into glue, then force it into drawing pin holes, brad marks or other tiny holes in wood; trim flush with a single-edged razor blade, sand the area smooth, and refinish the wood.

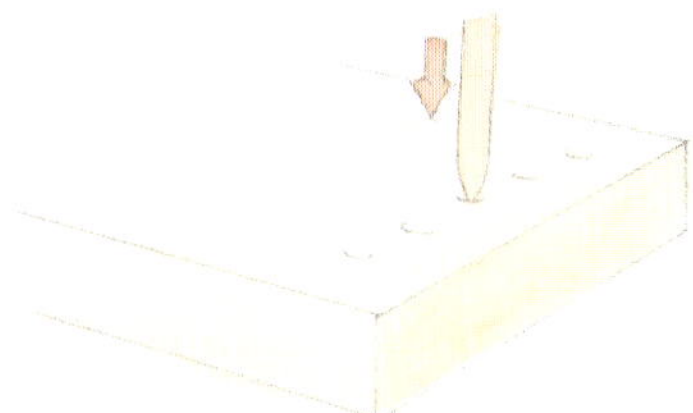

4. Sausage cooker. To make frying easier, thread two or three sausages at a time onto pairs of wooden toothpicks; they'll be easier to turn, and they'll brown more evenly.

Towel rack

1. Leaf storage. Keep extra table leaves behind a towel rack screwed to a cupboard wall or some other out-of-the-way place.

2. Spread hanger. Attach a sturdy towel rack to the back of a solid-wood bedroom or bathroom door to store the bedspread overnight.

3. Garage organizer. Mount one on a garage wall to store rags, refuse bags or drop cloths.

4. Reading rack. Place one on the wall alongside the toilet to hold newspapers and magazines.

Towels

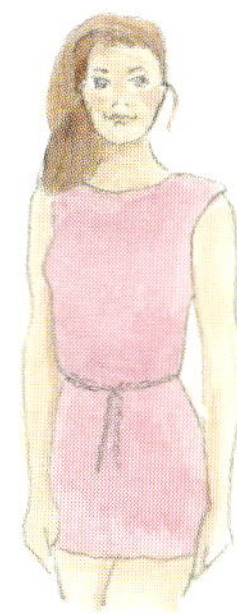

1. Beach dress. Stitch the long sides of two bath towels together, allowing for armholes at one end, then sew up one of the short sides, leaving room for your head.

2. Neck support pillow. Roll up a towel, wrap it with a scarf, and tie the ends with ribbon or yarn.

3. Antilocking device. You can drape a towel over the top of the bathroom door to prevent small children from locking themselves in. It will also prevent children catching their fingers in the door.

4. Sink cushion. During dishwashing, line the bottom of your kitchen sink with towelling to protect delicate crystal and china.

T-shirts

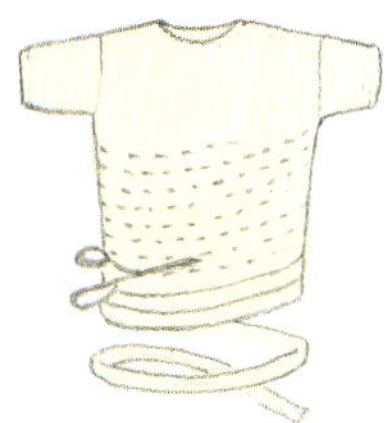

1. Rope. Remove the hem, then cut a two centimetre strip until you get to the sleeves. Use to tie packages.

2. Duster. They're soft and washable, and dust clings to them.

3. Filler. Cut your old T-shirts into strips and use them to stuff pillows and toys.

4. First aid. In an emergency you can use clean shirts as compresses to control heavy bleeding or as padding for various splints.

5. Plant tie. Cut old T-shirts into strips and tie vines and top-heavy plants to garden stakes.

Twist ties

1. Key coder. Using different colours, knot twist ties through the holes in keys so that you can pick out the one you want in a hurry.

2. Shoelace. If your child's shoelace breaks, keep her shoe on by putting twist ties in the eyelets.

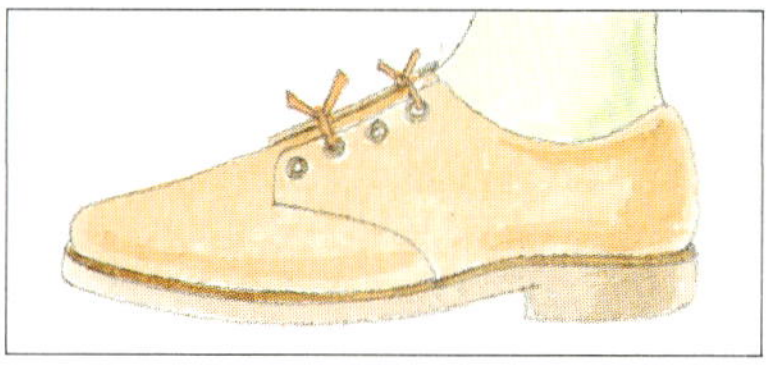

3. Cuff links. Pull the tie through so that the twist is inside the cuff.

4. Plant tie. Secure a drooping plant stem to a stake or hold vines to a trellis. Don't twist the ties too tight or you'll probably injure the stem and restrict its growth.

5. Craft aid. Use them as stitch markers or to hold various knit or crochet projects in place while you sew them together.

6. Binder. Hold sheets of loose-leaf paper together by inserting twist ties in the holes.

7. Car router. To prevent electrical wires from making contact with (and being damaged by) hot engine parts, use twist ties to direct their paths under the bonnet.

8. Ornament hanger. Use them to secure balls and other ornaments to the Christmas tree.

9. Reminder. Tie one around your finger if you're out of string.

Tyres

1. Wading pool. Drape a shower curtain over the centre of a large truck tyre and fill with water.

2. Doormat. Try cutting tyres into short strips with a hacksaw and wire together.

3. Planter. Plant tomatoes, potatoes, eggplants and peppers inside tyres laid on the ground – they'll protect the plants from the wind, and the dark rubber will warm the soil inside the tyre. With potatoes, as the vine grows, put another tyre on the stack, and fill up with soil and compost from the kitchen. Continue until the plant flowers and stops growing. Harvest the potatoes when the plant dies.

4. Greenhouse. Lay one on its side, plant seedlings, and cover with plastic wrap, ventilate and be sure to keep out of the sun.

5. Skid preventer. Glue or nail tyre strips to ramps, docks and stairs.

6. Fish environment. If you have a pond, weigh tyres down with rocks to create a pleasant residential neighbourhood for fish.

7. Rolling cylinder. Bolt several tyres of the same size together and use for practising your balancing act, or make several and hold races.

8. Swing. Drill holes in a tyre (so that rainwater can escape), paint it white (so that it won't get hot in summer), bolt two chains to it, and hang from a suitable tree.

9. Safety stand. For easy splitting, pack firewood logs tightly together, vertically, on the inside of an old tyre.

10. Bumper barrier. Nail tyre sections to the garage wall at the level of your car's bumper.

11. Retaining wall. Fill with soil and embed along a hillside; grow ground cover in between.

U

Umbrellas

1. Drying rack. Remove the fabric from the umbrella frame and hang upside down.

2. Seedling shield. An old open umbrella, with its handle removed, will protect seedlings from an unexpected spring frost.

3. Wall saver. Hold an open umbrella behind your house plants while you spray them.

4. Stake. Use the ribs from a broken umbrella as supports for plants.

5. Picnic cover. Keep flies off your food by removing the handle from an old umbrella and using the open frame to shield the dishes.

6. Trellis. Remove the fabric from an umbrella, insert the handle in the ground, and use to support creepers.

V

Vacuum cleaners

1. Air broom. Reverse the airflow to a vacuum hose and blow leaves and dirt from the garage, driveway or pavements. When dusting workshops or enclosed spaces with an airjet, wear a dust mask and eye protection, as well as a cap to keep your hair clean.

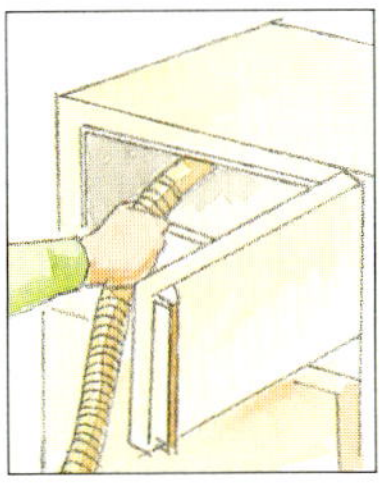

2. Defroster. Reverse the airflow on a vacuum and direct the stream of warm air to help eliminate the frost in your freezer.

Venetian blinds

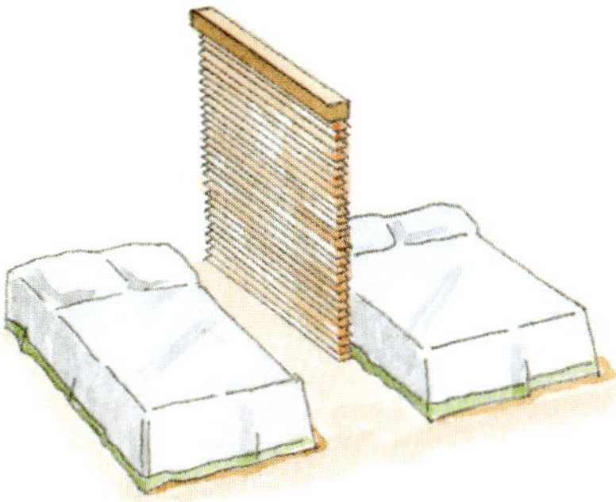

1. Room divider. Hang a row of blinds from a board attached to the ceiling to set off a dining area or den in your living room. Or, if your youngsters share a bedroom, you can use the blinds to partition a private area for each one.

2. Carpet protector. When painting a carpeted room, spread out a drop cloth and slide disassembled slats under the skirting board and over the edges of the cloth – they're just broad enough to catch errant drips.

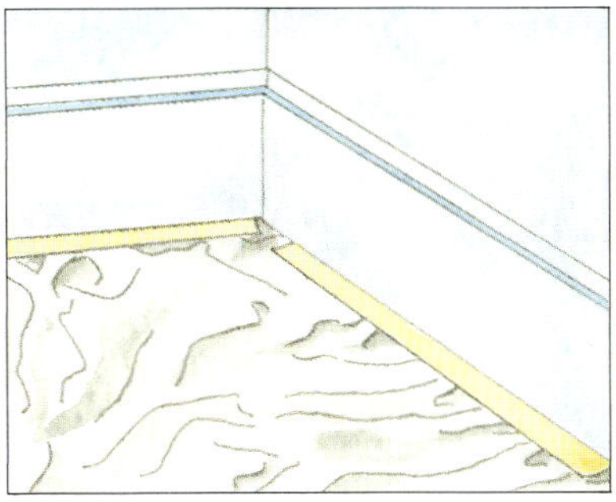

Vinegar

1. Pain reliever. If ice doesn't seem to ease the discomfort of a strain or sprain within 24 hours, apply hot vinegar compresses. If the pain persists, see your doctor.

2. Hand deodorant. Remove the smell of onions or fish on your hands by rinsing them with vinegar.

3. Kettle cleaner. Lime deposits in your tea kettle? Fill it with equal parts vinegar and water; bring to a boil and allow to stand overnight.

4. Transfer detacher. Give transfers an extra-heavy dose of vinegar and let it sink in. Then peel them off.

5. Grime remover. Rub a paste of vinegar and bicarbonate of soda into collar grime. Saturate perspiration stains with vinegar before laundering.

6. Brush softener. Revive old paintbrushes in a distilled white vinegar and water solution, then wash them in heavy-duty detergent.

7. Ironing aid. Remove mineral deposits from an old steam iron by filling it with a solution of equal parts white vinegar and water and letting it steam until dry; rinse the tank with plain water, then refill it and shake the water out through the steam holes.

8. Bath additive. To relieve aching muscles or itching skin, pour one cup cider vinegar into a warm bath.

9. Egg container. To poach an egg without having the white spread out too far, add one tablespoon vinegar to the water.

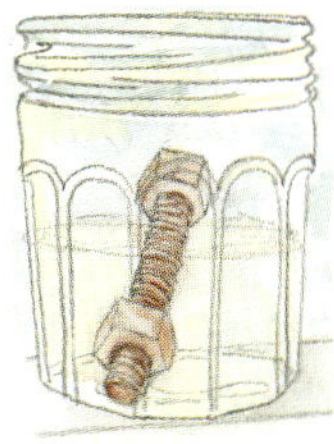

10. Rust remover. Soak a corroded bolt in a small container of vinegar for several days or until the rust begins to dissolve.

11. Laundry rinse. To brighten white clothes and get rid of detergent residue, soak them in five litres warm water with one cup white vinegar; follow with a clear-water rinse.

12. Hair treatment. Make dark hair extra shiny by rinsing it with a mixture of two cups water and one cup vinegar; follow with clear water.

13. Crease setter. Mix equal parts of white vinegar and water and apply to creases before pressing them in place. (Test first to see if the solution stains the fabric.)

14. Window-washer. Clean windows with a solution of two tablespoons vinegar in one litre warm water. Wash from top to bottom on the inside and from side to side on the outside, so that you can tell where there are streaks.

Vodka

1. Astringent. Apply some with cottonwool to close your pores and give your face a fresh, clean feeling.

2. Teething remedy. Rub a little vodka on a teething baby's gums.

3. Pipe cleaner. Soak a pipe cleaner in vodka to clean and freshen the interior of a pipe stem.

W

Wallpaper

1. Jigsaw puzzle. Cover cardboard with a piece of wallpaper and cut it into intricate shapes.

2. Liner. Use wallpaper strips in drawers or on shelves.

3. Place mat. Cut into a rectangle or an oval and spray with acrylic.
4. Screen. Why not customise a folding screen by covering it with wallpaper?
5. Book cover. Protect schoolbooks with leftover wallpaper.
6. Room co-ordinator. Use leftovers from covering the walls for decorating various canisters, planters, wastepaper baskets and shutters.
7. Wrapping paper. For an elegant-looking gift, why not cut wallpaper to fit the package?

Washers

1. Surface protector. When drilling holes into a finished surface, slip a rubber washer over the bit to protect the finish if the bit breaks.
2. Weight. Sew them into the hems of curtains.
3. Jewellery. Knot graduated sizes on nylon line.
4. Pull. Put one on the end of a string to turn a ceiling light on and off.
5. Sinker. Loop one or more metal washers to the end of your fishing line; change the weight according to the current and depth of the water.

Wastepaper baskets

1. Umbrella stand. Line a tall wastepaper basket with a plastic bag and keep it near the front or back door.
2. Sports equipment. Remove the bottom and attach the basket high on the family room wall. Using wadded paper or foam balls, play a game of indoor basketball.
3. Plant holder. Display a big plant in an attractive wastepaper basket.
4. Magazine rack. Keep reading material in one.
5. Vase. Use an attractive wastepaper basket to hold tall dried-flower arrangements.

Wax paper

1. Stamp saver. In humid weather you can keep stamps between sheets of wax paper to prevent them from sticking together.
2. Floor keeper. Clean and shine a floor between waxings by putting wax paper under the mop head.
3. Leaf preserver. Assemble colourful autumn leaves in a pleasing pattern on wax paper, cover with another sheet, then iron to seal; trim the paper around the leaves to any desired shape.
4. Super sealer. Place a piece over the opening of a jar before closing it.
5. Cheese easer. Fold a sheet of wax paper over a blunt knife to cut cheese cleanly and easily.
6. Kitchen buffer. For a nice shine, rub appliance exteriors and other surfaces with wax paper.

Weatherstripping

1. Gripper. Wrap flat weatherstripping around tool handles for a better and more comfortable grip.
2. Cleats. Glue felt weatherstripping to rubber boots to improve traction on slippery surfaces.
3. Scratch guard. Attach to the bottoms of rocking chairs, chair legs or sofa feet to prevent marking the floor.
4. Skid preventer. Attach strips to the bottoms of telephones and other lightweight appliances to keep them from sliding off tables and desktops.
5. Leak fixer. Use slivers of household weatherstripping to shim up dented or sagging motorcar weatherstripping, and prevent wind whistles and water leaks around the car's doors and boot.

Window blinds

1. Play mat. Put one down for kids to play on – it will protect the floor and give them a boundary for their activities. When playtime is over, roll up the blind for easy storage.
2. Canvas. Use an unrolled blind for a watercolour or pastel painting. Roll up to store your artwork neatly.
3. Crafts cloth. Cover the table with one to protect the surface.
4. Projection screen. View your movies or slides on a blind pulled down over a conveniently placed window or hung from a wall.
5. Room divider. Hang blinds from joists above a workshop so that they surround the workbench. Pull down the blinds to keep sawdust from flying all over.
6. Ground cloth. Keep an old window blind in the boot of your car. You can unroll it quickly when doing emergency work under the car to protect your clothes.

YZ

Yoghurt

1. Facial toner. Spread a thick coating of plain yoghurt all over your face; wait at least 15 minutes before removing it with lots of warm water.
2. Cleanser. Take off your make-up with plain yoghurt and facial tissues.

Zips

1. Valuables securer. Sew a zip across the inside pocket of a coat to keep credit cards, passport, traveller's cheques and other valuables safe.
2. Puppet mouth. Make a puppet out of an old sock by sewing on buttons for the eyes and nose and a small zip for the mouth.
3. Convertible jeans. Make cutoffs by carefully removing most of the legs from a pair of blue jeans, then reattach them with zips. Wear the cutoffs when you go hiking or biking on a hot day; zip on the legs in the evening or when it gets chilly.

4. RECYCLING & RENEWING

Instead of contributing to the ever-growing mountain of rubbish, why not recycle? Without much trouble at all, you can make good use of virtually anything – from an empty refrigerator box to an old road map to an extra picture frame. Along with the recycling projects, you'll find other ways to give your belongings new life – through simple renewal techniques for anything from card tables to lampshades, and much more.

All-weather sandals

Use an old tyre to make a pair of high-traction sandals you can wear over your shoes. Keep them in your car in case you have to negotiate a slippery stretch of muddy road on foot. Or hang them on the garage wall to wear when you have to carry your rubbish bins down a wet driveway.

To start, cut two sections from a tyre tread. Then nail them flat to a board or piece of plywood, tread side down, and outline your shoes on them with chalk, adding about 25 millimetres all around. Then draw a 25-millimetre square wing on each side at the back of the heel.

Detach the tyre and cut out the sandal. A table saw will do the job, though slowly. A quicker way is to drill 5-millimetre holes along the outline, then redrill them with a 10-millimetre bit. A table saw or utility knife will now easily finish the job.

Now use the drill and knife to cut a slit in each of the wings at the heel for a heel-and-ankle strap.

An old 20-millimetre-wide leather belt makes a good strap; you can trim a wider belt fairly easily with a craft or utility knife, but you'll have to buy a buckle to fit. Cut the belt 125 millimetres from the buckle end and thread it down through the slit in one of the heel wings – the right-handed wing for the right sandal, the left-handed one for the left sandal.

Cut about 300 millimetres from the other end of the belt (hold it over your ankle first to measure) and thread it through the other wing in the same way. Now cut a third piece long enough to fit around your heel with your shoe on. Use a leather punch to make corresponding holes in all three straps, then join all three with copper rivet sets. For the toe straps, drill two holes near the front of the sandal; then thread a leather thong through each hole and knot it at the side with two half-hitches. Be sure the thongs are long enough to be tied securely over the top of your shoe.

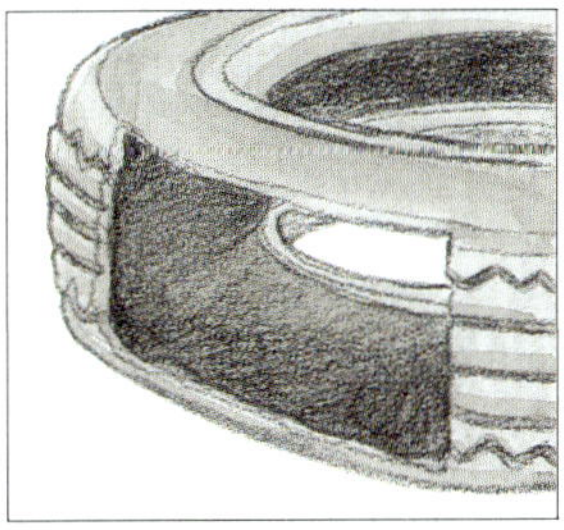

1. Use a heavy utility knife or table saw to cut a flat 300- x 450-mm piece of tyre tread. Scrub the treads clean.

2. Nail it tread side down and chalk an outline of your shoe 25 mm larger all around, adding wings at the heel. Cut it out.

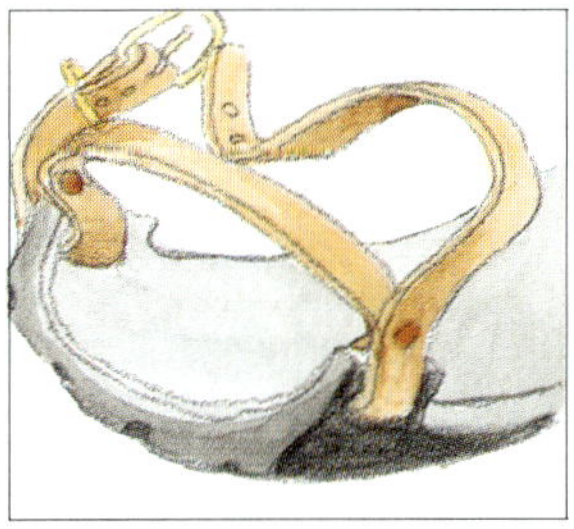

3. Cut slits in the wings and thread belt sections through. To hold them together, punch holes and install rivet sets.

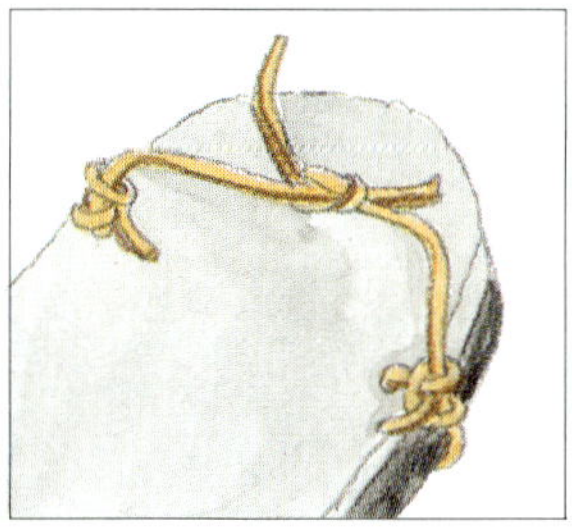

4. Drill holes at the front and thread leather thongs through them; knot with two half-hitches at the sides.

Aquarium/Herb garden

A dusty old fish tank, cleaned and spruced up, becomes a striking indoor herb garden in a few easy steps. Not only does it bring colour and vibrancy to your home, but it becomes a microcosm of life and growth. Rich black earth shows clearly through the glass walls and becomes a feature on its own. Above it, the plants form a forest of green and look more natural than they would in individual pots.

Herbs are a practical choice for this window garden, but the idea works just as well for ornamental purposes. You should consider planting freesias or tulips, flowering cacti, or even tufts of ornamental grass. Or why not sow some annuals for an unexpected show of colour in winter?

To start, fill the tank with water to check for leaks. If you find one, seal it with flexible epoxy glue or tubed silicon marine sealer. (Plan to turn that side of the finished garden to the window so that the repair won't show.) Wash with warm soapy water and rinse several times. Buff away fingerprints with a dry cloth (don't use window cleaner on the inside). If you plan to keep the garden on a wooden table, cover the bottom of the tank with felt.

If the tank still has its gravel, recycle it to use as a drainage base for the soil; just be sure to wash it well to remove slime and chemicals. Or buy new gravel or stones and spread a 25-millimetre layer over the bottom of the tank. Then top with a 25-millimetre layer of charcoal chips.

Fill the tank to within about 125 millimetres of the top with sterilized potting soil. Plant some healthy herbs from your local nursery and place the garden on a table or portable TV trolley next to a sunny window. Keep the soil moist but don't overwater.

Baby blankets/Bath mat

You can turn a few old baby blankets into a super-absorbent bath mat with the aid of an easy-to-make loom. Use five or six flannel or woollen blankets and don't worry about co-ordinating their colours – a rag rug look is what you're after.

First, put together a simple loom of 22- x 69-millimetre clear pine – cut two 825-millimetre lengths and two 575-millimetre ones. Use lap joints at the corners, making sure they're square; glue and secure the pieces with 20-millimetre nails driven from both sides.

On the face of the frame, trace a pencil line along the centre of each board. Then drive 50-millimetre oval wire nails about 10 millimetres deep along the lines, spacing them 25 millimetres apart on the long sides of the frame and 40 millimetres apart on the short sides. Make sure that the nails align with those on the opposite side and that they're secure enough to hold the strips of fabric you'll be weaving.

Now cut the baby blankets into 75-millimetre-wide strips and sew several strips together end to end. Have a sewing machine or needle and thread handy so that you can sew on more strips as you weave. Use your least stretchy blankets for the warp strips (the ones that you'll be attaching first, running lengthways on the loom) because they'll form the base through which the other strips are woven.

Begin by folding the end of your continuous strip in half lengthways (unfinished seams inward) and knotting it to the second nail on a 575-millimetre side of the loom (ignore the corner nails; you won't use them). Now stretch it to the nail on the opposite side, creasing the strip down the centre as you go. Loop it around and back to the next nail on the other side. Continue in this way, keeping the fabric tight and sewing on more strips as you need them, until you've reached the end. Tie off the strip on the last nail (be sure to knot it tightly).

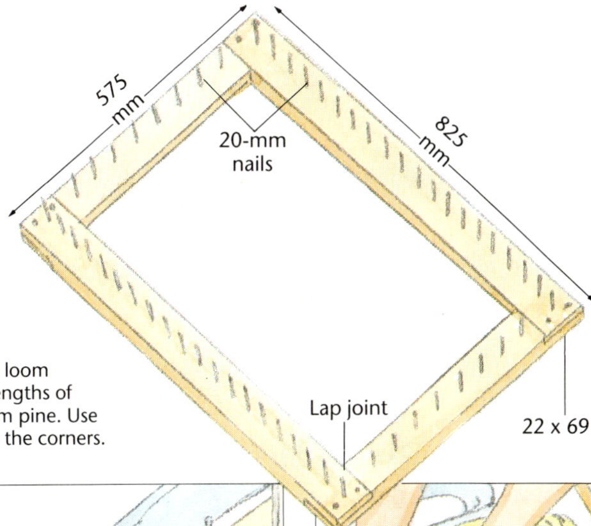

Construct a loom from four lengths of 22- x 69-mm pine. Use lap joints at the corners.

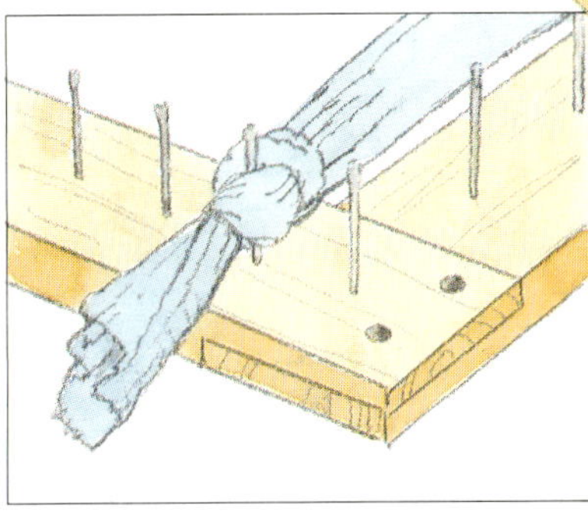

1. Fold blanket strips, sewn end to end, in half lengthways and tie one end to the second nail on the long side of the loom.

2. Loop the strip around the opposite nail, then continue working back and forth until you tie off on the last nail.

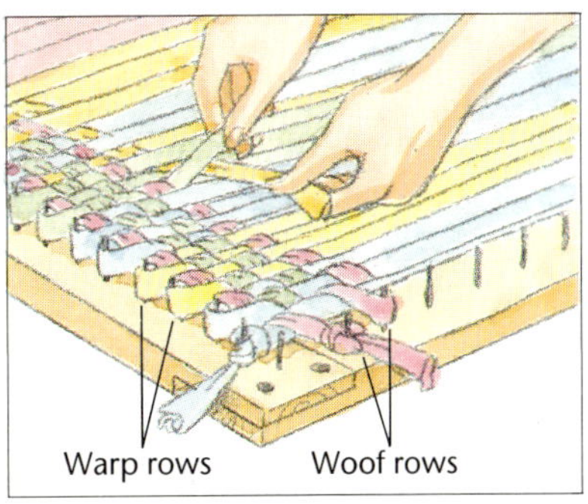

3. Weave the woof rows over and under the warp rows, using strips from stretchy blankets to make the job easier.

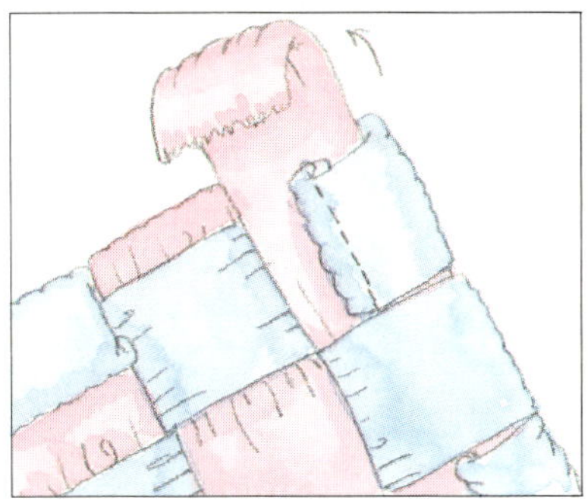

4. Untie the knots at the corner of the rug and trim the excess fabric. Hand-stitch the edges onto the underside of the rug.

Now you can start weaving. Use strips cut from stretchy blankets – they'll be easier to work through the warp. As before, fold the strip in half lengthways; this time, knot it to the second nail on the 825-millimetre side. Weave it through the warp strips to the nail on the opposite side, creasing it as you go. Loop it around and start back, adding more strips as you need them. As you work, push the strips as snugly as possible against one another. If the last few rows are hard to weave, use the end of a spoon to help push and pull them through. Knot the strip to the last nail.

Remove the rug from the loom by gently working it off the nails. Turn the rug over and untie the knots at the corners, trimming the excess fabric and hand-stitching the cut edges onto the underside of the rug.

Balusters/Table base

Replacing the banister on your stairs? Save four of the balusters to make a base for an occasional table. You can use plywood, timber or even the inverted saucer of a flowerpot as a footing; likewise, use whatever you like as a tabletop – a large metal tray, a marble slab, the discarded top of a small desk, or a cut-to-order wooden top that you finish yourself.

Most balusters are 600 millimetres long; occasional tables should stand 425 millimetres to 550 millimetres high. Cut the balusters to size, then paint, strip or stain them as you like.

An easily made footing is a circle of 18-millimetre plywood. Use a jigsaw to cut it about 300 millimetres in diameter. Stain or paint the footing to match the balusters and then finish the edge with a matching adhesive veneer tape.

Cut a 200-millimetre square of six-millimetre plywood to support the tabletop and draw a 110-millimetre square in the centre. Draw another 110-millimetre square in the centre of the footing. Then drill and countersink for 5,5-millimetre (No. 12) screws at each corner of both squares. Use 100-millimetre screws to attach the footing and 50-millimetre screws to attach the support.

For the sake of stability, don't choose a tabletop longer or wider than about 700 millimetres. Centre it on the support and attach it with brass carriage bolts, lag bolts or epoxy glue, depending on the material.

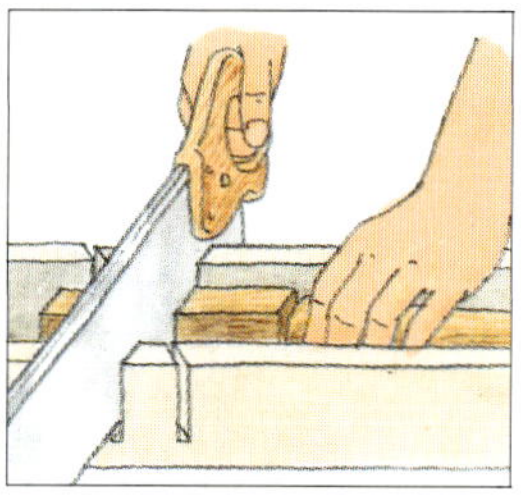

1. Saw the balusters to 375 to 500 mm – about 50 mm shorter than the desired height of your table.

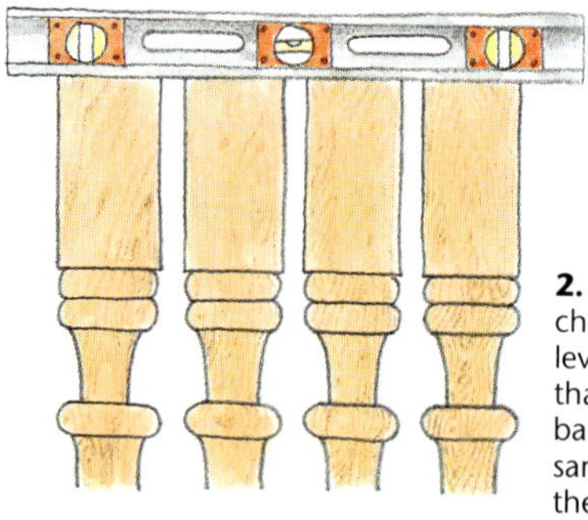

2. After sawing, check with a spirit level to make sure that the four balusters are the same height and the cuts are perfectly even.

3. Cut a 200-mm square from a piece of 6-mm plywood. With the aid of an edge guide, cut a 300-mm circle from 18-mm plywood.

4. Draw a 110-mm square in the centre of both pieces; drill and countersink at each corner for 5,5-mm (No.12) screws.

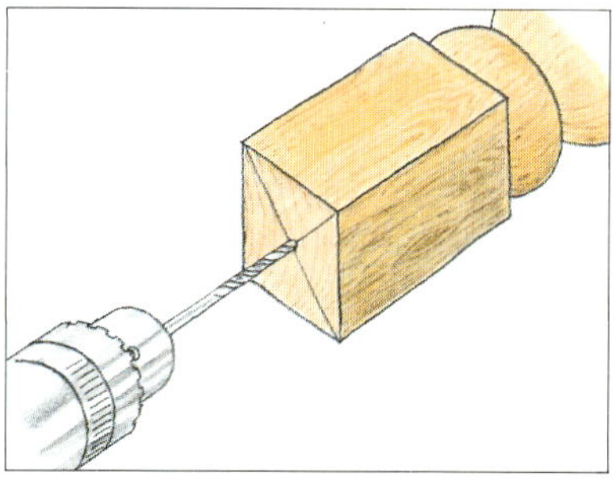

5. Use a straightedge to draw an X on the bottom and top of each baluster and drill a pilot hole exactly in the centre.

6. To assemble, drive 5,5-mm (No.12) flat-head screws through the plywood pieces and into the balusters. Then attach the top.

Bargeboard or skirting board/Wainscoting

Wainscoting, or panelling to the bottom of walls made from weathered bargeboards or fascia boards, gives a room a country feeling. The height can vary: 720 millimetres is traditional. Rounding exposed edges and sanding the top rail and the skirting board before varnishing makes dusting easier. Nail the siding to three stringers. Boards which meet doorframes or window frames may have to be bevelled to flush with them. For a baseboard or skirting board, rip a few of the boards to 75-millimetre widths, with square edges on both sides. For a cap rail, rip the bevelled edges 12 millimetres wider than the thickness of the siding. Nail to the wall with steel nails.

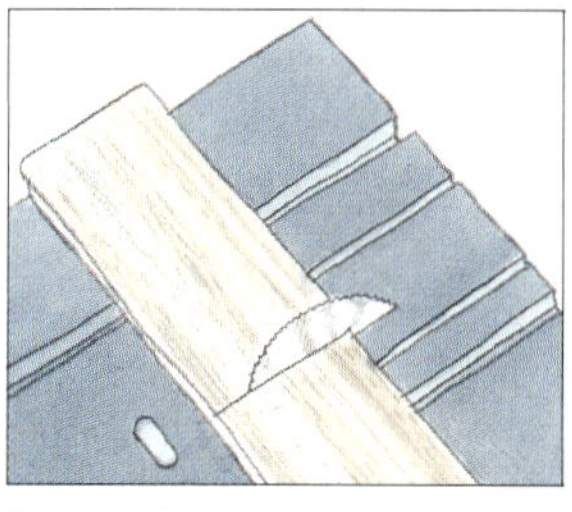

1. Cut off cracked tips of the boards, leaving firm timber not cracked by the elements.

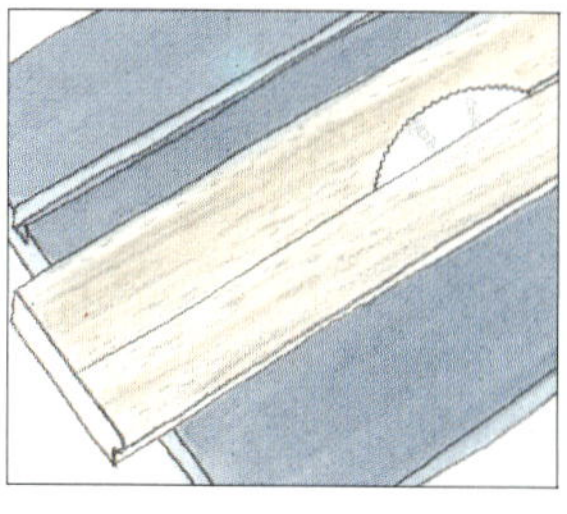

2. Rip planks to a uniform width desired. Rip bevelled edges for a cap rail.

Barrel/Garden irrigator

You can cut down substantially on water bills and save roof runoff for your garden with an old wooden barrel and a few brass plumbing fixtures. (An alternative to a wooden barrel is an asbestos water tank. These are available at some of the larger hardware stores, and are used extensively in rural areas to store drinking water.) In addition to the barrel, you'll need one PVC male elbow, with two locknuts and nylon washers, and a 15-millimetre brass hosebib cock with two nylon washers and a backnut.

Use a 16-millimetre wood bit to drill two holes in the barrel, one 200 millimetres from the top and the other an equal distance from the bottom. Then install the fittings; if the seals aren't watertight, caulk with silicone.

Set the barrel next to a downpipe, elevating it on concrete blocks to increase the water pressure. Cut the downpipe just above barrel level and affix one or two elbows, sold at roofing supply stores, to position the end over the lid. Cut a hole in the lid to admit the downpipe, making sure the seal is tight so that mosquitoes or other insects won't be able to breed in the stored water.

Now run a hose from the hosebib cock to the garden, connecting it firmly to a soaker hose set between rows of plants. Irrigation will be easy – just turn on the tap when you want to water your plants.

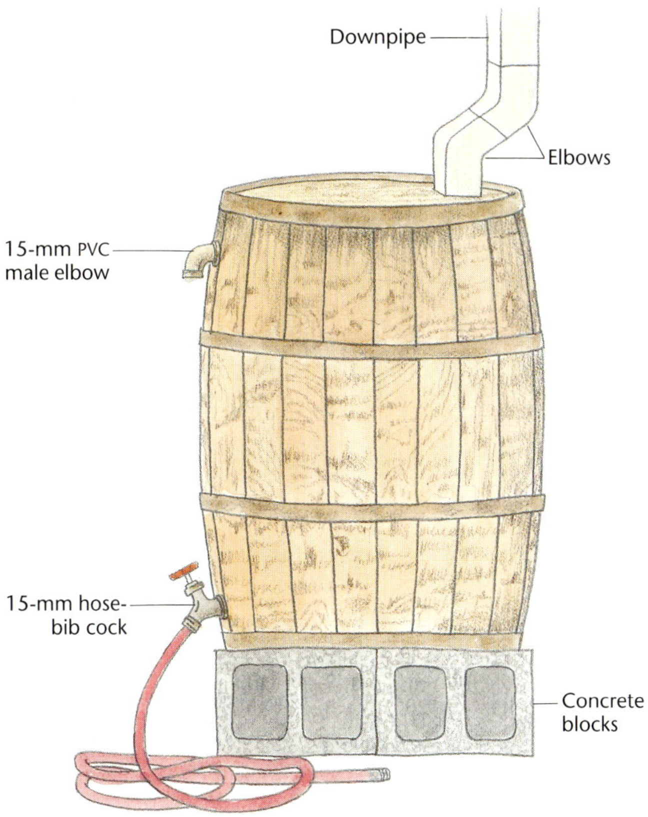

1. Drill 16-mm holes near the top and bottom of the barrel. Install a locknut in each, making sure they're watertight.

2. Screw a 15-mm PVC male elbow into the top hole to serve as an overflow pipe.

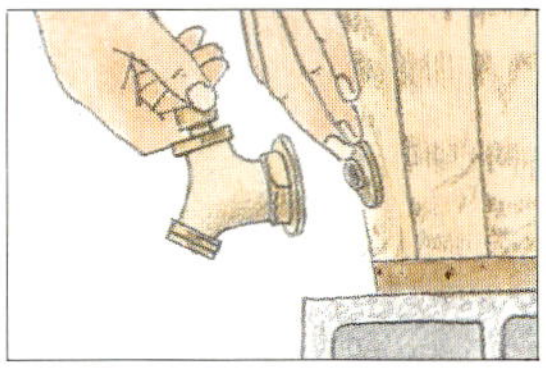

3. Screw a 15-mm hosebib cock onto the bottom hole, adding a nylon washer for a watertight seal.

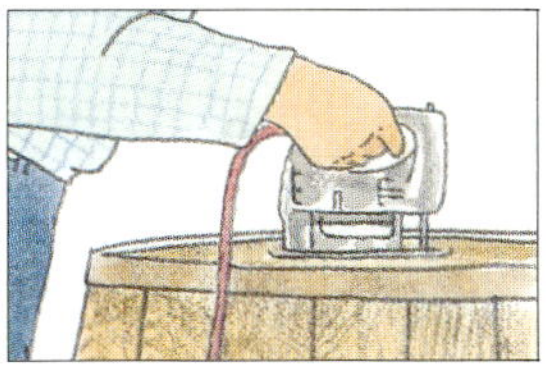

4. With a jigsaw, cut a square in the lid just large enough to admit the end of the downpipe.

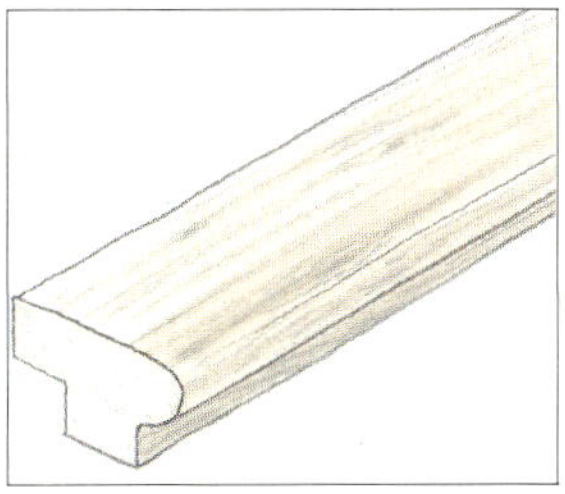

3. Rabbet the square edge of the cap rail sections deep enough to fit over the top of the wainscoting.

4. On plasterboard walls, wainscoting can replace board (as shown); on brick walls, nail stringers directly to the wall.

5. Nail boards to stringers with oval wire nails. Place top and bottom nails to be hidden by skirting board and cap rail.

6. Nail the baseboard sections to the bottom. Install the cap rail on top, nailing at an angle to each wall stud.

Beach towel/Wrap

With a few strips of Velcro, turn a beach towel into a towelling garment to wear over your bathing suit.

Any large towel – from a solid colour to a gaudy design – will do, although thin ones work better than those with heavy pile.

To get the proper fit, wrap the towel around you so that it's snug under the arms and it overlaps in front. With a felt-tip pen, mark three 100-millimetre strips as shown along both top edges. Then cut three pairs of 100-millimetre strips from 25-millimetre Velcro and stitch them onto the marks – and your beach wrap is ready to wear. Add a belt or brightly coloured fabric sash, if you like, to give it the look of a dress.

1. Make three marks on the outside top of the towel and three matching marks on the inside of the flap that will face them.

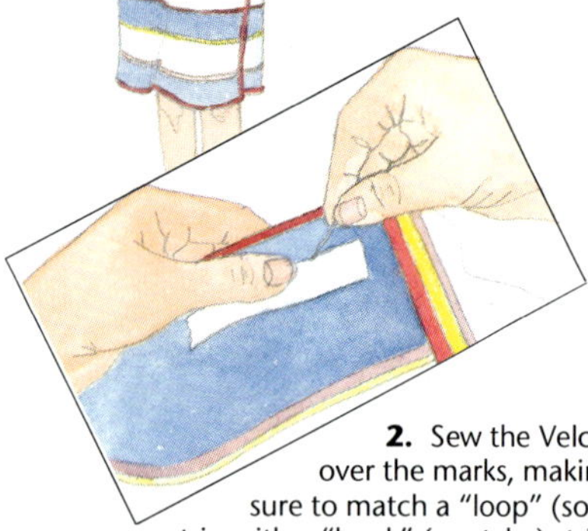

2. Sew the Velcro over the marks, making sure to match a "loop" (soft) strip with a "hook" (scratchy) strip.

3. The three pairs of Velcro strips should now line up and hold the towel securely in place as a wrap.

Bedspread/Wall hanging

Don't toss out that old, worn bedspread. An undamaged section with a complete design can be mounted on plywood as an attractive wall hanging (like the project which is shown here) or backed and stuffed as a large cushion. If the spread is a complete loss, you can store it in the garage to use as a painting drop cloth or a furniture pad for moving.

All you'll need for the wall hanging are some lengths of 12-millimetre plywood, a few drawing pins, a stapler and screw eyes and picture wire for hanging. Use drawing pins to make sure the fabric stays straight as you staple it to the back of the plywood. Staple one side first, then the opposite side, then the other two ends. Do the corners last, pulling them tight and folding neatly in place before stapling them down.

1. Measure off a section of bedspread that contains the complete picture or design that you want to mount and display; add 85 mm to all four sides and cut the section out.

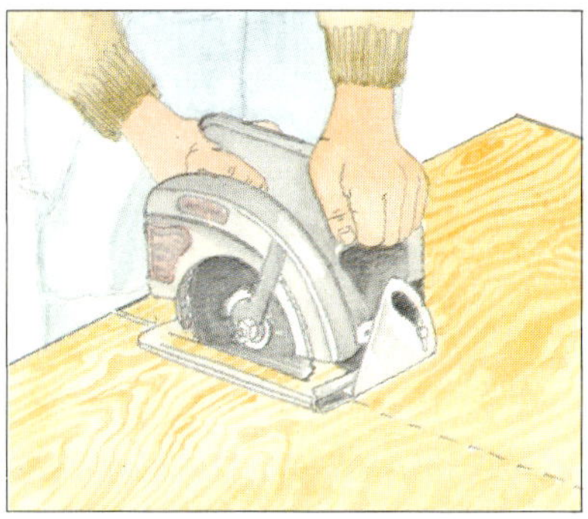

2. Cut a piece of 12-mm plywood 150 mm shorter and narrower than the cut-out fabric. Make sure all corners are square.

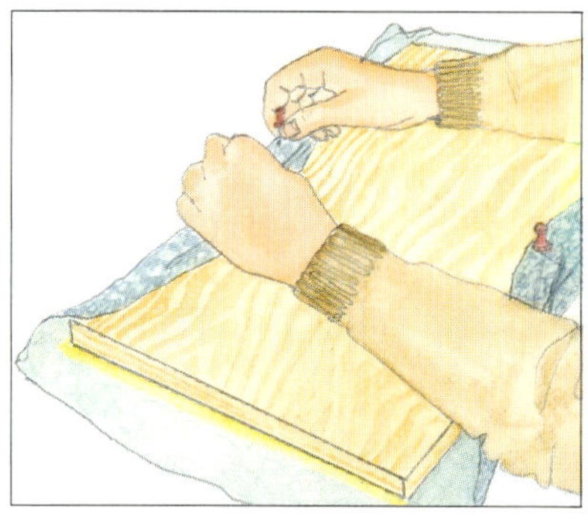

3. Lay the fabric face down, centre the plywood on it, pull it taut over the edges and secure with a drawing pin at each side.

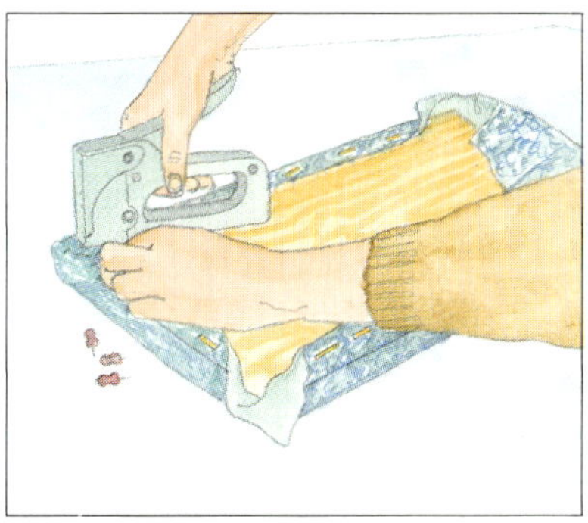

4. Staple fabric to the back of the board, leaving the corners open. Pull the corners tight, fold so that they lie flat, and staple.

5. Attach two screw eyes just below the top edge of the fabric, then thread with picture wire for hanging.

Bicycle/Exercise bike

If you have an old one-speed bicycle or the three-speed kind with the gears inside the rear hub, you can turn it into an exercise bike with this stand.

The base is a 140- x 500-millimetre rectangle of 18-millimetre plywood. The sides are two 375-millimetre equilateral triangles of the same material. You'll need four 75-millimetre corner braces; two 150-millimetre-long plates of steel, eight millimetres thick. A steel merchant will cut, bend, drill and countersink all the metal components, if your hardware shop cannot supply. Also buy 20 eight-millimetre machine screws, 35 millimetres long, with nuts and flat washers.

Make the tension rod from two screen door springs, on a 200-millimetre length of five-millimetre threaded rod and a large wooden spool. You'll also need two five-millimetre-thick eyebolts and a pair of S-hooks to secure the spring.

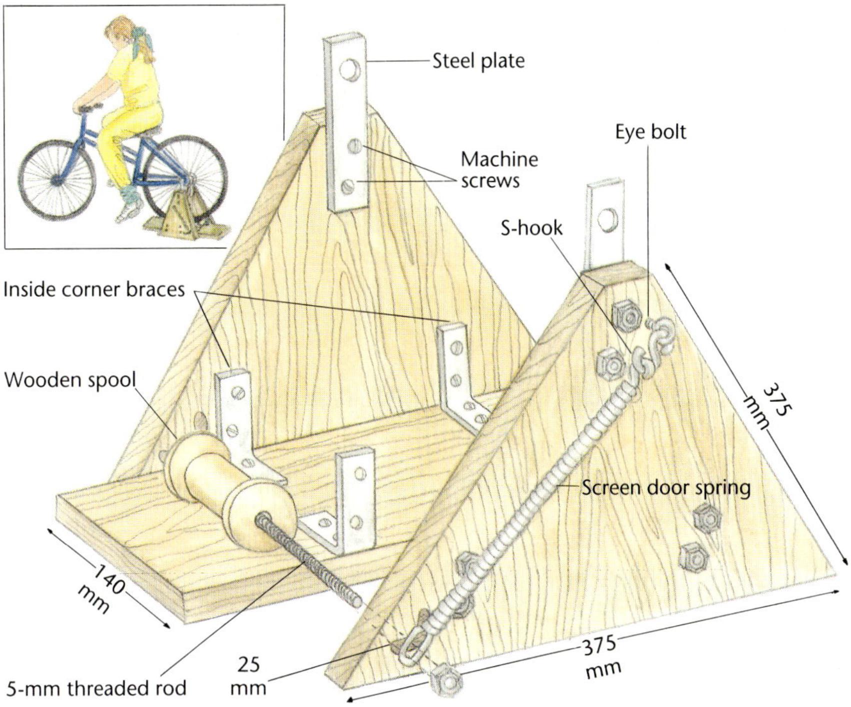

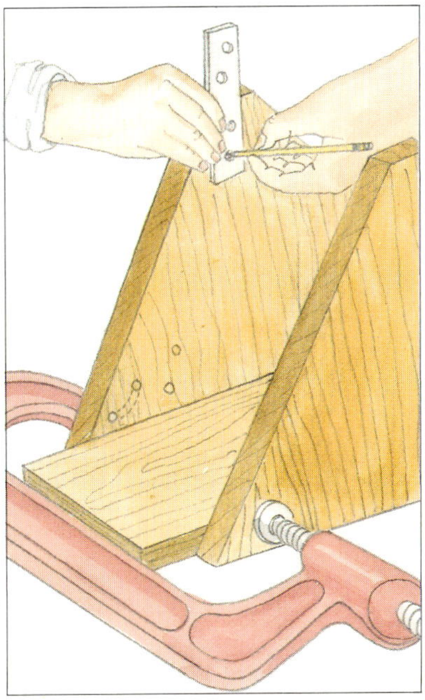

1. Cut the rectangle with the grain running the long way. Saw 25 millimetres off the top of each triangle. Clamp the pieces together with the grain of the triangles running straight up from the base. Position the hardware and mark the holes for drilling; place the steel plates so that the axle holes are 5 millimetres higher than the distance from your bike's axle to the ground.

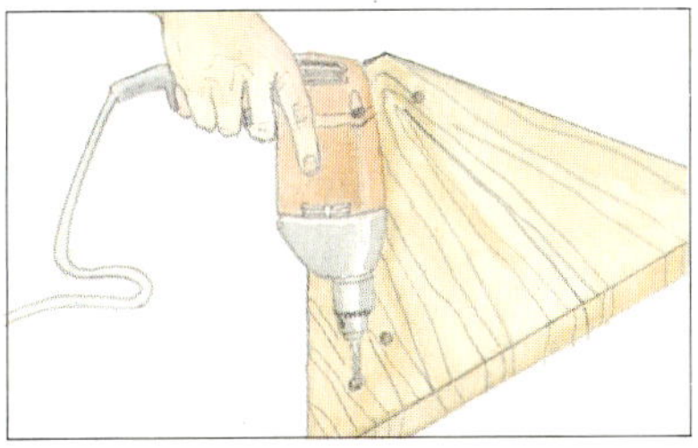

2. Drill and countersink an 8-mm hole near the top of each triangle as shown; at the opposite corner, cut a 25-mm slot for the tension rod (exact position depends on the size of the bike tyre). To cut the slots, drill two 5-mm holes and saw between them with a jigsaw.

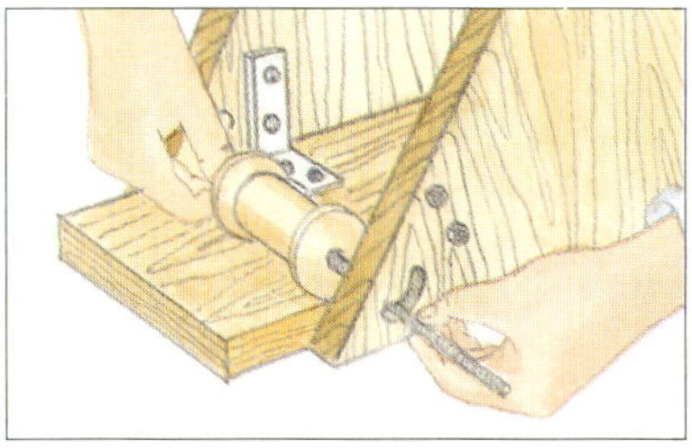

3. Drill 8-mm holes and assemble the stand with machine screws. Put an eye bolt in each 5-mm hole. Run the threaded rod through the 25-mm slots with the spool in the middle (you may need two smaller spools or two nuts to keep it positioned in the centre of the rod).

4. Use S-hooks to attach screen door springs to the eye bolts, then slip the springs over the ends of the threaded rod and secure with washers and nuts. If more tension is needed, shorten the top end of the spring with wire cutters and loop it around the S-hook two or three times.

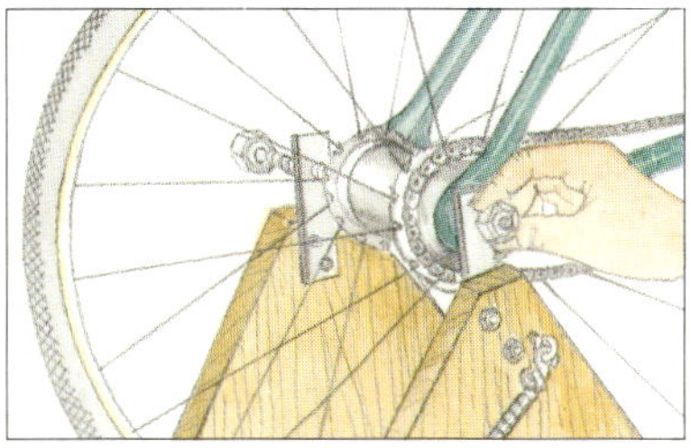

5. To place the bike on the stand, remove the rear wheel axle nuts. Loosen one set of bolts on one of the triangles so that you can fit the axle into the holes in the steel plates; retighten. Replace the axle nuts on the wheel, this time on the outside of the steel plates.

Birdhouse/Clock

Once the canaries have abandoned your birdhouse, bring it indoors and convert it into a unique wall clock. For the best effect, don't paint or stain it – weathered wood is part of the charm.

For the clock mechanism, buy an inexpensive mini-quartz type from a craft store or hobby shop. They run on AA or C batteries and are quite easy to install.

The kind of birdhouse that's designed to be nailed to a tree trunk is easiest to convert. If you have the two-sided hanging type, you can make two clocks from it – just saw it in half and mount each half on a board cut to size. If the birdhouse doesn't have a removable roof, hinge the back or bottom so that you can install the clock mechanism and change the battery.

To mark the hour positions, make a paper template as shown. Trace around the rim of a glass; make a mark at the 12, 3, 6 and 9 positions, then place two equidistant marks between each pair of numbers.

On the clock itself, shiny copper rivets can be glued in place to mark the hours, as shown here. To avoid drilling, use upholstery tacks or paint dots or numbers on the wood. As a finishing touch, why not glue a colourful carved bird to the perch?

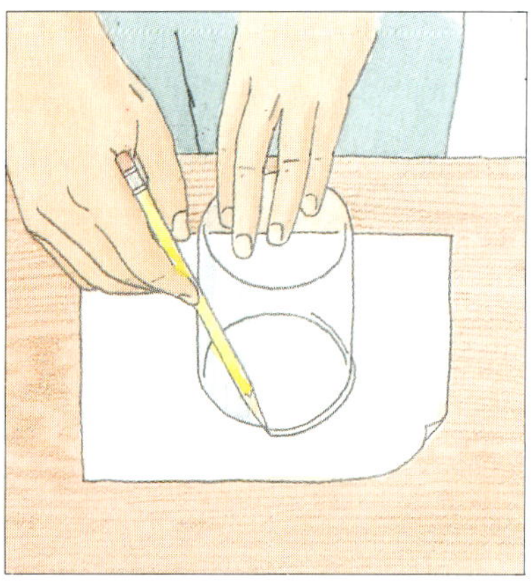

1. Draw a perfect circle on a piece of paper as a template for your clock face. Mark the hour positions.

2. Centre the template on the birdhouse and use a nail set to mark the positions of the centre hole and each hour.

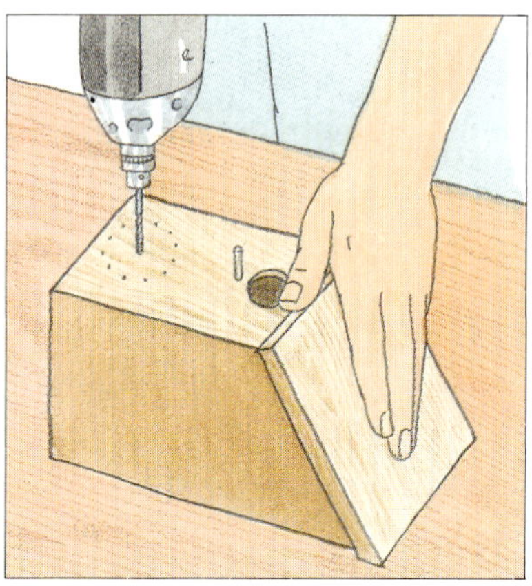

3. Drill the centre hole large enough to accept the clock shaft, the others the size of the rivets being used as hour markers.

4. Mount the clock in the birdhouse, and glue the rivets in place. Insert a battery, and hang the clock on the wall.

Blue jeans/Bag

When the legs of your jeans eventually wear out but the top part still has strong seams, you can transform the pants into a handy denim bag. Just cut off the legs and stitch the holes closed. Then add the kind of handle or straps that will turn the bag into a clothes peg or nail sack, sewing bag, shoulder bag or child's rucksack. (See also *Blue jeans*, p.290.)

1. Turn the jeans inside out and mark them for cutting about 50 mm below the crotch. Cut off the legs on the mark.

2. Sew the leg openings closed with two or three lines of straight stitches. Turn the jeans right side out and press.

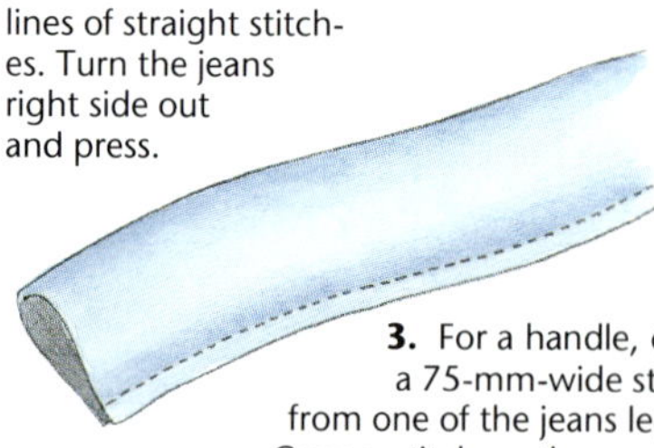

3. For a handle, cut a 75-mm-wide strip from one of the jeans legs. Crease, stitch on the wrong side, and turn inside out.

4. Sew 15 mm of the handle to the inside of the waistband at both sides. Use a cross-stitch for extra strength.

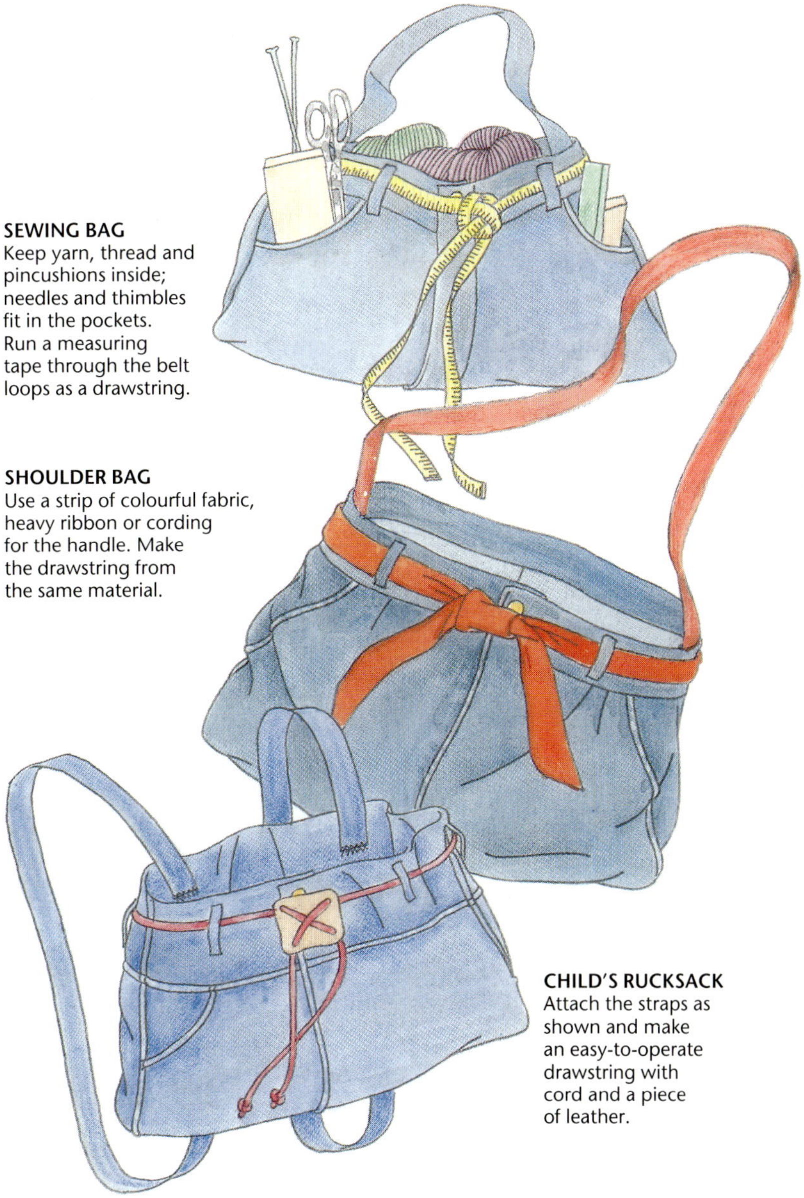

SEWING BAG
Keep yarn, thread and pincushions inside; needles and thimbles fit in the pockets. Run a measuring tape through the belt loops as a drawstring.

SHOULDER BAG
Use a strip of colourful fabric, heavy ribbon or cording for the handle. Make the drawstring from the same material.

CHILD'S RUCKSACK
Attach the straps as shown and make an easy-to-operate drawstring with cord and a piece of leather.

To turn the bag into a compact child's rucksack, first measure carefully for straps. Hold the bag against the child's back and then loop your measuring tape from the top of the bag, over the shoulders, and back to the bottom of the bag. Be sure to allow an extra 75 millimetres so that you can cross-stitch the straps to the inside of the waistband and the bottom of the back pockets. Rip open a few stitches in the bottom of the pockets and tuck the straps inside, then sew them in place.

To make a drawstring that even a little one can operate, cut a 25-millimetre square of heavy leather and drill or punch a four-millimetre hole in each corner. Run a long piece of strong cord through the belt loops in the rucksack, then through the top set of holes in the leather. Cross the cords to make an X, then thread them through the bottom holes. Knot the cord ends. Just pull on the cords to close the bag; to open it, hold the leather patch and tug at the part of the cord that runs through the belt loops.

Book/Jewellery safe

Foil thieves by turning a book into a small safe, and lining it up with the other books on your shelf.

Choose a hardcover book at least 40 millimetres thick. Glue all but the first few pages together with a mixture of three parts cold glue to one part water. Insert a sheet of wax paper between the first glued page and the loose ones; insert another between the last page and the back cover. Close the book, weight it down with several heavy volumes or some concrete blocks (don't skimp on the weight or the pages may wrinkle), and let dry overnight.

When the glue is dry, mark the section to be cut; leave at least a 25-millimetre margin at the edges. Drill starter holes in the corners and use a coping saw to remove the section. Glue the back cover in place and weight it down again.

For a finishing touch, line the cutout with satin or felt.

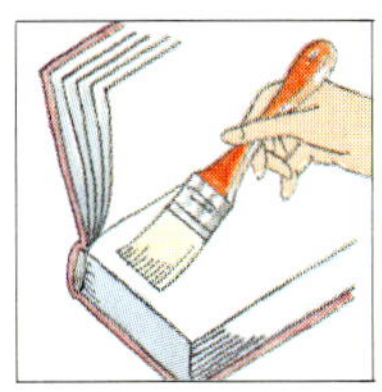

1. With a wide brush, apply glue sparingly to all pages except the first few.

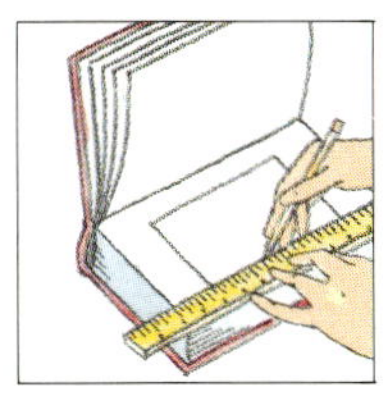

2. Leave a margin of at least 25 mm all around when you mark the section to be cut out.

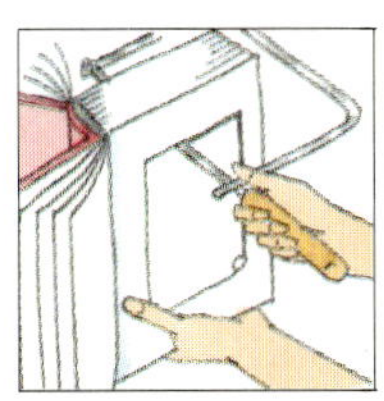

3. Drill starter holes in the corner and cut out the book section with a coping saw.

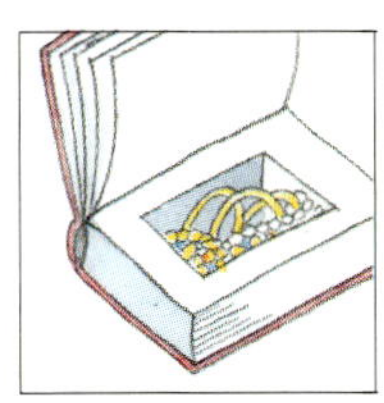

4. Glue down the back cover, then use white glue to line the cutout with satin or felt.

Brake drum/Forge or braai

For light metalwork – making your own fireplace tools or other wrought-iron implements – you can build a blacksmithing forge from the old brake drum of a truck. With a grid top, it doubles as a braai.

You'll also need the lid of an oil drum, three 900-millimetre lengths of 20-millimetre threaded steel pipe to use as legs, and three 20-millimetre flanges to hold them. For the blower assembly you'll need a length of 50-millimetre threaded pipe and matching flange, T-coupling, pipe cap and two brass nipples. Assemble the parts as shown. Connect the blower pipe to a motor-driven blower or an old-fashioned bellows. An old hair dryer will also do. Because the grate is made from the thin steel of an oil drum, you'll have to replace it occasionally. Other than that, your only maintenance will be removing the cap from the bottom of the centre pipe to clean out ashes.

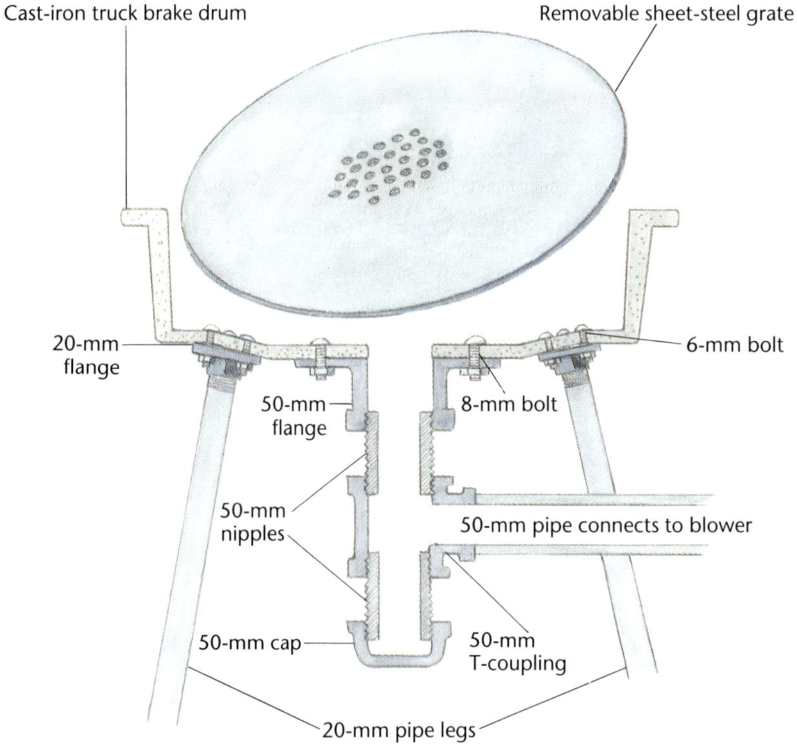

1. Drill holes and bolt three 20-mm flanges to the bottom of the brake drum to hold the threaded pipes that will be used as legs.

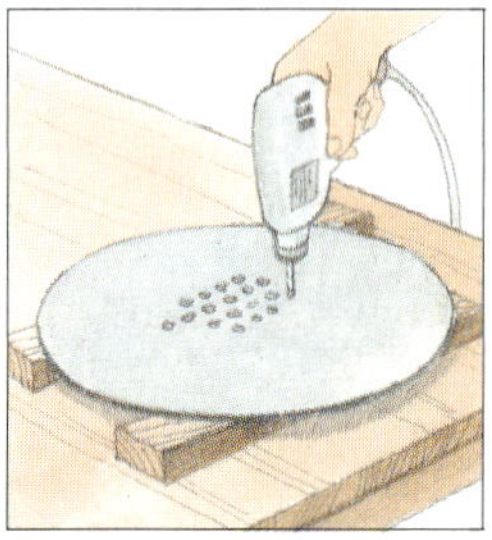

2. Use tin snips to cut the lid of an oil drum to fit inside the brake drum. Drill a few 5-mm holes in the centre to let in air.

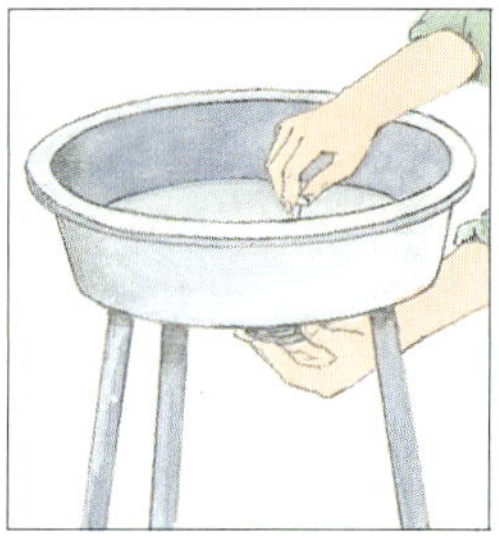

3. Attach a 50-mm flange to the bottom with 8-mm bolts. You should be able to bolt through the existing holes in the drum.

Cable spools/Child's table

The big wooden spools that hold cable or rope can make nifty furniture for kids. Turn a 600-millimetre spool and two 300-millimetre ones into a table and stools.

If the spool ends are secured with protruding dome-head screws, countersink them. Then attach three rubber feet to the bottom of each spool to keep it steady.

1. Lightly sand the spool ends and paint with alkyd semi-gloss. Apply an extra coat to the tabletop.

3. Trace the shape of the small spool ends on a sheet of foam rubber and cut out one piece for each seat.

Paint the spools' ends in a bright colour, such as red or yellow, and decorate the reels with thin rope as shown. Just spread cold glue randomly around the reel, nail down the end of the rope firmly at the inside base of the reel, and wrap, pushing each coil of the rope down tightly against the previous one.

If you find you have to use more than one piece of rope, secure the ends with tacks and remove them when the glue has dried.

For comfort, fit the two small spools with padded seats of foam rubber and fabric. If you want to cover the two or three holes in the centre of the tabletop (used for mounting the spools on rods), cut a piece of hardboard or plastic laminate the size of the tabletop and glue it down.

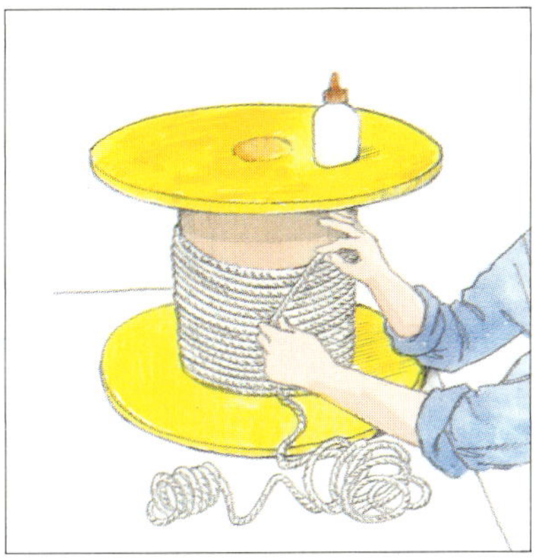

2. Spread cold glue on the centre reel of each spool and wrap rope around, securing the ends with tacks.

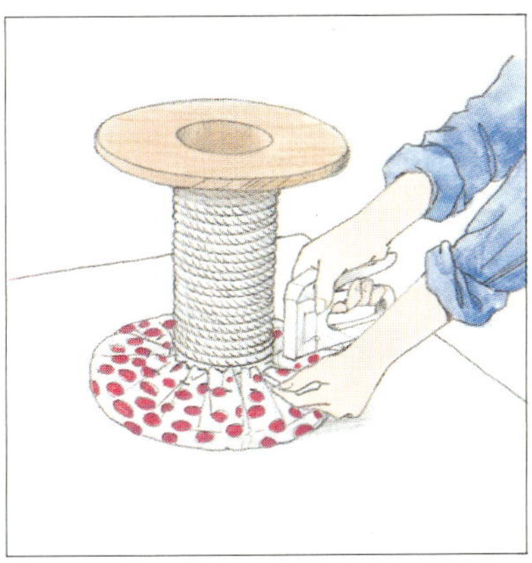

4. Centre the foam on fabric cut 100 mm larger all around, place the spools on top and staple the fabric down.

Candles/Luminaria

Save candle stubs to melt down, remould and turn into your own luminaria – decorative lanterns to place along your garden paths for special occasions.

Melt the candle stubs in a double boiler and use a slotted spoon to skim off the wicks that float to the surface. If you need more wax, buy some taper wax from a craft store, hardware outlet or hobby shop and add it to the stubs. Use old clean milk cartons for the moulds. For each lantern you'll need a 500 gram or one-kilogram coffee tin with the label removed. With a punch or chisel, punch the holes for the candlelight to shine through.

If you like, place a few luminaria in rock gardens or flower beds as well as on pathways.

1. Melt the candle stubs in a pan set in a larger pan filled with at least 50 ml of simmering water. Cut 1-litre- or 500-mm milk cartons down to 75 mm.

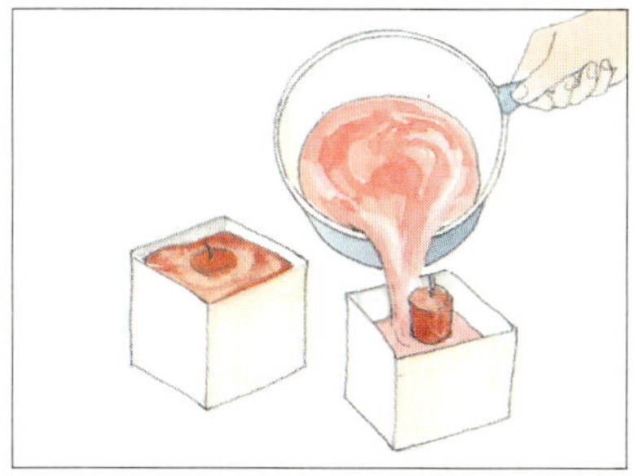

2. Pour 5 mm of wax into the bottom of each carton. Then hold a 75-mm candle stub upright in the middle until it stands by itself. Fill the carton to the top.

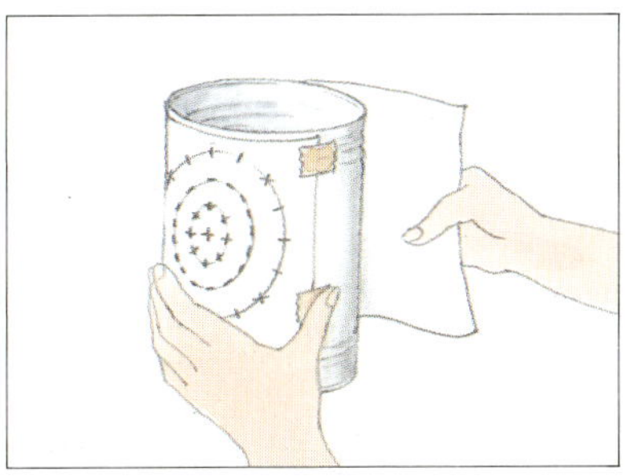

3. With the aid of a compass and straightedge, draw a series of geometric dot patterns on a piece of paper and tape the paper all the way around the tin.

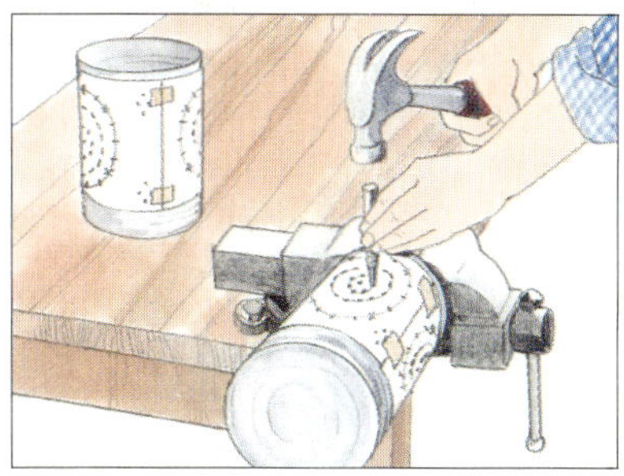

4. Clamp the end of a scrap of wood in a vice and slip the tin over it. Use a punch or chisel to punch out the design on all sides of the tin.

5. Peel the milk cartons from the candles, place a candle in each decorated tin, and line up the tins at the edge of the pathway to your front door.

Cardboard boxes/Table

Glued together, several sheets of corrugated cardboard are strong enough to make a lightweight piece of furniture that even children can move from place to place.

The carton that a refrigerator comes in, plus a smaller box or two, yields enough material to build the project shown here. Cut out matching sections with a utility knife and straightedge and use cold glue to sandwich them together in fours. Stack the sheets so that their corrugations run in alternating directions.

Your table can be any size or shape. Shown here is an occasional table 600 millimetres high by 750 millimetres across. The corners are trimmed for a decorative effect.

1. Draw four 750-mm squares and eight 500- x 600-mm rectangles on the cardboard and cut them out with a utility knife.

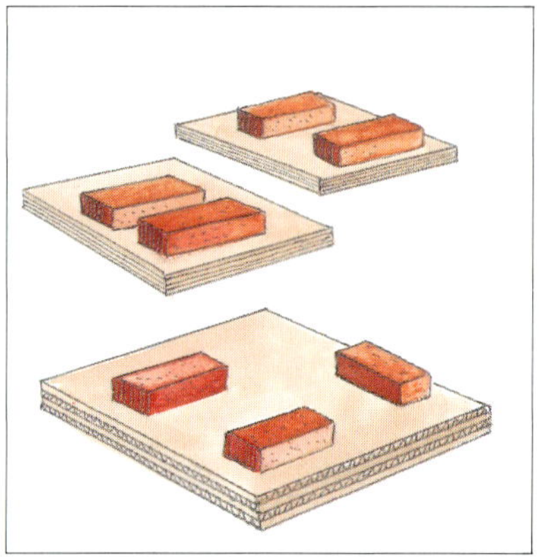

2. Glue the 750-mm squares together. Glue the rectangles together in two groups of four each. Weight down.

3. Cut a 300-mm slit in each rectangle just wide enough to enable the two parts to be fitted together to form a stand.

Cardboard boxes/Renewal

Use patterned adhesive plastic to turn a plain cardboard box into an attractive storage container.

The material comes in 450-millimetre-wide rolls. To determine how many you'll need, measure the five sides of the box you're covering (six if you're covering the lid) and add the measurements together. Then double the amount so that you can cover the inside, too.

Cover the inside bottom of the box first, cutting the paper an extra 10 millimetres all around. (To release the paper from its backing, roll a corner back and forth between your fingers.) Mitre the corners of the plastic by making a cut from the corner of the box outward, then a second cut at a 45° angle.

Next, use a single sheet to cover the outside bottom and both sides of both ends. Cut the plastic to the exact length and add 50 millimetres to the width so that you'll have an edge to fold over on each side. Fold the sheet in half and crease it across the middle so you can find the centre when you align the paper on the box.

Peel off two-thirds of the backing and lay the plastic down, adhesive side up. Centre the box on the crease and press down; then smooth the plastic up one end, slit the extra 50 millimetres at each side, and smooth it down the inside. Peel off the remaining backing and repeat the process on the other end. Press down the overlaps.

Cover the other two sides of the box in the same way (the bottom will have another thickness of paper for extra strength), but don't add any extra width; you won't need to fold over edges this time.

Always smooth the plastic from the centre. If the surface still has air bubbles, puncture them with a straight pin and flatten them.

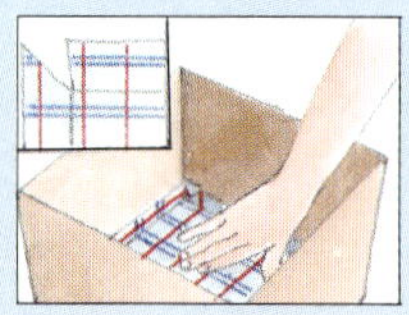

1. Cover the inside bottom, cutting the plastic with an extra 10 mm all the way around. Mitre the corners.

2. Cut a sheet to cover the outside bottom and two ends, inside and out, as shown. Add 50 mm to the width.

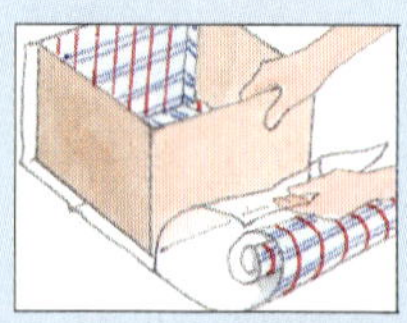

3. Peel most of the backing, centre box on plastic, and cover one end. Peel the rest and cover the other end.

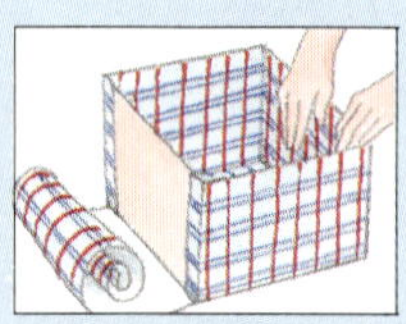

4. Slit the corners and fold the edges over. Cut a second sheet and cover the remaining two sides.

When you cut the slits in two of the sections to fit them together as a stand, make sure that the slits are the same length; otherwise the table will rock. And be sure to make them exactly as wide as the thickness of the glued cardboard. Just four strips of a single thickness of cardboard, folded lengthways and glued to the top edges of the stand, will enable you to attach the tabletop.

Cover the tabletop and stand with an adhesive plastic, such as NHP contact, in various patterns. Instead of going for imitation wood grain, why not try stripes, a solid bright colour, or a floral print? Another idea is to glue a collage of your own design onto the surface. Or, if the table is for children, use their crayon drawings and finger paintings for the collage.

4. Cut four 215- x 75-mm strips of cardboard, score lengthways, and bend in half. Glue to the stand and weight down.

5. Cut narrow strips of adhesive plastic to cover the edges of the cardboard, then cut pieces to cover the surfaces.

6. Apply glue to the cardboard strips on the stand, centre the tabletop, and weight it down until completely dry.

Ceramic tiles/Trivet

Glue some leftover tiles to a piece of 12-millimetre plywood, and you have a trivet that looks as good as the expensive ones which are usually sold in kitchen stores.

This one is made of four square ceramic tiles, four corner pieces and eight curved edging tiles. To ensure even joints, use spacers or matchsticks between the tiles as you cement them down; then remove them and apply grout.

Bevel the top edge of the plywood so that the curved edging tiles will fit. Then attach four rubber feet to the bottom – they'll keep the piece from sliding around as you apply adhesive to the surface. If you cannot find edging tiles, tile the edges square with mosaic tiles or strips of tile offcuts.

Before you start applying tile adhesive to the top of the plywood base, make sure that you position the tiles to check for fit.

Once you've glued down the tiles and finished grouting, turn the trivet upside down and fill the gaps at the edges with more adhesive.

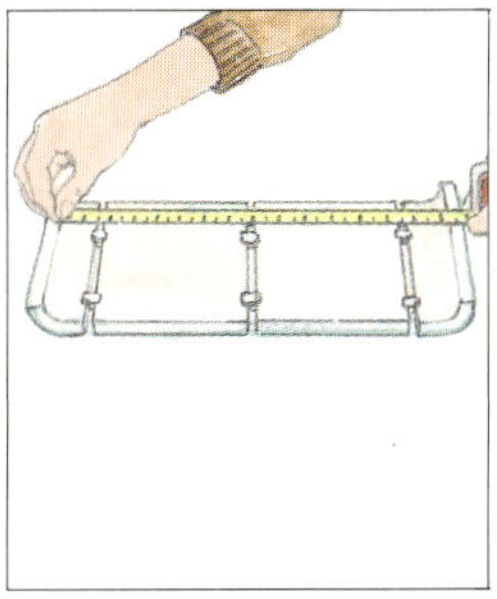

1. Insert spacers between two tiles and upside-down edging tiles. Measure the inside.

2. Cut the plywood 6 mm larger all around and use an orbital sander to bevel the top edge.

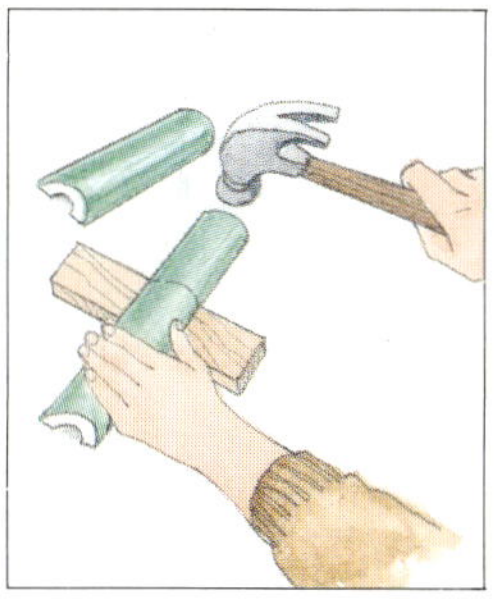

3. Mark and cut the edging tiles: score the glaze with a hacksaw, then break with a hammer.

4. Drive a nail into the centre point of the base. Use a notched trowel to cover the surface with adhesive.

5. Place the tiles around the nail. Remove the nail and insert matches or plastic spacers between the tiles.

6. Remove spacers and grout the joints, wiping away excess with a wet sponge. Buff when dry.

Chair/Rocking chair

Slot two hardwood rockers into the legs of an old straight chair to create a whole new piece of furniture.

First, enlarge the rocker pattern shown here, using 25-millimetre grid paper for an average-sized chair (300 to 350-millimetres between the front and the back legs). Then transfer it to a length of 12-millimetre hardwood for cutting.

Cut both rockers at the same time so that they will be identical. Clamp both pieces of wood together before rough cutting, then reclamp for simultaneous trimming and sanding.

Before you slot the chair legs for the rockers, make sure the chair will tilt at a comfortable angle by cutting about 12 millimetres off the back legs. Experiment with the angle by trimming the legs a little at a time.

The easiest way to cut the slots in the chair legs is with a dado head on your table saw. Position the rip fence so that the slots will be centred in the legs. Extend the fence to guide both legs by clamping a board to it (this will ensure that both legs are slotted at exactly the same angle). Make several passes, raising the dado in small increments. Remember that the slots must align exactly with the rockers, which, in turn, must be vertical. If the chair legs you are cutting are slanted, make the slots aligned and vertical by raising the opposite pair of legs with a board as you work.

If you cut the slots by hand, make sure that you use a backsaw or hacksaw and a chisel.

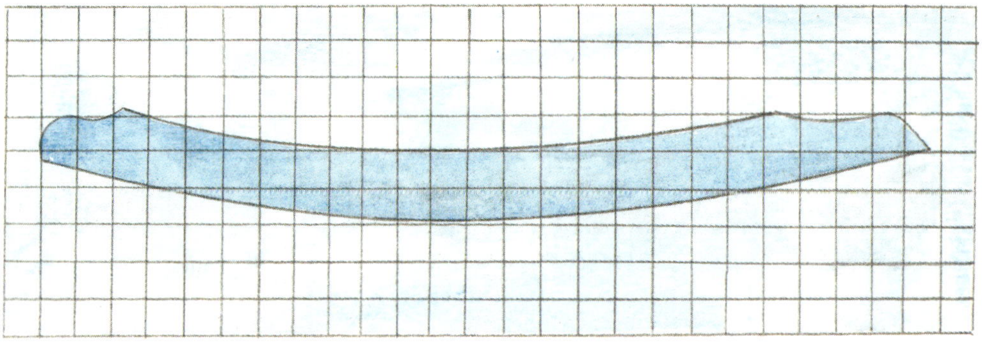

To make the wooden rockers for an average-sized chair whose front legs are 300 mm to 350 mm from the back legs, transfer this rocker pattern to 25-mm grid paper (use a straightedge and ruler to draw the grid yourself). For larger chairs, use a 30-mm grid; for smaller ones, use a 20-mm grid.

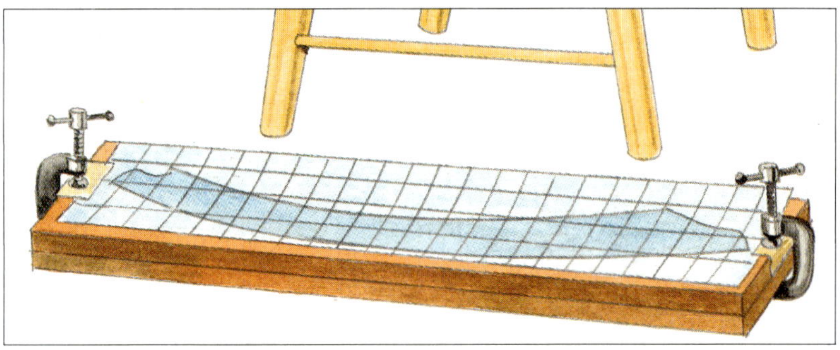

1. Firmly clamp two pieces of 12-mm hardwood together. Tape two sheets of carbon paper to the top piece, tape the rocker pattern over them, and transfer the pattern to the wood. Then rough-cut both pieces of wood at once.

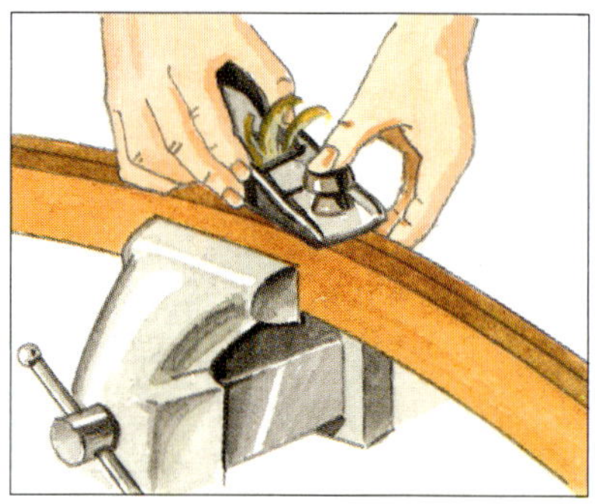

2. Reclamp the rough-cut rockers and shape them, using a spokeshave, plane and sandpaper.

3. Cut slots for the rockers in all four legs. Make them the exact width of a rocker and about 20 mm deep.

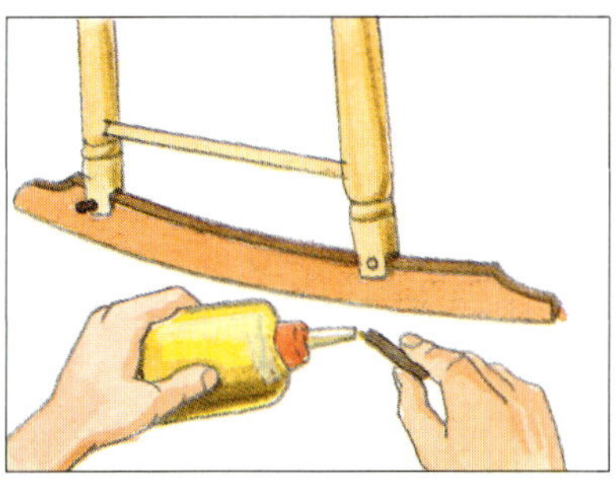

4. Place the rockers in the leg slots as shown and drill a 6-mm hole through each leg to receive a dowel pin.

5. Glue the pins in place, then trim them flush when the glue dries. Paint or stain the rockers to match the chair.

Chest of drawers/Bookcase

Do you have an old chest of drawers that's missing a drawer or two? Remove the back, insert some pine shelves, paint or refinish, and you have a free-standing, two-sided bookcase that makes an attractive room divider.

If the vertical space between the drawer supports is less than 200 millimetres, you'll have to pry out every other support to make the shelves tall enough for books. Leave one or two of the smaller spaces for magazines or extra-large books that can be laid on their sides.

Use wood filler on any holes, then finish the back of the chest and the shelves to match the front. Or paint the whole thing and stencil on a design (see below).

1. Remove the drawers and carefully pry the backing from the chest.

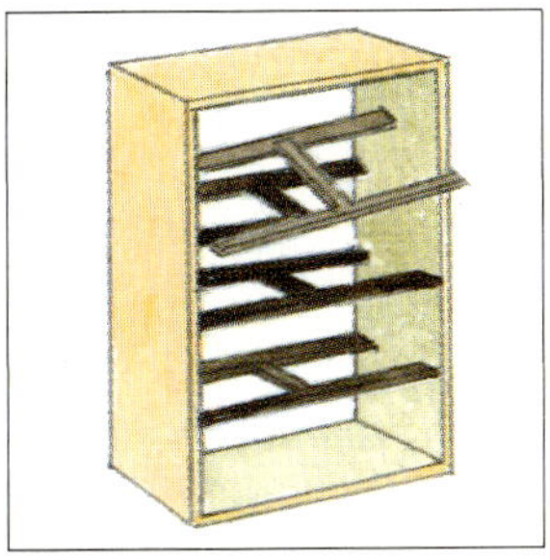

2. If necessary, remove every second support. Pry out the centre drawer rail.

3. Measure the inside for width and depth and cut shelves of 20-mm pine to size.

4. Drill and countersink for screws and secure the shelves to the supports.

Stencilling/Technique

Imperfect tables, chairs and chests, with their scratches and nicks, are the best candidates for stencilling. Painted in matt white or ivory and wiped down carefully with a thin stain to accentuate age marks, they become instant "antiques" onto which you can transfer any particular design you choose, from traditional African motifs to whimsical hearts and flowers.

Although stencils are sold at craft stores, you can make your own by tracing a design and enlarging it as shown. Just be sure to incorporate enough uncut sections, or "ties", to hold the stencil together.

Cut stencils from non-absorbent cardboard or waxed stencil paper. For paint, a quick-drying acrylic is ideal. Your work will look more professional if you buy a stencilling brush – round with stiff bristles.

If you're grouping many designs together, first work out your overall pattern on a piece of paper cut to the same size as your work surface. Then use it as a visual guide to position the stencils.

1. Choose a simple design from a pattern book or magazine. Use a sheet of carbon paper to trace the design onto another piece of paper. Then draw an evenly spaced grid on top of the tracing.

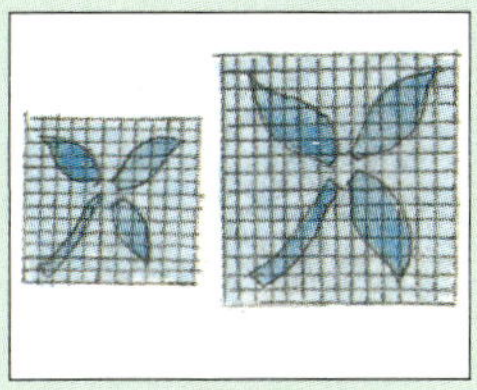

2. To enlarge your design to the desired size, use a ruler to draw a larger grid on a separate piece of paper and draw the design on it by carefully duplicating the pattern in each square of the smaller grid.

3. Using a sheet of carbon paper, transfer the design to the stencil board. Then cut out the design with a sharp craft knife, being sure to leave ties of at least 5 mm. Trim any ragged edges of the cutouts.

4. Position the stencil on the work surface and tape down the outside edges with masking tape. If you plan to use more than one colour, use more tape to cover the cutouts that will be painted later.

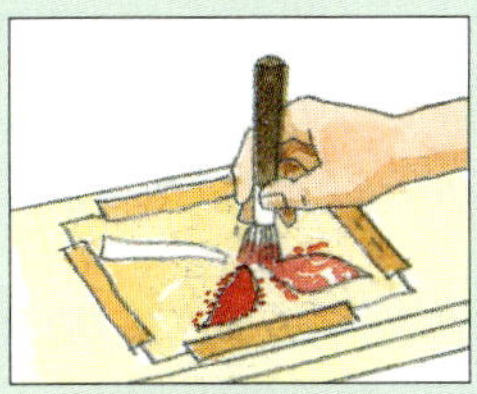

5. Dip your brush in the paint and blot it on a paper towel. Dab paint into each cutout with a quick up-and-down motion, working from the sides to the centre. Apply two light coats instead of one thick one.

6. Lift the stencil carefully and wipe any wet paint from the back before reusing it. When the stencilling is complete, allow the paint to dry overnight before applying a finishing coat of varnish or polyurethane.

Christmas cards/Decorations

Recycle your Christmas cards as seasonal decorations. Make little paper baskets, fill them with greenery or small ornaments, and hang them on the tree. Or create colourful place mats for a party table.

PAPER BASKETS

These colourful baskets make unusual Christmas tree ornaments. When you glue the paper strips together, first fold each strip in half, unfold, and use the crease as a centre mark so that the top of the basket will be even. And make sure the handle is long enough to fit around the end of a tree branch.

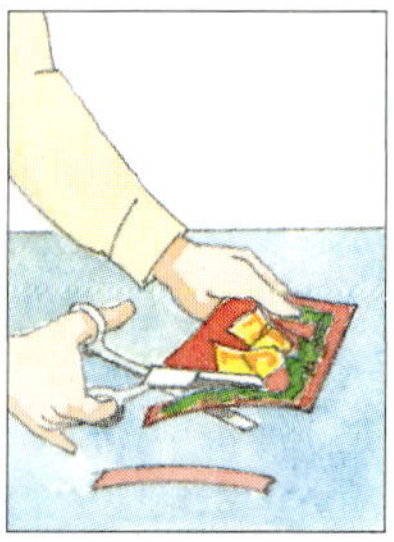

1. For each basket, mark off the fronts of the cards with a ruler and cut them into nine 12- x 200-mm strips. Then cut one 12- x 275-mm strip for a handle.

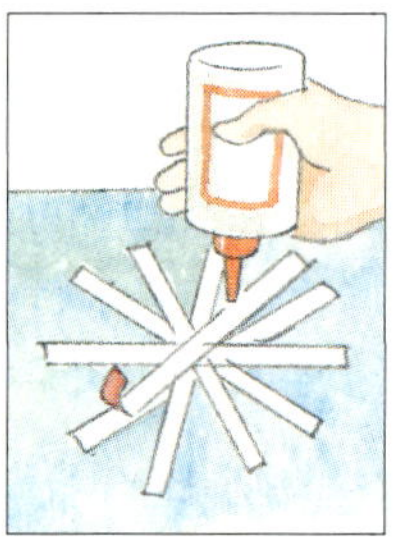

2. Use cold glue to join the centres of eight of the 200-mm strips. Stack them colour-side down, forming the spokes of a wheel; weight down firmly until the glue dries.

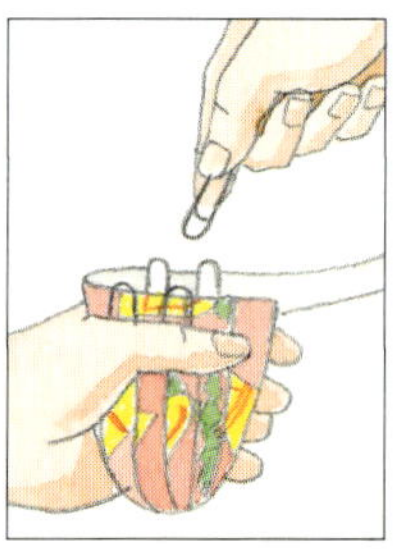

3. Cup the strips in your hand to make a basket. Glue the remaining 200-mm strip around the top and secure each strip with a paper clip until the glue dries.

4. Attach the 275-mm strip as a handle and let the glue dry. Then fill the basket with dried flowers or a bouquet of baby's breath before hanging on the tree.

PLACE MATS

Twenty to 25 cards are enough to make one 325-mm x 450-mm place mat with scalloped edges.

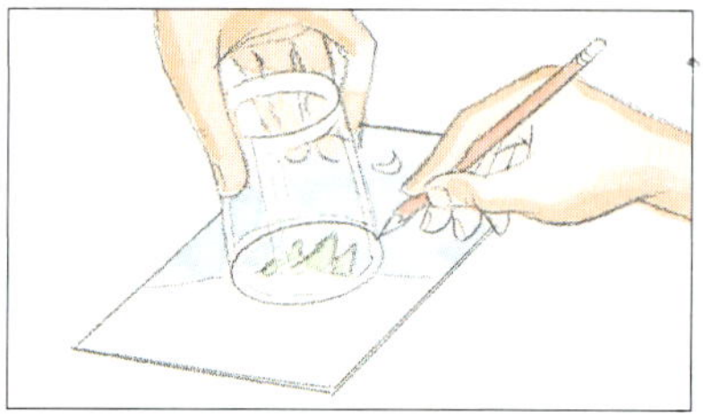

1. Use a compass or glass to trace 28 circles, each about 90 mm across, on the fronts of the cards. Cut them out.

2. Overlap 16 to 18 cutouts to form an oval on the sticky side of a 325- x 450-mm sheet of clear adhesive plastic. Fill the centre with the remaining cutouts.

3. Place clear adhesive plastic on top of the cards, sticky side down, and smooth from the middle to the edges.

4. With sharp scissors, trim away the excess adhesive plastic – both backing and top sheet – to finish the place mat.

Clothing/Rag rug

Instead of using old clothes as rags, cut them into strips and create a one-of-a-kind rug. Any lightweight fabric will do, from old shirts, skirts and shorts, to ties, ribbons and shoelaces – even string.

Besides the fabric strips, you'll need a three-count rug canvas, a latch hook to knot the strips on the canvas, and some 50-millimetre binding to finish off the edges.

Start by cutting the canvas to the desired size of your rug, adding an extra 25 millimetres all around. Then press masking tape over the edges to keep them from fraying as you work.

Cut your fabric into 12-millimetre strips 125 millimetres long (be sure that you do not cut on the bias or the strips will tend to fray). Then use the latch hook to knot them onto the rug canvas as shown, mixing the colours, textures and patterns for the most interesting effect.

When you've finished the rug, remove the masking tape, crease the binding over the extra 25 millimetres of canvas, and sew it on as close to the knots as possible.

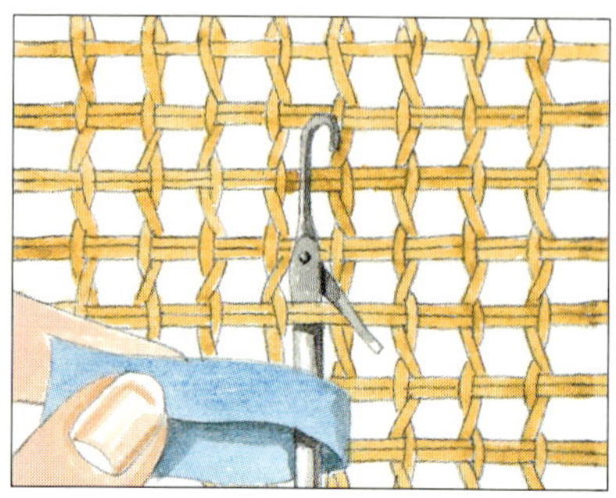

1. Hold the fabric strip around the shank of the latch hook and slip the tip under a strand of canvas. Flip the latch back.

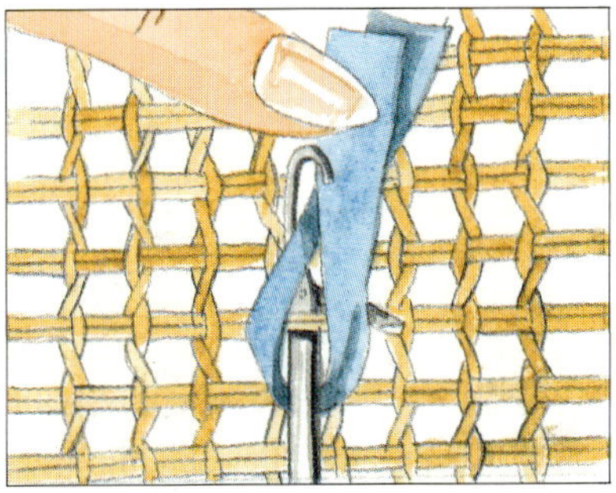

2. Still holding the fabric strip, and with the latch open, bring the ends of the strip up and into the open hook as shown.

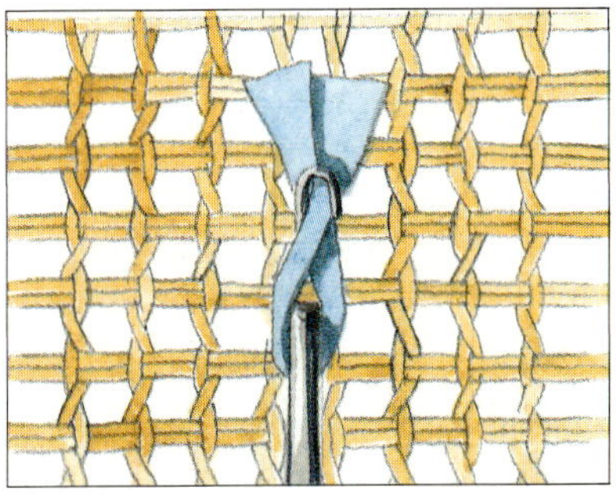

3. Carefully pull the hook across and under the strand. When the latch closes, release the fabric strip.

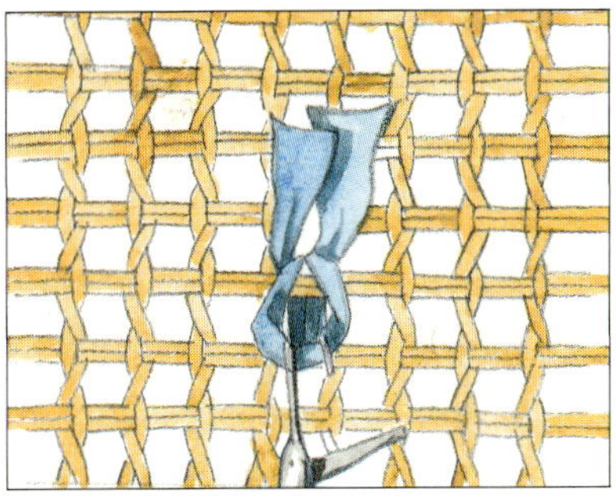

4. Continue to pull the hook across and under. The ends of the fabric strip will be pulled with the hook to form the knot.

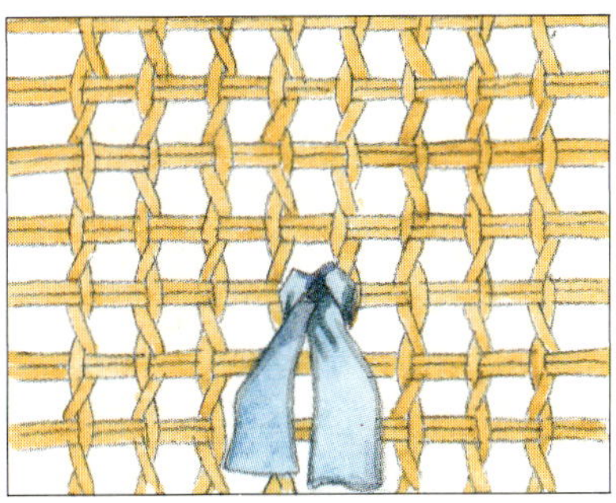

5. Tug on the ends of the fabric strip to tighten the knot.

Concrete block/Birdhouse

Chisel a hole in a concrete block to create an instant house for small garden birds. Just be sure not to make the hole larger than 35 millimetres or you'll attract starlings instead. And chisel slowly and carefully to keep the hole neat and round.

Use a square, hollow concrete block, which is smooth on four sides. Use a piece of pipe or a stout wooden pole as a stake to support the block one to two metres off the ground. Or try a shapely tree branch or a piece of driftwood for a more ornamental effect. Implant the stake at least 600 millimetres deep so that it won't blow over in the wind.

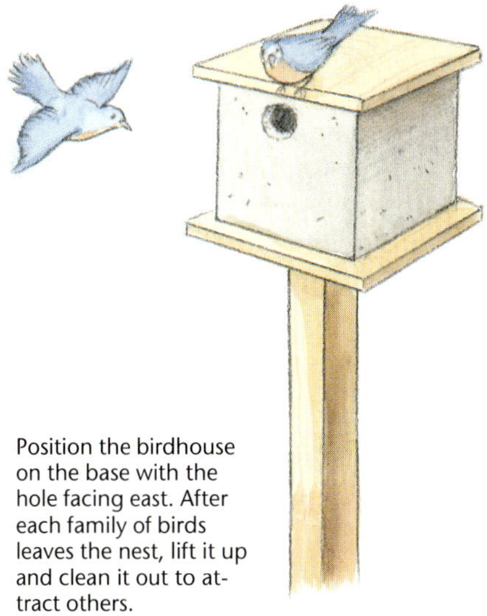

Position the birdhouse on the base with the hole facing east. After each family of birds leaves the nest, lift it up and clean it out to attract others.

1. Use a felt-tip pen to draw a 25-mm to 30-mm circle centred about 50 mm from the top of the concrete block. Make punch marks all the way around the circle with a sharp centre punch or large masonry nail.

2. Slowly drill all the way through the punch marks with a 5-mm masonry bit. Then use the centre punch or a nail and a hammer to carefully chisel out and enlarge the hole to a diameter of no more than 37 mm.

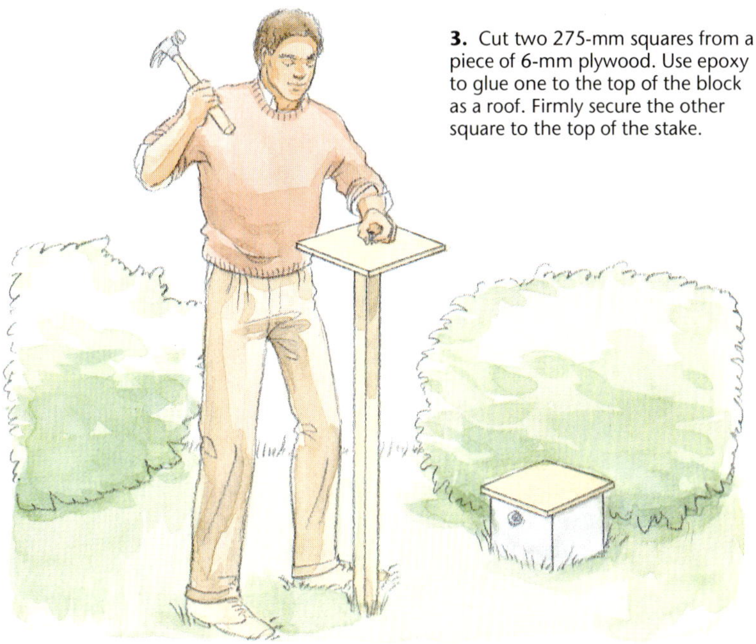

3. Cut two 275-mm squares from a piece of 6-mm plywood. Use epoxy to glue one to the top of the block as a roof. Firmly secure the other square to the top of the stake.

Deck chairs/Renewal

Deck chairs that have suffered from exposure to rain and sun can look like new with a little stain or paint and some bright new fabric.

Be careful as you pry out the staples when stripping the old fabric from the frames; gloves and protective goggles are both good ideas. Then sand the wood with medium sandpaper, paying special attention to any dark or rusty marks left by metal hardware. Paint or stain the frames as you prefer. If you use the chairs outdoors, finish with a coat of exterior polyurethane. Make sure that you choose heavy canvas or awning cloth (don't use synthetic fabric – it deteriorates in the sun). When you cut the fabric, allow a few centimetres extra to wrap around the back rails and seat frame; trim to the exact size just before you hem and staple. Pull the fabric tight as you staple.

1. Remove the old fabric by loosening the staples with a screwdriver, then pulling them out with pliers.

2. Wipe the wood with methylated spirits. If necessary sand and refinish with paint or stain and polyurethane.

3. Use the old fabric as a pattern for the new canvas. Or measure between rails and add 100 mm for stapling.

4. Hem the rough edges. With a heavy-duty stapler, secure the new seat and back panel to the frame.

Desk/Workbench

An old desk is a perfect base for a workbench, complete with storage drawers. Instead of blocking it up to raise the work surface to a comfortable level, build a new top of 18-millimetre plywood and 44- x 96-millimetre planking and cover it with a sheet of 6-millimetre hardboard. The hardboard should fit quite snugly into a recess at the top so that it doesn't need to be nailed down and can easily be replaced, if necessary.

Trim the edges all around with pine stock, making it six millimetres higher than the plywood surface to create a recess for the hardboard. Two pieces of 22- x 144-millimetre stock the same length as the plywood top will yield material for the front and back trim. Two lengths of 22 x 220 millimetres, 50 millimetres longer than the width of the plywood provide the side trim (end pieces).

1. Measure the desktop and cut two pieces of 18-mm plywood and one piece of 6-mm hardboard to its exact dimensions. Cut four 44- x 96-mm planks to the width of these panels and two more to the desired length of the cross braces.

4. Rip two 24-mm widths from the other 22- x 144-mm pieces of stock for the front and back top trim. Glue and nail them to the edges of the plywood so that they extend 6 mm above the surface, creating a recess for the hardboard work surface.

Doilies/Bowls

You can turn crocheted doilies into delicate, lacy bowls by simply stiffening them with a sugar-and-water solution. Use the smallest bowls as sweet dishes or for potpourri; larger ones make good fruit bowls and centrepiece holders.

This recipe is enough to convert one 225-millimetre doily. Mix fresh solution for each bowl.

As you dip a doily into the solution, squeeze it with your fingertips for even distribution; repeat two or three times and squeeze out the excess. For a mould place a bowl of the desired size upside down on a heavy towel.

When you want to restore the doily to its original form, just knead it under warm running water until it's no longer sticky, then wash with a mild detergent.

1. To make the stiffening solution, place ½ cup sugar in a large bowl and stir in ¼ cup boiling water. Stir for 3 minutes or until the mixture is almost opaque.

2. Dip a dry doily into the solution until it's thoroughly soaked. Squeeze out the excess and stretch it over the mould. Pin the edges to the towel with rustproof pins.

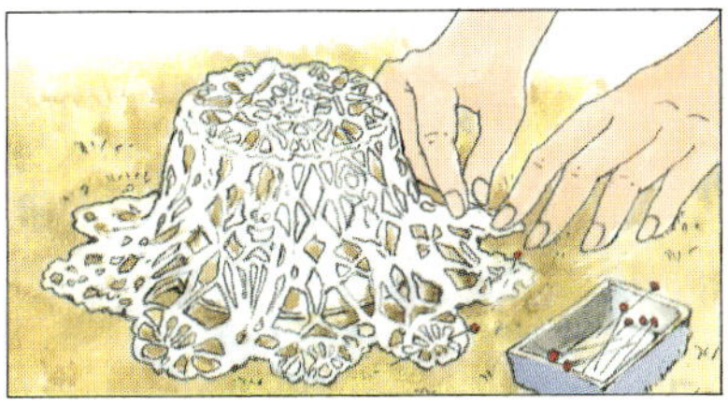

3. Let the doily dry for at least 6 hours. Then unpin it. Loosen it by wedging your fingers between the mould and the doily and working slowly around the perimeter.

4. Gently pull the loosened doily and the mould apart. To prevent small objects from falling through the holes in the bowl, line it with plastic wrap.

2. Set the 44- x 96-mm planks on edge, glue and nail to one of the plywood panels as shown – four vertically and two horizontally. Then glue and nail the other panel on top so that the planks are sandwiched between the plywood panels.

3. Cut two lengths of 22- x 144-mm stock the same length as the desktop. Rip one in half as bottom trim for the plywood. Hold the front piece in place before nailing to make sure that it doesn't interfere with opening the drawers; trim if necessary.

5. For end pieces, cut two lengths of 22- x 220-mm stock equal to the width of the plywood plus the trim. Glue and nail them in place so that they extend 6 mm above the top. The bottoms should overlap the existing desk by about 50 mm.

6. Rip a 37-mm width from the remainder of the 22- x 144-mm stock, and use it to trim the exposed ends of the 44- x 96-mm stock so that they are flush with the rest of the trim. Insert the hardboard top in the recess and attach a vice to the corner of the plywood top.

Doorknob/Ashtray

An old doorknob and a discarded pot lid make an unusual ashtray, complete with a centre post for stubbing out cigarettes or knocking the ashes from a pipe. Or, if you are a nonsmoker, you can use the tray as a sweet or nut dish.

Any kind of doorknob will do – you can try brass, ceramic or glass. Choose a pot lid of anodized aluminium or some other heat-resistant metal; a copper-coloured finish looks best.

For the base, use a square of hardwood. Cut a hole in the centre for the inverted pot lid to rest in. Once you've sanded and finished it, attach feet – brass drawer knobs make good ones – so that the knob spindle will clear the surface the ashtray is sitting on.

Assemble the pieces as shown after removing the handle from the lid and enlarging the hole to about 10 millimetres. Secure the spindle to the lid with a hose clamp – standard nuts won't fit. If the knob wobbles after assembly, use epoxy to glue it and its washer to the lid.

To make cigarette rests, use pliers to bend the lid flange.

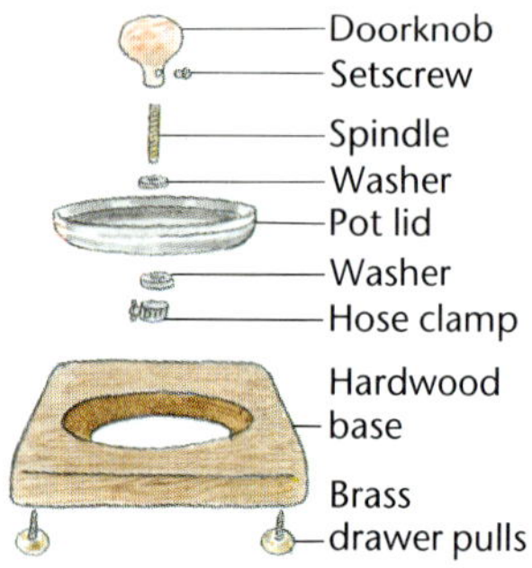

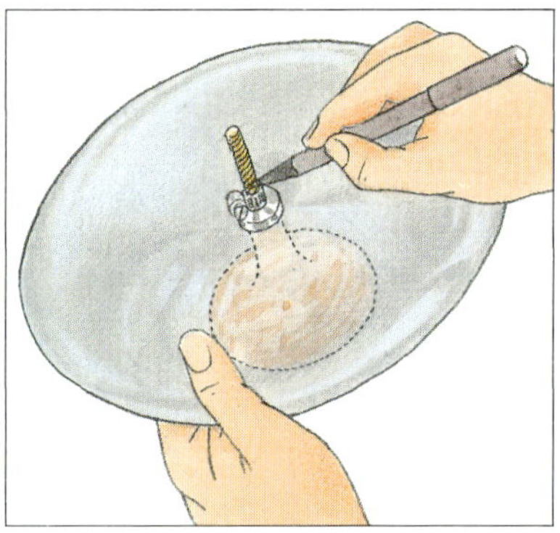

1. Drill a 10-mm hole in the centre of the lid and assemble the pieces to mark the spindle for cutting. Cut, reassemble, and apply epoxy if the doorknob wobbles.

2. Measure the diameter of the lid, add 50 mm, and cut a square of hardwood to this size. Then use a jigsaw to cut a hole about 25 millimetres smaller than the lid.

3. With a rasp or jigsaw, bevel the inside edges of the hardwood base at a 30° angle. Then round off the corners and sand the edges smooth.

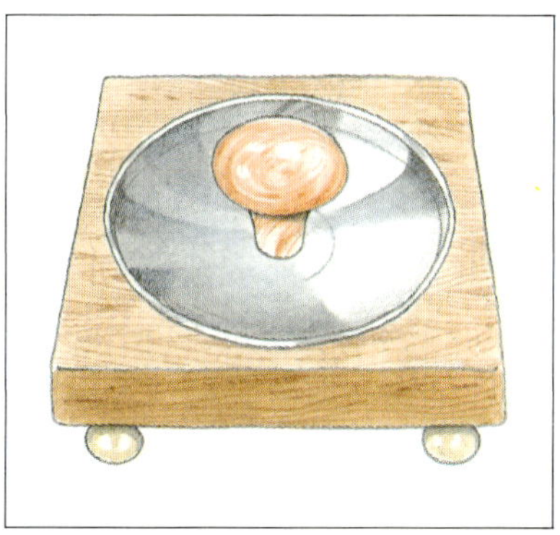

4. Stain the base and apply two coats of polyurethane. When it is dry, attach screw-in brass drawer knobs as feet and put the inverted pot lid in place.

Doors/Folding screen

Hinge two or three old doors together for a folding screen that can divide a room. Then try your hand at marbling (p.355) or stencilling (p.349) to turn your screen into a true original.

Buy double-action hinges the proper width for the doors. You'll also need some wood filler to level the old hinge mortises.

If the tops of the doors are out of alignment, place the unfolded screen across some workshop sawhorses. Clamp a board all the way across the top, flush with the lowest door, as a fence. Then trim the protruding tops with a circular saw.

1. Sand or strip the doors. Remove the old hinges and level the mortises by applying wood filler slightly higher than the surface. After it has set, sand it smooth.

2. Align the doors at the bottom and install double-action hinges 150 mm from the top and bottom. If the doors are heavy, install a third hinge in the middle.

Marbling/Technique

Give the walls, woodwork or furniture in your home the elegant look of marble with the following simple painting technique.

First, select six complementary shades of acrylic paint: one base colour, two "drift" colours, two "vein" colours and black or another colour that contrasts strongly with the others. At the same time, buy extender and thickener. Then sand your work surface smooth and clean it with a tack cloth. Apply two coats of the base colour, then spray on a clear matt acrylic sealer.

Use four paper plates as palettes – one for each phase of the painting.

1. Squeeze the two drift colours onto a paper plate with an even circular motion, then repeat the process with the extender and thickener. Tilt the plate back and forth until all of the ingredients run together but are not fully mixed. Wet a sponge, wring it out, and dip it into the paints. To paint, dab the surface gently but firmly, turning the sponge to make drifts as shown.

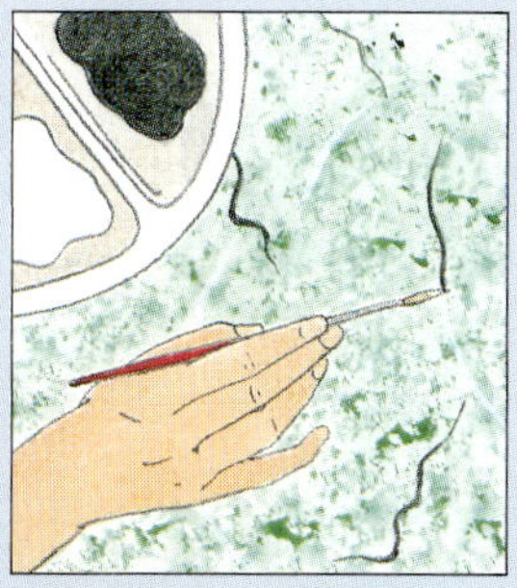

2. When the drift colours are completely dry, pour a small puddle of each vein colour onto another paper plate and mix each colour with extender and thickener. Then dip a fine brush into the paint; holding it loosely, choose a few of the drifts to outline with a combination of jagged and smooth strokes. Begin at the top end of a drift and move quickly down and around it.

3. To create a speckled effect over the drifts and veins of your marbled surface, dip an old toothbrush into the contrasting colour. Then flick a knife or your thumb across the bristles. Be careful not to overdo it – a few well-placed splatters should be enough. When the paint is completely dry, apply a couple of coats of matt-finish polyurethane to seal and protect the surface.

Drainpipe/Uplight

A lamp that shines up from the floor creates a dramatic effect of light and shadow, especially if it's placed indoors among potted plants. This kind of light is particularly effective on interior face-brick walls, giving a sense of warmth and coziness to a dining-room, lounge or bedroom. For an interior uplight that is as attractive as it is simple, you can easily convert an off cut of ceramic drainpipe.

All you need besides the drainpipe is a piece of 12-millimetre plywood and a lamp kit (sold at light fitting stores) that contains a socket, a threaded metal nipple, nuts and washers, flex, plug top and switch.

Cut a plywood disc to fit inside the tile, attach the lamp parts, and screw in a bulb. Turn the lamp on by simply plugging it in, or, if you prefer, install a line switch.

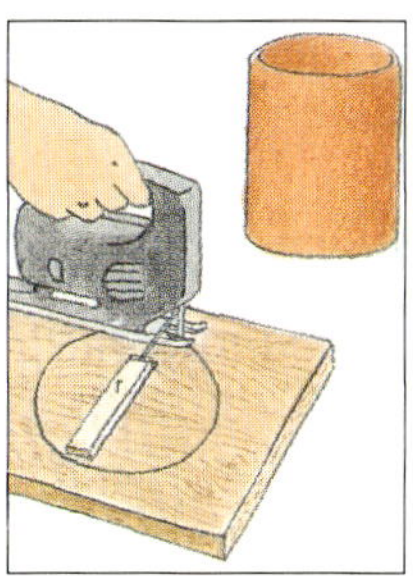

1. Measure the inside diameter of the drainpipe and cut a circle of 12-mm plywood to fit snugly into the pipe.

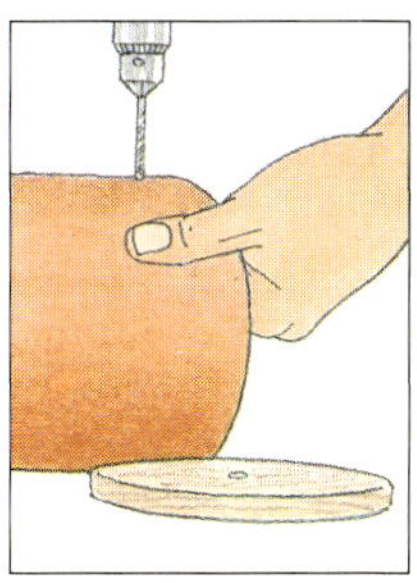

2. Drill a 10-mm hole in the centre of the plywood. Drill three 6-mm holes in the bottom of the pipe, 30 mm from the bottom, spaced equally on the circumference, and a fourth hole, for the flex, 36 mm from the end.

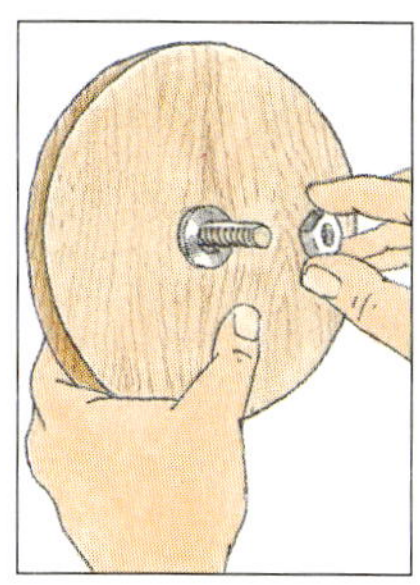

3. Insert a 25 mm-long 10-mm nipple into the centre hole and secure it with washers and nuts on each side.

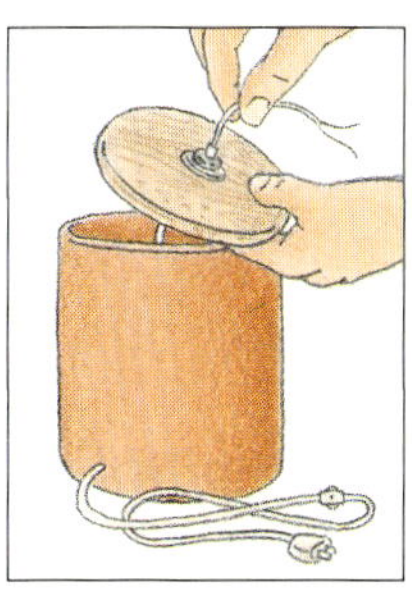

4. From the outside, thread the bare end of the lamp cord through the hole in the pipe, then up through the nipple.

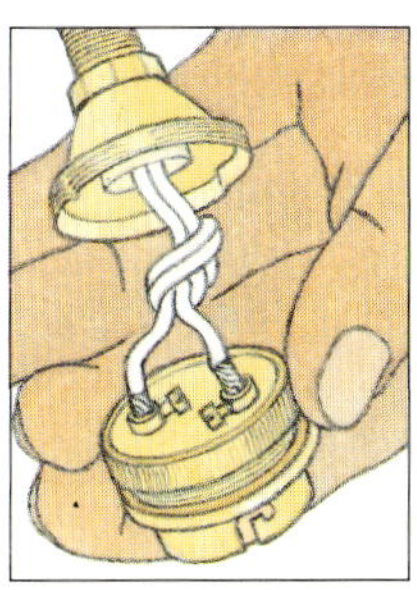

5. Strip and braid the wires and attach them firmly to their terminals in the disassembled light fitting. Knot insulated flex inside the fitting. Assemble and screw the socket onto the nipple, and bolt fitting to the plywood.

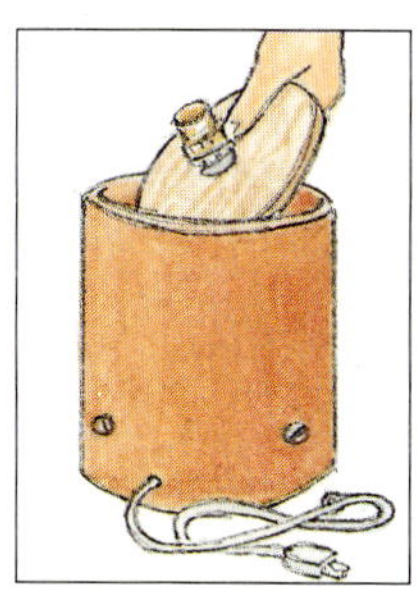

6. Turn the plywood disc on edge and wedge it down the pipe until opposite the three holes. Lock it in position using 20-mm panhead self-tapping screws. Plug in a bulb and plug in the lamp.

Drying rack/Tie rack

The top of an old drying rack makes a space-saving tie holder for your cupboard door. All you need are a couple of brass hinges and light-weight chains to put it in place. Then add a screw eye and hook to keep it up out of the way. Just make sure the rack is wide enough to attach to the stiles or side panels of your door; the centre section is too flimsy to support the hardware.

Start by removing the rack from the legs. Measure between the arms of the rack and cut a section of leg to size to use as an end piece. Cut the ends of the arms square if they are rounded or notched, then screw the end piece in place or join it with dowel pins. Sand and paint the rack or finish it to match the door.

Once you've screwed brass hinges into the end piece, attach a chain near the end of each arm of the rack and mount the rack at eye level on the back of the cupboard door. Fold the rack up and mark the positions of the chains on the door; then level the rack, hold the chains to the marks, and cut them to the appropriate length. Fix the chains securely to the door with screws.

Put a screw eye in the centre of the front dowel, then fold the rack flush with the door to position the hook.

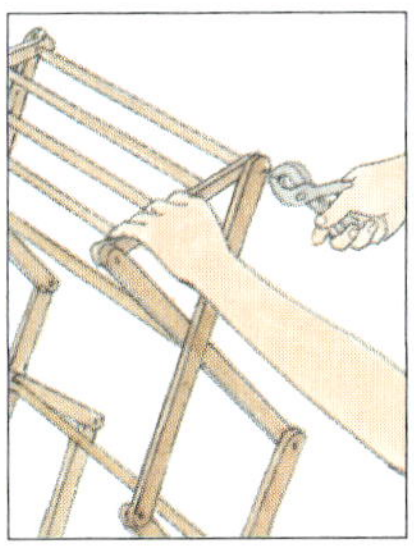

1. Free the top section of the drying rack from the accordion legs by removing the small brads or prying out the nails that hold it in place.

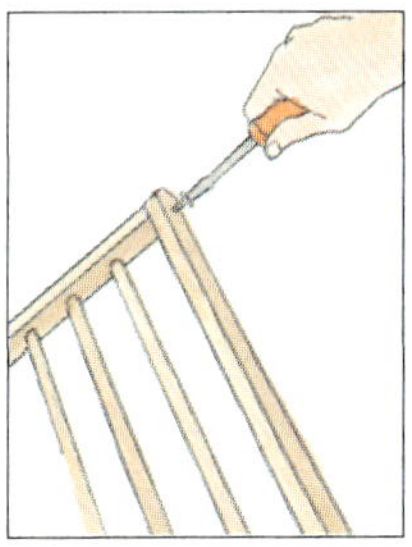

2. Cut a section from one of the rack legs. Drill and countersink for 4-mm (No.8) screws to attach it to the end of the arms as an end piece.

3. Attach hinges about 25 mm from each end of the end piece. Then secure chains near the other ends of the arms with 3-mm (No.4) screws.

4. Install a screw eye in the front dowel. Mark a level line on the cupboard door and mount the rack on it, screwing the hinges into the stiles or side panels.

5. Fold the rack against the door and mark the position of the chains. Then, using a spirit level, level the rack and cut the chains to the correct length.

6. Fold the rack flat against the door to mark the position for a screw hook. Then install it so that it engages the screw eye on the rack.

Eating utensils/Wind chime

For a charming wind chime with a surprisingly musical tone, use your old cutlery. Select a few silver-plated forks, spoons or knives; stainless-steel utensils don't have an appealing ring, and sterling silver is obviously too valuable a commodity for this kind of recycling.

Use a rubber mallet or a cloth-covered hammer to flatten the utensils on a block of wood. Then polish them so that the silver will glint in the sun. And be sure to have some extra forks on hand; bending the tines is

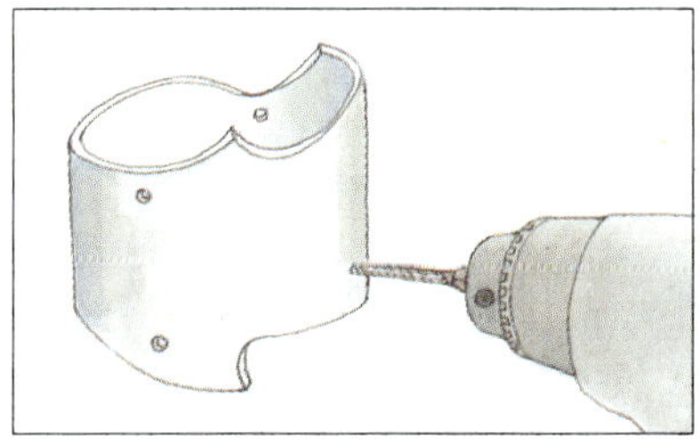

1. Cut a 100-mm section of PVC pipe and notch the edges. Drill two 4-mm holes exactly opposite each other about 12 mm from the top of the cylinder. At the other end, drill four equidistant holes.

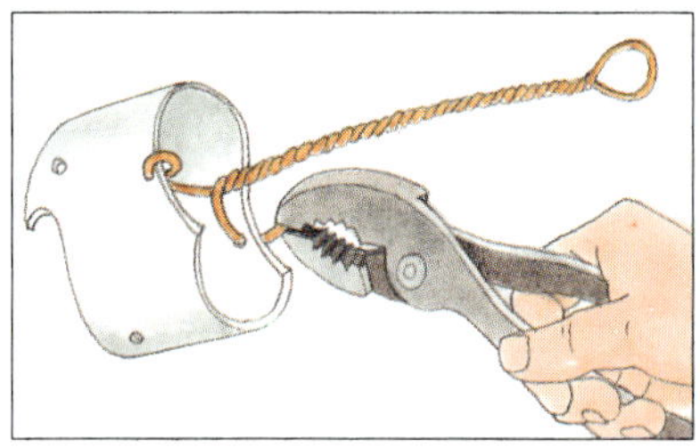

3. Remove the pipe. Thread the ends of the wires through the two top holes in the PVC cylinder, working from the inside, and use pliers to bend them over the top to secure.

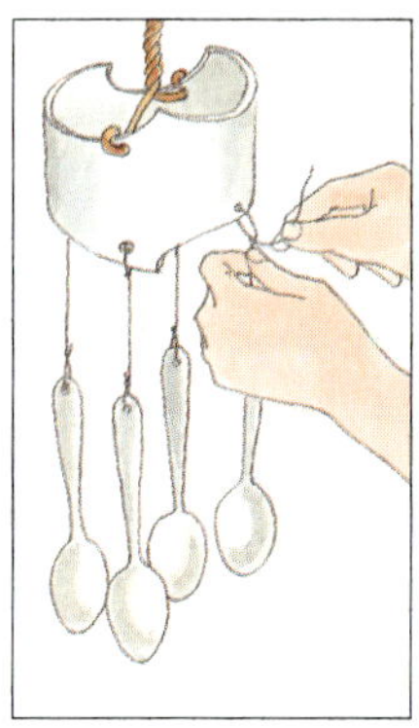

5. Drill a 4-mm hole 5 mm from the end of each utensil handle. Knot a 300-mm length of fishing line onto the end of each utensil, then hang the four spoons from the holes drilled in the PVC pipe.

tricky, and you will probably break a few before you get the hang of it.

Besides the utensils, you'll need a 100-millimetre length of 110-millimetre PVC pipe, some heavy-gauge copper wire, a small cylinder to use as a mandrel in shaping a hanging loop (12-millimetre pipe works fine), and some two-kilogram or stronger fishing line.

When cutting the PVC pipe, notch the lower edge or cut it in an irregular shape so that it will catch the wind and keep the chimes tinkling.

2. Cut a one-metre length of 12-gauge copper wire and fold it in half around a 12-mm pipe. Clamp the pipe in a vice and grip the wires 125 mm from the ends with locking-grip pliers. Twist until the wires are intertwined.

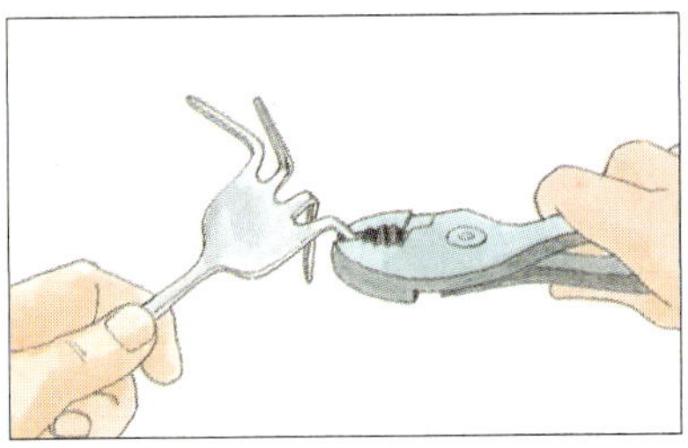

4. Flatten four spoons and a fork. With pliers, bend one of the middle tines of the fork to 90°; bend another in the opposite direction. Then bend the outer tines upward and sideways as shown.

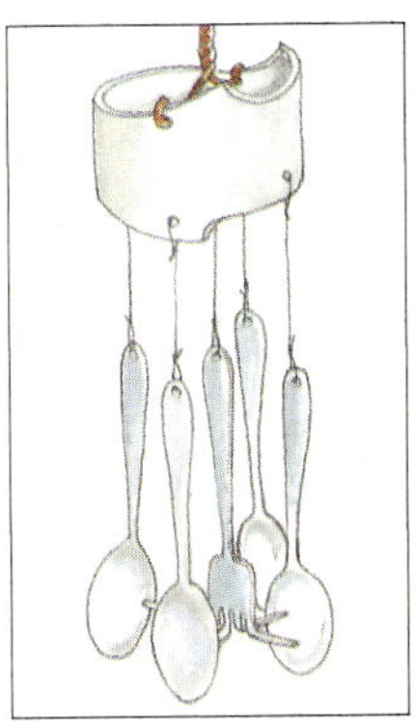

6. Hang the fork from the crotch of the copper wire hanger, positioning it so that its tines strike the bowls of the spoons. Trim the excess fishing line from the knots and hang the chime to catch the wind.

Fabric scraps/Serviettes & gift decorations

Use the leftover fabric from sewing projects to decorate jars of homemade preserves and other goodies. Your scraps can also be turned into small sacks to dress up the bottles of spirits or liqueur you're giving for Christmas. And several squares can be cut out of larger scraps with pinking shears – and left unhemmed – to make pretty fabric serviettes for parties and gifts. All three projects are easy enough for children to do.

JAR LID COVERS

These handmade fabric tops give your jars of homemade relishes and preserves the professional finish of those sold in speciality stores. Use traditional checked gingham for a country look or choose a solid colour and trim it with lace or rickrack. If you're distributing the jars as gifts, why not combine them in a basket with a few serviettes that match the lid covers.

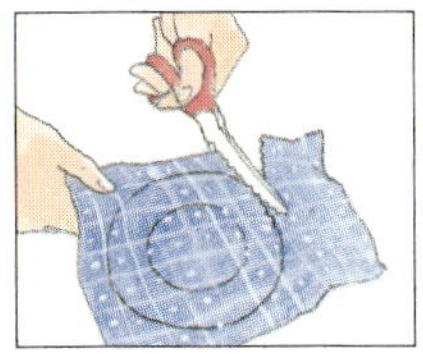

1. Trace the jar lid on the wrong side of the fabric, add 50 mm all around, and cut out with pinking shears.

2. Use cold glue to affix the trim. Secure the cover on the lid with a rubber band, then tie with ribbon.

SERVIETTES

Use these to complement your gifts of homemade treats. Or make several from different fabrics to use at a party or buffet. Although left unhemmed, the serviettes will stand up to four or five trips through the washing machine if you use pinking shears to help keep the edges from fraying.

Cut out a 250-mm square of cardboard and use chalk to trace around it on the wrong side of the fabric. Cut out with pinking shears and fold.

BOTTLE SACK

With a sewing machine, you can make one of these clever little gift sacks in less than five minutes. Use a running stitch on the wrong side of the fabric and turn the piece inside out so that the seam won't show.

Your finished product doesn't have to be used just for a bottle of Christmas cheer. Make sacks of different sizes for other gifts – toys for a child's birthday or kitchen gadgets for a bride-to-be. Decorate by gluing on a few felt cutouts or sequins, or use felt letters to form a name or greeting. Tie with a bow of ribbon or yarn.

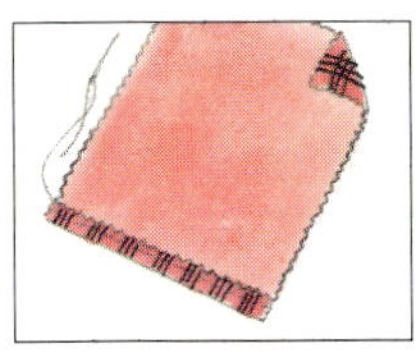

1. Cut a 325- x 375-mm piece of fabric, lay it face-down, and hem a short side by folding over 12 mm of material.

2. Fold in half lengthways, wrong side out. Press, then sew the long side and bottom with a running stitch.

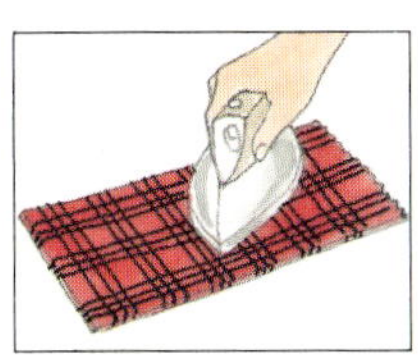

3. Turn right side out and press the seam flat. Put the bottle inside and tie at the neck with ribbon or yarn.

Fence/Headboard

To give your plain bed the look of a handsome antique, attach a section of decorative iron fencing to the frame as a headboard. Two gates can be bolted together to serve the purpose as well.

A hacksaw will probably be strong enough to cut the fencing to size; be sure to have several coarse blades (8 teeth per centimetre) on hand – they'll get blunt quickly. If the metal is too heavy to cut, take the fence to a body shop and have it trimmed with a cutting torch.

If your bed frame is already equipped with flanges for mounting a headboard, all you'll need are flat metal plates and some heavy gutter bolts. For a bed frame without the flanges, substitute inside corner braces (angle brackets) for the front mending plates.

1. Choose an attractive section of fencing and cut it to the width of your bed frame with a hacksaw equipped with a coarse blade; replace blades as necessary.

Folding table & chairs/Renewal

Give your patio furniture set a face-lift by painting the metal frames. Then re-cover the seats and tabletop with padding and a bright waterproof or vinyl fabric, and they'll look like new.

To start the job, turn the set over and remove the screws or metal tabs that hold the seats and tabletop in place (bend metal tabs straight with pliers for easy removal). Prepare the metal as shown, wipe down with methylated spirits, and spray-paint in a well-ventilated place. Prevent drip marks by applying two light coats instead of one heavy one.

If the seats are cardboard, use a standard office stapler to staple the foam padding and fabric to them; if they're wood, use a heavy-duty stapler. A glue gun will work, too.

Let the paint dry overnight. Then reassemble the table and chairs and finish them up with new rubber leg tips, available at hardware stores.

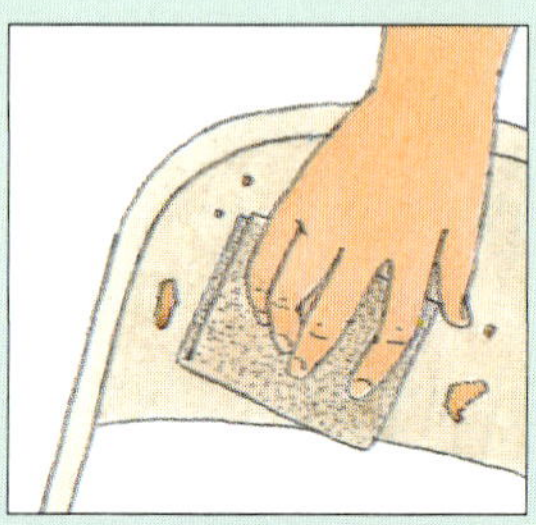

1. Scrub the metal frames with a wire brush and sand any rust spots with fine sandpaper. Then spray the spots with a metal primer.

2. Place the table frame and chairs in a well-ventilated place and clean with methylated spirits. Apply two light coats of spray-paint.

3. Cut 10-mm foam padding to the size of the tabletop and chair seats. Cut fabric 50 mm larger all around and place it face down.

4. Centre the padding, tabletop and seats on top of the fabric. Pull the fabric tight and staple it down. Reassemble table and chairs.

2. Scrub the fence headboard with a wire brush, wipe down with methylated spirits, and prime with metal primer. Spray-paint to match the decor of your bedroom.

3. Use 25-mm gutter bolts to clamp two flat metal plates together across three rods at both sides of the fence at the level of the bed frame; tighten well.

4. Use more bolts to attach the plates to the headboard brackets at the end of the frame; the brackets can be slotted to allow for adjustment.

Food storage container/Night light

You can turn a translucent plastic food storage container and an old lamp base into a decorative night light for a child's room or hallway. All you have to do is dismantle the base and cut down the spindle, reattach the socket and lamp cord, and secure the upside-down container on top with a nut and washer.

Best to use is a simply-designed lamp base with a flat top at least 75 millimetres across. To dismantle it, remove the lamp, unscrew the collar on the lampholding fitting, unscrew the locknuts clamping the wires in the fitting, and then unscrew the base of the lampholding fitting from the lamp base. Pull the electric cord out.

If your lamp spindle doesn't happen to have a threaded section at least 100 millimetres long, you can buy a threaded metal nipple at the nearest hardware store, along with two nuts and washers to fit it.

Choose a food storage container that has a snap-on or screw-lock lid. If you would prefer not to have to take the container off to reach the switch, just install a line switch on the cord. Once the night light is assembled, knot the cord just inside the base so that an accidental tug on the cord won't disconnect the wires from the socket.

Screw a 15-watt night-light bulb into the socket and snap on the upside-down container. If you prefer, embellish the top with transfers and install a line switch on the cord.

Be sure to drill vent holes in the plastic container and its lid. A 15-watt night-light bulb should provide enough illumination, but you can also use a 40-watt appliance bulb; just be sure it doesn't come too close to the top of the container, which will melt easily.

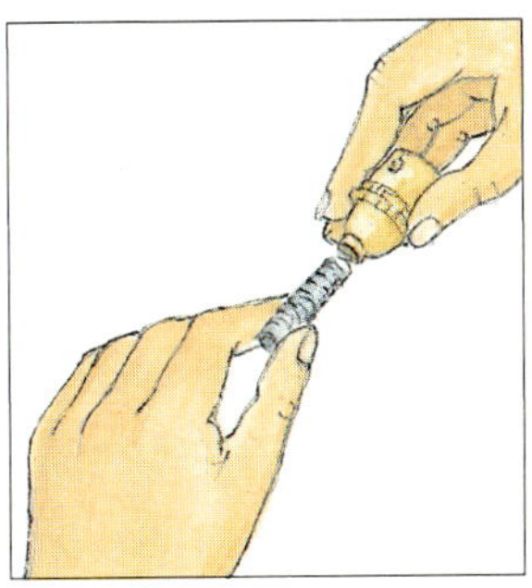

1. With a hacksaw, cut a 100-mm length from the threaded part of the nipple. Screw it into the hole in the metal base of the socket, leaving enough room for the wires that will pass through.

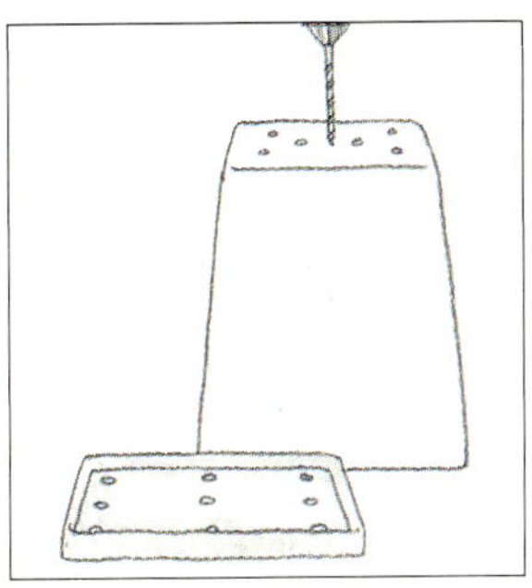

2. Drill a 10-mm hole in the centre of the lid of the food storage container, then drill four or five smaller vent holes around the edges. Drill five or six 6-mm vent holes in the bottom of the container.

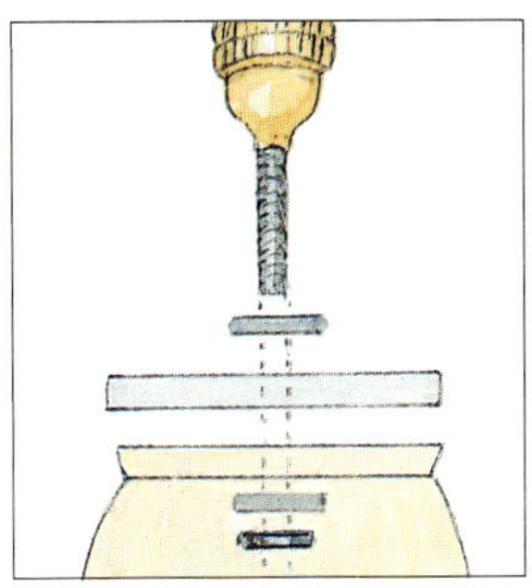

3. To assemble, push the bottom of the nipple through a washer, the upside-down lid of the food storage container, the base of the lamp and another washer. Secure with a nut.

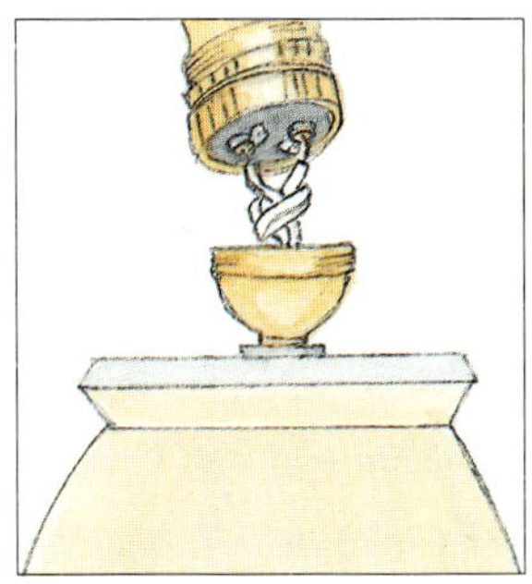

4. Push the stripped end of the electric cord through the bottom of the nipple and out the top, then connect the wires to the screws on the socket. Screw the socket together.

Freezer door/Dolly

To avoid accidents, remove the door before your dispose of an old refrigerator or freezer. Instead of carting it to the dump, put the door to good use: attach wheels and turn it into a dolly for moving heavy objects. Once you have removed the plastic shelf panel and rubber gasket from the door, all you have to do is screw on a sheet of plywood and attach four revolving casters and a rope. Then use it for moving heavy appliances such as fridges, stoves, large boxes or trunks. You can also use the dolly for ferrying several rubbish bins to the pavement at the same time.

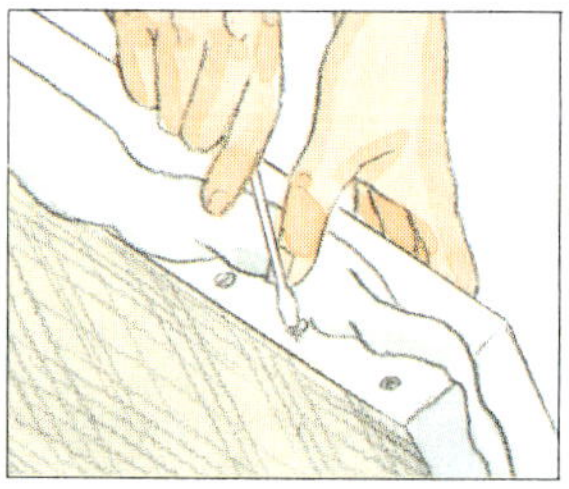

1. Remove the door handle. Unscrew and remove the rubber gasket and panel of shelves to expose the layer of insulating material and the metal frame that holds it in place.

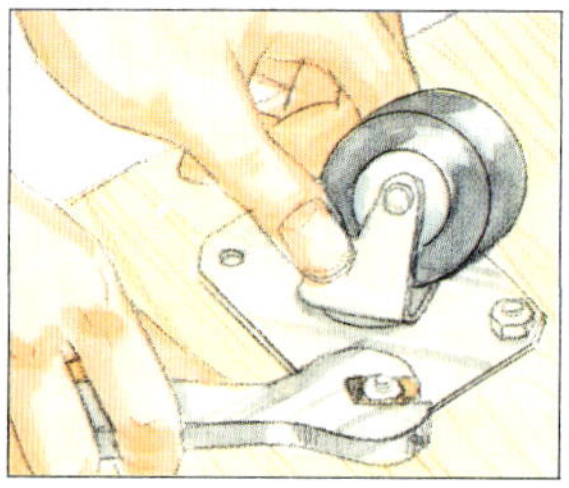

2. Cut a piece of 16-mm plywood the same size as the door. Position a caster 75 mm from each corner of the plywood and mark for drilling. Drill holes and bolt on the casters.

3. Place the plywood on the insulation side of the door, casters up, and drill holes around the edge and into the metal frame. Fasten the wood to the frame with 40-mm screws.

4. Drill 6-mm holes all the way through the plywood and door between the two front casters. Turn the dolly right side up, put 6-mm eye bolts in the holes, and tie a pull cord to the bolts.

Garden hose/Soaker hose

That leaky old garden hose that the dog has punctured can be a boon to your garden. Just drill more holes in it and use it as a soaker hose. It waters more deeply and gently than the usual spray or sprinkler – and more efficiently, as less water is lost to evaporation.

Place the hose next to plants – or, for an invisible watering system, bury it in a trench alongside. If you plan to use it to water shrubs or trees, save still more water by drilling holes only in the sections adjacent to the plants; the ground between will remain dry.

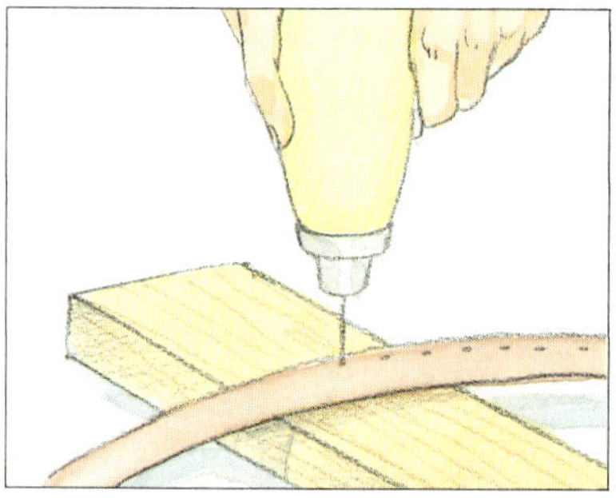

1. Place the hose on a piece of scrap wood and drill 2-mm holes all the way through, spacing them about 25 mm apart.

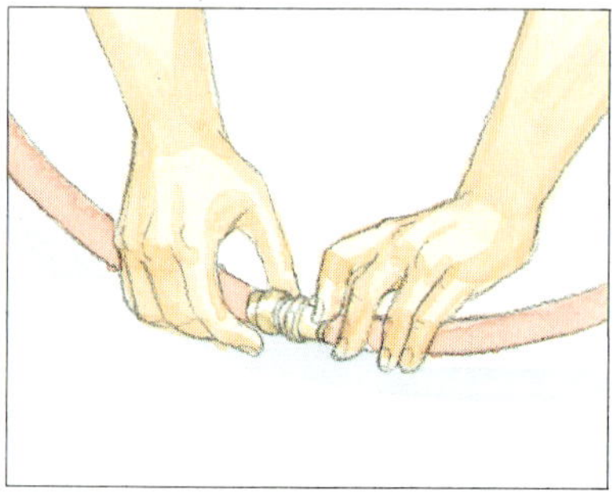

2. Attach the soaker hose to a standard hose with a plastic coupling that has two female receptors.

3. Seal off the end of the soaker hose with a plastic "stop" fitting. Place the hose next to plants you want to water or bury it in a trench alongside (don't damage roots when you dig). Adjust the water to a trickle and leave it on for 30 to 40 minutes.

Gramophone records/Planter

Do you have some old 45 rpm records gathering dust in the attic? Turn them into a novel reminder of the fifties with this blast-from-the-past planter.

You can also adapt these instructions to LP's to build a larger version. In either case, you'll need 11 records, but be sure to have plenty of extras on hand – the plastic breaks easily when drilled. Save the most nostalgic (or bizarre) titles for the four visible uprights; this project is meant to be a conversation piece after all.

Seven records – the top three of them slotted to accept the uprights – are glued together to form the base of the planter.

To make the job look neat, use a standard black silicone glue such as Bostik Car, which is sold at motor spares outlets.

Use a drill to cut the slots, moving the bit sideways along the edge of your masking-tape template. As you drill, the bit will heat up and collect plastic; push the residue off with a putty knife before it hardens.

To cut a flat edge on the uprights, first mark a deep line. Then bend the edge back and forth with flat-jaw pliers until the plastic breaks. When you cut the notches, use the side of your drill bit, cutting through the plastic as if you were using a knife.

To bend the edges of the uprights, mark deep lines exactly 144 millimetres apart. Preheat an electric curling iron for five minutes and place it against the outside of a line for 30 seconds. Then quickly align the line with the edge of a board and bend the record to a 90° angle.

Let the glue dry for at least 24 hours. Then place a saucer inside and add a potted house plant.

1. Cut a 144-mm square of cardboard, centre it exactly on a record, and mark a centred 50-mm line onto the record at each edge of the cardboard. Mark each line with a 50-mm strip of masking tape.

2. Clamp the record in a vice, protecting it with cardboard. Slowly drill along the inside edges of the tape strips with a 1,8-mm bit, using a piece of 22-mm x 96-mm plank as a brace and guide. Remove the tape.

3. Tape the record to two more, clamp them in the vice, and drill slots all the way through, using the slotted record as your guide. Smooth the inside edges of the slots with a nail file.

4. Glue all three records together, taking care to see that the slots are exactly aligned. After the glue has dried for at least eight hours, glue four more records to the bottom; let dry.

5. Select four more records and cut 4 mm off the bottom of each. Then cut a notch, about 6 mm deep, at each end of all the flat bottoms to create flanges that will fit into the slots in the base.

6. Glue two records into facing slots in the base. When the glue is dry, score the edges of the two remaining records and bend them to a 90° angle with an electric curling iron; then glue them in place.

Hangers/Renewal

Old wooden hangers – the kind with a single bar – can be transformed into colourful padded ones with a scrap of quilt batting and an easy-to-sew cover.

The puckered sleeve that fits over the hanger is usually made from silk. Sew three pieces of fabric together to make it, gathering two of them to form the decorative puckers. Finish off the hanger with a ribbon bow in a contrasting colour at the hook; you might want to tie on a small sachet as well, which will lightly perfume the whole cupboard.

The directions given here are for one standard 440-millimetre hanger.

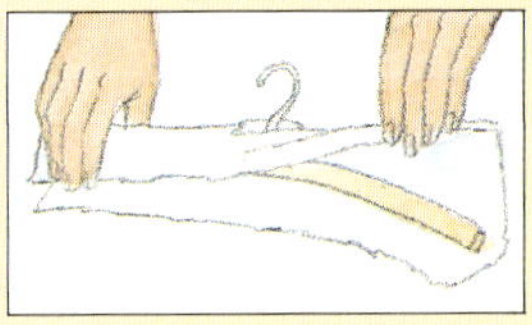

1. Cut the quilt batting to 250 mm x 450 mm. Cut an opening in the centre, stick the hook through, and wrap batting around the hanger. Secure with a basting stitch.

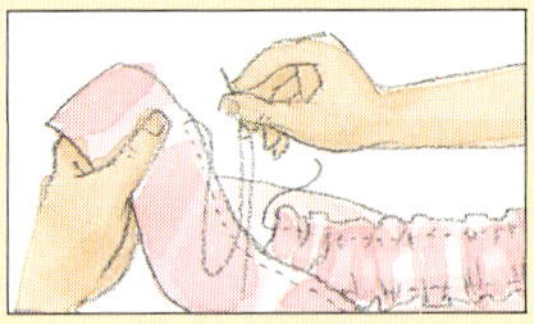

2. Cut fabric into three 125-mm-wide strips – two 300-mm-long top pieces and a 475-mm-long bottom piece. Sew a gathering stitch along the long sides of top pieces.

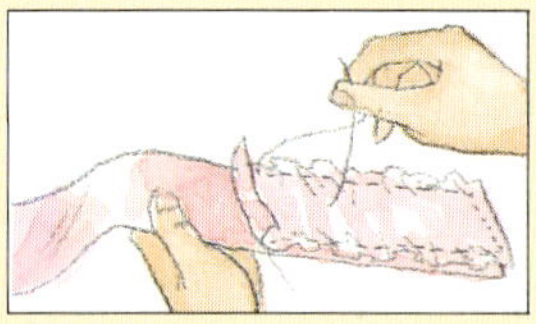

3. Lay the top pieces on the bottom piece, wrong side out. Arrange the puckers until the pieces fit together. Sew one of the top pieces to the bottom piece.

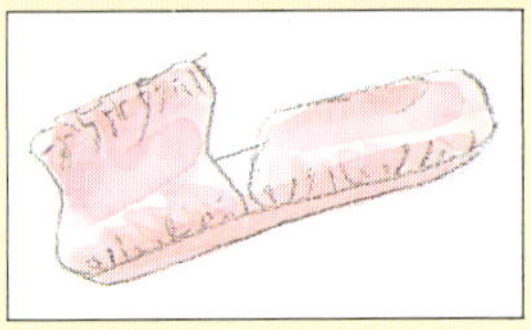

4. Sew the second top piece to the bottom, leaving most of one side open so that you can fit it over the hanger. Then turn this fabric sleeve right side out.

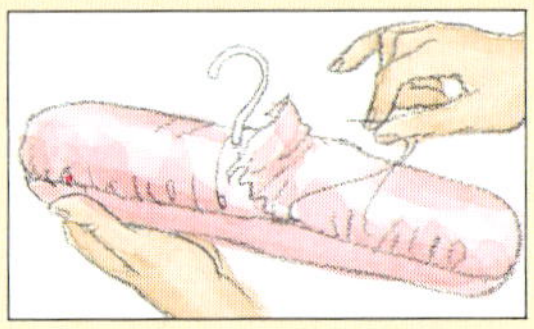

5. Gently pull the sleeve over both ends of the hanger. Hand-stitch the open side of the sleeve together. Stitch the top pieces together at the hook.

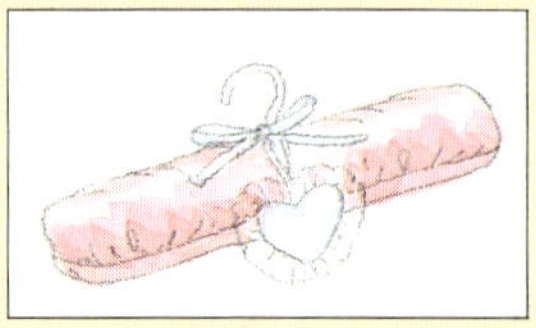

6. Tie a ribbon bow of a contrasting colour to the hook to decorate the hanger. Or, if you like, attach a small, lightly scented sachet with ribbon.

Irrigation hose/Safety barrier

You may wish to discourage cars from parking on your newly-grassed verge that you are struggling to cultivate. But in most urban areas it is illegal to erect fencing on the walkway. Firstly, one cannot obstruct pedestrian traffic, and secondly, sharp fencing poses a threat to cyclists, should they fall onto it.

Irrigation hose is frequently thrown away when new watering systems are installed. Measure your verge – you will need one metre of 25-millimetre hose for every one and a half metres. Using a section of steel piping and a two-kilogram hammer, bore holes 30 centimetres deep at intervals of one and a half metres along the edges of the grass. Be sure to ream the holes as truly vertical as possible. Slide and work one metre sections of piping into the holes.

The piping looks forbidding enough to discourage people from driving or parking on the verge – but should something collide with it, the piping will bend over harmlessly, without damaging anything.

To make the barrier show up at night, twist a turn of adhesive reflective tape (available from bicycle shops) around the top of each section.

1. Measure your verge – you will need roughly 1 m of piping for every 1,5 m of lawn, to discourage cars from intruding.

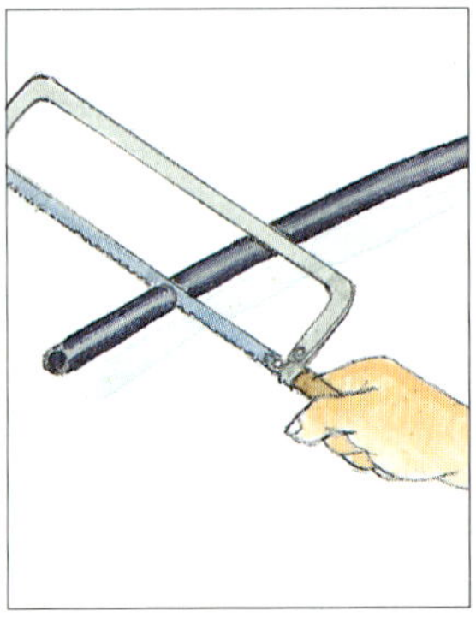

2. Peg a taut string along the line of the fence. This will make the job neat. Cut piping to length, using a hacksaw.

3. Hammer holes in the turf. Don't pierce the surface above water mains, usually in line with the water meter.

4. Work piping sections in, trim to the same height, and cap each piece of piping with a turn of reflective tape.

Lampshade/Renewal

If an old lampshade has started to become discoloured and splotched, give it a face-lift with a new fabric cover.

Don't remove the old fabric or paper from the shade – sew the new cover directly on top. To determine the amount of fabric you'll need, measure the bottom diameter of the shade and multiply by three and a half to get the length, then measure the height of the shade and add 55 millimetres to get the width.

Cut the fabric, sew it end to end, then pleat and stitch it as shown. To trim the top and bottom of the new shade, use double-fold bias binding, ribbon or braid.

1. Fold the fabric in half, wrong side out, and sew the ends together with a running stitch 12 mm from the edge. Turn the fabric right side out.

2. Place the cover over the shade and fold the top edge into pleats, securing each pleat with a straight pin. Be sure to tuck the seam into a pleat.

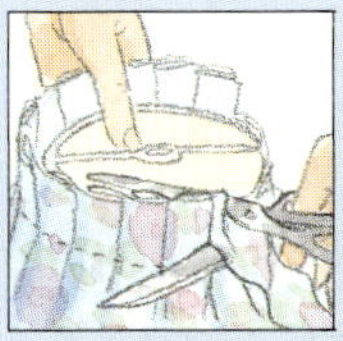

3. Remove the cover from the shade and stitch the pleats closed with a continuous running stitch 25 mm from the top edge. Remove the straight pins.

4. Pin the cover to the shade with clothes pegs, aligning the top stitch with the top edge. Then pleat the bottom. Remove and stitch 25 mm from the bottom edge.

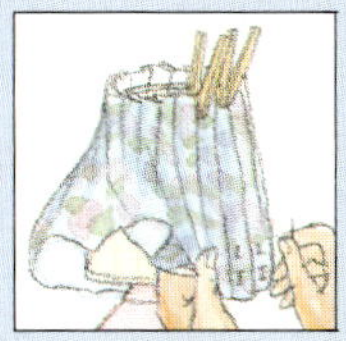

5. Again replace the cover, align the stitches with the edges of the shade, and use an overcast stitch to sew the cover to the shade. Cut off excess fabric.

6. To trim the shade and cover and conceal the stitches around the top and bottom edges, you should affix double-fold binding tape, ribbon or braid with cold glue.

Lattice/Window cover

Screen an unsightly view or filter bright sunlight with a piece of leftover wooden lattice. Edged with a wooden frame and painted to match the decor of your room, it makes an appealing change of pace from ordinary curtains or blinds.

Make the frame from 22- x 44-millimetre lengths of pine, then lock the lattice panel inside with thin strips ripped from plywood off cuts. If the cover doesn't fit snugly in the window frame, keep it in place with a couple of hooks on top and matching screw eyes on the window frame; this makes it easy to remove when you want to clean or open the window.

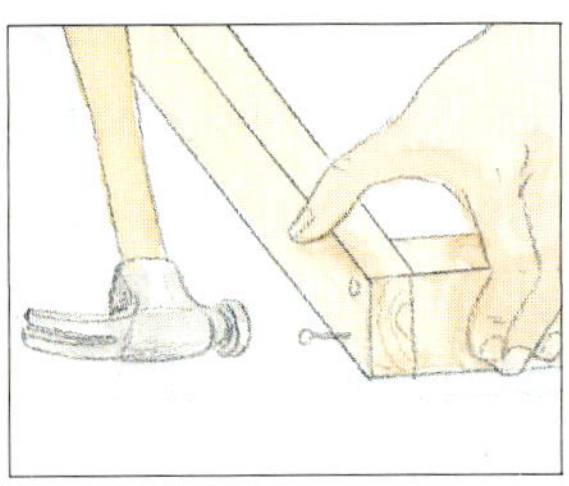

1. Measure the inside of the window and use 22- x 44-mm pine to build a frame to fit inside. Cut lattice panel to size.

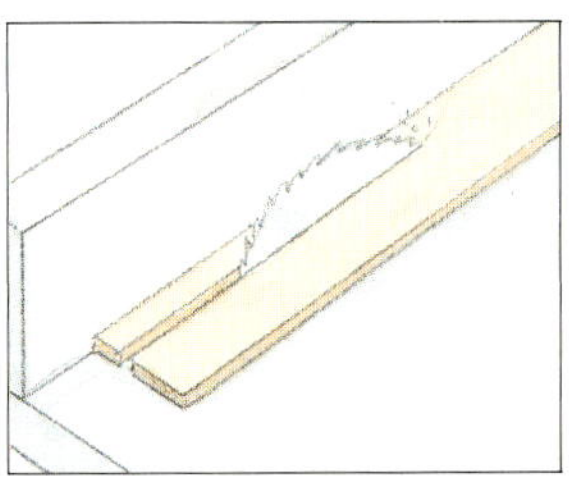

2. Rip eight thin widths of plywood off cuts to make the groove for holding the lattice in the frame.

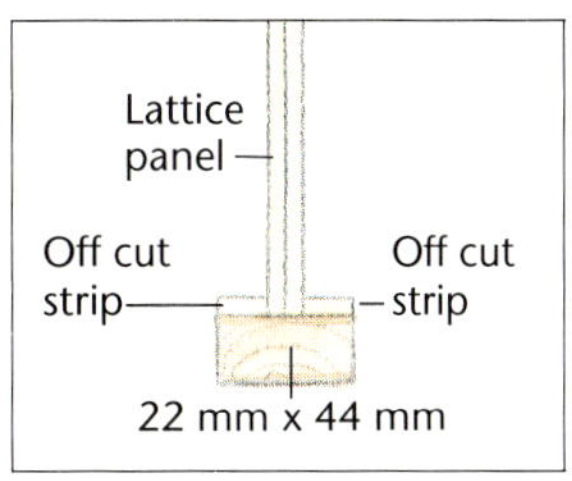

3. Nail and glue four of the strips inside the frame as shown. Insert the lattice panel and install the remaining strips.

4. Paint the window cover and attach two hooks to the top. Install matching screw eyes on the window frame.

Oil drums/Storage unit

1. Mark a large equilateral triangle on a piece of 12-mm plywood and cut it out. Stain or paint it if you like.

2. Draw a second triangle 75 mm inside the plywood base as a guideline; drill a pilot hole at the top.

3. Drill a hole in the exact centre of the bottom of a container and align it with the pilot hole.

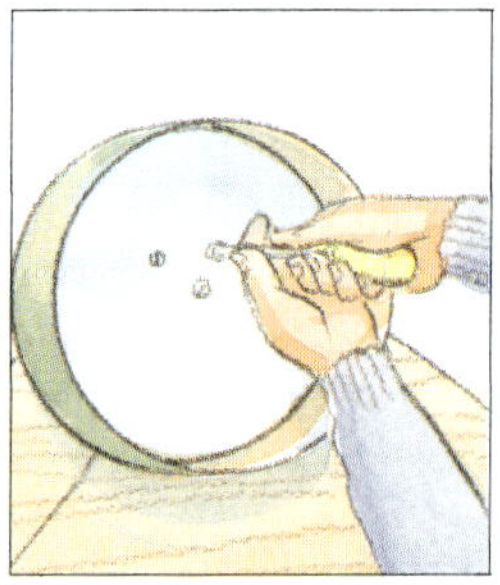

4. Attach it to the plywood with a screw and washer; place two more screws toward the point of the triangle.

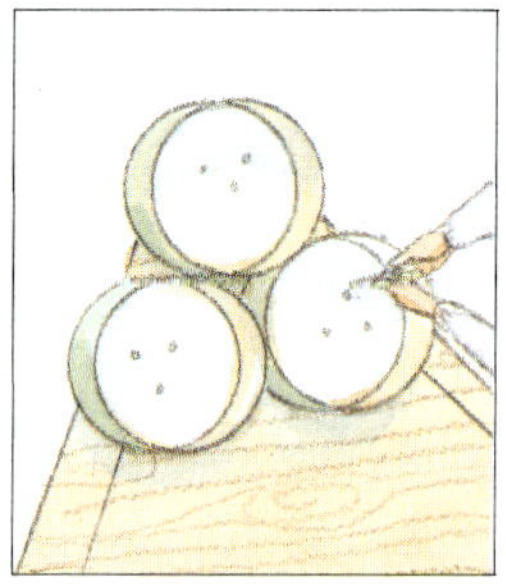

5. Position two more tins on the guideline, fitting snugly against the first. Attach them the same way.

6. Attach another row of three tins and a bottom row of four. Mount the unit to a wall with 50-mm screws.

Many people don't think twice about discarding their empty containers that could be put to good use for a variety of imaginative projects. This particular project shows that by recycling ordinary cylindrical containers you can create a storage unit which can be mounted in your garage or workshop. Quick and easy to make, it will prevent unwanted clutter.

Scout around your storage shed, garage, local hardware store or your nearest Chinese takeaway for 10 cylindrical cooking oil containers. Alternatively, ask your paint contractor or neighbours if they have any empty 25-litre paint tins.

First wash the tins thoroughly inside and out, and check that any sharp edges on their lips are pressed down so that they can't harm people or animals. Trim the lips of the tins with bookbinding tape or brown packing tape, then cover the tins with an appropriate adhesive patterned plastic shelving paper.

Then attach the tins to a triangular sheet of plywood. Make sure that you use the biggest washers you can lay your hands on, to spread the load on the base of the tin.

The dimensions naturally will vary according to the size of container used. To further strengthen the structure, pop-rivet the tins together where they touch.

When mounting the storage unit on the wall, use plastic wallplugs or an appropriate wooden dowel with a six-millimetre (No.14) screw, at least 50 millimetres long. Make sure that you use a big flat washer to spread the load evenly on the plywood.

If you intend to store very heavy objects, such as lead, iron or steel accessories in the drums, you should use steel expanding bolts to mount the unit.

HOMES FOR HENS

For another project, use square cooking oil containers to make laying boxes for hens. Clean the tins, check and trim the edges. Use one tin as a template to trace out a front door for the laying boxes on a plank of plywood at least 16 millimetres thick, or 22-millimetre pine stock about 150 millimetres wide. This can be nailed into the front of the tins, using 10-millimetre galvanized flat-headed clout nails. To make the tins easier to clean out, it can be hinged on two 50-millimetre butt hinges.

To hold the door closed on each laying box, fit a simple bolt on the top edge of each box door. The shaft slides through a hole drilled in the side of the tin.

For an even cheaper locking option, hold the door closed and drill horizontal shafts, six millimetres wide and 100 millimetres deep, through the metal and into the wood of each door. A 75-millimetre steel wire nail pushed into this hole will secure the door while the hens are a-laying. To fit a nail lock to the middle laying box of three in a row, stagger this box so that the edge is recessed or proud.

Pop-rivet the tins together, and screw or nail down the stack onto a wooden pallet, which you can often find abandoned in dumps.

Fill the boxes with straw or strips of newspaper, all of which make good compost when cleaned out and mixed with droppings.

Packing crate/Table

A rough, weather-beaten crate makes an interesting side table that fits perfectly with country-style decor. If weathered wood is not to your taste, sand and prime the crate; then paint it. Another alternative is bleaching the wood (p. 366).

Set the crate on its side to work on it. Drive in any loose nails and pull out rusty ones and replace them. Then cut a piece of 12-millimetre plywood to fit the top of the crate and nail four small plywood blocks to the underside to keep the top from shifting (you should place them just close enough to the edge to fit inside the crate).

Use a piece of hessian to make a no-sew tablecloth to complement your rustic table. Then, depending on its height and shape, top the table with a lamp and use it as a side table or place it in front of a couch as a coffee table with an arrangement of dried flowers.

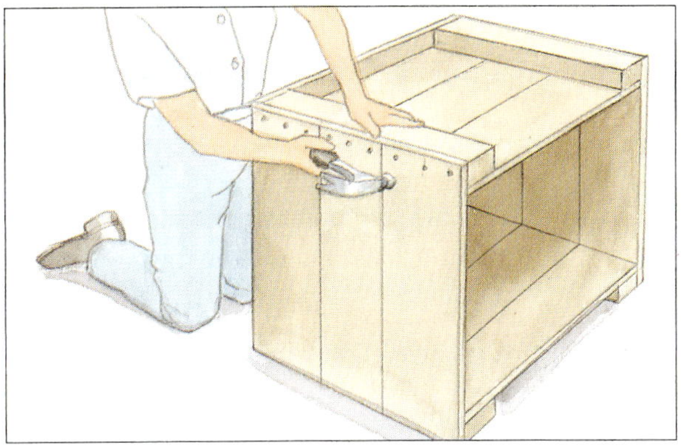

1. Hose down the crate; if necessary, use a scrubbing brush to remove dirt or peeling paint. Hammer raised nailheads into the wood and sand any rough corners that might snag carpeting.

2. Cut a piece of 12-mm plywood to fit the outside dimensions of the top of the crate. Then glue and nail small plywood blocks to the underside of the top.

3. Cut a piece of hessian or country-print heavy cotton fabric to fit the top. For a still more rustic look, pull several threads off the edges of the fabric to create a fringe on all four sides. Place the hessian over the table at an angle for best effect.

Packing crate/Bunny cage

Do you want to build a sturdy, dog-proof home for your children's pet rabbit, hamster or other small domestic animal? Ask a motor spares dealer or hardware dealer for a wooden crate – one made from low-quality, but highly durable waterproof plywood.

1. Measure and cut a sturdy plank the exact inside height of the open end of the crate, and nail this across to divide the open end vertically.
2. Nail another plank horizontally between this plank and the right-hand wall of the cage.
3. Using 10-mm U-shaped saddle nails, fix galvanized 25-mm chicken wire (for rabbits), or 10-mm mesh (for hamsters, white mice or rats) over the large opening and the upper of the two smaller ones.
4. Nail together a door frame to fit the lower right (or left) opening. Cover this with mesh. Using pliers, cut loops of coat hanger wire and hinge the cover on the cross strut above the small opening. Use the same wire to make a catch to secure the door to a saddle nail nailed into the base of the crate.
5. With 10-mm galvanized clout nails, fix an off cut of tar-paper or black plastic sheeting to the top for a waterproof roof.

You should place the cage on levelled bricks or cement blocks to keep it off the ground. If dogs are a problem, you could try raising the cage onto a stand nailed together from packing crate off cuts.

Wood bleaching/Technique

Stripping a piece of furniture will lighten it, but bleaching will make the wood look still fresher. This simple technique can transform a chair, picture frame or an entire room of panelling.

Wood is best bleached with hydrogen peroxide, which will do minimal damage to the wood. The action can be stopped using a 1:1 mixture of white vinegar and water. Whatever kind you choose, be sure to read the instructions carefully and wear rubber gloves and old clothing when you brush it on. The key to a good bleaching job is removing all the old finish. To test, wet the wood with water after you have stripped it. If the wood darkens evenly, it will bleach to an overall uniform colour; any areas that remain light must be stripped again.

Once the wood dries after the first application, it should be lighter. To make it lighter still, apply the solution two or three more times. But don't overdo it – after about four or five applications the wood may start to look grey and lifeless. If this happens, you can improve its appearance by wiping on a light stain to highlight the grain.

Protect the work area with newspapers covered with plastic refuse bags. Use an old brush to apply an even coat of bleach to the wood.

Paper towel tubes/Serviette rings

For some terrific-looking serviette rings, cut up paper towel tubes and cover them with fabric, bias binding or yarn. Children love to make the simpler ones, embellishing them with discarded costume jewellery or dried flowers. When you cut the tubes, take care not to mash the cylinder out of shape.

GATHERED FABRIC

Gather or pleat the fabric as you stitch little sleeves. These are sewn on only one end: if you prefer, you can cut the fabric in half lengthways and stitch both ends.

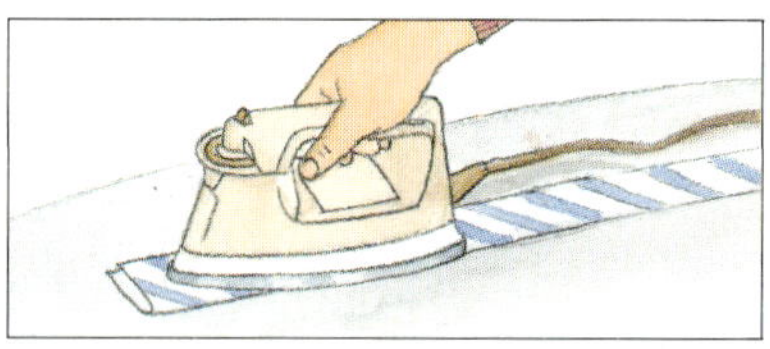

1. Cut a 50- x 225-mm piece of fabric, fold it in half lengthways, and press with an iron.

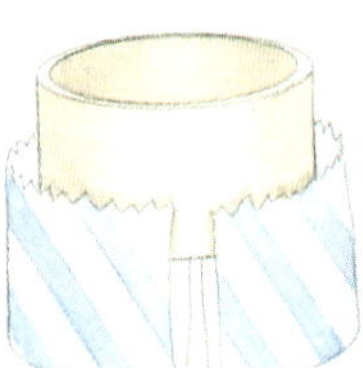

2. Cut a 37-mm section of paper towel tube with a single-edged razor blade and insert it into the fold.

3. Sew the cut edges of the fabric, gathering it as you go. Knot the last stitch and trim off the excess fabric.

BIAS BINDING

For a party, wrap each section of paper towel tube with a different bright colour.

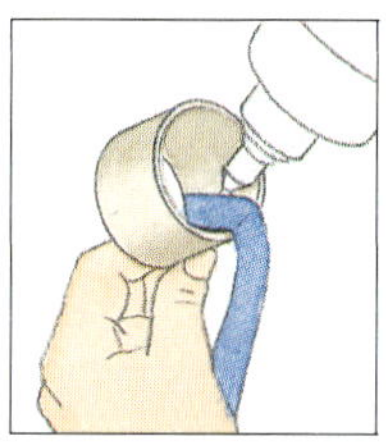

1. Glue a 1,25-m strip of bias binding inside the cylinder at a slight angle.

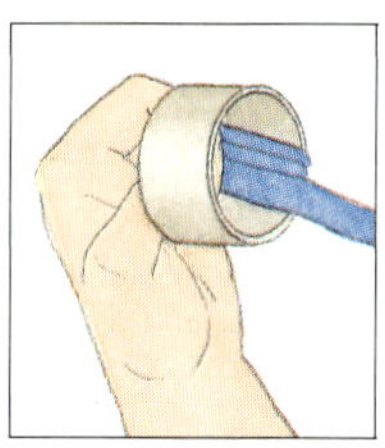

2. Wind the bias binding around the cylinder, slanting it slightly and overlapping half of each previous turn as you go.

3. Secure the last turn with a few stitches and attach a bauble to cover the thread.

YARN OR STRING

To make a slender row of knots at one edge of these serviette rings, wind to the left and tuck to the right (or vice versa). You should use a 1,25-m length of doubled yarn or string.

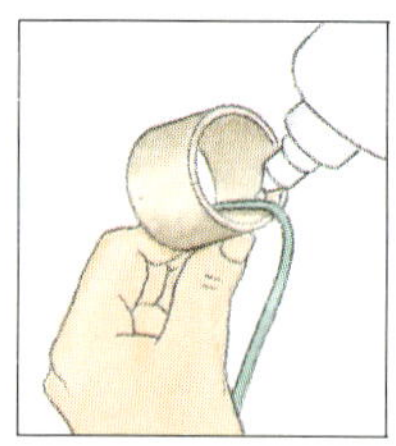

1. Glue the end of the doubled yarn to the inside of the cylinder and let the glue set. Begin winding over the top and up again.

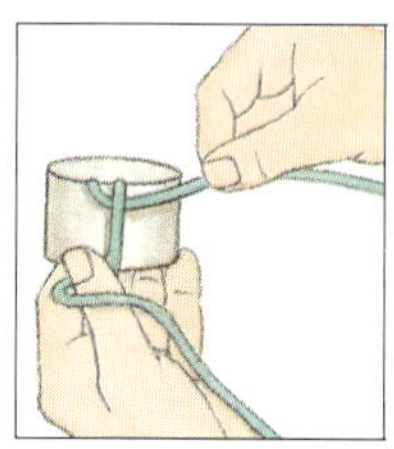

2. At each top turn, tuck the yarn under the previous loop and pull it out all the way. Continue winding to the left and tucking to the right.

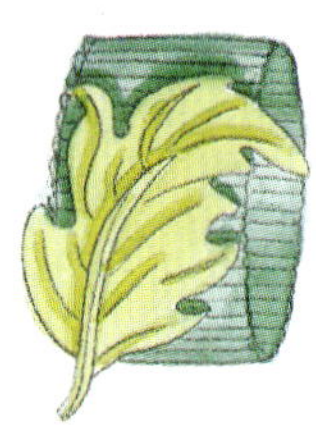

3. When you've covered the whole cylinder, sew down the last few loops with several stitches. Then decorate with jewellery.

Picket fence/Garden trellis

When you replace an old picket fence, save a section or two to use as a garden trellis. Lashed together to form an A-frame, two sections provide climbing space – and in hot climates, welcome shade – for beans, peas, tomatoes and cucumbers. Or you can attach one horizontal section to a planter box and use it on a patio or deck for climbing roses or jasmine.

A-FRAME TRELLIS

Use two equal sections of fencing to construct this simple trellis. If you don't want to bolt them together, try securing them with wire.

1. Cut two sections of fence (from 1,2 to 2,4 m), so that the rails extend about 50 mm beyond the pickets at each end. Then position the two sections to form an A-frame, positioning them so that the rails are flush against each other.

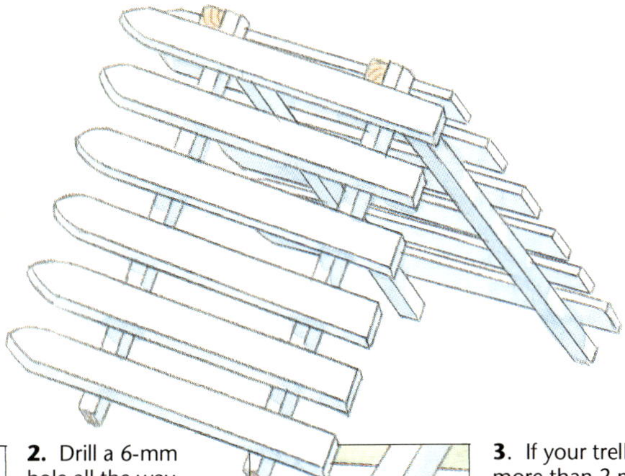

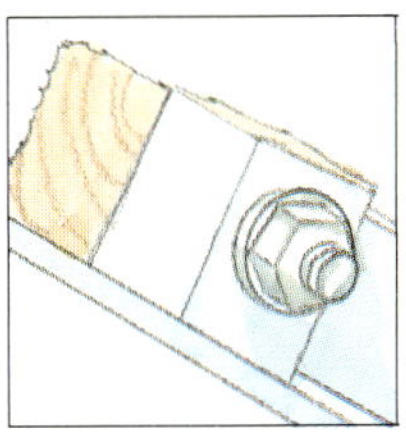

2. Drill a 6-mm hole all the way through the joined rails and fasten them together with 6-mm bolts; secure with nuts and washers.

3. If your trellis is more than 2 m high, anchor it by driving four wooden stakes in the ground and nailing the four rails to them.

PLANTER BOX TRELLIS

Use an existing planter box or make your own from any 22-mm x 297-mm stock (waterproof the wood first). Just be sure that the box is slightly longer than the section of fence you plan to use for the trellis.

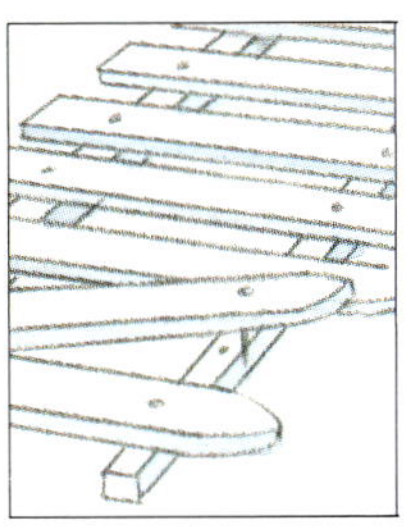

1. Cut a section of fence and pry off the bottom two pickets. For a uniform look, saw the pointed ends off. Sand rough areas and paint with several coats of exterior paint.

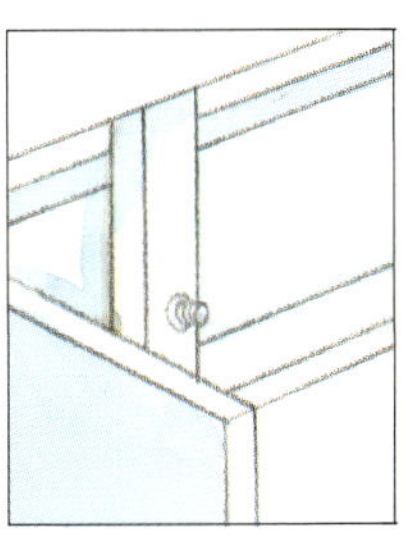

2. Position the exposed rails at the back of the box and drill 6-mm holes. Attach the fence with 6-mm bolts and fill the box with soil to keep it from tipping over.

Sanding/Technique

Are you having trouble sanding the various curves and crevices on a piece of furniture? Several common household items can become simple sanding aids.

TAPE

To make a sanding strip, cut a strip of duct, insulation or masking tape 150 millimetres longer than the sandpaper, and centre it on the back of the paper along one edge. Fold the extra tape over the grit side as handles, then cut the sandpaper to the width of the tape.

PLAYING CARDS

For hard-to-reach grooves or drawer tracks, use a deck of playing cards as a sanding block. Wrap the sandpaper around the deck, then push the edge of the deck against the irregular object you want to sand; your playing card "block" will take on the shape.

BLACKBOARD DUSTER

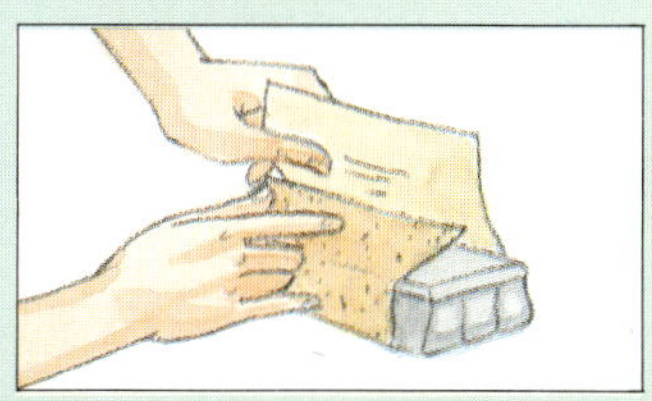

Wrap sandpaper around a blackboard duster when you sand large flat areas.

Picture frame/Serving tray

Old picture frames can become elegant and unusual trays in your home. Convert a large one to accommodate an entire coffee service. Or turn smaller frames into individual appetiser and dessert trays.

A piece of hardboard makes a sturdy bottom for your tray; top it with a thin sheet of cork. Or, for a more decorative tray, cover the hardboard with fabric and then with the original glass. Protect against seepage by running a bead of silicon sealer around the inside of the frame before putting the glass in place. You can use 25-millimetre brads to hold the hardboard in the frame. When you squeeze the brads in place, be sure to protect the frame with some cardboard. Finally, line the bottom of the tray with felt or another sheet or cork so that it won't scratch the surface of your table.

1. Remove the picture, glass and cardboard backing. Then cut a piece of 6-mm hardboard the same size as the backing. Or measure the interior length and width of the rabbet in the frame.

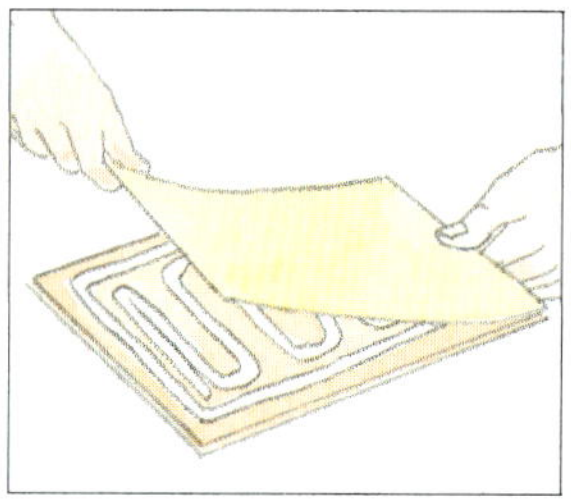

2. Glue a slightly larger sheet of cork to the top of the hardboard. Then, when the glue is completely dry, use a sharp utility knife to carefully trim the edges of the cork flush with the hardboard.

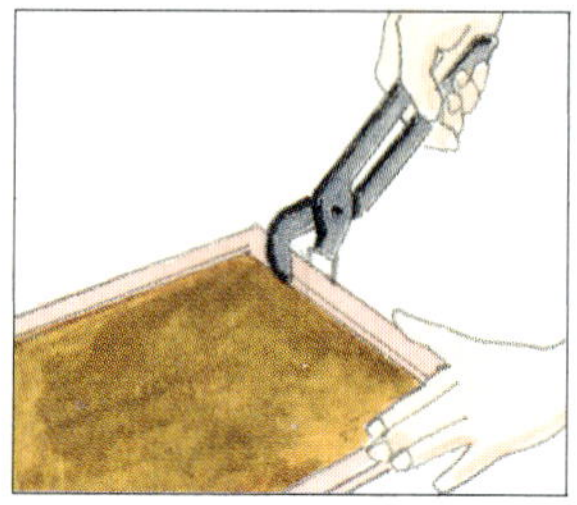

3. Mount the hardboard in the frame, cork side toward the front, and use locking-grip pliers to squeeze 25-mm brads into the frame at a slight angle. Put cardboard in the pliers' jaws to protect the frame.

4. Use a small hammer to tap down the protruding parts of the brads so that they hold the hardboard in place. Then line the bottom of the tray with a piece of felt or cork to prevent scratches.

Pill bottles/Spice rack

Save your glass or plastic pill bottles, especially the brown-tinted ones; they make perfect containers for dried herbs and spices. The ones shown here are chemist-type bottles, 45 millimetres across, like those that many vitamins come in. The rack, custom-built to hold eight of them, is made of 22- x 220-millimetre pine; if your carpentry skills are sufficient, you could use stinkwood or another hardwood. Stain or paint the rack as you like, or simply apply a wipe-on oil finish to the sanded wood. Or give the rack an interesting stippled look with a sponging technique.

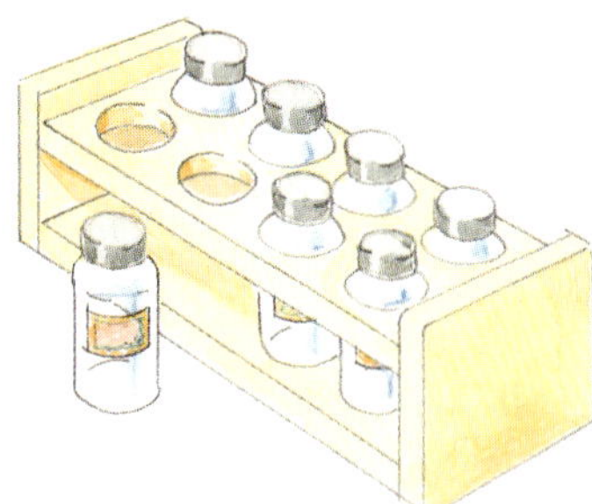

Adjust the size and position of the holes to accommodate the size of your bottles. The holes here measure 50 millimetres and the centres of each are 35 millimetres from the sides of a 250- x 130-millimetre plank. The four inside hole centres are 95 millimetres in from the ends of the boards. Cut the holes with a drill-mounted hole saw.

Wash the pill bottles thoroughly and make sure they're completely dry before you fill them with spices. Label each bottle with an adhesive file label, lettering it decoratively, or soak off the printed labels from old spice bottles in your kitchen.

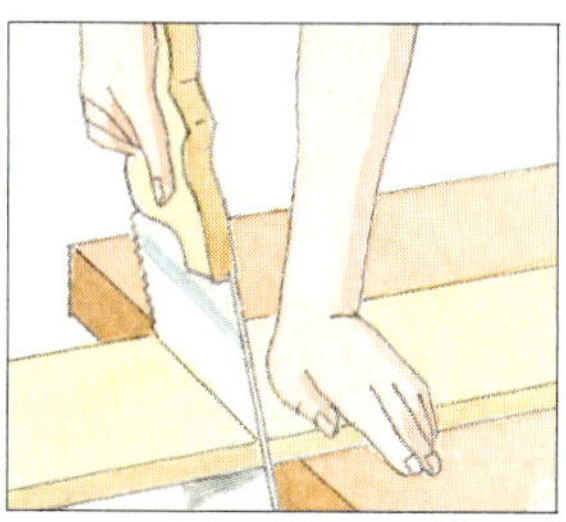

1. To construct the rack, cut two 250-mm lengths and two 105-mm lengths of 22- x 220-mm pine stock or a hardwood such as oak or stinkwood.

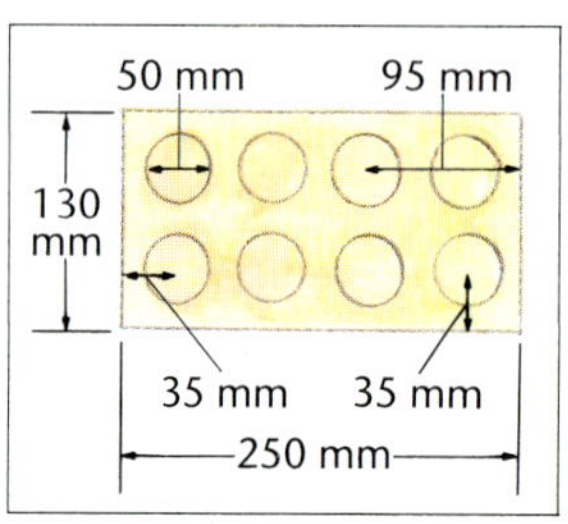

2. Mark the exact centres for eight holes on one of the 250-mm boards, taking care to space the holes evenly from the ends and sides.

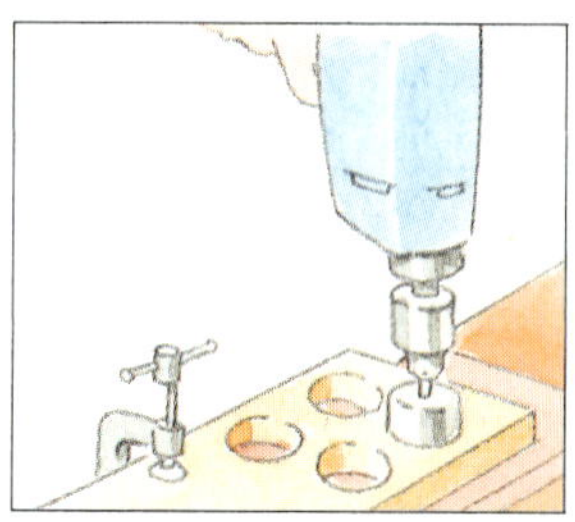

3. Clamp the board down on a piece of scrap wood. Use a hole saw to bore holes which are slightly larger than the diameter of your pill bottles.

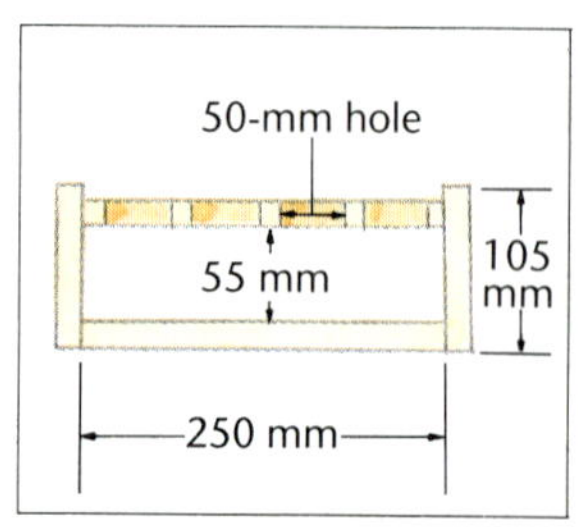

4. Assemble the rack with glue and oval wire nails, taking care to see that the nails do not protrude into the holes. Finish the wood as desired.

Quilt/Place mats

When an old quilt is worn beyond repair, cut out the undamaged sections and use them as place mats and pot holders. It's simply a matter of stitching extra-wide double-band bias binding around the edges.

For a set of place mats, you'll need quilted sections about 300 x 450 millimetres. To determine the length of bias binding you need for the edging, measure the perimeter of the piece and add 75 millimetres. Make pot holders 250 millimetres square; add 200 millimetres to the bias binding – enough to make a hanger hook.

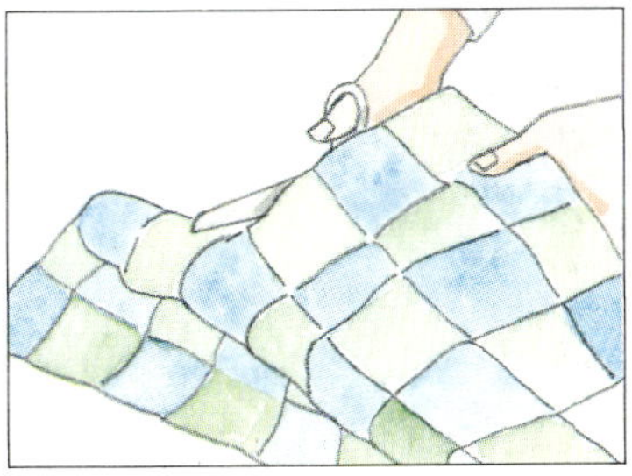

1. Cut out an undamaged section of quilt and measure the perimeter. Cut extra-wide double-band bias binding to the measurement, adding 75 mm for a place mat and 200 mm for a pot holder.

2. Unfold the bias binding at one end and stitch a 12-mm hem. Align the outside edge of the unfolded bias binding with the edge of the fabric and pin it down. Stitch the bias binding to the fabric along the first crease.

3. Pin and stitch the bias binding to the other three sides, one side at a time. Mitre the corners as you go. Then fold the end of the bias binding under and stitch a 12-mm hem. Remove the straight pins.

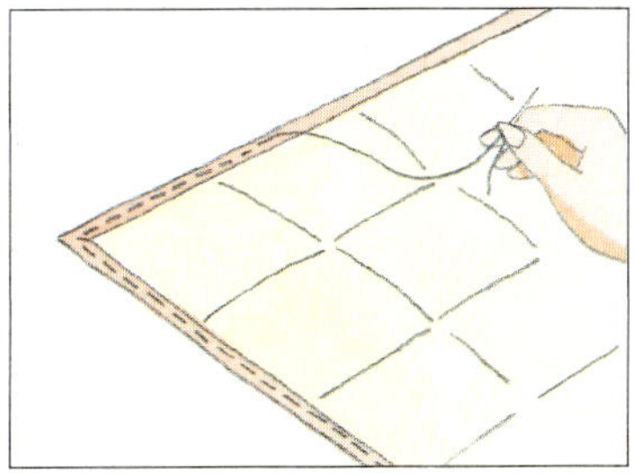

4. Fold the bias binding over the edge of the fabric so that there is a double fold of bias binding on the underside of the place mat. Sew it to the underside with a running stitch exactly down the middle of the fold.

Sponging/Technique

All it takes is a sponge (natural – not synthetic) and some acrylic paints to give an attractive stippled pattern to anything from a wooden spice rack (left) to a living room wall. (Remember that dishes are off-limits, however, unless you intend only to display them in a cupboard or on the wall.)

Start by choosing two or three colours that look good together – one for the base coat and another one or two for the sponged-on glaze. The base coat should be the lightest.

To keep the stipples neat and uniform, be sure to thin the glaze by mixing one part paint with two parts paint thinner or solvent. The more thinner you use, the lighter the glaze will be.

1. Choose a colour for the base coat that is lighter than the glaze. Paint it on and let it dry thoroughly.

2. Cut a sponge into 50- x 50-mm pieces. Drench a piece with the thinned glaze and squeeze out the excess.

3. Lightly dab the glaze onto the surface, rewetting the sponge often. After each application, dab the paint with a dry sponge.

4. When the paint is dry, spray it with a clear glaze or paint with matt-finish polyurethane to seal the surface.

Ribbons/Bag

Weave some old ribbons together to create a piece of silky material. Then, after lining the back, turn it into a one-of-a-kind clutch bag.

Hardly any sewing is involved; instead, weave the ribbons directly on top of a 300- x 475-millimetre piece of fusible interfacing, pinning the ends as you go. Then press with a hot iron. The work will tend to proceed even more smoothly if you place the interfacing on a padded surface, such as a folded towel or a clean scatter rug. Once you've lined the material and folded it into a bag, attach a press stud, catch or button and loop to keep it closed.

1. Cut enough 450-mm lengths of ribbon to measure 275 mm across when placed side by side. Pin both ends to the interfacing.

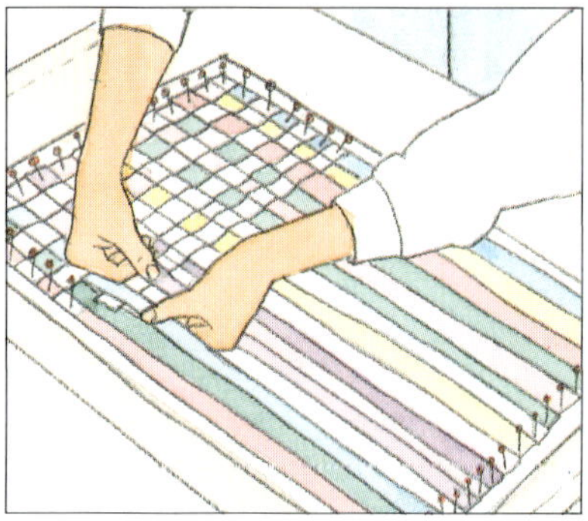

2. Cut several 275-mm ribbons and weave them through, pushing them tight and pinning each end as you go.

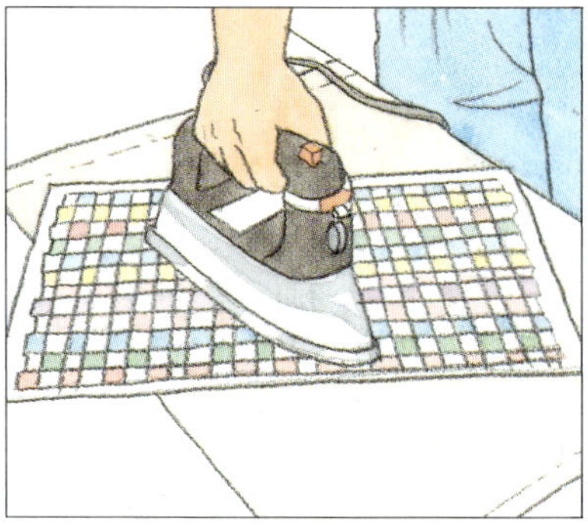

3. Remove the pins and fuse the ribbons to the interfacing with a hot iron. Then trim the material to 250 mm x 425 mm.

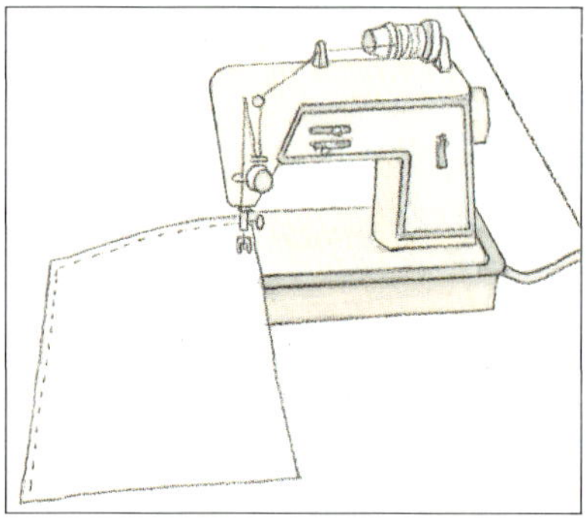

4. Turn the piece ribbon-side down on a 270-mm x 445-mm piece of lining fabric. Stitch around three sides as shown.

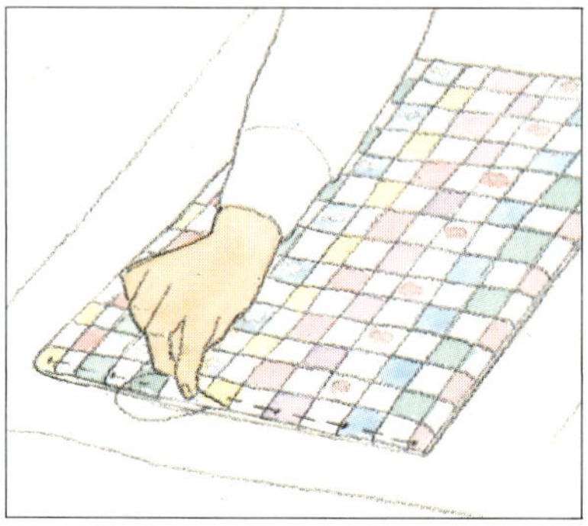

5. Turn the pieces right side out and stitch the fourth side by turning down the edge with a 6-mm seam.

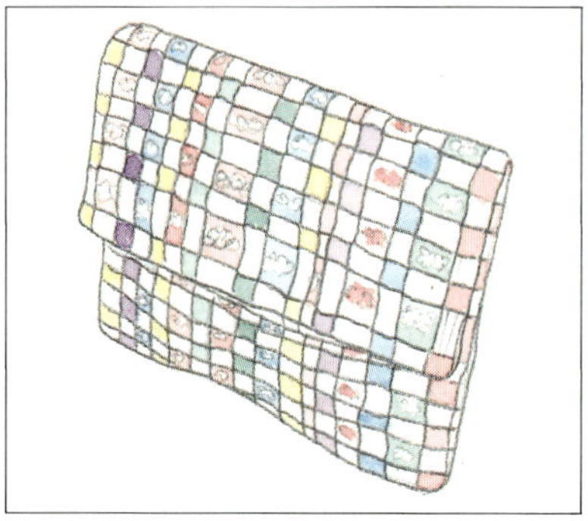

6. To make a bag, fold one end up 137 mm and stitch the edges to the lining. Fold the top flap over and sew on a catch.

Road maps/Paper trim

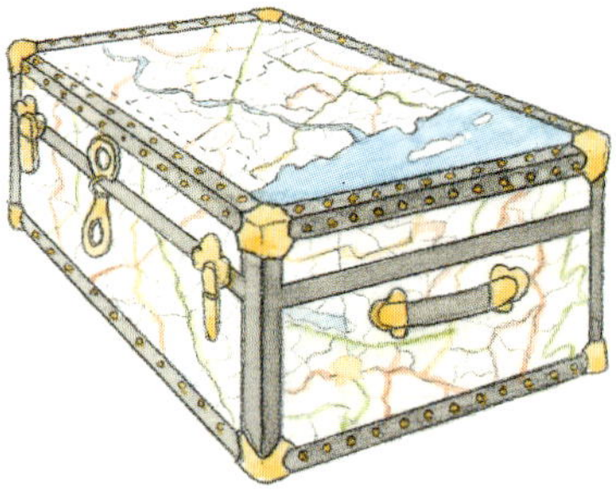

The most eye-catching paper for covering boxes, trunks or small wall areas may already be stashed away in your cupboard or store-room – old road maps! Once you've bought some vinyl paste and sizing for wallpaper, you'll find the paper is almost as easy to apply as the adhesive plastic sold

1. Thoroughly clean the surface to be covered and use a wide brush to prime it with wallpaper sizing. Let the sizing dry for at least three hours.

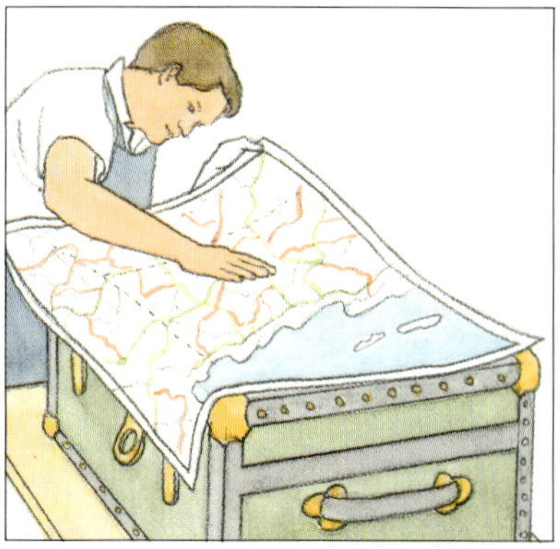

3. Position a sheet on the work surface, paste-side down, and use your hands to slowly smooth it from the centre toward the edges to prevent air bubbles.

in stores, especially if you let it lie flat for a while and press out the creases with a warm iron.

Road maps aren't the only material you can use for this decorative technique. Be imaginative and try navigation charts, vintage magazine covers – even sheet music.

Remember, however, that some paper is so thin that even a new razor blade can't trim it without fraying the edges. If this is the case, paste the paper down and let it dry properly before you start trimming (before the paste dries, use your fingernail to make an outline of the area to be cut).

If the surface you are about to cover has a pattern that might show through your cover, give it a coat or two of white paint and let it dry before priming with the sizing.

2. Spread vinyl paste onto the back of the paper with a small roller or paste brush. Temporarily fold the pasted sides of large sheets together until you need them.

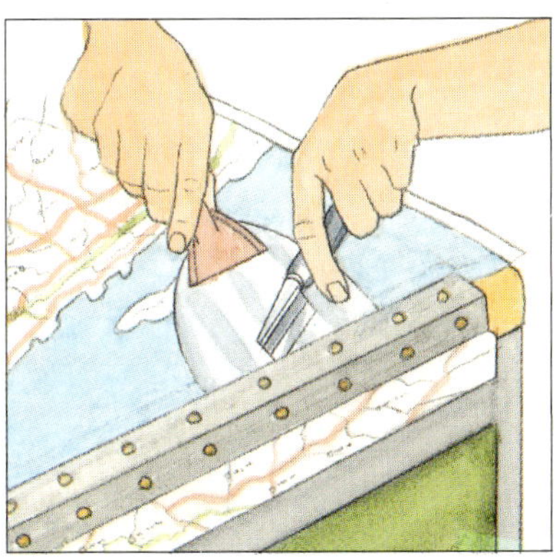

4. Trim the paper with a single-edged razor blade, using a wide putty knife as a guide. If the paper tears easily, wait until it is dry before trimming.

Cloth painting/Technique

Fabric paints, sold at craft stores and hobby shops, enable you to give new life to old T-shirts, jeans or tackies you might otherwise throw away. Paint colourful designs or emblazon the clothes with your name. Or use the paints to give your own touch to the ribbons you use for a handmade bag (p.370) or a table runner and serviettes (p.374).

These steps show you how to paint a piece of clothing. To decorate canvas tackies, make cardboard patterns of your designs and trace them onto the shoes with a pencil. Then fill in the designs with the fabric paints.

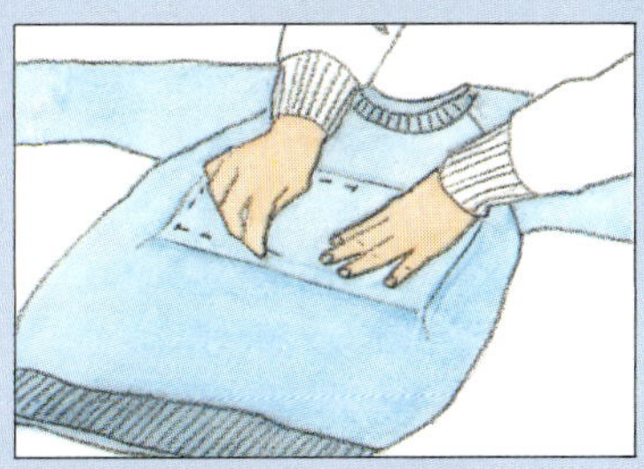

1. Insert a stiff piece of cardboard beneath the area to be painted and pin the corners to the cloth. Leave the cardboard in place as you sketch and paint your design.

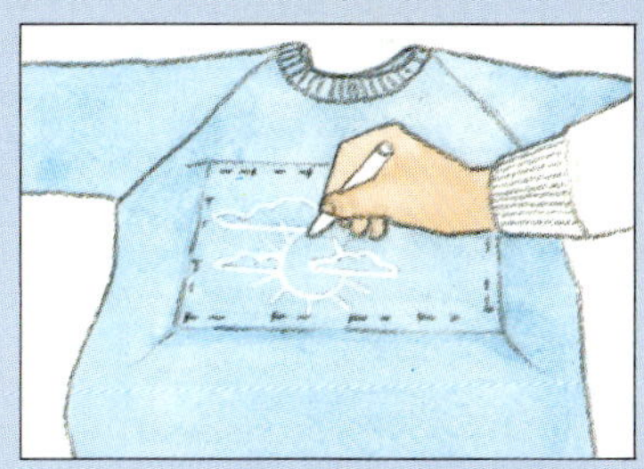

2. Use a piece of chalk to sketch out your design – white chalk for dark fabrics and coloured chalk for lighter colours and whites. Erase mistakes by rubbing lightly with a damp cloth.

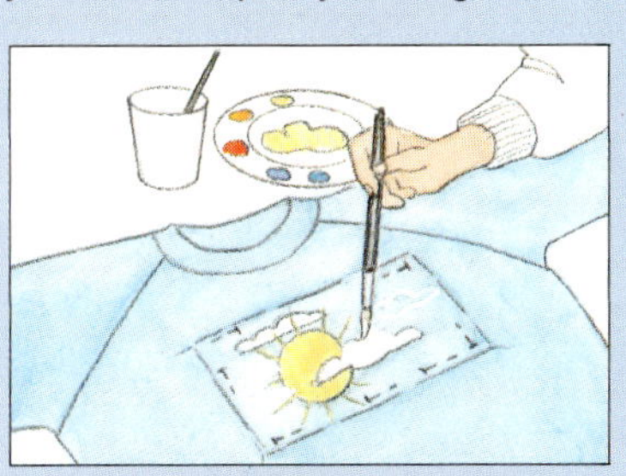

3. Paint your design with the fabric paints, using brushes of several different sizes for variety in strokes and shapes. Apply the paint sparingly and let it dry for at least 12 hours.

4. Remove cardboard, turn fabric wrong side out, and place a towel under the painted area. Press the wrong side of the painting with an iron at its hottest fabric setting.

Rolling pin/Key keeper

What to do with an old, battered rolling pin? Make a bracket of scrap wood and create a revolving bulletin board, of course. Mounted on the wall and adorned with a few cup hooks, paper clamps and alligator clips, it makes an ingenious board for your various keys, business cards and messages.

The bracket consists of a baseboard and two arms with 25-millimetre holes for the rolling pin handles. Use any scrap wood you have on hand and make it as decorative as you like: bevel the front edges of the arms with a rasp or a saw and incorporate a few scrolls and turns – or even some hand carving – into the entire piece. Drill and countersink for four screws to hold the pieces together.

Another idea is to saw grooves into the rolling pin itself. With your table saw set at 30°, the grooves will be angled downward to hold business or calling cards. Regular grooves, sawn both horizontally and vertically on the pin, can form a decorative pattern of squares in which you can centre the cup hooks and other holders. But be sure to use a fence to ensure that the grooves are as straight as possible.

Before you assemble the unit, stain or paint the bracket – and the rolling pin if you like (be aware, however, that the stains are not likely to match) – and apply two light coats of matt-finish polyurethane. Or try "pickling" the rolling pin and the bracket (p.373) for a still more interesting look.

Use screws to mount the unit to wall studs in a place where it will be seen often – near the back door or next to the phone.

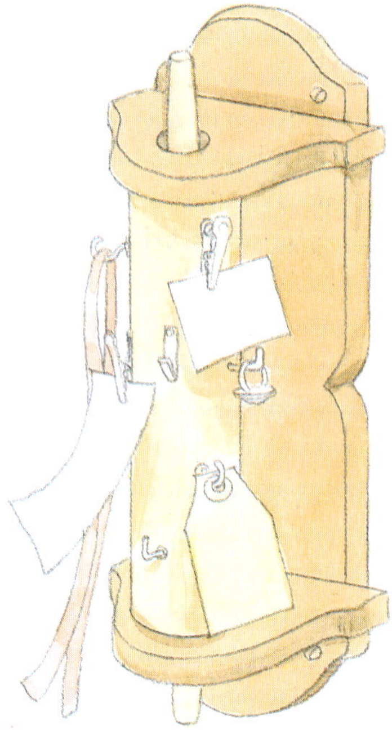

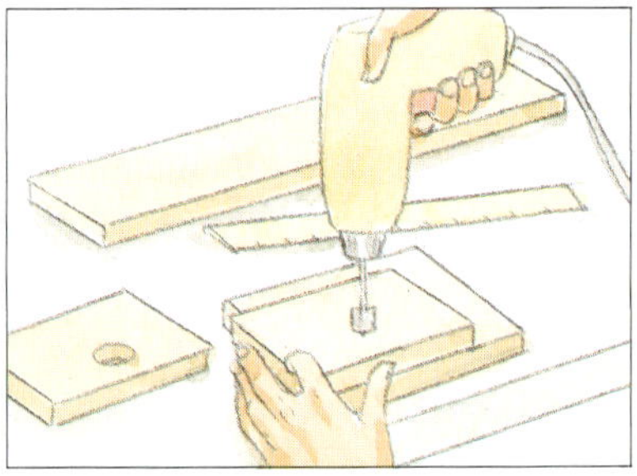

1. From a piece of 22-mm pine, cut a baseboard about 100 x 400 mm (or 25 mm longer than the length of your rolling pin). From the same stock, cut two 100- x 125-mm arms and drill a 25-mm hole centred about 37 mm from the long edge of each.

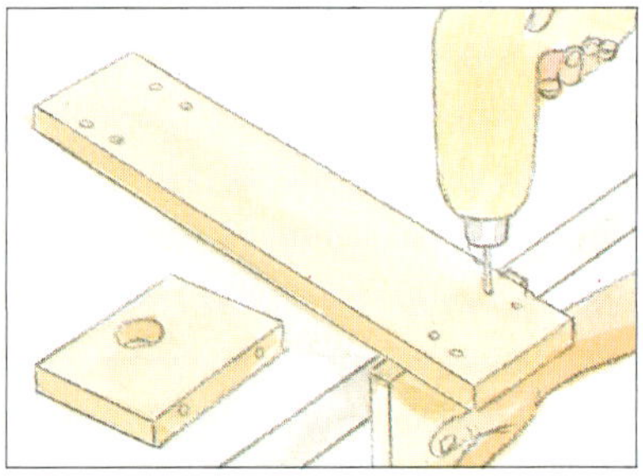

2. Drill and countersink two pilot holes at each end of the baseboard for the screws that will attach the unit to a wall. Position the arms and drill two pilot holes for screws through the baseboard into each arm.

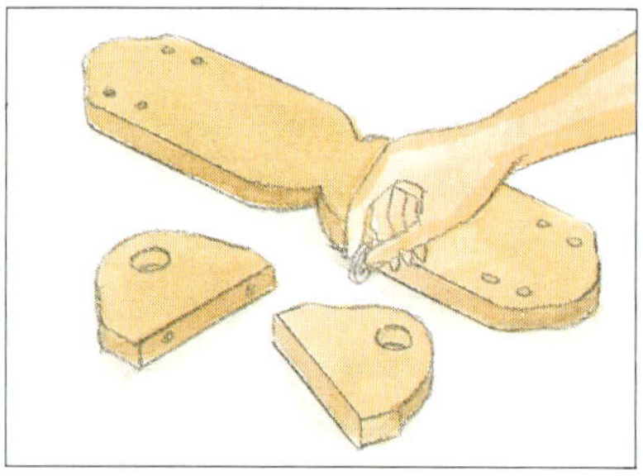

3. Bevel the edges of the wood; shape and decorate as you like. Sand and stain, then apply two coats of polyurethane, sanding lightly between coats. Glue a fibre washer to the hole in the lower arm so that the rolling pin will rotate more easily.

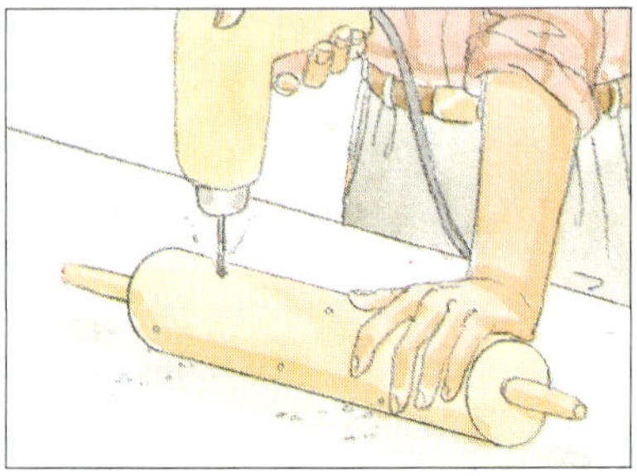

4. Predrill several holes for the cup hooks and screws on all sides of the rolling pin. Screw in the cup hooks and screws and hang paper clamps from the protruding screw heads. Attach alligator clips with smaller screws.

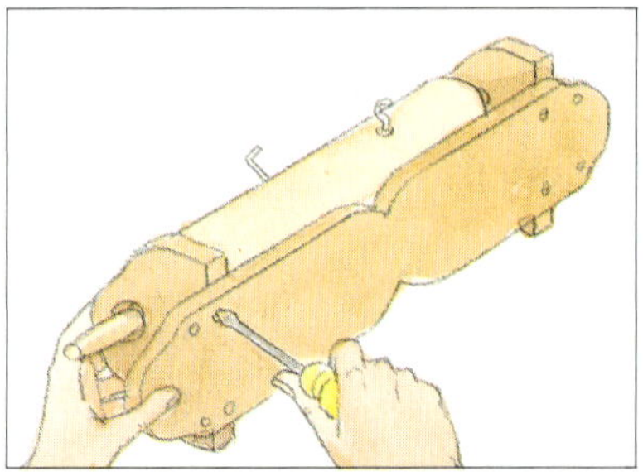

5. Attach the upper arm to the base from behind with flathead screws. Insert the top handle of the rolling pin through the hole, then place the lower arm over the bottom handle and attach with screws as shown.

6. Choose a spot in the kitchen or near the back door. Hold the unit against the wall at eye level and mark the positions of the holes on the wall, then drill for screws of suitable length. Fit to wall with plastic screw plugs.

Salad bowls/Bird feeder

Glass or wooden salad bowls of two different sizes make a clever bird feeder that has the added advantage of thwarting squirrels or other small animals. No feeder is entirely animal-proof, of course, but the slippery roof of this one makes it harder for furry thieves to reach the seed.

The two bowls, one of them upside down, are joined with a threaded rod and secured with nuts and washers. (For glass bowls, drill with a carbon-tipped glass or masonry bit.) To hang the feeder, bend the top of the rod into a hook (allow a few centimetres for the hook when you put the first nut in place) or attach a lamp hook with a nut.

The kinds of birds you attract depend on the positions of the bowls. Leave plenty of space between the bowls to attract large birds, or place them close together to limit the feed to smaller visitors.

1. Choose a large bowl as a roof and another about half the size, as a feeder. Drill a 6-mm hole through the centre of each, using scrap wood as backing.

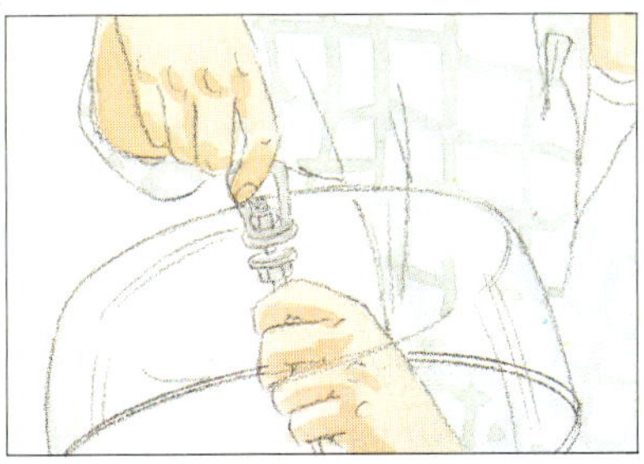

2. Place a nut near the end of a threaded rod, add a flat washer, and insert the rod through the inside of the large bowl. Secure with another washer and nut on top.

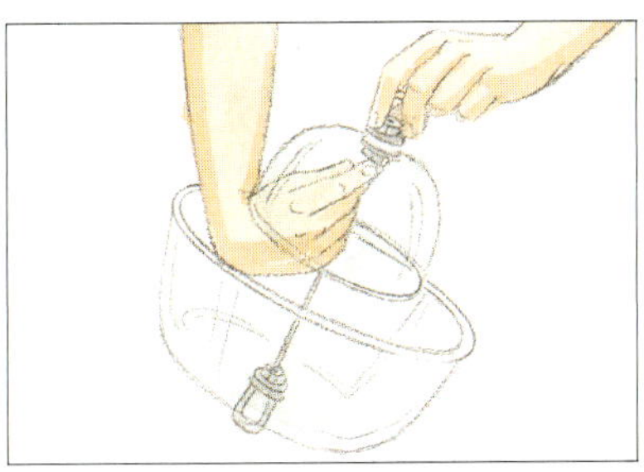

3. Place another nut and washer at the other end of the rod and secure the small bowl so that the insides of the two bowls face each other.

4. Bend the rod above the large bowl to form a hanging hook. Or attach a lamp hook with a nut. Then fill the small bowl with birdseed and hang the feeder outdoors.

Wood pickling/ Technique

Of all the methods for giving wood a washed, "pickled" look, this is the simplest. All that's involved is brushing on some oil-based paint and wiping it off with a coarse cloth.

Choose an off-white paint. Brush it onto a small area at a time and wipe it off with a smooth, even stroke. Depending on the colour of the wood and the effect you want, you may need to make more than one application after letting the previous one dry. Lightly sand the surface between coats. Then finish the wood with a light coat of satin-finish polyurethane to seal and protect.

1. Remove the old finish. If you want a smooth surface, apply a coat of sealer to fill the pores of the wood; let it dry completely.

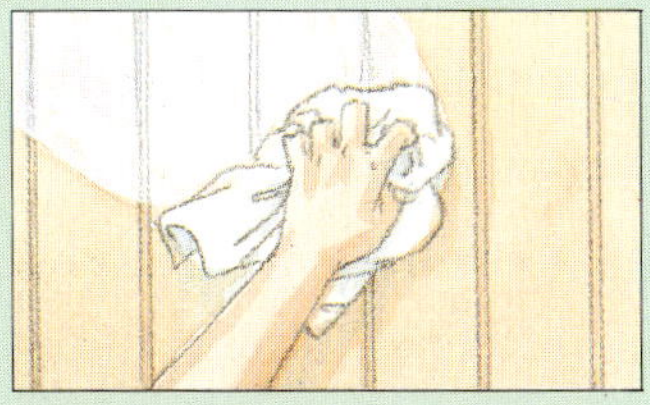

2. Use a wide brush to apply an off-white oil-based paint to a small area of the wood. Then wipe it off with a coarse rag.

3. If you need to apply a second coat, sand the surface lightly beforehand. Then finish with a coat of satin polyurethane.

Tablecloth/Runner & serviettes

Don't consign a stained or torn tablecloth to the rubbish bin. Instead, cut out an unmarred panel and hem it for use as a table runner; then cut out some smaller sections to turn into matching place mats or serviettes. If the cloth is lint-free linen, you can make dishcloths from it, too.

First cut your runner to a width of 375 millimetres. Cut place mats to 375 x 450 millimetres and serviettes in 400-millimetre squares (use coloured chalk as your marker for a white tablecloth, white chalk for dark fabric). After hemming, this will yield a 350-millimetre runner, 350 x 425-millimetre place mats and 375-millimetre square serviettes.

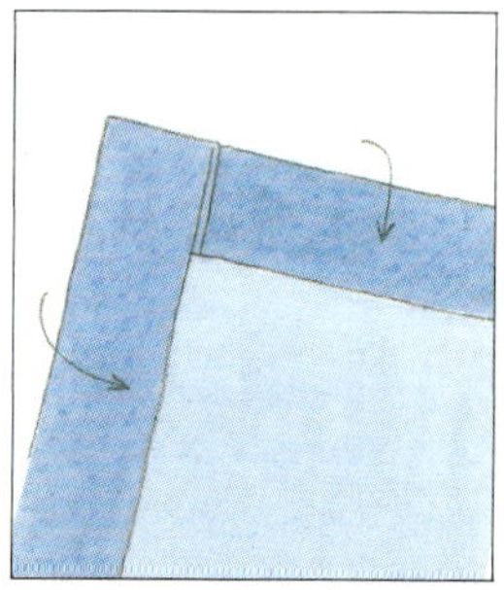

1. Cut a clean section of cloth. Fold the right side over 12 mm on all four sides and press with an iron.

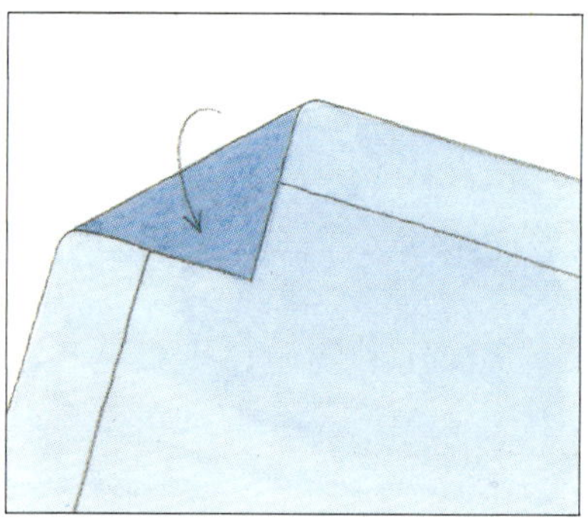

2. To mitre a corner, first fold the point back on itself and press with an iron to make a crease.

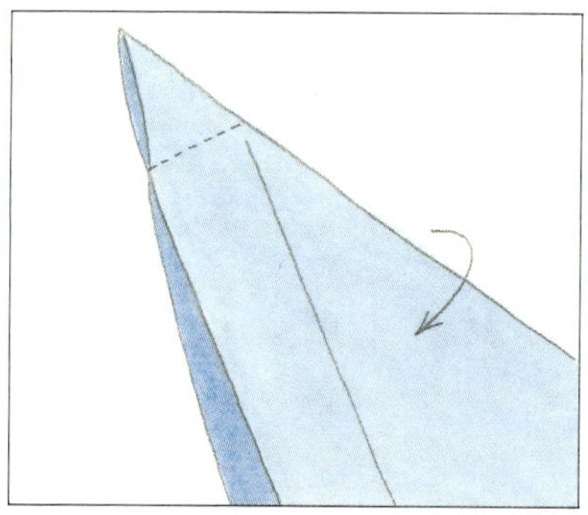

3. Unfold the corner, place the unfolded hem flaps together wrong side out, and stitch along the diagonal crease.

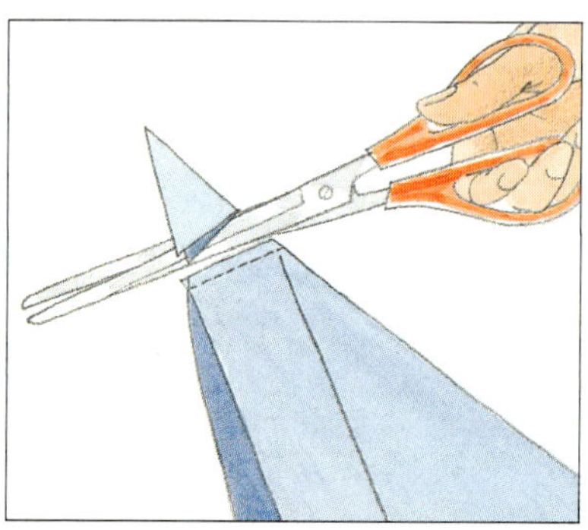

4. Trim the fabric just above the stitch. Turn the hem flaps right side out and straighten to form a neat corner.

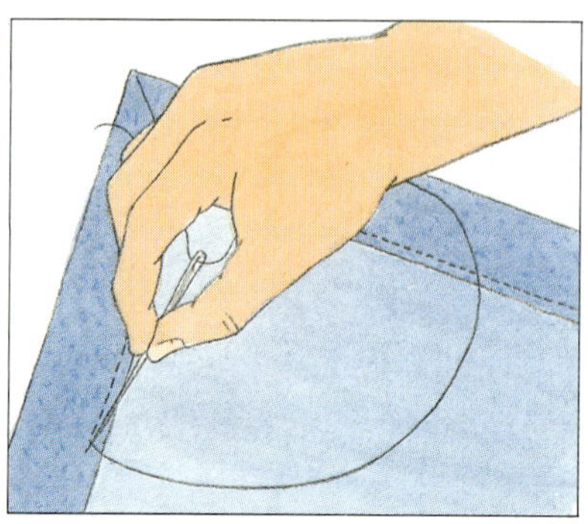

5. Stitch the adjoining hem flap down the edge and mitre the next corner when you come to it.

Tin cans/Containers

Here's the simplest recycling project of all: save tin cans and smarten them up with a coat of spray paint. Then use them as attractive containers for fudge, sweets and other treats. Or convert the kinds with snap-on plastic lids into money boxes – a simple and entertaining project for children. You can even glue a few painted tins together to make a desk organizer for your odds and ends.

For an interesting look, try flicking sand onto damp sprayed paint, and then respraying with a new colour. With a few coats this gives a rough splatter finish to the containers. Add interest by spraying without first shaking the paint – this can add bright splatters of colour.

DESK ORGANIZER

Choose tins of different sizes and shapes. Spray-paint the tins as at right, then put them together in any design you choose. Use a glue gun to attach the tins to one another with hot glue. Fill your stationery holder with pens, paper clips and erasers.

MONEY BOX

Use a tin that has a snap-on plastic lid. Spray-paint as at right; then, with a sharp utility knife, cut a three-millimetre slit in the centre of the lid. Let your child decorate the money box with stickers once the paint is dry – either placing a few figures in a ring around the tin or covering most of the surface with a colourful collage.

GIFT TINS

Use tins with snap-on plastic lids. Or make your own cover by cutting a piece of fabric with pinking shears and securing it with coloured string or yarn. Even plastic wrap is fine, especially if you dress it up with stick-on stars or other designs.

To make your gift tins look even neater, leave the metal rims unpainted (do the same with the desk organizer and money box, if you like). Just mask the rims with masking tape. As a bonus, the bottom circle of tape will keep the tin lifted off the surface and make painting easier.

1. To give your paint job a professional finish, protect the shiny metal rims with masking tape, then flick on sand before the paint dries and respray.

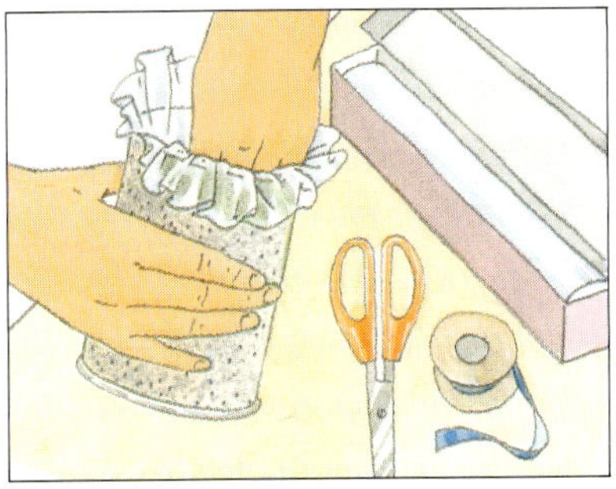

2. When the paint is dry, line the inside of the tin with plastic wrap. Once you've filled it, snap on the lid or secure a cover on top with a piece of yarn.

Spray-painting/Technique

Spray-painting small objects such as drawer knobs, wooden cutouts and doll's house furniture isn't easy. Just keeping them still in the force of the spray is usually a challenge. And if you place the objects on a flat, solid surface, you'll find that the overspray will bounce back onto whatever you're painting and cause drips. A cloud of overspray also tends to dull a high-gloss finish.

Here are some ways to solve the problem using a few common items that you probably already have around the house.

BED OF NAILS

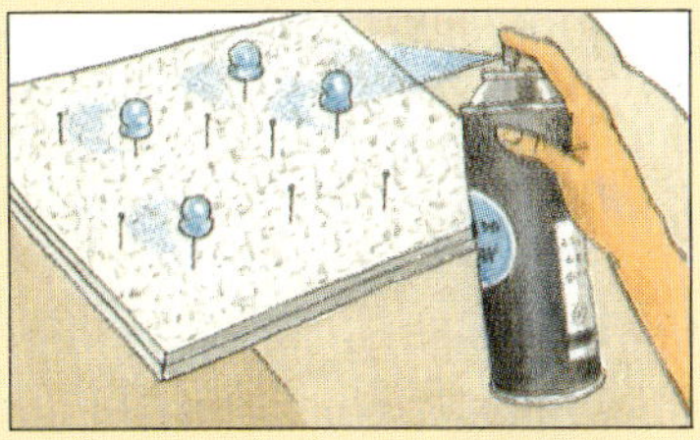

Tap finishing nails into a ceiling tile to act as little poles to support small objects. If the bottom of an object already has a recess – as a drawer knob has – it will stay on top of the head of the nail without a problem. If there's no recess, you'll need to reverse the position of the nail (drive it through the tile, pointed end up) and stick the sharp point far enough into the underside to keep the object from moving around in the force of the spray. Either way, supporting the object on a nail allows you to spray all sides and most of the underside at the same time.

PLATFORM

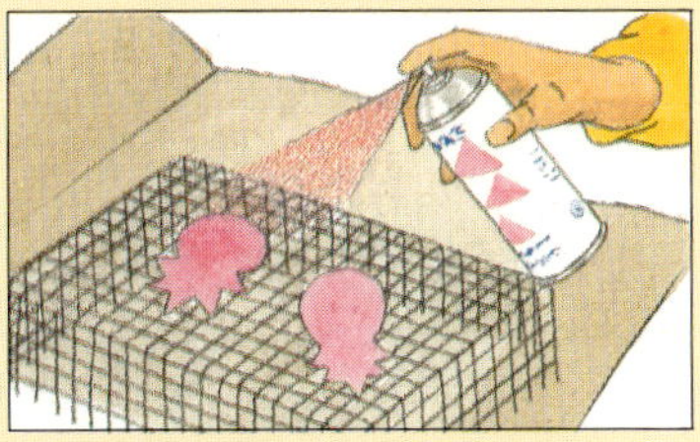

Bend a rectangular piece of coarse steel mesh or even chicken wire – into a rough box shape. The raised wire mesh makes a handy platform for spraying flat objects such as wooden and cardboard cutouts without having them stick to the surface. Spray-paint lightly; when one side is almost dry, turn the objects over and spray them on the other side.

To make the platform, choose a piece of mesh 300 to 600 millimetres long. Cut 100-millimetre squares from each corner, then bend the edges over to form sides. The wire is stiff enough to hold its shape by itself.

CARDBOARD SPRAYING BOOTH

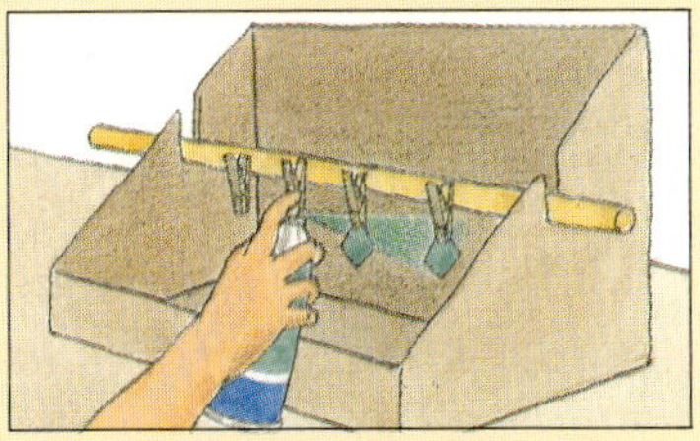

Make a nifty little spraying booth from an old cardboard box, a wooden dowel and some clothes pegs. The booth enables you to spray small objects from several angles and also neatens the job by effectively containing all the overspray.

Use a sharp utility knife to cut the box as shown. Cut two notches for the dowel near the top of the box, then glue the top ends of the clothes pegs (the ends that you pinch) to the dowel with epoxy. Clamp small objects in the clothes pegs and spray (don't overdo it; a couple of light coats will look neater than one heavy one). To spray the other side, simply pick up the dowel and turn it around. When the objects are dry, reclamp them upside down in the clothes pegs and spray again.

Tree branch/Post & door handle

Recycle some of Mother Nature's castoffs – fallen tree branches – as rustic signposts, post box supports or door handles for your home.

When you go to a wooded area to find your material, look for a fallen branch that's a little heavier than you think you'll need. Don't cut any trees in forestry or wilderness areas – this is illegal.

For a signpost, look for a large, straight branch and a couple of smaller ones to form a right-angle arm. An irregular board sawed from another branch can provide the sign that you'll hang from the post.

For a support for an old-style rural post box, choose a heavy branch with a natural crook at the top. The crook should fit within the bottom of your post box.

For a door handle, use a sharply curved or crooked branch small enough to fit in your hand. If you plan to leave the bark on, make sure it is smooth enough to be comfortable to the touch.

Use galvanized nails or brass screws for all three of these projects. And lengthen the life of the posts by treating the bottoms with wood preservative before you place them in the ground.

SIGNPOST

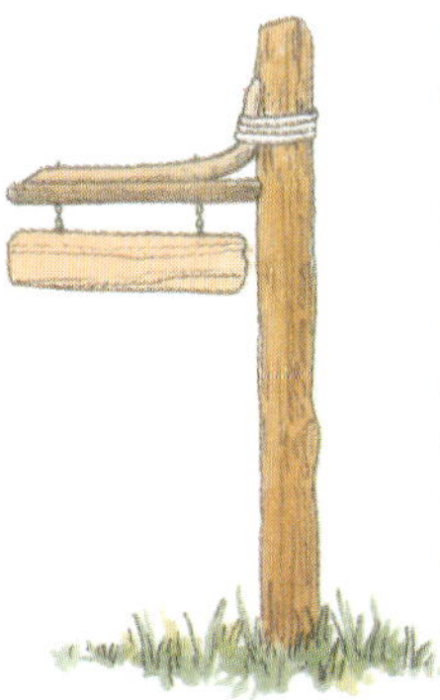

Choose a sturdy branch of one and a half to two metres long, then pick out two smaller ones for the arm that your sign will hang from. Drill a 25-50-millimetre hole near the top of the post and whittle the end of one straight small branch to fit snugly into the hole. Then brace the joint with a branch that has a natural curve; hold it in place with brass screws, and reinforce with a loop of rope. Attach two small chains to hang your sign.

POST BOX SUPPORT

Cut a plank to the size of the recess in the bottom of your post box. Then take it along when you search for a branch with a natural crook that will fit within the length of the board. Cut the crook to size.

Once you have securely implanted the branch in the ground and the concrete is completely dry, nail or screw the board to the two arms of the crook. Position the box on top and secure with nails driven into the holes in the flange.

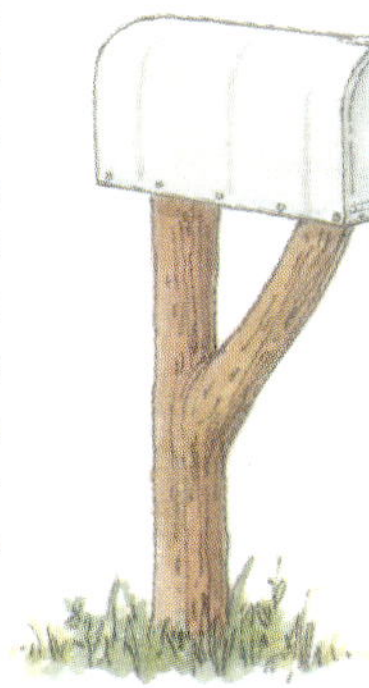

DOOR HANDLE

Find a branch you can get one of your hands around, and cut out a nicely curved 450-millimetre section. Saw or plane the rear side to make a flat surface for mounting the branch on a door. You can leave the bark as it is or strip it off; either way, the branch will eventually develop a nice patina from being handled.

Predrill two holes about 50 millimetres from each end. Position the branch on the door and mark for drilling, then attach with brass screws.

INSTALLING THE POST

1. Choose a fairly straight, heavy tree branch and measure the diameter. Multiply the diameter by three and dig a hole to at least that depth.

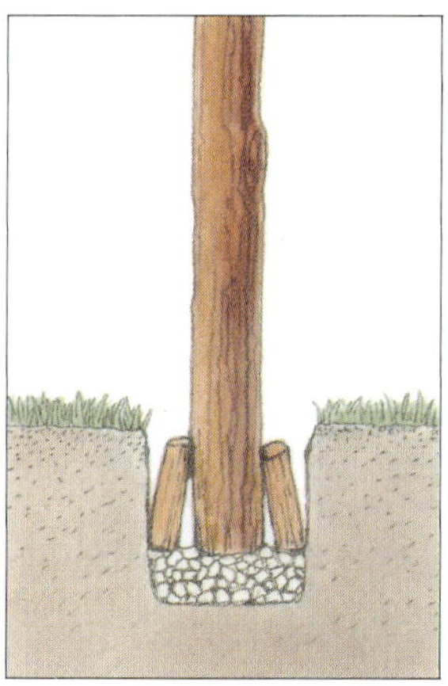

2. Add about 25 mm of stones to the hole and insert the post. Use two or three smaller pieces of wood to plumb it up and hold it in position.

3. Prepare a small bag of dry-mix concrete and fill the hole with it, forcing it around the pieces of wood and packing it just above ground level.

4. Using a trowel, smooth the concrete around the base of the post so that it tapers gently to the ground at an angle to shed rainwater.

Wicker furniture/Renewal

Don't retire wicker furniture to the attic or the rubbish dump just because a few spokes and strands are broken or unravelling. They are quite easily renewed.

Wicker is made from pliable plant fibres. Cane, reed and rattan are the most common of these – all are sold at craft stores. When you need to replace a piece, just snip off a sample and take it to the nearest store so that you can buy a replacement of exactly the same size.

You'll need binding cane, which is flat on one side, to replace the unravelling cane on chair legs. To replace broken spokes in chair seats, arms and backs, you will have to buy some reed spline.

You will also need a hammer, a pair of tin snips, some 12-millimetre wire brads, cold glue, masking tape and a bucket of warm water. Before you start, you should clean the piece of furniture properly. Take a soft brush and scrub with a mild detergent-and-water solution.

Rinse with a fine mist from a garden hose, using as little water as possible, then wipe dry. Another way to remove dust without damaging the wicker is to blow it away with an air hose.

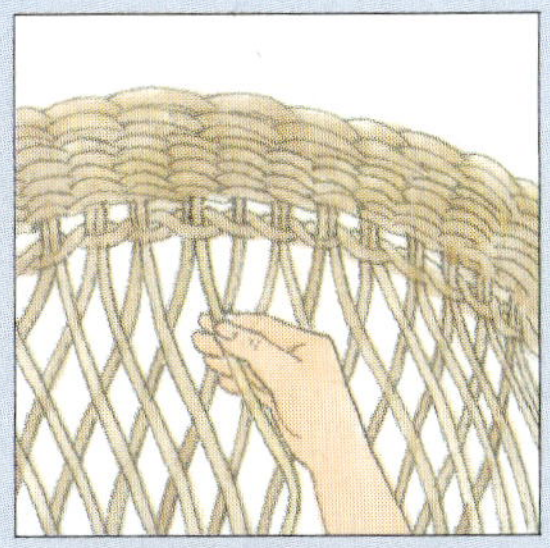

1. Soak replacement reeds in warm water for 10-20 minutes. Cut their tips to a point and weave into place.

2. To rewrap a chair leg, turn the piece upside down and secure binding cane to the top with a 12-mm wire brad.

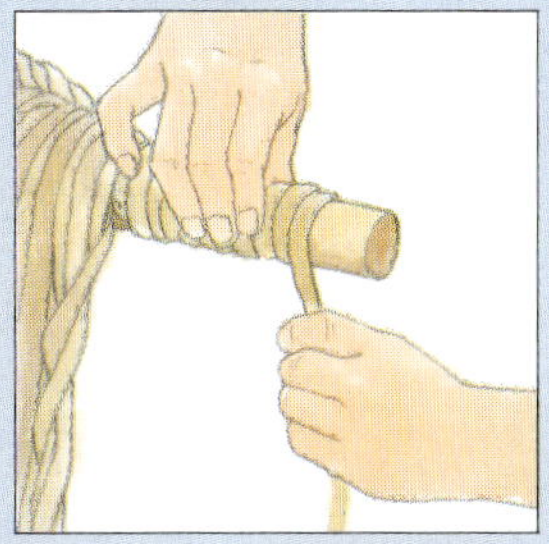

3. Wrap the cane tightly around the leg toward the bottom. Trim it with a knife when you reach the end.

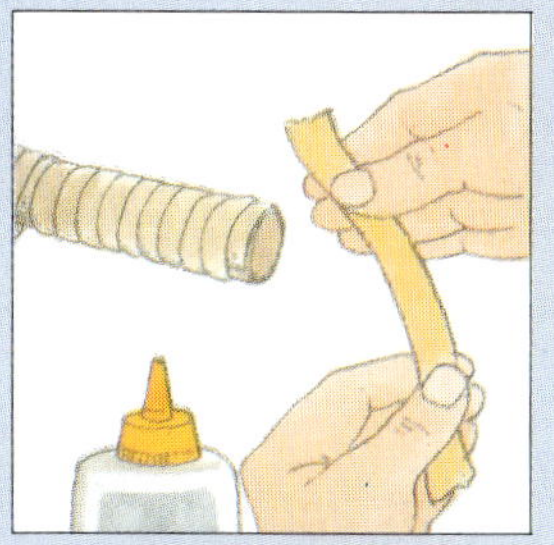

4. Apply cold glue to the end of the cane and tack down with a 12-mm brad. Secure with masking tape until dry.

Wine bottle/Lamp

A plain wine bottle makes a simple lamp base with clean lines. All you need to convert it to a bedside light is a lampholder, a 10-millimetre nipple and a length of flex.

Find a cork that fits tightly into the bottle, and drill out a 10-millimetre shaft, or buy a pre-drilled nylon cork with the shaft ready moulded. The wire goes through the bottle, and exits near the base. Drill a hole in the bottle through a tab of masking tape (to stop the bit wandering) using a six-millimetre masonry bit.

You will also need a length of nipple for the lampholder, harp, cord, plug top and line switch, and nuts to attach the lampholder to the bottle cork.

If the bottle is tall and slender (as some decorative containers are), it may need ballast. In that case, fill the bottle with marbles, pebbles, shells or sand. If the bottle glass is clear, you might want to use the coloured fish-tank gravel sold at pet shops.

Another way to make a tall bottle more stable is to detach the harp from the socket assembly and use a shade that snaps directly over the light bulb. This will lower the centre of gravity.

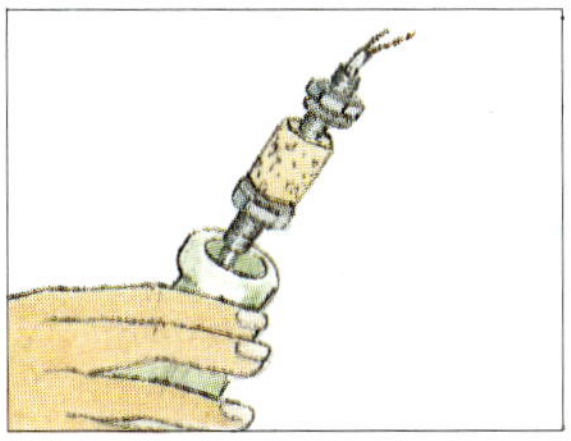

1. Drill a cork that fits snugly into your bottle. Insert the nipple and secure washers and nuts on both ends. Then twist the cork into the bottle.

2. Place the harp cradle over the nipple. Screw the socket base over the nipple and tighten the setscrew. Insert the cord through the socket base and strip the ends.

3. Attach the wire ends to the socket connections, wrapping clockwise before tightening the terminal screws. Install the socket cover and snap the assembly into the socket base.

4. Unscrew the finial on the harp, place a shade over the nipple, and replace the finial. Or, if the bottle is tall, remove the harp and use a shade that snaps over.

Wok lid/Hanging lamp

The shiny aluminium lid of a Chinese wok makes an elegant contemporary shade for a hanging lamp. All you have to do is drill a hole in the centre and rig up a hanging lamp socket. A small plastic locking collar on the flex above the fitting takes the weight of the fitting, so that the wires will not pull loose at all under stress.

Alternatively, drill a 10-millimetre hole and suspend the light on a length of metal nipple. Knot the cord inside the fitting to take the weight. (See *Drainpipe uplight,* p. 355.)

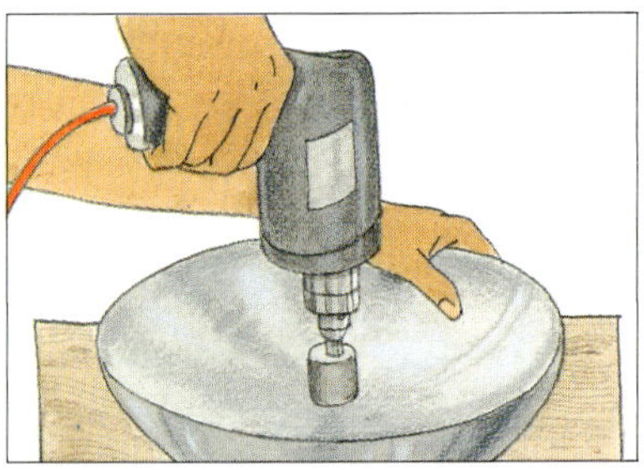

1. Remove the handle and place the inverted lid on a piece of scrap wood. Drill a 10-mm hole in the centre with a hole saw attached to your electric drill.

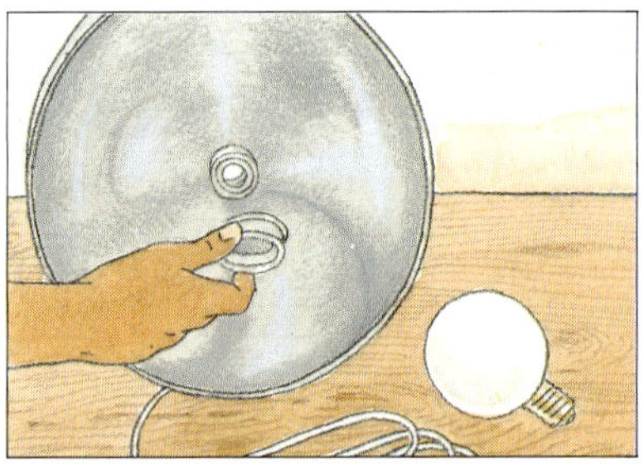

2. Insert the light socket into the hole and make sure that it is exactly centred. Then tighten the trim ring to lock it securely in place.

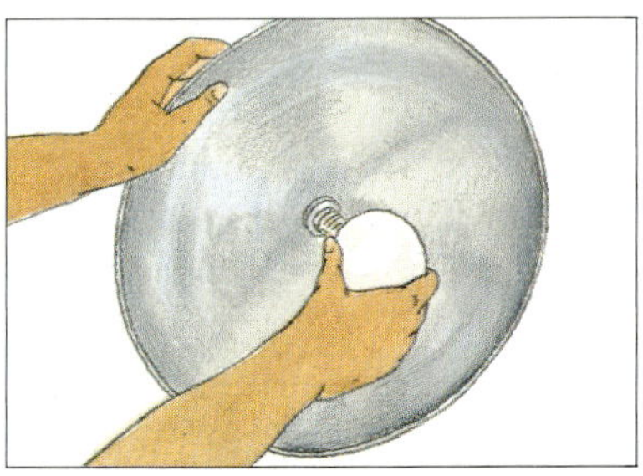

3. Screw a globe-shaped bulb into the socket. Install a hook in the ceiling where you want the fixture to hang and another hook in the ceiling above an outlet.

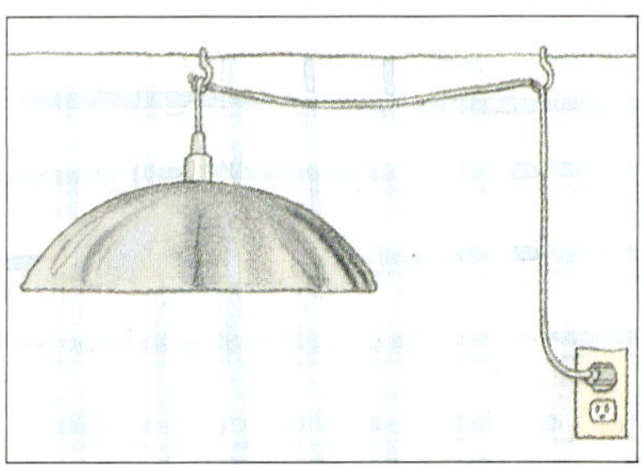

4. Hook the lamp cord over the ceiling hook and adjust the lamp to the desired height. Lead the cord to the second hook and then down to the outlet.

Potato printing/ Technique

Carve a design on a cut potato, dip it in paint, and use it as a print block. Your prints will have an attractive imperfection, reminiscent of child-art spontaneity.

Potato prints are ideal for customizing gift wrap (use ordinary white shelf paper and decorate it as you like), but don't confine them to paper. Print the designs on painted furniture (a chair back or the top of a wooden chest, for example), or on smaller wooden items such as the candle holders shown on p.379; then make sure you protect the design with a polyurethane finish.

If you're printing a row of the same design, cut a notch in the potato skin at the top of the design so that you can keep the prints aligned.

1. Cut a large potato in half and use a pencil to sketch your design on the surface. With a paring knife or artist's knife, carve 6-mm deep into the pulp to remove the sections that are not part of the design.

2. Saturate an ink pad with ink and press the potato firmly onto it. Clean up your design by trimming any rough edges that you see. Press the potato onto the surface you're printing, re-inking each time.

Wood scraps/Art board & candle holders

The leftover wood on your workshop floor doesn't have to end up as fireplace kindling. Instead, turn some of the end scraps into interesting little candle holders; just cut them to various heights, bore holes in the ends, and glue them together in any design you choose. Or use a piece of shelving stock and some elastic belting to craft an art board for a child. Both projects are easy to make, and both make terrific gifts.

ART BOARD

This child's art board, complete with handle, has enough room for four coloured markers. The drawing pad is secured by stapling the cardboard backing onto the board (use heavy-duty staples to make sure the pad stays in place).

When you staple down the strips of elastic belting to hold the markers, pull them tight before you insert the second staple, then neatly trim away the excess.

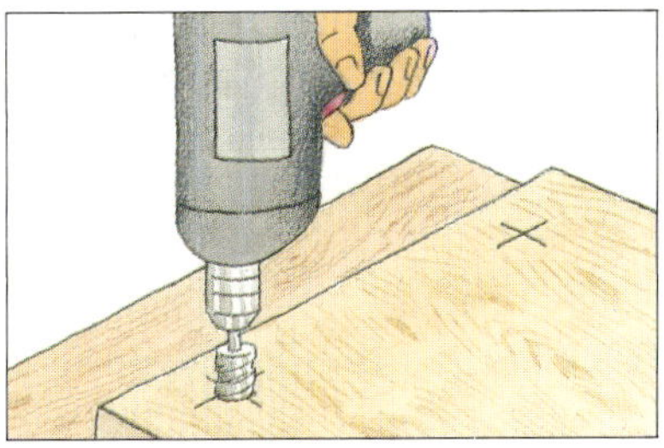

1. Cut 25- x 300-mm pine to a length of 450 mm. Drill a 25-mm hole 75 mm from one edge and 35 mm from the top.

2. Drill another 25-mm hole in the same position at the opposite side, then draw horizontal lines to connect the holes.

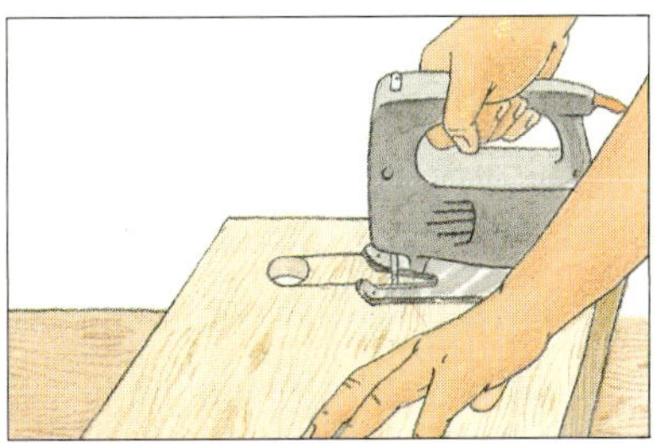

3. Use a coping saw or jigsaw to cut out the area between the holes to make a handle. Sand and apply a wipe-on finish.

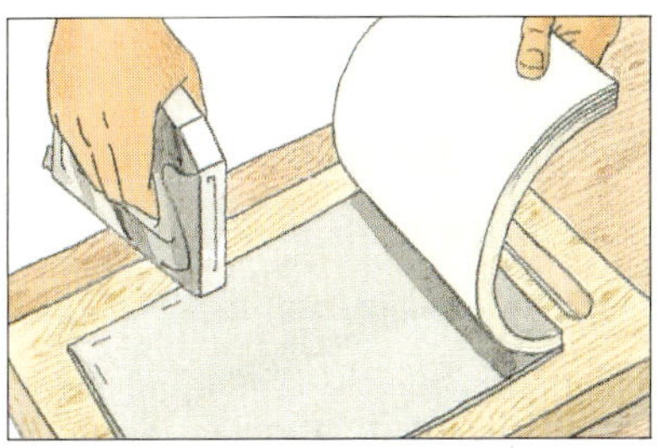

4. When the finish dries, centre a 200- x 275-mm drawing pad below the handle and staple down the cardboard back.

5. Staple the end of a piece of elastic belting just beneath the pad. Place a marker next to the staple.

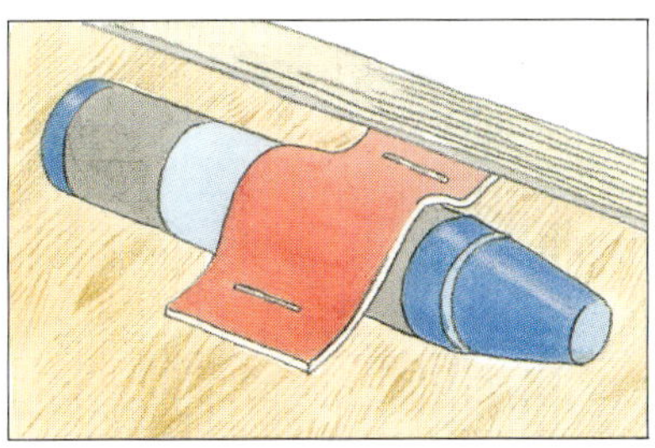

6. Pull the elastic over the marker and staple it to the other side. Make holders for three more markers in the same way.

CANDLE HOLDERS

The project shown here uses square pieces of wood, but you can use scraps of any shape. Half the fun is coming up with your own design.

Caution: These are best used for decoration only. If you burn candles in them, don't leave them unattended; a spluttering flame can ignite the wood.

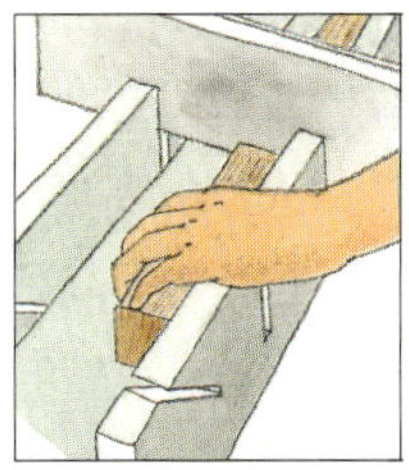

1. Rip pine scraps in half. Then cut these fairly square pieces into various lengths.

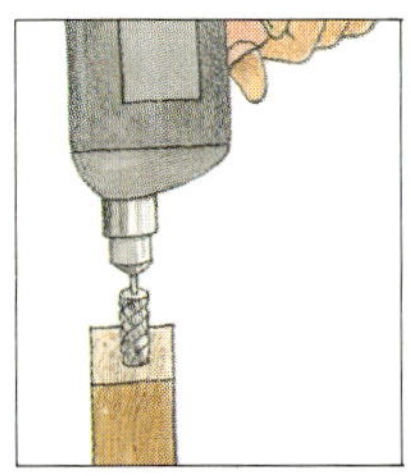

2. Check the diameter of the candles you plan to use and bore a hole the same size in the end of each piece of wood.

3. Sand the pieces smooth and use cold glue to attach them to each other, side by side. Clamp together until the glue dries.

4. Stain with a one-step wipe-on finish or paint as you like. Or, if you choose, leave the wood unfinished. Insert candles.

Wooden ladder/Toy box

To make handy storage for toys or other bulky objects, mount an old ladder horizontally on a wall and hang some brightly coloured canvas tote bags from its rungs. You'll need little more than screws, bolts and a couple of wooden supports.

A short section of ladder – five or six rungs – should be adequate, but the unit can be as long as you like. Clear 22-millimetre pine, ripped to a width of 55 mm, makes the best supports, since it most nearly matches the dimensions of most ladder rails. Make sure that the supports are no taller than 450 millimetres so that the toy-filled bags will be within easy reach of children.

Sand the ladder to remove splinters. Then use 75-millimetre screws to attach it to the length of wall it spans. If the unit is longer than one and a half metres, add a third support in the centre.

Canvas tote bags that measure about 400 x 550 millimetres are big enough to fill the spaces between the rungs. Secure them at each corner with a screw and washer, then screw each side to the centre of a rung. You can either remove the handles of the bags or drape them over the sides.

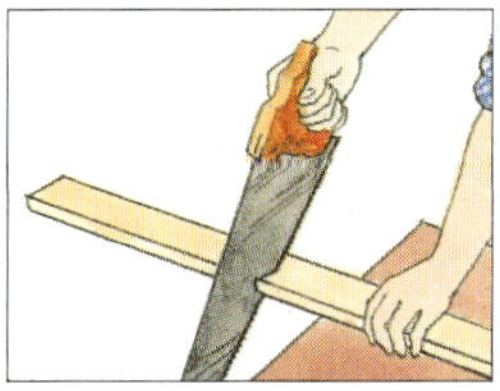

1. To make the supports for the ladder, saw two pieces of 22-mm clear pine stock to a width of 55 mm and a length of 250 mm.

2. Attach the supports near both ends of the ladder rail, using a 6- x 55-mm carriage bolt and a washer to secure each one.

3. Position the unit on the wall and attach with blue Rex wall anchors with a 6-mm (No.14) screw, at least 50 mm long.

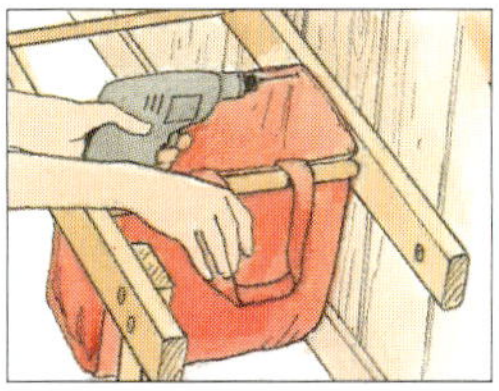

4. Hold a canvas tote bag between each set of rungs and drill 3-mm pilot holes in the corners and at the centre of both rungs.

5. Secure each canvas bag with screws and washers at all four corners and at the centre of the rungs.

6. If the bags lose their shape when filled with toys or other items, cut a piece of plywood to fit into each as a solid bottom.

Wrought iron/Renewal

Renewing wrought-iron patio furniture, stoep supports and handrails isn't as simple as just covering up the flaws with a coat of paint. First you have to remove rust spots and corrosion and fill the pitted areas.

When you buy your paints, make sure the primer and the top coat are manufactured by the same company. That way, you can be sure they'll be compatible.

1. Scrub the wrought iron with a wire brush, wetting it often. Use a beer can opener to remove rust and paint from small crevices.

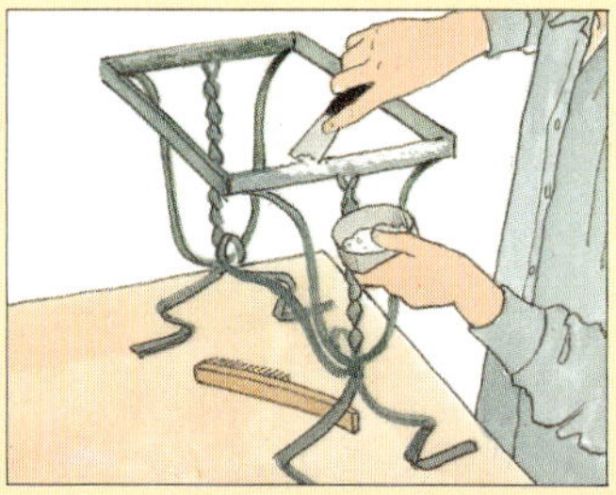

2. Use your fingers or a putty knife to fill pits and dents with a polyester base wood filler or an automotive body filler. Sand smooth when dry.

3. Paint with a rust-inhibiting primer. The next day, apply a top coat of oil or alkyd-base enamel. A high-gloss finish withstands weather best.

5. FORMULAS & RECIPES

Why pay more than you have to? Why pay for fancy packages, distribution costs and middlemen's profits when you can do it yourself with these foolproof formulas and recipes instead? They're easy and fun to make, they're just as good as, or better than, their commercial counterparts – and they'll save you money, too.

From African violet potting soil to yoghurt and mint sauce, all of the following formulas and recipes have been carefully tested. Uncommon ingredients have been marked with an asterisk (*) and appear alphabetically at the end of the section, together with the outlets at which they are generally available.

African violet potting soil

This potting soil is also well-suited to bromeliads, begonias, caladiums and most ferns.

*3 parts peat moss**
*2 parts vermiculite**
*1 part perlite**
5 tablespoons crushed eggshells
(or 5 teaspoons agricultural lime)
per 1,5 litres of mixture

Mix all the ingredients in a bucket. When repotting African violets, do not give the roots too much space – unless the roots thoroughly penetrate the soil, it will remain wet and the plant will rot. As a rule, the diameter of the pot should be one third that of the plant.

After-bath splash

A refreshing citrus-scented lotion.

½ cup witch hazel
4 teaspoons lemon juice

In a small bowl, combine the witch hazel and lemon juice. Shake well, then transfer to a covered jar and store in the refrigerator. Yield: 75 millilitres.

Aftershave

To soothe your skin and leave it smelling fresh.

2 cups witch hazel
*1 tablespoon glycerine**
1 tablespoon dried lavender
1 teaspoon dried rosemary
1 teaspoon ground cloves

Combine all the ingredients in a medium-sized bowl. Transfer to a lidded jar and refrigerate for 3 to 4 days, shaking occasionally to mix the ingredients. Strain before using. Will keep 1 to 2 months tightly covered and refrigerated. Yield: about 2 cups.

Air freshener

A spicy fragrance that will even get rid of strong odours such as onion.

¼ cup dried sage
½ cup crushed bay leaves
1 cup witch hazel

Mix all the ingredients in a large jar. Cover and leave, unrefrigerated, for 3 days. Strain, and pour the remaining liquid into a spray bottle, discarding the herbs. Yield: 1 cup.

Alikreukel

Alikreukels can be tough, but properly prepared they make a tasty dish. Use the following ingredients to prepare minced, sliced or chopped alikreukels. Remember that strict laws control the harvesting of alikreukels.

5 large alikreukels
salt water
butter
1–2 cloves garlic
black pepper
cooked rice
soya sauce (optional)

Bring a cooking pot of salt water (sea water if possible) to the boil. Place the alikreukels in the water, and allow to boil until the operculum (circular trapdoor at the opening of the shell) comes off easily (about 15 minutes). Remove the operculum and stomach. Chop or mince the alikreukels, and crush the cloves of garlic. Melt the butter in a heavy pan, add the crushed garlic, and gently fry the alikreukels for about 2 minutes. Add a dash of black pepper (and soya sauce for extra taste) and serve on a bed of rice.

For a variation, try cutting the alikreukels into thin slices. Pound the slices with a mallet to soften them, then fry with garlic and butter for about 2 minutes. Yield: 3 servings.

All-purpose cleaner

For extra help when removing tough stains from countertops, woodwork and tiles.

½ cup household ammonia
½ cup washing soda
7 cups warm water

1. In a 2-litre plastic jug, combine the ammonia, washing soda and 1 cup of the warm water. Cap the jug, shake briskly, then add the remaining warm water; label.
2. To use: mix ½ cup cleaner with about 7 litres hot water in a bucket. Before using on delicate surfaces, such as wallpaper, test on a small, inconspicuous area. Yield: 2 litres concentrated cleaner.

Almond butter

Are you getting tired of peanut butter? Here's a tasty new alternative that will please the whole family.

2 cups blanched almonds,
whole or slivered
2 tablespoons sunflower oil
½ teaspoon salt

1. Preheat the oven to 150°C. On an ungreased baking sheet, roast the nuts about 20 minutes or until they are lightly browned. Let cool and transfer to a blender or food processor. (For a chunkier spread, coarsely chop ⅓ cup nuts and set aside.)

2. Add the oil and salt and blend until creamy, working in batches, if necessary. (If chopped nuts were set aside, stir them in.) Transfer to a covered container. Will keep for about 1 month tightly covered and refrigerated. Yield: 1 cup.

Aluminium cleaner

This easy-to-make cleaner will remove unsightly tarnish and greasy film from your cookware.

½ cup cream of tartar
½ cup bicarbonate of soda
½ cup white vinegar
¼ cup soap powder

Combine the cream of tartar and the bicarbonate of soda in a medium-sized bowl. Add the vinegar and mix until the ingredients form a soft paste. Add the soap powder and transfer to a jar or bottle with a secure lid; label. To use, apply with a steel wool pad, then rinse off. Store out of the reach of children. Should keep 1 to 2 years. Yield: 1½ cups.

Antiperspirant

Here's a rose-scented spray that will keep you fresh and dry right through South Africa's sizzling summers.

1 cup water
1 cup witch hazel
*2 tablespoons alum**
*3 tablespoons rose water**

In a small bowl, mix together the water, witch hazel, alum and rose water. Transfer the mixture to a plastic spray bottle and use as needed. Yield: 500 millilitres.

Ant traps

Control unwanted ants in and around your home without using chemicals.

⅓ cup golden syrup
6 tablespoons sugar
6 tablespoons active dry yeast

Stir all the ingredients together in a small bowl until they form a smooth paste. Coat strips of cardboard with

the mixture or pour it into individual bottle caps, then place in and around infested areas.

Apple butter

This spicy, low-sugar spread will be sought after by the whole family, especially on picnic sandwiches in summer. The apples are cooked uncored and with their skins on because their pectin adds body to the butter.

2 kilograms assorted apples (Granny Smith, Golden Delicious), quartered
2 cups apple cider
1 vanilla pod, split
2 cinnamon sticks
4 whole cloves

1. Put the apples in a large heavy pot, cover, and cook over low heat for about 50 minutes or until they are soft. (The apples should contain enough moisture to prevent them from burning; if they do not, add a few tablespoons of water.)
2. Force the apples through a sieve into a large saucepan; discard the solids. Add the cider, vanilla pod, cinnamon sticks and the cloves; cook the mixture, uncovered, stirring frequently, over low heat for about 1 hour 15 minutes or until it is very thick.
3. Let the mixture cool slightly, then remove the vanilla pod, cinnamon and the cloves. While it is still warm, transfer the apple butter to hot, sterilized, 250-millilitre preserving jars and cover. Will keep 1 month refrigerated. Yield: 2½ cups.

Astringent

Tightens pores and helps remove excess oil from your skin.

½ lemon, sliced thinly
½ orange, sliced thinly
¾ cup witch hazel

Place the lemon and orange slices in a blender, add the witch hazel, and blend until the fruits are well pulverized – about 1 minute. Using a small strainer or cheesecloth, strain into a jar. Will keep 6 months refrigerated. Yield: ¾ cup.

Baby marrow bread

This rich, versatile loaf is good for breakfast, afternoon tea or dessert.

3 cups all-purpose flour
2 teaspoons baking powder
1 teaspoon salt
½ teaspoon bicarbonate of soda
1 teaspoon ground cinnamon
½ teaspoon ground allspice
2 eggs
1 cup sunflower oil
¾ cup sugar
½ cup firmly packed light brown sugar
2 tablespoons finely grated orange rind
2 tablespoons minced crystallized ginger
2 cups grated unpeeled baby marrows
1 cup coarsely chopped walnuts or pecan nuts

1. Preheat the oven to 180°C. Sift together the flour, baking powder, salt, bicarbonate of soda, cinnamon and allspice onto a sheet of wax paper; set aside.
2. In a large bowl, beat the eggs, oil, sugar, brown sugar, orange rind and ginger until well blended. Stir in the flour mixture, then fold in the grated baby marrows and nuts.
3. Pour the batter into two 23- x 12-centimetre loaf tins that have been greased and dusted with flour. Bake until a toothpick inserted in the centre comes out clean – 45 to 50 minutes. Cool 15 minutes in the tin on a wire

rack, then turn out and let cool to room temperature. Will keep 1 week wrapped in foil and refrigerated or 3 months in the freezer. Yield: 2 loaves.

Baby powder

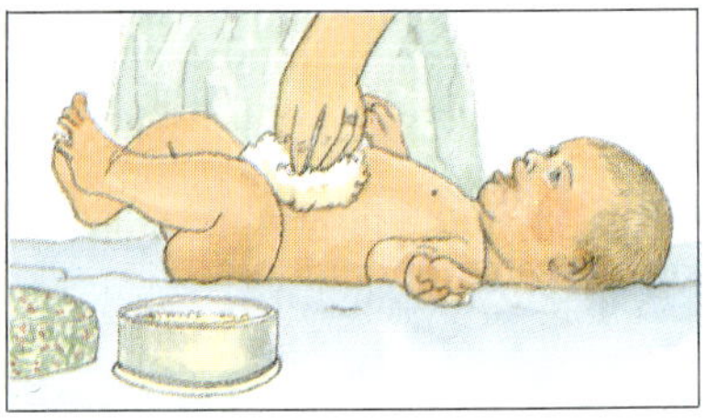

Keep your baby's tender, sensitive skin soft and dry. Be sure not to use on nappy rash.

*2 tablespoons dried camomile flowers, crumbled**
¼ cup cornflour
*1 tablespoon orrisroot**
*½ teaspoon alum**

In a small bowl, mix all the ingredients together. Store in flour shakers or old talcum powder boxes in a cool, dry place. Yield: ½ cup.

Barbecue sauce

A delicious sauce that goes well with beef, chicken or pork – especially at a braai. And with none of the preservatives which are found in most store-bought brands.

1 medium onion, peeled and finely chopped
¼ cup sunflower oil
1 cup tomato sauce
¾ cup water
2 tablespoons Worcestershire sauce
2 tablespoons sugar
¼ cup cider vinegar
2 tablespoons prepared mustard
1 teaspoon salt
½ teaspoon black pepper

Combine all the ingredients in a medium-sized saucepan. Simmer over low heat, uncovered, for 20 minutes; let cool. Will keep several days refrigerated in a clean glass jar with a tight-fitting lid or 6 months in the freezer. Yield: about 2½ cups.

Bath oil

Soothing and a great skin softener.

1 cup honey
2 cups milk
1 cup sea salt or plain salt
¼ cup bicarbonate of soda
½ cup baby oil

In a large bowl, combine the honey, milk, sea salt and bicarbonate of soda; stir well. Pour the mixture into a bathtub filled with warm water, add baby oil, and mix well.

Bath salts

To revitalize your tired muscles.

1 cup sea salt
1 cup bicarbonate of soda
1 cup inexpensive shampoo

Half fill a bathtub with warm water. Pour the ingredients into the bathtub, then add more water, swirling it around with your hand to spread out the bubbles.

Biltong

There are just as many recipes for biltong as there are biltong makers in South Africa. One basic rule applies: whichever recipe you use – choose good quality cuts of meat.

10 kilograms meat
2½ cups brown vinegar
⅓ cup brown sugar
*1¾ teaspoons ground saltpetre**
1¾ teaspoons bicarbonate of soda
2 teaspoons black pepper
3 tablespoons whole coriander seeds
1 cup salt

1. Cut the meat into strips and rub thoroughly with the vinegar, ensuring that all the meat is coated. Mix the sugar, saltpetre, bicarbonate of soda and pepper, and set aside. Roast the coriander seeds in a pan over medium heat, remove and mince until fine. Combine with the sugar mixture.
2. Place the thicker biltong strips at the bottom of an enamel container, cover with a layer of salt and then a layer of the spice mixture. Add successive layers of meat and seasoning, with the thinner strips on top. Add a final dressing of salt. Leave for about 12 hours. Remove the thinner strips at the top and then dip in hot water.
3. Dry the strips very well, then hang on S-shaped wire hooks. Take care to hang the pieces of biltong well apart so that air can circulate between them. After another 12 hours, remove the medium-sized biltong, treat as before, and hang. After 36 hours, the thick portions may be removed, treated and hung.
4. Leave the strips to hang until they are dry – this depends upon the temperature, air circulation and personal tastes. Yield: 4,25 kilograms biltong.

Bird treats

Keep your garden alive with the sound of birdsong.

1¾ cups lard
1 cup sesame seeds
1 cup hulled sunflower seeds
1 cup crushed savoury biscuits
⅓ cup raisins
¼ cup peanut butter

Using a double boiler, melt the lard over low heat. Let cool, then transfer to a medium-sized bowl. Mix in the sesame and sunflower seeds, biscuits and raisins. Add the peanut butter; stir until combined. Let the mixture harden by refrigerating overnight. Put in a bird feeder or hang in netting coarse enough to allow birds to penetrate it with their beaks. Yield: 1½ cups.

Bloody Mary mix

Eliminate guesswork; now you'll make a perfect drink every time.

4 cups tomato juice
2 tablespoons lime or lemon juice

2 tablespoons Worcestershire sauce
2 teaspoons horseradish sauce
1 teaspoon salt
¼ to ½ teaspoon Tabasco sauce

In a jug, mix all the ingredients; refrigerate. To use, stir well. Fill a balloon wineglass with ice, add a tot of vodka, and fill to the brim with the drink mix. Add a wedge of fresh lemon or lime and a celery stalk for stirring the drink. Will keep 4 days refrigerated. Yield: about 4¼ cups or enough for 6 Bloody Marys.

Braaied bananas

A delicious dessert to end a braai. They come ready packed in their own skins – just pop them onto the coals while you are eating your chops and boerewors.

6 large bananas
3 tablespoons butter or margarine, melted
2 tablespoons lemon juice
1 tablespoon brown sugar

1. First slice the bananas in half, lengthways, and brush the sliced surfaces with the melted butter or margarine. Sprinkle with the lemon juice and sugar.
2. Place the bananas, cut side down, on the hot part of the braai grill to sear. Then turn over and move to a cooler side of the grill. Bake until soft (about 20 minutes), then remove from their skins.

Whole, unpeeled bananas may be left to cook on the cool side of the grill for about 30 minutes. Peel and sprinkle with sugar and cinnamon.

Brass ager

Gives new brass an antique patina.

Lacquer thinner or paint remover
*15 grams liver of sulphur**
*60 grams copper sulphate**
9 litres warm water

1. Strip the brass piece using lacquer thinner.
2. Mix the liver of sulphur and half the water in a medium-sized bucket. In a second bucket, mix the copper sulphate and the remaining water. Be sure to use caution – copper sulphate is poisonous.
3. Using a hook to hold the brass, and gloves to protect your hands, quickly dip the piece in each solution in turn. Do not rinse between dippings. Repeat as often as desired. Rinse in clear water. When dry, scrub with extra-fine steel wool.

Brass & copper cleaner

This cleaner is tough enough to remove any grease or dirt.

½ cup all-purpose flour
½ cup salt
½ cup powdered detergent
¾ cup white vinegar
¼ cup lemon juice
½ cup very warm water

1. In a large glass bowl, mix the flour, salt and detergent well. Add the remaining ingredients and stir. Transfer the mixture to a large glass jar, close tightly and label. Store out of the reach of children.
2. To use, shake briskly, then pour some of the cleaner on cookware and rub with a dishcloth. For tough spots, scrub with an old toothbrush or a scouring pad (test first on an inconspicuous area). Rinse with water, dry, and polish with a soft cloth.

Breakfast cereal

Put nutritional punch into the start of your day – eat a breakfast cereal packed with minerals and vitamins. In this country a very popular breakfast cereal is muesli – a quick, nourishing meal that's high in protein and complex carbohydrates.

2 cups quick-cooking oats
*1 cup whole-wheat flakes or coarsely crumbled shredded wheat**
1 cup bran or bran cereal
1 cup wheat germ
1 cup any combination unsalted walnuts, almonds, pecan or cashew nuts, coarsely chopped
½ cup chopped, stoned dates
1 cup any combination chopped dried prunes, apricots, pears, apples or bananas
1 cup sultanas or raisins
1 cup instant non-fat dry milk

In a large bowl, combine the oats, wheat flakes or shredded wheat, bran, wheat germ and nuts. Add the dates and dried fruit and toss to coat with the oats mixture. Add the raisins and dry milk and mix thoroughly. This cereal will keep 2 months refrigerated in tightly sealed canisters. Yield: about 9½ cups.

Brownie mixture

It tastes better than store-bought.

3½ cups sugar
2½ cups all-purpose flour
1½ cups cocoa
2 teaspoons baking powder
1½ teaspoons salt
2 cups solid vegetable fat

In a large bowl, mix together the sugar, flour, cocoa, baking powder and salt. With a pastry blender or two knives, cut in the vegetable fat until the brownie mixture resembles bread crumbs, working in batches, if necessary. Will keep 6 weeks refrigerated in tightly covered canisters; 6 months in freezer containers. Yield: 9 cups or enough for 3 batches of 16 brownies. See below for cooking.

Brownies

For a delicious twist, make them with chocolate chips.

3 cups brownie mix (above)
2 large eggs
1 teaspoon vanilla essence
½ cup chocolate chips or chopped dark chocolate

1. Preheat the oven to 180°C. Place all the ingredients in a medium-sized bowl and mix thoroughly. Pour into a greased tin, smooth the surface and then bake for 30 minutes or until a fine skewer inserted into the centre comes out clean.
2. Place tin on a wire rack and allow to cool. Cut into squares and serve. Yield: 16 brownies.

Brown ink

Make your own with tea bags.

½ cup boiling water
5 tea bags
*1 teaspoon gum arabic**

In a medium-sized bowl, pour the water over the tea bags. Stir in the gum arabic and let steep until cool. Squeeze the tea bags to get all the tannic acid out. Use with a paintbrush or quill pen or any other type of writing utensil. Yield: ⅓ cup.

Bubble bath

A long soak will leave your skin sweet-smelling and soft.

2 cups liquid soap
2 cups inexpensive shampoo or dishwashing detergent
*¼ cup glycerine**
few drops of scented oil or perfume

In a small bowl, mix the soap with the shampoo, glycerine and scented oil. Transfer the bubbly mixture to a litre container, cover, and store in the bathroom. Add about 1 cup per bath. Yield: 1 litre.

Buttermilk rusks

A delicious treat for teatime.

1½ cups butter
2½ cups sugar
2 extra-large eggs
9 cups self-raising flour
2 tablespoons baking powder
2 cups buttermilk

1. Preheat the oven to 180°C.
2. Cream the butter and sugar, then beat in the eggs, one at a time. Sift the flour and baking powder and add to the butter mixture. Add the buttermilk (rinse out the carton with a little milk and add this as well). Mix together and knead lightly. Roll into 3-centimetre diameter balls, and pack them closely together in one layer in greased tins. Place in the centre of the oven and bake for 45 to 55 minutes. Remove the tins and turn the oven down to its lowest setting.
3. Separate the rusks and place on wire racks or cooled oven racks. Place them in the cool oven, with the door ajar, for 4 to 5 hours to dry out. Yield: 36 rusks.

Camomile astringent

Here's a gentle astringent that is especially good for oily skin.

4 cups water
½ cup chopped fresh mint or 2 tablespoons dried mint
*2 tablespoons dried camomile flowers, crumbled**

Place all the ingredients in a medium-sized saucepan and boil for 10 minutes. Remove from the heat and let steep for 5 minutes, then strain into a jar and screw on the lid. Will keep 2 weeks refrigerated. Apply with cottonwool.

Camomile tea

A relaxing beverage to help you get a good night's sleep.

2 tablespoons dried mint, crumbled
*2 tablespoons dried camomile flowers, crumbled**
1½ cups water
1 teaspoon honey
1 teaspoon lemon juice

In a small saucepan, boil the herbs in the water for 5 minutes. Then remove from the heat and let steep for 5 minutes. Strain and add the honey and lemon juice. If desired, reheat without boiling.

Canvas waterproofing

Paint on the surfaces of tents, awnings, car and boat covers to help prevent them rotting.

1 cup soya bean oil
½ cup turpentine

You can use a medium-sized bowl to mix together the soya bean oil and the turpentine. Store in a cool place, out of the reach of small children.

Cape brandy pudding

Serve this traditional Cape pudding on a cold winter's day. Good as a teatime treat as well.

250 grams dates, stoned
1 teaspoon bicarbonate of soda
1 cup boiling water
½ cup butter
1 cup sugar
2 eggs, beaten
2 cups flour
1 teaspoon baking powder
½ teaspoon salt
1 cup chopped walnuts

SYRUP
1¼ cups sugar
1½ tablespoons butter
¾ cup water
1 teaspoon vanilla essence
pinch salt
½ cup brandy

1. Cut up the dates and divide them into two equal portions. Add the bicarbonate of soda to one half, and pour the boiling water over it. Stir to mix, then leave to cool.
2. Cream together the butter and sugar, add the beaten eggs and mix well. Sift together the flour, baking powder and salt, and fold these into the butter mixture.
3. Add the second portion of dates and the nuts. Stir in the date and bicarbonate mixture and mix all the ingredients well.
4. Turn the batter into one large, ovenproof dish or two 22-centimetre tart tins. Bake for 45 minutes at 180°C.
5. Meanwhile, make the syrup by heating the sugar, butter and water together for 5 minutes. Remove from the heat and stir in the vanilla essence, salt and brandy. Pour this syrup over the hot pudding when it is taken from the oven. Serve hot or cold with cream.

Caramel corn

Make this on a dry day – the sugar may crystallize in high humidity.

20 cups unseasoned popped corn (about 1½ cups kernels)
1 cup golden syrup
¼ teaspoon salt
½ cup unsalted butter
2 teaspoons cider vinegar
1½ cups firmly packed light brown sugar
1 teaspoon vanilla essence
½ teaspoon bicarbonate of soda

1. Spread the popped corn in a large roasting tin or bowl or two 32- x 23- x 5-centimetre tins. Set aside.
2. In a medium-sized saucepan, mix the golden syrup, salt, butter, vinegar and sugar. Cook over a moderate heat, stirring occasionally, until the butter melts and the sugar dissolves; use a pastry brush to wipe down the sides of the saucepan.
3. Increase the heat slightly and place a sugar thermometer in the syrup. Cook, without stirring, until the mixture reaches the hard ball stage (130°C).
4. Remove the saucepan from the heat and stir in the vanilla essence and bicarbonate of soda. Pour the syrup over the popcorn and mix well with a wooden spoon. Allow to set on wax paper or shape the warm popcorn into tennis-ball-sized clusters; cool. Yield: about 24 popcorn balls.

Caraway cheese sticks

A tasty snack for nibbling on with pre-dinner drinks. You can make the dough ahead of time and bake them fresh as needed.

1 cup unsalted butter or margarine, at room temperature
2 cups grated Cheddar cheese
¼ teaspoon cayenne pepper
2 cups sifted all-purpose flour
½ teaspoon salt
2 tablespoons caraway seeds
1½ teaspoons dry mustard
1 egg beaten with
1 tablespoon water
2 tablespoons grated Parmesan cheese

1. In a large bowl, cream the butter and Cheddar cheese with an electric mixer. Beat in the cayenne pepper, flour, salt, caraway seeds and the dry mustard. Shape the dough into a flat patty, cover with plastic wrap or aluminium foil, and chill for about 2 hours. (At this point the dough can be kept 1 week refrigerated, 6 months in the freezer.)
2. Preheat the oven to 180°C. On a lightly floured surface, roll out the dough ½ centimetre thick. Using a sharp knife, cut into 5- x 1-centimetre strips. Place the strips, 1 centimetre apart, on an ungreased baking sheet. Brush each strip with the beaten egg mixture, then sprinkle with the grated Parmesan cheese.
3. Bake 10 to 12 minutes or until golden brown and crisp. Let the sticks cool 1 minute, then transfer to a wire rack. Will keep 2 days in an airtight container. Yield: 6 dozen sticks. (See also *Cheese crackers*, p.388.)

Car wash concentrate

For a clean, shiny car, here's a simple washing solution that comes straight out of the kitchen cupboard.

1 cup liquid dishwashing detergent
¾ cup washing powder
14 litres water

Mix the two detergents in a bottle. To use, combine ½ cup of the concentrate with the water. If a stronger solution is desired, slightly reduce the amount of water.

Car wax

To avoid overdrying, wax your car one section at a time. Make sure that your cloths are clean.

*½ cup melted ceresin wax**
*2 tablespoons melted beeswax**
2 cups turpentine
*1 tablespoon pine-needle oil**

In a double boiler, heat the ceresin wax and beeswax. Stir, then allow to cool just until the mixture starts to harden. Stir in the turpentine and pine-needle oil. To use, apply with a rag; polish with a soft cloth.

Cat food

A balanced supplement that fulfils the ongoing feline requirements for vitamins and trace minerals.

500 grams minced beef, cooked
125 grams beef or pork liver, cooked and diced
1 cup cooked rice (without added salt)
1 teaspoon sunflower oil
*1 teaspoon calcium carbonate**

Combine the ingredients in a medium-sized bowl. Mix thoroughly. Yield: 875 grams.

Cheese & walnut balls

A tasty change from plain cheese.

1/3 cup cream cheese
2/3 cup crumbled blue cheese
2/3 cup finely chopped walnuts

1. In a small mixing bowl, blend the cream and blue cheeses. Roll the mixture into 2,5-centimetre balls with your hands (use about 1 teaspoon for each one).
2. On a sheet of wax paper, roll the balls in the chopped walnuts. Will keep 1 week refrigerated on a plate covered with plastic wrap. To freeze, place the balls in a single layer on a plate and cover tightly with aluminium foil. When frozen, transfer to double plastic bags (one inside the other) and freeze; will keep 1 month. Yield: about 24.

Cheesecake

Here's a very popular, scrumptious tart, that will have your family scrambling for the last crumb. Both the crust and the filling complement each other for a great taste.

CRUMB CRUST

1½ cups digestive biscuit crumbs
¼ cup sugar
1/3 cup melted butter

FILLING

1 cup smooth cottage cheese
1 cup cream cheese
¾ cup caster sugar
2 tablespoons flour
1 teaspoon vanilla essence
1½ teaspoons grated lemon rind
1½ teaspoons grated orange rind
3 eggs
¼ cup thick cream

1. To make the crumb crust follow this procedure: In a small bowl, mix together the crumbs, sugar and butter. Stir well to moisten all the crumbs. Press the mixture firmly over the bottom and up the sides of a 24-centimetre springform tin, to about 1 centimetre from the top. Chill for about 10 minutes in the freezer to set the crust.
2. To make the filling: In a large bowl, cream the cheeses thoroughly with an electric mixer. Add the sugar, flour, vanilla essence and the lemon and orange rinds. Beat the ingredients well. Now add the eggs, one at a time, beating lightly after each addition and scraping down the sides of the bowl. Finally, add the cream, beat lightly, and pour the filling into the prepared tin.
3. Bake for 10 minutes at 250°C. Lower the temperature to 120°C and continue baking the filling for 1 hour 20 minutes. Place the cake in the tin on a wire rack and let cool gradually to room temperature. Cover and refrigerate at least 4 hours.
4. With a narrow spatula or knife, gently loosen the crumb crust from the sides of the tin. Remove the sides but not the bottom of the pan. Slice

and serve. Will keep for 2 days refrigerated; replace the sides of the tin and cover tightly. Will keep 1 month in the freezer; remove the sides of the tin but not the bottom and wrap tightly. Yield: 12 servings.

Cheese crackers

This light, flavourful snack is useful to keep on hand for unexpected guests dropping in for sundowners. Children love them too.

1 cup unsalted butter or margarine, at room temperature
2 cups grated Cheddar cheese
2 cups sifted all-purpose flour
½ teaspoon salt
¼ teaspoon cayenne pepper
1 egg beaten with
1 tablespoon water

1. In a large bowl, cream the butter and cheese with an electric mixer. Beat in the flour, salt and the cayenne pepper. Shape the dough into a flat patty, cover with plastic wrap, and chill for at least 2 hours. (If you wish to use the dough at a later stage, you can store it for about 3 or 4 days in the refrigerator, or for about 6 months in the freezer.)
2. Preheat the oven to 180°C. On a lightly floured surface, roll out the dough about ½ centimetre thick. Cut into any desired shape (a 6-centimetre scone cutter works well). Or use biscuit cutters of various shapes. Place the crackers on ungreased baking sheets and gently brush each one with the beaten egg.

3. For the best results you should bake the crackers for about 10 to 12 minutes or until they are crisp and golden. Let the crackers cool for 1 minute on the baking sheet, then transfer to a rack. The crackers will keep for up to 2 weeks in an airtight container. Yield: 4½ dozen 6-centimetre crackers.

Chilli sauce

Here's a taste to tantalise the palate. This sauce is a great accompaniment to hot chicken and beef dishes (and goes especially well with braaied meats). Make sure there's something cool to drink with your meal.

400 grams tomatoes
2 tins (400 grams each) tomato purée
1 large onion, peeled and grated
2 cloves garlic, crushed
¼ cup cider vinegar
1 tablespoon chilli powder
2 teaspoons salt
2 teaspoons sugar
⅛ teaspoon ground allspice
2 tablespoons cornflour
2 tablespoons cold water
a few drops of Tabasco sauce (optional)

1. Purée the tomatoes in a blender or food processor, transfer to a saucepan, and set over moderate heat. Add the remaining ingredients except the cornflour and water, and mix well.
2. Heat until bubbling, then stir the cornflour into the water and add to the mixture. Cook for 2 to 3 minutes, stirring constantly. Reduce the heat to low and simmer for 20 minutes.
3. Let the sauce cool to room temperature, then transfer to 500-millilitre containers, leaving 1 centimetre of space at the top, and cover. Will keep 1 week refrigerated in a covered jar. Yield: 5½ cups.

Chocolate sauce

Here's a perfect topping for vanilla ice cream. To give the sauce extra flavour, add chopped almonds.

2 tablespoons cocoa
3 tablespoons cold water
½ cup unsalted butter
300 grams dark chocolate
1 cup boiling water
1 cup firmly packed light brown sugar
¾ cup granulated sugar
½ cup golden syrup
¼ teaspoon salt
1 teaspoon vanilla essence

1. Dissolve the cocoa in the water. Melt the butter in a double boiler on a low heat. Add the cocoa and the chocolate, then stir in the boiling water, brown sugar, granulated sugar, golden syrup and salt.
2. Set the top half of the double boiler over moderate heat and boil the mixture, uncovered, for 5 minutes (boil for 7 minutes to make a thicker sauce that will harden the moment it hits ice cream). Remove from the heat and let cool to room temperature, then stir in the vanilla essence. Yield: 2½ cups.

Christmas snow

Are you dreaming of a white Christmas in South Africa's searing summer heat? Bring the white look of a northern hemisphere winter to your lounge by painting your own Christmas tree branches (and pine needles) with this easily made artificial snow.

2½ tablespoons powdered starch
1 cup water
2 cups soap powder
blue food colouring

In a medium-sized bowl, blend the starch and half the water to make a smooth thin cream. Add the soap powder and the rest of the water. Beat with a rotary egg beater until the mixture becomes very thick. With an eyedropper, add the food colouring, beating until the "snow" has an icy-white colour. After painting the snow on your Christmas tree, you can add some white glitter to give it a crystalline appearance.

Christmas tree fireproofer

Makes evergreens flame-resistant.

2 litres water
*½ cup ammonium sulphate**
*¼ cup boric acid**
*1 tablespoon borax**

Combine all the ingredients in a medium-sized bucket. Then use a large spray bottle to spritz the tree with the formula; pour the remainder into the tree stand.

Chutney

Quick to make and delicious with curried beef, lamb or chicken.

300 grams whole-fruit apricot or peach jam
½ teaspoon powdered garlic flakes
½ teaspoon ground ginger
½ teaspoon mustard powder
½ teaspoon salt

1/4 teaspoon ground coriander
1 tablespoon cider vinegar
1/4 cup seedless raisins (optional)

Mix all the ingredients in a small bowl. Store in a covered container. Will keep for 6 months refrigerated. Yield: 1½ cups.

Cinnamon tea

Good for relieving nausea.

*1 tablespoon dried camomile flowers, crumbled**
1 teaspoon whole cloves or
1/2 teaspoon ground cloves
1 cup boiling water
1 tablespoon ground cinnamon
1 teaspoon ground nutmeg

In a small pot, steep the camomile flowers and whole cloves in the water for about 15 minutes. (If you use ground cloves, do not add at this time.) Strain the flowers from the water with a tea strainer. Add the cinnamon and nutmeg (and the ground cloves, if used) and stir. Reheat in a mug in the microwave or in a small pot on the stove. Make fresh every time. You should phone your doctor if your nausea persists.

Cockroach exterminator

Get rid of the pests with this easy-to-make insecticide.

*2 tablespoons borax**
1 tablespoon flour
1½ teaspoons cocoa powder

Mix all the ingredients in a small bowl. Set out in bottle caps or other small, unsealed containers in areas where the cockroaches congregate. **Caution:** Keep out of the reach of pets and small children.

Cocktail sauce

Adds zest to seafood. For a hotter sauce, add more horseradish or Tabasco sauce.

1 cup tomato sauce or chilli sauce (p.389)
1 tablespoon prepared horseradish sauce
1 tablespoon lemon juice
1/2 teaspoon Worcestershire sauce
1/8 teaspoon Tabasco sauce

Combine all the ingredients in a small bowl. Cover and chill for 1 hour before serving. Will keep 1 month tightly covered and refrigerated. Yield: about 1 cup.

Coffee liqueur

Cheap and easy to make. Serve with ice cream or as an after-dinner drink.

1½ cups instant coffee powder
3 cups boiling water
6 cups sugar
1 vanilla pod
1 bottle (750 millilitres) vodka

In a large saucepan, dissolve the instant coffee in the water. Add the sugar and the vanilla pod, and set the saucepan over low heat, stirring with a wooden spoon until the mixture becomes syrupy. Remove from the heat, let cool, and stir in the vodka. Pour the mixture into a glass or earthenware jug, cap tightly, and let stand for at least 30 days before serving. Yield: about 2 litres.

Cold cream

A good, inexpensive moisturizer.

1 egg yolk, beaten
2 tablespoons lemon juice
1/2 cup olive oil
1/2 cup almond oil

Combine the egg yolk and the lemon juice in a small mixing bowl. Stirring constantly with a wire whisk, gradually add both oils until the mixture thickens. If the mixture is too thick, add more lemon juice.

Cologne

A lovely, light scent at a fraction of the cost of most commercial brands.

1 cup witch hazel
*1/2 cup dried lavender flowers**
1 tablespoon olive oil
1 cup distilled water
*3 drops oil of bergamot**

Pour the witch hazel into a jar and add the lavender and olive oil. Cover tightly for 2 days, shaking occasionally. Discard the lavender flowers, then add the water and oil of bergamot. Cap tightly.

Comb & brush cleaner

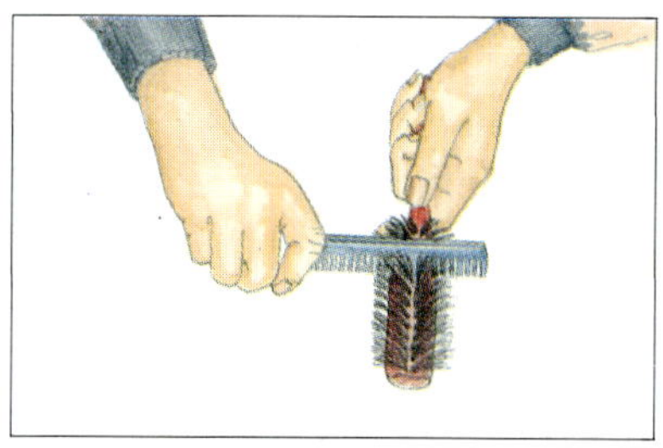

Removes oily residue.

1/2 cup household ammonia
1 litre water
1/2 teaspoon shampoo or mild detergent

Mix all the ingredients in a bowl. Add the comb and brush and let them soak in the formula for 5 to 10 minutes. Then remove from the solution, clean the comb with the brush, and vice versa. Rinse the brush and comb with water and let dry before using.

Cough syrup

Simple and effective for soothing a nagging cough.

3 tablespoons lemon juice
1 cup honey
¼ cup warm water

In a medium-sized bowl, combine the lemon juice and honey and slowly stir in the water. Store in the refrigerator until needed; take 1 or 2 tablespoons once every 3 hours to relieve bouts of coughing.

Cradle cap remedy

Here's a natural remedy for soothing and clearing baby's irritated scalp.

*50 grams dried, chopped comfrey root**
1 litre water

1. Place the comfrey root in the water in a medium-sized saucepan. Cover, bring to a boil, and simmer for 20 minutes. Strain and discard the comfrey root. Let the remaining liquid cool until tepid.
2. With a washcloth, gently work the rinse into the baby's scalp or use after a shampoo. Let it dry naturally on the scalp. Repeat the process nightly until the irritated area clears up. Will keep 4 days refrigerated; heat to skin temperature before using. Yield: 4 rinses.

Cream cheese dip

A refreshing accompaniment to fresh crudites and crackers.

1 cup cream (or cottage) cheese
2 tablespoons thick mayonnaise
2 tablespoons sour cream
1 tablespoon chopped chives
1 tablespoon chopped parsley
1 clove garlic, crushed
salt and pepper
1 tablespoon toasted sesame seeds

Mix all the ingredients, excluding the seeds. Season to taste, and pour into a decorative dish. Sprinkle the seeds over the dip and refrigerate until needed. Yield: 6 servings.

Creamed perlemoen

Cooked in the pressure cooker, this subtly flavoured dish from the sea is a delicious variation of the more conventional fried perlemoen.

1 kilogram cleaned and pounded perlemoen
2 cups dry white wine
juice of 1 lemon
salt
½ cup bread crumbs
2 tablespoons butter
¾ teaspoon ground nutmeg
1 tablespoon cornflour
½ cup milk

1. Soak the pounded perlemoen in the milk. Place in a pressure cooker with the wine and lemon juice. Seal and cook at high pressure for 5 minutes. Cool rapidly and remove the perlemoen, reserving the liquid.
2. Mince the perlemoen coarsely. Replace it in the pot with the bread crumbs, butter, nutmeg and salt, if needed. Simmer gently.
3. Mix the cornflour and water to form a smooth paste and add it to the fish mixture, stirring to thicken.
4. Serve on rice and garnish with lemon slices and a dash of cayenne pepper. Yield: 6 servings.

Crème de menthe

Surprisingly easy to make.

2 cups vodka
1 cup golden syrup
½ teaspoon peppermint essence
40 drops green colouring

Pour the vodka into a sterilized litre jar. Add the remaining ingredients, cover, and shake to mix. Serve as an after-dinner drink, add to chocolate sauces, or pour over ice cream. Yield: 3 cups.

Crème fraîche

Spoon over fresh berries or use as called for in recipes.

1 cup fresh cream
2 tablespoons sour cream, plain yoghurt or buttermilk

Stir the fresh cream and sour cream together in a medium-sized jar, and cover loosely with plastic wrap. Let stand at room temperature overnight or until thickened. Stir again and cover tightly. Refrigerate 2 hours before serving. Will keep 1 week refrigerated. Yield: 1 cup.

Crumb coating

Cheaper than store-bought and lower in sodium. Good with chicken or pork. Use the variation for fish.

2 cups sifted all-purpose flour
1 tablespoon paprika
2 teaspoons each dried marjoram and thyme, crumbled
4 teaspoons onion powder
1 teaspoon dried rosemary, crumbled
1 teaspoon salt

Put all the ingredients in a plastic or paper bag. Close it and shake to mix. Pour the mixture into a jar and cover tightly. Will keep 6 months in a cool, dark place. Yield: enough to coat 20 pork chops or 4 chickens.

Fish variation: To 2 cups all-purpose flour, add 2 teaspoons dried tarragon, 1 tablespoon dried dill, 2 teaspoons black pepper, 2 teaspoons parsley flakes, 2 teaspoons salt, 2 teaspoons onion powder and 1 teaspoon paprika. Proceed as directed above. Will keep 6 months in a cool, dark place. Yield: enough to coat 30 fish fillets or steaks.

Crumbed chicken

Low in fat and very tasty.

½ cup crumb coating
¼ cup sunflower oil
1,5 kilograms chicken, cut into 8 pieces

Preheat the oven to 180°C. Brush some of the sunflower oil onto a baking tin large enough to hold all the chicken pieces. Then brush each piece of chicken with oil. Put the crumb coating in a paper bag, add 2 chicken pieces, and shake until both pieces are evenly coated. Repeat until all the pieces are coated. Place the chicken pieces in the greased tin and bake, uncovered, until the chicken is no longer pink on the inside – about 1 hour; dark pieces may take an extra 5 to 10 minutes. Yield: 4 servings.

Crumbed fish

This simple recipe allows you to use the fish of your choice. It's easy to make and retains moisture.

¼ cup sunflower oil or melted butter
1 kilogram fish fillets or steaks
6 tablespoons crumb coating for fish

Preheat the oven to 180°C. Grease a baking sheet with some of the sunflower oil and then brush oil on both sides of each piece of fish. Spread the crumb coating on a sheet of wax paper and dredge the fish in it until well coated; shake off any excess. Arrange the fish on the greased baking sheet and bake until it flakes easily – 10 to 20 minutes depending on the thickness of each piece. Yield: 4 servings.

Crumbed pork chops

Great taste without any additives.

¼ cup sunflower oil
4 pork chops, trimmed
6 tablespoons crumb coating

Preheat the oven to 180°C. Brush some of the sunflower oil onto a baking tin large enough to hold all the chops. Brush each chop with oil. Put the crumb coating in a paper bag and shake each chop in the mixture until evenly coated. Place the chops in the greased tin and bake until they are no longer pink on the inside – 45 to 75 minutes, depending on the thickness of the chops. Yield: 4 servings.

Currant jelly sauce

Turns plain roasted chicken or game birds into dinner party fare.

½ cup redcurrant jelly
1 tablespoon lemon juice
1 teaspoon Dijon mustard
¼ teaspoon paprika

In a medium-sized saucepan, warm the jelly over moderate heat until it begins to melt. Stir in the lemon juice, then add the mustard and paprika. When heated, transfer the sauce to a medium-sized bowl and serve immediately.

Curry powder

Try this basic recipe. Then vary the ingredients to suit your own taste.

¼ cup ground coriander
2 tablespoons ground turmeric (borrie)
2 teaspoons each ground cumin, ginger and allspice
1 teaspoon each ground cinnamon, celery seed and black pepper
¼ teaspoon cayenne pepper

Thoroughly mix all the ingredients in a medium-sized bowl. Will keep 6 months in a glass jar at room temperature. Yield: ½ cup.

Cuticle cream

Softens cuticles and cures hangnails.

3 tablespoons paraffin
½ cup liquid paraffin
*1 tablespoon coconut oil**
*1 tablespoon glycerine**

1. In a double boiler, slowly heat the paraffin with the liquid paraffin and coconut oil until blended. Stir in the glycerine, remove from the heat, and let cool.

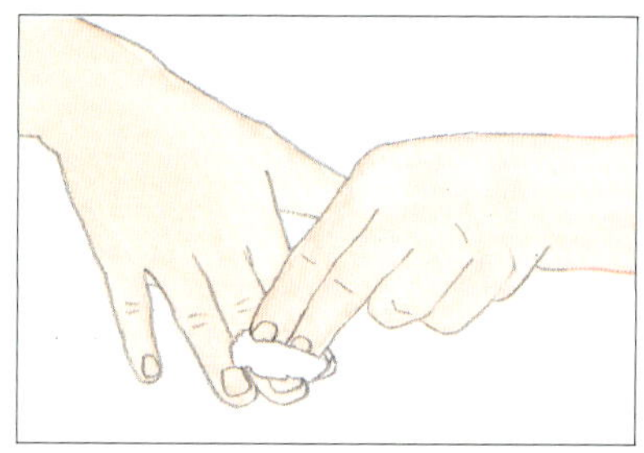

2. To use, apply directly to the cuticles with cottonwool. Or soak fingertips in the cream for about 5 minutes. Store in the refrigerator, labelled, where it will thicken.

Dandruff rinse

Combats itching and flaking.

1 cup witch hazel
1 tablespoon dried rosemary
1 tablespoon dried lavender
*1 tablespoon ground comfrey root**

Combine the witch hazel and the herbs in a medium-sized bowl and let steep for 2 days. Strain the herbs and discard. To use, massage the rinse

into the scalp and let dry. Then shampoo your hair. Store refrigerated in a covered jar.

Date & nut balls

Only minutes to make – and no baking required.

2 eggs, lightly beaten
1 cup dates, stoned and finely chopped
¾ cup sugar
1 cup walnuts or pecan nuts, finely chopped
2 cups rice crispies
1½ cups desiccated coconut

1. Place the eggs, dates and sugar in a medium-sized saucepan and cook over moderately low heat, stirring constantly, until the mixture thickens – about 5 minutes. Let cool for 5 minutes, then stir in the pecan nuts and rice crispies; let cool for 10 minutes longer.
2. Meanwhile, spread the coconut on a sheet of wax paper. Roll teaspoonfuls of the cooled date mixture into balls, and then roll in the coconut until well covered. Will keep 2 weeks refrigerated in airtight containers. Yield: 3 dozen.

Deodorant

Stay fresh all day without the chemicals or perfume found in many commercial products.

*4 teaspoons alum**
2 teaspoons bicarbonate of soda
1 cup witch hazel

Use a small mixing bowl from the kitchen, and stir the three ingredients together. Transfer to a spray bottle and apply to the skin immediately after bathing.

Diet cat food

A healthy regimen for cats.

1,25 kilograms beef liver or chicken liver, cooked and minced
2 cups cooked rice
2 teaspoons sunflower oil
*2 teaspoons calcium carbonate**

Put all the ingredients in a medium-sized bowl and mix well. Feed a 2,5-kilogram cat 125 grams daily, a 3- to 4-kilogram cat 180 grams daily, and one that weighs 5 kilograms or more 250 grams daily. The cat food will keep for up to 5 days in the refrigerator and for 3 months in the freezer. Cover tightly. Yield: 1,5 kilograms.

Diet dog food

Contains all the vitamins and minerals your pet needs.

250 grams lean minced beef
1 cup low-fat cottage cheese
4 cups cooked sliced carrots
4 cups cooked green beans
15 grams dry brewer's yeast

Fry the beef until no longer pink. Drain off the fat and allow to cool. Combine with the remaining ingredients in a medium-sized bowl. Feed a 2,5-kilogram dog 250 grams daily, a 5-kilogram dog 350 grams, a 10-kilogram dog 500 grams, a 20-kilogram dog 800 grams, a 30-kilogram dog 1,25 kilograms and a dog that weighs 40 kilograms or more 1,5 kilograms. Will keep in refrigerator (tightly sealed) for 5 days, and for 3 months in the freezer. Yield: 1,75 kilograms.

Disinfectant

Use on countertops and floors.

4 cups washing powder
12 cups hot water
*4 cups pine-needle oil**

1. Mix the washing powder and the water in a bucket and stir slowly until all the powder dissolves. If foam starts to surface, stop stirring and skim off the bubbles or wait until they melt. Gradually add the pine-needle oil; mix well.
2. To use, dilute the disinfectant with water, except when cleaning areas such as toilet bowls or dirty drains where bacteria flourish. Store in a jar with a tight-fitting lid, out of the reach of small children.

Dog biscuits

If you would like to give your pet something a little different from the traditional dog biscuits you get in the supermarket, try the following recipe. At least you will know what's in the dog biscuits.

1¾ cups dog food (below)
1 cup unprocessed bran
1 cup oats
½ cup sunflower oil

1. Preheat the oven to 100°C. Mash the dog food in a medium-sized bowl to remove all lumps, then mix in the bran and oats. Slowly add the oil, mixing to a pliable consistency that is easy to mould into patties or bone shapes. (You may find it necessary to use more or less oil than the recipe actually calls for.)
2. Bake for 3½ hours. Let cool and store in a covered tin. Will keep 1 month refrigerated. Yield: 16 medium-sized biscuits.

Dog food

If your pooch is looking undernourished, or is just plain bored with his usual fare, pamper him with this well-balanced diet.

500 grams minced beef
2 eggs, hard-boiled
4 cups cooked rice
6 slices white bread, crumbled
*2 teaspoons calcium carbonate**

Cook the meat in a covered pot until no longer pink, retaining the fat. Mix it thoroughly with the remaining ingredients in a medium-sized bowl. This mixture tends to be dry; to improve palatability add water (not milk). Feed a 2,5-kilogram dog about 125 grams daily, a 5-kilogram dog 180 grams, a 10-kilogram dog 350 grams, a 20-kilogram dog 750 grams, a 30-kilogram dog 1 kilogram and a dog that weighs 40 kilograms or more 1,3 kilograms. Yield: 1,5 kilograms.

Drain cleaner

Deodorizes drains and fights build-up in traps.

1 cup bicarbonate of soda
1 cup salt
¼ cup cream of tartar

1. Place all the ingredients in a covered jar and shake well to mix.
2. To use, pour ¼ cup directly down the drain, followed by 2 cups boiling water. After 1 minute, flush out with cool tap water. Repeat weekly. Be sure to store in a dry place in a tightly sealed container.

Dry carpet cleaner

Here's a cleaner that brightens rugs and adds a fresh scent.

2 cups bicarbonate of soda
½ cup cornflour
5 bay leaves, crumbled, and
1 teaspoon ground cloves or 1 cup potpourri (p.411)

1. In a covered container, mix all the ingredients well. Store in a safe place, away from children.
2. To use, shake well and sprinkle generously on the carpet. Leave for several hours (overnight if possible), keeping children and pets off the carpet. Vacuum thoroughly.

Dry shampoo

To avoid staining the bath mat, apply over the basin or bathtub.

2 tablespoons mealie meal
1 tablespoon ground almonds
*1½ tablespoons orrisroot**

Combine all the ingredients in a small mixing bowl. Massage 1 teaspoon into the scalp, then brush through the hair. Repeat the process, if necessary.

Ebonizer

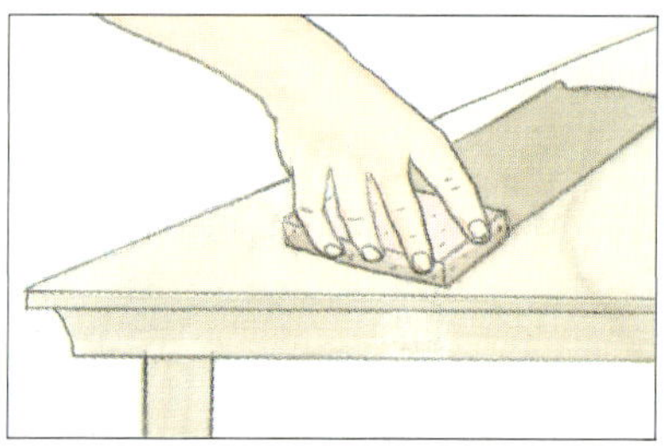

Effectively blackens any wood that contains tannin, such as mahogany, walnut or oak.

1 fine steel wool pad
2 cups cider vinegar

1. Put the steel wool pad in a small plastic or glass bowl; add the vinegar and allow to stand for several days or until the steel wool dissolves.
Caution: Do not cover the bowl; gas from the reaction between the vinegar and the steel wool could possibly cause it to explode.
2. To use, sponge the solution evenly onto a sanded wood surface. If a second coat is desired, wet the wood liberally but evenly with tap water and leave at least 1 hour before restaining. Allow to dry overnight before applying a finish.

Egg facial mask

Just three simple ingredients will help smooth your face and moisten dry skin, leaving you feeling refreshed. To enhance the benefits of applying regular facial masks, wash your face thoroughly at least twice a day.

1 egg
*½ cup coconut oil**
1 tablespoon honey

1. Beat the egg well in a small bowl. Slowly add the coconut oil and honey, beating until the mixture is the consistency of mayonnaise. Set an empty toilet paper roll upright in a bowl and pack the mask into it with a spoon. Freeze overnight.
2. To use, peel away some of the cardboard and rub the frozen stick over your face. After 5 or 10 minutes, rinse off with warm water. After using, cover the exposed end of the stick with plastic wrap and return to the freezer.

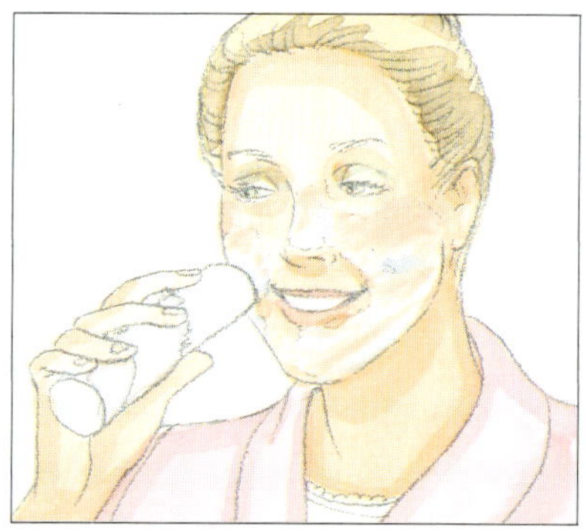

Facial mask

This facial not only revitalizes – it also helps remove impurities.

1 tablespoon instant non-fat dry milk
½ cucumber, peeled
1 teaspoon plain yoghurt

Purée the ingredients in a blender until smooth. Apply to your face, avoiding the area around the eyes, and let dry for about 20 minutes. Rinse off. It's best to mix a fresh batch for each use, but if a large quantity is desired, freeze in an ice cube tray; thaw enough for each use.

Facial scrub

Apply over a sink or bathtub.

1/3 cup mealie meal
2 tablespoons honey
1 tablespoon ground almonds or walnuts

Combine the ingredients in a small bowl, adding a little water if the mixture is too dry to apply easily. To use, pack onto your face and leave at least 5 minutes. Remove with warm water and a washcloth.

Fertilizer

General nutrition for most non-flowering house plants with foliage.

1 tablespoon Epsom salts
1 teaspoon bicarbonate of soda
*1/2 teaspoon saltpetre**
1/4 teaspoon household ammonia
4 litres warm water

Combine the Epsom salts, bicarbonate of soda, saltpetre and ammonia in a bowl. Dissolve the mixture in the warm water in a bucket. To use, apply once a month. For an acid-loving plant, you should add 4 drops white vinegar or 5 tablespoons black coffee per 4,5 litres fertilizer.

Fig bars

A delicious teatime treat.

DOUGH

3 cups sifted all-purpose flour
1/2 teaspoon salt
1/2 teaspoon ground cinnamon
2/3 cup butter or margarine
1/2 cup firmly packed light brown sugar
1/2 cup firmly packed dark brown sugar
2 egg whites
1 teaspoon vanilla essence

FILLING

1 3/4 cups finely chopped dried figs (about 11 figs)
1 cup water
2 tablespoons sugar
2 tablespoons lemon juice

1. Combine the flour, salt and cinnamon in a small bowl; set aside.
2. In a large mixing bowl, cream the butter and the light and dark brown sugar until light and fluffy. Beat in the egg whites and the vanilla essence, then slowly beat in the flour mixture. Shape the dough into a ball. Cover with plastic wrap and refrigerate for 2 to 3 hours.
3. Place the figs, water, sugar and lemon juice in a medium-sized saucepan. Cook over moderate heat, stirring constantly, until the mixture is thick – about 7 minutes. Allow to cool but don't chill.
4. Preheat the oven to 180°C. Place 1/4 of the dough between sheets of waxed paper and roll to a thickness of 3 millimetres. Slice the dough into 6- x 7,5-centimetre strips.
5. At the narrow end of each strip, place 2 level teaspoons of the filling. Roll the dough into bars and place 2,5 centimetres apart on 2 ungreased baking sheets. With a spatula, flatten them to 1 centimetre thick.
6. Bake in the centre of the oven for 12 to 14 minutes or until the bars are lightly browned. Transfer to a rack to cool. Will keep for 1 week in an airtight container at room temperature, and for 3 months in the freezer.

Finger paints

A colourful diversion to keep children occupied.

1 1/4 cups flour
1 cup water
*3 tablespoons glycerine**
assorted food colourings

Mix the flour and water in a medium-sized bowl. Divide the mixture equally among 3 small bowls. Stirring constantly, add 1 tablespoon glycerine to each batch, along with food colouring. Make fresh as needed.

Fire extinguisher

More effective than plain water; especially useful when leaving a campsite.

4 teaspoons bicarbonate of soda
4 teaspoons salt
2 litres water

Place the bicarbonate of soda and salt in a spray bottle. Add the water and combine thoroughly. To put out fires, aim the mixture at the base of the flames.

Fish stock

Use for soups and sauces.

1 kilogram fish heads, bones and trimmings
1 onion, peeled and sliced
1 carrot, peeled and sliced
1 stick celery, chopped
1 sprig each parsley, thyme and marjoram, tied together in a square of muslin
1 bay leaf
1,5 litres water
1/2 cup dry white wine
1 teaspoon salt

1. Rinse the fish well and place in a saucepan with the rest of the ingredients. Bring gently to the boil.
2. Remove the scum as it rises to the surface. When the surface is clear, half-cover the saucepan and simmer for about 30 minutes. Strain and allow to cool. Store in the refrigerator. Yield: 1,5 litres.

Fizzy fruit drink

A natural carbonated beverage filled with vitamins and free of refined sugar.

1/4 cup frozen orange, grape or apple juice concentrate
3/4 cup soda water
ice cubes

Pour the frozen juice concentrate into a glass. Add a few tablespoons of the soda water and stir until dissolved. Fill the glass with ice cubes, add the remaining soda, and mix well. Serve immediately. Yield: 1 serving.

Floral water

Here's a refreshing combination of oils that is lighter than cologne, with a sweet flowery scent.

*1 teaspoon lavender oil**
*1 teaspoon lemon oil**
*2 teaspoons jasmine oil**
*3 teaspoons bergamot oil**
*4 drops each clove, cinnamon and neroli oils**
*1 teaspoon musk oil**
2⅔ cups vodka
*¼ cup plus 4 teaspoons rose water**

Mix the oils and tincture of musk with ½ cup of the vodka. Gradually add the remaining vodka and the rose water, stirring constantly. Transfer the liquid to a bottle with a secure lid. Let stand 1 to 2 months to mature, shaking every few days. If the mixture gets cloudy, strain it through a coffee filter until clear. Make sure you store it in a tightly covered bottle out of the reach of small children.

Flypaper

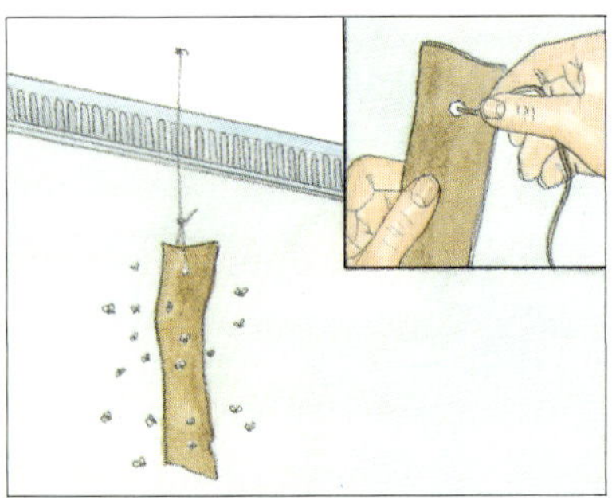

Easy to make and effective.

¼ cup golden syrup
1 tablespoon light or dark brown sugar
1 tablespoon sugar

Combine the ingredients in a small bowl. Pour over strips of brown paper and let soak overnight. To use, make a hole in one end of a strip, insert a string, and hang.

Fritters

Fritters, particularly pumpkin fritters, are popular in South Africa. Serve piping hot with cinnamon, sugar and lemon wedges.

450 grams peeled pumpkin
pinch of salt and sugar
½ cup flour
1 teaspoon baking powder
2 eggs
milk (optional)
3 tablespoons sunflower oil
3 tablespoons butter

1. Steam the pumpkin over boiling water with a little salt and sugar until it is soft.
2. Mix the pumpkin, flour, baking powder and eggs to form a batter of dropping consistency. Add a little milk if the mixture is too stiff.
3. Heat the oil and butter in a heavy frying pan and fry spoonfuls of the pumpkin mixture. Drain on brown paper or paper towels.
Variation: Substitute sweet potatoes. Yield: 6 servings.

Fruit compote

Keep dried fruit on hand and whip up a delicious dessert in no time.

1¼ cups (180 grams) dried, stoned prunes
⅔ cups (125 grams) raisins and sultanas
½ cup dried figs (100 grams)
½ cup (100 grams) dried apricots
1½ cups orange juice
⅓ cup water
¼ cup sugar
1 cinnamon stick, broken
¼ teaspoon ground ginger
⅛ teaspoon ground cloves
pinch black pepper
¾ teaspoon vanilla essence (optional)

1. Place all the ingredients except the vanilla in a medium-sized enamel or stainless steel saucepan. Set over high heat and bring to a boil; then reduce the heat to low, cover, and simmer for 25 to 30 minutes or until the fruit is tender.
2. Remove from the heat. Take out the pieces of cinnamon stick and discard. Let cool to room temperature and add the vanilla, if desired. Chill. You should serve with heavy cream or crème fraîche. Will keep for about 3 days tightly covered and refrigerated. Yield: 6 servings.

Furniture cleaner

Removes surface dirt and grime from finished wood.

1 cup boiled linseed oil
⅔ cup turpentine
⅔ cup white vinegar

Thoroughly mix all the ingredients in a large bowl. Apply to wood surfaces with a soft cloth, rubbing to remove dirt and excess polish. For badly caked-on dirt, use superfine steel wool. Store in a tightly covered jar out of the reach of children.

Gargle

Here's a simple way to soothe those sore throats that come with colds.

1 cup warm water
3 tablespoons cider vinegar
2 drops Tabasco sauce
pinch salt

Pour the water into a glass and add the remaining ingredients. Gargle as much as necessary. If the mixture is too sour, add another tablespoon water. Make only as much as needed at one time. If sore throat persists, consult a doctor.

Gedat milk

This Malay milk drink is usually served at prayer meetings on Thursday and Sunday nights after a funeral, but can be enjoyed at any time. Serve in small glasses.

½ teaspoon cardamom pods, pounded or bruised
1 cinnamon stick, slightly bruised
4 cups milk
pinch salt
4 teaspoons sugar
*a few drops of rose water**

Tie the cardamom and cinnamon in a muslin bag. Leave this bag in half the milk for about 5 minutes, then heat the milk to boiling point with the spice bag, salt and sugar. Remove from the heat, cover and allow the spices to draw for at least 15 minutes. Remove the bag. Add the remaining milk to the boiled milk. Strain and add a few drops of rose water.

Gentian root tonic

Perks up a declining appetite.

*2 to 4 teaspoons chopped dried gentian root**
2 cups water
2 teaspoons dried peppermint (optional)

In a small saucepan, bring the gentian root and water to a boil; reduce the heat and simmer for 15 minutes. Remove from the heat and add the peppermint, if desired. Cover and let steep for 5 minutes. Transfer to a cup. Let cool until lukewarm. Will keep 2 days tightly covered and refrigerated.

Gesmoorde snoek

This mouthwatering, traditional dish is very popular in the western Cape.

1 kilogram dried, salted snoek
3 onions, peeled and finely sliced
¼ cup butter
3 potatoes, peeled and diced
1 cup milk
salt and black pepper to taste
cayenne pepper (optional)

1. Soak the fish in cold water for 6 to 8 hours, changing the water after 3 hours. Drain and boil the fish in fresh water until tender (about 20 minutes).
2. Drain and flake the fish, using two forks. Discard the skin and all the bones.
3. Braise the onions lightly in the butter, then add the potatoes, milk and flaked fish. Cover tightly and simmer on a low heat until the potatoes are tender.
4. Season to taste, adding a shake of cayenne pepper if you are a spice fancier. An extra knob of butter may be added during cooking if required. Skinned and chopped tomatoes may also be added along with a teaspoon of sugar to counteract the tartness.
5. Most of the liquid should evaporate. The dish must be neither too moist nor too dry. Serve on a bed of rice. Yield: 4 to 6 servings.

Gingerbread

This delicious teatime cake is even better the day after baking.

2½ cups flour
1 teaspoon each ground cinnamon and ground ginger
½ teaspoon ground cloves
½ teaspoon salt
½ cup butter
¾ cup sugar
1 cup golden syrup
2 teaspoons bicarbonate of soda
1 cup boiling water
2 eggs, lightly beaten

1. Preheat the oven to 175°C. Sift together the flour, ground cinnamon, ground ginger, cloves and salt.
2. Blend the butter, sugar and syrup (or molasses, if you like).
3. Dissolve the bicarbonate of soda in the boiling water and add it to the butter mixture. Add the eggs and the dry ingredients.
4. Pour the mixture into a greased and floured 23- x 12-centimetre loaf tin, and bake for 1 hour, or use 2 smaller loaf tins, baking for 45 minutes. Serve sliced with butter. Yield: 8 servings.

Ginseng tea

The ginseng plant, which provides the main ingredient for this tea, has been used by the Chinese and Korean people for 5,000 years. It has been credited with increasing energy and relieving such problems as stress and headaches. Some users even attribute aphrodisiacal powers to ginseng.

1 cup water
*2 tablespoons ginseng extract**
1 teaspoon honey

Bring the water to a boil in a small saucepan, then add the ginseng and the honey. (For a sweeter tea, add more honey.) The ginseng tea may be reheated, although its flavour will decrease each time. Make it fresh as desired. Do not drink for more than 10 consecutive days.

Glass cleaner

This mixture enables you to clean even the dirtiest windows.

½ cup methylated spirits
½ cup household ammonia
7½ cups warm water

Pour the methylated spirits and ammonia into a bucket, then add the water and mix well. To use, transfer the cleaner to a spray bottle. Spritz the window with the cleaner and leave on for 30 seconds, then wipe the glass with newspaper, making sure to turn it frequently. Store tightly covered, out of reach of children.

Glue

Here's a waterproof binding mixture, that works effectively on most fabrics and paper.

6 tablespoons water
2 envelopes gelatine
2 tablespoons white vinegar
*2 teaspoons glycerine**

1. Bring the water to a boil in a small saucepan. Remove from the heat and stir in the gelatine until it dissolves. Pour in the vinegar and glycerine; stir well. Let cool, then transfer to a jar and cover tightly.
2. Apply the glue while warm. Will keep many months in a tightly sealed jar but will gel after a few days. Heat the jar in hot water before reusing.

Graham crackers

Here's a recipe for a traditional American favourite.

1 cup all-purpose flour
¼ cup whole-wheat flour
5 tablespoons sugar
½ teaspoon each salt and bicarbonate of soda
1 teaspoon baking powder
¼ teaspoon ground cinnamon
3 tablespoons chilled butter or margarine, in small pieces
¼ cup solid vegetable fat
2 tablespoons honey
1 tablespoon molasses
¼ cup water
1 teaspoon vanilla essence

1. In a medium-sized bowl, combine the all-purpose and whole-wheat flours, sugar, salt, bicarbonate of soda, baking powder and cinnamon. Work in the butter and the vegetable fat with a pastry blender or your fingertips until the mixture resembles coarse bread crumbs.
2. In a small bowl, mix the honey, molasses, water and vanilla essence. Sprinkle slowly over the dry ingredients, then toss with a fork until well blended. Form the dough into a ball (it may be crumbly, but don't add water). Cover with plastic wrap and chill for several hours.
3. Preheat the oven to 180°C. Cut the dough in half and leave to stand for 15 minutes at room temperature.
4. Lightly sprinkle a piece of wax paper with whole-wheat flour. Put a piece of the dough on top and flatten it with a rolling pin. Sprinkle the dough with more whole-wheat flour and cover with another sheet of wax paper. Roll out to form a rectangle measuring roughly 18 x 37 centimetres. If the dough breaks, pinch the pieces together with your fingers and continue rolling.

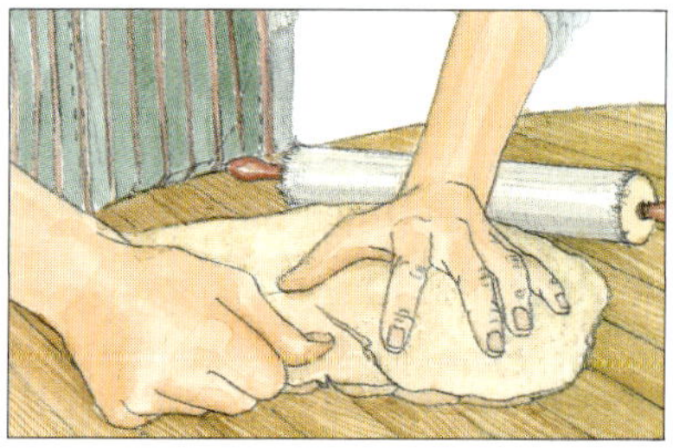

5. Peel off the top piece of wax paper, then use a fork to prick the dough at 1- to 2,5-centimetre intervals. Cut into 6-centimetre squares. With a spatula, transfer to a large, ungreased baking sheet, placing the squares close together.
6. Repeat the process with the remaining dough, rerolling and using the scraps. Bake the crackers on the centre rack of the oven for about 15 minutes or until lightly browned on the edges.
7. Let the crackers cool on a rack. They will keep 1 month in an airtight canister at room temperature or 6 months in a tightly covered container in the freezer.
8. Store at least 24 hours before serving. Yield: 24 to 28 crackers.

Grease solvent

Removes oil stains from your skin.

2 tablespoons liquid soap gel
3 tablespoons mealie meal
*1 teaspoon glycerine**

Combine the ingredients in a small bowl. Pour the mixture onto your hands and scrub until stains disappear; rinse off.

Gum arabic adhesive

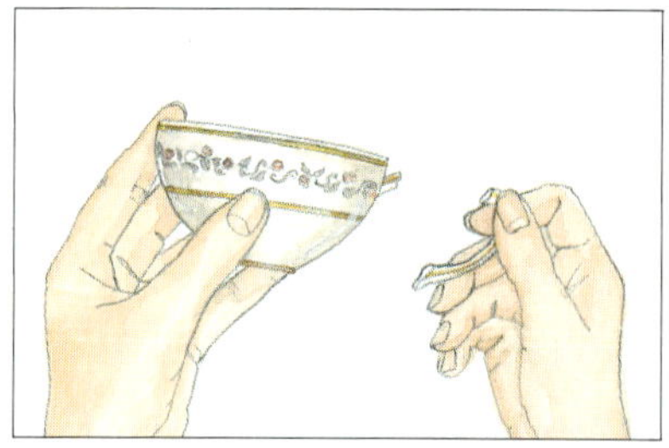

Use this adhesive to mend broken dishes and crockery.

*3 tablespoons gum arabic**
*1 tablespoon glycerine**
½ teaspoon water

In a small mixing bowl, thoroughly combine the ingredients. To use, apply a thin coating to each surface, fit the pieces together, and hold firmly in place until the glue dries – about 1 hour. Let dry at least 24 hours before washing or using the piece. The glue will keep 1 year in an airtight jar.

Hair conditioner

Softens dry hair and helps prevent split ends.

⅓ cup olive oil
⅓ cup sunflower oil
⅓ cup honey

Place all the ingredients in a small saucepan and set over low heat until just boiling. Remove from the heat and let cool for 5 minutes. Transfer to a 750-millilitre plastic spray bottle. Spray on hair and rub in thoroughly. Wet a towel with warm water and wrap around head for 1 hour. Shampoo to remove, then wash and style hair as usual. You should store in a cool, dry place.

Ham & cheese bread

A meal in itself. Make it ahead of time for lunchboxes or breakfast toast.

2 cups unsifted all-purpose flour
½ cup mealie meal
2¼ teaspoons baking powder
½ teaspoon salt
¼ teaspoon black pepper

¾ cup (125 grams) coarsely chopped ham
1 cup plus 2 tablespoons grated Parmesan cheese
¾ cup milk
⅓ cup olive oil
2 eggs

1. Preheat the oven to 190°C. In a large mixing bowl, sift together the flour, mealie meal, baking powder, salt and pepper. Stir in the chopped ham and 1 cup of the grated Parmesan cheese.

2. In a small bowl, whisk together the milk, olive oil and eggs. Add to the flour mixture and stir until just combined. Pour the batter into a greased 23- x 12,5- x 7,5-centimetre loaf tin. Sprinkle the remaining cheese on top and bake until a toothpick inserted in the middle comes out clean – 45 to 50 minutes. Set the tin on a wire rack and allow to cool for 20 minutes, then turn out. Serve warm or at room temperature. Will keep for 1 week covered with aluminium foil and refrigerated; 3 months wrapped tightly in aluminium foil in the freezer.

Hand treatment

Moisturizes and softens hands that are chapped and dry.

3 tablespoons finely ground almonds
*2 tablespoons dried comfrey root**
1 tablespoon chopped parsley
1 egg
1 tablespoon honey
*1 tablespoon glycerine**

Mix the ground almonds, comfrey root and parsley in a small bowl and set aside. In another bowl, combine the egg, honey and glycerine. Stir in 3 tablespoons of the almond mixture. Dip your hands in the concoction and gently massage it in, giving special attention to the area around the nails. Let it penetrate for about 30 minutes; rinse off with warm water. Will keep 5 days refrigerated.

Herbal face mask

Cleans skin and tightens pores.

1 tablespoon honey
1 egg
*1 teaspoon dried camomile flowers, crumbled**
1 teaspoon finely chopped fresh mint

Mix all the ingredients together in a small bowl. To use, apply the mixture to your face and neck. Let dry and rinse off with warm water.

Herbal ice cubes

For an upset stomach. The peppermint and bitters are soothing, and the ice cubes are easier to keep down than liquids.

1 cup water
1 peppermint tea bag
2 cups apple juice
1 teaspoon angostura bitters

1. Bring the water to a boil in a small saucepan. Add the tea bag, turn off the heat, and let steep for 10 minutes.
2. Discard the tea bag. Let the tea cool for 5 minutes, then stir in the remaining ingredients.
3. Transfer the mixture to an ice cube tray and place in the freezer until solidly frozen.
4. To use, suck or chew up to 3 ice cubes each hour or rub a little bit on your lips.
Caution: Call your doctor if vomiting lasts more than 24 hours or if it's unusually severe.

Herbal shampoo

Makes oily hair shiny and manageable. If hair needs conditioning, add the egg and milk.

4 tablespoons dried mint
1 tablespoon dried sage
1 cup water
⅓ cup baby shampoo
1 egg, beaten (optional)
⅓ cup milk (optional)

Place the herbs in a small saucepan, add the water, and bring to a full boil. Remove from the heat and let steep for 20 minutes. Strain and discard the herbs. In a jar, mix the baby shampoo with ¼ cup of the herbal water. Shampoo as usual.
Variation for dry hair: You can substitute 1 tablespoon dried comfrey root, 1 tablespoon dried rosemary and 1 tablespoon dried camomile for the dried mint and sage; proceed as directed.

Herb butters

Freeze them and enjoy the delicate flavour of fresh herbs all year long.

½ cup butter or margarine, at room temperature
¼ cup finely chopped dill or
2 tablespoons chopped tarragon or
3 tablespoons snipped chives or 1 to 3 cloves garlic, crushed
¼ teaspoon salt

Combine the butter with the herb or garlic and the salt in a small bowl. Refrigerate until firm enough to handle. Shape into a roll and cover with plastic wrap and aluminium foil. Or fill each section of an ice cube tray, cover with aluminium foil, and freeze. Will keep 5 days refrigerated, 4 months in the freezer. The dill butter is particularly good on grilled fish or vegetables; the tarragon butter, on steaks or poultry; the chive butter, on baked potatoes, scrambled eggs or fresh vegetables; the garlic butter, on hamburgers, steaks, lamb chops or seafood. Yield: 8 servings.

Herb dressing

For a stronger flavour to this dressing, you can add ½ teaspoon more herb dressing mix.

2 tablespoons herb dressing mix (p.400)
1½ cups warm water

2 tablespoons olive oil
5 tablespoons white vinegar or tarragon vinegar
2 cloves garlic, crushed

Mix the herb dressing mix with the warm water, olive oil, vinegar and the garlic in a small bowl. Whisk the ingredients together and leave the dressing at room temperature for about 30 minutes before using. Whisk again, then pour the desired amount over your salad. This dressing will keep 1 week tightly covered and refrigerated. Yield: 2 cups.

Herb dressing mix

This dressing mix has a fresh taste and no preservatives.

½ cup dried parsley
¼ cup each dried origanum, basil and marjoram, crumbled
¼ cup sugar
2 tablespoons fennel seed, crushed
2 tablespoons dry mustard
1 tablespoon black pepper

Place all the ingredients in a 1-litre glass jar. Cover the jar and shake thoroughly until well blended. The dressing mix will keep 6 weeks in a cool, dark, dry place. Yield: 2 cups.

Herbed cheese spread

As good as the imported brands and less costly.

1 cup cream cheese, drained
1 teaspoon chopped parsley
¼ teaspoon crushed garlic
¼ teaspoon salt
¼ teaspoon black pepper
¼ teaspoon lemon juice

To drain the cream cheese, place in a piece of muslin or a fine sieve and allow the moisture to seep out for an hour. Mix all the ingredients in a small bowl, cover, and refrigerate at least 2 hours to allow the flavours to blend. Will keep 7 days refrigerated in a tightly sealed container. To freeze, shape the cheese spread into a log and cover with plastic wrap, then aluminium foil. Will keep 3 months in the freezer.

Herbed rice

This rice dish can be served immediately, or kept for the next day. Contains less salt than packaged mixes and takes just minutes to make. An ideal accompaniment to grilled lamb cutlets, chicken or fish dishes.

2⅔ cups water
4 tablespoons herbed rice mix (below)
1⅓ cups uncooked white or brown rice
2 tablespoons unsalted butter or margarine

Bring the water to a boil in a large saucepan. Pour in the herbed rice mix and stir to combine. Add the rice and lower the heat until the water just simmers. Cover and cook white rice for 25 minutes or until tender; brown rice as directed on the package. Stir in the butter and serve the rice hot. Yield: 6 servings.

Herbed rice mix

This tasty herb mix can be used with either white or brown rice.

3 tablespoons dried onion flakes
1¼ teaspoons salt
1 bay leaf
¾ teaspoon dried basil
½ teaspoon paprika
½ teaspoon garlic flakes
⅛ teaspoon finely chopped dried lemon peel

Place all the ingredients in a plastic bag and shake vigorously to combine. Store in a tightly covered jar or canister in a cool kitchen cupboard or in the pantry. Yield: 4 tablespoons.

Horseradish sauce

Use sour cream and cider vinegar to give this sauce a special flavour.

1 cup sour cream
2 tablespoons cider vinegar
2 tablespoons horseradish sauce

Combine the ingredients and serve. Yield: 1¼ cups.

Hot dog relish

Exceptionally quick and easy.

1 large onion, peeled and finely chopped
2 tablespoons cider vinegar
2 tablespoons sugar
¼ teaspoon salt
125 grams bottled pimentos, drained and chopped

Mix all the ingredients in a medium-sized bowl. Let stand at room temperature for 30 minutes before serving. Will keep 1 week covered and refrigerated. Yield: 1 cup.

Hot pepper jelly

Serve with cold ham or pork.

2 medium-sized sweet red peppers, cored, seeded and chopped (about 1 cup)
*3 jalapeño peppers, cored, seeded and finely chopped**
2 cups cider vinegar
6½ cups sugar
*200 grams liquid pectin**

1. In a food processor or blender, process the peppers with 1 cup of the vinegar until finely minced.
2. Transfer the mixture to a large saucepan and add the sugar and remaining vinegar. Set over high heat and bring to a rolling boil. Then stir.
3. Remove the pan from the heat and skim the surface.
4. Stir in the pectin. Return the pan to the heat and bring to a boil for 1 minute. Repeat Step 3.
5. Pour the jelly into hot, sterilized 250-millilitre preserving jars. Wipe rims and seal. Will keep for 6 months. Yield: eight 250-millilitre jars.

House plant insecticide

Deal effectively with aphids, mealy bugs and thrips, those small insects which are difficult to remove by hand.

handful of tobacco (pipe or cigarette)
4 litres water
4 teaspoons liquid soap (p.403)

Steep the tobacco overnight in the water. Strain and discard the tobacco. Add the liquid soap to the water and mix well. To use, pour into spray bottles and thoroughly spray infested plants, wetting both the tops and bottoms of leaves. This treatment is most effective in warm weather. Do not apply to petunias, nicotiana, tomatoes or other plants that are susceptible to tobacco mosaic virus.

Caution: Test any new insecticide on a few small leaves before a full-scale application.

Ink

Buy lamp black in a tube at an art or craft store, or make it by holding a plate over a lit candle. Scrape the black soot which forms on the plate into a small bowl.

1 egg yolk
*1 teaspoon gum arabic**
½ cup honey
*½ teaspoon lamp black**
water

Mix the egg yolk, gum arabic and honey in a small bowl, and stir. Add the lamp black, and thin with a little water if necessary.

Insecticide

For shrubs, flowers and vegetables.

3 green chilli peppers
2 or 3 cloves garlic
¾ teaspoon liquid soap
3 cups water

Purée the peppers and garlic cloves in a blender. Transfer to a spray bottle, and add the liquid soap and water. Let stand 24 hours, strain, and spray onto infested plants.
Caution: Always test any new insecticide on a few small leaves before embarking on a full-scale application.

Insect repellent

Discourage mosquitoes, ticks and other biting pests.

¼ cup methylated spirits
*1½ teaspoons camphor**
*1½ teaspoons calcium chloride**

Place all the ingredients in a small bowl and stir until dissolved. To use, rub on exposed areas of skin before going outdoors.
Caution: Be careful not to use near the eyes. Discontinue if you notice a rash or other allergic reaction.

Jelly

More nutritious than commercial brands. Vary the sugar. according to the sweetness of the juice.

2 envelopes gelatine
6 to 8 tablespoons sugar
2 cups grape, apple or orange juice
1 cup chopped fruit (optional)

Mix the gelatine with the sugar in a small saucepan and slowly stir in ½ cup of the juice. Let stand for 5 minutes. Cook over moderately low heat, stirring, until the sugar and gelatine dissolve. Remove from the heat and stir in the remaining juice. Pour into a mould or bowl, let cool, cover, and refrigerate. When the gelatine is thick and syrupy, add the fresh fruit if desired. Chill until firmly set – about 3 hours. Will keep 2 days refrigerated. Yield: 4 servings.

Jewellery cleaner

For a sparkling effect, use this economical cleaner, made from traditional cleaning materials.

1 tablespoon dishwashing detergent
1 tablespoon washing soda (sodium carbonate)
1 tablespoon household ammonia
3 cups warm water

1. Combine the ingredients in a medium-sized bowl and pour into a glass jar. Label and cover. Be sure to store this jewellery cleaner out of the reach of children, as these household cleaning materials are very toxic.
2. To use, soak the jewellery in the solution for 1 to 10 minutes, depending on how heavily tarnished it is. If a piece has an intricate pattern or several cracks or crevices, swish it through the liquid vigorously. A toothbrush with soft bristles works especially well for cleaning large items. Wash an old mascara brush and use it to clean small, hard-to-reach spaces. Rinse and dry with a soft clean cloth. Before you immerse a valuable piece of jewellery, check that it will not be damaged – place a drop or two of the cleaner on an unobtrusive part of the piece, and watch for any reaction.

3. Don't soak pearls; rub them gently with a soft chamois cloth dampened in the solution.
Caution: Do not combine the cleaner with any substance containing chlorine bleach; together they produce hazardous fumes.

Koeksusters

A fête and bazaar favourite – sweet koeksusters dripping with syrup are always popular.

SYRUP

5 cups sugar
2 cups water
2 pieces fresh green ginger (5 centimetres each), peeled and crushed
½ teaspoon cream of tartar
pinch salt
grated rind and juice of 1 lemon

1. Put all the ingredients in a saucepan. Heat, stirring continuously, until the sugar has dissolved. Cover and boil for 1 minute.
2. Remove the lid and boil the syrup for another 5 minutes, but do not stir.
3. Remove the syrup from the heat, and allow to cool for at least 2 hours in a refrigerator – preferably overnight – it must be ice cold.

DOUGH

4 cups flour
½ teaspoon salt
2 tablespoons baking powder
5 tablespoons butter, grated
1 egg
1–1½ cups milk or water
sunflower oil for deep frying

1. Sift together the dry ingredients and rub in the grated butter with your fingertips, or cut the butter in with a pastry cutter.
2. Beat the egg, add 1 cup of the milk or water, and mix lightly with the dry ingredients to form a soft dough. Add more liquid if the dough is too stiff. Knead well until small bubbles form under the surface of the dough. Cover with a damp cloth and allow to stand for 30 minutes to 1 hour. Roll out the dough to a thickness of 1 centimetre.
3. Cut strips 1 centimetre wide and twist 2 strips together or plait 3 strips together, cutting the twisted or plaited lengths at 8-centimetre intervals and pinching the ends together.
4. Drop into deep, hot oil (180°C–190°C) – a cube of day-old bread should turn golden in a minute. Fry the koeksusters for 1–2 minutes or until golden brown. Turn the koeksusters over and fry on the other side until golden brown.
5. Remove and drain for a moment on paper towels, then plunge them into the ice-cold syrup. Remove from the syrup with a slotted spoon and allow excess syrup to drain back into the bowl, then drain the koeksusters on a wire rack.
Note: To ensure that the syrup stays icy cold – stand the syrup container in a bowl of ice cubes. Replace the ice cubes as they melt.

Laundry presoak

Penetrates heavily soiled spots.

¼ cup household ammonia
2 tablespoons bicarbonate of soda
1 tablespoon liquid detergent
1 litre water

1. Combine the ingredients in a jar and shake thoroughly. Transfer a part of the mixture to a spray bottle. Store the remaining portion in a clean 2-litre bottle. Label and store out of the reach of children and pets.
2. To use, spray soiled areas and let stand for 5 to 10 minutes; launder as usual. It may be necessary to repeat the process more than once.

Lawn fertilizer

A quick and easy springtime feeding for a green, healthy lawn.

1 cup Epsom salts
1 cup household ammonia
water

Combine the Epsom salts and ammonia in a clean jar. To use, mix 2 tablespoons of the mixture with 10 litres of water in a watering can, and sprinkle over 15 to 20 square metres of turf. Or, for use with a pressure sprayer, mix the entire batch with enough water to equal 1 litre total volume, and pour into the sprayer container. One litre of fertilizer will then cover 250 square metres of lawn. Water lightly so that the fertilizer will seep down into the soil.

Lawn fertilizer for autumn

Help grass roots get ready for spring.

2 cups Epsom salts
3 tablespoons baking powder
water

Mix the Epsom salts with the baking powder in a clean jar. To use, dissolve 2 tablespoons of the mixture with 5 litres of water in a watering can and sprinkle over 10 square metres of turf. Or, for application with a pressure sprayer, mix the entire batch with enough water to equal 1 litre total volume and pour into the sprayer container. This will cover 150 square metres of lawn.

Laxative

A gentle laxative that provides bulk.

1 tablespoon linseeds
150 millilitres cold water

Soak the seeds in the water overnight. Add them to your breakfast cereal. Or you can soak the seeds in 150 millilitres hot water for 2 hours, strain, drink the liquid sweetened with honey, and then eat the seeds.

Lemonade mix

For limeade, substitute the juice of fresh limes for the lemon juice.

4 cups fresh lemon juice (about 24 large lemons)
1 cup sugar
2 cups golden syrup

Stir all the ingredients together in a large bowl until the sugar dissolves. Pour into a screw-top jar, cover and store in the refrigerator. For each serving, shake well and add ¼ cup of the mix to ¾ cup water or soda water, and stir well. Add ice and a twist of lemon if desired. Will keep 2 weeks refrigerated. Yield: 24 servings.

Lemon curd

A versatile spread. Serve it in tart shells, as a filling for sponge cake or on toast. (For variety, substitute lime juice for the lemon juice.) Also makes a nice gift – pour into a jar and add a pretty frilled lid and label.

½ cup butter or margarine
2 cups sugar
⅔ cup fresh lemon juice (about 4 large lemons)
grated rind of 2 lemons
4 large eggs, lightly beaten
pinch salt

1. Melt the butter in a small saucepan over low heat. Remove from the heat and add the sugar, lemon juice, lemon rind, eggs and salt. Mix thoroughly. Cook over moderate heat, stirring constantly, until the mixture thickens – about 8 minutes. Do not let it boil.

2. Strain the mixture through a sieve into a bowl and discard the solids. Let cool for 5 minutes, then spoon the lemon curd into a clean jar and let cool to room temperature; cover. Will keep 1 month refrigerated. Yield: 2½ cups.

Lip balm

An inexpensive way to keep your lips soft in all kinds of weather.

1 tablespoon olive oil
*1 teaspoon glycerine**
2 tablespoons honey

Mix all the ingredients in a small bowl. To use, apply to chapped lips with your finger or a cottonwool bud. Use as often as necessary for chapped lips until condition improves. Store refrigerated in a tightly covered jar.

Liquid soap

Turn leftover bits of bar soap into a versatile cleaning agent.

2 cups grated soap flakes
4 litres water
*2 tablespoons glycerine**

Mix the ingredients together in a large, heavy-based pot. Place over a low heat, stirring occasionally, until the soap flakes have dissolved. Transfer to a storage container, cover tightly, and store out of the reach of children. Use as a hand soap or for general household cleaning chores.
Gel variation: For a thicker soap, use the same method but add only 2 litres of water.

Low-sodium mustard

Tasty without added salt. Ideal for people on a low-salt diet.

*⅓ cup mustard seed**
⅓ cup dry white wine
½ cup white vinegar
½ cup water
2 tablespoons honey
¼ teaspoon ground allspice
⅛ teaspoon each ground cinnamon and ginger

1. Mix the mustard seed, white wine and vinegar in a medium-sized bowl and let stand 3 hours at room temperature. Transfer to a food processor or blender and add the water, honey, allspice, cinnamon and ginger. Process until fairly smooth.

2. Place the mixture in the top of a double boiler over simmering water and cook, stirring occasionally, until thickened – 10 to 12 minutes. Pour into a hot, clean preserving jar and let cool to room temperature, then cover tightly. This low-sodium mustard will keep 1 year refrigerated. Yield: 2 cups. (See also *Mustard*, p.406.)

Make-up remover

An excellent way to moisturize skin. Add your own handmade labels and give jars of moisturizer to some of your friends as gifts.

*8 tablespoons beeswax**
450 millilitres liquid paraffin
300 millilitres water

1. Using a sharp kitchen knife or a grater, finely pare the beeswax. Place in the top of a double boiler with the liquid paraffin. Heat gently until melted. Allow to cool to 50°C, while separately heating the water to the same temperature.
2. When both temperatures are uniform, slowly add the water to the liquid paraffin and beeswax mixture, stirring continuously.
3. Leave the mixture to cool. When it begins to solidify, pour it into storage jars. Yield: 2½ cups.

Marble cleaner

A good non-abrasive cleaning agent. Ask your chemist for the ingredients.

*¾ cup sodium sulphate**
*¼ cup sodium sulphite**

Mix both ingredients in a small bowl. To use, sprinkle on marble and rub with a damp sponge, then wipe clean. Store in a tightly covered jar out of the reach of children. Yield: 2 cups.

Marsh mallow cough syrup

The orange juice helps to keep the syrup from crystallizing. For a tangier syrup, substitute the juice of 1 lemon for the orange juice.

*1½ to 2½ teaspoons chopped dried marsh mallow root**
2 cups water
2 cups sugar
¼ cup orange juice

In a small saucepan, stir the marsh mallow root into the water; bring to a boil over moderately high heat. Reduce the heat to low and simmer 20 minutes. Strain the decoction into another saucepan (you should have about 1 cup). Over low heat, slowly stir in the sugar, so that a thick syrup forms. Simmer another 5 minutes, making sure the grains dissolve completely. If the mixture gets too thick, stir in a little more water. Let cool slightly, then gradually add the orange juice and mix. Transfer to a container with a lid; cover when cool. Yield: about 3 cups.

Mealie meal bread

For a Mexican flavour, add to the batter ½ cup grated Cheddar cheese and 100 grams bottled, drained and chopped jalapeño peppers*.

2½ cups mealie meal mix
3 eggs, lightly beaten
1 cup water

Preheat the oven to 220°C. Place all the ingredients in a large bowl and mix well. Pour into a 20- x 20- x 5-centimetre baking tin and bake for about 17 minutes, or until a skewer inserted into the centre comes out clean. Cut into squares and serve hot with butter. To store, cover the tin tightly with aluminium foil. Will keep for 3 days refrigerated and 2 months in the freezer. Yield: 8 servings.

Mealie meal mix

Here's a real time-saver. You can have piping hot bread or muffins on the dining room table in minutes.

3 cups all-purpose flour
3 cups mealie meal
1½ cups instant non-fat dry milk
3 tablespoons sugar (optional)
3½ tablespoons baking powder
2½ teaspoons salt
¼ cup vegetable fat

Mix together all the dry ingredients in a large bowl. Using two knives or a pastry blender, cut in the vegetable fat until the mixture resembles coarse crumbs. Will keep 6 weeks refrigerated in covered containers. Yield: about 8 cups.

Mebos

Mebos is a very old Cape confection. Make it when apricots are plentiful.

1 kilogram well-ripened apricots
1 cup salt
3,5 litres water
*2 tablespoons slaked lime**
sugar for dipping and packing

1. Mix the salt and 8 cups of the water together and soak the apricots for 8 hours in this solution. Drain the fruit and remove the skins and pips.
2. Shape the apricots into flat rounds and spread them on racks to dry for 4-6 days. Cover with muslin to keep dust and insects at bay. Check that the air can circulate freely, and turn the fruit regularly. Bring the fruit inside if rain is threatening – moisture and humidity will ruin the fruit.
3. Alternatively, dry the fruit in a cool oven: 60°C for about 6 hours.
4. Dissolve the lime in the remaining 6 cups of water, and soak the apricots for 5 minutes in this solution. Dry slightly and dip in sugar. Pack the mebos in containers, layering the fruit with sugar. Yield: 250 grams mebos.

Melktert

A traditional South African teatime or dessert treat.

Uncooked puff pastry (bought or homemade)
3 extra-large eggs, separated
½ cup flour
3 tablespoons cornflour
⅓ cup sugar
600 millilitres (3 cups) milk
*1 stick cinnamon**
3 tablespoons butter
*ground cinnamon**

1. Preheat the oven to 230°C. Line a 25-centimetre pie plate with thinly rolled puff pastry. Paint the inside edge of the pastry lining with 2 teaspoons of egg white (taken from one of the three eggs). This will prevent the filling from pulling away from the crust. You should put the lined plate in the refrigerator while the filling is being prepared.
2. Scald milk and cinnamon stick. Mix the dry ingredients (setting aside one tablespoon sugar) in a saucepan. Stir the mixture into a paste with a little of the hot milk. When smooth, add the rest of the milk and the cinnamon stick, mix well, and bring to the boil, stirring continuously.
3. When the mixture has thickened, stir in the butter. Remove from the heat, add a little of the hot mixture to the egg yolks, and then carefully add the rest of the yolks to the mixture in the pot, stirring gently. Return to the heat for a minute. Allow to cool.
4. Beat the egg whites and remaining sugar until stiff. Fold thoroughly into the cooled milk mixture.
5. Spoon the filling into the pastry case, dust with cinnamon and bake in oven at 230°C for 10 to 15 minutes. Reduce the temperature to 180°C and bake for 20 minutes. Turn off the heat and leave for a further 5 minutes.

Mock chopped herring

This dish is a very tasty appetiser.

1 tin (215 grams) plain pilchards
1 apple, peeled and finely chopped
1 medium-sized onion, peeled and finely chopped
2 hard-boiled eggs, peeled and finely chopped
4 Marie biscuits, soaked in a little water
juice of ½ lemon
pinch salt

Garnish: 2 hard-boiled eggs, peeled and finely chopped parsley

1. Mash the pilchards thoroughly. Mix in the apple, chopped onion, eggs and the biscuits. Add lemon juice and salt to taste.
2. Place the mock chopped herring in an attractive bowl and garnish with the chopped hard-boiled eggs and parsley. Be sure to eat within a day or two. Yield: 1½ cups.

Mock mayonnaise

If you're watching your weight, here's an alternative to the commercial brands. There are only 76 kilojoules per tablespoon, and no cholesterol in this creamy spread. For a little spice, add a tablespoon of tomato sauce or Tabasco sauce.

2 cups cold water
2 tablespoons cornflour
¼ cup olive oil
¼ cup white vinegar
¼ cup plain low-fat yoghurt
2 teaspoons prepared mustard
1 teaspoon prepared horseradish sauce

1. Whisk together the water and cornflour in a small saucepan. Set over moderate heat and cook, stirring continuously, until the mixture comes to a boil. Boil for 1 or 2 minutes or until the mixture is clear. Transfer to a small bowl.
2. Whisk in the remaining ingredients in the order listed. Will keep 2 weeks tightly covered and refrigerated. Yield: about 2 cups.

Moisturizer

Softens skin and removes make-up. Applied moisturizers should generally last for about 10 hours.

1 tablespoon olive oil
*1 tablespoon coconut oil**
1 tablespoon sunflower oil
2 tablespoons mashed strawberries
1 or 2 drops vitamin E oil (optional)

Mix together the olive, coconut and sunflower oils in a small bowl, then stir in the strawberries. If desired, add the vitamin E oil. Store in the refrigerator in a covered jar.

Mosbolletjies

The leavening agent for mosbolletjies in South Africa was traditionally grape must (in Afrikaans, *mos*), but when must is not available, the yeast can be made from raisins.

1 cup raisins
3 cups cold water
½ teaspoon dried yeast
¼ cup warm water
15 cups flour, sifted
2½ cups sugar
1½ teaspoons salt
*1 tablespoon aniseed**
1½ cups butter or margarine, melted
3 cups lukewarm milk or an equal mixture of milk and water

For the glaze: 1 egg yolk, beaten with a pinch of sugar and 1 tablespoon milk

1. Crush the raisins and place in a saucepan with the cold water. Boil for 10 minutes, then allow to cool until lukewarm. Pour into a glass jar or enamel container with a tight-fitting lid. Dissolve the yeast in the warm water and stir into the raisin mixture. Stir well together and leave in a warm place for 24–48 hours, or until the raisins have risen to the top. Strain the raisin liquid (*must*).
2. Stir 250 grams of the flour into the must to form a smooth batter. Leave in a warm place for 3–4 hours, or until it is well fermented.
3. Sift together the rest of the flour, the sugar and salt, and add the aniseed. Form into a stiff dough with the must and flour mixture, the melted butter and enough of the milk (or milk and water mixture) to make a stiff dough. Knead the ingredients very well together.
4. Cover well and leave in a warm place overnight, or until the dough doubles in bulk. You don't have to knead it again.
5. Carefully shape the dough into buns, and pack into greased loaf tins. Lightly cover, and allow to rise in a warm place until doubled in bulk. Brush with the egg yolk, sugar and milk glaze, bake for 1 hour at 180°C. Turn out and break apart.

Suggestion: Serve either hot with butter, or make rusks by drying out the buns in a very slow oven (about 140°C). Store in an airtight container. Yield: 50 buns.

Mouthwash

If mint is not to your liking, substitute other flavours until you find the taste you like best.

2 cups water
3 teaspoons fresh or dried parsley
2 teaspoons whole cloves
*2 teaspoons ground cinnamon**
2 teaspoons peppermint essence

Boil the water in a small saucepan, then remove from the heat. Add the remaining ingredients and let steep. Strain. Will keep 2 weeks tightly covered and refrigerated.

Mushroom barley soup

For heartier soup, add sautéed mushrooms or leftover meat or chicken.

5 cups water
1 recipe mushroom barley soup mix (below)
1 tin (400 grams) whole peeled tomatoes with juice
1 small carrot, peeled, halved lengthways, and thinly sliced

Bring the water to a boil over moderately high heat in a medium-sized saucepan. Add the mix, tomatoes (breaking them up with a spoon) and carrot. When the mixture returns to a boil, turn the heat to low and let simmer, covered, until the barley is tender – about 30 minutes. Remove from the heat and let stand, covered, at room temperature for 10 minutes. Remove the bay leaf and serve. Yield: 4 servings (1½ cups each).

Mushroom barley soup mix

Great to have on hand, especially on a cold winter's day.

25 grams dried mushrooms
½ cup dried pearl barley
2 tablespoons dried onion flakes
1 teaspoon ground sage
1 teaspoon dried marjoram, crumbled
1 small bay leaf
1 teaspoon salt
½ teaspoon garlic flakes
¼ teaspoon black pepper

Rub the mushrooms with paper towels to remove any surface dirt, then break into small pieces, discarding any tough stems. Place in a plastic bag or small container, add the remaining ingredients, seal tightly, and shake to mix. This dry mixture will keep 6 months in a tightly covered container at room temperature. Yield: 4 servings soup (1½ cups each).

Mustard

Hot and spicy. Good with cold meats or on sandwiches or hot dogs.

*⅓ cup mustard seed**
3 tablespoons dry mustard
½ cup cider vinegar
½ cup dark beer
2 cloves garlic, finely chopped
¼ cup firmly packed light brown sugar
¾ teaspoon salt
½ teaspoon ground ginger
¼ teaspoon ground allspice

1. Mix the mustard seed, dry mustard and vinegar in a small bowl. Cover with plastic wrap and let stand 3 hours at room temperature.
2. Place the remaining ingredients in a small saucepan, add the mustard mixture, and stir well. Bring to a boil over moderate heat, then reduce the heat to low and let simmer 5 minutes, stirring occasionally. Remove from the heat and transfer to a clean, hot preserving jar. Seal tightly and cool to room temperature. Will keep 1 month tightly covered and refrigerated. Yield: 1 cup.

Mustard plaster

A folk remedy for relieving chest congestion due to colds.

1 tablespoon dry mustard
¼ cup flour (for adults) or 6 tablespoons flour (for children)
lukewarm water

1. Sift together the mustard and flour in a medium-sized bowl. Slowly add just enough water to make a paste. Spread the plaster on a piece of muslin big enough to cover the chest area. Place another piece of muslin on top.
2. To use, make sure the skin is dry, then place the mustard plaster on the chest. Check frequently and, when the skin begins turning red, usually after 10 to 20 minutes, remove the plaster. (Do not use for more than 30 minutes at a time.) Rub the area with Vaseline to hold in the heat. Use the plaster twice a day until the congestion clears up.
Caution: Try the plaster on a small patch of skin to test for an allergy.

Naartjie ice cream

Serve this tangy, refreshing ice cream on a hot summer's day. For an elegant dinner party dessert, garnish with crystallized violets and mint leaves. Pour a few drops of Van der Hum liqueur over the ice cream immediately before serving.

8 medium-sized naartjies
1 cup caster sugar
250 millilitres water
juice of half a lemon
1 egg yolk
250 millilitres thick cream

1. Peel the naartjies and squeeze 250 millilitres of juice from the naartjie pulp. Set aside ¼ of the rind.
2. Boil the sugar and water in a saucepan over high heat for 10 minutes to make a syrup. Remove and allow to cool.
3. Stir the naartjie and lemon juices into the syrup. Beat the egg yolk and stir into the syrup. Return to the heat and cook gently for 5 minutes, stirring continuously.
4. Cool, pour into a container, cover with a lid, and place in the freezing compartment of the refrigerator until lightly set.
5. Grate the rind of 2 of the naartjies and beat the cream until stiff. Break the frozen syrup into a bowl and beat with a fork until it has an even texture. Beat in the cream and rind until the colour is uniform and the rind evenly distributed. Spoon back into the container, cover with a lid and freeze for 2½ hours.
6. Turn out the mixture once more and beat until the texture is even, then replace in the freezer.
7. For a different presentation, remove the pulp from 6 of the naartjies by scooping it out. Serve the ice cream in the empty naartjie shells with the lids placed on top at an angle. Yield: 6 servings.

Nappy rash ointment

Ease baby's skin problems. As is the case with all homemade skin preparations, you should first test for an allergic reaction on a small patch of skin.

*1 tablespoon dried chickweed**
*1 tablespoon dried marsh mallow root**
*1 tablespoon dried comfrey root**
*⅛ teaspoon dried and ground goldenseal root**
*1 cup sweet almond oil**
*50 grams beeswax**

Combine all the ingredients except the beeswax in a medium-sized saucepan. Cook over a moderately low heat until soft, 5 to 10 minutes. Add the beeswax and keep cooking until the beeswax melts completely. Strain through muslin into a small glass jar, seal and refrigerate until solid. Apply when changing a nappy. Yield: 20 applications.

Caution: If the rash doesn't disappear after 3 or 4 applications, phone your doctor and ask whether or not to continue the treatment.

Newspaper preservative

Newspaper clippings are usually of great sentimental value. They won't yellow as long as they're kept out of direct sunlight, and you soak them in this preservative.

2 litres soda water, at room temperature
2 milk of magnesia tablets

Pour the soda water into a medium-sized bowl and add the milk of magnesia tablets. Let them dissolve overnight, then pour 5 millimetres of preservative into a baking pan. Lay the clippings out flat in the solution until they are saturated, then remove. Let them dry on a flat surface, and remember to keep them out of direct sunlight at all times. Yield: 2 litres preserving solution.

No-fry chicken

This method of cooking chicken results in crusty, moist meat without all the mess and kilojoules of deep fat. For a less spicy dish, omit the ginger and Tabasco sauce.

1/4 teaspoon dried origanum
1/4 teaspoon ground ginger
1/2 teaspoon dried basil
1 clove garlic, crushed
2 tablespoons all-purpose flour
1/2 teaspoon salt
750 grams skinless, filleted chicken breasts
2 tablespoons milk
1/8 teaspoon Tabasco sauce
1 cup branflakes or cornflakes, coarsely crumbled

1. Preheat the oven to 180°C. Put the origanum, ginger, basil, garlic, flour and salt into a paper bag and shake to mix. Place the chicken in the bag and shake until evenly coated with the mixture.

2. In a soup plate, combine the milk and Tabasco sauce. Place the cereal crumbs on a plate. Dip each breast in the milk mixture, then roll in the crumbs until coated all over.

3. Spray a cake rack with non-stick cooking spray or wipe with oil. Place the chicken on top and set the rack on a baking tray. Bake, uncovered, until the breasts are no longer pink on the inside – about 15 minutes. You should serve hot or at room temperature. Yield: 4 servings.

Nose drops

Relieves stuffed nasal passages. If you don't have distilled water, let tap water stand overnight in a shallow bowl to allow the chlorine to escape.

1 teaspoon salt
2 cups distilled water

Mix the salt with the water. Transfer to an atomizer and spray into your nose. Or place a tablespoon in the palm of your hand and inhale. Use alone or before using decongestant drops such as ephedrine.

Onion cough syrup

A soothing and aromatic remedy.

2 medium onions, thinly sliced
1 cup honey
1/2 cup warm water
1 tot vodka (optional)
juice of 1 lemon

Place the onions in a medium-sized bowl. Pour the honey, water and vodka (if desired) over them and let the mixture stand overnight in the refrigerator. Strain the liquid, discarding the onions, and transfer to a bottle; cover tightly. Will keep 1 week refrigerated. Take 2 teaspoons every 3 to 4 hours. Yield: 1½ cups.

Ostrich eggs

Fresh ostrich eggs can be bought in some specialized shops. For an unusual dish, try scrambled ostrich egg.

1 whole egg
water or skim milk (half the volume of the egg)
salt and black pepper to taste
3 tablespoons butter or margarine

1. Make a hole in one end of the egg and shake the contents into a bowl. Beat the egg with the water (or skim milk), and add the salt and pepper.

2. Melt butter or margarine in a large frying pan and when bubbly, pour in the egg mixture. As the egg begins to cook, use a large spoon to lift layers of it, and fold them over (do not stir with a fork).

3. When the egg is cooked, but still slightly moist, transfer it onto plates. Traditionally, this is served with a spoonful of *moskonfyt*, a syrupy jam which is made from grapes. If *moskonfyt* is not available, use a commercial brand of grape jam instead.

4. To keep egg mixture fresh, refrigerate in a sealed container. A fresh, uncooked egg in its shell will keep, refrigerated, for 4-6 weeks. Yield: 8 servings.

Pancakes

For variety, add ½ cup strawberries or sliced bananas to the batter, then proceed as directed.

2 cups scone mix (see p.414)
2 large eggs, lightly beaten
1 cup water or milk

Place the scone mix in a large bowl and stir in the eggs and milk until just blended; do not overmix. (The batter should be slightly lumpy.) Heat a well-oiled large, heavy pan over moderate heat until hot but not smoking. Spoon about ¼ cup batter per pancake into the pan and cook until bubbles form across the top – about 2 minutes. Turn the pancakes, and cook 2 minutes longer. Serve immediately with butter and honey or syrup. Yield: 10 to 12 pancakes.

Papier-mâché

A good way to make inexpensive birthday and holiday gifts.

1 cup flour
⅔ cup water
newspaper strips (about 4 centimetres wide)

1. Mix the flour and water in a medium-sized bowl. It should be the consistency of thick glue. If a thicker mixture is desired, add more flour.
2. Dip each strip separately in the paste and gently pull it through your fingers to remove any excess. Then apply to a surface you want to cover. (Clay, cartons, bottles or any disposable containers make a good base.) Repeat until well covered.
3. When dry, decorate with poster paint. For a longer-lasting and harder surface, coat with clear varnish after the paint dries. The more coats of varnish, the stronger the papier-mâché object will be.

Paste

An all-purpose paste, excellent for papier-mâché projects.

1½ cups flour
½ cup sugar
1 cup cold water
2 cups boiling water
*1 tablespoon alum**
*1 teaspoon oil of cinnamon**

Combine the flour and sugar in a large saucepan and slowly stir in the cold water. Add the boiling water gradually, then bring the mixture to a boil, stirring constantly. When the mixture is thick, remove from the heat and stir in the alum and oil of cinnamon. Store in a tightly sealed container. Thin, if necessary, with boiling water.

Peach jam

Natural fruit juices are the primary sweetener in this low-sugar preserve. It's best made when peaches are in season and bursting with flavour.

1,5 kilograms ripe clingstone peaches
3 strips orange peel, 1 centimetre x 5 centimetres each
⅔ cup fresh orange juice
⅔ cup unsweetened white grape juice
⅔ cup firmly packed light brown sugar
1 tablespoon fresh lemon juice
¼ teaspoon ground ginger

1. Bring a large saucepan of water to a boil over moderate heat. Drop the peaches in, 2 or 3 at a time, and boil for 30 seconds. Remove with a slotted spoon and rinse with cold water to cool. Peel off the skins, remove the pits, and coarsely chop.
2. Transfer the peaches to a large saucepan, add the remaining ingredients, and set over moderate heat. Let the mixture boil slowly, stirring frequently, until it thickens and

reaches 105°C on a sugar thermometer – about 30 minutes.
3. Discard the orange rind and transfer the jam to hot, sterilized preserving jars. Cover and let cool to room temperature. Will keep 2 months refrigerated. Yield: 3 cups.

Peanut butter

Pure, delicious and easy to make.

2 cups salted dry-roasted peanuts
1 tablespoon plus 1 teaspoon sunflower oil

1. For creamy peanut butter, process the peanuts with the oil in a food processor or blender until creamy, working in batches if necessary. Stop the machine occasionally and scrape down the sides.
2. To make chunky peanut butter, coarsely chop about ⅓ cup of the peanuts in a blender or food processor and set aside. Process the remaining peanuts with the oil until creamy, then stir in the coarsely chopped peanuts. Will keep for 1 month refrigerated in a covered jar. Yield: 1 cup.

Peanut butter bars

A protein-packed snack. For extra crunch, add the unsalted peanuts.

½ cup sugar
1 cup golden syrup
1 jar (350 grams) crunchy peanut butter
4 cups rice crispies
1 cup coarsely chopped unsalted peanuts (optional)

In a very large saucepan over moderate heat, bring the sugar, syrup and peanut butter to a boil, stirring constantly. (Watch carefully to make sure the mixture does not burn on the bottom of the pan.) Remove from the heat and mix in the remaining ingredients. Press into a well-greased 32,5- x 23- x 5-centimetre baking pan and let cool to room temperature. Cut into 2,5- x 5-centimetre bars and serve. Store in a tightly covered container. Will keep 1 week at room temperature, 2 weeks refrigerated, and up to 3 months in the freezer. Yield: 54 bars (2,5 x 5 centimetres each).

Periwinkles with garlic butter

Make sure you comply with the strict regulations which apply to the harvesting of periwinkles.

50 periwinkles
water or dry wine to cover
salt
4 cloves garlic, crushed
1/3 cup butter

Soak the periwinkles in fresh water for 30 minutes. Wash thoroughly and poach in salted boiling water or wine for 5 minutes. Drain. When cool, pick the periwinkles out of the shells with a pin. Discard the hard "trap door" and stomach. Mix the garlic well with the butter. Serve the periwinkles with the garlic butter and slices of fresh whole-wheat bread.

Peppermint tea

Ease a stuffy nose or stimulate a sluggish digestive system with this soothing herbal tea.

*1/3 cup dried peppermint leaves**
1 cup water
1 tablespoon grated lemon and orange rind
2 teaspoons crème de menthe liqueur
1 teaspoon honey

Put the peppermint leaves in the water and bring to a boil in a small saucepan; remove pan from the heat and let the tea steep for 10 minutes. Strain the liquid and add more hot water, if needed, to make 1 cup. Add the grated lemon rind, grated orange rind, crème de menthe and honey. Make the tea fresh every time.

Perfume

A nice spicy scent at a bargain price.

1/2 cup witch hazel
1/4 cup whole cloves
*1 teaspoon orrisroot**

Mix the witch hazel and cloves in a small jar; add the orrisroot. Cap the jar and shake; let stand for 2 days, stirring occasionally. Strain the liquid, discarding the solids, and transfer it to a jar; cover tightly. To use, dab on behind your ears or on wrists. Store out of the reach of small children.

Pesto

An easy-to-prepare sauce that goes well with pasta or potatoes. Or mix it with mayonnaise to make a dip for raw vegetables. It freezes well, too.

2 cups loosely packed fresh basil leaves, washed and patted dry with paper towels
1/2 cup olive oil
2 cloves garlic, crushed
3 tablespoons pine nuts or chopped almonds
1/2 teaspoon salt
1/2 cup grated Parmesan cheese

Put all the ingredients except the cheese in a blender or a food processor and purée until smooth; if using a blender, stop frequently and push the mixture down with a rubber spatula. Stir in the cheese (the mixture will be very thick). Stir in 2 or 3 tablespoons water and serve. Will keep 1 week refrigerated or 6 months in the freezer. Yield: about 1 cup or enough for 500 grams of pasta.

Parsley variation: For a lighter sauce, omit the pine nuts and substitute 1 cup fresh parsley for 1 cup of the basil.

Pine potpourri

Bring the scent of the forest indoors.

1/2 cup lavender or lemon leaves
1/2 cup snipped pine needles
1/2 cup miniature pine cones
*1/2 cup rose hips**
*2 teaspoons orrisroot**
*2 drops pine-needle oil**

Mix the lavender or lemon leaves, pine needles, pine cones and rose hips in a large bowl. Add the orrisroot and oil and stir well. Transfer to a decorative container.

Pizza

A quick low-kilojoule, low-fat version of the old favourite. For variety, top with sautéed mushrooms, cooked crumbled sausage, steamed spinach or asparagus.

DOUGH

1/2 cup flour or 1/4 cup flour and 1/4 cup whole-wheat flour
1/8 teaspoon salt
1 1/2 teaspoons baking powder
3 to 4 tablespoons water

TOPPING

1/3 cup pizza sauce
1/4 cup grated mozzarella cheese
1/2 large green pepper, seeded and sliced
1 tablespoon chopped fresh basil leaves (optional)

1. Combine the flour, salt and the baking powder in a small bowl. Add the water and stir with a fork until the dough comes together, adding a few teaspoons more water if necessary. Knead the dough until smooth – about 2 minutes. Shape it into a ball, cover with a clean dishcloth, and let rest 5 minutes.

2. Roll the dough into a 25-centimetre circle, using flour as needed to prevent it from sticking.

3. Preheat the griller. Brush a medium-sized non-stick pan lightly with sunflower oil and set over moderate heat until very hot – about 1 minute. Add the dough and cook until the underside is dry and flecked with brown spots – 2 to 3 minutes. (The dough will puff up in spots, but the sauce will cover them up.)

4. Transfer to an ungreased baking tray, and spread the sauce evenly over the crust. Sprinkle with the cheese and top with the seeded and sliced green pepper rings.

5. Grill 10 centimetres from the heat until the sauce is bubbling and the cheese has melted – 2 to 3 minutes. Before serving, sprinkle with the chopped basil leaves if desired. Serve immediately. Yield: 4 slices.

Play dough

A good modelling dough for children. It can also be used to make Christmas tree decorations.

1/2 cup table salt (do not use rock or sea salt)
1/2 cup hot water
1/2 cup cold water
1/2 cup cornflour
2 drops food colouring (optional)

1. Mix the salt and hot water in a large saucepan and bring to a boil over high heat.

2. Place the cold water in a small bowl and stir in the cornflour: mix well. Add the drops of food colouring, if desired.

3. Add the cornflour mixture to the boiling salt water and stir vigorously to keep it from forming lumps. Cook over low heat, stirring constantly, until the mixture is stiff.

4. Remove from the heat and, using a large spoon, carefully turn the mixture onto a breadboard. Let cool, then knead until smooth. Use immediately or wrap in plastic wrap and store in an airtight container. If desired, clay models can be preserved by air-drying at room temperature for 3 days or by baking for 2 hours at 100°C.

5. To make Christmas tree decorations, roll out the dough 5 millimetres thick, then use biscuit cutters to make a variety of shapes. Using a toothpick, make a hole at the top of each one where a string or wire can be inserted. Bake at 100°C for 2 hours. Decorate as desired.

Pomander

Gives a fresh fruity scent to cupboards and drawers.

180 grams whole cloves
1 apple, lemon, lime or orange
*2 tablespoons orrisroot**
*2 tablespoons ground cinnamon**

Push the cloves into the fruit you've chosen, placing them so close together that none of the skin is exposed. In a medium-sized bowl, mix the orrisroot and cinnamon; roll the clove-studded fruit in this mixture until it is completely coated. Wrap in muslin or netting. Hang in the cupboard or wrap in tissue paper and put in a drawer.

Potato sausage

A delicious way to stretch meat, and much less fatty than most sausage.

750 grams potatoes, peeled and sliced
2 large onions, peeled and finely chopped (2 cups)
2 medium-sized tart apples (such as Granny Smith), peeled, cored and finely chopped
3 cloves garlic, finely chopped
2 tablespoons olive oil
500 grams veal mince
500 grams pork mince
1 1/2 tablespoons prepared mustard
4 teaspoons salt
1 1/2 teaspoons black pepper
1 1/2 teaspoons ground sage
1 teaspoon ground allspice
1/4 teaspoon ground nutmeg
1 1/2 tablespoons sunflower oil

1. Bring a large saucepan of salted water to a boil over moderate heat and cook the potatoes until tender – about 20 minutes. Let cool, then mash the potatoes until smooth; set aside.

2. In a large heavy pan, heat the olive oil over moderate heat. When the oil is hot, add the onions, apple and garlic. Cook, stirring occasionally, until soft – 15 to 20 minutes.

3. Combine the remaining ingredients, except the sunflower oil, in a large mixing bowl. Add the mashed potatoes and the onion mixture; mix well. Using a pastry bag, stuff the mixture into casings to form link sausages. Or add 3 eggs to the mixture and form into small patties.

4. To cook, warm the sunflower oil in a large pan over moderate heat. Add the sausage and cook until lightly browned and cooked through – about 15 minutes for link sausages, 4 minutes on each side for the patties. Add more oil if necessary. Will keep for about 3 months in the freezer (make sure you thaw before cooking). Yield: 2 kilograms.

Potjiekos

Here's a tasty recipe for this favourite South African dish. Once all these ingredients are in your potjie, you can sit back and relax for 2 hours.

1 kilogram neck of lamb, sawn into slices, and excess fat removed
500 grams lamb shanks, sawn into slices
1 tablespoon cake flour
1 tablespoon sunflower oil
1 tablespoon butter
2 onions, peeled and chopped
1 tablespoon chopped root ginger
1½ teaspoons salt
freshly ground pepper to taste
4 cardamom pods, crushed
*1 cinnamon stick**
1 bay leaf
1 kilogram pumpkin (boerpampoen, if possible), cut into wedges and peeled
250 grams sweet potatoes, peeled and sliced
⅔ cup meat stock
1 tablespoon lemon juice

1. Slash the edges of the meat to prevent curling during cooking and dredge the slices in flour. Heat the oil and butter in the potjie and brown the meat by adding it gradually to the pot.
2. Add the onions and sauté until they are transparent. Add the ginger, salt, pepper, cardamom pods, cinnamon and bay leaf. Arrange the pumpkin and sweet potatoes on top of the meat. Heat stock and lemon juice and pour over the meat and vegetables.
3. Cover, and simmer over a small fire for 1½ to 2 hours, or until the meat and vegetables are tender.

Potpourri

Bring the wonderful aroma of garden flowers inside your home.

10 marigold blossoms
6 scented geranium leaves
5 rose blossoms
2 teaspoons dried lavender
*2 teaspoons orrisroot**
*2 drops rose oil**

Combine all the ingredients in a medium-sized bowl. Then set out in bathrooms, living rooms or bedrooms for a sweet flowery scent.

Potted Blaauwkrantz

Surprise your guests with this potted local cheese.

1⅓ cups mellow Blaauwkrantz
5 tablespoons unsalted butter, softened
¼ teaspoon ground mace
½ teaspoon freshly made English mustard

Mash the cheese and the butter. Add the mace and mustard and mix to a creamy consistency. Pack into little pots, pressing the cheese down well. Will keep 1 week in the refrigerator. Yield: 275 grams.

Potting soil

Use to plant or repot house plants.

10 litres sterilized garden soil
*10 litres peat moss**
*10 litres perlite**
*½ cup dolomitic limestone**
or 1½ cups crushed eggshells
*3 tablespoons superphosphate**
1 tablespoon 2:3:2 fertilizer

Sift all the ingredients through a sieve made with shadecloth, which will eliminate any pebbles and twigs. Store in a covered container. (See also *African violet potting soil*, p.382; *Soilless potting mix*, p.415.)

Poultice

Fades bruises and relieves the pain and inflammation of an assortment of strains and sprains.

*30 grams comfrey root**
*30 grams dried wintergreen leaves**
1 litre water

1. In a medium-sized saucepan, combine the herbs and water and bring to a boil over high heat. Reduce the heat to low and simmer 5 minutes. Pour through a sieve, drain off the water and reserve the herbs.
2. Dampen a 30-centimetre-square towel in warm water and place the herbs in the centre. Fold the towel over the herbs and place the poultice on the bruise. Leave on until the herbs have cooled. Reheat and use once a day until symptoms subside.

Pretzels

These soft pretzels are a delicious change from the packaged variety. Serve as a snack or with soup.

1¼ cups warm water
4 teaspoons sugar
1 envelope active dry yeast
1 teaspoon salt
¾ cup bread flour
2½ cups all-purpose flour
1 litre water, at room temperature
3 tablespoons bicarbonate of soda
1 tablespoon coarse salt or
1 teaspoon table salt

1. In a small bowl, combine ½ cup of the warm water with 1 teaspoon of the sugar and the yeast. Let stand until bubbly – about 10 minutes.
2. Put the remaining ¾ cup warm water in the bowl of an electric mixer or food processor along with the salt and bread flour and 1 cup of the all-purpose flour. Beat on medium-low speed until well blended – about 1 minute. Add the yeast mixture and beat 4 to 5 minutes longer. Then stir in the remaining flour.
3. On a floured surface, knead the dough until very smooth – about 5 minutes. Add more flour if the dough is too sticky. Form into a ball, place in an ungreased bowl, and cover with a dishcloth. Let the dough rise until doubled in bulk – about 45 minutes to 1 hour.
4. Preheat the oven to 220°C. Punch the dough down, cut into 12 equal pieces, and cover with a dishcloth. Roll each piece, stretching it as you do so, into a rope about 50 centimetres

long. Twist each rope into a pretzel shape, then lay on a lightly floured surface. Cover all the pretzels with a cloth and let rise until not quite doubled – about 20 minutes.

5. In a medium-sized enamelled or stainless steel saucepan, combine the remaining litre water, the bicarbonate of soda and the remaining 3 teaspoons sugar. Bring to a simmer over moderately low heat. Place 3 pretzels in the water and cook for 20 seconds on each side, flipping them gently with a large slotted spoon. As you remove each pretzel, let it drain over the saucepan for a few seconds, then place on a dishcloth. Repeat until all the pretzels have been cooked and drained, then transfer them, top side up, onto baking sheets coated with non-stick cooking spray and sprinkle with the salt.

6. Bake in the centre of the oven until nicely browned – about 15 minutes. Serve warm or at room temperature. Yield: 12 pretzels.

Pudding

For vanilla, add a few grains of nutmeg along with the milk. For chocolate, add 3 tablespoons cocoa to the pudding mix and proceed as directed.

1 cup pudding mix (below)
1 cup milk
1 cup water
2 teaspoons vanilla essence
1 egg, lightly beaten
1 tablespoon butter or margarine, cut into small pieces

1. Place the pudding mix in a medium-sized heavy saucepan and gradually whisk in the milk and water. Cook, stirring constantly, over moderate heat until the mixture thickens – 3 to 5 minutes. Cook, still stirring, 1½ minutes more.

2. Remove from the heat. In a small bowl, stir the vanilla essence into the egg. Whisk in about ½ cup of the hot mixture, stir, then whisk in another ½ cup. Pour the egg mixture into the saucepan and whisk until combined. Whisk in the butter.

3. Strain the pudding into a bowl, cool a few minutes, then spoon into dessert dishes. Cover with plastic wrap and refrigerate for several hours before serving. Will keep 2 days refrigerated. Yield: 4 servings.

Pudding mix

Better tasting than store-bought and takes only minutes to make. Keep it on hand for emergencies.

3 cups instant non-fat dry milk
1½ cups sugar
1½ cups cornflour, measured without packing
1½ teaspoons salt

Using a whisk, combine all the ingredients in a large bowl. Store in a closed container or canister. Will keep 3 months refrigerated. Yield: 6 cups or 24 servings.

Puffed pancake

Impressive looking and easy.

2 large eggs
½ cup sifted all-purpose flour
½ cup milk
¼ teaspoon ground nutmeg
½ teaspoon salt
¼ cup butter or margarine, melted
1 tablespoon icing sugar (optional)
*½ teaspoon ground cinnamon (optional)**

Preheat the oven to 200°C. Lightly beat the eggs in a medium-sized bowl, then beat in the flour, milk, nutmeg and salt until just blended. Do not overbeat. Cover the bottom of a 32- x 23- x 5-centimetre baking dish with the melted butter, then pour in the batter. Place in the centre of the oven and bake until puffed and golden brown – about 20 minutes. If desired, mix the sugar and cinnamon together and sprinkle over the pancake just before serving. Cut into 2 or 4 equal pieces and serve with honey or syrup and a small jug of melted butter if desired. Yield: 2-4 servings.

Raspberry liqueur

Intensely flavoured, with a rich, red hue – delicious over vanilla-flavoured sorbet or ice cream.

¾ cup sugar
½ cup water
2 cups fresh raspberries
3 strips lemon peel (1,25 x 5 centimetres each)
½ vanilla pod, split
1 teaspoon lemon juice
1½ cups vodka

1. Combine the sugar and water in a medium-sized heavy saucepan. Add the raspberries, lemon peel and vanilla pod, and cook over low heat until the sugar dissolves.

2. Raise the heat to medium-low and boil 3 minutes, then cover. Let stand 30 minutes. Strain through a muslin-lined sieve (you should get about 1½ cups liquid). Discard the lemon peel and vanilla pod.

3. Stir in the lemon juice and vodka, pour into a bottle or some other container, and cover tightly; let cool. The liqueur may be served immediately. Will keep 1 month in a refrigerator. Serve chilled or at room temperature. Yield: 3 cups.

Raspberry syrup

Delicious on strawberry, banana or plain pancakes and waffles.

4 cups fresh raspberries
2 thin strips lemon peel (2,5 x 7,5 centimetres each)
3 cups water
3 cups sugar
1 tablespoon lemon juice

1. In a large saucepan, crush the berries with a wooden spoon. Add the peel and 1 cup water. Bring to a sim-

mer over moderate heat. Reduce heat to very low and allow to simmer, uncovered, for 5 minutes.
2. Pour the berries into a muslin-lined strainer and squeeze out all the juice – about 2 cups. Set the juice aside and discard the pulp.
3. Boil the remaining 2 cups water and the sugar in a large saucepan, stirring constantly until the sugar dissolves and the solution is clear. With a pastry brush, wash down the sides of the pan. Keep boiling, without stirring, until a sugar thermometer gives a temperature reading of 132°C.
4. Add the raspberry mixture: boil, uncovered for 1 minute. Cool the syrup and add the lemon juice. Will keep for 1 month refrigerated. Yield: about 3½ cups.

Refrigerator deodorizer

Works better and quicker than plain bicarbonate of soda. Buy regular charcoal briquettes from your supermarket and use a hammer or brick to crush them into small chunks.

½ cup crushed charcoal
½ cup bicarbonate of soda
2 tablespoons powdered orange or lemon peel
*1 tablespoon ground cloves or cinnamon**
2 tablespoons vanilla essence
old, clean pantihose, cut into 5-centimetre squares
45 centimetres porous fabric, (towelling, loose-weave cotton or muslin), cut into 5-centimetre squares
string or ribbon, cut into 20-centimetre lengths for tying and hanging

1. Combine the charcoal, bicarbonate of soda, citrus peel and cloves in a medium-sized glass or enamel bowl. Sprinkle in the vanilla, stir to mix, and let stand 1 hour.
2. Put 2 tablespoons of the mixture in the centre of a pantihose square, fold it up and put this packet in the centre of a square of bright fabric. Tie the corners together firmly with the string or ribbon.
3. To use, tie a packet in an inconspicuous spot in the refrigerator or freezer. Or tie onto a shelf inside the door. For longer life, sprinkle with a few drops of vanilla essence and add 1 teaspoon bicarbonate of soda after 10 or 12 weeks. Yield: 9 packets.

Rejuvenating skin cream

For smooth, fresher-looking skin.

2 capsules (400 IU's each) vitamin E
1 tablespoon honey
*1 tablespoon coconut oil**
*1 tablespoon rose water**
1 tablespoon olive oil

Remove the vitamin E from the capsules and place with the remaining ingredients in a small bowl; mix well. To use, apply to the skin with cottonwool. Store tightly covered in the refrigerator.

Rooibos refresher

Try this caffeine-free drink on a hot summer's day.

4 cups boiling water
8 level teaspoons rooibos tea
ice cubes
sugar to taste
mint leaves or lemon slices

Pour the boiling water onto the tea leaves and leave to steep for a few minutes, then strain. Cool first or pour directly onto the ice cubes. Add sugar, if you wish, and garnish with mint leaves or lemon slices. Yield: 4 cups.

Rose petal lotion

Use this sweet-smelling rinse to remove any traces of soap after washing your face.

1 tablespoon dried rosemary or 2 tablespoons fresh rosemary
*2 tablespoons dried camomile flowers**
4 cups water
2 tablespoons dried or fresh rose petals

Combine all the ingredients in a small glass or enamelled pan and boil, uncovered, over moderate heat for 10 minutes. Let cool to room temperature. Strain and transfer the liquid to a bottle with a lid. To use, dab on with cottonwool or transfer to a spray bottle and spray on the skin. Rinse off. Will keep 2 months tightly covered and refrigerated.

Rum balls

A tasty treat you can make without cooking. A nice gift.

1¾ cups fine vanilla wafer crumbs
1 cup pecan nuts, finely ground
1 cup unsifted icing sugar
¼ cup cocoa
3 tablespoons golden syrup
¼ cup light or dark rum
⅓ cup sifted icing sugar

Put all the ingredients except the sifted icing sugar in a medium-sized bowl and mix well, using your hands if necessary. Roll the mixture into 2,5-centimetre balls, then dredge in the sifted sugar. The rum balls will keep 10 days in airtight containers at room temperature. Yield: about 3½ dozen.

Russian-style beetroot

This salad takes 20 minutes to make.

2 tablespoons butter or margarine
2 medium beetroot, coarsely grated
2 tablespoons lemon juice
1 teaspoon salt
pinch black pepper
½ cup water

Heat the butter in a frying pan. Add all the ingredients. Cover and cook over moderately low heat for 20 minutes, stirring from time to time. Add more water if necessary, but there should be no liquid left at the end of the cooking time.

Sachet

Tuck in drawers to give your clothes a fresh scent.

10 bay leaves, crumbled
2 tablespoons each dried sage, origanum, basil, thyme and lavender flowers, crumbled
3 tablespoons dried rosemary, crumbled
*¼ cup orrisroot**

Combine all the ingredients in a medium-sized bowl. Then place 3 tablespoons of the mixture on a 10- x 10-centimetre piece of muslin. Tie the corners together with a ribbon.

Sambals

Sambals are traditional Cape Malay relishes which are served as accompaniments, usually for curries. Allow 1–2 tablespoons per person. This cucumber sambal is very popular.

2 fresh cucumbers, peeled and coarsely grated
2 teaspoons salt
1 clove garlic, crushed
1 teaspoon sugar
4 teaspoons vinegar
2 green chillies, seeded and sliced

1. Grate the cucumber and sprinkle with salt. Allow to stand for at least 30 minutes to draw out the water. Squeeze to remove all the water. Add the garlic, sugar and vinegar to the cucumber pulp. Add the chillies sparingly, tasting as you go along, and remember not to touch your eyes with chillies on your hands. Serve the same day. Yield: 2 cups, depending on the size of the cucumbers.

2. A quick banana sambal can be made by slicing as many bananas as you will need and adding diced red pepper, salt, marjoram (preferably freshly chopped leaves) and lemon juice. Serve immediately.

Sausage

Hot and spicy taste with less fat than most commercial sausages and none of the preservatives. For a milder sausage, eliminate the Tabasco sauce.

1 teaspoon salt
a few drops of Tabasco sauce
¼ teaspoon black pepper
1 teaspoon dried sage, crumbled
½ teaspoon each dried marjoram and summer savory, crumbled
½ teaspoon ground coriander
500 grams pork mince

1. Mix all the herbs and spices in a small bowl. Place the pork in a large bowl, sprinkle the mixture over it, and combine.

2. Shape into a cylinder about 20 centimetres long. Cover with plastic wrap, then aluminium foil. Refrigerate for several hours to allow the seasonings to blend.

3. Cut the sausage into 1-centimetre slices, place in an ungreased pan, and sauté over moderate heat until cooked through and lightly browned – about 10 minutes on each side. Will keep 3 days tightly wrapped in aluminium foil and refrigerated; 2 months in the freezer.

Scone mix

Use it to whip up scones, pancakes or waffles in a flash.

6 cups all-purpose flour (or 3 cups cake flour and 3 cups whole-wheat flour)
3½ tablespoons baking powder
1 cup instant non-fat dry milk
1 tablespoon salt
1 cup vegetable fat

In a large bowl, combine the flour, baking powder, dry milk and salt. Mix well. With a pastry blender, cut in the vegetable fat until the mixture resembles bread crumbs. Will keep 6 weeks in a closed container at room temperature. Yield: about 8 cups. (See also *Scones*, below; *Pancakes*, p.408; *Waffles*, p.418.)

Scones

So quick to prepare and good to eat, you'll want to make them often.

2 cups scone mix (above)
½ cup water or milk

1. Preheat the oven to 220°C. In a medium-sized bowl, stir the scone mix and water with a fork until just blended. Do not over-stir.

2. On a lightly floured surface, gently knead the dough 10 times; roll out to a thickness of 1 centimetre. Cut into 5-centimetre rounds. Bake on an ungreased baking sheet for 10 to 12 minutes or until golden brown. Serve hot. Yield: 10 scones.

Scouring powder

Cleans kitchen utensils, sinks, pots and pans – but don't use on items that have a high polish.

¼ cup powdered soap
*1 tablespoon powdered borax**
*1 tablespoon soda ash**
*7 tablespoons fine pumice**

Place all the ingredients in a medium-sized bowl and mix well. Strain through a fine sieve. To use, wet the surface to be cleaned with warm water, sprinkle on the powder, and wash thoroughly with a wet cloth or sponge. Rinse with clear water and dry with a dishcloth.

Scratch remover

For use on metal or glass surfaces.

*¼ cup glycerine**
*¼ cup jeweller's rouge**
¼ cup water

Mix all the ingredients in a medium-sized glass or plastic jar until they form a smooth paste. To use, apply to the scratched areas with a clean cloth and rub in. Rinse with clear water. To fill in deeper scratches, repeat the process several times until the scratch has disappeared. Store in a tightly covered jar.

Seed-starting soil

A potting mix that's free of soil-borne diseases. Make it in the summer so that it can be sun-dried. All these ingredients, except the eggshells, are available at your local nursery.

16 litres garden soil
*8 litres peat moss**
8 litres river sand
*1 tablespoon dolomitic limestone**
or 3 tablespoons crushed eggshells
*3 tablespoons superphosphate**

Blend the soil, peat moss and sand, then pass through a 50-millimetre shadecloth sieve. Add the limestone and superphosphate. To use, pour the mixture into nursery-type black plastic containers. Water until the soil is saturated, then seal in a clear plastic bag and set in a sunny spot for several weeks. If sealed tightly when stored in the tool shed or garage, the bags of soil should remain disease-free until the following spring.

Shampoo enhancer

Try this shampoo for normal and dry hair. The egg conditions the hair; the lemon juice makes it shine.

1 egg
1 teaspoon lemon juice or cider vinegar
3 tablespoons mild, unscented shampoo

Mix the ingredients in a small bowl. Then shampoo into hair and rinse well with warm water.

Shellac

It's best to make your own because commercial brands have only a 6-week shelf life and may have deteriorated by the time you buy them.

*¾ cup shellac flakes**
*1 cup ethyl alcohol**

Place the shellac flakes in a 500 millilitre jar, then pour in the alcohol. Cover and let stand 8 hours or overnight, shaking every few hours, until all the flakes have dissolved. Stir well, then apply with a brush. To apply with a rag or spray gun, the mixture will have to be thinned. Add more alcohol until the desired consistency is reached. The shellac will keep for at least 6 weeks stored in a tightly covered container.
Caution: Keep out of the reach of children at all times.

Shrub fertilizer

For acid-loving plants like azaleas, rhododendrons and camellias, substitute granite dust for the wood ash.

4 cups coffee grounds
*1 cup bonemeal**
*1 cup wood ash**

Place all the ingredients in a bucket and mix well. To use, scatter evenly over the ground shaded by the plant, using about 500 grams of fertilizer for each 30 centimetres of the diameter – a shrub that shades an area 1 metre in diameter should get about 1,5 kilograms of fertilizer.

Skin cleanser

Clears out oil-clogged facial pores.

1 teaspoon milk
1 teaspoon honey
1 tablespoon ground almonds

Combine all the ingredients in a small bowl. Using your hands or a washcloth, apply the mixture to your face and rub lightly for a minute or two. Rinse. Mix fresh every time. Discontinue use immediately if there is any allergic reaction.

Smoked snoek dip

Serve chips, savoury biscuits, pitta bread or raw vegetables with this dip.

250 grams smoked snoek
1 clove garlic, crushed
1 thick slice whole-wheat bread
¼ cup natural yoghurt
2 tablespoons lemon juice
¼ cup sunflower oil
salt (optional) and freshly ground black pepper

Skin the snoek and remove the bones. Flake the fish and place in the bowl of a food processor or blender with the garlic. Remove the crusts from the bread, crumble it into the yoghurt and mash them together.

Add this mixture to the snoek and blend them together. Add the lemon juice, then gradually add the sunflower oil. Beat all these ingredients well together. Add pepper to taste and salt only if it is needed. Refrigerate. Yield: 6 servings.

Soap bubbles

An inexpensive, safe and fun diversion for children.

½ cup dishwashing detergent
1 cup water
2 drops food colouring

Mix all the ingredients together in a jar and cover. Use a bubble pipe or a store-bought or homemade bubble wand. Store at room temperature in a tightly covered jar. Yield: 1½ cups.

Soilless potting mix

Better for house plants than garden soil because it's free of soil-borne insects and weed seed.

*16 litres peat moss**
*16 litres perlite**
*½ cup dolomitic limestone**
or 1½ cups crushed eggshells
*1 tablespoon superphosphate**
*or 2 tablespoons bonemeal**
½ cup 2:3:2 fertilizer

Strain the peat moss and perlite through a sieve into a large bucket.

Add the limestone, superphosphate and fertilizer and mix thoroughly. Yield: 1 bushel.

Sousboontjies

Serve as an accompaniment to any meat dish or as part of a salad table.

500 grams butter or sugar beans
2 cups water
½ cup vinegar
⅓ cup sugar
¾ teaspoon salt
1½ tablespoons butter

Soak the beans overnight. Cook them slowly in the water until they are tender. Drain and add the vinegar, sugar, salt and butter, adjusting the amounts used according to your own taste. Press a few of the beans to a pulp to thicken the sauce. Allow to cool and store in sterilized containers in the refrigerator. Yield: 10–12 servings.

Spanspek (sweet melon) ice

Light, refreshing and gratifyingly low in kilojoules.

1 tablespoon gelatine
3 tablespoons cold water
2 spanspeks (500 grams each), peeled, seeded and coarsely chopped
¼ cup each orange juice and honey
1 tablespoon lemon juice
2 teaspoons finely grated orange rind

1. In a small saucepan, soften the gelatine in the cold water for about 5 minutes. Set over a low heat and stir until dissolved – about 3 minutes.
2. In a food processor or blender, purée the spanspeks in batches and transfer to a medium-sized bowl. Stir in the gelatine, orange juice, honey, lemon juice and orange rind until well mixed. Pour the mixture into a 23-centimetre-square dish, cover tightly with plastic wrap, and freeze until firm – 2 to 4 hours.
3. In a food processor or blender, purée the spanspek ice in batches until smooth but not liquefied; re-freeze. Will keep for up to 3 days in the freezer. Yield: about 2 cups.

Watermelon variation: Follow the directions above, but eliminate the orange rind and orange juice and substitute the flesh of a 1,5 kilogram watermelon, seeded and coarsely chopped, for the spanspek. Use ½ cup syrup instead of the honey and increase the lemon juice to 2 tablespoons. You should store as directed for the spanspek ice.

Starch

This recipe is very simple, cheap and quick. Use 1 tablespoon cornflour for a light starch; up to 3 tablespoons for a heavier finish.

1 to 3 tablespoons cornflour
2 cups cold water

Mix the cornflour and water in a spray bottle that gives a fine spray mist. Store out of the reach of children. To use, shake well, spray the area to be starched, then iron immediately.

Strawberry preserves

Not as sweet as commercial brands. For the best flavour, be sure to choose firm, ripe strawberries.

½ cup sugar
½ cup fresh orange juice
1 kilogram strawberries, washed and hulled
2 large sweet apples (such as Golden Delicious), peeled, cored and coarsely chopped

1. Combine the sugar and orange juice in a large glass or enamel bowl. Add the hulled strawberries and toss to coat. Let stand for about ½ hour at room temperature.
2. Transfer the mixture to a large non-aluminium saucepan, add the apples, and set over moderately high heat. Cook, uncovered, for about 45 minutes or until thick and glossy – 105°C on a sugar thermometer.
3. Pour the preserves into hot, sterilized preserving jars. Cover, let cool to room temperature, then refrigerate. The strawberry preserves will keep for about 2 months refrigerated. Yield: 2¾ cups.

Stywe pap

Also known as putu, this filling dish is a traditional favourite among many thousands of South Africans. Made of mealie meal, stywe pap can be eaten either for breakfast or with a braai. One reason for its popularity is that it can be served as an accompaniment to a wide range of dishes. A variation of stywe pap is known as *krummelpap,* meaning "crumbly" pap.

300 grams coarsely ground mealie meal
½ teaspoon salt
3 cups boiling water

Pour the mealie meal and salt into a pot with the boiling water and stir well. Cover and turn the heat down to its lowest setting. After 20-30 minutes, turn off the heat and allow the mixture to cool slowly on the hot plate for about 20 minutes.

For breakfast, serve with milk and sugar or serve at a braai with boerewors. Use the pap to mop up gravy.

Sunburn soother

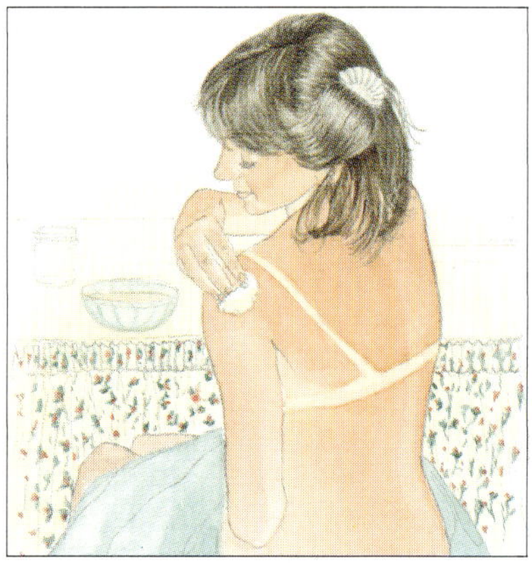

Tired of expensive, cosmetic brands to soothe your sunburn? Here's a natural remedy you can prepare in a flash when you return from a harsh day out in the sun. It takes the bite out of a mild burn.

4 tea bags
2 cups fresh mint leaves or
1 cup dried mint
4 cups water

Place all the ingredients in a medium-sized saucepan and bring to a boil over high heat. Reduce the heat to low and simmer for about 5 minutes. Remove from the heat and let steep for 15 minutes. To use, strain the liquid into a jar, discarding the tea and mint, and then let cool. Dab the mixture on sunburned areas with cotton-wool or a washcloth. Or pour the liquid into warm bath water; then remove the tea from the bags and tie it, along with the mint, in a piece of muslin and drop into the bath. Soak in the mixture for 10 to 15 minutes. Repeat as necessary.

Tameletjie

This traditional Malay sweet, once sold by vendors on the streets of Cape Town, is quick and easy to make. It was originally made with pine nuts, but almonds or coconut can be successfully used instead.

2 cups sugar
1 cup water
almonds, desiccated coconut or pine nuts

Boil the sugar and water until the mixture is a caramel colour. Continue boiling until it starts to foam. Add a sprinkling of chopped almonds, coconut or pine nuts. Pour the mixture into a greased flat 23-centimetre-square tin, and mark off in squares. Cool and then cut. Yield: 400 grams.

Tile and grout cleaner

Here's an effective formula that will help you to eliminate the grimy soap film that often forms on and between bathroom tiles.

½ cup bicarbonate of soda
⅓ cup household ammonia
¼ cup white vinegar
7 cups warm water

Combine the ingredients in a 5-litre plastic jug, cover, and swish to mix. Label the container and store it out of the reach of children. For small jobs, fill a pump-type container with the solution; spray directly onto the tile surface, then wipe with a damp sponge or cloth.
Caution: Do not mix this cleaner with anything containing bleach.

Toilet bowl cleaner

Use this cleaner regularly to keep your toilet sparkling clean.

1 tablespoon household ammonia
*1 cup hydrogen peroxide**
2 litres water

Mix the ingredients in a bucket, then pour the solution slowly into the toilet. Let stand for 30 minutes, then scrub the inside of the bowl and flush. For stubborn stains, allow the solution to remain in the bowl for several hours. Yield: 2 litres.

Tomato sauce

Much fresher-tasting than commercial brands, this sauce makes a nice gift. To prevent the tomato sauce from splattering as it cooks, put a wire mesh splatter shield over the pot.

4 tins (400 grams each) tomato purée
2 bay leaves
1 teaspoon celery seed
*1 teaspoon mustard seed**
1 teaspoon whole allspice
*1 stick cinnamon**
½ teaspoon peppercorns
1½ teaspoons salt
1 cup white vinegar
1 cup sugar

1. In a large, deep saucepan set over moderate heat, cook the tomato purée, uncovered, at a slow boil for 1½ hours, stirring occasionally. Tie the bay leaves, seeds and spices in a piece of muslin and add to the saucepan, then add the salt. Set the lid askew, reduce the heat to low, and simmer 30 minutes longer.
2. Remove the spice bag and add the vinegar and sugar. Increase the heat to moderate and cook, uncovered, at a slow boil, stirring often, until very thick – about 1½ hours. At the end of the cooking time, you may have to stir constantly to prevent scorching.
3. Ladle the piping hot tomato sauce into 2 hot, sterilized 500-millilitre preserving jars, leaving 3 millimetres head space. Wipe the rims and seal. Will keep 1 month refrigerated. Yield: about 4 cups.

Toothpaste

Leaves a fresh taste in your mouth.

¼ cup each arrowroot, powdered orrisroot* and water*
½ teaspoon each oil of cinnamon and oil of cloves**
*1 teaspoon ground sage**

Mix all the ingredients in a small bowl. If the paste is too thick, add more water until the desired consistency is reached. Use as needed. Store at room temperature in a tightly covered jar. Yield: ½ cup.

Veal patties with tomatoes

These delicious patties will bring your guests back for seconds.

1 onion, finely chopped
4 tablespoons sunflower oil
2 ripe red tomatoes, skinned and chopped
1 clove garlic, crushed
1 teaspoon dried origanum
50 grams fresh bread crumbs
500 grams veal mince
3 tablespoons chopped fresh parsley
1 egg
salt and freshly ground black pepper
sifted flour

1. Fry the onion in one tablespoon of the oil until pale and golden.
2. Add the tomatoes, garlic and origanum. Cover the pan and cook for 5 minutes, then remove the cover and boil rapidly over a high heat until the liquid has been greatly reduced.
3. Transfer contents of the pan to a mixing bowl. Add the bread crumbs, veal, parsley and egg, and season with salt and pepper. Mix well.
4. Form the mixture into round patties, dredge them with sifted flour, and then slowly brown them in the remaining oil for about 15 minutes. Yield: 6 servings.

Vegetable and chicken mix

Here's a simple way to make a great, nutritious meal.

3 medium-sized potatoes, peeled and diced
6 rashers bacon, cut into strips
1 small onion, peeled and finely chopped
½ cup chopped spring onions
¾ cup diced celery
2 cups diced cooked chicken
⅔ cup cream
½ teaspoon salt
¼ teaspoon black pepper

1. Bring lightly salted water to a boil in a saucepan. Add the potatoes, put the lid askew on the saucepan, and cook for 5 minutes.
2. Meanwhile, cook the bacon in a heavy, medium-sized frying pan over moderately high heat until crisp – about 5 minutes. Drain the bacon on paper towels and reserve. Pour off half the bacon fat. Drain the potatoes.
3. Raise the heat to high and add the potatoes, onion, spring onions, celery and chicken to the pan. Sauté, stirring, to brown all the ingredients slightly – about 3 minutes.
4. Lower the heat to moderately high. Add half the cream, pressing down on the mixture. Cook until dry, scraping the crust that forms into the mixture. Repeat with the rest of the cream. This should take about 12 minutes altogether.
5. Add the salt and pepper, and crumble the bacon over the top. Serve with peas, broccoli or other green vegetables. Yield: 6 servings.

Vegetable fertilizer

This fertilizer not only helps vegetables – it's a real boost to your garden flowers as well.

*1 part dried poultry manure or 5 parts dried horse manure**
*1 part bonemeal**
*1 part wood ash**

Mix all the ingredients together. Spread over the garden soil at a rate of 2,5 kilograms per 9 square metres.

Vinyl upholstery cleaner

Never apply leather cleaner to vinyl upholstery; use this gentle solution instead.

¼ cup washing powder
½ cup bicarbonate of soda
2 cups warm water

Mix the detergent and bicarbonate of soda together and add to the water. To use, moisten a rough-textured cloth with the solution and rub the vinyl surface with it, concentrating on the arms, seat and headrest; rinse well and wipe dry. Yield: 2½ cups.

Waffles

You can make these in minutes.

2 large eggs, separated
1¾ cups scone mix (p.414)
1 cup water or milk
3 tablespoons butter or margarine, melted

1. Preheat a waffle iron. In a large mixing bowl, lightly beat the egg yolks. Add the scone mix, water and butter and stir just enough to moisten. In a medium-sized bowl, beat the egg whites until stiff peaks form. Gently fold into the batter until just blended.
2. Cook according to the waffle iron manufacturer's directions. Serve with butter and syrup if desired. Yield: 5 waffles (20 x 10 centimetres each).

Walnut and date crackles

Walnuts are the magic ingredients in this mouth-watering combination. Peanuts can be used as an alternative.

2 cups corn- or branflakes
¾ cup stoned dates
½ cup walnuts
2 tablespoons honey
2½ teaspoons butter or margarine, softened
2 teaspoons lemon juice
3 tablespoons icing sugar

1. Put the cornflakes, dates and walnuts into a blender or a food processor, and whirl until well chopped. Or crush the cereal with your hands, and chop the dates and nuts.
2. In a bowl, combine the cereal mixture with the honey, butter and lemon juice. Knead until well mixed, then roll into 2-centimetre balls.
3. Sprinkle the sugar on a sheet of waxed paper, and roll the balls in the sugar. Store in an airtight container. Yield: 24 balls.

Walnut butter

Serve on crackers or in sandwiches; particularly good with apple butter.

2 cups walnuts
1 teaspoon sunflower oil
½ teaspoon salt

Preheat the oven to 150°C. Spread the walnuts on an ungreased baking tray and bake, uncovered, until lightly browned – about 20 minutes; let cool. If a chunky butter is desired, coarsely chop ¼ cup of the nuts and set aside. Transfer the remaining nuts to a blender or food processor. Add the oil and salt and process until creamy, working in batches if necessary, then add the chopped nuts if desired. Will keep 1 month tightly covered and refrigerated. Yield: 1 cup.

Walnut dreams

Give the family a special treat with these tasty biscuits.

8 teaspoons butter, softened
¼ cup icing sugar, unsifted
1 teaspoon vanilla essence
1 cup sifted flour
pinch ground nutmeg
pinch salt
¾ cup finely chopped walnuts

1. Preheat the oven to 150°C. In a mixing bowl, cream the butter and sugar with an electric mixer at medium speed until light and fluffy. Stir in the vanilla essence, flour, nutmeg, salt and walnuts.
2. Roll the dough into 2-centimetre balls. Place them 3 centimetres apart on a greased baking tray, pressing each ball with the heel of your hand to a thickness of 1 centimetre.
3. Bake, uncovered, for about 20 minutes, or until the bottoms are golden brown. Cool on a wire rack. Yield: 18 biscuits.

Walnut sauce

A superb topping for ice cream.

¾ cup golden syrup
½ cup maple syrup
¼ cup water
¼ cup sugar
1¼ cups coarsely chopped walnuts

Place the golden syrup, maple syrup, water and sugar in a small heavy saucepan and bring to a boil over moderately high heat, stirring constantly. Add the walnuts, turn the heat to low, and simmer, partially covered, 30 minutes. Do not stir. Let cool, then pour into a clean 500-millilitre jar. Will keep 4 months tightly covered and refrigerated. Yield: 500 millilitres.

Waterblommetjie bredie

A hearty South African favourite.

500 grams waterblommetjies
1 tablespoon sunflower oil
700 grams fat mutton, chopped into 2-centimetre pieces
2 onions, peeled and thinly sliced
salt and black pepper
1 teaspoon sugar
1 cup dry white wine
450 grams potatoes, thinly sliced
1 cooking apple, thinly sliced
1 cup water

1. Wash the waterblommetjies well. Soak in salted water for an hour, then rinse and chop roughly. Heat the oil in a saucepan and brown the meat, a few pieces at a time.
2. Add the onions, salt, pepper and sugar and stir.
3. Add the waterblommetjies, wine, potato slices, apple and water, and simmer for 1½ to 2 hours until the meat is tender. Yield: 4 servings.

Waterblommetjie soup

Here's an unusual method of cooking with waterblommetjies.

500 grams waterblommetjies
3 tablespoons butter
1 onion, peeled and thinly sliced
3 cups chicken stock
juice of 1 lemon
½ cup sour cream
salt and freshly ground black pepper

Garnish: snipped chives or parsley

1. Wash the waterblommetjies well, and soak in salty water for an hour before chopping roughly. Heat the butter in a saucepan and cook the onion until softened.
2. Add the waterblommetjies and stock. Half cover with the lid and cook for 15–20 minutes until the waterblommetjies are tender.
3. Purée, then reheat. Add the lemon juice, then stir in the cream. Allow to heat through. Season with salt and pepper. Garnish with chives or snipped parsley.

Watercolours

Here's an easy-to-make substitute for the commercial product that you can make in your own kitchen.

1 tablespoon white or cider vinegar
2 tablespoons bicarbonate of soda
1 tablespoon cornflour
*½ teaspoon glycerine**
2 drops food colouring
1 teaspoon water

Mix the vinegar and bicarbonate of soda together in a small bowl; add the cornflour and glycerine when the soda stops foaming. Stir in the food colouring and add the water if the solution seems too thick. Store in a tightly covered jar in your pantry for later use. Yield: ¼ cup.

Watercress stuffing

Here's an ideal stuffing for poultry. Assemble it while your chicken is roasting, and bake it on a shelf above the bird.

1 teaspoon butter or margarine
1 medium-sized onion, peeled and finely chopped
2 sticks celery, finely chopped
1 bunch watercress, finely chopped
2 cups diced dry bread
½ teaspoon salt

1. Preheat the oven to 180°C. Melt the butter or margarine in a medium-sized pan over moderate heat. Add the onion and celery, and cook, uncovered, for 10 minutes, or until the vegetables are soft.
2. Stir in the watercress and cook, stirring, for 3 minutes. Add the bread and salt, and toss to mix. Spoon the mixture into a buttered shallow casserole dish and bake, uncovered, for 15 minutes. Yield: 4 servings.

Watercress tossed with radishes and pear

Try spicy, peppery watercress in this tossed salad. You'll get a change in flavour as well as a bonus in nutrition – watercress is far richer than lettuce in protein, calcium and vitamin C.

1 bunch watercress
1 small onion, peeled and thinly sliced
12 radishes, thinly sliced
1 medium-sized firm, ripe pear, peeled, cored and thinly sliced
3 tablespoons sunflower oil
1 tablespoon lemon juice
¼ teaspoon salt
½ teaspoon prepared French mustard

1. Wash the watercress and dry it with paper towelling. Cut off and discard the stem ends, tear the watercress into bite-sized pieces, and place in a serving bowl. Add the onion, radishes and pear slices.
2. In a small bowl, mix the oil, lemon juice, salt and mustard. Pour over the salad, and serve. Yield: 4 servings.

Watermelon konfyt

Don't toss away the peel after the watermelon has been eaten – use it to make a delicious preserve.

1 kilogram watermelon peel
5 teaspoons slaked lime or 3 tablespoons bicarbonate of soda*
7 litres water
5 cups sugar
4 teaspoons lemon juice
pinch salt
4-centimetre piece of fresh green ginger, bruised

1. To obtain the peel, cut the watermelon into slices, remove the flesh and cut off the hard green rind. Cut the remaining white fleshy peel into squares and prick well on both sides.
2. Soak the peel overnight in a solution made from lime or bicarbonate of soda and 5 litres of the water. This ensures that the konfyt is tender yet crisp. Rinse the peel thoroughly, soak in fresh water for 2 hours, then drain.
3. Place the pieces in boiling water one at a time so that the water does not stop boiling. Boil uncovered until just tender (20–30 minutes) – test by piercing with a matchstick.
4. Prepare a syrup by combining the sugar, 2 litres of water, lemon juice, salt and ginger in a saucepan over a low heat. When all the sugar has dissolved, bring the mixture to the boil. Place the peel in the syrup and boil rapidly until the pieces are tender and translucent and the syrup is thick (1–1½ hours).
5. Pack the peel into hot, dry sterilized jars, fill with syrup and make sure that you seal immediately. Yield: 4 jars of 500 millilitres.

Watermelon sherbet

This refreshing summer dessert has only 365 kilojoules per serving.

½ cup sugar
8 heaped cups of 1-centimetre watermelon cubes
fresh mint leaves

1. Sprinkle the sugar over the watermelon cubes. Place the cubes in plastic bags and freeze for at least 4 hours. Purée the frozen watermelon in a food processor until fluffy.
2. Spoon the sherbet into dessert glasses, garnish with mint and serve immediately. Yield: 8 servings.

Wax finish for raw wood

Meant for raw wood, such as exposed beams – not for use over a finish.

1 cup turpentine
*1 cup melted beeswax**
1 cup boiled linseed oil

Warm the turpentine in the top of a double boiler; stir in the beeswax until it dissolves, then add the oil. Remove from the heat and brush the warm mixture on raw wood. Allow to dry and buff with a clean soft cloth.

Caution: Because this formula uses flammable materials, take care to see that the mixture does not overheat or spill on a hot surface.

Wheatless brownies

Chocolate treats that are both wheat- and milk-free.

⅓ cup margarine, at room temperature
1 cup firmly packed light brown sugar
2 eggs, lightly beaten
50 grams dark chocolate, melted
50 grams semisweet chocolate, melted
1 teaspoon vanilla essence
⅔ cup unsifted rice flour
½ teaspoon baking powder
¼ teaspoon salt
½ cup coarsely chopped pecan nuts or walnuts

1. Preheat the oven to 180°C. Cream the margarine and sugar in a large bowl. Add all the remaining ingredients except the nuts, and stir until smooth. Stir in the nuts, then pour the batter into a greased 20-centimetre-square baking tin.
2. Bake uncovered until the edges pull away slightly from the sides of the tin and a toothpick inserted into the centre comes out clean – about ½ hour. Cool the brownies in the tin on a wire rack, then cut into squares. Will keep 3 days stored in an airtight container. These make an ideal gift for someone who is allergic to wheat or milk. Yield: 16 brownies.

Whipped cream substitute

This recipe is much lower in saturated fat than those toppings made with heavy cream.

1 tin (150 grams) evaporated milk
2 tablespoons cold water
1 teaspoon gelatine
2 tablespoons sugar
*3 tablespoons corn oil**

1. Pour the milk into an empty ice-cube tray or a shallow dish and place in the freezer. When crystals form around the edges – about 20 minutes – the milk is cold enough to whip.
2. Meanwhile, place the water in a small heatproof dish and add the gelatine without stirring. Heat 2,5 centimetres of water in a small saucepan, remove from the heat, and place the dish of water and gelatine in it. Let stand until the gelatine dissolves – about 5 minutes. Remove the dish from the water, stir the gelatine solution, and let cool.
3. In a medium-sized bowl, beat the milk until stiff peaks form. Gradually add the sugar, then the corn oil, then the gelatine mixture. Continue beating the mixture until stiff peaks form again. Cover the bowl with foil and place in the freezer for 10 minutes, then transfer to the refrigerator. The mixture will become stiff; stir to soften it before serving. Will keep 3 days covered with foil and refrigerated. Yield: 4 servings.

Whipped cream topping

A quick and easy way to ensure that whipped cream remains firm and does not separate.

½ teaspoon gelatine
1 tablespoon cold water
1 cup fresh cream
½ teaspoon vanilla essence
pinch salt
1 tablespoon sugar (optional)

1. Sprinkle the gelatine over the water in a small ovenproof glass or ceramic bowl, then stand the bowl in 2 centimetres of hot water in a saucepan. Let it stand until the gelatine dissolves. Remove the bowl from the water, and let the mixture cool for about 1 minute.
2. Whip the cream until almost stiff, then add the dissolved gelatine mixture, the vanilla essence and salt, and the sugar, if used, and continue to whip until the cream is stiff. Cover and refrigerate. Just before serving, beat with a spoon to blend.

If the cream is very fresh, it will keep in the refrigerator for 4 days.

White sauce

For a much richer sauce, add 2 tablespoons butter or margarine during the last minute of cooking and stir until melted.

¼ cup white sauce mix (below)
1 cup skim or whole milk

Place the white sauce mix in a medium-sized saucepan and gradually whisk in the milk. Set the pan over moderate heat and cook, stirring constantly, for about 2 minutes or until the mixture thickens. Then reduce the heat to low and simmer, stirring constantly, 2 minutes more. This sauce is best made fresh whenever it is needed. Yield: 1 cup.

CHEESE VARIATION
Proceed as directed, but add ½ cup or more grated mature Cheddar cheese, a dash or two of Worcestershire sauce and a pinch of cayenne pepper in the last 2 minutes of cooking. Serve on broccoli, cauliflower, potatoes or other vegetables.

CURRY VARIATION
Add 1 teaspoon curry powder to the white sauce mix and proceed as directed. Serve with roast chicken, poached fish fillets or eggs.

MUSHROOM VARIATION
At the end of the cooking time, add 1 cup chopped mushrooms that have been sautéed in butter. Serve with chicken or vegetables.

MUSTARD VARIATION
Stir in 2 tablespoons Dijon or spicy brown mustard along with the milk and proceed as directed. Serve with ham or pork chops.

PAPRIKA VARIATION
Add 1 or more tablespoons paprika to the white sauce mix and proceed as directed. Serve with veal or chicken.

PARSLEY VARIATION
Add 2 tablespoons finely chopped parsley after adding the milk and proceed as directed. Serve with carrots or any fish dish.

White sauce mix

A low-fat version of the classic recipe in an easy-to-use mix.

1 cup flour
1 cup instant non-fat dry milk
1½ teaspoons salt

Combine all the ingredients in a jar, cover, and store at room temperature. Yield: 2 cups dry mix or enough for 8 cups sauce.

Whitewash

A cheap coating that must be re-applied frequently. Excellent for farm buildings because the lime is germicidal. For interior use only.

*2,5 kilograms hydrated lime**
4 litres water, at room temperature
750 grams salt
2 litres warm water

In a large tub, mix the lime with the room-temperature water and let stand overnight. Meanwhile, dissolve the salt in the warm water. Add the salt water to the lime mixture and stir well. For colouring, add powdered pigment if desired. Store tightly covered. Yield: 10,5 litres.

Windscreen cleaner

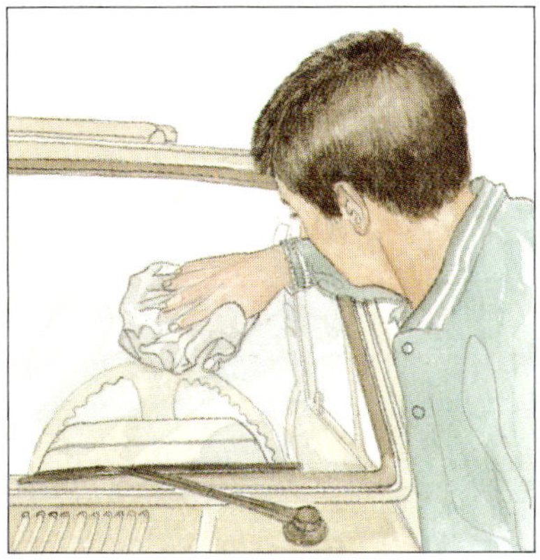

Effective for removing dried insects.

½ cup powdered chalk
¼ cup bicarbonate of soda
1 cup diatomaceous earth
enough water to make a paste

Combine the ingredients in a small bowl or other container and stir slowly until a paste is formed. Apply the mixture to the dirty windscreen with a sponge, then polish with a dry, lint-free cloth. Yield: 1½ cups.

Winter fruit salad

Give this winter fruit salad a distinctive South African flavour by adding Van der Hum liqueur.

3 oranges
2 bananas
1 green apple
1 red apple
1 yellow apple
1 pear
½ papino
½ pineapple
1 tablespoon Van der Hum liqueur

1. Pour the juice of 2 of the oranges into a bowl. Peel and slice the third

orange into thin segments. Peel and slice the bananas and toss in the orange juice.
2. Wash and core the apples (do not peel), and slice thinly. Toss in the orange juice.
3. Add cubes of pear, papino and pineapple, and pour in the liqueur. Toss gently and chill.

Yellow rice

Traditionally served with bobotie, try this tasty rice with other dishes.

4 tablespoons butter
5 teaspoons sunflower oil
1 cup long-grained rice
3 cups boiling water
2 teaspoons turmeric
1 teaspoon salt
2 teaspoons sugar
½ cup seedless raisins

1. Heat the butter and oil and add the rice. Cook, stirring constantly, for 10 minutes, or until transparent.
2. Mix together the boiling water, turmeric, salt and sugar. Pour this mixture into the rice when it has become transparent. Mix well, cover the pan and turn the heat to low.
3. After about 15 minutes, sprinkle the raisins on top of the rice. Cover the pan again and cook for another 10–15 minutes until all the water has been absorbed. Stir the rice and raisins together gently. Yield: 4 servings.

Yellow squash casserole

You can prepare this dish a few hours ahead of the meal. Be sure to keep covered and refrigerated until you are ready to cook.

4 teaspoons butter or margarine
1 large onion, peeled and finely chopped
500 grams Hubbard or butternut squash
1 egg, lightly beaten
1 cup grated mature Cheddar cheese
pinch ground nutmeg
pinch salt
pinch black pepper
⅓ cup fine dry bread crumbs

1. Preheat the oven to 220°C. Melt 3 teaspoons of the butter in a large frying pan over moderate heat. Add the onion and cook, covered, for 5 minutes, or until soft.
2. Meanwhile, cut the squash into 6-millimetre slices. If they are large, quarter them. Add the squash to the onion, cover, and cook for 3 minutes or until just tender.
3. In a bowl, blend the egg, cheese, nutmeg, salt and pepper, and the marjoram and thyme if used. Remove the squash from the heat, and blend in the egg and cheese mixture.
4. Pour into a buttered 5-centimetre deep casserole dish, top with the bread crumbs, and dot with the remaining butter. Bake, uncovered, for 10 minutes, or until bubbly, then grill for 2 minutes, or until golden brown. Yield: 4 servings.

Yoghurt

For rich yoghurt, use a mixture of whole milk and cream. For a healthy substitute for sour cream, you can use low-fat milk.

1 litre milk
¼ cup store-bought plain yoghurt

1. Pour the milk into a small saucepan, prop a sugar thermometer inside, and heat to 82°C. Allow the milk to cool to 40°C.
2. Stir in the yoghurt and pour the mixture into glass jars. Cap the jars and place in a pan of warm water (40°C–44°C) along with the sugar thermometer. Allow the yoghurt to incubate for a period of about 5 to 6 hours, adding hot water as needed to maintain the water temperature. Or set the saucepan on top of the stove and check the temperature often. The yoghurt is ready when it retains the impression of a spoon which is pressed into the surface. Remove the jars from the saucepan and refrigerate for up to 1 week. Yield: 4 containers.
Caution: The temperature is important. The milk must be heated to just below boiling point in order to destroy the bacteria which prevent formation of the yoghurt.

Yoghurt & Greek cucumber salad

Here's a delightful salad that takes just 10 minutes to prepare.

2 medium cucumbers, peeled, seeded and diced
1 cup thick plain yoghurt
1 clove garlic, peeled and crushed
1 tablespoon fresh dill, chopped, or 1½ teaspoons dried dill
2 teaspoons white wine vinegar
½ teaspoon salt

1. Combine the cucumbers, yoghurt, garlic, dill, vinegar and salt in a bowl. Mix the ingredients well, cover and place in the refrigerator.
2. Serve the salad chilled.

Yoghurt & honey dressing

Use homemade or bought yoghurt to make this dressing for a fruit salad.

1 teaspoon lemon rind
2 tablespoons lemon juice
1 tablespoon sunflower oil
½ cup plain yoghurt
2 tablespoons honey
¼ teaspoon paprika
dash of Tabasco sauce
¼ teaspoon salt

Put all the ingredients into a jar, cap the jar securely and shake vigorously; or whisk in a bowl. Store in the refrigerator, but shake again just before serving. Yield: 1 cup.

Yoghurt & mint sauce

Here's a family favourite that's ideal served with a hot or spicy dish.

1½ cups thick plain yoghurt
6 heaped tablespoons chopped, fresh mint
2-3 cloves garlic, peeled and crushed with 1 level teaspoon salt
pinch of sugar
black pepper to taste

Whisk all the ingredients together in a bowl with plenty of black pepper. Alternatively, blend the ingredients in a food processor or liquidizer. Chill until needed. Yield: 1½ cups.

Where to find uncommon ingredients

The following uncommon ingredients (identified with an asterisk in the *Formulas and recipes* section) are listed along with the outlets at which they are usually available.

Almond oil – Health food stores and certain craft shops
Alum – Pharmacies
Ammonium sulphate – Supermarkets
Aniseed – Supermarkets
Arrowroot – Supermarkets
Beeswax – Pharmacies
Bergamot oil – Health food stores and certain craft shops
Bonemeal – Nurseries and garden centres
Borax – Supermarkets
Boric acid – Supermarkets
Calcium carbonate – Pharmacies
Calcium chloride – Pharmacies
Camomile flowers – Health food stores and certain craft shops
Camphor – Health food stores and pharmacies
Ceresin wax – Pharmacies
Chickweed – Health food stores and certain craft shops
Cinnamon oil – Health food stores
Clove oil – Health food stores and certain craft shops
Coconut oil – Pharmacies and supermarkets
Comfrey root – Health food stores and certain pharmacies
Corn oil – Supermarkets
Copper sulphate – Pharmacies
Diatomaceous earth – Nurseries and plant departments of hardware stores
Dolomitic limestone – Nurseries and some hardware stores
Ethyl alcohol – Pharmacies
Gentian root – Health food stores
Ginseng extract – Health food stores and certain pharmacies
Glycerine – Supermarkets and pharmacies
Goldenseal root – Health food stores and certain craft shops
Gum arabic – Art suppliers and hardware stores
Hydrogen peroxide – Pharmacies
Jalapeño peppers – Supermarkets
Jasmine oil – Health food stores and certain craft shops
Jeweller's rouge – Jewellers' suppliers
Lamp black – Art and craft shops
Lavender oil – Health food stores
Lemon oil – Health food stores and certain craft shops
Lime, hydrated – Hardware stores and building materials suppliers
Lime, slaked – Pharmacies
Liquid pectin – Supermarkets and pharmacies
Liver of sulphur – Pharmacies
Manure, dried – Nurseries
Marsh mallow root – Health food stores
Musk oil – Health food stores and certain craft shops
Neroli oils – Health food stores and certain craft shops
Oil of bergamot – Health food stores, some pharmacies and certain craft shops
Oil of cloves – Health food stores
Orrisroot – Health food stores and certain craft shops
Peat moss – Nurseries and garden centres
Peppermint leaves – Health food stores
Perlite – Nurseries and hardware stores
Pine-needle oil – Health food stores and some craft shops
Pumice – Pharmacies
Rose hips – Health food stores
Rose oil – Health food stores and certain craft shops
Rose water – Pharmacies
Saltpetre – Supermarkets
Shellac flakes – Hardware stores
Soda ash – Supermarkets
Sodium sulphate – Pharmacies
Sodium sulphite – Pharmacies
Superphosphate – Nurseries and garden centres
Vermiculite – Nurseries and hardware stores
Whole-wheat flakes, shredded wheat – Health food stores and some supermarkets
Wintergreen leaves – Health food stores
Wood ash – Nurseries and some garden centres

INDEX

D

G

M

N

Q

R

U

V

W

Y

Z

CREDITS & ACKNOWLEDGMENTS

Bantam Doubleday Dell Publishing Group Inc.
The Doubleday Cookbook by Jean Anderson and Elaine Hanna. Copyright © 1975 by Doubleday, a division of the Bantam Doubleday Dell Publishing Group Inc. Reprinted by permission.

Dover Publications, Inc.
The Standard Book of Quilt Making and Collecting by Marguerite Ickis. Copyright © 1949 by Marguerite Ickis. Reprinted by permission.

Harmony Books, A Division of Crown Publishers, Inc.
Natural Child Care by Maribeth Riggs. Copyright © 1989 by Maribeth Riggs and Rita Aero. Reprinted by permission.

Harper & Row Publishers, Inc.
Better Than Store-Bought by Helen Witty and Elizabeth Schneider Colchie. Copyright © 1979 by Helen Witty and Elizabeth Schneider Colchie. *Scarne's Encyclopedia of Games* by John Scarne. Copyright © 1973 by John Scarne Games Inc. *Cheaper & Better: Homemade Alternatives to Store-Bought Goods* by Nancy Birnes. Copyright © 1987 by Shadow Lawn Press, Inc. Reprinted by permission.

Little, Brown and Company
The Town & Country Cookbook by James Villas. Copyright © 1985 by James Villas. Reprinted by permission.

Mark Morris Associates Topeka, Kansas
High Quality Maintenance Diet of Dogs and Cats. Reprinted by permission.

New American Library, A Division of Penguin USA Inc.
Deliciously Simple: Quick and Easy, Low-Sodium, Low-Fat, Low-Cholesterol, Low-Sugar Meals by Harriet Roth. Copyright © 1986 by Harriet Roth. Reprinted by permission.

The New York Public Library, Picture Collection

Times Books, A Division of Quadrangle/ The New York Times Book Co., Inc.
The Grass Roots Cookbook by Jean Anderson. Copyright © 1974 by Jean Anderson. Reprinted by permission.

Zondervan Corporation
Play It! by Wayne Rice and Mike Yaconelli. Copyright © 1986 by Youth Specialities, Inc. Reprinted by permission.

CONSULTANTS
Ron Alford
Jean Anderson
Richard Asa
David A Barnebl, Sr VP
Paine Webber
Jennifer Birckmayer
Walter F Burghardt Jr, DVM, PhD
John J Byrne, MD, FACS
Al Carrell
John T Cavanaugh, MS, PT/ATC
Russell B Clanahan
John L Costa, MD, FAAP
Sheila Danko
Seymour Diamond, MD
Michael M Dresdner
Ben T Etheridge
Michele C Fisher, PhD, RD
Todd P Forte
Michael S Frank, MD
Jim Fremont
Alan French, MBA, MM
Dora Galitzki
Bernard Gladstone
Leon Grabowski
Ray Greenley
Walter A Grub, Jr
Elizabeth Hall
Wade A Hoyt
Robert E Hueter, PhD
Marjorie Grossman Jaffe
John Karl
Roberta Ann Kaseman
William J Keller, PhD
Carolyn Klass
Steven Lamm, MD
Frances La Rosa
Walter LeStrange, RN, MPH
Scott Lewis
Cynthia J MacKay, MD
Jim McCann
Jean McLean
Janet E Meleney
John Mulligan, Assistant Fire Commissioner, New York Fire Department
Mary E Purchase, PhD
Ruth Raimon-Wilson
Maureen Reardon
Marilyn S Rogers
Gertrude Rowland
Lauren B Scheib
Gerry Schremp
Victor J Selmanowitz, MD
Frances E Shanahan
Leonard A Sipes, Jr, MS
Stanley H Smith
Joanne Tunney Stack, JD
Eric Stand
Marjabelle Young Stewart
Martha Strohl
Valerie Sutton
John Warde
Paul Weissler, SAE
Stephanie Whalen
Thomas A Wilson, DDS
Donald E Witten, National Weather Service

SPECIAL THANKS
American Health and Beauty Aids Institute
American Society of Travel Agents, Inc.
Carole Collins
Cleveland Pharmacy
Consumer Communications Group
Carol Ennis
Gerald Ferguson
Lester Harrison
Home Owner
Melanie Hulse
Det. Bernard Jacobs
Lothian Lynas
National Institute on Ageing
Natural Remedies Centre
Naturama
Rosemary Nelson
Rieses Delicatessen
Reynolds Metal Co.
Kelly Riley
Ruth Savolaine
Salt Institute
The Soap and Detergent Association
The Softness Group
Wardkiss Homecare

Reproduction by Fotoplate (Pty) Ltd, Cape Town
Printing and Binding by CTP Book Printers (Pty) Ltd, Cape Town